New York State
Juvenile Rights Practice
Handbook

Current through
Chapter 519, Laws of 2016

Looseleaf
Law Publications, Inc.

43-08 162nd Street
Flushing, NY 11358
www.LooseleafLaw.com
800-647-5547

**New York State
Juvenile Rights Practice
Handbook**

978-1-60885-011-2

**Current through
Chapter 519 Laws of 2016**

Table of Contents

FAMILY COURT ACT

In Its Entirety

Part I

43-08 162nd Street
Flushing, NY 11358
www.LooseleafLaw.com   800-647-5547

FAMILY COURT ACT

ARTICLE 1
Family Court Established

Part 1
Applicability of Act and Creation of Court

§111.   Title of act.
The title of this act is "the family court act of the state of New York." It may be cited as "The Family Court Act."

§112.   Applicability.
The family court act applies in all counties of the state of New York.

§113.   Establishment of court.
The family court of the state of New York is established in each county of the state as part of the unified court system for the state.

§114.   "Exclusive original jurisdiction".
When used in this act, "exclusive original jurisdiction" means that the proceedings over which the family court is given such jurisdiction must be originated in the family court in the manner prescribed by this act. The provisions of this act shall in no way limit or impair the jurisdiction of the supreme court as set forth in section seven of article six of the constitution of the state of New York.

§115.   Jurisdiction of family court.
(a) The family court has exclusive original jurisdiction over
(i) abuse and neglect proceedings, as set forth in article ten;
(ii) support proceedings, as set forth in article four;
(iii) proceedings to determine paternity and for the support of children born out-of-wedlock, as set forth in article five;
(iv) proceedings to permanently terminate parental rights to guardianship and custody of a child: (A) by reason of permanent neglect, as set forth in part one of article six of this act and paragraph (d) of subdivision four of section three hundred eighty-four-b of the social services law, (B) by reason

of mental illness, intellectual disability and severe or repeated child abuse, as set forth in paragraphs (c) and (e) of subdivision four of section three hundred eighty-four-b of the social services law, and (C) by reason of the death of one or both parents, where no guardian of the person of the child has been lawfully appointed, or by reason of abandonment of the child for a period of six months immediately prior to the filing of the petition, where a child is under the jurisdiction of the family court as a result of a placement in foster care by the family court pursuant to article ten or ten-A of this act or section three hundred fifty-eight-a of the social services law, unless the court declines jurisdiction pursuant to section three hundred eighty-four-b of the social services law;

(Eff.5/25/16,Ch.37,L.2016)

(v) proceedings concerning whether a person is in need of supervision, as set forth in article seven; and

(vi) proceedings concerning juvenile delinquency as set forth in article three.

(b) The family court has such other jurisdiction as is set forth in this act, including jurisdiction over habeas corpus proceedings and over applications for support, maintenance, a distribution of marital property and custody in matrimonial actions when referred to the family court by the supreme court, conciliation proceedings, and proceedings concerning physically handicapped and mentally defective or retarded children.

(c) The family court has such other jurisdiction as is provided by law, including but not limited to: proceedings concerning adoption and custody of children, as set forth in parts two and three of article six of this act; proceedings concerning the uniform interstate family support act, as set forth in article five-B of this act; proceedings concerning children in foster care and care and custody of children, as set forth in sections three hundred fifty-eight-a and three hundred eighty-four-a of the social services law and article ten-A of this act; proceedings concerning former foster children as set forth in article ten-B of this act; proceedings concerning destitute children, as set forth in article ten-C of this act; proceedings concerning guardianship and custody of children by reason of the death of, or abandonment or surrender by, the parent or parents, as set forth in sections three hundred eighty-three-c, three hundred eighty-four and paragraphs (a) and (b) of subdivision four of section three hundred eighty-four-b of the social services law; proceedings concerning standby guardianship and guardianship of the person as set forth in part four of article six of this act and article seventeen of the surrogate's court procedure act; and proceedings concerning the interstate compact on juveniles as set forth in chapter one hundred fifty-five of the laws of nineteen hundred fifty-five, as amended, the interstate compact on the placement of children, as set forth in section three hundred seventy-four-a of the social services law, and the uniform child custody jurisdiction and enforcement act, as set forth in article five-A of the domestic relations law.

(d) Notwithstanding subdivisions (a) through (c) of this section, jurisdiction of the family court and tribal courts of Indian tribes designated by the Secretary of the Interior over those child custody proceedings provided for in articles three, seven, ten and ten-A of this act and sections three hundred fifty-eight-a and three hundred eighty-four-b of the social services law involving Indian children as defined in subdivision thirty-six of section two of the social services law shall be subject to the terms and conditions set forth in applicable sections of title twenty-five of the United States code; provided that tribal courts of Indian tribes designated as such by the state of New York shall have jurisdiction over such child custody proceedings involving Indian children to the same extent as federally designated Indian tribes upon the approval of the state office of children and family services pursuant to section thirty-nine of the social services law.

(e) The family court has concurrent jurisdiction with the criminal court over all family offenses as defined in article eight of this act.

(f) The family court has jurisdiction to direct the commencement of proceedings to suspend the driving privileges, recreational licenses and permits, and license, permit, registration or authority to practice of persons who are delinquent in their child or combined child and spousal support obligations or persons who have failed, after receiving appropriate notice, to comply with summonses, subpoenas or warrants relating to paternity and child support proceedings as set forth in sections four hundred fifty-eight-a, four hundred fifty-eight-b, four hundred fifty-eight-c, five hundred forty-eight-a, five hundred forty-eight-b, and five forty-eight-c of this act. Such jurisdiction shall include jurisdiction over all boards, departments, authorities or offices of the state for the purposes of implementing such section.

§116. Religion of custodial persons and agencies.

(a) Whenever a child is remanded or committed by the court to any duly authorized association, agency, society or institution, other than an institution supported and controlled by the state or a subdivision thereof, such commitment must be made, when practicable, to a duly authorized association, agency, society or institution under the control of persons of the same religious faith or persuasion as that of the child.

(b) Whenever any child thus committed is placed by any such association, agency, society or institution in a family, or in the home, or in the custody, of any person other than that of its birth or adopted parent or parents, or when so placed or paroled directly by the court, such placement or parole must, when practicable, be with or in the custody of a person or persons of the same religious faith or persuasion as that of the child.

(c) In appointing guardians of children, except guardians ad litem, and in granting orders of adoption of children, the court must, when practicable, appoint only as such guardians, and only give custody through adoption to, persons of the same religious faith or persuasion as that of the child.

(d) The provisions of paragraphs (a), (b) and (c) of this section shall be interpreted literally, so as to assure that in the care, protection, guardianship, discipline or control of any child his religious faith shall be preserved and protected by the court. But this section shall not be construed so as to prevent the remanding of a child, during the pendency of a proceeding, to a place of detention designated by rules of court nor to the placing of a child in a hospital or similar institution for necessary treatment.

(e) The words "when practicable" as used in this section shall be interpreted as being without force or effect if there is a proper or suitable person of the same religous faith or persuasion as that of the child available for appointment as guardian, or to be designated as custodian, or to whom control may be given, or to whom orders of adoption may be granted; or if there is a duly authorized association, agency, society or institution under the control of persons of the same religious faith or persuasion as that of the child, at the time available and willing to assume the responsibility for the custody of or control over any such child.

(f) If a child is placed in the custody, or under the supervision or control, of a person or of persons of a religious faith or persuasion different from that of the child, or if a guardian of a child is appointed whose religious faith or persuasion is different from that of the child, or if orders of adoption are granted to a person or persons whose religious faith is different from that of the child adopted, or if a child is remanded or committed to a duly authorized association, agency, society or institution, or to any other place, which is under the control of persons of a religious faith or persuasion different from that of the child, the court shall state or recite the facts which impel it to make such disposition and such statement shall be made a part of the minutes of the proceeding.

(g) The provisions of subdivisions (a), (b), (c), (d), (e) and (f) of this section shall, so far as consistent with the best interests of the child, and where practicable, be applied so as to give effect to the religious wishes of the birth mother, if the child is born out-of-wedlock, or if born in-wedlock, the religious wishes of the birth parents of the child, or if only one of the birth parents of an in-wedlock child is then living, the religious wishes of the birth parent then living. Religious wishes of a birth parent shall include wishes that the child be placed in the same religion as the birth parent or in a different religion from the birth parent or with indifference to religion or with religion a subordinate consideration. Expressed religious wishes of a birth parent shall mean those which have been set forth in a writing signed by the birth parent, except that, in a non-agency adoption, such writing shall be an affidavit of the birth parent. In the absence of expressed religious wishes, as defined in this subdivision, determination of the religious wishes, if any, of the birth parent, shall be made upon the other facts of the particular case, and, if there is no evidence to the contrary, it shall be presumed that the birth parent wishes the child to be reared in the religion of the birth parent.

§117. Parts of court.

(a) There is hereby established in the family court a "child abuse part". Such part shall be held separate from all other proceedings of the court, and shall have jurisdiction over all proceedings in the family court involving abused children, and shall be charged with the immediate protection of these children. All cases involving abuse shall be originated in or be transferred to this part from other parts as they are made known to the court unless there is or was before the court a proceeding involving any members of the same family or household, in which event the judge who heard said proceeding may hear the case involving abuse. Consistent with its primary purpose, nothing in this section is intended to prevent the child abuse part from hearing other cases.

(b) For every juvenile delinquency proceeding under article three involving an allegation of an act committed by a person which, if done by an adult, would be a crime (i) defined in sections 125.27 (murder in the first degree); 125.25 (murder in the second degree); 135.25 (kidnapping in the first degree); or 150.20 (arson in the first degree) of the penal law committed by a person thirteen, fourteen or fifteen years of age; or such conduct committed as a sexually motivated felony, where authorized pursuant to section 130.91 of the penal law; (ii) defined in sections 120.10 (assault in the first degree); 125.20 (manslaughter in the first degree); 130.35 (rape in the first degree); 130.50 (criminal sexual act in the first degree); 135.20 (kidnapping in the second degree), but only where the abduction involved the use or threat of use of deadly physical force; 150.15 (arson in the second degree); or 160.15 (robbery in the first degree) of the penal law committed by a person thirteen, fourteen or fifteen years of age; or such conduct committed as a sexually motivated felony, where authorized pursuant to section 130.91 of the penal law; (iii) defined in the penal law as an attempt to commit murder in the first or second degree or kidnapping in the first degree committed by a person thirteen, fourteen or fifteen years of age; or such conduct committed as a sexually motivated felony, where authorized pursuant to section 130.91 of the penal law; (iv) defined in section 140.30 (burglary in the first degree); subdivision one of section 140.25 (burglary in the second degree); subdivision two of section 160.10 (robbery in the second degree) of the penal law; or section 265.03 of the penal law, where such machine gun or such firearm is possessed on school grounds, as that phrase is defined in subdivision fourteen of section 220.00 of the penal law committed by a person fourteen or fifteen years of age; or such conduct committed as a sexually motivated felony, where authorized pursuant to section 130.91 of the penal law; (v) defined in section 120.05 (assault in the second degree) or 160.10 (robbery in the second degree) of the penal law committed by a person fourteen or fifteen years of age but only where there has been a prior finding by a court that such person has previously committed an act which, if committed by an adult, would be the crime of assault in the second degree, robbery in the second degree or any designated felony act specified in clause (i), (ii) or (iii) of this subdivision regardless of the age of such person at the time of the commission of the prior act; or (vi) other than a misdemeanor, committed by a person at least seven but less than sixteen years of age, but only where there has been two prior findings by the court that such person has committed a prior act which, if committed by an adult would be a felony:

(i) There is hereby established in the family court in the city of New York at least one "designated felony act part." Such part or parts shall be held separate from all other proceedings of the court, and shall have jurisdiction over all proceedings involving such an allegation. All such proceedings shall be originated in or be transferred to this part from other parts as they are made known to the court.

(ii) Outside the city of New York, all proceedings involving such an allegation shall have a hearing preference over every other proceeding in the court, except proceedings under article ten.

(c) The chief administrator of the courts may establish one or more separate support parts in each family court for the purpose of expediting support proceedings instituted pursuant to articles four, five and five-A of this act. Where such separate support parts are established, all such proceedings shall be originated in or be transferred to this part or parts as they are made known to the court and shall be heard by support magistrates in accordance with section four hundred thirty-nine of this act.

(d) The appellate division of the supreme court in each department may provide, in accordance with the standards and policies established by the administrative board of the judicial conference, that the family court in counties within its department shall or may be organized into such other parts, if any, as may be appropriate.

§118. Seal.

The seal of the family court consists of an engraving of the arms of the state of New York and the words "Family Court of the State of New York" followed by the name of the county in which the family court using the seal is located.

§119. Definitions.

When used in this act and unless the specific context indicates otherwise:

(a) "Duly authorized association, agency, society or institution" means any institution supported or controlled by the state or by a subdivision thereof; any social services official of this state; or an association, agency, society, or institution, duly empowered to care for children, which

(i) is incorporated under the laws of this state;

(ii) actually has its place of business or home within the state; and

(iii) is approved, visited, inspected and supervised by the department of family assistance, or which shall submit and consent to the approval, visitation, inspection and supervision of the department of family assistance.

(b) "Person legally responsible for the child's care" includes the child's custodian, guardian or any other person responsible for the child's care at the relevant time.

(c) The term "infant" or "minor" means a person who has not attained the age of eighteen years.

§120. Expenses of the court.

(a) All salaries of the judicial and non-judicial personnel of the court and all other expenses of the court whatsoever, except as provided in subdivision (b), shall within the city of New York, be a city charge and in the counties outside the city of New York, a county charge; provided however, that the final determination of the itemized estimates of the annual financial needs of the court shall be made by the appropriate governing bodies of such counties and the city of New York in the manner provided in article seven-a of the judiciary law, and section twenty-nine of article six of the constitution.

(b) Salaries of support magistrates appointed in proceedings to compel support pursuant to section four hundred thirty-nine of this act shall be a state charge payable out of funds appropriated to the office of court administration for that purpose.

Part 2
Number, Appointment, Term and Compensation of
Judges Within the City of New York

§121. Number of judges.

The family court within the city of New York shall consist of fifty-six judges, effective January first, two thousand fifteen. There shall be at least one family court judge resident in each county of the city of New York.

§122. Continuance in office.

The justices of the domestic relations court of the city of New York in office on the effective date of this act, shall for the remainder of the term of their appointment continue in office as judges of the family court in the county within the city of New York in which they reside.

§123. Appointment by mayor.

The mayor of the city of New York shall appoint the judges of the family court in counties within the city of New York for a term of ten years.

§124. Eligibility for appointment.

No person, other than one who holds such office at the effective date of this act, may assume the office of judge of the family court within the city of New York unless he has been admitted to practice law in this state at least ten years prior to the date of such appointment. In making such appointments, the mayor of the city of New York shall select persons who are especially qualified for the court's work by reason of their character, personality, tact, patience and common sense.

§126. Vacancies.

When a vacancy occurs, otherwise than by expiration of term on the last day of any year, in the office of judge of the family court in a county within the city of New York, the vacancy shall be filled by appointment of the mayor of the city of New York for the unexpired term.

Part 3
Number, Election, Term and Compensation of
Judges Not Within the City of New York

§131. Number of judges.

The number of judges of the family court for each county outside the city of New York shall be as follows:

(a) in each county in which there was a separate office or offices of judge of the children's court authorized by law on the thirty-first day of August nineteen hundred sixty-two, the number of judges of the family court for such county shall be equal to the number of offices so authorized except those authorized by certificate filed pursuant to subdivision two of section four of the children's court act of the state of New York subsequent to March first, nineteen hundred sixty-two; and, effective May fifteenth, nineteen hundred sixty-three, there shall be a separate office of judge of the family court for the county of Niagara; and, effective May fifteenth, nineteen hundred sixty-three, there shall be a separate office of judge of the family court for the county of Ulster; and, effective January first, nineteen hundred sixty-four, there shall be a separate office of judge of the family court for the county of St. Lawrence; and, effective January first, nineteen hundred sixty-five, there shall be a separate office of judge of the family court for the county of Chautauqua; and, effective January first, nineteen hundred sixty-seven, there shall be a separate office of judge of the family court for the county of Oneida; and, effective January first, nineteen hundred sixty-five, there shall be a separate office of judge of the family court for the county of Jefferson; and, effective January first, nineteen hundred sixty-six, there shall be a separate office of judge of the family court for the county of Rockland:

(b) in the other counties except the counties of Chautauqua, Jefferson and Oneida, a judge of the county court shall act as and discharge the duties of judge of the family court;

(c) in the counties of Chautauqua, Jefferson and Oneida, upon the expiration of the term of office of the special county judge who was continued as a judge of the family court pursuant to section one hundred thirty-two of this act, or if there was no special county judge in office on the effective date of this act, a judge of the county court of each such county shall act as and discharge the duties of judge of the family court.

(d) In the county of Nassau there shall be eight family court judges and the number of such judges now existing in said county is hereby increased accordingly.

(e) In the county of Monroe there shall be six family court judges and the number of such judges now existing in said county is hereby increased accordingly; in the county of Erie there shall be six family court judges and the number of such judges now existing in said county is hereby increased accordingly. In the county of Albany there shall be a total of three family court judges and the number of such judges now existing in such county is hereby increased accordingly.

(f) In the county of Onondaga there shall be three additional family court judges and the number of such judges now existing in such county is hereby increased accordingly. The compensation of each such additional family court judge shall be the same as the compensation of existing family court judges in such county.

(g) There shall be a separate office of judge of the family court for the counties of Oswego and Sullivan and the compensation payable for each such separate office of judge of the family court shall be twenty-five thousand dollars per annum. In the county of Saratoga there shall be an additional family court judge and the number of such judges now existing in such county is hereby increased accordingly. The compensation of such additional family court judge shall be the same as the compensation of the existing family court judge in such county.

(h) In the county of Westchester there shall be three additional family court judges and the number of such judges now existing is hereby increased accordingly. The compensation of each additional family court judge shall be the same as the existing family court judge in such county.

(i) In the county of Schenectady there shall be one additional family court judge and the number of such judges now existing is hereby increased accordingly. The compensation of the additional family court judge shall be the same as the existing family court judge in such county.

(j) In the county of Genesee there shall be one additional family court judge and the number of such judges now existing is hereby increased accordingly. The compensation of the additional family court judge shall be the same as the existing family court judge in such county.

(k) In the county of Rockland there shall be one additional family court judge and the number of such judges now existing is hereby increased accordingly. The compensation of the additional family court judge shall be the same as the existing family court judge in such county.

(l) In the county of Dutchess there shall be two additional family court judges and the number of such judges now existing is hereby increased accordingly. The compensation of the additional family court judges shall be the same as the compensation paid to each of the existing family court judges in such county pursuant to section two hundred twenty-one-e of the judiciary law.

(m) In the county of Niagara there shall be one additional family court judge and the number of such judges now existing is hereby increased accordingly. The compensation of the additional family court judge shall be the same as the existing family court judge in such county.

(n) In the county of Ulster there shall be one additional family court judge and the number of such judges now existing is hereby increased accordingly. The compensation of the additional family court judge shall be the same as the existing family court judge in such county.

(o) In the county of Oneida there shall be two additional family court judges making a total of three family court judges in such county. The number of such judges now existing in such county is hereby increased accordingly. The compensation of the additional family court judges shall be the same as the compensation of the existing family court judge in such county.

(p) In the county of Suffolk there shall be four additional family court judges making a total of ten family court judges in such county. The number of such judges now existing in such county is hereby increased accordingly. The compensation of each such family court judge shall be the same as the compensation of existing family court judges in such county.

(q) In the county of Rensselaer, there shall be one additional family court judge and the number of judges now existing is hereby increased accordingly. The compensation of the additional family court judge shall be the same as the existing family court judge in such county.

(r) In the county of Orange there shall be three additional family court judges, making a total of four family court judges, and the number of such judges now existing is hereby increased accordingly. The compensation of each such additional family court judge shall be the same as the compensation paid to each of the existing family court judges in such county.

(s) In the county of Broome there shall be a total of three family court judges and the number of such judges now existing is hereby increased accordingly. The compensation of such additional family court judge shall be the same as the compensation paid to each of the existing family court judges in such county.

(t) There shall be a separate office of judge of the family court for the county of Clinton and the compensation payable for such separate office of judge of the family court shall be the same as the compensation payable to the judge of the county court of Clinton county.

(u) There shall be an additional family court judge for each of the following counties: Albany, Broome, Chautauqua, Franklin, Nassau, Oneida, Oswego, Schenectady, Suffolk, Ulster and Westchester. The compensation of each such additional family court judge shall be the same as the compensation paid to each existing family court judge in the county for which it is established or, if there is no separately-elected family court judge in such county, the same as the compensation paid to a judge of the county court in such county.

(v) There shall be an additional family court judge for each of the following counties: Delaware, Dutchess, Erie, Monroe, and Warren. The compensation of each such additional family court judge shall be the same as the compensation paid to each existing family court judge in the county for which it is established or, if there is no separately-elected family court judge in such county, the same as the compensation paid to a judge of the county court in such county.

§132. Continuance in office.

The special county judges of the counties of Broome, Chautauqua, Jefferson, Oneida and Rockland and the judges of the children's courts in all counties outside the city of New York in office at midnight on August thirty-first, nineteen hundred sixty-two, shall be judges of the family court in and for the county in which they hold office for the remainder of the terms for which they were elected or appointed.

§133. Vacancies.

When a vacancy occurs, otherwise than by expiration of term, in the office of judge of the family court in a county not within the city of New York, the vacancy shall be filled for a full term at the next general election held not less than three months after such vacancy occurs and, until the vacancy shall be so filled, the governor by and with the advice and consent of the senate, if the senate shall be in session, or, if the senate not be in session, the governor may fill such vacancy by an appointment which shall continue until and including the last day of December next after the election at which the vacancy shall be filled.

§134. Eligibility for office.

No person, other than one who holds such office on the effective date of this act may serve in the office of judge of the family court unless he or she has been admitted to practice law in the state of New York for at least ten years as of the date he or she commences the duties of office.

§135. Term of office.

The term of office of a judge elected to the family court in a county outside the city of New York is ten years.

§137. County judge designated as family court judge.

In each county referred to in subdivisions (b) and (c) of section one hundred thirty-one of this act in which there is more than one county judge, the appellate division of the supreme court of the judicial department in which such county is located shall designate and may revoke any designation of, one or more of the county judges within the county to act as and discharge the duties of family court judge.

§138. Additional compensation for designated judge.

Any additional compensation for a judge designated under section one hundred thirty-seven to act and discharge the duties of family court judge shall be as provided by law.

Part 4
Family Court Judges

§141. Findings.

This act defines the conditions on which the family court may intervene in the life of a child, parent and spouse. Once these conditions are satisfied, the court is given a wide range of powers for dealing with the complexities of family life so that its action may fit the particular needs of those before it. The judges of the court are thus given a wide discretion and grave responsibilities.

The people of the state of New York have concluded that legal training and experience should be required before any person may assume the office of family court judge and so provided in section twenty, paragraph a, of the judiciary article of the constitution of the state of New York. Judges of the family court should also be familiar with areas of learning and practice that often are not supplied by the practice of law.

§142. Authority to visit school or institution.

Judges of the family court may officially visit any school or institution to which any person within the jurisdiction of the court of which he is an officer may be remanded or committed, and the authorities responsible for paying their respective salaries are authorized and required to approve and pay the necessary traveling expenses incurred by such judges in making such visits.

§143. Authority to attend meetings of association.

Judges discharging the duties of family court judge may attend conferences and meetings of the association of judges of the family court, and the fiscal authorities responsible for paying their respective salaries are authorized and required to approve and pay the necessary traveling expenses incurred by such judges in attending such conferences and meetings, if within the authorized appropriation.

§144. Activity in community organizations.

Any judge discharging the duties of family court judge is authorized to serve as an officer or member of the governing body of any corporation or association organized and maintained exclusively for religious, charitable, benevolent, or educational purposes.

§145. Liability of judge.

Any family court judge who in good faith issues process in any proceeding under this act shall not be liable therefor unless it is shown that his action in so doing was malicious or a deliberate abuse of his discretion.

§146. Temporary assignment of judges.

Nothing in this act is intended to prevent the temporary assignment of family court judges by the appropriate administrative judge to counties other than the one to which they were elected or appointed for the purpose of meeting a temporary need for judicial personnel or for greater contact between courts.

Part 5
General Powers

§151.   Judges as magistrates.

Judges of the family court are magistrates.

§152.   Power to administer oaths.

(a) Each family court judge may administer oaths and take acknowledgments, and may designate an official of his court so to do.

(b) In conducting a hearing under this act, a judge may dispense with the formality of placing a minor under oath before taking his testimony.

§153.   Subpoena, warrant and other process to compel attendance.

The family court may issue a subpoena or in a proper case a warrant or other process to secure or compel the attendance of an adult respondent or child or any other person whose testimony or presence at a hearing or proceeding is deemed by the court to be necessary, and to admit to, fix or accept bail, or parole him pending the completion of the hearing or proceeding. The court is also authorized to issue a subpoena duces tecum in accordance with the applicable provisions of the civil practice act and, upon its effective date, in accordance with the applicable provisions of the CPLR. A judge of the family court is also authorized to hear and decide motions relating to child support subpoenas issued pursuant to section one hundred eleven-p of the social services law.

§153-a.   Warrant of arrest; when and how executed.

(a) A warrant of arrest may be executed on any day of the week, and at any hour of the day or night.

(b) Unless encountering physical resistance, flight or other factors rendering normal procedure impractical, the arresting police officer must inform the subject named therein that a warrant for his arrest for attendance at the proceeding designated therein has been issued. Upon request of such subject, the police officer must show him the warrant if he has it in his possession. The officer need not have the warrant in his possession, and, if he has not, he must show it to the subject upon request as soon after the arrest as possible.

(c) In order to effect the arrest, the police officer may use such physical force as is justifiable pursuant to section 35.30 of the penal law.

(d) In order to effect the arrest, the police officer may enter any premises in which he reasonably believes the subject named therein to be present. Before such entry, he must give, or make reasonable effort to give, notice of his authority and purpose to an occupant thereof.

(e) If the officer, after giving such notice, is not admitted, he may enter such premises, and by a breaking if necessary.

§153-b. Service of process request for order of protection.
Whenever a petitioner requests an order of protection or temporary order of protection or files for an extension of such order or a petition or motion for modification or a violation of such an order under any article of this act:

(a) the summons and the petition and, if one has been issued, the temporary order of protection, order of protection issued upon a default, or a copy or copies thereof, may be served on any day of the week, and at any hour of the day or night;

(b) a peace officer, acting pursuant to his or her special duties, or a police officer shall, upon receipt, serve or provide for the service of the summons and the petition together with any associated papers and, if one has been issued, the temporary order of protection, or order of protection issued upon a default and shall not charge a fee for such service, including, but not limited to, fees as provided under section eight thousand eleven of the civil practice law and rules;

(c) if a temporary order of protection has been issued, or an order of protection has been issued upon a default, unless the party requesting the order states on the record that she or he will arrange for other means for service or deliver the order to a peace or police officer directly for service, the court shall immediately deliver a copy of the temporary order of protection or order of protection together with any associated papers that may be served simul-taneously including the summons and petition, to a peace officer, acting pursuant to his or her special duties and designated by the court, or to a police officer as defined in paragraph (b) or (d) of subdivision thirty-four of section 1.20 of the criminal procedure law, or to any other county or municipal officer who may be directed to effect service under section two hundred fifty-five of this act, or, in the city of New York, to a designated representative of the police department of the city of New York. Any peace or police officer or designated person receiving a temporary order of protection or an order of protection as provided in this section shall serve or provide for the service thereof together with any associated papers that may be served simultaneously, at any address designated therewith, including the summons and petition if not previously served. Service of such temporary order of protection, or order of protection, and associated papers, shall insofar as practicable, be achieved promptly. An officer or designated person obliged to perform service pursuant to this section, and his or her employer, shall not be liable for damages resulting from the failure to achieve service where, having made a reasonable effort, such officer is unable to locate and serve the temporary order of protection or order of protection at any address provided by the party requesting the order;

(d) Where the temporary order of protection or order of protection and papers, if any, have been served, such officer or designated person shall provide the court with an affirmation, certificate or affidavit of service when the temporary order of protection or order of protection has been served, and shall provide notification of the date and time of such service to the statewide computer registry established pursuant to section two hundred twenty-one-a of the executive law. A statement subscribed by the officer or designated person, and affirmed by him or her to be true under the penalties of perjury, stating the papers served, the date, time, address or in the event there is no address, place, and manner of service, the name and a brief physical description of the party served, shall be proof of the service of the summons, petition and temporary order of protection or order of protection.

*(e) Notwithstanding any other provision of law, all orders of protection and temporary orders of protection issued pursuant to this act along with any associated papers that may be served simultaneously may, for the purposes of section one hundred sixty-eight of this article, be transmitted by facsimile transmission or electronic means and may be transmitted by facsimile transmission or electronic means for expedited service in accordance with the provisions of this section. For purposes of this section, "facsimile transmission" and "electronic means" shall be as defined in subdivision (f) of rule twenty-one hundred three of the civil practice law and rules.

*(e) where an officer or designated person obliged to perform service pursuant to this section is unable to complete service of the temporary order of protection or order of protection such officer or designated person shall provide the court with proof of attempted service of the temporary order of protection or order of protection with information regarding the dates, times, locations and manner of attempted service. An affirmation, certificate or affidavit of service with a statement subscribed by the officer or designated person, and affirmed by him or her to be true under the penalties of perjury, stating the name of the party and the papers attempted to be served on said person, and for each attempted service, the date, time, address or in the event there is no address, place, and manner of attempted service, shall be proof of attempted service.

§153-c. **Temporary order of protection.**
(a) Any person appearing at family court when the court is open requesting a temporary order of protection under any article of this act shall be entitled to file a petition without delay on the same day such person first appears at the family court, and a hearing on that request shall be held on the same day or the next day that the family court is open following the filing of such petition.

(b) As provided in this section, the chief administrator of the courts, with the approval of the administrative board of the courts, may promulgate rules to establish and implement a pilot program for the filing of petitions for temporary orders of protection by electronic means and for the issuance of such orders ex parte by audio-visual means in order to accommodate litigants for whom attendance at court to file for, and obtain, emergency relief would constitute an undue hardship or to accommodate litigants, for whom traveling to and appearing in the courthouse to obtain emergency relief, creates a risk of harm to such litigant.

(1) Definitions. As used in this section:
(i) "Electronic means" means any method of transmission of information between computers or other machines designed for the purpose of sending and receiving such transmissions, and which allows the recipient to reproduce the information transmitted in a tangible medium of expression.

(ii) "Independent audio-visual system" means an electronic system for the transmission and receiving of audio and visual signals, encompassing encoded signals, frequency domain multiplexing or other suitable means to preclude the unauthorized reception and decoding of the signals by commercially available television receivers, channel converters, or other available receiving devices.

(iii) "Electronic appearance" means an appearance in which one or more of the parties are not present in the court, but in which, by means of an independent audio-visual system, all of the participants are simultaneously able to see and hear reproductions of the voices and images of the judge, counsel, parties, witnesses, if any and other participants.

*Two subdivisions "(e)" enacted by the laws of 2010.

(2) Development of a pilot program. A plan for a pilot program pursuant to this section shall be developed by the chief administrator of the courts or his or her delegate in consultation with one or more local programs providing assistance to victims of domestic violence, the office for the prevention of domestic violence, and attorneys who represent family offense petitions. The plan shall include, but is not limited to:

(i) identification of one or more family justice centers or organizations or agencies or other sites outside of the local family court that are equipped with, or have access to, an independent audio-visual system and electronic means for filing documents that are compatible with the equipment in the local family court, with consideration given to the location of such site or sites and available resources; and

(ii) identification of one or more licensed and certified organizations, agencies or entities with advocates for victims of domestic violence who are trained, and available to assist petitioners in preparing and filing petitions for temporary orders of protection and in their electronic appearances before the family court to obtain such orders; and

(iii) identification of the existing resources available in local family courts for the implementation and oversight of the pilot program; and

(iv) delineation of procedures for filing of the petitions and documents, if any, by electronic means, swearing in the petitioners and any witnesses, preparation of a verbatim transcription of testimony presented and a record of evidence adduced and prompt transmission of any orders issued to the petitioners; and

(v) a timetable for implementation of the pilot program and plan for informing the public of its availability; and

(vi) a description of data to be collected in order to evaluate and, if necessary, make recommendations for improvements to the pilot program.

(3) Filing by electronic means. In conjunction with an electronic appearance under this section, petitioners for ex parte temporary orders of protection may, with the assistance of trained advocates, commence the proceedings by filing petitions by electronic means.

(i) A petitioner who seeks a temporary order of protection ex parte by use of an electronic appearance must file a petition in advance of such appearance and may do so by electronic means. The petitioner shall set forth the circumstances in which traveling to or appearing in the courthouse would constitute an undue hardship, or create a risk of harm to the petitioner. In granting or denying the relief sought by the petitioner, the court shall state the names of all participants, and whether it is granting or denying an appearance by electronic means and the basis for such determination; provided, however, that nothing in this section shall be construed to compel a party to file a petition or other document by electronic means or to testify by means of an electronic appearance.

(ii) Nothing in this section shall affect or change any existing laws governing the service of process, including requirements for personal service, or the sealing and confidentiality of court records in family court proceedings, or access to court records by the parties to such proceedings.

(4) (i) All electronic appearances by petitioners seeking temporary orders of protection ex parte under this section shall be strictly voluntary and the consent of such petitioners shall be given on the record at the commencement of each appearance.

(ii) Appearances taken through the use of an electronic appearance under this section shall be recorded and preserved for transcription. Documentary evidence, if any, referred to by a party or witness or the court may be transmitted and submitted and introduced by electronic means.

§154. State-wide process.

(a) The family court may send process or other mandates in any matter in which it has jurisdiction into any county of the state for service or execution in like manner and with the same force and effect as similar process or mandates of county courts as provided by law.

(b) In a proceeding to establish paternity or to establish, modify or enforce support, the court may send process without the state in the same manner and with the same effect as process sent within the state in the exercise of personal jurisdiction over any person subject to the jurisdiction of the court under section three hundred one or three hundred two of the civil practice law and rules or under section 580-201 of article five-B of the family court act, notwithstanding that such person is not a resident or domiciliary of the state.

(c) In a proceeding arising under article four, five, six, eight or ten of this act in which an order of protection is sought or in which a violation of an order of protection is alleged, the court may send process without the state in the same manner and with the same effect as process sent within the state in the exercise of personal jurisdiction over any person, subject to the jurisdiction of the court under section three hundred one or three hundred two of the civil practice law and rules, notwithstanding that such person is not a resident or domiciliary of the state, so long as: (1) the act or acts giving rise to the application for issuance or enforcement of the order of protection occurred within the state; and (2) the applicant for the order of protection resides or is domiciled in the state or has substantial contacts in the state, including but not limited to, presence on a regular basis in the state. Upon good cause shown, the court may issue a temporary order of protection in accordance with article four, five, six, eight or ten of this act. Where personal jurisdiction over a non-resident or non-domiciliary respondent would not be obtainable but for this subdivision, the papers to be served shall include a conspicuous notice that the exercise of such jurisdiction is limited to the issue of the order of protection. Where service of a petition and summons upon a non-resident or non-domiciliary respondent is required, such service shall be made at least twenty days before the return date. Where service is effected on an out-of-state respondent and the respondent defaults by failing to appear, the court may on its own motion, or upon application of any party or the attorney for the child, proceed to a hearing with respect to issuance or enforcement of the order of protection. Nothing in this section shall be construed to affect or alter the exercise of personal jurisdiction with respect to issues other than the order of protection.

§154-a. Service of petition.

In every proceeding in family court, a copy of the petition filed therein shall be served upon the respondent at the time of service of process or, if that is not practicable, at the first court appearance by respondent.

§154-b.   Order of protection; answer and counter-claims; confidentiality of address.

1. In every proceeding under articles four, five, six and eight of this act in which an order of protection is requested, the respondent may file with the

court an answer to the petition and a counter-claim. A counter-claim shall be heard in the same manner as a petition and may be heard on the return date of the petition, provided that the counter-claim is served on the petitioner no later than five days prior to the return date and said counter-claim and proof of service is filed with the court. The petitioner may file and serve a reply to the counter-claim. A denial of the allegations of the counter-claim shall be presumed if the petitioner does not file and serve a reply.

2. (a) Notwithstanding any other provision of law, in any proceeding under article four, five, five-b, six, eight or ten of this act, whether or not an order of protection or temporary order of protection is sought or has been sought in the past, the court may, upon its own motion or upon the motion of any party or the child's attorney, authorize any party or the child to keep his or her address confidential from any adverse party or the child, as appropriate, in any pleadings or other papers submitted to the court, where the court finds that disclosure of such address or other identifying information would pose an unreasonable risk to the health or safety of a party or the child. Pending such a finding, any address or other identifying information of the child or party seeking confidentiality shall be safeguarded and sealed in order to prevent its inadvertent or unauthorized use or disclosure.

(b) Notwithstanding any other provision of law, if a party and a child has resided or resides in a residential program for victims of domestic violence as defined in section four hundred fifty-nine-a of the social services law, the present address of such party and of the child and the address of the residential program for victims of domestic violence shall not be revealed.

(c) Upon such authorization, the court shall designate the clerk of the court or such other disinterested person as it deems appropriate, with consent of such disinterested person, as the agent for service of process for the party whose address is to remain confidential and shall notify the adverse party of such designation in writing. The clerk or disinterested person designated by the court shall, when served with process on behalf of the party whose address is to remain confidential, promptly notify such party whose address is to remain confidential and forward such process to him or her.

(d) In any case in which such confidentiality authorization is made, the party whose address is to remain confidential shall inform the clerk of the court or disinterested person designated by the court of any change in address for purposes of receipt of service of process or any papers.

§154-c. Orders of protection; procedural requirements.

1. Expiration dates. Any order of protection or temporary order of protection issued under articles four, five, six and eight of this act shall plainly state the date that such order expires.

2. Modifications of orders of protection. Except as provided in subdivision two of section one hundred fifty-four-d of this act, any motion to vacate or modify any order of protection or temporary order of protection issued under this act shall be on notice to the non-moving party and the child's attorney, if any.

3. Pleadings and requisite findings. No order of protection may direct any party to observe conditions of behavior unless: (i) the party requesting the order of protection has served and filed a petition or counter-claim in accordance with article four, five, six or eight of this act and, (ii) the court has made a finding on the record that such party is entitled to issuance of the order of protection which may result from a judicial finding of fact, judicial

acceptance of an admission by the party against whom the order was issued or judicial finding that the party against whom the order is issued has given knowing, intelligent and voluntary consent to its issuance. Nothing herein shall be deemed to limit or restrict the authority of the court to issue a temporary order of protection on an ex parte basis.

§154-d. Emergency powers; local criminal courts.
1. Issuance of temporary orders of protection. Upon the request of the petitioner, a local criminal court may on an ex parte basis issue a temporary order of protection pending a hearing in family court, provided that a sworn affidavit, certified in accordance with subdivision one of section 100.30 of the criminal procedure law is submitted: (i) alleging that the family court is not in session; (ii) alleging that a family offense, as defined in subdivision one of section eight hundred twelve of this act or subdivision one of section 530.11 of the criminal procedure law, has been committed; (iii) alleging that a family offense petition has been filed or will be filed in family court on the next day the court is in session; and (iv) showing good cause. Upon appearance in a local criminal court, the petitioner shall be advised that he or she may continue with the proceeding either in family court or, upon the filing of a local criminal court accusatory instrument, in criminal court or both. Upon issuance of a temporary order of protection where petitioner requests that it be returnable in family court, the local criminal court shall transfer the matter forthwith to the family court and shall make the matter returnable in family court on the next day the family court is in session, or as soon thereafter as practicable, but in no event more than four calendar days after issuance of the order. The local criminal court, upon issuing a temporary order of protection returnable in family court pursuant to this subdivision shall immediately forward in a manner designed to ensure arrival before the return date set in the order, a copy of the temporary order of protection and sworn affidavit to the family court and shall provide a copy of such temporary order of protection to the petitioner; provided, however, that if the temporary order of protection and affidavit are transmitted by facsimile or other electronic means, the original order and affidavit shall be forwarded to the family court immediately thereafter. Any temporary order of protection issued pursuant to this subdivision shall be issued to the respondent and copies shall be filed as required in subdivisions six and eight of section 530.12 of the criminal procedure law for orders of protection issued pursuant to such section. Any temporary order of protection issued pursuant to this subdivision shall plainly state the date that such order expires which, in the case of an order returnable in family court, shall be not more than four calendar days after its issuance, unless sooner vacated or modified by the family court. A petitioner requesting a temporary order of protection returnable in family court pursuant to this subdivision in a case in which a family court petition has not been filed shall be informed that such temporary order of protection shall expire as provided for herein, unless the petitioner files a petition pursuant to subdivision one of section eight hundred twenty-one of this act on or before the return date in family court and the family court issues a temporary order of protection as authorized under article eight of this act. Nothing in this subdivision shall limit or restrict the petitioner's right to proceed directly and without court referral in either a criminal or family court, or both, as provided for in section one hundred fifteen of this act and section 100.07 of the criminal procedure law.

2. Modifications of orders of protection or temporary orders of protection. Upon the request of the petitioner, a local criminal court may on an ex parte basis modify a temporary order of protection or order of protection which has been issued under article four, five, six or eight of this act pending a hearing in family court, provided that a sworn affidavit, verified in accordance with subdivision one of section 100.30 of the criminal procedure law, is submitted: (i) alleging that the family court is not in session and (ii) showing good cause, including a showing that the existing order is insufficient for the purposes of protection of the petitioner, the petitioner's child or children or other members of the petitioner's family or household. The local criminal court shall make the matter regarding the modification of the order returnable in family court on the next day the family court is in session, or as soon thereafter as practicable, but in no event more than four calendar days after issuance of the modified order. The local criminal court shall immediately forward, in a manner designed to ensure arrival before the return date set in the order, a copy of the modified order if any and sworn affidavit to the family court and shall provide a copy of such modified order, if any, and affidavit to the petitioner; provided, however, that if the modified order and affidavit are transmitted to the family court by facsimile or other electronic means, the original copy of such modified order and affidavit shall be forwarded to the family court immediately thereafter. Any modified temporary order of protection or order of protection issued pursuant to this subdivision shall be issued to the respondent, and copies shall be filed as provided in subdivisions six and eight of section 530.12 of the criminal procedure law for orders of protection issued pursuant to such section.

§154-e. Orders of protection; filing and enforcement of out-of-state orders.
A valid order of protection or temporary order of protection issued by a court of competent jurisdiction in another state, territorial or tribal jurisdiction shall be accorded full faith and credit and enforced under article eight of this act as if it were issued by a court within the state for as long as the order remains in effect in the issuing jurisdiction in accordance with sections two thousand two hundred sixty-five and two thousand two hundred sixty-six of title eighteen of the United States Code.
1. An order issued by a court of competent jurisdiction in another state, territorial or tribal jurisdiction shall be deemed valid if:
a. the issuing court had personal jurisdiction over the parties and over the subject matter under the law of the issuing jurisdiction;
b. the person against whom the order was issued had reasonable notice and an opportunity to be heard prior to issuance of the order; provided, however, that if the order was a temporary order of protection issued in the absence of such person, that notice had been given and that an opportunity to be heard had been provided within a reasonable period of time after the issuance of the order; and
c. in the case of orders of protection or temporary orders of protection issued against both a petitioner and respondent, the order or portion thereof sought to be enforced was supported by: (i) a pleading requesting such order, including, but not limited to, a petition, cross-petition or counterclaim; and (ii) a judicial finding that the requesting party is entitled to the issuance of the order which may result from a judicial finding of fact, judicial acceptance of an admission by the party against whom the order was issued or judicial finding that the party against whom the order was issued had given knowing, intelligent and voluntary consent to its issuance.

2. Notwithstanding the provisions of article fifty-four of the civil practice law and rules, an order of protection or temporary order of protection issued by a court of competent jurisdiction in another state, territorial or tribal jurisdiction, accompanied by a sworn affidavit that upon information and belief such order is in effect as written and has not been vacated or modified, may be filed without fee with the clerk of the family court, who shall transmit information regarding such order to the statewide registry of orders of protection and warrants established pursuant to section two hundred twenty-one-a of the executive law; provided, however, that such filing and registry entry shall not be required for enforcement of the order.

§155. Arrested adult.
1. If an adult respondent is arrested under this act when the family court is not in session, he or she shall be taken to the most accessible magistrate and arraigned. The production of a warrant issued by the family court, a certificate of warrant, a copy or a certificate of the order of protection or temporary order of protection, an order of protection or temporary order of protection, or a record of such warrant or order from the statewide computer registry established pursuant to section two hundred twenty-one-a of the executive law shall be evidence of the filing of an information, petition or sworn affidavit, as provided in section one hundred fifty-four-d of this article. Upon consideration of the bail recommendation, if any, made by the family court and indicated on the warrant or certificate of warrant, the magistrate shall thereupon commit such respondent to the custody of the sheriff, as defined in subdivision thirty-five of section 1.20 of the criminal procedure law, admit to, fix or accept bail, or parole him or her for hearing before the family court, subject to the provisions of subdivision four of section 530.11 of the criminal procedure law concerning arrests upon a violation of an order of protection.
2. If no warrant, order of protection or temporary order of protection has been issued by the family court, whether or not an information or petition has been filed, and an act alleged to be a family offense as defined in section eight hundred twelve of this act is the basis of an arrest, the magistrate shall permit the filing of an information, accusatory instrument or sworn affidavit as provided for in section one hundred fifty-four-d of this article, verified in accordance with subdivision one of section 100.30 of the criminal procedure law, alleging facts in support of a petition pursuant to article eight of this act. The magistrate shall thereupon commit such respondent to the custody of the sheriff, as defined in subdivision thirty-five of section 1.20 of the criminal procedure law, admit to, fix or accept bail, or parole such respondent for hearing before the family court and/or appropriate criminal court.
3. The protected party in whose favor the order of protection or temporary order of protection is issued may not be held to violate an order issued in his or her favor nor may such protected party be arrested for violating such order.

§155-a. Admission to bail.
A desk officer in charge at a police station, county jail or police headquarters, or any of his or her superior officers, may, in such place, take cash bail for his or her appearance before the appropriate court the next morning from any person arrested pursuant to a warrant issued by the family court; provided that such arrest occurs between eleven o'clock in the morning and eight o'clock the next morning, except that in the city of New York bail shall be taken between two o'clock in the afternoon and eight o'clock the next

morning. The amount of such cash bail shall be the amount fixed in the warrant of arrest.

§156. Contempts.

The provisions of the judiciary law relating to civil and criminal contempts shall apply to the family court in any proceeding in which it has jurisdiction under this act or any other law, and a violation of an order of the family court in any such proceeding which directs a party, person, association, agency, institution, partnership or corporation to do an act or refrain from doing an act shall be punishable under such provisions of the judiciary law, unless a specific punishment or other remedy for such violation is provided in this act or any other law.

§157. Interpretation of this part.

If there is any conflict between the application of any provision of this part to any proceeding under this act and any provision of the article of this act governing the proceeding, the article governing the proceeding controls.

§158. Protective custody of material witness; duration.

(a) The family court may place in protective custody a person under sixteen years of age who is a material witness, as provided by law. (b) No order of protective custody under paragraph (a) may extend for a period of more than fourteen days. For good cause shown, the court may renew the order for additional periods of fourteen days, but the total period of protective custody under this part may not exceed forty-two days.

Part 6
General Provisions Concerning Hearings

§161. Days and hours court open; availability of judge.

(a) The days and hours the court is open shall be as provided by rule of court.

(b) For purposes of sections seven hundred twenty-eight and one thousand twenty-two of this act, rules of court may authorize a judge other than a judge of the family court to perform the functions of a family court judge under those sections.

(c) For purposes of subdivision (a) of section four hundred thirty, subdivision (a) of section five hundred fifty, subdivision (a) of section six hundred fifty-five, subdivision (a) of section seven hundred forty, subdivision one of section eight hundred twenty-eight and subdivision (a) of section one thousand twenty-nine of this act, any magistrate is authorized to perform the functions of a family court judge as prescribed in such sections.

§162. Waiting room for children.
So far as possible a waiting room with a competent person in charge shall be provided for the care of children brought to the family court under this act.

§163. Separate hearing when child appears.
Any case under this act in which children are directly involved or appear shall be heard separately and apart from the hearing of cases against adults, and, where practicable, room separate and apart from a regular court room shall be provided for the use of the family court, together with suitable quarters for the use of the judge, probation officers and other employees of the court.

§164. Judicial notice of matters of law; proof of statutes, decrees and decisions of another state or county.
The provisions of the civil practice law and rules and any rules regulating judicial notice and authentication and proof of records shall, unless otherwise prescribed by this act, apply to proceedings under this act to the extent that they are appropriate to the proceedings involved.

§165. Procedure.
(a) Where the method of procedure in any proceeding in which the family court has jurisdiction is not prescribed by this act, the procedure shall be in accord with rules adopted by the administrative board of the judicial conference or, if none has been adopted, with the provisions of the civil practice act to the extent they are suitable to the proceeding involved. Upon the effective date of the CPLR, where the method of procedure in any proceeding in which the family court has jurisdiction is not prescribed, the provisions of the civil practice law and rules shall apply to the extent that they are appropriate to the proceedings involved.

(b) In any proceeding commenced pursuant to the provisions of the social services law in which the family court has exercised jurisdiction, the provisions of articles one, two and eleven of the family court act shall apply to the extent that they do not conflict with the specific provisions of the social services law.

§166. Privacy of records.
The records of any proceeding in the family court shall not be open to indiscriminate public inspection. However, the court in its discretion in any case may permit the inspection of any papers or records. Any duly authorized agency, association, society or institution to which a child is committed may cause an inspection of the record of investigation to be had and may in the discretion of the court obtain a copy of the whole or part of such record.

§167. Effect of personal appearance.
Whenever a person, whether adult or child, to whom a summons shall have been directed shall physically appear before the court on the return day of such summons, it shall be conclusively presumed that the summons was duly served upon such person in accordance with the provisions of this act unless such person or some one in his behalf shall on such return day make objection to the manner of service.

§168. Notice of order of protection.
1. In any case in which an order of protection or temporary order of protection has been made by the family court, the clerk of the court shall issue

a copy of such order to the petitioner and respondent and to any other person affected by the order. The presentation of a copy of an order of protection or temporary order of protection or a warrant or a certificate of warrant to any peace officer, acting pursuant to his special duties, or police officer shall constitute authority for him to arrest a person charged with violating the terms of such order of protection or temporary order of protection and bring such person before the court and, otherwise, so far as lies within his power, to aid in securing the protection such order was intended to afford, provided, however, that any outstanding, unexpired certificate of order of protection or temporary order of protection shall have the same force and effect as a copy of such order or temporary order.

2. A copy of an order of protection or temporary order of protection shall be filed by the clerk of the court with the sheriff's office or police department in the county in which the petitioner resides, or, if the petitioner resides within a city, with the police department of such city. A copy of such order of protection or temporary order of protection may from time to time be filed by the clerk of the court with any other police department or sheriff's office having jurisdiction of the residence, work place and school of anyone intended to be protected by such order. A copy of the order of protection or temporary order of protection may also be filed by the petitioner with any appropriate police department or sheriff's office having jurisdiction. Any subsequent amendment or revocation of such order shall be filed in the same manner as herein provided. Any outstanding, unexpired certificate or order of protection or temporary order of protection shall be filed in the same manner as a copy of an order of protection or temporary order of protection.

3. Any order of protection or temporary order of protection issued by the family court shall bear, in a conspicuous manner, the language, as the case may be, "this order constitutes an order of protection" or "this order constitutes a temporary order of protection", on the front page of said order. The order of protection or temporary order of protection shall also contain the following notice: "This order of protection will remain in effect even if the protected party has, or consents to have, contact or communication with the party against whom the order is issued. This order of protection can only be modified or terminated by the court. The protected party cannot be held to violate this order nor be arrested for violating this order.". The absence of such language shall not affect the validity of such order.

Part 7
Proceeding in Counties Other than Original County

§171. Enforcement or modification of orders in other county.

Except for proceedings for enforcement or modification of an order of probation in cases brought under article three or seven of this act, which shall be subject to the terms of subdivision two of section one hundred seventy-six of this part, a lawful order of the family court in any county may be enforced or modified in that county or in the family court in any other county in which the party affected by the order resides or is found.

§172. Commencement of enforcement and modification proceedings in other county.

An enforcement or modification proceeding commenced in the family court in a county other than that in which the order was made is commenced by a petition alleging that fact in addition to the facts required under this act for enforcement or modification orders. An original or certified copy of the order sought to be enforced or modified shall be attached to the petition.

§173. Transfer of papers to other county.

If the family court in which an enforcement or modification proceeding is brought under this article does not transfer it under section one hundred seventy-four of this part, it shall advise the family court that issued the order sought to be enforced or modified of the commencement of such proceedings and shall request that court to forward to it by electronic or other means a copy of all or any of the papers with respect to the order sought to be enforced or modified. The requested court shall forthwith comply with the request.

§174. Transfer of proceedings to another county.

The family court in a county may for good cause transfer a proceeding to a family court in any other county where the proceeding might have been originated and shall transfer a proceeding laying venue in the wrong county to a family court in any county where the proceeding might have been originated.

§175. Violation of probation in other county.

Except for cases brought under articles three and seven of this act which shall be subject to the terms of subdivision two of section one hundred seventy-six of this part, if an act or omission which constitutes a violation of the terms of probation allegedly occurs in a county other than the one in which the order of probation was made, the family court in either county may hear the allegation of a violation of the terms of probation and proceed in accordance with the provisions of this act.

§176. Inter-county probation.

1. Transfer of probation supervision. Where a person placed on probation resides in another jurisdiction within the state at the time of the order of disposition, the family court which placed him or her on probation may, and, in the case of orders of probation issued under article three or seven of this act, shall transfer probation supervision to the probation department in the jurisdiction in which the person resides. Where, after a probation disposition is pronounced, a probationer relocates to another jurisdiction within the state, the family court which placed him or her on probation may, and, in the case of orders of probation issued under article three or seven of this act, shall transfer probation supervision to the probation department in the jurisdiction of the probationer's new residence. Upon completion of a transfer of probation supervision as authorized pursuant to this subdivision, the probation department in

the receiving jurisdiction shall assume all powers and duties of the probation department in the jurisdiction of the family court which placed the probationer on probation. Any transfer under this subdivision must be in accordance with rules adopted by the commissioner of the division of criminal justice services.

2. For all cases brought under article three or seven of this act, where probation supervision has been transferred under subdivision one of this section, the family court in the receiving jurisdiction shall hear any proceedings to enforce or modify the order of probation, unless the receiving family court determines that there is good cause to return the proceeding to the sending family court for adjudication, in which case the proceeding shall be returned to the sending family court for adjudication.

3. For the purpose of this section, "jurisdiction" shall mean a county or the city of New York.

ARTICLE 2
Administration, Medical Examinations, Attorneys for Children, Auxiliary Services

Part 1
Administration

§211. Administration and operation of family court.
The administration and operation of the family court shall be in accord with article seven-a of the judiciary law.

§212. Rules of court.
(a) The administrative board of the judicial conference shall prepare rules of court when required by this act and may prepare rules of court when authorized by this act. To the extent practicable, any rule of court prepared under this act shall apply uniformly throughout the state of New York.

(b) In exercising its responsibilities under paragraph (a), the administrative board may designate a committee of judges of the family court and of such consultants as it deems appropriate to draft rules for approval by the administrative board.

§213. Reports to administrative board, legislature and governor.
(a) In addition to any reports required by the administrative board of the judicial conference under article seven-a of the judiciary law, the administrative board shall, as soon as practicable, require the family court in each county

to include in its reports to the administrative board and the administrative board shall include in its annual report to the legislature information, by county, showing:

(i) the number of children temporarily removed under section one thousand twenty-two before the filing of a petition, the number of children temporarily removed without court order under section ten hundred twenty-four of this act, and the period of time between such removal and the filing of a petition;

(ii) the number of children temporarily removed under section one thousand twenty-seven after the filing of a petition and the period of time that passed after such removal until its termination;

(iii) the number of placements under section one thousand fifty-two by person, agency or institution in which the placement is made, and the number of orders extending the period of placement;

(iv) the number of children released and the number detained under sections seven hundred twenty-eight and 307.4;

(v) the number of alleged juvenile delinquents released and the number detained under section 320.5 and the number of alleged persons in need of supervision released and detained under section seven hundred thirty-nine, and the duration of the detention in both groups;

(vi) the number of adjudicated juvenile delinquents placed under section 353.3 and the number of adjudicated persons in need of supervision placed under section seven hundred fifty-six by person, agency or institution in which the placement is made, and the number of orders extending the period of placement;

(vii) the number of adjudicated juvenile delinquents put on probation under section 353.2 and the number of adjudicated persons in need of supervision put on probation under section seven hundred fifty-seven and the duration of such probation;

(viii) the number, nature and disposition of cases involving child abuse under article ten of this act, including total number of new cases, their nature, whether heard by the child abuse part, the age and sex of the children involved, the type of petitioner, the number of children temporarily removed both before and after the filing of a petition, the length of time and number of adjournments between the filing of a petition and the fact-finding hearing, the number of cases that are dismissed, withdrawn, sustained and admitted to, the length of time and number of adjournments between the fact-finding hearing and the dispositional hearing, and the final disposition of such cases.

(b) Rules of court shall as soon as practicable implement this section by prescribing appropriate forms for reports and may require such additional information as may be appropriate. The administrative board of the judicial conference may request the state department of corrections and community supervision and the state department of social welfare to assist it in the preparation and processing of reports under this section, and those departments, when so requested, shall render such assistance as is possible.

§214. Chief administrator to prescribe forms; electronic filing in family court.

(a) The chief administrator of the courts shall promulgate a uniform, statewide petition for adoption and may prescribe such other forms as may be proper for the efficient and just administration of this act, including forms for petitions, summons, warrants, subpoenas, undertakings, and orders authorized by this act.

(b) (i) Notwithstanding any other provision of law, the chief administrator, with the approval of the administrative board of the courts, may promulgate rules authorizing a program in the use of electronic means ("e-filing") in the family court for: (1) the origination of proceedings in such court, and (2) the filing and service of papers in pending proceedings.

(ii) (1) Except as otherwise provided in this paragraph, participation in this program shall be strictly voluntary and will take place only upon consent of all parties in the proceeding; except that failure of a party or other person who is entitled to notice of the proceedings to consent to participation shall not bar any other party from filing and serving papers by electronic means upon the court or any other party or person entitled to receive notice of such proceeding who has consented to participation. Filing a petition with the court by electronic means for the purpose of originating a proceeding shall not require the consent of any other party; provided, however, that upon such filing, a party to such proceeding and any attorney for such person shall be permitted to immediately review and obtain copies of such documents and papers if such person or attorney would have been authorized by law to review or obtain copies of such documents and papers if they had been filed with the court in paper form.

No party shall be compelled, directly or indirectly, to participate in e-filing. All parties shall be notified clearly, in plain language, about their options to participate in e-filing. Where a party is not represented by counsel, the clerk shall explain such party's options for electronic filing in plain language, including the option for expedited processing, and shall inquire whether he or she wishes to participate, provided however the unrepresented litigant may participate in the program only upon his or her request, which shall be documented in the case file, after said party has been presented with sufficient information in plain language concerning the program.

(2) In the rules promulgated pursuant to paragraph (i) of this subdivision, the chief administrator may eliminate the requirement of consent to participation in this program in family courts of not more than six counties for:

(A) the filing with the court of a petition originating a juvenile delinquency proceeding under article three of this act by a presentment agency as defined in section 301.2 of such act;

(B) the filing with the court of a petition originating in a proceeding to determine abuse or neglect pursuant to article ten of this act by a child protective agency, as defined in section one thousand twelve of such act; and

(C) the filing and service of papers in proceedings specified in clauses (A) and (B) of this subparagraph where, pursuant to such clauses, such proceedings were originated in the court by electronic filing.

Notwithstanding the foregoing, the chief administrator shall not eliminate the requirement of consent to participation without the consent of each authorized presentment agency, child protective agency of an affected county, the family court bar providing representation to parents, and the family court bar providing representation to children (as represented by the head of each legal services organization representing parents and/or children, the head of each public defender organization, and president of the local bar association as applicable) in any county in which such elimination shall apply.

Notwithstanding the foregoing, the chief administrator may not eliminate the requirement of consent to participation in a county hereunder until he or she shall have provided all persons or organizations, or their representative or representatives, who regularly appear in proceedings in the family court of such county, in which proceedings the requirement of consent is to be eliminated, with reasonable notice and an opportunity to submit comments with respect thereto and shall have given due consideration to all such comments, nor until he or she shall have consulted with the members of the advisory committee continued pursuant to subparagraph (vi) of paragraph (t) of subdivision two of section two hundred twelve of the judiciary law.

(c) Where the chief administrator eliminates the requirement of consent as provided in subparagraph two of paragraph (ii) of subdivision (b) of this section, he or she shall afford counsel the opportunity to opt out of the program, via presentation of a prescribed form to be filed with the clerk of the court where the proceeding is pending. Said form shall permit an attorney to opt out of participation in the program under any of the following circumstances, in which event, he or she will not be compelled to participate:

(i) Where the attorney certifies in good faith that he or she lacks the computer hardware and/or connection to the internet and/or scanner or other device by which documents may be converted to an electronic format; or

(ii) Where the attorney certifies in good faith that he or she lacks the requisite knowledge in the operation of such computers and/or scanners necessary to participate. For the purposes of this paragraph, the knowledge of any employee of an attorney, or any employee of the attorney's law firm, office or business who is subject to such attorney's direction, shall be imputed to the attorney.

Notwithstanding the foregoing provisions of this paragraph: (A) where a party or a person entitled to notice of the proceedings is not represented by counsel, the court shall explain such party's options for electronic filing in plain language, including the option for expedited processing, and shall inquire whether he or she wishes to participate, provided however, the unrepresented litigant may participate in the program only upon his or her request, which shall be documented in the case file, after said party has been presented with sufficient information in plain language concerning the program; (B) a party who is not represented by counsel who has chosen to participate in the program shall be afforded the opportunity to opt out of the program for any reason via presentation of a prescribed form to be filed with the clerk of the court where the proceeding is pending; and (C) a court may exempt any attorney from being required to participate in the program upon application for such exemption, showing good cause therefor.

(d) For purposes of this section, "electronic means" shall be as defined in subdivision (f) of rule twenty-one hundred three of the civil practice law and rules.

(e) Notwithstanding any provision of this chapter, no paper or document that is filed by electronic means in a proceeding in family court shall be available for public inspection on-line. Subject to the provisions of existing laws governing the sealing and confidentiality of court records, nothing herein shall prevent the unified court system from sharing statistical information that does not include any papers or documents filed with the action.

(f) Nothing in this section shall affect or change any existing laws governing the sealing and confidentiality of court records in family court proceedings or access to court records by the parties to such proceedings, nor shall this section be construed to compel a party to file a sealed document by electronic means.

(g) Nothing in this section shall affect or change existing laws governing service of process, nor shall this section be construed to abrogate existing personal service requirements as set forth in this act and the civil practice law and rules.

§215. Continuance in office of non-judicial personnel.

(a) Officers and employees of the domestic relations court of the city of New York shall, to the extent practicable, be transferred to the family court in counties within the city of New York in accord with article seven-a of the judiciary law. To the extent practicable, those assigned to a division of the domestic relations court located in a particular county shall be assigned to the family court in that county.

(b) Officers and employees of the children's court in each county outside the city of New York shall, to the extent practicable, be transferred to the family court in their respective counties in accord with article seven-a of the judiciary law.

§216-a. Clerk of court.

There shall be a clerk of court for the family court in each county. The clerk of court shall keep the court records and seal and have such other responsibilities as may be provided in accord with article seven-a of the judiciary law.

§216-b. Petition forms.

The clerk of the court shall give petition forms to any person requesting them.

§216-c. Preparation of petitions.

(a) Whenever a petitioner is not represented by counsel, any person who assists in the preparation of a petition shall include all allegations presented by the petitioner.

(b) No clerk of the court or probation officer may prevent any person who wishes to file a petition from having such petition filed with the court immediately.

(c) If there is a question regarding whether or not the family court has jurisdiction of the matter, the petition shall be prepared and the clerk shall file the petition and refer the petition to the court for determination of all issues including the jurisdictional question.

(d) This section shall not be applicable to juvenile delinquency proceedings.

§217. Orders; filing and service.

1. An order shall be in writing and signed with the judge's signature or initials by the judge who made it. The form of such order shall be promulgated by the chief administrator of the courts pursuant to section two hundred fourteen of this article.

2. The original of an order of the family court shall be filed with the clerk of the family court in the county in which the family court making the order is located.

3. The court shall file or direct the filing of an order within twenty days of the decision of the court. If the court directs that such order be settled on notice, such twenty day period shall commence on the date on which such order is settled.

4. The court shall direct service of a copy of an order in whatever manner it deems appropriate. If the court makes no direction, the applicable provisions of the civil practice law and rules shall apply. Where the clerk of the court is directed to serve such order, the clerk shall note in the court record the manner and date of service and the person to whom such order was served.

Part 2
Support Bureau; Duties to Cooperate

§221. Support collection unit; local probation department.

1. When referred to in this chapter, the support collection unit designated by the appropriate social services district, shall be deemed to refer to any support collection unit established by a social services district pursuant to the provisions of section one hundred eleven-h of the social services law, or to a local public agency, where such agency is responsible for the performance of all the functions of the support collection unit pursuant to an agreement under the provisions of section one hundred eleven-h of the social services law.

2. The local probation department shall be responsible for providing services to the family court, in accordance with the provisions of subdivision six of section two hundred fifty-six of the executive law.

§228. Cooperation by banks and other fiduciary institutions.

Banks and other fiduciary institutions are authorized and required to report to the court, when so requested, full information relative to any fund therein deposited by a petitioner or respondent in a proceeding under articles four or five of this act.

§229. Cooperation by employer.

Employers are authorized and required to report to the court, when so requested, full information as to the earnings of a petitioner or respondent in a proceeding under articles four or five of this act.

Part 3
Medical Examinations and Treatment

§231. Jurisdiction over intellectually disabled children.

If it shall appear to the court that any child within its jurisdiction is intellectually disabled, the court may cause such child to be examined as provided in the mental hygiene law and if found to be intellectually disabled as therein defined, may commit such child in accordance with the provisions of such law.   (Eff.5/25/16,Ch.37,L.2016)

§232. Jurisdiction over children with physical disabilities.

(a) The family court has jurisdiction over children with physical disabilities.

(b) "Child with physical disabilities" means a person under twenty-one years of age who, by reason of a physical disability, whether congenital or acquired by accident, injury or disease, is or may be expected to be totally or partially incapacitated for education or for remunerative occupation, as provided in the education law, or has a physical disability, as provided in section two thousand five hundred eighty-one of the public health law.

(c) (1) Whenever a parent or other person who has been ordered to contribute to the cost of medical service authorized pursuant to section two thousand five hundred eighty-two of the public health law refuses to or fails to make such contribution, the health commissioner or the medical director of the program for children with physical disabilities, as the case may be, may institute a proceeding in the family court to compel such contribution. In any case where an order has been granted pursuant to section 556-18.0 or section 17-121 of the administrative code of the city of New York the department of health, under the conditions specified in such section, may institute a proceeding in the family court to compel the parents of a child for whom care, treatment, appliances or devices have been ordered pursuant to such section, or other persons legally chargeable with the support of such child, to contribute such portion of the expense of such care, treatment, appliances or devices as may be just, by payments in installments or otherwise.

(2) A parent or other person who has been ordered by the commissioner of health of a county or part-county health district, the medical director of a county program for children with physical disabilities, or the department of health of the city of New York, to contribute to the cost of medical service authorized under section two thousand five hundred eighty-two of the public health law, may petition the family court to review such order and determine the extent, if any, of his financial liability. In any such proceeding, the court may by order require such parent or other person to pay part or all of the expense of such service in a lump sum or in such weekly or monthly installments as the court may decide.

§233. Medical services.
Whenever a child within the jurisdiction of the court appears to the court to be in need of medical, surgical, therapeutic, or hospital care or treatment, a suitable order may be made therefor.

§234. Compensation and liability for support and care in counties outside the city of New York.
(a) Whenever a child is detained, placed or committed under the provisions of this act to an authorized agency, or to any person other than his parent and is retained in accordance with the rules of the state board of social welfare, compensation for his care and maintenance shall be a charge on the county. The compensation paid by the county for care and maintenance of the child may be charged back to a city or town in the county in accordance with and to the extent permitted by the provisions of the social services law. All bills for such care and maintenance to be paid from public funds shall be paid by the county treasurer from moneys appropriated for public assistance and care in the county social services district by warrant of the commissioner of social services.

(b) The court may, after issuance and service of an order to show cause upon the parent or other person having the duty under the law to support such child, adjudge that such parent or other person shall pay to the court such sum as will cover in whole or in part the support of such child, and willful failure to pay such sum may, in the discretion of the court, be punished as for a criminal contempt of court. When a person liable to such payment on order, as herein provided, is before the court in the proceeding relating to the commitment or placement, a formal order to show cause may be dispensed with in the discretion of the court.

(c) (i) The social services district from which the detention, placement or commitment is made shall be entitled to be reimbursed by another social services district for its expenditures for care and maintenance of the child, if, and to the extent that, it would have been entitled to be reimbursed therefor by such other district had the care been provided under and pursuant to the provisions of the social services law. The commissioner of social services of the social services district from which the commitment was made may enforce repayment from the other social services district in accordance with the provisions of the social services law.

(ii) In accordance with the provisions of the social services law and the rules and regulations of the state department of social services relating to state charges, and from funds available to the state department of social services therefor, the state shall reimburse the social services district for the full cost of care and maintenance of the child, in the event the child is a state charge as defined by the social services law.

§235. **Compensation and liability for support and care in counties within the city of New York.**

(a) Upon the detention, placement or commitment of a child by the family court in a county within the city of New York to a public or private institution other than a shelter maintained and conducted by a society for the prevention of cruelty to children, the department of social services of the city of New York shall investigate the ability of the parent of the child, or other person legally chargeable, to contribute in whole or in part to the expense incurred by the city of New York on account of the maintenance of such child.

(b) If in the opinion of the department of social services such parent or legal custodian is able to contribute in whole or in part the commissioner of social services shall thereupon institute a proceeding in the family court to compel such parent or person legally chargeable to contribute such portion of such expense on account of maintenance of such child as shall be proper and just.

§236. **Powers of the family court with regard to certain handicapped children.**

1. This section shall apply for:

(a) services provided to children with handicapping conditions as defined in subdivision one of section forty-four hundred one of the education law who were not eligible, prior to September first, nineteen hundred eighty-six, for educational services during July and August pursuant to article seventy-three, eighty-five, eighty-seven, eighty-eight or eighty-nine of the education law;

(b) for services provided to children with handicapping conditions who meet all the criteria of subdivision one of section forty-four hundred one of the education law except that such children are under the age of five and are not entitled to attend public schools without the payment of tuition pursuant to section thirty-two hundred two of the education law and that such children are also not eligible for educational services pursuant to article seventy-three, eighty-five, eighty-seven, eighty-eight or eighty-nine of the education law;

(c) for services provided to children with handicapping conditions who meet all the criteria of subdivision one of section forty-four hundred one of the education law except that such children are five years of age or under and: (i) are first eligible to attend public school in the nineteen hundred eighty-seven--eighty-eight or the nineteen hundred eighty-eight--eighty-nine school year but are not eligible for educational services pursuant to the education law during the months of July and August, nineteen hundred eighty-seven or nineteen hundred eighty-eight, or (ii) are not eligible to commence a state appointment pursuant to article eighty-five, eighty-seven or eighty-eight of the education law during the months of July and August;

(d) for services provided during the nineteen hundred eighty-nine--ninety school year, pursuant to the provisions of subdivision six of section forty-four hundred ten of the education law;

(e) for services provided prior to July first, nineteen hundred ninety-one to children with handicapping conditions who met the criteria of subdivision one of section forty-four hundred one of the education law except that such children were three years of age or under and (i) were not eligible for services pursuant to section forty-four hundred ten of such law, or (ii) were not eligible for services through a state appointment pursuant to article eighty-five, eighty-seven or eighty-eight of such law; and

**(f) for services provided on or after July first, nineteen hundred ninety-one to children with handicapping conditions who meet the criteria of subdivision one of section forty-four hundred one of the education law except that such children are three years of age or under and (i) are not eligible for services pursuant to section forty-four hundred ten of such law, or who are first eligible for services pursuant to such section whose parents or persons in parental relationship elect to have them continue to be eligible to receive services pursuant to this section through August thirty-first of the calendar year in which the child turns three or (ii) are not eligible for services through a state appointment pursuant to article eighty-five, eighty-seven or eighty-eight of such law.

*(f) for services provided to children with handicapping conditions who meet the criteria of subdivision one of section forty-four hundred one of the education law and who, on or before June thirtieth, nineteen hundred ninety-three, are receiving services or who, as of July first, nineteen hundred ninety-three, have petitioned for services pursuant to this section prior to such date and which complete petition has not been denied prior to October first, nineteen hundred ninety-three and whose parent has elected to continue the provision of such services until the child is no longer an eligible child under title II-A of article twenty-five of the public health law or is eligible for services pursuant to section forty-four hundred ten of the education law.

(g) Notwithstanding any other provision of this section, this section shall not apply for services to children who were not receiving services prior to July first, nineteen hundred ninety-three, or who, as of July first, nineteen hundred ninety-three, have petitioned for services prior to July first, nineteen hundred ninety-three and whose complete petition has been denied prior to October first, nineteen hundred ninety-three.

2. Whenever such a child within the jurisdiction of the court pursuant to this section appears to the court to be in need of special educational services as provided in section forty-four hundred six of the education law, including transportation, tuition or maintenance, a suitable order may be made for the education of such child in its home, a hospital, or other suitable institution, and the expenses thereof, when approved by the court and duly audited, shall be a charge upon the county or the city of New York thereof wherein the child is domiciled at the time application is made to the court for such order.

There are two subdivisions "(f)."

3. (a) Every such order for services to be provided after September first, nineteen hundred eighty-six which provides for the transportation of a child shall further require that such transportation shall be provided by the county or the city of New York, as the case may be, and, that the city of New York may delegate the authority to provide such transportation to the board of education or the city school district of such city.

(b) Such order shall further require that such transportation shall be provided within thirty days of the issuance of such order, and, shall be provided as part of a municipal cooperation agreement, as part of a contract awarded to the lowest responsible bidder in accordance with the provisions of section one hundred three of the general municipal law, or as part of a contract awarded pursuant to an evaluation of proposals to the extent authorized by paragraphs e and f of subdivision fourteen of section three hundred five of the education law and otherwise consistent with the provisions of this subdivision, and that buses and vehicles utilized in the performance of such contract shall meet the minimum requirements for school age children as established by the commissioner of transportation.

Part 4
Attorneys for Children

§241. Findings and purpose.
This act declares that minors who are the subject of family court proceedings or appeals in proceedings originating in the family court should be represented by counsel of their own choosing or by assigned counsel. This declaration is based on a finding that counsel is often indispensable to a practical realization of due process of law and may be helpful in making reasoned determinations of fact and proper orders of disposition. This part establishes a system of attorneys for children who often require the assistance of counsel to help protect their interests and to help them express their wishes to the court. Nothing in this act is intended to preclude any other interested person from appearing by counsel.

§242. Attorney for the child.
As used in this act, "attorney for the child" refers to an attorney admitted to practice law in the state of New York and designated under this part to represent minors pursuant to section two hundred forty-nine of this act.

§243. Designation.
(a) The office of court administration may enter into an agreement with a legal aid society for the society to provide attorneys to represent children in the family court or appeals in proceedings originating in the family court in a county having a legal aid society.

(b) The appellate division of the supreme court for the judicial department in which a county is located may, upon determining that a county panel designated pursuant to subdivision (c) of this section is not sufficient to afford appropriate services of attorneys for children, enter into an agreement, subject to regulations as may be promulgated by the administrative board of the courts, with any qualified attorney or attorneys to serve as attorneys for children for the family court or appeals in proceedings originating in the family court in that county.

(c) The appellate division of the supreme court for the judicial department in which a county is located may designate a panel of attorneys for children for the family court and appeals in proceedings originating in the family court in that county, subject to the approval of the administrative board of the courts. For this purpose, such appellate division may invite a bar association to recommend qualified persons for consideration by the appellate division in making its designation, subject to standards as may be promulgated by such administrative board.

§244. Duration of designation.

(a) An agreement pursuant to subdivision (a) of section two hundred forty-three of this chapter may be terminated by the office of court administration by serving notice on the society sixty days prior to the effective date of the termination.

(b) No designations pursuant to subdivision (c) of section two hundred forty-three may be for a term of more than one year, but successive designations may be made. The appellate division proceeding pursuant to subdivision (c) of section two hundred forty-three, may at any time increase or decrease the number of attorneys for children designated in any county and may rescind any designation at any time, subject to the approval of the office of court administration.

§245. Compensation.

(a) If the office of court administration proceeds pursuant to subdivision (a) of section two hundred forty-three of this chapter, the agreement shall provide that the society shall be reimbursed on a cost basis for services rendered under the agreement. The agreement shall contain a general plan for the organization and operation of the program for the provision of attorneys for children by the respective legal aid society, approved by the administrative board, and the office of court administration may require such reports as it deems necessary from the society.

(b) If an appellate division proceeds pursuant to subdivision (b) of such section two hundred forty-three, the agreement may provide that the attorney or attorneys shall be reimbursed on a cost basis for services rendered under the agreement. The agreement shall contain a general plan for the organization and operation of the program for the provision of attorneys for children by the respective attorney or attorneys, and the appellate division may require such reports as it deems necessary from the attorney or attorneys.

(c) If an appellate division proceeds pursuant to subdivision (c) of such section two hundred forty-three, attorneys for children shall be compensated and allowed expenses and disbursements in the same amounts established by subdivision three of section thirty-five of the judiciary law.

§246. Supervision by administrative board.

The administrative board of the judicial conference may prescribe standards for the exercise of the powers granted to the appellate divisions under this part and may require such reports as it deems desirable.

§248. Appropriations.

The costs of attorneys for children under section two hundred forty-five shall be payable by the state of New York within the amounts appropriated therefor.

§249. Appointment of attorney for child.

*(a) In a proceeding under article three, seven, ten, ten-A or ten-C of this act or where a revocation of an adoption consent is opposed under section one hundred fifteen-b of the domestic relations law or in any proceeding under section three hundred fifty-eight-a, three hundred eighty-three-c, three hundred eighty-four or three hundred eighty-four-b of the social services law or when a minor is sought to be placed in protective custody under section one hundred fifty-eight of this act or in any proceeding where a minor is detained under or governed by the interstate compact for juveniles established pursuant to section five hundred one-e of the executive law, the family court shall appoint an attorney to represent a minor who is the subject of the proceeding or who is sought to be placed in protective custody, if independent legal representation is not available to such minor. In any proceeding to extend or continue the placement of a juvenile delinquent or person in need of supervision pursuant to section seven hundred fifty-six or 353.3 of this act or any proceeding to extend or continue a commitment to the custody of the commissioner of mental health or the commissioner of people with developmental disabilities pursuant to section 322.2 of this act, the court shall not permit the respondent to waive the right to be represented by counsel chosen by the respondent, respondent's parent, or other person legally responsible for the respondent's care, or by assigned counsel. In any proceeding under article ten-B of this act, the family court shall appoint an attorney to represent a youth, under the age of twenty-one, who is the subject of the proceeding, if independent legal representation is not available to such youth. In any other proceeding in which the court has jurisdiction, the court may appoint an attorney to represent the child, when, in the opinion of the family court judge, such representation will serve the purposes of this act, if independent legal counsel is not available to the child. The family court on its own motion may make such appointment.

(Effective until 9/1/20,Ch.195,L.2015)

*(a) In a proceeding under article three, seven, ten, ten-A or ten-C of this act or where a revocation of an adoption consent is opposed under section one hundred fifteen-b of the domestic relations law or in any proceeding under section three hundred fifty-eight-a, three hundred eighty-three-c, three hundred eighty-four or three hundred eighty-four-b of the social services law or when a minor is sought to be placed in protective custody under section one hundred fifty-eight of this act, the family court shall appoint an attorney to represent a minor who is the subject of the proceeding or who is sought to be placed in protective custody, if independent legal representation is not available to such minor. In any proceeding to extend or continue the placement of a juvenile delinquent or person in need of supervision pursuant to section seven hundred fifty-six or 353.3 of this act or any proceeding to extend or continue a commitment to the custody of the commissioner of mental health or the commissioner

of mental retardation and developmental disabilities pursuant to section 322.2 of this act, the court shall not permit the respondent to waive the right to be represented by counsel chosen by the respondent, respondent's parent, or other person legally responsible for the respondent's care, or by assigned counsel. In any proceeding under article ten-B of this act, the family court shall appoint an attorney to represent a youth, under the age of twenty-one, who is the subject of the proceeding, if independent legal representation is not available to such youth. In any other proceeding in which the court has jurisdiction, the court may appoint an attorney to represent the child, when, in the opinion of the family court judge, such representation will serve the purposes of this act, if independent legal counsel is not available to the child. The family court on its own motion may make such appointment.   *(Eff.9/1/20,Ch.195,L.2015)*

(b) In making an appointment of an attorney for a child pursuant to this section, the court shall, to the extent practicable and appropriate, appoint the same attorney who has previously represented the child. Notwithstanding any other provision of law, in a proceeding under article three of this act following an order of removal made pursuant to article seven hundred twenty-five of the criminal procedure law, the court shall, wherever practicable, appoint the same counsel who represented the juvenile offender in the criminal proceedings.

§249-a.   Waiver of counsel.

A minor who is a subject of a juvenile delinquency or person in need of supervision proceeding *or in any proceeding where a minor is detained under or governed by the interstate compact for juveniles established pursuant to section five hundred one-e of the executive law* shall be presumed to lack the requisite knowledge and maturity to waive the appointment of an attorney. This presumption may be rebutted only after an attorney has been appointed and the court determines after a hearing at which the attorney appears and participates and upon clear and convincing evidence that (a) the minor understands the nature of the charges, the possible dispositional alternatives and the possible defenses to the charges, (b) the minor possesses the maturity, knowledge and intelligence necessary to conduct his or her own defense, and (c) waiver is in the best interest of the minor.   *(Material in Italics Expires 9/1/20,Ch.195,L.2015)*

§249-b.   Rules of court.

(a) The chief administrator of the courts, pursuant to paragraph (e) of subdivision two of section two hundred twelve of the judiciary law, shall promulgate court rules for attorneys for children. Such court rules shall:

1. prescribe workload standards for attorneys for children, including maximum numbers of children who can be represented at any given time, in order to ensure that children receive effective assistance of counsel comporting with legal and ethical mandates, the complexity of the proceedings affecting each client to which the attorney is assigned, and the nature of the court appearance likely to be required for each individual client; and

2. provide for the development of training programs with the input of and in consultation with the state office for the prevention of domestic violence. Such training programs must include the dynamics of domestic violence and its effect on victims and on children, and the relationship between such dynamics and the issues considered by the court, including, but not limited to, custody, visitation and child support. Such training programs along with the providers of such training must be approved by the office of court administration following consultation with and input from the state office for the prevention of domestic violence; and

3. require that all attorneys for children, including new and veteran attorneys, receive initial and ongoing training as provided for in this section.

(b) Appointments of attorneys for children under section two hundred forty-nine of this part shall be in conformity with the rules.

Part 5
Auxiliary Services

§251. Medical examinations.

(a) After the filing of a petition under this act over which the family court appears to have jurisdiction, the court may order any person within its jurisdiction and the parent or other person legally responsible for the care of any child within its jurisdiction to be examined by a physician, psychiatrist or psychologist appointed or designated for that purpose by the court when such an examination will serve the purposes of this act, the court may remand any such person for physical or psychiatric examination to, or direct such person to appear for such examination at:

(1) the department of health of the city of New York, if the court is located in a county within the city of New York, or

(2) a hospital maintained by the county in which the court is located, if the court is in a county outside the city of New York, or

(3) a hospital maintained by the state of New York, or

(4) a qualified private institution approved for such purpose by the local social services department.

Provided, however, that, outside of the city of New York, if the court shall order a psychiatric examination of any such person, the court may direct the director of an institution in the department of mental hygiene serving the institutional district in which the court is located to cause such examination to be made. Such director shall be afforded an opportunity to be heard before the court makes any such direction. The director may designate a member of the staff of the institution or any psychiatrist in the state to make the examination. The psychiatrist shall forthwith examine such person. The examination may be made in the place where the person may be or the court may remand such person to, or otherwise direct that such person appear at, such institution or to a hospital or other place for such examination. During the time such person is at such institution for examination, the director may administer or cause to be administered to such person such psychiatric, medical or other therapeutic treatment as in the director's discretion should be administered. The chief administrator of the courts shall prescribe the form of an order for examination. Upon completion of the examination, the director shall transmit to the court the report of the psychiatrist who conducted the examination.

(b) Except for examinations conducted pursuant to section 322.1 of this act where the family court determines that an inpatient examination is necessary, or those ordered after a fact-finding hearing has been completed under article three or seven of this act and the court determines according to the criteria in subdivision three of section 320.5 or subdivision (a) of section seven hundred thirty-nine of this act that the child should be detained pending disposition, or unless otherwise consented to by the adult to be examined or by the attorney representing the respondent, all examinations pursuant to this section shall be conducted on an outpatient basis. An order for remand after a fact-finding hearing under article three or seven of this act shall include findings on the record supporting the need for examination in a residential facility and a determination that it is the most appropriate facility. Remands for examinations shall be for a period determined by the facility, which shall not exceed thirty days, except that, upon motion by the person detained on its own motion, the court may, for good cause shown, terminate the remand at any time.

(c) Nothing in this section shall preclude the issuance of an order by the family court pursuant to section 9.43 of the mental hygiene law for emergency admission for immediate care, observation and treatment of a person before the court or pursuant to section twenty-one hundred twenty of the public health law for commitment for care and maintenance of a person before the court.

§252. Probation service.

(a) The family court in each county shall have a probation service. This service may include volunteer probation officers when necessary, provided they have the qualifications required of salaried officers, but no such volunteer probation officer shall be a chief probation officer or receive pay from public funds for his services.

(b) The methods, organization, and responsibilities of the probation service shall be defined by rule of court, which shall not be inconsistent with any provision of law.

(c) When there is a sufficient number of probation officers of the same religious faith as that of a child to be placed on probation, the child shall be placed on probation with a probation officer of the same religious faith as that of the child.

(d) The probation service shall be available to assist the court and participate in all proceedings under this act, including supervision of the family or individual family members pending final disposition of a child protection proceeding under article ten.

*§252-a. Fees.

(a) Notwithstanding any other provision of law, every county, including the city of New York, may adopt a local law authorizing its probation department which is ordered to conduct an investigation pursuant to section six hundred fifty-three of this act, to be entitled to a fee of not less than fifty dollars and not more than five hundred dollars from the parties in such proceeding for performing such investigation. Such fee shall be based on the party's ability to pay the fee and the schedule for payment shall be fixed by the court issuing the order for investigation, pursuant to the guidelines issued by the office of probation and correctional alternatives, and may in the discretion of the court be waived when the parties lack sufficient means to pay the fee. The court shall apportion the fee between the parties based upon the respective financial circumstances of the parties and the equities of the case.

(b) Fees pursuant to this section shall be paid directly to the local probation department to be retained and utilized for local probation services, and shall not be considered by the office of probation and correctional alternatives when determining state aid pursuant to section two hundred forty-six of the executive law.   *(Expires 9/1/17,Ch.55.L.2015)

§253. Auxiliary services.

The family court in any county shall have such other auxiliary services as will serve the purposes of this act and as are within its authorized appropriation.

§254. Presentation by corporation counsel, county attorney or district attorney.

(a) The family court or the appropriate appellate division of the supreme court may request the corporation counsel of the city of New York or the appropriate county attorney to present the case in support of the petition when, in the opinion of the family court or appellate division such presentation will serve the purposes of the act. When so requested, the corporation counsel or county attorney shall present the case in support of the petition and assist in all stages of the proceedings, including appeals in connection therewith. Nothing herein shall be deemed to affect the provisions of section five hundred thirty-five of this chapter.

(b) In all cases involving abuse, the corporation counsel of the city of New York and outside the city of New York, the appropriate district attorney shall be a necessary party to the proceeding.

§254-a. Procedure for district attorney presentation.

1. The county attorney and the district attorney of a county, and the corporation counsel of the city of New York and the district attorney of any county in such city, may enter into an agreement whereby the district attorney shall present the case in support of the petition in which a designated felony act has been alleged.

2. Where such agreement has been entered into, in the case of a respondent who is alleged to have done two or more acts which, if done by an adult, would constitute joinable offenses pursuant to subdivision two of section 200.20 of the criminal procedure law, the district attorney shall present the juvenile delinquency petition with respect to all such acts, notwithstanding less than all of such acts constitute designated felony acts.

3. Where such agreement has been entered into, the district attorney shall also present petitions which have been filed against all respondents who are accused of participating, in concert, in the commission of a designated felony act, notwithstanding less than all of such respondents are charged with having committed a designated felony act. Such petition shall be adjudicated in a single fact-finding hearing, unless the court orders separate fact-finding hearings for good cause shown.

4. When presenting cases the district attorney shall have the same powers under this act as the corporation counsel or county attorney and shall assist in all stages of the proceedings including appeals in connection therewith.

5. Such agreement shall be subject to the approval in the city of New York of its mayor, and outside the city of the respective county executive, if there be one, otherwise, the board of supervisors.

6. The district attorney may elect to present the petition against a respondent, who was the defendant in a criminal proceeding removed to the family court pursuant to article seven hundred twenty-five of the criminal

procedure law, when a proceeding under article three is commenced as a result of the order of removal.

§255. Cooperation of officials and organizations.

It is hereby made the duty of, and the family court or a judge thereof may order, any state, county, municipal and school district officer and employee to render such assistance and cooperation as shall be within his legal authority, as may be required, to further the objects of this act provided, however, that with respect to a school district an order made pursuant to this section shall be limited to requiring the performance of the duties imposed upon the school district and board of education or trustees thereof pursuant to sections four thousand five, forty-four hundred two and forty-four hundred four of the education law, to review, evaluate, recommend, and determine the appropriate special services or programs necessary to meet the needs of a handicapped child, but shall not require the provisions of a specific special service or program, and such order shall be made only where it appears to the court or judge that adequate administrative procedure to require the performance of such duties is not available. It is hereby made the duty of and the family court or judge thereof may order, any agency or other institution to render such information, assistance and cooperation as shall be within its legal authority concerning a child who is or shall be under its care, treatment, supervision or custody as may be required to further the objects of this act. The court is authorized to seek the cooperation of, and may use, within its authorized appropriation therefor, the services of all societies or organizations, public or private, having for their object the protection or aid of children or families, including family counselling services, to the end that the court may be assisted in every reasonable way to give the children and families within its jurisdiction such care, protection and assistance as will best enhance their welfare.

§256. Visitation, inspection and supervision by state department of social services or board of social welfare.

Any child placed or committed under order of the court shall be subject to such visitation, inspection and supervision as the state board of social welfare or department of social services shall provide for or require.

Part 6
Counsel for Indigent Adults in
Family Court Proceedings

Section
261.   Legislative findings and purpose.
262.   Assignment of counsel for indigent persons.

§261. Legislative findings and purpose.

Persons involved in certain family court proceedings may face the infringements of fundamental interests and rights, including the loss of a child's society and the possibility of criminal charges, and therefore have a constitutional right to counsel in such proceedings. Counsel is often indispensable to a practical realization of due process of law and may be helpful to the court in making reasoned determinations of fact and proper orders of disposition. The purpose of this part is to provide a means for implementing the right to assigned counsel for indigent persons in proceedings under this act.

§262. Assignment of counsel for indigent persons.

(a) Each of the persons described below in this subdivision has the right to the assistance of counsel. When such person first appears in court, the judge shall advise such person before proceeding that he or she has the right to be represented by counsel of his or her own choosing, of the right to have an adjournment to confer with counsel, and of the right to have counsel assigned by the court in any case where he or she is financially unable to obtain the same:

(i) the respondent in any proceeding under article ten or ten-A of this act and the petitioner in any proceeding under part eight of article ten of this act;

(ii) the petitioner and the respondent in any proceeding under article eight of this act;

(iii) the respondent in any proceeding under part three of article six of this act;

(iv) the parent or person legally responsible, foster parent, or other person having physical or legal custody of the child in any proceeding under article ten or ten-A of this act or section three hundred fifty-eight-a, three hundred eighty-four or three hundred eighty-four-b of the social services law, and a non-custodial parent or grandparent served with notice pursuant to paragraph (e) of subdivision two of section three hundred eighty-four-a of the social services law;

(v) the parent of any child seeking custody or contesting the substantial infringement of his or her right to custody of such child, in any proceeding before the court in which the court has jurisdiction to determine such custody;

(vi) any person in any proceeding before the court in which an order or other determination is being sought to hold such person in contempt of the court or in willful violation of a previous order of the court, except for a contempt which may be punished summarily under section seven hundred fifty-five of the judiciary law;

(vii) the parent of a child in any adoption proceeding who opposes the adoption of such child.

(viii) the respondent in any proceeding under article five of this act in relation to the establishment of paternity.

(ix) in a proceeding under article ten-C of this act:

(1) a parent or caretaker as such terms are defined in section one thousand ninety-two of this act;

(2) an interested adult as such term is defined in section one thousand ninety-two of this act provided that:

(A) the child alleged to be destitute in the proceeding held pursuant to article ten-C of this act was removed from the care of such interested adult;

(B) the child alleged to be destitute in the proceeding held pursuant to article ten-C of this act resides with the interested adult; or

(C) the child alleged to be destitute in the proceeding held pursuant to article ten-C of this act resided with such interested adult immediately prior to the filing of the petition under article ten-C of this act;

(3) any interested adult as such term is defined in section one thousand ninety-two of this act or any person made a party to the article ten-C proceeding pursuant to subdivision (c) of section one thousand ninety-four of this act for whom the court orders counsel appointed pursuant to subdivision (d) of section one thousand ninety-four of this act.

(b) Assignment of counsel in other cases. In addition to the cases listed in subdivision (a) of this section, a judge may assign counsel to represent any adult in a proceeding under this act if he determines that such assignment of counsel is mandated by the constitution of the state of New York or of the United States, and includes such determination in the order assigning counsel;

(c) Implementation. Any order for the assignment of counsel issued under this part shall be implemented as provided in article eighteen-B of the county law.

ARTICLE 3
Juvenile Delinquency

Part 1
Jurisdiction and Preliminary Procedures

§301.1. Purpose.

The purpose of this article is to establish procedures in accordance with due process of law (a) to determine whether a person is a juvenile delinquent and

(b) to issue an appropriate order of disposition for any person who is adjudged a juvenile delinquent. In any proceeding under this article, the court shall consider the needs and best interests of the respondent as well as the need for protection of the community.

§301.2. Definitions.
As used in this article, the following terms shall have the following meanings:

1. "Juvenile delinquent" means a person over seven and less than sixteen years of age, who, having committed an act that would constitute a crime if committed by an adult, (a) is not criminally responsible for such conduct by reason of infancy, or (b) is the defendant in an action ordered removed from a criminal court to the family court pursuant to article seven hundred twenty-five of the criminal procedure law.

2. "Respondent" means the person against whom a juvenile delinquency petition is filed pursuant to section 310.1. Provided, however, that any act of the respondent required or authorized under this article may be performed by his or her attorney unless expressly provided otherwise.

3. "Detention" means the temporary care and maintenance of children away from their own homes, as defined in section five hundred two of the executive law. Detention of a person alleged to be or adjudicated as a juvenile delinquent shall be authorized only in a facility certified by the division for youth as a detention facility pursuant to section five hundred three of the executive law.

4. "Secure detention facility" means a facility characterized by physically restricting construction, hardware and procedures.

5. "Non-secure detention facility" means a facility characterized by the absence of physically restricting construction, hardware and procedures.

6. "Fact-finding hearing" means a hearing to determine whether the respondent or respondents committed the crime or crimes alleged in the petition or petitions.

7. "Dispositional hearing" means a hearing to determine whether the respondent requires supervision, treatment or confinement.

8. "Designated felony act" means an act which, if done by an adult, would be a crime: (i) defined in sections 125.27 (murder in the first degree); 125.25 (murder in the second degree); 135.25 (kidnapping in the first degree); or 150.20 (arson in the first degree) of the penal law committed by a person thirteen, fourteen or fifteen years of age; or such conduct committed as a sexually motivated felony, where authorized pursuant to section 130.91 of the penal law; (ii) defined in sections 120.10 (assault in the first degree); 125.20 (manslaughter in the first degree); 130.35 (rape in the first degree); 130.50 (criminal sexual act in the first degree); 130.70 (aggravated sexual abuse in the first degree); 135.20 (kidnapping in the second degree) but only where the abduction involved the use or threat of use of deadly physical force; 150.15 (arson in the second degree) or 160.15 (robbery in the first degree) of the penal law committed by a person thirteen, fourteen or fifteen years of age; or such conduct committed as a sexually motivated felony, where authorized pursuant to section 130.91 of the penal law; (iii) defined in the penal law as an attempt to commit murder in the first or second degree or kidnapping in the first degree committed by a person thirteen, fourteen or fifteen years of age; or such conduct committed as a sexually motivated felony, where authorized pursuant to section 130.91 of the penal law; (iv) defined in section 140.30 (burglary in the first degree); subdivision one of section 140.25 (burglary in the second

degree); subdivision two of section 160.10 (robbery in the second degree) of the penal law; or section 265.03 of the penal law, where such machine gun or such firearm is possessed on school grounds, as that phrase is defined in subdivision fourteen of section 220.00 of the penal law committed by a person fourteen or fifteen years of age; or such conduct committed as a sexually motivated felony, where authorized pursuant to section 130.91 of the penal law; (v) defined in section 120.05 (assault in the second degree) or 160.10 (robbery in the second degree) of the penal law committed by a person fourteen or fifteen years of age but only where there has been a prior finding by a court that such person has previously committed an act which, if committed by an adult, would be the crime of assault in the second degree, robbery in the second degree or any designated felony act specified in paragraph (i), (ii), or (iii) of this subdivision regardless of the age of such person at the time of the commission of the prior act; or (vi) other than a misdemeanor committed by a person at least seven but less than sixteen years of age, but only where there has been two prior findings by the court that such person has committed a prior felony.

9. "Designated class A felony act" means a designated felony act defined in paragraph (i) of subdivision eight.

10. "Secure facility" means a residential facility in which the respondent may be placed under this article, which is characterized by physically restricting construction, hardware and procedures, and is designated as a secure facility by the division for youth.

11. "Restrictive placement" means a placement pursuant to section 353.5.

12. "Presentment agency" means the agency or authority which pursuant to section two hundred fifty-four or two hundred fifty-four-a is responsible for presenting a juvenile delinquency petition.

13. "Incapacitated person" means a respondent who, as a result of mental illness, or intellectual or developmental disability as defined in subdivisions twenty and twenty-two of section 1.03 of the mental hygiene law, lacks capacity to understand the proceedings against him or her or to assist in his or her own defense. *(Eff. 5/25/16, Ch. 37, L. 2016)*

14. Any reference in this article to the commission of a crime includes any act which, if done by an adult, would constitute a crime.

15. "Aggravated circumstances" shall have the same meaning as the definition of such term in subdivision (j) of section one thousand twelve of this act.

16. "Permanency hearing" means an initial hearing or subsequent hearing held in accordance with the provisions of this article for the purpose of reviewing the foster care status of the respondent and the appropriateness of the permanency plan developed by the commissioner of social services or the office of children and family services.

17. "Designated educational official" shall mean (a) an employee or representative of a school district who is designated by the school district or (b) an employee or representative of a charter school or private elementary or secondary school who is designated by such school to receive records pursuant to this article and to coordinate the student's participation in programs which may exist in the school district or community, including: non-violent conflict resolution programs, peer mediation programs and youth courts, extended day programs and other school violence prevention and intervention programs which may exist in the school district or community. Such notification shall be kept separate and apart from such student's school records and shall be

accessible only by the designated educational official. Such notification shall not be part of such student's permanent school record and shall not be appended to or included in any documentation regarding such student and shall be destroyed at such time as such student is no longer enrolled in the school district. At no time shall such notification be used for any purpose other than those specified in this subdivision.

§301.3. Applicability of article to actions and matters occurring before and after effective date.

1. The provisions of this article apply exclusively to:

(a) all juvenile delinquency actions and proceedings commenced upon or after the effective date thereof and all appeals and other post-judgment proceedings relating or attaching thereto; and

(b) all matters of juvenile delinquency procedure prescribed in this article which do not constitute a part of any particular action or case, occurring upon or after such effective date.

2. The provisions of this article apply to:

(a) all juvenile delinquency actions and proceedings commenced prior to the effective date thereof but still pending on such date; and

(b) all appeals and other post-judgment proceedings commenced upon or after such effective date which relate or attach to juvenile delinquency actions and proceedings commenced or concluded prior to such effective date provided that, if application of such provisions in any particular case would not be feasible or would work injustice, the provisions of article seven pertaining to juvenile delinquency actions apply thereto, as such article seven read immediately prior to the effective date of this article.

3. The provisions of this article do not impair or render ineffectual any proceedings or procedural matters which occurred prior to the effective date thereof.

§301.4. Separability clause.

If any clause, sentence, paragraph, section or part of this article shall be adjudged by any court of competent jurisdiction to be invalid, such judgment shall not affect, impair, or invalidate the remainder thereof, but shall be confined in its operation to the clause, sentence, paragraph, section or part thereof directly involved in the controversy in which such judgment shall have been rendered.

§302.1. Jurisdiction.

1. The family court has exclusive original jurisdiction over any proceeding to determine whether a person is a juvenile delinquent.

2. In determining the jurisdiction of the court the age of such person at the time the delinquent act allegedly was committed is controlling.

§302.2. Statute of limitations.

A juvenile delinquency proceeding must be commenced within the period of limitation prescribed in section 30.10 of the criminal procedure law or, unless the alleged act is a designated felony as defined in subdivision eight of section 301.2, commenced before the respondent's eighteenth birthday, whichever occurs earlier. When the alleged act constitutes a designated felony as defined in subdivision eight of section 301.2 such proceeding must be commenced within such period of limitation or before the respondent's twentieth birthday, whichever occurs earlier.

§302.3. Venue.
1. Juvenile delinquency proceedings shall be originated in the county in which the act or acts referred to in the petition allegedly occurred. For purposes of determining venue, article twenty of the criminal procedure law shall apply.
2. Upon motion of the respondent or the appropriate presentment agency the family court in which the proceedings have been originated may order, for good cause shown, that the proceeding be transferred to another county. If the order is issued after motion by the presentment agency, the court may impose such conditions as it deems equitable and appropriate to ensure that the transfer does not subject the respondent to an unreasonable burden in making his defense.
3. Any motion made pursuant to subdivision two by the respondent shall be made within the time prescribed by section 332.2. Any such motion by a presentment agency must be based upon papers stating the ground therefor and must be made within thirty days from the date that the action was originated unless such time is extended for good cause shown.
4. Except for designated felony act petitions, after entering a finding pursuant to subdivision one of section 345.1, and prior to the commencement of the dispositional hearing the court may, in its discretion and for good cause shown, order that the proceeding be transferred to the county in which the respondent resides. The court shall not order such a transfer, however, unless it grants the respondent and the presentment agency an opportunity to state on the record whether each approves or disapproves of such a transfer and the reasons therefor. The court shall take into consideration the provisions of subdivisions two and three of section 340.2 in determining such transfer.

§303.1. Criminal procedure law.
1. The provisions of the criminal procedure law shall not apply to proceedings under this article unless the applicability of such provisions are specifically prescribed by this act.
2. A court may, however, consider judicial interpretations of appropriate provisions of the criminal procedure law to the extent that such interpretations may assist the court in interpreting similar provisions of this article.

§303.2. Double jeopardy.
The provisions of article forty of the criminal procedure law concerning double jeopardy shall apply to juvenile delinquency proceedings.

§303.3. Defenses.
The provisions of articles twenty-five, thirty-five and forty and section 30.05 of the penal law shall be applicable to juvenile delinquency proceedings.

§304.1. Detention.
1. A facility certified by the state division for youth as a juvenile facility must be operated in conformity with the regulations of the state division for youth and shall be subject to the visitation and inspection of the state board of social welfare.
2. No child to whom the provisions of this article may apply shall be detained in any prison, jail, lockup, or other place used for adults convicted of

crime or under arrest and charged with crime without the approval of the state division for youth in the case of each child and the statement of its reasons therefor. The state division for youth shall promulgate and publish the rules which it shall apply in determining whether approval should be granted pursuant to this subdivision.

3. The detention of a child under ten years of age in a secure detention facility shall not be directed under any of the provisions of this article.

4. A detention facility which receives a child under subdivision four of section 305.2 shall immediately notify the child's parent or other person legally responsible for his care or, if such legally responsible person is unavailable the person with whom the child resides, that he has been placed in detention.

§304.2. Temporary order of protection.

(1) Upon application by the presentment agency, the court may issue a temporary order of protection against a respondent for good cause shown, ex parte or upon notice, at any time after a juvenile is taken into custody, pursuant to section 305.1 or 305.2 or upon the issuance of an appearance ticket pursuant to section 307.1 or upon the filing of a petition pursuant to section 310.1.

(2) A temporary order of protection may contain any of the provisions authorized on the making of an order of protection under section 352.3.

(3) A temporary order of protection is not a finding of wrongdoing.

(4) A temporary order of protection may remain in effect until an order of disposition is entered.

§305.1. Custody by a private person.

1. A private person may take a child under the age of sixteen into custody in cases in which he may arrest an adult for a crime under section 140.30 of the criminal procedure law.

2. Before taking such child under the age of sixteen into custody, a private person must inform the child of the cause thereof and require him to submit, except when he is taken into custody on pursuit immediately after the commission of a crime.

3. After taking such child into custody, a private person must take the child, without unnecessary delay, to the child's home, to a family court, or to a police officer or peace officer.

§305.2. Custody by a peace officer or a police officer without a warrant.

1. For purposes of this section, the word "officer" means a peace officer or a police officer.

2. An officer may take a child under the age of sixteen into custody without a warrant in cases in which he may arrest a person for a crime under article one hundred forty of the criminal procedure law.

3. If an officer takes such child into custody or if a child is delivered to him under section 305.1, he shall immediately notify the parent or other person legally responsible for the child's care, or if such legally responsible person is unavailable the person with whom the child resides, that the child has been taken into custody.

4. After making every reasonable effort to give notice under subdivision three, the officer shall:

(a) release the child to the custody of his parents or other person legally responsible for his care upon the issuance in accordance with section 307.1 of a family court appearance ticket to the child and the person to whose custody the child is released; or

(b) forthwith and with all reasonable speed take the child directly, and without his first being taken to the police station house, to the family court located in the county in which the act occasioning the taking into custody allegedly was committed, unless the officer determines that it is necessary to question the child, in which case he may take the child to a facility designated by the chief administrator of the courts as a suitable place for the questioning of children or, upon the consent of a parent or other person legally responsible for the care of the child, to the child's residence and there question him for a reasonable period of time; or

(c) take the child to a place certified by the office of children and family services as a juvenile detention facility for the reception of children; or

(d) take the child who such officer has decided to take into custody in accordance with this section or section 305.1 of this part for violating the provisions of section 230.00 of the penal law, to an available short-term safe house as defined in subdivision two of section four hundred forty-seven-a of the social services law; or

(e) take the child, if it appears that such child is a sexually exploited child as defined in paragraph (a), (c) or (d) of subdivision one of section four hundred forty-seven-a of the social services law, to an available short-term safe house, but only if the child consents to be taken.

5. If such child has allegedly committed a designated felony act as defined in subdivision eight of section 301.2, and the family court in the county is in session, the officer shall forthwith take the child directly to such family court, unless the officer takes the child to a facility for questioning in accordance with paragraph (b) of subdivision four. If such child has not allegedly committed a designated felony act and such family court is in session, the officer shall either forthwith take the child directly to such family court, unless the officer takes the child to a facility for questioning in accordance with paragraph (b) of subdivision four or release the child in accordance with paragraph (a) of subdivision four.

6. In all other cases, and in the absence of special circumstances, the officer shall release the child in accordance with paragraph (a) of subdivision four.

7. A child shall not be questioned pursuant to this section unless he and a person required to be notified pursuant to subdivision three if present, have been advised:

(a) of the child's right to remain silent;

(b) that the statements made by the child may be used in a court of law;

(c) of the child's right to have an attorney present at such questioning; and

(d) of the child's right to have an attorney provided for him without charge if he is indigent.

8. In determining the suitability of questioning and determining the reasonable period of time for questioning such a child, the child's age, the presence or absence of his parents or other persons legally responsible for his care and notification pursuant to subdivision three shall be included among relevant considerations.

§306.1. Fingerprinting of certain alleged juvenile delinquents.

1. Following the arrest of a child alleged to be a juvenile delinquent, or the filing of a delinquency petition involving a child who has not been arrested, the arresting officer or other appropriate police officer or agency shall take or cause to be taken fingerprints of such child if:

(a) the child is eleven years of age or older and the crime which is the subject of the arrest or which is charged in the petition constitutes a class A or B felony; or

(b) the child is thirteen years of age or older and the crime which is the subject of the arrest or which is charged in the petition constitutes a class C, D or E felony.

2. Whenever fingerprints are required to be taken pursuant to subdivision one, the photograph and palmprints of the arrested child may also be taken.

3. The taking of fingerprints, palmprints, photographs, and related information concerning the child and the facts and circumstances of the acts charged in the juvenile delinquency proceeding shall be in accordance with standards established by the commissioner of the division of criminal justice services and by applicable provisions of this article.

4. Upon the taking of fingerprints pursuant to subdivision one the appropriate officer or agency shall, without unnecessary delay, forward such fingerprints to the division of criminal justice services and shall not retain such fingerprints or any copy thereof. Copies of photographs and palmprints taken pursuant to this section shall be kept confidential and only in the exclusive possession of such law enforcement agency, separate and apart from files of adults.

§306.2. Fingerprinting; duties of the division of criminal justice services.

1. Upon receipt of fingerprints taken pursuant to section 306.1, the division of criminal justice services shall retain such fingerprints distinctly identifiable from adult criminal records except as provided in section 354.1, and shall not release such fingerprints to a federal depository or to any person except as authorized by this act. The division shall promulgate regulations to protect the confidentiality of such fingerprints and related information and to prevent access thereto, by, and the distribution thereof to, persons not authorized by law.

2. Upon receipt of such fingerprints, the division of criminal justice services shall classify them and search its records for information concerning an adjudication or pending matter involving the person arrested. The division shall promptly transmit to such forwarding officer or agency a report containing any information on file with respect to such person's previous adjudications and pending matters or a report stating that the person arrested has no previous record according to its files. Notwithstanding the foregoing, where the division has not received disposition information within two years of an arrest, the division shall, until such information or up-to-date status information is received, withhold the record of that arrest and any related activity in disseminating criminal history information.

3. Upon receipt of a report of the division of criminal justice services pursuant to this section, the recipient office or agency must promptly transmit two copies of such report to the family court in which the proceeding may be originated and two copies thereof to the presentment agency who shall furnish a copy thereof to counsel for the respondent.

§307.1. Family court appearance ticket.

1. A family court appearance ticket is a written notice issued and subscribed by a peace officer or police officer, a probation service director or his designee or the administrator responsible for operating a detention facility or his designee, directing a child and his parent or other person legally responsible for his care to appear, without security, at a designated probation service on a

specified return date in connection with the child's alleged commission of the crime or crimes specified on such appearance ticket. The form of a family court appearance ticket shall be prescribed by rules of the chief administrator of the courts.

2. If the crime alleged to have been committed by the child is a designated felony as defined by subdivision eight of section 301.2, the return date shall be no later than seventy-two hours excluding Saturdays, Sundays and public holidays after issuance of such family court appearance ticket. If the crime alleged to have been committed by such child is not a designated felony, the return date shall be no later than fourteen days after the issuance of such appearance ticket.

3. A copy of the family court appearance ticket shall be forwarded by the issuing person or agency to the complainant, respondent, respondent's parent, and appropriate probation service within twenty-four hours after its issuance.

§307.2.   Appearance ticket procedures.

1. If a child fails to appear on the return date specified on a family court appearance ticket, the probation service may refer the matter forthwith to the appropriate presentment agency or may, in its discretion, attempt to secure the attendance of the child. Upon exercise of its discretion, probation services shall take appropriate action under law including, but not limited to, written notification to the child and parent or other person legally responsible for his care or telephone communications with the child and parent or other person legally responsible for his care. Efforts to secure the attendance of the child shall not extend beyond seven days subsequent to such return date and the probation service must refer the matter to the appropriate presentment agency within such period. Upon referral, the presentment agency may take whatever action it deems appropriate, including the filing of a petition pursuant to section 311.1.

2. If the complainant fails to appear on the return date specified on such appearance ticket, the probation service may, in its discretion, attempt to secure his voluntary attendance. Upon exercise of its discretion, probation services may take appropriate action under law including, but not limited to, written notification to the complainant or telephone communications with the complainant. Efforts to secure the voluntary attendance of such person shall not extend beyond seven days subsequent to such return date and the probation service shall refer the matter to the appropriate presentment agency within such period. Upon referral, the presentment agency may take whatever action it deems appropriate, including the issuance of a subpoena or the filing of a petition pursuant to section 311.1.

3. If a petition is filed subsequent to the issuance of an appearance ticket the appearance ticket shall be made part of the probation service file.

§307.3.   Rules of court authorizing release before filing of petition.

1. The agency responsible for operating a detention facility pursuant to section two hundred eighteen-a of the county law, five hundred ten-a of the executive law or other applicable provisions of law, shall release a child in custody before the filing of a petition to the custody of his parents or other person legally responsible for his care, or if such legally responsible person is unavailable, to a person with whom he resides, when the events occasioning the taking into custody do not appear to involve allegations that the child committed a delinquent act.

2. When practicable such agency may release a child before the filing of a petition to the custody of his parents or other person legally responsible for his care, or if such legally responsible person is unavailable, to a person with whom he resides, when the events occasioning the taking into custody appear to involve allegations that the child committed a delinquent act.

3. If a child is released under this section, the child and the person legally responsible for his care shall be issued a family court appearance ticket in accordance with section 307.1.

4. If the agency for any reason does not release a child under this section, such child shall be brought before the appropriate family court within seventy-two hours or the next day the court is in session, whichever is sooner. Such agency shall thereupon file an application for an order pursuant to section 307.4 and shall forthwith serve a copy of the application upon the appropriate presentment agency. Nothing in this subdivision shall preclude the adjustment of suitable cases pursuant to section 308.1.

§307.4.   Hearing following detention.

1. If a child in custody is brought before a judge of the family court before a petition is filed upon a written application pursuant to subdivision four of section 307.3, the judge shall hold a hearing for the purpose of making a preliminary determination of whether the court appears to have jurisdiction over the child.

2. At such hearing the court must appoint an attorney to represent the child pursuant to the provisions of section two hundred forty-nine if independent legal representation is not available to such child.

3. The provisions of sections 320.3 and 341.2 shall apply at such hearing.

4. After such hearing, the judge shall order the release of the child to the custody of his parent or other person legally responsible for his care if:

(a) the court does not appear to have jurisdiction, or

(b) the events occasioning the taking into custody do not appear to involve allegations that the child committed a delinquent act, or

(c) the events occasioning the taking into custody appear to involve acts which constitute juvenile delinquency, unless the court finds and states facts and reasons which would support a detention order pursuant to section 320.5.

5. Such hearing shall be held within seventy-two hours of the time detention commenced or the next day the court is in session, whichever is sooner.

6. The appropriate presentment agency shall present the application at a hearing pursuant to this section.

7. A petition shall be filed and a probable-cause hearing held under section 325.1 within four days of the conclusion of a hearing under this section. If a petition is not filed within four days the child shall be released.

8. Upon a finding of facts and reasons which support a detention order pursuant to section 320.5 of this chapter, the court shall also determine and state in any order directing detention:

(a) whether the continuation of the child in the child's home would be contrary to the best interests of the child based upon, and limited to, the facts and circumstances available to the court at the time of the hearing held in accordance with this section; and

(b) where appropriate and consistent with the need for protection of the community, whether reasonable efforts were made prior to the date of the court hearing that resulted in the detention order issued in accordance with this section to prevent or eliminate the need for removal of the child from his or her home or, if the child had been removed from his or her home prior to the initial appearance, where appropriate and consistent with the need for protection of the community, whether reasonable efforts were made to make it possible for the child to safely return home.

§308.1. Rules of court for preliminary procedure.

1. Rules of court shall authorize and determine the circumstances under which the probation service may confer with any person seeking to have a juvenile delinquency petition filed, the potential respondent and other interested persons concerning the advisability of requesting that a petition be filed.

2. Except as provided in subdivisions three and four of this section, the probation service may, in accordance with rules of court, adjust suitable cases before a petition is filed. The inability of the respondent or his or her family to make restitution shall not be a factor in a decision to adjust a case or in a recommendation to the presentment agency pursuant to subdivision six of this section. Nothing in this section shall prohibit the probation service or the court from directing a respondent to obtain employment and to make restitution from the earnings from such employment. Nothing in this section shall prohibit the probation service or the court from directing an eligible person to complete an education reform program in accordance with section four hundred fifty-eight-l of the social services law.

3. The probation service shall not adjust a case in which the child has allegedly committed a designated felony act unless it has received the written approval of the court.

4. The probation service shall not adjust a case in which the child has allegedly committed a delinquent act which would be a crime defined in section 120.25, (reckless endangerment in the first degree), subdivision one of section 125.15, (manslaughter in the second degree), subdivision one of section 130.25, (rape in the third degree), subdivision one of section 130.40, (criminal sexual act in the third degree), subdivision one or two of section 130.65, (sexual abuse in the first degree), section 135.65, (coercion in the first degree), section 140.20, (burglary in the third degree), section 150.10, (arson in the third degree), section 160.05, (robbery in the third degree), subdivision two, three or four of section 265.02, (criminal possession of a weapon in the third degree), section 265.03, (criminal possession of a weapon in the second degree), or section 265.04, (criminal possession of a dangerous weapon in the first degree) of the penal law where the child has previously had one or more adjustments of a case in which such child allegedly committed an act which would be a crime specified in this subdivision unless it has received written approval from the court and the appropriate presentment agency.

5. The fact that a child is detained prior to the filing of a petition shall not preclude the probation service from adjusting a case; upon adjusting such a case the probation service shall notify the detention facility to release the child.

6. The probation service shall not transmit or otherwise communicate to the presentment agency any statement made by the child to a probation officer. However, the probation service may make a recommendation regarding adjustment of the case to the presentment agency and provide such information, including any report made by the arresting officer and record of previous adjustments and arrests, as it shall deem relevant.

7. No statement made to the probation service prior to the filing of a petition may be admitted into evidence at a fact-finding hearing or, if the proceeding is transferred to a criminal court, at any time prior to a conviction.

8. The probation service may not prevent any person who wishes to request that a petition be filed from having access to the appropriate presentment agency for that purpose.

9. Efforts at adjustment pursuant to rules of court under this section may not extend for a period of more than two months without leave of the court, which may extend the period for an additional two months.

10. If a case is not adjusted by the probation service, such service shall notify the appropriate presentment agency of that fact within forty-eight hours or the next court day, whichever occurs later.

11. The probation service may not be authorized under this section to compel any person to appear at any conference, produce any papers, or visit any place.

12. The probation service shall certify to the division of criminal justice services and to the appropriate police department or law enforcement agency whenever it adjusts a case in which the potential respondent's fingerprints were taken pursuant to section 306.1 in any manner other than the filing of a petition for juvenile delinquency for an act which, if committed by an adult, would constitute a felony, provided, however, in the case of a child eleven or twelve years of age, such certification shall be made only if the act would constitute a class A or B felony.

13. The provisions of this section shall not apply where the petition is an order of removal to the family court pursuant to article seven hundred twenty-five of the criminal procedure law.

§310.1.   Originating a juvenile delinquency proceeding.

1. A proceeding to adjudicate a person a juvenile delinquent is originated by the filing of a petition.

2. Only a presentment agency may originate a juvenile delinquency proceeding.

3. If the appropriate agency does not originate a proceeding within thirty days of receipt of notice from the probation service pursuant to subdivision ten of section 308.1, it shall notify in writing the complainant of that fact.

§310.2.   Speedy trial.

After a petition has been filed, or upon the signing of an order of removal pursuant to section 725.05 of the criminal procedure law, the respondent is entitled to a speedy fact-finding hearing.

§311.1.   The petition; definition and contents.

1. A petition originating a juvenile delinquency proceeding is a written accusation by an authorized presentment agency.

2. A petition shall charge at least one crime and may, in addition, charge in separate counts one or more other crimes, provided that all such crimes are joinable in accord with section 311.6.

3. A petition must contain:

(a) the name of the family court in which it is filed;

(b) the title of the action;

(c) the fact that the respondent is a person under sixteen years of age at the time of the alleged act or acts;

(d) a separate accusation or count addressed to each crime charged, if there be more than one;

(e) the precise crime or crimes charged;

(f) a statement in each count that the crime charged was committed in a designated county;

(g) a statement in each count that the crime charged therein was committed on, or on or about, a designated date, or during a designated period of time;

(h) a plain and concise factual statement in each count which, without allegations of an evidentiary nature, asserts facts supporting every element of the crime charged and the respondent's commission thereof with sufficient precision to clearly apprise the respondent of the conduct which is the subject of the accusation;

(i) the name or names, if known, of other persons who are charged as co-respondents in the family court or as adults in a criminal court proceeding in the commission of the crime or crimes charged;

(j) a statement that the respondent requires supervision, treatment or confinement; and

(k) the signature of the appropriate presentment attorney.

4. A petition shall be verified in accordance with the civil practice law and rules and shall conform to the provisions of section 311.2.

5. If the petition alleges that the respondent committed a designated felony act, it shall so state, and the term "designated felony act petition" shall be prominently marked thereon. Certified copies of prior delinquency findings shall constitute sufficient proof of such findings for the purpose of filing a designated felony petition. If all the allegations of a designated felony act are dismissed or withdrawn or the respondent is found to have committed crimes which are not designated felony acts, the term "designated felony act petition" shall be stricken from the petition.

6. The form of petition shall be prescribed by the chief administrator of the courts. A petition shall be entitled "In the Matter of", followed by the name of the respondent.

7. When an order of removal pursuant to article seven hundred twenty-five of the criminal procedure law is filed with the clerk of the court, such order and those pleadings and proceedings, other than the minutes of any hearing inquiry or trial, grand jury proceeding, or of any plea accepted or entered, held in this action that has not yet been transcribed shall be transferred with it and shall be deemed to be a petition filed pursuant to subdivision one of section 310.1 containing all of the allegations required by this section notwithstanding that such allegations may not be set forth in the manner therein prescribed. Where the order or the grand jury request annexed to the order specifies an act that is a designated felony act, the clerk shall annex to the order a sufficient statement and marking to make it a designated felony act petition. The date such order is filed with the clerk of the court shall be deemed the date a petition was filed under this article. For purposes of service in accord with section 312.1, however, only the order of removal shall be deemed the petition. All minutes of any hearing inquiry or trial held in this action, the minutes of any grand jury proceeding and the minutes of any plea accepted and entered shall be transferred to the family court within thirty days.

§311.2.   Sufficiency of petition.
A petition, or a count thereof, is sufficient on its face when:
1. it substantially conforms to the requirements prescribed in section 311.1; and
2. the allegations of the factual part of the petition, together with those of any supporting depositions which may accompany it, provide reasonable cause to believe that the respondent committed the crime or crimes charged; and
3. non-hearsay allegations of the factual part of the petition or of any supporting depositions establish, if true, every element of each crime charged and the respondent's commission thereof.

§311.3.   Petition; fact-finding hearings.
1. When two or more respondents are charged in separate petitions with the same crime or crimes the court shall conduct a single or consolidated fact-finding hearing. The court, however, upon motion of a respondent or the presentment agency, may, in its discretion and for good cause shown, order that any respondent be granted a fact-finding hearing separate from the other respondents. Such motion must be made within the period prescribed in section 332.2.
2. If such petitions, in addition to charging the same crime or crimes against the different respondents, charge other crimes not common to all, the court may nevertheless conduct a single fact-finding hearing for the crime or crimes common to all.

§311.4.   Substitution of petition or finding.
1. At any time in the proceedings the court, upon motion of a respondent or its own motion, may, with the consent of the presentment agency and with the consent of the respondent, substitute a petition alleging that the respondent is in need of supervision for a petition alleging that the respondent is a juvenile delinquent.
2. At the conclusion of the dispositional hearing the court, upon motion of the respondent or its own motion, may in its discretion and with the consent of the respondent, substitute a finding that the respondent is a person in need of supervision for a finding that the respondent is a juvenile delinquent.
3. In any proceeding under this article based upon an arrest for an act of prostitution, there is a presumption that the respondent meets the criteria as a victim of a severe form of trafficking as defined in section 7105 of title 22 of the United States Code (Trafficking Victims Protection Act of 2000). Upon the motion of the respondent, without the consent of the presentment agency, a petition alleging that the respondent is in need of supervision shall be substituted for the delinquency petition. If, however, the respondent has been previously adjudicated as a juvenile delinquent under this article for an act which would be a crime pursuant to article two hundred thirty of the penal law, if the respondent was an adult, or expresses a current unwillingness to cooperate with specialized services for sexually exploited youth, continuing with the delinquency proceeding shall be within the court's discretion. The necessary findings of fact to support the continuation of the delinquency proceeding shall be reduced to writing and made part of the court record. If, subsequent to issuance of a substitution order under this subdivision and prior to the conclusion of the fact finding hearing on the petition alleging that the respondent is a person in need of supervision, the respondent is not in substantial compliance with a lawful order of the court, the court may, in its discretion, substitute the original petition alleging that the respondent is a

juvenile delinquent for the petition alleging that the respondent is in need of supervision.

§311.5. Amendment of the petition.

1. At any time before or during the fact-finding hearing, the court may, upon application of the presentment agency and with notice to the respondent and an opportunity to be heard, order the amendment of a petition with respect to defects, errors or variances from the proof relating to matters of form, time, place, names of persons and the like, when such amendment does not tend to prejudice the respondent on the merits. Upon permitting such an amendment, the court must, upon application of the respondent, order any adjournment which may be necessary to accord the respondent an adequate opportunity to prepare his defense.

2. A petition may not be amended for the purpose of curing:
(a) a failure to charge or state a crime; or
(b) legal insufficiency of the factual allegations; or
(c) a misjoinder of crimes.

§311.6. Joinder, severance and consolidation.

1. Two crimes are joinable and may be included as separate counts in the same petition when:
(a) they are based upon the same act or upon the same criminal transaction, as that term is defined in subdivision two; or
(b) even though based upon different criminal transactions, such crimes, or the criminal transactions underlying them, are of such nature that either proof of the first crime would be material and admissible as evidence in chief upon a fact-finding hearing of the second, or proof of the second would be material and admissible as evidence in chief upon a fact-finding hearing of the first; or
(c) even though based upon different criminal transactions, and even though not joinable pursuant to paragraph (b), such crimes are defined by the same or similar statutory provisions and consequently are the same or similar in law.

2. "Criminal transaction" means conduct which establishes at least one crime, and which is comprised of two or more or a group of acts either:
(a) so closely related and connected in point of time and circumstance of commission as to constitute a single criminal incident; or
(b) so closely related in criminal purpose or objective as to constitute elements or integral parts of a single criminal venture.

3. In any case where two or more crimes or groups of crimes charged in a petition are based upon different criminal transactions, and where their joinability rests solely upon the fact that such crimes, or as the case may be at least one offense of each group, are the same or similar in law, as prescribed in paragraph (c) of subdivision one, the court, in the interest of justice and for good cause shown, may upon application of either the respondent or the presentment agency order that any one of such crimes or groups of crimes be tried separately from the other or others, or that two or more thereof be tried together but separately from two or more others thereof. Such application must be made within the period prescribed in section 332.2.

4. When two or more petitions against the same respondent charge different crimes of a kind that are joinable in a single petition pursuant to subdivision one, the court may, upon application of either the presentment agency or respondent order that such petitions be consolidated and treated as a single petition for trial purposes. Such application must be made within the period

prescribed in section 332.2. If the respondent requests consolidation with respect to crimes which are, pursuant to paragraph (a) of subdivision one, of a kind that are joinable in a single petition by reason of being based upon the same act or criminal transaction, the court must order such consolidation unless good cause to the contrary be shown.

§312.1.   Issuance and service of summons.

1. After a petition has been filed, the court may cause a copy thereof and a summons to be issued, requiring the respondent personally and his parent or other person legally responsible for his care, or, if such legally responsible person is not available, a person with whom he resides, to appear for the initial appearance as defined by section 320.1 at a time and place named. The summons shall be signed by a judge or by the clerk of the court.

2. Service of a summons and petition shall be made by delivery of a true copy thereof to the person summoned at least twenty-four hours before the time stated therein for appearance.

3. If after reasonable effort, personal service as provided in subdivision two is not made, the court may at any stage in the proceedings make an order providing for service in any manner the court directs.

§312.2.   Issuance of a warrant.

1. The court may issue a warrant, directing that the respondent personally or other person legally responsible for his or her care or, if such legally responsible person is not available, a person with whom he or she resides, be brought before the court, when a petition has been filed and it appears that:

(a) a summons cannot be served; or

(b) such person has refused to obey a summons or family court appearance ticket; or

(c) the respondent or other person is likely to leave the jurisdiction; or

(d) a summons, in the court's opinion, would be ineffectual; or

(e) a respondent has failed to appear.

2. Upon issuance of a warrant due to the respondent's failure to appear for a scheduled court date, the court shall adjourn the matter to a date certain within thirty days for a report on the efforts made to secure the respondent's appearance in court. The court may order that the person legally responsible for the respondent's care or, if such legally responsible person is not available, a person with whom the respondent resides, appear on the adjourned date. Upon receiving the report, for good cause, the court may order further reports and may require further appearances of the person legally responsible for the respondent's care or, if such person legally responsible is not available, a person with whom the respondent resides. Upon receiving the initial or any subsequent report, the court shall set forth in writing its findings of fact as to the efforts, if any, made up to that date to secure the respondent's appearance in court.

§315.1.   Motion to dismiss; defective petition.

1. A petition or a count thereof is defective when:

(a) it does not substantially conform to the requirements stated in sections 311.1 and 311.2; provided that a petition may not be dismissed as defective, but must instead be amended when the defect or irregularity is of a kind that may be cured by amendment pursuant to section 311.5, and where the presentment agency moves to so amend; or

(b) the allegations demonstrate that the court does not have jurisdiction of the crime charged; or

(c) the statute defining the crime charged is unconstitutional or otherwise invalid.

2. An order dismissing a petition as defective may be issued upon motion of the respondent or of the court itself.

3. A motion to dismiss under this section must be made within the time provided for in section 332.2.

§315.2. Motion to dismiss in furtherance of justice.

1. A petition or any part or count thereof may at any time be dismissed in furtherance of justice when, even though there may be no basis for dismissal as a matter of law, such dismissal is required as a matter of judicial discretion by the existence of some compelling further consideration or circumstances clearly demonstrating that a finding of delinquency or continued proceedings would constitute or result in injustice. In determining whether such compelling further consideration or circumstances exist, the court shall, to the extent applicable, examine and consider, individually and collectively, the following:

(a) the seriousness and circumstances of the crime;

(b) the extent of harm caused by the crime;

(c) any exceptionally serious misconduct of law enforcement personnel in the investigation and arrest of the respondent or in the presentment of the petition;

(d) the history, character and condition of the respondent;

(e) the needs and best interest of the respondent;

(f) the need for protection of the community; and

(g) any other relevant fact indicating that a finding would serve no useful purpose.

2. An order dismissing a petition in the interest of justice may be issued upon motion of the presentment agency, the court itself or of the respondent. Upon issuing such an order, the court must set forth its reasons therefor upon the record.

3. Such a motion brought by the presentment agency or the respondent must be in writing and may be filed at any time subsequent to the filing of the petition. Notice of the motion shall be served upon the opposing party not less than eight days prior to the return date of the motion. Answering affidavits shall be served at least two days prior to the return date of such motion.

§315.3. Adjournment in contemplation of dismissal.

1. Except where the petition alleges that the respondent has committed a designated felony act, the court may at any time prior to the entering of a finding under section 352.1 and with the consent of the respondent order that the proceeding be "adjourned in contemplation of dismissal". An adjournment in contemplation of dismissal is an adjournment of the proceeding, for a period not to exceed six months, with a view to ultimate dismissal of the petition in furtherance of justice. Upon issuing such an order, providing such terms and conditions as the court deems appropriate, the court must release the respondent. The court may, as a condition of an adjournment in contemplation of dismissal order, in cases where the record indicates that the consumption of alcohol may have been a contributing factor, require the respondent to attend and complete an alcohol awareness program established pursuant to of subdivision (a) of section 19.07 of the mental hygiene law. The court may, as a condition of an adjournment in contemplation of dismissal order, in cases

where the record indicates that the respondent is an eligible person as defined in section four hundred fifty-eight-l of the social services law and has allegedly committed an eligible offense as defined in such section, direct the respondent to attend and complete an education reform program established pursuant to section four hundred fifty-eight-l of the social services law. Upon ex parte motion by the presentment agency, or upon the court's own motion, made at the time the order is issued or at any time during its duration, the court may restore the matter to the calendar. If the proceeding is not restored, the petition is, at the expiration of the order, deemed to have been dismissed by the court in furtherance of justice.

2. Rules of court shall define the permissible terms and conditions which may be included in an order that the proceeding be adjourned in contemplation of dismissal; such permissible terms and conditions may include supervision by the probation service, a requirement that the respondent cooperate with a mental health, social services or other appropriate community facility or agency to which the respondent may be referred and a requirement that the respondent comply with such other reasonable conditions as the court shall determine to be necessary or appropriate to ameliorate the conduct which gave rise to the filing of the petition or to prevent placement with the commissioner of social services or the division for youth.

3. An order adjourning a petition in contemplation of dismissal may be issued upon motion of the presentment agency, the court itself, or the respondent. Upon issuing such an order, the court must set forth its reasons therefor upon the record.

Part 2
Initial Appearance and Probable Cause Hearing

§320.1.   The initial appearance; definition.
When used in this article "initial appearance" means the proceeding on the date the respondent first appears before the court after a petition has been filed and any adjournments thereof, for the purposes specified in section 320.4.

§320.2.   The initial appearance; timing; adjournment and appointment of counsel.
1. If the respondent is detained, the initial appearance shall be held no later than seventy-two hours after a petition is filed or the next day the court is in session, whichever is sooner. If the respondent is not detained, the initial appearance shall be held as soon as practicable and, absent good cause shown,

within ten days after a petition is filed. If a warrant for the respondent's arrest has been issued pursuant to section 312.2 of this article due to the respondent's failure to appear for an initial appearance of which he or she had notice, computation of the time within which the initial appearance must be held shall exclude the period extending from the date the court issues the warrant to the date the respondent is returned pursuant to the warrant or appears voluntarily; provided, however, no period of time may be excluded hereunder unless the respondent's location cannot be determined by the exercise of due diligence or, if the respondent's location is known, his or her presence in court cannot be obtained by the exercise of due diligence. In determining whether due diligence has been exercised, the court shall consider, among other factors, the report presented to the court pursuant to subdivision two of section 312.2 of this article.

2. At the initial appearance the court must appoint an attorney to represent the respondent pursuant to the provisions of section two hundred forty-nine if independent legal representation is not available to such respondent.

3. The initial appearance may be adjourned for no longer than seventy-two hours or until the next court day, whichever is sooner, to enable an attorney for the respondent to appear before the court.

4. The clerk of the court shall notify the presentment agency and any attorney for the respondent of the initial appearance date.

§320.3.   Notice of rights.

At the time the respondent first appears before the court, the respondent and his or her parent or other person legally responsible for his or her care shall be advised of the respondent's right to remain silent and of his or her right to be represented by counsel chosen by him or her or by an attorney assigned by the court. Provided, however, that in the event of the failure of the respondent's parent or other person legally responsible for his care to appear, after reasonable and substantial effort has been made to notify such parent or responsible person of the commencement of the proceeding and such initial appearance, the court shall appoint an attorney for the respondent.

§320.4.   The initial appearance; procedures.

1. At the initial appearance the court must inform the respondent, or cause him to be informed in its presence, of the charge or charges contained in the petition, and the presentment agency must cause the respondent and his or her counsel to be furnished with a copy of the petition.

2. At the initial appearance the court shall determine:
(a) whether detention is necessary pursuant to section 320.5; and
(b) whether the case should be referred to the probation service pursuant to section 320.6; and
(c) if the child is detained, the date of the probable-cause hearing pursuant to section 325.1 unless such hearing has already been held; and
(d) the date of the fact-finding hearing; and
(e) such other issues as may be properly before it.

§320.5.   The initial appearance; release or detention.

1. At the initial appearance, the court in its discretion may release the respondent or direct his detention.

2. Rules of court shall define permissible terms and conditions of release. The court may in its discretion release the respondent upon such terms and conditions as it deems appropriate. The respondent shall be given a written copy of any such

terms and conditions. The court may modify or enlarge such terms and conditions at any time prior to the expiration of the respondent's release.

3. (a) The court shall not direct detention unless available alternatives to detention, including conditional release, would not be appropriate, and the court finds that unless the respondent is detained:

(i) there is a substantial probability that he or she will not appear in court on the return date; or

(ii) there is a serious risk that he or she may before the return date commit an act which if committed by an adult would constitute a crime.

(b) Any finding directing detention pursuant to paragraph (a) of this subdivision made by the court shall state the facts, the level of risk the youth was assessed pursuant to a detention risk assessment instrument approved by the office of children and family services, and the reasons for such finding including, if a determination is made to place a youth in detention who was assessed at a low or medium risk on such a risk assessment instrument, the particular reasons why detention was determined to be necessary.

(c) If the court makes a finding that detention is necessary pursuant to subparagraphs (i) and (ii) of paragraph (a) of this subdivision, the court may consider, where applicable, as a condition of release, electronic monitoring of the respondent, if such electronic monitoring would significantly reduce the substantial probability that the respondent would not return to court on the return date, or the serious risk that the respondent may before the return date commit an act that if committed by an adult would constitute a crime.

(d) If the respondent may be a sexually exploited child as defined in subdivision one of section four hundred forty-seven-a of the social services law, the court may direct the respondent to an available short-term safe house as a condition of release.

4. At the initial appearance the presentment agency may introduce the respondent's previous delinquency findings entered by a family court. If the respondent has been fingerprinted for the current charge pursuant to section 306.1, the presentment agency may also introduce the fingerprint records maintained by the division of criminal justice services. The clerk of court and the probation service shall cooperate with the presentment agency in making available the appropriate records. At the conclusion of the initial appearance such fingerprint records shall be returned to the presentment agency and shall not be made a part of the court record.

5. Upon a finding of facts and reasons which support a detention order pursuant to subdivision three of this section, the court shall also determine and state in any order directing detention:

(a) whether the continuation of the respondent in the respondent's home would be contrary to the best interests of the respondent based upon, and limited to, the facts and circumstances available to the court at the time of the initial appearance; and

(b) where appropriate and consistent with the need for protection of the community, whether reasonable efforts were made prior to the date of the court appearance that resulted in the detention order issued in accordance with this section to prevent or eliminate the need for removal of the respondent from his or her home or, if the respondent had been removed from his or her home prior to the initial appearance, where appropriate and consistent with the need for protection of the community, whether reasonable efforts were made to make it possible for the respondent to safely return home.

§320.6. The initial appearance; referral to the probation service.
1. If the petition alleges the commission of a designated felony act or the commission of a crime enumerated in subdivision four of section 308.1, the probation service shall make a recommendation to the court at the initial appearance regarding the suitability of adjusting the case pursuant to section 308.1.
2. At the initial appearance the court may, with the consent of the victim or complainant and the respondent, refer a case to the probation service for adjustment services. In the case of a designated felony petition the consent of the presentment agency shall also be required to refer a case to probation services for adjustment services.
3. If the court refers a case to the probation service pursuant to this section and the probation service adjusts the case, the petition shall be dismissed.
4. If such case is referred to the probation service, the provisions of section 308.1, except subdivision thirteen thereof, shall apply.

§321.1. Entry of an admission or a denial.
1. At the initial appearance the respondent shall admit or deny each charge contained in the petition unless the petition is dismissed or the proceeding otherwise terminated.
2. If the respondent refuses to admit or deny each such charge or remains mute, the court must enter a denial in his behalf as to any charge neither admitted nor denied.

§321.2. Admissions to part of a petition; admissions concerning other petitions.
1. A respondent may as a matter of right enter an admission to those allegations in the petition which are determinable at the fact-finding hearing.
2. Where the petition charges but one crime, a respondent may, with the consent of the court and the appropriate presentment agency, enter an admission of a lesser included crime as defined in section 1.20 of the criminal procedure law.
3. Where the petition charges more than one crime in separate counts a respondent may, with the consent of the court and the appropriate presentment agency, enter an admission to part of the petition or a lesser included crime upon the condition that such admission constitutes a complete disposition of these allegations in the petition which are determinable at the fact-finding hearing.

§321.3. Acceptance of an admission.
1. The court shall not consent to the entry of an admission unless it has advised the respondent of his right to a fact-finding hearing. The court shall also ascertain through allocution of the respondent and his parent or other person legally responsible for his care, if present, that (a) he committed the act or acts to which he is entering an admission, (b) he is voluntarily waiving his right to a fact-finding hearing, and (c) he is aware of the possible specific dispositional orders. The provisions of this subdivision shall not be waived.
2. Upon consenting to the entry of an admission pursuant to this section, the court must state the reasons for granting such consent.
3. Upon the entry of an admission pursuant to this section the court shall enter an appropriate order pursuant to section 345.1 and schedule a dispositional hearing pursuant to section 350.1.

§321.4. Withdrawal of an admission or denial.

1. A respondent who has entered a denial of a petition may as a matter of right withdraw such denial at any time before the conclusion of the fact-finding hearing and enter an admission to the entire petition.

2. At any time prior to the entry of a finding under section 352.1 the court in its discretion may permit a respondent who has entered an admission to the entire petition or to part of the petition to withdraw such admission, and in such event the entire petition as it existed at the time of the admission shall be restored.

§322.1. Incapacitated person; examination reports.

1. At any proceeding under this article, the court must issue an order that the respondent be examined as provided herein when it is of the opinion that the respondent may be an incapacitated person. Notwithstanding the provisions of this or any other law, the court may direct that the examination be conducted on an outpatient basis when the respondent is not in custody at the time the court issues an order of examination. The court shall order that two qualified psychiatric examiners as defined in subdivision seven of section 730.10 of the criminal procedure law examine the respondent to determine if he is mentally ill, mentally retarded or developmentally disabled.

2. If an order of examination has been issued pursuant to subdivision one, the proceedings shall be adjourned until the examination reports have been filed with the court. Every such report shall be filed within ten days after entry of such order. Upon a showing of special circumstances and a finding that a longer period is necessary to complete the examination and report, the court may extend the time for filing the examination report.

3. Each report shall state the examiner's opinion as to whether the respondent is or is not an incapacitated person, the nature and extent of his examination and, if he finds the respondent is an incapacitated person, his diagnosis and prognosis and a detailed statement of the reasons for his opinion by making particular reference to those aspects of the proceedings wherein the respondent lacks capacity to understand or to assist in his own defense. The chief administrator of the courts shall prescribe the form for the examination report.

§322.2. Proceedings to determine capacity.

1. Upon the receipt of examination reports ordered under section 322.1 of this act, the court shall conduct a hearing to determine whether the respondent is an incapacitated person. The respondent, the counsel for the respondent, the presentment agency and the commissioner of mental health or the commissioner of developmental disabilities, as appropriate, shall be notified of such hearing at least five days prior to the date thereof and afforded an opportunity to be heard. *(Eff.5/25/16,Ch.37,L.2016)*

2. If the court finds that the respondent is not an incapacitated person, it shall continue the delinquency proceedings.

3. If the court finds that the respondent is an incapacitated person, the court shall schedule a hearing to determine whether there is probable cause to believe that the respondent committed a crime. The order of proceeding at such hearing shall conform to section 325.2.

4. If the court finds that there is probable cause to believe that the respondent committed a misdemeanor, the respondent shall be committed to the custody of the appropriate commissioner for a reasonable period not to

exceed ninety days. The court shall dismiss the petition on the issuance of the order of commitment.

5. (a) If the court finds that there is probable cause to believe that the respondent committed a felony, it shall order the respondent committed to the custody of the commissioner of mental health or the commissioner of developmental disabilities for an initial period not to exceed one year from the date of such order. Such period may be extended annually upon further application to the court by the commissioner having custody or his or her designee. Such application must be made not more than sixty days prior to the expiration of such period on forms that have been prescribed by the chief administrator of the courts. At that time, the commissioner must give written notice of the application to the respondent, the counsel representing the respondent and the mental hygiene legal service if the respondent is at a residential facility. Upon receipt of such application, the court must conduct a hearing to determine the issue of capacity. If, at the conclusion of a hearing conducted pursuant to this subdivision, the court finds that the respondent is no longer incapacitated, he or she shall be returned to the family court for further proceedings pursuant to this article. If the court is satisfied that the respondent continues to be incapacitated, the court shall authorize continued custody of the respondent by the commissioner for a period not to exceed one year. Such extensions shall not continue beyond a reasonable period of time necessary to determine whether the respondent will attain the capacity to proceed to a fact finding hearing in the foreseeable future but in no event shall continue beyond the respondent's eighteenth birthday. *(Eff.5/25/16,Ch.37,L.2016)*

(b) If a respondent is in the custody of the commissioner upon the respondent's eighteenth birthday, the commissioner shall notify the clerk of the court that the respondent was in his custody on such date and the court shall dismiss the petition.

(c) If the court finds that there is probable cause to believe that the respondent has committed a designated felony act, the court shall require that treatment be provided in a residential facility within the appropriate office of the department of mental hygiene.

(d) The commissioner shall review the condition of the respondent within forty-five days after the respondent is committed to the custody of the commissioner. He or she shall make a second review within ninety days after the respondent is committed to his or her custody. Thereafter, he or she shall review the condition of the respondent every ninety days. The respondent and the counsel for the respondent, shall be notified of any such review and afforded an opportunity to be heard. The commissioner having custody shall apply to the court for an order dismissing the petition whenever he or she determines that there is a substantial probability that the respondent will continue to be incapacitated for the foreseeable future. At the time of such application the commissioner must give written notice of the application to the respondent, the presentment agency and the mental hygiene legal service if the respondent is at a residential facility. Upon receipt of such application, the court may on its own motion conduct a hearing to determine whether there is substantial probability that the respondent will continue to be incapacitated for the foreseeable future, and it must conduct such hearing if a demand therefor is made by the respondent or the mental hygiene legal service within ten days from the date that notice of the application was given to them. The respondent may apply to the court for an order of dismissal on the same ground.

6. Any order pursuant to this section dismissing a petition shall not preclude an application for voluntary or involuntary care and treatment in a facility of the appropriate office of the department of mental hygiene pursuant to the provisions of the mental hygiene law. Unless the respondent is admitted pursuant to such an application he shall be released.

7. If the commissioner having custody of a child committed to a residential facility determines at any time that such child may be more appropriately treated in a non-residential facility, he may petition the family court for a hearing. If the court finds after a hearing that treatment in a non-residential facility would be more appropriate for such child, the court shall modify its order of commitment to authorize transfer of such child to a non-residential facility. Application for such a hearing may be made by the respondent.

8. If the commissioner having custody of the child determines at any time that such child is not an incapacitated person, he shall petition the court for a hearing. The respondent and the presentment agency shall be notified of such hearing within twenty-four hours of the scheduling of such hearing and afforded an opportunity to be heard. Application for such a hearing may be made by the respondent. If the court finds after the hearing that the child is no longer incapacitated, he shall be returned to the family court for further proceedings pursuant to this article.

9. Time spent by the respondent in the custody of a commissioner of an office within the department of mental hygiene or in a local hospital or detention facility pending transfer to the custody of the commissioner after a finding of incapacity, shall be credited and applied towards the period of placement specified in a dispositional order on the original petition.

§325.1.   The probable-cause hearing; time.

1. At the initial appearance, if the respondent denies a charge contained in the petition and the court determines that he shall be detained for more than three days pending a fact-finding hearing, the court shall schedule a probable-cause hearing to determine the issues specified in section 325.3.

2. Such probable-cause hearing shall be held within three days following the initial appearance or within four days following the filing of a petition, whichever occurs sooner.

3. For good cause shown, the court may adjourn the hearing for no more than an additional three court days.

4. The respondent may waive the probable-cause hearing, but the fact that the respondent is not ready for a fact-finding hearing shall not be deemed such a waiver.

5. Where the petition consists of an order of removal pursuant to article seven hundred twenty-five of the criminal procedure law, unless the removal was pursuant to subdivision three of section 725.05 of such law and the respondent was not afforded a probable cause hearing pursuant to subdivision three of section 180.75 of such law for a reason other than his waiver thereof pursuant to subdivision two of section 180.75 of such law, the petition shall be deemed to be based upon a determination that probable cause exists to believe the respondent is a juvenile delinquent and the respondent shall not be entitled to any further inquiry on the subject of whether probable cause exists. After the filing of any such petition the court must, however, exercise independent, de novo discretion with respect to release or detention as set forth in section 320.5.

§325.2.   The probable-cause hearing; order of proceeding.
1. The order of a probable-cause hearing held pursuant to section 325.1 or 322.2 shall be as follows:

(a) the presentment agency must call and examine witnesses and offer evidence in support of the charge;

(b) the respondent may, as a matter of right, testify in his own behalf; if the respondent so testifies, his testimony may not be introduced against him in any future proceeding, except to impeach his testimony at such future proceeding as inconsistent prior testimony;

(c) upon request of the respondent, the court shall, except for good cause shown, permit him to call and examine other witnesses or to produce other evidence in his behalf.

2. Each witness, whether called by the presentment agency or by the respondent, must, unless he would be authorized to give unsworn evidence at a fact-finding hearing, testify under oath. Each witness, including any respondent testifying in his own behalf, may be cross-examined.

3. Only non-hearsay evidence shall be admissible to demonstrate reasonable cause to believe that the respondent committed a crime; except that reports of experts and technicians in professional and scientific fields and sworn statements of the kinds admissible at a hearing upon a felony complaint in a criminal court may be admitted, unless the court determines, upon application of the respondent, that such hearsay evidence is, under the particular circumstances of the case, not sufficiently reliable, in which case the court shall require that the witness testify in person and be subject to cross-examination.

4. Such hearing should be completed at one session. In the interest of justice, however, it may be adjourned by the court, but no such adjournment may be for more than one court day.

§325.3.   The probable-cause hearing; determination.
1. At the conclusion of a probable-cause hearing held pursuant to section 325.1 the court shall determine in accordance with the evidentiary standards applicable to a hearing on a felony complaint in a criminal court:

(a) whether it is reasonable to believe that a crime was committed; and

(b) whether it is reasonable to believe that the respondent committed such crime.

2. The court shall state on the record the section or sections of the penal law or other law which it is reasonable to believe the respondent violated.

3. If the court finds that there is reasonable cause pursuant to subdivision one, it shall further determine whether continued detention is necessary pursuant to section 320.5.

4. If the court does not find that there is reasonable cause to believe that a crime was committed and that the respondent committed it, the case shall be adjourned and the respondent released from detention. If the court or the presentment agency cannot hold a probable cause hearing within the limits of subdivision two of section 325.1, the court may dismiss the petition without prejudice or for good cause shown adjourn the hearing and release the respondent pursuant to section 320.5.

Part 3
Discovery

§330.1.   Bill of particulars.

1. Definitions. (a) "Bill of particulars" is a written statement by the presentment agency specifying, as required by this section, items of factual information which are not recited in the petition and which pertain to the offense charged and including the substance of each respondent's conduct encompassed by the charge which the presentment agency intends to prove at a fact-finding hearing on its direct case, and whether the presentment agency intends to prove that the respondent acted as principal or accomplice or both. However, the presentment agency shall not be required to include in the bill of particulars matters of evidence relating to how the presentment agency intends to prove the elements of the offense charged or how the presentment agency intends to prove any item of factual information included in the bill of particulars.

(b) "Request for a bill of particulars" is a written request served by respondent upon the presentment agency, without leave of the court, requesting a bill of particulars, specifying the items of factual information desired, and alleging that respondent cannot adequately prepare or conduct his defense without the information requested.

2. Bill of particulars upon request. Upon a timely request for a bill of particulars by a respondent against whom a petition is pending, the presentment agency shall within fifteen days of the service of the request or as soon thereafter as is practicable, serve upon the respondent or his or her attorney and file with the court, the bill of particulars, except to the extent the presentment agency shall have refused to comply with the request pursuant to subdivision four of this section. If the respondent is detained, the court shall direct the filing of the bill of particulars on an expedited basis and prior to the commencement of the fact-finding hearing.

3. Timeliness of request. A request for a bill of particulars shall be timely if made within thirty days after the conclusion of the initial appearance and before commencement of the fact-finding hearing. If the respondent is not represented by counsel, and has requested an adjournment to retain counsel or to have counsel appointed, the thirty-day period shall commence, for the purposes of a request for a bill of particulars by the respondent, on the date counsel initially appeared on respondent's behalf. However, the court may direct compliance with a request for a bill of particulars that, for good cause shown, could not have been made within the time specified.

4. Request refused. The presentment agency may refuse to comply with the request for a bill of particulars or any portion of the request for a bill of

particulars to the extent it reasonably believes that the item of factual information requested is not authorized to be included in a bill of particulars, or that such information is not necessary to enable the respondent adequately to prepare or conduct his defense, or that a protective order would be warranted or that the demand is untimely. Such refusal shall be made in a writing, which shall set forth the grounds of such belief as fully as possible, consistent with the reason for the refusal. Within fifteen days of the request or as soon thereafter as practicable, the refusal shall be served upon the respondent and a copy shall be filed with the court.

5. Court ordered bill of particulars. Where a presentment agency has timely served a written refusal pursuant to subdivision four of this section and upon motion, made in writing, of a respondent, who has made a request for a bill of particulars and whose request has not been complied with in whole or in part, the court must, to the extent a protective order is not warranted, order the presentment agency to comply with the request if it is satisfied that the items of factual information requested are authorized to be included in a bill of particulars, and that such information is necessary to enable the respondent adequately to prepare or conduct his defense and, if the request was untimely, a finding of good cause for the delay. Where a presentment agency has not timely served a written refusal pursuant to subdivision four of this section the court must, unless it is satisfied that the presentment agency has shown good cause why such an order should not be issued, issue an order requiring the presentment agency to comply or providing for any other order authorized by subdivision one of section 331.6.

6. Motion procedure. A motion for a bill of particulars shall be made as prescribed in section 332.1. Upon an order granting a motion pursuant to this section, the presentment agency must file with the court a bill of particulars, reciting every item of information designated in the order, and serve a copy thereof upon the respondent. Pending such filing and service, the fact-finding hearing is stayed.

7. Protective order.

(a) The court may, upon motion of the presentment agency, or of any affected person, or upon determination of a motion of respondent for a court-ordered bill of particulars, or upon its own initiative, issue a protective order denying, limiting, conditioning, delaying or regulating the bill of particulars for good cause, including constitutional limitations, danger to the integrity of physical evidence or a substantial risk of physical harm, intimidation, economic reprisal, bribery or unjustified annoyance or embarrassment to any person or an adverse effect upon the legitimate needs of law enforcement, including the protection of the confidentiality of informants, or any other factor or set of factors which outweighs the need for the bill of particulars.

(b) An order limiting, conditioning, delaying or regulating the bill of particulars may, among other things, require that any material copied or derived therefrom be maintained in the exclusive possession of the attorney for the respondent and be used for the exclusive purpose of preparing for the defense of the juvenile delinquency proceeding.

8. Amendment. At any time before commencement of the fact-finding hearing, the presentment agency may, without leave of the court, serve upon respondent and file with the court an amended bill of particulars. At any time during the fact-finding hearing, upon application of the presentment agency and with notice to the respondent and an opportunity for him to be heard, the court

must, upon finding that no undue prejudice will accrue to respondent and that the presentment agency has acted in good faith, permit the presentment agency to amend the bill of particulars. Upon any amendment of the bill of particulars, the court must, upon application of respondent, order an adjournment of the fact-finding hearing or any other action it deems appropriate which may, by reason of the amendment, be necessary to accord the respondent an adequate opportunity to defend.

§330.2. Suppression of evidence.

1. A respondent in a juvenile delinquency proceeding may make a motion to suppress evidence in accordance with sections 710.20 and 710.60 of the criminal procedure law.

2. Whenever the presentment agency intends to offer at a fact-finding hearing evidence described in section 710.20 or subdivision one of section 710.30 of the criminal procedure law, such agency must serve upon respondent notice of such intention. Such notice must be served within fifteen days after the conclusion of the initial appearance or before the fact-finding hearing, whichever occurs first, unless the court, for good cause shown, permits later service and accords the respondent a reasonable opportunity to make a suppression motion thereafter. If the respondent is detained, the court shall direct that such notice be served on an expedited basis.

3. When a motion to suppress evidence is made before the commencement of the fact-finding hearing, the fact-finding hearing shall not be held until the determination of the motion.

4. After the pre-trial determination and denial of the motion, if the court is satisfied, upon a showing by the respondent, that additional pertinent facts have been discovered by the respondent which could not have been discovered by the respondent with reasonable diligence before determination of the motion, it may permit him to renew. Such motion to renew shall be made prior to the commencement of the fact-finding hearing, unless the additional pertinent facts were discovered during the fact-finding hearing.

5. Upon granting a motion to suppress evidence, the court must order that the evidence in question be excluded. When the order excludes tangible property unlawfully taken from the respondent's possession, and when such property is not otherwise subject to lawful retention, the court may, upon request of the respondent, further order that such property be restored to him.

6. An order finally denying a motion to suppress evidence may be reviewed upon an appeal from an ensuing finding of delinquency, notwithstanding the fact that such finding is entered upon an admission made by the respondent, unless the respondent, upon an admission, expressly waives his right to appeal.

7. A motion to suppress evidence is the exclusive method of challenging the admissibility of evidence upon the grounds specified in this section, and a respondent who does not make such a motion waives his right to judicial determination of any such contention.

8. In the absence of service of notice upon a respondent as prescribed in this section, no evidence of a kind specified in subdivision two may be received against him at the fact-finding hearing unless he has, despite the lack of such notice, moved to suppress such evidence and such motion has been denied.

9. An order granting a motion to suppress evidence shall be deemed an order of disposition appealable under section eleven hundred twelve. In taking such an appeal the presentment agency must file, in addition to a notice of appeal, a statement alleging that the deprivation of the use of the evidence ordered

suppressed has rendered the sum of the proof available to the presentment agency either: (a) insufficient as a matter of law, or (b) so weak in its entirety that any reasonable possibility of proving the allegations contained in the petition has been effectively destroyed. If the respondent is in detention he shall be released pending such appeal unless the court, upon conducting a hearing, enters an order continuing detention. An order continuing detention under this subdivision may be stayed by the appropriate appellate division.

10. The taking of an appeal by the presentment agency pursuant to subdivision nine constitutes a bar to the presentment of the petition involving the evidence ordered suppressed, unless and until such suppression is reversed upon appeal and vacated.

§331.1. **Discovery; definition of terms.**
The following definitions are applicable to this section and sections 331.2 through 331.7.

1. "Demand to produce" means a written notice served by and on a party, without leave of the court, demanding to inspect property pursuant to section 331.2 or 331.3 and giving reasonable notice of the time at which the demanding party wishes to inspect the property designated.

2. "Attorneys' work product" means property to the extent that it contains the opinions, theories or conclusions of the presentment agency, counsel for the respondent or members of their staffs.

3. "Property" means any existing tangible personal or real property, including but not limited to, books, records, reports, memoranda, papers, photographs, tapes or other electronic recordings, articles of clothing, fingerprints, blood samples, fingernail scrapings or handwriting specimens, but excluding attorneys' work product.

4. "Co-respondent" means a person whose name appears in the petition pursuant to paragraph (i) of subdivision three of section 311.1.

§331.2. **Discovery; upon demand of a party.**
1. Except to the extent protected by court order, upon a demand to produce by a respondent, the presentment agency shall disclose to the respondent and make available for inspection, photography, copying or testing, the following property:

(a) any written, recorded or oral statement of the respondent, or by a co-respondent, made, other than in the course of the criminal transaction, to a public servant engaged in law enforcement activity or to a person then acting under his direction or in cooperation with him;

(b) any transcript of testimony relating to the proceeding pending against the respondent, given by the respondent, or by a co-respondent, before any grand jury;

(c) any written report or document, or portion thereof, concerning a physical or mental examination, or scientific test or experiment, relating to the proceeding which was made by, or at the request or direction of a public servant engaged in law enforcement activity or which was made by a person whom the presentment agency intends to call as a witness at a hearing, or which the presentment agency intends to introduce at a hearing;

(d) any photograph or drawing relating to the proceeding which was made or completed by a public servant engaged in law enforcement activity, or which was made by a person whom the presentment agency intends to call as a witness at a hearing, or which the presentment agency intends to introduce at a hearing;

(e) any other property obtained from the respondent or a co-respondent;

(f) any tapes or other electronic recordings which the presentment agency intends to introduce at the fact-finding hearing, irrespective of whether such recording was made during the course of the criminal transaction;

(g) anything required to be disclosed, prior to the fact-finding hearing, to the respondent by the presentment agency, pursuant to the constitution of this state or of the United States; and

(h) the approximate date, time and place of the offense charged and of respondent's arrest.

2. (a) The presentment agency shall make a diligent, good faith effort to ascertain the existence of property demanded pursuant to subdivision one and to cause such property to be made available for discovery where it exists but is not within the presentment agency's possession, custody or control; provided, that the presentment agency shall not be required to obtain by subpoena duces tecum demanded material which the respondent may thereby obtain.

(b) In any case in which the property includes grand jury testimony, the presentment agency shall forthwith request that the district attorney provide a transcript of such testimony; upon receiving such a request, the district attorney shall promptly apply to the appropriate criminal court, with written notice to the presentment agency and the respondent, for a written order pursuant to section three hundred twenty-five of the judiciary law releasing a transcript of testimony to the presentment agency.

3. Except to the extent protected by court order, upon demand to produce by the presentment agency, the respondent shall disclose and make available for inspection, photography, copying or testing, subject to constitutional limitations:

(a) any written report or document, or portion thereof, concerning a physical examination, or scientific test, experiment, or comparison, made by or at the request or direction of, the respondent, if the respondent intends to introduce such report or document at a hearing, or if the respondent has filed a notice of defense of mental disease or defect pursuant to section 335.1 and such report or document relates thereto, or if such report or document was made by a person, other than respondent, whom respondent intends to call as a witness at a hearing; and

(b) any photograph, drawing, tape or other electronic recording which the respondent intends to introduce at a hearing.

4. Except to the extent protected by court order, upon demand to produce by the presentment agency, a respondent who has served a written notice, under section 335.1, of intention to rely upon the defense of mental disease or defect shall disclose and make available for inspection, photography, copying or testing, subject to constitutional limitations, any written report or document, or portion thereof, concerning a mental examination made by or at the request or direction of the respondent.

5. The respondent shall make a diligent good faith effort to make such property available for discovery pursuant to subdivisions three and four where it exists but the property is not within his possession, custody or control, provided that the respondent shall not be required to obtain by subpoena duces tecum demanded material that the presentment agency may thereby obtain.

6. Notwithstanding the provisions of subdivisions one through five, the presentment agency or the respondent, as the case may be, may refuse to disclose any information which he reasonably believes is not discoverable by

a demand to produce, or for which he reasonably believes a protective order pursuant to section 331.5 would be warranted. Such refusal shall be made in writing, which shall set forth the grounds of such belief as fully as possible, consistent with the objective of the refusal. The writing shall be served upon the demanding party and a copy shall be filed with the court.

§331.3. Discovery; upon court order.
1. Upon motion of respondent the court, (a) must order discovery as to any material not disclosed upon a demand pursuant to section 331.2, if it finds that the presentment agency's refusal to disclose such material is not justified; (b) must, unless it is satisfied that the presentment agency has shown good cause why such an order should not be issued, order discovery or any other order authorized by subdivision one of section 331.6 as to any material not disclosed upon demand pursuant to section 331.2 where the presentment agency has failed to serve a timely written refusal pursuant to subdivision six of section 331.2; and (c) may order discovery with respect to any other property which the presentment agency intends to introduce at the fact-finding hearing, upon a showing by the respondent that discovery with respect to such property is material to the preparation of his defense, and that the request is reasonable. Upon granting the motion pursuant to paragraph (c) hereof, the court shall, upon motion of the presentment agency showing such to be material to the preparation of its case and that the request is reasonable, condition its order of discovery by further directing discovery by the presentment agency of property, of the same kind or character as that authorized to be inspected by the respondent which he intends to introduce at the fact-finding hearing.
2. Upon motion of the presentment agency, and subject to constitutional limitation, the court; (a) must order discovery as to any property not disclosed upon a demand pursuant to section 331.2, if it finds that the respondent's refusal to disclose such material is not justified; and (b) may order the respondent to provide non-testimonial evidence. Such order may, among other things, require the respondent to:
(i) appear in a line-up;
(ii) speak for identification by witness or potential witness;
(iii) be fingerprinted, provided that the respondent is subject to fingerprinting pursuant to this article;
(iv) pose for photographs not involving reenactment of an event, provided the respondent is subject to fingerprinting pursuant to this article;
(v) permit the taking of samples of blood, hair or other materials from his body in a manner not involving an unreasonable intrusion thereof or a risk of serious physical injury thereto;
(vi) provide specimens of his handwriting; and
(vii) submit to a reasonable physical or medical inspection of his body.
This subdivision shall not be construed to limit, expand, or otherwise affect the issuance of a similar court order, as may be authorized by law, before the filing of a petition consistent with such rights as the respondent may derive from this article, the constitution of this state or of the United States.
3. An order pursuant to this section may be denied, limited or conditioned as provided in section 331.5.

§331.4.   Discovery; of prior statements and history of witnesses.

1. At the commencement of the fact-finding hearing, the presentment agency shall, subject to a protective order, make available to the respondent:

(a) any written or recorded statement, including any testimony before a grand jury and any examination videotaped pursuant to section 190.32 of the criminal procedure law, made by a person whom the presentment agency intends to call as a witness at the fact-finding hearing, and which relates to the subject matter of the witness's testimony. When such a statement includes grand jury testimony, the presentment agency shall request that the district attorney provide a transcript of testimony prior to the commencement of the fact-finding hearing; upon receiving such a request, the district attorney shall promptly apply to the appropriate criminal court, with written notice to the presentment agency and the respondent, for a written order pursuant to section three hundred twenty-five of the judiciary law releasing a transcript of testimony to the presentment agency;

(b) a record of judgment of conviction of a witness the presentment agency intends to call at the fact-finding hearing if such record is known by the presentment agency to exist;

(c) the existence of any pending criminal action against a witness the presentment agency intends to call at the fact-finding hearing, if the pending criminal action is known by the presentment agency to exist.

The provisions of paragraphs (b) and (c) shall not be construed to require the presentment agency to fingerprint a witness or otherwise cause the division of criminal justice services or other law enforcement agency or court to issue a report concerning a witness.

2. At the conclusion of the presentment agency's direct case and before the commencement of the respondent's direct case, the respondent shall, subject to a protective order, make available to the presentment agency (a) any written or recorded statement made by a person other than the respondent whom the respondent intends to call as a witness at the fact-finding hearing and which relates to the subject matter of the witness's testimony; (b) a record of judgment of conviction of a witness, other than the respondent, the respondent intends to call at a hearing if the record of conviction is known by the respondent to exist; and (c) the existence of any pending criminal action against a witness, other than the respondent, the respondent intends to call at a hearing, if the pending criminal action is known by the respondent to exist.

3. Subject to a protective order, at a pre-fact-finding hearing held upon a motion pursuant to section 330.2, at which a witness is called to testify, each party at the conclusion of the direct examination of each of its witnesses, shall, upon request of the other party, make available to that party to the extent not previously disclosed:

(a) any written or recorded statement, including any testimony before a grand jury, made by such witness other than the respondent, which relates to the subject matter of the witness's testimony. When such a statement includes grand jury testimony, the presentment agency shall request that the district attorney provide a transcript of testimony prior to the commencement of the pre-fact-finding hearing; upon receiving such a request, the district attorney shall promptly apply to the appropriate criminal court, with written notice to the presentment agency and the respondent, for a written order pursuant to section three hundred twenty-five of the judiciary law releasing a transcript of testimony to the presentment agency;

(b) a record of a judgment of conviction of such witness other than the respondent if the record of conviction is known by the presentment agency or respondent, as the case may be, to exist; and

(c) the existence of any pending criminal action against such witness other than the respondent, if the pending criminal action is known by the presentment agency or respondent, as the case may be, to exist.

§331.5. Discovery; protective orders, continuing duty to disclose.

1. The court may, upon motion of either party, or of any affected person, or upon determination of a motion of either party for an order of discovery, or upon its own initiative, issue a protective order denying, limiting, conditioning, delaying or regulating discovery for good cause, including constitutional limitations, danger to the integrity of physical evidence or a substantial risk of physical harm, intimidation, economic reprisal, bribery or unjustified annoyance or embarrassment to any person or an adverse effect upon the legitimate needs of law enforcement, including the protection of the confidentiality of informants, or any other factor or set of factors which outweighs the usefulness of the discovery.

2. An order limiting, conditioning, delaying or regulating discovery may, among other things, require that any material copied or derived therefrom be maintained in the exclusive possession of the attorney for the discovering party and be used for the exclusive purpose of preparing for the defense or presentment of the action.

3. A motion for a protective order shall suspend discovery of the particular matter in dispute.

4. If, after complying with the provisions of sections 331.2 through 331.7 or an order pursuant thereto, a party finds, either before or during the fact-finding hearing, additional material subject to discovery or covered by such order, he shall promptly comply with the demand or order, refuse to comply with the demand where refusal is authorized, or apply for a protective order pursuant to this section.

§331.6. Discovery; sanctions.

1. If, during the course of discovery proceedings, the court finds that a party has failed to comply with any of the provisions of sections 331.2 through 331.7, the court may order such party to permit discovery of the property not previously disclosed, grant a continuance, issue a protective order, prohibit the introduction of certain evidence or the calling of certain witnesses or take any other appropriate action.

2. The failure of the presentment agency to call as a witness a person specified in subdivision one of section 331.2 or any party to introduce disclosed material at the fact-finding hearing shall not, by itself constitute grounds for any sanction or for adverse comment thereupon by any party.

§331.7. Discovery; demand and motion procedure.

1. If the respondent is in detention:

(a) a demand to produce shall be made within seven days after the conclusion of the initial appearance or prior to the commencement of the fact-finding hearing, whichever occurs sooner, unless the court grants an extension for good cause shown;

(b) a refusal to comply with a demand to produce shall be made within five days of the service of the demand to produce, but for good cause may be made thereafter;

(c) absent a refusal to comply with a demand to produce, compliance with such demand shall be made within seven days of the service of the demand or as soon thereafter as practicable. The court, however, may order compliance within a shorter period of time.

2. If the respondent is not in detention:

(a) a demand to produce shall be made within fifteen days after the conclusion of the initial appearance unless extended for good cause shown, but in no event later than the commencement of the fact-finding hearing;

(b) a refusal to comply with a demand to produce shall be made within fifteen days of the service of the demand to produce, but for good cause may be made thereafter;

(c) absent a refusal to comply with a demand to produce, compliance with such demand shall be made within fifteen days of the service of the demand or as soon thereafter as practicable.

3. If the respondent is not in detention, a motion by the presentment agency for discovery shall be made within thirty days after the conclusion of the initial appearance, but for good cause shown may be made at any time before commencement of the fact-finding hearing. If the respondent is in detention such motion shall be made within fourteen days after the conclusion of the initial appearance or prior to the commencement of the fact-finding hearing, whichever occurs sooner.

4. A motion by a respondent for discovery shall be made as prescribed in section 332.2.

5. Where the interests of justice so require, the court may permit a party to a motion for an order of discovery or a protective order, or other affected person, to submit papers or to testify ex parte or in camera. Any such papers and transcripts of such testimony shall be sealed, but shall constitute a part of the record on appeal. If practical, a judge who receives papers or testimony in camera shall refer the case to a different judge of the same court to preside at the fact-finding hearing.

§332.1. Pre-trial motions; definition.

"Pre-trial motion" as used in this article means any motion by a respondent which seeks an order of the court:

1. transferring a proceeding pursuant to section 302.3; or

2. granting a separate fact-finding hearing pursuant to section 311.3; or

3. granting separate fact-finding hearings or consolidating petitions pursuant to section 311.6; or

4. dismissing a petition pursuant to section 315.1; or

5. granting a bill of particulars pursuant to section 330.1; or

6. granting discovery pursuant to section 331.3; or

7. suppressing the use at the fact-finding hearing of any evidence pursuant to section 330.2; or

8. dismissing a petition, or any count thereof, on the ground that the respondent has been denied a speedy fact-finding hearing contrary to section 310.2; or

9. dismissing a petition, or any count thereof, on the ground that the proceeding is untimely, pursuant to section 302.2; or

10. dismissing a petition, or any count thereof, on the ground that the proceeding is barred in accordance with the laws applicable pursuant to section 303.2.

§332.2.   Pre-trial motions; procedure.

1. Except as otherwise expressly provided in this article, all pre-trial motions shall be filed within thirty days after the conclusion of the initial appearance and before commencement of the fact-finding hearing, or within such additional times as the court may fix upon application of the respondent made prior to entering a finding pursuant to section 345.1. If the respondent is not represented by counsel and has requested an adjournment to retain counsel or to have counsel appointed, such thirty-day period shall commence on the date counsel initially appears on the respondent's behalf. A motion made pursuant to subdivision eight of section 332.1 must be made prior to the commencement of a fact-finding hearing or the entry of an admission.

2. All pre-trial motions with supporting affidavits, exhibits and memoranda of law, if any, shall be included within the same set of motion papers wherever practicable, and shall be made returnable on the same date, unless the respondent shows that it would be prejudicial to the defense were a single judge to consider all such motions. Where one motion seeks to provide the basis for making another motion, it shall be deemed impracticable to include both motions in the same set of motion papers.

3. Notwithstanding the provisions of subdivisions one and two, the court must entertain and decide on its merits, at any time before the conclusion of the fact-finding hearing, any appropriate motion based upon grounds of which the respondent could not, with due diligence, have been previously aware, or which, for other good cause, could not reasonably have raised within the period specified in subdivision one. Any other pre-trial motions made after such thirty day period may be summarily denied, but the court, in the interest of justice and for good cause shown may, in its discretion, at any time before a finding is entered, entertain and dispose of the motion on the merits.

4. If the respondent is detained, the court shall hear and determine pre-trial motions on an expedited basis.

§335.1.   Notice of defense of mental disease or defect.

Evidence of mental disease or defect of the respondent excluding his responsibility under this article is not admissible at the fact-finding hearing unless the respondent serves upon the presentment agency and files with the court a written notice of intention to rely upon such defense. Such notice must be served and filed before the fact-finding hearing and not more than thirty days after the conclusion of the initial appearance, whichever is sooner. In the interest of justice and for good cause shown, however, the court may permit such service and filing to be made at any later time prior to the conclusion of the fact-finding hearing.

§335.2.   Notice of alibi.

1. At any time not more than fifteen days after the conclusion of the initial appearance and before the fact-finding hearing the presentment agency may serve upon the respondent and file a copy thereof with the court, a demand that if the respondent intends to offer a defense that at the time of the commission of the crime charged he was at some place or places other than the scene of the crime, and to call witnesses in support of such defense, he must within ten days of service of such demand, serve upon such agency, and file a copy thereof with the court, a "notice of alibi", reciting; (a) the place or places where the respondent claims to have been at the time in question, and (b) the names, the residential addresses, the places of employment and the addresses thereof of

every such alibi witness upon whom he intends to rely. For good cause shown, the court may extend the period for service of the notice.

2. Within a reasonable time after receipt of the respondent's witness list but not later than ten days before the fact-finding hearing, the presentment agency must serve upon the respondent and file a copy thereof with the court, a list of witnesses such agency proposes to offer in rebuttal to discredit the respondent's alibi at the trial together with the residential addresses, the places of employment and the addresses thereof of any such rebuttal witnesses. A witness who will testify that the respondent was at the scene of the crime is not such an alibi rebuttal witness. For good cause shown, the court may extend the period for service.

3. If at the trial the respondent calls such an alibi witness without having served the demanded notice of alibi, or if having served such a notice he calls a witness not specified therein, the court may exclude any testimony of such witness relating to the alibi defense. The court may in its discretion receive such testimony, but before doing so, it must, upon application of the presentment agency, grant a reasonable adjournment.

4. Similarly, if the presentment agency fails to serve and file a list of any rebuttal witnesses, the provisions of subdivision three shall reciprocally apply.

5. Both the respondent and the presentment agency shall be under a continuing duty to promptly disclose the names and addresses of additional witnesses which come to the attention of either party subsequent to filing his witness list as provided in this section.

Part 4
The Fact-finding Hearing

§340.1.　　Time of fact-finding hearing.

1. If the respondent is in detention and the highest count in the petition charges the commission of a class A, B, or C felony, the fact-finding hearing shall commence not more than fourteen days after the conclusion of the initial appearance except as provided in subdivision four. If the respondent is in detention and the highest count in such petition is less than a class C felony the

fact-finding hearing shall commence no more than three days after the conclusion of the initial appearance except as provided in subdivision four.

2. If the respondent is not in detention the fact-finding hearing shall commence not more than sixty days after the conclusion of the initial appearance except as provided in subdivision four.

3. For the purposes of this section, in any case where a proceeding has been removed to the family court pursuant to an order issued pursuant to section 725.05 of the criminal procedure law, the date specified in such order for the defendant's appearance in the family court shall constitute the date of the initial appearance.

4. The court may adjourn a fact-finding hearing:

(a) on its own motion or on motion of the presentment agency for good cause shown for not more than three days if the respondent is in detention and not more than thirty days if the respondent is not in detention; provided, however, that if there is probable cause to believe the respondent committed a homicide or a crime which resulted in a person being incapacitated from attending court, the court may adjourn the hearing for a reasonable length of time; or

(b) on motion by the respondent for good cause shown for not more than thirty days; or

(c) on its own motion for not more than six months if the proceeding has been adjourned in contemplation of dismissal pursuant to section 315.3.

5. The court shall state on the record the reason for any adjournment of the fact-finding hearing.

6. Successive motions to adjourn a fact-finding hearing shall not be granted in the absence of a showing, on the record, of special circumstances; such circumstances shall not include calendar congestion or the status of the court's docket or backlog.

7. For purposes of this section, if a warrant for the respondent's arrest has been issued pursuant to section 312.2 of this article due to the respondent's failure to appear for a scheduled fact-finding hearing, computation of the time within which such hearing must take place shall exclude the period extending from the date of issuance of the bench warrant for respondent's arrest because of his or her failure to appear to the date the respondent subsequently appears in court pursuant to a bench warrant or appears voluntarily; provided, however, no period of time may be excluded hereunder unless the respondent's location cannot be determined by the exercise of due diligence or, if the respondent's location is known, his or her presence in court cannot be obtained by the exercise of due diligence. In determining whether due diligence has been exercised, the court shall consider, among other factors, the report presented to the court pursuant to subdivision two of section 312.2 of this article.

§340.2. Presiding judge.

1. The judge who presides at the commencement of the fact-finding hearing shall continue to preside until such hearing is concluded and an order entered pursuant to section 345.1 unless a mistrial is declared.

2. The judge who presides at the fact-finding hearing or accepts an admission pursuant to section 321.3 shall preside at any other subsequent hearing in the proceeding, including but not limited to the dispositional hearing.

3. Notwithstanding the provisions of subdivision two, the rules of the family court shall provide for the assignment of the proceeding to another judge of the court when the appropriate judge cannot preside:

(a) by reason of illness, disability, vacation or no longer being a judge of the court in that county; or

(b) by reason of removal from the proceeding due to bias, prejudice or similar grounds; or

(c) because it is not practicable for the judge to preside.

4. The provisions of this section shall not be waived.

§341.1.   Exclusion of general public.

The general public may be excluded from any proceeding under this article and only such persons and the representatives of authorized agencies as have a direct interest in the case shall be admitted thereto.

§341.2.   Presence of respondent and his or her parent.

1. The respondent and his or her counsel shall be personally present at any hearing under this article and at the initial appearance.

2. If a respondent conducts himself or herself in so disorderly and disruptive a manner that the hearing cannot be carried on with the respondent in the courtroom, the court may order a recess for the purpose of enabling the respondent's parent or other person responsible for his or her care and the respondent's counsel to exercise full efforts to assist the respondent to conduct himself or herself so as to permit the proceedings to resume in an orderly manner. If such efforts fail, the respondent may be removed from the courtroom if, after he or she is warned by the court that he or she will be removed, he or she continues such disorderly and disruptive conduct. Such time shall not extend beyond the minimum period necessary to restore order.

3. The respondent's parent or other person responsible for his or her care shall be present at any hearing under this article and at the initial appearance. However, the court shall not be prevented from proceeding by the absence of such parent or person if reasonable and substantial effort has been made to notify such parent or other person and if the respondent and his or her counsel are present.

§342.1.   The fact-finding hearing; order of procedure.

The order of the fact-finding hearing shall be as follows:

1. The court shall permit the parties to deliver opening addresses. If both parties deliver opening addresses, the presentment agency's address shall be delivered first.

2. The presentment agency must offer evidence in support of the petition.

3. The respondent may offer evidence in his defense.

4. The presentment agency may offer evidence in rebuttal of the respondent's evidence, and the respondent may then offer evidence in rebuttal of the presentment agency's evidence. The court may in its discretion permit the parties to offer further rebuttal or surrebuttal evidence in this pattern. In the interest of justice, the court may permit either party to offer evidence upon rebuttal which is not technically of a rebuttal nature but more properly a part of the offering party's original case.

5. At the conclusion of the evidence, the respondent shall have the right to deliver a summation.

6. The presentment agency shall then have the right to deliver a summation.

7. The court must then consider the case and enter a finding.

§342.2.   Evidence in fact-finding hearings; required quantum.

1. Only evidence that is competent, material and relevant may be admitted at a fact-finding hearing.

2. Any determination at the conclusion of a fact-finding hearing that a respondent committed an act or acts which if committed by an adult would be a crime must be based on proof beyond a reasonable doubt.

3. An order of removal pursuant to a direction authorized by sections 220.10, 310.85 and 330.25 of the criminal procedure law constitutes proof beyond a reasonable doubt and a determination that the respondent did the act or acts specified therein in accordance with section 725.05 of the criminal procedure law.

§343.1. Rules of evidence; testimony given by children.

1. Any person may be a witness in a delinquency proceeding unless the court finds that, by reason of infancy or mental disease or defect, he does not possess sufficient intelligence or capacity to justify reception of his evidence.

2. Every witness more than nine years old may testify only under oath unless the court is satisfied that such witness cannot, as a result of mental disease or defect, understand the nature of an oath. A witness less than nine years old may not testify under oath unless the court is satisfied that he or she understands the nature of an oath. If under either of the above provisions, a witness is deemed to be ineligible to testify under oath, the witness may nevertheless be permitted to give unsworn evidence if the court is satisfied that the witness possesses sufficient intelligence and capacity to justify the reception thereof.

3. A respondent may not be found to be delinquent solely upon the unsworn evidence given pursuant to subdivision two.

*4. A child witness may give testimony in accordance with the provisions of article sixty-five of the criminal procedure law, provided such child is declared vulnerable in accordance with subdivision one of section 65.10 of such law. A child witness means a person fourteen years old or less who is or will be called to testify in any proceeding concerning an act defined in article one hundred thirty of the penal law or section 255.25, 255.26 or 255.27 of such law, which act would constitute a crime if committed by an adult. The provisions of this subdivision shall expire and be deemed repealed on the same date as article sixty-five of the criminal procedure law expires and is deemed repealed pursuant to section five of chapter five hundred five of the laws of nineteen hundred eighty-five, as from time to time, amended.   *(Repealed Eff.9/1/17,Ch.55,L.2015)*

§343.2. Rules of evidence; corroboration of accomplice testimony.

1. A respondent may not be found to be delinquent upon the testimony of an accomplice unsupported by corroborative evidence tending to connect the respondent with the commission of the crime or crimes charged in the petition.

2. An "accomplice" means a witness in a juvenile delinquency proceeding who, according to evidence adduced in such proceeding, may reasonably be considered to have participated in:

(a) the crime charged; or

(b) a crime based on the same or some of the same facts or conduct which constitutes the crime charged in the petition.

3. A witness who is an accomplice as defined in subdivision two is no less such because a proceeding, conviction or finding of delinquency against him would be barred or precluded by some defense or exemption such as infancy, immunity or previous prosecution amounting to a collateral impediment to such proceeding, conviction or finding, not affecting the conclusion that such

witness engaged in the conduct constituting the crime with the mental state required for the commission thereof.

§343.3. Rules of evidence; identification by means of previous recognition in absence of present identification.

1. In any juvenile delinquency proceeding in which the respondent's commission of a crime is in issue, testimony as provided in subdivision two may be given by a witness when:

(a) such witness testifies that:

(i) he observed the person claimed by the presentment agency to be the respondent either at the time and place of the commission of the crime or upon some other occasion relevant to the case; and

(ii) on a subsequent occasion he observed, under circumstances consistent with such rights as an accused person may derive under the constitution of this state or of the United States, a person whom he recognized as the same person whom he had observed on the first incriminating occasion; and

(iii) he is unable at the proceeding to state, on the basis of present recollection, whether or not the respondent is the person in question; and

(b) it is established that the respondent is in fact the person whom the witness observed and recognized on the second occasion. Such fact may be established by testimony of another person or persons to whom the witness promptly declared his recognition on such occasion.

2. Under circumstances prescribed in subdivision one, such witness may testify at the proceeding that the person whom he observed and recognized on the second occasion is the same person whom he observed on the first or incriminating occasion. Such testimony, together with the evidence that the respondent is in fact the person whom the witness observed and recognized on the second occasion, constitutes evidence in chief.

§343.4. Rules of evidence; identification by means of previous recognition, in addition to present identification.

In any juvenile delinquency proceeding in which the respondent's commission of a crime is in issue, a witness who testifies that: (a) he observed the person claimed by the presentment agency to be the respondent either at the time and place of the commission of the crime or upon some other occasion relevant to the case, and (b) on the basis of present recollection, the respondent is the person in question, and (c) on a subsequent occasion he observed the respondent, under circumstances consistent with such rights as an accused person may derive under the constitution of this state or of the United States, and then also recognized him as the same person whom he had observed on the first or incriminating occasion, may, in addition to making an identification of the respondent at the delinquency proceeding on the basis of present recollection as the person whom he observed on the first or incriminating occasion, also describe his previous recognition of the respondent and testify that the person whom he observed on such second occasion is the same person whom he had observed on the first or incriminating occasion. Such testimony constitutes evidence in chief.

§343.5. Rules of evidence; impeachment of own witness by proof of prior contradictory statement.

1. When, upon examination by the party who called him, a witness in a delinquency proceeding gives testimony upon a material issue of the case which tends to disprove the position of such party, such party may introduce

evidence that such witness has previously made either a written statement signed by him or an oral statement under oath contradictory to such testimony.

2. Evidence concerning a prior contradictory statement introduced pursuant to subdivision one may be received only for the purpose of impeaching the credibility of the witness with respect to his testimony upon the subject, and does not constitute evidence in chief.

3. When a witness has made a prior signed or sworn statement contradictory to his testimony in a delinquency proceeding upon a material issue of the case, but his testimony does not tend to disprove the position of the party who called him and elicited such testimony, evidence that the witness made such prior statement is not admissible, and such party may not use such prior statement for the purpose of refreshing the recollection of the witness in a manner that discloses its contents to the court.

§344.1. Rules of evidence; proof of previous conviction or delinquency finding.

1. If in the course of a juvenile delinquency proceeding, any witness, including a respondent, is properly asked whether he was previously convicted of a specified offense and answers in the negative or in an equivocal manner, the party adverse to the one who called him may independently prove such conviction. If in response to proper inquiry whether he has ever been convicted of any offense the witness answers in the negative or in an equivocal manner, the adverse party may independently prove any previous conviction.

2. If a respondent in a juvenile delinquency proceeding, through the testimony of a witness other than respondent called by him, offers evidence of his good character, the presentment agency may independently prove any previous finding of delinquency of the respondent for a crime the commission of which would tend to negate any character trait or quality attributed to the respondent in such witness' testimony.

§344.2. Rules of evidence; statements of respondent; corroboration.

1. Evidence of a written or oral confession, admission, or other statement made by a respondent with respect to his participation or lack of participation in the crime charged, may not be received in evidence against him in a juvenile delinquency proceeding if such statement was involuntarily made.

2. A confession, admission or other statement is "involuntarily made" by a respondent when it is obtained from him:

(a) by any person by the use or threatened use of physical force upon the respondent or another person, or by means of any other improper conduct or undue pressure which impaired the respondent's physical or mental condition to the extent of undermining his ability to make a choice whether or not to make a statement; or

(b) by a public servant engaged in law enforcement activity or by a person then acting under his direction or in cooperation with him:

(i) by means of any promise or statement of fact, which promise or statement creates a substantial risk that the respondent might falsely incriminate himself; or

(ii) in violation of such rights as the respondent may derive from the constitution of this state or of the United States; or

(iii) in violation of section 305.2.

3. A child may not be found to be delinquent based on the commission of any crime solely upon evidence of a confession or admission made by him without additional proof that the crime charged has been committed.

§344.3.   Rules of evidence; psychiatric testimony in certain cases.

When, in connection with a defense of mental disease or defect, a psychiatrist or licensed psychologist who has examined the respondent testifies at the fact-finding hearing concerning the respondent's mental condition at the time of the conduct charged to constitute a crime, he must be permitted to make a statement as to the nature of the examination, the diagnosis of the mental condition of the respondent and his opinion as to the extent, if any, to which the capacity of the respondent to know or appreciate the nature and consequences of such conduct, or its wrongfulness, was impaired as a result of mental disease or defect at that time. The psychiatrist must be permitted to make any explanation reasonably serving to clarify his diagnosis and opinion, and may be cross-examined as to any matter bearing on his competency or credibility or the validity of his diagnosis or opinion.

§344.4.   Rules of evidence; admissibility of evidence of victim's sexual conduct in sex offense cases.

Evidence of a victim's sexual conduct shall not be admissible in a juvenile delinquency proceeding for a crime or an attempt to commit a crime defined in article one hundred thirty of the penal law unless such evidence:

1. proves or tends to prove specific instances of the victim's prior sexual conduct with the accused; or

2. proves or tends to prove that the victim has been convicted of an offense under section 230.00 of the penal law within three years prior to the sex offense which is the subject of the juvenile delinquency proceeding; or

3. rebuts evidence introduced by the presentment agency of the victim's failure to engage in sexual intercourse, oral sexual conduct, anal sexual conduct or sexual contact during a given period of time; or

4. rebuts evidence introduced by the presentment agency which proves or tends to prove that the accused is the cause of pregnancy or disease of the victim, or the source of semen found in the victim; or

5. is determined by the court after an offer of proof by the accused, or such hearing as the court may require, and a statement by the court of its findings of fact essential to its determination, to be relevant and admissible in the interests of justice.

§345.1.   Orders.

1. If the allegations of a petition or specific counts of a petition concerning the commission of a crime or crimes are established, the court shall enter an appropriate order and schedule a dispositional hearing pursuant to section 350.1. The order shall specify the count or counts of the petition upon which such order is based and the section or sections of the penal law or other law under which the act or acts so stated would constitute a crime if committed by an adult. If the respondent or respondents are found to have committed a designated felony act, the order shall so state.

2. If the allegations of a petition or specific counts of a petition under this article are not established, the court shall enter an order dismissing the petition or specific counts therein.

§346.1.   Fact-finding hearing; removal.

Where the proceeding was commenced by the filing of an order of removal pursuant to a direction authorized by section 220.10, 310.85 or 330.25 of the criminal procedure law, the requirements of a fact-finding hearing shall be deemed to have been satisfied upon the filing of the order and no further fact-finding hearing need be held; provided, however, that where any specification required by subdivision five of section 725.05 of the criminal procedure law is not clear, the court may examine such records or hold such hearing as it deems necessary to clarify said specification.

§347.1. Required testing of the respondent in certain proceedings.

1. (a) In any proceeding where the respondent is found pursuant to section 345.1 or 346.1 of this article, to have committed a felony offense enumerated in any section of article one hundred thirty of the penal law, or any subdivision of section 130.20 of such law, for which an act of "sexual intercourse", "oral sexual conduct" or "anal sexual conduct", as those terms are defined in section 130.00 of the penal law, is required as an essential element for the commission thereof, the court must, upon a request of the victim, order that the respondent submit to human immunodeficiency (HIV) related testing. The testing is to be conducted by a state, county, or local public health officer designated by the order. Test results, which shall not be disclosed to the court, shall be communicated to the respondent and the victim named in the order in accordance with the provisions of section twenty-seven hundred eighty-five-a of the public health law.

(b) For the purposes of this section, the term "victim" means the person with whom the respondent engaged in an act of "sexual intercourse", "oral sexual conduct" or "anal sexual conduct", as those terms are defined in section 130.00 of the penal law, where such conduct with such victim was the basis for the court's finding that the respondent committed acts constituting one or more of the offenses specified in paragraph (a) of this subdivision.

2. Any request made by the victim pursuant to this section must be in writing, filed with the court and provided by the court to the defendant and his or her counsel. The request must be filed with the court prior to or within ten days after the filing of an order in accordance with section 345.1 or 346.1 of this article, provided that, for good cause shown, the court may permit such request to be filed at any time prior to the entry of an order of disposition.

3. Any requests, related papers and orders made or filed pursuant to this section, together with any papers or proceedings related thereto, shall be sealed by the court and not made available for any purpose, except as may be necessary for the conduct of judicial proceedings directly related to the provisions of this section. All proceedings on such requests shall be held in camera.

4. The application for an order to compel a respondent to undergo an HIV related test may be made by the victim but, if the victim is an infant or incompetent person, the application may also be made by a representative as defined in section twelve hundred one of the civil practice law and rules. The application must state that (a) the applicant was the victim of the offense, enumerated in paragraph (a) of subdivision one of this section, which the court found the defendant to have committed; and (b) the applicant has been offered counseling by a public health officer and been advised of (i) the limitations on the information to be obtained through an HIV test on the proposed subject; (ii) current scientific assessments of the risk of transmission of HIV from the exposure he or she may have experienced; and (iii) the need for the applicant to undergo HIV related testing to definitively determine his or her HIV status.

5. The court shall conduct a hearing only if necessary to determine if the applicant is the victim of the offense the respondent was found to have committed. The court ordered test must be performed within fifteen days of the

date on which the court ordered the test, provided however that whenever the respondent is not tested within the period prescribed by the court, the court must again order that the respondent undergo an HIV related test.

6. (a) Test results shall be disclosed subject to the following limitations, which shall be specified in any order issued pursuant to this section:

(i) disclosure of confidential HIV related information shall be limited to that information which is necessary to fulfill the purpose for which the order is granted;

(ii) disclosure of confidential HIV related information shall be limited to the person making the application; redisclosure shall be permitted only to the victim, the victim's immediate family, guardian, physicians, attorneys, medical or mental health providers and to his or her past and future contacts to whom there was or is a reasonable risk of HIV transmission and shall not be permitted to any other person or the court.

(b) Unless inconsistent with this section, the court's order shall direct compliance with and conform to the provisions of article twenty-seven-F of the public health law. Such order shall include measures to protect against disclosure to others of the identity and HIV status of the applicant and of the person tested and may include such other measures as the court deems necessary to protect confidential information.

7. Any failure to comply with the provisions of this section or section twenty-seven hundred eighty-five-a of the public health law shall not impair the validity of any order of disposition entered by the court.

8. No information obtained as a result of a consent, hearing or court order for testing issued pursuant to this section nor any information derived therefrom may be used as evidence in any criminal or civil proceeding against the respondent which relates to events that were the basis for the respondent's conviction, provided however that nothing herein shall prevent prosecution of a witness testifying in any court hearing held pursuant to this section for perjury pursuant to article two hundred ten of the penal law.

Part 5
The Dispositional Hearing

§350.1. Time of dispositional hearing.

1. If the respondent is detained and has not been found to have committed a designated felony act the dispositional hearing shall commence not more than ten days after the entry of an order pursuant to subdivision one of section 345.1, except as provided in subdivision three.

2. In all other cases, the dispositional hearing shall commence not more than fifty days after entry of an order pursuant to subdivision one of section 345.1, except as provided in subdivision three.

3. The court may adjourn the dispositional hearing:

(a) on its own motion or on motion of the presentment agency for good cause shown for not more than ten days; or

(b) on motion by the respondent for good cause shown for not more than thirty days.

4. The court shall state on the record the reason for any adjournment of the dispositional hearing.

5. Successive motions to adjourn a dispositional hearing beyond the limits enumerated in subdivision one or two shall not be granted in the absence of a showing, on the record, of special circumstances; special circumstances shall not include calendar congestion or the status of the court's docket or backlog.

§350.2. Order of removal.

1. Where the proceeding has been commenced by the filing of an order of removal pursuant to a direction authorized by sections 220.10, 310.85 and 330.25 of the criminal procedure law, the date of filing in the family court shall be deemed for purposes of section 350.1 to be the date of the entry of an order pursuant to subdivision one of section 345.1.

2. The clerk of court shall calendar an appearance to be held within seven days from the date the order of removal was filed. At such appearance the court shall schedule a dispositional hearing in accordance with section 350.1 and determine such other issues as may properly be before it.

§350.3. Dispositional hearings; evidence and required quantum of proof - appearance of presentment agency.

1. Only evidence that is material and relevant may be admitted during a dispositional hearing.

2. An adjudication at the conclusion of a dispositional hearing must be based on a preponderance of the evidence.

3. The presentment agency shall appear at the dispositional hearing.

§350.4. Order of procedure.

The order of the dispositional hearing shall be as follows:

1. The court, with the consent of the parties, may direct the probation service to summarize its investigation report if one has been prepared and, in its discretion, deliver any further statement concerning the advisability of specific dispositional alternatives.

2. The court may in its discretion call witnesses, including the preparer of probation reports or diagnostic studies, to offer evidence concerning the advisability of specific dispositional alternatives. Such witnesses may be cross-examined by the presentment agency and the respondent.

3. The presentment agency may call witnesses to offer such evidence, including the preparer of a probation report or a diagnostic study.

4. The respondent may call witnesses, to offer such evidence, including the preparer of a probation report or a diagnostic study.

5. The court may permit the presentment agency or respondent to offer such rebuttal or surrebuttal evidence as it may deem appropriate.

6. The presentment agency may deliver a statement concerning the advisability of specific dispositional alternatives.

7. The respondent may deliver such a statement.

8. The court shall then permit rebuttal statements by both the presentment agency and the respondent.

9. The court shall then consider the case and enter a dispositional order.

§351.1. Probation, investigation and diagnostic assessment.

1. Following a determination that a respondent has committed a designated felony act and prior to the dispositional hearing, the judge shall order a probation investigation and a diagnostic assessment. For the purposes of this article, the probation investigation shall include, but not be limited to, the history of the juvenile including previous conduct, the family situation, any previous psychological and psychiatric reports, school adjustment, previous social assistance provided by voluntary or public agencies and the response of the juvenile to such assistance. For the purposes of this article, the diagnostic assessment shall include, but not be limited to, psychological tests and psychiatric interviews to determine mental capacity and achievement, emotional stability and mental disabilities. It shall include a clinical assessment of the situational factors that may have contributed to the act or acts. When feasible, expert opinion shall be rendered as to the risk presented by the juvenile to others or himself, with a recommendation as to the need for a restrictive placement.

2. Following a determination that a respondent committed a crime and prior to the dispositional hearing, the court shall order a probation investigation and may order a diagnostic assessment.

*2-a. (a) In a social services district operating an approved juvenile justice services close to home initiative pursuant to section four hundred four of the social services law, the local probation department shall develop and submit to the office of children and family services for prior approval a validated pre-dispositional risk assessment instrument and any risk assessment process. The office shall share a copy of any such instrument and process with the office of probation and correctional alternatives and any expert consulting with the office pursuant to this section. Such department shall periodically revalidate any approved pre-dispositional risk assessment instrument. The department shall conspicuously post information about the instrument on its website, including but not limited to, the name of the instrument; the name and contact information of the person, institution or company that developed such instrument; what the instrument is intended to measure; the types of factors and information the instrument takes into consideration; the process by which the instrument is used in both the pre-disposition investigation and dispositional phase of a hearing; the purpose for the instrument and how the instrument informs the recommendation in the pre-dispositional investigation report; links to independent research and studies about the instrument as well as its own validation analysis relating to the instrument, when available; the most recent date the instrument was validated and the date the next re-validation process is anticipated to begin. The department shall confer with appropriate stakeholders, including but not limited to, attorneys for children, presentment agencies and the family court, prior to revising any validated pre-dispositional risk assessment instrument or process. Such department shall provide any approved pre-dispositional risk assessment instrument and process to the temporary president of the senate and the speaker of the assembly. Any revised pre-dispositional risk assessment instrument shall be subject to periodic empirical validation and to the approval of the office of children and family services. The office of children and family services shall consult with individuals with professional research experience and expertise in criminal justice; social work; juvenile justice; and applied mathematics, psychometrics and/or statistics to assist the office in determining the methods it will use to: approve the department's validated and revalidated pre-dispositional risk assessment instrument and process; and analyze the effectiveness of the use of such instrument and process in accomplishing their intended goals; and analyze, to the greatest extent possible, any disparate impact on dispositional outcomes for juveniles based on race, sex, national origin, economic status, and any other constitutionally protected class, regarding the use of such instrument. The office shall consult with such individuals regarding whether it is appropriate to attempt to analyze whether there is any such disparate impact based on sexual orientation and, if so, the best methods to conduct such analysis. The office shall take into consideration any recommendations given by such individuals involving improvements that could be made to such instrument and process. The department shall provide training on the approved instrument and any approved process to the applicable family courts, presentment agency, and court appointed attorneys for respondents.

(b) Once an initial validated risk assessment instrument and any risk assessment process have been approved by the office of children and family services in consultation with the office of probation and correctional alternatives, the local probation department shall provide the applicable supervising family court judge with a copy of the validated risk assessment instrument and any such process along with the letter from the office of children and family services approving the instrument and process, if applicable, and indicating the date the instrument and any such process shall be effective, provided that such effective date shall be at least thirty days after such notification.

(c) Commencing on the effective date of a validated pre-dispositional risk assessment instrument and any approved process and thereafter, each probation investigation ordered under subdivision two of this section shall include the results of the validated risk assessment of the respondent and process, if any; and a respondent shall not be placed in accordance with section 353.3 or 353.5 of this part unless the court has received and given due consideration to the results of such validated risk assessment and any approved process and made the findings required pursuant to paragraph (f) of subdivision two of section 352.2 of this part.

(d) Notwithstanding any other provision of law to the contrary, data necessary for completion of a pre-dispositional risk assessment instrument may be shared among law enforcement, probation, courts, detention administrations, detention providers, presentment agencies, and the attorney for the child upon retention or appointment solely for the purpose of accurate completion of such risk assessment instrument. A copy of the completed pre-dispositional risk assessment instrument shall be made available to the attorney for the respondent and the applicable court.

(e) The local probation department shall provide the office of probation and correctional alternatives with information regarding the use of the pre-dispositional risk assessment instrument and any risk assessment process in the time and manner required by the office. The office may require that such data be submitted to the office electronically. The office shall not commingle any such information with any criminal history database. The office shall share such information with the office of children and family services. The office of children and family services shall use and share such information only for the purposes of this section and in accordance with this section. Such information shall be shared and received in a manner that protects the confidentiality of such information. The sharing, use, disclosure and redisclosure of such information to any person, office, or other entity not specifically authorized to receive it pursuant to this section or any other law is prohibited.

(f) The family courts shall provide the office of children and family services with such information, in the time and manner required by the office, as is necessary for the office to determine the validity and efficacy of any pre-dispositional risk assessment instrument and process submitted to the office for approval under this subdivision and to analyze any disparate impact on dispositional outcomes for juveniles in accordance with paragraph (a) of this subdivision. The office shall use and share such information only for the purposes of this section and in accordance with this section. Such information shall be shared and received in a manner that protects the confidentiality of such information. The sharing, use, disclosure and redisclosure of such information to any person, office, or other entity not specifically authorized to receive it pursuant to this section or any other law is prohibited.

(g) The office of probation and correctional alternatives shall promulgate regulations, in consultation with the office of children and family services, regarding the role of local probation departments in the completion and use of the pre-dispositional risk assessment instrument and in the risk assessment process.   *(Repealed 3/31/18,Ch.57,L.2012)*

*2-b. The office of children and family services shall develop a validated pre-dispositional risk assessment instrument and any risk assessment process for juvenile delinquents. The office shall periodically revalidate any approved pre-dispositional risk assessment instrument. The office shall conspicuously post any approved pre-dispositional risk assessment instrument and any risk assessment process on its website and shall confer with appropriate stakeholders, including but not limited to, attorneys for children, presentment agencies and the family court, prior to revising any validated pre-dispositional risk assessment instrument or process. Any such revised pre-dispositional risk assessment instrument shall be subject to periodic empirical validation. The office of children and family services shall consult with individuals with professional research experience and expertise in criminal justice; social work; juvenile justice; and applied mathematics, psychometrics and/or statistics to assist the office in determining the method it will use to: develop, validate and revalidate such pre-dispositional risk assessment instrument; develop the risk assessment process; and analyze the effectiveness of the use of such pre-dispositional risk assessment instrument and process in accomplishing their intended goals; and analyze, to the greatest extent possible, any disparate impact on dispositional outcomes for juveniles based on race, sex, national origin, economic status, and any other constitutionally protected class, regarding the use of such instrument. The office shall consult with such individuals regarding whether it is appropriate to attempt to analyze whether there is any such disparate impact based on sexual orientation and, if so, the best methods to conduct such analysis. The office shall take into consideration any recommendations given by such individuals involving improvements that could be made to such instrument and process. The office also shall consult with local probation departments in the development of the validated pre-dispositional risk assessment instrument and the revalidation of such instrument. The office of children and family services shall provide training on the instrument and any process to the family courts, local probation departments, presentment agencies and court appointed attorneys for respondents. The office may determine that a pre-dispositional risk assessment instrument and any process in use pursuant to subdivision two-a of section 351.1 of this part may continue to be used pursuant to such subdivision instead of requiring the use of any instrument or process developed pursuant to this subdivision.

(a) Once an initial validated risk assessment instrument and risk assessment process have been developed, the office of children and family services shall provide the supervising family court judges and local probation departments with copies of the validated risk assessment instrument and process and notify them of the effective date of the instrument and process, which shall be at least six months after such notification.

(b) Commencing on the effective date of a validated risk assessment instrument and any risk assessment process and thereafter, each probation investigation ordered under subdivision two of this section shall include the results of the validated risk assessment of the respondent and process, if any; and a respondent shall not be placed in accordance with section 353.3 or 353.5 of this part unless the court has received and given due consideration to the results of such validated risk assessment and any process and made the findings required pursuant to paragraph (g) of subdivision two of section 352.2 of this part.

(c) Notwithstanding any other provision of law to the contrary, data necessary for completion of a pre-dispositional risk assessment instrument may be shared among law enforcement, probation, courts, detention administrations, detention providers, presentment agencies and the attorney for the child upon retention or appointment solely for the purpose of accurate completion of such risk assessment instrument, and a copy of the completed pre-dispositional risk assessment instrument shall be made available to the attorney for the respondent and applicable court.

(d) Local probation departments shall provide the office of probation and correctional alternatives with information regarding use of the pre-dispositional risk assessment instrument and any risk assessment process in the time and manner required by the office. The office may require that such data be submitted to the office electronically. The office shall not commingle any such information with any criminal history database. The office shall share such information with the office of children and family services. The office of children and family services shall use and share such information only for the purposes of this section and in accordance with this section. Such information shall be shared and received in a manner that protects the confidentiality of such information. The sharing, use, disclosure and redisclosure of such information to any person, office, or other entity not specifically authorized to receive it pursuant to this section or any other law is prohibited.

(e) Law enforcement and the family courts shall provide the office of children and family services with such information, in the time and manner required by the office, as is necessary for the office to develop, validate and revalidate any such pre-dispositional risk assessment instrument and process and to analyze any disparate impact on dispositional outcomes for juveniles in accordance with this section. The office shall use and share such information only for the purposes of this section and share it in accordance with this section. Such information shall be shared and received in a manner that protects the confidentiality of such information. The sharing, use, disclosure and redisclosure of such information to any person, office, or other entity not specifically authorized to receive it pursuant to this section or any other law is prohibited.

(f) The office of probation and correctional alternatives shall promulgate regulations, in consultation with the office of children and family services, regarding the role of local probation departments in the completion and use of the pre-dispositional risk assessment instrument and in the risk assessment process. *(Repealed 3/31/18,Ch.57,L.2012)*

3. A child shall not be placed in accord with section 353.3 unless the court has ordered a probation investigation prior to the dispositional hearing; a child shall not be placed in accord with section 353.4 unless the court has ordered a diagnostic assessment prior to such hearing.

4. When it appears that such information would be relevant to the findings of the court or the order of disposition, each investigation report prepared pursuant to this section shall contain a victim impact statement which shall include an analysis of the victim's version of the offense, the extent of injury or economic loss or damage to the victim, including the amount of unreimbursed medical expenses, if any, and the views of the victim relating to disposition including the amount of restitution sought by the victim, subject to availability of such information. In the case of a homicide or where the victim is unable to assist in the preparation of the victim impact statement, the information may be acquired from the victim's family. Nothing contained in this section shall be interpreted to require that a victim or his or her family supply information for the preparation of an investigation report or that the dispositional hearing should be delayed in order to obtain such information.

5. (a) All diagnostic assessments and probation investigation reports shall be submitted to the court and made available by the court for inspection and copying by the presentment agency and the respondent at least five court days prior to the commencement of the dispositional hearing. All such reports shall be made available by the court for inspection and copying by the presentment agency and the respondent in connection with any appeal in the case.

(b) The victim impact statement shall be made available to the victim or the victim's family by the presentment agency prior to sentencing.

6. All reports or memoranda prepared or obtained by the probation service for the purpose of a dispositional hearing shall be deemed confidential information furnished to the court and shall be subject to disclosure solely in accordance with this section or as otherwise provided for by law. Except as provided under section 320.5 such reports or memoranda shall not be furnished to the court prior to the entry of an order pursuant to section 345.1.

7. The probation services which prepare the investigation reports shall be responsible for the collection and transmission to the office of probation and correctional alternatives, of data on the number of victim impact statements prepared. Such information shall be transmitted annually to the office of victim services and included in the office's biennial report pursuant to subdivision twenty-one of section six hundred twenty-three of the executive law.

§352.1. Findings.

1. If, upon the conclusion of the dispositional hearing, the court determines that the respondent requires supervision, treatment or confinement, the court

shall enter a finding that such respondent is a juvenile delinquent and order an appropriate disposition pursuant to section 352.2.

2. If, upon the conclusion of the dispositional hearing, the court determines that the respondent does not require supervision, treatment or confinement, the petition shall be dismissed.

§352.2. Order of disposition.
1. Upon the conclusion of the dispositional hearing, the court shall enter an order of disposition:
(a) conditionally discharging the respondent in accord with section 353.1; or
(b) putting the respondent on probation in accord with section 353.2; or
(c) continuing the proceeding and placing the respondent in accord with section 353.3; or
(d) placing the respondent in accord with section 353.4; or
(e) continuing the proceeding and placing the respondent under a restrictive placement in accord with section 353.5.
2. (a) In determining an appropriate order the court shall consider the needs and best interests of the respondent as well as the need for protection of the community. If the respondent has committed a designated felony act the court shall determine the appropriate disposition in accord with section 353.5. In all other cases the court shall order the least restrictive available alternative enumerated in subdivision one which is consistent with the needs and best interests of the respondent and the need for protection of the community.
(b) In an order of disposition entered pursuant to section 353.3 or 353.4 of this chapter, or where the court has determined pursuant to section 353.5 of this chapter that restrictive placement is not required, which order places the respondent with the commissioner of social services or with the office of children and family services for placement with an authorized agency or class of authorized agencies or in such facilities designated by the office of children and family services as are eligible for federal reimbursement pursuant to title IV-E of the social security act, the court in its order shall determine
(i) that continuation in the respondent's home would be contrary to the best interests of the respondent; or in the case of a respondent for whom the court has determined that continuation in his or her home would not be contrary to the best interests of the respondent, that continuation in the respondent's home would be contrary to the need for protection of the community;
(ii) that where appropriate, and where consistent with the need for protection of the community, reasonable efforts were made prior to the date of the dispositional hearing to prevent or eliminate the need for removal of the respondent from his or her home, or if the child was removed from his or her home prior to the dispositional hearing, where appropriate and where consistent with the need for safety of the community, whether reasonable efforts were made to make it possible for the child to safely return home. If the court determines that reasonable efforts to prevent or eliminate the need for removal of the child from the home were not made but that the lack of such efforts was appropriate under the circumstances, or consistent with the need for protection of the community, or both, the court order shall include such a finding; and
(iii) in the case of a child who has attained the age of sixteen, the services needed, if any, to assist the child to make the transition from foster care to independent living.

(c) For the purpose of this section, when an order is entered pursuant to section 353.3 or 353.4 of this article, reasonable efforts to prevent or eliminate the need for removing the respondent from the home of the respondent or to make it possible for the respondent to return safely to the home of the respondent shall not be required where the court determines that:

(1) the parent of such respondent has subjected the respondent to aggravated circumstances, as defined in subdivision fifteen of section 301.2 of this article;

(2) the parent of such child has been convicted of (i) murder in the first degree as defined in section 125.27 or murder in the second degree as defined in section 125.25 of the penal law and the victim was another child of the parent; or (ii) manslaughter in the first degree as defined in section 125.20 or manslaughter in the second degree as defined in section 125.15 of the penal law and the victim was another child of the parent, provided, however, that the parent must have acted voluntarily in committing such crime;

(3) the parent of such child has been convicted of an attempt to commit any of the foregoing crimes, and the victim or intended victim was the child or another child of the parent; or has been convicted of criminal solicitation as defined in article one hundred, conspiracy as defined in article one hundred five or criminal facilitation as defined in article one hundred fifteen of the penal law for conspiring, soliciting or facilitating any of the foregoing crimes, and the victim or intended victim was the child or another child of the parent;

(4) the parent of such respondent has been convicted of assault in the second degree as defined in section 120.05, assault in the first degree as defined in section 120.10 or aggravated assault upon a person less than eleven years old as defined in section 120.12 of the penal law, and the commission of one of the foregoing crimes resulted in serious physical injury to the respondent or another child of the parent;

(5) the parent of such respondent has been convicted in any other jurisdiction of an offense which includes all of the essential elements of any crime specified in subparagraph two, three or four of this paragraph, and the victim of such offense was the respondent or another child of the parent; or

(6) the parental rights of the parent to a sibling of such respondent have been involuntarily terminated; unless the court determines that providing reasonable efforts would be in the best interests of the child, not contrary to the health and safety of the child, and would likely result in the reunification of the parent and the child in the foreseeable future. The court shall state such findings in its order.

If the court determines that reasonable efforts are not required because of one of the grounds set forth above, a permanency hearing shall be held pursuant to section 355.5 of this article within thirty days of the finding of the court that such efforts are not required. The social services official or the office of children and family services, where the respondent was placed with such office, shall subsequent to the permanency hearing make reasonable efforts to place the respondent in a timely manner and to complete whatever steps are necessary to finalize the permanent placement of the respondent as set forth in the permanency plan approved by the court. If reasonable efforts are determined by the court not to be required because of one of the grounds set forth in this paragraph, the social services official may file a petition for termination of parental rights in accordance with section three hundred eighty-four-b of the social services law.

(d) For the purposes of this section, in determining reasonable efforts to be made with respect to the respondent, and in making such reasonable efforts, the respondent's health and safety shall be the paramount concern.

(e) For the purpose of this section, a sibling shall include a half-sibling.

*(f)(1) In a social services district operating an approved juvenile justice services close to home initiative pursuant to section four hundred four of the social services law, upon the effective date of a risk assessment instrument and any risk assessment process that have been approved by the office of children and family services pursuant to subdivision two-a of section 351.1 of this part, the court shall give due consideration to the results of the validated risk assessment and any such process provided to the court pursuant to such subdivision when determining the appropriate disposition for the respondent.

(2) Any order of the court directing the placement of a respondent into a residential program shall state:

     (i) the level of risk the youth was assessed at pursuant to the validated risk assessment instrument; and

     (ii) if a determination is made to place a youth in a higher level of placement than appears warranted based on such risk assessment instrument and any approved risk assessment process, the particular reasons why such placement was determined to be necessary for the protection of the community and to be consistent with the needs and best interests of the respondent; and

     (iii) that a less restrictive alternative that would be consistent with the needs and best interests of the respondent and the need for protection of the community is not available.   *(Repealed 3/31/18,Ch.57,L.2012)*

*(g)(i) Once a validated risk assessment instrument and any risk assessment process is a required part of each probation investigation ordered under subdivision two of section 351.1 of this part and provided to the court in accordance with subdivision two-b of such section, the court shall give due consideration to the results of such validated risk assessment and any such process when determining the appropriate disposition for the respondent.

     (ii) Any order of the court directing the placement of a respondent into a residential program shall state:

     (A) the level of risk the youth was assessed pursuant to the validated risk assessment instrument; and

     (B) if a determination is made to place a youth in a higher level of placement than appears warranted based on such risk assessment instrument and any risk assessment process, the particular reasons why such placement was determined to be necessary for the protection of the community and to be consistent with the needs and best interests of the respondent; and

     (C) that a less restrictive alternative that would be consistent with the needs and best interests of the respondent and the need for protection of the community is not available.   *(Repealed 3/31/18,Ch.57,L.2012)*

3. The order shall state the court's reasons for the particular disposition, including, in the case of a restrictive placement pursuant to section 353.5, the specific findings of fact required in such section.

§352.3. Order of protection.

(1) Upon the issuance of an order pursuant to section 315.3 or the entry of an order of disposition pursuant to section 352.2, a court may enter an order of protection against any respondent for good cause shown. The order may require that the respondent:

(a) stay away from the home, school, business or place of employment of the victims of the alleged offense; or

(b) refrain from harassing, intimidating, threatening or otherwise interfering with the victim or victims of the alleged offense and such members of the family or household of such victim or victims as shall be specifically named by the court in such order; or

(c) refrain from intentionally injuring or killing, without justification, any companion animal the respondent knows to be owned, possessed, leased, kept or held by the person protected by the order or a minor child residing in such person's household. "Companion animal", as used in this subdivision, shall have the same meaning as in subdivision five of section three hundred fifty of the agriculture and markets law.

(1-a) Upon the issuance of an order pursuant to section 315.3 or the entry of an order of disposition pursuant to section 352.2, a court may, for good cause shown, enter an order of protection against any respondent requiring that the respondent refrain from engaging in conduct, against any designated witness specifically named by the court in such order, that would constitute intimidation of a witness pursuant to section 215.15, 215.16 or 215.17 of the penal law or an attempt thereof, provided that the court makes a finding that the respondent did previously, or is likely to in the future, intimidate or attempt to intimidate such witness in such manner.

(2) An order of protection shall remain in effect for the period specified by the court, but shall not exceed the period of time specified in any order of disposition or order adjourning a proceeding in contemplation of dismissal.

§353.1.　Conditional discharge.

1. The court may conditionally discharge the respondent if the court, having regard for the nature and circumstances of the crime and for the history, character and condition of the respondent, is of the opinion that consistent with subdivision two of section 352.2, neither the public interest nor the ends of justice would be served by a placement and that probation supervision is not appropriate. The court may, as a condition of a conditional discharge, in cases where the record indicates the respondent qualifies as an eligible person and has been adjudicated for an eligible offense as defined in section four hundred fifty-eight-l of the social services law, require the respondent to attend and complete an education reform program established pursuant to section four hundred fifty-eight-l of the social services law.

2. When the court orders a conditional discharge the respondent shall be released with respect to the finding upon which such order is based without placement or probation supervision but subject, during the period of conditional discharge, to such conditions enumerated in subdivision two of section 353.2, as the court may determine. The court shall order the period of conditional discharge authorized by subdivision three and shall specify the conditions to be complied with. The court may modify or enlarge the conditions at any time prior to the expiration or termination of the period of conditional discharge. Such action may not, however, be taken unless the respondent is personally present, except that the respondent need not be present if the modification consists solely of the elimination or relaxation of one or more conditions.

3. The maximum period of a conditional discharge shall not exceed one year.

4. The respondent must be given a written copy of the conditions at the time a conditional discharge is ordered or modified, provided, however, that

whenever the respondent has not been personally present at the time of a modification, the court shall notify the respondent in writing within twenty days after such modification, specifying the nature of the elimination or relaxation of any condition and the effective date thereof. A copy of such conditions must be filed with and become part of the record of the case.

5. A finding that the respondent committed an additional crime after a conditional discharge has been ordered and prior to expiration and termination of the period of such order constitutes a ground for revocation of such order irrespective of whether such fact is specified as a condition of the order.

§353.2. Probation.

1. The court may order a period of probation if the court, having regard for the nature and circumstances of the crime and the history, character and condition of the respondent, is of the opinion that:

(a) placement of respondent is not or may not be necessary;

(b) the respondent is in need of guidance, training or other assistance which can be effectively administered through probation; and

(c) such disposition is consistent with the provisions of subdivision two of section 352.2.

2. When ordering a period of probation or a conditional discharge pursuant to section 353.1, the court may, as a condition of such order, require that the respondent:

(a) attend school regularly and obey all rules and regulations of the school;

(b) obey all reasonable commands of the parent or other person legally responsible for the respondent's care;

(c) abstain from visiting designated places or associating with named individuals;

(d) avoid injurious or vicious activities;

(e) co-operate with a mental health, social services or other appropriate community facility or agency to which the respondent is referred;

(f) make restitution or perform services for the public good pursuant to section 353.6, provided the respondent is over ten years of age;

(g) except when the respondent has been assigned to a facility in accordance with subdivision four of section five hundred four of the executive law, in cases wherein the record indicates that the consumption of alcohol by the respondent may have been a contributing factor, attend and complete an alcohol awareness program established pursuant to section 19.25 of the mental hygiene law; and

(h) comply with such other reasonable conditions as the court shall determine to be necessary or appropriate to ameliorate the conduct which gave rise to the filing of the petition or to prevent placement with the commissioner of social services or the division for youth.

3. When ordering a period of probation, the court may, as a condition of such order, further require that the respondent:

(a) meet with a probation officer when directed to do so by that officer and permit the officer to visit the respondent at home or elsewhere;

(b) permit the probation officer to obtain information from any person or agency from whom respondent is receiving or was directed to receive diagnosis, treatment or counseling;

(c) permit the probation officer to obtain information from the respondent's school;

(d) co-operate with the probation officer in seeking to obtain and in accepting employment, and supply records and reports of earnings to the officer when requested to do so;

(e) obtain permission from the probation officer for any absence from respondent's residence in excess of two weeks; and

(f) with the consent of the division for youth, spend a specified portion of the probation period, not exceeding one year, in a non-secure facility provided by the division for youth pursuant to article nineteen-G of the executive law.

4. A finding that the respondent committed an additional crime after probation supervision has been ordered and prior to expiration or termination of the period of such order constitutes a ground for revocation of such order irrespective of whether such fact is specified as a condition of such order.

5. The respondent must be given a written copy of the conditions at the time probation supervision is ordered. A copy of such conditions must be filed with and become part of the record of the case.

6. The maximum period of probation shall not exceed two years. If the court finds at the conclusion of the original period and after a hearing that exceptional circumstances require an additional year of probation, the court may continue the probation for an additional year.

§353.3. Placement.

1. In accordance with section 352.2 of this part, the court may place the respondent in his or her own home or in the custody of a suitable relative or other suitable private person or the commissioner of the local social services district or the office of children and family services pursuant to article nineteen-G of the executive law, subject to the orders of the court.

2. *Where the respondent is placed with the commissioner of the local social services district, the court may (i) in a social services district operating an approved juvenile justice services close to home initiative pursuant to section four hundred four of the social services law, direct the commissioner to provide services necessary to meet the needs of the respondent, provided that such services are authorized or required to be made available pursuant to the approved plan to implement a juvenile justice close to home initiative then in effect and the commissioner shall notify the court and the attorney for the respondent of the authorized agency that such respondent was placed in; or (ii) in a social services district that is not operating an approved juvenile justice services close to home initiative pursuant to section four hundred four of the social services law, direct the commissioner to place him or her with an authorized agency or class of authorized agencies; and if the court finds that the respondent placed with a social services district pursuant to this subdivision is a sexually exploited child as defined in subdivision one of section four hundred forty-seven-a of the social services law, the court may place such respondent in an available long-term safe house. Unless the dispositional order provides otherwise, the court so directing shall include one of the following alternatives to apply in the event that the commissioner is unable to so place the respondent: *(Repealed 3/31/18,Ch.57,L.2012)*

(a) the commissioner shall apply to the court for an order to stay, modify, set aside, or vacate such directive pursuant to the provisions of section 355.1 of this part; or

(b) the commissioner shall return the respondent to the family court for a new dispositional hearing and order.

*2-a. Notwithstanding any inconsistent provision of law to the contrary, and pursuant to subdivision two of this section in a district operating an approved juvenile justice services close to home initiative pursuant to section four hundred four of the social services law:

(a) beginning on the effective date of the district's approved plan that only covers juvenile delinquents placed in non-secure settings, the court may only place the respondent:

(i) in the custody of the commissioner of the local social services district for placement in a non-secure level of care; or

(ii) in the custody of the commissioner of the office of children and family services for placement in a limited secure or secure level of care; and

(b) beginning on the effective date of the district's approved plan to implement programs for youth placed in limited secure settings, the court may only place the respondent:

(i) in the custody of the commissioner of the local social services district for placement in:

(A) a non-secure level of care;

(B) a limited secure level of care; or

(C) either a non-secure or limited secure level of care, as determined by such commissioner; or

(ii) in the custody of the commissioner of the office of children and family services for placement in a secure level of care.
*(Repealed 3/31/18,Ch.57,L.2012)

3. Where the respondent is placed with the office of children and family services, the court shall, unless it directs the office to place him or her with an authorized agency or class of authorized agencies, including if the court finds that the respondent is a sexually exploited child as defined in subdivision one of section four hundred forty-seven-a of the social services law, an available long-term safe house pursuant to subdivision four of this section, authorize the office to do one of the following:

(a) place the respondent in a secure facility without a further hearing at any time or from time to time during the first sixty days of residency in office of children and family services facilities. Notwithstanding the discretion of the office to place the respondent in a secure facility at any time during the first sixty days of residency in a* office of children and family services facility, the respondent may be placed in a non-secure facility. In the event that the office desires to transfer a respondent to a secure facility at any time after the first sixty days of residency in office facilities, a hearing shall be held pursuant to subdivision three of section five hundred four-a of the executive law; or

(b) place the respondent in a limited secure facility. The respondent may be transferred by the office to a secure facility after a hearing is held pursuant to section five hundred four-a of the executive law; provided, however, that during the first twenty days of residency in office facilities, the respondent shall not be transferred to a secure facility unless the respondent has committed an act or acts which are exceptionally dangerous to the respondent or to others; or

(c) place the respondent in a non-secure facility. No respondent placed pursuant to this paragraph may be transferred by the office of children and family services to a secure facility.

4. Where the respondent is placed with the office of children and family services, the court may direct the office to place the respondent with an authorized agency or class of authorized agencies, including, if the court finds

*(So in original. Probably should read "an".)

that the respondent is a sexually exploited child as defined in subdivision one of section four hundred forty-seven-a of the social services law, an available long-term safe house, and in the event the office is unable to so place the respondent or, discontinues the placement with the authorized agency, the respondent shall be deemed to have been placed with the office pursuant to paragraph (b) or (c) of subdivision three of this section. In such cases, the office shall notify the court, presentment agency, respondent's attorney and parent or other person responsible for the respondent's care, of the reason for discontinuing the placement with the authorized agency and the level and location of the youth's placement.

5. If the respondent has committed a felony the initial period of placement shall not exceed eighteen months. If the respondent has committed a misdemeanor such initial period of placement shall not exceed twelve months. If the respondent has been in detention pending disposition, the initial period of placement ordered under this section shall be credited with and diminished by the amount of time spent by the respondent in detention prior to the commencement of the placement unless the court finds that all or part of such credit would not serve the needs and best interests of the respondent or the need for protection of the community.

6. The court may at any time conduct a hearing in accordance with section 355.1 of this part concerning the need for continuing a placement.

7. The place in which or the person with whom the respondent has been placed under this section shall submit a report to the court, respondent's attorney of record, and presentment agency at the conclusion of the placement period, except as provided in paragraphs (a) and (b) of this subdivision. Such report shall include recommendations and such supporting data as is appropriate. The court may extend a placement pursuant to section 355.3 of this part.

(a) Where the respondent is placed pursuant to subdivision two or three of this section and where the agency is not seeking an extension of the placement pursuant to section 355.3 of this part, such report shall be submitted not later than thirty days prior to the conclusion of the placement.

(b) Where the respondent is placed pursuant to subdivision two or three of this section and where the agency is seeking an extension of the placement pursuant to section 355.3 of this part and a permanency hearing pursuant to section 355.5 of this part, such report shall be submitted not later than sixty days prior to the date on which the permanency hearing must be held and shall be annexed to the petition for a permanency hearing and extension of placement.

(c) Where the respondent is placed pursuant to subdivision two or three of this section, such report shall contain a plan for the release, or conditional release (pursuant to section five hundred ten-a of the executive law), of the respondent to the custody of his or her parent or other person legally responsible, or to another permanency alternative as provided in paragraph (d) of subdivision seven of section 355.5 of this part. If the respondent is subject to article sixty-five of the education law or elects to participate in an educational program leading to a high school diploma, such plan shall include, but not be limited to, the steps that the agency with which the respondent is placed has taken and will be taking to facilitate the enrollment of the respondent in a school or educational program leading to a high school diploma following release, or, if such release occurs during the summer recess, upon the commencement of the next school term. If the respondent is not subject to article sixty-five of the education law and does not elect to participate in an educational program leading to a high school diploma, such plan shall include, but not be limited to, the steps that the agency with which the respondent is placed has taken and will be taking to assist the respondent to become gainfully employed or enrolled in a vocational program following release.

8. In its discretion, the court may recommend restitution or require services for the public good pursuant to section 353.6 of this part in conjunction with an order of placement.

*9. If the court places a respondent with the office of children and family services, or with a social services district with an approved plan to implement a juvenile justice services close to home initiative under section four hundred four of the social services law, pursuant to this section after finding that such respondent committed a felony, the court may, in its discretion, further order that such respondent shall be confined in a residential facility for a minimum period set by the order, not to exceed six months.   *(Repealed 3/31/18,Ch.57,L.2012)*

10. A placement pursuant to this section with the commissioner of the local social services district shall not be directed in any detention facility, but the court may direct detention pending transfer to a placement authorized and ordered under this section for no more than thirty days after the order of placement is made or in a city of one million or more, for no more than fifteen days after such order of placement is made. Such direction shall be subject to extension pursuant to subdivision three of section three hundred ninety-eight of the social services law.

§353.4. Transfer of certain juvenile delinquents.

1. If at the conclusion of the dispositional hearing and in accordance with section 352.2 of this act the court finds that the respondent has a mental illness, or intellectual or developmental disability, as defined in section 1.03 of the mental hygiene law, which is likely to result in serious harm to himself or herself or others, the court may issue an order placing such respondent with the office of children and family services or, with the consent of the local commissioner, with a local commissioner of social services. Any such order shall direct the temporary transfer for admission of the respondent to the custody of either the commissioner of mental health or the commissioner of developmental disabilities who shall arrange the admission of the respondent to the appropriate facility of the department of mental hygiene. The director of a hospital operated by the office of mental health may, subject to the provisions of section 9.51 of the mental hygiene law, transfer a person admitted to the hospital pursuant to this subdivision to a residential treatment facility for children and youth, as that term is defined in section 1.03 of the mental hygiene law, if care and treatment in such a facility would more appropriately meet the needs of the respondent. Persons temporarily transferred to such custody under this provision may be retained for care and treatment for a period of up to one year and whenever appropriate shall be transferred back to the office of children and family services pursuant to the provisions of section five hundred nine of the executive law or transferred back to the local commissioner of social services. Within thirty days of such transfer back, application shall be made by the office of children and family services or the local commissioner of social services to the placing court to conduct a further dispositional hearing at which the court may make any order authorized under section 352.2 of this act, except that the period of any further order of disposition shall take into account the period of placement hereunder. Likelihood to result in serious harm

shall mean (a) substantial risk of physical harm to himself or herself as manifested by threats or attempts at suicide or serious bodily harm or other conduct demonstrating he or she is dangerous to himself or herself or (b) a substantial risk of physical harm to other persons as manifested by homicidal or other violent behavior by which others are placed in reasonable fear of serious bodily harm.

2. (a) Where the order of disposition is for a restrictive placement under section 353.5 of this act if the court at the dispositional hearing finds that the respondent has a mental illness, or intellectual or developmental disability, as defined in section 1.03 of the mental hygiene law, which is likely to result in serious harm to himself or herself or others, the court may, as part of the order of disposition, direct the temporary transfer, for a period of up to one year, of the respondent to the custody of the commissioner of mental health or of developmental disabilities who shall arrange for the admission of the respondent to an appropriate facility under his or her jurisdiction within thirty days of such order. The director of the facility so designated by the commissioner shall accept such respondent for admission.

(b) Persons transferred to the office of mental health or of the office for people with developmental disabilities, pursuant to this subdivision, shall be retained by such office for care and treatment for the period designated by the court. At any time prior to the expiration of such period, if the director of the facility determines that the child is no longer mentally ill or no longer in need of active treatment, the responsible office shall make application to the family court for an order transferring the child back to the office of children and family services. Not more than thirty days before the expiration of such period, there shall be a hearing, at which time the court may:

(i) extend the temporary transfer of the respondent for an additional period of up to one year to the custody of the commissioner of mental health or the commissioner of developmental disabilities pursuant to this subdivision; or

(ii) continue the restrictive placement of the respondent in the custody of the office of children and family services.

(c) During such temporary transfer, the respondent shall continue to be under restrictive placement with the office of children and family services. Whenever the respondent is transferred back to the office of children and family services the conditions of the placement as set forth in section 353.5 shall apply. Time spent by the respondent in the custody of the commissioner of mental health or the commissioner of developmental disabilities shall be credited and applied towards the period of placement.

3. No dispositional hearing at which proof of a mental disability as defined in section 1.03 of the mental hygiene law is to be offered shall be completed until the commissioner of mental health or commissioner of developmental disabilities, as appropriate, have been notified and afforded an opportunity to be heard at such dispositional hearing.   *(Eff.5/25/16,Ch.37,L.2016)*

4. No order of disposition placing the respondent in accordance with this section shall be entered except upon clear and convincing evidence which shall include the testimony of two examining physicians as provided in section two hundred fifty-one.

5. If the respondent has been in detention pending disposition, the initial period of placement ordered under this section shall be credited with and diminished by the amount of time spent by the respondent in detention prior to the commencement of the placement unless the court finds that all or part of

such credit would not serve the needs and best interests of the respondent or the need for protection of the community.

§353.5. Designated felony acts; restrictive placement.

1. Where the respondent is found to have committed a designated felony act, the order of disposition shall be made within twenty days of the conclusion of the dispositional hearing and shall include a finding based on a preponderance of the evidence as to whether, for the purposes of this article, the respondent does or does not require a restrictive placement under this section, in connection with which the court shall make specific written findings of fact as to each of the elements set forth in paragraphs (a) through (e) in subdivision two as related to the particular respondent. If the court finds that a restrictive placement under this section is not required, the court shall enter any other order of disposition provided in section 352.2. If the court finds that a restrictive placement is required, it shall continue the proceeding and enter an order of disposition for a restrictive placement. Every order under this section shall be a dispositional order, shall be made after a dispositional hearing and shall state the grounds for the order.

2. In determining whether a restrictive placement is required, the court shall consider:

(a) the needs and best interests of the respondent;

(b) the record and background of the respondent, including but not limited to information disclosed in the probation investigation and diagnostic assessment;

(c) the nature and circumstances of the offense, including whether any injury was inflicted by the respondent or another participant;

(d) the need for protection of the community; and

(e) the age and physical condition of the victim.

3. Notwithstanding the provisions of subdivision two, the court shall order a restrictive placement in any case where the respondent is found to have committed a designated felony act in which the respondent inflicted serious physical injury, as that term is defined in subdivision ten of section 10.00 of the penal law, upon another person who is sixty-two years of age or more.

*4. When the order is for a restrictive placement in the case of a youth found to have committed a designated class A felony act,

(a) the order shall provide that:

(i) the respondent shall be placed with the office of children and family services for an initial period of five years. If the respondent has been in detention pending disposition, the initial period of placement ordered under this section shall be credited with and diminished by the amount of time spent by the respondent in detention prior to the commencement of the placement unless the court finds that all or part of such credit would not serve the needs and best interests of the respondent or the need for protection of the community.

(ii) the respondent shall initially be confined in a secure facility for a period set by the order, to be not less than twelve nor more than eighteen months provided, however, where the order of the court is made in compliance with subdivision five of this section, the respondent shall initially be confined in a secure facility for eighteen months.

(iii) after the period set under subparagraph (ii) of this paragraph, the respondent shall be placed in a residential facility for a period of twelve months; provided, however, that if the respondent has been placed from a family court in a social services district operating an approved juvenile justice services close to home initiative pursuant to section four hundred four of the social services law, once the time frames in subparagraph (ii) of this paragraph are met:

(A) beginning on the effective date of such a social services district's plan that only covers juvenile delinquents placed in non-secure settings, if the office of children and family services concludes, based on the needs and best interests of the respondent and the need for protection for the community, that a non-secure level of care is appropriate for the respondent, such office shall file a petition pursuant to paragraph (b) or (c) of subdivision two of section 355.1 of this part to have the respondent placed with the applicable local commissioner of social services; and

(B) beginning on the effective date of such a social services district's plan that covers juvenile delinquents placed in limited secure settings, if the office of children and family services concludes, based on the needs and best interests of the respondent and the need for protection for the community, that a non-secure or limited secure level of care is appropriate for the respondent, such office shall file a petition pursuant to paragraph (b) or (c) of subdivision two of section 355.1 of this part to have the respondent placed with the applicable local commissioner of social services.

(C) If the respondent is placed with the local commissioner of social services in accordance with clause (A) or (B) of this subparagraph, the remainder of the provisions of this section shall continue to apply to the respondent's placement.

(iv) the respondent may not be released from a secure facility or transferred to a facility other than a secure facility during the period provided in subparagraph (ii) of this paragraph, nor may the respondent be released from a residential facility during the period provided in subparagraph (iii) of this paragraph. No home visits shall be permitted during the period of secure confinement set by the court order or one year, whichever is less, except for emergency visits for medical treatment or severe illness or death in the family. All home visits must be accompanied home visits:

(A) while a youth is confined in a secure facility, whether such confinement is pursuant to a court order or otherwise;

(B) while a youth is confined in a residential facility other than a secure facility within six months after confinement in a secure facility; and

(C) while a youth is confined in a residential facility other than a secure facility in excess of six months after confinement in a secure facility unless two accompanied home visits have already occurred. An "accompanied home visit" shall mean a home visit during which the youth shall be accompanied at all times while outside the secure or residential facility by appropriate personnel of the office of children and family services or, if applicable, a local social services district which operates an approved juvenile justice services close to home initiative pursuant to section four hundred four of the social services law.

(b) Notwithstanding any other provision of law, during the first twelve months of the respondent's placement, no motion, hearing or order may be made, held or granted pursuant to section 355.1; provided, however, that during such period a motion to vacate the order may be made pursuant to such section, but only upon grounds set forth in section 440.10 of the criminal procedure law.

(c) During the placement or any extension thereof:

(i) after the expiration of the period provided in subparagraph (iii) of paragraph (a) of this subdivision, the respondent shall not be released from a residential facility without the written approval of the office of children and family services or, if applicable, a social services district operating an approved juvenile justice services close to home initiative pursuant to section four hundred four of the social services law.

(ii) the respondent shall be subject to intensive supervision whenever not in a secure or residential facility.

(iii) the respondent shall not be discharged from the custody of the office of children and family services, or, if applicable, a social services district operating an approved juvenile justice services close to home initiative pursuant to section four hundred four of the social services law, unless a motion therefor under section 355.1 is granted by the court, which motion shall not be made prior to the expiration of three years of the placement.

(iv) unless otherwise specified in the order, the office of children and family services or, if applicable, a social services district operating an approved juvenile justice services close to home initiative pursuant to section four hundred four of the social services law shall report in writing to the court not less than once every six months during the placement on the status, adjustment and progress of the respondent.

(d) Upon the expiration of the initial period of placement, or any extension thereof, the placement may be extended in accordance with section 355.3 on a petition of any party or the office of children and family services or, if applicable, a social services district operating an approved juvenile justice services close to home initiative pursuant to section four hundred four of the social services law, after a dispositional hearing, for an additional period not to exceed twelve months, but no initial placement or extension of placement under this section may continue beyond the respondent's twenty-first birthday.

(e) The court may also make an order pursuant to subdivision two of section 353.4.   *(Repealed 3/31/18,Ch.57,L.2012)*

*5. When the order is for a restrictive placement in the case of a youth found to have committed a designated felony act, other than a designated class A felony act,

(a) the order shall provide that:

(i) the respondent shall be placed with the office of children and family services for an initial period of three years. If the respondent has been in detention pending disposition, the initial period of placement ordered under this section shall be credited with and diminished by the amount of time spent by the respondent in detention prior to the commencement of the placement unless the court finds that all or part of such credit would not serve the needs and best interests of the respondent or the need for protection of the community.

(ii) the respondent shall initially be confined in a secure facility for a period set by the order, to be not less than six nor more than twelve months.

(iii) after the period set under subparagraph (ii) of this paragraph, the respondent shall be placed in a residential facility for a period set by the order, to be not less than six nor more than twelve months; provided, however, that if the respondent has been placed from a family court in a social services district operating an approved juvenile justice services close to home initiative pursuant to section four hundred four of the social services law, once the time frames in subparagraph (ii) of this paragraph are met:

(A) beginning on the effective date of such a social services district's plan that only covers juvenile delinquents placed in non-secure settings, if the office of children and family services concludes, based on the needs and best interests of the respondent and the need for protection for the community, that a non-secure level of care is appropriate for the respondent, such office shall file a petition pursuant to paragraph (b) or (c) of subdivision two of section 355.1 of this part to have the respondent placed with the applicable local commissioner of social services; and

(B) beginning on the effective date of such a social services district's plan to implement programs for youth placed in limited secure settings, if the office of children and family services concludes, based on the needs and best interests of the respondent and the need for protection for the community, that a non-secure or limited secure level of care is appropriate for the respondent, such office shall file a petition pursuant to paragraph (b) or (c) of subdivision two of section 355.1 of this part to have the respondent placed with the applicable local commissioner of social services.

(C) If the respondent is placed with a local commissioner of social services in accordance with clause (A) or (B) of this subparagraph, the remainder of the provisions of this section shall continue to apply to the respondent's placement.

(iv) the respondent may not be released from a secure facility or transferred to a facility other than a secure facility during the period provided by the court pursuant to subparagraph (ii) of this paragraph, nor may the respondent be released from a residential facility during the period provided by the court pursuant to subparagraph (iii) of this paragraph. No home visits shall be permitted during the period of secure confinement set by the court order or one year, whichever is less, except for emergency visits for medical treatment or severe illness or death in the family. All home visits must be accompanied home visits:

(A) while a youth is confined in a secure facility, whether such confinement is pursuant to a court order or otherwise;

(B) while a youth is confined in a residential facility other than a secure facility within six months after confinement in a secure facility; and

(C) while a youth is confined in a residential facility other than a secure facility in excess of six months after confinement in a secure facility unless two accompanied home visits have already occurred. An "accompanied home visit" shall mean a home visit during which the youth shall be accompanied at all times while outside the secure or residential facility by appropriate personnel of the office of children and family services or, if applicable, a social services district operating an approved juvenile justice close to home initiative pursuant to section four hundred four of the social services law.

(b) Notwithstanding any other provision of law, during the first six months of the respondent's placement, no motion, hearing or order may be made, held or granted pursuant to section 355.1; provided, however, that during such period a motion to vacate the order may be made pursuant to such section, but only upon grounds set forth in section 440.10 of the criminal procedure law.

(c) During the placement or any extension thereof:

(i) after the expiration of the period provided in subparagraph (iii) of paragraph (a) of this subdivision, the respondent shall not be released from a residential facility without the written approval of the office of children and family services or, if applicable, a social services district operating an approved juvenile justice services close to home initiative pursuant to section four hundred four of the social services law.

(ii) the respondent shall be subject to intensive supervision whenever not in a secure or residential facility.

(iii) the respondent shall not be discharged from the custody of the office of children and family services, or, if applicable, a social services district operating an approved juvenile justice services close to home initiative pursuant to section four hundred four of the social services law.

(iv) unless otherwise specified in the order, the office of children and family services or, if applicable, a social services district operating an approved juvenile justice services close to home initiative pursuant to section four hundred four of the social services law shall report in writing to the court not less than once every six months during the placement on the status, adjustment and progress of the respondent.

(d) Upon the expiration of the initial period of placement or any extension thereof, the placement may be extended in accordance with section 355.3 upon petition of any party or the office of children and family services or, if applicable, a social services district operating an approved juvenile justice services close to home initiative pursuant to section four hundred four of the social services law, after a dispositional hearing, for an additional period not to exceed twelve months, but no initial placement or extension of placement under this section may continue beyond the respondent's twenty-first birthday.

(e) The court may also make an order pursuant to subdivision two of section 353.4. *(Repealed 3/31/18,Ch.57,L.2012)*

6. When the order is for a restrictive placement in the case of a youth found to have committed any designated felony act and such youth has been found by a court to have committed a designated felony act on a prior occasion, regardless of the age of such youth at the time of commission of such prior act, the order of the court shall be made pursuant to subdivision four.

7. If the dispositional hearing has been adjourned on a finding of specific circumstances pursuant to subdivision six* of section 350.1 while the respondent is in detention, where a restrictive placement is subsequently ordered, time spent by the respondent in detention during such additional adjournment shall be credited and applied against any term of secure confinement ordered by the court pursuant to subdivision four or five. *(So in original)*

*8. The office of children and family services or, if applicable, the social services district operating an approved close to home initiative pursuant to section four hundred four of the social services law, shall retain the power to continue the confinement of the youth in a secure or other residential facility, as applicable, beyond the periods specified by the court, within the term of the placement. *(Repealed 3/31/18,Ch.57,L.2012)*

§353.6. Restitution.

1. At the conclusion of the dispositional hearing in cases involving respondents over ten years of age the court may:

(a) recommend as a condition of placement, or order as a condition of probation or conditional discharge, restitution in an amount representing a fair and reasonable cost to replace the property, repair the damage caused by the respondent or provide the victim with compensation for unreimbursed medical expenses, not, however, to exceed one thousand five hundred dollars. In the case of a placement, the court may recommend that the respondent pay out of his or her own funds or earnings the amount of replacement, damage or unreimbursed medical expenses, either in a lump sum or in periodic payments in amounts set by the agency with which he or she is placed, and in the case of probation or conditional discharge, the court may require that the respondent pay out of his or her own funds or earnings the amount of replacement, damage or unreimbursed medical expenses, either in a lump sum or in periodic payments in amounts set by the court; and/or

(b) order as a condition of placement, probation, or conditional discharge, services for the public good including in the case of a crime involving willful, malicious, or unlawful damage or destruction to real or personal property maintained as a cemetery plot, grave, burial place, or other place of interment of human remains, services for the maintenance and repair thereof, taking into consideration the age and physical condition of the respondent.

2. If the court recommends restitution or requires services for the public good in conjunction with an order of placement pursuant to section 353.3 or 353.5, the placement shall be made only to an authorized agency, including the division for youth, which has adopted rules and regulations for the supervision of such a program, which rules and regulations, except in the case of the division for youth, shall be subject to the approval of the state department of social services. Such rules and regulations shall include, but not be limited to provisions:

(i) assuring that the conditions of work, including wages, meet the standards therefor prescribed pursuant to the labor law;

(ii) affording coverage to the respondent under the workers' compensation law as an employee of such agency, department, division or institution;

(iii) assuring that the entity receiving such services shall not utilize the same to replace its regular employees; and

(iv) providing for reports to the court not less frequently than every six months.

3. If the court requires restitution or services for the public good as a condition of probation or conditional discharge, it shall provide that an agency or person supervise the restitution or services and that such agency or person report to the court not less frequently than every six months. Upon the written notice submitted by a school district to the court and the appropriate probation department or agency which submits probation recommendations or reports to the court, the court may provide that such school district shall supervise the performance of services for the public good.

4. The court, upon receipt of the reports provided for in subdivisions two and three may, on its own motion or the motion of the agency, probation service or the presentment agency, hold a hearing pursuant to section 355.1 to determine whether the dispositional order should be modified.

§354.1.   Retention and destruction of fingerprints of persons alleged to
           be juvenile delinquents.

1. If a person whose fingerprints, palmprints or photographs were taken pursuant to section 306.1 or was initially fingerprinted as a juvenile offender and the action is subsequently removed to a family court pursuant to article seven hundred twenty-five of the criminal procedure law is adjudicated to be a juvenile delinquent for a felony, the family court shall forward or cause to be forwarded to the division of criminal justice services notification of such adjudication and such related information as may be required by such division, provided, however, in the case of a person eleven or twelve years of age such

notification shall be provided only if the act upon which the adjudication is based would constitute a class A or B felony.

2. If a person whose fingerprints, palmprints or photographs were taken pursuant to section 306.1 or was initially fingerprinted as a juvenile offender and the action is subsequently removed to family court pursuant to article seven hundred twenty-five of the criminal procedure law has had all petitions disposed of by the family court in any manner other than an adjudication of juvenile delinquency for a felony, but in the case of acts committed when such person was eleven or twelve years of age which would constitute a class A or B felony only, all such fingerprints, palmprints, photographs, and copies thereof, and all information relating to such allegations obtained by the division of criminal justice services pursuant to section 306.1 shall be destroyed forthwith. The clerk of the court shall notify the commissioner of the division of criminal justice services and the heads of all police departments and law enforcement agencies having copies of such records, who shall destroy such records without unnecessary delay.

3. If the appropriate presentment agency does not originate a proceeding under section 310.1 for a case in which the potential respondent's fingerprints were taken pursuant to section 306.1, the presentment agency shall serve a certification of such action upon the division of criminal justice services, and upon the appropriate police department or law enforcement agency.

4. If, following the taking into custody of a person alleged to be a juvenile delinquent and the taking and forwarding to the division of criminal justice services of such person's fingerprints but prior to referral to the probation department or to the family court, an officer or agency, elects not to proceed further, such officer or agency shall serve a certification of such election upon the division of criminal justice services.

5. Upon certification pursuant to subdivision twelve of section 308.1 or subdivision three or four of this section, the department or agency shall destroy forthwith all fingerprints, palmprints, photographs, and copies thereof, and all other information obtained in the case pursuant to section 306.1. Upon receipt of such certification, the division of criminal justice services and all police departments and law enforcement agencies having copies of such records shall destroy them.

6. If a person fingerprinted pursuant to section 306.1 and subsequently adjudicated a juvenile delinquent for a felony, but in the case of acts committed when such a person was eleven or twelve years of age which would constitute a class A or B felony only, is subsequently convicted of a crime, all fingerprints and related information obtained by the division of criminal justice services pursuant to such section and not destroyed pursuant to subdivisions two, five and seven or subdivision twelve of section 308.1 shall become part of such division's permanent adult criminal record for that person, notwithstanding section 381.2 or 381.3.

7. When a person fingerprinted pursuant to section 306.1 and subsequently adjudicated a juvenile delinquent for a felony, but in the case of acts committed when such person was eleven or twelve years of age which would constitute a class A or B felony only, reaches the age of twenty-one, or has been discharged from placement under this act for at least three years, whichever occurs later, and has no criminal convictions or pending criminal actions which ultimately terminate in a criminal conviction, all fingerprints, palmprints, photographs, and related information and copies thereof obtained pursuant to section 306.1 in the possession of the division of criminal justice services, any police department, law enforcement agency or any other agency shall be destroyed forthwith. The division of criminal justice services shall notify the agency or

agencies which forwarded fingerprints to such division pursuant to section 306.1 of their obligation to destroy those records in their possession. In the case of a pending criminal action which does not terminate in a criminal conviction, such records shall be destroyed forthwith upon such determination.

§354.2. Duties of counsel.

1. If the court has entered a dispositional order pursuant to section 352.2, it shall be the duty of the respondent's counsel to promptly advise such respondent and his or her parent or other person responsible for his or her care in writing of the right to appeal to the appropriate appellate division of the supreme court, the time limitations involved, the manner of instituting an appeal and obtaining a transcript of the testimony and the right to apply for leave to appeal as a poor person if he or she is unable to pay the cost of an appeal. It shall be the further duty of such counsel to explain to the respondent and his or her parent or person responsible for his or her care the procedures for instituting an appeal, the possible reasons upon which an appeal may be based and the nature and possible consequences of the appellate process.

2. It shall also be the duty of such counsel to ascertain whether the respondent wishes to appeal and, if so, to serve and file the necessary notice of appeal.

3. If the respondent has been permitted to waive the appointment of counsel pursuant to section two hundred forty-nine-a, it shall be the duty of the court to provide the notice and explanation pursuant to subdivision one and, if the respondent indicates that he or she wishes to appeal, the clerk of the court shall file and serve the notice of appeal.

§355.1. New hearing; staying, modifying or terminating an order.

1. Upon a showing of a substantial change of circumstances, the court may on its own motion or on motion of the respondent or his parent or person responsible for his care:

(a) grant a new fact-finding or dispositional hearing; or

(b) stay execution of, set aside, modify, terminate or vacate any order issued in the course of a proceeding under this article.

2. An order issued under section 353.3, may, upon a showing of a substantial change of circumstances, be set aside, modified, vacated or terminated upon motion of the commissioner of social services or the office of children and family services with whom the respondent has been placed.

(a)(i) For a social services district that only has an approved plan to implement programs for juvenile delinquents placed in non-secure settings as part of an approved juvenile justice services close to home initiative pursuant to section four hundred four of the social services law, beginning on the effective date of that plan, if the district determines that placement in a limited secure facility is appropriate and consistent with the need for protection of the community and the needs and best interests of the respondent placed into its care, the social services district shall file a petition to transfer the custody of the respondent to the office of children and family services, and shall provide a copy of such petition to such office, the respondent, the attorney for the respondent and the respondent's parent or legal guardian. The court shall render a decision whether the juvenile delinquent should be transferred to the office within seventy-two hours, excluding weekends and public holidays. The family court shall, after allowing the office of children and family services and the attorney for the respondent, after notice having been given, an opportunity to be heard, grant such a petition only if the court determines, and states in its written order, the reasons why a limited secure placement is necessary and consistent with the needs and best interests of the respondent and the need for protection of the community.

(ii) For a social services district with an approved plan or approved plans that cover juvenile delinquents placed in non-secure or in non-secure and in limited secure settings as part of an approved juvenile justice services close to home initiative pursuant to section four hundred four of the social services law, beginning on the effective date of the plan, if the district determines that a secure level of placement is appropriate and consistent with the need for protection of the community and the needs and best interests of the respondent placed into its care, the social services district shall file a petition to transfer the custody of the respondent to the office of children and family services, and shall provide a copy of such petition to such office, the respondent, the attorney for the respondent and the respondent's parent or legal guardian. The court shall render a decision whether the youth should be transferred within seventy-two hours, excluding weekends and public holidays. The family court shall, after allowing the office of children and family services and the attorney for the respondent, after notice having been given, an opportunity to be heard, grant such a petition only if the court determines, and states in its written order, that the youth needs a secure level of placement because:

(A) the respondent has been shown to be exceptionally dangerous to himself or herself or to other persons. Exceptionally dangerous behavior may include, but is not limited to, one or more serious intentional assaults, sexual assaults or setting fires; or

(B) the respondent has demonstrated by a pattern of behavior that he or she needs a more structured setting and the social services district has considered the appropriateness and availability of a transfer to an alternative non-secure or limited secure facility. Such behavior may include, but is not limited to: disruptions in facility programs; continuously and maliciously destroying property; or, repeatedly committing or inciting other youth to commit assaultive or destructive acts.

(iii) The court may order that the respondent be housed in a local secure detention facility on an interim basis pending its final ruling on the petition filed pursuant to this paragraph.

(b) The following provisions shall apply if the office of children and family services files a petition with a family court in a social services district with an approved juvenile justice services close to home initiative pursuant to section four hundred four of the social services law to transfer, within the first ninety days that such plan is effective, to such district a respondent placed in the office's care pursuant to either section 353.3 or 353. 5 of this part:

(i) Such a petition shall be provided to the respondent, the attorney for the respondent and the respondent's parent or legal guardian. If the district only has an approved plan that covers juvenile delinquents placed in non-secure settings, the family court shall grant such a petition, without a hearing, unless the attorney for the respondent, after notice, objects to the transfer on the basis that the respondent needs to be placed with the office or the family court determines that there is insufficient information in the petition to grant the transfer without a hearing. The family court shall grant the petition unless the court determines, and states in its written order, the reasons why placement with the office is necessary and consistent with the needs and best interests of the respondent and the need for protection of the community.

(ii) If the district has an approved plan or approved plans that cover juvenile delinquents placed in non-secure and in limited secure settings, for the first ninety days that the plan that covers juvenile delinquents in limited secure settings is effective, the family court shall grant such a petition, without a hearing, unless the attorney for the respondent, after notice, objects to the transfer on the basis that the respondent needs to be placed with the office or the family court determines that there is insufficient information in the petition to grant the transfer without a hearing. The family court shall grant the petition unless the court determines, and states in its written order, the reasons why placement with the office is necessary and consistent with the needs and best interests of the respondent and the need for protection of the community.

(c) Beginning ninety-one days after the effective date a social services district's plan to implement programs for juvenile justice services close to home initiative pursuant to section four hundred four of the social services law, if the office of children and family services files a petition to transfer to such district a respondent placed in the office's care pursuant to either section 353.3 or 353.5 of this part from a family court in such a social services district, the office shall provide a copy of the petition to the social services district, the attorney for the respondent and the presentment agency. (i) If the district only has an approved plan that covers juvenile delinquents placed in non-secure settings, the family court shall, after allowing the social services district, the attorney for the respondent and the presentment agency an opportunity to be heard, grant a petition filed pursuant to this subparagraph unless the court determines, and states in its written order, the reasons why a secure or limited secure placement is necessary and consistent with the needs and best interests of the respondent and the need for protection of the community.

(ii) If the district has an approved plan or approved plans that cover juvenile delinquents placed in non-secure and limited secure settings, beginning ninety-one days after the effective date of the plan that covers juvenile delinquents placed in limited secure settings, the family court, after allowing the social services district, the attorney for the respondent and the presentment agency an opportunity to be heard, shall grant a petition filed pursuant to this subparagraph, unless the court determines, and states in its written order, the reasons why a secure placement is necessary and consistent with the needs and best interests of the respondent and the need for protection of the community.

3. If the court issues a new order of disposition under this section the date such order expires shall not be later than the expiration date of the original order.

§355.2. Motion procedures.

1. A motion for relief pursuant to section 355.1 must be in writing and must state the specific relief requested. If the motion is based upon the existence or occurrence of facts, the motion papers must contain sworn allegations thereof; such sworn allegations may be based upon personal knowledge of the affiant or upon information and belief, provided that in the latter event the affidavit must state the sources of such information and the grounds of such belief.

2. Notice of such motion, including the court's own motion, shall be served upon the respondent, the presentment agency and the commissioner of social services or the division for youth having custody of the respondent. Motions shall be noticed in accordance with the civil practice law and rules.

3. Each party to the motion shall have the right to oral argument and the court shall conduct a hearing to resolve any material question of fact.

4. Regardless of whether a hearing is conducted, the court, upon determining the motion, must set forth on the record its findings of fact, its conclusions of law and the reasons for its determination.

5. If the motion is denied, a motion requesting the same or similar relief cannot be filed for a period of ninety days after such denial, unless the order of denial permits renewal at an earlier time.

§355.3 Extension of placement.

1. In any case in which the respondent has been placed pursuant to section 353.3 the respondent, the person with whom the respondent has been placed, the commissioner of social services, or the division for youth may petition the court to extend such placement. Such petition shall be filed at least sixty days prior to the expiration of the period of placement, except for good cause shown but in no event shall such petition be filed after the original expiration date.

2. The court shall conduct a hearing concerning the need for continuing the placement. The respondent, the presentment agency and the agency with whom the respondent has been placed shall be notified of such hearing and shall have the opportunity to be heard thereat. If the petition is filed within sixty days prior to the expiration of the period of placement, the court shall first determine at such hearing whether good cause has been shown. If good cause is not shown, the court shall dismiss the petition.

3. The provisions of sections 350.3 and 350.4 shall apply at such hearing.

4. At the conclusion of the hearing the court may, in its discretion, order an extension of the placement for not more than one year. The court must consider and determine in its order:

(i) that where appropriate, and where consistent with the need for the protection of the community, reasonable efforts were made to make it possible for the respondent to safely return to his or her home;

(ii) in the case of a respondent who has attained the age of sixteen, the services needed, if any, to assist the child to make the transition from foster care to independent living; and

(iii) in the case of a child placed outside New York state, whether the out-of-state placement continues to be appropriate and in the best interests of the child.

5. Pending final determination of a petition to extend such placement filed in accordance with the provisions of this section, the court may, on its own motion or at the request of the petitioner or respondent, enter one or more temporary orders extending a period of placement for a period not to exceed thirty days upon satisfactory proof showing probable cause for continuing such placement and that each temporary order is necessary. The court may order additional temporary extensions, not to exceed a total of fifteen days, if the court is unable to conclude the hearing within the thirty day temporary extension period. In no event shall the aggregate number of days in extensions granted or ordered under this subdivision total more than forty-five days. The petition shall be dismissed if a decision is not rendered within the period of placement or any temporary extension thereof.

6. Successive extensions of placement under this section may be granted, but no placement may be made or continued beyond the respondent's eighteenth birthday without the child's consent and in no event past the child's twenty-first birthday.

§355.4. Provisions for routine medical, dental and mental health services and treatment.

1. At the conclusion of the dispositional hearing pursuant to this article, where the respondent is to be placed with the office of children and family services or a social services district, the court shall inquire as to whether the parents or legal guardian of the youth, if present, will consent for the office or the district to provide routine medical, dental and mental health services and treatment.

2. Notwithstanding subdivision one of this section, where the court places a youth with the office of children and family services or a social services district pursuant to this article and no medical consent has been obtained prior to an order of disposition, the placement order shall be deemed to grant consent for the office or the district to provide for routine medical, dental and mental health services and treatment to such youth so placed.

3. Subject to regulations of the department of health, routine medical, dental and mental health services and treatment is defined for the purposes of this section to mean any routine diagnosis or treatment, including without limitation the administration of medications or nutrition, the extraction of bodily fluids for analysis, and dental care performed with a local anesthetic. Routine mental health treatment shall not include psychiatric administration of medication unless it is part of an ongoing mental health plan or unless it is otherwise authorized by law.

4. (a) At any time during placement or at an extension of placement hearing, a parent or legal guardian may make a motion objecting to routine medical, dental or mental health services and treatment being provided to such youth as authorized under the provisions of subdivision one of this section.

(b) Such notice of motion shall be served on the youth, the presentment agency and the division not less than seven days prior to the return date of the motion. The persons on whom the notice of motion is served shall answer the motion not less than two days before the return date. On examining the motion and answer and, in its discretion, after hearing argument, the court shall enter an order, granting or denying the motion.

5. Nothing in this section shall preclude a youth from consenting on his or her own behalf to any medical, dental or mental health service and treatment where otherwise authorized by law to do so, or the division for youth from petitioning the court pursuant to section two hundred thirty-three of this act, as appropriate.

§355.5. Permanency hearing.

1. For the purposes of this section the term "non-secure facility" means a facility operated by an authorized agency in accordance with an operating certificate issued pursuant to the social services law or a facility, not including a secure or limited secure facility, with a capacity of twenty-five beds or less operated by the office of children and family services in accordance with section five hundred four of the executive law. The term shall not include a limited secure facility within a social services district operating an approved juvenile justice services close to home initiative pursuant to section four hundred four of the social services law.   *(Repealed 3/31/18,Ch.57,L.2012)*

2. Where a respondent is placed with a commissioner of social services or the office of children and family services pursuant to section 353.3 of this article for a period of twelve or fewer months and resides in a foster home or non-secure facility;

(a) The initial permanency hearing shall be held no later than twelve months after the respondent who was placed with a commissioner of social services or the office of children and family services entered foster care and such permanency hearing shall be held in conjunction with an extension of placement hearing held pursuant to section 355.3 of this article.

(b) Subsequent permanency hearings shall be held no later than every twelve months following the respondent's initial permanency hearing and shall be held in conjunction with an extension of placement hearing held pursuant to section 355.3 of this article.

3. Where a respondent is placed with a commissioner of social services or the office of children and family services pursuant to section 353.3 of this article for a period in excess of twelve months and resides in a foster home or in a non-secure facility;

(a) the initial permanency hearing shall be held no later than twelve months after the respondent who was placed with a commissioner of social services or the office of children and family services entered foster care.

(b) subsequent permanency hearings shall be held no later than every twelve months following the respondent's initial twelve months in placement; provided, however, that they shall be held in conjunction with an extension of placement hearing held pursuant to section 355.3 of this article.

4. For the purposes of this section, the respondent shall be considered to have entered foster care sixty days after the respondent was removed from his or her home pursuant to this article.

5. A petition for an initial or subsequent permanency hearing shall be filed by the office of children and family services or by the commissioner of social services with whom the respondent was placed. Such petition shall be filed no later than sixty days prior to the end of the month in which an initial or subsequent permanency hearing must be held, as directed in subdivision two of this section.

6. The foster parent caring for the respondent or any pre-adoptive parent or relative providing care for the respondent shall be provided with notice of any permanency hearing held pursuant to this section by the office of children and family services or the commissioner of social services with whom the respondent was placed. Such foster parent, pre-adoptive parent and relative shall have the right to be heard at any such hearing; provided, however, no such foster parent, pre-adoptive parent or relative shall be construed to be a party to the hearing solely on the basis of such notice and right to be heard. The failure of the foster parent, pre-adoptive parent, or relative caring for the child to appear at a permanency hearing shall constitute a waiver of the right to be heard and such failure to appear shall not cause a delay of the permanency hearing nor shall such failure to appear be a ground for the invalidation of any order issued by the court pursuant to this section.

7. At the permanency hearing, the court must consider and determine in its order:

(a) where appropriate, that reasonable efforts were made to make it possible for the respondent to return safely to his or her home, or if the permanency plan for the respondent is adoption, guardianship or another permanent living arrangement other than reunification with the parent or parents of the respondent, that reasonable efforts were made to make and finalize such alternate permanent placement including consideration of appropriate in-state and out-of-state placements;

(b) in the case of a respondent who has attained the age of fourteen, (i) the services needed, if any, to assist the respondent to make the transition from foster care to successful adulthood; and (ii)(A) that the permanency plan developed for the respondent, and any revision or addition to the plan, shall be developed in consultation with the respondent and, at the option of the respondent, with up to two members of the respondent's permanency planning team who are selected by the respondent and who are not a foster parent of, or case worker, case planner or case manager for, the child, except that the local commissioner of social services with custody of the respondent or the commissioner of the office of children and family services if such office has custody of the respondent may reject an individual selected by the respondent if such commissioner has good cause to believe that the individual would not act in the best interests of the respondent, and (B) that one individual so selected by the respondent may be designated to be the respondent's advisor and, as necessary, advocate, with respect to the application of the reasonable and prudent parent standard;   *(Eff.4/4/16,Ch.54,L.2016)*

(c) in the case of a respondent placed outside of this state, whether the out-of-state placement continues to be appropriate and in the best interests of the respondent;

(d) with regard to the completion of placement ordered by the court pursuant to section 353.3 or 355.3 of this part: whether and when the respondent: (i) will be returned to the parent; (ii) should be placed for adoption with the local commissioner of social services filing a petition for termination of parental rights; (iii) should be referred for legal guardianship; (iv) should be placed permanently with a fit and willing relative; or (v) should be placed in another planned permanent living arrangement with a significant connection to an adult willing to be a permanency resource for the respondent if the respondent is age sixteen or older and (A) the office of children and family services or the local commissioner of social services has documented to the court: (1) the intensive, ongoing, and, as of the date of the hearing, unsuccessful efforts made to return the respondent home or secure a placement for the respondent with a fit and willing relative including adult siblings, a legal guardian, or an adoptive parent, including through efforts that utilize search technology including social media to find biological family members for children, (2) the steps being taken to ensure that (I) the respondent's foster family home or child care facility is following the reasonable and prudent parent standard in accordance with guidance provided by the United States department of health and human services, and (II) the respondent has regular, ongoing opportunities to engage in age or developmentally appropriate activities including by consulting with the respondent in an age-appropriate manner about the opportunities of the respondent to participate in activities; and (B) the office of children and family services or the local commissioner of social services has documented to the court and the court has determined that there are compelling reasons for determining that it continues to not be in the best interest of the respondent to return home, be referred for termination of parental rights and placed for adoption, placed with a fit and willing relative, or placed with a legal guardian; and (C) the court has made a determination explaining why, as of the date of this hearing, another planned living arrangement with a significant connection to an adult willing to be a permanency resource for the respondent is the best permanency plan for the respondent; and

(e) with regard to the completion or extension of placement ordered by the court pursuant to section 353.3 or 355.3 of this article, the steps that must be taken by the agency with which the respondent is placed to implement the plan for release or conditional release submitted pursuant to paragraph (c) of subdivision seven of section 353.3 of this article, including consideration of appropriate in-state and out-of-state placements, the adequacy of such plan and any modifications that should be made to such plan.

8. At the permanency hearing, the court shall consult with the respondent in an age-appropriate manner regarding the permanency plan for the respondent; provided, however, that if the respondent is age sixteen or older and the requested permanency plan for the respondent is placement in another planned permanent living arrangement with a significant connection to an adult willing to be a permanency resource for the respondent, the court must ask the respondent about the desired permanency outcome for the respondent.

9. The court shall not reduce or terminate the placement of the respondent prior to the completion of the period of placement ordered by the court pursuant to section 353.3 or 355.3 of this article.

Part 6
Post-dispositional Procedures

§360.1.   Jurisdiction and supervision of respondent placed on probation.

1. A respondent who is placed on probation shall remain under the legal jurisdiction of the court pending expiration or termination of the period of the order of probation.

2. The probation service shall supervise the respondent during the period of such legal jurisdiction.

3. If at any time during the period of probation the court has reasonable cause to believe that the respondent has violated a condition of the probation order, it may issue a search order. A search order is an order directed to a probation officer authorizing such officer to search the person of the respondent or any personal property which he owns or which is in his possession.

4. In executing a search order pursuant to this section, a probation officer may be assisted by a police officer.

§360.2.   Petition of violation.

1. If at any time during the period of an order of probation or conditional discharge the probation service has reasonable cause to believe that the respondent has violated a condition thereof, it may file a petition of violation.

2. The petition must be verified and subscribed by the probation service or the appropriate presentment agency. Such petition must stipulate the condition or conditions of the order violated and a reasonable description of the time, place and manner in which the violation occurred. Non-hearsay allegations of the factual part of the petition or of any supporting depositions must establish, if true, every violation charged.

3. The court must promptly take reasonable and appropriate action to cause the respondent to appear before it for the purpose of enabling the court to make a determination with respect to the alleged violation. Such action may include the issuance of a summons under section 312.1 or the issuance of a warrant under section 312.2.

4. If a petition is filed under subdivision one, the period of probation as prescribed by section 353.2 or conditional discharge as prescribed by section 353.1 shall be interrupted as of the date of the filing of the petition. Such interruption shall continue until a final determination as to the petition has been made by the court pursuant to a hearing held in accordance with section 360.3 or until such time as the respondent reaches the maximum age of acceptance into an office of children and family services facility.

5. If the court determines that there was no violation of probation or conditional discharge by the respondent, the period of interruption shall be credited to the period of probation or conditional discharge, as applicable.

§360.3.   Hearing on violation.

1. The court may not revoke an order of probation or conditional discharge unless:

(a) the court has found that the respondent has violated a condition of such order; and

(b) the respondent has had an opportunity to be heard. The respondent is entitled to a hearing in accordance with this section promptly after a petition of violation has been filed.

2. At the time of his first appearance following the filing of a petition of violation the court must:

(a) advise the respondent of the contents of the petition and furnish him with a copy thereof;

(b) determine whether the respondent should be released or detained pursuant to section 320.5; and

(c) ask the respondent whether he wishes to make any statement with respect to the violation. If the respondent makes a statement, the court may accept it and base its decision thereon; the provisions of subdivision two of section 321.3 shall apply in determining whether a statement should be accepted. If the court does not accept such statement or if the respondent does not make a statement, the court shall proceed with the hearing. Upon request, the court shall grant a reasonable adjournment to the respondent to enable him to prepare for the hearing.

3. At such hearing, the court may receive any relevant, competent and material evidence. The respondent may cross-examine witnesses and may present evidence on his own behalf.

4. The respondent is entitled to counsel at all stages of a proceeding under this section and the court shall advise him of such right at the outset of the proceeding.

5. The presentment agency shall present the petition in all stages of this part.

6. At the conclusion of the hearing the court may revoke, continue or modify the order of probation or conditional discharge. If the court revokes the order, it shall order a different disposition pursuant to section 352.2. If the court continues the order of probation or conditional discharge, it shall dismiss the petition of violation.

§365.1.   Appeal; authorized as of right.

1. An appeal to the appropriate appellate division may be taken as of right by the respondent from any order of disposition under this article in accordance with article eleven.

2. An appeal to the appropriate appellate division may be taken as of right by the presentment agency from the following orders of the family court:

(a) an order dismissing a petition prior to the commencement of a fact-finding hearing; or

(b) an order of disposition, but only upon the ground that such order was invalid as a matter of law; or

(c) an order suppressing evidence entered before the commencement of the fact-finding hearing pursuant to section 330.2, provided that such presentment agency files a statement pursuant to subdivision nine of section 330.2.

§365.2. Appeal by permission.

An appeal may be taken by the respondent, in the discretion of the appropriate appellate division, from any other order under this article.

§365.3. Notice of appeal.

1. An appeal shall be taken by filing a written notice of appeal, in duplicate, with the clerk of the family court in which the order was entered.

2. If the respondent is the appellant, he must also serve a copy of such notice of appeal upon the appropriate presentment agency.

3. If the presentment agency is the appellant, it must serve a copy of such notice of appeal upon the respondent and upon the attorney who last appeared for him or her in the family court.

4. Following the filing with him of the notice of appeal in duplicate, the clerk of the family court must endorse upon such instruments the filing date and must transmit the duplicate notice of appeal to the clerk of the appropriate appellate division of the supreme court.

Part 7
Securing Testimony and Records

Section
370.1.   Securing the attendance of witnesses; securing certain testimony.
375.1.   Order upon termination of a delinquency action in favor of the respondent.
375.2.   Motion to seal after a finding.
375.3.   Expungement of court records.

§370.1. Securing the attendance of witnesses; securing certain testimony.

1. The provisions of article six hundred twenty of the criminal procedure law concerning the securing of attendance of witnesses by material witness order shall apply to proceedings under this article.

2. Article six hundred sixty, six hundred seventy and six hundred eighty of the criminal procedure law concerning the securing of testimony for use in a subsequent proceeding, the use of testimony given in a previous proceeding and the examination of witness by commission shall apply to proceedings under this article.

3. The provisions of the uniform act to secure attendance of witnesses from without the state in criminal cases, as incorporated in article six hundred forty of the criminal procedure law, shall apply to proceedings under this article.

§375.1. Order upon termination of a delinquency action in favor of the respondent.

1. Upon termination of a delinquency proceeding against a respondent in favor of such respondent, unless the presentment agency upon written motion with not less than eight days notice to such respondent demonstrates to the satisfaction of the court that the interests of justice require otherwise or the court on its own motion with not less than eight days notice to such respondent

determines that the interest of justice require otherwise and states the reason for such determination on the record, the clerk of the court shall immediately notify the counsel for the child, the director of the appropriate presentment agency, and the heads of the appropriate probation department and police department or other law enforcement agency, that the proceeding has terminated in favor of the respondent and, unless the court has directed otherwise, that the records of such action or proceeding, other than those destroyed pursuant to section 354.1 of this act, shall be sealed. Upon receipt of such notification all official records and papers, including judgments and orders of the court, but not including public court decisions or opinions or records and briefs on appeal, relating to the arrest, the prosecution and the probation service proceedings, including all duplicates or copies thereof, on file with the court, police agency, probation service and presentment agency shall be sealed and not made available to any person or public or private agency. Such records shall remain sealed during the pendency of any motion made pursuant to this subdivision.

2. For the purposes of subdivision one, a delinquency proceeding shall be considered terminated in favor of a respondent where:

(a) the petition is withdrawn; or

(b) the petition is dismissed under section 315.1 or 315.2 and the presentment agency has not appealed from such order or the determination of an appeal or appeals from such order has been against the presentment agency; or

(c) the petition has been deemed to have been dismissed under section 315.3 and the presentment agency has not appealed from such order or the determination of an appeal or appeals from such order has been against the presentment agency; or

(d) the petition is dismissed without prejudice under subdivision four of section 325.3 and the presentment agency has not appealed from such order or the determination of an appeal or appeals from such order has been against the presentment agency; or

(e) the entire petition has been dismissed under subdivision two of section 345.1; or

(f) the petition is dismissed under subdivision two of section 352.1; or

(g) prior to the filing of a petition, the probation department has adjusted the case or terminated the case without adjustment; or

(h) prior to the filing of a petition the presentment agency chooses not to proceed to petition; or

(i) the petition is dismissed pursuant to a motion made in accordance with subdivision eight, nine or ten of section 332.1.

3. Records sealed pursuant to subdivision one shall be made available to the respondent or his designated agent and the records and papers of a probation service shall be available to any probation service for the purpose of complying with subdivision four of section 308.1.

4. If prior to the filing of a petition the presentment agency elects not to commence a delinquency action it shall serve a certification of such disposition upon the appropriate probation service and the appropriate police department or law enforcement agency, which, upon receipt thereto, shall comply with the provision of subdivision one in the same manner as is required with respect to an order of the court.

5. If the probation service adjusts a delinquency case it shall serve a certification of such disposition upon the appropriate police department or law enforcement agency which, upon receipt thereof, shall comply with the

provisions of subdivision one in the same manner as is required thereunder with respect to an order of a court.

6. A respondent in whose favor a delinquency proceeding was terminated prior to the effective date of this section may upon motion apply to the court, upon not less than twenty days notice to the presentment agency, for an order granting him the relief set forth in subdivision one, and such order shall be granted unless the presentment agency demonstrates to the satisfaction of the court that the interests of justice require otherwise. A respondent in whose favor a delinquency action or proceeding was terminated as defined by subdivisions four and five, prior to the effective date of this section, may apply to the appropriate presentment agency or probation service for a certification as described in such subdivisions granting him the relief set forth therein and such certification shall be granted by such presentment agency or probation service.

§375.2.   Motion to seal after a finding.
1. If an action has resulted in a finding of delinquency pursuant to subdivision one of section 352.1, other than a finding that the respondent committed a designated felony act, the court may, in the interest of justice and upon motion of the respondent, order the sealing of appropriate records pursuant to subdivision one of section 375.1.
2. Such motion must be in writing and may be filed at any time subsequent to the entering of such finding. Notice of such motion shall be served upon the presentment agency not less than eight days prior to the return date of the motion. Answering affidavits shall be served at least two days before such time.
3. The court shall state on the record its reasons for granting or denying the motion.
4. If such motion is denied, it may not be renewed for a period of one year, unless the order of denial permits renewal at an earlier time.
5. The court shall not order the sealing of any record except as prescribed by this section or section 375.1.
6. Such a motion cannot be filed until the respondent's sixteenth birthday.

§375.3.   Expungement of court records.
Nothing contained in this article shall preclude the court's use of its inherent power to order the expungement of court records.

Part 8
General Provisions

Section
380.1.   Nature and effect of adjudication.
381.1.   Transfer of records and information to institutions and agencies.
381.2.   Use of records in other courts.
381.3.   Use of police records.
385.1.   Reports.
385.2.   Consolidation of records within a city having a population of one million or more.

§380.1.   Nature and effect of adjudication.
1. No adjudication under this article may be denominated a conviction and no person adjudicated a juvenile delinquent shall be denominated a criminal by reason of such adjudication.
2. No adjudication under this article shall operate as a forfeiture of any right or privilege or disqualify any person from holding any public office or receiving any license granted by public authority. Such adjudication shall not

operate as a disqualification of any person to pursue or engage in any lawful activity, occupation, profession or calling.

3. Except where specifically required by statute, no person shall be required to divulge information pertaining to the arrest of the respondent or any subsequent proceeding under this article; provided, however, whenever a person adjudicated a juvenile delinquent has been placed with the office of children and family services pursuant to section 353.3 of this article, and is thereafter enrolled as a student in a public or private elementary or secondary school, the court that has adjudicated such person shall provide notification of such adjudication to the designated educational official of the school in which such person is enrolled as a student. Such notification shall be used by the designated educational official only for purposes related to the execution of the student's educational plan, where applicable, successful school adjustment and reentry into the community. Such notification shall be kept separate and apart from such student's school records and shall be accessible only by the designated educational official. Such notification shall not be part of such student's permanent school record and shall not be appended to or included in any documentation regarding such student and shall be destroyed at such time as such student is no longer enrolled in the school district. At no time shall such notification be used for any purpose other than those specified in this subdivision.

4. Notwithstanding any other provision of law, where a finding of juvenile delinquency has been entered, upon request, the records pertaining to such case shall be made available to the commissioner of mental health or the commissioner of developmental disabilities, as appropriate; the case review panel; and the attorney general pursuant to section 10.05 of the mental hygiene law.

(Eff.5/25/16,Ch.37,L.2016)

§381.1. Transfer of records and information to institutions and agencies.

Whenever a person is placed with an institution suitable for placement of a person adjudicated a juvenile delinquent maintained by the state or any subdivision thereof or to an authorized agency including the division for youth, the family court placing such person shall forthwith transmit a copy of the orders of the family court pursuant to sections 352.1 and 352.2 and of the probation report and all other relevant evaluative records in the possession of the family court and probation department related to such person, including but not limited to any diagnostic, educational, medical, psychological and psychiatric records with respect to such person to such institution or agency, notwithstanding any contrary provision of law.

§381.2. Use of records in other courts.

1. Neither the fact that a person was before the family court under this article for a hearing nor any confession, admission or statement made by him to the court or to any officer thereof in any stage of the proceeding is admissible as evidence against him or his interests in any other court.

2. Notwithstanding the provisions of subdivision one, another court, in imposing sentence upon an adult after conviction may receive and consider the records and information on file with the family court, unless such records and information have been sealed pursuant to section 375.1.

§381.3.   Use of police records.

1. All police records relating to the arrest and disposition of any person under this article shall be kept in files separate and apart from the arrests of adults and shall be withheld from public inspection.

2. Notwithstanding the provisions of subdivision one, the family court in the county in which the petition was adjudicated may, upon motion and for good cause shown, order such records open:

   (a) to the respondent or his parent or person responsible for his care; or

   (b) if the respondent is subsequently convicted of a crime, to a judge of the court in which he was convicted, unless such record has been sealed pursuant to section 375.1.

3. An order issued under subdivision two must be in writing.

§385.1.   Reports.

1. In addition to reports filed pursuant to section two hundred thirteen, the chief administrator of the courts shall include in its annual report to the legislature and the governor information, by county, showing the total number of delinquency cases filed under this article, the precise crime or crimes charged in such petitions by penal law section, the number of respondents included in such petitions, the number of cases heard in the designated felony parts, the age of the alleged victim by crime, the length of time and number of adjournments between the filing of a petition and the conclusion of the fact-finding process, the number of cases dismissed by the court, the number withdrawn, the number admitted to in whole or in part, the number of contested fact-finding hearings and their result, the precise crime, if any, found to have been committed, the length of time and number of adjournments between the fact-finding hearing and the conclusion of the dispositional hearing and the final precise disposition of such cases. Designated felony cases shall be separately reported by each event or fact enumerated in this section. Cases removed from criminal courts shall also be separately reported by each event and fact enumerated in this section.

2. The office of probation and correctional alternatives shall include in its annual report to the legislature and the governor information, by county, showing the total number of delinquency cases adjusted prior to filing.

§385.2.   Consolidation of records within a city having a population of one million or more.

Notwithstanding any other provision of law, in a city having a population of one million or more, an index of the records of the local probation departments located in the counties comprising such city for proceedings under article three shall be consolidated and filed in a central office for use by the family court and local probation service in each such county. After consultation with the state administrative judge, the commissioner of the division of criminal justice services in consultation with the director of the office of probation and correctional alternatives shall specify the information to be contained in such index and the organization of such consolidated file.

ARTICLE 4
Support Proceedings

Part 1
Jurisdiction and Duties of Support

§411. Jurisdiction.

The family court has exclusive original jurisdiction over proceedings for support or maintenance under this article and in proceedings under article five-B of this act, known as the uniform interstate family support act. On its own motion, the court may at any time in the proceedings also direct the filing of a neglect petition in accord with article ten of this act.

§412. Married person's duty to support spouse.

1. A married person is chargeable with the support of his or her spouse and, except where the parties have entered into an agreement pursuant to section four hundred twenty-five of this article providing for support, the court, upon application by a party, shall make its award for spousal support pursuant to the provisions of this part.

2. For purposes of this section, the following definitions shall be used:

(a) "payor" shall mean the spouse with the higher income.

(b) "payee" shall mean the spouse with the lower income.

(c) "income" shall mean income as defined in the child support standards act and codified in section two hundred forty of the domestic relations law and section four hundred thirteen of this article without subtracting spousal support actually paid or to be paid to a spouse that is a party to the instant action pursuant to subclause (C) of clause (vii) of subparagraph five of paragraph (b) of subdivision one-b of section two hundred forty of the domestic relations law and subclause (C) of clause (vii) of subparagraph five of paragraph (b) of subdivision one of section four hundred thirteen of this article.

(d) "income cap" shall mean up to and including one hundred seventy-five thousand dollars of the payor's annual income; provided, however, beginning January thirty-first, two thousand sixteen and every two years thereafter, the income cap amount shall increase by the sum of the average annual percentage changes in the consumer price index for all urban consumers (CPI-U) as published by the United States department of labor bureau of labor statistics for the prior two years multiplied by the then income cap and then rounded to the nearest one thousand dollars. The office of court administration shall determine and publish the income cap.

(e) "guideline amount of spousal support" shall mean the sum derived by the application of subdivision three or four of this section.

(f) "self-support reserve" shall mean the self-support reserve as defined in the child support standards act and codified in section two hundred forty of the domestic relations law and section four hundred thirteen of this article.

(g) "agreement" shall have the same meaning as provided in subdivision three of part B of section two hundred thirty-six of the domestic relations law.

3. Where the payor's income is lower than or equal to the income cap, the court shall determine the guideline amount of spousal support as follows:

(a) Where child support will be paid for children of the marriage and where the payor as defined in this section is also the non-custodial parent pursuant to the child support standards act:

(1) the court shall subtract twenty-five percent of the payee's income from twenty percent of the payor's income.

(2) the court shall then multiply the sum of the payor's income and the payee's income by forty percent.

(3) the court shall subtract the payee's income from the amount derived from subparagraph two of this paragraph.

(4) the court shall determine the lower of the two amounts derived by subparagraphs one and three of this paragraph.

(5) the guideline amount of spousal support shall be the amount determined by subparagraph four of this paragraph except that, if the amount determined by subparagraph four of this paragraph is less than or equal to zero, the guideline amount of spousal support shall be zero dollars.

(6) spousal support shall be calculated prior to child support because the amount of spousal support shall be subtracted from the payor's income and added to the payee's income as part of the calculation of the child support obligation.

(b) Where child support will not be paid for children of the marriage, or where child support will be paid for children of the marriage but the payor as defined in this section is the custodial parent pursuant to the child support standards act:

(1) the court shall subtract twenty percent of the payee's income from thirty percent of the payor's income.

(2) the court shall then multiply the sum of the payor's income and the payee's income by forty percent.

(3) the court shall subtract the payee's income from the amount derived from subparagraph two of this paragraph.

(4) the court shall determine the lower of amounts derived by subparagraphs one and three of this paragraph.

(5) the guideline amount of spousal support shall be the amount determined by subparagraph four of this paragraph except that, if the amount determined by subparagraph four of this paragraph is less than or equal to zero, the guideline amount of spousal support shall be zero dollars.

(6) if child support will be paid for children of the marriage but the payor as defined in this section is the custodial parent pursuant to the child support standards act, spousal support shall be calculated prior to child support because the amount of spousal support shall be subtracted from the payor's income and added to the payee's income as part of the calculation of the child support obligation.

4. Where the payor's income exceeds the income cap, the court shall determine the guideline amount of spousal support as follows:

(a) the court shall perform the calculations set forth in subdivision three of this section for the income of the payor up to and including the income cap; and

(b) for income exceeding the cap, the amount of additional spousal support awarded, if any, shall be within the discretion of the court which shall take into consideration any one or more of the factors set forth in paragraph (a) of subdivision six of this section; and

(c) the court shall set forth the factors it considered and the reasons for its decision in writing or on the record. Such decision, whether in writing or on the record, may not be waived by either party or counsel.

5. Notwithstanding the provisions of this section, where the guideline amount of spousal support would reduce the payor's income below the self-support reserve for a single person, the guideline amount of spousal support shall be the difference between the payor's income and the self-support reserve. If the payor's income is below the self-support reserve, there shall be a rebuttable presumption that no spousal support is awarded.

6. (a) The court shall order the guideline amount of spousal support up to the cap in accordance with subdivision three of this section, unless the court finds that the guideline amount of spousal support is unjust or inappropriate, which finding shall be based upon consideration of any one or more of the following factors, and adjusts the guideline amount of spousal support accordingly based upon consideration of the following factors:

(1) the age and health of the parties;

(2) the present or future earning capacity of the parties, including a history of limited participation in the workforce;

(3) the need of one party to incur education or training expenses;

(4) the termination of a child support award during the pendency of the spousal support award when the calculation of spousal support was based upon child support being awarded which resulted in a spousal support award lower than it would have been had child support not been awarded;

(5) the wasteful dissipation of marital property, including transfers or encumbrances made in contemplation of a support proceeding without fair consideration;

(6) the existence and duration of a pre-marital joint household or a pre-support proceedings separate household;

(7) acts by one party against another that have inhibited or continue to inhibit a party's earning capacity or ability to obtain meaningful employment. Such acts include but are not limited to acts of domestic violence as provided in section four hundred fifty-nine-a of the social services law;

(8) the availability and cost of medical insurance for the parties;

(9) the care of children or stepchildren, disabled adult children or stepchildren, elderly parents or in-laws provided during the marriage that inhibits a party's earning capacity;

(10) the tax consequences to each party;

(11) the standard of living of the parties established during the marriage;

(12) the reduced or lost earning capacity of the payee as a result of having forgone or delayed education, training, employment or career opportunities during the marriage;

(13) the contributions and services of the payee as a spouse, parent, wage earner and homemaker and to the career or career potential of the other party;

(14) any other factor which the court shall expressly find to be just and proper.

(b) Where the court finds that the guideline amount of spousal support is unjust or inappropriate and the court adjusts the guideline amount of spousal support pursuant to this subdivision, the court shall set forth, in a written decision or on the record, the guideline amount of spousal support, the factors it considered, and the reasons that the court adjusted the guideline amount of spousal support. Such decision, whether in writing or on the record, shall not be waived by either party or counsel.

(c) Where either or both parties are unrepresented, the court shall not enter a spousal support order unless the court informs the unrepresented party or parties of the guideline amount of spousal support.

7. When a party has defaulted and/or the court makes a finding at the time of trial that it was presented with insufficient evidence to determine income, the court shall order the spousal support award based upon the needs of the payee or the standard of living of the parties prior to commencement of the spousal support proceeding, whichever is greater. Such order may be retroactively modified upward without a showing of change in circumstances upon a showing of substantial newly discovered evidence.

8. In any action or proceeding for modification of an order of spousal support existing prior to the effective date of the chapter of the laws of two thousand fifteen which amended this section, brought pursuant to this article, the spousal support guidelines set forth in this section shall not constitute a change of circumstances warranting modification of such spousal support order.

9. In any action or proceeding for modification where spousal support or maintenance was established in a written agreement providing for spousal support made pursuant to section four hundred twenty-five of this article or made pursuant to subdivision three of part B of section two hundred thirty-six of the domestic relations law entered into prior to the effective date of the chapter of the laws of two thousand fifteen which amended this section, brought pursuant to this article, the spousal support guidelines set forth in this section shall not constitute a change of circumstances warranting modification of such spousal support order.

10. The court may modify an order of spousal support upon a showing of a substantial change in circumstances. Unless so modified, any order for spousal support issued pursuant to this section shall continue until the earliest to occur of the following:

(a) a written stipulation or agreement between the parties;

(b) an oral stipulation or agreement between the parties entered into on the record in open court;

(c) issuance of a judgment of divorce or other order in a matrimonial proceeding;

(d) the death of either party.

§413. Parents' duty to support child.

1. (a) Except as provided in subdivision two of this section, the parents of a child under the age of twenty-one years are chargeable with the support of such child and, if possessed of sufficient means or able to earn such means, shall be required to pay for child support a fair and reasonable sum as the court may determine. The court shall make its award for child support pursuant to the provisions of this subdivision. The court may vary from the amount of the basic child support obligation determined pursuant to paragraph (c) of this subdivision only in accordance with paragraph (f) of this subdivision.

(b) For purposes of this subdivision, the following definitions shall be used:

(1) "Basic child support obligation" shall mean the sum derived by adding the amounts determined by the application of subparagraphs two and three of paragraph (c) of this subdivision except as increased pursuant to subparagraphs four, five, six and seven of such paragraph.

(2) "Child support" shall mean a sum to be paid pursuant to court order or decree by either or both parents or pursuant to a valid agreement between the parties for care, maintenance and education of any unemancipated child under the age of twenty-one years.

(3) "Child support percentage" shall mean:

(i) seventeen percent of the combined parental income for one child;

(ii) twenty-five percent of the combined parental income for two children;

(iii) twenty-nine percent of the combined parental income for three children;

(iv) thirty-one percent of the combined parental income for four children; and

(v) no less than thirty-five percent of the combined parental income for five or more children.

(4) "Combined parental income" shall mean the sum of the income of both parents.

(5) "Income" shall mean, but shall not be limited to, the sum of the amounts determined by the application of clauses (i), (ii), (iii), (iv), (v) and (vi) of this subparagraph reduced by the amount determined by the application of clause (vii) of this subparagraph:

(i) gross (total) income as should have been or should be reported in the most recent federal income tax return. If an individual files his/her federal income tax return as a married person filing jointly, such person shall be required to prepare a form, sworn to under penalty of law, disclosing his/her gross income individually;

(ii) to the extent not already included in gross income in clause (i) of this subparagraph, investment income reduced by sums expended in connection with such investment;

(iii) to the extent not already included in gross income in clauses (i) and (ii) of this subparagraph, the amount of income or compensation voluntarily deferred and income received, if any, from the following sources:

(A) workers' compensation,

(B) disability benefits,

(C) unemployment insurance benefits,

(D) social security benefits,

(E) veterans benefits,

(F) pensions and retirement benefits,

(G) fellowships and stipends,

(H) annuity payments, and

(I) alimony or maintenance actually paid or to be paid to a spouse who is a party to the instant action pursuant to an existing court order or contained in the order to be entered by the court, or pursuant to a validly executed written agreement, in which event the order or agreement shall provide for a specific adjustment, in accordance with this subdivision, in the amount of child support payable upon the termination of alimony or maintenance to such spouse; provided, however, that the specific adjustment in the amount of child support is without prejudice to either party's right to seek a modification in accordance with subdivision three of section four hundred fifty-one of this article. In an action or proceeding to modify an order of child support, including an order incorporating without merging an agreement, issued prior to the effective date of this subclause, the provisions of this subclause shall not, by themselves, constitute a substantial change of circumstances pursuant to paragraph (a) of subdivision three of section four hundred fifty-one of this article.

(iv) at the discretion of the court, the court may attribute or impute income from, such other resources as may be available to the parent, including, but not limited to:

(A) non-income producing assets,

(B) meals, lodging, memberships, automobiles or other perquisites that are provided as part of compensation for employment to the extent that such perquisites constitute expenditures for personal use, or which expenditures directly or indirectly confer personal economic benefits,

(C) fringe benefits provided as part of compensation for employment, and

(D) money, goods, or services provided by relatives and friends;

(v) an amount imputed as income based upon the parent's former resources or income, if the court determines that a parent has reduced resources or income in order to reduce or avoid the parent's obligation for child support;

(vi) to the extent not already included in gross income in clauses (i) and (ii) of this subparagraph, the following self-employment deductions attributable to self-employment carried on by the taxpayer:

(A) any depreciation deduction greater than depreciation calculated on a straight-line basis for the purpose of determining business income or investment credits, and

(B) entertainment and travel allowances deducted from business income to the extent said allowances reduce personal expenditures;

(vii) the following shall be deducted from income prior to applying the provisions of paragraph (c) of this subdivision:

(A) unreimbursed employee business expenses except to the extent said expenses reduce personal expenditures,

(B) alimony or maintenance actually paid to a spouse not a party to the instant action pursuant to court order or validly executed written agreement,

(C) alimony or maintenance actually paid or to be paid to a spouse who is a party to the instant action pursuant to an existing court order or contained in the order to be entered by the court, or pursuant to a validly executed written agreement, in which event the order or agreement shall provide for a specific adjustment, in accordance with this subdivision, in the amount of child support payable upon the termination of alimony or maintenance to such spouse; provided, however, that the specific adjustment in the amount of child support is without prejudice to either party's right to seek a modification in accordance with subdivision three of section four hundred fifty-one of this article. In an action or proceeding to modify an order of child support, including an order incorporating without merging an agreement, issued prior to the effective date of this subclause, the provisions of this subclause shall not, by themselves, constitute a substantial change of circumstances pursuant to paragraph (a) of subdivision three of section four hundred fifty-one of this article.

(D) child support actually paid pursuant to court order or written agreement on behalf of any child for whom the parent has a legal duty of support and who is not subject to the instant action,

(E) public assistance,

(F) supplemental security income,

(G) New York city or Yonkers income or earnings taxes actually paid, and

(H) federal insurance contributions act (FICA) taxes actually paid.

(6) "Self-support reserve" shall mean one hundred thirty-five percent of the poverty income guidelines amount for a single person as reported by the federal department of health and human services. For the calendar year nineteen hundred eighty-nine, the self-support reserve shall be eight thousand sixty-five dollars. On March first of each year, the self-support reserve shall be revised to reflect the annual updating of the poverty income guidelines as reported by the federal department of health and human services for a single person household.

(c) The amount of the basic child support obligation shall be determined in accordance with the provision of this paragraph:

(1) The court shall determine the combined parental income.

(2) The court shall multiply the combined parental income up to the amount set forth in paragraph (b) of subdivision two of section one hundred eleven-i of the social services law by the appropriate child support percentage and such amount shall be prorated in the same proportion as each parent's income is to the combined parental income.

(3) Where the combined parental income exceeds the dollar amount set forth in subparagraph two of this paragraph, the court shall determine the amount of child support for the amount of the combined parental income in excess of such dollar amount through consideration of the factors set forth in paragraph (f) of this subdivision and/or the child support percentage.

(4) Where the custodial parent is working, or receiving elementary or secondary education, or higher education or vocational training which the court determines will lead to employment, and incurs child care expenses as a result thereof, the court shall determine reasonable child care expenses and such child care expenses, where incurred, shall be prorated in the same proportion as each parent's income is to the combined parental income. Each parent's pro rata share of the child care expenses shall be separately stated and added to the sum of subparagraphs two and three of this paragraph.

(5) The court shall determine the parties' obligation to provide health insurance benefits pursuant to section four hundred sixteen of this part and to pay cash medical support as provided under this subparagraph.

(i) "Cash medical support" means an amount ordered to be paid toward the cost of health insurance provided by a public entity or by a parent through an employer or organization, including such employers or organizations which are self insured, or through other available health insurance or health care coverage plans, and/or for other health care expenses not covered by insurance.

(ii) Where health insurance benefits pursuant to paragraph one and subparagraphs (i) and (ii) of paragraph two of subdivision (e) of section four hundred sixteen of this part are determined by the court to be available, the cost of providing health insurance benefits shall be prorated between the parties in the same proportion as each parent's income is to the combined parental income. If the custodial parent is ordered to provide such benefits, the non-custodial parent's pro rata share of such costs shall be added to the basic support obligation. If the non-custodial parent is ordered to provide such benefits, the custodial parent's pro rata share of such costs shall be deducted from the basic support obligation.

(iii) Where health insurance benefits pursuant to paragraph one and subparagraphs (i) and (ii) of paragraph two of subdivision (e) of section four hundred sixteen of this part are determined by the court to be unavailable, if the child or children are determined eligible for coverage under the medical assistance program established pursuant to title eleven of article five of the social services law, the court shall order the non-custodial parent to pay cash medical support as follows:

(A) In the case of a child or children authorized for managed care coverage under the medical assistance program, the lesser of the amount that would be required as a family contribution under the state's child health insurance plan pursuant to title one-A of article twenty-five of the public health law for the child or children if they were in a two-parent household with income equal to the combined income of the non-custodial and custodial parents or the premium paid by the medical assistance program on behalf of the child or children to the managed care plan. The court shall separately state the non-custodial parent's monthly obligation. The non-custodial parent's cash medical support obligation under this clause shall not exceed five percent of his or her gross income, or the difference between the non-custodial parent's income and the self-support reserve, whichever is less.

(B) In the case of a child or children authorized for fee-for-service coverage under the medical assistance program other than a child or children described in item (A) of this clause, the court shall determine the non-custodial parent's maximum annual cash medical support obligation, which shall be equal to the lesser of the monthly amount that would be required as a family contribution under the state's child health insurance plan pursuant to title one-A of article twenty-five of the public health law for the child or children if they were in a two-parent household with income equal to the combined income of the non-custodial and custodial parents times twelve months or the number of months that the child or children are authorized for fee-for-service coverage during any year. The court shall separately state in the order the non-custodial parent's maximum annual cash medical support obligation and, upon proof to the court that the non-custodial parent, after notice of the amount due, has failed to pay the public entity for incurred health care expenses, the court shall order the non-custodial parent to pay such incurred health care expenses up to the maximum annual cash medical support obligation. Such amounts shall be support arrears/past due support and shall be subject to any remedies as provided by law for the enforcement of support arrears/past due support. The total annual amount that the non-custodial parent is ordered to pay under this clause shall not exceed five percent of his or her gross income or the difference between the non-custodial parent's income and the self-support reserve, whichever is less.

(C) The court shall order cash medical support to be paid by the non-custodial parent for health care expenses of the child or children paid by the medical assistance program prior to the issuance of the court's order. The amount of such support shall be calculated as provided under item (A) or (B) of this clause, provided that the amount that the non-custodial parent is ordered to pay under this item shall not exceed five percent of his or her gross income or the difference between the non-custodial parent's income and the self-support reserve, whichever is less, for the year when the expense was incurred. Such amounts shall be support arrears/past due support and shall be subject to any remedies as provided by law for the enforcement of support arrears/past due support.

(iv) Where health insurance benefits pursuant to paragraph one and subparagraphs (i) and (ii) of paragraph two of subdivision (e) of section four hundred sixteen of this part are determined by the court to be unavailable, and the child or children are determined eligible for coverage under the state's child health insurance plan pursuant to title one-A of article twenty-five of the public health law, the court shall prorate each parent's share of the cost of the family contribution required under such child health insurance plan in the same proportion as each parent's income is to the combined parental income, and state the amount of the non-custodial parent's share in the order. The total amount of cash medical support that the non-custodial parent is ordered to pay under this clause shall not exceed five percent of his or her gross income, or the difference between the non-custodial parent's income and the self-support reserve, whichever is less.

(v) In addition to the amounts ordered under clause (ii), (iii), or (iv) of this subparagraph, the court shall pro rate each parent's share of reasonable health care expenses not reimbursed or paid by insurance, the medical assistance program established pursuant to title eleven of article five of the social services law, or the state's child health insurance plan pursuant to title one-A of article twenty-five of the public health law, in the same proportion as each parent's income is to the combined parental income, and state the non-custodial parent's share as a percentage in the order. The non-custodial parent's pro rata share of such health care expenses determined by the court to be due and owing shall be support arrears/past due support and shall be subject to any remedies provided by law for the enforcement of support arrears/past due support. In addition, the court may direct that the non-custodial parent's pro rata share of such health care expenses be paid in one sum or in periodic sums, including direct payment to the health care provider.

(vi) Upon proof by either party that cash medical support pursuant to clause (ii), (iii), (iv) or (v) of this subparagraph would be unjust or inappropriate pursuant to paragraph (f) of subdivision one of this section, the court shall:

    (A) order the parties to pay cash medical support as the court finds just and appropriate, considering the best interests of the child; and

    (B) set forth in the order the factors it considered, the amount calculated under this subparagraph, the reason or reasons the court did not order such amount, and the basis for the amount awarded.

(6) Where the court determines that the custodial parent is seeking work and incurs child care expenses as a result thereof, the court may determine reasonable child care expenses and may apportion the same between the custodial and non-custodial parent. The non-custodial parent's share of such expenses shall be separately stated and paid in a manner determined by the court.

(7) Where the court determines, having regard for the circumstances of the case and of the respective parties and in the best interests of the child, and as justice requires, that the present or future provision of post-secondary, private, special, or enriched education for the child is appropriate, the court may award educational expenses. The non-custodial parent shall pay educational expenses, as awarded, in a manner determined by the court, including direct payment to the educational provider.

(d) Notwithstanding the provisions of paragraph (c) of this subdivision, where the annual amount of the basic child support obligation would reduce the non-custodial parent's income below the poverty income guidelines amount for a single person as reported by the federal department of health and human services, the basic child support obligation shall be twenty-five dollars per month; provided, however, that if the court finds that such basic child support obligation is unjust or inappropriate, which finding shall be based upon considerations of the factors set forth in paragraph (f) of this subdivision, then the court shall order the non-custodial parent to pay such amount of the child support as the court finds just and appropriate. Notwithstanding the provisions of paragraph (c) of this subdivision, where the annual amount of the basic child support obligation would reduce the non-custodial parent's income below the self-support reserve but not below the poverty income guidelines amount for a single person as reported by the federal department of health and human services, the basic child support obligation shall be fifty dollars per month or the difference between the non-custodial parent's income and the self-support reserve, whichever is greater, in addition to any amounts that the court may, in its discretion, order in accordance with subparagraphs four, five, six and/or seven of paragraph (c) of this subdivision.

(e) Where a parent is or may be entitled to receive non-recurring payments from extraordinary sources not otherwise considered as income pursuant to this section, including but not limited to:

(1) Life insurance policies;

(2) Discharges of indebtedness;

(3) Recovery of bad debts and delinquency amounts;

(4) Gifts and inheritances; and

(5) Lottery winnings,

the court, in accordance with paragraphs (c), (d) and (f) of this subdivision may allocate a proportion of the same to child support, and such amount shall be paid in a manner determined by the court.

(f) The court shall calculate the basic child support obligation, and the non-custodial parent's pro rata share of the basic child support obligation. Unless the court finds that the non-custodial parents's pro-rata share of the basic child support obligation is unjust or inappropriate, which finding shall be based upon consideration of the following factors:

(1) The financial resources of the custodial and non-custodial parent, and those of the child;

(2) The physical and emotional health of the child and his/her special needs and aptitudes;

(3) The standard of living the child would have enjoyed had the marriage or household not been dissolved;

(4) The tax consequences to the parties;

(5) The non-monetary contributions that the parents will make toward the care and well-being of the child;

(6) The educational needs of either parent;

(7) A determination that the gross income of one parent is substantially less than the other parent's gross income;

(8) The needs of the children of the non-custodial parent for whom the non-custodial parent is providing support who are not subject to the instant action and whose support has not been deducted from income pursuant to subclause (D) of clause (vii) of subparagraph five of paragraph (b) of this subdivision, and the financial resources of any person obligated to support such children, provided, however, that this factor may apply only if the resources available to support such children are less than the resources available to support the children who are subject to the instant action;

(9) Provided that the child is not on public assistance (i) extraordinary expenses incurred by the non-custodial parent in exercising visitation, or (ii) expenses incurred by the non-custodial parent in extended visitation provided

that the custodial parent's expenses are substantially reduced as a result thereof; and

(10) Any other factors the court determines are relevant in each case, the court shall order the non-custodial parent to pay his or her pro rata share of the basic child support obligation, and may order the non-custodial parent to pay an amount pursuant to paragraph (e) of this subdivision.

(g) Where the court finds that the non-custodial parent's pro rata share of the basic child support obligation is unjust or inappropriate, the court shall order the non-custodial parent to pay such amount of child support as the court finds just and appropriate, and the court shall set forth, in a written order, the factors it considered; the amount of each party's pro rata share of the basic child support obligation; and the reasons that the court did not order the basic child support obligation. Such written order may not be waived by either party or counsel; provided, however, and notwithstanding any other provision of law, including but not limited to section four hundred fifteen of this part, the court shall not find that the non-custodial parent's pro rata share of such obligation is unjust or inappropriate on the basis that such share exceeds the portion of a public assistance grant which is attributable to a child or children. Where the non-custodial parent's income is less than or equal to the poverty income guidelines amount for a single person as reported by the federal department of health and human services, unpaid child support arrears in excess of five hundred dollars shall not accrue.

(h) A validly executed agreement or stipulation voluntarily entered into between the parties after the effective date of this subdivision presented to the court for incorporation in an order or judgment shall include a provision stating that the parties have been advised of the provisions of this subdivision and that the basic child support obligation provided for therein would presumptively result in the correct amount of child support to be awarded. In the event that such agreement or stipulation deviates from the basic child support obligation, the agreement or stipulation must specify the amount that such basic child support obligation would have been and the reason or reasons that such agreement or stipulation does not provide for payment of that amount. Such provision may not be waived by either party or counsel. Nothing contained in this subdivision shall be construed to alter the rights of the parties to voluntarily enter into validly executed agreements or stipulations which deviate from the basic child support obligation provided such agreements or stipulations comply with the provisions of this paragraph. The court shall, however, retain discretion with respect to child support pursuant to this section. Any court order or judgment incorporating a validly executed agreement or stipulation which deviates from the basic child support obligation shall set forth the court's reasons for such deviation.

(i) Where either or both parties are unrepresented, the court shall not enter an order or judgment other than a temporary order pursuant to section two hundred thirty-seven of the domestic relations law, that includes a provision for child support unless the unrepresented party or parties have received a copy of the child support standards chart promulgated by the commissioner of the office of temporary and disability assistance pursuant to subdivision two of section one hundred eleven-i of the social services law. Where either party is in receipt of child support enforcement services through the local social services district, the local social services district child support enforcement unit shall advise such party of the amount derived from application of the child support percentage and that such amount serves as a starting point for the determination of the child support award, and shall provide such party with a copy of the child support standards chart.

(j) In addition to financial disclosure required in section four hundred twenty-four-a of this article, the court may require that the income and/or expenses of either party be verified with documentation including, but not limited to, past and present income tax returns, employer statements, pay stubs, corporate, business, or partnership books and records, corporate and business tax returns, and receipts for expenses or such other means of verification as the court determines appropriate. Nothing herein shall affect any party's right to pursue discovery pursuant to this chapter, the civil practice law and rules, or the family court act.

(k) When a party has defaulted and/or the court is otherwise presented with insufficient evidence to determine gross income, the court shall order child support based upon the needs or standard of living of the child, whichever is greater. Such order may be retroactively modified upward, without a showing of change in circumstances.

(l) In any action or proceeding for modification of an order of child support existing prior to the effective date of this paragraph, brought pursuant to this article, the child support standards set forth in paragraphs (a) through (k) of this subdivision shall not constitute grounds for modification of such support order; provided, however, that (1) where the circumstances warrant modification of such order, or (2) where any party objects to an adjusted child support order made or proposed at the direction of the support collection unit pursuant to section one hundred eleven-h or one hundred eleven-n of the social services law, and the court is reviewing the current order of child support, such standards shall be applied by the court in its determination with regard to the request for modification or disposition of an objection to an adjusted child support order made or proposed by a support collection unit. In applying such standards, when the order to be modified incorporates by reference or merges with a validly executed separation agreement or stipulation of settlement, the court may consider, in addition to the factors set forth in paragraph (f) of this subdivision, the provisions of such agreement or stipulation concerning property distribution, distributive award and/or maintenance in determining whether the amount calculated by using the standards would be unjust or inappropriate.

2. Nothing in this article shall impose any liability upon a person to support the adopted child of his or her spouse, if such child was adopted after the adopting spouse is living separate and apart from the non-adopting spouse pursuant to a legally recognizable separation agreement or decree under the domestic relations law. Such liability shall not be imposed for so long as the spouses remain separate and apart after the adoption.

3. a. One-time adjustment of child support orders issued prior to September fifteenth, nineteen hundred eighty-nine. Any party to a child support order issued prior to September fifteenth, nineteen hundred eighty-nine on the behalf of a child in receipt of public assistance or child support services pursuant to section one hundred eleven-g of the social services law may request that the support collection unit undertake one review of the order for adjustment purposes pursuant to section one hundred eleven-h of the social services law. A hearing on the adjustment of such order shall be granted upon the objection of either party pursuant to the provisions of this section. An order shall be adjusted if as of the date of the support collection unit's review of the correct amount of child support as calculated pursuant to the provisions of this section would deviate by at least

ten percent from the child support ordered in the last permanent support order of the court. Additionally, a new support order shall be issued upon a showing that the current order of support does not provide for the health care needs of the child through insurance or otherwise. Eligibility of the child for medical assistance shall not relieve any obligation the parties otherwise have to provide for the health care needs of the child. The support collection unit's review of a child support order shall be made on notice to all parties to the current support order and shall be subject to the provisions of section four hundred twenty-four-a of this article. Nothing herein shall be deemed in any way to limit, restrict, expand or impair the rights of any party to file for a modification of a child support order as is otherwise provided by law.

b. Upon receipt of an adjustment finding and where appropriate a proposed order in conformity with such finding filed by either party or by the support collection unit, a party shall have thirty-five days from the date of mailing of the adjustment finding and proposed adjusted order, if any, to submit to the court identified thereon specific written objections to such finding and proposed order.

(1) If specific written objections are submitted by either party or by the support collection unit, a hearing shall be scheduled by the court on notice to the parties and the support collection unit, who shall have the right to be heard by the court and to offer evidence in support of or in opposition to adjustment of the support order.

(2) The party filing the specific written objections shall bear the burden of going forward and the burden of proof; provided, however, that if the support collection unit has failed to provide the documentation and information required by subdivision fourteen of section one hundred eleven-h of the social services law, the court shall first require the support collection unit to furnish such documents and information to the parties and the court.

(3) If the court finds by a preponderance of the evidence that the specific written objections have been proven, the court shall recalculate or readjust the proposed adjusted order accordingly or, for good cause, shall remand the order to the support collection unit for submission of a new proposed adjusted order. Any readjusted order so issued by the court or resubmitted by the support collection unit following remand by the court shall be effective as of the date the proposed adjusted order would have been effective had no written objections been filed.

(4) If the court finds that the specific written objections have not been proven by a preponderance of the evidence, the court shall immediately issue the adjusted order, which shall be effective as of the date the order would have been effective had no written objections been filed.

(5) If the determination of the specific written objections has been made by a family court support magistrate, the parties shall be permitted to obtain judicial review of such determination by filing timely written objections pursuant to subdivision (e) of section four hundred thirty-nine of this act.

(6) If the court receives no specific written objections to the support order within thirty-five days of the mailing of the proposed order, the clerk of the court shall immediately issue the order without any further review, modification, or other prior action by the court or any judge or support magistrate thereof, and the clerk shall immediately transmit copies of the order of support to the parties and to the support collection unit.

c. A motion to vacate an order of support adjusted pursuant to this section may be made no later than forty-five days after an adjusted support order is executed by the court where no specific written objections to the proposed order have been timely received by the court. Such motion shall be granted only upon a determination by the court issuing such order that personal jurisdiction was not timely obtained over the moving party.

4. On-going cost of living adjustment of child support orders issued prior to September fifteenth, nineteen hundred eighty-nine. Any party to a child support order issued prior to September fifteenth, nineteen hundred eighty-nine on the behalf of a child in receipt of public assistance or child support services pursuant to section one hundred eleven-g of the social services law may request that the support collection unit review the order for a cost of living adjustment in accordance with the provisions of section four hundred thirteen-a of this article.

§413-a.   Review and cost of living adjustment of child support orders.

1. Request. Any party to a child support order issued on behalf of a child in receipt of public assistance, or child support enforcement services pursuant to section one hundred eleven-g of the social services law, may request that the support collection unit review the order for cost of living adjustment purposes pursuant to section one hundred eleven-n of the social services law.

2. Adjustment process. (a) A cost of living adjustment shall be made by the support collection unit with respect to an order of support under review if the sum of the annual average changes of the consumer price index for all urban consumers (CPI-U), as published annually by the United States department of labor bureau of labor statistics, is ten percent or greater.

(b) The cost of living adjustment and adjusted child support obligation amount as calculated by the review shall be reflected on the adjusted order issued by the support collection unit and mailed to the parties by first class mail. The child support obligation amount contained in the adjusted order shall be due and owing on the date the first payment is due under the terms of the order of support which was reviewed and adjusted occurring on or after the effective date of the adjusted order.

(c) The support collection unit shall provide a copy of the adjusted order to the court which issued the most recent order of support, which shall append it to the order.

3. Objection process. (a) An objection to a cost of living adjustment, as reflected in an adjusted order issued by a support collection unit, may be made to the court by either party to the order, or by the support collection unit, and shall be submitted to the court in writing within thirty-five days from the date of mailing of the adjusted order. A copy of the written objection shall be provided by the objecting party to the other party and to the support collection unit.

(b) Where such objections are timely filed, the cost of living adjustment shall not take effect, and a hearing on the adjustment of such order shall be granted pursuant to the provisions of this section, which shall result in either:

(1) the issuance by the court of a new order of support in accordance with the child support standards as set forth in section four hundred thirteen of this article; or

(2) where application of the child support standards as set forth in section four hundred thirteen of this article results in a determination that no adjustment is appropriate, an order of no adjustment.

(c) Any order of support made by the court under this section shall occur without the requirement for proof or showing of a change in circumstances.

(d) The court shall conduct the hearing and make its determination no later than forty-five days from the date it receives an objection. If the order under review does not provide for health insurance benefits for the child, the court shall make a determination regarding such benefits pursuant to section four hundred sixteen of this part. The clerk of the court shall immediately transmit copies of the order of support or order of no adjustment issued by the court pursuant to this subdivision to the parties and the support collection unit. Where a hearing results in the issuance of a new order of support, the effective date of the court order shall be the earlier of the date of the court determination or the date the cost of living adjustment would have been effective had it not been challenged.

(e) Where no objection has been timely raised to a cost of living adjustment as reflected in an adjusted order, such adjustment shall become final without further review by the court or any judge or support magistrate thereof.

4. Modification of orders. Nothing herein shall be deemed in any way to limit, restrict, expand or impair the rights of any party to file for a modification of a child support order as is otherwise provided by law.

5. Notice. Parties eligible for adjustment of child support orders shall receive notice of the right to review such orders as follows:

(a) All applications or motions by the support collection unit or by persons seeking support enforcement services through the support collection unit for the establishment, modification, enforcement, violation or adjustment of child support orders shall on their face in conspicuous type state:

NOTE: (1) A COURT ORDER OF SUPPORT RESULTING FROM A PROCEEDING COMMENCED BY THIS APPLICATION (PETITION) SHALL BE ADJUSTED BY THE APPLICATION OF A COST OF LIVING ADJUSTMENT AT THE DIRECTION OF THE SUPPORT COLLECTION UNIT NO EARLIER THAN TWENTY-FOUR MONTHS AFTER SUCH ORDER IS ISSUED, LAST MODIFIED OR LAST ADJUSTED, UPON THE REQUEST OF ANY PARTY TO THE ORDER OR PURSUANT TO PARAGRAPH (2) BELOW. SUCH COST OF LIVING ADJUSTMENT SHALL BE ON NOTICE TO BOTH PARTIES WHO, IF THEY OBJECT TO THE COST OF LIVING ADJUSTMENT, SHALL HAVE THE RIGHT TO BE HEARD BY THE COURT AND TO PRESENT EVIDENCE WHICH THE COURT WILL CONSIDER IN ADJUSTING THE CHILD SUPPORT ORDER IN ACCORDANCE WITH SECTION FOUR HUNDRED THIRTEEN OF THE FAMILY COURT ACT, KNOWN AS THE CHILD SUPPORT STANDARDS ACT.

(2) A PARTY SEEKING SUPPORT FOR ANY CHILD(REN) RECEIVING FAMILY ASSISTANCE SHALL HAVE A CHILD SUPPORT ORDER REVIEWED AND ADJUSTED AT THE DIRECTION OF THE SUPPORT COLLECTION UNIT NO EARLIER THAN TWENTY-FOUR MONTHS AFTER SUCH ORDER IS ISSUED, LAST MODIFIED OR LAST ADJUSTED BY THE SUPPORT COLLECTION UNIT, WITHOUT FURTHER APPLICATION BY ANY PARTY. ALL PARTIES WILL RECEIVE A COPY OF THE ADJUSTED ORDER.

(3) WHERE ANY PARTY FAILS TO PROVIDE, AND UPDATE UPON ANY CHANGE, THE SUPPORT COLLECTION UNIT WITH A CURRENT ADDRESS, AS REQUIRED BY SECTION FOUR HUNDRED FORTY-THREE OF THE FAMILY COURT ACT, TO WHICH AN ADJUSTED ORDER CAN BE SENT, THE SUPPORT OBLIGATION AMOUNT

CONTAINED THEREIN SHALL BECOME DUE AND OWING ON THE DATE THE FIRST PAYMENT IS DUE UNDER THE TERMS OF THE ORDER OF SUPPORT WHICH WAS REVIEWED AND ADJUSTED OCCURRING ON OR AFTER THE EFFECTIVE DATE OF THE ADJUSTED ORDER, REGARDLESS OF WHETHER OR NOT THE PARTY HAS RECEIVED A COPY OF THE ADJUSTED ORDER.

(b) All court orders of support payable through a support collection unit shall on their face in conspicuous type state:

NOTE: (1) THIS ORDER OF CHILD SUPPORT SHALL BE ADJUSTED BY THE APPLICATION OF A COST OF LIVING ADJUSTMENT AT THE DIRECTION OF THE SUPPORT COLLECTION UNIT NO EARLIER THAN TWENTY-FOUR MONTHS AFTER THIS ORDER IS ISSUED, LAST MODIFIED OR LAST ADJUSTED, UPON THE REQUEST OF ANY PARTY TO THE ORDER OR PURSUANT TO PARAGRAPH (2) BELOW. UPON APPLICATION OF A COST OF LIVING ADJUSTMENT AT THE DIRECTION OF THE SUPPORT COLLECTION UNIT, AN ADJUSTED ORDER SHALL BE SENT TO THE PARTIES WHO, IF THEY OBJECT TO THE COST OF LIVING ADJUSTMENT, SHALL HAVE THIRTY-FIVE (35) DAYS FROM THE DATE OF MAILING TO SUBMIT A WRITTEN OBJECTION TO THE COURT INDICATED ON SUCH ADJUSTED ORDER. UPON RECEIPT OF SUCH WRITTEN OBJECTION, THE COURT SHALL SCHEDULE A HEARING AT WHICH THE PARTIES MAY BE PRESENT TO OFFER EVIDENCE WHICH THE COURT WILL CONSIDER IN ADJUSTING THE CHILD SUPPORT ORDER IN ACCORDANCE WITH THE CHILD SUPPORT STANDARDS ACT.

(2) A RECIPIENT OF FAMILY ASSISTANCE SHALL HAVE THE CHILD SUPPORT ORDER REVIEWED AND ADJUSTED AT THE DIRECTION OF THE SUPPORT COLLECTION UNIT NO EARLIER THAN TWENTY-FOUR MONTHS AFTER SUCH ORDER IS ISSUED, LAST MODIFIED OR LAST ADJUSTED WITHOUT FURTHER APPLICATION OF ANY PARTY. ALL PARTIES WILL RECEIVE NOTICE OF ADJUSTMENT FINDINGS.

(3) WHERE ANY PARTY FAILS TO PROVIDE, AND UPDATE UPON ANY CHANGE, THE SUPPORT COLLECTION UNIT WITH A CURRENT ADDRESS, AS REQUIRED BY SECTION FOUR HUNDRED FORTY-THREE OF THE FAMILY COURT ACT, TO WHICH AN ADJUSTED ORDER CAN BE SENT, THE SUPPORT OBLIGATION AMOUNT CONTAINED THEREIN SHALL BECOME DUE AND OWING ON THE DATE THE FIRST PAYMENT IS DUE UNDER THE TERMS OF THE ORDER OF SUPPORT WHICH WAS REVIEWED AND ADJUSTED OCCURRING ON OR AFTER THE EFFECTIVE DATE OF THE ORDER, REGARDLESS OF WHETHER OR NOT THE PARTY HAS RECEIVED A COPY OF THE ADJUSTED ORDER.

§415. Duties to support recipient of public assistance or welfare and patients in institutions in the department of mental hygiene.

Except as otherwise provided by law, the spouse or parent of a recipient of public assistance or care or of a person liable to become in need thereof or of a patient in an institution in the department of mental hygiene, if of sufficient ability, is responsible for the support of such person or patient, provided that a parent shall be responsible only for the support of his child or children who have not attained the age of twenty-one years. In its discretion, the court may require any such person to contribute a fair and reasonable sum for the support of such relative and may apportion the costs of such support among such persons as may be just and appropriate in view of the needs of the petitioner and the other circumstances of the case and their respective means. Step-parents shall in like manner be responsible for the support of children under the age of twenty-one years.

§416. Elements of support; provisions for accident, life and health insurance benefits.

(a) The court may include in the requirements for an order for support the providing of necessary shelter, food, clothing, care, medical attention, expenses of confinement, the expense of education, payment of funeral expenses, and other proper and reasonable expenses.

(b) The court may also order a party to purchase, maintain, or assign a policy of accident insurance or insurance on the life of either party and designate in the case of life insurance, the person or persons on whose behalf the petition is brought or in the case of accident insurance, the insured party as irrevocable beneficiaries during a period of time fixed by the court. The obligation to provide such insurance shall cease upon the termination of such party's duty to provide support.

(c) Every support order shall provide that if any legally responsible relative currently, or at any time in the future, has health insurance benefits available that may be extended or obtained to cover any person on whose behalf the petition is brought, such responsible relative is required to exercise the option of additional coverage in favor of such person whom he or she is legally responsible to support and to execute and deliver to such person any forms, notices, documents, or instruments to assure timely payment of any health insurance claims for such person.

(d) As used in this section, the following terms shall have the following meanings: (1) "Health insurance benefits" means any medical, dental, optical and prescription drugs and health care services or other health care benefits that may be provided for a dependent through an employer or organization, including such employers or organizations which are self insured, or through other available health insurance or health care coverage plans.

(2) "Available health insurance benefits" means any health insurance benefits that are reasonable in cost and that are reasonably accessible to the person on whose behalf the petition is brought. Health insurance benefits that are not reasonable in cost or whose services are not reasonably accessible to such person shall be considered unavailable.

(3) When the person on whose behalf the petition is brought is a child in accordance with subdivision (e) of this section, health insurance benefits shall be considered "reasonable in cost" if the cost of health insurance benefits does not exceed five percent of the combined parental gross income. The cost of health insurance benefits shall refer to the cost of the premium and deductible attributable to adding the child or children to existing coverage or the difference between such costs for self-only and family coverage. Provided, however, the presumption that the health insurance benefits are reasonable in cost may be rebutted upon a finding that the cost is unjust or inappropriate which finding shall be based on the circumstances of the case, the cost and comprehensiveness of the health insurance benefits for which the child or children may otherwise be eligible, and the best interests of the child or

children. In no instance shall health insurance benefits be considered "reasonable in cost" if a parent's share of the cost of extending such coverage would reduce the income of that parent below the self-support reserve. Health insurance benefits are "reasonably accessible" if the child lives within the geographic area covered by the plan or lives within thirty minutes or thirty miles of travel time from the child's residence to the services covered by the health insurance benefits or through benefits provided under a reciprocal agreement; provided, however, this presumption may be rebutted for good cause shown including, but not limited to, the special health needs of the child. The court shall set forth such finding and the reasons therefor in the order of support.

(e) When the person on whose behalf the petition is brought is a child, the court shall consider the availability of health insurance benefits to all parties and shall take the following action to insure that health insurance benefits are provided for the benefit of the child:

(1) Where the child is presently covered by health insurance benefits, the court shall direct in the order of support that such coverage be maintained, unless either parent requests the court to make a direction for health insurance benefits coverage pursuant to paragraph two of this subdivision.

(2) Where the child is not presently covered by health insurance benefits, the court shall make its determination as follows:

(i) If only one parent has available health insurance benefits, the court shall direct in the order of support that such parent provide health insurance benefits.

(ii) If both parents have available health insurance benefits the court shall direct in the order of support that either parent or both parents provide such health insurance. The court shall make such determination based on the circumstances of the case, including, but not limited to, the cost and comprehensiveness of the respective health insurance benefits and the best interests of the child.

(iii) If neither parent has available health insurance benefits, the court shall direct in the order of support that the custodial parent apply for the state's child health insurance plan pursuant to title one-A of article twenty-five of the public health law and the medical assistance program established pursuant to title eleven of article five of the social services law. A direction issued under this subdivision shall not limit or alter either parent's obligation to obtain health insurance benefits at such time as they become available as required pursuant to subdivision (c) of this section. Nothing in this subdivision shall alter or limit the authority of the medical assistance program to determine when it is considered cost effective to require a custodial parent to enroll a child in an available group health insurance plan pursuant to paragraphs (b) and (c) of subdivision one of section three hundred sixty-seven-a of the social services law.

(f) The cost of providing health insurance benefits or benefits under the state's child health insurance plan or the medical assistance program, pursuant to subdivision (e) of this section, shall be deemed cash medical support, and the court shall determine the obligation of either or both parents to contribute to the cost thereof pursuant to subparagraph five of paragraph (c) of subdivision one of section four hundred thirteen of this part.

(g) The court shall provide in the order of support that the legally responsible relative immediately notify the other party, or the other party and the support collection unit when the order is issued on behalf of a child in receipt of public assistance and care or in receipt of services pursuant to section one hundred eleven-g of the social services law, of any change in health insurance benefits, including any termination of benefits, change in the health insurance benefit carrier, premium, or extent and availability of existing or new benefits.

(h) Where the court determines that health insurance benefits are available, the court shall provide in the order of support that the legally responsible relative immediately enroll the eligible dependents named in the order who are otherwise eligible for such benefits without regard to any seasonal enrollment restrictions. The support order shall further direct the legally responsible relative to maintain such benefits as long as they remain available to such relative. Such order shall further direct the legally responsible relative to assign all insurance reimbursement payments for health care expenses incurred for his or her eligible dependents to the provider of such services or the party actually having incurred and satisfied such expenses, as appropriate.

(i) When the court issues an order of child support or combined child and spousal support on behalf of persons in receipt of public assistance and care or in receipt of services pursuant to section one hundred eleven-g of the social services law, such order shall further direct that the provision of health care benefits shall be immediately enforced pursuant to section fifty-two hundred forty-one of the civil practice law and rules.

(j) When the court issues an order of child support or combined child and spousal support on behalf of persons other than those in receipt of public assistance and care or in receipt of services pursuant to section one hundred eleven-g of the social services law, the court shall also issue a separate order which shall include the necessary direction to ensure the order's characterization as a qualified medical child support order as defined by section six hundred nine of the employee retirement income security act of 1974 (29 USC 1169). Such order shall: (i) clearly state that it creates or recognizes the existence of the right of the named dependent to be enrolled and to receive benefits for which the legally responsible relative is eligible under the available group health plans, and shall clearly specify the name, social security number and mailing address of the legally responsible relative, and of each dependent to be covered by the order; (ii) provide a clear description of the type of coverage to be provided by the group health plan to each such dependent or the manner in which the type of coverage is to be determined; and (iii) specify the period of time to which the order applies. The court shall not require the group health plan to provide any type or form of benefit or option not otherwise provided under the group health plan except to the extent necessary to meet the requirements of a law relating to medical child support described in section one thousand three hundred and ninety-six g-1 of title forty-two of the United States code.

(k) Upon a finding that a legally responsible relative wilfully failed to obtain health insurance benefits in violation of a court order, such relative will be presumptively liable for all health care expenses incurred on behalf of such dependents from the first date such dependents were eligible to be enrolled to receive health insurance benefits after the issuance of the order of support directing the acquisition of such coverage.

§417. Child of ceremonial marriage.

A child born of parents who at any time prior or subsequent to the birth of said child shall have entered into a ceremonial marriage shall be deemed the legitimate child of both parents for all purposes of this article regardless of the validity of such marriage.

§418.   Genetic marker and DNA tests; admissibility of records or reports of test results; costs of tests.

(a) The court, on its own motion or motion of any party, when paternity is contested, shall order the mother, the child and the alleged father to submit to one or more genetic marker or DNA marker tests of a type generally acknowledged as reliable by an accreditation body designated by the secretary of the federal department of health and human services and performed by a laboratory approved by such an accreditation body and by the commissioner of health or by a duly qualified physician to aid in the determination of whether the alleged father is or is not the father of the child. No such test shall be ordered, however, upon a written finding by the court that it is not in the best interests of the child on the basis of res judicata, equitable estoppel or the presumption of legitimacy of a child born to a married woman. The record or report of the results of any such genetic marker or DNA test shall be received in evidence, pursuant to subdivision (e) of rule forty-five hundred eighteen of the civil practice law and rules where no timely objection in writing has been made thereto. Any order pursuant to this section shall state in plain language that the results of such test shall be admitted into evidence, pursuant to rule forty-five hundred eighteen of the civil practice law and rules absent timely objections thereto and that if such timely objections are not made, they shall be deemed waived and shall not be heard by the court. If the record or report of results of any such genetic marker or DNA test or tests indicate at least a ninety-five percent probability of paternity, the admission of such record or report shall create a rebuttable presumption of paternity, and, if unrebutted, shall establish the paternity of and liability for the support of a child pursuant to this article and article five of this act.

(b) Whenever the court directs a genetic marker or DNA test pursuant to this section, a report made as provided in subdivision (a) of this section may be received in evidence pursuant to rule forty-five hundred eighteen of the civil practice law and rules if offered by any party.

(c) The cost of any test ordered pursuant to subdivision (a) of this section shall be, in the first instance, paid by the moving party. If the moving party is financially unable to pay such cost, the court may direct any qualified public health officer to conduct such test, if practicable; otherwise, the court may direct payment from the funds of the appropriate local social services district. In its order of disposition, however, the court may direct that the cost of any such test be apportioned between the parties according to their respective abilities to pay or be assessed against the party who does not prevail on the issue of paternity, unless such party is financially unable to pay.

Part 2
Venue and Preliminary Procedure

§421. Venue.

Proceedings to compel support under this article may be originated in the county in which one of the parties resides or is domiciled at the time of the filing of the petition. Upon application, the family court may change the place of trial of a proceeding in accordance with article five of the civil practice law and rules.

§422. Persons who may originate proceedings.

(a) A husband, wife, child, or relative in need of public assistance or care may originate a proceeding under this article to compel a person chargeable with the support to support the petitioner as required by law. A social services official may originate a proceeding under this article if so authorized by section one hundred and two of the social services law. The commissioner of mental health may originate a proceeding under this article when authorized by article forty-three of the mental hygiene law. A parent or guardian, of a child, or other person in loco parentis, or a representative of an incorporated charitable or philanthropic society having a legitimate interest in the petitioner, or, when the petitioner is unable because of his physical or mental condition to file a petition, a guardian ad litem, or a committee, conservator, next friend or other person appointed by the court, may file a petition in behalf of a dependent relative.

(b) Any party to a decree of divorce, separation, or annulment may originate a proceeding to enforce or modify a decree of the supreme court or a court of competent jurisdiction, not of the state of New York, as is provided in part six of this article.

§423. Petition; prior demand not required.

Proceedings under this article are commenced by the filing of a petition, which may be made on information and belief. The petitioner need not make a demand upon the respondent for support as a condition precedent to the filing of a petition for support. Any such petition for the establishment, modification and/or enforcement of a child support obligation for persons not in receipt of family assistance, which contains a request for child support enforcement services completed in a manner as specified in section one hundred eleven-g of the social services law, shall constitute an application for such services.

§424. Probation services.

1. A local probation service may provide services to a party seeking to establish, modify or enforce a support obligation where there is a contract with the appropriate social services district for the performance of support collection services under section one hundred eleven-h of the social services law.

2. A local probation service may provide services to persons ordered to pay support seeking to modify such orders.

3. The probation service may not prevent any person who wishes to file a petition under this article from having access to the court for that purpose nor may the probation service compel any person to appear at any conference, produce any papers or visit any place.

§424-a. Compulsory financial disclosure.
Except as provided herein:
(a) in all support proceedings in family court, there shall be compulsory disclosure by both parties of their respective financial states, provided, however, that this requirement shall not apply to a social services official who is a party in any support proceeding under this act. No showing of special circumstances shall be required before such disclosure is ordered and such disclosure may not be waived by either party or by the court. A sworn statement of net worth shall be filed with the clerk of the court on a date to be fixed by the court, no later than ten days after the return date of the petition. As used in this part, the term "net worth" shall mean the amount by which total assets including income exceed total liabilities including fixed financial obligations. It shall include all income and assets of whatsoever kind and nature and wherever situated and shall include a list of all assets transferred in any manner during the preceding three years, or the length of the marriage, whichever is shorter, provided, however, that transfers in the routine course of business which resulted in an exchange of assets of substantially equivalent value need not be specifically disclosed where such assets are otherwise identified in the statement of net worth. All such sworn statements of net worth shall be accompanied by a current and representative paycheck stub and the most recently filed state and federal income tax returns including a copy of the W-2(s) wage and tax statement(s) submitted with the returns. In addition, both parties shall provide information relating to any and all group health plans available to them for the provision of care or other medical benefits by insurance or otherwise for the benefit of the child or children for whom support is sought, including all such information as may be required to be included in a qualified medical child support order as defined in section six hundred nine of the employee retirement income security act of 1974 (29 USC 1169) including, but not limited to:
(i) the name and last known mailing address of each party and of each dependent to be covered by the order;
(ii) the identification and a description of each group health plan available for the benefit or coverage of the disclosing party and the child or children for whom support is sought;
(iii) a detailed description of the type of coverage available from each group health plan for the potential benefit of each such dependent;
(iv) the identification of the plan administrator for each such group health plan and the address of such administrator;
(v) the identification numbers for each such group health plan; and
(vi) such other information as may be required by the court;
(b) when a respondent fails, without good cause, to file a sworn statement of net worth, a current and representative paycheck stub and the most recently filed state and federal income tax returns, including a copy of the W-2(s) wage and tax statement submitted with the returns, or to provide information relating to all group health plans available for the provision of care or other medical benefits by insurance or otherwise for the benefit of the disclosing party and the child or children for whom support is sought, as provided in subdivision (a) of this section, the court on its own motion or on application shall grant the relief demanded in the petition or shall order that, for purposes of the support proceeding, the respondent shall be precluded from offering evidence as to respondent's financial ability to pay support;

(c) when a petitioner other than a social services official fails, without good cause to file a sworn statement of net worth, a current and representative paycheck stub and the most recently filed state and federal income tax returns, as provided in subdivision (a) of this section, the court may on its own motion or upon application of any party adjourn such proceeding until such time as the petitioner files with the court such statements and tax returns. The provisions of this subdivision shall not apply to proceedings establishing temporary support or proceedings for the enforcement of a support order or support provision of a separation agreement or stipulation.

§425. Agreement to support.

If an agreement for the support of the petitioner is brought about, it must be reduced to writing and submitted to the family court or a support magistrate appointed pursuant to section four hundred thirty-nine of this act for approval. If the court or support magistrate approves it, the court without further hearing may thereupon enter an order for the support of the petitioner by the respondent in accordance with the agreement, which shall be binding upon the respondent and shall in all respects be a valid order as though made after process had been issued out of the court. The court record shall show that such order was made upon agreement.

§426. Issuance of summons.

(a) On the filing of a petition under this article, the court may cause a copy of the petition and a summons to be issued, requiring the respondent to show cause why the order of support and other and further relief prayed for by the petition should not be made.

(b) The summons shall contain or have attached thereto a notice stating: (i) that a respondent's failure to appear shall result in entry of an order of default; (ii) that the respondent must provide the court with proof of his or her income and assets; (iii) that a temporary or permanent order of support will be made on the return date of the summons; and (iv) that a respondent's failure to appear may result in the suspension of his or her driving privileges; state professional, occupational and business licenses; and recreational licenses and permits.

§427. Service of summons.

(a) Personal service of a summons and petition may be made by delivery of a true copy thereof to the person summoned at least eight days before the time stated therein for appearance; or by delivery of a true copy thereof to a person of suitable age and discretion at the actual place of business, dwelling place or usual place of abode of the person to be served and by mailing a true copy thereof to the person to be served at his last known residence at least eight days before the time stated in the summons for appearance; proof of service shall identify such person of suitable age and discretion and state the date, time and place of service.

(b) If after reasonable effort, personal service is not made, the court may at any stage in the proceedings make an order providing for substituted service in the manner provided for substituted service in the civil practice law and rules.

(c) In any case, whether or not service is attempted under subdivision (a) or (b) of this section, service of a summons and petition under this section may be effected by mail alone to the last known address of the person to be served.

Service by mail alone shall be made at least eight days before the time stated in the summons for appearance. If service is by mail alone, the court will enter an order of support by default if there is proof satisfactory to the court that the respondent had actual notice of the commencement of the proceeding which may be established upon sufficient proof that the summons and petition were in fact mailed by certified mail and signed for at the respondent's correct street address or signed for at the post office. If service by certified mail at the respondent's correct street address cannot be accomplished, service pursuant to subdivisions one, two, three or four of section three hundred eight of the civil practice law and rules shall be deemed good and sufficient service. Upon failure of the respondent to obey a summons served in accordance with the provisions of this section by means other than mail alone, the court will enter an order of support by default. Such order of support shall be made pursuant to the provisions set forth in section four hundred thirteen of this article. The respondent shall have the right to make a motion for relief from such default order within one year from the date such order was entered.

§428. Issuance of warrant; certificate of warrant.

(a) The court may issue a warrant, directing that the respondent be arrested, brought before the court, when a petition is presented to the court under section four hundred twenty-three and it appears that

(i) the summons cannot be served, or

(ii) the respondent has failed to obey the summons; or

(iii) the respondent is likely to leave the jurisdiction; or

(iv) a summons, in the court's opinion, would be ineffectual; or

(v) the safety of the petitioner is endangered; or

(vi) a respondent on bail or on parole has failed to appear.

(b) The petitioner may not serve a warrant upon the respondent, unless the court itself grants such permission upon the application of the petitioner. The clerk of the court may issue to the petitioner or to the representative of an incorporated charitable or philanthropic society having a legitimate interest in the family a certificate stating that a warrant for the respondent has been issued by the court. The presentation of such certificate by said petitioner or representative to any peace officer, acting pursuant to his special duties, or police officer authorizes him to arrest the respondent and take him to court.

(c) A certificate of warrant expires ninety days from the date of issue but may be renewed from time to time by the clerk of the court.

(d) Rules of court shall provide that a record of all unserved warrants be kept and that periodic reports concerning unserved warrants be made.

§429. Sequestration of respondent's property.

Where in a proceeding under this article it appears to the court that the respondent is not within the state, or cannot be found therein, or is concealing himself or herself therein, so that process cannot be personally served upon the respondent, the court may at any time and from time to time make any order or orders without notice directing the sequestration of his or her property, both real and personal and whether tangible or intangible, within the state, and may appoint a receiver thereof, or by injunction or otherwise take the same into its possession and control. The property thus sequestered and the income therefrom may be applied in whole or in part and from time to time, under the direction of the court and as justice may require, to the payment of such sum or sums as the court may deem it proper to award, by order, and during the pendency of the proceeding or at the termination thereof, for the education or maintenance of any of the children of a marriage, or for the support of a spouse, or for his or her expenses in bringing and carrying on said proceeding; and if the rents and profits of the real estate, together with the other property so sequestered, be insufficient to pay the sums of money required, the court, upon such terms and conditions as it may prescribe, may direct the mortgage or sale of sufficient of said real estate to pay such sums. The court may appoint the petitioning spouse receiver or sequestrator in such cases. The court may authorize such spouse to use and occupy, free of any liability for rent or use and occupation or otherwise, any house or other suitable property of the respondent spouse as a dwelling for himself or herself with or without the children of the marriage, and may likewise turn over to the petitioning spouse for the use of such spouse with or without the children of the marriage any chattel or chattels of the respondent spouse. The relief herein provided for is in addition to any and every other remedy to which a spouse may be entitled under the law.

§430. Temporary order of protection.

(a) Upon the filing of a petition under this article, the court for good cause shown may issue a temporary order of protection which may contain any of the provisions authorized on the making of an order of protection under section four hundred forty-six.

(b) A temporary order of protection is not a finding of wrongdoing.

(c) The court may issue or extend a temporary order of protection ex parte or on notice simultaneously with the issuance of a warrant, directing that the respondent be arrested and brought before the court pursuant to section four hundred twenty-eight of this article.

Part 3
Hearing

Section
431.   Preliminary procedure on warrant.
432.   Procedure before court.
433.   Hearing.
434.   Order for temporary child support.
434-a. Order for temporary spousal support.
435.   Procedure; adjournment; confidentiality of requests.
436.   Competence of spouse.
437.   Presumption of sufficient means.
437-a. Referral to work programs.
438.   Counsel fees.
439.   Support magistrates.
439-a. Expedited process.

§431. Preliminary procedure on warrant.

(a) When a respondent is taken into custody pursuant to a warrant issued by a family court in New York city under section four hundred twenty-eight, he shall be taken before the court issuing the warrant if the respondent is taken into custody in New York city. If the respondent is taken into custody in a county not within New York city, he shall be taken before a family judge in that county.

(b) When a respondent is taken into custody pursuant to a warrant issued by a family court in a county not within the city of New York, he shall be taken before the court issuing the warrant if the respondent is taken into custody in the county in which the court sits. If the respondent is taken into custody in a different county, he shall be brought before a family court judge in that county.

§432. Procedure before court.

The court before whom the respondent is taken under section four hundred thirty-one may require an undertaking to appear or in default thereof may place the respondent in custody until the hearing commences.

§433. (a)* Hearing. Upon the return of the summons or when a respondent is brought before the court pursuant to a warrant, the court shall proceed to hear and determine the case. The respondent shall be informed of the contents of the petition, advised of his right to counsel, and shall be given opportunity to be heard and to present witnesses. The court may exclude the public from the court room in a proper case.

(b) If the initial return of a summons or warrant is before a judge of the court, when support is an issue, the judge must make an immediate order, either temporary or permanent with regard to support. If a temporary order is made, the court shall refer the issue of support to a support magistrate for final determination pursuant to sections four hundred thirty-nine and four hundred thirty-nine-a of this act. Procedures shall be established by the chief administrator of the courts which shall provide for the disposition of all support matters or a referral to a support magistrate prior to the conclusion of a respondent's first appearance before the court. Such procedures shall provide for referral of support issues by appropriate clerical staff of the family court at any time after a petition has been presented to the court.

(c) In any proceeding under this article, the court may permit a party or a witness to be deposed or to testify by telephone, audio-visual means, or other electronic means at a designated family court or other location:

(i) where such party or witness resides in a county other than that of the family court where the case is pending and that of any contiguous county; provided, however, that for the purposes of this section, the five counties of New York city shall be treated as one county;

(ii) where such party or witness is presently incarcerated and will be incarcerated on the date on which the hearing or deposition is scheduled and is not expected to be released within a reasonable period of time after the date on which the hearing or deposition is scheduled; or

(iii) where the court determines that it would be an undue hardship for such party or witness to testify or to be deposed at the family court where the case is pending.

(d) Any such deposition or testimony taken by telephone, audio-visual means or other electronic means in accordance with subdivision (c) of this section shall be recorded and preserved for transcription. Where a party or witness is deposed or testifies by telephone, audio-visual or other electronic means pursuant to this section, documentary evidence referred to by a party or witness or the court may be transmitted by facsimile, telecopier, or other electronic means and may not be excluded from evidence by reason of an objection based on the means of transmission. The chief administrator of the courts shall promulgate rules to facilitate the taking of testimony by telephone, audio-visual means or other electronic means.

§434. Order for temporary child support.

The court shall make an order for temporary child support pending a final determination, in an amount sufficient to meet the needs of the child, without a showing of immediate or emergency need. The court shall make an order for

---

*So in original.

temporary child support notwithstanding that information with respect to income and assets of the respondent may be unavailable. Where such information is available, the court may make an award for temporary child support pursuant to the formula set forth in subdivision one of section four hundred thirteen of this article.

§434-a.   Order for temporary spousal support.

The court may make an order for temporary spousal support pending a final determination, notwithstanding that information with respect to income and assets of the respondent may be unavailable.

§435.   Procedure; adjournment; confidentiality of requests.

(a) Hearings are conducted by the court without a jury. The court may adjourn the hearing to enable it to make inquiry into the surroundings, conditions and capacities of the child, into the financial abilities and responsibilities of both parents and for other proper cause. If the court so adjourns the hearing, it may require the respondent to give an undertaking to appear or in default thereof may commit him until the hearing resumes.

(b) Hearings are conducted without a jury. The support magistrate may adjourn the hearing in order to make inquiry into the surroundings, conditions and capacities of the child and into the financial abilities and responsibilities of both parents and for other proper cause including a referral of issues required to be determined by a judge. If the support magistrate so adjourns the hearing, the support magistrate shall make a temporary order of support, pending a final determination, and may require the respondent to give an undertaking to appear or in default thereof may, subject to the provisions in section four hundred thirty-nine of this act and confirmation by a judge, commit him or her until the hearing resumes. The support magistrate shall enter an order of support on default if the respondent fails to answer or appear after having been properly served.

(c) Reports prepared by the probation service for use by the court at any time prior to the making of an order of disposition shall be deemed confidential information furnished to the court which the court in a proper case may, in its discretion, withhold from or disclose in whole or in part to the support magistrate, child's attorney, counsel, party in interest, or other appropriate person. Such reports may not be made available to the court prior to a determination that the respondent is liable under this article for the support of the petitioner.

§436.   Competence of spouse.

Wives and husbands are competent witnesses against each other in a hearing under section four hundred thirty-three and may testify to non-access in such a hearing.

§437.   Presumption of sufficient means.

A respondent is prima facie presumed in a hearing under section four hundred thirty-three and section four hundred fifty-four to have sufficient means to support his or her spouse and children under the age of twenty-one years.

§437-a.   Referral to work programs.

In any proceeding to establish, decrease or enforce an order of support, if the support obligor is unemployed, the court may require the support obligor to seek employment, or to participate in job training, employment counseling or other programs designed to lead to employment provided such programs are available. The court shall not require the support obligor to seek employment or to participate in job training, employment counseling, or other programs designed to lead to employment under this section if the support obligor is in receipt of supplemental security income or social security disability benefits.

§438. Counsel fees.

(a) In any proceeding under this article, including proceedings for support of a spouse and children, or for support of children only, or at any hearing to modify or enforce an order entered in that proceeding or a proceeding to modify a decree of divorce, separation, or annulment, including an appeal under article eleven, the court may allow counsel fees at any stage of the proceeding, to the attorney representing the spouse, former spouse or person on behalf of children.

(b) In any proceeding for failure to obey any lawful order compelling payment of support of a spouse or former spouse and children, or of children only, the court shall, upon a finding that such failure was willful, order respondent to pay counsel fees to the attorney representing the petitioner or person on behalf of the children. Representation by an attorney pursuant to paragraph (b) of subdivision nine of section one hundred eleven-b of the social services law shall not preclude an award of counsel fees to an applicant which would otherwise be allowed under this section.

§439. Support magistrates.

*(a) The chief administrator of the courts shall provide, in accordance with subdivision (f) of this section, for the appointment of a sufficient number of support magistrates to hear and determine support proceedings. Except as hereinafter provided, support magistrates shall be empowered to hear, determine and grant any relief within the powers of the court in any proceeding under this article, articles five, five-A, and five-B and sections two hundred thirty-four and two hundred thirty-five of this act, and objections raised pursuant to section five thousand two hundred forty-one of the civil practice law and rules. Support magistrates shall not be empowered to hear, determine and grant any relief with respect to issues specified in section four hundred fifty-five of this article, issues of contested paternity involving claims of equitable estoppel, custody, visitation including visitation as a defense, and orders of protection or exclusive possession of the home, which shall be referred to a judge as provided in subdivision (b) or (c) of this section. Where an order of filiation is issued by a judge in a paternity proceeding and child support is in issue, the judge, or support magistrate upon referral from the judge, shall be authorized to immediately make a temporary or final order of support, as applicable. A support magistrate shall have the authority to hear and decide motions and issue summonses and subpoenas to produce persons pursuant to section one hundred fifty-three of this act, hear and decide proceedings and issue any order authorized by subdivision (g) of section five thousand two hundred forty-one of the civil practice law and rules, issue subpoenas to produce prisoners pursuant to section two thousand three hundred two of the civil practice law and rules and make a determination that any person before the support magistrate is in violation of an order of the court as authorized by section one hundred fifty-six of this act subject to confirmation by a judge of the court who shall impose any punishment for such violation as provided by law. A determination by a support magistrate that a person is in willful violation of an order under subdivision three of section four hundred fifty-four of this article and

that recommends commitment shall be transmitted to the parties, accompanied by findings of fact, but the determination shall have no force and effect until confirmed by a judge of the court. *(Expires and reverts 8/31/17,Ch.29,L.2015)*

*(a) The chief administrator of the courts shall provide, in accordance with subdivision (f) of this section, for the appointment of a sufficient number of support magistrates to hear and determine support proceedings. Except as hereinafter provided, support magistrates shall be empowered to hear, determine and grant any relief within the powers of the court in any proceeding under this article, articles five, five-A, and five-B and sections two hundred thirty-four and two hundred thirty-five of this act, and objections raised pursuant to section five thousand two hundred forty-one of the civil practice law and rules. Support magistrates shall not be empowered to hear, determine and grant any relief with respect to issues specified in section four hundred fifty-five of this article, issues of contested paternity involving claims of equitable estoppel, custody, visitation including visitation as a defense, and orders of protection or exclusive possession of the home, which shall be referred to a judge as provided in subdivision (b) or (c) of this section. Where an order of filiation is issued by a judge in a paternity proceeding and child support is in issue, the judge, or support magistrate upon referral from the judge, shall be authorized to immediately make a temporary or final order of support, as applicable. A support magistrate shall have the authority to hear and decide motions and issue summonses and subpoenas to produce persons pursuant to section one hundred fifty-three of this act, hear and decide proceedings and issue any order authorized by subdivision (g) of section five thousand two hundred forty-one of the civil practice law and rules, issue subpoenas to produce prisoners pursuant to section two thousand three hundred two of the civil practice law and rules and make a determination that any person before the support magistrate is in violation of an order of the court as authorized by section one hundred fifty-six of this act subject to confirmation by a judge of the court who shall impose any punishment for such violation as provided by law. A determination by a support magistrate that a person is in willful violation of an order under subdivision three of section four hundred fifty-four of this article and that recommends commitment shall be transmitted to the parties, accompanied by findings of fact, but the determination shall have no force and effect until confirmed by a judge of the court. *(Eff.8/31/17,Ch.29,L.2015)*

(b) In any proceeding to establish paternity which is heard by a support magistrate, the support magistrate shall advise the mother and putative father of the right to be represented by counsel and shall advise the mother and putative father of their right to blood grouping or other genetic marker or DNA tests in accordance with section five hundred thirty-two of this act. The support magistrate shall order that such tests be conducted in accordance with section five hundred thirty-two of this act. The support magistrate shall be empowered to hear and determine all matters related to the proceeding including the making of an order of filiation pursuant to section five hundred forty-two of this act, provided, however, that where the respondent denies paternity and paternity is contested on the grounds of equitable estoppel, the support magistrate shall not be empowered to determine the issue of paternity, but shall transfer the proceeding to a judge of the court for a determination of the issue of paternity. Where an order of filiation is issued by a judge in a paternity proceeding and child support is in issue, the judge, or support magistrate upon referral from the judge, shall be authorized to immediately make a temporary or final order of support, as applicable. Whenever an order of filiation is made by a support magistrate, the support magistrate also shall make a final or temporary order of support.

(c) The support magistrate, in any proceeding in which issues specified in section four hundred fifty-five of this act, or issues of custody, visitation, including visitation as a defense, orders of protection or exclusive possession of the home are present or in which paternity is contested on the grounds of equitable estoppel, shall make a temporary order of support and refer the proceeding to a judge. Upon determination of such issue by a judge, the judge may make a final determination of the issue of support, or immediately refer the proceeding to a support magistrate for further proceedings regarding child support or other matters within the authority of the support magistrate.

(d) Rules of evidence shall be applicable in proceedings before a support magistrate. A support magistrate shall have the power to issue subpoenas, to administer oaths and to direct the parties to engage in and permit such disclosure as will expedite the disposition of issues. The assignment of proceedings and matters to support magistrates, the conduct of the trial before a support magistrate, the contents and filing of a support magistrate's findings of fact and decision and all matters incidental to proceedings before support magistrates shall be in accordance with rules provided for by the chief administrator of the courts. Proceedings held before a support magistrate may be recorded mechanically as provided by the chief administrator of the courts. A transcript of such proceeding may be made available in accordance with the rules of the chief administrator of the courts.

(e) The determination of a support magistrate shall include findings of fact and, except with respect to a determination of a willful violation of an order under subdivision three of section four hundred fifty-four of this article where commitment is recommended as provided in subdivision (a) of this section, a final order which shall be entered and transmitted to the parties. Specific written objections to a final order of a support magistrate may be filed by either party with the court within thirty days after receipt of the order in court or by personal service, or, if the objecting party or parties did not receive the order in court or by personal service, thirty-five days after mailing of the order to such party or parties. A party filing objections shall serve a copy of such objections upon the opposing party, who shall have thirteen days from such service to serve and file a written rebuttal to such objections. Proof of service upon the opposing party shall be filed with the court at the time of filing of objections and any rebuttal. Within fifteen days after the rebuttal is filed, or the time to file such rebuttal has expired, whichever is applicable, the judge, based upon a review of the objections and the rebuttal, if any, shall (i) remand one or more issues of fact to the support magistrate, (ii) make, with or without holding a new hearing, his or her own findings of fact and order, or (iii) deny the objections. Pending review of the objections and the rebuttal, if any, the order of the support magistrate shall be in full force and effect and no stay of such order shall be granted. In the event a new order is issued, payments made by the respondent in excess of the new order shall be applied as a credit to future support obligations. The final order of a support magistrate, after objections and the rebuttal, if any, have been reviewed by a judge, may be appealed pursuant to article eleven of this act.

(f) The chief administrator shall promulgate written rules for the selection, appointment, reappointment, compensation and training of support magistrates, who shall be attorneys admitted to the practice of law in this state for at least three years and who shall be knowledgeable with respect to the family court and federal and state support law and programs. Support magistrates shall be appointed on a full-time basis for a term of three years and may be reappointed for subsequent terms which shall be five years in length, except that the rules promulgated hereunder may permit the appointment of an acting support magistrate to serve during a support magistrate's authorized leave of absence. Where it is determined that the employment of a full-time support magistrate is not required, one or more counties may agree to share the services of a full-time support magistrate or a support magistrate may be appointed to serve within one or more counties on a part-time basis.

§439-a. Expedited process.

(a) When used in this section, expedited process means a process in effect in the family court which reduces the processing time of support order establishment and enforcement efforts from the date of successful service of process on the respondent to the date on which a support obligation or enforcement order is entered, the petition is voluntarily withdrawn or the petition is dismissed on the merits or for lack of jurisdiction of the respondent, by the referral of proceedings to support magistrates appointed and qualified under section four hundred thirty-nine of this article and exercising the powers set forth in such section.

(b) The chief administrator shall assign a sufficient number of support magistrates to ensure that such expedited process shall conform to the requirements of such case processing as set forth in federal statutes and regulations promulgated by the federal secretary of health and human services.

(c) The use of an expedited process shall be required (i) in any county which has a population of four hundred thousand or more or which is wholly within a city and (ii) in any county which has a population of less than four hundred thousand and for which the state has not been granted an exemption from the federal expedited process required by federal statutes and regulations of the federal secretary of health and human services.

(d) The chief administrator of the courts may request of the state commissioner of social services that an exemption from use of an expedited process as required by this section and section four hundred thirty-nine of this article in counties which are not wholly within a city and which have a population of less than four hundred thousand be applied for from the federal secretary of health and human services pursuant to federal statutes and regulations providing for waivers from the federal expedited process requirements. The chief administrator of the courts shall, upon making such a request, provide such information in the possession of the office of court administration which supports an exemption from use of an expedited process to the state commissioner of social services. Upon receipt of such a request from the chief administrator of the courts, the state commissioner of social services with the approval of the local commissioner of social services may apply to the federal secretary of health and human services for exemption from use of an expedited process. If application for such exemption is made, the state commissioner of social services shall, promptly upon receiving notification from the federal department of health and human services, inform the chief administrator of the courts and the local commissioners of social services of the granting or denial of any such application.

Part 4
Orders

§440. Order of support.

1. (a) Any support order made by the court in any proceeding under the provisions of article five-B of this act, pursuant to a reference from the supreme court under section two hundred fifty-one of the domestic relations law or under the provisions of article four, five or five-A of this act (i) shall direct that payments of child support or combined child and spousal support collected on behalf of persons in receipt of services pursuant to section one hundred eleven-g of the social services law, or on behalf of persons in receipt of public assistance be made to the support collection unit designated by the appropriate social services district, which shall receive and disburse funds so paid; or (ii) shall be enforced pursuant to subdivision (c) of section five thousand two hundred forty-two of the civil practice law and rules at the same time that the court issues an order of support; and (iii) shall in either case, except as provided for herein, be effective as of the earlier of the date of the filing of the petition therefor, or, if the children for whom support is sought are in receipt of public assistance, the date for which their eligibility for public assistance was effective. Any retroactive amount of support due shall be support arrears/past due support and shall be paid in one sum or periodic sums, as the court directs, and any amount of temporary support which has been paid to be taken into account in calculating any amount of such retroactive support due. In addition, such retroactive child support shall be enforceable in any manner provided by law including, but not limited to, an execution for support enforcement pursuant to subdivision (b) of section fifty-two hundred forty-one of the civil practice law and rules. When a child receiving support is a public assistance recipient, or the order of support is being enforced or is to be enforced pursuant to section one hundred eleven-g of the social services law, the court shall establish the amount of retroactive child support and notify the parties that such amount shall be enforced by the support collection unit pursuant to an execution for support enforcement as provided for in subdivision (b) of section fifty-two hundred forty-one of the civil practice law and rules, or in such periodic payments as would have been authorized had such an execution been issued. In such case, the court shall not direct the schedule of repayment of retroactive support. Where such direction is for child support and paternity has been established by a voluntary acknowledgment of paternity as defined in section forty-one hundred thirty-five-b of the public health law, the court shall inquire of the parties whether the acknowledgment has been duly filed, and unless satisfied that it has been so filed shall require the clerk of the court to file such acknowledgment with the appropriate registrar within five business days. The court shall not direct that support payments be made to the support collection unit unless the child, who is the

subject of the order, is in receipt of public assistance or child support services pursuant to section one hundred eleven-g of the social services law. Any such order shall be enforceable pursuant to section fifty-two hundred forty-one or fifty-two hundred forty-two of the civil practice law and rules, or in any other manner provided by law. Such orders or judgments for child support and maintenance shall also be enforceable pursuant to article fifty-two of the civil practice law and rules upon a debtor's default as such term is defined in paragraph seven of subdivision (a) of section fifty-two hundred forty-one of the civil practice law and rules. The establishment of a default shall be subject to the procedures established for the determination of a mistake of fact for income executions pursuant to subdivision (e) of section fifty-two hundred forty-one of the civil practice law and rules. For the purposes of enforcement of child support orders or combined spousal and child support orders pursuant to section five thousand two hundred forty-one of the civil practice law and rules, a "default" shall be deemed to include amounts arising from retroactive support. Where permitted under federal law and where the record of the proceedings contains such information, such order shall include on its face the social security number and the name and address of the employer, if any, of the person chargeable with support provided, however, that failure to comply with this requirement shall not invalidate such order.

(b) (1) When the court issues an order of child support or combined child and spousal support on behalf of persons in receipt of public assistance or in receipt of services pursuant to section one hundred eleven-g of the social services law, the support collection unit shall issue an income execution immediately for child support or combined spousal and child support, and shall issue an execution for medical support enforcement in accordance with the provisions of the order of support unless:

(i) the court finds and sets forth in writing the reasons that there is good cause not to require immediate income withholding; or

(ii) when the child is not in receipt of public assistance, a written agreement providing for an alternative arrangement has been reached between the parties. Such written agreement may include an oral stipulation made on the record resulting in a written order. For purposes of this paragraph, good cause shall mean substantial harm to the debtor. The absence of an arrearage or the mere issuance of an income execution shall not constitute good cause. When an immediate income execution or an execution for medical support enforcement is issued by the support collection unit, such execution shall be issued pursuant to section five thousand two hundred forty-one of the civil practice law and rules, except that the provisions thereof relating to mistake of fact, default and any other provisions which are not relevant to the issuance of an execution pursuant to this paragraph shall not apply; provided, however, that if the support collection unit makes an error in the issuance of an execution pursuant to this paragraph, and such error is to the detriment of the debtor, the support collection unit shall have thirty days after notification by the debtor to correct the error. Where permitted under federal law and where the record of the proceedings contains such information, such order shall include on its face the social security number and the name and address of the employer, if any, of the person chargeable with support; provided, however, that failure to comply with this requirement shall not invalidate such order. When the court determines that there is good cause not to immediately issue an income execution or when the parties agree to an alternative arrangement as provided in this paragraph, the court shall provide expressly in the order of support that the support collection unit shall not issue an immediate income execution. Notwithstanding any such order, the support collection unit shall issue an income execution for support enforcement when the debtor defaults on the support obligation, as defined in section five thousand two hundred forty-one of the civil practice law and rules. When an income execution for support enforcement is issued pursuant to this paragraph, such income execution shall supersede any income deduction order previously issued for enforcement of the same support order pursuant to subdivision (c) of section five thousand two hundred forty-two of the civil practice law and rules, whereupon such income deduction order shall cease to have further effect.

(2) When the court issues an order of child support or combined child and spousal support on behalf of persons other than those in receipt of public assistance or in receipt of services pursuant to section one hundred eleven-g of the social services law, the court shall issue an income deduction order pursuant to subdivision (c) of section five thousand two hundred forty-two of the civil practice law and rules at the same time at which it issues the order of support. The court shall enter the income deduction order unless the court finds and sets forth in writing:

(i) the reasons that there is good cause not to require immediate income withholding; or

(ii) that an agreement providing for an alternative arrangement has been reached between the parties. Such agreement may include a written agreement or an oral stipulation, made on the record, that results in a written order. For purposes of this paragraph, good cause shall mean substantial harm to the debtor. The absence of an arrearage or the mere issuance of an income deduction order shall not constitute good cause. Where permitted under federal law and where the record of the proceedings contains such information, the order shall include on its face the social security number and the name and address of the employer, if any, of the person chargeable with support; provided, however, that failure to comply with this requirement shall not invalidate the order. When the court determines that there is good cause not to immediately issue an income deduction order or when the parties agree to an alternative arrangement as provided in this paragraph, the court shall not issue an income deduction order. In addition, the court shall make provisions for health insurance benefits in accordance with the requirements of section four hundred sixteen of this article.

(c) Any order of support issued on behalf of a child in receipt of family assistance or child support enforcement services pursuant to section one hundred eleven-g of the social services law shall be subject to review and adjustment by the support collection unit pursuant to section one hundred eleven-n of the social services law, section two hundred forty-c of the domestic relations law and section four hundred thirteen-a of this article. Such review and adjustment shall be in addition to any other activities undertaken by the support collection unit relating to the establishment, modification, and enforcement of support orders payable to such unit.

2. The court shall require any person chargeable with support under the provisions of article five-B of this act or under any support order made pursuant to a reference from the supreme court under section two hundred fifty-one of the domestic relations law or in any proceeding under the provisions of article four, five or five-A of this act to provide his or her social security number, the name and address of his or her employer and to report any changes of employer or change in employment status affecting compensation

received, including rate of compensation or loss of employment, to the support collection unit designated by the appropriate social services district and to keep such support collection unit advised of his or her current employer and current employment status; provided, however, that a social security number may be required only where permitted under federal law.

3. The amount of support determined in accordance with the statewide child support standards, as set forth in section four hundred thirteen of this act, shall constitute prima facie evidence of the ability of any person chargeable with support in accordance with the provisions of article three-A of the domestic relations law or under any support order made pursuant to a reference from the supreme court under section two hundred fifty-one of the domestic relations law or in any proceeding under the provisions of article four, five or five-A of this chapter to support or contribute such amount towards the support of his or her children.

4. Any support order made by the court in any proceeding under the provisions of article five-B of this act, pursuant to a reference from the supreme court under section two hundred fifty-one of the domestic relations law or under the provisions of this article or article five or five-A of this act shall include, on its face, a notice printed or typewritten in a size equal to at least eight point bold type:

(a) informing the respondent that a willful failure to obey the order may, after court hearing, result in commitment to jail for a term not to exceed six months for contempt of court, and

(b) informing the parties of their right to seek a modification of the child support order upon a showing of:

(i) a substantial change in circumstances; or

(ii) that three years have passed since the order was entered, last modified or adjusted; or

(iii) there has been a change in either party's gross income by fifteen percent or more since the order was entered, last modified, or adjusted; however, if the parties have specifically opted out of subparagraph (ii) or (iii) of this paragraph in a validly executed agreement or stipulation, then that basis to seek modification does not apply.

5. The court shall direct that a copy of any child support or combined child and spousal support order issued by the court on or after the first day of October, nineteen hundred ninety-eight, in any proceeding pursuant to a reference from the supreme court under section two hundred fifty-one of the domestic relations law or under the provisions of article four, five, five-A or five-B of this act be provided promptly to the state case registry established pursuant to subdivision four-a of section one hundred eleven-b of the social services law.

6. Any order of support made by the court shall provide for health insurance benefits pursuant to section four hundred sixteen of this article.

§441. Order dismissing petition.

If the allegations of a petition under this article are not established by competent proof, the court shall dismiss the petition. If a neglect petition was filed in the support proceeding, the court retains jurisdiction over the neglect petition whether or not it dismisses the support petition.

§442. Order of support by a spouse.

If the court finds after a hearing that a husband or wife is chargeable under section four hundred twelve with the support of his or her spouse and is possessed of sufficient means or able to earn such means, the court shall make an order requiring the husband or wife to pay weekly or at other fixed periods a fair and reasonable sum for or towards the support of the other spouse. The court shall require the spouse chargeable with support to make his or her residence known at all times should he or she move from the address last known to the court by reporting such change to the support collection unit designated by the appropriate social services district. Failure to report such change shall subject him or her to the provisions of section four hundred fifty-four of this act.

§443. Order of support by parent.

If the court finds after a hearing that a parent is chargeable under section four hundred thirteen of this act with the support of his or her child and is possessed of sufficient means or able to earn such means, the court shall make an order requiring the parent to pay weekly or at other fixed periods a fair and reasonable sum for or towards the support of such child. Where permitted under federal law and where the record of the proceedings contains such information, the court shall also require the social security number of such parent to be affixed to such order; provided, however, that no such order shall be invalid because of the omission of such number. Where the record of the proceedings contains such information, such order shall also include on its face the name and address of the employer, if any, of the person chargeable with support provided, however, that failure to comply with this requirement shall not invalidate such order. Where the order of child support or combined child and spouse support is made on behalf of persons in receipt of public assistance or in receipt of services pursuant to section one hundred eleven-g of the social services law, the court shall require each party to provide, and update upon any change, the following information to the court by reporting such change to the support collection unit designated by the appropriate social services district: social security number, residential and mailing addresses, telephone number, driver's license number; and name, address and telephone number of the parties' employers. Due process requirements for notice and service of process for subsequent hearings are met, with respect to such party, upon sending written notice by first class mail to the most recent residential address on record with the support collection unit; or by sending by first class mail written notice to the most recent employer address on record with the support collection unit, if a true copy thereof also is sent by first class mail to the most recent residential address on record with the support collection unit. Any such order issued on or after the first day of October, nineteen hundred ninety-nine shall also include, where available, the social security number of each child on whose behalf support has been ordered. Failure to report such changes shall subject the parent to the provisions of section four hundred fifty-four of this act.

§445. Order of support by relative; duration.

(a) If the court finds after a hearing that a relative, including a step-parent, should be held responsible under section four hundred fifteen for support, the court in its discretion may make an order requiring such person to contribute a fair and reasonable sum for the support of such person.

(b) For good cause shown, the court may at any time terminate or modify an order made under this section.

§446. Order of protection.

The court may make an order of protection in assistance or as a condition of any other order made under this part. The order of protection may set forth reasonable conditions of behavior to be observed for a specified time by the petitioner or respondent or both. No order of protection may direct any party to observe conditions of behavior unless the party requesting the order of protection has served and filed a petition or counter-claim in accordance with section one hundred fifty-four-b of this act. Such an order may require the petitioner or the respondent:

(a) to stay away from the home, school, business or place of employment of any other party, the other spouse, the other parent or the child, and to stay away from any other specific location designated by the court;

(b) to permit a parent, or a person entitled to visitation by a court order or a separation agreement, to visit the child at stated periods;

(c) to refrain from committing a family offense, as defined in subdivision one of section eight hundred twelve of this act, or any criminal offense against the child or against the other parent or against any person to whom custody of the child is awarded, or from harassing, intimidating or threatening such persons;

(d) to permit a designated party to enter the residence during a specified period of time in order to remove personal belongings not in issue in this proceeding or in any other proceeding or action under this act or the domestic relations law;

(e) to refrain from acts of commission or omission that create an unreasonable risk to the health, safety or welfare of a child;

(f) to participate in an educational program and to pay the costs thereof if the person has the means to do so, provided however that nothing contained herein shall be deemed to require payment of the costs of any such program by the state or any political subdivision thereof;

(g) to provide, either directly or by means of medical and health insurance, for expenses incurred for medical care and treatment arising from the incident or incidents forming the basis for the issuance of the order.

(h) 1. to refrain from intentionally injuring or killing, without justification, any companion animal the respondent knows to be owned, possessed, leased, kept or held by the person protected by the order or a minor child residing in such person's household.

2. "Companion animal", as used in this section, shall have the same meaning as in subdivision five of section three hundred fifty of the agriculture and markets law;

(i) 1. to promptly return specified identification documents to the protected party, in whose favor the order of protection or temporary order of protection is issued; provided, however, that such order may: (A) include any appropriate provision designed to ensure that any such document is available for use as evidence in this proceeding, and available if necessary for legitimate use by the party against whom such order is issued; and (B) specify the manner in which such return shall be accomplished.

2. For purposes of this subdivision, "identification document" shall mean any of the following: (A) exclusively in the name of the protected party: birth certificate, passport, social security card, health insurance or other benefits card, a card or document used to access bank, credit or other financial accounts or records, tax returns, any driver's license, and immigration documents including but not limited to a United States permanent resident card and

employment authorization document; and (B) upon motion and after notice and an opportunity to be heard, any of the following, including those that may reflect joint use or ownership, that the court determines are necessary and are appropriately transferred to the protected party: any card or document used to access bank, credit or other financial accounts or records, tax returns, and any other identifying cards and documents; and

(j) to observe such other conditions as are necessary to further the purposes of protection.

The court may also award custody of the child, during the term of the order of protection to either parent, or to an appropriate relative within the second degree. Nothing in this section gives the court power to place or board out any child or to commit a child to an institution or agency. In making orders of protection, the court shall so act as to insure that in the care, protection, discipline and guardianship of the child his religious faith shall be preserved and protected. Notwithstanding the foregoing provisions, an order of protection, or temporary order of protection where applicable, may be entered against a former spouse and persons who have a child in common, regardless of whether such persons have been married or have lived together at any time, or against a member of the same family or household as defined in subdivision one of section eight hundred twelve of this act. In addition to the foregoing provisions, the court may issue an order, pursuant to section two hundred twenty-seven-c of the real property law, authorizing the party for whose benefit any order of protection has been issued to terminate a lease or rental agreement pursuant to section two hundred twenty-seven-c of the real property law.

In any proceeding pursuant to this article, a court shall not deny an order of protection, or dismiss an application for such an order, solely on the basis that the acts or events alleged are not relatively contemporaneous with the date of the application or the conclusion of the action. The duration of any temporary order shall not by itself be a factor in determining the length or issuance of any final order.

The protected party in whose favor the order of protection or temporary order of protection is issued may not be held to violate an order issued in his or her favor nor may such protected party be arrested for violating such order.

§446-a. Firearms; surrender and license suspension, revocation and ineligibility.

Upon the issuance of an order of protection or temporary order of protection, or upon a violation of such order, the court shall make a determination regarding the suspension and revocation of a license to carry, possess, repair or dispose of a firearm or firearms, ineligibility for such a license and the surrender of firearms in accordance with section eight hundred forty-two-a of this act.

§447. Order of visitation.

(a) In the absence of an order of custody or of visitation entered by the supreme court, the court may make an order of custody or of visitation, in accordance with subdivision one of section two hundred forty of the domestic relations law, requiring one parent to permit the other to visit the children at stated periods without an order of protection, even where the parents are divorced and the support order is for a child only.

(b) Any order of the family court under this section shall terminate when the supreme court makes an order of custody or of visitation concerning the children, unless the supreme court continues the order of the family court.

§448. Enforcement by income deduction.

Orders of support shall be enforceable pursuant to section fifty-two hundred forty-one or fifty-two hundred forty-two of the civil practice law and rules, or in any other manner provided by law. The family court is hereby authorized to enter an order with respect to an income deduction, in accordance with the provisions of section fifty-two hundred forty-two of the civil practice law and rules, in any support proceeding under the provisions of article five-B of this act under any support order made pursuant to a reference from the supreme court under section two hundred fifty-one of the domestic relations law or in any support proceeding under the provisions of article four, five or five-A of this act.

§449. Effective date of order of support.

1. Any order of spousal support made under this article shall be effective as of the date of the filing of the petition therefor, and any retroactive amount of support due shall be paid in one sum or periodic sums, as the court shall direct, to the petitioner, to the custodial parent or to third persons. Any amount of temporary support which has been paid shall be taken into account in calculating any amount of retroactive support due.

2. Any order of child support made under this article shall be effective as of the earlier of the date of the filing of the petition therefor, or, if the children for whom support is sought are in receipt of public assistance, the date for which their eligibility for public assistance was effective. Any retroactive amount of support due shall be support arrears/past-due support and shall be paid in one sum or periodic sums, as the court shall direct, to the petitioner, to the custodial parent or to third persons. Any amount of temporary support which has been paid shall be taken into account in calculating any amount of retroactive support due. In addition, such retroactive child support shall be enforceable in any manner provided by law including, but not limited to, an execution for support enforcement pursuant to subdivision (b) of section fifty-two hundred forty-one of the civil practice law and rules.

Part 5
Compliance with Orders

§451. Continuing jurisdiction.

1. Except as provided in article five-B of this act, the court has continuing jurisdiction over any support proceeding brought under this article until its

judgment is completely satisfied and may modify, set aside or vacate any order issued in the course of the proceeding, provided, however, that the modification, set aside or vacatur shall not reduce or annul child support arrears accrued prior to the making of an application pursuant to this section. The court shall not reduce or annul any other arrears unless the defaulting party shows good cause for failure to make application for relief from the judgment or order directing payment prior to the accrual of the arrears, in which case the facts and circumstances constituting such good cause shall be set forth in a written memorandum of decision. A modification may increase support payments nunc pro tunc as of the date of the initial application for support based on newly discovered evidence. Any retroactive amount of support due shall be paid and be enforceable as provided in section four hundred forty of this article. Upon an application to set aside or vacate an order of support, no hearing shall be required unless such application shall be supported by affidavit and other evidentiary material sufficient to establish a prima facie case for the relief requested.

2. A proceeding to modify an order of support shall be commenced by the filing of a petition which shall allege facts sufficient to meet one or more of the grounds enumerated in subdivision three of this section.

3. (a) The court may modify an order of child support, including an order incorporating without merging an agreement or stipulation of the parties, upon a showing of a substantial change in circumstances. Incarceration shall not be a bar to finding a substantial change in circumstances provided such incarceration is not the result of non-payment of a child support order, or an offense against the custodial parent or child who is the subject of the order or judgment.

(b) In addition, unless the parties have specifically opted out of the following provisions in a validly executed agreement or stipulation entered into between the parties, the court may modify an order of child support where:

(i) three years have passed since the order was entered, last modified or adjusted; or

(ii) there has been a change in either party's gross income by fifteen percent or more since the order was entered, last modified, or adjusted. A reduction in income shall not be considered as a ground for modification unless it was involuntary and the party has made diligent attempts to secure employment commensurate with his or her education, ability, and experience.

§453. Petition; violation of court order.

Proceedings under this part shall be originated by the filing of a petition containing an allegation that the respondent has failed to obey a lawful order of this court.

(a) Persons who may originate and prosecute proceedings. The original petitioner, the support collection unit on behalf of persons in receipt of public assistance or in receipt of services pursuant to section one hundred eleven-g of the social services law, or any person to whom the order is payable expressly or who may originate proceedings under section four hundred twenty-two of this article may originate and prosecute a proceeding under this part.

(b) Issuance of summons. Upon the filing of a petition under this part, the court may cause a copy of the petition and a summons to be issued, requiring the respondent to show cause why he should not be dealt with in accordance with section four hundred fifty-four of this part. The summons shall include on its face, printed or typewritten in a size equal to at least eight point bold type, a notice, warning the respondent that a failure to appear in court may result in immediate arrest, and that, after an appearance in court, a finding that the respondent willfully failed to obey the order may result in commitment to jail for a term not to exceed six months, for contempt of court. The notice shall also advise the respondent of the right to counsel, and the right to assigned counsel, if indigent.

(c) Service of summons. Upon the issuance of a summons, the provisions of section four hundred twenty-seven of this article shall apply, except that no order of commitment may be entered upon the default in appearance by the respondent if service has been made by mail alone notwithstanding proof of actual notice of the commencement of the proceeding.

(d) Issuance of warrant. The court may issue a warrant, directing that the respondent be arrested and brought before the court, pursuant to section four hundred twenty-eight of this article.

§454. Powers of the court on violation of a support order.

1. If a respondent is brought before the court for failure to obey any lawful order of support and if, after hearing, the court is satisfied by competent proof that the respondent has failed to obey any such order, the court may use any or all of the powers conferred upon it by this part. The court has the power to use any or all enforcement powers in every proceeding brought for violation of a court order under this part regardless of the relief requested in the petition.

2. Upon a finding that a respondent has failed to comply with any lawful order of support:

(a) the court shall enter a money judgment under section four hundred sixty of this article; and

(b) the court may make an income deduction order for support enforcement under section fifty-two hundred forty-two of the civil practice law and rules;

(c) the court may require the respondent to post an undertaking under section four hundred seventy-one of this article;

(d) the court may make an order of sequestration under section four hundred fifty-seven of this article.

(e) the court may suspend the respondent's driving privileges pursuant to section four hundred fifty-eight-a of this article.

(f) the court may suspend the respondent's state professional or business license pursuant to section four hundred fifty-eight-b of this article;

(g) the court may suspend the recreational license or licenses of the respondent pursuant to section four hundred fifty-eight-c of this article.

(h) the court may require the respondent, if the persons for whom the respondent has failed to pay support are applicants for or recipients of public assistance, to participate in work activities as defined in title nine-B of article five of the social services law. Those respondents ordered to participate in work activities need not be applicants for or recipients of public assistance.

(i) except as otherwise provided in paragraph (h) of this subdivision, the court may require the respondent to participate in job training, employment counseling or other programs designed to lead to employment if authorized pursuant to section four hundred thirty-seven-a of this article provided such programs are available.

3. Upon a finding by the court that a respondent has willfully failed to obey any lawful order of support, the court shall order respondent to pay counsel fees to the attorney representing petitioner pursuant to section four hundred thirty-eight of this act and may in addition to or in lieu of any or all of the powers conferred in subdivision two of this section or any other section of law:

(a) commit the respondent to jail for a term not to exceed six months. For purposes of this subdivision, failure to pay support, as ordered, shall constitute prima facie evidence of a willful violation. Such commitment may be served upon certain specified days or parts of days as the court may direct, and the court may, at any time within the term of such sentence, revoke such suspension and commit the respondent for the remainder of the original sentence, or suspend the remainder of such sentence. Such commitment does not prevent the court from subsequently committing the respondent for failure thereafter to comply with any such order; or

(b) require the respondent to participate in a rehabilitative program if the court determines that such participation would assist the respondent in complying with such order of support and access to such a program is available. Such rehabilitative programs shall include, but not be limited to, work preparation and skill programs, non-residential alcohol and substance abuse programs and educational programs; or

(c) place the respondent on probation under such conditions as the court may determine and in accordance with the provisions of the criminal procedure law.

4. The court shall not deny any request for relief pursuant to this section unless the facts and circumstances constituting the reasons for its determination are set forth in a written memorandum of decision.

*5. The court may review a support collection unit's denial of a challenge made by a support obligor pursuant to paragraph (d) of subdivision twelve of section one hundred eleven-b of the social services law if objections thereto are filed by a support obligor who has received notice that the office of temporary and disability assistance intends to notify the department of motor vehicles that the support obligor's driving privileges are to be suspended. Specific written objections to a support collection unit's denial may be filed by the support obligor within thirty-five days of the mailing of the notice of the support collection unit's denial. A support obligor who files such objections shall serve a copy of the objections upon the support collection unit, which shall have ten days from such service to file a written rebuttal to such objections and a copy of the record upon which the support collection unit's denial was made, including all documentation submitted by the support obligor. Proof of service shall be filed with the court at the time of filing of objections and any rebuttal. The court's review shall be based upon the record and submissions of the support obligor and the support collection unit upon which the support collection unit's denial was made. Within forty-five days after the rebuttal, if any, is filed, the court shall

(i) deny the objections and remand to the support collection unit or

(ii) affirm the objections if the court finds the determination of the support collection unit is based upon a clearly erroneous determination of fact or error of law, whereupon the court shall direct the support collection unit not to notify the department of motor vehicles to suspend the support obligor's driving privileges. Provisions set forth herein relating to procedures for appeal to the family court by individuals subject to suspension of driving privileges for failure to pay child support shall apply solely to such cases and not affect or modify any other procedure for review or appeal of administrative enforcement of child support requirements. *(Repealed 8/31/17,Ch.29,L.2015)*

§455. Commitment.

1. The court may at any time suspend an order of commitment upon such reasonable conditions, if any, as the court deems appropriate to carry out the

purposes of this article without placing the respondent on probation or may place him on probation under such conditions as the court may determine and in accordance with the provisions of the criminal procedure law. For good cause shown, the court may at any time revoke the suspension of the order of commitment.

2. Except as provided in article five-B of this act, any respondent against whom an order of commitment has been issued, if financially unable to comply with any lawful order issued under this article, upon such notice to such parties as the court may direct, may make application to the court for an order relieving him or her of payments directed in such order and the commitment order. The court, upon the hearing on such application, if satisfied by competent proof that the respondent is financially unable to comply with such order may, upon a showing of good cause until further order of the court, modify such order and relieve the respondent from the commitment order. No such modification shall reduce or annul unpaid sums or installments accrued prior to the making of such application unless the defaulting party shows good cause for failure to make application for relief from the order directing payment prior to the accrual of such arrears. Such modification may increase the amount to be paid pursuant to a lawful order issued under this article nunc pro tunc based on newly discovered evidence.

3. Whenever, upon application to the court by an interested party, it appears to the satisfaction of the court that any person, who has been relieved totally or partially from making any payment pursuant to the provisions of this section, is no longer financially unable to comply with the order to make such payment, then the court may, upon a showing of good cause modify or revoke its order relieving such person totally or partially from making such payment.

4. Notwithstanding any inconsistent provision of this article, the provision of any order issued under this article requiring the payment of money by one spouse for the support of the other shall be suspended and inoperative so far as punishment for contempt is concerned during the period in which the defaulting spouse is imprisoned pursuant to any order adjudging him or her in contempt for failure to comply with any provision in such order.

5. Any respondent may assert his or her financial inability to comply with the directions contained in an order issued under this article or an order or judgment entered in a matrimonial action or in an action for the enforcement in this state of a judgment in a matrimonial action rendered in another state, as a defense in a proceeding instituted against him or her under subdivision one of section four hundred fifty-four of this article or under the judiciary law to punish him or her for failure to comply with such directions. If the court, upon the hearing of such contempt proceeding, is satisfied by competent proof that the respondent is financially unable to comply with such order or judgment, it may, in its discretion, until further order of the court, make an order modifying such order or judgment and denying the application to punish the respondent for contempt; provided, however, that if an order or judgement for child support issued by another state is before the court solely for enforcement, the court may only modify the order in accordance with article five-B of this act. No such modification shall reduce or annul arrears accrued prior to the making of such application for modification unless the defaulting party shows good cause for failure to make application for relief from the order or judgment directing such payment prior to the accrual of such arrears.

Such modification may increase such support nunc pro tunc as of the date of the application based on newly discovered evidence. Any retroactive amount of support due shall be paid in one sum or periodic sums, as the court shall direct, taking into account any amount of temporary support which has been paid.

§456. Probation.

(a) No person may be placed on probation under this article unless the court makes an order to that effect, either at the time of the making of an order of support or under section four hundred fifty-four. The period of probation may continue so long as an order of support, order of protection or order of visitation applies to such person.

(b) The court may at any time, where circumstances warrant it, revoke an order of probation. Upon such revocation, the probationer shall be brought to court, which may, without further hearing, make any order that might have been made at the time the order of probation was made.

§457. Order of sequestration on failure to obey support order.

If an order of support is made under this article and the respondent has failed to obey it and either leaves or threatens to leave the state, the court on application may issue an order of sequestration of his property within the state, providing that such property may be taken, sequestered and applied in like manner as is provided in section four hundred twenty-nine.

§458-a. Enforcement of arrears; Suspension of driving privileges.

(a) If the respondent has accumulated support arrears equivalent to or greater than the amount of support due pursuant to court order for a period of four months, the court may order the department of motor vehicles to suspend the respondent's driving privileges, and if such order issues, the respondent may apply to the department of motor vehicles for a restricted use license pursuant to section five hundred thirty of the vehicle and traffic law. The court may at any time upon payment of arrears or partial payment of arrears by the respondent order the department of motor vehicles to terminate the suspension of respondent's driving privileges. For purposes of determining whether a support obligor has accumulated support arrears equivalent to or greater than the amount of support due for a period of four months, the amount of any retroactive support, other than periodic payments of retroactive support which are past due, shall not be included in the calculation of support arrears pursuant to this section.

(b) If the respondent, after receiving appropriate notice, fails to comply with a summons, subpoena or warrant relating to a paternity or child support proceeding, the court may order the department of motor vehicles to suspend the respondent's driving privileges. The court may subsequently order the department of motor vehicles to terminate the suspension of the respondent's driving privileges; however, the court shall order the termination of such suspension when the court is satisfied that the respondent has fully complied with the requirements of all summonses, subpoenas and warrants relating to a paternity or child support proceeding. Nothing in this subdivision shall authorize the court to terminate the respondent's suspension of driving privileges except as provided in this subdivision.

(c) The provisions of subdivision (a) of this section shall not apply to:

(i) respondents who are receiving public assistance or supplemental security income; or

(ii) respondents whose income as defined by subparagraph five of paragraph (b) of subdivision one of section four hundred thirteen of this act falls below the self-support reserve as defined by subparagraph six of paragraph (b) of subdivision one of section four hundred thirteen of this act; or

(iii) respondents whose income as defined by subparagraph five of paragraph (b) of subdivision one of section four hundred thirteen of this act remaining after the payment of the current support obligation would fall below the self-support reserve as defined by subparagraph six of paragraph (b) of subdivision one of section four hundred thirteen of this act.

(d) The court's discretionary decision not to suspend driving privileges shall not have any res judicata effect or preclude any other agency with statutory authority to direct the department of motor vehicles to suspend driving privileges.

§458-b.   Child support proceedings and enforcement of arrears; suspension of state professional, occupational and business licenses.

(a) If the respondent has accumulated support arrears equivalent to or greater than the amount of support due pursuant to court order for a period of four months and the court has determined that the respondent is licensed, permitted or registered by or with a board, department, authority or office of this state to conduct a trade, business, profession or occupation, the court may order such board, department, authority or office to commence proceedings as required by law regarding the suspension of such license, permit, registration or authority to practice and to inform the court of the actions it has taken pursuant to such proceedings. For purposes of determining whether a respondent has accumulated support arrears equivalent to or greater than the amount of support due for a period of four months, the amount of any retroactive support, other than periodic payments of retroactive support which are past due, shall not be included in the calculation of support arrears pursuant to this section.

(b) If the respondent after receiving appropriate notice, fails to comply with a summons, subpoena or warrant relating to a paternity or child support proceeding, and the court has determined that the respondent is licensed, permitted or registered by or with a board, department, authority or office of this state or one of its political subdivisions or instrumentalities to conduct a trade, business, profession or occupation, the court may order such board, department, authority or office to commence proceedings as required by law regarding the suspension of such license, permit, registration or authority to practice and to inform the court of the actions it has taken pursuant to such proceeding. The court may subsequently order such board, department, authority or office to terminate the suspension of the respondent's license, permit, registration or authority to practice; however, the court shall order the termination of such suspension when the court is satisfied that the respondent has fully complied with the requirements of all summonses, subpoenas and warrants relating to a paternity or child support proceeding.

(c) If the court determines that the suspension of the license, permit or registration of the respondent would create an extreme hardship to either the licensee, permittee or registrant or to persons whom he or she serves, the court may, in lieu of suspension, suspend the order described in subdivision (a) of this section to the licensing entity for a period not to exceed one year. If on or before the expiration of this period the court has not received competent proof presented at hearing that the respondent is in full compliance with his or her support obligation and has fully complied with all summons, subpoenas and warrants relating to a paternity or child support proceeding, the court shall cause the suspension of the order to be removed and shall further cause such order to be served upon the licensing entity.

(d) The provisions of subdivision (a) of this section shall not apply to:

(i) respondents who are receiving public assistance or supplemental security income; or

(ii) respondents whose income as defined by subparagraph five of paragraph (b) of subdivision one of section four hundred thirteen of this act falls below the self-support reserve as defined by subparagraph six of paragraph (b) of subdivision one of section four hundred thirteen of this act; or

(iii) respondents whose income as defined by subparagraph five of paragraph (b) of subdivision one of section four hundred thirteen of this act remaining after the payment of the current support obligation would fall below the self-support reserve as defined by subparagraph six of paragraph (b) of subdivision one of section four hundred thirteen of this act.

(e) The court shall inform the respondent that competent proof for purposes of proving payment to a licensing entity shall be a certified check, notice issued by the court, or notice from a support collection unit where the order is for payment to the support collection unit.

§458-c. **Child support proceedings and enforcement of arrears; suspension of recreational licenses.**

(a) If the respondent has accumulated support arrears equivalent to or greater than the amount of support due pursuant to court order for a period of four months, the court may order any agency responsible for the issuance of a recreational license to suspend or refuse to reissue a license to the respondent, or deny application for such license by the respondent. For purposes of determining whether a respondent has accumulated support arrears equivalent to or greater than the amount of support due for a period of four months, the amount of any retroactive support, other than periodic payments of retroactive support which are past due, shall not be included in the calculation of support arrears pursuant to this section.

(b) If the respondent, after receiving appropriate notice, fails to comply with a summons, subpoena, or warrant relating to a paternity or child support proceeding, the court may order any agency responsible for the issuance of a recreational license to suspend or to refuse to reissue a license to the respondent or to deny application for such license by the respondent. The court may subsequently order such agency to terminate the adverse action regarding the respondent's license; however, the court shall order the termination of such suspension or other adverse action when the court is satisfied that the respondent has fully complied with the requirements of all summons, subpoenas, and warrants relating to a paternity or child support proceeding.

(c) The provisions of subdivision (a) of this section shall not apply to:

(i) respondents who are receiving public assistance or supplemental security income; or

(ii) respondents whose income as defined by subparagraph five of paragraph (b) of subdivision one of section four hundred thirteen of this act falls below the self-support reserve as defined by subparagraph six of paragraph (b) of subdivision one of section four hundred thirteen of this article; or

(iii) respondents whose income as defined by subparagraph five of paragraph (b) of subdivision one of section four hundred thirteen of this article remaining after the payment of the current support obligation would fall below the self-support reserve as defined by subparagraph six of paragraph (b) of subdivision one of section four hundred thirteen of this article.

§459. Additional arrears.

If a respondent has failed to obey a lawful order under this article the party seeking enforcement may amend the petition to include any additional arrears which have accrued from the commencement of such enforcement proceeding up to the date of the hearing, provided that written notice of the intention to so amend has been given eight days previously.

§460. Entry and docketing of a money judgment.

1. Where the family court enters an order:

(a) requiring any party to provide for the support of another party, or child, or both; or

(b) providing for the support or maintenance of a spouse or former spouse, or child, or both, on a referral from the supreme court in an action for divorce, separation, annulment or a proceeding for the determination of the custody of a minor by writ of habeas corpus or by petition and order to show cause; or

(c) enforcing or modifying an order or decree of a court of competent jurisdiction not of the state of New York providing for the support of the petitioner and/or child support; or

(d) awarding support under article five-B of this act; or

(e) awarding counsel fees under this act;

and the party defaults in paying any sum of money due as required by the order directing the payment thereof, the court, without regard to the amount due, shall make an order directing the entry of judgment for the amount of child support arrears, together with costs and disbursements. The court shall make an order directing the entry of judgment for the amount of arrears of any other payments so directed, together with costs and disbursements, unless the defaulting party shows good cause for failure to make application for relief from the judgment or order directing such payment prior to the accrual of such arrears. The court shall not make an order reducing or cancelling such arrears unless the facts and circumstances constituting good cause are set forth in a written memorandum of decision. The application for such order shall be made upon such notice to the party or other person as the court may direct. Such judgment shall provide for the payment of interest on the amount of any arrears if the default was willful, in that the defaulting party knowingly, consciously and voluntarily disregarded the obligation under a lawful court order. Such interest shall be computed from the date on which the payment was due, at the prevailing rate of interest on judgments as provided in the civil practice law and rules.

2. A certified copy of the order directing the entry of a money judgment shall be entered in the office of the clerk of the county in which the proceeding was commenced. Said clerk shall docket the same in the book kept by him for the docketing of judgments as if said order were a transcript of a judgment directed for the amount designated in the order. An order docketed under this subdivision shall have the same effect as a docketed judgment entered in the supreme court within the county where it is docketed and may be enforced by execution or in any other manner provided by law for the collection of a money judgment.

3. The relief provided for herein shall be in addition to any and every other remedy which may be provided under the law including, but not limited to, the remedies provided under the provisions of section four hundred fifty-four of this

act and sections fifty-two hundred forty-one and fifty-two hundred forty-two of the civil practice law and rules; provided that when a judgment for such arrears has been entered pursuant to this section, such judgment shall not thereafter be subject to modification or be affected by the provisions of section four hundred sixty-two of this act. After the entry of any order hereunder, the judgment creditor shall not thereafter be entitled to collect, by any form of remedy, any greater portion of such arrears than that represented by the order so entered.

Part 6
Effect of Action for Separation,
Divorce or Annulment

Section
461. Duty to support child after separation agreement, separation, or termination of marriage.
462. Effect of support order in matrimonial action on duration of family court support order for child.
463. Effect of separation agreement on duty to support a spouse.
464. Effect of pendency of action for divorce, separation or annulment on petition for support of a spouse.
465. Effect of denial of support in action for separation.
466. Effect of granting of support in action for divorce, separation or annulment.
467. Referral by supreme court of applications to fix custody in action for divorce, separation or annulment.
469. Rules of court; venue.

§461. Duty to support child after separation agreement, separation, or termination of marriage.

(a) A separation agreement, a decree of separation, and a final decree or judgment terminating a marriage relationship does not eliminate or diminish either parent's duty to support a child of the marriage under section four hundred thirteen of this article. In the absence of an order of the supreme court or of another court of competent jurisdiction requiring support of the child, the family court may entertain a petition and make an order for its support.

(b) If an order of the supreme court or of another court of competent jurisdiction requires support of the child, the family court may:

(i) entertain an application to enforce the order requiring support; or

(ii) entertain an application to modify such order as provided under subdivision two of section four hundred fifty-one of this article, unless the order of the supreme court provides that the supreme court retains exclusive jurisdiction to enforce or modify the order.

(c) In an action for divorce, separation or annulment in the supreme court, the supreme court on its own motion or on motion of one of the parties may refer an application for temporary or permanent support or both of a child of the marriage to the family court. If the supreme court so refers the application, the family court shall have jurisdiction to determine the application with the same powers possessed by the supreme court and the family court's disposition of the application shall be an order of the family court appealable only under article eleven of this act.

§462. Effect of support order in matrimonial action on duration of family court support order for child.

Any order of the family court requiring support of a child terminates when the supreme court makes an order in an action for divorce, separation or annulment providing for the support of the child, unless the supreme court continues the order of the family court.

§463. Effect of separation agreement on duty to support a spouse.

A separation agreement does not preclude the filing of a petition and the making of an order under section four hundred forty-five of this article for support of a spouse who is likely to become in need of public assistance or care.

§464. Effect of pendency of action for divorce, separation or annulment on petition for support of a spouse.

(a) In a matrimonial action in the supreme court, the supreme court on its own motion or on motion of either spouse may refer to the family court an application for temporary or permanent support, or for maintenance or a distribution of marital property. If the supreme court so refers an application, the family court has jurisdiction to determine the application with the same powers possessed by the supreme court and the family court's disposition of the application is an order of the family court appealable only under article eleven of this act.

(b) In the absence of an order of referral under paragraph (a) of this section and in the absence of an order by the supreme court granting temporary or permanent support or maintenance, the family court during the pendency of such action may entertain a petition and may make an order under section four hundred forty-five of this article for a spouse who is likely to become in need of public assistance or care.

§465. Effect of denial of support in action for separation.

After final adjudication of an action for separation in which the supreme court denies support to a spouse, the family court may entertain a petition and make an order for support of such spouse

(a) under section four hundred forty-two of this article if in the opinion of the family court the circumstances of the parties have changed, or

(b) under section four hundred forty-five of this article if it is shown to the satisfaction of the family court that the petitioner is likely to become in need of public assistance or care.

§466. Effect of granting of support in action for divorce, separation or annulment.

(a) The supreme court may provide in an order or decree granting temporary or permanent support or maintenance in an action for divorce, separation or annulment that only the family court may entertain an application to enforce or, upon a showing to the family court that there has been a subsequent change of circumstance and that modification is required, to modify such order or decree. If the supreme court so provides, the family court shall entertain such an application and any disposition by the family court of the application is an order of the family court appealable only under article eleven of this act.

(b) The supreme court may provide in an order or decree granting alimony, maintenance or support in an action for divorce, separation or annulment that the order or decree may be enforced or modified only in the supreme court. If the supreme court so provides, the family court may not entertain an application to enforce or modify an order or decree of the supreme court involving the parties to the action.

(c) If the supreme court enters an order or decree granting alimony, maintenance or support in an action for divorce, separation or annulment and if the supreme court does not exercise the authority given under subdivision (a) or (b) of this section; or if a court of competent jurisdiction not of the state of

New York shall enter an order or decree granting alimony, maintenance or support in any such action, the family court may

(i) entertain an application to enforce the order or decree granting alimony or maintenance, or

(ii) entertain an application to modify the order or decree granting alimony or maintenance on the ground that there has been a subsequent change of circumstances and that modification is required.

§467. Referral by supreme court of applications to fix custody in action for divorce, separation or annulment.

(a) In an action for divorce, separation or annulment, the supreme court may refer to the family court the determination of applications to fix temporary or permanent custody or visitation, applications to enforce judgments and orders of custody or visitation, and applications to modify judgments and orders of custody which modification may be granted only upon a showing to the family court that there has been a subsequent change of circumstances and that modification is required.

(b) In the event no such referral has been made and unless the supreme court provides in the order or judgment awarding custody or visitation in an action for divorce, separation or annulment, that it may be enforced or modified only in the supreme court, the family court may:

(i) determine an application to enforce the order or judgment awarding custody or visitation, or

(ii) determine an application to modify the order or judgment awarding custody or visitation upon a showing that there has been a subsequent change of circumstances and modification is required.

(c) In any determination of an application pursuant to this section, the family court shall have jurisdiction to determine such applications, in accordance with subdivision one of section two hundred forty of the domestic relations law, with the same powers possessed by the supreme court, and the family court's disposition of any such application is an order of the family court appealable only under article eleven of this act.

§469. Rules of court; venue.

(a) Rules of court under section four hundred twenty-four of this article may be made applicable with such modifications, if any, as may be appropriate to the determination of applications referred to the family court by the supreme court under part six of this article.

(b) The supreme court referring an application to the family court under part six may designate a county within the judicial district as the county in which the application is to be determined. If the supreme court does not designate the county, section four hundred twenty-one of this article applies.

(c) Section four hundred twenty-one of this article applies in determining the county in which an application under section four hundred sixty-one, section four hundred sixty-six or section six hundred fifty-four may be heard.

Part 7
Undertaking

§471. Undertaking for support and cash deposits.

The court may in its discretion require either a written undertaking with sufficient surety approved by the court or may require that cash be posted to secure compliance by the respondent with the order for support for such period. Such undertaking shall be for a definite period, not to exceed three years, and the required amount of the principal of such undertaking shall not exceed the total payments for support required for three years and shall be so stated in the order for support. After hearing and for good cause shown, the court may extend an undertaking requirement by requiring a new undertaking similar to the original undertaking. The respondent may deposit cash with the clerk, or when the court so orders, with the support collection unit designated by the appropriate social services district, when the order for support directs payments to such unit. When such cash has been deposited with the support collection unit and the respondent fails to make any payment, when due, within such period, payment shall be made by the support collection unit to the petitioner out of such cash. When cash is posted as security, as herein provided, the person or persons so posting such cash shall at the expiration of the period for which such security shall have been ordered be entitled to the return of such cash less any amount which shall have been paid therefrom to the petitioner by reason of any default or defaults in payments on the part of the respondent. The form of the undertaking and the form and manner of justification of the surety shall conform to the rules of court.

§472. Undertaking to be filed.

If the property securing the undertaking consists of real estate, the undertaking shall be filed with the county clerk of the county in which the real estate is located and the same shall constitute a lien upon the real estate specified in the undertaking. The county clerk of each county is hereby directed to accept such undertakings for filing and to provide proper and sufficient books and indexes wherein the same shall be entered.

§473. Substitution of surety.

The court may at any time thereafter, before or after there has been a default, if all arrears have been paid in case there shall have been a default on such undertaking, accept a new undertaking in lieu of the original undertaking, and the court shall enter an order discharging such undertaking.

§474. Default.

A default in the terms of the order shall constitute a breach of the undertaking. When there has been a default the court shall cause an affidavit to be drawn, verified and filed by any person familiar with the facts. The surety shall thereupon be personally served, or served by registered mail at the address given in the undertaking or subsequent address furnished by said surety in writing, with notice of such default and shall be required to attend at the court on a day certain and show cause why judgment should not be entered on the undertaking and the amount thereof applied to the relief of the petitioner for the amount in default. If the surety appears and pays the amount in arrears the court may remit the forfeiture. Inability to serve the surety shall not be prejudicial to the renewal of proceedings against the respondent.

§475. Procedure as to defaults.
If the surety contests the default the court shall hear and determine the issue. In the event that the court finds that a default has been suffered, it shall make an order specifying the amount in default and forfeiting the undertaking or cash deposit to the extent of such default. A certified copy of such order shall be filed in the county clerk's office with a certified copy of the undertaking and thereupon the said clerk shall docket the same in the book kept by the clerk for the docketing of judgments, as if the same was a transcript of a judgment directed for the amount of such sum in default. The certified copy of the undertaking and of the order shall be the judgment record. Such judgment shall be a lien on all of the real estate and collectible out of the real and personal property of the surety. An execution may be issued to collect the amount thereof in the same manner as upon a judgment recovered in any court of record.

§476. Forfeitures applied to support of petitioner.
(a) All sums collected from the surety by judgment as well as forfeited cash deposits shall be applied by the clerk of court to the support of the petitioners for whose benefit the order for support was made. Subsequent defaults shall be proceeded upon in the same manner until the amount of the principal of the undertaking or the cash deposited has been recovered in full.

(b) Where the respondent, or any one in his behalf, shall have deposited with the court monies as surety for compliance with the terms of the order of support and the respondent shall have died, the court may make an order directing the payment to the petitioner of all monies still in possession of the court in conformance with the order of support.

§477. Surrender of respondent by surety.
A surety may at any time surrender a respondent to the court. The respondent shall thereupon be dealt with as provided in the order for support. If the arrears on the order for support with interest thereon are paid in full, the court may make an order discharging the surety of any further liability and directing the return of the balance of the cash on deposit to the person entitled thereto.

§478. Termination of surety's liability.
Whenever the liability on an undertaking has ceased, the court shall make an order to that effect. Upon receipt of a certified copy of the order, the county clerk shall discharge of record the lien of the undertaking.

§479. When new security required.
After an undertaking has been given or cash has been deposited and it shall appear upon proof by affidavit either
(a) that a judgment entered upon default can not be collected; or
(b) that the liability of the surety has ceased; or
(c) that the money deposited has been applied in full; or
(d) that personal service cannot be effected upon the surety or the person depositing the cash; or
(e) if for any reason the court shall find that there is not sufficient security, the court may issue a summons requiring the respondent to appear or a warrant for the arrest of the respondent, and require him to give new or additional security. In default thereof the court may commit him under the original order in the manner hereinabove provided.

ARTICLE 5
Paternity Proceedings

Part 1
Jurisdiction and Duties to Support

§511. Jurisdiction.

Except as otherwise provided, the family court has exclusive original jurisdiction in proceedings to establish paternity and, in any such proceedings in which it makes a finding of paternity, to order support and to make orders of custody or of visitation, as set forth in this article. On its own motion, the court may at any time in the proceedings also direct the filing of a neglect petition in accord with the provisions of article ten of this act. In accordance with the provisions of section one hundred eleven-b of the domestic relations law, the surrogate's court has original jurisdiction concurrent with the family court to determine the issues relating to the establishment of paternity.

§512. Definitions.

When used in this article,

(a) The phrase "child born out of wedlock" refers to a child who is begotten and born out of lawful matrimony.

(b) The word "child" refers to a child born out of wedlock.

(c) The word "mother" refers to the mother of a child born out of wedlock.

(d) The word "father" refers to the father of a child born out-of-wedlock.

§513. Obligation of parents.

Subject to the provisions of paragraph (f) of subdivision six of section three hundred ninety-eight of the social services law, each parent of a child born out of wedlock is chargeable with the support of such child including the child's funeral expenses and, if possessed of sufficient means or able to earn such means, shall be required to pay child support. A court shall make an award for child support pursuant to subdivision one of section four hundred thirteen of this act.

§514. Liability of father to mother.

The father is liable for the reasonable expenses of the mother's confinement and recovery and such reasonable expenses in connection with her pregnancy as determined by the court; provided, however, where the mother's confinement, recovery and expenses in connection with her pregnancy were paid under the medical assistance program on the mother's behalf, the father may be liable to the social services district furnishing such medical assistance and to the state department of health for medical assistance so expended. Such expenses, including such expenses paid by the medical assistance program on the mother's behalf, shall be deemed cash medical support and the court shall determine the obligation of the parties to contribute to the cost thereof pursuant to subparagraph five of paragraph (c) of subdivision one of section four hundred thirteen of this act.

§515.　Governmental obligation to child.

In case of the neglect or inability of the parents to provide for the support and education of the child, it shall be supported by the county, city or town chargeable therewith under the provisions of the social welfare law.

§516-a.　Acknowledgment of paternity.

(a) An acknowledgment of paternity executed pursuant to section one hundred eleven-k of the social services law or section four thousand one hundred thirty-five-b of the public health law shall establish the paternity of and liability for the support of a child pursuant to this act. Such acknowledgment must be reduced to writing and filed pursuant to section four thousand one hundred thirty-five-b of the public health law with the registrar of the district in which the birth occurred and in which the birth certificate has been filed. No further judicial or administrative proceedings are required to ratify an unchallenged acknowledgment of paternity.

(b) (i) Where a signatory to an acknowledgment of paternity executed pursuant to section one hundred eleven-k of the social services law or section four thousand one hundred thirty-five-b of the public health law had attained the age of eighteen at the time of execution of the acknowledgment, the signatory may seek to rescind the acknowledgment by filing a petition with the court to vacate the acknowledgment within the earlier of sixty days of the date of signing the acknowledgment or the date of an administrative or a judicial proceeding (including, but not limited to, a proceeding to establish a support order) relating to the child in which the signatory is a party. For purposes of this section, the ''date of an administrative or a judicial proceeding'' shall be the date by which the respondent is required to answer the petition.

(ii) Where a signatory to an acknowledgment of paternity executed pursuant to section one hundred eleven-k of the social services law or section four thousand one hundred thirty-five-b of the public health law had not attained the age of eighteen at the time of execution of the acknowledgment, the signatory may seek to rescind the acknowledgment by filing a petition with the court to vacate the acknowledgment anytime up to sixty days after the signatory's attaining the age of eighteen years or sixty days after the date on which the respondent is required to answer a petition (including, but not limited to, a petition to establish a support order) relating to the child in which the signatory is a party, whichever is earlier; provided, however, that the signatory must have been advised at such proceeding of his or her right to file a petition to vacate the acknowledgment within sixty days of the date of such proceeding.

(iii) Where a petition to vacate an acknowledgment of paternity has been filed in accordance with paragraph (i) or (ii) of this subdivision, the court shall order genetic marker tests or DNA tests for the determination of the child's paternity. No such test shall be ordered, however, upon a written finding by the court that it is not in the best interests of the child on the basis of res judicata, equitable estoppel, or the presumption of legitimacy of a child born to a married woman. If the court determines, following the test, that the person who signed the acknowledgment is the father of the child, the court shall make a finding of paternity and enter an order of filiation. If the court determines that the person who signed the acknowledgment is not the father of the child, the acknowledgment shall be vacated.

(iv) After the expiration of the time limits set forth in paragraphs (i) and (ii) of this subdivision, any of the signatories to an acknowledgment of paternity may challenge the acknowledgment in court by alleging and proving fraud, duress, or material mistake of fact. If the petitioner proves to the court that the acknowledgment of paternity was signed under fraud, duress, or due to a material mistake of fact, the court shall then order genetic marker tests or DNA tests for the determination of the child's paternity. No such test shall be ordered, however, upon a written finding by the court that it is not in the best interests of the child on the basis of res judicata, equitable estoppel, or the presumption of legitimacy of a child born to a married woman. If the court determines, following the test, that the person who signed the acknowledgment is the father of the child, the court shall make a finding of paternity and enter an order of filiation. If the court determines that the person who signed the acknowledgment is not the father of the child, the acknowledgment shall be vacated.

(v) If, at any time before or after a signatory has filed a petition to vacate an acknowledgment of paternity pursuant to this subdivision, the signatory dies or becomes mentally ill or cannot be found within the state, neither the proceeding nor the right to commence the proceeding shall abate but may be commenced or continued by any of the persons authorized by this article to commence a paternity proceeding.

(c) Neither signatory's legal obligations, including the obligation for child support arising from the acknowledgment, may be suspended during the challenge to the acknowledgment except for good cause as the court may find. If the court vacates the acknowledgment of paternity, the court shall immediately provide a copy of the order to the registrar of the district in which the child's birth certificate is filed and also to the putative father registry operated by the department of social services pursuant to section three hundred seventy-two-c of the social services law. In addition, if the mother of the child who is the subject of the acknowledgment is in receipt of child support services pursuant to title six-A of article three of the social services law, the court shall immediately provide a copy of the order to the child support enforcement unit of the social services district that provides the mother with such services.

(d) A determination of paternity made by any other state, whether established through an administrative or judicial process or through an acknowledgment of paternity signed in accordance with that state's laws, must be accorded full faith and credit pursuant to section 466(a)(11) of title IV-D of the social security act (42 U.S.C. § 666(a)(11)).

§517.   Time for instituting proceedings.

Proceedings to establish the paternity of a child may be instituted during the pregnancy of the mother or after the birth of the child, but shall not be brought after the child reaches the age of twenty-one years, unless paternity has been acknowledged by the father in writing or by furnishing support.

§518.　Effect of death, absence, or mental illness of mother.

If, at any time before or after a petition is filed, the mother dies or becomes mentally ill or cannot be found within the state, neither the proceeding nor the right to commence the proceeding shall abate but may be commenced or continued by any of the persons authorized by this article to commence a paternity proceeding.

§519.　Effect of death, absence or mental illness of putative father.

If, at any time before or after a petition if filed, the putative father dies, or becomes mentally ill or cannot be found within the state, neither the proceeding nor the right to commence the proceeding shall necessarily abate but may be commenced or continued by any of the persons authorized by this article to commence a paternity proceeding where:

(a) the putative father was the petitioner in the paternity proceeding; or,

(b) the putative father acknowledged paternity of the child in open court; or,

(c) a genetic marker or DNA test had been administered to the putative father prior to his death; or,

(d) the putative father has openly and notoriously acknowledged the child as his own.

Part 2
Venue and Preliminary Procedure

§521.　Venue.

Proceedings to establish paternity may be originated in the county where the mother or child resides or is found or in the county where the putative father resides or is found. The fact that the child was born outside of the state of New York does not bar a proceeding to establish paternity in the county where the putative father resides or is found or in the county where the mother resides or the child is found.

§522.　Persons who may originate proceedings.

Proceedings to establish the paternity of the child and to compel support under this article may be commenced by the mother, whether a minor or not, by a person alleging to be the father, whether a minor or not, by the child or child's guardian or other person standing in a parental relation or being the next of kin of the child, or by any authorized representative of an incorporated society doing charitable or philanthropic work, or if the mother or child is or is likely to become a public charge on a county, city or town, by a public welfare official of the county, city or town where the mother resides or the child is found. If a proceeding is originated by a public welfare official and thereafter withdrawn or dismissed without consideration on the merits, such withdrawal or dismissal shall be without prejudice to other persons.

§523. Petition.

Proceedings are commenced by the filing of a verified petition, alleging that the person named as respondent, or the petitioner if the petitioner is a person alleging to be the child's father, is the father of the child and petitioning the court to issue a summons or a warrant, requiring the respondent to show cause why the court should not enter a declaration of paternity, an order of support, and such other and further relief as may be appropriate under the circumstances. The petition shall be in writing and verified by the petitioner. Any such petition for the establishment of paternity or the establishment, modification and/or enforcement of a child support obligation for persons not in receipt of family assistance, which contains a request for child support enforcement services completed in a manner as specified in section one hundred eleven-g of the social services law, shall constitute an application for such services.

§524. Issuance of summons.

(a) On receiving a petition sufficient in law commencing a paternity proceeding, the court shall cause a summons to be issued, requiring the respondent to show cause why the declaration of paternity, order of filiation, order of support and other and further relief prayed for by the petition should not be made.

(b) The summons shall contain or have attached thereto a notice stating:

(i) that the respondent's failure to appear shall result in the default entry of an order of filiation by the court upon proof of respondent's actual notice of the commencement of the proceeding; and

(ii) that a respondent's failure to appear may result in the suspension of his or her driving privileges; state professional, occupational and business licenses; and sporting licenses and permits.

§525. Service of summons.

(a) Personal service of summons and petition shall be made by delivery of a true copy thereof to the person to be summoned at least eight days before the time stated therein for appearance; or by delivery of a true copy thereof to a person of suitable age and discretion at the actual place of business, dwelling place or usual place of abode of the person to be served and by mailing a true copy thereof to the person to be served at his last known residence at least eight days before the time stated in the summons for appearance; proof of service shall identify such person of suitable age and discretion and state the date, time and place of service. If so requested by one acting on behalf of the respondent or by a parent or other person legally responsible for his care, the court shall not proceed with the hearing or proceeding earlier than eight days after such service.

(b) If after reasonable effort, personal service is not made, the court may at any stage in the proceedings make an order providing for substituted service in the manner provided for substituted service in the civil practice law and rules.

(c) In any case, whether or not service is attempted under subdivision (a) or (b) of this section, service of a summons and petition under this section may be effected by mail alone to the last known address of the person to be served. Service by mail alone shall be made at least eight days before the time stated in the summons for appearance. If service is by mail alone, the court will enter an order of filiation by default if there is proof satisfactory to the court that the respondent had actual notice of the commencement of the proceeding, which may be established upon sufficient proof that the summons and petition were in fact mailed by certified mail and signed for at the respondent's correct street address or signed for at the post office. If service by certified mail at the respondent's correct street address cannot be accomplished, service pursuant to subdivision one, two, three or four of section three hundred eight of the civil practice law and rules shall be deemed good and sufficient service. Upon failure of the respondent to obey a summons served in accordance with the provisions of this section by means other than mail alone, the court will enter an order of filiation by default. The respondent shall have the right to make a motion for relief from such default order within one year from the date such order was entered.

§526. Issuance of warrant.

The court may issue a warrant, directing that the respondent be arrested and brought before the court, when a petition is presented to the court under section five hundred twenty-three and it appears that

(a) the summons cannot be served; or

(b) the respondent has failed to obey the summons; or

(c) the respondent is likely to leave the jurisdiction; or

(d) a summons, in the court's opinion, would be ineffectual; or

(e) the safety of the petitioner is endangered; or

(f) a respondent on bail or on parole has failed to appear.

§527. Preliminary procedure on warrant.

(a) When a respondent is taken into custody pursuant to a warrant issued by a family court in a county in New York city under section five hundred twenty-six, he or she shall be taken before the court issuing the warrant if the respondent is taken into custody in New York city. If the respondent is taken into custody in a county not within New York city, he or she shall be taken before a family court judge in that county.

(b) When a respondent is taken into custody pursuant to a warrant issued by a family court in a county not within the city of New York, he or she shall be taken before the court issuing the warrant if the respondent is taken into custody in the county in which the court sits. If the respondent is taken into custody in a different county, he or she shall be brought before a family court judge in that county.

§528. Procedure before court.

The court before whom the respondent is taken under section five hundred twenty-seven may require an undertaking to appear or in default thereof may place the respondent in custody.

Part 3
Hearings

§531. Hearing.

The trial shall be by the court without a jury. The mother or the alleged father shall be competent to testify but the respondent shall not be compelled to testify. If the mother is married both she and her husband may testify to non-access. If the respondent shall offer testimony of access by others at or about the time charged in the complaint, such testimony shall not be competent or admissible in evidence except when corroborated by other facts and circumstances tending to prove such access. The court may exclude the general public from the room where the proceedings are heard and may admit only persons directly interested in the case, including officers of the court and witnesses.

§531-a. Testimony by telephone, audio-visual means or other electronic means.

(a) In any proceeding under this article, the court may permit a party or a witness to be deposed or to testify by telephone, audio-visual means, or other electronic means at a designated family court or other location:

(i) where such party or witness resides in a county other than that of the family court where the case is pending and that of any contiguous county; provided, however, that for the purposes of this section, the five counties of New York city shall be treated as one county;

(ii) where such party or witness is presently incarcerated and will be incarcerated on the date on which the hearing or deposition is scheduled and is not expected to be released within a reasonable period of time after the date on which the hearing is scheduled; or

(iii) where the court determines that it would be an undue hardship for such party or witness to testify or to be deposed at the family court where the case is pending.

(b) Any such deposition or testimony taken by telephone, audio-visual means or other electronic means in accordance with subdivision (a) of this section shall be recorded and preserved for transcription. Where a party or witness is deposed or testifies by telephone, audio-visual or other electronic means pursuant to this section, documentary evidence referred to by a party or witness or the court may be transmitted by facsimile, telecopier, or other electronic means and may not be excluded from evidence by reason of an objection based on the means of transmission. The chief administrator of the courts shall promulgate rules to facilitate the taking of testimony by telephone, audio-visual means or other electronic means.

§532. Genetic marker and DNA tests; admissibility of records or reports of test results; costs of tests.

(a) The court shall advise the parties of their right to one or more genetic marker tests or DNA tests and, on the court's own motion or the motion of any party, shall order the mother, her child and the alleged father to submit to one or more genetic marker or DNA tests of a type generally acknowledged as reliable by an accreditation body designated by the secretary of the federal department of health and human services and performed by a laboratory approved by such an accreditation body and by the commissioner of health or by a duly qualified physician to aid in the determination of whether the alleged father is or is not the father of the child. No such test shall be ordered, however, upon a written finding by the court that it is not in the best interests of the child on the basis of res judicata, equitable estoppel, or the presumption of legitimacy of a child born to a married woman. The record or report of the results of any such genetic marker or DNA test ordered pursuant to this section or pursuant to section one hundred eleven-k of the social services law shall be received in evidence by the court pursuant to subdivision (e) of rule forty-five hundred eighteen of the civil practice law and rules where no timely objection in writing has been made thereto and that if such timely objections are not made, they shall be deemed waived and shall not be heard by the court. If the record or report of the results of any such genetic marker or DNA test or tests indicate at least a ninety-five percent probability of paternity, the admission of such record or report shall create a rebuttable presumption of paternity, and shall establish, if unrebutted, the paternity of and liability for the support of a child pursuant to this article and article four of this act.

(b) Whenever the court directs a genetic marker or DNA test pursuant to this section, a report made as provided in subdivision (a) of this section may be received in evidence pursuant to rule forty-five hundred eighteen of the civil practice law and rules if offered by any party.

(c) The cost of any test ordered pursuant to subdivision (a) of this section shall be, in the first instance, paid by the moving party. If the moving party is financially unable to pay such cost, the court may direct any qualified public health officer to conduct such test, if practicable; otherwise, the court may direct payment from the funds of the appropriate local social services district. In its order of disposition, however, the court may direct that the cost of any such test be apportioned between the parties according to their respective abilities to pay or be assessed against the party who does not prevail on the issue of paternity, unless such party is financially unable to pay.

§533. Adjournment on application of party.

The court, on application of either party, may for good cause shown grant such adjournments as may be necessary. If an adjournment is granted upon the request of either party, the court may require the respondent to give an undertaking for appearance.

§534. Adjournment on motion of court.

On its own motion, the court may adjourn the hearing after it has made a finding of paternity to enable it to make inquiry into the surroundings, conditions and capacities of the child, into the financial abilities and responsibilities of both parents or for other proper cause. If the court so adjourns the hearing, it may require the respondent to give an undertaking to appear.

§535. Counsel for social services commissioner.

(a) The corporation counsel of the city of New York shall represent the social services commissioner of such city in all proceedings under this article in which the commissioner is the petitioner.

(b) In any county outside the city of New York in which attorneys have been appointed pursuant to section sixty-six of the social services law, such attorneys may represent the social services commissioner of such county in all proceedings under this article in which the commissioner is the petitioner.

(c) Except as provided in subdivision (b) of this section, in any county outside the city of New York, the county attorney, or an attorney designated by the county executive, if there be one, otherwise by the board of supervisors, shall represent the social services commissioner of the county in all proceedings under this article in which the commissioner is the petitioner.

§536. Counsel fees.

Once an order of filiation is made, the court in its discretion may allow counsel fees to the attorney for the prevailing party, if he or she is unable to pay such counsel fees. Representation by an attorney pursuant to paragraph (b) of subdivision nine of section one hundred eleven-b of the social services law shall not preclude an award of counsel fees to an applicant which would otherwise be allowed under this section.

Part 4
Orders

§541. Order dismissing petition.

If the court finds the male party is not the father of the child, it shall dismiss the petition. If a neglect petition was filed in the paternity proceeding, the court retains jurisdiction over the neglect petition whether or not it dismisses the paternity petition.

§542. Order of filiation.

(a) If the court finds the male party is the father of the child, it shall make an order of filiation, declaring paternity. Such order shall contain the social security number of the declared father.

(b) If the respondent willfully fails to appear before the court subsequent to the administration and analysis of a genetic marker test or DNA test administered pursuant to sections four hundred eighteen and five hundred thirty-two of this act or section one hundred eleven-k of the social services law, and if such test does not exclude the respondent as being the father of the child or the court determines that there exists clear and convincing evidence of paternity, the court shall enter an order of temporary support notwithstanding that paternity of such child has not been established nor an order of filiation entered against the respondent. The respondent shall be prospectively relieved from liability for support under such order of temporary support upon the respondent's appearance before the court.

(c) If the respondent willfully fails to comply with an order made by either the court pursuant to sections four hundred eighteen and five hundred thirty-two of this act or by a social services official or designee pursuant to section one hundred eleven-k of the social services law, and willfully fails to appear before the court when otherwise required, the court shall enter an order of temporary support notwithstanding that paternity of the subject child has not been established nor an order of filiation entered against the respondent. The respondent shall be prospectively relieved from liability for support under such order of temporary support upon the respondent's compliance with such order and subsequent appearance before the court.

§543. Transmission of order of filiation.

When an order of filiation is made, the clerk of the court shall forthwith transmit to the state commissioner of health on a form prescribed by him a written notification as to such order, together with such other facts as may assist in identifying the birth record of the person whose paternity was in issue. When it appears to the clerk that the person whose paternity was established was born in New York city, he shall forthwith transmit the written notification aforesaid to the commissioner of health of the city of New York instead of to the state commissioner of health.

§544. Transmission of abrogation of filiation order.

If an order of filiation is abrogated by a later judgment or order of the court that originally made the order or by another court on appeal, that fact shall be immediately communicated in writing by the clerk of the court that originally made the order of filiation to the state commissioner of health on a form prescribed by him. If notice of the order was given to the commissioner of health of New York city, notice of abrogation shall be transmitted to him.

§545. Order of support by parents.

1. In a proceeding in which the court has made an order of filiation, the court shall direct the parent or parents possessed of sufficient means or able to earn such means to pay weekly or at other fixed periods a fair and reasonable sum according to their respective means as the court may determine and apportion for such child's support and education, until the child is twenty-one. The order shall be effective as of the earlier of the date of the application for an order of filiation, or, if the children for whom support is sought are in receipt of public assistance, the date for which their eligibility for public assistance was effective. Any retroactive amount of child support shall be support arrears/past-due support and shall be paid in one sum or periodic sums as the court shall direct, taking into account any amount of temporary support which has been paid. In addition, such retroactive child support shall be enforceable in any manner provided by law including, but not limited to, an execution for support enforcement pursuant to subdivision (b) of section fifty-two hundred forty-one of the civil practice law and rules. The court shall direct such parent to make his or her residence known at all times should he or she move from the address last known to the court by reporting such change to the support collection unit designated by the appropriate social services district. The order shall contain the social security numbers of the named parents. The order may also direct each parent to pay an amount as the court may determine and apportion for the support of the child prior to the making of the order of filiation, and may direct each parent to pay an amount as the court may determine and apportion for the funeral expenses if the child has died. The necessary expenses incurred by or for the mother in connection with her confinement and recovery and such expenses in connection with the pregnancy of the mother shall be deemed cash medical support, and the court shall determine the obligation of either or both parents to contribute to the cost thereof pursuant to subparagraph five of paragraph (c) of subdivision one of section four hundred thirteen of this act. In addition, the court shall make

provisions for health insurance benefits in accordance with the requirements of section four hundred sixteen of this act.

2. The court, in its discretion, taking into consideration the means of the father and his ability to pay and the needs of the child, may direct the payment of a reasonable sum or periodic sums to the mother as reimbursement for the needs of the child accruing from the date of the birth of the child to the date of the application for an order of filiation.

§546. Payment to parent or support collection unit.

(a) The court may require the payment to be made to the parent having custody of the child or to the support collection unit as designated by the appropriate social services district.

(b) The support collection unit as designated by the appropriate social services district shall report to the court as the court may direct, the amounts received and paid over.

§547. Substitution of trustee.

The court, on motion of a party or otherwise, may at any time for good cause shown substitute another trustee for the one designated and acting.

§548. Compliance with orders.

The provisions of part five and part seven of article four of this act apply when an order is issued under this article.

§548-a. Paternity or child support proceedings; suspension of driving privileges.

(a) If the respondent, after receiving appropriate notice, fails to comply with a summons, subpoena or warrant relating to a paternity or child support proceeding, the court may order the department of motor vehicles to suspend the respondent's driving privileges.

(b) The court may subsequently order the department of motor vehicles to terminate the suspension of the respondent's driving privileges; however, the court shall order the termination of such suspension when the court is satisfied that the respondent has fully complied with the requirements of all summonses, subpoenas and warrants relating to a paternity or child support proceeding.

§548-b. Paternity or child support proceedings; suspension of state professional, occupational and business licenses.

(a) If the respondent, after receiving appropriate notice, fails to comply with a summons, subpoena or warrant relating to a paternity or child support proceeding, and the court has determined that the respondent is licensed, permitted or registered by or with a board, department, authority or office of this state or one of its political subdivisions or instrumentalities to conduct a trade, business, profession or occupation, the court may order such board, department, authority or office to commence proceedings as required by law regarding the suspension of such license, permit, registration or authority to practice and to inform the court of the actions it has taken pursuant to such proceeding.

(b) The court may subsequently order such board, department, authority or office to terminate the suspension of the respondent's license, permit, registration or authority to practice; however, the court shall order the termination of such suspension when the court is satisfied that the respondent has fully complied with all summons, subpoenas and warrants relating to a paternity or child support proceeding.

§548-c. **Paternity or child support proceedings; suspension of recreational licenses.**

If the respondent, after receiving appropriate notice, fails to comply with a summons, subpoena, or warrant relating to a paternity or child support proceeding, the court may order any agency responsible for the issuance of a recreational license to suspend or to refuse to reissue a license to the respondent or to deny application for such license by the respondent. The court may subsequently order such agency to terminate the adverse action regarding the respondent's license; however, the court shall order the termination of such suspension or other adverse action when the court is satisfied that the respondent has fully complied with the requirements of all summons, subpoenas, and warrants relating to a paternity or child support proceeding.

§549. **Order of visitation.**

(a) If an order of filiation is made or if a paternity agreement or compromise is approved by the court, in the absence of an order of custody or of visitation entered by the supreme court the family court may make an order of custody or of visitation, in accordance with subdivision one of section two hundred forty of the domestic relations law, requiring one parent to permit the other to visit the child or children at stated periods.

(b) Any order of the family court under this section shall terminate when the supreme court makes an order of custody or of visitation concerning the child or children, unless the supreme court continues the order of the family court.

§550. **Temporary order of protection.**

(a) Upon the filing of a petition or counter-claim under this article, the court for good cause shown may issue a temporary order of protection which may contain any of the provisions authorized on the making of an order of protection under section five hundred fifty-one.

(b) A temporary order of protection is not a finding of wrongdoing.

(c) The court may issue or extend a temporary order of protection ex parte or on notice simultaneously with the issuance of a warrant directing that the respondent be arrested and brought before the court pursuant to section five hundred twenty-six of this article. Notwithstanding the foregoing provisions, an order of protection, or temporary order of protection where applicable, may be entered against a former spouse and persons who have a child in common, regardless of whether such persons have been married or have lived together at any time, or against a member of the same family or household as defined in subdivision one of section eight hundred twelve of this act.

§551. **Order of protection.**

The court may make an order of protection in assistance or as a condition of any other order made under this article. The order of protection may set forth reasonable conditions of behavior to be observed for a specified time by the petitioner or respondent or both. No order of protection may direct any party to observe conditions of behavior unless the party requesting the order of protection has served and filed a petition or counter-claim in accordance with section one hundred fifty-four-b of this act. Such an order may require the petitioner or the respondent:

(a) to stay away from the home, school, business or place of employment of any other party, the other parent, or the child, and to stay away from any other specific location designated by the court;

(b) to permit a parent, or a person entitled to visitation by a court order or a separation agreement to visit the child at stated periods;

(c) to refrain from committing a family offense, as defined in subdivision one of section eight hundred twelve of this act, or any criminal offense against the child or against the other parent or against any person to whom custody of the child is awarded, or from harassing, intimidating or threatening such persons;

(d) to permit a designated party to enter the residence during a specified period of time in order to remove personal belongings not in issue in this proceeding or in any other proceeding or action under this act or the domestic relations law;

(e) to refrain from acts of commission or omission that create an unreasonable risk to the health, safety or welfare of a child;

(f) to participate in an educational program and to pay the costs thereof if the person has the means to do so, provided, however, that nothing contained herein shall be deemed to require payment of the costs of any such program by the state or any political subdivision thereof;

(g) to provide, either directly or by means of medical and health insurance, for expenses incurred for medical care and treatment arising from the incident or incidents forming the basis for the issuance of the order;

(h) to pay the reasonable counsel fees and disbursements involved in obtaining or enforcing the order of the person who is protected by such order if such order is issued or enforced, whether or not an order of filiation is made;

(i) 1. to refrain from intentionally injuring or killing, without justification, any companion animal the respondent knows to be owned, possessed, leased, kept or held by the person protected by the order or a minor child residing in such person's household.

2. "Companion animal", as used in this section, shall have the same meaning as in subdivision five of section three hundred fifty of the agriculture and markets law;

(j) 1. to promptly return specified identification documents to the protected party, in whose favor the order of protection or temporary order of protection is issued; provided, however, that such order may: (A) include any appropriate provision designed to ensure that any such document is available for use as evidence in this proceeding, and available if necessary for legitimate use by the party against whom such order is issued; and (B) specify the manner in which such return shall be accomplished.

2. For purposes of this subdivision, "identification document" shall mean any of the following: (A) exclusively in the name of the protected party: birth certificate, passport, social security card, health insurance or other benefits card, a card or document used to access bank, credit or other financial accounts or records, tax returns, any driver's license, and immigration documents including but not limited to a United States permanent resident card and employment authorization document; and (B) upon motion and after notice and an opportunity to be heard, any of the following, including those that may reflect joint use or ownership, that the court determines are necessary and are appropriately transferred to the protected party: any card or document used to access bank, credit or other financial accounts or records, tax returns, and any other identifying cards and documents; and

(k) to observe such other conditions as are necessary to further the purposes of protection.

The court may also award custody of the child, during the term of the order of protection to either parent, or to an appropriate relative within the second degree. Nothing in this section gives the court power to place or board out any child or to commit a child to an institution or agency. In making orders of protection, the court shall so act as to insure that in the care, protection, discipline and guardianship of the child his religious faith shall be preserved and protected.

Notwithstanding the foregoing provisions, an order of protection, or temporary order of protection where applicable, may be entered against a former spouse and persons who have a child in common, regardless of whether such persons have been married or have lived together at any time, or against a member of the same family or household as defined in subdivision one of section eight hundred twelve of this act.

In any proceeding pursuant to this article, a court shall not deny an order of protection, or dismiss an application for such an order, solely on the basis that the acts or events alleged are not relatively contemporaneous with the date of the application or the conclusion of the action. The duration of any temporary order shall not by itself be a factor in determining the length or issuance of any final order.

The protected party in whose favor the order of protection or temporary order of protection is issued may not be held to violate an order issued in his or her favor nor may such protected party be arrested for violating such order.

§552. Firearms; surrender and license suspension, revocation and ineligibility.

Upon the issuance of an order of protection or temporary order of protection, or upon a violation of such order, the court shall make a determination regarding the suspension and revocation of a license to carry, possess, repair or dispose of a firearm or firearms, ineligibility for such a license and the surrender of firearms in accordance with section eight hundred forty-two-a of this act.

Part 5
Related Proceedings

§561. Proceedings to compel support by mother.

Proceedings may be initiated under article four of this act to compel a mother who fails to support her child to do so in accord with the provisions of article four of this act.

§562. Proceedings to compel support by mother and father.

Proceedings to compel a father who does not deny paternity of a child and the mother of the child to support the child may be instituted in accord with the provisions of article four of this act, unless an agreement or compromise is made in accord with section five hundred seventeen.

§563. Paternity and support proceedings combined; apportionment.

When a proceeding to establish paternity is initiated under this article, the court on its own motion or on motion of any person qualified under article four of this act to file a support petition may direct the filing of a petition under article four to compel the mother to support her child. If the court enters an order of filiation, it may apportion the costs of the support and education of the child between the parents according to their respective means and responsibilities.

§564. Order of filiation in other proceedings.

(a) In any proceeding in the family court, whether under this act or under any other law, if there is an allegation or statement in a petition that a person is the father of a child who is a party to the proceeding or also is a subject of the proceeding and if it shall appear that the child is a child born out-of-wedlock, the court may make an order of filiation declaring the paternity of the child in accordance with the provisions of this section.

(b) The court may make such an order of filiation if (1) both parents are before the court, (2) the father waives both the filing of a petition under section five hundred twenty-three of this act and the right to a hearing under section five hundred thirty-three of this act, and (3) the court is satisfied as to the paternity of the child from the testimony or sworn statements of the parents.

(c) The court may in any such proceeding in its discretion direct either the mother or any other person empowered under section five hundred twenty-two of this act to file a verified petition under section five hundred twenty-three of this act.

(d) The provisions of part four of this article five shall apply to any order of filiation made under this section. The court may in its discretion direct a severance of proceedings upon such order of filiation from the proceeding upon the petition referred to in subdivision (a) of this section.

(e) For the purposes of this section the term "petition" shall include a complaint in a civil action, an accusatory instrument under the criminal procedure law, a writ of habeas corpus, a petition for supplemental relief, and any amendment in writing of any of the foregoing.

§565. A proceeding to challenge testing directive.

The court is authorized to hear and decide motions to challenge a directive by the department of social services requiring a party to submit to genetic testing, pursuant to section one hundred eleven-k of the social services law. Nothing contained in this section shall be deemed to preclude the authority of a local social services district from filing a petition pursuant to this article.

ARTICLE 5-A
Special Provisions Relating to
Enforcement of Support
and Establishment of Paternity

Section
571.   Enforcement of support and establishment of paternity.

§571. Enforcement of support and establishment of paternity.

1. Any inconsistent provision of this law or any other law notwithstanding, in cases where a social services official has accepted, on behalf of the state and a social services district, an assignment of support rights from a person applying for or receiving family assistance in accordance with the provisions

of the social services law, the social services official or an authorized representative of the state is authorized to bring a proceeding or proceedings in the family court pursuant to article four of this act to enforce such support rights and, when appropriate or necessary, to establish the paternity of a child pursuant to article five of this act.

2. The official who brings such a proceeding and the attorney representing him shall be deemed to represent the interests of all persons, officials and agencies having an interest in the assignment. The court shall determine, in accordance with applicable provisions of law, whether such person is a necessary party to the proceeding and whether independent counsel need be appointed to represent any party to the assignment or any other person having an interest in the support right.

3. (a) Any support order made by the court in such a proceeding shall direct that payments be made directly to the support collection unit, as designated by the appropriate social services district, so long as there is in effect an assignment of support rights to such district. Further, the order shall provide that when the person or family no longer receives public assistance, payments shall continue to be made to the support collection unit, unless the person or family requests otherwise. When the person or family is no longer receiving public assistance, the social services district shall notify the parties to the order that the person or family upon request to the social services official and without further judicial intervention may receive support payments directly. If such a request is made, the person paying support shall be so notified and shall be informed that unless such person applies for an order pursuant to section four hundred forty of this act within thirty days, the person or family may receive such payments directly.

(b) The entry of an order of support under this section shall not preclude an assignor who is no longer receiving public assistance from instituting a support proceeding and receiving a hearing de novo on the amount of support to which the assignor is entitled at that time.

4. Any order for support made by the court in such a proceeding shall specify the amount of support to be paid on behalf of the spouse, if any, and the amount to be paid on behalf of each child.

5. In cases where a support agreement or compromise is entered into between a social services official and the absent parent, the social services official may petition the court for approval of such agreement or compromise in accordance with the provisions of section four hundred twenty-five of this chapter, which provisions shall apply thereto.

6. In cases where an order for support has been made by a family court and upon notification to the court that an assignment of support rights has thereafter been made to the social services official responsible for furnishing family assistance, payments pursuant to such order shall be made to such official until he or she notifies the court of the termination of the assignment.

7. Any inconsistent provision of the law notwithstanding, the provision of this section shall also apply to cases brought in accordance with title six-A of article three of the social services law involving persons who are not applicants for or recipients of family assistance.

8. Any other inconsistent provision of law notwithstanding, if an applicant for or recipient of family assistance is pregnant, and a proceeding to establish paternity has been filed, and the allegation of paternity is denied by the respondent there shall be a stay of all paternity proceedings until sixty days after the birth of the child.

9. Any order of support made pursuant to this section shall be effective as of the date of the application therefor, and any retroactive amount of support shall be paid in one sum or periodic sums as the court shall direct, taking into account any amount of temporary support which has been paid.

10. (a) When a person has applied for and is receiving public assistance and care and an assignment of support rights has been made or has applied for and is receiving child support enforcement services pursuant to section one hundred eleven-g of the social services law, or is receiving such services in another state, and such person has an existing order of support which does not direct that support payments be made to the support collection unit, the social services district shall, upon notice to the parties and without further judicial intervention, direct that support payments be made directly to the appropriate support collection unit.

(b) When a child is in foster care, in this state or in another state, and where there is an existing order for the support of such child which does not direct that support payments be made to the support collection unit, the social services district shall, upon notice to the parties and without further judicial intervention, direct that support payments be made directly to the appropriate support collection unit.

11. A support order of another state payable to a support collection unit as a result of a notice pursuant to this section or through a court order shall be deemed to be an order on behalf of persons receiving services under title six-A of article three of the social services law and shall be enforceable in the same manner as such orders.

ARTICLE 5-B
Uniform Interstate Family Support Act

Part 1
General Provisions

§580-101.   Short title.

This article may be cited as the "uniform interstate family support act" or "UIFSA".

§580-102.   Definitions.

In this article:

(1) "Child" means an individual, whether over or under the age of majority, who is or is alleged to be owed a duty of support by the individual's parent or

who is or is alleged to be the beneficiary of a support order directed to the parent.

(2) "Child support order" means a support order for a child, including a child who has attained the age of majority under the law of the issuing state or foreign country.

(3) "Convention" means the Convention on the International Recovery of Child Support and Other Forms of Family Maintenance, concluded at The Hague on November twenty-third, two thousand seven.

(4) "Duty of support" means an obligation imposed or imposable by law to provide support for a child, spouse, or former spouse, including an unsatisfied obligation to provide support.

(5) "Foreign country" means a country, including a political subdivision thereof, other than the United States, that authorizes the issuance of support orders and:

(i) which has been declared under the law of the United States to be a foreign reciprocating country;

(ii) which has established a reciprocal arrangement for child support with this state as provided in section 580-308 of this article;

(iii) which has enacted a law or established procedures for the issuance and enforcement of support orders which are substantially similar to the procedures under this article; or

(iv) in which the Convention is in force with respect to the United States.

(6) "Foreign support order" means a support order of a foreign tribunal.

(7) "Foreign tribunal" means a court, administrative agency or quasi-judicial entity of a foreign country which is authorized to establish, enforce or modify support orders, or to determine parentage of a child. The term includes a competent authority under the Convention.

(8) "Home state" means the state or foreign country in which a child lived with a parent or a person acting as parent for at least six consecutive months immediately preceding the time of filing of a petition or comparable pleading for support and, if a child is less than six months old, the state or foreign country in which the child lived from birth with any of them. A period of temporary absence of any of them is counted as part of the six-month or other period.

(9) "Income" includes earnings or other periodic entitlements to money from any source and any other property subject to withholding for support as defined by section five thousand two hundred forty-one of the civil practice law and rules.

(10) "Income withholding order" means an order or other legal process directed to an obligor's employer, an income payor as defined by section five thousand two hundred forty-one or five thousand two hundred forty-two of the civil practice law and rules, or other debtor to withhold support from the income of the obligor.

(11) "Initiating tribunal" means the tribunal of a state or foreign country from which a petition or comparable pleading is forwarded or in which a petition or comparable pleading is filed for forwarding to another state or foreign country.

(12) "Issuing foreign country" means the foreign country in which a tribunal issues a support order or a judgment determining parentage of a child.

(13) "Issuing state" means the state in which a tribunal issues a support order or a judgment determining parentage of a child.

(14) "Issuing tribunal" means the tribunal of a state or foreign country that issues a support order or a judgment determining parentage of a child.

(15) "Law" includes decisional and statutory law and rules and regulations having the force of law.

(16) "Obligee" means:

(i) an individual to whom a duty of support is or is alleged to be owed or in whose favor a support order or a judgment determining parentage of a child has been issued;

(ii) a foreign country, state or political subdivision of a state to which the rights under a duty of support or support order have been assigned or which has independent claims based on financial assistance provided to an individual obligee in place of child support;

(iii) an individual seeking a judgment determining parentage of the individual's child; or

(iv) a person that is a creditor in a proceeding under part seven of this article.

(17) "Obligor" means an individual, or the estate of a decedent that:

(i) owes or is alleged to owe a duty of support;

(ii) is alleged but has not been adjudicated to be a parent of a child;

(iii) is liable under a support order; or

(iv) is a debtor in a proceeding under part seven of this article.

(18) "Outside this state" means a location in another state or a country other than the United States, whether or not the country is a foreign country.

(19) "Person" means an individual, corporation, business trust, estate, trust, partnership, limited liability company, association, joint venture, public corporation, government or governmental subdivision, agency or instrumentality, or any other legal or commercial entity.

(20) "Record" means information that is inscribed on a tangible medium or that is stored in an electronic or other medium and is retrievable in perceivable form.

(21) "Register" means to file in a tribunal of this state a support order or judgment determining parentage of a child issued in another state or a foreign country.

(22) "Registering tribunal" means a tribunal in which a support order or judgment determining parentage of a child is registered.

(23) "Responding state" means a state in which a petition or comparable pleading for support or to determine parentage of a child is filed or to which a petition or comparable pleading is forwarded for filing from another state or a foreign country.

(24) "Responding tribunal" means the authorized tribunal in a responding state or foreign country.

(25) "Spousal-support order" means a support order for a spouse or former spouse of the obligor.

(26) "State" means a state of the United States, the District of Columbia, Puerto Rico, the United States Virgin Islands, or any territory or insular possession under the jurisdiction of the United States. The term includes an Indian nation or tribe.

(27) "Support enforcement agency" means a public official, governmental entity or private agency authorized to:

(i) seek enforcement of support orders or laws relating to the duty of support;

(ii) seek establishment or modification of child support;

(iii) request determination of parentage of a child;

(iv) attempt to locate obligors or their assets; or

(v) request determination of the controlling child support order.

(28) "Support order" means a judgment, decree, order, decision or directive, whether temporary, final or subject to modification, issued in a state or foreign country for the benefit of a child, a spouse or a former spouse, which provides for monetary support, health care, arrearages, retroactive support or reimbursement for financial assistance provided to an individual obligee in place of child support. The term may include related costs and fees, interest, income withholding, automatic adjustment, reasonable attorney's fees and other relief.

(29) "Tribunal" means a court, administrative agency, or quasi-judicial entity authorized to establish, enforce, or modify support orders or to determine parentage of a child.

§580-103. State tribunal and state support enforcement agencies.

(a) The family court is the tribunal of this state.

(b) The office of temporary and disability assistance and/or a social services district as defined in subdivision seven of section two of the social services law are the support enforcement agencies of this state.

§580-104. Remedies cumulative.

(a) Remedies provided by this article are cumulative and do not affect the availability of remedies under other law or the recognition of a foreign support order on the basis of comity.

(b) This article does not:

(1) provide the exclusive method of establishing or enforcing a support order under the law of this state; or

(2) grant a tribunal of this state jurisdiction to render judgment or issue an order relating to child custody or visitation in a proceeding under this article.

§580-105. Application of the article to a resident of a foreign country and foreign support proceedings.

(a) A tribunal of this state shall apply parts one through six of this article and, as applicable, part seven of this article, to a support proceeding involving:

(1) a foreign support order;

(2) a foreign tribunal; or

(3) an obligee, obligor, or child residing in a foreign country.

(b) A tribunal of this state that is requested to recognize and enforce a support order on the basis of comity may apply the procedural and substantive provisions of parts one through six of this article.

(c) Part seven of this article applies only to a support proceeding under the convention. In such a proceeding, if a provision of part seven of this article is inconsistent with parts one through six of this article, part seven of this article controls.

Part 2
Jurisdiction

§580-201. Bases for jurisdiction over nonresident.

(a) In a proceeding to establish or enforce a support order or to determine parentage of a child, a tribunal of this state may exercise personal jurisdiction over a nonresident individual or the individual's guardian or conservator if:

(1) the individual is personally served with a summons and petition within this state;

(2) the individual submits to the jurisdiction of this state by consent, by entering a general appearance, or by filing a responsive document or other action having the effect of waiving any contest to personal jurisdiction;

(3) the individual resided with the child in this state;

(4) the individual resided in this state and provided prenatal expenses or support for the child;

(5) the child resides in this state as a result of the acts or directives of the individual;

(6) the individual engaged in sexual intercourse in this state and the child may have been conceived by that act of intercourse;

(7) the individual asserted parentage of a child in the putative father registry maintained in this state by the office of children and family services; or

(8) there is any other basis consistent with the constitutions of this state and the United States for the exercise of personal jurisdiction.

(b) The bases of personal jurisdiction set forth in subdivision (a) of this section or in any other law of this state may not be used to acquire personal jurisdiction for a tribunal of this state to modify a child support order of another state unless the requirements of section 580-611 of this article are met, or, in the case of a foreign support order, unless the requirements of section 580-615 of this article are met.

§580-202. Duration of personal jurisdiction.

Personal jurisdiction acquired by a tribunal of this state in a proceeding under this article or other law of this state relating to a support order continues as long as a tribunal of this state has continuing, exclusive jurisdiction to modify its order or continuing jurisdiction to enforce its order as provided by sections 580-205, 580-206 and 580-211 of this part.

§580-203. Initiating and responding tribunal of state.

Under this article, a tribunal of this state may serve as an initiating tribunal to forward proceedings to a tribunal of another state, and as a responding tribunal for proceedings initiated in another state or a foreign country.

§580-204. Simultaneous proceedings.

(a) A tribunal of this state may exercise jurisdiction to establish a support order if the petition or comparable pleading is filed after a pleading is filed in another state or a foreign country only if:

(1) the petition or comparable pleading in this state is filed before the expiration of the time allowed in the other state or the foreign country for filing a responsive pleading challenging the exercise of jurisdiction by the other state or the foreign country;

(2) the contesting party timely challenges the exercise of jurisdiction in the other state or the foreign country; and

(3) if relevant, this state is the home state of the child.

(b) A tribunal of this state may not exercise jurisdiction to establish a support order if the petition or comparable pleading is filed before a petition or comparable pleading is filed in another state or a foreign country if:

(1) the petition or comparable pleading in the other state or foreign country is filed before the expiration of the time allowed in this state for filing a responsive pleading challenging the exercise of jurisdiction by this state;

(2) the contesting party timely challenges the exercise of jurisdiction in this state; and

(3) if relevant, the other state or foreign country is the home state of the child.

§580-205.   Continuing exclusive jurisdiction to modify child support order.

(a) A tribunal of this state that has issued a child support order consistent with the law of this state has and shall exercise continuing, exclusive jurisdiction to modify its child support order if the order is the controlling order and:

(1) at the time of the filing of a request for modification this state is the residence of the obligor, the individual obligee or the child for whose benefit the support order is issued; or

(2) even if this state is not the residence of the obligor, the individual obligee or the child for whose benefit the support order is issued, the parties consent in a record or in open court that the tribunal of this state may continue to exercise jurisdiction to modify its order.

(b) A tribunal of this state that has issued a child support order consistent with the law of this state may not exercise continuing, exclusive jurisdiction to modify the order if:

(1) all of the parties who are individuals file consent in a record with the tribunal of this state that a tribunal of another state that has jurisdiction over at least one of the parties who is an individual or that is located in the state of residence of the child may modify the order and assume continuing, exclusive jurisdiction; or

(2) its order is not the controlling order.

(c) If a tribunal of another state has issued a child support order pursuant to the Uniform Interstate Family Support Act or a law substantially similar to that act which modifies a child support order of a tribunal of this state, tribunals of this state shall recognize the continuing, exclusive jurisdiction of the tribunal of the other state.

(d) A tribunal of this state that lacks continuing, exclusive jurisdiction to modify a child support order may serve as an initiating tribunal to request a tribunal of another state to modify a support order issued in that state.

(e) A temporary support order issued ex parte or pending resolution of a jurisdictional conflict does not create continuing, exclusive jurisdiction in the issuing tribunal.

§580-206. Continuing jurisdiction to enforce child support order.
(a) A tribunal of this state that has issued a child support order consistent with the law of this state may serve as an initiating tribunal to request a tribunal of another state to enforce:
(1) the order if the order is the controlling order and has not been modified by a tribunal of another state that assumed jurisdiction pursuant to the Uniform Interstate Family Support Act; or
(2) a money judgment for arrears of support and interest on the order accrued before a determination that an order of a tribunal of another state is the controlling order.
(b) A tribunal of this state having continuing jurisdiction over a support order may act as a responding tribunal to enforce the order.

§580-207. Determination of controlling child support order.
(a) If a proceeding is brought under this article and only one tribunal has issued a child support order, the order of that tribunal controls and must be recognized.
(b) If a proceeding is brought under this article, and two or more child support orders have been issued by tribunals of this state, another state or a foreign country with regard to the same obligor and same child, a tribunal of this state having personal jurisdiction over both the obligor and individual obligee shall apply the following rules and by order shall determine which order controls and must be recognized:
(1) If only one of the tribunals would have continuing, exclusive jurisdiction under this article, the order of that tribunal controls.
(2) If more than one of the tribunals would have continuing, exclusive jurisdiction under this article:
(i) an order issued by a tribunal in the current home state of the child controls; or
(ii) if an order has not been issued in the current home state of the child, the order most recently issued controls.
(3) If none of the tribunals would have continuing, exclusive jurisdiction under this article, the tribunal of this state shall issue a child support order, which controls.
(c) If two or more child support orders have been issued for the same obligor and same child, upon request of a party who is an individual or that is a support enforcement agency, a tribunal of this state having personal jurisdiction over both the obligor and the obligee who is an individual shall determine which order controls under subdivision (b) of this section. The request may be filed with a registration for enforcement or registration for modification pursuant to part six of this article, or may be filed as a separate proceeding.
(d) A request to determine which is the controlling order must be accompanied by a copy of every child support order in effect and the applicable record of payments. The requesting party shall give notice of the request to each party whose rights may be affected by the determination.
(e) The tribunal that issued the controlling order under subdivision (a), (b) or (c) of this section has continuing jurisdiction to the extent provided in section 580-205 or 580-206 of this part.
(f) A tribunal of this state that determines by order which is the controlling order under paragraph one or two of subdivision (b) or subdivision (c) of this section, or that issues a new controlling order under paragraph three of subdivision (b) of this section, shall state in that order:

(1) the basis upon which the tribunal made its determination;

(2) the amount of prospective support, if any; and

(3) the total amount of consolidated arrears and accrued interest, if any, under all of the orders after all payments made are credited as provided by section 580-209 of this part.

(g) Within thirty days after issuance of an order determining which is the controlling order, the party obtaining the order shall file a certified copy of it in each tribunal that issued or registered an earlier order of child support. A party or support enforcement agency obtaining the order that fails to file a certified copy is subject to appropriate sanctions by a tribunal in which the issue of failure to file arises. The failure to file does not affect the validity or enforceability of the controlling order.

(h) An order that has been determined to be the controlling order, or a judgment for consolidated arrears of support and interest, if any, made pursuant to this section must be recognized in proceedings under this article.

§580-208. Child support orders for two or more obligees.

In responding to registrations or petitions for enforcement of two or more child support orders in effect at the same time with regard to the same obligor and different individual obligees, at least one of which was issued by a tribunal of another state or a foreign country, a tribunal of this state shall enforce those orders in the same manner as if the orders had been issued by a tribunal of this state.

§580-209. Credit for payments.

A tribunal of this state shall credit amounts collected for a particular period pursuant to any child support order against the amounts owed for the same period under any other child support order for support of the same child issued by a tribunal of this state, another state, or a foreign country.

§580-210. Application of article to nonresident subject to personal jurisdiction.

A tribunal of this state exercising personal jurisdiction over a nonresident in a proceeding under this article, under other law of this state relating to a support order, or recognizing a foreign support order may receive evidence from outside this state pursuant to section 580-316 of this article, communicate with a tribunal outside this state pursuant to section 580-317 of this article and obtain discovery through a tribunal outside this state pursuant to section 580-318 of this article. In all other respects, parts three through six of this article do not apply, and the tribunal shall apply the procedural and substantive law of this state.

§580-211. Continuing exclusive jurisdiction to modify spousal-support order.

(a) A tribunal of this state issuing a spousal-support order consistent with the law of this state has continuing, exclusive jurisdiction to modify the spousal-support order throughout the existence of the support obligation.

(b) A tribunal of this state may not modify a spousal-support order issued by a tribunal of another state or a foreign country having continuing, exclusive jurisdiction over that order under the law of that state or foreign country.

(c) A tribunal of this state that has continuing, exclusive jurisdiction over a spousal-support order may serve as:

(1) an initiating tribunal to request a tribunal of another state to enforce the spousal-support order issued in this state; or

(2) a responding tribunal to enforce or modify its own spousal-support order.

Part 3
Civil Provisions of General Application

§580-301.   Proceedings under article.

(a) Except as otherwise provided in this article, this part applies to all proceedings under this article.

(b) An individual petitioner or a support enforcement agency may initiate a proceeding authorized under this article by filing a petition in an initiating tribunal for forwarding to a responding tribunal or by filing a petition or a comparable pleading directly in a tribunal of another state or a foreign country which has or can obtain personal jurisdiction over the respondent.

§580-302.   Proceeding by a minor parent.

A minor parent, or a guardian or other legal representative of a minor parent, may maintain a proceeding on behalf of or for the benefit of the minor's child.

§580-303.   Application of law of state.

Except as otherwise provided in this article, a responding tribunal of this state shall:

1. apply the procedural and substantive law generally applicable to similar proceedings originating in this state and may exercise all powers and provide all remedies available in those proceedings; and

2. determine the duty of support and the amount payable in accordance with the law and support guidelines of this state.

§580-304.   Duties of initiating tribunal.

(a) Upon the filing of a petition authorized by this article, an initiating tribunal of this state shall forward the petition and its accompanying documents:

(1) to the responding tribunal or appropriate support enforcement agency in the responding state; or

(2) if the identity of the responding tribunal is unknown, to the state information agency of the responding state with a request that they be forwarded to the appropriate tribunal and that receipt be acknowledged.

(b) If requested by the responding tribunal, a tribunal of this state shall issue a certificate or other document and make findings required by the law of the responding state. If the responding tribunal is in a foreign country, upon request the tribunal of this state shall specify the amount of support sought, convert that amount into the equivalent amount in the foreign currency under applicable official or market exchange rate as publicly reported, and provide any other documents necessary to satisfy the requirements of the responding foreign tribunal.

§580-305. Duties and powers of responding tribunal.

(a) When a responding tribunal of this state receives a petition or comparable pleading from an initiating tribunal or directly pursuant to subdivision (b) of section 580-301 of this part, it shall cause the petition or pleading to be filed and notify the petitioner where and when it was filed.

(b) A responding tribunal of this state, to the extent not prohibited by other law, may do one or more of the following:

(1) establish or enforce a support order, modify a child support order, determine the controlling child support order or determine parentage of a child;

(2) order an obligor to comply with a support order, specifying the amount and the manner of compliance;

(3) order income withholding;

(4) determine the amount of any arrearages, and specify a method of payment;

(5) enforce orders by civil or criminal contempt, or both;

(6) set aside property for satisfaction of the support order;

(7) place liens and order execution on the obligor's property;

(8) order an obligor to keep the tribunal informed of the obligor's current residential address, electronic-mail address, telephone number, employer, address of employment and telephone number at the place of employment;

(9) issue a warrant for an obligor who has failed after proper notice to appear at a hearing ordered by the tribunal and enter the warrant in any local and state computer systems for criminal warrants;

(10) order the obligor to seek appropriate employment by specified methods;

(11) award reasonable attorney's fees and other fees and costs; and

(12) grant any other available remedy.

(c) A responding tribunal of this state shall include in a support order issued under this article, or in the documents accompanying the order, the calculations on which the support order is based.

(d) A responding tribunal of this state may not condition the payment of a support order issued under this article upon compliance by a party with provisions for visitation.

(e) If a responding tribunal of this state issues an order under this article, the tribunal shall send a copy of the order to the petitioner and the respondent and to the initiating tribunal, if any.

(f) If requested to enforce a support order, arrears, or judgment or modify a support order stated in a foreign currency, a responding tribunal of this state shall convert the amount stated in the foreign currency to the equivalent amount in dollars under the applicable official or market exchange rate as publicly reported.

§580-306.   Inappropriate tribunal.

If a petition or comparable pleading is received by an inappropriate tribunal of this state, the tribunal shall forward the pleading and accompanying documents to an appropriate tribunal of this state or another state and notify the petitioner where and when the pleading was sent.

§580-307.   Duties of support enforcement agency.

(a) A support enforcement agency of this state, upon request, shall provide services to a petitioner in a proceeding under this article.

(b) A support enforcement agency of this state that is providing services to the petitioner shall:

(1) take all steps necessary to enable an appropriate tribunal of this state, another state or a foreign country to obtain jurisdiction over the respondent;

(2) request an appropriate tribunal to set a date, time and place for a hearing;

(3) make a reasonable effort to obtain all relevant information, including information as to income and property of the parties;

(4) within ten days, exclusive of Saturdays, Sundays and legal holidays, after receipt of notice in a record from an initiating, responding or registering tribunal, send a copy of the notice to the petitioner;

(5) within ten days, exclusive of Saturdays, Sundays and legal holidays, after receipt of communication in a record from the respondent or the respondent's attorney, send a copy of the communication to the petitioner; and

(6) notify the petitioner if jurisdiction over the respondent cannot be obtained.

(c) A support enforcement agency of this state that requests registration of a child support order in this state for enforcement or for modification shall make reasonable efforts:

(1) to ensure that the order to be registered is the controlling order; or

(2) if two or more child support orders exist and the identity of the controlling order has not been determined, to ensure that a request for such a determination is made in a tribunal having jurisdiction to do so.

(d) A support enforcement agency of this state that requests registration and enforcement of a support order, arrears or judgment stated in a foreign currency shall convert the amounts stated in the foreign currency into the equivalent amounts in dollars under the applicable official or market exchange rate as publicly reported.

(e) A support enforcement agency of this state shall issue or request a tribunal of this state to issue a child support order and an income withholding order that redirect payment of current support, arrears, and interest if requested to do so by a support enforcement agency of another state pursuant to section 580-319 of this part.

(f) This article does not create or negate a relationship of attorney and client or other fiduciary relationship between a support enforcement agency or the attorney for the agency and the individual being assisted by the agency.

§580-308.   Duty of certain state officials.

(a) If the attorney general determines that the support enforcement agency is neglecting or refusing to provide services to an individual, the attorney general may order the agency to perform its duties under this article or may provide those services directly to the individual.

(b) The commissioner of temporary and disability assistance may determine that a foreign country has established a reciprocal arrangement for child support with this state and take appropriate action for notification of the determination.

§580-309. Private counsel.

An individual may employ private counsel to represent the individual in proceedings authorized by this article.

§580-310. Duties of state information agency.

(a) The office of temporary and disability assistance is the state information agency under this article.

(b) The state information agency shall:

(1) compile and maintain a current list, including addresses, of the tribunals in this state which have jurisdiction under this article and any support enforcement agencies in this state and transmit a copy to the state information agency of every other state;

(2) maintain a register of names and addresses of tribunals and support enforcement agencies received from other states;

(3) forward to the appropriate tribunal in the county in this state in which the obligee who is an individual or the obligor resides, or in which the obligor's property is believed to be located, all documents concerning a proceeding under this article received from another state or a foreign country; and

(4) obtain information concerning the location of the obligor and the obligor's property within this state not exempt from execution, by such means as postal verification and federal or state locator services, examination of telephone directories, requests for the obligor's address from employers and examination of governmental records, including, to the extent not prohibited by other law, those relating to real property, vital statistics, law enforcement, taxation, motor vehicles, driver's licenses and social security.

§580-311. Pleadings and accompanying documents.

(a) In a proceeding under this article, a petitioner seeking to establish a support order, to determine parentage of a child or to register and modify a support order of a tribunal of another state or a foreign country must file a petition. Unless otherwise ordered under section 580-312 of this part, the petition or accompanying documents must provide, so far as known, the name, residential address and social security numbers of the obligor and the obligee or the parent and alleged parent, and the name, sex, residential address, social security number and date of birth of each child for whose benefit support is sought or whose parentage is to be determined. Unless filed at the time of registration, the petition must be accompanied by a copy of any support order known to have been issued by another tribunal. The petition may include any other information that may assist in locating or identifying the respondent.

(b) The petition must specify the relief sought. The petition and accompanying documents must conform substantially with the requirements imposed by the forms mandated by federal law for use in cases filed by a support enforcement agency.

§580-312. Nondisclosure of information in exceptional circumstances.
If a party alleges in an affidavit or a pleading under oath that the health, safety or liberty of a party or child would be jeopardized by disclosure of specific identifying information, that information must be sealed and may not be disclosed to the other party or the public. After a hearing in which a tribunal takes into consideration the health, safety or liberty of the party or child, the tribunal may order disclosure of information that the tribunal determines to be in the interest of justice.

§580-313. Costs and fees.
(a) The petitioner may not be required to pay a filing fee or other costs.

(b) If an obligee prevails, a responding tribunal of this state may assess against an obligor filing fees, reasonable attorney's fees, other costs, and necessary travel and other reasonable expenses incurred by the obligee and the obligee's witnesses. The tribunal may not assess fees, costs or expenses against the obligee or the support enforcement agency of either the initiating or responding state or foreign country, except as provided by other law. Attorney's fees may be taxed as costs, and may be ordered paid directly to the attorney, who may enforce the order in the attorney's own name. Payment of support owed to the obligee has priority over fees, costs, and expenses.

(c) The tribunal shall order the payment of costs and reasonable attorney's fees if it determines that a hearing was requested primarily for delay. In a proceeding under part six of this article, a hearing is presumed to have been requested primarily for delay if a registered support order is confirmed or enforced without change.

§580-314. Limited immunity of petitioner.
(a) Participation by a petitioner in a proceeding under this article before a responding tribunal, whether in person, by private attorney or through services provided by the support enforcement agency, does not confer personal jurisdiction over the petitioner in another proceeding.

(b) A petitioner is not amenable to service of civil process while physically present in this state to participate in a proceeding under this article.

(c) The immunity granted by this section does not extend to civil litigation based on acts unrelated to a proceeding under this article committed by a party while physically present in this state to participate in the proceeding.

§580-315. Nonparentage as defense.
A party whose parentage of a child has been previously determined by or pursuant to law may not plead nonparentage as a defense to a proceeding under this article.

§580-316. Special rules of evidence and procedure.
(a) The physical presence of a nonresident party who is an individual in a tribunal of this state is not required for the establishment, enforcement or modification of a support order, or the rendition of a judgment determining parentage of a child.

(b) An affidavit, a document substantially complying with federally mandated forms or a document incorporated by reference in any of them, which would not be excluded under the hearsay rule if given in person, is admissible in evidence if given under penalty of perjury by a party or witness residing outside this state.

(c) A copy of the record of child support payments certified as a true copy of the original by the custodian of the record may be forwarded to a responding tribunal. The copy is evidence of facts asserted in it, and is admissible to show whether payments were made.

(d) Copies of bills for testing for parentage of a child, and for prenatal and postnatal health care of the mother and child, furnished to the adverse party at least ten days before trial, are admissible in evidence to prove the amount of the charges billed and that the charges were reasonable, necessary and customary.

(e) Documentary evidence transmitted from outside this state to a tribunal of this state by telephone, telecopier or other electronic means that do not provide an original record may not be excluded from evidence on an objection based on the means of transmission.

(f) In a proceeding under this article, a tribunal of this state shall permit a party or witness residing outside this state to be deposed or to testify under penalty of perjury by telephone, audiovisual means or other electronic means at a designated tribunal or other location. A tribunal of this state shall cooperate with other tribunals in designating an appropriate location for the deposition or testimony.

(g) If a party called to testify at a civil hearing refuses to answer on the ground that the testimony may be self-incriminating, the trier of fact may draw an adverse inference from the refusal.

(h) A privilege against disclosure of communications between spouses does not apply in a proceeding under this article.

(i) The defense of immunity based on the relationship of husband and wife or parent and child does not apply in a proceeding under this article.

(j) A voluntary acknowledgment of paternity, certified as a true copy, is admissible to establish parentage of the child.

§580-317. Communications between tribunals.

A tribunal of this state may communicate with a tribunal outside this state in a record or by telephone, electronic mail or other means, to obtain information concerning the laws, the legal effect of a judgment, decree or order of that tribunal, and the status of a proceeding. A tribunal of this state may furnish similar information by similar means to a tribunal outside this state.

§580-318. Assistance with discovery.

A tribunal of this state may:

1. request a tribunal outside this state to assist in obtaining discovery; and

2. upon request, compel a person over which it has jurisdiction to respond to a discovery order issued by a tribunal outside this state.

§580-319. Receipt and disbursement of payments.

(a) A support enforcement agency or tribunal of this state shall disburse promptly any amounts received pursuant to a support order, as directed by the order. The agency or tribunal shall furnish to a requesting party or tribunal of another state or a foreign country a certified statement by the custodian of the record of the amounts and dates of all payments received.

(b) If neither the obligor, nor the obligee who is an individual, nor the child resides in this state, upon request from a support enforcement agency of this state or another state, a support enforcement agency or a tribunal of this state shall:

(1) direct that the support payment be made to the support enforcement agency in the state in which the obligee is receiving services; and

(2) issue and send to the obligor's employer a conforming income withholding order or an administrative notice of change of payee, reflecting the redirected payments.

(c) A support enforcement agency of this state receiving redirected payments from another state pursuant to a law similar to subdivision (b) of this section shall furnish to a requesting party or tribunal of the other state a certified statement by the custodian of the record of the amount and dates of all payments received.

Part 4
Establishment of Support Order or Determination of Parentage

§580-401.   Establishment of support order.
(a) If a support order entitled to recognition under this article has not been issued, a responding tribunal of this state with personal jurisdiction over the parties may issue a support order if:

(1) the individual seeking the order resides outside this state; or

(2) the support enforcement agency seeking the order is located outside this state.

(b) The tribunal may issue a temporary child support order if the tribunal determines that such an order is appropriate and the individual ordered to pay is:

(1) a presumed father of the child;

(2) petitioning to have his paternity adjudicated;

(3) identified as the father of the child through genetic testing;

(4) an alleged father who has declined to submit to genetic testing;

(5) shown by clear and convincing evidence to be the father of the child;

(6) an acknowledged father as provided by applicable state law;

(7) the mother of the child; or

(8) an individual who has been ordered to pay child support in a previous proceeding and the order has not been reversed or vacated.

(c) Upon finding, after notice and opportunity to be heard, that an obligor owes a duty of support, the tribunal shall issue a support order directed to the obligor and may issue other orders pursuant to section 580-305 of this article.

§580-402.   Proceeding to determine parentage.
A tribunal of this state authorized to determine parentage of a child may serve as a responding tribunal in a proceeding to determine parentage of a child brought under this article or a law or procedure substantially similar to this article.

Part 5
Enforcement of Support Order Without Registration

§580-501. Employer's receipt of income withholding order of another state.

An income withholding order issued in another state may be sent by or on behalf of the obligee, or by the support enforcement agency, to the person defined as the obligor's employer or income payor under section five thousand two hundred forty-one of the civil practice law and rules or other debtor (for purposes of this part and section 580-605 of this article, employer shall also include income payor or other debtor) without first filing a petition or comparable pleading or registering the order with a tribunal of this state.

§580-502. Employer's compliance with income withholding order of another state.

(a) Upon receipt of an income withholding order, the obligor's employer shall immediately provide a copy of the order to the obligor.

(b) The employer shall treat an income withholding order issued in another state which appears regular on its face as if it had been issued by a tribunal of this state.

(c) Except as otherwise provided in subdivision (d) of this section and section 580-503 of this part, the employer shall withhold and distribute the funds as directed in the withholding order by complying with terms of the order which specify:

(1) the duration and amount of periodic payments of current child support, stated as a sum certain;

(2) the person designated to receive payments and the address to which the payments are to be forwarded;

(3) medical support, whether in the form of periodic cash payment, stated as a sum certain, or ordering the obligor to provide health insurance coverage for the child under a policy available through the obligor's employment;

(4) the amount of periodic payments of fees and costs for a support enforcement agency, the issuing tribunal and the obligee's attorney, stated as sums certain; and

(5) the amount of periodic payments of arrearages and interest on arrearages, stated as sums certain.

(d) An employer shall comply with the law of the state of the obligor's principal place of employment for withholding from income with respect to:

(1) the employer's fee for processing an income withholding order;

(2) the maximum amount permitted to be withheld from the obligor's income; and

(3) the times within which the employer must implement the withholding order and forward the child support payment.

§580-503. Compliance with multiple income withholding orders.

If an obligor's employer receives two or more income withholding orders with respect to the earnings of the same obligor, the employer satisfies the terms of the orders if the employer complies with the law of the state of the obligor's principal place of employment to establish the priorities for withholding and allocating income withheld for two or more child support obligees.

§580-504. Immunity from civil liability.

An employer that complies with an income withholding order issued in another state in accordance with this part is not subject to civil liability to an individual or agency with regard to the employer's withholding of child support from the obligor's income.

§580-505.   Penalties for noncompliance.

An employer that willfully fails to comply with an income withholding order issued in another state and received for enforcement is subject to the same penalties that may be imposed for noncompliance with an order issued by a tribunal of this state.

§580-506.   Contest by obligor.

(a) An obligor may contest the validity or enforcement of an income withholding order issued in another state and received directly by an employer in this state by registering the order in a tribunal of this state and filing a contest to that order as provided in part six of this article, or otherwise contesting the order in the same manner as if the order had been issued by a tribunal of this state.

(b) The obligor shall give notice of the contest to:

(1) a support enforcement agency providing services to the obligee;

(2) each employer that has directly received an income withholding order relating to the obligor; and

(3) the person designated to receive payments in the income withholding order or, if no person is designated, to the obligee.

§580-507.   Administrative enforcement of orders.

(a) A party or support enforcement agency seeking to enforce a support order or an income withholding order, or both, issued in another state or a foreign support order may send the documents required for registering the order to a support enforcement agency of this state.

(b) Upon receipt of the documents, the support enforcement agency, without initially seeking to register the order, shall consider and, if appropriate, use any administrative procedure authorized by the law of this state to enforce a support order or an income withholding order, or both. If the obligor does not contest administrative enforcement, the order need not be registered. If the obligor contests the validity or administrative enforcement of the order, the support enforcement agency shall register the order pursuant to this article.

Part 6
Registration, Enforcement and Modification of Support Order

Subpart

A.   Registration and enforcement of support order.
B.   Contest of validity or enforcement.
C.   Registration and modification of child support order of another state.
D.   Registration and modification of foreign child support order.

Subpart A
Registration and Enforcement of Support Order

Section

§580-601.   Registration of order for enforcement.

A support order or income withholding order issued in another state or a foreign support order may be registered in this state for enforcement.

**§580-602.	Procedure to register order for enforcement.**

(a) Except as otherwise provided in section 580-706 of this article, a support order or income withholding order of another state or a foreign support order may be registered in this state by sending the following records to the appropriate tribunal in this state:

(1) a letter of transmittal to the tribunal requesting registration and enforcement;

(2) two copies, including one certified copy, of the order to be registered, including any modification of the order;

(3) a sworn statement by the person requesting registration or a certified statement by the custodian of the records showing the amount of any arrearage;

(4) the name of the obligor and, if known:

(i) the obligor's address and social security number;

(ii) the name and address of the obligor's employer and any other source of income of the obligor; and

(iii) a description and the location of property of the obligor in this state not exempt from execution; and

(5) except as otherwise provided in section 580-312 of this article, the name and address of the obligee and, if applicable, the person to whom support payments are to be remitted.

(b) On receipt of a request for registration, the registering tribunal shall cause the order to be filed as an order of a tribunal of another state or a foreign support order, together with one copy of the documents and information, regardless of their form.

(c) A petition or comparable pleading seeking a remedy that must be affirmatively sought under other law of this state may be filed at the same time as the request for registration or later. The pleading must specify the grounds for the remedy sought.

(d) If two or more orders are in effect, the person requesting registration shall:

(1) furnish to the tribunal a copy of every support order asserted to be in effect in addition to the documents specified in this section;

(2) specify the order alleged to be the controlling order, if any; and

(3) specify the amount of consolidated arrears, if any.

(e) A request for a determination of which is the controlling order may be filed separately or with a request for registration and enforcement or for registration and modification. The person requesting registration shall give notice of the request to each party whose rights may be affected by the determination.

**§580-603.	Effect of registration for enforcement.**

(a) A support order or income withholding order issued in another state or a foreign support order is registered when the order is filed in the registering tribunal of this state.

(b) A registered support order issued in another state or a foreign country is enforceable in the same manner and is subject to the same procedures as an order issued by a tribunal of this state.

(c) Except as otherwise provided in this article, a tribunal of this state shall recognize and enforce, but may not modify, a registered support order if the issuing tribunal had jurisdiction.

§580-604.   Choice of law.

(a) Except as otherwise provided in subdivision (d) of this section, the law of the issuing state or foreign country governs:

(1) the nature, extent, amount and duration of current payments under a registered support order;

(2) the computation and payment of arrearages and accrual of interest on the arrearages under the support order; and

(3) the existence and satisfaction of other obligations under the support order.

(b) In a proceeding for arrears under a registered support order, the statute of limitation of this state or of the issuing state or foreign country, whichever is longer, applies.

(c) A responding tribunal of this state shall apply the procedures and remedies of this state to enforce current support and collect arrears and interest due on a support order of another state or a foreign country registered in this state.

(d) After a tribunal of this state or another state determines which is the controlling order and issues an order consolidating arrears, if any, a tribunal of this state shall prospectively apply the law of the state or foreign country issuing the controlling order, including its law on interest on arrears, on current and future support, and on consolidated arrears.

Subpart B
Contest of Validity or Enforcement

Section

§580-605.   Notice of registration of order.

(a) When a support order or income withholding order issued in another state or a foreign support order is registered, the registering tribunal of this state shall notify the nonregistering party. The notice must be accompanied by a copy of the registered order and the documents and relevant information accompanying the order.

(b) A notice must inform the nonregistering party:

(1) that a registered support order is enforceable as of the date of registration in the same manner as an order issued by a tribunal of this state;

(2) that a hearing to contest the validity or enforcement of the registered order must be requested within twenty days after notice unless the registered order is under section 580-707 of this article;

(3) that failure to contest the validity or enforcement of the registered order in a timely manner will result in confirmation of the order and enforcement of the order and the alleged arrearages; and

(4) of the amount of any alleged arrearages.

(c) If the registering party asserts that two or more orders are in effect, a notice must also:

(1) identify the two or more orders and the order alleged by the registering party to be the controlling order and the consolidated arrears, if any;

(2) notify the nonregistering party of the right to a determination of which is the controlling order;

(3) state that the procedures provided in subdivision (b) of this section apply to the determination of which is the controlling order; and

(4) state that failure to contest the validity or enforcement of the order alleged to be the controlling order in a timely manner may result in confirmation that the order is the controlling order.

(d) Upon registration of an income withholding order for enforcement, the support enforcement agency or the registering tribunal shall notify the obligor's employer pursuant to section five thousand two hundred forty-one or five thousand two hundred forty-two of the civil practice law and rules.

§580-606.   Procedure to contest validity or enforcement of registered support order.

(a) A nonregistering party seeking to contest the validity or enforcement of a registered support order in this state shall request a hearing within the time required by section 580-605 of this subpart. The nonregistering party may seek to vacate the registration, to assert any defense to an allegation of noncompliance with the registered order, or to contest the remedies being sought or the amount of any alleged arrearages pursuant to section 580-607 of this subpart.

(b) If the nonregistering party fails to contest the validity or enforcement of the registered support order in a timely manner, the order is confirmed by operation of law.

(c) If a nonregistering party requests a hearing to contest the validity or enforcement of the registered support order, the registering tribunal shall schedule the matter for hearing and give notice to the parties of the date, time, and place of the hearing.

§580-607.   Contest of registration or enforcement.

(a) A party contesting the validity or enforcement of a registered support order or seeking to vacate the registration has the burden of proving one or more of the following defenses:

(1) the issuing tribunal lacked personal jurisdiction over the contesting party;

(2) the order was obtained by fraud;

(3) the order has been vacated, suspended, or modified by a later order;

(4) the issuing tribunal has stayed the order pending appeal;

(5) there is a defense under the law of this state to the remedy sought;

(6) full or partial payment has been made;

(7) the statute of limitation under section 580-604 of this part precludes enforcement of some or all of the alleged arrearages; or

(8) the alleged controlling order is not the controlling order.

(b) If a party presents evidence establishing a full or partial defense under subdivision (a) of this section, a tribunal may stay enforcement of a registered support order, continue the proceeding to permit production of additional relevant evidence, and issue other appropriate orders. An uncontested portion of the registered support order may be enforced by all remedies available under the law of this state.

(c) If the contesting party does not establish a defense under subdivision (a) of this section to the validity or enforcement of a registered support order, the registering tribunal shall issue an order confirming the order.

§580-608.   Confirmed order.
Confirmation of a registered support order, whether by operation of law or after notice and hearing, precludes further contest of the order with respect to any matter that could have been asserted at the time of registration.

Subpart C
Registration and Modification of Child Support Order

§580-609.   Procedure to register child support order of another state for modification.
A party or support enforcement agency seeking to modify, or to modify and enforce a child support order issued in another state shall register that order in this state in the same manner provided in sections 580-601 through 580-608 of this part if the order has not been registered. A petition for modification may be filed at the same time as a request for registration, or later. The pleading must specify the grounds for modification.

§580-610.   Effect of registration for modification.
A tribunal of this state may enforce a child support order of another state registered for purposes of modification, in the same manner as if the order had been issued by a tribunal of this state, but the registered support order may be modified only if the requirements of section 580-611 or 580-613 of this subpart have been met.

§580-611.   Modification of child support order of another state.
(a) If section 580-613 of this subpart does not apply, upon petition a tribunal of this state may modify a child support order issued in another state which is registered in this state if, after notice and hearing, the tribunal finds that:
(1) the following requirements are met:
(i) neither the child, nor the obligee who is an individual, nor the obligor resides in the issuing state;
(ii) a petitioner who is a nonresident of this state seeks modification; and
(iii) the respondent is subject to the personal jurisdiction of the tribunal of this state; or
(2) this state is the residence of the child, or a party who is an individual is subject to the personal jurisdiction of the tribunal of this state, and all of the parties who are individuals have filed consents in a record in the issuing tribunal for a tribunal of this state to modify the support order and assume continuing, exclusive jurisdiction.
(b) Modification of a registered child support order is subject to the same requirements, procedures, and defenses that apply to the modification of an order issued by a tribunal of this state and the order may be enforced and satisfied in the same manner.

(c) A tribunal of this state may not modify any aspect of a child support order that may not be modified under the law of the issuing state, including the duration of the obligation of support. If two or more tribunals have issued child support orders for the same obligor and same child, the order that controls and must be so recognized under section 580-207 of this article establishes the aspects of the support order which are nonmodifiable.

(d) In a proceeding to modify a child support order, the law of the state that is determined to have issued the initial controlling order governs the duration of the obligation of support. The obligor's fulfillment of the duty of support established by that order precludes imposition of a further obligation of support by a tribunal of this state.

(e) On the issuance of an order by a tribunal of this state modifying a child support order issued in another state, the tribunal of this state becomes the tribunal having continuing, exclusive jurisdiction.

(f) Notwithstanding subdivisions (a) through (e) of this section and subdivision (b) of section 580-201 of this article, a tribunal of this state retains jurisdiction to modify an order issued by a tribunal of this state if:

(1) one party resides in another state; and

(2) the other party resides outside the United States.

§580-612. **Recognition of order modified in another state.**

If a child support order issued by a tribunal of this state is modified by a tribunal of another state which assumed jurisdiction pursuant to the Uniform Interstate Family Support Act, a tribunal of this state:

(a) may enforce its order that was modified only as to arrears and interest accruing before the modification;

(b) may provide appropriate relief for violations of its order which occurred before the effective date of the modification; and

(c) shall recognize the modifying order of the other state, upon registration, for the purpose of enforcement.

§580-613. **Jurisdiction to modify child-support order of another state when individual parties reside in this state.**

(a) If all of the parties who are individuals reside in this state and the child does not reside in the issuing state, a tribunal of this state has jurisdiction to enforce and to modify the issuing state's child support order in a proceeding to register that order.

(b) A tribunal of this state exercising jurisdiction under this section shall apply the provisions of parts one and two of this article, this part and the procedural and substantive law of this state to the proceeding for enforcement or modification. Parts three, four, five, seven and eight of this article do not apply.

§580-614. **Notice to issuing tribunal of modification.**

Within thirty days after issuance of a modified child support order, the party obtaining the modification shall file a certified copy of the order with the issuing tribunal that had continuing, exclusive jurisdiction over the earlier order, and in each tribunal in which the party knows the earlier order has been registered. A party who obtains the order and fails to file a certified copy is subject to appropriate sanctions by a tribunal in which the issue of failure to file arises. The failure to file does not affect the validity or enforceability of the modified order of the new tribunal having continuing, exclusive jurisdiction.

Subpart D
Registration and Modification of Foreign Child Support Order

§580-615.   Jurisdiction to modify child support order of foreign country.

(a) Except as otherwise provided in section 580-711 of this article, if a foreign country lacks or refuses to exercise jurisdiction to modify its child support order pursuant to its laws, a tribunal of this state may assume jurisdiction to modify the child support order and bind all individuals subject to the personal jurisdiction of the tribunal whether the consent to modification of a child support order otherwise required of the individual pursuant to section 580-611 of this part has been given or whether the individual seeking modification is a resident of this state or of the foreign country.

(b) An order issued by a tribunal of this state modifying a foreign child support order pursuant to this section is the controlling order.

§580-616.   Procedure to register child support order of foreign country for modification.

A party or support enforcement agency seeking to modify, or to modify and enforce, a foreign child support order not under the Convention may register that order in this state under sections 580-601 through 580-608 of this part if the order has not been registered. A petition for modification may be filed at the same time as a request for registration, or at another time. The petition must specify the grounds for modification.

Part 7
Support Proceedings under Convention

§580-701.   Definitions.

In this part:

1. "Application" means a request under the Convention by an obligee or obligor, or on behalf of a child, made through a central authority for assistance from another central authority.

2. "Central authority" means the entity designated by the United States or a foreign country described in paragraph (iv) of subdivision five of section 580-102 of this article to perform the functions specified in the Convention.

3. "Convention support order" means a support order of a tribunal of a foreign country described in paragraph (iv) of subdivision five of section 580-102 of this article.

4. "Direct request" means a petition filed by an individual in a tribunal of this state in a proceeding involving an obligee, obligor or child residing outside the United States.

5. "Foreign central authority" means the entity designated by a foreign country described in paragraph (iv) of subdivision five of section 580-102 of this article to perform the functions specified in the Convention.

6. "Foreign support agreement":
   (i) means an agreement for support in a record that:
   (a) is enforceable as a support order in the country of origin;
   (b) has been:
      (A) formally drawn up or registered as an authentic instrument by a foreign tribunal; or
      (B) authenticated by, or concluded, registered or filed with a foreign tribunal; and
   (c) may be reviewed and modified by a foreign tribunal; and
   (ii) includes a maintenance arrangement or authentic instrument under the convention.

7. "United States central authority" means the secretary of the United States department of health and human services.

§580-702. Applicability.
This part applies only to a support proceeding under the Convention. In such a proceeding, if a provision of this part is inconsistent with parts one through six of this article, this part controls.

§580-703. Relationship of office of temporary and disability assistance to United States central authority.
The office of temporary and disability assistance is recognized as the agency designated by the United States central authority to perform specific functions under the Convention; provided, however, that a social services district of this state may perform any function authorized under state law.

§580-704. Initiation by state support enforcement agencies of support proceeding under Convention.
(a) In a support proceeding under this part, the support enforcement agencies of this state shall:
   (1) transmit and receive applications; and
   (2) initiate or facilitate the institution of a proceeding regarding an application in a tribunal of this state.

(b) The following support proceedings are available to an obligee under the Convention:
   (1) recognition or recognition and enforcement of a foreign support order;
   (2) enforcement of a support order issued or recognized in this state;
   (3) establishment of a support order if there is no existing order, including, if necessary, determination of parentage of a child;

(4) establishment of a support order if recognition of a foreign support order is refused under paragraph two, four or nine of subdivision (b) of section 580-708 of this part;

(5) modification of a support order of a tribunal of this state; and

(6) modification of a support order of a tribunal of another state or a foreign country.

(c) The following support proceedings are available under the Convention to an obligor against which there is an existing support order:

(1) recognition of an order suspending or limiting enforcement of an existing support order of a tribunal of this state;

(2) modification of a support order of a tribunal of this state; and

(3) modification of a support order of a tribunal of another state or a foreign country.

(d) A tribunal of this state may not require security, bond or deposit, however described, to guarantee the payment of costs and expenses in proceedings under the Convention.

§580-705.   Direct request.

(a) A petitioner may file a direct request seeking establishment or modification of a support order or determination of parentage of a child. In the proceeding, the law of this state applies.

(b) A petitioner may file a direct request seeking recognition and enforcement of a support order or support agreement. In the proceeding, sections 580-706 through 580-713 of this part apply.

(c) In a direct request for recognition and enforcement of a Convention support order or foreign support agreement:

(1) a security, bond or deposit is not required to guarantee the payment of costs and expenses; and

(2) an obligee or obligor that in the issuing country has benefited from free legal assistance is entitled to benefit, at least to the same extent, from any free legal assistance provided for by the law of this state under the same circumstances.

(d) A petitioner filing a direct request is not entitled to assistance from the state child support agencies.

(e) This part does not prevent the application of laws of this state that provide simplified, more expeditious rules regarding a direct request for recognition and enforcement of a foreign support order or foreign support agreement.

§580-706.   Registration of Convention support order.

(a) Except as otherwise provided in this part, a party who is an individual or a support enforcement agency seeking recognition of a Convention support order shall register the order in this state as provided in part six of this article.

(b) Notwithstanding section 580-311 and subdivision (a) of section 580-602 of this article, a request for registration of a Convention support order must be accompanied by:

(1) a complete text of the support order or an abstract or extract of the support order drawn up by the issuing foreign tribunal, which may be in the form recommended by the Hague Conference on Private International Law;

(2) a record stating that the support order is enforceable in the issuing country;

(3) if the respondent did not appear and was not represented in the proceedings in the issuing country, a record attesting, as appropriate, either that

the respondent had proper notice of the proceedings and an opportunity to be heard or that the respondent had proper notice of the support order and an opportunity to be heard in a challenge or appeal on fact or law before a tribunal;

(4) a record showing the amount of arrears, if any, and the date the amount was calculated;

(5) a record showing a requirement for automatic adjustment of the amount of support, if any, and the information necessary to make the appropriate calculations; and

(6) if necessary, a record showing the extent to which the applicant received free legal assistance in the issuing country.

(c) A request for registration of a Convention support order may seek recognition and partial enforcement of the order.

(d) A tribunal of this state may vacate the registration of a Convention support order without the filing of a contest under section 580-707 of this part only if, acting on its own motion, the tribunal finds that recognition and enforcement of the order would be manifestly incompatible with public policy.

(e) The tribunal shall promptly notify the parties of the registration or the order vacating the registration of a Convention support order.

§580-707. Contest of registered Convention support order.

(a) Except as otherwise provided in this part, sections 580-605 through 580-608 of this article apply to a contest of a registered Convention support order.

(b) A party contesting a registered Convention support order shall file a contest not later than thirty days after notice of the registration, but if the contesting party does not reside in the United States, the contest must be filed not later than sixty days after notice of the registration.

(c) If the nonregistering party fails to contest the registered Convention support order by the time specified in subdivision (b) of this section, the order is enforceable.

(d) A contest of a registered Convention support order may be based only on grounds set forth in section 580-708 of this part. The contesting party bears the burden of proof.

(e) In a contest of a registered Convention support order, a tribunal of this state:

(1) is bound by the findings of fact on which the foreign tribunal based its jurisdiction; and

(2) may not review the merits of the order.

(f) A tribunal of this state deciding a contest of a registered Convention support order shall promptly notify the parties of its decision.

(g) A challenge or appeal, if any, does not stay the enforcement of a Convention support order unless there are exceptional circumstances.

§580-708. Recognition and enforcement of registered Convention support order.

(a) Except as otherwise provided in subdivision (b) of this section, a tribunal of this state shall recognize and enforce a registered Convention support order.

(b) The following grounds are the only grounds on which a tribunal of this state may refuse recognition and enforcement of a registered Convention support order:

(1) recognition and enforcement of the order is manifestly incompatible with public policy, including the failure of the issuing tribunal to observe

minimum standards of due process, which include notice and an opportunity to be heard;

(2) the issuing tribunal lacked personal jurisdiction consistent with section 580-201 of this article;

(3) the order is not enforceable in the issuing country;

(4) the order was obtained by fraud in connection with a matter of procedure;

(5) a record transmitted in accordance with section 580-706 of this part lacks authenticity or integrity;

(6) a proceeding between the same parties and having the same purpose is pending before a tribunal of this state and that proceeding was the first to be filed;

(7) the order is incompatible with a more recent support order involving the same parties and having the same purpose if the more recent support order is entitled to recognition and enforcement under this article in this state;

(8) payment, to the extent alleged arrears have been paid in whole or in part;

(9) in a case in which the respondent neither appeared nor was represented in the proceeding in the issuing foreign country:

(i) if the law of that country provides for prior notice of proceedings, the respondent did not have proper notice of the proceedings and an opportunity to be heard; or

(ii) if the law of that country does not provide for prior notice of the proceedings, the respondent did not have proper notice of the order and an opportunity to be heard in a challenge or appeal on fact or law before a tribunal; or

(10) the order was made in violation of section 580-711 of this part.

(c) If a tribunal of this state does not recognize a Convention support order under paragraph two, four or nine of subdivision (b) of this section:

(1) the tribunal may not dismiss the proceeding without allowing a reasonable time for a party to request the establishment of a new Convention support order; and

(2) the state child support agency shall take all appropriate measures to request a child support order for the obligee if the application for recognition and enforcement was received under section 580-704 of this part.

§580-709.   Partial enforcement.

If a tribunal of this state does not recognize and enforce a Convention support order in its entirety, it shall enforce any severable part of the order. An application or direct request may seek recognition and partial enforcement of a Convention support order.

§580-710.   Foreign support agreement.

(a) Except as otherwise provided in subdivisions (c) and (d) of this section, a tribunal of this state shall recognize and enforce a foreign support agreement registered in this state.

(b) An application or direct request for recognition and enforcement of a foreign support agreement must be accompanied by:

(1) a complete text of the foreign support agreement; and

(2) a record stating that the foreign support agreement is enforceable as an order of support in the issuing country.

(c) A tribunal of this state may vacate the registration of a foreign support agreement only if, acting on its own motion, the tribunal finds that recognition and enforcement would be manifestly incompatible with public policy.

(d) In a contest of a foreign support agreement, a tribunal of this state may refuse recognition and enforcement of the agreement if it finds:

(1) recognition and enforcement of the agreement is manifestly incompatible with public policy;

(2) the agreement was obtained by fraud or falsification;

(3) the agreement is incompatible with a support order involving the same parties and having the same purpose in this state, another state, or a foreign country if the support order is entitled to recognition and enforcement under this article in this state; or

(4) the record submitted under subdivision (b) of this section lacks authenticity or integrity.

(e) A proceeding for recognition and enforcement of a foreign support agreement must be suspended during the pendency of a challenge to or appeal of the agreement before a tribunal of another state or a foreign country.

§580-711.   Modification of Convention child support order.

(a) A tribunal of this state may not modify a Convention child support order if the obligee remains a resident of the foreign country where the support order was issued unless:

(1) the obligee submits to the jurisdiction of a tribunal of this state, either expressly or by defending on the merits of the case without objecting to the jurisdiction at the first available opportunity; or

(2) the foreign tribunal lacks or refuses to exercise jurisdiction to modify its support order or issue a new support order.

(b) If a tribunal of this state does not modify a Convention child support order because the order is not recognized in this state, subdivision (c) of section 580-708 of this part applies.

§580-712.   Personal information; limit on use.

Personal information gathered or transmitted under this part may be used only for the purposes for which it was gathered or transmitted.

§580-713.   Record in original language; English translation.

A record filed with a tribunal of this state under this part must be in the original language and, if not in English, must be accompanied by an English translation.

Part 8
Interstate Rendition

Section
580-801   Grounds for rendition.
580-802   Conditions of rendition.

§580-801.   Grounds for rendition.

(a) For purposes of this part, "governor" includes an individual performing the functions of governor or the executive authority of a state covered by this article.

(b) The governor of this state may:

(1) demand that the governor of another state surrender an individual found in the other state who is charged criminally in this state with having failed to provide for the support of an obligee; or

(2) on the demand of the governor of another state, surrender an individual found in this state who is charged criminally in the other state with having failed to provide for the support of an obligee.

(c) A provision for extradition of individuals not inconsistent with this article applies to the demand even if the individual whose surrender is demanded was not in the demanding state when the crime was allegedly committed and has not fled therefrom.

§580-802.　Conditions of rendition.

(a) Before making a demand that the governor of another state surrender an individual charged criminally in this state with having failed to provide for the support of an obligee, the governor of this state may require a prosecutor of this state to demonstrate that at least sixty days previously the obligee had initiated proceedings for support pursuant to this article or that the proceeding would be of no avail.

(b) If, under this article or a law substantially similar to this article, the governor of another state makes a demand that the governor of this state surrender an individual charged criminally in that state with having failed to provide for the support of a child or other individual to whom a duty of support is owed, the governor may require a prosecutor to investigate the demand and report whether a proceeding for support has been initiated or would be effective. If it appears that a proceeding would be effective but has not been initiated, the governor may delay honoring the demand for a reasonable time to permit the initiation of a proceeding.

(c) If a proceeding for support has been initiated and the individual whose rendition is demanded prevails, the governor may decline to honor the demand. If the petitioner prevails and the individual whose rendition is demanded is subject to a support order, the governor may decline to honor the demand if the individual is complying with the support order.

Part 9
Miscellaneous Provisions

§580-901.　Uniformity of application and construction.

In applying and construing this uniform act, consideration must be given to the need to promote uniformity of the law with respect to its subject matter among states that enact it.

§580-902.　Severability.

If any provision of this article or its application to any person or circumstance is held invalid, the invalidity does not affect other provisions or applications of this article which can be given effect without the invalid provision or application, and to this end the provisions of this article are severable.

§580-903.   Effective date.
This article shall take effect on January first, two thousand sixteen; provided, however, that if it shall become a law after January first, two thousand sixteen, it shall be deemed to have been in full force and effect on and after January first, two thousand sixteen; and provided further, that the provisions of this article shall apply to any action or proceeding filed or order issued on or before the effective date of this article.

ARTICLE 6
Permanent Termination of Parental Rights,
Adoption, Guardianship and Custody

Part 1
Permanent Termination of Parental Custody
by Reason of Permanent Neglect

§611.   Permanently neglected child; purpose of part.
The purpose of this part is to provide the procedures for proceedings initiated in family court, pursuant to section three hundred eighty-four-b of the social services law, for the commitment of the guardianship and custody of a child upon the ground that the child is a permanently neglected child. As used in this part "permanently neglected child" shall mean permanently neglected child as defined in subdivision seven of section three hundred eighty-four-b of the social services law, and unless the context requires otherwise, the provisions of such section three hundred eighty-four-b shall be deemed applicable requirements in addition to the procedures contained in this part. All references in this part to petitions and proceedings initiated "under this part" shall be deemed references to petitions and proceedings initiated under section three hundred eighty-four-b of the social services law upon the ground that the child is a permanently neglected child.

§614. Originating proceeding for the commitment of the guardianship and custody of a permanently neglected child.

1. A proceeding for the commitment of the guardianship and custody of a child on the ground of permanent neglect is originated by a petition, alleging:

(a) the child is a person under eighteen years of age;

(b) the child is in the care of an authorized agency;

(c) the authorized agency has made diligent efforts to encourage and strengthen the parental relationship and specifying the efforts made or that such efforts would be detrimental to the best interests of the child and specifying the reasons therefor;

(d) the parent or custodian, notwithstanding the agency's efforts, has failed for a period of either at least one year or fifteen out of the most recent twenty-two months following the date such child came into the care of an authorized agency substantially and continuously or repeatedly to maintain contact with or plan for the future of the child, although physically and financially able to do so; and

(e) the best interests of the child require that the guardianship and custody of the child be committed to an authorized agency or to a foster parent authorized to originate this proceeding under section one thousand eighty-nine of this act.

2. Where the petitioner is not the authorized agency, allegations relating to the efforts of the authorized agency may be made upon information and belief.

§616. Issuance of summons.

On the filing of a petition under this part, the court may cause a copy of the petition and a summons to be issued, requiring the parent to show cause why the court should not enter an order committing the guardianship and custody of the child to the petitioner for the reason that the child is permanently neglected.

§617. Service of summons.

(a) Service of a summons and petition under this part shall be made by delivery of a true copy thereof to the person summoned at least twenty days before the time stated therein for appearance. If so requested by the parent or other person legally responsible for the child's care, the court may extend the time for appearance and answer.

(b) If after reasonable effort, personal service is not made, such substituted service or service by publication as may be ordered by the judge shall be sufficient.

(c) Personal service within or without the state or in a foreign country shall be made in accordance with the provisions of section three hundred seven of the surrogate's court procedure act, as the same may be amended from time to time, with respect to service of a citation.

(d) Service of the summons and other process with a notice as specified herein by publication shall be made in accordance with the provisions of CPLR 316, provided, however, that a single publication of the summons or other process with a notice as specified herein in only one newspaper designated in the order shall be sufficient. In no event shall the whole petition be published. The petition shall be delivered to the person summoned at the first court appearance pursuant to section one hundred fifty-four-a of this chapter. The notice to be published with the summons or other process shall state:

1. the date, time, place and purpose of the proceeding,

2. that upon failure of the person summoned to appear, all of his or her parental rights in the child may be terminated, and

3. that his or her failure to appear shall constitute a denial of his or her interest in the child, which denial may result, without further notice, in the transfer or commitment of the child's care, custody or guardianship or in the child's adoption in this or any subsequent proceeding in which such care, custody or guardianship or adoption may be at issue.

§622. Definition of "fact-finding hearing".

When used in this part, "fact-finding hearing" means in the case of a petition for the commitment of the guardianship and custody of a child, a hearing to determine whether the allegations required by paragraphs (a), (b), (c), and (d) of subdivision one of section six hundred fourteen are supported by clear and convincing proof.

§623. Definition of "dispositional hearing".

When used in this part, "dispositional hearing" means a hearing to determine what order of disposition should be made in accordance with the best interests of the child. Where the disposition ordered is the commitment of guardianship and custody in accordance with section six hundred thirty-four of this part, an initial freed child permanency hearing and all subsequent permanency hearings shall be held in accordance with article ten-A of this act.

§624. Evidence.

Only competent, material and relevant evidence may be admitted in a fact-finding hearing; only material and relevant evidence may be admitted in a dispositional hearing. Evidence of parental contact or of failure to maintain contact with a child subsequent to the date of the filing of a petition under this part shall be inadmissible in the fact-finding hearing. Such evidence may be admitted in the dispositional hearing but shall not, of itself, be sufficient as a matter of law to preclude or require an order committing the guardianship and custody of the child.

§625. Sequence of hearings.

(a) Upon completion of the fact-finding hearing, the dispositional hearing may commence immediately after the required findings are made; provided, however, that if all parties consent the court may, upon motion of any party or upon its own motion, dispense with the dispositional hearing and make an order of disposition on the basis of competent evidence admitted at the fact-finding hearing. Where the disposition ordered is the commitment of guardianship and custody in accordance with section six hundred thirty-four of this part, an initial freed child permanency hearing and all subsequent permanency hearings shall be held in accordance with article ten-A of this act.

(b) Reports prepared by the probation service or a duly authorized agency for use by the court prior to the making of an order of disposition shall be deemed confidential information furnished to the court which the court in a proper case may, in its discretion, withhold from or disclose in whole or in part to the child's attorney, counsel, party in interest, or other appropriate person. Such reports may not be furnished to the court prior to the completion of a fact-finding hearing, but may be used in a dispositional hearing or in the making of an order of disposition without a dispositional hearing pursuant to subdivision (a) of this section.

§626. Adjournments.

(a) The court may adjourn a fact-finding hearing or a dispositional hearing for good cause shown on its own motion or on motion made on behalf of the child, or on motion of the parent or other person responsible for the care of the child.

(b) At the conclusion of a fact-finding hearing and after it has made findings required before a dispositional hearing may commence, the court may adjourn the proceedings to enable it to make inquiry into the surroundings, conditions, and capacities of the persons involved in the proceedings.

§631. Disposition on adjudication of permanent neglect.

At the conclusion of a dispositional hearing on a petition for the commitment of the guardianship and custody of a child, the court shall enter an order of disposition:

(a) dismissing the petition in accord with section six hundred thirty-two; or

(b) suspending judgment in accord with section six hundred thirty-three; or

(c) committing the guardianship and custody of the child in accord with section six hundred thirty-four; provided, however, that an order of disposition committing the guardianship and custody of the child may not be entered after the child's eighteenth birthday, unless the child consents.

An order of disposition shall be made, pursuant to this section, solely on the basis of the best interests of the child, and there shall be no presumption that such interests will be promoted by any particular disposition.

§632. Order dismissing petition.

(a) If the allegations of a petition under this part are not established, the court shall dismiss the petition.

(b) If a motion or application has been made in the course of a proceeding under this part to reconsider an underlying order of placement or commitment, or upon the court's own motion on notice to all parties, the court retains jurisdiction to dispose of that motion or application regardless of whether it dismisses the petition.

§633. Suspended judgment.

(a) Rules of court shall define permissible terms and conditions of a suspended judgment. These terms and conditions shall relate to the acts or omissions of the parent or other person responsible for the care of the child.

(b) The maximum duration of a suspended judgment under this section is one year, unless the court finds at the conclusion of that period that exceptional circumstances require an extension of that period for one additional period of up to one year. Successive extensions may not be granted.

(c) The order of suspended judgment must set forth the duration, terms and conditions of the suspended judgment, and must contain a date certain for a court review not later than thirty days prior to the expiration of the period of suspended judgment. The order of suspended judgment must also state in conspicuous print that a failure to obey the order may lead to its revocation and to the issuance of an order terminating parental rights and committing the guardianship and custody of the child to an authorized agency for the purposes of adoption. A copy of the order of suspended judgment, along with the current permanency plan, must be furnished to the respondent.

(d) Not later than sixty days before the expiration of the period of suspended judgment, the petitioner shall file a report with the family court and all parties, including the respondent and his or her attorney, the child's attorney and intervenors, if any, regarding the respondent's compliance with the terms of suspended judgment. The report shall be reviewed by the court on the scheduled court date. Unless a motion or order to show cause has been filed prior to the expiration of the period of suspended judgment alleging a violation or seeking an extension of the period of the suspended judgment, the terms of the disposition of suspended judgment shall be deemed satisfied and an order committing the guardianship and custody of the child shall not be entered.

(e) If, prior to the expiration of the period of the suspended judgment, a motion or order to show cause is filed that alleges a violation of the terms and conditions of the suspended judgment, or that seeks to extend the period of the suspended judgment for an additional period of up to one year, then the period of the suspended judgment is tolled until entry of the order that disposes of the motion or order to show cause.

(f) Upon finding that the respondent has violated the terms and conditions of the order of suspended judgment, the court may enter an order revoking the order of suspended judgment and terminating the parental rights of the respondent or, where such extension is in the best interests of the child, extend the period of suspended judgment for an additional period of up to one year, if no prior extension has been granted.

(g) If an order of suspended judgment has been satisfied or has been extended, but the child nonetheless remains in foster care pursuant to a placement under article ten of this act or section three hundred fifty-eight-a of the social services law, a permanency hearing shall be completed as previously scheduled pursuant to section one thousand eighty-nine of this act, but no later than six months after the completion of the last permanency hearing. If guardianship and custody of the child have been transferred to the authorized agency upon an order revoking the order of suspended judgment, a permanency hearing shall be completed pursuant to paragraph one of subdivision (a) of section one thousand eighty-nine of this act immediately following, but in no event later than sixty days after, the earlier of the court's statement of its order on the record or issuance of its written order.

§634. Commitment of guardianship and custody; further orders.

The court may enter an order under section six hundred thirty-one committing the guardianship and custody of the child to the petitioner on such conditions, if any, as it deems proper.

Part 1-A
Modification of Disposition;
Restoration of Parental Rights

§635. Petition to restore parental rights.

A petition to modify a disposition ordered pursuant to subdivision (c) of section six hundred thirty-one of this article or paragraph (a) of subdivision three of section three hundred eighty-four-b of the social services law in order to restore parental rights may be filed in accordance with this part where the following conditions are met:

(a) the order committing guardianship and custody of the child had been issued two or more years prior to the date of filing of the petition under this section; and

(b) the order committing guardianship and custody of the child had been based upon an adjudication upon grounds enumerated in paragraph (b), (c) or (d) of subdivision four of section three hundred eighty-four-b of the social services law; and

(c) the petition alleges that the petitioner or petitioners and the respondent or respondents in the proceeding in which guardianship and custody had been committed consent to the relief requested in the petition or that the petitioner or petitioners withheld consent to the relief requested in the petition without good cause; and

(d) the child is fourteen years of age or older, remains under the jurisdiction of the family court, has not been adopted, does not have a permanency goal of adoption and consents to the relief requested in the petition.

§636. Originating a proceeding to restore parental rights; service and venue.

(a) A proceeding to modify the disposition in order to restore parental rights may be originated by the filing of a petition by the child's attorney, by the agency or individual to whom guardianship and custody of the child had been committed or by the respondent or respondents in the termination of parental rights proceeding. The petition shall be served upon the child's attorney, the agency or individual to whom guardianship and custody of the child had been committed and the respondent or respondents in the termination of parental rights proceeding, as well as the attorney or attorneys who represented the respondent or respondents in the termination of parental rights proceeding. A certified copy of the order committing guardianship and custody shall be attached to the petition.

(b) Upon the filing of a petition under this part, the court may cause a summons to be issued to the child, the agency or individual to whom guardianship and custody of the child had been committed and the respondent or respondents in the termination of parental rights proceeding. The summons shall be served in accordance with section six hundred seventeen of this article, accompanied by a copy of the petition and the certified order of commitment sought to be modified.

(c) The petition shall be filed before the court that exercised jurisdiction over the most recent permanency proceeding involving the child and shall be assigned, wherever practicable, to the family court judge who presided over that proceeding or the proceeding to terminate parental rights.

(d) Wherever practicable, the child shall be represented by the same attorney that represented the child in the most recent permanency proceeding and the parent or parents shall be represented by the same attorney or attorneys who represented the parent or parents in the termination of parental rights proceeding. Where this is not practicable, or where the court grants a request by the attorney or attorneys to be relieved, the court shall immediately assign a new attorney or attorneys, as applicable.

§637. Burden of proof, disposition and findings.

(a) The petitioner shall have the burden of proof by clear and convincing evidence that restoration of parental rights is in the child's best interests, that the requirements of section six hundred thirty-five of this part have been met and that all of the parties and the child have consented or, if the petitioner in the proceeding in which guardianship and custody have been committed failed to consent to the relief requested, that such failure was without good cause.

(b) The court shall state on the record the reason or reasons for its disposition of the petition. The court may make the following orders of disposition:

(i) The court may grant the petition, modify the order of disposition previously entered in the termination of parental rights proceeding and transfer guardianship and custody of the child to the birth parent or parents, provided, however, that the findings of fact rendered pursuant to section six hundred twenty-two of this article or subdivision four of section three hundred eighty-four-b of the social services law that formed the basis for the adjudication terminating parental rights shall remain; or

(ii) The court may dismiss the petition, in which case the commitment of guardianship and custody of the child to the authorized agency or individual would continue and a permanency hearing would be required to be held as scheduled in accordance with article ten-A of this act; or

(iii) The court may grant the petition conditionally for a designated period of up to six months, during which time guardianship and custody of the child shall remain with the local social services district or authorized agency while the child may visit with, or be placed on a trial discharge with, the birth parent or parents. The court shall direct the district or agency to supervise the child's birth parent or parents, develop a reunification plan and provide appropriate transitional services to the child and birth parent or parents and report to the parties, attorney for the child and the court not later than thirty days prior to the expiration of the designated period. The court shall schedule the proceeding to be heard prior to the expiration of the designated period and shall determine whether to grant the petition permanently in accordance with paragraph (i) of this subdivision or dismiss the petition in accordance with paragraph (ii) of this subdivision. The court shall state its reasons for its determination. If the petition is permanently granted, the child's custody and guardianship shall be transferred to the birth parent or parents. If the child has been removed from the custody of the birth parent or parents prior to the expiration of the designated period by reason of a report of suspected child abuse or maltreatment, the court shall schedule the proceeding to be heard on notice to the parties and attorney for the child, may terminate the trial discharge and may dismiss the petition in accordance with paragraph (ii) of this subdivision.

Part 2
Adoption

Section
641.   Jurisdiction over adoption proceedings.
642.   Rules of court.

§641.   Jurisdiction over adoption proceedings.

The family court has original jurisdiction concurrent with the surrogate's courts over adoption proceedings under article seven of the domestic relations law.

§642.   Rules of court.

Rules of court, not inconsistent with any provision of article seven of the domestic relations law, may authorize the probation service to interview such persons and obtain such data as will aid the court in determining a petition under that article.

Part 3
Custody

§651. Jurisdiction over habeas corpus proceedings and petitions for custody and visitation of minors.

(a) When referred from the supreme court or county court to the family court, the family court has jurisdiction to determine, in accordance with subdivision one of section two hundred forty of the domestic relations law and with the same powers possessed by the supreme court in addition to its own powers, habeas corpus proceedings and proceedings brought by petition and order to show cause, for the determination of the custody or visitation of minors.

(b) When initiated in the family court, the family court has jurisdiction to determine, in accordance with subdivision one of section two hundred forty of the domestic relations law and with the same powers possessed by the supreme court in addition to its own powers, habeas corpus proceedings and proceedings brought by petition and order to show cause, for the determination of the custody or visitation of minors, including applications by a grandparent or grandparents for visitation or custody rights pursuant to section seventy-two or two hundred forty of the domestic relations law.

(c) When initiated in the family court pursuant to a petition under part eight of article ten of this act or section three hundred fifty-eight-a of the social services law, the family court has jurisdiction to enforce or modify orders or judgments of the supreme court relating to the visitation of minors in foster care, notwithstanding any limitation contained in subdivision (b) of section four hundred sixty-seven of this act.

(c-1) Where a proceeding filed pursuant to article ten or ten-A of this act is pending at the same time as a proceeding brought in the family court pursuant to this article, the court presiding over the proceeding under article ten or ten-A of this act may jointly hear the hearing on the custody and visitation petition under this article and the dispositional hearing on the petition under article ten or the permanency hearing under article ten-A of this act; provided, however, the court must determine the custody and visitation petition in accordance with the terms of this article.

(d) With respect to applications by a grandparent or grandparents for visitation or custody rights, made pursuant to section seventy-two or two hundred forty of the domestic relations law, with a child remanded or placed in the care of a person, official, agency or institution pursuant to the provisions of article ten of this act, the applicant, in such manner as the court shall prescribe, shall serve a copy of the application upon the social services official having care and custody of such child, and the child's attorney, who shall be afforded an opportunity to be heard thereon.

(e) 1. Permanent and initial temporary orders of custody or visitation. Prior to the issuance of any permanent or initial temporary order of custody or visitation, the court shall conduct a review of the decisions and reports listed in paragraph three of this subdivision.

2. Successive temporary orders of custody or visitation. Prior to the issuance of any successive temporary order of custody or visitation, the court shall conduct a review of the decisions and reports listed in paragraph three of this subdivision, unless such a review has been conducted within ninety days prior to the issuance of such order.

3. Decisions and reports for review. The court shall conduct a review of the following:

(i) related decisions in court proceedings initiated pursuant to article ten of this act, and all warrants issued under this act; and

(ii) reports of the statewide computerized registry of orders of protection established and maintained pursuant to section two hundred twenty-one-a of the executive law, and reports of the sex offender registry established and maintained pursuant to section one hundred sixty-eight-b of the correction law.

4. Notifying counsel and issuing orders. Upon consideration of decisions pursuant to article ten of this act, and registry reports and notifying counsel involved in the proceeding, or in the event of a self-represented party, notifying such party of the results thereof, including any court appointed attorney for children, the court may issue a temporary, successive temporary or final order of custody or visitation.

5. Temporary emergency order. Notwithstanding any other provision of the law, upon emergency situations, including computer malfunctions, to serve the best interest of the child, the court may issue a temporary emergency order for custody or visitation in the event that it is not possible to timely review decisions and reports on registries as required pursuant to paragraph three of this subdivision.

6. After issuing a temporary emergency order. After issuing a temporary emergency order of custody or visitation, the court shall conduct reviews of the decisions and reports on registries as required pursuant to paragraph three of this subdivision within twenty-four hours of the issuance of such temporary emergency order. Should such twenty-four hour period fall on a day when court is not in session, then the required reviews shall take place the next day the court is in session. Upon reviewing decisions and reports the court shall notify associated counsel, self-represented parties and attorneys for children pursuant to paragraph four of this subdivision and may issue temporary or permanent custody or visitation orders.

7. Feasibility study. The commissioner of the office of children and family services, in conjunction with the office of court administration, is hereby authorized and directed to examine, study, evaluate and make recommendations concerning the feasibility of the utilization of computers in family courts which are connected to the statewide central register of child abuse and maltreatment established and maintained pursuant to section four hundred twenty-two of the social services law, as a means of providing family courts with information regarding parties requesting orders of custody or visitation. Such commissioner shall make a preliminary report to the governor and the legislature of findings, conclusions and recommendations not later than January thirty-first, two thousand nine, and a final report of findings, conclusions and recommendations not later than June first, two thousand nine, and shall submit with the reports

such legislative proposals as are deemed necessary to implement the commissioner's recommendations.

(f) Military service by parent; effect on child custody orders.

1. During the period of time that a parent is activated, deployed or temporarily assigned to military service, such that the parent's ability to continue as a joint caretaker or the primary caretaker of a minor child is materially affected by such military service, any orders issued pursuant to this section, based on the fact that the parent is activated, deployed or temporarily assigned to military service, which would materially affect or change a previous judgment or order regarding custody of that parent's child or children as such judgment or order existed on the date the parent was activated, deployed, or temporarily assigned to military service, shall be subject to review pursuant to paragraph three of this subdivision. Any relevant provisions of the Service Member's Civil Relief Act shall apply to all proceedings governed by this section.

2. During such period, the court may enter an order to modify custody if there is clear and convincing evidence that the modification is in the best interests of the child. An attorney for the child shall be appointed in all cases where a modification is sought during such military service. Such order shall be subject to review pursuant to paragraph three of this subdivision. When entering an order pursuant to this section, the court shall consider and provide for, if feasible and if in the best interests of the child, contact between the military service member and his or her child including, but not limited to, electronic communication by e-mail, webcam, telephone, or other available means. During the period of the parent's leave from military service, the court shall consider the best interests of the child when establishing a parenting schedule, including visiting and other contact. For such purpose, a "leave from military service" shall be a period of not more than three months.

3. Unless the parties have otherwise stipulated or agreed, if an order is issued pursuant to this subdivision, the return of the parent from active military service, deployment or temporary assignment shall be considered a substantial change in circumstances. Upon the request of either parent, the court shall determine on the basis of the child's best interests whether the custody judgment or order previously in effect should be modified.

4. This subdivision shall not apply to assignments to permanent duty stations or permanent changes of station.

§651-a. Reports of child abuse and maltreatment; admissibility.

In any proceeding brought pursuant to this section to determine the custody or visitation of minors, a report made to the statewide central register of child abuse and maltreatment, pursuant to title six of article six of the social services law, or a portion thereof, which is otherwise admissible as a business record pursuant to rule forty-five hundred eighteen of the civil practice law and rules shall not be admissible in evidence, notwithstanding such rule, unless an investigation of such report conducted pursuant to title six of article six of the social services law has determined that there is some credible evidence of the alleged abuse or maltreatment, that the subject of the report has been notified that the report is indicated. In addition, if such report has been reviewed by the state commissioner of social services or his designee and has been determined to be unfounded, it shall not be admissible in evidence. If such report has been so reviewed and has been amended to delete any finding, each such deleted finding shall not be admissible. If the state commissioner of social services or his designee has amended the report to add any new finding, each such new finding, together with any portion of the original report not deleted by the commissioner or his designee, shall be admissible if it meets the other requirements of this section and is otherwise admissible as a business record. If such a report, or portion thereof, is admissible in evidence but is uncorroborated, it shall not be sufficient to make a fact finding of abuse or maltreatment in such proceeding. Any other evidence tending to support the reliability of such report shall be sufficient corroboration.

§652. Jurisdiction over applications to fix custody in matrimonial actions on referral from supreme court.

(a) When referred from the supreme court to the family court, the family court has jurisdiction to determine, with the same powers possessed by the supreme court, applications to fix temporary or permanent custody and applications to modify judgments and orders of custody or visitation in actions and proceedings for marital separation, divorce, annulment of marriage and dissolution of marriage. Applications to modify judgments and orders of custody may be granted by the family court under this section only upon the showing to the family court that there has been a subsequent change of circumstances and that modification is required.

(b) In the event no such referral has been made and unless the supreme court provides in the order or judgment awarding custody or visitation in an action for divorce, separation or annulment, that it may be enforced or modified only in the supreme court, the family court may:

(i) determine an application to enforce the order or judgment awarding custody or visitation, or

(ii) determine an application to modify the order or judgment awarding custody or visitation upon a showing that there has been a subsequent change of circumstances and modification is required.

(c) In any determination of an application pursuant to this section, the family court shall have jurisdiction to determine such applications, in accordance with subdivision one of section two hundred forty of the domestic relations law, with the same powers possessed by the supreme court, and the family court's disposition of any such application is an order of the family court appealable only under article eleven of this act.

§653. Rules of court.

Rules of court, not inconsistent with any law, may authorize the probation service to interview such persons and obtain such data as will aid the court in determining a habeas corpus or custody proceeding under section six hundred fifty-one.

§655. Temporary order of protection.

(a) Upon the filing of a petition or counter-claim under this article, the court for good cause shown may issue a temporary order of protection which may contain any of the provisions authorized on the making of an order of protection under section six hundred fifty-six of this article.

(b) A temporary order of protection is not a finding of wrongdoing.

(c) The court may issue or extend a temporary order of protection ex parte or on notice simultaneously with the issuance of a warrant directing that the respondent be arrested and brought before the court pursuant to section six hundred seventy-one of this article.

(d) The court shall not require anyone seeking a temporary order of protection under this section to first request that child protective services investigate the allegations or to first request permission to file a petition under article ten of this act.

Notwithstanding the foregoing provisions, an order of protection, or temporary order of protection where applicable, may be entered against a former spouse and persons who have a child in common, regardless of whether such persons have been married or have lived together at any time, or against a member of the same family or household as defined in subdivision one of section eight hundred twelve of this act.

§656. Order of protection.

The court may make an order of protection and an order of probation in assistance or as a condition of any other order made under this part. The order of protection may set forth reasonable conditions of behavior to be observed for a specific time by any petitioner or any respondent, and shall specify if an order of probation is in effect. No order of protection may direct any party to observe conditions of behavior unless the party requesting the order of protection has served and filed a petition or counter-claim in accordance with section one hundred fifty-four-b of this act. Such an order may require the petitioner or the respondent:

(a) to stay away from the home, school, business or place of employment of any other party, the other spouse or parent, or the child, and to stay away from any other specific location designated by the court;

(b) to permit a parent, or a person entitled to visitation by a court order or a separation agreement, to visit the child at stated periods;

(c) to refrain from committing a family offense, as defined in subdivision one of section eight hundred twelve of this act, or any criminal offense against the child or against the other parent or against any person to whom custody of the child is awarded, or from harassing, intimidating or threatening such persons;

(d) to permit a designated party to enter the residence during a specified period of time in order to remove personal belongings not in issue in this pro-ceeding or in any other proceeding or action under this act or the domestic rela-tions law;

(e) to refrain from acts of commission or omission that create an unreasonable risk to the health, safety or welfare of a child;

(f) to participate in an educational program and to pay the costs thereof if the person has the means to do so, provided however that nothing contained herein shall be deemed to require payment of the costs of any such program by the state or any political subdivision thereof;

(g) to provide, either directly or by means of medical and health insurance, for expenses incurred for medical care and treatment arising from the incident or incidents forming the basis for the issuance of the order;

(h) to pay the reasonable counsel fees and disbursements involved in obtaining or enforcing the order of the person who is protected by such order if such order is issued or enforced;

(i) 1. to refrain from intentionally injuring or killing, without justification, any companion animal the respondent knows to be owned, possessed, leased, kept or held by the petitioner or a minor child residing in the household.

2. "Companion animal", as used in this section, shall have the same meaning as in subdivision five of section three hundred fifty of the agriculture and markets law;

(j) 1. to promptly return specified identification documents to the protected party, in whose favor the order of protection or temporary order of protection is issued; provided, however, that such order may: (A) include any appropriate provision designed to ensure that any such document is available for use as evidence in this proceeding, and available if necessary for legitimate use by the party against whom such order is issued; and (B) specify the manner in which such return shall be accomplished.

2. For purposes of this subdivision, "identification document" shall mean any of the following: (A) exclusively in the name of the protected party: birth certificate, passport, social security card, health insurance or other benefits card, a card or document used to access bank, credit or other financial accounts or records, tax returns, any driver's license, and immigration documents including but not limited to a United States permanent resident card and employment authorization document; and (B) upon motion and after notice and an opportunity to be heard, any of the following, including those that may reflect joint use or ownership, that the court determines are necessary and are appropriately transferred to the protected party: any card or document used to access bank, credit or other financial accounts or records, tax returns, and any other identifying cards and documents; and

(k) to observe such other conditions as are necessary to further the purposes of protection.

The court shall not require anyone seeking an order of protection under this section to first request that child protective services investigate the allegations or to first request permission to file a petition under article ten of this act.

Notwithstanding the foregoing provisions, an order of protection, or temporary order of protection where applicable, may be entered against a former spouse and persons who have a child in common, regardless of whether such persons have been married or have lived together at any time, or against a member of the same family or household as defined in subdivision one of section eight hundred twelve of this act.

In addition to the foregoing provisions, the court may issue an order, pursuant to section two hundred twenty-seven-c of the real property law, authorizing the party for whose benefit any order of protection has been issued to terminate a lease or rental agreement pursuant to section two hundred twenty-seven-c of the real property law.

In any proceeding pursuant to this article, a court shall not deny an order of protection, or dismiss an application for such an order, solely on the basis that the acts or events alleged are not relatively contemporaneous with the date of the application or the conclusion of the action. The duration of any temporary order shall not by itself be a factor in determining the length or issuance of any final order.

The protected party in whose favor the order of protection or temporary order of protection is issued may not be held to violate an order issued in his or her favor nor may such protected party be arrested for violating such order.

§656-a. Firearms; surrender and license suspension, revocation and ineligibility.

Upon the issuance of an order of protection or temporary order of protection, or upon a violation of such order, the court shall make a determination regarding the suspension and revocation of a license to carry, possess, repair or dispose of a firearm or firearms, ineligibility for such a license and the surrender of firearms in accordance with section eight hundred forty-two-a of this act.

§657. Certain provisions relating to the guardianship and custody of children by persons who are not the parents of such children.

(a) Notwithstanding any provision of the law to the contrary, a person possessing a lawful order of guardianship or custody of a minor child, who is not the parent of such child, may enroll such child in public school in the applicable school district where he or she and such child reside. Upon application for enrollment of a minor child by a guardian or custodian who is not the parent of such child, a public school shall enroll such child for such time as the child resides with the guardian or custodian in the applicable school district, upon verification that the guardian or custodian possess a lawful order of guardianship or custody for such child and that the guardian or custodian and the child properly reside in the same household within the school district.

(b) Notwithstanding any provision of law to the contrary, persons possessing a lawful order of custody of a child who are not a parent of such child shall have the same right to enroll and receive coverage for such child in their employer based health insurance plan and to assert the same legal rights under such employer based health insurance plans as persons who possess lawful orders of guardianship of the person for a child pursuant to rule twelve hundred ten of the civil practice laws and rules, article seventeen of the surrogate's court procedure act, or part 4 of this article.

(c) Notwithstanding any other provision of law to the contrary, persons possessing a lawful order of guardianship of a child shall have the right and responsibility to make decisions, including issuing any necessary consents, regarding the child's protection, education, care and control, health and medical needs, and the physical custody of the person of the child. Provided, however, that nothing in this subdivision shall be construed to limit the ability of a child to consent to his or her own medical care as may be otherwise provided by law.

Part 4
Guardianship

§661. Jurisdiction.

When initiated in the family court, such court has like jurisdiction and authority to determine as county and surrogates courts in proceedings regarding the guardianship of the person of a minor or infant and permanent guardianship of a child. Such jurisdiction shall apply as follows:

(a) Guardianship of the person of a minor or infant. When making a determination regarding the guardianship of the person of a minor or infant, the provisions of the surrogate's court procedure act shall apply to the extent they are applicable to guardianship of the person of a minor or infant and do not conflict with the specific provisions of this act. For purposes of appointment of a guardian of the person pursuant to this part, the terms infant or minor shall include a person who is less than twenty-one years old who consents to the appointment or continuation of a guardian after the age of eighteen.

(b) Permanent guardianship of a child. Where the guardianship and custody of a child have been committed to an authorized agency pursuant to section six hundred fourteen of this article, or section three hundred eighty-three-c, section three hundred eighty-four or section three hundred eighty-four-b of the social services law, or where both parents of a child whose consent to the adoption of the child would have been required pursuant to section one hundred eleven of the domestic relations law or who were entitled to notice of an adoption proceeding pursuant to section one hundred eleven-a of the domestic relations law are dead, the court may appoint a permanent guardian of a child if the court finds that such appointment is in the best interests of the child. The provisions of the surrogate's court procedure act shall apply to the extent that they are applicable to a proceeding for appointment of a permanent guardian of a child and do not conflict with the specific provisions of this act. Such permanent guardian of a child shall have the right and responsibility to make decisions, including issuing any necessary consents, regarding the child's protection, education, care and control, health and medical needs, and the physical custody of the person of the child, and may consent to the adoption of the child. Provided, however, that nothing in this subdivision shall be construed to limit the ability of a child to consent to his or her own medical care as may be otherwise provided by law.

(c) Special provisions in relation to guardianship of a foster child. Where the permanency goal for a foster child who is the subject of a proceeding under article ten or ten-A of this act is referral for legal guardianship, a petition under this article filed by a fit and willing relative or other suitable person shall be filed with the court before whom the most recent proceeding under article ten or ten-A of this act is pending. The court presiding over the proceeding pursuant to article ten or ten-A of this act may consolidate the hearing of the guardianship petition or permanent guardianship petition filed by such relative or other suitable person with the dispositional hearing under article ten of this act or a permanency hearing under article ten-A of this act, as applicable. In granting such a petition, the court must make such order in accordance with the procedures and make the findings enumerated in section one thousand fifty-five-b or one thousand eighty-nine-a of this act, as applicable.

§662. Rules of court.
Rules of court, not inconsistent with any law, may authorize the probation service to interview such persons and obtain such data as will aid the court in exercising its power under section six hundred sixty-one.

§663. Guardian of person to file copy of order of appointment.
Upon the appointment and qualification of guardian of the person of a minor as provided in section six hundred sixty-one of this act, letters of guardianship shall thereupon issue from this court.

§664. Recording in camera interviews of infants.
(a) The court shall not conduct an in camera interview of an infant in any action or proceeding to fix temporary or permanent custody or to modify judgments and orders of custody concerning marital separation, divorce, annulment of marriage and dissolution of marriage unless a stenographic record of such interview is made.

(b) If an appeal is taken to the appellate division from a judgment or order of the court on any such action or proceeding, the stenographic record of any such interview shall be made a part of the record and forwarded under seal to the appellate division.

Part 5
Warrant

§671. Issuance of warrant; certificate of warrant.

(a) The court may issue a warrant, directing that the respondent be arrested, brought before the court, when a petition is presented to the court under sections six hundred fourteen, six hundred fifty-one, six hundred fifty-four, six hundred fifty-five and six hundred fifty-six of this article or section three hundred eighty-four-b of the social services law and it appears that:

(i) the summons cannot be served; or

(ii) the respondent has failed to obey the summons; or

(iii) the respondent is likely to leave the jurisdiction; or

(iv) a summons, in the court's opinion, would be ineffectual; or

(v) the safety of the petitioner or child is endangered; or

(vi) a respondent on bail or on parole has failed to appear.

(b) The petitioner may not serve a warrant upon the respondent unless the court itself grants such permission upon the application of the petitioner. The clerk of the court may issue to the petitioner or to the representative of an incorporated charitable or philanthropic society having a legitimate interest in the family a certificate stating that a warrant for the respondent has been issued by the court. The presentation of such certificate by said petitioner or representative to any peace officer, acting pursuant to his special duties, or police officer authorizes him to arrest the respondent and take him to court.

(c) A certificate of warrant expires ninety days from the date of issue but may be renewed from time to time by the clerk of the court.

(d) Rules of court shall provide that a record of all unserved warrants be kept and that periodic reports concerning unserved warrants be made.

ARTICLE 7
Proceedings Concerning
Whether a Person Is in Need of Supervision

Part 1
Jurisdiction

§711. Purpose.

The purpose of this article is to provide a due process of law (a) for considering a claim that a person is in need of supervision and (b) for devising an appropriate order of disposition for any person adjudged in need of supervision.

§712. Definitions.

As used in this article, the following terms shall have the following meanings:

(a) "Person in need of supervision". A person less than eighteen years of age who does not attend school in accordance with the provisions of part one of article sixty-five of the education law or who is incorrigible, ungovernable or habitually disobedient and beyond the lawful control of a parent or other person legally responsible for such child's care, or other lawful authority, or who violates the provisions of section 221.05 or 230.00 of the penal law, or who appears to be a sexually exploited child as defined in paragraph (a), (c) or (d) of subdivision one of section four hundred forty-seven-a of the social services law, but only if the child consents to the filing of a petition under this article.

(b) "Detention". The temporary care and maintenance of children away from their own homes as defined in section five hundred two of the executive law.

(c) "Secure detention facility". A facility characterized by physically restricting construction, hardware and procedures.

(d) "Non-secure detention facility". A facility characterized by the absence of physically restricting construction, hardware and procedures.

(e) "Fact-finding hearing". A hearing to determine whether the respondent did the acts alleged to show that he violated a law or is incorrigible, ungovernable or habitually disobedient and beyond the control of his parents, guardian or legal custodian.

(f) "Dispositional hearing". A hearing to determine whether the respondent requires supervision or treatment.

(g) "Aggravated circumstances". Aggravated circumstances shall have the same meaning as the definition of such term in subdivision (j) of section one thousand twelve of this act.

(h) "Permanency hearing". A hearing held in accordance with paragraph (b) of subdivision two of section seven hundred fifty-four or section seven hundred fifty-six-a of this article for the purpose of reviewing the foster care status of the respondent and the appropriateness of the permanency plan developed by the social services official on behalf of such respondent.

(i) "Diversion services". Services provided to children and families pursuant to section seven hundred thirty-five of this article for the purpose of avoiding the need to file a petition or direct the detention of the child. Diversion services shall include: efforts to adjust cases pursuant to this article before a petition is filed, or by order of the court, after the petition is filed but before fact-finding is commenced; and preventive services provided in accordance with section four hundred nine-a of the social services law to avert the placement of the child into foster care, including crisis intervention and respite services. Diversion services may also include, in cases where any person is seeking to file a petition that alleges that the child has a substance use disorder or is in need of immediate detoxification or substance use disorder services, an assessment for substance use disorder; provided, however, that notwithstanding any other provision of law to the contrary, the designated lead agency shall not be required to pay for all or any portion of the costs of such assessment or substance use disorder or detoxification services, except in cases where medical assistance for needy persons may be used to pay for all or any portion of the costs of such assessment or services.

(j) "Substance use disorder". The misuse of, dependence on, or addiction to alcohol and/or legal or illegal drugs leading to effects that are detrimental to the person's physical and mental health or the welfare of others.

(k) "Assessment for substance use disorder". Assessment by a provider that has been certified by the office of alcoholism and substance abuse services of a person less than eighteen years of age where it is alleged that the youth is suffering from a substance use disorder which could make a youth a danger to himself or herself or others.

(*l*) "A substance use disorder which could make a youth a danger to himself or herself or others". A substance use disorder that is accompanied by the dependence on, or the repeated use or abuse of, drugs or alcohol to the point of intoxication such that the person is in need of immediate detoxification or other substance use disorder services.

(m) "Substance use disorder services". Substance use disorder services shall have the same meaning as provided for in section 1.03 of the mental hygiene law.

§713. Jurisdiction.

The family court has exclusive original jurisdiction over any proceeding involving a person alleged to be a person in need of supervision.

§714. Determination of age.

(a) In determining the jurisdiction of the court under section seven hundred thirteen the age of the respondent at the time the need for supervision allegedly arose is controlling.

(b) If the respondent is within the jurisdiction of the court, but the proceedings were initiated after the respondent's eighteenth birthday, the family court shall dismiss a petition to determine whether a person is in need of supervision.

§716. Substitution of petition.

On its own motion and at any time in the proceedings, the court may substitute a neglect petition under article ten for a petition to determine whether a person is in need of supervision.

§717. Venue.

Proceedings under this article are originated in the county in which the act or acts referred to in the petition allegedly occurred. On motion made on behalf of the respondent or by his parent or other person legally responsible for his care or on the court's motion, and for good cause shown, the court may transfer the proceedings to another county.

§718. Return of run away.

(a) A peace officer, acting pursuant to such peace officer's special duties, or a police officer may return to a parent or other person legally responsible for such child's care any child under the age of eighteen who has run away from home without just cause or who, in the reasonable conclusion of the officer, appears to have run away from home without just cause. For purposes of this action, a police officer or peace officer may reasonably conclude that a child has run away from home when the child refuses to give his or her name or the name and address of a parent or other person legally responsible for such child's care or when the officer has reason to doubt that the name or address given are the actual name and address of the parent or other person legally responsible for the child's care.

(b) A peace officer, acting pursuant to the peace officer's special duties, or a police officer is authorized to take a youth who has run away from home or who, in the reasonable opinion of the officer, appears to have run away from home, to a facility certified or approved for such purpose by the office of children and family services, if the peace officer or police officer is unable, or if it is unsafe, to return the youth to his or her home or to the custody of his or her parent or other person legally responsible for his or her care. Any such facility receiving a youth shall inform a parent or other person responsible for such youth's care.

(c) If a child placed pursuant to this article in the custody of a commissioner of social services or an authorized agency shall run away from the custody of such commissioner or authorized agency, any peace officer, acting pursuant to his special duties, or police officer may apprehend, restrain, and return such child to such location as such commissioner shall direct or to such authorized agency and it shall be the duty of any such officer to assist any representative of the commissioner or agency to take into custody any such child upon the request of such representative.

Part 2
Custody and Detention

§720. Detention.

1. No child to whom the provisions of this article may apply, shall be detained in any prison, jail, lockup, or other place used for adults convicted of crime or under arrest and charged with a crime.

2. The detention of a child in a secure detention facility shall not be directed under any of the provisions of this article.

3. Detention of a person alleged to be or adjudicated as a person in need of supervision shall, except as provided in subdivision four of this section, be authorized only in a foster care program certified by the office of children and family services, or a certified or approved family boarding home, or a non-secure detention facility certified by the office and in accordance with section seven hundred thirty-nine of this article. The setting of the detention shall take into account (a) the proximity to the community in which the person alleged to be or adjudicated as a person in need of supervision lives with such person's parents or to which such person will be discharged, and (b) the existing educational setting of such person and the proximity of such setting to the location of the detention setting.

4. Whenever detention is authorized and ordered pursuant to this article, for a person alleged to be or adjudicated as a person in need of supervision, a

family court in a city having a population of one million or more shall, notwithstanding any other provision of law, direct detention in a foster care facility established and maintained pursuant to the social services law. In all other respects, the detention of such a person in a foster care facility shall be subject to the identical terms and conditions for detention as are set forth in this article and in section two hundred thirty-five of this act.

5. (a) The court shall not order or direct detention under this article, unless the court determines that there is no substantial likelihood that the youth and his or her family will continue to benefit from diversion services and that all available alternatives to detention have been exhausted; and

(b) Where the youth is sixteen years of age or older, the court shall not order or direct detention under this article, unless the court determines and states in its order that special circumstances exist to warrant such detention.

(c) If the respondent may be a sexually exploited child as defined in subdivision one of section four hundred forty-seven-a of the social services law, the court may direct the respondent to an available short-term safe house as defined in subdivision two of section four hundred forty-seven-a of the social services law as an alternative to detention.

§723.   Duties of private person before and after taking into custody.

(a) Before taking into custody, a private person must inform the person to be taken into custody of the cause thereof and require him to submit.

(b) After taking into custody, a private person must take the person, without unnecessary delay, to his home, to a family court judge or deliver him to a peace officer, who is acting pursuant to his special duties, or a police officer.

§724.   Duties of police officer or peace officer after taking into custody or on delivery by private person.

(a) If a peace officer or a police officer takes into custody or if a person is delivered to him under section seven hundred twenty-three, the officer shall immediately notify the parent or other person legally responsible for his care, or the person with whom he is domiciled, that he has been taken into custody.

(b) After making every reasonable effort to give notice under paragraph (a), the officer shall

(i) release the youth to the custody of his or her parent or other person legally responsible for his or her care upon the written promise, without security, of the person to whose custody the youth is released that he or she will produce the youth before the lead agency designated pursuant to section seven hundred thirty-five of this article in that county at a time and place specified in writing; or

(ii) forthwith and with all reasonable speed take the youth directly, and without first being taken to the police station house, to the designated lead agency located in the county in which the act occasioning the taking into custody allegedly was done, unless the officer determines that it is necessary to question the youth, in which case he or she may take the youth to a facility designated by the chief administrator of the courts as a suitable place for the questioning of youth or, upon the consent of a parent or other person legally responsible for the care of the youth, to the youth's residence and there question him or her for a reasonable period of time; or

(iii) take a youth in need of crisis intervention or respite services to an approved runaway program or other approved respite or crisis program; or

(iv) take the youth directly to the family court located in the county in which the act occasioning the taking into custody was allegedly done, provided that the officer affirms on the record that he or she attempted to exercise the options identified in paragraphs (i), (ii) and (iii) of this subdivision, was unable to exercise these options, and the reasons therefor.

(c) In the absence of special circumstances, the officer shall release the child in accord with paragraph (b) (i).

(d) In determining what is a "reasonable period of time" for questioning a child, the child's age and the presence or absence of his parents or other person legally responsible for his care shall be included among the relevant considerations.

§725. Summons or warrant on failure to appear.

The family court before which a person failed to produce a child pursuant to a written promise given under section seven hundred twenty-four may issue a summons requiring the child and the person who failed to produce him to appear at the court at a time and place specified in the summons or may issue a warrant for either or both of them, directing that either or both be brought to the court at a time and place specified in the warrant.

§727. Rules of court authorizing release before filing of petition.

(a) The agency responsible for operating a detention facility or in a city of one million or more, the agency responsible for operating a foster care facility, may release a child in custody before the filing of a petition to the custody of his parents or other relative, guardian or legal custodian when the events occasioning the taking into custody appear to involve a petition to determine whether a person is in need of supervision rather than a petition to determine whether a person is a juvenile delinquent.

(b) When a release is made under this section such release may, but need not, be conditioned upon the giving of a recognizance in accord with section seven hundred twenty-four (b) (i).

(c) If the probation service for any reason does not release a child under this section, the child shall promptly be brought before a judge of the court, if practicable, and section seven hundred twenty-eight shall apply.

§728. Discharge, release or detention by judge after hearing and before filing of petition in custody cases.

(a) If a child in custody is brought before a judge of the family court before a petition is filed, the judge shall hold a hearing for the purpose of making a preliminary determination of whether the court appears to have jurisdiction over the child. At the commencement of the hearing, the judge shall advise the child of his or her right to remain silent, his or her right to be represented by counsel of his or her own choosing, and of the right to have an attorney assigned in accord with part four of article two of this act. The judge must also allow the child a reasonable time to send for his or her parents or other person or persons legally responsible for his or her care, and for counsel, and adjourn the hearing for that purpose.

(b) After hearing, the judge shall order the release of the child to the custody of his parent or other person legally responsible for his care if the court does not appear to have jurisdiction.

(c) An order of release under this section may, but need not, be conditioned upon the giving of a recognizance in accord with sections seven hundred twenty-four (b) (i).

(d) Upon a finding of facts and reasons which support a detention order pursuant to this section, the court shall also determine and state in any order directing detention:

(i) that there is no substantial likelihood that the youth and his or her family will continue to benefit from diversion services and that all available alternatives to detention have been exhausted; and

(ii) whether continuation of the child in the child's home would be contrary to the best interests of the child based upon, and limited to, the facts and circumstances available to the court at the time of the hearing held in accordance with this section; and

(iii) where appropriate, whether reasonable efforts were made prior to the date of the court hearing that resulted in the detention order, to prevent or eliminate the need for removal of the child from his or her home or, if the child had been removed from his or her home prior to the court appearance pursuant to this section, where appropriate, whether reasonable efforts were made to make it possible for the child to safely return home; and

(iv) whether the setting of the detention takes into account the proximity to the community in which the person alleged to be or adjudicated as a person in need of supervision lives with such person's parents or to which such person will be discharged, and the existing educational setting of such person and the proximity of such setting to the location of the detention setting.

§729. Duration of detention before filing of petition or hearing.

No person may be detained under this article for more than seventy-two hours or the next day the court is in session, whichever is sooner, without a hearing under section seven hundred twenty-eight.

Part 3
Preliminary Procedure

§732. Originating proceeding to adjudicate need for supervision.

A proceeding to adjudicate a person to be in need of supervision is originated by the filing of a petition, alleging:

(a) (i) the respondent is an habitual truant or is incorrigible, ungovernable, or habitually disobedient and beyond the lawful control of his or her parents, guardian or lawful custodian, or has been the victim of sexual exploitation as defined in subdivision one of section four hundred forty-seven-a of the social services law, and specifying the acts on which the allegations are based and the time and place they allegedly occurred. Where habitual truancy is alleged or the petitioner is a school district or local educational agency, the petition shall also include the steps taken by the responsible school district or local educational agency to improve the school attendance and/or conduct of the respondent;

(ii) the respondent was under eighteen years of age at the time of the specified acts;

(iii) the respondent requires supervision or treatment; and

(iv) the petitioner has complied with the provisions of section seven hundred thirty-five of this article; or

(b) the respondent appears to be a sexually exploited child as defined in paragraph (a), (c) or (d) of subdivision one of section four hundred forty-seven-a of the social services law but only if the child consents to the filing of a petition under this article.

§733. Persons who may originate proceedings.

The following persons may originate a proceeding under this article:

(a) a peace officer, acting pursuant to his special duties, or a police officer;

(b) the parent or other person legally responsible for his care;

(c) any person who has suffered injury as a result of the alleged activity of a person alleged to be in need of supervision, or a witness to such activity;

(d) the recognized agents of any duly authorized agency, association, society or institution; or

(e) the presentment agency that consented to substitute a petition alleging the person is in need of supervision for a petition alleging, that the person is a juvenile delinquent pursuant to section 311.4.

§735. Preliminary procedure; diversion services.

(a) Each county and any city having a population of one million or more shall offer diversion services as defined in section seven hundred twelve of this article to youth who are at risk of being the subject of a person in need of supervision petition. Such services shall be designed to provide an immediate response to families in crisis, to identify and utilize appropriate alternatives to detention and to divert youth from being the subject of a petition in family court. Each county and such city shall designate either the local social services district or the probation department as lead agency for the purposes of providing diversion services.

(b) The designated lead agency shall:

(i) confer with any person seeking to file a petition, the youth who may be a potential respondent, his or her family, and other interested persons, concerning the provision of diversion services before any petition may be filed; and

(ii) diligently attempt to prevent the filing of a petition under this article or, after the petition is filed, to prevent the placement of the youth into foster care; and

(iii) assess whether the youth would benefit from residential respite services; and

(iv) determine whether alternatives to detention are appropriate to avoid remand of the youth to detention; and

(v) determine whether an assessment of the youth for substance use disorder by an office of alcoholism and substance abuse services certified provider is necessary when a person seeking to file a petition alleges in such petition that the youth is suffering from a substance use disorder which could make the youth a danger to himself or herself or others. Provided, however, that notwithstanding any other provision of law to the contrary, the designated lead agency shall not be required to pay for all or any portion of the costs of such assessment or for any substance use disorder or detoxification services, except in cases where medical assistance for needy persons may be used to pay for all or any portion of the costs of such assessment or services. The office of alcoholism and substance abuse services shall make a list of its certified providers available to the designated lead agency.

(c) Any person or agency seeking to file a petition pursuant to this article which does not have attached thereto the documentation required by subdivision (g) of this section shall be referred by the clerk of the court to the designated lead agency which shall schedule and hold, on reasonable notice to the potential petitioner, the youth and his or her parent or other person legally responsible for his or her care, at least one conference in order to determine the factual circumstances and determine whether the youth and his or her family should receive diversion services pursuant to this section. Diversion services shall include clearly documented diligent attempts to provide appropriate services to the youth and his or her family unless it is determined that there is no substantial likelihood that the youth and his or her family will benefit from further diversion attempts. Notwithstanding the provisions of section two hundred sixteen-c of this act, the clerk shall not accept for filing under this part any petition that does not have attached thereto the documentation required by subdivision (g) of this section.

(d) Diversion services shall include documented diligent attempts to engage the youth and his or her family in appropriately targeted community-based services, but shall not be limited to:

(i) providing, at the first contact, information on the availability of or a referral to services in the geographic area where the youth and his or her family are located that may be of benefit in avoiding the need to file a petition under this article; including the availability, for up to twenty-one days, of a residential respite program, if the youth and his or her parent or other person legally responsible for his or her care agree, and the availability of other non-residential crisis intervention programs such as family crisis counseling or alternative dispute resolution programs or an educational program as defined in section four hundred fifty-eight-l of the social services law.

(ii) scheduling and holding at least one conference with the youth and his or her family and the person or representatives of the entity seeking to file a petition under this article concerning alternatives to filing a petition and services that are available. Diversion services shall include clearly documented diligent attempts to provide appropriate services to the youth and his or her family before it may be determined that there is no substantial likelihood that the youth and his or her family will benefit from further attempts.

(iii) where the entity seeking to file a petition is a school district or local educational agency, the designated lead agency shall review the steps taken by the school district or local educational agency to improve the youth's attendance and/or conduct in school and attempt to engage the school district or local educational agency in further diversion attempts, if it appears from review that such attempts will be beneficial to the youth.

(e) The designated lead agency shall maintain a written record with respect to each youth and his or her family for whom it considers providing or provides diversion services pursuant to this section. The record shall be made available to the court at or prior to the initial appearance of the youth in any proceeding initiated pursuant to this article.

(f) Efforts to prevent the filing of a petition pursuant to this section may extend until the designated lead agency determines that there is no substantial likelihood that the youth and his or her family will benefit from further attempts. Efforts at diversion pursuant to this section may continue after the filing of a petition where the designated lead agency determines that the youth and his or her family will benefit from further attempts to prevent the youth from entering foster care.

(g) (i) The designated lead agency shall promptly give written notice to the potential petitioner whenever attempts to prevent the filing of a petition have terminated, and shall indicate in such notice whether efforts were successful. The notice shall also detail the diligent attempts made to divert the case if a determination has been made that there is no substantial likelihood that the youth will benefit from further attempts. No persons in need of supervision petition may be filed pursuant to this article during the period the designated lead agency is providing diversion services. A finding by the designated lead agency that the case has been successfully diverted shall constitute presumptive evidence that the underlying allegations have been successfully resolved in any petition based upon the same factual allegations. No petition may be filed pursuant to this article by the parent or other person legally responsible for the youth where diversion services have been terminated because of the failure of the parent or other person legally responsible for the youth to consent to or actively participate.

(ii) The clerk of the court shall accept a petition for filing only if it has attached thereto the following:

(A) if the potential petitioner is the parent or other person legally responsible for the youth, a notice from the designated lead agency indicating there is no bar to the filing of the petition as the potential petitioner consented to and actively participated in diversion services; and

(B) a notice from the designated lead agency stating that it has terminated diversion services because it has determined that there is no substantial likelihood that the youth and his or her family will benefit from further attempts, and that the case has not been successfully diverted.

(h) No statement made to the designated lead agency or to any agency or organization to which the potential respondent has been referred, prior to the filing of the petition, or if the petition has been filed, prior to the time the respondent has been notified that attempts at diversion will not be made or have been terminated, or prior to the commencement of a fact-finding hearing if attempts at diversion have not terminated previously, may be admitted into evidence at a fact-finding hearing or, if the proceeding is transferred to a criminal court, at any time prior to a conviction.

§736. Issuance of summons.

(1) On the filing of a petition under this article, the court may cause a copy of the petition and a summons to be issued, requiring the respondent and his parent or other person legally responsible for his care, or with whom he is domiciled, to appear at the court at a time and place named to answer the petition. The summons shall be signed by the court or by the clerk or deputy clerk of the court. If those on whom a summons must be served are before the court at the time of the filing of a petition, the provisions of part four of this article shall be followed.

(2) In proceedings originated pursuant to subdivision (b) of section seven hundred thirty-three of this article, the court shall cause a copy of the petition and notice of the time and place to be heard to be served upon any parent of the respondent or other person legally responsible for the respondent's care who

has not signed the petition, provided that the address of such parent or other person legally responsible is known to the court or is ascertainable by the court. Such petition shall include a notice that, upon placement of the child in the care and custody of the department of social services or any other agency, said parent may be named as a respondent in a child support proceeding brought pursuant to article four of this act. Service shall be made by the clerk of the court by mailing such notice and petition by ordinary first class mail to such parent or other person legally responsible at such person's last known residence.

(3) In proceedings originated pursuant to subdivision (a), (c), (d) or (e) of section seven hundred thirty-three of this article, the court shall cause a copy of the petition and notice of the time and place to be heard to be served upon each parent of the respondent or other person legally responsible for the respondent's care, provided that the address of such parent or other person legally responsible is known to the court or is ascertainable by the court. Service shall be made by the clerk of the court by mailing such notice and petition by ordinary first class mail to such parent or other person legally responsible at such person's last known residence.

§737. Service of summons.

(a) Service of a summons and petition shall be made by delivery of a true copy thereof to the person summoned at least twenty-four hours before the time stated therein for appearance. If so requested by one acting on behalf of the respondent or by a parent or other person legally responsible for his care, the court shall not proceed with the hearing or proceeding earlier than three days after such service.

(b) If after reasonable effort, personal service is not made, the court may at any stage in the proceedings make an order providing for substituted service in the manner provided for substituted service in civil process in courts of record.

§738. Issuance of warrant for respondent or other person legally responsible for care.

The court may issue a warrant, directing that the respondent or other person legally responsible for his care or with whom he is domiciled be brought before the court, when a petition is filed with the court under this article and it appears that

(a) the summons cannot be served; or

(b) the respondent or other person has refused to obey the summons; or

(c) the respondent or other person is likely to leave the jurisdiction; or

(d) a summons, in the court's opinion, would be ineffectual; or

(e) a respondent on bail or on parole has failed to appear.

A warrant issued for a respondent under this section shall expire at the end of six months from the date of its issuance, unless extended for an additional period of not more than six months upon application by the petitioner for good cause shown.

§739. Release or detention after filing of petition and prior to order of disposition.

(a) After the filing of a petition under section seven hundred thirty-two of this part, the court in its discretion may release the respondent or direct his or her detention. If the respondent may be a sexually exploited child as defined in subdivision one of section four hundred forty-seven-a of the social services law, the court may direct the respondent to an available short-term safe house as an alternative to detention. However, the court shall not direct detention unless it finds and states the facts and reasons for so finding that unless the respondent is detained there is a substantial probability that the respondent will not appear in court on the return date and all available alternatives to detention have been exhausted.

(b) Unless the respondent waives a determination that probable cause exists to believe that he is a person in need of supervision, no detention under this section may last more than three days (i) unless the court finds, pursuant to the evidentiary standards applicable to a hearing on a felony complaint in a criminal court, that such probable cause exists, or (ii) unless special circumstances exist, in which cases such detention may be extended not more than an additional three days exclusive of Saturdays, Sundays and public holidays.

(c) Upon a finding of facts and reasons which support a detention order pursuant to subdivision (a) of this section, the court shall also determine and state in any order directing detention:

(i) whether continuation of the respondent in the respondent's home would be contrary to the best interests of the respondent based upon, and limited to, the facts and circumstance available to the court at the time of the court's determination in accordance with this section; and

(ii) where appropriate, whether reasonable efforts were made prior to the date of the court order directing detention in accordance with this section, to prevent or eliminate the need for removal of the respondent from his or her home or, if the respondent had been removed from his or her home prior to the court appearance pursuant to this section, where appropriate, whether reasonable efforts were made to make it possible for the respondent to safely return home.

§740. Temporary order of protection.

(a) Upon the filing of a petition under this article, the court for good cause shown may issue a temporary order of protection which may contain any of the provisions authorized on the making of an order of protection under section seven hundred fifty-nine.

(b) A temporary order of protection is not a finding of wrongdoing.

(c) The court may issue or extend a temporary order of protection ex parte or on notice simultaneously with the issuance of a warrant directing that the respondent be arrested and brought before the court pursuant to section seven hundred thirty-eight of this part.

Part 4
Hearings

§741. Notice of rights; general provision.

(a) At the initial appearance of a respondent in a proceeding and at the commencement of any hearing under this article, the respondent and his or her parent or other person legally responsible for his or her care shall be advised of the respondent's right to remain silent and of the respondent's right to be represented by counsel chosen by him or her or his or her parent or other person legally responsible for his or her care, or by an attorney assigned by the court under part four of article two. Provided, however, that in the event of the failure of the respondent's parent or other person legally responsible for his or her care to appear, after reasonable and substantial effort has been made to notify such parent or responsible person of the commencement of the proceeding and such initial appearance, the court shall appoint an attorney for the respondent and shall, unless inappropriate also appoint a guardian ad litem for such respondent, and in such event, shall inform the respondent of such rights in the presence of such attorney and any guardian ad litem.

(b) The general public may be excluded from any hearing under this article and only such persons and the representatives of authorized agencies admitted thereto as have a direct interest in the case.

(c) At any hearing under this article, the court shall not be prevented from proceeding by the absence of the respondent's parent or other person responsible for his or her care if reasonable and substantial effort has been made to notify such parent or responsible person of the occurrence of the hearing and if the respondent and his or her attorney are present. The court shall, unless inappropriate, also appoint a guardian ad litem who shall be present at such hearing and any subsequent hearing.

§741-a. Notice and right to be heard.
The foster parent caring for the child or any pre-adoptive parent or relative providing care for the respondent shall be provided with notice of any permanency hearing held pursuant to this article by the social services official. Such foster parent, pre-adoptive parent or relative shall have the right to be heard at any such hearing; provided, however, no such foster parent, pre-adoptive parent or relative shall be construed to be a party to the hearing solely on the basis of such notice and right to be heard. The failure of the foster parent, pre-adoptive parent, or relative caring for the child to appear at a permanency hearing shall constitute a waiver of the right to be heard and such failure to appear shall not cause a delay of the permanency hearing nor shall such failure to appear be a ground for the invalidation of any order issued by the court pursuant to this section.

§742. Diversion attempts.
(a) Whenever a petition is filed pursuant to this article, the lead agency designated pursuant to section seven hundred thirty-five of this article shall file a written report with the court indicating any previous actions it has taken with respect to the case.

(b) At the initial appearance of the respondent, the court shall review any termination of diversion services pursuant to such section, and the documentation of diligent attempts to provide appropriate services and determine whether such efforts or services provided are sufficient and may, subject to the provisions of section seven hundred forty-eight of this article, order that additional diversion attempts be undertaken by the designated lead agency. The court may order the youth and the parent or other person legally responsible for the youth to participate in diversion services. If the designated lead agency thereafter determines that the case has been successfully resolved, it shall so notify the court, and the court shall dismiss the petition.

§743. Acceptance of an admission.

(a) Before accepting an admission, the court shall advise the respondent of his or her right to a fact-finding hearing. The court shall also ascertain through allocution of the respondent and his or her parent or person legally responsible for his or her care, if present, that the respondent:

(i) committed the act or acts to which an admission is being entered;

(ii) is voluntarily waiving his or her right to a fact-finding hearing; and

(iii) is aware of the possible specific dispositional orders. The provisions of this subdivision shall not be waived.

(b) Upon acceptance of an admission, the court shall state the reasons for its determination and shall enter a fact-finding order. The court shall schedule a dispositional hearing in accordance with subdivision (b) or (c) of section seven hundred forty-nine of this part.

§744. Evidence in fact-finding hearings; required quantum.

(a) Only evidence that is competent, material and relevant may be admitted in a fact-finding hearing.

(b) Any determination at the conclusion of a fact-finding hearing that a respondent did an act or acts must be based on proof beyond a reasonable doubt. For this purpose, an uncorroborated confession made out of court by a respondent is not sufficient.

§745. Evidence in dispositional hearings; required quantum of proof.

(a) Only evidence that is material and relevant may be admitted during a dispositional hearing.

(b) An adjudication at the conclusion of a dispositional hearing must be based on a preponderance of the evidence.

§746. Sequence of hearings.

Upon completion of the fact-finding hearing the dispositional hearing may commence immediately after the required findings are made.

§747. Time of fact-finding hearing.

A fact-finding hearing shall commence not more than three days after the filing of a petition under this article if the respondent is in detention.

§748. Adjournment of fact-finding hearing.

(a) If the respondent is in detention, the court may adjourn a fact-finding hearing

(i) on its own motion or on motion of the petitioner for good cause shown for not more than three days;

(ii) on motion on behalf of the respondent or by his parent or other person legally responsible for his care for good cause shown, for a reasonable period of time.

(b) Successive motions to adjourn a fact-finding hearing may be granted only under special circumstances.

(c) The court shall state on the record the reason for any adjournment of the fact-finding hearing.

§749. Adjournment after fact-finding hearing or during dispositional hearing.

(a) (i) Upon or after a fact-finding hearing, the court may, upon its own motion or upon a motion of a party to the proceeding, order that the proceeding be "adjourned in contemplation of dismissal". An adjournment in contemplation of dismissal is an adjournment of the proceeding, for a period not to exceed six months with a view to ultimate dismissal of the petition in furtherance of justice. Upon issuing such an order, upon such permissible terms and conditions as the rules of court shall define, the court must release the individual.

(ii) The court may, as a condition of an adjournment in contemplation of dismissal order:

(A) in cases where the record indicates that the consumption of alcohol may have been a contributing factor, require the respondent to attend and complete an alcohol awareness program established pursuant to section 19.25 of the mental hygiene law; or

(B) in cases where the record indicates that cyberbullying or sexting was the basis of the petition, require an eligible person to complete an education reform program in accordance with section four hundred fifty-eight-l of the social services law.

(iii) Upon application of the petitioner, or upon the court's own motion, made at any time during the duration of the order, the court may restore the matter to the calendar. If the proceeding is not so restored, the petition is at the expiration of the order, deemed to have been dismissed by the court in furtherance of justice.

(b) On its own motion, the court may adjourn the proceedings on conclusion of a fact-finding hearing or during a dispositional hearing to enable it to make inquiry into the surroundings, conditions and capacities of the respondent. An adjournment on the court's motion may not be for a period of more than ten days if the respondent is detained, in which case not more than a total of two such adjournments may be granted in the absence of special circumstances. If the respondent is not detained, an adjournment may be for a reasonable time, but the total number of adjourned days may not exceed two months.

(c) On motion on behalf of the respondent or by his parent or other person legally responsible for his care, the court may adjourn the proceedings on conclusion of a fact finding hearing or during a dispositional hearing for a reasonable period of time.

§750. Probation reports; probation investigation and diagnostic assessment.

1. All reports or memoranda prepared or obtained by the probation service shall be deemed confidential information furnished to the court and shall be subject to disclosure solely in accordance with this section or as otherwise provided for by law. Except as provided in section seven hundred thirty-five of this article, such reports or memoranda shall not be furnished to the court prior to the completion of the fact-finding hearing and the making of the required findings.

2. After the completion of the fact-finding hearing and the making of the required findings and prior to the dispositional hearing, the reports or memoranda prepared or obtained by the probation service and furnished to the court shall be made available by the court for examination and copying by the child's counsel or by the respondent if he or she is not represented by counsel. All diagnostic assessments and probation investigation reports shall be submitted to the court at least five court days prior to the commencement of the dispositional hearing. In its discretion the court may except from disclosure a part or parts of the reports or memoranda which are not relevant to a proper disposition, or sources of

information which have been obtained on a promise of confidentiality, or any other portion thereof, disclosure of which would not be in the interest of justice. In all cases where a part or parts of the reports or memoranda are not disclosed, the court shall state for the record that a part or parts of the reports or memoranda have been excepted and the reasons for its action. The action of the court excepting information from disclosure shall be subject to review on any appeal from the order of disposition. If such reports or memoranda are made available to the respondent or his or her counsel, they shall also be made available to the counsel presenting the petition pursuant to section two hundred fifty-four and, in the court's discretion, to any other attorney representing the petitioner.

Part 5
Orders

§751. Order dismissing petition.

If the allegations of a petition under this article are not established, the court shall dismiss the petition. The court may in its discretion dismiss a petition under this article, in the interests of justice where attempts have been made to adjust the case as provided for in sections seven hundred thirty-five and seven hundred forty-two of this article and the probation service has exhausted its efforts to successfully adjust such case as a result of the petition's failure to provide reasonable assistance to the probation service.

§752. Findings.

If the allegations of a petition under this article are established in accord with part three, the court shall enter an order finding that the respondent is a person in need of supervision. The order shall state the grounds for the finding and the facts upon which it is based.

§754. Disposition on adjudication of person in need of supervision.

1. Upon an adjudication of person in need of supervision, the court shall enter an order of disposition:

(a) Discharging the respondent with warning;

(b) Suspending judgment in accord with section seven hundred fifty-five;

(c) Continuing the proceeding and placing the respondent in accord with section seven hundred fifty-six; provided, however, that the court shall not place the respondent in accord with section seven hundred fifty-six where the respondent is sixteen years of age or older, unless the court determines and states in its order that special circumstances exist to warrant such placement; or

(d) Putting the respondent on probation in accord with section seven hundred fifty-seven.

The court may order an eligible person to complete an education reform program in accordance with section four hundred fifty-eight-l of the social services law, as part of a disposition pursuant to paragraph (a), (b) or (d) of this subdivision.

2. (a) The order shall state the court's reasons for the particular disposition. If the court places the child in accordance with section seven hundred fifty-six of this part, the court in its order shall determine: (i) whether continuation in the child's home would be contrary to the best interest of the child and where appropriate, that reasonable efforts were made prior to the date of the dispositional hearing held pursuant to this article to prevent or eliminate the need for removal of the child from his or her home and, if the child was removed from his or her home prior to the date of such hearing, that such removal was in the child's best interest and, where appropriate, reasonable efforts were made to make it possible for the child to return safely home. If the court determines that reasonable efforts to prevent or eliminate the need for removal of the child from the home were not made but that the lack of such efforts was appropriate under the circumstances, the court order shall include such a finding; and (ii) in the case of a child who has attained the age of fourteen, the services needed, if any, to assist the child to make the transition from foster care to independent living. Nothing in this subdivision shall be construed to modify the standards for directing detention set forth in section seven hundred thirty-nine of this article.

(b) For the purpose of this section, reasonable efforts to prevent or eliminate the need for removing the child from the home of the child or to make it possible for the child to return safely to the home of the child shall not be required where the court determines that:

(i) the parent of such child has subjected the child to aggravated circumstances, as defined in subdivision (g) of section seven hundred twelve of this article;

(ii) the parent of such child has been convicted of (A) murder in the first degree as defined in section 125.27 or murder in the second degree as defined in section 125.25 of the penal law and the victim was another child of the parent; or (B) manslaughter in the first degree as defined in section 125.20 or manslaughter in the second degree as defined in section 125.15 of the penal law and the victim was another child of the parent, provided, however, that the parent must have acted voluntarily in committing such crime;

(iii) the parent of such child has been convicted of an attempt to commit any of the crimes set forth in subparagraphs (i) and (ii) of this paragraph, and the victim or intended victim was the child or another child of the parent; or has been convicted of criminal solicitation as defined in article one hundred, conspiracy as defined in article one hundred five or criminal facilitation as defined in article one hundred fifteen of the penal law for conspiring, soliciting or facilitating any of the foregoing crimes, and the victim or intended victim was the child or another child of the parent;

(iv) the parent of such child has been convicted of assault in the second degree as defined in section 120.05, assault in the first degree as defined in section 120.10 or aggravated assault upon a person less than eleven years old as defined in section 120.12 of the penal law, and the commission of one of the foregoing crimes resulted in serious physical injury to the child or another child of the parent;

(v) the parent of such child has been convicted in any other jurisdiction of an offense which includes all of the essential elements of any crime specified in subparagraph (ii), (iii) or (iv) of this paragraph, and the victim of such offense was the child or another child of the parent; or

(vi) the parental rights of the parent to a sibling of such child have been involuntarily terminated; unless the court determines that providing reasonable efforts would be in the best interests of the child, not contrary to the health and safety of the child, and would likely result in the reunification of the parent and the child in the foreseeable future. The court shall state such findings in its order.

If the court determines that reasonable efforts are not required because of one of the grounds set forth above, a permanency hearing shall be held within thirty days of the finding of the court that such efforts are not required. At the permanency hearing, the court shall determine the appropriateness of the permanency plan prepared by the social services official which shall include whether and when the child: (A) will be returned to the parent; (B) should be placed for adoption with the social services official filing a petition for termination of parental rights; (C) should be referred for legal guardianship; (D) should be placed permanently with a fit and willing relative; or (E) should be placed in another planned permanent living arrangement with a significant connection to an adult willing to be a permanency resource for the child if the child is age sixteen or older and if the requirements of subparagraph (E) of paragraph (iv) of subdivision (d) of section seven hundred fifty-six-a of this part have been met. The social services official shall thereafter make reasonable efforts to place the child in a timely manner and to complete whatever steps are necessary to finalize the permanent placement of the child as set forth in the permanency plan approved by the court. If reasonable efforts are determined by the court not to be required because of one of the grounds set forth in this paragraph, the social services official may file a petition for termination of parental rights in accordance with section three hundred eighty-four-b of the social services law.

(c) For the purpose of this section, in determining reasonable efforts to be made with respect to a child, and in making such reasonable efforts, the child's health and safety shall be the paramount concern.

(d) For the purpose of this section, a sibling shall include a half-sibling.

§755. Suspended judgment.

(a) Rules of court shall define permissible terms and conditions of a suspended judgment. The court may order as a condition of a suspended judgment restitution or services for public good pursuant to section seven hundred fifty-eight-a, and, except when the respondent has been assigned to a facility in accordance with subdivision four of section five hundred four of the executive law, in cases wherein the record indicates that the consumption of alcohol by the respondent may have been a contributing factor, the court may order attendance at and completion of an alcohol awareness program established pursuant to section 19.25 of the mental hygiene law.

(b) The maximum duration of any term or condition of a suspended judgment is one year, unless the court finds at the conclusion of that period that exceptional circumstances require an additional period of one year.

§756. Placement.

(a) (i) For purposes of section seven hundred fifty-four, the court may place the child in its own home or in the custody of a suitable relative or other suitable private person or a commissioner of social services, subject to the orders of the court.

(ii) Where the child is placed with the commissioner of the local social services district, the court may direct the commissioner to place the child with an authorized agency or class of authorized agencies, including, if the court finds that the respondent is a sexually exploited child as defined in subdivision one of section four hundred forty-seven-a of the social services law, an available long-term safe house. Unless the dispositional order provides otherwise, the court so directing shall include one of the following alternatives to apply in the event that the commissioner is unable to so place the child:

(1) the commissioner shall apply to the court for an order to stay, modify, set aside, or vacate such directive pursuant to the provisions of section seven hundred sixty-two or seven hundred sixty-three; or

(2) the commissioner shall return the child to the family court for a new dispositional hearing and order.

(b) Placements under this section may be for an initial period of twelve months. The court may extend a placement pursuant to section seven hundred fifty-six-a. In its discretion, the court may recommend restitution or require services for public good pursuant to section seven hundred fifty-eight-a in conjunction with an order of placement. For the purposes of calculating the initial period of placement, such placement shall be deemed to have commenced sixty days after the date the child was removed from his or her home in accordance with the provisions of this article. If the respondent has been in detention pending disposition, the initial period of placement ordered under this section shall be credited with and diminished by the amount of time spent by the respondent in detention prior to the commencement of the placement unless the court finds that all or part of such credit would not serve the best interests of the respondent.

(c) A placement pursuant to this section with the commissioner of social services shall not be directed in any detention facility, but the court may direct detention pending transfer to a placement authorized and ordered under this section for no more than than fifteen days after such order of placement is made. Such direction shall be subject to extension pursuant to subdivision three of section three hundred ninety-eight of the social services law, upon written documentation to the office of children and family services that the youth is in need of specialized treatment or placement and the diligent efforts by the commissioner of social services to locate an appropriate placement.

§756-a.   Extension of placement.

(a) In any case in which the child has been placed pursuant to section seven hundred fifty-six, the child, the person with whom the child has been placed or the commissioner of social services may petition the court to extend such placement. Such petition shall be filed at least sixty days prior to the expiration of the period of placement, except for good cause shown, but in no event shall such petition be filed after the original expiration date.

(b) The court shall conduct a permanency hearing concerning the need for continuing the placement. The child, the person with whom the child has been placed and the commissioner of social services shall be notified of such hearing and shall have the right to be heard thereat.

(c) The provisions of section seven hundred forty-five shall apply at such permanency hearing. If the petition is filed within sixty days prior to the expiration of the period of placement, the court shall first determine at such permanency hearing whether good cause has been shown. If good cause is not shown, the court shall dismiss the petition.

(d) At the conclusion of the permanency hearing the court may, in its discretion, order an extension of the placement for not more than one year. The court must consider and determine in its order:

(i) where appropriate, that reasonable efforts were made to make it possible for the child to safely return to his or her home, or if the permanency plan for the child is adoption, guardianship or some other permanent living arrangement other than reunification with the parent or parents of the child, reasonable efforts are being made to make and finalize such alternate permanent placement including consideration of appropriate in-state and out-of-state placements;

(ii) in the case of a child who has attained the age of fourteen, (A) the services needed, if any, to assist the child to make the transition from foster care to successful adulthood; and (B)(1) that the permanency plan developed for the child, and any revision or addition to the plan shall be developed in consultation with the child and, at the option of the child, with up to two additional members of the child's permanency planning team who are selected by the child and who are not a foster parent of, or case worker, case planner or case manager for, the child, except that the local commissioner of social services with custody of the child may reject an individual so selected by the child if such commissioner has good cause to believe that the individual would not act in the best interests of the child, and (2) that one individual so selected by the child may be designated to be the child's advisor and, as necessary, advocate with respect to the application of the reasonable and prudent parent standard;   *(Eff.4/4/16,Ch.54,L2016)*

(iii) in the case of a child placed outside New York state, whether the out-of-state placement continues to be appropriate and in the best interests of the child;

(iv) whether and when the child: (A) will be returned to the parent; (B) should be placed for adoption with the social services official filing a petition for termination of parental rights; (C) should be referred for legal guardianship; (D) should be placed permanently with a fit and willing relative; or (E) should be placed in another planned permanent living arrangement with a significant connection to an adult willing to be a permanency resource for the child if the child is age sixteen or older and (1) the social services official has documented to the court: (I) intensive, ongoing, and, as of the date of the hearing, unsuccessful efforts made by the social services district to return the child home or secure a placement for the child with a fit and willing relative including adult siblings, a legal guardian, or an adoptive parent, including through efforts that utilize search technology including social media to find biological family members for children, (II) the steps the social services district is taking to ensure that (A) the child's foster family home or child care facility is following the reasonable and prudent parent standard in accordance with guidance provided by the United States department of health and human services, and (B) the child has regular, ongoing opportunities to engage in age or developmentally appropriate activities including by consulting with the child in an age-appropriate manner about the opportunities of the child to participate in activities; and (2) the social services district has documented to the court and the court has determined that there are compelling reasons for determining that it continues to not be in the best interest of the child to return home, be referred for termination of parental rights and placed for adoption, placed with a fit and willing relative, or placed with a legal guardian; and (3) the court has made a determination explaining why, as of the date of the hearing, another planned living arrangement with a significant connection to an adult willing to be a permanency resource for the child is the best permanency plan for the child; and

(v) where the child will not be returned home, consideration of appropriate in-state and out-of-state placements.

(d-1) At the permanency hearing, the court shall consult with the respondent in an age-appropriate manner regarding the permanency plan; provided, however, that if the respondent is age sixteen or older and the requested permanency plan for the respondent is placement in another planned permanent living arrangement with a significant connection to an adult willing to be a permanency resource for the respondent, the court must ask the respondent about the desired permanency outcome for the respondent.

(e) Pending final determination of a petition to extend such placement filed in accordance with the provisions of this section, the court may, on its own motion or at the request of the petitioner or respondent, enter one or more temporary orders extending a period of placement not to exceed thirty days upon satisfactory proof showing probable cause for continuing such placement and that each temporary order is necessary. The court may order additional temporary extensions, not to exceed a total of fifteen days, if the court is unable to conclude the hearing within the thirty day temporary extension period. In no event shall the aggregate number of days in extensions granted or ordered under this subdivision total more than forty-five days. The petition shall be dismissed if a decision is not rendered within the period of placement or any temporary extension thereof. Notwithstanding any provision of law to the contrary, the initial permanency hearing shall be held within twelve months of the date the child was placed into care pursuant to section seven hundred fifty-six of this article and no later than every twelve months thereafter. For the purposes of this section, the date the child was placed into care shall be sixty days after the child was removed from his or her home in accordance with the provisions of this section.

(f) Successive extensions of placement under this section may be granted, but no placement may be made or continued beyond the child's eighteenth birthday without his or her consent and in no event past his or her twenty-first birthday.

§757. Probation.

(a) Rules of court shall define permissible terms and conditions of probation.

(b) The maximum period of probation shall not exceed one year. If the court finds at the conclusion of the original period that exceptional circumstances require an additional year of probation, the court may continue probation for an additional year.

(c) The court may order as a condition of probation restitution or services for public good pursuant to section seven hundred fifty-eight-a.

(d) In cases wherein the record indicates that the consumption of alcohol by the respondent may have been a contributing factor, the court may order as a condition of probation attendance at and completion of an alcohol awareness program established pursuant to section 19.25 of the mental hygiene law.

§758-a. Restitution.

1. In cases involving acts of infants over ten and less than sixteen years of age, the court may

(a) recommend as a condition of placement, or order as a condition of probation or suspended judgment, restitution in an amount representing a fair and reasonable cost to replace the property or repair the damage caused by the infant, not, however, to exceed one thousand dollars. In the case of a placement, the court may recommend that the infant pay out of his or her own funds or earnings the amount of replacement or damage, either in a lump sum or in periodic payments in amounts set by the agency with which he is placed, and in the case of probation or suspended judgment, the court may require that the infant pay out of his or her own funds or earnings the amount of replacement or damage, either in a lump sum or in periodic payments in amounts set by the court; and/or

(b) order as a condition of placement, probation, or suspended judgment, services for the public good including in the case of a crime involving willful, malicious, or unlawful damage or destruction to real or personal property maintained as a cemetery plot, grave, burial place, or other place of interment of human remains, services for the maintenance and repair thereof, taking into consideration the age and physical condition of the infant.

2. If the court recommends restitution or requires services for the public good in conjunction with an order of placement pursuant to section seven hundred fifty-six, the placement shall be made only to an authorized agency which has adopted rules and regulations for the supervision of such a program, which rules and regulations shall be subject to the approval of the state department of social services. Such rules and regulations shall include, but not be limited to provisions (i) assuring that the conditions of work, including wages, meet the standards therefor prescribed pursuant to the labor law; (ii) affording coverage to the child under the workers' compensation law as an employee of such agency, department or institution; (iii) assuring that the entity receiving such services shall not utilize the same to replace its regular employees; and (iv) providing for reports to the court not less frequently than every six months, unless the order provides otherwise.

3. If the court requires restitution or services for the public good as a condition of probation or suspended judgment, it shall provide that an agency or person supervise the restitution or services and that such agency or person report to the court not less frequently than every six months, unless the order provides otherwise. Upon the written notice sent by a school district to the court and the appropriate probation department or agency which submits probation recommendations or reports to the court, the court may provide that such school district shall supervise the performance of services for the public good.

4. The court, upon receipt of the reports provided for in subdivision two or three of this section may, on its own motion or the motion of any party or the agency, hold a hearing to determine whether the placement should be altered or modified.

§759. Order of protection.

The court may make an order of protection in assistance or as a condition of any order issued under this article. The order of protection may set forth reasonable conditions of behavior to be observed for a specified time by a person who is before the court and is a parent or other person legally responsible for the child's care or the spouse of the parent or other person legally responsible for the child's care, or respondent or both. Such an order may require any such person

(a) to stay away from the home, school, business or place of employment of any other party, the other spouse, the other parent or the child, and to stay away from any other specific location designated by the court;

(b) to permit a parent, or a person entitled to visitation by a court order or a separation agreement, to visit the child at stated periods;

(c) to refrain from committing a family offense, as defined in subdivision one of section eight hundred twelve of this act, or any criminal offense against the child or against the other parent or against any person to whom custody of the child is awarded, or from harassing, intimidating or threatening such persons;

(d) to permit a designated party to enter the residence during a specified period of time in order to remove personal belongings not in issue in this proceeding or in any other proceeding or action under this act or the domestic relations law;

(e) to refrain from acts of commission or omission that create an unreasonable risk to the health, safety or welfare of a child;

(f) to participate in family counseling or other professional counseling activities, or other services, including alternative dispute resolution services conducted by an authorized person or an authorized agency to which the youth has been referred or placed, deemed necessary for the rehabilitation of the youth, provided that such family counseling, other counseling activity or other necessary services are not contrary to such person's religious beliefs;

(g) to provide, either directly or by means of medical and health insurance, for expenses incurred for medical care and treatment arising from the incident or incidents forming the basis for the issuance of the order.

(h) 1. to refrain from intentionally injuring or killing, without justification, any companion animal the respondent knows to be owned, possessed, leased, kept or held by the person protected by the order or a minor child residing in such person's household.

2. "Companion animal", as used in this section, shall have the same meaning as in subdivision five of section three hundred fifty of the agriculture and markets law.

(i) to observe such other conditions as are necessary to further the purposes of protection.

The court may also award custody of the child, during the term of the order of protection to either parent, or to an appropriate relative within the second degree. Nothing in this section gives the court power to place or board out any child to an institution or agency. In making orders of protection, the court shall so act as to insure that in the care, protection, discipline and guardianship of the child his religious faith shall be preserved and protected.

Notwithstanding the foregoing provisions, an order of protection, or temporary order of protection where applicable, may be entered against a former spouse and persons who have a child in common, regardless of whether such persons have been married or have lived together at any time, or against a member of the same family or household as defined in subdivision one of section eight hundred twelve of this act.

In any proceeding pursuant to this article, a court shall not deny an order of protection, or dismiss an application for such an order, solely on the basis that the acts or events alleged are not relatively contemporaneous with the date of the application or the conclusion of the action. The duration of any temporary order shall not by itself be a factor in determining the length or issuance of any final order.

The protected party in whose favor the order of protection or temporary order of protection is issued may not be held to violate an order issued in his or her favor nor may such protected party be arrested for violating such order.

§760. Duties of counsel.

1. If the court has entered a dispositional order pursuant to section seven hundred fifty-four, it shall be the duty of the respondent's counsel to promptly advise such respondent and if his or her parent or other person responsible for his or her care is not the petitioner, such parent or other person responsible for his or her care, in writing of the right to appeal to the appropriate appellate division of the supreme court, the time limitations involved, the manner of instituting an appeal and obtaining a transcript of the testimony and the right to apply for leave to appeal as a poor person if he or she is unable to pay the cost of an appeal. It shall be the further duty of such counsel to explain to the respondent and if his or her parent or other person responsible for his or her care is not the petitioner, such parent or person responsible for his or her care, the procedures for instituting an appeal, the possible reasons upon which an appeal may be based and the nature and possible consequences of the appellate process.

2. It shall also be the duty of such counsel to ascertain whether the respondent wishes to appeal and, if so, to serve and file the necessary notice of appeal.

3. If the respondent has been permitted to waive the appointment of counsel pursuant to section two hundred forty-nine-a, it shall be the duty of the court to provide the notice and explanation pursuant to subdivision one and, if the respondent indicates that he or she wishes to appeal, the clerk of the court shall file and serve the notice of appeal.

Part 6
New Hearing and Reconsideration of Orders

§761. New hearing.

On its own motion or on motion of any interested person acting on behalf of the respondent, the court may for good cause grant a new fact-finding or dispositional hearing under this article.

§762. Staying, modifying, setting aside or vacating order.

For good cause, the court on its own motion or on motion of any interested person acting on behalf of the respondent may stay execution of, arrest, set aside, modify or vacate any order issued in the course of a proceeding under this article.

§763. Notice of motion.

Notice of motion under sections seven hundred sixty-one or seven hundred sixty-two, including the court's own motion, shall be served upon parties and any agency or institution having custody of the child not less than seven days prior to the return date of the motion. The persons on whom the notice of motion is served shall answer the motion not less than two days before the return date. On examining the motion and answer and, in its discretion, after hearing argument, the court shall enter an order, granting or denying the motion.

§764. Petition to terminate placement.

Any parent or guardian or duly authorized agency or next friend of a person placed under section seven hundred fifty-six may petition to the court for an order terminating the placement. The petition must be verified and must show:

(a) that an application for release of the respondent was made to the duly authorized agency with which the child was placed;

(b) that the application was denied or was not granted within thirty days from the day application was made; and

(c) the grounds for the petition.

§765. Service of petition; answer.

A copy of a petition under section seven hundred sixty-four shall be served promptly upon the duly authorized agency or the institution having custody of the person, whose duty it is to file an answer to the petition within five days from the day of service.

§766. Examination of petition and answer; hearing.

The court shall promptly examine the petition and answer. If the court concludes that a hearing should be had, it may proceed upon due notice to all concerned to hear the facts and determine whether continued placement serves the purposes of this article. If the court concludes that a hearing need not be had, it shall enter an order granting or denying the petition.

§767. Orders on hearing.

(a) If the court determines after hearing that continued placement serves the purposes of this article, it shall deny the petition. The court may, on its own motion, reduce the duration of the placement, change the agency in which the child is placed, or direct the agency to make such other arrangements for the person's care and welfare as the facts of the case may require.

(b) If the court determines after hearing that continued placement does not serve the purposes of this article, the court shall discharge the person from the custody of the agency and may place the person on probation or under the supervision of the court.

§768. Successive petitions.

If a petition under section seven hundred sixty-four is denied, it may not be renewed for a period of ninety days after the denial, unless the order of denial permits renewal at an earlier time.

Part 7
Compliance with Orders

§771. Discontinuation of treatment by agency or institution.
If an authorized agency in which a person is placed under section seven hundred fifty-six
(a) discontinues or suspends its work; or
(b) is unwilling to continue to care for the person for the reason that support by the state of New York or one of its political subdivisions has been discontinued; or
(c) so fundamentally alters its program that the person can no longer benefit from it, the person shall be returned by the agency to the court which entered the order of placement.

§772. Action on return from agency or institution.
If a person is returned to the court under section seven hundred seventy-one, the court may make any order that might have been made at the time the order of placement was made, except that the maximum duration authorized for any such order shall be decreased by the time spent in placement.

§773. Petition for transfer for incorrigibility.
Any institution, society or agency in which a person was placed under section seven hundred fifty-six may petition to the court which made the order of placement for transfer of that person to a society or agency, governed or controlled by persons of the same religious faith or persuasion as that of the child, where practicable, or, if not practicable, to some other suitable institution, or to some other suitable institution on the ground that such person
(a) is incorrigible and that his or her presence is seriously detrimental to the welfare of the applicant institution, society, agency or other persons in its care, or
(b) after placement by the court was released on parole or probation from such institution, society or agency and a term or condition of the release was willfully violated. The petition shall be verified by an officer of the applicant institution, society or agency and shall specify the act or acts bringing the person within this section.

§774. Action on petition for transfer.
On receiving a petition under section seven hundred seventy-three, the court may proceed under sections seven hundred thirty-seven, seven hundred thirty-eight or seven hundred thirty-nine with respect to the issuance of a summons or warrant and sections seven hundred twenty-seven and seven hundred twenty-nine govern questions of detention and failure to comply with a promise to appear. Due notice of the petition and a copy of the petition shall also be served personally or by mail upon the office of the locality chargeable for the support of the person involved and upon the person involved and his parents and other persons.

§775. Order on hearing.
(a) After hearing a petition under section seven hundred seventy-three, the court may:
(i) dismiss the petition;
(ii) grant the petition, making such placement, if the court was authorized to make such placement upon the original adjudication; or
(iii) terminate the prior order of placement and either discharge the respondent or place him on probation.

(b) If the court grants the petition and orders placement, the respondent shall thereupon be transferred to the custody of the person, agency or institution provided by the court's order.

§776. Failure to comply with terms and conditions of suspended judgment.

A respondent brought before the court for failure to comply with reasonable terms and conditions of an order of suspended judgment shall be subject to section seven hundred seventy-nine-a of this part. If, after hearing, the court determines by competent proof that the respondent without just cause failed to comply with such terms and conditions, the court may adjourn the matter for a new dispositional hearing in accordance with subdivision (b) or (c) of section seven hundred forty-nine of this article. The court may revoke the order of suspended judgment and proceed to make any order that might have been made at the time judgment was suspended.

§777. Failure to comply with terms of placement at home.

If a person placed in his own home subject to orders of the court leaves home without the court's permission, he may be brought before the court and if, after hearing, the court is satisfied by competent proof that the respondent left home without just cause, the court may revoke the order of placement and proceed to make any order that might have been made at the time the order of placement was made. It may also continue the order of placement and, on due notice and after hearing, enter an order of protection for the duration of the placement.

§778. Failure to comply with terms of placement in authorized agency.

If a person is placed in the custody of a suitable institution in accord with section seven hundred fifty-six and leaves the institution without permission of the superintendent or person in charge and without permission of the court, and if, after hearing, the court is satisfied by competent proof that the respondent left the institution without just cause, the court may revoke the order of placement and proceed to make any order that might have been made at the time the order of placement was made, or any order authorized under section seven hundred fifty-six.

§779. Jurisdiction and supervision of respondent placed on probation; failure to comply with terms of probation.

(a) A respondent who is placed on probation in accordance with section seven hundred fifty-seven of this article shall remain under the legal jurisdiction of the court pending expiration or termination of the period of probation.

(b) The probation service shall supervise the respondent during the period of such legal jurisdiction.

(c) A respondent brought before the court for failure to comply with reasonable terms and conditions of an order of probation issued under section seven hundred fifty-seven of this article shall be subject to section seven hundred seventy-nine-a of this article. If, after a hearing pursuant to such section, the court determines by competent proof that the respondent without just cause failed to comply with such terms and conditions, the court may adjourn the matter for a new dispositional hearing in accordance with subdivision (b) or (c) of section seven hundred forty-nine of this article. The court may revoke the order of probation and proceed to make any order that might have been made at the time the order of probation was entered.

§779-a. **Petition and hearing on violation of order of probation or suspended judgment.**

(a) If, at any time during the period of probation, the petitioner, probation service or appropriate presentment agency has reasonable cause to believe the respondent has violated a condition of the disposition, the petitioner, probation service or appropriate presentment agency may file a violation petition.

(b) The petition must be verified and subscribed by the petitioner, probation service or the appropriate presentment agency. The petition must specify the condition or conditions of the order violated and a reasonable description of the date, time, place and specific manner in which the violation occurred. Non-hearsay allegations of the factual part of the petition or of any supporting depositions must establish, if true, every violation charged.

(c) Upon the filing of a violation petition, the court must promptly take reasonable and appropriate action to cause the respondent to appear before it for the purpose of enabling the court to make a final determination with respect to the alleged delinquency. Where the respondent is on probation pursuant to section seven hundred fifty-seven of this article, the time for prompt court action shall not be construed against the probation service when the respondent has absconded from probation supervision and the respondent's whereabouts are unknown. The court must be notified promptly of the circumstances of any such probationers.

(d) If a petition is filed under subdivision (a) of this section and the petition satisfies the requirements of subdivision (b) of this section, the period of probation or suspended judgment prescribed by section seven hundred fifty-five or seven hundred fifty-seven of this article shall be interrupted as of the date of the filing of the petition. Such interruption shall continue until a final determination of the petition or until such time as the respondent reaches the maximum age of acceptance into placement with the commissioner of social services. If the court dismisses the violation petition, the period of interruption shall be credited to the period of probation or suspended judgment.

(e) Hearing on violation. (i) The court may not revoke an order of probation or suspended judgment unless the court has found by competent proof that the respondent has violated a condition of such order in an important respect and without just cause and that the respondent has had an opportunity to be heard. The respondent is entitled to a hearing promptly after a violation petition has been filed. The respondent is entitled to counsel at all stages of the proceeding and may not waive representation by counsel except as provided in section two hundred forty-nine-a of this act.

(ii) At the time of the respondent's first appearance following the filing of a violation petition, the court must:

(A) advise the respondent of the contents of the petition and furnish a copy to the respondent;

(B) advise the respondent that he or she is entitled to counsel at all stages of a proceeding under this section and appoint an attorney pursuant to section two hundred forty-nine of this act if independent legal representation is not available to the respondent. If practicable, the court shall appoint the same attorney who represented the respondent in the original proceedings under this article; and

(C) determine whether the respondent should be released or detained pursuant to section seven hundred twenty of this article.

(iii) Upon request, the court shall grant a reasonable adjournment to the respondent to prepare for the hearing.

(iv) At the hearing, the court may receive any evidence that is relevant, competent and material. The respondent may cross-examine witnesses and present evidence on his or her own behalf. The court's determination must be based upon competent evidence.

(v) At the conclusion of the hearing, the court may adjourn the matter for a new dispositional hearing in accordance with subdivision (b) or (c) of section seven hundred forty-nine of this article. The court may revoke, continue or modify the order of probation or suspended judgment. If the court revokes the order, it shall order a different disposition pursuant to subdivision one of section seven hundred fifty-four of this article and shall make findings in accordance with subdivision two of such section. If the court continues the order of probation or suspended judgment, it shall dismiss the petition of violation.

§780. Failure to comply with order of protection.

If any person is brought before the court for failure to comply with the terms and conditions of an order of protection properly issued under this article and applicable to him and if, after hearing, the court is satisfied by competent proof that that person without just cause failed to comply with such terms and conditions, the court may modify or revoke the order of protection, or commit said person, if he willfully violated the order, to jail for a term not to exceed six months, or both. The court may suspend an order of commitment under this section on condition that the said person comply with the order of protection.

§780-a. Firearms; surrender and license suspension, revocation and ineligibility.

Upon the issuance of an order of protection or temporary order of protection, or upon a violation of such order, the court shall make a determination regarding the suspension and revocation of a license to carry, possess, repair or dispose of a firearm or firearms, ineligibility for such a license and the surrender of firearms in accordance with section eight hundred forty-two-a of this act.

Part 8
Effect of Proceedings

Section
781.   Nature of adjudication.
782.   Effect of adjudication.
782-a. Transfer of records and information to institutions and agencies.
783.   Use of record in other court.
783-a. Consolidation of records within a city having a population of one million or more.
784.   Use of police records.

§781. Nature of adjudication.

No adjudication under this article may be denominated a conviction, and no person adjudicated a person in need of supervision under this article shall be denominated a criminal by reason of such adjudication.

§782. Effect of adjudication.

No adjudication under this article shall operate as a forfeiture of any right or privilege or disqualify any person from subsequently holding public office or receiving any license granted by public authority.

§782-a.   **Transfer of records and information to institutions and agencies.**
Whenever a person is placed with an institution suitable for the placement of a person adjudicated in need of supervision maintained by the state or any subdivision thereof or to an authorized agency, the family court so placing such person shall forthwith transmit a copy of the orders of the family court pursuant to sections seven hundred fifty-two and seven hundred fifty-four, and of the probation report and all other relevant evaluative records in the possession of the family court and probation department related to such child, including but not limited to any diagnostic, educational, medical, psychological and psychiatric records with respect to such person to such institution or agency, notwithstanding any contrary provision of law.

§783.   **Use of record in other court.**
Neither the fact that a person was before the family court under this article for a hearing nor any confession, admission or statement made by him to the court or to any officer thereof in any stage of the proceeding is admissible as evidence against him or his interests in any other court. Another court, in imposing sentence upon an adult after conviction, may receive and consider the records and information on file with the family court concerning such person when he was a child.

§783-a.   **Consolidation of records within a city having a population of one million or more.**
Notwithstanding any other provision of law, in a city having a population of one million or more, an index of the records of the local probation departments located in the counties comprising such city for proceedings under article seven shall be consolidated and filed in a central office for use by the family court and local probation service in each such county. After consultation with the state administrative judge, the commissioner of the division of criminal justice services, in consultation with the director of the office of probation and correctional alternatives shall specify the information to be contained in such index and the organization of such consolidated file.

§784.   **Use of police records.**
All police records relating to the arrest and disposition of any person under this article shall be kept in files separate and apart from the arrests of adults and shall be withheld from public inspection, but such records shall be open to inspection upon good cause shown by the parent, guardian, next friend or attorney of that person upon the written order of a judge of the family court in the county in which the order was made or, if the person is subsequently convicted of a crime, of a judge of the court in which he was convicted.

ARTICLE 8
Family Offenses Proceedings

Part
1. **Jurisdiction.**
2. **Preliminary procedure.**
3. **Hearing.**
4. **Orders.**

Part 1
Jurisdiction

§812. Procedures for family offense proceedings.

1. Jurisdiction. The family court and the criminal courts shall have concurrent jurisdiction over any proceeding concerning acts which would constitute disorderly conduct, harassment in the first degree, harassment in the second degree, aggravated harassment in the second degree, sexual misconduct, forcible touching, sexual abuse in the third degree, sexual abuse in the second degree as set forth in subdivision one of section 130.60 of the penal law, stalking in the first degree, stalking in the second degree, stalking in the third degree, stalking in the fourth degree, criminal mischief, menacing in the second degree, menacing in the third degree, reckless endangerment, criminal obstruction of breathing or blood circulation, strangulation in the second degree, strangulation in the first degree, assault in the second degree, assault in the third degree, an attempted assault, identity theft in the first degree, identity theft in the second degree, identity theft in the third degree, grand larceny in the fourth degree, grand larceny in the third degree or coercion in the second degree as set forth in subdivisions one, two and three of section 135.60 of the penal law between spouses or former spouses, or between parent and child or between members of the same family or household except that if the respondent would not be criminally responsible by reason of age pursuant to section 30.00 of the penal law, then the family court shall have exclusive jurisdiction over such proceeding. Notwithstanding a complainant's election to proceed in family court, the criminal court shall not be divested of jurisdiction to hear a family offense proceeding pursuant to this section. In any proceeding pursuant to this article, a court shall not deny an order of protection, or dismiss a petition, solely on the basis that the acts or events alleged are not relatively contemporaneous with the date of the petition, the conclusion of the fact-finding or the conclusion of the dispositional hearing. For purposes of this article, "disorderly conduct" includes disorderly conduct not in a public place. For purposes of this article, "members of the same family or household" shall mean the following:

(a) persons related by consanguinity or affinity;

(b) persons legally married to one another;

(c) persons formerly married to one another regardless of whether they still reside in the same household;

(d) persons who have a child in common regardless of whether such persons have been married or have lived together at any time; and

(e) persons who are not related by consanguinity or affinity and who are or have been in an intimate relationship regardless of whether such persons have lived together at any time. Factors the court may consider in determining whether a relationship is an "intimate relationship" include but are not limited to: the nature or type of relationship, regardless of whether the relationship is sexual in nature; the frequency of interaction between the persons; and the duration of the relationship. Neither a casual acquaintance nor ordinary fraternization between two individuals in business or social contexts shall be deemed to constitute an "intimate relationship".

2. Information to petitioner or complainant. The chief administrator of the courts shall designate the appropriate persons, including, but not limited to district attorneys, criminal and family court clerks, corporation counsels, county attorneys, victims assistance unit staff, probation officers, warrant officers, sheriffs, police officers or any other law enforcement officials, to inform any petitioner or complainant bringing a proceeding under this article, before such proceeding is commenced, of the procedures available for the institution of family offense proceedings, including but not limited to the following:

(a) That there is concurrent jurisdiction with respect to family offenses in both family court and the criminal courts;

(b) That a family court proceeding is a civil proceeding and is for the purpose of attempting to stop the violence, end the family disruption and obtain protection. Referrals for counseling, or counseling services, are available through probation for this purpose;

(c) That a proceeding in the criminal courts is for the purpose of prosecution of the offender and can result in a criminal conviction of the offender;

(d) That a proceeding or action subject to the provisions of this section is initiated at the time of the filing of an accusatory instrument or family court petition, not at the time of arrest, or request for arrest, if any;

(f) That an arrest may precede the commencement of a family court or a criminal court proceeding, but an arrest is not a requirement for commencing either proceeding; provided, however, that the arrest of an alleged offender shall be made under the circumstances described in subdivision four of section 140.10 of the criminal procedure law;

(g) That notwithstanding a complainant's election to proceed in family court, the criminal court shall not be divested of jurisdiction to hear a family offense proceeding pursuant to this section.

3. Official responsibility. No official or other person designated pursuant to subdivision two of this section shall discourage or prevent any person who wishes to file a petition or sign a complaint from having access to any court for that purpose.

4. Official forms. The chief administrator of the courts shall prescribe an appropriate form to implement subdivision two of this section.

5. Notice. Every police officer, peace officer or district attorney investigating a family offense under this article shall advise the victim of the availability of a shelter or other services in the community, and shall immediately give the victim written notice of the legal rights and remedies available to a victim of a family offense under the relevant provisions of the criminal procedure law, the family court act and the domestic relations law. Such notice shall be available in English and Spanish and, if necessary, shall be delivered orally and shall include but not be limited to the following statement:

"If you are the victim of domestic violence, you may request that the officer assist in providing for your safety and that of your children, including providing information on how to obtain a temporary order of protection. You may also request that the officer assist you in obtaining your essential personal effects and locating and taking you, or assist in making arrangement to take you, and your children to a safe place within such officer's jurisdiction, including but not limited to a domestic violence program, a family member's or a friend's residence, or a similar place of safety. When the officer's jurisdiction is more than a single county, you may ask the officer to take you or make arrangements to take you and your children to a place of safety in the county where the incident occurred. If you or your children are in need of medical treatment, you have the right to request that the officer assist you in obtaining such medical treatment. You may request a copy of any incident reports at no cost from the law enforcement agency. You have the right to seek legal counsel of your own choosing and if you proceed in family court and if it is determined that you cannot afford an attorney, one must be appointed to represent you without cost to you.

You may ask the district attorney or a law enforcement officer to file a criminal complaint. You also have the right to file a petition in the family court when a family offense has been committed against you. You have the right to have your petition and request for an order of protection filed on the same day you appear in court, and such request must be heard that same day or the next day court is in session. Either court may issue an order of protection from conduct constituting a family offense which could include, among other provisions, an order for the respondent or defendant to stay away from you and your children. The family court may also order the payment of temporary child support and award temporary custody of your children. If the family court is not in session, you may seek immediate assistance from the criminal court in obtaining an order of protection.

The forms you need to obtain an order of protection are available from the family court and the local criminal court (the addresses and telephone numbers shall be listed). The resources available in this community for information relating to domestic violence, treatment of injuries, and places of safety and shelters can be accessed by calling the following 800 numbers (the statewide English and Spanish language 800 numbers shall be listed and space shall be provided for local domestic violence hotline telephone numbers).

Filing a criminal complaint or a family court petition containing allegations that are knowingly false is a crime."

The division of criminal justice services in consultation with the state office for the prevention of domestic violence shall prepare the form of such written notice consistent with the provisions of this section and distribute copies thereof to the appropriate law enforcement officials pursuant to subdivision nine of section eight hundred forty-one of the executive law. Additionally, copies of such notice shall be provided to the chief administrator of the courts to be distributed to victims of family offenses through the family court at such time as such persons first come before the court and to the state department of health for distribution to all hospitals defined under article twenty-eight of the public health law. No cause of action for damages shall arise in favor of any person by reason of any failure to comply with the provisions of this subdivision except upon a showing of gross negligence or willful misconduct.

§813. Transfer to criminal court.

1. At any time prior to a finding on the petition the court may, with the consent of the petitioner and upon reasonable notice to the district attorney, who shall have an opportunity to be heard, order that any matter which is the subject of a proceeding commenced pursuant to this article be prosecuted as a criminal action in an appropriate criminal court if the court determines that the interests of justice so require.

2. The court may simultaneously with the transfer of any matter to the appropriate criminal court, issue or continue a temporary order of protection

which, notwithstanding any other provision of law, shall continue in effect, absent action by the appropriate criminal court pursuant to subdivision three of section 530.12 of the criminal procedure law, until the defendant is arraigned upon an accusatory instrument filed pursuant to this section in such criminal court.

3. Nothing herein shall be deemed to limit or restrict a petitioner's rights to proceed directly and without court referral in either criminal or family court, or both, as provided for in section one hundred fifteen of this act and section 100.07 of the criminal procedure law.

§814. Rules of court regarding concurrent jurisdiction.

The chief administrator of the courts pursuant to paragraph (e) of subdivision two of section two hundred twelve of the judiciary law shall promulgate rules to facilitate record sharing and other communication between the criminal and family courts, subject to applicable provisions of the criminal procedure law and the family court act pertaining to the confidentiality, expungement and sealing of records, where such courts exercise concurrent jurisdiction over family offense proceedings.

§814-a. Uniform forms.

The chief administrator of the courts, shall promulgate appropriate uniform temporary orders of protection and orders of protection forms, applicable to proceedings under this article, to be used throughout the state. Such forms shall be promulgated and developed in a manner to ensure the compatability of such forms with the statewide computerized registry established pursuant to section two hundred twenty-one-a of the executive law.

§815. Transcript of family offense proceedings; request by district attorney.

The court shall, upon the written request of a district attorney stating that such transcript is necessary in order to conduct a criminal investigation or prosecution involving the petitioner or respondent, provide a copy of the transcript of any proceedings under this article, to such district attorney. Such transcript shall not be redisclosed except as necessary for such investigation or prosecution.

§817. Support, paternity and child protection.

On its own motion and at any time in proceedings under this article, the court may direct the filing of a child protective petition under article ten of this chapter, a support petition under article four, or a paternity petition under article five of this act and consolidate the proceedings.

§818. Venue.

Proceedings under this article may be originated in the county in which the act or acts referred to in the petition allegedly occurred or in which the family or household resides or in which any party resides. For the purposes of this section, residence shall include any residential program for victims of domestic violence, as defined in subdivision four of section four hundred fifty-nine-a of the social services law, or facility which provides shelter to homeless persons or families on an emergency or temporary basis.

Part 2
Preliminary Procedure

§821. Originating proceedings.

1. A proceeding under this article is originated by the filing of a petition containing the following:

(a) An allegation that the respondent assaulted or attempted to assault his or her spouse, or former spouse, parent, child or other member of the same family or household or engaged in disorderly conduct, harassment, sexual misconduct, forcible touching, sexual abuse in the third degree, sexual abuse in the second degree as set forth in subdivision one of section 130.60 of the penal law, stalking, criminal mischief, menacing, reckless endangerment, criminal obstruction of breathing or blood circulation, strangulation, identity theft in the first degree, identity theft in the second degree, identity theft in the third degree, grand larceny in the fourth degree, grand larceny in the third degree or coercion in the second degree as set forth in subdivisions one, two and three of section 135.60 of the penal law, toward any such person;

(b) The relationship of the alleged offender to the petitioner;

(c) The name of each and every child in the family or household and the relationship of the child, if any, to the petitioner and to the respondent;

(d) A request for an order of protection or the use of the court's conciliation procedures; and

(e) An allegation as to whether any accusatory instrument alleging an act specified in paragraph (a) of this subdivision has been verified with respect to the same act alleged in the petition. Appended to the copy of the petition provided to the petitioner shall be a copy of the notice described in subdivision five of section eight hundred twelve of this article.

2. When family court is not in session, an arrest and initial appearance by the defendant or respondent may be in a criminal court, as provided in sections one hundred fifty-four-d and one hundred fifty-five of this act.

§821-a. Preliminary procedure.

1. Upon the filing of a petition under this article, the court shall advise the petitioner of the right to retain legal representation or if indigent, the right to have counsel appointed pursuant to section two hundred sixty-two of this act.

2. Upon the filing of a petition under this article, the court may:

(a) issue a summons pursuant to section eight hundred twenty-six of this part or issue a warrant pursuant to section eight hundred twenty-seven of this part;

(b) issue a temporary order of protection in favor of the petitioner and, where appropriate, the petitioner's children or any other children residing in the petitioner's household, pursuant to section eight hundred twenty-eight of this part.

3. Where the respondent is brought before the court pursuant to a summons under section eight hundred twenty-six of this part or a warrant issued under section eight hundred twenty-seven of this part, or where a respondent

voluntarily appears before the court after such summons or warrant has been issued, the court shall:

(a) advise the parties of the right to retain legal representation or, if indigent, the right to have counsel appointed pursuant to section two hundred sixty-two of this act;

(b) advise the respondent of the allegations contained in the petition before the court; and

(c) provide the respondent with a copy of such petition; and the court may:

(i) order the release of the respondent on his or her own recognizance pending further appearances as required by the court;

(ii) direct that the respondent post bail in a manner authorized pursuant to section one hundred fifty-five-a of this act in an amount set by the court; or

(iii) issue a commitment order directing that the respondent be remanded to the custody of the county sheriff or other appropriate law enforcement official until such time as bail is posted as required by the court.

4. Where the court directs that the respondent post bail or that the respondent be committed to the custody of a law enforcement official as provided for herein, and the respondent fails to post bail or otherwise remains in custody, a hearing shall be held without unreasonable delay but in no event later than one hundred twenty hours after the arrest of the respondent or in the event that a Saturday, Sunday, or legal holiday occurs during such custody, one hundred forty-four hours after the arrest of the respondent, to determine upon material and relevant evidence whether sufficient cause exists to keep the respondent in custody. If the court determines that sufficient cause does not exist or if no hearing is timely held, the respondent shall immediately be released on the respondent's own recognizance.

5. (a) At such time as the petitioner first appears before the court, the court shall advise the petitioner that the petitioner may: continue with the hearing and disposition of such petition in the family court; or have the allegations contained therein heard in an appropriate criminal court; or proceed concurrently in both family and criminal court.

(b) Where the petitioner seeks to have the petition heard and determined in the family court, the court shall set the matter down for further proceedings pursuant to the provisions of this article. Nothing herein shall be deemed to limit or restrict petitioner's rights to seek to proceed directly in either criminal or family court, or both, as provided for in section one hundred fifteen of this act and section 100.07 of the criminal procedure law.

6. When both parties first appear before the court, the court shall inquire as to the existence of any other orders of protection involving the parties.

§822. Person who may originate proceedings.

(a) Any person in the relation to the respondent of spouse, or former spouse, parent, child, or member of the same family or household;

(b) A duly authorized agency, association, society, or institution;

(c) A peace officer, acting pursuant to his special duties, or a police officer;

(d) A person on the court's own motion.

§823. Rules of court for preliminary procedure.

(a) Rules of court may authorize the probation service

(i) to confer with any person seeking to file a petition, the potential petitioner and other interested persons concerning the advisability of filing a petition under this article, and

(ii) to attempt through conciliation and agreement informally to adjust suitable cases before a petition is filed over which the court apparently would have jurisdiction.

(b) The probation service may not prevent any person who wishes to file a petition under this article from having access to the court for that purpose.

(c) Efforts at adjustment pursuant to rules of court under this section may not extend for a period of more than two months without leave of a judge of the court, who may extend the period for an additional sixty days. Two successive extensions may be granted under this section.

(d) The probation service may not be authorized under this section to compel any person to appear at any conference, produce any papers, or visit any place.

(e) If agreement to cease offensive conduct is reached, it must be reduced to writing and submitted to the family court for approval. If the court approves it, the court without further hearing may thereupon enter an order of protection in accordance with the agreement, which shall be binding upon the respondent and shall in all respects be a valid order. The court record shall show that such order was made upon agreement.

§824. Admissibility of statements made during preliminary conference.

No statement made during a preliminary conference may be admitted into evidence at a fact-finding hearing under this act or in a criminal court at any time prior to conviction.

§825. Issuance of summons.

On the filing of a petition under this article, the court may cause a copy of the petition and a summons to be issued, requiring the respondent to appear at the court at a time and place to answer the petition.

§826. Service of summons.

(a) Unless the court issues a warrant pursuant to section eight hundred twenty-seven of this part, service of a summons and petition shall be made by delivery of a true copy thereof to the person summoned at least twenty-four hours before the time stated therein for appearance. If so requested by the respondent, the court shall not proceed with the hearing or proceeding earlier than three days after such service.

(b) If after reasonable effort, personal service is not made, the court may at any stage in the proceedings make an order providing for substituted service in the manner provided for substituted service in civil process in courts of record.

§827. Issuance of warrant; certificate of warrant.

(a) The court may issue a warrant, directing that the respondent be brought before the court, when a petition is presented to the court under section eight hundred twenty-one and it appears that

(i) the summons cannot be served; or

(ii) the respondent has failed to obey the summons; or

(iii) the respondent is likely to leave the jurisdiction; or

(iv) a summons, in the court's opinion, would be ineffectual; or

(v) the safety of the petitioner is endangered; or

(vi) the safety of a child is endangered; or

(vii) aggravating circumstances exist which require the immediate arrest of the respondent. For the purposes of this section aggravating circumstances shall mean physical injury or serious physical injury to the petitioner caused by the respondent, the use of a dangerous instrument against the petitioner by the respondent, a history of repeated violations of prior orders of protection by the respondent, prior convictions for crimes against the petitioner by the respondent or the exposure of any family or household member to physical injury by the respondent and like incidents, behaviors and occurrences which to the court constitute an immediate and ongoing danger to the petitioner, or any member of the petitioner's family or household.

(b) The petitioner may not serve a warrant upon the respondent, unless the court itself grants such permission upon the application of the petitioner. The clerk of the court may issue to the petitioner or to the representative of an incorporated charitable or philanthropic society having a legitimate interest in the family a certificate stating that a warrant for the respondent has been issued by the court. The presentation of such certificate by said petitioner or representative to any peace officer, acting pursuant to his special duties, or police officer authorizes him to arrest the respondent and take him to court.

(c) A certificate of warrant expires ninety days from the date of issue but may be renewed from time to time by the clerk of the court.

(d) Rules of court shall provide that a record of all unserved warrants be kept and that periodic reports concerning unserved warrants be made.

§828. Temporary order of protection; temporary order for child support.

1. (a) Upon the filing of a petition or counter-claim under this article, the court for good cause shown may issue a temporary order of protection, which may contain any of the provisions authorized on the making of an order of protection under section eight hundred forty-two, provided that the court shall make a determination, and the court shall state such determination in a written decision or on the record, whether to impose a condition pursuant to this subdivision, provided further, however, that failure to make such a determination shall not affect the validity of such order of protection. In making such determination, the court shall consider, but shall not be limited to consideration of, whether the temporary order of protection is likely to achieve its purpose in the absence of such a condition, conduct subject to prior orders of protection, prior incidents of abuse, extent of past or present injury, threats, drug or alcohol abuse, and access to weapons.

(b) Upon the filing of a petition under this article, or as soon thereafter as the petitioner appears before the court, the court shall advise the petitioner of the right to proceed in both the family and criminal courts, pursuant to the provisions of section one hundred fifteen of this act.

2. A temporary order of protection is not a finding of wrongdoing.

3. The court may issue or extend a temporary order of protection ex parte or on notice simultaneously with the issuance of a warrant, directing that the respondent be arrested and brought before the court, pursuant to section eight hundred twenty-seven of this article.

4. Notwithstanding the provisions of section eight hundred seventeen of this article the court may, together with a temporary order of protection issued pursuant to this section, issue an order for temporary child support, in an amount sufficient to meet the needs of the child, without a showing of immediate or emergency need. The court shall make an order for temporary child support notwithstanding that information with respect to income and assets of the respondent may be unavailable. Where such information is available, the court may make an award for temporary child support pursuant

to the formula set forth in subdivision one of section four hundred thirteen of this act. An order making such award shall be deemed to have been issued pursuant to article four of this act. Upon making an order for temporary child support pursuant to this subdivision, the court shall advise the petitioner of the availability of child support enforcement services by the support collection unit of the local department of social services, to enforce the temporary order and to assist in securing continued child support, and shall set the support matter down for further proceedings in accordance with article four of this act.

Where the court determines that the respondent has employer-provided medical insurance, the court may further direct, as part of an order of temporary support under this subdivision, that a medical support execution be issued and served upon the respondent's employer as provided for in section fifty-two hundred forty-one of the civil practice law and rules.

Part 3
Hearing

Section
832.   Definition of "fact-finding hearing".
833.   Definition of "dispositional hearing".
834.   Evidence.
835.   Sequence of hearings.
836.   Adjournments.
838.   Petitioner and respondent may have friend or relative present.

§832. Definition of "fact-finding hearing".

When used in this article, "fact-finding hearing" means a hearing to determine whether the allegations of a petition under section eight hundred twenty-one are supported by a fair preponderance of the evidence.

§833. Definition of "dispositional hearing".

When used in this article, "dispositional hearing" means in the case of a petition under this article a hearing to determine what order of disposition should be made.

§834. Evidence.

Only competent, material and relevant evidence may be admitted in a fact-finding hearing; only material and relevant evidence may be admitted in a dispositional hearing.

§835. Sequence of hearings.

(a) Upon completion of the fact-finding hearing, the dispositional hearing may commence immediately after the required findings are made.

(b) Reports prepared by the probation service for use by the court at any time prior to the making of an order of disposition shall be deemed confidential information furnished to the court which the court in a proper case may, in its discretion, withhold from or disclose in whole or in part to the child's attorney, counsel, party in interest, or other appropriate person. Such reports may not be furnished to the court prior to the completion of a fact-finding hearing, but may be used in a dispositional hearing.

§836. Adjournments.

(a) The court may adjourn a fact-finding hearing or a dispositional hearing for good cause shown on its own motion or on motion of either party.

(b) At the conclusion of a fact-finding hearing and after it has made findings required before a dispositional hearing may commence, the court may adjourn the proceedings to enable it to make inquiry into the surroundings, conditions, and capacities of the persons involved in the proceedings.

§838. Petitioner and respondent may have friend or relative present.

Unless the court shall find it undesirable, the petitioner shall be entitled to a non-witness friend, relative, counselor or social worker present in the court room. This section does not authorize any such person to take part in the proceedings. However, at any time during the proceeding, the court may call such person as a witness and take his or her testimony. Unless the court shall find it undesirable, the respondent shall be entitled to a non-witness friend, relative, counselor or social worker present in the court room in the event such respondent is not represented by legal counsel. This section does not authorize any such person to take part in the proceedings. However, at any time during the proceeding, the court may call such person as a witness and take his or her testimony.

Part 4
Orders

§841. Orders of disposition.

At the conclusion of a dispositional hearing under this article, the court may enter an order:

(a) dismissing the petition, if the allegations of the petition are not established; or

(b) suspending judgment for a period not in excess of six months; or

(c) placing the respondent on probation for a period not exceeding one year, and requiring respondent to participate in a batterer's education program designed to help end violent behavior, which may include referral to drug and alcohol counseling, and to pay the costs thereof if respondent has the means to do so, provided however that nothing contained herein shall be deemed to require payment of the costs of any such program by the petitioner, the state or any political subdivision thereof; or

(d) making an order of protection in accord with section eight hundred forty-two of this part; or

(e) directing payment of restitution in an amount not to exceed ten thousand dollars. An order of restitution may be made in conjunction with any order of disposition authorized under subdivisions (b), (c), or (d) of this section. In no case shall an order of restitution be issued where the court determines that the respondent has already paid such restitution as part of the disposition or settlement of another proceeding arising from the same act or acts alleged in the petition before the court.

No order of protection may direct any party to observe conditions of behavior unless the party requesting the order of protection has served and filed a petition or counter-claim in accordance with section one hundred fifty-four-b of this act. Nothing in this section shall preclude the issuance of a temporary order of protection ex parte, pursuant to section eight hundred twenty-eight of this article.

Nothing in this section shall preclude the issuance of both an order of probation and an order of protection as part of the order of disposition.

Notwithstanding the foregoing provisions, an order of protection, or temporary order of protection where applicable, may be entered against a former spouse and persons who have a child in common, regardless of whether such persons have been married or have lived together at any time, or against a member of the same family or household as defined in subdivision one of section eight hundred twelve of this article.

§842. Order of protection.

An order of protection under section eight hundred forty-one of this part shall set forth reasonable conditions of behavior to be observed for a period not in excess of two years by the petitioner or respondent or for a period not in excess of five years upon (i) a finding by the court on the record of the existence of aggravating circumstances as defined in paragraph (vii) of subdivision (a) of section eight hundred twenty-seven of this article; or (ii) a finding by the court on the record that the conduct alleged in the petition is in violation of a valid order of protection. Any finding of aggravating circumstances pursuant to this section shall be stated on the record and upon the order of protection. The court may also, upon motion, extend the order of protection for a reasonable period of time upon a showing of good cause or consent of the parties. The fact that abuse has not occurred during the pendency of an order shall not, in itself, constitute sufficient ground for denying or failing to extend the order. The court must articulate a basis for its decision on the record. The duration of any temporary order shall not by itself be a factor in determining the length or issuance of any final order. Any order of protection issued pursuant to this section shall specify if an order of probation is in effect. Any order of protection issued pursuant to this section may require the petitioner or the respondent:

(a) to stay away from the home, school, business or place of employment of any other party, the other spouse, the other parent, or the child, and to stay away from any other specific location designated by the court, provided that the court shall make a determination, and shall state such determination in a written decision or on the record, whether to impose a condition pursuant to this subdivision, provided further, however, that failure to make such a determination shall not affect the validity of such order of protection. In making such determination, the court shall consider, but shall not be limited to consideration of, whether the order of protection is likely to achieve its purpose in the absence of such a condition, conduct subject to prior orders of protection, prior incidents of abuse, extent of past or present injury, threats, drug or alcohol abuse, and access to weapons;

(b) to permit a parent, or a person entitled to visitation by a court order or a separation agreement, to visit the child at stated periods;

(c) to refrain from committing a family offense, as defined in subdivision one of section eight hundred twelve of this act, or any criminal offense against the child or against the other parent or against any person to whom custody of the child is awarded, or from harassing, intimidating or threatening such persons;

(d) to permit a designated party to enter the residence during a specified period of time in order to remove personal belongings not in issue in this proceeding or in any other proceeding or action under this act or the domestic relations law;

(e) to refrain from acts of commission or omission that create an unreasonable risk to the health, safety or welfare of a child;

(f) to pay the reasonable counsel fees and disbursements involved in obtaining or enforcing the order of the person who is protected by such order if such order is issued or enforced;

(g) to require the respondent to participate in a batterer's education program designed to help end violent behavior, which may include referral to drug and alcohol counselling, and to pay the costs thereof if the person has the means to do so, provided however that nothing contained herein shall be deemed to require payment of the costs of any such program by the petitioner, the state or any political subdivision thereof;

(h) to provide, either directly or by means of medical and health insurance, for expenses incurred for medical care and treatment arising from the incident or incidents forming the basis for the issuance of the order;

(i) 1. to refrain from intentionally injuring or killing, without justification, any companion animal the respondent knows to be owned, possessed, leased, kept or held by the petitioner or a minor child residing in the household. 2. "Companion animal", as used in this section, shall have the same meaning as in subdivision five of section three hundred fifty of the agriculture and markets law;

(j) 1. to promptly return specified identification documents to the protected party, in whose favor the order of protection or temporary order of protection is issued; provided, however, that such order may: (A) include any appropriate provision designed to ensure that any such document is available for use as evidence in this proceeding, and available if necessary for legitimate use by the party against whom such order is issued; and (B) specify the manner in which such return shall be accomplished.

2. For purposes of this subdivision, "identification document" shall mean any of the following: (A) exclusively in the name of the protected party: birth certificate, passport, social security card, health insurance or other benefits card, a card or document used to access bank, credit or other financial accounts or records, tax returns, any driver's license, and immigration documents including but not limited to a United States permanent resident card and employment authorization document; and (B) upon motion and after notice and an opportunity to be heard, any of the following, including those that may reflect joint use or ownership, that the court determines are necessary and are appropriately transferred to the protected party: any card or document used to access bank, credit or other financial accounts or records, tax returns, and any other identifying cards and documents; and

(k) to observe such other conditions as are necessary to further the purposes of protection.

The court may also award custody of the child, during the term of the order of protection to either parent, or to an appropriate relative within the second degree. Nothing in this section gives the court power to place or board out any child or to commit a child to an institution or agency.

Notwithstanding the provisions of section eight hundred seventeen of this article, where a temporary order of child support has not already been issued, the court may in addition to the issuance of an order of protection pursuant to this section, issue an order for temporary child support in an amount sufficient to meet the needs of the child, without a showing of immediate or emergency need. The court shall make an order for temporary child support notwithstanding that information with respect to income and assets of the respondent may be unavailable. Where such information is available, the court may make an award for temporary child support pursuant to the formula set forth in subdivision one of section four hundred thirteen of this act. Temporary orders of support issued pursuant to this article shall be deemed to have been issued pursuant to section four hundred thirteen of this act.

Upon making an order for temporary child support pursuant to this subdivision, the court shall advise the petitioner of the availability of child support enforcement services by the support collection unit of the local department of social services, to enforce the temporary order and to assist in securing continued child support, and shall set the support matter down for further proceedings in accordance with article four of this act.

Where the court determines that the respondent has employer-provided medical insurance, the court may further direct, as part of an order of temporary support under this subdivision, that a medical support execution be issued and served upon the respondent's employer as provided for in section fifty-two hundred forty-one of the civil practice law and rules.

In any proceeding in which an order of protection or temporary order of protection or a warrant has been issued under this section, the clerk of the court shall issue to the petitioner and respondent and his counsel and to any other person affected by the order a copy of the order of protection or temporary order of protection and ensure that a copy of the order of protection or temporary order of protection be transmitted to the local correctional facility where the individual is or will be detained, the state or local correctional facility where the individual is or will be imprisoned, and the supervising probation department or the department of corrections and community supervision where the individual is under probation or parole supervision.

Notwithstanding the foregoing provisions, an order of protection, or temporary order of protection where applicable, may be entered against a former spouse and persons who have a child in common, regardless of whether such persons have been married or have lived together at any time, or against a member of the same family or household as defined in subdivision one of section eight hundred twelve of this article.

In addition to the foregoing provisions, the court may issue an order, pursuant to section two hundred twenty-seven-c of the real property law, authorizing the party for whose benefit any order of protection has been issued to terminate a lease or rental agreement pursuant to section two hundred twenty-seven-c of the real property law.

The protected party in whose favor the order of protection or temporary order of protection is issued may not be held to violate an order issued in his or her favor nor may such protected party be arrested for violating such order.

§842-a. **Suspension and revocation of a license to carry, possess, repair or dispose of a firearm or firearms pursuant to section 400.00 of the penal law and ineligibility for such a license; order to surrender firearms.**

1. Suspension of firearms license and ineligibility for such a license upon the issuance of a temporary order of protection. Whenever a temporary order of

protection is issued pursuant to section eight hundred twenty-eight of this article, or pursuant to article four, five, six, seven or ten of this act:

(a) the court shall suspend any such existing license possessed by the respondent, order the respondent ineligible for such a license, and order the immediate surrender pursuant to subparagraph (f) of paragraph one of subdivision a of section 265.20 and subdivision six of section 400.05 of the penal law, of any or all firearms owned or possessed where the court receives information that gives the court good cause to believe that: (i) the respondent has a prior conviction of any violent felony offense as defined in section 70.02 of the penal law; (ii) the respondent has previously been found to have willfully failed to obey a prior order of protection and such willful failure involved (A) the infliction of physical injury, as defined in subdivision nine of section 10.00 of the penal law, (B) the use or threatened use of a deadly weapon or dangerous instrument as those terms are defined in subdivisions twelve and thirteen of section 10.00 of the penal law, or (C) behavior constituting any violent felony offense as defined in section 70.02 of the penal law; or (iii) the respondent has a prior conviction for stalking in the first degree as defined in section 120.60 of the penal law, stalking in the second degree as defined in section 120.55 of the penal law, stalking in the third degree as defined in section 120.50 of the penal law or stalking in the fourth degree as defined in section 120.45 of such law; and

(b) the court shall where the court finds a substantial risk that the respondent may use or threaten to use a firearm unlawfully against the person or persons for whose protection the temporary order of protection is issued, suspend any such existing license possessed by the respondent, order the respondent ineligible for such a license, and order the immediate surrender pursuant to subparagraph (f) of paragraph one of subdivision a of section 265.20 and subdivision six of section 400.05 of the penal law, of any or all firearms owned or possessed.

2. Revocation or suspension of firearms license and ineligibility for such a license upon the issuance of an order of protection. Whenever an order of protection is issued pursuant to section eight hundred forty-one of this part, or pursuant to article four, five, six, seven or ten of this act:

(a) the court shall revoke any such existing license possessed by the respondent, order the respondent ineligible for such a license, and order the immediate surrender pursuant to subparagraph (f) of paragraph one of subdivision a of section 265.20 and subdivision six of section 400.05 of the penal law, of any or all firearms owned or possessed where the court finds that the conduct which resulted in the issuance of the order of protection involved (i) the infliction of physical injury, as defined in subdivision nine of section 10.00 of the penal law, (ii) the use or threatened use of a deadly weapon or dangerous instrument as those terms are defined in subdivisions twelve and thirteen of section 10.00 of the penal law, or (iii) behavior constituting any violent felony offense as defined in section 70.02 of the penal law; and

(b) the court shall, where the court finds a substantial risk that the respondent may use or threaten to use a firearm unlawfully against the person or persons for whose protection the order of protection is issued, (i) revoke any such existing license possessed by the respondent, order the respondent ineligible for such a license and order the immediate surrender pursuant to subparagraph (f) of paragraph one of subdivision a of section 265.20 and subdivision six of section 400.05 of the penal law, of any or all firearms owned or possessed or (ii) suspend or continue to suspend any such existing license possessed by the respondent, order the respondent ineligible for such a license, and order the immediate surrender pursuant to subparagraph (f) of paragraph one of subdivision a of section 265.20 and subdivision six of section 400.05 of the penal law, of any or all firearms owned or possessed.

3. Revocation or suspension of firearms license and ineligibility for such a license upon a finding of a willful failure to obey an order of protection or temporary order of protection. Whenever a respondent has been found, pursuant to section eight hundred forty-six-a of this part to have willfully failed to obey an order of protection or temporary order of protection issued pursuant to this act or the domestic relations law, or by this court or by a court of competent jurisdiction in another state, territorial or tribal jurisdiction, in addition to any other remedies available pursuant to section eight hundred forty-six-a of this part:

(a) the court shall revoke any such existing license possessed by the respondent, order the respondent ineligible for such a license, and order the immediate surrender pursuant to subparagraph (f) of paragraph one of subdivision a of section 265.20 and subdivision six of section 400.05 of the penal law, of any or all firearms owned or possessed where the willful failure to obey such order involves (i) the infliction of physical injury, as defined in subdivision nine of section 10.00 of the penal law, (ii) the use or threatened use of a deadly weapon or dangerous instrument as those terms are defined in subdivisions twelve and thirteen of section 10.00 of the penal law, or (iii) behavior constituting any violent felony offense as defined in section 70.02 of the penal law; or (iv) behavior constituting stalking in the first degree as defined in section 120.60 of the penal law, stalking in the second degree as defined in section 120.55 of the penal law, stalking in the third degree as defined in section 120.50 of the penal law or stalking in the fourth degree as defined in section 120.45 of such law; and

(b) the court shall where the court finds a substantial risk that the respondent may use or threaten to use a firearm unlawfully against the person or persons for whose protection the order of protection was issued, (i) revoke any such existing license possessed by the respondent, order the respondent ineligible for such a license, whether or not the respondent possesses such a license, and order the immediate surrender pursuant to subparagraph (f) of paragraph one of subdivision a of section 265.20 and subdivision six of section 400.05 of the penal law, of any or all firearms owned or possessed or (ii) suspend any such existing license possessed by the respondent, order the respondent ineligible for such a license, and order the immediate surrender of any or all firearms owned or possessed.

4. Suspension. Any suspension order issued pursuant to this section shall remain in effect for the duration of the temporary order of protection or order of protection, unless modified or vacated by the court.

5. Surrender. (a) Where an order to surrender one or more firearms has been issued, the temporary order of protection or order of protection shall specify the place where such firearms shall be surrendered, shall specify a date and time by which the surrender shall be completed and, to the extent possible, shall describe such firearms to be surrendered and shall direct the authority receiving such surrendered firearms to immediately notify the court of such surrender.

(b) The prompt surrender of one or more firearms pursuant to a court order issued pursuant this section shall be considered a voluntary surrender for purposes of subparagraph (f) of paragraph one of subdivision a of section

265.20 of the penal law. The disposition of any such firearms shall be in accordance with the provisions of subdivision six of section 400.05 of the penal law.

(c) The provisions of this section shall not be deemed to limit, restrict or otherwise impair the authority of the court to order and direct the surrender of any or all pistols, revolvers, rifles, shotguns or other firearms owned or possessed by a respondent pursuant to this act.

6. Notice. (a) Where an order of revocation, suspension or ineligibility has been issued pursuant to this section, any temporary order of protection or order of protection issued shall state that such firearm license has been suspended or revoked or that the respondent is ineligible for such license, as the case may be.

(b) The court revoking or suspending the license, ordering the respondent ineligible for such license, or ordering the surrender of any firearm shall immediately notify the statewide registry of orders of protection and the duly constituted police authorities of the locality of such action.

(c) The court revoking or suspending the license or ordering the defendant ineligible for such license shall give written notice thereof without unnecessary delay to the division of state police at its office in the city of Albany.

(d) Where an order of revocation, suspension, ineligibility, or surrender is modified or vacated, the court shall immediately notify the statewide registry of orders of protection and the duly constituted police authorities of the locality concerning such action and shall give written notice thereof without unnecessary delay to the division of state police at its office in the city of Albany.

7. Hearing. The respondent shall have the right to a hearing before the court regarding any revocation, suspension, ineligibility or surrender order issued pursuant to this section, provided that nothing in this subdivision shall preclude the court from issuing any such order prior to a hearing. Where the court has issued such an order prior to a hearing, it shall commence such hearing within fourteen days of the date such order was issued.

8. Nothing in this section shall delay or otherwise interfere with the issuance of a temporary order of protection.

§843. Rules of court.

Rules of court shall define permissible terms and conditions of any order issued under section eight hundred forty-one, paragraphs (b), (c) and (d).

§844. Reconsideration and modification.

For good cause shown, the family court may after hearing reconsider and modify any order issued under paragraphs (b), (c) and (d) of section eight hundred forty-one.

§846. Petition; violation of court order.

Proceedings under this part shall be originated by the filing of a petition containing an allegation that the respondent has failed to obey a lawful order of this court or an order of protection issued by a court of competent jurisdiction of another state, territorial or tribal jurisdiction.

(a) Persons who may originate proceedings. The original petitioner, or any person who may originate proceedings under section eight hundred twenty-two of this article, may originate a proceeding under this part.

(a-1) The protected party in whose favor the order of protection or temporary order of protection is issued may not be held to violate an order issued in his or her favor nor may such protected party be arrested for violating such order.

(b) Issuance of summons. (i) Upon the filing of a petition under this part, the court may cause a copy of the petition and summons to be issued requiring the respondent to show cause why respondent should not be dealt with in accordance with section eight hundred forty-six-a of this part. The summons shall include on its face, printed or typewritten in a size equal to at least eight point bold type, a notice warning the respondent that a failure to appear in court may result in immediate arrest, and that, after an appearance in court, a finding that the respondent willfully failed to obey the order may result in commitment to jail for a term not to exceed six months, for contempt of court. The notice shall also advise the respondent of the right to counsel, and the right to assigned counsel, if indigent.

(ii) Upon the filing of a petition under this part alleging a violation of a lawful order of this or any other court, as provided in this section, the court may, on its own motion, or on motion of the petitioner:

(A) hear the violation petition and take such action as is authorized under this article; or

(B) retain jurisdiction to hear and determine whether such violation constitutes contempt of court, and transfer the allegations of criminal conduct constituting such violation to the district attorney for prosecution pursuant to section eight hundred thirteen of this article; or

(C) transfer the entire proceeding to the criminal court pursuant to section eight hundred thirteen of this article.

(c) Service of summons. Upon issuance of a summons, the provisions of section eight hundred twenty-six of this article shall apply, except that no order of commitment may be entered upon default in appearance by the respondent if service has been made pursuant to subdivision (b) of such section.

(d) Issuance of warrant. The court may issue a warrant, directing that the respondent be arrested and brought before the court, pursuant to section eight hundred twenty-seven of this article.

§846-a. Powers on failure to obey order.

If a respondent is brought before the court for failure to obey any lawful order issued under this article or an order of protection or temporary order of protection issued pursuant to this act or issued by a court of competent jurisdiction of another state, territorial or tribal jurisdiction and if, after hearing, the court is satisfied by competent proof that the respondent has willfully failed to obey any such order, the court may modify an existing order or temporary order of protection to add reasonable conditions of behavior to the existing order, make a new order of protection in accordance with section eight hundred forty-two of this part, may order the forfeiture of bail in a manner consistent with article five hundred forty of the criminal procedure law if bail has been ordered pursuant to this act, may order the respondent to pay the petitioner's reasonable and necessary counsel fees in connection with the violation petition where the court finds that the violation of its order was willful, and may commit the respondent to jail for a term not to exceed six months. Such commitment may be served upon certain specified days or parts of days as the court may direct, and the court may, at any time within the term of such sentence, revoke such suspension and commit the respondent for the remainder of the original sentence, or suspend the remainder of such sentence. If the court determines that the willful failure to obey such order involves violent behavior constituting the crimes of menacing, reckless endangerment, assault or attempted assault and if such a respondent is licensed to carry, possess, repair and dispose of firearms pursuant to section 400.00 of the penal law, the court may also immediately revoke such license and may arrange for the immediate surrender pursuant to subparagraph (f) of paragraph one of subdivision a of section 265.20 and subdivision six of section 400.05 of the penal law, and disposal of any firearm such respondent owns or possesses. If the willful failure to obey such order involves the infliction of physical injury as defined in subdivision nine of section 10.00 of the penal law or the use or threatened use of a deadly weapon or dangerous instrument, as those terms are defined in subdivisions twelve and thirteen of section 10.00 of the penal law, such revocation and immediate surrender pursuant to subparagraph (f) of paragraph one of subdivision a of section 265.20 and subdivision six of section 400.05 of the penal law six and disposal of any firearm owned or possessed by respondent shall be mandatory, pursuant to subdivision eleven of section 400.00 of the penal law.

§847.   Procedures for violation of orders of protection; certain cases.
An assault, attempted assault or other family offense as defined in section eight hundred twelve of this article which occurs subsequent to the issuance of an order of protection under this article shall be deemed a new offense for which the petitioner may file a petition alleging a violation of an order of protection or file a new petition alleging a new family offense and may seek to have an accusatory instrument filed in a criminal court, as authorized by section one hundred fifteen of this act.

ARTICLE 9
Conciliation Proceedings
Part
1. Purpose and jurisdiction.
2. Procedure.

Part 1
Purpose and Jurisdiction
Section
911.   Purpose.
912.   Jurisdiction.
913.   Support and family offense proceedings.
914.   No effect on marital status.
915.   Confidentiality of statements.

§911.   Purpose.
This article is designed to implement section thirteen-c, subdivision six, of article six of the constitution by making available an informal conciliation procedure to those whose marriage is in trouble.

§912.   Jurisdiction.
The family court has original jurisdiction over conciliation proceedings under this article.

§913.   Support and family offense proceedings.
On its own motion and at any time in a proceeding under this article, the court may direct the filing of a support petition under article four or a family offense petition under article eight of this act.

§914. No effect on marital status.

The family court in a proceeding under this article may not issue any order affecting the marital status of the petitioner or of the petitioner's spouse or relieving either of any marital obligation.

§915. Confidentiality of statements.

All statements made in proceedings under this article are confidential and shall not be admissible in evidence in any subsequent proceeding or action.

Part 2
Procedure

§921. Originating proceeding.

A spouse may originate a conciliation proceeding under this article by filing a petition stating that his or her marriage is in difficulty and that the conciliation services of the family court are needed.

§922. Preliminary procedure.

The probation service is authorized to confer with a potential petitioner and may invite the potential petitioner's spouse and any other interested person to attend such conferences as appear to be advisable in conciliating the spouses. The probation service is also authorized after the filing of a petition to confer with the petitioner and to invite the petitioner's spouse to attend such conferences as appear to be advisable in conciliating the spouses.

§923. Referral to voluntary agency.

(a) The probation service may recommend to the petitioner and to the petitioner's spouse that they consult with interested voluntary social or religious agencies in the community. If they consent, the service may thereupon refer them to any such interested voluntary agency.

(b) The probation service may not prevent any person from having access to the court for the purpose of having conciliation proceedings under this article.

§924. Attendance at conference.

If the petitioner's spouse does not attend a conference to which he or she has been invited after the filing of a petition under section nine hundred twenty-one, the petitioner may apply to the court for an order directing the petitioner's spouse to attend a conciliation conference. The court may enter an order directing the petitioner's spouse to appear in court on not less than five days' notice and, if the court concludes after hearing that it will serve the purposes of this article to require attendance at a conference, may direct the petitioner's spouse to attend a conference.

§925. Continuation of proceeding.

If the petitioner's spouse attends a conference to which he or she has been invited under section nine hundred twenty-two or has been directed to attend under section nine hundred twenty-four and thereafter does not attend any conciliation conference, the court, on due notice to both spouses, may hold a hearing to determine whether the proceeding should be continued. If it concludes that conciliation under the auspices of the family court is not feasible, it may refer the parties to interested voluntary social or religious agencies in the community and shall terminate the proceeding under this article. If it concludes that further efforts at conciliation under this article should be undertaken, it may direct the spouses to attend another conciliation conference.

§926. Duration of proceeding.

Unless both spouses consent to the continuation of a conciliation proceeding under this article, it terminates ninety days after the filing of the petition.

ARTICLE 10
Child Protective Proceedings

Part
1. Jurisdiction.
2. Temporary removal and preliminary orders.
3. Preliminary procedure.
4. Hearings.
5. Orders.
6. New hearing and reconsideration of orders.
7. Compliance with orders.
8. Visitation of minors in foster care.

Part I
Jurisdiction

§1011. Purpose.

This article is designed to establish procedures to help protect children from injury or mistreatment and to help safeguard their physical, mental, and emotional well-being. It is designed to provide a due process of law for determining when the state, through its family court, may intervene against the wishes of a parent on behalf of a child so that his needs are properly met.

§1012. Definitions.

When used in this article and unless the specific context indicates otherwise:

(a) "Respondent" includes any parent or other person legally responsible for a child's care who is alleged to have abused or neglected such child;

(b) "Child" means any person or persons alleged to have been abused or neglected, whichever the case may be;

(c) "A case involving abuse" means any proceeding under this article in which there are allegations that one or more of the children of, or the legal responsibility of, the respondent are abused children;

(d) "Drug" means any substance defined as a controlled substance in section thirty-three hundred six of the public health law;

(e) "Abused child" means a child less than eighteen years of age whose parent or other person legally responsible for his care

(i) inflicts or allows to be inflicted upon such child physical injury by other than accidental means which causes or creates a substantial risk of death, or serious or protracted disfigurement, or protracted impairment of physical or emotional health or protracted loss or impairment of the function of any bodily organ, or

(ii) creates or allows to be created a substantial risk of physical injury to such child by other than accidental means which would be likely to cause death or serious or protracted disfigurement, or protracted impairment of physical or emotional health or protracted loss or impairment of the function of any bodily organ, or

(iii) commits, or allows to be committed an offense against such child defined in article one hundred thirty of the penal law; allows, permits or encourages such child to engage in any act described in sections 230.25, 230.30 and 230.32 of the penal law; commits any of the acts described in sections 255.25, 255.26 and 255.27 of the penal law; or allows such child to engage in acts or conduct described in article two hundred sixty-three of the penal law provided, however, that (a) the corroboration requirements contained in the penal law and (b) the age requirement for the application of article two hundred sixty-three of such law shall not apply to proceedings under this article.

(f) "Neglected child" means a child less than eighteen years of age

(i) whose physical, mental or emotional condition has been impaired or is in imminent danger of becoming impaired as a result of the failure of his parent or other person legally responsible for his care to exercise a minimum degree of care

(A) in supplying the child with adequate food, clothing, shelter or education in accordance with the provisions of part one of article sixty-five of the education law, or medical, dental, optometrical or surgical care, though financially able to do so or offered financial or other reasonable means to do so; or

(B) in providing the child with proper supervision or guardianship, by unreasonably inflicting or allowing to be inflicted harm, or a substantial risk thereof, including the infliction of excessive corporal punishment; or by misusing a drug or drugs; or by misusing alcoholic beverages to the extent that he loses self-control of his actions; or by any other acts of a similarly serious nature requiring the aid of the court; provided, however, that where the respondent is voluntarily and regularly participating in a rehabilitative program, evidence that the respondent has repeatedly misused a drug or drugs or alcoholic beverages to the extent that he loses self-control of his actions shall not establish that the child is a neglected child in the absence of evidence establishing that the child's physical, mental or emotional condition has been impaired or is in imminent danger of becoming impaired as set forth in paragraph (i) of this subdivision; or

(ii) who has been abandoned, in accordance with the definition and other criteria set forth in subdivision five of section three hundred eighty-four-b of the social services law, by his parents or other person legally responsible for his care.

(g) "Person legally responsible" includes the child's custodian, guardian, any other person responsible for the child's care at the relevant time. Custodian may include any person continually or at regular intervals found in the same household as the child when the conduct of such person causes or contributes to the abuse or neglect of the child.

(h) "Impairment of emotional health" and "impairment of mental or emotional condition" includes a state of substantially diminished psychological or intellectual functioning in relation to, but not limited to, such factors as failure to thrive, control of aggressive or self-destructive impulses, ability to think and reason, or acting out or misbehavior, including incorrigibility, ungovernability or habitual truancy; provided, however, that such impairment must be clearly attributable to the unwillingness or inability of the respondent to exercise a minimum degree of care toward the child.

(i) "Child protective agency" means the child protective service of the appropriate local department of social services or such other agencies with whom the local department has arranged for the provision of child protective services under the local plan for child protective services or an Indian tribe that has entered into an agreement with the state department of social services pursuant to section thirty-nine of the social services law to provide child protective services.

(j) "Aggravated circumstances" means where a child has been either severely or repeatedly abused, as defined in subdivision eight of section three hundred eighty-four-b of the social services law; or where a child has subsequently been found to be an abused child, as defined in paragraph (i) or (iii) of subdivision (e) of this section, within five years after return home following placement in foster care as a result of being found to be a neglected child, as defined in subdivision (f) of this section, provided that the respondent or respondents in each of the foregoing proceedings was the same; or where the court finds by clear and convincing evidence that the parent of a child in foster care has refused and has failed completely, over a period of at least six months from the date of removal, to engage in services necessary to eliminate the risk of abuse or neglect if returned to the parent, and has failed to secure services on his or her own or otherwise adequately prepare for the return home and, after being informed by the court that such an admission could eliminate the requirement that the local department of social services provide reunification services to the parent, the parent has stated in court under oath that he or she intends to continue to refuse such necessary services and is unwilling to secure such services independently or otherwise prepare for the child's return home; provided, however, that if the court finds that adequate justification exists for the failure to engage in or secure such services, including but not limited to a lack of child care, a lack of transportation, and an inability to attend services that conflict with the parent's work schedule, such failure shall not constitute an aggravated circumstance; or where a court has determined a child five days old or younger was abandoned by a parent with an intent to wholly abandon such child and with the intent that the child be safe from physical injury and cared for in an appropriate manner.

(k) "Permanency hearing" means a hearing held in accordance with section one thousand eighty-nine of this act for the purpose of reviewing the foster care status of the child and the appropriateness of the permanency plan developed by the social services district or agency.

(*l*) "Parent" means a person who is recognized under the laws of the state of New York to be the child's legal parent.

(m) "Relative" means any person who is related to the child by blood, marriage or adoption and who is not a parent, putative parent or relative of a putative parent of the child.

(n) "Suitable person" means any person who plays or has played a significant positive role in the child's life or in the life of the child's family.

§1013. Jurisdiction.

(a) The family court has exclusive original jurisdiction over proceedings under this article alleging the abuse or neglect of a child.

(b) For the protection of children, the family court has jurisdiction over proceedings under this article notwithstanding the fact that a criminal court also has or may be exercising jurisdiction over the facts alleged in the petition or complaint.

(c) In determining the jurisdiction of the court under this article, the age of the child at the time the proceedings are initiated is controlling.

(d) In determining the jurisdiction of the court under this article, the child need not be currently in the care or custody of the respondent if the court otherwise has jurisdiction over the matter.

§1014. Transfer to and from family court; concurrent proceedings.

(a) The family court may transfer upon a hearing any proceedings originated under this article to an appropriate criminal court or may refer such proceeding to the appropriate district attorney if it concludes, that the processes of the family court are inappropriate or insufficient. The family court may continue the proceeding under this article after such transfer or referral and if the proceeding is continued, the family court may enter any preliminary order, as authorized by section one thousand twenty-seven, in order to protect the interests of the child pending a final order of disposition.

(b) Any criminal complaint charging facts amounting to abuse or neglect under this article may be transferred by the criminal court in which the complaint was made to the family court in the county in which the criminal court is located, unless the family court has transferred the proceeding to the criminal court. The family court shall then, upon a hearing, determine what further action is appropriate. After the family court makes this determination, any criminal complaint may be transferred back to the criminal court, with or without retention of the proceeding in the family court, or may be retained solely in the family court, or if there appears to be no basis for the complaint, it may be dismissed by the family court. If the family court determines a petition should be filed, proceedings under this act shall be commenced as soon as practicable.

(c) Nothing in this article shall be interpreted to preclude concurrent proceedings in the family court and a criminal court.

(d) In any hearing conducted by the family court under this section, the court may grant the respondent or potential respondent testimonial immunity in any subsequent criminal court proceeding.

§1015. Venue.

(a) Proceedings under this article may be originated in the county in which the child resides or is domiciled at the time of the filing of the petition or in the county in which the person having custody of the child resides or is domiciled.

For the purposes of this section, residence shall include a dwelling unit or facility which provides shelter to homeless persons or families on an emergency or temporary basis.

(b) If in another proceeding under this act the court directs the filing of an abuse or neglect petition, the venue provision of the article under which the other proceeding is brought and the provisions of part seven of article one shall apply.

§1015-a. Court-ordered services.

In any proceeding under this article, the court may order a social services official to provide or arrange for the provision of services or assistance to the child and his or her family to facilitate the protection of the child, the rehabilitation of the family and, as appropriate, the discharge of the child from foster care. Such order shall not include the provision of any service or assistance to the child and his or her family which is not authorized or required to be made available pursuant to the comprehensive annual services program plan then in effect. In any order issued pursuant to this section the court may require a social services official to make periodic progress reports to the court on the implementation of such order. Nothing in such order shall preclude any party from exercising its rights under this article or any other provision of law relating to the return of the care and custody of the child by a social services official to the parent, parents or guardian. Violation of such order shall be subject to punishment pursuant to section seven hundred fifty-three of the judiciary law.

§1016. Appointment of attorney for the child.

The court shall appoint an attorney to represent a child who has been allegedly abused or neglected upon the earliest occurrence of any of the following: (i) the court receiving notice, pursuant to paragraph (iv) of subdivision (b) of section one thousand twenty-four of this act, of the emergency removal of the child; (ii) an application for an order for removal of the child prior to the filing of a petition, pursuant to section one thousand twenty-two of this act; or (iii) the filing of a petition alleging abuse or neglect pursuant to this article.

Whenever an attorney has been appointed by the family court pursuant to section two hundred forty-nine of this act to represent a child in a proceeding under this article, such appointment shall continue without further court order or appointment during (i) an order of disposition issued by the court pursuant to section one thousand fifty-two of this article directing supervision, protection or suspending judgment, or any extension thereof; (ii) an adjournment in contemplation of dismissal as provided for in section one thousand thirty-nine of this article or any extension thereof; or (iii) the pendency of the foster care placement ordered pursuant to section one thousand fifty-two of this article. All notices and reports required by law shall be provided to such attorney for the child. Such appointment shall terminate upon the expiration of such order, unless another appointment of an attorney for the child has been made by the court or unless such attorney makes application to the court to be relieved of his or her appointment. Upon approval of such application to be relieved, the court shall immediately appoint another attorney for the child to whom all notices and reports required by law shall be provided.

The attorney for the child shall be entitled to compensation pursuant to applicable provisions of law for services rendered up to and including disposition of the petition. The attorney for the child shall, by separate application, be entitled to compensation for services rendered subsequent to the disposition of the petition.

Nothing in this section shall be construed to limit the authority of the court to remove the attorney for the child from his or her assignment.

§1017. Placement of children.

1. In any proceeding under this article, when the court determines that a child must be removed from his or her home, pursuant to part two of this article, or placed, pursuant to section one thousand fifty-five of this article:

(a) the court shall direct the local commissioner of social services to conduct an immediate investigation to locate any non-respondent parent of the child and any relatives of the child, including all of the child's grandparents, all relatives or suitable persons identified by any respondent parent or any non-respondent parent and any relative identified by a child over the age of five as a relative who plays or has played a significant positive role in his or her life. The local commissioner shall inform them in writing of the pendency of the proceeding and of the opportunity for non-respondent parents to seek temporary release of the child under this article or custody under article six of this act or for relatives to seek to become foster parents or to provide free care under this article or to seek custody pursuant to article six of this act; or for suitable persons to become foster parents or provide free care under this article or to seek guardianship pursuant to article six of this act. Uniform statewide rules of court shall specify the contents of the notice consistent with the provisions of this section. The local commissioner of social services shall report the results of such investigation, or investigations to the court and parties, including the attorney for the child. The local commissioner shall also record the results of the investigation or investigations, including, but not limited to, the name, last known address, social security number, employer's address and any other identifying information to the extent known regarding any non-respondent parent, in the uniform case record maintained pursuant to section four hundred nine-f of the social services law. For the purpose of this section, "non-respondent parent" shall include a person entitled to notice of the pendency of the proceeding and of the right to intervene as an interested party pursuant to subdivision (d) of section one thousand thirty-five of this article, and a non-custodial parent entitled to notice and the right to enforce visitation rights pursuant to subdivision (e) of section one thousand thirty-five of this article.

(b) The court shall also direct the local commissioner of social services to conduct an investigation to locate any person who is not recognized to be the child's legal parent and does not have the rights of a legal parent under the laws of the state of New York but who (i) has filed with a putative father registry an instrument acknowledging paternity of the child, pursuant to section 4-1.2 of the estates, powers and trusts law, or (ii) has a pending paternity petition, or (iii) has been identified as a parent of the child by the child's other parent in a written sworn statement. The local commissioner of social services shall report the results of such investigation to the court and parties, including the attorney for the child.

(c) The court shall determine:

(i) whether there is a non-respondent parent, relative or suitable person with whom such child may appropriately reside; and

(ii) in the case of a relative or suitable person, whether such individual seeks approval as a foster parent pursuant to the social services law for the purposes of providing care for such child, or wishes to provide free care for the child during the pendency of any orders pursuant to this article.

2. The court shall, upon receipt of the report of the investigation ordered pursuant to subdivision one of this section:

(a) where the court, after a review of the reports of the sex offender registry established and maintained pursuant to section one hundred sixty-eight-b of the correction law, reports of the statewide computerized registry of orders of protection established and maintained pursuant to section two hundred twenty-one-a of the executive law, related decisions in court proceedings under this article and all warrants issued under this act, determines that the child may appropriately reside with a non-respondent parent or other relative or suitable person, either:

(i) grant a temporary order of custody or guardianship to such non-respondent parent, relative or suitable person pursuant to a petition filed under article six of this act pending further order of the court, or at disposition of the proceeding, grant a final order of custody or guardianship to such non-respondent parent, relative or suitable person pursuant to article six of this act and section one thousand fifty-five-b of this article; or

(ii) temporarily release the child directly to such non-respondent parent or temporarily place the child with a relative or suitable person pursuant to this article during the pendency of the proceeding or until further order of the court, whichever is earlier and conduct such other and further investigations as the court deems necessary. The court may direct the commissioner of social services, pursuant to regulations of the office of children and family services, to commence an investigation of the home of such non-respondent parent, relative or suitable person within twenty-four hours and to report the results to the court and the parties, including the attorney for the child. If the home of a non-respondent parent, relative or suitable person, is found unqualified as appropriate for the temporary release or placement of the child under this article, the local commissioner shall report such fact and the reasons therefor to the court and the parties, including the attorney for the child, forthwith; or

(iii) remand or place the child, as applicable, with the local commissioner of social services and direct such commissioner to have the child reside with such relative or suitable person and further direct such commissioner pursuant to regulations of the office of children and family services, to commence an investigation of the home of such relative or other suitable person within twenty-four hours and thereafter approve such relative or other suitable person, if qualified, as a foster parent. If such home is found to be unqualified for approval, the local commissioner shall report such fact and the reasons thereafter to the court and the parties, including the attorney for the child, forthwith.

(b) where the court determines that a suitable non-respondent parent or other person related to the child cannot be located, remand or place the child with a suitable person, pursuant to subdivision (b) of section one thousand twenty-seven or subdivision (a) of section one thousand fifty-five of this article, or remand or place the child in the custody of the local commissioner of social services pursuant to subdivision (b) of section one thousand twenty-seven or subdivision (a) of section one thousand fifty-five of this article. The court in its discretion may direct that such commissioner have the child reside in a specific certified foster home where the court determines that such placement is in furtherance of the child's best interests.

3. An order temporarily releasing a child to a non-respondent parent or parents, or temporarily placing a child with a relative or relatives or other

suitable person or persons pursuant to subparagraph (ii) of paragraph (a) of subdivision two of this section or remanding or placing a child with a local commissioner of social services to reside with a relative or relatives or suitable person or persons as foster parents pursuant to subparagraph (iii) of paragraph (a) of subdivision two of this section may not be granted unless the person or persons to whom the child is released, remanded or placed submits to the jurisdiction of the court with respect to the child. The order shall set forth the terms and conditions applicable to such person or persons and child protective agency, social services official and duly authorized agency with respect to the child and may include, but may not be limited to, a direction for such person or persons to cooperate in making the child available for court-ordered visitation with respondents, siblings and others and for appointments with and visits by the child protective agency, including visits in the home and in-person contact with the child protective agency, social services official or duly authorized agency, and for appointments with the child's attorney, clinician or other individual or program providing services to the child during the pendency of the proceeding. The court also may issue a temporary order of protection under subdivision (f) of section one thousand twenty-two, section one thousand twenty-three or section one thousand twenty-nine of this article and an order directing that services be provided pursuant to section one thousand fifteen-a of this part.

4. Nothing in this section shall be deemed to limit, impair or restrict the ability of the court to remove a child from his or her home as authorized by law, or the right of a party to a hearing pursuant to section ten hundred twenty-eight of this article.

§1018. Conferencing and mediation.

In any proceeding initiated pursuant to this article, the court may, at its discretion, authorize the use of conferencing or mediation at any point in the proceedings to further a plan for the child that fosters the child's health, safety, and well-being. Such conferencing or mediation may involve interested relatives or other adults who are significant in the life of the child.

Part 2
Temporary Removal and Preliminary Orders

Section

§1021. Temporary removal with consent.

A peace officer, acting pursuant to his or her special duties, or a police officer or an agent of a duly authorized agency, association, society or institution may temporarily remove a child from the place where he or she is residing with the written consent of his or her parent or other person legally responsible for his or her care, if the child is suspected to be an abused or neglected child under this article. The officer or agent shall, coincident with consent or removal, give written notice to the parent or other person legally responsible for the child's care of the right to apply to the family court for the return of the child pursuant to section one thousand twenty-eight of this article, and of the right to be represented by counsel and the procedures for those who are indigent to obtain counsel in proceedings brought pursuant to this article. Such notice shall also include the name, title, organization, address and telephone number of the person removing the child; the name, address and telephone number of the authorized agency to which the child will be taken, if available; and the telephone number of the person to be contacted for visits with the child. A copy of the instrument whereby the parent or legally responsible person has given such consent to such removal shall be appended to the petition alleging abuse or neglect of the removed child and made a part of the permanent court record of the proceeding. A copy of such instrument and notice of the telephone number of the child protective agency to contact to ascertain the date, time and place of the filing of the petition and of the hearing that will be held pursuant to section one thousand twenty-seven of this article shall be given to the parent or legally responsible person. Unless the child is returned sooner, a petition shall be filed within three court days from the date of removal. In such a case, a hearing shall be held no later than the next court day after the petition is filed and findings shall be made as required pursuant to section one thousand twenty-seven of this article.

§1022. Preliminary orders of court before petition filed.

(a) (i) The family court may enter an order directing the temporary removal of a child from the place where he or she is residing before the filing of a petition under this article, if

(A) the parent or other person legally responsible for the child's care is absent or, though present, was asked and refused to consent to the temporary removal of the child and was informed of an intent to apply for an order under this section and of the information required by section one thousand twenty-three of this part; and

(B) the child appears so to suffer from the abuse or neglect of his or her parent or other person legally responsible for his or her care that his or her immediate removal is necessary to avoid imminent danger to the child's life or health; and

(C) there is not enough time to file a petition and hold a preliminary hearing under section one thousand twenty-seven of this part.

(ii) When a child protective agency applies to a court for the immediate removal of a child pursuant to this subdivision, the court shall calendar the matter for that day and shall continue the matter on successive subsequent court days, if necessary, until a decision is made by the court.

(iii) In determining whether temporary removal of the child is necessary to avoid imminent risk to the child's life or health, the court shall consider and determine in its order whether continuation in the child's home would be contrary to the best interests of the child and where appropriate, whether reasonable efforts were made prior to the date of application for the order directing such temporary removal to prevent or eliminate the need for removal of the child from the home. If the court determines that reasonable efforts to prevent or eliminate the need for removal of the child from the home were not made but that the lack of such efforts was appropriate under the circumstances, the court order shall include such a finding.

(iv) If the court determines that reasonable efforts to prevent or eliminate the need for removal of the child from the home were not made but that such efforts were appropriate under the circumstances, the court shall order the child protective agency to provide or arrange for the provision of appropriate services or assistance to the child and the child's family pursuant to section one thousand fifteen-a of this article or subdivision (c) of this section.

(v) The court shall also consider and determine whether imminent risk to the child would be eliminated by the issuance of a temporary order of protection, pursuant to section one thousand twenty-nine of this part, directing the removal of a person or persons from the child's residence.

(vi) Any order directing the temporary removal of a child pursuant to this section shall state the court's findings with respect to the necessity of such removal, whether the respondent was present at the hearing and, if not, what notice the respondent was given of the hearing, whether the respondent was represented by counsel, and, if not, whether the respondent waived his or her right to counsel.

(vii) At the conclusion of a hearing where it has been determined that a child should be removed from his or her parent or other person legally responsible, the court shall set the date certain for an initial permanency hearing pursuant to paragraph two of subdivision (a) of section one thousand eighty-nine of this act. The date certain shall be included in the written order issued pursuant to subdivision (b) of this section and shall set forth the date certain scheduled for the permanency hearing.

(b) Any written order pursuant to this section shall be issued immediately, but in no event later than the next court day following the removal of the child. The order shall specify the facility to which the child is to be brought. Except for good cause shown or unless the child is sooner returned to the place where he or she was residing, a petition shall be filed under this article within three court days of the issuance of the order. The court shall hold a hearing pursuant to section one thousand twenty-seven of this part no later than the next court day following the filing of the petition if the respondent was not present, or was present and unrepresented by counsel, and has not waived his or her right to counsel, for the hearing pursuant to this section.

(c) The family court, before the filing of a petition under this article, may enter an order authorizing the provision of services or assistance, including authorizing a physician or hospital to provide emergency medical or surgical procedures, if

(i) such procedures are necessary to safeguard the life or health of the child; and

(ii) there is not enough time to file a petition and hold a preliminary hearing under section one thousand twenty-seven. Where the court orders a social services official to provide or contract for services or assistance pursuant to this section, such order shall be limited to services or assistance authorized or required to be made available pursuant to the comprehensive annual services program plan then in effect.

(d) The person removing the child shall, coincident with removal, give written notice to the parent or other person legally responsible for the child's care of the right to apply to the family court for the return of the child pursuant to section one thousand twenty-eight of this act, the name, title, organization, address and telephone number of the person removing the child, the name and telephone number of the child care agency to which the child will be taken, if available, the telephone number of the person to be contacted for visits with the child, and the information required by section one thousand twenty-three of this act. Such notice shall be personally served upon the parent or other person at the residence of the child provided, that if such person is not present at the child's residence at the time of removal, a copy of the notice shall be affixed to the door of such residence and a copy shall be mailed to such person at his or her last known place of residence within twenty-four hours after the removal of the child. If the place of removal is not the child's residence, a copy of the notice shall be personally served upon the parent or person legally responsible for the child's care forthwith, or affixed to the door of the child's residence and mailed to the parent or other person legally responsible for the child's care at his or her last known place of residence within twenty-four hours after the removal. The form of the notice shall be prescribed by the chief administrator of the courts.

(e) Nothing in this section shall be deemed to require that the court order the temporary removal of a child as a condition of ordering services or assistance, including emergency medical or surgical procedures pursuant to subdivision (c) of this section.

(f) The court may issue a temporary order of protection pursuant to section ten hundred twenty-nine of this article as an alternative to or in conjunction with any other order or disposition authorized under this section.

§1022-a. Preliminary orders; notice and appointment of counsel.

At a hearing held pursuant to section one thousand twenty-two of this part at which the respondent is present, the court shall advise the respondent and any non-respondent parent who is present of the allegations in the application and shall appoint counsel for each in accordance with section two hundred sixty-two of this act, unless waived.

§1023. Procedure for issuance of temporary order.

Any person who may originate a proceeding under this article may apply for, or the court on its own motion may issue, an order of temporary removal under section one thousand twenty-two or one thousand twenty-seven or an order for the provision of services or assistance, including emergency medical or surgical procedures pursuant to subdivision (c) of section one thousand twenty-two, or a temporary order of protection pursuant to section ten hundred twenty-nine. The applicant or, where designated by the court, any other appropriate person, shall make every reasonable effort, with due regard for any necessity for immediate protective action, to inform the parent or other person legally responsible for the child's care of the intent to apply for the order, of the date and the time that the application will be made, the address of the court where the application will be made, of the right of the parent or other person legally responsible for the child's care to be present at the application and at any hearing held thereon and, of the right to be represented by counsel, including procedures for obtaining counsel, if indigent.

§1024. Emergency removal without court order.

(a) A peace officer, acting pursuant to his or her special duties, police officer, or a law enforcement official, or a designated employee of a city or county department of social services shall take all necessary measures to protect a child's life or health including, when appropriate, taking or keeping a child in protective custody, and any physician shall notify the local department of social services or appropriate police authorities to take custody of any child such physician is treating, without an order under section one thousand twenty-two of this article and without the consent of the parent or other person legally responsible for the child's care, regardless of whether the parent or other person legally responsible for the child's care is absent, if (i) such person has reasonable cause to believe that the child is in such circumstance or condition that his or her continuing in said place of residence or in the care and custody of the parent or person legally responsible for the child's care presents an imminent danger to the child's life or health; and

(ii) there is not time enough to apply for an order under section one thousand twenty-two of this article.

(b) If a person authorized by this section removes or keeps custody of a child, he shall (i) bring the child immediately to a place approved for such purpose by the local social services department, unless the person is a physician treating the child and the child is or will be presently admitted to a hospital, and

(ii) make every reasonable effort to inform the parent or other person legally responsible for the child's care of the facility to which he has brought the child, and

(iii) give, coincident with removal, written notice to the parent or other person legally responsible for the child's care of the right to apply to the family court for the return of the child pursuant to section one thousand twenty-eight of this act, and of the right to be represented by counsel in proceedings brought pursuant to this article and procedures for obtaining counsel, if indigent. Such notice shall also include the name, title, organization, address and telephone number of the person removing the child, the name, address, and telephone number of the authorized agency to which the child will be taken, if available, the telephone number of the person to be contacted for visits with the child, and the information required by section one thousand twenty-three of this act. Such notice shall be personally served upon the parent or other person at the residence of the child provided, that if such person is not present at the child's residence at the time of removal, a copy of the notice shall be affixed to the door of such residence and a copy shall be mailed to such person at his or her last known place of residence within twenty-four hours after the removal of the child. If the place of removal is not the child's residence, a copy of the notice shall be personally served upon the parent or person legally responsible for the child's care forthwith, or affixed to the door of the child's residence and mailed to the parent or other person legally responsible for the child's care at his or her last known place of residence within twenty-four hours after the removal. An affidavit of such service shall be filed with the clerk of the court within twenty-four hours of serving such notice exclusive of weekends and holidays pursuant to the provisions of this section. The form of the notice shall be prescribed by the chief administrator of the courts. Failure to file an affidavit of service as required by this subdivision shall not constitute grounds for return of the child.

(iv) inform the court and make a report pursuant to title six of the social services law, as soon as possible.

(c) Any person or institution acting in good faith in the removal or keeping of a child pursuant to this section shall have immunity from any liability, civil or criminal, that might otherwise be incurred or imposed as a result of such removal or keeping.

(d) Where the physician keeping a child in his custody pending action by the local department of social services or appropriate police authorities does so in his capacity as a member of the staff of a hospital or similar institution, he shall notify the person in charge of the institution, or his designated agent, who shall then become responsible for the further care of such child.

(e) Any physician keeping a child in his custody pursuant to this section shall have the right to keep such child in his custody until such time as the custody of the child has been transferred to the appropriate police authorities or the social services official of the city or county in which the physician maintains his place of business. If the social services official receives custody of a child pursuant to the provisions of this section, he shall promptly inform the parent or other person responsible for such child's care and the family court of his action.

§1026. Action by the appropriate person designated by the court and child protective agency upon emergency removal.

(a) The appropriate person designated by the court or a child protective agency when informed that there has been an emergency removal of a child from his or her home without court order shall

(i) make every reasonable effort to communicate immediately with the child's parent or other person legally responsible for his or her care, and

(ii) except in cases involving abuse, cause a child thus removed to be returned, if it concludes there is not an imminent risk to the child's health in so doing. In cases involving abuse, the child protective agency may recommend to the court that the child be returned or that no petition be filed.

(b) The child protective agency may, but need not, condition the return of a child under this section upon the giving of a written promise, without security, of the parent or other person legally responsible for the child's care that he or she will appear at the family court at a time and place specified in the recognizance and may also require him or her to bring the child with him or her.

(c) If the child protective agency for any reason does not return the child under this section after an emergency removal pursuant to section one thousand twenty-four of this part on the same day that the child is removed, or if the child protective agency concludes it appropriate after an emergency removal pursuant to section one thousand twenty-four of this part, it shall cause a petition to be filed under this part no later than the next court day after the child was removed. The court may order an extension, only upon good cause shown, of up to three court days from the date of such child's removal. A hearing shall be held no later than the next court day after the petition is filed and findings shall be made as required pursuant to section one thousand twenty-seven of this part.

§1027. Hearing and preliminary orders after filing of petition.

(a) (i) In any case where the child has been removed without court order or where there has been a hearing pursuant to section one thousand twenty-two of this part at which the respondent was not present, or was not represented by counsel and did not waive his or her right to counsel, the family court shall hold a hearing. Such hearing shall be held no later than the next court day after the filing of a petition to determine whether the child's interests require protection, including whether the child should be returned to the parent or other person legally responsible, pending a final order of disposition and shall continue on successive court days, if necessary, until a decision is made by the court.

(ii) In any such case where the child has been removed, any person originating a proceeding under this article shall, or the attorney for the child may apply for, or the court on its own motion may order, a hearing at any time after the petition is filed to determine whether the child's interests require protection pending a final order of disposition. Such hearing must be scheduled for no later than the next court day after the application for such hearing has been made.

(iii) In any case under this article in which a child has not been removed from his or her parent or other person legally responsible for his or her care, any person originating a proceeding under this article or the attorney for the child may apply for, or the court on its own motion may order, a hearing at any time after the petition is filed to determine whether the child's interests require protection, including whether the child should be removed from his or her parent or other person legally responsible, pending a final order of disposition. Such hearing must be scheduled for no later than the next court day after the application for such hearing has been made.

(iv) Notice of a hearing shall be provided pursuant to section one thousand twenty-three of this part.

(b) (i) Upon such hearing, if the court finds that removal is necessary to avoid imminent risk to the child's life or health, it shall remove or continue the removal of the child. If the court makes such a determination that removal is necessary, the court shall immediately inquire as to the status of any efforts made by the local social services district to locate relatives of the child, including any non-respondent parent and all of the child's grandparents, as required pursuant to section one thousand seventeen of this article. The court shall also inquire as to whether the child, if over the age of five, has identified any relatives who play or have played a significant positive role in his or her life and whether any respondent parent or any non-respondent parent has identified any suitable relatives. Such inquiry shall include whether any relative who has been located has expressed an interest in becoming a foster parent for the child or in seeking custody or care of the child. Upon completion of such inquiry, the court shall remand or place the child:

(A) with the local commissioner of social services and the court may direct such commissioner to have the child reside with a relative or other suitable person who has indicated a desire to become a foster parent for the child and further direct such commissioner, pursuant to regulations of the office of children and family services, to commence an investigation of the home of such relative or other suitable person within twenty-four hours and thereafter expedite approval or certification of such relative or other suitable person, if qualified, as a foster parent. If such home is found to be unqualified for approval or certification, the local commissioner shall report such fact to the court forthwith so that the court may make a placement determination that is in the best interests of the child;

(B) to a place approved for such purpose by the social services district; or

(C) with a relative or suitable person other than the respondent.

(ii) Such order shall state the court's findings which support the necessity of such removal, whether the respondent was present at the hearing and, if not, what notice the respondent was given of the hearing, and, where a pre-petition removal has occurred, whether such removal took place pursuant to section one thousand twenty-one, one thousand twenty-two or one thousand twenty-four of this part. If the parent or other person legally responsible for the child's care is physically present at the time the child is removed, and has not previously been served with the summons and petition, the summons and petition shall be served upon such parent or person coincident with such removal. If such parent or person is not physically present at the time the child is removed, service of the summons and petition shall be governed by section one thousand thirty-six of this article. In determining whether removal or continuing the removal of a child is necessary to avoid imminent risk to the child's life or health, the court shall consider and determine in its order whether continuation in the child's home would be contrary to the best interests of the child and where appropriate, whether reasonable efforts were made prior to the date of the hearing held under subdivision (a) of this section to prevent or eliminate the need for removal of the child from the home and, if the child was removed from his or her home prior to the date of the hearing held under subdivision (a) of this section, where appropriate, that reasonable efforts were made to make it possible for the child to safely return home.

(iii) If the court determines that reasonable efforts to prevent or eliminate the need for removal of the child from the home were not made but that the lack of such efforts was appropriate under the circumstances, the court order shall include such a finding.

(iv) If the court determines that reasonable efforts to prevent or eliminate the need for removal of the child from the home were not made but that such efforts were appropriate under the circumstances, the court shall order the child protective agency to provide or arrange for the provision of appropriate services or assistance to the child and the child's family pursuant to section one thousand fifteen-a or as enumerated in subdivision (c) of section one thousand twenty-two of this article, notwithstanding the fact that a petition has been filed.

(v) The court shall also consider and determine whether imminent risk to the child would be eliminated by the issuance of a temporary order of protection, pursuant to section one thousand twenty-nine of this part, directing the removal of a person or persons from the child's residence.

(c) Upon such hearing, the court may, for good cause shown, issue a preliminary order of protection which may contain any of the provisions authorized on the making of an order of protection under section one thousand fifty-six of this act.

(d) Upon such hearing, the court may, for good cause shown, release the child to his or her parent or other person legally responsible for his or her care, pending a final order of disposition, in accord with subparagraph (ii) of paragraph (a) of subdivision two of section one thousand seventeen of this article.

(e) Upon such hearing, the court may authorize a physician or hospital to provide medical or surgical procedures if such procedures are necessary to safeguard the child's life or health.

(f) If the court grants or denies a preliminary order requested pursuant to this section, it shall state the grounds for such decision.

(g) In all cases involving abuse the court shall order, and in all cases involving neglect the court may order, an examination of the child pursuant to section two hundred fifty-one of this act or by a physician appointed or designated for the purpose by the court. As part of such examination, the physician shall arrange to have colored photographs taken as soon as practical of the areas of trauma visible on such child and may, if indicated, arrange to have a radiological examination performed on the child. The physician, on the completion of such examination, shall forward the results thereof together with the color photographs to the court ordering such examination. The court may dispense with such examination in those cases which were commenced on the basis of a physical examination by a physician. Unless colored photographs have already been taken or unless there are no areas of visible trauma, the court shall arrange to have colored photographs taken even if the examination is dispensed with.

(h) At the conclusion of a hearing where it has been determined that a child should be removed from his or her parent or other person legally responsible, the court shall set a date certain for an initial permanency hearing pursuant to paragraph two of subdivision (a) of section one thousand eighty-nine of this act. The date certain shall be included in the written order issued pursuant to subdivision (b) of this section and shall set forth the date certain scheduled for the permanency hearing. A copy of such order shall be provided to the parent or other person legally responsible for the child's care.

§1027-a. Placement of siblings; contact with siblings.

(a) When a social services official removes a child pursuant to this part, such official shall place such child with his or her minor siblings or half-siblings who have been or are being remanded to or placed in the care and custody of such official unless, in the judgment of such official, such placement is contrary to the best interests of the children. Placement with siblings or half-siblings shall be presumptively in the child's best interests unless such placement would be contrary to the child's health, safety, or welfare. If such placement is not immediately available at the time of the removal of the child, such official shall provide or arrange for the provision of such placement within thirty days.

(b) If placement of a child removed pursuant to this part together with his or her minor siblings is not in the best interests of the child, the social services official shall arrange appropriate and regular contact by the child with his or her minor siblings and half-siblings unless such contact would not be in the child's and the siblings' best interests.

(c) If a child removed pursuant to this part is not placed together or afforded regular contact with his or her siblings, the child, through his or her attorney or through a parent on his or her behalf, may move for an order regarding placement or contact. The motion shall be served upon: (i) the respondent in the proceeding under this article; (ii) the local social services official having the care of the child; (iii) other persons having care, custody and control of the child, if any; (iv) the parents or other persons having care, custody and control of the siblings to be visited or with whom contact is sought; (v) any non-respondent parent in the proceeding under this article; (vi) such sibling himself or herself if ten years of age or older; and (vii) such sibling's attorney, if any. For purposes of this section, "siblings" shall include half-siblings and those who would be deemed siblings or half-siblings but for the termination of parental rights or death of a parent. The court may order that the child be placed together with or have regular contact with his or her siblings if the court determines it to be in the best interests of the child and his or her siblings.

(Eff.11/16/16,Ch.242,L.2016)

§1028. Application to return child temporarily removed.

(a) Upon the application of the parent or other person legally responsible for the care of a child temporarily removed under this part or upon the application of the child's attorney for an order returning the child, the court shall hold a hearing to determine whether the child should be returned (i) unless there has been a hearing pursuant to section one thousand twenty-seven of this article on the removal of the child at which the parent or other person legally responsible for the child's care was present and had the opportunity to be represented by counsel, or (ii) upon good cause shown. Except for good cause shown, such hearing shall be held within three court days of the application and shall not be adjourned. Upon such hearing, the court shall grant the application, unless it finds that the return presents an imminent risk to the child's life or health. If a parent or other person legally responsible for the care of a child waives his or her right to a hearing under this section, the court shall advise such person at that time that, notwithstanding such waiver, an application under this section may be made at any time during the pendency of the proceedings.

(b) In determining whether temporary removal of the child is necessary to avoid imminent risk to the child's life or health, the court shall consider and determine in its order whether continuation in the child's home would be contrary to the best interests of the child and where appropriate, whether reasonable efforts were made prior to the date of the hearing to prevent or eliminate the need for removal of the child from the home and where appropriate, whether reasonable efforts were made after removal of the child to make it possible for the child to safely return home.

(c) If the court determines that reasonable efforts to prevent or eliminate the need for removal of the child from the home were not made but that the lack of such efforts was appropriate under the circumstances, the court order shall include such a finding.

(d) If the court determines that reasonable efforts to prevent or eliminate the need for removal of the child from the home were not made but that such efforts were appropriate under the circumstances, the court shall order the child protective agency to provide or arrange for the provision of appropriate services or assistance to the child and the child's family pursuant to section one thousand fifteen-a or as enumerated in subdivision (c) of section one thousand twenty-two of this article, notwithstanding the fact that a petition has been filed.

(e) The court may issue a temporary order of protection pursuant to section ten hundred twenty-nine of this article as an alternative to or in conjunction with any other order or disposition authorized under this section.

(f) The court shall also consider and determine whether imminent risk to the child would be eliminated by the issuance of a temporary order of protection, pursuant to section ten hundred twenty-nine of this article, directing the removal of a person or persons from the child's residence.

§1028-a. Application of a relative to become a foster parent.

(a) Upon the application of a relative to become a foster parent of a child in foster care, the court shall, subject to the provisions of this subdivision, hold a hearing to determine whether the child should be placed with a relative in foster care. Such hearing shall only be held if:

(i) the relative is related within the third degree of consanguinity to either parent;

(ii) the child has been temporarily removed under this part, or placed pursuant to section one thousand fifty-five of this article, and placed in non-relative foster care;

(iii) the relative indicates a willingness to become the foster parent for such child and has not refused previously to be considered as a foster parent or custodian of the child, provided, however, that an inability to provide immediate care for the child due to a lack of resources or inadequate housing, educational or other arrangements necessary to care appropriately for the child shall not constitute a previous refusal;

(iv) the local social services district has refused to place the child with the relative for reasons other than the relative's failure to qualify as a foster parent pursuant to the regulations of the office of children and family services; and

(v) the application is brought within six months from the date the relative received notice that the child was being removed or had been removed from his or her home and no later than twelve months from the date that the child was removed.

(b) The court shall give due consideration to such application and shall make the determination as to whether the child should be placed in foster care with the relative based on the best interests of the child.

(c) After such hearing, if the court determines that placement in foster care with the relative is in the best interests of the child, the court shall direct the local commissioner of social services, pursuant to regulations of the office of children and family services, to commence an investigation of the home of the relative within twenty-four hours and thereafter expedite approval or certification of such relative, if qualified, as a foster parent. No child, however, shall be placed with a relative prior to final approval or certification of such relative as a foster parent.

§1029.   Temporary order of protection.

(a) The family court, upon the application of any person who may originate a proceeding under this article, for good cause shown, may issue a temporary order of protection, before or after the filing of such petition, which may contain any of the provisions authorized on the making of an order of protection under section one thousand fifty-six. If such order is granted before the filing of a petition and a petition is not filed under this article within ten days from the granting of such order, the order shall be vacated. In any case where a petition has been filed and an attorney for the child has been appointed, such attorney may make application for a temporary order of protection pursuant to the provisions of this section.

(b) A temporary order of protection is not a finding of wrongdoing.

(c) The court may issue or extend a temporary order of protection ex parte or on notice simultaneously with the issuance of a warrant directing that the respondent be arrested and brought before the court pursuant to section ten hundred thirty-seven of this article.

(d) Nothing in this section shall: (i) limit the power of the court to order removal of a child pursuant to this article where the court finds that there is imminent danger to a child's life or health; or (ii) limit the authority of authorized persons to remove a child without a court order pursuant to section one thousand twenty-four of this article; or (iii) be construed to authorize the court to award permanent custody of a child to a parent or relative pursuant to a temporary order of protection.

§1030.   Order of visitation by a respondent.

(a) A respondent shall have the right to reasonable and regularly scheduled visitation with a child in the temporary custody of a social services official pursuant to this part or pursuant to subdivision (d) of section one thousand fifty-one of this article, unless limited by an order of the family court.

(b) A respondent who has not been afforded such visitation may apply to the court for an order requiring the local social services official having temporary custody of the child pursuant to this part or pursuant to subdivision (d) of section one thousand fifty-one of this article, to permit the respondent to visit the child at stated periods. Such application shall be made upon notice to the local social services official and to any attorney appointed to represent the child, who shall be afforded an opportunity to be heard thereon.

(c) A respondent shall be granted reasonable and regularly scheduled visitation unless the court finds that the child's life or health would be endangered thereby, but the court may order visitation under the supervision of an employee of a local social services department upon a finding that such supervised visitation is in the best interest of the child.

(d) An order made under this section may be modified by the court for good cause shown, upon application by any party or the child's attorney, and upon notice of such application to all other parties and the child's attorney, who shall be afforded an opportunity to be heard thereon.

(e) An order made under this section shall terminate upon the entry of an order of disposition pursuant to part five of this article.

Part 3
Preliminary Procedure

§1031. Originating proceeding to determine abuse or neglect.

(a) A proceeding under this article is originated by the filing of a petition in which facts sufficient to establish that a child is an abused or neglected child under this article are alleged.

(b) Allegations of abuse and neglect may be contained in the same petition. Where more than one child is the legal responsibility of the respondent, it may be alleged in the same petition that one or more children are abused children, or that one or more children are neglected children, or both.

(c) On its own motion and at any time in the proceedings, the court may substitute for a petition to determine abuse a petition to determine neglect if the facts established are not sufficient to make a finding of abuse, as defined by this article.

(d) A proceeding under this article may be originated by a child protective agency pursuant to section one thousand thirty-two, notwithstanding that the child is in the care and custody of such agency. In such event, the petition shall allege facts sufficient to establish that the return of the child to the care and custody of his parent or other person legally responsible for his care would place the child in imminent danger of becoming an abused or neglected child.

(e) In any case where a child has been removed prior to the filing of a petition, the petition alleging abuse or neglect of said child shall state the date and time of the removal, the circumstances necessitating such removal, whether the removal occurred pursuant to section ten hundred twenty-one, ten hundred twenty-two or ten hundred twenty-four of this act, and if the removal occurred without court order, the reason there was not sufficient time to obtain a court order pursuant to section ten hundred twenty-two of this act.

(f) A petition alleging abuse shall contain a notice in conspicuous print that a fact-finding that a child is severely or repeatedly abused as defined in subdivision eight of section three hundred eighty-four-b of the social services law, by clear and convincing evidence, could constitute a basis to terminate parental rights in a proceeding pursuant to section three hundred eighty-four-b of the social services law.

§1032. Persons who may originate proceedings.

The following may originate a proceeding under this article:
(a) a child protective agency, or
(b) a person on the court's direction.

§1033. Access to the court for the purpose of filing a petition.

Any person seeking to file a petition at the court's direction, pursuant to subdivision (b) of section one thousand thirty-two shall have access to the court for the purpose of making an ex parte application therefor. Nothing in this section, however, is intended to prevent a family court judge from requiring such person to first report to an appropriate child protective agency.

§1033-a. Initial appearance.

For the purposes of this section, "initial appearance" means the proceeding on the date the respondent first appears before the court after the petition has been filed and any adjournments thereof.

§1033-b. Initial appearance; procedures.

1. (a) At the initial appearance, the court shall appoint an attorney to represent the interests of any child named in a petition who is alleged to be abused or neglected, unless an attorney has already been appointed for such child pursuant to section one thousand sixteen of this act.

(b) At the initial appearance, the court shall advise the respondent of the allegations in the petition and further advise the respondent of the right to an adjournment of the proceeding in order to obtain counsel. The recitation of such rights shall not be waived except that the recitation of the allegations in the petition may be waived upon the consent of the counsel for the respondent and such counsel's representation on the record that he or she has explained such allegations to the respondent and has provided the respondent with a copy of the petition and the respondent's acknowledgement of receipt of the petition and such explanation.

(c) At the initial appearance, the court shall appoint counsel for indigent respondents pursuant to section two hundred sixty-two of this act.

(d) In any case where a child has been removed, the court shall advise the respondent of the right to a hearing, pursuant to section ten hundred twenty-eight of this act, for the return of the child and that such hearing may be requested at any time during the proceeding. The recitation of such rights shall not be waived.

(e) At the initial appearance, the court shall inquire of the child protective agency whether such agency intends to prove that the child is a severely or repeatedly abused child as defined in subdivision eight of section three hundred eighty-four-b of the social services law, by clear and convincing evidence. Where the agency advises the court that it intends to submit such proof, the court shall so advise the respondent.

§1034. Power to order investigations.

1. A family court judge may order the child protective service of the appropriate social services district to conduct a child protective investigation as described by the social services law and report its findings to the court:

(a) in any proceedings under this article, or

(b) in order to determine whether a proceeding under this article should be initiated.

2. (a)(i) Before a petition is filed and where there is reasonable cause to suspect that a child or children's life or health may be in danger, child protective services may seek a court order based upon:

(A) a report of suspected abuse or maltreatment under title six of article six of the social services law as well as any additional information that a child protective investigator has learned in the investigation; and

(B) the fact that the investigator has been unable to locate the child named in the report or any other children in the household or has been denied access to the child or children in the household sufficient to determine their safety; and

(C) the fact that the investigator has advised the parent or other persons legally responsible for the child or children that, when denied sufficient access to the child or other children in the household, the child protective investigator may consider seeking an immediate court order to gain access to the child or children without further notice to the parent or other persons legally responsible.

(ii) Where a court order has been requested pursuant to this paragraph the court may issue an order under this section requiring that the parent or other persons legally responsible for the child or children produce the child or children at a particular location which may include a child advocacy center, or to a particular person for an interview of the child or children, and for observation of the condition of the child, outside of the presence of the parent or other person responsible.

(b)(i) Before a petition is filed and where there is probable cause to believe that an abused or neglected child may be found on the premises, child protective services may seek a court order based upon:

(A) a report of suspected abuse or maltreatment under title six of article six of the social services law as well as any additional information that a child protective investigator has learned in the investigation; and

(B) the fact that the investigator has been denied access to the home of the child or children in order to evaluate the home environment; and

(C) the fact that the investigator has advised the parent or other person legally responsible for the child or children that, when denied access to the home environment, the child protective investigator may consider seeking an immediate court order to gain access to the home environment without further notice to the parent or other person legally responsible.

(ii) Where a court order has been requested pursuant to this paragraph the court may issue an order under this section authorizing the person conducting the child protective investigation to enter the home in order to determine whether such child or children are present and/or to conduct a home visit and evaluate the home environment of the child or children.

(c) The procedure for granting an order pursuant to this subdivision shall be the same as for a search warrant under article six hundred ninety of the criminal procedure law. If an order is issued in accordance with this subdivision the court shall specify which action may be taken and by whom in the order.

(d) In determining if such orders shall be made, the court shall consider all relevant information, including but not limited to:

    (i) the nature and seriousness of the allegations made in the report;

    (ii) the age and vulnerability of the child or children;

    (iii) the potential harm to the child or children if a full investigation is not completed;

    (iv) the relationship of the source of the report to the family, including the source's ability to observe that which has been alleged; and

    (v) the child protective or criminal history, if any, of the family and any other relevant information that the investigation has already obtained.

(e) The court shall assess which actions are necessary in light of the child or children's safety, provided, however, that such actions shall be the least intrusive to the family.

(f) The court shall be available at all hours to hear such requests by the social services district which shall be permitted to make such requests either in writing or orally, pursuant to section 690.36 of the criminal procedure law, in person to the family court during hours that the court is open and orally by telephone or in person, pursuant to section 690.36 of the criminal procedure law, to a family court judge when the court is not open. While the request is being made, law enforcement shall remain where the child or children are or are believed to be present if the child protective services investigator has requested law enforcement assistance. Provided, however, that law enforcement may not enter the premises where the child or children are believed to be present without a search warrant or another constitutional basis for such entry.

(g) Where the court issues an order under this section, the child protective investigator shall within three business days prepare a report to the court detailing his or her findings and any other actions that have been taken pertaining to the child named in the report and any other children in the household.

(h) Nothing in this section shall limit the court's authority to issue any appropriate order in accordance with the provisions of this article after a petition has been filed.

§1035. Issuance of summons; notice to certain interested persons and intervention.

(a) On the filing of a petition under this article where the child has been removed from his or her home, unless a warrant is issued pursuant to section one thousand thirty-seven of this part, the court shall cause a copy of the petition and a summons to be issued the same day the petition is filed, clearly marked on the face thereof "Child Abuse Case", as applicable, requiring the parent or other person legally responsible for the child's care or with whom he or she had been residing to appear at the court within three court days to answer the petition, unless a shorter time for a hearing to occur is prescribed in part two of this article.

(b) In a proceeding to determine abuse or neglect, the summons shall contain a statement in conspicuous print informing the respondent that:

(i) the proceeding may lead to the filing of a petition under the social services law for the termination of respondent's parental rights and commitment of guardianship and custody of the child for the purpose of adoption; and

(ii) if the child is placed and remains in foster care for fifteen of the most recent twenty-two months, the agency may be required by law to file a petition for termination of respondent's parental rights and commitment of guardianship and custody of the child for the purposes of adoption.

(c) On the filing of a petition under this article where the child has not been removed from his or her home, the court shall forthwith cause a copy of the petition and a summons to be issued, clearly marked on the face thereof "Child Abuse Case", as applicable, requiring the parent or other person legally responsible for the child's care or with whom the child is residing to appear at the court to answer the petition within seven court days. The court may also require the person thus summoned to produce the child at the time and place named.

(d) Where the respondent is not the child's parent, service of the summons and petition shall also be ordered on both of the child's parents; where only one of the child's parents is the respondent, service of the summons and petition shall also be ordered on the child's other parent. The summons and petition shall be accompanied by a notice of pendency of the child protective proceeding advising the parents or parent of the right to appear and participate in the proceeding as an interested party intervenor for the purpose of seeking temporary and permanent release of the child under this article or custody of the child under article six of this act, and to participate thereby in all arguments and hearings insofar as they affect the temporary release or custody of the child during fact-finding proceedings, and in all phases of dispositional proceedings. The notice shall also advise the parent or parents of the right to counsel, including assigned counsel, pursuant to section two hundred sixty-two of this act, and also indicate that:

(i) upon good cause, the court may order an investigation pursuant to section one thousand thirty-four of this part to determine whether a petition should be filed naming such parent or parents as respondents;

(ii) if the court determines that the child must be removed from his or her home, the court may order an investigation to determine whether the non-respondent parent or parents would be suitable custodians for the child; and

(iii) if the child is placed and remains in foster care for fifteen of the most recent twenty-two months, the agency may be required by law to file a petition for termination of the parental rights of the parent or parents and commitment of guardianship and custody of the child for the purposes of adoption, even if the parent or parents were not named as a respondent or as respondents in the child abuse or neglect proceeding.

(e) The summons, petition and notice of pendency of a child protective proceeding served on the child's non-custodial parent in accordance with subdivision (d) of this section shall, if applicable, be served together with a notice that the child was removed from his or her home by a social services official. Such notice shall also include the name and address of the official to whom temporary custody of the child has been transferred, the name and address of the agency or official with whom the child has been temporarily placed, if different, and shall advise such parent of the right to request temporary and permanent custody and to seek enforcement of visitation rights with the child as provided for in part eight of this article.

(f) The child's adult sibling, grandparent, aunt or uncle not named as respondent in the petition, may, upon consent of the child's parent appearing in the proceeding, or where such parent has not appeared then without such consent, move to intervene in the proceeding as an interested party intervenor for the purpose of seeking temporary or permanent custody of the child, and upon the granting of such motion shall be permitted to participate in all arguments and hearings insofar as they affect the temporary custody of the child during fact-finding proceedings, and in all phases of dispositional proceedings. Such motions for intervention shall be liberally granted.

§1036. Service of summons.

(a) Except as provided for in subdivision (c) of this section, in cases involving abuse, the petition and summons shall be served within two court days after their issuance. If they cannot be served within that time, such fact shall be reported to the court with the reasons thereof within three court days after their issuance and the court shall thereafter issue a warrant in accordance with the provisions of section one thousand thirty-seven. The court shall also, unless dispensed with for good cause shown, direct that the child be brought before the court. Issuance of a warrant shall not be required where process is sent without the state as provided for in subdivision (c) of this section.

(b) Service of a summons and petition shall be made by delivery of a true copy thereof to the person summoned at least twenty-four hours before the time stated therein for appearance.

(c) In cases involving either abuse or neglect, the court may send process without the state in the same manner and with the same effect as process sent within the state in the exercise of personal jurisdiction over any person subject to the jurisdiction of the court under section three hundred one or three hundred two of the civil practice law and rules, notwithstanding that such person is not a resident or domiciliary of the state, where the allegedly abused or neglected child resides or is domiciled within the state and the alleged abuse or neglect occurred within the state. In cases involving abuse where service of a petition and summons upon a non-resident or non-domiciliary respondent is required, such service shall be made within ten days after its issuance. If service can not be effected in ten days, an extension of the period to effect service may be granted by the court for good cause shown upon application of any party or the child's attorney. Where service is effected on an out of state respondent and the respondent defaults by failing to appear to answer the petition, the court may on its own motion, or upon application of any party or the child's attorney proceed to a fact finding hearing thereon.

(d) If after reasonable effort, personal service is not made, the court may at any stage in the proceedings make an order providing for substituted service in the manner provided for substituted service in civil process in courts of record.

§1037. Issuance of warrant and reports to court.

(a) The court may issue a warrant directing the parent, or other person legally responsible for the child's care or with whom he is residing to be brought before the court, when a petition is filed with the court under this article and it appears that

(i) the summons cannot be served; or

(ii) the summoned person has refused to obey the summons; or

(iii) the parent or other person legally responsible for the child's care is likely to leave the jurisdiction; or

(iv) a summons, in the court's opinion, would be ineffectual; or

(v) the safety of the child is endangered; or

(vi) the safety of a parent, person legally responsible for the child's care or with whom he is residing, foster parent or temporary custodian is endangered.

(b) When issuing a warrant under this section, the court may also direct that the child be brought before the court.

(c) In any case involving abuse, the warrant shall be clearly marked on the face thereof "Child Abuse Case". If a warrant is not executed within two court days of its issuance, such fact shall be reported to the court within three court days of its issuance. Rules of court shall provide that reports of unexecuted warrants issued under this article shall be periodically made to the court.

(d) In a proceeding to determine abuse, the warrant shall contain a statement clearly marked on the face thereof, that the proceeding could lead to a proceeding under the social services law for the commitment of guardianship and custody of the child and that the rights of the respondent with respect to said child may be terminated in such proceeding under such law.

§1038. Records and discovery involving abuse and neglect.

(a) Each hospital and any other public or private agency having custody of any records, photographs or other evidence relating to abuse or neglect, upon the subpoena of the court, the corporation counsel, county attorney, district attorney, counsel for the child, or one of the parties to the proceeding, shall be required to send such records, photographs or evidence to the court for use in any proceeding relating to abuse or neglect under this article. Notwithstanding any other provision of law to the contrary, service of any such subpoena on a hospital may be made by certified mail, return receipt requested, to the director of the hospital. The court shall establish procedures for the receipt and safeguarding of such records.

(b) Pursuant to a demand made under rule three thousand one hundred twenty of the civil practice law and rules, a petitioner or social services official shall provide to a respondent or the child's attorney any records, photographs or other evidence demanded relevant to the proceeding, for inspection and photocopying. The petitioner or social services official may delete the identity of the persons who filed reports pursuant to section four hundred fifteen of the social services law, unless such petitioner or official intends to offer such reports into evidence at a hearing held pursuant to this article. The petitioner or social services official may move for a protective order to withhold records, photographs or evidence which will not be offered into evidence and the disclosure of which is likely to endanger the life or health of the child.

(c) A respondent or the child's attorney may move for an order directing that any child who is the subject of a proceeding under this article be made available for examination by a physician, psychologist or social worker selected by such party or the child's attorney. In determining the motion, the court shall consider the need of the respondent or child's attorney for such examination to assist in the preparation of the case and the potential harm to the child from the examination. Nothing in this section shall preclude the parties from agreeing upon a person to conduct such examination without court order.

Any examination or interview, other than a physical examination, of a child who is the subject of a proceeding under this article, for the purposes of offering expert testimony to a court regarding the sexual abuse of the child, as such term is defined by section one thousand twelve of this article, may, in the discretion of the court, be videotaped in its entirety with access to be provided to the court, the child's attorney and all parties. In determining whether such examination or interview should be videotaped, the court shall consider the effect of the videotaping on the reliability of the examination, the effect of the videotaping on the child and the needs of the parties, including the attorney for the child, for the videotape. Prior to admitting a videotape of an examination or interview into evidence, the person conducting such examination or the person operating the video camera shall submit to the court a verified statement confirming that such videotape is a complete and unaltered videographic record of such examination of the child. The proponent of entry of the videotape into evidence must establish that the potential prejudicial effect is substantially outweighed by the probative value of the videotape in assessing the reliability of the validator in court. Nothing in this section shall in any way affect the admissibility of such evidence in any other court proceeding. The chief administrator of the courts shall promulgate regulations protecting the confidentiality and security of such tapes, and regulating the access thereto, consistent with the provisions of this section.

(d) Unless otherwise proscribed by this article, the provisions and limitations of article thirty-one of the civil practice law and rules shall apply to proceedings under this article. In determining any motion for a protective order, the court shall consider the need of the party for the discovery to assist in the preparation of the case and any potential harm to the child from the discovery. The court shall set a schedule for discovery to avoid unnecessary delay.

§1038-a. Discovery; upon court order.
Upon motion of a petitioner or attorney for the child, the court may order a respondent to provide nontestimonial evidence, only if the court finds probable cause that the evidence is reasonably related to establishing the allegations in a petition filed pursuant to this article. Such order may include, but not be limited to, provision for the taking of samples of blood, urine, hair or other materials from the respondent's body in a manner not involving an unreasonable intrusion or risk of serious physical injury to the respondent.

§1039. Adjournment in contemplation of dismissal.
(a) Prior to or upon a fact-finding hearing, the court may upon a motion by the petitioner with the consent of the respondent and the child's attorney or upon its own motion with the consent of the petitioner, the respondent and the child's attorney, order that the proceeding be "adjourned in contemplation of dismissal". Under no circumstances shall the court order any party to consent to an order under this section. The court may make such order only after it has apprised the respondent of the provisions of this section and it is satisfied that the respondent understands the effect of such provisions.

(b) An adjournment in contemplation of dismissal is an adjournment of the proceeding for a period not to exceed one year with a view to ultimate dismissal of the petition in furtherance of justice. Upon the consent of the petitioner, the respondent and the child's attorney, the court may issue an order extending such period for such time and upon such conditions as may be agreeable to the parties.

(c) Such order may include terms and conditions agreeable to the parties and to the court, provided that such terms and conditions shall include a requirement that the child and the respondent be under the supervision of a child protective agency during the adjournment period. In any order issued pursuant to this section, such agency shall be directed to make a progress report to the court, the parties and the child's attorney on the implementation of such order, no later than ninety days after the issuance of such order, unless the court determines that the facts and circumstances of the case do not require such reports to be made. The child protective agency shall make further reports to the court, the parties and the child's attorney in such manner and at such times as the court may direct.

(d) Upon application of the respondent, the petitioner, the child's attorney or upon the court's own motion, made at any time during the duration of the order, if the child protective agency has failed substantially to provide the respondent with adequate supervision or to observe the terms and conditions of the order, the court may direct the child protective agency to observe such terms and conditions and provide adequate supervision or may make any order authorized pursuant to section two hundred fifty-five of this act.

(e) Upon application of the petitioner or the child's attorney, or upon the court's own motion, made at any time during the duration of the order, the court may restore the matter to the calendar, if the court finds after a hearing that the respondent has failed substantially to observe the terms and conditions of the order or to cooperate with the supervising child protective agency. In such event, unless the parties consent to an order pursuant to section one thousand fifty-one of this act or unless the petition is dismissed upon the consent of the petitioner, the court shall thereupon proceed to a fact-finding hearing under this article no later than sixty days after such application unless such period is extended by the court for good cause shown.

(f) If the proceeding is not so restored to the calendar, the petition is, at the expiration of the adjournment period, deemed to have been dismissed by the court in furtherance of justice unless an application is pending pursuant to subdivision (e) of this section. If such application is granted the petition shall not be dismissed and shall proceed in accordance with the provisions of such subdivision (e).

(g) Notwithstanding the provisions of this section, the court, may, at any time prior to dismissal of the petition pursuant to subdivision (f), issue an order authorized pursuant to section one thousand twenty-seven.

§1039-a. **Procedures following adjournment in contemplation of dismissal.**
The local child protective service shall notify the child's attorney of an indicated report of child abuse or maltreatment in which the respondent is a subject of the report or another person named in the report, as such terms are defined in section four hundred twelve of the social services law, while any order issued pursuant to section one thousand thirty-nine or extension thereof remains in effect.

§1039-b. **Termination of reasonable efforts.**
(a) In conjunction with, or at any time subsequent to, the filing of a petition under section ten hundred thirty-one of this chapter, the social services official may file a motion upon notice requesting a finding that reasonable efforts to return the child to his or her home are no longer required.

(b) For the purpose of this section, reasonable efforts to make it possible for the child to return safely to his or her home shall not be required where the court determines that:

(1) the parent of such child has subjected the child to aggravated circumstances, as defined in subdivision (j) of section ten hundred twelve of this article;

(2) the parent of such child has been convicted of (i) murder in the first degree as defined in section 125.27 or murder in the second degree as defined in section 125.25 of the penal law and the victim was another child of the parent; or (ii) manslaughter in the first degree as defined in section 125.20 or manslaughter in the second degree as defined in section 125.15 of the penal law and the victim was another child of the parent, provided, however, that the parent must have acted voluntarily in committing such crime;

(3) the parent of such child has been convicted of an attempt to commit any of the foregoing crimes, and the victim or intended victim was the child or another child of the parent; or has been convicted of criminal solicitation as defined in article one hundred, conspiracy as defined in article one hundred five or criminal facilitation as defined in article one hundred fifteen of the penal law for conspiring, soliciting or facilitating any of the foregoing crimes, and the victim or intended victim was the child or another child of the parent;

(4) the parent of such child has been convicted of assault in the second degree as defined in section 120.05, assault in the first degree as defined in section 120.10 or aggravated assault upon a person less than eleven years old as defined in section 120.12 of the penal law, and the commission of one of the foregoing crimes resulted in serious physical injury to the child or another child of the parent;

(5) the parent of such child has been convicted in any other jurisdiction of an offense which includes all of the essential elements of any crime specified in paragraph two, three or four of this subdivision, and the victim of such offense was the child or another child of the parent; or

(6) the parental rights of the parent to a sibling of such child have been involuntarily terminated; unless the court determines that providing reasonable efforts would be in the best interests of the child, not contrary to the health and safety of the child, and would likely result in the reunification of the parent and the child in the foreseeable future. The court shall state such findings in its order.

(c) If the court determines that reasonable efforts are not required because of one of the grounds set forth above, a permanency hearing shall be held within thirty days of the finding of the court that such efforts are not required. At the permanency hearing, the court shall determine the appropriateness of the permanency plan prepared by the social services official which shall include whether or when the child:

(i) will be returned to the parent;

(ii) should be placed for adoption with the social services official filing a petition for termination of parental rights;

(iii) should be referred for legal guardianship;

(iv) should be placed permanently with a fit and willing relative; or

(v) should be placed in another planned permanent living arrangement with a significant connection to an adult willing to be a permanency resource for the child if the child is age sixteen or older and if the requirements of clause (E) of subparagraph (i) of paragraph two of subdivision (d) of section one thousand eighty-nine of this chapter have been met. The social services official shall thereafter make reasonable efforts to place the child in a timely manner, including consideration of appropriate in-state and out-of-state placements, and to complete whatever steps are necessary to finalize the permanent placement of the child as set forth in the permanency plan approved by the court. If reasonable efforts are determined by the court not to be required because of one of the grounds set forth in this paragraph, the social services official may file a petition for termination of parental rights in accordance with section three hundred eighty-four-b of the social services law.

(d) For the purpose of this section, in determining reasonable effort to be made with respect to a child, and in making such reasonable efforts, the child's health and safety shall be the paramount concern; and

(e) For the purpose of this section, a sibling shall include a half-sibling.

§1040. Notice and right to be heard.

The foster parent caring for the child or any pre-adoptive parent or relative providing care for the child shall be provided with notice of any permanency hearing held pursuant to this article by the social services official. Such foster parent, pre-adoptive parent or relative shall have the right to be heard at any such hearing; provided, however, no such foster parent, pre-adoptive parent or relative shall be construed to be a party to the hearing solely on the basis of such notice and right to be heard. The failure of the foster parent, pre-adoptive parent, or relative caring for the child to appear at a permanency hearing shall constitute a waiver of the right to be heard and such failure to appear shall not cause a delay of the permanency hearing nor shall such failure to appear be a ground for the invalidation of any order issued by the court pursuant to this section.

Part 4
Hearings

Section
1041. Required findings concerning notice.
1042. Effect of absence of parent or other person responsible for care.
1043. Hearings not open to the public.
1044. Definition of "fact-finding hearing".
1045. Definition of "dispositional hearing".
1046. Evidence.
1047. Sequence of hearings.
1048. Adjournments.
1049. Special consideration in certain cases.

§1041. Required findings concerning notice.

No factfinding hearing may commence under this article unless the court enters a finding:

(a) that the parent or other person legally responsible for the child's care is present at the hearing and has been served with a copy of the petition; or

(b) if the parent or other person legally responsible for the care of the child is not present, that every reasonable effort has been made to effect service under section ten hundred thirty-six or ten hundred thirty-seven.

§1042. Effect of absence of parent or other person responsible for care.

If the parent or other person legally responsible for the child's care is not present, the court may proceed to hear a petition under this article only if the child is represented by counsel. The parent or other person legally responsible for the child's care shall be served with a copy of the order of disposition with written notice of its entry pursuant to section one thousand thirty-six of this article. Within one year of such service or substituted service pursuant to section one thousand thirty-six of this article, the parent or other person legally responsible for the child's care may move to vacate the order of disposition and schedule a rehearing. Such motion shall be granted on an affidavit showing such relationship or responsibility and a meritorious defense to the petition, unless the court finds that the parent or other person willfully refused to appear at the hearing, in which case the court may deny the motion.

§1043. Hearings not open to the public.

The general public may be excluded from any hearing under this article and only such persons and the representatives of authorized agencies admitted thereto as have an interest in the case.

§1044. Definition of "fact-finding hearing".

When used in this article, "fact-finding hearing" means a hearing to determine whether the child is an abused or neglected child as defined by this article.

§1045. Definition of "dispositional hearing".

When used in this article, "dispositional hearing" means a hearing to determine what order of disposition should be made.

§1046. Evidence.

(a) In any hearing under this article and article ten-A of this act:

(i) proof of the abuse or neglect of one child shall be admissible evidence on the issue of the abuse or neglect of any other child of, or the legal responsibility of, the respondent; and

(ii) proof of injuries sustained by a child or of the condition of a child of such a nature as would ordinarily not be sustained or exist except by reason of the acts or omissions of the parent or other person responsible for the care of such child shall be prima facie evidence of child abuse or neglect, as the case may be, of the parent or other person legally responsible; and

(iii) proof that a person repeatedly misuses a drug or drugs or alcoholic beverages, to the extent that it has or would ordinarily have the effect of producing in the user thereof a substantial state of stupor, unconsciousness, intoxication, hallucination, disorientation, or incompetence, or a substantial impairment of judgment, or a substantial manifestation of irrationality, shall be prima facie evidence that a child of or who is the legal responsibility of such person is a neglected child except that such drug or alcoholic beverage misuse shall not be prima facie evidence of neglect when such person is voluntarily and regularly participating in a recognized rehabilitative program; and

(iv) any writing, record or photograph, whether in the form of an entry in a book or otherwise, made as a memorandum or record of any condition, act, transaction, occurrence or event relating to a child in an abuse or neglect proceeding of any hospital or any other public or private agency shall be admissible in evidence in proof of that condition, act, transaction, occurrence or event, if the judge finds that it was made in the regular course of the business of any hospital, or any other public or private agency and that it was in the regular course of such business to make it, at the time of the act, transaction, occurrence or event, or within a reasonable time thereafter. A certification by the head of or by a responsible employee of the hospital or agency that the writing, record or photograph is the full and complete record of said condition, act, transaction, occurrence or event and that it was made in the regular course of the business of the hospital or agency and that it was in the regular course of such business to make it, at the time of the condition, act, transaction, occurrence or event, or within a reasonable time thereafter, shall be prima facie evidence of the facts contained in such certification. A certification by someone other than the head of the hospital or agency shall be accompanied by a photocopy of a delegation of authority signed by both the head of the hospital or agency and by such other employee. All other circumstances of the making of the memorandum, record or photograph, including lack of personal knowledge of the maker, may be proved to affect its weight, but they shall not affect its admissibility; and

(v) any report filed with the statewide central register of child abuse and maltreatment by a person or official required to do so pursuant to section four hundred thirteen of the social services law shall be admissible in evidence; and

(vi) previous statements made by the child relating to any allegations of abuse or neglect shall be admissible in evidence, but if uncorroborated, such statements shall not be sufficient to make a fact-finding of abuse or neglect. Any other evidence tending to support the reliability of the previous statements, including, but not limited to the types of evidence defined in this subdivision shall be sufficient corroboration. The testimony of the child shall not be necessary to make a fact-finding of abuse or neglect; and

(vii) neither the privilege attaching to confidential communications between husband and wife, as set forth in section forty-five hundred two of the civil practice law and rules, nor the physician-patient and related privileges, as set forth in section forty-five hundred four of the civil practice law and rules, nor the psychologist-client privilege, as set forth in section forty-five hundred seven of the civil practice law and rules, nor the social worker-client privilege, as set forth in section forty-five hundred eight of the civil practice law and rules, nor the rape crisis counselor-client privilege, as set forth in section forty-five hundred ten of the civil practice law and rules, shall be a ground for excluding evidence which otherwise would be admissible.

(viii) proof of the "impairment of emotional health" or "impairment of mental or emotional condition" as a result of the unwillingness or inability of the respondent to exercise a minimum degree of care toward a child may include competent opinion or expert testimony and may include proof that such impairment lessened during a period when the child was in the care, custody or supervision of a person or agency other than the respondent.

(b) In a fact-finding hearing: (i) any determination that the child is an abused or neglected child must be based on a preponderance of evidence;

(ii) whenever a determination of severe or repeated abuse is based upon clear and convincing evidence, the fact-finding order shall state that such determination is based on clear and convincing evidence; and

(iii) except as otherwise provided by this article, only competent, material and relevant evidence may be admitted.

(c) In a dispositional hearing and during all other stages of a proceeding under this article, except a fact-finding hearing, and in permanency hearings and all other proceedings under article ten-A of this act, only material and relevant evidence may be admitted.

§1047. Sequence of hearings.

(a) Upon completion of the fact-finding hearing, the dispositional hearing may commence immediately after the required findings are made.

(b) Reports prepared by the probation service or a duly authorized association, agency, society or institution for use by the court at any time for the making of an order of disposition shall be deemed confidential information furnished to the court which the court shall make available for inspection and copying by all counsel. The court may, in its discretion, withhold from disclosure, a part or parts of the reports which are not relevant to a proper disposition, or sources of information which have been obtained on a promise of confidentiality, or any other portion thereof, disclosure of which would not be in the interests of justice or in the best interests of the child. In all cases where a part or parts of the reports are not disclosed, the court shall state for the record that a part or parts of the reports have been excepted and the reasons for its action. The action of the court excepting information from disclosure shall be subject to review on appeal from the order of disposition. Such reports may not be furnished to the court prior to the completion of a fact-finding hearing, but may be used in a dispositional hearing.

§1048. Adjournments.

(a) The court may adjourn a fact-finding hearing or a dispositional hearing for good cause shown on its own motion, or on motion of the corporation counsel, county attorney or district attorney, or on motion of the petitioner or on motion of the child or on his behalf or of the parent or other person legally responsible for the care of the child. If so requested by the parent or other person legally responsible for the care of the child, the court shall not proceed with a fact-finding hearing earlier than three days after service of summons and petition, unless emergency medical or surgical procedures are necessary to safeguard the life or health of the child.

(b) At the conclusion of a fact-finding hearing and after the court has made findings required before a dispositional hearing may commence, the court may on its own motion or motion of the respondent, the petitioner or the child's attorney order a reasonable adjournment of the proceedings to enable the court to make inquiry into the surroundings, conditions and capacities of the persons involved in the proceedings.

(c) Whenever a child has been remanded to the care of an agency or institution under section ten hundred fifty-one of this article, notice of any dispositional hearing shall be served upon the agency or institution with whom the child was placed and upon the agency supervising the care of the child on behalf of the agency with whom the child was placed. Service of notice of the adjourned hearing shall be made in such manner and on such notice as the court may, in its discretion, prescribe. Any such agency or institution served with notice pursuant to this subdivision may apply to the court for leave to be heard.

§1049. Special consideration in certain cases.

In scheduling hearings and investigations, the court shall give priority to proceedings under this article involving abuse or in which a child has been removed from home before a final order of disposition. Any adjournment granted in the course of such a proceeding should be for as short a time as is practicable.

Part 5
Orders

§1051. Sustaining or dismissing petition.

(a) If facts sufficient to sustain the petition are established in accord with part four of this article, or if all parties and the attorney for the child consent, the court shall, subject to the provisions of subdivision (c) of this section, enter an order finding that the child is an abused child or a neglected child and shall state the grounds for the finding.

(b) If the proof does not conform to the specific allegations of the petition, the court may amend the allegations to conform to the proof; provided, however, that in such case the respondent shall be given reasonable time to prepare to answer the amended allegations.

(c) If facts sufficient to sustain the petition under this article are not established, or if, in a case of alleged neglect, the court concludes that its aid is not required on the record before it, the court shall dismiss the petition and shall state on the record the grounds for the dismissal.

(d) If the court makes a finding of abuse or neglect, it shall determine, based upon the facts adduced during the fact-finding hearing and any other additional facts presented to it, whether a preliminary order pursuant to section one thousand twenty-seven is required to protect the child's interests pending a final order of disposition. The court shall state the grounds for its determination. In addition, a child found to be abused or neglected may be removed and remanded to a place approved for such purpose by the local social services department or be placed in the custody of a suitable person, pending a final order of disposition, if the court finds that there is a substantial probability that the final order of disposition will be an order of placement under section one thousand fifty-five. In determining whether substantial probability exists, the court shall consider the requirements of subdivision (b) of section one thousand fifty-two.

(e) If the court makes a finding of abuse, it shall specify the paragraph or paragraphs of subdivision (e) of section one thousand twelve of this act which it finds have been established. If the court makes a finding of abuse as defined in paragraph (iii) of subdivision (e) of section one thousand twelve of this act, it shall make a further finding of the specific sex offense as defined in article one hundred thirty of the penal law. In addition to a finding of abuse, the court may enter a finding of severe abuse or repeated abuse, as defined in subparagraphs (i), (ii) and (iii) of paragraph (a) or subparagraphs (i) and (ii) of paragraph (b) of subdivision eight of section three hundred eighty-four-b of the social services law, which shall be admissible in a proceeding to terminate parental rights pursuant to paragraph (e) of subdivision four of section three hundred eighty-four-b of the social services law; provided, however, that a finding of severe or repeated abuse under this section may be made against any respondent as defined in subdivision (a) of section one thousand twelve of this act. If the court makes such additional finding of severe abuse or repeated abuse, the court shall state the grounds for its determination, which shall be based upon clear and convincing evidence.

(f) Prior to accepting an admission to an allegation or permitting a respondent to consent to a finding of neglect or abuse, the court shall inform the respondent that such an admission or consent will result in the court making a fact-finding order of neglect or abuse, as the case may be, and shall further inform the respondent of the potential consequences of such order, including but not limited to the following:

(i) that the court will have the power to make an order of disposition, which may include an order placing the subject child or children in foster care until completion of the initial permanency hearing scheduled pursuant to section one thousand eighty-nine of this act and subject to successive extensions of placement at any subsequent permanency hearings;

(ii) that the placement of the children in foster care may, if the parent fails to maintain contact with or plan for the future of the child, lead to proceedings for the termination of parental rights and to the possibility of adoption of the child if the child remains in foster care for fifteen of the most recent twenty-two months, the agency may be required by law to file a petition to terminate parental rights;

(iii) that the report made to the state central register of child abuse and maltreatment upon which the petition is based will remain on file until ten years after the eighteenth birthday of the youngest child named in such report, that the respondent will be unable to obtain expungement of such report, and that the existence of such report may be made known to employers seeking to screen employee applicants in the field of child care, and to child care agencies if the respondent applies to become a foster parent or adoptive parent.

Any finding upon such an admission or consent made without such notice being given by the court shall be vacated upon motion of any party. In no event shall a person other than the respondent, either in person or in writing, make an admission or consent to a finding of neglect or abuse.

§1052. Disposition on adjudication.

(a) At the conclusion of a dispositional hearing under this article, the court shall enter an order of disposition directing one or more of the following:

(i) suspending judgment in accord with section one thousand fifty-three of this part; or

(ii) releasing the child to a non-respondent parent or parents or legal custodian or custodians or guardian or guardians, who is not or are not respondents in the proceeding, in accord with section one thousand fifty-four of this part; or

(iii) placing the child in accord with section one thousand fifty-five of this part; or

(iv) making an order of protection in accord with section one thousand fifty-six of this part; or

(v) releasing the child to the respondent or respondents or placing the respondent or respondents under supervision, or both, in accord with section one thousand fifty-seven of this part; or

(vi) granting custody of the child to a respondent parent or parents, a relative or relatives or a suitable person or persons pursuant to article six of this act and section one thousand fifty-five-b of this part; or

(vii) granting custody of the child to a non-respondent parent or parents pursuant to article six of this act.

However, the court shall not enter an order of disposition combining placement of the child under paragraph (iii) of this subdivision with a disposition under paragraph (i) or (ii) of this subdivision. An order granting custody of the child pursuant to paragraph (vi) or (vii) of this subdivision shall not be combined with any other disposition under this subdivision.

(b) (i) The order of the court shall state the grounds for any disposition made under this section. If the court places the child in accord with section one thousand fifty-five of this part, the court in its order shall determine:

(A) whether continuation in the child's home would be contrary to the best interests of the child and where appropriate, that reasonable efforts were made prior to the date of the dispositional hearing held pursuant to this article to prevent or eliminate the need for removal of the child from his or her home and if the child was removed from the home prior to the date of such hearing, that such removal was in the child's best interests and, where appropriate, reasonable efforts were made to make it possible for the child to safely return home. If the court determines that reasonable efforts to prevent or eliminate the need for removal of the child from the home were not made but that the lack of such efforts was appropriate under the circumstances, the court order shall include such a finding, or if the permanency plan for the child is adoption, guardianship or another permanent living arrangement other than reunification with the parent or parents of the child, the court order shall include a finding that reasonable efforts, including consideration of appropriate in-state and out-of-state placements, are being made to make and finalize such alternate permanent placement.

For the purpose of this section, reasonable efforts to prevent or eliminate the need for removing the child from the home of the child or to make it possible for the child to return safely to the home of the child shall not be required where, upon motion with notice by the social services official, the court determines that:

(1) the parent of such child has subjected the child to aggravated circumstances, as defined in subdivision (j) of section one thousand twelve of this article;

(2) the parent of such child has been convicted of (i) murder in the first degree as defined in section 125.27 or murder in the second degree as defined in section 125.25 of the penal law and the victim was another child of the parent; or (ii) manslaughter in the first degree as defined in section 125.20 or manslaughter in the second degree as defined in section 125.15 of the penal law and the victim was another child of the parent, provided, however, that the parent must have acted voluntarily in committing such crime;

(3) the parent of such child has been convicted of an attempt to commit any of the foregoing crimes, and the victim or intended victim was the child or another child of the parent; or has been convicted of criminal solicitation as defined in article one hundred, conspiracy as defined in article one hundred five or criminal facilitation as defined in article one hundred fifteen of the penal law for conspiring, soliciting or facilitating any of the foregoing crimes, and the victim or intended victim was the child or another child of the parent;

(4) the parent of such child has been convicted of assault in the second degree as defined in section 120.05, assault in the first degree as defined in section 120.10 or aggravated assault upon a person less than eleven years old as defined in section 120.12 of the penal law, and the commission of one of the foregoing crimes resulted in serious physical injury to the child or another child of the parent;

(5) the parent of such child has been convicted in any other jurisdiction of an offense which includes all of the essential elements of any crime specified in clause two, three or four of this subparagraph, and the victim of such offense was the child or another child of the parent; or

(6) the parental rights of the parent to a sibling of such child have been involuntarily terminated; unless the court determines that providing reasonable efforts would be in the best interests of the child, not contrary to the health and safety of the child, and would likely result in the reunification of the parent and the child in the foreseeable future. The court shall state such findings in its order.

(7) If the court determines that reasonable efforts are not to be required because of one of the grounds set forth above, a permanency hearing shall be held within thirty days of the finding of the court that such efforts are not required. At the permanency hearing, the court shall determine the appropriateness of the permanency plan prepared by the social services official which shall include whether or when the child: (i) will be returned to the parent; (ii) should be placed for adoption with the social services official filing a petition for termination of parental rights; (iii) should be referred for legal guardianship; (iv) should be placed permanently with a fit and willing relative; or (v) should be placed in another planned permanent living arrangement that includes a significant connection to an adult willing to be a permanency resource for the child, if the child is age sixteen or older and if the requirements of clause (E) of subparagraph (i) of paragraph two of subdivision (d) of section one thousand eighty-nine of the chapter have been met. The social services official shall thereafter make reasonable efforts to place the child in a timely manner, including consideration of appropriate in-state and out-of-state placements, and to complete whatever steps are necessary to finalize the permanent placement of the child as set forth in the permanency plan approved by the court. If reasonable efforts are determined by the court not to be required because of one of the grounds set forth in this paragraph, the social services official may file a petition for termination of parental rights in accordance with section three hundred eighty-four-b of the social services law.

For the purpose of this section, in determining reasonable effort to be made with respect to a child, and in making such reasonable efforts, the child's health and safety shall be the paramount concern.

For the purpose of this section, a sibling shall include a half-sibling;

(B) if the child has attained the age of sixteen, the services needed, if any, to assist the child to make the transition from foster care to independent living. Where the court finds that the local department of social services has not made reasonable efforts to prevent or eliminate the need for placement, and that such efforts would be appropriate, it shall direct the local department of social services to make such efforts pursuant to section one thousand fifteen-a of this article, and shall adjourn the hearing for a reasonable period of time for such purpose when the court determines that additional time is necessary and appropriate to make such efforts; and

(C) whether the local social services district made a reasonable search to locate relatives of the child as required pursuant to section one thousand seventeen of this article. In making such determination, the court shall consider whether the local social services district engaged in a search to locate any non-respondent parent and whether the local social services district attempted to locate all of the child's grandparents, all suitable relatives identified by any respondent parent and any non-respondent parent and all relatives identified by a child over the age of five as relatives who play or have played a significant positive role in the child's life.

(ii) The court shall also consider and determine whether the need for placement of the child would be eliminated by the issuance of an order of protection, as provided for in paragraph (iv) of subdivision (a) of this section, directing the removal of a person or persons from the child's residence. Such determination shall consider the occurrence, if any, of domestic violence in the child's residence.

(c) Prior to granting an order of disposition pursuant to subdivision (a) of this section following an adjudication of child abuse, as defined in paragraph (i) of subdivision (e) of section ten hundred twelve of this act or a finding of a felony sex offense as defined in sections 130.25, 130.30, 130.35, 130.40, 130.45, 130.50, 130.65 and 130.70 of the penal law, the court shall advise the respondent that any subsequent adjudication of child abuse, as defined in paragraph (i) of subdivision (e) of section one thousand twelve of this act or any subsequent finding of a felony sex offense as defined in those sections of the penal law herein enumerated, arising out of acts of the respondent may result in the commitment of the guardianship and custody of the child or another child pursuant to section three hundred eighty-four-b of the social services law. The order in such cases shall contain a statement that any subsequent adjudication of child abuse or finding of a felony sex offense as described herein may result in the commitment of the guardianship and custody of the child, or another child pursuant to section three hundred eighty-four-b of the social services law.

§1052-a. Post-dispositional procedures.

The local child protective service shall notify the child's attorney of an indicated report of child abuse or maltreatment in which the respondent is a subject of the report or another person named in the report, as such terms are defined in section four hundred twelve of the social services law, while any order issued pursuant to paragraph (i), (iii), (iv) or (v) of subdivision (a) of section one thousand fifty-two remains in effect against the respondent.

§1052-b. Duties of counsel.

1. If the court has entered a dispositional order pursuant to section one thousand fifty-two it shall be the duty of the respondent's counsel promptly to advise such respondent in writing of his or her right to appeal to the appropriate appellate division of the supreme court, the time limitations involved, the manner of instituting an appeal and obtaining a transcript of the testimony and the right to apply for leave to appeal as a poor person if the respondent is unable to pay the cost of an appeal. It shall be the further duty of such counsel to explain to the respondent the procedures for instituting an appeal, the possible reasons upon which an appeal may be based and the nature and possible consequences of the appellate process.

2. It also shall be the duty of such counsel to ascertain whether the respondent wishes to appeal and, if so, to serve and file the necessary notice of appeal.

§1052-c. Duty to report investigations to locate non-respondent parents or relatives.

Upon a determination by the court to enter an order of disposition placing the child in accordance with section one thousand fifty-five of this part, the court shall immediately require the local social services district to report to the court the results of any investigation to locate any non-respondent parent or relatives of the child, including all of the child's grandparents, all suitable relatives identified by any respondent parent and any non-respondent parent and all relatives identified by a child over the age of five as relatives who play or have played a significant positive role in the child's life, as required pursuant to section one thousand seventeen of the article. Such report shall include whether any non-respondent parent has expressed an interest in seeking custody of the child or whether any relative who has been located has expressed an interest in becoming a foster parent for the child or in seeking custody or care of the child.

§1053. Suspended judgment.

(a) Rules of court shall define permissible terms and conditions of a suspended judgment. These terms and conditions shall relate to the acts or omissions of the parent or other person legally responsible for the care of the child.

(b) The maximum duration of any term or condition of a suspended judgment is one year, unless the court finds at the conclusion of that period, upon a hearing, that exceptional circumstances require an extension thereof for an additional year.

(c) Except as provided for herein, in any order issued pursuant to this section, the court may require the child protective agency to make progress reports to the court, the parties, and the child's attorney on the implementation of such order. Where the order of disposition is issued upon the consent of the parties and the child's attorney, such agency shall report to the court, the parties and the child's attorney no later than ninety days after the issuance of the order, unless the court determines that the facts and circumstances of the case do not require such report to be made.

§1054. Release to non-respondent parent or legal custodian or guardian.

(a) An order of disposition may release the child for a designated period of up to one year to a non-respondent parent or parents or a person or persons who had been the child's legal custodian or guardian at the time of the filing of the petition, and who is not or are not respondents in the proceeding under this article. An order under this section may be extended upon a hearing for a period of up to one year for good cause.

(b) The court may require the person or persons to whom the child is released under this section to submit to the jurisdiction of the court with respect to the child for the period of the disposition or an extension thereof. The order may include, but is not limited to, a direction for such person or persons to cooperate in making the child available for court-ordered visitation with respondents, siblings and others and for appointments with and visits by the child protective agency, including visits in the home and in-person contact with the child protective agency, social services official or duly authorized agency, and for appointments with the child's attorney, clinician or other individual or program providing services to the child. The order shall set forth the terms and conditions applicable to such non-respondent and child protective agency, social services official and duly authorized agency with respect to the child.

(c) In conjunction with an order releasing the child to a non-respondent parent, legal custodian or guardian under this subdivision, the court may also issue any or all of the following orders: an order of supervision of a respondent parent under section one thousand fifty-seven, an order directing that services be provided to the respondent parent under section one thousand fifteen-a or an order of protection under section one thousand fifty-six of this article. An order of supervision of the respondent entered under this subdivision may be extended upon a hearing for a period of up to one year for good cause.

(d) Except as provided for herein, in any order issued pursuant to this section, the court may require the child protective agency to make progress reports to the court, the parties, and the child's attorney on the implementation of such order. Where the order of disposition is issued upon the consent of the parties and the child's attorney, such agency shall report to the court, the parties and the child's attorney no later than ninety days after the issuance of the order and no later than sixty days prior to the expiration of the order, unless the court determines that the facts and circumstances of the case do not require such report to be made.

§1055. Placement.

(a) (i) For purposes of section one thousand fifty-two of this part the court may place the child in the custody of a relative or other suitable person pursuant to this article, or of the local commissioner of social services or of such other officer, board or department as may be authorized to receive children as public charges, or a duly authorized association, agency, society or in an institution suitable for the placement of a child. The court may also place a child who it finds to be a sexually exploited child as defined in subdivision one of section four hundred forty-seven-a of the social services law with the local commissioner of social services for placement in an available long-term safe house. The court may also place the child in the custody of the local commissioner of social services and may direct such commissioner to have the child reside with a relative or other suitable person who has indicated a desire to become a foster parent for the child and further direct such commissioner, pursuant to regulations of the office of children and family services, to commence an investigation of the home of such relative or other suitable person within twenty-four hours and thereafter expedite approval or certification of such relative or other suitable person, if qualified, as a foster parent. If such home is found to be unqualified for approval or certification, the local commissioner shall report such fact to the court forthwith so that the court may make a placement determination that is in the best interests of the child.

(ii) An order placing a child directly with a relative or other suitable person pursuant to this part may not be granted unless the relative or other suitable person consents to the jurisdiction of the court. The court may place the person with whom the child has been directly placed under supervision of a child protective agency, social services official or duly authorized agency during the pendency of the proceeding. The court also may issue an order of protection under section one thousand fifty-six of this part. An order of supervision issued pursuant to this subdivision shall set forth the terms and conditions that the relative or suitable person must meet and the actions that the child protective agency, social services official or duly authorized agency must take to exercise such supervision.

(b) (i) The court shall state on the record its findings supporting the placement in any order of placement made under this section. The order of placement shall include, but not be limited to:

(A) a description of the visitation plan;

(B) a direction that the respondent or respondents shall be notified of the planning conference or conferences to be held pursuant to subdivision three of section four hundred nine-e of the social services law, of their right to attend the conference, and of their right to have counsel or another representative or companion with them;

(C) a date certain for the permanency hearing, which may be the previously-scheduled date certain, but in no event more than eight months from the date of removal of the child from his or her home. Provided, however, that if there is a sibling or half-sibling of the child who was previously removed from the home pursuant to this article, the date certain for the permanency hearing shall be the date certain previously scheduled for the sibling or half-sibling of the child who was the first child removed from the home, where such sibling or half-sibling has a permanency hearing date certain scheduled within the next eight months, but in no event later than eight months from the date of removal of the child from his or her home;

(D) a notice that if the child remains in foster care for fifteen of the most recent twenty-two months, the agency may be required by law to file a petition to terminate parental rights. A copy of the court's order and the service plan shall be given to the respondent; and

*(E) where the permanency goal is return to the parent and it is anticipated that the child may be finally discharged to his or her parent before the next scheduled permanency hearing, the court may provide the local social services district with authority to finally discharge the child to the parent without further court hearing, provided that ten days prior written notice is served upon the court and child's attorney. If the court on its own motion or the child's attorney on motion to the court does not request the matter to be brought for review before final discharge, no further permanency hearings will be required. The local social services district may also discharge the child on a trial basis to the parent unless the court has prohibited such trial discharge or unless the court has conditioned such trial discharge on another event. For the purposes of this section, trial discharge shall mean that the child is physically returned to the parent while the child remains in the care and custody of the local social services district. Permanency hearings shall continue to be held for any child who has returned to his or her parents on a trial discharge. Where the permanency goal for a child aging out of foster care is another planned permanent living arrangement that includes a significant connection to an adult willing to be a permanency resource for the child, the local social services district may also discharge the child on a trial basis to the planned permanent living arrangements, unless the court has prohibited or otherwise conditioned such a trial discharge. Trial discharge for a child aging out of foster care shall mean that a child is physically discharged but the local social services district retains care and custody or custody and guardianship of the child and there remains a date certain for the scheduled permanency hearing. Children placed under this section shall be placed until the court completes the initial permanency hearing scheduled pursuant to article ten-A of this act. Should the court determine pursuant to article ten-A of this act that placement shall be extended beyond completion of the scheduled permanency hearing, such extended placement and any such successive extensions of placement shall expire at the completion of the next scheduled permanency hearing, unless the court shall determine, pursuant to article ten-A of this act, to continue to extend such placement.   *Separately amended; cannot be put together

*(E) where the permanency goal is return to the parent and it is anticipated that the child may be finally discharged to his or her parent before the next scheduled permanency hearing, the court may provide the local social services district with authority to finally discharge the child to the parent

without further court hearing, provided that ten days prior written notice is served upon the court and the attorney for the child. If the court on its own motion or the attorney for the child on motion to the court does not request the matter to be brought for review before final discharge, no further permanency hearings will be required. The local social services district may also discharge the child on a trial basis to the parent unless the court has prohibited such trial discharge or unless the court has conditioned such trial discharge on another event. For the purposes of this section, trial discharge shall mean that the child is physically returned to the parent while the child remains in the care and custody of the local social services district. Permanency hearings shall continue to be held for any child who has returned to his or her parents on a trial discharge. Where the permanency goal for a youth aging out of foster care is another planned permanent living arrangement that includes a significant connection to an adult willing to be a permanency resource for the youth, the local social services district may also discharge the youth on a trial basis to the planned permanent living arrangements, unless the court has prohibited or otherwise conditioned such a trial discharge. Trial discharge for a youth aging out of foster care shall mean that a youth is physically discharged but the local social services district retains care and custody or custody and guardianship of the youth and there remains a date certain for the scheduled permanency hearing. Trial discharge for a youth aging out of foster care may be extended at each scheduled permanency hearing, until the child reaches the age of twenty-one, if a child over the age of eighteen consents to such extension. Prior to finally discharging a youth aging out of foster care to another planned permanent living arrangement, the local social services official shall give the youth notice of the right to apply to reenter foster care within the earlier of twenty-four months of the final discharge or the youth's twenty-first birthday in accordance with article ten-B of this act. Such notice shall also advise the youth that reentry into foster care will only be available where the former foster care youth has no reasonable alternative to foster care and consents to enrollment in and attendance at an appropriate educational or vocational program in accordance with paragraph two of subdivision (a) of section one thousand ninety-one of this act. Children placed under this section shall be placed until the court completes the initial permanency hearing scheduled pursuant to article ten-A of this act. Should the court determine pursuant to article ten-A of this act that placement shall be extended beyond completion of the scheduled permanency hearing, such extended placement and any such successive extensions of placement shall expire at the completion of the next scheduled permanency hearing, unless the court shall determine, pursuant to article ten-A of this act, to continue to extend such placement.

Separately amended; cannot be put together

(ii) Upon placing a child under the age of one, who has been abandoned, with a local commissioner of social services, the court shall, where either of the parents do not appear after due notice, include in its order of disposition pursuant to section one thousand fifty-two of this part, a direction that such commissioner shall promptly commence a diligent search to locate the child's non-appearing parent or parents or other known relatives who are legally responsible for the child, and to commence a proceeding to commit the guardianship and custody of such child to an authorized agency pursuant to section three hundred eighty-four-b of the social services law, six months from the date that care and custody of the child was transferred to the commissioner, unless there has been communication and visitation between such child and such parent or parents or other known relatives or persons legally responsible for the child. In addition to such diligent search the local commissioner of social services shall provide written notice to the child's parent or parents or other known relatives or persons legally responsible as provided for in this paragraph. Such notice shall be served upon such parent or parents or other known relatives or persons legally responsible in the manner required for service of process pursuant to section six hundred seventeen of this act. Information regarding such diligent search, including, but not limited to, the name, last known address, social security number, employer's address and any other identifying information to the extent known regarding the non-appearing parent, shall be recorded in the uniform case record maintained pursuant to section four hundred nine-f of the social services law.

(iii) Notice as required by paragraph (ii) of this subdivision shall state:

(A) that the local commissioner of social services shall initiate a proceeding to commit the guardianship and custody of the subject child to an authorized agency and that such proceeding shall be commenced six months from the date the child was placed in the care and custody of such commissioner with such date to be specified in the notice;

(B) that there has been no visitation and communication between the parent and the child since the child has been placed with the local commissioner of social services and that if no such visitation and communication with the child occurs within six months of the date the child was placed with such commissioner the child will be deemed an abandoned child as defined in section three hundred eighty-four-b of the social services law and a proceeding will be commenced to commit the guardianship and custody of the subject child to an authorized agency;

(C) that it is the legal responsibility of the local commissioner of social services to reunite and reconcile families whenever possible and to offer services and assistance for that purpose;

(D) the name, address and telephone number of the caseworker assigned to the subject child who can provide information, services and assistance with respect to reuniting the family;

(E) that it is the responsibility of the parent, relative or other person legally responsible for the child to visit and communicate with the child and that such visitation and communication may avoid the necessity of initiating a petition for the transfer of custody and guardianship of the child. Such notice shall be printed in both Spanish and English and contain in conspicuous print and in plain language the information set forth in this paragraph.

(c) In addition to or in lieu of an order of placement made pursuant to subdivision (b) of this section, the court may make an order directing a child protective agency, social services official or other duly authorized agency to undertake diligent efforts to encourage and strengthen the parental relationship when it finds such efforts will not be detrimental to the best interests of the child. Such efforts shall include encouraging and facilitating visitation with the child by the parent or other person legally responsible for the child's care. Such order may include a specific plan of action for such agency or official including, but not limited to, requirements that such agency or official assist the parent or other person responsible for the child's care in obtaining adequate housing, employment, counseling, medical care or psychiatric treatment. Such order shall also include encouraging and facilitating visitation with the child by the non-custodial parent and grandparents who have obtained orders pursuant to part eight of this article, and may include encouraging and facilitating visitation with the child by the child's siblings. The order may incorporate an order, if any, issued pursuant to subdivision (c) of section one thousand twenty-seven-a or one thousand eighty-one of this article, provided that such visitation or contact is in the best interests of the child and his or her siblings. For purposes of this section, "siblings" shall include half-siblings and those who would be deemed siblings or half-siblings but for the termination of parental rights of death of a parent. Nothing in this subdivision shall be deemed to limit the authority of the court to make an order pursuant to section two hundred fifty-five of this act.   *(Eff.11/16/16,Ch.242,L.2016)*

(d) In addition to or in lieu of an order of placement made pursuant to subdivision (b) of this section, the court may make an order directing a social services official or other duly authorized agency to institute a proceeding to legally free the child for adoption, if the court finds reasonable cause to believe that grounds therefor exist. Upon a failure by such official or agency to institute such a proceeding within ninety days after entry of such order, the court shall permit the foster parent or parents in whose home the child resides to institute such a proceeding unless the social services official or other duly authorized agency caring for the child, for good cause shown and upon due notice to all parties to the proceeding, has obtained a modification or extension of such order, or unless the court has reasonable cause to believe that such foster parent or parents would not obtain approval of their petition to adopt the children in a subsequent adoption proceeding.

(e) No placement may be made or continued under this section beyond the child's eighteenth birthday without his or her consent and in no event past his or her twenty-first birthday. However, a former foster care youth under the age of twenty-one who was previously discharged from foster care due to a failure to consent to continuation of placement may make a motion pursuant to section one thousand ninety-one of this act to return to the custody of the local commissioner of social services or other officer, board or department authorized to receive children as public charges. In such motion, the youth must consent to enrollment in and attendance at a vocational or educational program in accordance with paragraph two of subdivision (a) of section one thousand ninety-one of this act.

(f) If a child is placed in the custody of the local commissioner of social services or other officer, board or department authorized to receive children as public charges, such person shall provide for such child as authorized by law, including, but not limited to section three hundred ninety-eight of the social services law.

(g) If the parent or person legally responsible for the care of any such child or with whom such child resides receives public assistance and care, any portion of which is attributable to such child, a copy of the order of the court providing for the placement of such child from his or her home shall be furnished to the appropriate social services official, who shall reduce the public assistance and care furnished such parent or other person by the amount attributable to such child, provided, however, that when the child service plan prepared pursuant to section four hundred nine-e of the social services law includes a goal of discharge of the child to the parent or person legally responsible for the care of the child or other member of the household, such social services official shall not, to the extent that federal reimbursement is available therefor, reduce the portion attributable to such child which is intended to meet the cost of shelter and fuel for heating.

(h) Any order made under this section shall be suspended upon the entry of an order of disposition with respect to a child whose custody and guardianship have been committed pursuant to section three hundred eighty-four-b of the social services law, and shall expire upon the expiration of the time for appeal of such order or upon the final determination of any such appeal and any subsequent appeals authorized by law; provided, however, that where custody and guardianship have been committed pursuant to section three hundred eighty-four-b of the social services law or where the child has been surrendered pursuant to section three hundred eighty-three-c or three hundred eighty-four of the social services law, the child shall nonetheless be deemed to continue in foster care until such time as an adoption or other alternative living arrangement is finalized. A permanency hearing or hearings regarding such child shall be conducted in accordance with article ten-A of this act. Nothing in this subdivision shall cause such order of placement to be suspended or to expire with respect to any parent or other person whose consent is required for an adoption against whom an order of disposition committing guardianship and custody of the child has not been made.

(i) In making an order under this section, the court may direct a local commissioner of social services to place the subject child together with minor siblings or half-siblings who have been placed in the custody of the commissioner, or to provide or arrange for regular visitation and other forms of communication between such child and siblings where the court finds that such placement or visitation and communication is in the child's best interests. Placement or regular visitation and communication with siblings or half-siblings shall be presumptively in the child's best interests unless such placement or visitation and communication would be contrary to the child's health, safety or welfare, or the lack of geographic proximity precludes or prevents visitation.

§1055-a. Substantial failure of a material condition of surrender; enforcement of a contact agreement.

(a) In case of a substantial failure of a material condition in a surrender executed pursuant to section three hundred eighty-three-c of the social services law prior to finalization of the adoption of the child, the court shall possess continuing jurisdiction in accordance with subdivision six of such section to rehear the matter upon the filing of a petition by the authorized agency, the parent or the attorney for the child or whenever the court deems necessary. In such case, the authorized agency shall notify the parent, unless such notice is expressly waived by a statement written by the parent and appended to or included in such instrument, the attorney for the child and the court that approved the surrender within twenty days of any substantial failure to comply with a material condition of the surrender prior to the finalization of the adoption of the child. In such case, the authorized agency shall file a petition on notice to the parent unless notice is expressly waived by a statement written by the parent and appended to or included in such instrument and the attorney for the child in accordance with this section within thirty days of such failure, except for good cause shown, in order for the court to review such failure and, where necessary, to hold a hearing; provided, however, that in the absence of such filing, the parent and/or attorney for the child may file such a petition at any time up to sixty days after notification of the failure. Such petition filed by a parent or child's attorney must be filed prior to the adoption of the child.

(b) If an agreement for continuing contact and communication pursuant to paragraph (b) of subdivision two of section three hundred eighty-three-c of the social services law is approved by the court, and the child who is the subject of the approved agreement has not yet been adopted, any party to the approved agreement may file a petition with the family court in the county where the agreement was approved to enforce such agreement. A copy of the approved agreement shall be annexed to such petition. The court shall enter an order enforcing communication or contact pursuant to the terms and conditions of the agreement unless the court finds that enforcement would not be in the best interests of the child.

(c) Nothing in this section shall limit the rights and remedies available to the parties and the attorney for the child pursuant to section one hundred twelve-b of the domestic relations law with respect to a failure to comply with a material condition of a surrender subsequent to the finalization of the adoption of the child.

§1055-b. Custody or guardianship with a parent or parents, relatives or suitable persons pursuant to article six of this act or guardianship with relatives or suitable persons pursuant to article seventeen of the surrogate's court procedure act.

(a) Custody or guardianship with respondent parent or parents, relatives or suitable persons. At the conclusion of the dispositional hearing under this article, the court may enter an order of disposition granting custody or guardianship of the child to a respondent parent or parents, as defined in subdivision (1) of section one thousand twelve of this article, or a relative or relatives or other suitable person or persons pursuant to article six of this act or an order of guardianship of the child to a relative or relatives or suitable person or persons under article seventeen of the surrogate's court procedure act if the following conditions have been met:

(i) the respondent parent or parents, relative or relatives or suitable person or persons has or have filed a petition for custody or guardianship of the child pursuant to article six of this act or, in the case of a relative or relatives or suitable person or persons, a petition for guardianship of the child under article seventeen of the surrogate's court procedure act; and

(ii) the court finds that granting custody or guardianship of the child to such person or persons is in the best interests of the child and that the safety of the child will not be jeopardized if the respondent or respondents under the child protective proceeding are no longer under supervision or receiving services. In determining whether the best interests of the child will be promoted by the granting of guardianship of the child to a relative who has cared for the child as a foster parent, the court shall give due consideration to the permanency goal of the child, the relationship between the child and the relative, and whether the relative and the social services district have entered into an agreement to provide kinship guardianship assistance payments for the child to the relative under title ten of article six of the social services law, and, if so, whether the fact-finding hearing pursuant to section one thousand fifty-one of this part and a permanency hearing pursuant to section one thousand eighty-nine of this chapter have occurred and whether compelling reasons exist for determining that the return home of the child and the adoption of the child are not in the best interests of the child and are, therefore, not appropriate permanency options; and

(iii) the court finds that granting custody or guardianship of the child to the respondent parent, relative or suitable person under article six of this act or granting guardianship of the child to the relative or suitable person under article seventeen of the surrogate's court procedure act will provide the child with a safe and permanent home; and

(iv) all parties to the child protective proceeding consent to the granting of custody or guardianship under article six of this act or the granting of guardianship under article seventeen of the surrogate's court procedure act; or, if any of the parties object to the granting of custody or guardianship, the court has made the following findings after a joint dispositional hearing on the child protective petition and the petition under article six of this act or under article seventeen of the surrogate's court procedure act:

(A) if a relative or relatives or suitable person or persons have filed a petition for custody or guardianship and a parent or parents fail to consent to the granting of the petition, the court finds that the relative or relatives or suitable person or persons have demonstrated that extraordinary circumstances exist that support granting an order of custody or guardianship to the relative or relatives or suitable person or persons and that the granting of the order will serve the child's best interests; or

(B) if a relative or relatives or suitable person or persons have filed a petition for custody or guardianship and a party other than the parent or parents fail to consent to the granting of the petition, the court finds that granting custody or guardianship of the child to the relative or relatives or suitable person or persons is in the best interests of the child; or

(C) if a respondent parent has filed a petition for custody under article six of this act and a party who is not a parent of the child objects to the granting of the petition, the court finds either that the objecting party has failed to establish extraordinary circumstances, or, if the objecting party has established extraordinary circumstances, that granting custody to the petitioning respondent parent would nonetheless be in the child's best interests; or

(D) if a respondent parent has filed a petition for custody under article six of this act and the other parent fails to consent to the granting of the petition, the court finds that granting custody to the petitioning respondent parent is in the child's best interests.

(a-1) Custody and visitation petition of non-respondent parent under article six of this act. Where a proceeding filed by a non-respondent parent pursuant to article six of this act is pending at the same time as a proceeding brought in the family court pursuant to this article, the court presiding over the proceeding under this article may jointly hear the permanency hearing and the hearing on the custody and visitation petition under article six of this act; provided however, the court must determine the non-respondent parent's custody petition filed under article six of this act in accordance with the terms of that article.

(a-2) Custody and visitation petition of non-respondent parent under section two hundred forty of the domestic relations law. Where a proceeding brought in the supreme court involving the custody of, or right to visitation with, any child of a marriage is pending at the same time as a proceeding brought in the family court pursuant to this article, the court presiding over the proceeding under this article may jointly hear the permanency hearing and, upon referral from the supreme court, the hearing to resolve the matter of custody or visitation in the proceeding pending in the supreme court; provided however, the court must determine the non-respondent parent's custodial rights in accordance with the terms of paragraph (a) of subdivision one of section two hundred forty of the domestic relations law.

(b) An order made in accordance with the provisions of this section shall set forth the required findings as described in subdivision (a) of this section where applicable, including, if the guardian and the local department of social services have entered into an agreement to provide kinship guardianship assistance payments for the child to the relative under title ten of article six of the social services law, that a fact-finding hearing pursuant to section one thousand fifty-one of this part and a permanency hearing pursuant to section one thousand eighty-nine of this chapter have occurred, and the compelling reasons that exist for determining that the return home of the child and the adoption of the child are not in the best interests of the child and are, therefore, not appropriate permanency options for the child, and shall constitute the final disposition of the child protective proceeding. Notwithstanding any other provision of law, the court shall not issue an order of supervision nor may the court require the local department of social services to provide services to the respondent or respondents when granting custody or guardianship pursuant to article six of this act under this section or granting guardianship under article seventeen of the surrogate's court procedure act.

(c) As part of the order granting custody or guardianship pursuant to article six of this act or granting guardianship under article seventeen of the surrogate's court procedure act, the court may require that the local department of social services and the attorney for the child receive notice of, and be made parties to, any subsequent proceeding to modify the order of custody or guardianship granted pursuant to the article six proceeding or the order of guardianship granted pursuant to article seventeen of the surrogate's court procedure act; provided, however, if the guardian and the local department of social services had entered into an agreement to provide kinship guardianship assistance payments for the child to the relative under title ten of article six of the social services law, the order must require that the local department of social services and the attorney for the child receive notice of, and be made parties to, any such subsequent proceeding regarding custody or guardianship of the child.

(d) An order entered in accordance with this section shall conclude the court's jurisdiction over the proceeding held pursuant to this article and the court shall not maintain jurisdiction over the parties for the purposes of permanency hearings held pursuant to article ten-A of this act.

(e) The court shall hold age appropriate consultation with the child, however, if the youth has attained fourteen years of age, the court shall ascertain his or her preference for a suitable guardian. Notwithstanding any other section of law, where the youth is over the age of eighteen, he or she shall consent to the appointment of a suitable guardian.

§1056. Order of protection.
1. The court may make an order of protection in assistance or as a condition of any other order made under this part. Such order of protection shall remain in effect concurrently with, shall expire no later than the expiration date of, and may be extended concurrently with, such other order made under this part, except as provided in subdivision four of this section. The order of protection may set forth reasonable conditions of behavior to be observed for a specified time by a person who is before the court and is a parent or a person legally responsible for the child's care or the spouse of the parent or other person

legally responsible for the child's care, or both. Such an order may require any such person

(a) to stay away from the home, school, business or place of employment of the other spouse, parent or person legally responsible for the child's care or the child, and to stay away from any other specific location designated by the court;

(b) to permit a parent, or a person entitled to visitation by a court order or a separation agreement, to visit the child at stated periods;

(c) to refrain from committing a family offense, as defined in subdivision one of section eight hundred twelve of this act, or any criminal offense against the child or against the other parent or against any person to whom custody of the child is awarded, or from harassing, intimidating or threatening such persons;

(d) to permit a designated party to enter the residence during a specified period of time in order to remove personal belongings not in issue in this proceeding or in any other proceeding or action under this act or the domestic relations law;

(e) to refrain from acts of commission or omission that create an unreasonable risk to the health, safety and welfare of a child;

(f) to provide, either directly or by means of medical and health insurance, for expenses incurred for medical care and treatment arising from the incident or incidents forming the basis for the issuance of the order;

(g) 1. to refrain from intentionally injuring or killing, without justification, any companion animal the respondent knows to be owned, possessed, leased, kept or held by the person protected by the order or a minor child residing in such person's household.

2. "Companion animal", as used in this section, shall have the same meaning as in subdivision five of section three hundred fifty of the agriculture and markets law;

(h) 1. to promptly return specified identification documents to the protected party, in whose favor the order of protection or temporary order of protection is issued; provided, however, that such order may: (A) include any appropriate provision designed to ensure that any such document is available for use as evidence in this proceeding, and available if necessary for legitimate use by the party against whom such order is issued; and (B) specify the manner in which such return shall be accomplished.

2. For purposes of this subdivision, "identification document" shall mean any of the following: (A) exclusively in the name of the protected party: birth certificate, passport, social security card, health insurance or other benefits card, a card or document used to access bank, credit or other financial accounts or records, tax returns, any driver's license, and immigration documents including but not limited to a United States permanent resident card and employment authorization document; and (B) upon motion and after notice and an opportunity to be heard, any of the following, including those that may reflect joint use or ownership, that the court determines are necessary and are appropriately transferred to the protected party: any card or document used to access bank, credit or other financial accounts or records, tax returns, and any other identifying cards and documents; and

(i) to observe such other conditions as are necessary to further the purposes of protection.

2. The court may also award custody of the child, during the term of the order of protection to either parent, or to an appropriate relative within the

second degree. Nothing in this section gives the court power to place or board out any child or to commit a child to an institution or agency. In making orders of protection, the court shall so act as to insure that in the care, protection, discipline and guardianship of the child his religious faith shall be preserved and protected.

3. Notwithstanding the foregoing provisions, an order of protection, or temporary order of protection where applicable, may be entered against a former spouse and persons who have a child in common, regardless of whether such persons have been married or have lived together at any time, or against a member of the same family or household as defined in subdivision one of section eight hundred twelve of this act.

4. The court may enter an order of protection independently of any other order made under this part, against a person who was a member of the child's household or a person legally responsible as defined in section one thousand twelve of this chapter, and who is no longer a member of such household at the time of the disposition and who is not related by blood or marriage to the child or a member of the child's household. An order of protection entered pursuant to this subdivision may be for any period of time up to the child's eighteenth birthday and upon such conditions as the court deems necessary and proper to protect the health and safety of the child and the child's caretaker.

5. The court may issue an order, pursuant to section two hundred twenty-seven-c of the real property law, authorizing the party for whose benefit any order of protection has been issued to terminate a lease or rental agreement pursuant to section two hundred twenty-seven-c of the real property law.

6. In any proceeding pursuant to this article, a court shall not deny an order of protection, or dismiss an application for such an order, solely on the basis that the acts or events alleged are not relatively contemporaneous with the date of the application or the conclusion of the action. The duration of any temporary order shall not by itself be a factor in determining the length or issuance of any final order.

7. The protected party in whose favor the order of protection or temporary order of protection is issued may not be held to violate an order issued in his or her favor nor may such protected party be arrested for violating such order.

§1056-a. Firearms; surrender and license suspension, revocation and ineligibility.

Upon the issuance of an order of protection or temporary order of protection, or upon a violation of such order, the court shall make an order in accordance with section eight hundred forty-two-a of this act.

§1057. Release of the child to the respondent or respondents; supervision of the respondent or respondents.

(a) The court may release the child to the respondent or respondents for a period of up to one year, which may be extended pursuant to subdivision (d) of this section.

(b) In conjunction with an order releasing a child under this section or an order under paragraph (ii), (iii) or (iv) of subdivision (a) of section one thousand fifty-two of this part, the court may place the respondent or respondents under supervision of a child protective agency or of a social services official or duly authorized agency. An order of supervision entered under this section shall set forth the terms and conditions of such supervision that the respondent or respondents must meet and the actions that the child protective agency, social services official or duly authorized agency must take to exercise such supervision.

(c) Except as provided for herein, in any order issued pursuant to subdivision (a) or (b) of this section, the court may require the child protective agency to make progress reports to the court, the parties, and the child's attorney on the implementation of such order. Where the order of disposition is issued upon the consent of the parties and the child's attorney, such agency shall report to the court, the parties and the child's attorney no later than ninety days after the issuance of the order and no later than sixty days prior to the expiration of the order, unless the court determines that the facts and circumstances of the case do not require such report to be made. Uniform statewide rules of court shall define permissible terms and conditions of supervision of the respondent or respondents under this section.

(d) The duration of any period of release of the child to the respondent or respondents or supervision of the respondent or respondents or both shall be for an initial period of no more than one year. The court may at the expiration of that period, upon a hearing and for good cause shown, extend such release or supervision or both for a period of up to one year.

§1058. Expiration of orders.

No later than sixty days prior to the expiration of an order issued pursuant to paragraph (i), (ii), (iv), or (v) of subdivision (a) of section one thousand fifty-two of this part or prior to the conclusion of the period of an adjournment in contemplation of dismissal pursuant to section one thousand thirty-nine of this article, where no application has been made seeking extension of such orders or adjournments and, with respect to an adjournment in contemplation of dismissal, no violations of the court's order are before the court, the child protective agency shall, whether or not the child has been or will be returned to the family, report to the court, the parties, including any non-respondent parent and the child's attorney on the status and circumstances of the child and family and any actions taken or contemplated by such agency with respect to such child and family.

Part 6
New Hearing and Reconsideration of Orders

§1061. Staying, modifying, setting aside or vacating order.

For good cause shown and after due notice, the court on its own motion, on motion of the corporation counsel, county attorney or district attorney or on motion of the petitioner, or on motion of the child or on his behalf, or on motion of the parent or other person responsible for the child's care may stay execution, of arrest, set aside, modify or vacate any order issued in the course of a proceeding under this article.

§1062. Motion to terminate placement.

Any interested person acting on behalf of a child placed under section one thousand fifty-five of this article, the child's parent, or the person legally responsible for the child may make a motion to the court for an order terminating the placement. The motion must:

(a) show that an application for the child's return to his or her home was made to an appropriate person in the place in which the child was placed;

(b) show that the application was denied or was not granted within thirty days from the day application was made; and

(c) be accompanied by a sworn affidavit stating the grounds for the motion.

§1063. Service of motion; answer.

A copy of a motion under section one thousand sixty-two of this part shall promptly be served by regular mail upon the duly authorized agency or the institution having custody of the child and upon the child's attorney, each of whose duty it is to file an answer to the motion within five days of the receipt of the motion.

§1064. Examination of motion and answers; hearing.

The court shall promptly examine the motion and answers. If the court concludes that a hearing should be had, it may proceed upon due notice to all concerned to hear the facts and determine whether continued placement serves the purposes of this article. If the court concludes that a hearing need not be had, it shall enter an order granting or denying the motion.

§1065. Orders on hearing.

(a) If the court determines after hearing that continued placement serves the purposes of this article, it shall deny the motion. The court may, on its own motion, determine a schedule for the return of the child, change the agency or institution in which the child is placed, or direct the agency or institution to make such other arrangements for the child's care and welfare as the facts of the case may require.

(b) If the court determines after hearing that continued placement does not serve the purposes of this article, the court shall discharge the child from the custody of the agency or the institution in accord with section one thousand fifty-four of this article.

§1066. Successive motions.

If a motion under section one thousand sixty-two of this part is denied, it may not be renewed for a period of ninety days after the denial, unless the order of denial permits renewal at an earlier time.

§1067. Discontinuation of treatment by agency or institution.

A child placed with an authorized agency under section one thousand fifty-five shall be returned to the court which entered the order of placement, if the agency

(a) discontinues or suspends its work; or

(b) is unwilling to continue to care for the child for the reason that support by the state of New York or one of its political subdivisions has been discontinued; or

(c) so fundamentally alters its program that the child can no longer benefit from it.

§1068. Action on return from agency or institution.

If a person is returned to the court under section one thousand sixty-seven of this part, the court may make any order that might have been made at the time of the order of placement.

§1069. Rules of court.

Rules of court may authorize an agency with which a child is placed pursuant to section three hundred fifty-five to arrange for the child's care by another person or authorized agency. In the event such an arrangement is made, the agency making the arrangement shall, within one week of the making of the arrangement, advise the court of the change and reason therefor.

Part 7
Compliance with Orders

Section

§1071. Failure to comply with terms and conditions of suspended judgment.

If, prior to the expiration of the period of the suspended judgment, a motion or order to show cause is filed that alleges that a parent or other person legally responsible for a child's care violated the terms and conditions of a suspended judgment issued under section one thousand fifty-three of this article, the period of the suspended judgment shall be tolled pending disposition of the motion or order to show cause. If, after hearing, the court is satisfied by competent proof that the parent or other person violated the order of suspended judgment, the court may revoke the suspension of judgment and enter any order that might have been made at the time judgment was suspended.

§1072. Failure to comply with terms and conditions of supervision.

If, prior to the expiration of the period of an order of supervision pursuant to section one thousand fifty-four or one thousand fifty-seven of this article, a motion or order to show cause is filed that alleges that a parent or other person legally responsible for a child's care violated the terms and conditions of an order of supervision issued under section one thousand fifty-four or one thousand fifty-seven of this article, the period of the order of supervision shall be tolled pending disposition of the motion or order to show cause. If, after hearing, the court is satisfied by competent proof that the parent or other person violated the order of supervision willfully and without just cause, the court may:

(a) revoke the order of supervision or of protection and enter any order that might have been made at the time the order of supervision or of protection was made, or

(b) commit the parent or other person who willfully and without just cause violated the order to jail for a term not to exceed six months.

§1073. Effect of running away from place of placement.

If a child placed under section one thousand fifty-five runs away from the place of placement the court may, after hearing, revoke the order of placement and make any order, including an order of placement, that might have been made at the time the order of placement was made. The court may require that the child be present at such hearing and shall appoint an attorney to represent him or her.

§1074. Release from responsibility under order of placement.

Those responsible for the operation of a place where a child has been placed under section one thousand fifty-five may petition the court for leave to return the child to the court and for good cause shown be released from responsibility under the order of placement. After hearing, the court may grant the petition and make any order, including an order of placement, that might have been made at the time the order of placement was made.

§1075. Special duties of attorney for the child.

In addition to all other duties and responsibilities necessary to the representation of a child who is the subject of a proceeding under this article, an attorney for a child shall upon receipt of a report from a child protective agency pursuant to sections one thousand thirty-nine, one thousand thirty-nine-a, one thousand fifty-two-a, one thousand fifty-three, one thousand fifty-four, one thousand fifty-five, one thousand fifty-seven and one thousand fifty-eight, review the information contained therein and make a determination as to whether there is reasonable cause to suspect that the child is at risk of further abuse or neglect or that there has been a substantive violation of a court order. Where the attorney for the child makes such a determination, the attorney shall apply to the court for appropriate relief pursuant to section one thousand sixty-one. Nothing contained in this section shall relieve a child protective agency or social services official of its duties pursuant to this act or the social services law.

Part 8
Visitation of Minors in Foster Care

§1081. Visitation rights.

1. A non-custodial parent or grandparent shall have the visitation rights with a child remanded or placed in the care of a social services official pursuant to this article as conferred by order of the family court or by any order or judgment of the supreme court, or by written agreement between the parents as described in section two hundred thirty-six of the domestic relations law, subject to the provisions of section one thousand eighty-two of this part.

2. (a) A non-custodial parent or any grandparent or grandparents who have not been afforded the visitation rights described in subdivision one of this section, shall have the right to petition the court for enforcement of visitation rights with a child remanded or placed in the care of a social services official pursuant to this article, as such visitation rights have been conferred by order of the family court or by any order or judgment of the supreme court, or by written agreement between the parents as described in section two hundred thirty-six of the domestic relations law.

(b) A child remanded or placed in the care of a social services official pursuant to this article shall have the right to move for visitation and contact with his or her siblings. The siblings of a child remanded or placed in the care of a social services official pursuant to this article shall have a right to petition the court for visitation and contact with such child. For purposes of this section, "siblings" shall include half-siblings and those who would be deemed siblings or half-siblings but for the termination of parental rights or death of a parent.

(Eff.11/16/16,Ch.242,L.2016)

3. (a) The petition by a non-custodial parent shall allege that such parent has visitation rights conferred by order of the family court or by any order or judgment of the supreme court or by written agreement between the parents as described in section two hundred thirty-six of the domestic relations law, shall have a copy of such order, judgment or agreement attached thereto, shall request enforcement of such rights pursuant to this part, and shall state, when known by the petitioner, that visitation rights with the child by any grandparent or grandparents have been conferred by order of the supreme court or family court pursuant to section seventy-two or two hundred forty of the domestic relations law, and shall provide the name and address of such grandparent or grandparents.

(b) A petition by a grandparent or grandparents shall allege that such grandparent or grandparents have been granted visitation rights with the child pursuant to section seventy-two or two hundred forty of the domestic relations law, or subdivision (b) of section six hundred fifty-one of this act, shall have a copy of such order or judgment attached thereto, and shall request enforcement of such rights pursuant to this part.

(c) A motion by a child remanded or placed in the care of a social services official pursuant to this article or a petition by a sibling of such child shall allege that visitation and contact would be in the best interests of both the child who has been remanded or placed and the child's sibling. *(Eff.11/16/16,Ch.242,L.2016)*

4. (a) A petition filed under paragraphs (a) or (b) of subdivision three of this section shall be served upon the respondent in a proceeding under this article, the local social services official having the care of the child, any grandparent or grandparents named in the petition as having visitation rights conferred by court order pursuant to section seventy-two or two hundred forty of the domestic relations law, and upon the child's attorney. The petition shall be served in such manner as the court may direct.

(b) A petition or motion filed under paragraph (c) of subdivision three of this section shall be served upon: (i) the respondent in the proceeding under this article; (ii) the local social services official having the care of the child; (iii) other persons having care, custody and control of the child, if any; (iv) the parents or other persons having care, custody and control of the sibling to be visited or with whom contact is sought; (v) any non-respondent parent in the proceeding under this article; (vi) such sibling himself or herself if ten years of age or older; and (vii) such sibling's attorney, if any. The petition or motion shall be served in such manner as the court may direct. *(Eff.11/16/16,Ch.242,L.2016)*

5. (a) Upon receipt of a petition filed under paragraphs (a) or (b) of subdivision three of this section, the court shall, subject to the provisions of section one thousand eighty-two of this part, require that any order of a family court or order or judgment of the supreme court, or any agreement between the parents as described in subdivision one of this section, granting visitation rights to the non-custodial parent, grandparent or grandparents, be incorporated in any preliminary order or order of placement made under this article to the

extent that such order, judgment or agreement confers visitation rights. In any case where a dispositional hearing has not been held or will not be held within thirty days of the filing of such petition the court shall order the person, official, agency or institution caring for the child pursuant to this article to comply with such part of the order, judgment or agreement granting visitation rights.

(b) Upon receipt of a petition or motion filed under paragraph (c) of subdivision three of this section, the court shall determine, after giving notice and an opportunity to be heard to persons served under subdivision four of this section, whether visitation and contact would be in the best interests of the child and his or her sibling. The court's determination may be included in the dispositional order issued pursuant to section one thousand fifty-two of this article.

(c) Violation of an order issued under this section shall be punishable pursuant to section seven hundred fifty-three of the judiciary law.

(Eff.11/16/16,Ch.242,L.2016)

§1082. Approval, modification or denial of visitation rights.

1. (a) Upon receipt of a petition pursuant to subdivision four of section one thousand eighty-one of this part, the local department of social services shall make inquiry of the state central register of child abuse and maltreatment to determine whether or not the petitioner is a subject of an indicated report of child abuse or maltreatment, as such terms are defined in section four hundred twelve of the social services law, and shall further ascertain whether or not the petitioner is a respondent in a proceeding under this article whereby the child with whom visitation is sought has been allegedly abused or neglected or has been adjudicated as an abused or neglected child.

(b) The department, the child's attorney and the respondent in a proceeding under this article, shall have the right to be heard with respect to a petition for an order to enforce visitation rights under this part.

2. Where the local department of social services or the child's attorney opposes a petition described in section one thousand eighty-one of this part, the department or the child's attorney as appropriate shall serve and file an answer to the petition. The court shall, upon the filing of such answer, set a date for a hearing on such petition and shall notify the parents, grandparent or grandparents, the department and the child's attorney of such hearing date.

3. Whenever a hearing described in subdivision two of this section is to be held within ten court days of a dispositional hearing authorized under this article, the court may in its discretion hear such petition as part of such dispositional hearing.

4. In any hearing under this section, the court shall approve such petition unless the court finds upon competent, relevant and material evidence that enforcement of visitation rights as described in the order, judgment or agreement would endanger the child's life or health. Upon such a finding, the court shall make an order denying such petition or make such other order affecting enforcement of visitation rights as the court deems to be in the best interests of the child.

5. (a) Where a petition is approved pursuant to this section the parties may agree in writing to an alternative schedule of visitation equivalent to and consistent with the original or modified visitation order or agreement where such alternative schedule reflects changed circumstances of the parties and is consistent with the best interests of the child.

(b) In the absence of such an agreement between the parties, the court may, in its discretion, order an alternative schedule of visitation as defined herein, where it determines that such schedule is necessary to facilitate visitation and to protect the best interests of the child.

§1083. Duration of orders affecting visitation rights.

1. Where an order of the court has been made incorporating an order, judgment or agreement conferring visitation rights with a child on a non-custodial parent or grandparent into a dispositional order under this article, or where the court otherwise orders compliance by a person, official, agency or institution caring for the child, with an order, judgment or agreement granting visitation rights, such order shall remain in effect for the length of time the child remains in such care pursuant to this article, unless such order is subsequently modified by the court for good cause shown.

2. Where the court makes an order denying a petition seeking enforcement of visitation rights or makes an order modifying visitation rights, pursuant to the provisions of section one thousand eighty-two of this part, such order shall remain in effect for the length of time the child is placed with a person, official, agency or institution caring for the child pursuant to this article, unless such order is subsequently modified by the court for good cause shown.

§1084. Out-of-wedlock children; paternity.

No visitation right shall be enforceable under this part concerning any person claiming to be a parent of an out-of-wedlock child without an adjudication of the paternity of such person by a court of competent jurisdiction, or without an acknowledgement of the paternity of such person executed pursuant to applicable provisions of law.

§1085. Visitation and custody rights unenforceable; murder of parent, custodian, guardian, or child.

1. No visitation or custody order shall be enforceable under this part by a person who has been convicted of murder in the first or second degree in this state, or convicted of an offense in another jurisdiction which, if committed in this state, would constitute either murder in the first or second degree, of a parent, legal custodian, legal guardian, sibling, half-sibling or step-sibling of the child unless:

(i) (A) such child is of suitable age to signify assent and such child assents to such visitation or custody; or

(B) if such child is not of suitable age to signify assent the child's custodian or legal guardian assents to such order; or

(C) the person who has been convicted of murder in the first or second degree, or an offense in another jurisdiction which if committed in this state, would constitute either murder in the first or second degree, can prove by a preponderance of the evidence that:

(1) he or she, or a family or household member of either party, was a victim of domestic violence by the victim of such murder; and

(2) the domestic violence was causally related to the commission of such murder; and

(ii) the court finds that such visitation or custody is in the best interest of the child.

2. Pending determination of a petition for visitation or custody such child shall not visit and no person shall visit, with such child present, such person,

legal guardian or legal custodian who has been convicted of murder in the first or second degree in this state, or an offense in another jurisdiction which, if committed in this state, would constitute either murder in the first or second degree, of the other parent, legal guardian, legal custodian, sibling, half-sibling or step-sibling of such child, without the consent of such child's custodian or legal guardian.

3. Nothing contained in this section shall be construed to require a court, without petition from any of the interested parties, to review a previously issued order of visitation or custody or denial of such petition.

4. For the purposes of making a determination pursuant to subparagraph (C) of paragraph (i) of subdivision one of this section, the court shall not be bound by the findings of fact, conclusions of law or ultimate conclusion as determined by the proceedings leading to the conviction of murder in the first or second degree in this state or of an offense in another jurisdiction which, if committed in this state, would constitute murder in either the first or second degree, of a parent, legal guardian, legal custodian, sibling, half-sibling or step-sibling of a child who is the subject of the proceeding. In all proceedings under this section, an attorney shall be appointed for the child.

ARTICLE 10-A
Permanency Hearings for Children
Placed out of Their Homes

§1086. Purpose.

The purpose of this article is to establish uniform procedures for permanency hearings for all children who are placed in foster care pursuant to section three hundred fifty-eight-a, three hundred eighty-four or three hundred eighty-four-a of the social services law or pursuant to section one thousand twenty-two, one thousand twenty-seven, one thousand fifty-two, one thousand eighty-nine, one thousand ninety-one, one thousand ninety-four or one thousand ninety-five of this act; children who are directly placed with a relative pursuant to section one thousand seventeen or one thousand fifty-five of this act; and children who are freed for adoption. It is meant to provide children placed out of their homes timely and effective judicial review that promotes permanency, safety and well-being in their lives.

§1087. Definitions.

When used in this article, the following terms shall have the following meanings:

(a) "Child" shall mean a person under the age of eighteen who is placed in foster care pursuant to section three hundred fifty-eight-a, three hundred eighty-four or three hundred eighty-four-a of the social services law or pursuant to section one thousand twenty-two, one thousand twenty-seven, one thousand fifty-two, one thousand eighty-nine, one thousand ninety-one, one thousand ninety-four or one thousand ninety-five of this act; or directly placed with a relative pursuant to section one thousand seventeen or one thousand fifty-five of this act; or who has been freed for adoption or a person between the ages of eighteen and twenty-one who has consented to continuation in foster care or trial discharge status; or a former foster care youth under the age of twenty-one for whom a court has granted a motion to permit the former foster care youth to return to the custody of the local commissioner of social services or other officer, board or department authorized to receive children as public charges.

(b) "Child freed for adoption" shall mean a person whose custody and guardianship has been committed to an authorized agency pursuant to section three hundred eighty-three-c, three hundred eighty-four, or three hundred eighty-four-b of the social services law. Such category shall include a person whose parent or parents have died during the period in which the child was in foster care and for whom there is no surviving parent who would be entitled to notice or consent pursuant to section one hundred eleven or one hundred eleven-a of the domestic relations law. Such category shall not include a child who has been freed for adoption with respect to one parent but who has another parent whose consent to an adoption is required pursuant to section one hundred eleven of the domestic relations law.

(c) "Foster care" shall mean care provided by an authorized agency to a child in a foster family, free or boarding home; agency boarding home; group home; child care institution, health care facility or any combination thereof.

(d) "Agency" means an authorized agency as defined in paragraphs (a) and (b) of subdivision ten of section three hundred seventy-one of the social services law, to which the care and custody or custody and guardianship of a child has been transferred or committed.

(e) "Permanency hearing report" shall mean a sworn report submitted by the social services district to the court and the parties prior to each permanency hearing regarding the health and well-being of the child, the reasonable efforts that have been made since the last hearing to promote permanency for the child, and the recommended permanency plan for the child.

§1088. Continuing court jurisdiction.

If a child is placed pursuant to section three hundred fifty-eight-a, three hundred eighty-four, or three hundred eighty-four-a of the social services law, or pursuant to section one thousand seventeen, one thousand twenty-two, one thousand twenty-seven, one thousand fifty-two, one thousand eighty-nine, one thousand ninety-one, one thousand ninety-four or one thousand ninety-five of this act, or directly placed with a relative pursuant to section one thousand seventeen or one thousand fifty-five of this act; or if the child is freed for adoption pursuant to section three hundred eighty-three-c, three hundred eighty-four or three hundred eighty-four-b of the social services law, the case shall remain on the court's calendar and the court shall maintain jurisdiction over the case until the child is discharged from placement and all orders regarding supervision, protection or services have expired. The court shall rehear the matter whenever it deems necessary or desirable, or upon motion by any party entitled to notice in proceedings under this article, or by the attorney for the child, and whenever a permanency hearing is required by this article. While the court maintains jurisdiction over the case, the provisions of section one thousand thirty-eight of this act shall continue to apply. The court shall also maintain jurisdiction over a case for purposes of hearing a motion to permit a former foster care youth under the age of twenty-one who was discharged from foster care due to a failure to consent to continuation of placement to return to the custody of the local commissioner of social services or other officer, board or department authorized to receive children as public charges.

§1089. Permanency hearings.

(a) Scheduling, commencement and completion of permanency hearings.

(1) Children freed for adoption. (i) At the conclusion of the dispositional hearing at which the child was freed for adoption in a proceeding pursuant to section three hundred eighty-three-c, three hundred eighty-four or three hundred eighty-four-b of the social services law, the court shall set a date certain for the initial freed child permanency hearing and advise all parties in court of the date set, except for the respondent or respondents. The permanency hearing shall be commenced no later than thirty days after the hearing at which the child was freed and shall be completed within thirty days, unless the court determines to hold the permanency hearing immediately upon completion of the hearing at which the child was freed, provided adequate notice has been given.

(ii) At the conclusion of the hearing pursuant to section one thousand ninety-one of this act where the court has granted the motion for a former foster care youth who was discharged from foster care due to a failure to consent to continuation of placement to return to the custody of the local commissioner of social services or other officer, board or department authorized to receive children as public charges, the court shall set a date certain for a permanency hearing and advise all parties in court of the date set. The permanency hearing shall be commenced no later than thirty days after the hearing at which the former foster care youth was returned to foster care.

(2) All other permanency hearings. At the conclusion of the hearing pursuant to section one thousand twenty-two, one thousand twenty-seven, one thousand fifty-two, one thousand eighty-nine, one thousand ninety-one, one thousand ninety-four or one thousand ninety-five of this act at which the child was remanded or placed and upon the court's approval of a voluntary placement instrument pursuant to section three hundred fifty-eight-a of the social services law, the court shall set a date certain for an initial permanency hearing, advise all parties in court of the date set and include the date in the order. Orders issued in subsequent court hearings prior to the permanency hearing, including, but not limited to, the order of placement issued pursuant to section one thousand fifty-five of this act, shall include the date certain for the permanency hearing. The initial permanency hearing shall be commenced no later than six months from the date which is sixty days after the child was removed from his or her home; provided, however, that if a sibling or half-sibling of the child has previously been removed from the home and has a permanency hearing date certain scheduled within the next eight months, the permanency hearing for each child subsequently removed from the home shall be scheduled on the same date certain that has been set for the first child removed from the home, unless such sibling or half-sibling has been removed from the home pursuant to article three or seven of this act. The permanency hearing shall be completed within thirty days of the scheduled date certain.

(3) Subsequent permanency hearings for a child who continues in out-of-home placement or who is freed for adoption shall be scheduled for a date certain which shall be no later than six months from the completion of the

previous permanency hearing and such subsequent permanency hearings shall be completed within thirty days of the date certain set for such hearings.

(b) Notice of permanency hearings. (1) No later than fourteen days before the date certain for a permanency hearing scheduled pursuant to this section, the local social services district shall serve the notice of the permanency hearing and the permanency hearing report by regular mail upon:

(i) the child's parent, including any non-respondent parent, unless the parental rights of the parent have been terminated or surrendered and any other person legally responsible for the child's care at the most recent address or addresses known to the local social services district or agency, and the foster parent in whose home the child currently resides, each of whom shall be a party to the proceeding;

(ii) the agency supervising the care of the child on behalf of the social services district with whom the child was placed, the child's attorney, and the attorney for the respondent parent; and

(iii) the attorney for the child   *(Eff.12/22/15,Ch.14,L.2016)*

(1-a) If the child is age ten or older, no later than fourteen days before the date certain for a permanency hearing scheduled pursuant to this section, the local social services district shall serve the notice of the permanency hearing by regular mail upon the child. Nothing herein shall be deemed to prevent an attorney for the child from consulting with the child about the child's participation in the permanency hearing as required by section one thousand ninety-a of this article prior to the service of the notice required pursuant to this paragraph.   *(Eff.12/22/15,Ch.14,L.2016)*

(2) The notice and the permanency hearing report shall also be provided to any pre-adoptive parent or relative providing care for the child and shall be submitted to the court. The notice of the permanency hearing only shall be provided to a former foster parent in whose home the child previously had resided for a continuous period of twelve months in foster care, if any, unless the court, on motion of any party or on its own motion, dispenses with such notice on the basis that such notice would not be in the child's best interests. However, such pre-adoptive parent, relative, or former foster parent, on the basis of such notice, shall have the right to be heard but shall not be a party to the permanency hearing. The failure of such pre-adoptive parent, relative or former foster parent to appear at a permanency hearing shall constitute a waiver of the right to be heard. Such failure to appear shall not cause a delay of the permanency hearing nor be a ground for the invalidation of any order issued by the court pursuant to this section.

(c) Content of the permanency hearing report. The permanency hearing report shall include, but need not be limited to, up-to-date and accurate information regarding:

(1) the child's current permanency goal, which may be:

(i) return to the parent or parents;

(ii) placement for adoption with the local social services official filing a petition for termination of parental rights;

(iii) referral for legal guardianship;

(iv) permanent placement with a fit and willing relative; or

(v) placement in another planned permanent living arrangement that includes a significant connection to an adult who is willing to be a permanency resource for the child if the child is age sixteen or older, including documentation of: (A) intensive, ongoing, and, as of the date of the hearing, unsuccessful efforts to return the child home or secure a placement for the child with a fit and willing relative including adult siblings, a legal guardian, or an adoptive parent, including through efforts that utilize search technology including social media to find biological family members for children, (B) the steps being taken to ensure that (I) the child's foster family home or child care facility is following the reasonable and prudent parent standard in accordance with the guidance provided by the United States department of health and human services, and (II) the child has regular, ongoing opportunities to engage in age or developmentally appropriate activities including by consulting with the child in an age-appropriate manner about the opportunities of the child to participate in activities, and (C) the compelling reasons for determining that it continues to not be in the best interests of the child to be returned home, placed for adoption, placed with a legal guardian, or placed with a fit and willing relative;

(2) the health, well-being, and status of the child since the last hearing including:

(i) a description of the child's health and well-being;

(ii) information regarding the child's current placement;

(iii) an update on the educational and other progress the child has made since the last hearing including a description of the steps that have been taken by the local social services district or agency to enable prompt delivery of appropriate educational and vocational services to the child, including, but not be limited to:

(A) where the child is subject to article sixty-five of the education law or elects to participate in an educational program leading to a high school diploma, the steps that the local social services district or agency has taken to promptly enable the child to be enrolled or to continue enrollment in an appropriate school or educational program leading to a high school diploma;

(B) where the child is eligible to be enrolled in a pre-kindergarten program pursuant to section thirty-six hundred two-e of the education law, the steps that the local social services district or agency has taken to promptly enable the child to be enrolled in an appropriate pre-kindergarten program, if available;

(C) where the child is under three years of age and is involved in an indicated case of child abuse or neglect, or where the local social services district suspects that the child may have a disability as defined in subdivision five of section twenty-five hundred forty-one of the public health law or if the child has been found eligible to receive early intervention or special educational services prior to or during the foster care placement, in accordance with title two-A of article twenty-five of the public health law or article eighty-nine of the education law, the steps that the local social services district or agency has taken to make any necessary referrals of the child for early intervention, pre-school special educational or special educational evaluations or services, as appropriate, and any available information regarding any evaluations and services which are being provided or are scheduled to be provided in accordance with applicable law; and

(D) where the child is at least sixteen and not subject to article sixty-five of the education law and elects not to participate in an educational program leading to a high school diploma, the steps that the local social services district has taken to assist the child to become gainfully employed or enrolled in a vocational program;

(iv) a description of the visitation plan or plans describing the persons with whom the child visits, including any siblings, and the frequency, duration and quality of the visits;

(v) where a child has attained the age of fourteen, a description of the services and assistance that are being provided to enable the child to learn independent living skills; and

(vi) a description of any other services being provided to the child;

(3) the status of the parent, including:

(i) the services that have been offered to the parent to enable the child to safely return home;

(ii) the steps the parent has taken to use the services;

(iii) any barriers encountered to the delivery of such services;

(iv) the progress the parent has made toward reunification; and

(v) a description of any other steps the parent has taken to comply with and achieve the permanency plan, if applicable.

(4) a description of the reasonable efforts to achieve the child's permanency plan that have been taken by the local social services district or agency since the last hearing. The description shall include:

(i) unless the child is freed for adoption or there has been a determination by a court that such efforts are not required pursuant to section one thousand thirty-nine-b of this act, the reasonable efforts that have been made by the local social services district or agency to eliminate the need for placement of the child and to enable the child to safely return home, including a description of any services that have been provided;

(ii) where the permanency plan is adoption, guardianship, placement with a fit and willing relative or another planned permanent living arrangement other than return to parent, the reasonable efforts that have been made by the local social services district or agency to make and finalize such alternate permanent placement, including a description of any services that have been provided and a description of the consideration of appropriate in-state and out-of-state placements;

(iii) where return home of the child is not likely, the reasonable efforts that have been made by the local social services district or agency to evaluate and plan for another permanent plan, including consideration of appropriate in-state and out-of-state placements, and any steps taken to further a permanent plan other than return to the child's parent; or

(iv) where a child has been freed for adoption, a description of the reasonable efforts that will be taken to facilitate the adoption of the child; and

(5) the recommended permanency plan including:

(i) a recommendation regarding whether the child's current permanency goal should be continued or modified, the reasons therefor, and the anticipated date for meeting the goal;

(ii) a recommendation regarding whether the child's placement should be extended and the reasons for the recommendation;

(iii) any proposed changes in the child's current placement, trial discharge or discharge that may occur before the next permanency hearing;

(iv) a description of the steps that will be taken by the local social services district or agency to continue to enable prompt delivery of appropriate educational and vocational services to the child in his or her current placement and during any potential change in the child's foster care placement, during any trial discharge, and after discharge of the child in accordance with the plans for the child's placement until the next permanency hearing;

(v) whether any modification to the visitation plan or plans is recommended and the reasons therefor;

(vi) where a child has attained the age of fourteen or will attain the age of fourteen before the next permanency hearing, a description of the services and assistance that will be provided to enable the child to learn independent living skills;

(vii) where a child has been placed outside this state, whether the out-of-state placement continues to be appropriate, necessary and in the best interests of the child;

(viii) where return home of the child is not likely, the efforts that will be made to evaluate or plan for another permanent plan, including consideration of appropriate in-state and out-of-state placements; and

(ix) in the case of a child who has been freed for adoption:

(A) a description of services and assistance that will be provided to the child and the prospective adoptive parent to expedite the adoption of the child;

(B) information regarding the child's eligibility for adoption subsidy pursuant to title nine of article six of the social services law; and

(C) if the child is over age fourteen and has voluntarily withheld his or her consent to an adoption, the facts and circumstances regarding the child's decision to withhold consent and the reasons therefor.

(d) Evidence, court findings and order. The provisions of subdivisions (a) and (c) of section one thousand forty-six of this act shall apply to all proceedings under this article. The permanency hearing shall include an age appropriate consultation with the child; provided, however that if the child is age sixteen or older and the requested permanency plan for the child is placement in another planned permanent living arrangement with a significant connection to an adult willing to be a permanency resource for the child, the court must ask the child about the desired permanency outcome for the child. At the conclusion of each permanency hearing, the court shall, upon the proof adduced, and in accordance with the best interests and safety of the child, including whether the child would be at risk of abuse or neglect if returned to the parent or other person legally responsible, determine and issue its findings, and enter an order of disposition in writing:

(1) directing that the placement of the child be terminated and the child returned to the parent or other person legally responsible for the child's care with such further orders as the court deems appropriate; or

(2) where the child is not returned to the parent or other person legally responsible:

(i) whether the permanency goal for the child should be approved or modified and the anticipated date for achieving the goal. The permanency goal may be determined to be:

(A) return to parent;

(B) placement for adoption with the local social services official filing a petition for termination of parental rights;

(C) referral for legal guardianship;

(D) permanent placement with a fit and willing relative; or

(E) placement in another planned permanent living arrangement that includes a significant connection to an adult willing to be a permanency resource for the child if the child is age sixteen or older and the court has determined that as of the date of the permanency hearing, another planned permanency living arrangement with a significant connection to an adult willing to be a permanency resource for the child is the best permanency plan for the child and there are compelling reasons for determining that it continues to not be in the best interests of the child to return home, be referred for termination of parental rights and placed for adoption, placed with a fit and willing relative, or placed with a legal guardian;

(ii) placing the child in the custody of a fit and willing relative or other suitable person, or continuing the placement of the child until the completion of the next permanency hearing, provided, however, that no placement may be continued under this section beyond the child's eighteenth birthday without his or her consent and in no event past the child's twenty-first birthday; provided, however, that a former foster youth who was previously discharged from foster care due to a failure to consent to continuation of placement may be returned to the custody of the local commissioner of social services or other officer, board or department authorized to receive children as public charges if the court has granted the motion of the former foster care youth or local social services official upon a finding that the youth has no reasonable alternative to foster care and has consented to enrollment in and attendance at a vocational or educational program in accordance with section one thousand ninety-one of this act;

(iii) determining whether reasonable efforts have been made to effectuate the child's permanency plan as follows:

(A) unless the child is freed for adoption or there has been a determination by a court that such efforts are not required pursuant to section one thousand thirty-nine-b of this act, whether reasonable efforts have been made to eliminate the need for placement of the child and to enable the child to safely return home;

(B) where the permanency plan is adoption, guardianship, placement with a fit and willing relative or another planned permanent living arrangement other than return to parent, whether reasonable efforts have been made to make and finalize such alternate permanent placement, including consideration of appropriate in-state and out-of-state placements;

(iv) where return home of the child is not likely, what efforts should be made to evaluate or plan for another permanent plan, including consideration of appropriate in-state and out-of-state placements;

(v) the steps that must be taken by the local social services official or agency to implement the educational and vocational program components of the permanency hearing report submitted pursuant to subdivision (c) of this section, and any modifications that should be made to such plan;

(vi) specifying the date certain for the next scheduled permanency hearing;

(vii) where placement of the child is extended, such order shall also include:

(A) a description of the visitation plan or plans;

(B) where the child is not freed for adoption, a direction that the child's parent or parents, including any non-respondent parent or other person legally responsible for the child's care shall be notified of the planning conference or conferences to be held pursuant to subdivision three of section four hundred nine-e of the social services law and notification of their right to attend such conference or conferences and their right to have counsel or another representative with them;

(C) where the child is not freed for adoption, a direction that the parent or other person legally responsible for the child's care keep the local social services district or agency apprised of his or her current whereabouts and a current mailing address;

(D) where the child is not freed for adoption, a notice that if the child remains in foster care for fifteen of the most recent twenty-two months, the local social services district or agency may be required by law to file a petition to terminate parental rights;

(E) where a child has been freed for adoption and is over age fourteen and has voluntarily withheld his or her consent to an adoption, the facts and circumstances with regard to the child's decision to withhold consent and the reasons therefor;

(F) where a child has been placed outside of this state, whether the out-of-state placement continues to be appropriate, necessary and in the best interests of the child;

(G) where a child has or will before the next permanency hearing reach the age of fourteen, (I) the services and assistance necessary to assist the child in learning independent living skills to assist the child to make the transition from foster care to successful adulthood; and (II) A. that the permanency plan developed for the child in foster care who has attained the age of fourteen, and any revision or addition to the plan, shall be developed in consultation with the child and, at the option of the child, with up to two members of the child's permanency planning team who are selected by the child and who are not a foster parent of, or the case worker, case planner or case manager for, the child except that the local commissioner of social services with custody of the child may reject an individual so selected by the child if such local commissioner has good cause to believe that the individual would not act in the best interests of the child, and B. that one individual so selected by the child may be designated to be the child's advisor and, as necessary, advocate, with respect to the application of the reasonable and prudent parent standard to the child; and *(Eff.4/4/16,Ch.54,L.2016)*

(viii) any other findings or orders that the court deems appropriate, which may include:

(A) Whether the court should issue any orders for services in the manner specified in section one thousand fifteen-a of this act in order to achieve the permanency plan and, if so, what services should be ordered.

(B) Where a child has been freed for adoption, the order may also:

(I) direct that such child be placed for adoption in the foster family home where he or she resides or has resided or with any other suitable person or persons;

(II) direct the local social services district to provide services or assistance to the child and the prospective adoptive parent authorized or required to be made available pursuant to the comprehensive annual services program plan then in effect. Such order shall include, where appropriate, the evaluation of eligibility for adoption subsidy pursuant to title nine of article six of the social services law, but shall not require the provision of such subsidy. Violation of such an order shall be subject to punishment pursuant to section seven hundred fifty-three of the judiciary law; and

(III) recommend that the office of children and family services investigate the facts and circumstances concerning the discharge of responsibilities for the care and welfare of such child by a local social services district pursuant to section three hundred ninety-five of the social services law; and

(IV) recommend that the attorney for the child, local social services district or agency file a petition pursuant to part one-A of article six of this act to restore the parental rights of a child who has been freed for adoption.

*(C) Where the permanency goal is return to parent and it is anticipated that the child may be returned home before the next scheduled permanency hearing, the court may provide the local social services district with authority to finally discharge the child to the parent without further court hearing,

provided that ten days prior written notice is served upon the court and child's attorney. If the court on its own motion or the child's attorney on motion to the court does not request the matter to be brought for review before final discharge, no further permanency hearings will be required. The local social services district may also discharge the child on a trial basis to the parent unless the court has prohibited such trial discharge or unless the court has conditioned such trial discharge on another event. For the purposes of this section, trial discharge shall mean that the child is physically returned to the parent while the child remains in the care and custody of the local social services district. Permanency hearings shall continue to be held for any child who has returned to his or her parents on a trial discharge. Where the permanency goal for a child aging out of foster care is another planned permanent living arrangement that includes a significant connection to an adult willing to be a permanency resource for the child, the local social services district may also discharge the child on a trial basis to the planned permanent living arrangements, unless the court has prohibited or otherwise conditioned such a trial discharge. Trial discharge for a child aging out of foster care shall mean that a child is physically discharged but the local social services district retains care and custody or custody and guardianship of the child and there remains a date certain for the scheduled permanency hearing.

*NB Sep amd; cannot be put together

*(C) Where the permanency goal is return to parent and it is anticipated that the child may be returned home before the next scheduled permanency hearing, the court may provide the local social services district with authority to finally discharge the child to the parent without further court hearing, provided that ten days prior written notice is served upon the court and attorney for the child. If the court on its own motion or the attorney for the child on motion to the court does not request the matter to be brought for review before final discharge, no further permanency hearings will be required. The local social services district may also discharge the child on a trial basis to the parent unless the court has prohibited such trial discharge or unless the court has conditioned such trial discharge on another event. For the purposes of this section, trial discharge shall mean that the child is physically returned to the parent while the child remains in the care and custody of the local social services district. Permanency hearings shall continue to be held for any child who has returned to his or her parents on a trial discharge. Where the permanency goal for a youth aging out of foster care is another planned permanent living arrangement that includes a significant connection to an adult willing to be a permanency resource for the youth, the local social services district may also discharge the youth on a trial basis to the planned permanent living arrangements, unless the court has prohibited or otherwise conditioned such a trial discharge. Trial discharge for a youth aging out of foster care shall mean that the youth is physically discharged but the local social services district retains care and custody or custody and guardianship of the child and there remains a date certain for the scheduled permanency hearing. Trial discharge for a youth aging out of foster care may be extended at each scheduled permanency hearing, until the youth reaches the age of twenty-one, if a youth over the age of eighteen consents to such extension. Prior to finally discharging a youth aging out of foster care to another planned permanent living arrangement, the local social services official shall give the youth notice of the right to apply to reenter foster care within the earlier of twenty-four months of the final discharge or the youth's twenty-first birthday in accordance

with article ten-B of this act. Such notice shall also advise the youth that reentry into foster care will only be available where the former foster care youth has no reasonable alternative to foster care and consents to enrollment in and attendance at an appropriate educational or vocational program in accordance with paragraph two of subdivision (a) of section one thousand ninety-one of this act.   *NB Sep amd; cannot be put together.*

(D) The court may make an order of protection in the manner specified by section one thousand fifty-six of this act in assistance or as a condition of any other order made under this section. The order of protection may set forth reasonable conditions of behavior to be observed for a specified period of time by a person before the court.

(E) Where the court finds reasonable cause to believe that grounds for termination of parental rights exist, the court may direct the local social services district or other agency to institute a proceeding to legally free the child for adoption pursuant to section three hundred eighty-four-b of the social services law. Upon a failure by such agency to institute such proceeding within ninety days after entry of such order, the court shall permit the foster parent or parents in whose home the child resides to institute such a proceeding unless the local social services district or other agency, for good cause shown and upon due notice to all the parties to the proceeding, has obtained a modification or extension of such order, or unless the court has reasonable cause to believe that such foster parent or parents would not obtain approval of their petition to adopt the child in a subsequent adoption proceeding.

(F) The court may make an order directing a local social services district or agency to undertake diligent efforts to encourage and strengthen the parental relationship when it finds such efforts will not be detrimental to the best interests of the child and there has been no prior court finding that such efforts are not required. Such efforts shall include encouraging and facilitating visitation with the child by the parent or other person legally responsible for the child's care. Such order may include a specific plan of action for the local social services district or agency including, but not limited to, requirements that such agency assist the parent or other person legally responsible for the child's care in obtaining adequate housing, employment, counseling, medical care or psychiatric treatment. Such order shall also include encouraging and facilitating visitation with the child by the noncustodial parent and grandparents who have the right to visitation pursuant to section one thousand eighty-one of this act. Such order may also include encouraging and facilitating visitation with the child by the child's siblings and may incorporate an order, if any, issued pursuant to section one thousand twenty-seven-a or one thousand eighty-one of this act. For purposes of this section, "siblings" shall include half-siblings and those who would be deemed siblings or half-siblings but for the termination of parental rights or death of a parent. Nothing in this subdivision shall be deemed to limit the authority of the court to make an order pursuant to section two hundred fifty-five of this act.   *(Eff.11/16/16,Ch.242,L.2016)*

(G) Except as provided for herein, in any order issued pursuant to this section, the court may require the local social services district or agency to make progress reports to the court, the parties, and the child's attorney on the implementation of such order.

(H) Where a child freed for adoption has not been placed in a prospective adoptive home and the court has entered an order of disposition directing that the child be placed for adoption or directing the provision of services or assistance to the child and the agency charged with the guardianship and custody of the child fails, prior to the next scheduled permanency hearing, to comply with such order, the court at the time of such hearing may, in the best interests of the child, enter an order committing the guardianship and custody of the child to another authorized agency or may make any other order authorized pursuant to section two hundred fifty-five of this act.

(e) Service of court order and permanency hearing report. A copy of the court order which includes the date certain for the next permanency hearing and the permanency hearing report as approved, adjusted, or modified by the court, shall be given to the parent or other person legally responsible for the child.

§1089-a. **Custody or guardianship with a parent or parents, a relative or relatives or a suitable person or persons pursuant to article six of this act or guardianship of a relative or relatives or a suitable person or persons pursuant to article seventeen of the surrogate's court procedure act.**

(a) Where the permanency plan is placement with a fit and willing relative or a respondent parent, the court may issue an order of custody or guardianship in response to a petition filed by a respondent parent, relative or suitable person seeking custody or guardianship of the child under article six of this act or an order of guardianship of the child under article seventeen of the surrogate's court procedure act. A petition for custody or guardianship may be heard jointly with a permanency hearing held pursuant to this article. An order of custody or guardianship issued in accordance with this subdivision will result in termination of all pending orders issued pursuant to this article or article ten of this act if the following conditions have been met:

(i) the court finds that granting custody to the respondent parent or parents, relative or relatives or suitable person or persons or guardianship of the child to the relative or relatives or suitable person or persons is in the best interests of the child and that the termination of the order placing the child pursuant to article ten of this act will not jeopardize the safety of the child. In determining whether the best interests of the child will be promoted by the granting of guardianship of the child to a relative who has cared for the child as a foster parent, the court shall give due consideration to the permanency goal of the child, the relationship between the child and the relative, and whether the relative and the local department of social services have entered into an agreement to provide kinship guardianship assistance payments for the child to the relative under title ten of article six of the social services law, and, if so, whether a fact-finding hearing pursuant to section one thousand fifty-one of this chapter has occurred, and whether compelling reasons exist for determining that the return home of the child and the adoption of the child are not in the best interests of the child and are, therefore, not appropriate permanency options; and

(ii) the court finds that granting custody to the respondent parent or parents, relative or relatives or suitable person or persons or guardianship of the child to the relative or relatives or suitable person or persons will provide the child with a safe and permanent home; and

(iii) the parents, the attorney for the child, the local department of social services, and the foster parent of the child who has been the foster parent for the child for one year or more consent to the issuance of an order of custody or guardianship under article six of this act or the granting of guardianship under article seventeen of the surrogate's court procedure act and the termination of the order of placement pursuant to this article or article ten of this act; or, if any of the parties object to the granting of custody or guardianship, the court has made the following findings after a joint hearing on the permanency of the child and the petition under article six of this act or article seventeen of the surrogate's court procedure act:

(A) if a relative or relatives or suitable person or persons have filed a petition for custody or guardianship and a parent or parents fail to consent to the granting of the petition, the court finds that the relative or relatives or suitable person or persons have demonstrated that extraordinary circumstances exist that support granting an order of custody or guardianship under article six of this act or the granting of guardianship under article seventeen of the surrogate's court procedure act to the relative or relatives or suitable person or persons and that the granting of the order will serve the child's best interests; or

(B) if a relative or relatives or suitable person or persons have filed a petition for custody or guardianship and the local department of social services, the attorney for the child, or the foster parent of the child who has been the foster parent for the child for one year or more objects to the granting of the petition, the court finds that granting custody or guardianship of the child to the relative or relatives or suitable person or persons is in the best interests of the child; or

(C) if a respondent parent has filed a petition for custody under article six of this act and a party who is not a parent of the child objects to the granting of the petition, the court finds either that the objecting party has failed to establish extraordinary circumstances, or, if the objecting party has established extraordinary circumstances, that granting custody to the petitioning respondent parent would nonetheless be in the child's best interests; or

(D) if a respondent parent has filed a petition for custody under article six of this act and the other parent fails to consent to the granting of the petition, the court finds that granting custody to the petitioning respondent parent is in the child's best interests.

(a-1) Custody and visitation petition of non-respondent parent under article six of this act. Where a proceeding filed by a non-respondent parent pursuant to article six of this act is pending at the same time as a proceeding brought in the family court pursuant to this article, the court presiding over the proceeding under this article may jointly hear the permanency hearing and the hearing on the custody and visitation petition under article six of this act; provided however, the court must determine the non-respondent parent's custody petition filed under article six of this act in accordance with the terms of that article.

(a-2) Custody and visitation petition of non-respondent parent under section two hundred forty of the domestic relations law. Where a proceeding brought in the supreme court involving the custody of, or right to visitation with, any child of a marriage is pending at the same time as a proceeding brought in the family court pursuant to this article, the court presiding over the proceeding under this article may jointly hear the permanency hearing and, upon referral from the supreme court, the hearing to resolve the matter of custody or visitation in the proceeding pending in the supreme court; provided however, the court must determine the non-respondent parent's custodial rights in accordance with the terms of paragraph (a) of subdivision one of section two hundred forty of the domestic relations law.

(b) An order made in accordance with the provisions of this section shall set forth the required findings as described in subdivision (a) of this section, where applicable, including, if the guardian and local department of social services have entered into an agreement to provide kinship guardianship assistance payments for the child to the relative under title ten of article six of the social services law, that a fact-finding hearing pursuant to section one thousand fifty-one of this chapter and a permanency hearing pursuant to section one thousand eighty-nine of this part have occurred, and the compelling reasons that exist for determining that the return home of the child are not in the best interests of the child and are, therefore, not appropriate permanency options for the child, and shall result in the termination of any orders in effect pursuant to article ten of this act or pursuant to this article. Notwithstanding any other provision of law, the court shall not issue an order of supervision nor may the court require the local department of social services to provide services to the respondent or respondents when granting custody or guardianship pursuant to article six of this act under this section or the granting of guardianship under article seventeen of the surrogate's court procedure act in accordance with this section.

(c) As part of the order granting custody or guardianship in accordance with this section pursuant to article six of this act or the granting of guardianship under article seventeen of the surrogate's court procedure act, the court may require that the local department of social services and the attorney for the child receive notice of, and be made parties to any subsequent proceeding to modify the order of custody or guardianship granted pursuant to the article six proceeding; provided, however, if the guardian and the local department of social services have entered into an agreement to provide kinship guardianship assistance payments for the child to the relative under title ten of article six of the social services law, the order must require that the local department of social services and the attorney for the child receive notice of, and be made parties to, any such subsequent proceeding involving custody or guardianship of the child.

(d) Any order entered pursuant to this section shall conclude the court's jurisdiction over the article ten proceeding and the court shall not maintain jurisdiction over the proceeding for further permanency hearings.

(e) The court shall hold age appropriate consultation with the child, however, if the youth has attained fourteen years of age, the court shall ascertain his or her preference for a suitable guardian or custodian. Notwithstanding any other section of law, where the youth is over the age of eighteen, he or she shall consent to the appointment of a suitable guardian or custodian.

§1090. Representation of parties.

(a) If an attorney for the child has been appointed by the family court in a proceeding pursuant to this article or section three hundred fifty-eight-a, three hundred eighty-three-c, three hundred eighty-four, or three hundred eighty-four-b of the social services law, or article ten, ten-B or ten-C of this act, the appointment of the attorney for the child shall continue without further court order or appointment, unless another appointment of an attorney for the child has been made by the court, until the child is discharged from placement and all orders regarding supervision, protection or services have expired. The attorney for the child shall also represent the child without further order or appointment in any proceedings under article ten-B or ten-C of this act. All notices, reports and motions required by law shall be provided to such attorney. The attorney for the child may be relieved of his or her representation upon application to the court for termination of the appointment. Upon approval of the application, the court shall immediately appoint another attorney to whom all notices, reports, and motions required by law shall be provided.

(b) The appointment of an attorney for the respondent parent or parents pursuant to section two hundred sixty-two of this act shall continue without further order of the court. The appointment shall expire upon the expiration of the time for appeal of an order of disposition against the respondent parent committing custody and guardianship of the child pursuant to section three hundred eighty-four-b of the social services law or upon final determination of any appeal or subsequent appeals authorized by law, or upon entry of an order approving a surrender pursuant to the provisions of section three hundred eighty-three-c of the social services law. All notices, reports and motions required by law shall be served upon the attorney for the respondent parent or parents. The attorney may be relieved of his or her representation upon application to the court for termination of the appointment. If the application is approved, the court shall immediately appoint another attorney for the respondent parent or parents pursuant to section two hundred sixty-two of this act upon whom all notices, reports, and motions required by law shall be provided.

§1090-a. Participation of children in their permanency hearings.

(a) (1) As provided for in subdivision (d) of section one thousand eighty-nine of this article, the permanency hearing shall include an age appropriate consultation with the child.

(2) Except as otherwise provided for in this section, children age ten and over have the right to participate in their permanency hearings and a child may only waive such right following consultation with his or her attorney.

(3) Nothing in this section shall be deemed to limit the ability of a child under the age of ten years old from participating in his or her permanency hearing. Additionally, nothing herein shall be deemed to require an attorney for the child to make a motion to allow for such participation. The court shall have the discretion to determine the manner and extent to which any particular child under the age of ten may participate in his or her permanency hearing based on the best interests of the child.

(b)(1) A child age fourteen and older shall be permitted to participate in person in all or any portion of his or her permanency hearing in which he or she chooses to participate.

(2) For children who are at least ten years of age and less than fourteen years of age, the court may, on its own motion or upon the motion of the local social services district, limit the child's participation in any portion of a permanency hearing or limit the child's in person participation in any portion of a permanency hearing upon a finding that doing so would be in the best interests of the child. In making a determination pursuant to this paragraph the court shall consider the child's assertion of his or her right to participate and may also consider factors including, but not limited to, the impact that contact with other persons who may attend the permanency hearing would have on the child, the nature of the content anticipated to be discussed at the permanency hearing, whether attending the hearing would cause emotional detriment to the child, and the child's age and maturity level. If the court determines that limiting a child's in person participation is in his or her best interests, the court shall make alternative methods of participation available, which may include bifurcating the permanency hearing, participation by telephone or other available electronic means, or the issuance of a written statement to the court.

(c) Except as otherwise provided for in this section, a child who has chosen to participate in his or her permanency hearing shall choose the manner in which he or she shall participate, which may include participation in person, by telephone or available electronic means, or the issuance of a written statement to the court.

(d)(1) For children who are age ten and over, the attorney for the child shall consult with the child regarding whether the child would like to assert his or her right to participate in the permanency hearing and if so, the extent and manner in which he or she would like to participate.

(2) The attorney for the child shall notify the attorneys for all parties and the court at least ten days in advance of the scheduled hearing whether or not the child is asserting his or her right to participate, and if so, the manner in which the child has chosen to participate.

(3) (i) The court shall grant an adjournment whenever necessary to accommodate the right of a child to participate in his or her permanency hearing in accordance with the provisions of this section.

(ii) Notwithstanding paragraph two of this subdivision, the failure of an attorney for the child to notify the court of the request of a child age ten or older to participate in his or her permanency hearing shall not be grounds to prevent such child from participating in his or her permanency hearing unless a finding to limit the child's participation is made in accordance with paragraph two of subdivision (b) of this section.

(4) Notwithstanding any other provision of law to the contrary, upon the consent of the attorney for the child, the court may proceed to conduct a permanency hearing if the attorney for the child has not conducted a meaningful consultation with the child regarding his or her participation in the permanency hearing if the court finds that:

(i) The child lacks the mental capacity to consult meaningfully with his or her attorney and cannot understand the nature and consequences of the permanency hearing as a result of a significant cognitive limitation as determined by a health or mental health professional or educational professional as part of a committee on special education and such limitation is documented in the court record or the permanency hearing report;

(ii) The attorney for the child has made diligent and repeated efforts to consult with the child and the child was either unresponsive, unreachable, or declined to consult with his or her attorney; provided, however that the failure of a foster parent or agency to cooperate in making the child reachable or available shall not be grounds to proceed without consulting with the child;

(iii) At the time consultation was attempted, the child was absent without leave from foster care; or

(iv) Demonstrative evidence that other good cause exists and cannot be alleviated in a timely manner.

(e) If an adjournment is granted pursuant to paragraph three of subdivision (d) of this section, the court may, upon its own motion or upon the motion of any party or the attorney for the child, make a finding that reasonable efforts have been made to effectuate the child's approved permanency plan as set forth in subparagraph (iii) of paragraph two of subdivision (d) of section one thousand eighty-nine of this article; such finding shall be made in a written order.

(f) Nothing in this section shall contravene the requirements contained in subparagraph (ii) of paragraph one of subdivision (a) of section one thousand eighty-nine of this article that the permanency hearing be completed within thirty days of the scheduled date certain.

(g) Nothing in this section shall be construed to compel a child who does not wish to participate in his or her permanency hearing to do so.

(Eff.12/22/15,Ch.14,L.2016)

ARTICLE 10-B
Former Foster Care Youth Re-entry Proceedings

Section
1091. Motion to return to foster care placement.

§1091. Motion to return to foster care placement.

A motion to return a former foster care youth under the age of twenty-one, who was discharged from foster care due to a failure to consent to continuation of placement, to the custody of the local commissioner of social services or other officer, board or department authorized to receive children as public charges, may be made by such former foster care youth, or by a local social services official upon the consent of such former foster care youth, if there is a compelling reason for such former foster care youth to return to foster care; provided however, that the court shall not entertain a motion filed after twenty-four months from the date of the first final discharge that occurred on or after the former foster care youth's eighteenth birthday.

(a) A motion made pursuant to this section by a social services official shall be made by order to show cause. Such motion shall show by affidavit or other evidence that:

(1) the former foster care youth has no reasonable alternative to foster care;

(2) the former foster care youth consents to enrollment in and attendance at an appropriate educational or vocational program, unless evidence is submitted that such enrollment or attendance is unnecessary or inappropriate, given the particular circumstances of the youth;

(3) re-entry into foster care is in the best interests of the former foster care youth; and

(4) the former foster care youth consents to the re-entry into foster care.

(b) A motion made pursuant to this section by a former foster care youth shall be made by order to show cause or ten days notice to the social services official. Such motion shall show by affidavit or other evidence that:

(1) the requirements outlined in paragraphs one, two and three of subdivision (a) of this section are met; and

(2) the applicable local social services district consents to the re-entry of such former foster care youth, or if the applicable local social services district refuses to consent to the re-entry of such former foster care youth and that such refusal is unreasonable.

(c) (1) If at any time during the pendency of a proceeding brought pursuant to this section the court finds a compelling reason that it is in the best interests of the former foster care youth to be returned immediately to the custody of the local commissioner of social services or other officer, board or department authorized to receive children as public charges pending a final decision on the motion, the court may issue a temporary order returning the youth to the custody of the local commissioner of social services or other officer, board or department authorized to receive children as public charges.

(2) Where the local social services district has refused to consent to the re-entry of a former foster care youth, and where it is alleged pursuant to

paragraph two of subdivision (b) of this section, that such refusal by such social services district is unreasonable, the court shall grant a motion made pursuant to subdivision (b) of this section if the court finds and states in writing that the refusal by the local social services district is unreasonable. For purposes of this section, a court shall find that a refusal by a local social services district to allow a former foster care youth to re-enter care is unreasonable if:

(i) the youth has no reasonable alternative to foster care;

(ii) the youth consents to enrollment in and attendance at an appropriate educational or vocational program, unless the court finds a compelling reason that such enrollment or attendance is unnecessary or inappropriate, given the particular circumstances of the youth; and

(iii) re-entry into foster care is in the best interests of the former foster youth.

(3) Upon making a determination on a motion filed pursuant to this section, where a motion has previously been granted pursuant to this section, in addition to the applicable findings required by this section, the court shall grant the motion to return a former foster care youth to the custody of the local commissioner of social services or other officer, board or department authorized to receive children as public charges only:

(i) upon a finding that there is a compelling reason for such former foster care youth to return to care;

(ii) if the court has not previously granted a subsequent motion for such former foster care youth to return to care pursuant to this paragraph; and

(iii) upon consideration of the former foster care youth's compliance with previous orders of the court, including the youth's previous participation in an appropriate educational or vocational program, if applicable.

ARTICLE 10-C
DESTITUTE CHILDREN

§1092. Definitions.

When used in this article unless the specific context indicates otherwise:

(a) "destitute child" shall mean a child under the age of eighteen who is in a state of want or suffering due to lack of sufficient food, clothing, shelter, or medical or surgical care and:

(1) does not fit within the definition of an "abused child" or a "neglected child" as such terms are defined in section one thousand twelve of this act; and

(2) is without any parent or caretaker available to sufficiently care for him or her, due to:

(i) the death of a parent or caretaker; or

(ii) the incapacity or debilitation of a parent or caretaker, where such incapacity or debilitation would prevent such parent or caretaker from being able to knowingly and voluntarily enter into a written agreement to transfer the care and custody of said child pursuant to section three hundred fifty-eight-a or three hundred eighty-four-a of the social services law; or

(iii) the inability of the commissioner of social services to locate any parent or caretaker, after making reasonable efforts to do so; or

(iv) a parent or caretaker being physically located outside of the state of New York and the commissioner of social services is or has been unable to return the child to such parent or caretaker while or after making reasonable efforts to do so, unless the lack of such efforts is or was appropriate under the circumstances.

(b) "parent" shall mean any living biological or adoptive parent of the child whose rights have not been terminated or surrendered.

(c) "caretaker" shall mean a person or persons, other than a parent of a child alleged or adjudicated to be a destitute child pursuant to this article, who possesses a valid, current court order providing him or her with temporary or permanent guardianship or temporary or permanent custody of said child.

(d) "permanency hearing" shall mean a hearing in accordance with article ten-A of this act, as defined in subdivision (k) of section one thousand twelve of this act.

(e) "commissioner of social services" shall mean the commissioner of the local department of social services or, in a city having a population of one million or more, the administration for children's services.

(f) "Interested adult" shall mean a person or persons over the age of eighteen, other than a parent or caretaker, who, at the relevant time resided with and had responsibility for the day-to-day care of a child alleged or adjudicated to be destitute.

§1093. Originating proceedings.

(a) Filing of the petition. Only a commissioner of social services may originate a proceeding under this article. A proceeding under this article may be originated by the filing of a petition alleging that the child is a destitute child as defined by section one thousand ninety-two of this article. A commissioner of social services, who accepts the care and custody of a child appearing to be a destitute child, shall provide for such child as authorized by law, including but not limited to section three hundred ninety-eight of the social services law, and shall file a petition pursuant to this section within fourteen days upon accepting the care and custody of such child.

(b) Venue. A petition under this article shall be filed in the family court located in the county where the child resides or is found; provided however, that upon the motion of any party or the attorney for the child, the court may transfer a petition filed under this article to a county the court deems to be more appropriate under the circumstances, including, but not limited to, a county located within a jurisdiction where the child is domiciled or has another significant nexus.

(c) Contents of the petition. (1) The petition shall allege upon information and belief:

(i) the manner, date and circumstance under which the child became known to the petitioner;

(ii) the child's date of birth, if known;

(iii) that the child is a destitute child as defined in subdivision (a) of section one thousand ninety-two of this article and the basis for the allegation;

(iv) the identity of the parent or parents of the child in question, if known;

(v) whether the parent or parents of the child are living or deceased, if known;

(vi) the whereabouts and last known address for the parent or parents, if known;

(vii) the identity of a caretaker or interested adult, if known;

(viii) the efforts, if any, which were made prior to the filing of the petition to prevent any removal of the child from the home and if such efforts were not made, the reasons such efforts were not made; and

(ix) the efforts, if any, which were made prior to the filing of the petition to allow the child to return or remain safely home, and if such efforts were not made, the reasons such efforts were not made.

(2) The petition shall contain a notice in conspicuous print providing that if the child remains in foster care for fifteen of the most recent twenty-two months, the agency may be required by law to file a petition to terminate parental rights.

(d) Service of summons. (1) Upon the filing of a petition under this article, if a living parent, caretaker or interested adult is identified in the petition, the court shall cause a copy of the petition and a summons to be issued the same day the petition is filed, requiring such parent, caretaker or interested adult to appear in court on the return date to answer the petition. If the court deems a person a party to the proceeding pursuant to subdivision (c) of section one thousand ninety-four of this article and if such person is not before the court, the court shall cause a copy of the petition and a summons requiring such person to appear in court on the return date be served on such person.

(2) Service of a summons and petition under this article shall be made by delivery of a true copy thereof to the person summoned at least twenty-four hours before the time stated therein for appearance.

(3) The court may send process without the state in the same manner and with the same effect as process sent within the state in the exercise of personal jurisdiction over any person subject to the jurisdiction of the court under section three hundred one or three hundred two of the civil practice law and rules, notwithstanding that such person is not a resident or domiciliary of the state. Where service is effected outside of the state of New York on a parent, caretaker, interested adult or person made a party to the proceeding pursuant to subdivision (c) of section one thousand ninety-four of this article and such person defaults by failing to appear to answer the petition, the court may on its own motion, or upon application of any party or the attorney for the child proceed to a hearing pursuant to section one thousand ninety-five of this article.

(4) If after reasonable effort, personal service is not made, the court may at any stage in the proceedings make an order providing for substituted service in the manner provided for substituted service in civil process in courts of record.

§1094. Initial appearance and preliminary proceedings.

(a) At the initial appearance, the court shall:

(1) appoint an attorney to represent the child in accordance with section two hundred forty-nine of this act, and appoint an attorney to represent a parent, caretaker or interested adult in accordance with paragraph (ix) of subdivision (a) of section two hundred sixty-two of this act, if he or she is financially unable to obtain counsel;

(2) (i) if any parent, caretaker or interested adult enters an appearance, determine whether the child may safely remain in or return to his or her home and, if appropriate, order services to assist the family toward that end; provided however, that such order shall not include the provision of any service or assistance to the child and his or her family which is not authorized or required to be made available pursuant to the comprehensive annual services program plan then in effect;

(ii) determine whether temporary care is necessary to avoid risk to the child's life or health and whether it would be contrary to the welfare of the child to continue in, or return to his or her own home, and, if so, whether the child should be placed in the temporary care and custody of a relative or other suitable person or in the temporary care and custody of the commissioner of social services;

(iii) upon a determination that the child should be temporarily placed:

(A) direct the petitioner to investigate whether there are any parents, caretakers or interested adults not named in the petition or any other relatives or other suitable persons with whom the child may safely reside and, if so, direct the child to reside temporarily in their care; and

(B) if a relative or other suitable person seeks approval to care for the child as a foster parent, direct the petitioner to commence an investigation into the home of such relative and thereafter approve such relative or other suitable person, if qualified, as a foster parent; provided, however, that if such home is found to be unqualified for approval, the petitioner shall report such fact to the court forthwith and, in the case of a relative who seeks approval to care for the child as a foster parent, the relative may proceed in accordance with section one thousand twenty-eight-a of this act.

(3) set a date certain for the fact finding and disposition hearing pursuant to section one thousand ninety-five of this article and, if the child is temporarily placed, set a date certain for the initial permanency hearing pursuant to paragraph two of subdivision (a) of section one thousand eighty-nine of this act. The date certain for the initial permanency hearing shall be no later than eight months from the date the social services official accepted care of the child;

(4) determine whether reasonable efforts were made prior to the placement of the child into foster care to prevent or eliminate the need for removal of the child from his or her home, and if such efforts were not made whether the lack of such efforts were appropriate under the circumstances; determine, where appropriate, if reasonable efforts were made to make it possible for the child to remain in or return safely home; and

(5) include the findings made pursuant to paragraphs one through four of this subdivision in a written order.

(b)(1) Any parent or caretaker, or interested adult from whose care the child has been removed, or the child's attorney may request a hearing to determine whether a child who has been removed from his or her home should be returned and, if so, whether services should be ordered to facilitate such return; provided however, that such order shall not include the provision of any service or assistance to the child and his or her family which is not authorized or required to be made available pursuant to the comprehensive annual services program plan then in effect. Except for good cause shown, the hearing shall be held within three court days of the request and shall not be adjourned. The court shall grant the application for return of the child unless it finds that the return presents an imminent risk to the child's life or health. If imminent risk to the child is found, the court may make orders in accordance with paragraph two of subdivision (a) of this section, including, but not limited to, directions for investigations of relatives or other suitable persons with whom the child may safely reside.

(2) In determining whether temporary removal of the child is necessary to avoid imminent risk to the child's life or health, the court shall consider and determine in its order whether continuation in the child's home would be contrary to the best interests of the child and where appropriate, whether

reasonable efforts were made prior to the date of the hearing to prevent or eliminate the need for removal of the child from the home and where appropriate, whether reasonable efforts were made after removal of the child to make it possible for the child to safely return home.

(3) If the court determines that reasonable efforts to prevent or eliminate the need for removal of the child from the home were not made but that the lack of such efforts was appropriate under the circumstances, the court order shall include such a finding and the basis for such finding.

(4) If the court determines that reasonable efforts to allow a child to safely return home were not made subsequent to the removal of the child but that the lack of such efforts was appropriate under the circumstances, the court order shall include such a finding and the basis for such finding.

(c) (1) The court may upon its own motion or the motion of any person, deem a person not named in the petition who has a significant connection to the child alleged to be destitute, a party to the proceeding, if such person consents to being added as a party, and such action is appropriate under the circumstances

(2) If the court deems a person a party pursuant to paragraph (i) of this subdivision and such person is not before the court, the court shall cause a copy of the petition and a summons requiring such person to appear in court on the return date be served on such person in accordance with subdivision (d) of section one thousand ninety-three of this article.

(d) The court may, if it deems appropriate, appoint counsel for an interested adult or another person named as a party to the proceeding pursuant to subdivision (c) of this section, if such adult or person is financially unable to obtain counsel.

§1095. Fact finding and disposition.

(a) No fact finding hearing may commence under this article unless the court enters a finding that all parties are present at the hearing and have been served with a copy of the petition, provided however, that if any party is or are living but are not present, that the court may proceed if every reasonable effort has been made to effect service under subdivision (d) of section one thousand ninety-three of this article.

(b) The court shall sustain the petition and make a finding that a child is destitute if, based upon a preponderance of competent, material and relevant evidence presented, the court finds that the child meets the definition of a destitute child as described in subdivision (a) of section one thousand ninety-two of this article. If the proof does not conform to the specific allegations of the petition, the court may amend the allegations to conform to the proof if no party objects to such conformation.

(c) If the court finds that the child does not meet such definition of a destitute child or that the aid of the court is not required, the court shall dismiss the petition, and if applicable, return a child who was placed in the temporary care of the commissioner of social services to any parent, caretaker or interested adult; provided, however, that if the court finds that the child may be in need of protection under article ten of this act, the court may request the commissioner of social services to conduct a child protective investigation in accordance with subdivision one of section one thousand thirty-four of this act. The court shall state the grounds for any finding under this subdivision.

(d) If the court sustains the petition pursuant to subdivision (b) of this section, it may immediately convene a dispositional hearing or may adjourn the proceeding for further inquiries to be made prior to disposition provided however, that if a petition pursuant to article six of this act has been filed by a person or persons seeking custody or guardianship of the child, or if a petition pursuant to article seventeen of the surrogate's court procedure act seeking guardianship of the child has been filed, the court shall consolidate the dispositional hearing with a hearing under section one thousand ninety-six of this article, unless consolidation would not be appropriate under the circumstances. If the court does not consolidate such dispositional proceedings it shall hold the dispositional hearing under this section in abeyance pending the disposition of the petition filed pursuant to article six of this act or article seventeen of the surrogate's court procedure act. Based upon material and relevant evidence presented at the dispositional hearing, the court shall enter an order of disposition stating the grounds for its order and directing one of the following alternatives:

(1) placing the child in the care and custody of the commissioner of social services; or

(2) granting an order of custody or guardianship to relatives or suitable persons pursuant to a petition under article six of this act or guardianship of the child to a relative or suitable person under article seventeen of the surrogate's court procedure act and in accordance with section one thousand ninety-six of this article.

(e) If the child has been placed pursuant to paragraph one of subdivision (d) of this section, the court shall include the following in its order:

(1) a date certain for the permanency hearing in accordance with paragraph two of subdivision (a) of section one thousand eighty-nine of this act;

(2) a description of the plan for the child to visit with his or her parent or parents unless contrary to the child's best interests;

(3) a direction that the child be placed together with or, at minimum, to visit and have regular communication with, his or her siblings, if any, unless contrary to the best interests of the child and/or the siblings;

(4) a direction that the child's parent or parents be notified of any planning conferences to be held pursuant to subdivision three of section four hundred nine-e of the social services law, of their right to attend such conferences and to have counsel or another representative or companion with them;

(5) if the child is or will be fourteen or older by the date of the permanency hearing, the services and assistance that may be necessary to assist the child in learning independent living skills; and

(6) a notice that, if the child remains in foster care for fifteen of the most recent twenty-two months, the agency may be required by law to file a petition to terminate parental rights.

(f) If the child has been placed pursuant to paragraph one of subdivision (d) of this section, the provisions of part eight of article ten of this act shall be applicable.

(g) If the court makes an order pursuant to paragraph one of subdivision (d) of this section, the court may include a direction for the commissioner of social services to provide or arrange for services or assistance, limited to those authorized or required to be made available under the comprehensive annual services program plan then in effect, to ameliorate the conditions that formed the basis for the fact-finding under this section and, if the child has been placed in the care and custody of the commissioner of social services, to facilitate the child's permanency plan.

§1096. Custody or guardianship with relatives or suitable persons pursuant to article six of this act or article seventeen of the surrogate's court procedure act.

(a) At the conclusion of a hearing held pursuant to section one thousand ninety-five of this article, the court may enter an order of disposition granting custody or guardianship of the child to a relative or suitable person under article six of this act or guardianship of the child to a relative or suitable person under article seventeen of the surrogate's court procedure act if:

(1) the relative or suitable person has filed a petition for custody or guardianship of the child pursuant to article six of this act or guardianship of the child pursuant to article seventeen of the surrogate's court procedure act; and

(2) the court finds that granting custody or guardianship of the child to the relative or suitable person is in the best interests of the child; and

(3) the court finds that granting custody or guardianship of the child to the relative or suitable person under article six of this act or guardianship of the child to a relative or suitable person under article seventeen of the surrogate's court procedure act will provide the child with a safe and permanent home; and

(4) all parties to the destitute child proceeding consent to the granting of custody or guardianship under article six of this act or article seventeen of the surrogate's court procedure act; or

(5) after a consolidated fact finding and dispositional hearing on the destitute child petition and the petition under article six of this act or article seventeen of the surrogate's court procedure act:

(i) if a parent or parents fail to consent to the granting of custody or guardianship under article six of this act or guardianship under article seventeen of the surrogate's court procedure act, the court finds that extraordinary circumstances exist that support granting an order of custody or guardianship under article six of this act or guardianship under article seventeen of the surrogate's court procedure act; or

(ii) if the parent or parents consent and a party other than a parent fails to consent to the granting of custody or guardianship under article six of this act or guardianship under article seventeen of the surrogate's court procedure act, the court finds that granting custody or guardianship of the child to the relative or suitable person is in the best interests of the child.

(b) An order made in accordance with the provisions of this section shall set forth the required findings as described in subdivision (a) of this section and shall constitute the final disposition of the destitute child proceeding. Notwithstanding any other provision of law, the court shall not issue an order of supervision nor may the court require the local department of social services to provide services to the parent, parents, caretaker or interested adult when granting custody or guardianship pursuant to article six of this act or guardianship under article seventeen of the surrogate's court procedure act under this section.

(c) As part of the order granting custody or guardianship pursuant to article six of this act or guardianship pursuant to article seventeen of the surrogate's court procedure act, the court may require that the local department of social services and the attorney for the child receive notice of and be made parties to any subsequent proceeding to modify such order of custody or guardianship.

(d) An order entered in accordance with this section shall conclude the court's jurisdiction over the proceeding held pursuant to this article and the court shall not maintain jurisdiction over the parties for the purposes of permanency hearings held pursuant to article ten-A of this act.

ARTICLE 11
Appeals

§1111. Appeals to appellate division.

An appeal may be taken to the appellate division of the supreme court of the judicial department in which the family court whose order is appealed from is located.

§1112. Appealable orders.

a. An appeal may be taken as of right from any order of disposition and, in the discretion of the appropriate appellate division, from any other order under this act. An appeal from an intermediate or final order in a case involving abuse or neglect may be taken as of right to the appellate division of the supreme court. Pending the determination of such appeal, such order shall be stayed where the effect of such order would be to discharge the child, if the family court or the court before which such appeal is pending finds that such a stay is necessary to avoid imminent risk to the child's life or health. A preference in accordance with rule five thousand five hundred twenty-one of the civil practice law and rules shall be afforded, without the necessity of a motion, for appeals under article three; parts one and two of article six; articles seven, ten, and ten-A of this act; and sections three hundred fifty-eight-a, three hundred eighty-three-c, three hundred eighty-four, and three hundred eighty-four-b of the social services law.

b. In any proceeding pursuant to article ten of this act or in any proceeding pursuant to article ten-A of this act that originated as a proceeding under article ten of this act where the family court issues an order which will result in the return of a child previously remanded or placed by the family court in the custody of someone other than the respondent, such order shall be stayed until five p.m. of the next business day after the day on which such order is issued unless such stay is waived by all parties to the proceeding by written stipulation or upon the record in family court. Nothing herein shall be deemed to affect the discretion of a judge of the family court to stay an order returning a child to the custody of a respondent for a longer period of time than set forth in this subdivision.

§1113. Time of appeal.

An appeal under this article must be taken no later than thirty days after the service by a party or the child's attorney upon the appellant of any order from which the appeal is taken, thirty days from receipt of the order by the appellant in court or thirty-five days from the mailing of the order to the appellant by the clerk of the court, whichever is earliest.

All such orders shall contain the following statement in conspicuous print: "Pursuant to section 1113 of the family court act, an appeal must be taken within thirty days of receipt of the order by appellant in court, thirty-five days from the mailing of the order to the appellant by the clerk of the court, or thirty days after service by a party or attorney for the child upon the appellant, whichever is earliest." When service of the order is made by the court, the time to take an appeal shall not commence unless the order contains such statement and there is an official notation in the court record as to the date and the manner of service of the order.

§1114. Effect of appeal; stay.
(a) The timely filing of a notice of appeal under this article does not stay the order from which the appeal is taken.

(b) Except as provided in subdivision (d) of this section, a justice of the appellate division to which an appeal is taken may stay execution of the order from which the appeal is taken on such conditions, if any, as may be appropriate.

(c) If the order appealed from is an order of support under articles four or five, the stay may be conditioned upon the giving of sufficient surety by a written undertaking approved by such judge of the appellate division, that during the pendency of the appeal, the appellant will pay the amount specified in the order to the family court from whose order the appeal is taken. The stay may further provide that the family court (i) shall hold such payments in escrow, pending determination of the appeal or (ii) shall disburse such payments or any part of them for the support of the petitioner or other person for whose benefit the order was made.

(d) Any party to a child protective proceeding, or the attorney for the child, may apply to a justice of the appellate division for a stay of an order issued pursuant to part two of article ten of this chapter returning a child to the custody of a respondent. The party applying for the stay shall notify the attorneys for all parties and the attorney for the child of the time and place of such application. If requested by any party present, oral argument shall be had on the application, except for good cause stated upon the record. The party applying for the stay shall state in the application the errors of fact or law allegedly committed by the family court. A party applying to the court for the granting or continuation of such stay shall make every reasonable effort to obtain a complete transcript of the proceeding before the family court.

If a stay is granted, a schedule shall be set for an expedited appeal.

§1115. Notices of appeal.
An appeal as of right shall be taken by filing the original notice of appeal with the clerk of the family court in which the order was made and from which the appeal is taken.

A notice of appeal shall be served on any adverse party as provided for in subdivision one of section five thousand five hundred fifteen of the civil practice law and rules and upon the child's attorney, if any. The appellant shall file two copies of such notice, together with proof of service, with the clerk of the family court who shall forthwith transmit one copy of such notice to the clerk of the appropriate appellate division or as otherwise required by such appellate division.

§1116. **Printed case and brief not required.**

In appeals under this article, a printed case on appeal or a printed brief shall not be required.

§1117. **Costs.**

When costs and disbursements on an appeal in a proceeding instituted by a social services official are awarded to the respondent, they shall be a county charge and be paid by the county.

§1118. **Applicability of civil practice law and rules.**

The provisions of the civil practice law and rules apply where appropriate to appeals under this article, provided, however, that the fees required by section eight thousand twenty-two of the civil practice law and rules shall not be required where the attorney for the appellant or attorney for the movant, as applicable, certifies that such appellant or movant has been assigned counsel or an attorney for a child pursuant to section two hundred forty-nine, two hundred sixty-two or eleven hundred twenty of this act or section seven hundred twenty-two of the county law, or is represented by a legal aid society or a legal services program or other nonprofit organization, which has as its primary purpose the furnishing of legal services to indigent persons, or by private counsel working on behalf of or under the auspices of such society or organization. Where the attorney for the appellant or the attorney for the movant certifies in accordance with procedures established by the appropriate appellate division that the appellant or movant has been represented in family court by assigned counsel or an attorney for a child, pursuant to section two hundred forty-nine, two hundred sixty-two or eleven hundred twenty of this act or section seven hundred twenty-two of the county law, or is represented by a legal aid society or legal services program or some other nonprofit organization, which has as its primary purpose the furnishing of legal services to indigent persons, or by private counsel working on behalf or under the auspices of such society or organization, and that the appellant, who has indicated an intention to appeal, or movant, continues to be eligible for assignment of counsel and, in the case of counsel assigned to represent an adult party, continues to be indigent, the appellant or movant shall be presumed eligible for poor person relief pursuant to section eleven hundred one of the civil practice law and rules and for assignment of counsel on appeal without further motion. The appointment of counsel and granting of poor person relief by the appellate division shall continue for the purpose of filing a notice of appeal or motion for leave to appeal to the court of appeals.

§1119. **Effective date.**

This act shall take effect September first, nineteen hundred sixty-two.

§1120. **Counsel for parties and children on appeal.**

(a) Upon an appeal in a proceeding under this act, the appellate division to which such appeal is taken, or is sought to be taken, shall assign counsel to any person upon a showing that such person is one of the persons described in section two hundred sixty-two of this act and is financially unable to obtain independent counsel or upon certification by an attorney in accordance with section eleven hundred eighteen of this article. The appellate division to which such appeal is taken, or is sought to be taken, may in its discretion assign counsel to any party to the appeal. Counsel assigned under this section shall be compensated and shall receive reimbursement for expenses reasonably incurred in the same manner provided by section seven hundred twenty-two-b of the county law. The appointment of counsel by the appellate division shall continue for the purpose of filing a notice of appeal or motion for leave to appeal to the court of appeals. Counsel may be relieved of his or her representation upon application to the court to which the appeal is taken for termination of the appointment, by the court on its own motion or, in the case of a motion for leave to appeal to the court of appeals, upon application to the appellate division. Upon termination of the appointment of counsel for an indigent party the court shall promptly appoint another attorney.

(b) Whenever an attorney has been appointed by the family court pursuant to section two hundred forty-nine of this act to represent a child in a proceeding described therein, the appointment shall continue without further court order or appointment where (i) the attorney on behalf of the child files a notice of appeal, or (ii) where a party to the original proceeding files a notice of appeal. The attorney for the child may be relieved of his representation upon application to the court to which the appeal is taken for termination of the appointment. Upon approval of such application the court shall appoint another attorney for the child.

(c) An appellate court may appoint an attorney to represent a child in an appeal in a proceeding originating in the family court where an attorney was not representing the child at the time of the entry of the order appealed from or at the time of the filing of the motion for permission to appeal and when independent legal representation is not available to such child.

(d) Nothing in this section shall be deemed to relieve attorneys for children of their duties pursuant to subdivision one of sections 354.2 and seven hundred sixty of this act.

(e) An attorney appointed or continuing to represent a child under this section shall be compensated and shall receive reimbursement for expenses reasonably incurred in the same manner provided by section thirty-five of the judiciary law.

(f) In any case where an attorney is or shall be representing a child in an appellate proceeding pursuant to subdivision (b) or (c) of this section, such attorney shall be served with a copy of the notice of appeal.

§1121. Special procedures.

1. Consistent with the provisions of sections 354.2, seven hundred sixty and one thousand fifty-two-b of this act the provisions of this section shall apply to appeals taken from orders issued pursuant to articles three, seven, ten and ten-A and parts one and two of article six of this act, and pursuant to sections three hundred fifty-eight-a, three hundred eighty-three-c, three hundred eighty-four, and three hundred eighty-four-b of the social services law.

2. Upon the filing of such order, it shall be the duty of counsel to the parties and the child to promptly advise the parties in writing of the right to appeal to the appropriate appellate division of the supreme court, the time limitations involved, the manner of instituting an appeal and obtaining a transcript of the testimony and the right to apply for leave to appeal as a poor person if the party is unable to pay the cost of an appeal. It shall be the further duty of such counsel to explain to the client the procedures for instituting an appeal, the possible reasons upon which an appeal may be based and the nature and possible consequences of the appellate process.

3. It shall also be the duty of such counsel to ascertain whether the party represented by such attorney wishes to appeal and, if so, to serve and file the necessary notice of appeal and, as applicable, to apply for leave to appeal as a poor person, to file a certification of continued eligibility for appointment of counsel pursuant to section eleven hundred eighteen of this article, and to submit such other documents as may be required by the appropriate appellate division.

4. If the party has been permitted to waive the appointment of counsel appointed pursuant to section two hundred forty-nine-a or two hundred sixty-two of this act, it shall be the duty of the court to advise the party of the right to the appointment of counsel for the purpose of filing an appeal.

5. Where a party wishes to appeal, it shall also be the duty of such counsel, where appropriate, to apply for assignment of counsel for such party pursuant to applicable provisions of this act, the judiciary law and the civil practice law and rules, and to file a certification of continued eligibility for appointment of counsel and, in the case of counsel assigned to represent an adult party, continued indigency, pursuant to section one thousand one hundred eighteen of this article and to submit such other documents as may be required by the appropriate appellate division.

6. (a) Except as provided for herein, counsel for the appellant shall, no later than ten days after filing the notice of appeal, request preparation of the transcript of the proceeding appealed therefrom.

(b) Counsel assigned or appointed pursuant to article eleven of the civil practice law and rules or section eleven hundred twenty of this act shall, no later than ten days after receipt of notice of such appointment, request preparation of the transcript of the proceeding appealed from.

(c) In any case where counsel is assigned or appointed pursuant to paragraph (b) of this subdivision subsequent to the filing of the notice of appeal, such counsel shall, within ten days of such assignment or appointment, request preparation of the transcript of the proceeding appealed from.

(d) Where the appellant is seeking relief to proceed as a poor person pursuant to article eleven of the civil practice law and rules, the transcript of the proceeding appealed from shall be requested within ten days of the order determining the motion.

7. Such transcript shall be completed within thirty days from the receipt of the request of the appellant. Where such transcript is not completed within such time period, the court reporter or director of the transcription service responsible for the preparation of the transcript shall notify the administrative judge of the appropriate judicial district. Such administrative judge shall establish procedures to effectuate the timely preparation of such transcript. The appellate divisions may establish additional procedures to effectuate the timely preparation of transcripts. The appellate division shall establish procedures to ensure the expeditious filing and service of the appellant's brief, the answering brief and any reply brief, which may include scheduling orders. The appellant shall perfect the appeal within sixty days of receipt of the transcript of the proceeding appealed from or within any different time that the appellate division has by rule prescribed for perfecting such appeals under subdivision (c) of rule five thousand five hundred thirty of the civil practice law and rules or as otherwise specified by the appellate division. Such sixty day or other prescribed period may be extended by the appellate division for good cause shown upon written application to the appellate division showing merit to the appeal and a reasonable ground for an extension of time. Upon the granting of

such an extension of time the appellate division shall issue new specific deadlines by which the appellant's brief, the answering brief and any reply brief must be filed and served.

§1122. Filing of papers on appeal to the appellate division by electronic means.

Notwithstanding any other provision of law, the appellate division in each judicial department may promulgate rules authorizing a program in the use of electronic means for the taking and perfection of appeals in accordance with the provisions of section twenty-one hundred twelve of the civil practice law and rules. For purposes of this section, "electronic means" shall be as defined in subdivision (f) of rule twenty-one hundred three of the civil practice law and rules. Provided however, such rules shall not require an unrepresented party or any attorney who furnishes a certificate specified in paragraph (i) or (ii) of subdivision (c) of section two hundred fourteen of this chapter to take or perfect an appeal by electronic means. Provided further, however, before promulgating any such rules, the appellate division in each judicial department shall consult with the chief administrator of the courts and shall provide an opportunity for review and comment by all those who are or would be affected including city, state, county and women's bar associations; institutional legal service providers; not-for-profit legal service providers; attorneys assigned pursuant to article eighteen-B of the county law; unaffiliated attorneys who regularly appear in proceedings that are or have been affected by the programs that have been implemented or who may be affected by promulgation of rules concerning the use of the electronic filing program in the appellate division of any judicial department; and any other persons in whose county a program has been implemented in any of the courts therein as deemed to be appropriate by any appellate division. To the extent practicable, rules promulgated by the appellate division in each judicial department pursuant to this section shall be uniform.

ARTICLE 12
Separability

Section
1211.   Separability.

§1211. Separability.

If any provision of this act or the application thereof to any person or circumstances is held to be invalid, the remainder of the act and the application of such provision to other persons or circumstances shall not be affected thereby.

UNIFORM RULES
for the
FAMILY COURT

Part II

43-08 162nd Street
Flushing, NY 11358
www.LooseleafLaw.com   800-647-5547

UNIFORM RULES FOR N.Y.S. TRIAL COURTS

Part 205
Uniform Rules for the Family Court

§205.1 Application of Part; waiver; additional rules; definitions.

(a) Application. This Part shall be applicable to all proceedings in the Family Court.

(b) Waiver. For good cause shown, and in the interests of justice, the court in a proceeding may waive compliance with any of the rules in this Part, other than sections 205.2 and 205.3, unless prohibited from doing so by statute or by a rule of the Chief Judge.

(c) Additional rules. Local court rules, not inconsistent with law or with these rules, shall comply with Part 9 of the Rules of the Chief Judge (22 NYCRR Part 9).

(d) Statutory applicability. The provisions of this Part shall be construed consistent with the Family Court Act, the Domestic Relations Law and, where applicable, the Social Services Law. Matters not covered by these rules or the foregoing statutes are governed by the Civil Practice Law and Rules.

(e) Definitions.

(1) Chief Administrator of the Courts in this Part also includes a designee of the administrator.

(2) Unless otherwise defined in this Part, or the context otherwise requires, all terms used in this Part shall have the same meaning as they have in the Family Court Act, the Domestic Relations Law, the Social Services Law and the Civil Practice Law and Rules, as applicable.

§205.2 Terms and parts of court.

(a) Terms of court. A term of court is a four-week session of court, and there shall be 13 terms of court in a year, unless otherwise provided in the annual schedule of terms established by the Chief Administrator of the Courts, which also shall specify the dates of such terms.

(b) Parts of court. A part of court is a designated unit of the court in which specified business of the court is to be conducted by a judge or quasi-judicial officer. There shall be such parts of court, including those mandated by statute, as may be authorized from time to time by the Chief Administrator of the Courts.

§205.3 Individual assignment system; structure.

(a) General. There shall be established for all proceedings heard in the Family Court an individual assignment system which provides for the continuous supervision of each proceeding by a single judge or, where appropriate, a single support magistrate. For the purposes of this Part, the word judge shall include a support magistrate, where appropriate. Except as otherwise may be authorized by the Chief Administrator or by these rules, every proceeding shall be assigned and heard pursuant to the individual assignment system.

(b) Assignments. Proceedings shall be assigned to a judge of the court upon the filing with the court of the first document in the case. Assignments shall be made by the clerk of the court pursuant to a method of random selection authorized by the Chief Administrator. The judge thereby assigned shall be known as the "assigned judge" with respect to that matter and, except as otherwise provided in subdivision (c) of this section or by law, shall conduct all further proceedings therein.

(c) Exceptions.

(1) Where the requirements of matters already assigned to a judge are such as to limit the ability of the judge to handle additional cases, the Chief Administrator may authorize that new assignments to the judge be suspended until the judge is able to handle additional cases.

(2) The Chief Administrator may authorize the establishment in any court of special categories of proceedings for assignment to judges specially assigned to hear such proceedings. Where more than one judge is specially assigned to hear a particular category of proceeding, the assignment of such proceedings to the judges so assigned shall be at random.

(3) Matters requiring immediate disposition may be assigned to a judge designated to hear such matters when the assigned judge is not available.

(4) The Chief Administrator may authorize the transfer of any proceeding and any matter relating to a proceeding from one judge to another in accordance with the needs of the court.

(5) Assignment of cases to judges pursuant to this section shall be consistent with section 205.27 of this Part.

(6) Multiple proceedings involving members of the same family shall be assigned to be heard by a single judge to the extent feasible and appropriate, including, but not limited to, child protective, foster care placement, family offense and custody proceedings.

(7) Where a child is under the jurisdiction of the Family Court as a result of a placement in foster care pursuant to Article 10 or 10-A of the Family Court Act or section 358-a of the Social Services Law, a judicial surrender, or a petition for the termination of parental rights, approval of an extra-judicial surrender or adoption of the child, shall be assigned, wherever practicable, to the Family Court judge who last presided over the child's proceeding.

§205.4 Access to Family Court proceedings.

(a) The Family Court is open to the public. Members of the public, including the news media, shall have access to all courtrooms, lobbies, public waiting areas and other common areas of Family Court otherwise open to individuals having business before the court.

(b) The general public or any person may be excluded from a courtroom only if the judge presiding in the courtroom determines, on a case-by-case basis based upon supporting evidence, that such exclusion is warranted in that case. In exercising this inherent and statutory discretion, the judge may consider, among other factors, whether:

(1) the person is causing or is likely to cause a disruption in the proceedings;

(2) the presence of the person is objected to by one of the parties, including the attorney for the child, for a compelling reason;

(3) the orderly and sound administration of justice, including the nature of the proceeding, the privacy interests of individuals before the court, and the need for protection of the litigants, in particular, children, from harm, requires that some or all observers be excluded from the courtroom;

(4) less restrictive alternatives to exclusion are unavailable or inappropriate to the circumstances of the particular case.

Whenever the judge exercises discretion to exclude any person or the general public from a proceeding or part of a proceeding in Family Court, the judge shall make findings prior to ordering exclusion.

(c) When necessary to preserve the decorum of the proceedings, the judge shall instruct representatives of the news media and others regarding the permissible use of the courtroom and other facilities of the court, the assignment of seats to representatives of the news media on an equitable basis, and any other matters that may affect the conduct of the proceedings and the well-being and safety of the litigants therein.

(d) Audio-visual coverage of Family Court facilities and proceedings shall be governed by Parts 29 and 131 of this Title.

(e) Nothing in this section shall limit the responsibility and authority of the Chief Administrator of the Courts, or the administrative judges with the approval of the Chief Administrator of the Courts, to formulate and effectuate such reasonable rules and procedures consistent with this section as may be necessary and proper to ensure that the access by the public, including the press, to proceedings in the Family Court shall comport with the security needs of the courthouse, the safety of persons having business before the court and the proper conduct of court business.

§205.5 Privacy of Family Court records.

Subject to limitations and procedures set by statute and case law, the following shall be permitted access to the pleadings, legal papers formally filed in a proceeding, findings, decisions and orders and, subject to the provisions of CPLR 8002, transcribed minutes of any hearing held in the proceeding:

(a) the petitioner, presentment agency and adult respondent in the Family Court proceeding and their attorneys;

(b) when a child is either a party to, or the child's custody may be affected by, the proceeding:

(1) the parents or persons legally responsible for the care of that child and their attorneys;

(2) the guardian, guardian ad litem and attorney for that child;

(3) an authorized representative of the child protective agency involved in the proceeding or the probation service;

(4) an agency to which custody has been granted by an order of the Family Court and its attorney;

(5) an authorized employee or volunteer of a Court Appointed Special Advocate program appointed by the Family Court to assist in the child's case in accordance with Part 44 of the Rules of the Chief Judge.

(c) a representative of the State Commission on Judicial Conduct, upon application to the appropriate Deputy Chief Administrator, or his or her designee, containing an affirmation that the commission is inquiring into a complaint under article 2-A of the Judiciary Law, and that the inquiry is subject to the confidentiality provisions of said article;

(d) in proceedings under articles 4, 5, 6 and 8 of the Family Court Act in which temporary or final orders of protection have been issued:

(1) where a related criminal action may, but has not yet been commenced, a prosecutor upon affirmation that such records are necessary to conduct an investigation of prosecution; and

(2) where a related criminal action has been commenced, a prosecutor or defense attorney in accordance with procedures set forth in the Criminal Procedure Law provided, however, that prosecutors may request transcripts of Family Court proceedings in accordance with section 815 of the Family Court Act, and provided further that any records or information disclosed pursuant to this subdivision must be retained as confidential and may not be redisclosed except as necessary for such investigation or use in the criminal action; and

(e) another court when necessary for a pending proceeding involving one or more parties or children who are or were the parties in, or subjects of, a proceeding in the Family Court pursuant to article 4, 5, 6, 8 or 10 of the Family Court Act. Only certified copies of pleadings and orders in, as well as information regarding the status of, such Family Court proceeding may be transmitted without court order pursuant to this section. Any information or records disclosed pursuant to this subdivision may not be redisclosed except as necessary to the pending proceeding.

Where the Family Court has authorized that the address of a party or child be kept confidential in accordance with Family Court Act, section 154-b(2), any record or document disclosed pursuant to this section shall have such address redacted or otherwise safeguarded.

§205.6 Periodic reports.

Reports on forms to be furnished by the Office of Court Administration shall be filed with that office by the Family Court in each county, as follows:

(a) On or before the 20th day of each term, a report shall be filed in the Office of Court Administration for each of the following instances in which an order of disposition was entered in the preceding month:

(1) every proceeding instituted under article 10 of the Family Court Act; and

(2) every proceeding instituted under article 7 of the Family Court Act.

(b) No later than five calendar days thereafter, a separate weekly account for the preceding week ending Sunday shall be filed in the Office of Court Administration concerning:

(1) new cases;

(2) assignment of judges;

(3) appearances of counsel; and

(4) judicial activity;

unless the requirement therefor is otherwise specifically suspended, in whole or in part, by the Office of Court Administration.

(c) On or before the 20th day of the first term of each year, an inventory of the cases pending as of the first day of the first term of that year shall be filed in the Office of Court Administration, and an inventory of pending cases shall also be filed at such other times as may be specified by the Office of Court Administration.

§205.7 Papers filed in court; docket number; prefix; forms.

(a) The forms set forth in Chapter IV of Subtitle D of this Title, designated "Forms of the Family Court of the State of New York" and "Adoption Forms of the Family Court and Surrogate's Court of the State of New York," respectively, shall be the official forms of the court and shall, in substantially the same form as set forth, be uniformly used throughout the State. Examples of these forms shall be available at the clerk's office of any Family Court.

(b) The prefixes for the docket numbers assigned to Family Court proceedings shall be:

A	Adoption
As	Adoption Surrender
B	Commitment of guardianship and custody (§§ 384, 384-b, Social Services Law)
C	Conciliation
D	Delinquency (including transfers from criminal courts)
E	Designated felony delinquency (including transfers from criminal courts)
F	Support
G	Guardianship (§ 661, Family Court Act)
K	Foster care review
L	Approval of foster care placement
M	Consent to marry
N	Neglect or child abuse (child protective proceeding)
O	Family offenses
P	Paternity
R	Referred from Supreme Court (except delinquency)
S	Person in need of supervision
U	Uniform Interstate Family Support Law
V	Custody of minors (§ 651, Family Court Act)
W	Material witness
Z	Miscellaneous

(c) Proceedings for extensions of placement in Person in Need of Supervision and juvenile delinquency proceedings and for permanency hearings in child protective and voluntary foster care proceedings pursuant to Article 10-A of the Family Court Act shall bear the prefix and docket number of the original proceeding in which the placement was made. Permanency hearings pursuant to Family Court Act Article 10-A regarding children freed for adoption shall bear the prefix and docket number of the proceeding or proceedings in which the child was freed: the surrender and/or termination of parental rights proceedings. Permanency reports submitted pursuant to Article 10-A shall not be considered new petitions.

(d) The case docket number shall appear on the outside cover and first page to the right of the caption of every paper tendered for filing in the proceeding. Each such cover and first page also shall contain an indication of the county of venue and a brief description of the nature of the paper and, where the case has been assigned to an individual judge, shall contain the name of the assigned judge to the right of caption. In addition to complying with the provisions of CPLR 2101, every paper filed in court shall have annexed thereto appropriate proof of service on all parties where required, and every paper, other than an exhibit or a printed official form promulgated in accordance with section 214 of the Family Court Act, shall contain writing on one side only and, if typewritten, shall have at least double space between each line, except for quotations and the names and addresses of attorneys appearing in the action, and shall have at least one-inch margins.

§205.7-a. Electronic Transmission of Orders of Protection.

(a) Unless the party requesting an order of protection or temporary order of protection states on the record that he or she is making alternative arrangements for service or is delivering the order to the law enforcement agency directly, the Family Court may transmit the order of protection or temporary order of protection, together with any associated papers to be served simultaneously, to such agency by facsimile or other electronic means, as defined in subdivision (f) of rule 2103 of the Civil Practice Law and Rules, so that such agency may provide expedited service in accordance with subdivision (c) of section one hundred fifty-three-b of the Family Court Act and subdivision (3-a) of section 240 of the Domestic Relations Law.

(b) Proof of service must be provided to the Court pursuant to subdivision (d) of section 153-b of the Family Court Act and subdivision (3-a) of section 240 of the Domestic Relations Law. No fees may be charged by the agency for such service. Such transmission shall constitute the filing required by section one hundred sixty-eight of the Family Court Act.

§205.7-b. Pilot programs for the filing of petitions for temporary orders of protection by electronic means and the issuance of such orders by audio-visual means.

(a) The chief administrator of the courts may establish and implement a plan for one or more pilot programs for the filing of petitions ex parte for temporary orders of protection by electronic means, and for the conduct of proceedings and the issuance of such orders by audio-visual means in order to accommodate litigants for whom attendance at court to file for and obtain emergency relief would constitute an undue hardship, or to accommodate litigants for whom traveling to and appearing in the courthouse to obtain emergency relief creates a risk of harm to such litigant. In developing this plan, the chief administrator shall strive for programs that are regionally diverse, and shall take into consideration the availability of public transportation, population density, and the availability of suitable program facilities.

(b) In planning pilot programs, the chief administrator will consult with one or more local programs providing assistance to victims of domestic violence, the office for the prevention of domestic violence, and attorneys who represent family offense petitioners.

(c) The plan shall include, but not be limited to:

(i) identification of family justice centers or other organizations or appropriate sites outside of the local family court that are equipped with or have access to suitable audio-visual and electronic equipment for participation in a pilot program;

(ii) identification of licensed and certified organizations, agencies or entities with advocates for victims of domestic violence who are trained and available to assist persons filing for orders under a pilot program;

(iii) assessment of family court and other court system resources;

(iv) delineation of procedures for filing of petitions and supporting documents by electronic means, swearing in petitioners and witnesses, preparation of transcriptions of testimony and a record of evidence adduced, and prompt transmission of orders to petitioners;

(v) a timetable for implementation and public notice of pilot programs.

(vi) a description of data to be collected to evaluate and improve pilot programs.

(d) The procedures of each pilot program shall provide that:

(i) All electronic appearances by petitioners seeking temporary orders of protection ex parte by electronic appearance in a pilot program shall be voluntary, and the consent of participating petitioners will be stated on the record at the commencement of each appearance.

(ii) Petitioners seeking temporary orders of protection ex parte by electronic appearance in a pilot program must file a petition in advance of such appearance, and may do so by electronic means with the assistance of trained advocates. The petition shall set forth the circumstances in which a courthouse appearance would constitute undue hardship or create a risk of harm to the petitioner. Documentary evidence referred to by a party or witness or the court may be transmitted, submitted, and introduced by electronic means.

(iii) In granting or denying relief sought in a petition, the court shall state the names of all participants, and whether it is granting or denying an appearance by electronic means, and the basis for such determination.

(iv) Parties shall not be compelled to file a petition or document by electronic means or to testify by electronic appearance.

(v) Electronic appearances shall be recorded and preserved for transcription.

(vi) The pilot program shall not affect or change any existing laws governing the service of process (including requirements for personal service), or the sealing and confidentiality of court records in family court proceedings, or access to family court records.

(e) The chief administrator shall maintain a current and publicly-available listing of sites where petitioners may make applications and appearances under pilot programs pursuant to this section.   *(A.O.88-16,Eff.3/1/16)*

§205.8 Submission of papers to judge.

All papers for signature or consideration of the court shall be presented to the clerk of the court in the appropriate courtroom or clerk's office, except that when the clerk is unavailable or the judge so directs, papers may be submitted to the judge and a copy filed with the clerk at the first available opportunity. All papers for any judge which are filed in the clerk's office shall be promptly delivered to the judge by the clerk. The papers shall be clearly addressed to the judge for whom they are intended and prominently show the nature of the papers, the title and docket number of the proceeding in which they are filed, the judge's name and the name of the attorney or party submitting them.

§205.9 Miscellaneous proceedings.

All proceedings for which the procedure has not been prescribed by provisions of the Family Court Act, the Domestic Relations Law or the Social Services Law, including but not limited to, proceedings involving consent to marry, interstate compact on juveniles and material witnesses, shall be commenced by the filing of a petition and shall require the entry of a written order.

§205.10 Notice of appearance.

Each attorney appearing in a proceeding is required to file a written notice of appearance on or before the time of the attorney's first appearance in court or no later than 10 days after appointment or retainer, whichever is sooner. The notice shall contain the attorney's name, office address and telephone number, and the name of the person on whose behalf he or she is appearing.

§205.11 Service and filing of motion papers.

Where motions are required to be on notice:

(a) The motion shall be made returnable at such hour as the assigned judge directs.

(b) At the time of service of the notice of motion, the moving party shall serve copies of all affidavits and briefs upon all of the attorneys for the parties or upon the parties appearing pro se. The answering party shall serve copies of all affidavits and briefs as required by CPLR 2214. Affidavits shall be for a statement of the relevant facts, and briefs shall be for a statement of the relevant law. Unless otherwise directed by the court, answering and reply affidavits and all papers required to be furnished to the court by the Family Court Act or CPLR 2214(c) must be filed no later than the time of argument or submission of the motion.

(c) The assigned judge may determine that any or all motions in that proceeding shall be orally argued and may direct that moving and responding papers shall be filed with the court prior to the time of argument.

(d) Unless oral argument has been requested by a party and permitted by the court, or directed by the court, motion papers received by the clerk of the court on or before the return date shall be deemed submitted as of the return date. A party requesting oral argument shall set forth such request in its notice of motion or on the first page of the answering papers, as the case may be. A party requesting oral argument on a motion brought on by an order to show cause shall do so as soon as practicable before the time the motion is to be heard.

(e) Hearings on motions shall be held when required by statute or ordered by the assigned judge in the judge's discretion.

§205.12   Conference.

(a) In any proceeding, a conference or conferences shall be ordered by the court as required as soon as practicable after the proceeding has been assigned.

(b) The matters which may be considered at such conference may include, but are not limited to:

(1) completion of discovery;

(2) filing of motions;

(3) argument or hearing of motions;

(4) fixing a date for fact-finding and dispositional hearings;

(5) clarification and limitation of issues;

(6) amendment of pleadings or bills of particulars;

(7) admissions of fact;

(8) stipulations as to admissibility of documents;

(9) completion or modification of financial disclosure;

(10) possibilities for settlement; and

(11) identification of expert and fact witnesses.

(c) Where parties are represented by counsel, an attorney thoroughly familiar with the action and authorized to act on behalf of the party or accompanied by a person empowered to act on behalf of the party represented shall appear at such conference.

(d) At the conclusion of a conference, the court shall make a written order, including its directions to the parties as well as stipulations of counsel. Alternatively, in the court's discretion, all directions of the court and stipulations of counsel shall be formally placed on the record.

§205.13   Engagement of counsel.

No adjournment shall be granted on the ground of engagement of counsel except in accordance with Part 125 of the Rules of the Chief Administrator of the Courts (22 NYCRR Part 125).

§205.14   Time limitations for proceedings involving custody or visitation.

In any proceeding brought pursuant to sections 467, 651 or 652 of the Family Court Act to determine temporary or permanent custody or visitation, once a hearing or trial is commenced, it shall proceed to conclusion within 90 days.

§205.15   Submission of orders for signature.

Proposed orders, with proof of service on all parties, must be submitted for signature unless otherwise directed by the court within thirty days after the signing and filing of the decision directing that the order be settled or submitted. Proposed orders in child protective proceedings and permanency hearings pursuant to Articles 10 and 10-A of the Family Court Act, respectively, must be submitted for signature immediately, but in no event later than 14 days of the earlier of the Court's oral announcement of its decision or signing and filing of its decision, unless otherwise directed by the Court, provided, however, that proposed orders pursuant to section 1022 of the Family Court Act must be submitted for signature immediately, but in no event later than the next court date following the removal of the child. Orders in termination of parental rights proceedings pursuant to Article 6 of the Family Court Act or section 384-b of the Social Services Law shall be settled not more than 14 days after the earlier of the Family Court's oral announcement of its decision or signing and filing of its decision.

§205.16   Motion for judicial determination that reasonable efforts are not required for child in foster care.

(a) This section shall govern any motion for a judicial determination, pursuant to section 352.2(2)(c), 754(2)(b), 1039-b or 1052(b) of the Family Court Act or section 358-a(3)(b) of the Social Services Law, that reasonable efforts to prevent or eliminate the need for removal of the child from the home or to make it possible to reunify the child with his or her parents are not required.

(b) A motion for such a determination shall be filed in writing on notice to the parties, including the attorney for the child, on the form officially promulgated by the Chief Administrator of the Courts and set forth in Chapter IV of Subtitle D of this Title and shall contain all information required therein.

§205.17   Permanency hearings for child in foster care, children directly placed with relatives or other suitable persons and children freed for adoption.

(a) This section shall govern all permanency hearings conducted pursuant to article 10-A of the Family Court Act.

(b) Scheduling for dates certain; deadlines for submitting permanency reports.

(1) The first court order remanding a child into foster care or into direct placement with a relative or other suitable person in a proceeding pursuant to article 10 or approving a voluntary placement instrument pursuant to section 358-a of the Social Services Law must contain a date certain for the initial permanency hearing pursuant to article 10-A of the Family Court Act, which must be not later than eight months from the date of removal of the child from his or her home. If the child has a sibling or half-sibling removed from the home, whose permanency hearing is scheduled before this Court, the date certain shall be the same as the date certain for the sibling's or half-sibling's permanency hearing, unless the sibling or half-sibling was removed on a juvenile delinquency or person in need of supervision petition or unless either sibling has been freed for adoption.

(2) A permanency hearing with respect to a child who has been freed for adoption shall be scheduled for a date certain not more than 30 days after the earlier of the Family Court's oral announcement of its decision or the signing and filing of its decision freeing the child for adoption.

(3) In any case in which the court has made a determination, pursuant to section 1039-b or 1052(b) of the Family Court Act or section 358- a(3)(b) of the Social Services Law, that reasonable efforts to reunify the child with his or her parents are not required, a permanency hearing must be scheduled for a date certain within 30 days of the determination and the originally scheduled date shall be cancelled. In such a case, a permanency hearing report shall be transmitted to the parties and counsel, including the child's attorney, on an expedited basis as directed by the court.

(4) Each permanency hearing order must contain a date certain for the next permanency hearing, which shall be not more than six months following the completion of the permanency hearing, except as provided in paragraph (3) of this subdivision. Except with respect to a child freed for adoption, if the child has a sibling or half-sibling removed from the home, whose permanency hearing is scheduled before this Court, the date certain shall be the same as the date certain for the sibling's or half-sibling's permanency hearing, unless the

sibling or half-sibling was removed on a juvenile delinquency or person in need of supervision petition or unless either sibling has been freed for adoption.

(5) If the child has been adopted or has been the subject of a final order of discharge or custody or guardianship by the scheduled date certain, the permanency hearing shall be cancelled and the petitioner shall promptly so notify the court, all parties and their attorneys, including the child's attorney, as well as all individuals required to be notified of the hearing pursuant to Family Court Act, section 1089.

(c) Required notice and transmittal of permanency reports. Except in cases involving children freed for adoption, in addition to sending the permanency hearing report and accompanying papers to the respondent parents' last-known address and to their attorneys not less than 14 days in advance of the hearing date, the petitioner shall make reasonable efforts to provide actual notice of the permanency hearing to the respondent parents through any additional available means, including, but not limited to, case-work, service and visiting contacts. Additionally, not less than 14 days in advance of the hearing date, the petitioner shall send a notice of the permanency hearing and the report and accompanying documents to the non-respondent parent(s) and the foster parent or parents caring for the child, each of whom shall be a party, and to the child's attorney. Petitioner shall also send the notice and report to a pre-adoptive parent or relative providing care for the child and shall send a notice, but not the report, to former foster parents who cared for the child in excess of one year unless the court has dispensed with such notice in accordance with paragraph two of subdivision (b) of section 1089 of the Family Court Act. The court shall give such persons an opportunity to be heard, but they shall not be considered parties and their failures to appear shall not constitute cause to delay the hearing. As provided in subdivision (d) of this section, the petitioner shall submit on or before the return date documentation of the notice or notices given to the respondent and non-respondent parents, their attorneys, the child's attorney, and any present or former foster parent, pre-adoptive parent or relative.

(d) Required papers to be submitted.

(1) A sworn permanency report shall be submitted on the form officially promulgated by the Chief Administrator of the Courts and set forth in Chapter IV of Subtitle D of this Title, and shall contain all information required by section 1089 of the Family Court Act.

(2) The permanency report shall be accompanied by additional reports and documents as directed by the court, which may include, but not be limited to, periodic school report cards, photographs of the child, clinical evaluations and prior court orders in related proceedings.

(3) The copy of the report submitted to the Family Court must be sworn and must be accompanied by a list of all persons and addresses to whom the report and/or notice of the permanency hearing were sent. Except as otherwise directed by the Family Court, the list containing the addresses shall be kept confidential and shall not be part of the court record that may be subject to disclosure pursuant to section 205.5 of this Title. The copies of the permanency hearing report required to be sent to the parties and their attorneys, including the child's attorney, not less than 14 days prior to the scheduled date certain need not be sworn so long as the verification accompanying the Family Court's sworn copy attests to the fact that the copies transmitted were identical in all other respects to the court's sworn copy.

(e) In any permanency hearing under Article 10-A of the Family Court Act, the child shall be represented by an attorney and the Family Court shall consider the child's position regarding the child's permanency plan.

§205.18 to 205.19 [Reserved]

§205.20 Designation of a facility for the questioning of children in custody (juvenile delinquency).

(a) The district administrative judge in each judicial district outside the City of New York and the administrative judge for the Family Court within the City of New York, or a designee, shall arrange for the inspection of any facility within the judicial district proposed for designation as suitable for the questioning of children pursuant to section 305.2 of the Family Court Act, and if found suitable, the district administrative judge or the administrative judge for the Family Court within the City of New York, as appropriate, shall recommend its designation to the Chief Administrator of the Courts.

(b) Every recommendation to the Chief Administrator of the Courts shall include:

(1) the room number or identification, the type of facility in which the room is located, the address and the hours of access;

(2) the name of the police or other law enforcement agency, department of probation, Family Court judge or other interested person or agency which proposed the designation of the particular facility;

(3) a signed and dated copy of the report of inspection of the proposed facility, made at the direction of the district administrative judge or the administrative judge for the Family Court within the City of New York; and

(4) the factors upon which the recommendation is based.

(c) Any facility recommended for designation as suitable for the questioning of children shall be separate from areas accessible to the general public and adult detainees.

(d) Insofar as possible, the district administrative judge or the administrative judge for the Family Court within the City of New York, in making a recommendation for designation, shall seek to assure an adequate number and reasonable geographic distribution of designated questioning facilities, and that:

(1) the room is located in a police facility or in a governmental facility not regularly or exclusively used for the education or care of children;

(2) the room presents an office-like, rather than a jail-like, setting;

(3) the room is clean and well maintained;

(4) the room is well lit and heated;

(5) there are separate toilet facilities for children or, in the alternative, procedures insuring the privacy and safety of the children when in use;

(6) there is a separate entrance for children or, in the alternative, there are procedures which minimize public exposure and avoid mingling with the adult detainees;

(7) a person will be in attendance with the child whenever the room is in use as a questioning facility, such person to be a policewoman or other qualified female person when the child is a female; and

(8) any other factors relevant to suitability for designation are considered.

(e) The appropriate district administrative judge or the administrative judge for the Family Court within the City of New York, or a designee, when notified of any material physical change in a facility designated for the questioning of children, shall arrange for the reinspection of such facility concerning its continued suitability for designation.

(f) A current list of facilities designated for the questioning of children within each judicial district and within the City of New York shall be maintained by the district administrative judge and the administrative judge for the Family Court within the City of New York, and shall be kept for easy public inspection in each Family Court in that judicial district and within the City of New York. A current statewide list shall be maintained in the office of the Chief Administrator of the Courts. These lists shall be kept available for public inspection.

§205.21   Authorization to detention agency for release of a child taken into custody before the filing of a petition (juvenile delinquency).

(a) When a child is brought to a detention facility prior to the filing of a petition, pursuant to section 305.2 of the Family Court Act, the agency responsible for operating the detention facility is authorized to release the child before the filing of a petition when the events that occasioned the taking into custody do not appear to involve allegations that the child committed a delinquent act.

(b) If the events occasioning the taking into custody do appear to involve allegations that the child committed a delinquent act, the agency is authorized to release the child where practicable and issue an appearance ticket in accordance with section 307.1 of the Family Court Act, unless special circumstances exist which require the detention of the child, including whether:

(1) there is a substantial probability that the child will not appear or be produced at the appropriate probation service at a specified time and place; or

(2) there is a serious risk that, before the petition is filed, the child may commit an act which, if committed by an adult, would constitute a crime; or

(3) the alleged conduct by the child involved the use or threatened use of violence; or

(4) there is reason to believe that a proceeding to determine whether the child is a juvenile delinquent or juvenile offender is currently pending.

(c) Any child released pursuant to this rule shall be released to the custody of his or her parent or other person legally responsible for his or her care, or if such legally responsible person is unavailable, to a person with whom he or she resides.

§205.22   Preliminary probation conferences and procedures (juvenile delinquency).

(a) The probation service shall conduct preliminary conferences with any person seeking to have a juvenile delinquency petition filed, the potential respondent and other interested persons, including the complainant or victim, on the same day that such persons appear at a probation service pursuant to section 305.2(4)(a), 307.1 or 320.6 of the Family Court Act, concerning the advisability of requesting that a juvenile delinquency petition be filed and in order to gather information needed for a determination of the suitability of the case for adjustment. The probation service shall permit any participant who is represented by a lawyer to be accompanied by the lawyer at any preliminary conference.

(b) During the preliminary probation conferences, the probation service shall ascertain, from the person seeking to have a juvenile delinquency petition filed, a brief statement of the underlying events and, if known to that person, a brief statement of factors that would be of assistance to the court in determining whether the potential respondent should be detained or released in the event that a petition is filed.

(c) In order to determine whether the case is suitable for the adjustment process, the probation service shall consider the following circumstances, among others:

(1) the age of the potential respondent; and

(2) whether the conduct of the potential respondent allegedly involved:

(i) an act or acts causing or threatening to cause death, substantial pain or serious physical injury to another;

(ii) the use or knowing possession of a dangerous instrument or deadly weapon;

(iii) the use or threatened use of violence to compel a person to engage in sexual intercourse, deviant sexual intercourse or sexual contact;

(iv) the use or threatened use of violence to obtain property;

(v) the use or threatened use of deadly physical force with the intent to restrain the liberty of another;

(vi) the intentional starting of a fire or the causing of an explosion which resulted in damage to a building;

(vii) a serious risk to the welfare and safety of the community; or

(viii) an act which seriously endangered the safety of the potential respondent or another person;

(3) whether there is a substantial likelihood that a potential respondent will not appear at scheduled conferences with the probation service or with an agency to which he or she may be referred;

(4) whether there is a substantial likelihood that the potential respondent will not participate in or cooperate with the adjustment process;

(5) whether there is a substantial likelihood that, in order to adjust the case successfully, the potential respondent would require services that could not be administered effectively in less than four months;

(6) whether there is a substantial likelihood that the potential respondent will, during the adjustment process:

(i) commit an act which, if committed by an adult, would be a crime; or

(ii) engage in conduct that endangers the physical or emotional health of the potential respondent or a member of the potential respondent's family or household; or

(iii) harass or menace the complainant, victim or person seeking to have a juvenile delinquency petition filed, or a member of that person's family or household, where demonstrated by prior conduct or threats;

(7) whether there is pending another proceeding to determine whether the potential respondent is a person in need of supervision, a juvenile delinquent or a juvenile offender;

(8) whether there have been prior adjustments or adjournments in contemplation of dismissal in other juvenile delinquency proceedings;

(9) whether there has been a prior adjudication of the potential respondent as a juvenile delinquent or juvenile offender;

(10) whether there is a substantial likelihood that the adjustment process would not be successful unless the potential respondent is temporarily removed from his or her home and that such removal could not be accomplished without invoking the court process; and

(11) whether a proceeding has been or will be instituted against another person for acting jointly with the potential respondent.

(d) At the first appearance at a conference by each of the persons listed in subdivision (a) of this section, the probation service shall inform such person concerning the function and limitations of, and the alternatives to, the adjustment process, and that:

(1) he or she has the right to participate in the adjustment process;

(2) the probation service is not authorized to and cannot compel any person to appear at any conference, produce any papers or visit any place;

(3) the person seeking to have a juvenile delinquency petition filed is entitled to have access to the appropriate presentment agency at any time for the purpose of requesting that a petition be filed under article 3 of the Family Court Act;

(4) the adjustment process may continue for a period of two months and may be extended for an additional two months upon written application to the court and approval thereof;

(5) statements made to the probation service are subject to the confidentiality provisions contained in section 308.1(6) and (7) of the Family Court Act; and

(6) if the adjustment process is commenced but is not successfully concluded, the persons participating therein may be notified orally or in writing of that fact and that the case will be referred to the appropriate presentment agency; oral notification will be confirmed in writing.

(e) If the adjustment process is not commenced:

(1) the record of the probation service shall contain a statement of the grounds therefor; and

(2) the probation service shall give written notice to the persons listed in subdivision (a) of this section who have appeared that:

(i) the adjustment process will not be commenced;

(ii) the case will be referred to the appropriate presentment agency; and

(iii) they are entitled to have access to the presentment agency for the purpose of requesting that a petition be filed under article 3 of the Family Court Act.

§205.23 Duties of the probation service and procedures relating to the adjustment process (juvenile delinquency).

(a) Upon a determination by the probation service that a case is suitable for the adjustment process, it shall include in the process the potential respondent and any other persons listed in section 205.22(a) of this Part who wish to participate therein. The probation service shall permit any participant who is represented by a lawyer to be accompanied by the lawyer at any conference.

(b) If an extension of the period of the adjustment process is sought, the probation service shall apply in writing to the court and shall set forth the services rendered to the potential respondent, the date of commencement of those services, the degree of success achieved, the services proposed to be rendered and a statement by the assigned probation officer that, in the judgment of such person, the matter will not be successfully adjusted unless an extension is granted.

(c) The probation service may discontinue the adjustment process if, at any time:

(1) the potential respondent or the person seeking to have a juvenile delinquency petition filed requests that it do so; or

(2) the potential respondent refuses to cooperate with the probation service or any agency to which the potential respondent or a member of his or her family has been referred.

(d) If the adjustment process is not successfully concluded, the probation service shall notify all the persons who participated therein in writing:

(1) that the adjustment process has not been successfully concluded;

(2) that the appropriate presentment agency will be notified within 48 hours or the next court day, whichever occurs later; and

(3) that access may be had to the presentment agency to request that a petition be filed;

and, in addition to the above, shall notify the potential respondent in writing of the reasons therefor.

(e) The case record of the probation service required to be kept pursuant to section 243 of the Executive Law and the regulations promulgated thereunder shall contain a statement of the grounds upon which:

(1) the adjustment process was commenced but was not successfully concluded; or

(2) the adjustment process was commenced and successfully concluded.

§205.24 Terms and conditions of order adjourning a proceeding in contemplation of dismissal in accordance with section 315.3 of the Family Court Act.

(a) An order adjourning a proceeding in contemplation of dismissal pursuant to section 315.3 of the Family Court Act shall be related to the alleged or adjudicated acts or omissions of respondent and shall contain at least one of the following terms and conditions directing the respondent to:

(1) attend school regularly and obey all rules and regulations of the school;

(2) obey all reasonable commands of the parent or other person legally responsible for respondent's care;

(3) avoid injurious or vicious activities;

(4) abstain from associating with named individuals;

(5) abstain from visiting designated places;

(6) abstain from the use of alcoholic beverages, hallucinogenic drugs, habit-forming drugs not lawfully prescribed for the respondent's use, or any other harmful or dangerous substance;

(7) cooperate with a mental health, social services or other appropriate community facility or agency to which the respondent is referred;

(8) restore property taken from the complainant or victim, or replace property taken from the complainant or victim, the cost of said replacement not to exceed $1,500;

(9) repair any damage to, or defacement of, the property of the complainant or victim, the cost of said repair not to exceed $1,500;

(10) cooperate in accepting medical or psychiatric diagnosis and treatment, alcoholism or drug abuse treatment or counseling services and permit an agency delivering that service to furnish the court with information concerning the diagnosis, treatment or counseling;

(11) attend and complete an alcohol awareness program established pursuant to section 19.25 of the Mental Hygiene Law;

(12) abstain from disruptive behavior in the home and in the community;

(13) abstain from any act which, if done by an adult, would be an offense; and

(14) comply with such other reasonable terms and conditions as may be permitted by law and as the court shall determine to be necessary or

appropriate to ameliorate the conduct which gave rise to the filing of the petition or to prevent placement with the Commissioner of Social Services or the Office of Children and Family Services.

(b) An order adjourning a proceeding in contemplation of dismissal pursuant to section 315.3 of the Family Court Act may direct that the probation service supervise respondent's compliance with the terms and conditions of said order, and may set a time or times at which the probation service shall report to the court, orally or in writing, concerning compliance with the terms and conditions of said order.

(c) A copy of the order setting forth the terms and conditions imposed, and the duration thereof, shall be furnished to the respondent and to the parent or other person legally responsible for the respondent.

§205.25 Terms and conditions of order releasing respondent in accordance with section 320.5 of the Family Court Act.

(a) An order releasing a respondent at the initial appearance in accordance with section 320.5 of the Family Court Act may contain one or more of the following terms and conditions, directing the respondent to:

(1) attend school regularly;

(2) abstain from any act which, if done by an adult, would be an offense;

(3) observe a specified curfew, which must be reasonable in relation to the ends sought to be achieved and narrowly drawn;

(4) participate in a program duly authorized as an alternative to detention; or

(5) comply with such other reasonable terms and conditions as the court shall determine to be necessary or appropriate.

(b) A copy of the order setting forth terms and conditions imposed, and the duration thereof, shall be furnished at the time of issuance to the respondent and, if present, to the parent or other person legally responsible for the respondent.

§205.26 Procedure when remanded child absconds.

(a) When a child absconds from a facility to which he or she was duly remanded, written notice of that fact shall be given within 48 hours, by an authorized representative of the facility, to the clerk of the court from which the remand was made. The notice shall state the name of the child, the docket number of the pending proceeding in which the child was remanded, the date on which the child absconded and the efforts made to locate and secure the return of the child. Every order of remand shall include a direction embodying the requirements of this subdivision.

(b) Upon receipt of the written notice of absconding, the clerk shall cause the proceeding to be placed on the court calendar no later than the next court day for such action as the court may deem appropriate, and shall give notice of such court date to the presentment agency and appointed or privately retained counsel for the child.

§205.27 Procedure for assignment, in accordance with section 340.2(3) of the Family Court Act, of a proceeding to another judge when the appropriate judge cannot preside.

Except for proceedings transferred in accordance with section 302.3(4) of the Family Court Act, when a judge who has presided at the fact-finding hearing, or accepted an admission pursuant to section 321.3 of such act in a juvenile delinquency proceeding, cannot preside at another subsequent hearing, including the dispositional hearing, for the reasons set forth in section 340.2(3), the assignment of the proceeding to another judge of the court shall be made as authorized by the Chief Administrator of the Courts.

§205.28 Procedures for compliance with Adoption and Safe Families Act (juvenile delinquency proceeding).

(a) Pre-petition and pretrial detention; required findings. In any case in which detention is ordered by the court pursuant to section 307.4 or 320.5 of the Family Court Act, the court shall make additional, specific written findings regarding the following issues:

(1) whether the continuation of the respondent in his or her home would be contrary to his or her best interests; and

(2) where appropriate and consistent with the need for protection of the community, whether reasonable efforts were made, prior to the date of the court hearing that resulted in the detention order, to prevent or eliminate the need for removal of the respondent from his or her home, or, if the respondent had been removed from his or her home prior to the initial appearance, where appropriate and consistent with the need for protection of the community, whether reasonable efforts were made to make it possible for the respondent to safely return home.

The court may request the presentment agency and the local probation department to provide information to the court to aid in its determinations and may also consider information provided by the child's attorney.

(b) Motion for an order that reasonable efforts are not required. A motion for a judicial determination, pursuant to section 352.2(2)(c) of the Family Court Act, that reasonable efforts to prevent or eliminate the need for removal of the respondent from his or her home or to make it possible to reunify the respondent with his or her parents are not required, shall be governed by section 205.16 of this Part.

(c) Placement; required findings. In any case in which the court is considering ordering placement pursuant to section 353.3 or 353.4 of the Family Court Act, the presentment agency, local probation department, local commissioner of social services and New York State Office of Children and Family Services shall provide information to the court to aid in its required determination of the following issues:

(1) whether continuation in the respondent's home would be contrary to the best interests of the respondent, and, in the case of a respondent for whom the court has determined that continuation in his or her home would not be contrary to the best interests of the respondent, whether continuation in the respondent's home would be contrary to the need for protection of the community;

(2) whether, where appropriate and where consistent with the need for protection of the community, reasonable efforts were made, prior to the date of the dispositional hearing, to prevent or eliminate the need for removal of the respondent from his or her home, and, if the respondent was removed from his or her home prior to the dispositional hearing, where appropriate and where consistent with the need for protection of the community, whether reasonable efforts were made to make it possible for the respondent to return home safely. If the court determines that reasonable efforts to prevent or eliminate the need for removal of the respondent from the home were not made, but that the lack of such efforts was appropriate under the circumstances, or consistent with the

need for protection of the community, or both, the court order shall include such a finding;

(3) in the case of a respondent who has attained the age of 16, the services needed, if any, to assist the respondent to make the transition from foster care to independent living; and

(4) in the case of an order of placement specifying a particular authorized agency or foster care provider, the position of the New York State Office of Children and Family Services or local department of social services, as applicable, regarding such placement.

(d) Permanency hearing; extension of placement.

(1) A petition for a permanency hearing and, if applicable, an extension of placement, pursuant to sections 355.3 and 355.5 of the Family Court Act, shall be filed at least 60 days prior to the expiration of one year following the respondent's entry into foster care; provided, however, that if the Family Court makes a determination, pursuant to section 352.2(2)(c) of the Family Court Act, that reasonable efforts are not required to prevent or eliminate the need for removal of the respondent from his or her home or to make it possible to reunify the respondent with his or her parents, the permanency hearing shall be held within 30 days of such finding and the petition for the permanency hearing shall be filed and served on an expedited basis as directed by the court.

(2) Following the initial permanency hearing in a case in which the respondent remains in placement, a petition for a subsequent permanency hearing and, if applicable, extension of placement, shall be filed at least 60 days prior to the expiration of one year following the date of the preceding permanency hearing.

(3) The permanency petition shall include, but not be limited to, the following: the date by which the permanency hearing must be held; the date by which any subsequent permanency petition must be filed; the proposed permanency goal for the child; the reasonable efforts, if any, undertaken to achieve the child's return to his or her parents or other permanency goal; the visitation plan for the child and his or her sibling or siblings and, if parental rights have not been terminated, for his or her parent or parents; and current information regarding the status of services ordered by the court to be provided, as well as other services that have been provided, to the child and his or her parent or parents.

(4) In all cases, the permanency petition shall be accompanied by the most recent service plan containing, at minimum: the child's permanency goal and projected time-frame for its achievement; the reasonable efforts that have been undertaken and are planned to achieve the goal; impediments, if any, that have been encountered in achieving the goal; and the services required to achieve the goal. Additionally, the permanency petition shall contain or have annexed to it a plan for the release or conditional release of the child, as required by section 353.3(7) of the Family Court Act.

§205.29   Transfers of proceedings for disposition; required documents.

Whenever the court makes an order pursuant to section 302.3 of the Family Court Act transferring a juvenile delinquency proceeding for disposition to the Family Court in the county where the respondent resides, the clerk of the sending court shall immediately transmit by electronic means all available records concerning the case, including, but not limited to, the petition, order of fact-finding, any reports regarding the respondent contained in the court file, the transcript of the plea allocution by the respondent, the court activity reports and any other orders made by the sending court. Any documents or orders not immediately available for such transmission shall be expeditiously prepared and forwarded by the sending court no later than forty-eight (48) hours from the date of the order of transfer.

§205.30   Preliminary probation conferences and procedures (support).

(a) Any person except a commissioner of social services, a social services official or a person who is receiving paternity and support services pursuant to section 111-g of the Social Services Law, seeking to file a petition for support under article 4 of the Family Court Act, may first be referred to the probation service concerning the advisability of filing a petition.

(b) The probation service shall be available to meet and confer concerning the advisability of filing a petition with the person seeking to file a petition for support, the potential respondent and any other interested person no later than the next regularly scheduled court day. The probation service shall permit any participant who is represented by a lawyer to be accompanied at any preliminary conference by the lawyer, who shall be identified by the probation officer to the other party, and shall not discourage any person from seeking to file a petition.

(c) At the first appearance at a conference by each of the persons listed in subdivision (b) of this section, the probation service shall inform such person concerning the function and limitations of, and the alternative to, the adjustment process, and that:

(1) the purpose of the adjustment process is to discover whether it will be possible to arrive at a voluntary agreement for support without filing a petition;

(2) the person seeking to file a petition for support is entitled to request that the probation service confer with him or her, the potential respondent and any other interested person concerning the advisability of filing a petition for support under article 4 of the Family Court Act;

(3) if the assistance of the probation service is not requested or, if requested, is subsequently declined, the person seeking to file a petition for support is entitled to have access to the court at any time for that purpose and may proceed to file a petition for support;

(4) the probation service is not authorized to, and shall not, compel any person, including the person seeking support, to appear at any conference, produce any papers or visit any place;

(5) the adjustment process must commence within 15 days from the date of the request for a conference, may continue for a period of two months from the date of that request, and may be extended for an additional 60 days upon written application to the court containing the consent of the person seeking to file a petition;

(6) if the adjustment process is not successful, the persons participating therein shall be notified in writing of that fact and that the person seeking to file a petition for support is entitled to access to the court for that purpose; and

(7) if the adjustment of the matter results in a voluntary agreement for support of the petitioner and any dependents:

(i) it shall be reduced to writing by the probation service, signed by both parties to it, and submitted to the Family Court for approval;

(ii) if the court approves it, the court may, without further hearing, enter an order for support pursuant to section 425 of the Family Court Act in accordance with the agreement;

(iii) the order when entered shall be binding upon the parties and shall in all respects be a valid order, and the Family Court may entertain a proceeding for enforcement of the order should there not be compliance with the order; and

(iv) unless the agreement is submitted to the Family Court and an order is issued, the Family Court will not entertain a proceeding for the enforcement of the agreement should the agreement not be complied with.

(d) If the adjustment process is not commenced, the probation service shall give written notice to the persons listed in subdivision (b) of this section that:

(1) the adjustment process will not be commenced, and the reasons therefor;

(2) the person seeking to file a petition for support is entitled to access to the court for that purpose; and

(3) if applicable, the adjustment process was not commenced on the ground that the court would not have jurisdiction over the case, and the question of the court's jurisdiction may be tested by filing a petition.

§205.31   Duties of the probation service and procedures relating to the adjustment process (support).

(a) If the assistance of the probation service is requested by the person seeking to file a petition for support, and it appears that it may be possible to arrive at a voluntary agreement for support, the adjustment process shall commence within 15 days from the date of request, and shall include the person seeking to file a petition for support, the potential respondent and any other person listed in subdivision (b) of section 205.30 of this Part who wishes to participate therein. The probation service shall permit any participant who is represented by a lawyer to be accompanied at any conference by the lawyer, who shall be identified by the probation officer to the other party, and shall not discourage any person from seeking to file a petition.

(b) If an extension of the period of the adjustment process is sought, the probation service shall apply in writing to the court and shall set forth the services rendered, the date of commencement of those services, the degree of success achieved and the services proposed to be rendered. The application shall set forth the reasons why, in the opinion of the assigned probation officer, additional time is needed to adjust the matter, and shall contain the signed consent of the person seeking to file a petition for support.

(c) The probation service shall discontinue its efforts at adjustment if, at any time:

(1) the person seeking to file a petition for support or the potential respondent requests that it do so; or

(2) it appears to the probation service that there is no reasonable likelihood that a voluntary agreement for support will result.

(d) If the adjustment process is not successfully concluded, the probation service shall notify all the persons who participated therein, in writing:

(1) that the adjustment process has not been successfully concluded and the reasons therefor; and

(2) that the person seeking to file a petition for support is entitled to access to the court for that purpose.

(e) If the adjustment process results in an agreement for the support of the petitioner and any dependents:

(1) it shall be reduced to writing by the probation service, shall be signed by both parties to it, and shall be submitted to the court, together with a petition for approval of the agreement and a proposed order incorporating the agreement; and

(2) if the agreement is approved by the court, a copy of the order shall be furnished by the probation service to the person seeking to file a petition for support and the potential respondent, in person if they are present, and by mail if their presence has been dispensed with by the court.

§205.32 Support magistrates.

(a) Qualifications. Support magistrates shall be appointed by the Chief Administrator of the Courts to hear and determine support proceedings in Family Court pursuant to section 439 of the Family Court Act. They shall be attorneys admitted to the practice of law in New York for at least five years and shall be knowledgeable with respect to Family Court procedure, family law and Federal and State support law and programs.

(b) Term.

(1) Support magistrates shall be appointed as nonjudicial employees of the Unified Court System on a full-time basis for a term of three years and, in the discretion of the Chief Administrator, may be reappointed for subsequent terms, provided that if the Chief Administrator determines that the employment of a full-time support magistrate is not required in a particular court, the services of a full-time support magistrate may be shared by one or more counties or a support magistrate may be appointed to serve within one or more counties on a part-time basis.

(2) In the discretion of the Chief Administrator, an acting support magistrate may be appointed to serve during a support magistrate's authorized leave of absence. In making such appointment, the provisions for selection of support magistrates set forth in subdivision (c) of this section may be modified by the Chief Administrator as appropriate to the particular circumstances.

(3) A support magistrate shall be subject to removal or other disciplinary action pursuant to the procedure set forth in section 25.29(b) of the Rules of the Chief Judge (22 NYCRR 25.29[b]).

(c) Selection of support magistrates.

(1) The district administrative judge for the judicial district in which the county or counties where the support magistrate is authorized to serve is located, or the administrative judge for the courts in Nassau County or the administrative judge for the courts in Suffolk County, if the support magistrate is authorized to serve in either of those counties, or the administrative judge for the Family Court within the City of New York, if the support magistrate is to serve in New York City, shall:

(i) publish an announcement inviting applications from the bar in any of the following media: the law journal serving the affected county or counties, a newspaper of general circulation, or the Unified Court System's website; and

(ii) communicate directly with bar associations in the affected county or counties to invite applicants to apply.

(2) The announcements and communications shall set forth the qualifications for selection as contained in subdivision (a) of this section, the compensation, the term of appointment and requirements concerning restrictions on the private practice of law.

(3) A committee consisting of an administrative judge, a judge of the Family Court and a designee of the Chief Administrator shall screen each applicant for qualifications, character and ability to handle the support magistrate responsibilities, and shall forward the names of recommended nominees, with a summary of their qualifications, to the Chief Administrator, who shall make the appointment. The appointment order shall indicate the court or courts in

which the support magistrate shall serve. The Chief Administrator further may authorize temporary assignments to additional courts.

(d) Training. The Chief Administrator shall authorize such training for support magistrates as appropriate to ensure the effective performance of their duties.

(e) Compensation and expenses. Compensation for support magistrates shall be fixed by the Chief Administrator. Support magistrates shall be entitled to reimbursement of actual and necessary travel expenses in accordance with the rules governing the reimbursement of the travel expenses of nonjudicial court employees of the State of New York.

§205.33   Assignment of support magistrates.

The supervising judge of the Family Court in the county in which the support magistrate will serve, or the deputy administrative judge for the Family Court within the City of New York, if the support magistrate is to serve in New York City, shall assign support magistrates as required by the needs of the courts, in conformance with law and in conformance with section 205.3 of this Part.

§205.34   Referrals to support magistrates.

(a) A summons or warrant in support proceedings shall be made returnable by the clerk of the court before a support magistrate in the first instance, unless otherwise provided by the court. A net worth statement form prescribed by the Chief Administrator shall be appended by the clerk to the summons to be served upon the respondent and shall be given to the petitioner upon the filing of the petition.

(b) Whenever the parties are before a judge of the court when support is an issue, the judge shall make an immediate order, either temporary or permanent, with respect to support. If a temporary order is made, the court shall refer the issues of support to a support magistrate.

(c) The above provisions shall apply to initial determinations of support, subsequent modification or violation proceedings, and support proceedings referred to Family Court by the Supreme Court pursuant to part 6 of article 4 of the Family Court Act.

§205.35   Conduct of hearing.

(a) Unless otherwise specified in the order of reference, the support magistrate shall conduct the hearing in the same manner as a court trying an issue without a jury in conformance with the procedures set forth in the Civil Practice Law and Rules and with section 205.3 of this Part.

(b) If a full or partial agreement is reached between the parties during the hearing, it shall be placed on the record and, if approved, shall be incorporated into an order, which shall be duly entered.

(c) The support magistrate shall require the exchange and filing of affidavits of financial disclosure.

§205.36   Findings of fact; transmission of findings of fact and other information; quarterly reports.

(a) Findings of fact shall be in writing and shall include, where applicable, the income and expenses of each party, the basis for liability for support and an assessment of the needs of the children. The findings of fact shall be set forth on a form prescribed by the Chief Administrator. A copy of the findings of fact shall accompany the order of support.

(b) At the time of the entry of the order of support, the clerk of the court shall cause a copy of the findings of fact and order of support to be served either in person or by mail upon the parties to the proceeding or their attorneys. When the findings and order are transmitted to a party appearing pro se, they shall be accompanied by information about the objection process, including the requirements for a transcript, the time limitations governing the filing of objections and rebuttals, and the necessity for affidavits of service on the opposing party of all papers filed with the court.

(c) Each support magistrate shall file with the Chief Administrator, in such form as may be required, a quarterly report indicating the matters that have been pending undecided before such support magistrate for a period of 30 days after final submission, and the reasons therefor.

§205.37   Recording of hearings; objections.

(a) Hearings may be recorded mechanically. Any equipment used for such mechanical recording or for the production of such recording shall have the prior approval of the Chief Administrator of the Courts.

(b) Mechanical recordings shall be appropriately and clearly identified with the name of the case, docket number and date of hearing for storage and retrieval with proper precautions taken for security and preservation of confidentiality. Where hearings are recorded mechanically, the clerk of the court shall provide a means for the making of a duplicate recording or for an alternative method for preparation of a transcript where required by a judge reviewing objections to an order of a support magistrate or when requested by a party.

(c) A transcript of the proceeding before the support magistrate shall be prepared where required by the judge to whom objections have been submitted for review, in which event costs of duplication and of transcript preparation shall be borne by the objecting party. Either party may request a duplicate recording or transcript, in which event costs of duplication of the recording or preparation of the transcript shall be borne by the requesting party. A transcript shall bear the certification of the transcriber that the transcript is a true and accurate transcription of the proceeding. A party who is financially unable to pay the cost of the duplicate recording or the preparation of a transcript may seek leave of the court to proceed as a poor person pursuant to article 11 of the Civil Practice Law and Rules.

(d) Objections to the order of the support magistrate and rebuttals thereto shall be accompanied by an affidavit of service on the opposing party.

§205.38   Record and report of unexecuted warrants issued pursuant to section 428 of the Family Court Act.

(a) The clerk of court for the Family Court in each county shall obtain and keep a record of executed warrants issued pursuant to section 428 of the Family Court Act.

(b) At the end of each six-month period, on the first of January and on the first of July in each year, a report concerning all unexecuted warrants issued pursuant to section 428 of the Family Court Act shall be made and filed with the Office of Court Administration, on a form to be supplied by the Office of Court Administration.

§205.39   Authority of probation when there is a failure to obey a lawful order of the court (support).

(a) The probation service, at the request of the petitioner, is authorized to confer with the respondent and the petitioner whenever any respondent fails to obey a lawful order of the court made under article 4 of the Family Court Act or an order of support made under article 5 of the Family Court Act concerning the existence of the violation, the reason for it and the likelihood that there will be compliance in the future. The probation service shall permit any participant who is represented by a lawyer to be accompanied at any conference by the lawyer, who shall be identified by the probation officer to the other party, and shall not discourage any person from seeking to file a petition to enforce compliance.

(b) Before holding any conference pursuant to subdivision (a) of this section:

(1) the probation service shall notify the respondent in writing that:

(i) the probation service is willing to confer with the respondent and must hear from the respondent within seven days if a conference is to be held; and

(ii) the petitioner is entitled to petition the court to enforce compliance with the order;

(2) a copy of this notice shall be furnished to the petitioner; and

(3) if the respondent does not communicate with the probation service within seven days, the probation service shall advise the petitioner that he or she may petition the court to enforce compliance with the order.

(c) If, at a conference held pursuant to subdivision (a) of this section, it shall appear to the probation service that the failure to comply with the order was not willful and that there is a substantial likelihood that compliance with the order will result, the probation service is authorized to adjust the matter informally. An existing order may not be modified by informal adjustment without the filing of a petition for such modification and the approval of the court thereof. Efforts at adjustment pursuant to this subdivision shall not extend beyond the conference held pursuant to subdivision (a) of this section.

(d) The probation service is not authorized to, and shall not, discuss with the petitioner or the respondent:

(1) the advisability or likely outcome of filing a petition to enforce compliance with the order; or

(2) the amount of arrears that would be awarded or cancelled by the court if a petition to enforce the order were filed.

§205.40   Preliminary probation conferences and procedures upon a referral from Supreme Court (support).

(a) When an application is referred to the Family Court by the Supreme Court pursuant to part 6 of article 4 of the Family Court Act, the parties may first be referred to the probation service, which shall inform them at the first conference concerning the function and limitations of and the alternatives to the adjustment process in accordance with section 205.30(c) of this Part.

(b) The probation service, at the request of either party to the proceeding, shall be available to meet with the parties and other interested persons no later than the next regularly scheduled court day concerning the willingness of the parties to resolve those issues by voluntary agreement. The probation service shall permit any participant who is represented by a lawyer to be accompanied at any preliminary conference by the lawyer, who shall be identified by the probation officer to the other party, and shall not discourage any person from seeking to file a petition.

§205.41 Duties of the probation service and procedures relating to the adjustment process upon referral from Supreme Court (support).

(a) If the assistance of the probation service is requested by either party to the proceeding, efforts at adjustment shall commence within 15 days from the date of the request and may continue for a period of two months from the date of request. The court may extend the adjustment process for an additional 60 days upon written application containing the consent of the person seeking to file a petition.

(b) The probation service shall permit any participant who is represented by a lawyer to be accompanied at any conference by the lawyer, who shall be identified by the probation officer to the other party.

(c) If an extension of the period of the adjustment process is sought, the probation service shall apply in writing to the court and shall set forth the services rendered, the date of commencement of those services, the degree of success achieved and the services proposed to be rendered. The application shall set forth the reasons why, in the opinion of the assigned probation officer, additional time is needed to adjust the matter, and shall contain the signed consent of the parties and a statement by the probation officer that there is a substantial likelihood that a voluntary agreement would be reached if an extension were granted.

(d) The probation service shall discontinue the adjustment process if, at any time:

(1) either party requests that it do so; or

(2) it appears to the probation service that there is no substantial likelihood that a voluntary agreement will result.

(e) If the adjustment process is not successfully concluded, the probation service shall notify the persons who participated therein in writing:

(1) that the adjustment process has not been successfully concluded, and the reasons therefor;

(2) that either party is entitled to access to the court to have the issues which have been referred determined at a fact-finding hearing.

(f) If the adjustment process results in a voluntary agreement on the issues referred:

(1) it shall be reduced to writing by the probation service, shall be signed by both parties to it, and shall be submitted to the court, together with a petition for approval of the agreement and a proposed order incorporating the agreement;

(2) if the agreement is approved by the court, a copy of the order made by the court shall be furnished by the probation service to the parties, in person if they are present, and by mail if their presence has been dispensed with by the court.

§205.42 Submission by support collection units of proposed adjusted orders of support.

(a) A submission by a support collection unit pursuant to section 413 of the Family Court Act for adjustment of a child support order shall include the following, which shall be submitted on forms promulgated by the Chief Administrator of the Courts:

(1) an affidavit from the support collection unit, with findings in support of adjustment;

(2) a proposed adjusted order of support; and

(3) a notice to the parties of the proposed adjusted order and of the rights of the parties, including the addresses of the court and the support collection unit. The documents set forth in this subdivision shall be filed with the clerk of the court within 10 days of mailing to the parties, together with an affidavit of service of these documents upon the parties.

(b) Where a written objection is received by the clerk of the court within 35 days of mailing to the parties of the documents set forth in subdivision (a) of this section, the court shall schedule a hearing upon notice to the support collection unit and the parties.

(c) Where no timely objection is received by the court, the court shall sign the order upon the court's being satisfied that the requirements of sections 111-h of the Social Services Law and 413 of the Family Court Act have been met, and shall transmit copies of the order to the support collection unit for service on the parties. Absent unusual circumstances, the court shall sign the order or dismiss the application within 10 business days after the conclusion of the 35-day objection period.

§205.43   Hearings to determine willful nonpayment of child support.

(a) A petition that alleges a willful violation or seeks enforcement of an order of support shall be scheduled as soon as possible for a first appearance date in Family Court but in no event more than 30 days of the filing of the violation or enforcement petition.

(b) After service is made, the judge or support magistrate must commence a hearing to determine a willful violation within 30 days of the date noticed in the summons. The hearing must be concluded within 60 days of its commencement.

(c) Neither party shall be permitted more than one adjournment to secure counsel, except for good cause shown.

(d) On the scheduled hearing date on the issue of willfulness, the hearing may not be adjourned except for the following reasons:

(1) actual engagement of counsel pursuant to Part 125 of this Title;

(2) illness of a party; or

(3) other good cause shown.

No adjournment shall be in excess of 14 days.

(e) If a willfulness hearing has commenced and must be continued, the adjourned date shall be within seven court days.

(f) Upon the conclusion of a willfulness hearing in a case heard by a support magistrate, the support magistrate shall issue written findings of fact within five court days.

(g) In a case heard by a support magistrate, if the support magistrate makes a finding of willfulness, the written findings shall include the following:

(1) the specific facts upon which the finding of willfulness is based;

(2) the specific amount of arrears established and a money judgment for such amount. An award of attorney's fees may be issued with the findings or at a later date after the case is heard by the Family Court judge;

(3) a recommendation regarding the sanctions that should be imposed, including a recommendation whether the sanction of incarceration is recommended; and

(4) a recommendation, as appropriate, regarding a specific dollar amount to be paid or a specific plan to repay the arrears.

(h) In a case heard by a support magistrate, if counsel is assigned, the assignment shall continue through the confirmation proceeding before the Family Court judge without further order of the court.

(i) In a case heard by a support magistrate, a Family Court judge may confirm the findings of the support magistrate by adopting his or her findings and recommendations in whole or in part. Alternatively, the Family Court judge may modify or refuse to confirm the findings and recommendations and may refer the matter back to the support magistrate for further proceedings. The court may, if necessary, conduct an evidentiary hearing.

§205.44   Testimony by telephone, audio-visual or other electronic means in child support and paternity cases.

(a) This section shall govern applications for testimony to be taken by telephone, audio-visual means or other electronic means in accordance with sections 433, 531-a and 580-316 of the Family Court Act.

(b) A party or witness seeking to testify by telephone, audio-visual means or other electronic means must complete an application on the form officially promulgated by the Chief Administrator of the Courts and set forth in Chapter IV of Subtitle D of this Title and, except for good cause shown, must file such application with the court not less than three days in advance of the hearing date. The applicant shall attempt to arrange to provide such testimony at a designated tribunal or the child support enforcement agency, as defined in the Federal Social Security Act (42 U.S.C. title IV-D) in that party's state, or county if within the State. The court may permit the testimony to be taken at any suitable location acceptable to the court, including but not limited to, the party's or witness' counsel's office, personal residence or place of business.

(c) The applicant must provide all financial documentation ordered to be disclosed by the court pursuant to section 424 or 580-316 of the Family Court Act, as applicable, before he or she will be permitted to testify by telephone, audio-visual means or other electronic means. The financial documentation may be provided by personal delivery, mailing, fascimile, telecopier or any other electronic means that is acceptable to the court.

(d) The court shall transmit a copy of its decision by mail, fascimile, telecopier, or electronic means to the applicant and the parties. The court shall state its reasons in writing for denying any request to appear by telephone, audio-visual means or other electronic means.

§205.45 to 205.47 [Reserved]

§205.48   Judicial and extra-judicial surrenders; required papers and putative father determination.

(a) In addition to the judicial or extra-judicial surrender instrument and, if applicable, the post-adoption contact agreement and petition for approval of an extra-judicial surrender, the petitioner shall submit a copy of the child's birth certificate and the adoption information registry birth parent registration consent form as required by sections 383-c and 384 of the Social Services Law and subdivision 10 of section 4138-c of the Public Health Law.

(b) Where the surrender is by the birth mother:

(1) The petitioner shall also submit:

(i) the response from the putative father registry that is current within 60 days prior to the filing of the surrender proceeding;

(ii) a sworn written statement, if any, by the mother naming the father; and

(iii) a sworn written statement by the caseworker setting forth information regarding any putative father whose consent to adopt is required by section 111 of the Domestic Relations Law or who is entitled to notice of an adoption pursuant to section 111-a of the Domestic Relations Law.

(2) Where a determination has not yet been made by the court regarding any putative father whose consent to adopt is required or who is entitled to notice of an adoption, the proceeding shall be referred to the Family Court judge on the date of filing or the next court date for a determination regarding who must be notified of the surrender proceeding, Except for good cause shown or unless the putative father has previously defaulted in a termination of parental rights proceeding regarding the child, the surrender proceeding shall not be scheduled for execution of a judicial surrender or approval of an extrajudicial surrender, as applicable, until a determination regarding required notices and consents have been made by the Court.

§205.49   Termination of parental rights; required papers; venue; putative father determination.

(a) This section shall apply to petitions filed pursuant to Part 1 of Article Six of the Family Court Act and section 384-b of the Social Services Law.

(b) The petitioner shall submit a copy of the child's birth certificate with the petition.

(c) Where the petition is filed to terminate the birth mother's rights:

(1) The petitioner shall also submit:

(i) the response from the putative father registry that is current within 60 days prior to the filing of the termination of parental rights proceeding;

(ii) a sworn written statement, if any, by the mother naming the father; and

(iii) a sworn written statement by the caseworker setting forth information regarding any putative father who is entitled to notice of the proceeding pursuant to section 384-c of the social services law.

(2) Where a determination has not yet been made by the court regarding any putative father who is entitled to notice of the proceeding pursuant to section 384-c of the social services law, the petition shall be referred to the Family Court judge on the date of filing or the next court date for a determination regarding who must be notified of the proceeding, Except for good cause shown, the petition shall not be scheduled for a fact-finding hearing until a determination regarding required notices has been made by the court.

(d) Where a child is under the jurisdiction of the Family Court as a result of a placement in foster care pursuant to Article 10 or 10-A of the Family Court Act or section 358-a of the social services law, the petition regarding termination of parental rights to the child shall be assigned , wherever practicable, to the Family Court judge who last presided over the child's child protective, foster care placement or permanency proceeding or over a termination of parental rights proceeding involving the child's other parent. Where the petition has been filed regarding such a child either before a different judge in a different court or before a court in a different county, the petitioner shall so indicate in the petition and the petitioner's attorney shall file an affirmation on a uniform form promulgated by the Chief Administrator of the Courts attesting to the reasons for, and circumstances regarding, such filing. The court in which the petition has been filed shall stay the proceeding for not more than 30 days in order to communicate with the Family Court judge who presided over the child's most recent child protective, foster care placement or permanency hearing or the termination of parental rights or surrender for adoption proceeding involving the child's other parent, and in order to afford the parties and child's attorney in the respective proceedings an opportunity to be heard orally, in person or by telephone, or in writing.

Pursuant to paragraph (c-1) of subdivision three of section 384-b of the Social Services Law, the Family Court judge who presided over the child's case shall determine whether the termination of parental rights petition should be transferred or should be heard in the court in which it has been filed and shall record that determination on a uniform form promulgated by the Chief Administrator of the Courts. This determination shall be incorporated by the court in which the termination of parental rights petition has been filed into an order on a uniform form promulgated by the Chief Administrator of the Courts either retaining or transferring the petition. If the termination of parental rights petition is to be transferred, the transfer must take place forthwith, but in no event more than 35 days after the filing of the petition.

§205.50 Terms and conditions of order suspending judgment in accordance with section 633 of the Family Court Act or section 384-b(8)(c) of the Social Services Law.

(a) An order suspending judgment entered pursuant to section 631 of the Family Court Act or section 384-b(8)(c) of the Social Services Law shall be related to the adjudicated acts or omissions of respondent and shall contain at least one of the following terms and conditions requiring respondent to:

(1) sustain communication of a substantial nature with the child by letter or telephone at stated intervals;

(2) maintain consistent contact with the child, including visits or outings at stated intervals;

(3) participate with the authorized agency in developing and effectuating a plan for the future of the child;

(4) cooperate with the authorized agency's court-approved plan for encouraging and strengthening the parental relationship;

(5) contribute toward the cost of maintaining the child if possessed of sufficient means or able to earn such means;

(6) seek to obtain and provide proper housing for the child;

(7) cooperate in seeking to obtain and in accepting medical or psychiatric diagnosis or treatment, alcoholism or drug abuse treatment, employment or family counseling or child guidance, and permit information to be obtained by the court from any person or agency from whom the respondent is receiving or was directed to receive such services; and

(8) satisfy such other reasonable terms and conditions as the court shall determine to be necessary or appropriate to ameliorate the acts or omissions which gave rise to the filing of the petition.

(b) The order shall set forth the duration, terms and conditions of the suspended judgment and shall contain a date certain for review of respondent's compliance not less than 30 days in advance of the expiration of the suspended judgment. The suspended judgment may last for up to one year and may, if exceptional circumstances warrant, be extended by the Court for one additional period of up to one year. A copy of the order, along with a current service plan, shall be furnished to the respondent. The order shall contain a written statement informing the respondent that a failure to obey the order may lead to its revocation and to the issuance of an order for the commitment of the guardianship and custody of a child. Where the child is in foster care, the order shall set forth the visitation plan for the child and the respondent, as well as for the child and his or her sibling or siblings, if any, and shall require the agency to notify the respondent of case conferences. The order shall further contain a determination in accordance with subdivision 12 of section 384-b of the Social Services Law of the existence of any person or persons to whom notice of an adoption would be required pursuant to section 111-b of the Domestic Relations Law and, if so, whether such person or persons were given notice of the termination of parental rights proceeding and whether such person or persons appeared.

(c) Not later than 60 days in advance of the expiration of the period of suspended judgment, the petitioner shall file a report with the Family Court and all parties, including the respondent and his or her attorney, the child's attorney and intervenors, if any, regarding the respondent's compliance with the terms and conditions of the suspended judgment. The court may set additional times at which the respondent or the authorized agency caring for the child shall report to the court regarding compliance with the terms and conditions of the suspended judgment.

(d) If a respondent fails to comply with the terms and conditions of an order suspending judgment made pursuant to section 631 of the Family Court Act or section 384-b(8)(c) of the Social Services Law:

(1) a motion or order to show cause seeking the revocation of the order may be filed;

(2) the affidavit accompanying the motion or order to show cause shall contain a concise statement of the acts or omissions alleged to constitute noncompliance with the order;

(3) the motion or order to show cause shall be served upon the respondent by mail at the last known address or as directed by the court and shall be served upon all attorneys, the child's attorney and intervenors, if any;

(4) during the pendency of the motion or order to show cause, the period of the suspended judgment is tolled; and

(5) if, after a hearing or upon the respondent's admission, the court is satisfied that the allegations of the motion or order to show cause have been established and upon a determination of the child's best interests, the court may modify, revise or revoke the order of suspended judgment or if exceptional circumstances warrant and the suspended judgment has not already been extended, the court may extend the suspended judgment for an additional period of up to one year.

(e) The court may at any time, upon notice and opportunity to be heard to the parties, their attorneys and the child's attorney, revise, modify or enlarge the terms and conditions of a suspended judgment previously imposed.

(f) If the child remains in foster care during the pendency of a suspended judgment or after a suspended judgment has been deemed satisfied or if guardianship and custody have been transferred to the agency as a result of a revocation of the suspended judgment, a permanency hearing must be scheduled for a date certain and must be completed immediately following or not more than 60 days after the earlier of the Family Court's oral announcement of its decision or signing and filing of its written order. Subsequent permanency hearings must be held as required by section 1089 of the Family

Court Act at intervals of not more than six months from the date of completion of the prior permanency hearing.

§205.51 Proceedings involving custody of a Native American child.

In any proceeding in which the custody of a child is to be determined, the petition shall set forth whether the child is a Native American child subject to the Indian Child Welfare Act of 1978 (25 USC 1901-1963) and the Court shall proceed further, as appropriate, in accordance with the provisions of that act.

§205.52 Adoption rules; application; timing and venue of filing of petition.

(a) Sections 205.53 through 205.55 of this Part shall be applicable to all agency and private-placement adoption proceedings in Family Court.

(b) In any agency adoption, a petition may be filed to adopt a child who is the subject of a termination of parental rights proceeding and whose custody and guardianship has not yet been committed to an authorized agency, provided that:

(1) the adoption petition is filed in the same court where the termination of parental rights proceeding is pending; and

(2) the adoption petition, supporting documents and the fact of their filing shall not be provided to the judge before whom the petition for termination of parental rights is pending until such time as fact-finding is concluded under that petition.

(c) Where a child is under the jurisdiction of the Family Court as a result of a placement in foster care pursuant to Article 10 or 10-A of the Family Court Act or section 358-a of the social services law, the adoption petition regarding the child shall be assigned , wherever practicable, to the Family Court judge who last presided over the child's child protective, foster care placement, permanency, surrender or termination of parental rights proceeding. Where the adoption petition has been filed regarding such a child either before a different judge in a different court or before a court in a different county, the petitioner shall so indicate in the petition and the petitioner's attorney shall file an affirmation by the attorney for the petitioner on a uniform form promulgated by the Chief Administrator of the Courts attesting to the reasons for, and circumstances regarding, such filing. The court in which the adoption petition has been filed shall stay the proceeding for not more than 30 days in order to communicate with the Family Court judge who presided over the child's most recent child protective, foster care placement, permanency, termination of parental rights or surrender proceeding, and afford the agency attorney and child's attorney in the respective proceedings an opportunity to be heard orally, in person or by telephone, or in writing. Pursuant to section 113 of the Domestic Relations Law, the Family Court judge who presided over the child's case shall determine whether the adoption petition should be transferred or should be heard in the court in which it has been filed and shall record that determination on a uniform form promulgated by the Chief Administrator of the Courts. This determination shall be incorporated by the court in which the adoption petition has been filed into an order on a uniform form promulgated by the Chief Administrator of the Courts either retaining or transferring the petition. If the adoption petition is to be transferred, the transfer must take place forthwith, but in no event more than 35 days after the filing of the petition.

§205.53   Papers required in an adoption proceeding.

(a) All papers submitted in an adoption proceeding shall comply with section 205.7 of this Part.

(b) In addition to those papers required by the Domestic Relations Law, the following papers, unless otherwise dispensed with by the court, shall be submitted and filed prior to the placement of any adoption proceeding on the calendar:

(1) a certified copy of the birth certificate of the adoptive child;

(2) an affidavit or affidavits by an attorney admitted to practice in the State of New York or, in the discretion of the court, by a person other than an attorney who is known to the court, identifying each of the parties;

(3) a certified marriage certificate, where the adoptive parents are husband and wife or where an individual adoptive parent is the spouse of the birth parent;

(4) a certified copy of a decree or judgment, where an adoptive parent's marriage has been terminated by decree or judgment;

(5) a certified death certificate, where an adoptive or birth parent's marriage has been terminated by death or where it is alleged that consent or notice is not required because of death;

(6) a proposed order of adoption;

(7) a copy of the attorney's affidavit of financial disclosure filed with the Office of Court Administration pursuant to section 603.23, 691.23, 806.14 or 1022.33 of this Title; and either an attorney's affirmation that the affidavit has been personally delivered or mailed in accordance with such rules or the dated receipt from the Office of Court Administration;

(8) an affidavit of financial disclosure from the adoptive parent or parents, and from any person whose consent to the adoption is required by law, setting forth the following information:

(i) name, address and telephone number of the affiant;

(ii) status of the affiant in the proceeding and relationship, if any, to the adoptive child;

(iii) docket number of the adoption proceeding;

(iv) the date and terms of every agreement, written or otherwise, between the affiant and any attorney pertaining to any fees, compensation or other remuneration paid or to be paid by or on behalf of the adoptive parents or the birth parents, directly or indirectly, including but not limited to retainer fees on account of or incidental to the placement or adoption of the child or assistance in arrangements for such placement or adoption;

(v) the total amount of fees, compensation or other remuneration to be paid to such attorney by the affiant, directly or indirectly, including the date and amounts of each payment already made, if any, on account of or incidental to the placement or adoption of the child or assistance in arrangements for such placement or adoption;

(vi) the name and address of any other person, agency, association, corporation, institution, society or organization who received or will receive any fees, compensation or other remuneration from the affiant, directly or indirectly, on account of or incidental to the birth or care of the adoptive child, the pregnancy or care of the adoptive child's birth mother or the placement or adoption of the child and on account of or incidental to assistance in arrangements for such placement or proposed adoption; the amount of each such fee, compensation or other remuneration; and the reason for or services rendered, if any, in connection with each such fee, compensation or other remuneration; and

(vii) the name and address of any person, agency, association, corporation, society or organization who has or will pay the affiant any fee, compensation or other remuneration, directly or indirectly, on account of or incidental to the birth or care of the adoptive child, the pregnancy or care of the adoptive child's birth mother, or the placement or adoption of the child and on account of or incidental to assistance in arrangements for such placement or adoption; the amount of each such fee, compensation or other remuneration; and the reason for or services rendered, if any, in connection with each such fee, compensation or other remuneration;

(9) in the case of an adoption from an authorized agency in accordance with title 2 of article 7 of the Domestic Relations Law, a copy of the criminal history summary report made by the New York State Office of Children and Family Services to the authorized agency pursuant to section 378-a of the Social Services Law regarding the criminal record or records of the prospective adoptive parent or parents and any adult over the age of 18 currently residing in the home, including fingerprint-based records of the national crime information databases, as defined in section 534(e)(3)(A) of Title 28 of the United States Code, as well as a report from the New York State Central Registry of Child Abuse and Maltreatment regarding any indicated reports regarding the prospective adoptive parent or parents and any adult over the age of 18 currently residing in the home and from the child abuse and maltreatment registry, if any, of any state in which the prospective adoptive parents and any adult over the age of 18 have resided during the five years immediately prior to the filing of the petition;

(10) in the case of an adoption from an authorized agency, an affidavit by the attorney for the agency attesting to the fact that no appeal from a surrender, surrender revocation or termination of parental rights proceeding is pending in any court and that a notice of entry of the final order of disposition of the surrender, surrender revocation or termination of parental rights proceeding had been served upon the child's attorney, the attorneys for the respondent parents or the parents themselves, if they were self-represented, as well as any other parties;

(11) in the case of an adoption from an authorized agency in which a post-adoption contact agreement has been approved by the Family Court in conjunction with a surrender of the child, a copy of the post-adoption contact agreement, as well as the order of the Court that approved the agreement as being in the child's best interests, and

(12) in the case of an adoption petition filed either before a different judge in a different court or a court in a different county regarding a child under the jurisdiction of the Family Court as a result of a placement in foster care pursuant to Article 10 or 10-A of the Family Court Act or section 358-a of the Social Services Law, an affirmation by the attorney for the petitioner on a uniform form promulgated by the Chief Administrator of the Courts attesting to the reasons for, and circumstances regarding, such filing.

(13) in the case of an adoption petition filed with consents by a birth parent or parents as required by section 111 of the Domestic Relations Law, the adoption information registry birth parent registration consent form required by sections 112 and 115-b of the Domestic Relations Law and subdivision 10 of section 4138-c of the Public Health Law.

(c) Prior to the signing of an order of adoption, the court may in its discretion require the filing of a supplemental affidavit by the adoptive parent or parents, any person whose consent to the adoption is required, the authorized agency and the attorney for any of the aforementioned, setting forth any additional information pertaining to allegations in the petition or in any affidavit filed in the proceeding.

§205.54   Investigation by disinterested person; adoption.

(a) The probation service or an authorized agency or disinterested person is authorized to, and at the request of the court, shall, interview such persons and obtain such data as will aid the court in determining the truth and accuracy of an adoption petition under article 7 of the Domestic Relations Law, including the allegations set forth in the schedule annexed to the petition pursuant to section 112(3) of that law and such other facts as are necessary to a determination of the petition.

(b) The adoptive parent or parents and other persons concerned with the proceeding shall be notified of the date, time and place of any interview by a disinterested person or authorized agency designated by the court in accordance with sections 112 and 116 of the Domestic Relations Law.

(c) The written report of the investigation conducted pursuant to subdivision (a) of this section shall be submitted to the court within 30 days from the date on which it was ordered, or earlier as the court may direct, unless, for good cause, the court shall grant an extension for a reasonable period of time not to exceed an additional 30 days.

§205.55   Special applications.

All applications, including applications to dispense with statutorily required personal appearances, the period of residence of a child, or the period of waiting after filing of the adoption petition, shall be made in writing and shall be accompanied by affidavits setting forth the reasons for the application and all facts relevant thereto.

§205.56   Investigation by disinterested person; custody; guardianship.

(a) The probation service or an authorized agency or disinterested person is authorized to, and at the request of the court, shall interview such persons and obtain such data as will aid the court in:

(1) determining custody in a proceeding under section 467 or 651 of the Family Court Act;

(2) exercising its power under section 661 of the Family Court Act to appoint a guardian of the person of a minor under the jurisdiction of the court.

(b) The written report of the investigation conducted pursuant to subdivision (a) of this section shall be submitted to the court within 30 days from the date on which it was ordered, or earlier as the court may direct, unless, for good cause, the court shall grant an extension for a reasonable period of time not to exceed an additional 30 days.

§205.57   Petition for guardianship by adoptive parent.

(a) When a petition for temporary guardianship has been filed by an adoptive parent or parents pursuant to section 115-c of the Domestic Relations Law, the clerk of the court in which the petition has been filed shall distribute a written notice to the adoptive parents and lawyers who have appeared, and to the Commissioner of Social Services or the Director of the Probation Service, as appropriate, indicating that:

(1) a petition for adoption must be filed in the court in which the application for temporary guardianship has been brought within 45 days from the date of the signing of the consent to the adoption;

(2) any order or decree of temporary guardianship will expire no later than nine months following its issuance or upon the entry of a final order of adoption whichever is sooner, unless, upon application to the court, it is extended for good cause; and

(3) any order or decree of temporary guardianship will terminate upon withdrawal or denial of a petition to adopt the child, unless the court orders a continuation of such order or decree.

(b) In addition to and without regard to the date set for the hearing of the petition, the clerk of the court shall calendar the case for the 45th day from the date of the signing of the consent to the adoption. If no petition for adoption has been filed by the 45th day, the court shall schedule a hearing and shall order the appropriate agency to conduct an investigation forthwith, if one had not been ordered previously.

§205.58 Proceedings for certification as a qualified adoptive parent or parents.

(a) Where the petition in a proceeding for certification as a qualified adoptive parent or parents alleges that petitioner or petitioners will cause a preplacement investigation to be undertaken, the petition shall include the name and address of the disinterested person by whom such investigation will be conducted.

(b) The report of the disinterested person conducting the preplacement investigation shall be filed by such person directly with the court, with a copy of such report delivered simultaneously to the applicant or applicants.

(c) The court shall order a report (1) from the statewide central register of child abuse and maltreatment setting forth whether the child or the petitioner is, or petitioners are, the subject of or another person named in an indicated report, as such terms are defined in section 412 of the Social Services Law, filed with such register; and (2) from the New York State Division of Criminal Justice Services setting forth any existing criminal record of such petitioner or petitioners, in accordance with section 115-d(3-a) of the Domestic Relations Law; provided, however, that where the petitioner(s) have been fingerprinted pursuant to section 378-a of the Social Services Law, the authorized agency in possession of a current criminal history summary report from the New York State Office of Children and Family Services may be requested to provide such report to the court in lieu of a report from the New York State Division of Criminal Justice Services.

§205.59 Calendaring of proceedings for adoption from an authorized agency.

Proceedings for adoption from an authorized agency shall be calendared as follows:

(a) Within 60 days of the filing of the petition and documents specified in section 112-a of the Domestic Relations Law, the court shall schedule a review of said petition and documents to take place to determine if there is adequate basis for approving the adoption.

(b) If such basis is found, the court shall schedule the appearance of the adoptive parent(s) and child before the court, for approval of the adoption, within 30 days of the date of the review.

(c) If, upon the court's review, the court finds that there is not an adequate basis for approval of the adoption, the court shall direct such further hearings, submissions or appearances as may be required, and the proceeding shall be adjourned as required for such purposes.

§205.60   Designation of a facility for the questioning of children in custody (PINS).

Designation of facilities for the questioning of children pursuant to section 724(b)(ii) of the Family Court Act shall be in accordance with section 205.20 of this Part.

§205.61   Authorization to release a child taken into custody before the filing of a petition (PINS).

When a child is brought to a detention facility pursuant to section 724(b)(iii) of the Family Court Act, the administrator responsible for operating the detention facility is authorized, before the filing of a petition, to release the child to the custody of a parent or other relative, guardian or legal custodian when the events that occasioned the taking into custody appear to involve a petition to determine whether the child is a person in need of supervision rather than a petition to determine whether the child is a juvenile delinquent.

§205.62   Preliminary conferences and procedures (PINS).

(a) Any person seeking to originate a proceeding under Article 7 of the Family Court Act to determine whether a child is a person in need of supervision shall first be referred to the designated lead diversion agency, which may be either the probation service or the local department of social services. The clerk shall not accept any petition for filing that does not have attached the notification from the lead diversion agency required by section 735 of the Family Court Act and, in the case of a petition filed by a school district or school official, documentation of the efforts made by the school district or official to remediate the child's school problems.

(b) The lead diversion agency shall begin to conduct preliminary conferences with the person seeking to originate the proceeding, the potential respondent and any other interested person, on the same day that such persons are referred to the diversion agency in order to gather information needed to assist in diversion of the case from petition, detention and placement through provision of or referral for services. The diversion agency shall permit any participant who is represented by a lawyer to be accompanied by the lawyer at any preliminary conference.

(c) During the preliminary conferences, the diversion agency shall ascertain, from the person seeking to originate the proceeding, a brief statement of the underlying events, an assessment of whether the child would benefit from diversion services, respite care and other alternatives to detention and, if known to that person, a brief statement of the factors that would be of assistance to the court in determining whether the potential respondent should be detained or released in the event that a petition is filed. Such factors include whether there is a substantial probability that the respondent would not be likely to appear in court if released, whether he or she would be likely to benefit from diversion services, whether all available alternatives to detention have been exhausted and, in the case of a child 16 years of age or older, whether special circumstances exist warranting detention. The diversion agency shall also gather information to aid the court in its determination of whether remaining in the home would be contrary to the child's best interests and, where appropriate, whether reasonable efforts were made to prevent or eliminate the need for removal of the child from his or her home.

(d) At the first appearance at a conference by each of the persons listed in subdivision (b) of this section, the diversion agency shall inform such person concerning the function of the diversion process and that:

(1) he or she has the right to participate in the diversion process;

(2) the diversion agency is not authorized to and cannot compel any person to appear at any conference, produce any papers or visit any place, but if the person seeking to originate the proceeding does not cooperate with the diversion agency, he or she will not be able to file a petition. The court may direct the parties to cooperate with the diversion agency even after a petition has been filed;

(3) statements made to the diversion agency are subject to the confidentiality provisions contained in section 735 of the Family Court Act;

(4) if the diversion process is not successfully concluded for reasons other than the noncooperation of the person seeking to originate the proceeding, the diversion agency shall notify the person seeking to originate the proceeding in writing of that fact and that the person seeking to originate the proceeding is entitled to access to the court for the purpose of filing a petition; oral notification shall be confirmed in writing.

(e) If the diversion process is not successfully concluded, the diversion agency shall notify all the persons who participated therein, in writing, of that fact and of the reasons therefor, including a description of the services offered and efforts made to avert the filing of a petition. The notification shall be appended to the petition.

§205.63 [Repealed]

§205.64   Procedure when remanded child absconds (PINS).

(a) When a child absconds from a facility to which he or she was remanded pursuant to section 739 of the Family Court Act, written notice of that fact shall be given within 48 hours by an authorized representative of the facility to the clerk of the court from which the remand was made. The notice shall state the name of the child, the docket number of the pending proceeding in which the child was remanded, the date on which the child absconded, and the efforts made to secure the return of the child. Every order of remand pursuant to section 739 shall include a direction embodying the requirements of this subdivision.

(b) Upon receipt of the written notice of absconding, the clerk shall cause the proceeding to be placed on the court calendar no later than the next court day for such action as the court may deem appropriate and shall give notice of such court date to the petitioner, presentment agency and appointed or privately retained counsel for the child.

§205.65   Terms and conditions of order adjourning a proceeding in contemplation of dismissal entered in accordance with section 749(a) of the Family Court Act (PINS).

(a) An order adjourning a proceeding in contemplation of dismissal pursuant to section 749(a) of the Family Court Act shall contain at least one of the following terms and conditions directing the respondent to:

(1) attend school regularly and obey all rules and regulations of the school;

(2) obey all reasonable commands of the parent or other person legally responsible for the respondent's care;

(3) avoid injurious or vicious activities;

(4) abstain from associating with named individuals;

(5) abstain from visiting designated places;

(6) abstain from the use of alcoholic beverages, hallucinogenic drugs, habit-forming drugs not lawfully prescribed for the respondent's use, or any other harmful or dangerous substance;

(7) cooperate with a mental health or other appropriate community facility to which the respondent is referred;

(8) restore property taken from the petitioner, complainant or victim, or replace property taken from the petitioner, complainant or victim, the cost of said replacement not to exceed $1,500;

(9) repair any damage to, or defacement of, the property of the petitioner, complainant or victim, the cost of said repair not to exceed $1,500;

(10) cooperate in accepting medical or psychiatric diagnosis and treatment, alcoholism or drug abuse treatment or counseling services, and permit an agency delivering that service to furnish the court with information concerning the diagnosis, treatment or counseling;

(11) attend and complete an alcohol awareness program established pursuant to section 19.25 of the Mental Hygiene Law;

(12) abstain from disruptive behavior in the home and in the community; or

(13) comply with such other reasonable terms and conditions as may be permitted by law and as the court shall determine to be necessary or appropriate to ameliorate the conduct which gave rise to the filing of the petition.

(b) An order adjourning a proceeding in contemplation of dismissal pursuant to section 749(b) of the Family Court Act may set a time or times at which the probation service shall report to the court, orally or in writing, concerning compliance with the terms and conditions of said order.

(c) A copy of the order setting forth the terms and conditions imposed and the duration thereof shall be furnished to the respondent and to the parent or other person legally responsible for the respondent.

§205.66   Terms and conditions of order in accordance with section 755 or 757 of the Family Court Act (PINS).

(a) An order suspending judgment entered pursuant to section 755 of the Family Court Act shall be reasonably related to the adjudicated acts or omissions of the respondent and shall contain at least one of the following terms and conditions directing the respondent to:

(1) attend school regularly and obey all rules and regulations of the school;

(2) obey all reasonable commands of the parent or other person legally responsible for the respondent's care;

(3) avoid injurious or vicious activities;

(4) abstain from associating with named individuals;

(5) abstain from visiting designated places;

(6) abstain from the use of alcoholic beverages, hallucinogenic drugs, habit-forming drugs not lawfully prescribed for the respondent's use, or any other harmful or dangerous substance;

(7) cooperate with a mental health or other appropriate community facility to which the respondent is referred;

(8) make restitution or perform services for the public good;

(9) restore property taken from the petitioner, complainant or victim, or replace property taken from the petitioner, complainant or victim, the cost of said replacement not to exceed $1,000;

(10) repair any damage to, or defacement of, the property of the petitioner, complainant or victim, the cost of said repair not to exceed $1,000;

(11) abstain from disruptive behavior in the home and in the community;

(12) cooperate in accepting medical or psychiatric diagnosis and treatment, alcoholism or drug abuse treatment or counseling services, and permit an agency delivering that service to furnish the court with information concerning the diagnosis, treatment or counseling;

(13) attend and complete an alcohol awareness program established pursuant to section 19.25 of the Mental Hygiene Law;

(14) in a case in which respondent has been adjudicated for acts of willful, malicious, or unlawful damage to real or personal property maintained as a cemetery plot, grave, burial place or other place of internment of human remains, provide restitution by performing services for the maintenance and repair of such property; or

(15) comply with such other reasonable terms and conditions as the court shall determine to be necessary or appropriate to ameliorate the conduct which gave rise to the filing of a petition.

(b) An order placing the respondent on probation in accordance with section 757 of the Family Court Act shall contain at least one of the following terms and conditions, in addition to any of the terms and conditions set forth in subdivision (a) of this section, directing the respondent to:

(1) meet with the assigned probation officer when directed to do so by that officer;

(2) permit the assigned probation officer to visit the respondent at home or at school;

(3) permit the assigned probation officer to obtain information from any person or agency from whom the respondent is receiving or was directed to receive diagnosis, treatment or counseling;

(4) permit the assigned probation officer to obtain information from the respondent's school;

(5) cooperate with the assigned probation officer in seeking to obtain and in accepting employment and employment counseling services;

(6) submit records and reports of earnings to the assigned probation officer when requested to do so by that officer;

(7) obtain permission from the assigned probation officer for any absence from the county or residence in excess of two weeks; or

(8) attend and complete an alcohol awareness program established pursuant to section 19.25 of the Mental Hygiene Law;

(9) do or refrain from doing any other specified act of omission or commission that, in the opinion of the court, is necessary and appropriate to implement or facilitate the order placing the respondent on probation.

(c) An order entered pursuant to section 754 of the Family Court Act may set a time or times at which the probation service shall report to the court, orally or in writing, concerning compliance with the terms and conditions of said order.

(d) A copy of the order setting forth the terms and conditions imposed and the duration thereof shall be furnished to the respondent and to the parent or other person legally responsible for the respondent.

§205.67　Procedures for compliance with Adoption and Safe Families Act (Persons in Need of Supervision proceeding).

(a) Pretrial detention; required findings. In any case in which detention is ordered by the court pursuant to section 728 or 739 of the Family Court Act, the court shall make additional, specific written findings regarding the following issues:

(1) whether the continuation of the respondent in his or her home would be contrary to his or her best interests; and

(2) whether reasonable efforts, where appropriate, were made, prior to the date of the court hearing that resulted in the detention order, to prevent or eliminate the need for removal of the respondent from his or her home, or, if the respondent had been removed from his or her home prior to such court hearing, whether reasonable efforts, where appropriate, were made to make it possible for the respondent to safely return home.

The court may request the petitioner, presentment agency, if any, and the local probation department to provide information to the court to aid in its determinations and may also consider information provided by the child's attorney.

(b) Motion for an order that reasonable efforts are not required. A motion for a judicial determination, pursuant to section 754(2)(b) of the Family Court Act, that reasonable efforts to prevent or eliminate the need for removal of the respondent from his or her home or to make it possible to reunify the respondent with his or her parents are not required shall be governed by section 205.16 of this Part.

(c) Placement; required findings. In any case in which the court is considering ordering placement pursuant to section 756 of the Family Court Act, the petitioner, presentment agency, if any, local probation department and local commissioner of social services shall provide information to the court to aid in its required determination of the following issues:

(1) whether continuation in the respondent's home would be contrary to his or her best interests, and, if the respondent was removed from his or her home prior to the date of such hearing, whether such removal was in his or her best interests;

(2) whether reasonable efforts, where appropriate, were made, prior to the date of the dispositional hearing, to prevent or eliminate the need for removal of the respondent from his or her home, and, if the respondent was removed from his or her home prior to the date of such hearing, whether reasonable efforts, where appropriate, were made to make it possible for the respondent to return safely home. If the court determines that reasonable efforts to prevent or eliminate the need for removal of the respondent from his or her home were not made, but that the lack of such efforts was appropriate under the circumstances, the court order shall include such a finding;

(3) in the case of a respondent who has attained the age of 16, the services needed, if any, to assist the respondent to make the transition from foster care to independent living; and

(4) in the case of an order of placement specifying a particular authorized agency or foster care provider, the position of the local commissioner of social services regarding such placement.

(d) Permanency hearing; extension of placement.

(1) A petition for a permanency hearing and, if applicable, an extension of placement, pursuant to section 756-a of the Family Court Act, shall be filed at least 60 days prior to the expiration of one year following the respondent's

entry into foster care; provided, however, that if the Family Court makes a determination, pursuant to section 754(2)(b) of the Family Court Act, that reasonable efforts are not required to prevent or eliminate the need for removal of the respondent from his or her home or to make it possible to reunify the respondent with his or her parents, the permanency hearing shall be held within 30 days of such finding and the petition for the permanency hearing shall be filed and served on an expedited basis as directed by the court.

(2) Following the initial permanency hearing in a case in which the respondent remains in placement, a petition for a subsequent permanency hearing and, if applicable, extension of placement, shall be filed at least 60 days prior to the expiration of one year following the date of the preceding permanency hearing.

(3) The permanency petition shall include, but not be limited to, the following: the date by which the permanency hearing must be held; the date by which any subsequent permanency petition must be filed; the proposed permanency goal for the child; the reasonable efforts, if any, undertaken to achieve the child's return to his or her parents and other permanency goal; the visitation plan for the child and his or her sibling or siblings and, if parental rights have not been terminated, for his or her parent or parents; and current information regarding the status of services ordered by the court to be provided, as well as other services that have been provided, to the child and his or her parent or parents.

(4) In all cases, the permanency petition shall be accompanied by the most recent service plan containing, at minimum: the child's permanency goal and projected time-frame for its achievement; the reasonable efforts that have been undertaken and are planned to achieve the goal; impediments, if any, that have been encountered in achieving the goal; the services required to achieve the goal; and a plan for the release or conditional release of the child, including information regarding steps to be taken to enroll the child in a school or, as applicable, vocational program.

§205.68 to 205.69 [Reserved]

§205.70 Designation of persons to inform complainant of procedures available for the institution of family offense proceedings.

Pursuant to section 812 of the Family Court Act, the following persons are hereby designated to inform any petitioner or complainant seeking to bring a proceeding under article 8 of the Family Court Act of the procedures available for the institution of these proceedings, before such proceeding or action is commenced:

(a) within the City of New York:

(1) the commanding officer of the police precinct wherein the offense is alleged to have occurred; or

(2) any police officer attached to such precinct who is designated by such commanding officer;

(b) outside the City of New York:

(1) the commanding officer of any law enforcement agency providing police service in the county wherein the offense is alleged to have occurred; or

(2) any police officer attached to such law enforcement agency who is designated by such commanding officer;

(c) the district attorney, corporation counsel or county attorney in the county wherein the offense is alleged to have occurred, or any assistant district attorney, assistant corporation counsel or assistant county attorney who is designated by such district attorney, corporation counsel or county attorney;

(d) any probation officer in the employ of the State of New York, or any political subdivision thereof, providing probation service in the criminal court or in the intake unit of the Family Court in the county in which a proceeding may be instituted;

(e) the clerk of the Family Court and the clerk of the criminal court located in the county in which the proceeding may be instituted, or any clerk in that court designated by such clerk of the family or criminal court; and

(f) judges of all local criminal courts outside the City of New York having jurisdiction over the alleged offense.

§205.71 Preliminary probation conferences and procedures (family offenses).

(a) Any person seeking to file a family offense petition under article 8 of the Family Court Act may first be referred to the probation service concerning the advisability of filing a petition.

(b) Upon such referral, the probation service shall inform such person:

(1) concerning the procedures available for the institution of family offense proceedings, including the information set forth in subdivision 2 of section 812 of the Family Court Act; and

(2) that the person seeking to file a family offense petition is entitled to request that the probation service confer with him or her, the potential respondent and any other interested person concerning the advisability of filing a petition requesting:

(i) an order of protection;

(ii) a temporary order of protection; or

(iii) the use of the court's conciliation procedure.

(c) March 11, 2009 seeking to file a family offense petition, shall commence conducting preliminary conferences concerning the advisability of filing a petition with that person, the potential respondent and any other interested person no later than the next regularly scheduled court day. The probation service shall permit any participant who is represented by a lawyer to be accompanied at any preliminary conference by the lawyer, who shall be identified by the probation officer to the other party, and shall not discourage any person from seeking to file a petition.

(d) At the first appearance at a conference by each of the persons listed in subdivision (c) of this section, the probation service shall inform such person concerning the function and limitations of, and the alternatives to, the adjustment process, and that:

(1) the purpose of the adjustment process is to attempt through conciliation and agreement to arrive at a cessation of the conduct forming the basis of the family offense complaint without filing a petition in court;

(2) the probation service may confer with the persons listed in subdivision (c) of this section if it shall appear to the probation service that:

(i) there is a reasonable likelihood that the adjustment process will result in a cessation of the conduct forming the basis of the family offense complaint; and

(ii) there is no reasonable likelihood that the potential respondent will, during the period of the adjustment, inflict or threaten to inflict physical injury on the person seeking to obtain relief, or any other member of the same family or household, if the filing of a petition is delayed;

(3) the probation service is not authorized to, and shall not, compel any person, including the person seeking to file a family offense petition, to appear at any conference, produce any papers or visit any place;

(4) the person seeking to file a family offense petition is entitled to request that the probation service confer with him or her, the potential respondent and any other interested person concerning the advisability of filing a family offense petition under article 8 of the Family Court Act;

(5) if the assistance of the probation service is not requested or, if requested, is subsequently declined, the person seeking to file a family offense petition is entitled to have access to the court at any time, even after having consented to an extension of the adjustment period, and may proceed to file a family offense petition;

(6) no statements made during any preliminary conference with the probation service may be admitted into evidence at a fact-finding hearing held in the Family Court or at any proceeding conducted in a criminal court at any time prior to conviction;

(7) the adjustment process must commence within seven days from the date of the request for a conference, may continue for a period of two months from the date of that request and may be twice extended by the court for two periods of up to 60 days each upon written application to the court containing the consent and signature of the person seeking to file a family offense petition;

(8) if a petition is filed, a temporary order of protection may be issued for good cause shown, and unless a petition is filed, the court may not issue any order of protection;

(9) if the adjustment process is not successful, the persons participating therein shall be notified in writing of that fact, and that the person seeking to file a family offense petition is entitled to access to the court for that purpose;

(10) if the matter has been successfully adjusted, the persons participating therein shall be notified in writing of that fact; and

(11) if the adjustment of the matter results in a voluntary agreement concerning the cessation of the offensive conduct forming the basis of the family offense complaint:

(i) it shall be reduced to writing by the probation service, signed by both parties to it and submitted to the Family Court for approval;

(ii) if the court approves it, the court may, without further hearing, enter an order of protection pursuant to section 823 of the Family Court Act in accordance with the agreement; and

(iii) the order when entered shall be binding on the respondent and shall in all respects be a valid order.

(e) If the adjustment process is not commenced, the probation service shall give written notice to the persons listed in subdivision (c) of this section that:

(1) the adjustment process was not commenced, and the reasons therefor;

(2) the person seeking to file a family offense petition is entitled to access to the court for that purpose; and

(3) if applicable, the adjustment process was not commenced on the ground that the court would not have jurisdiction over the case, and the person seeking to file a family offense petition may test the question of the court's jurisdiction by filing a petition.

§205.72 Duties of the probation service and procedures relating to the adjustment process (family offenses).

(a) If the assistance of the probation service is requested by the person seeking to file a family offense petition, the adjustment process shall commence within seven days from the request. The probation service shall permit any participant who is represented by a lawyer to be accompanied at any conference by the lawyer, who shall be identified by the probation officer to the other party, and shall not discourage any person from seeking to file a petition.

(b) If an extension of the period of the adjustment process is sought, the probation service shall, with the written consent of the person seeking to file a family offense petition, apply in writing to the court and shall set forth the services rendered, the date of commencement of those services, the degree of success achieved, the services proposed to be rendered and a statement by the assigned probation officer: that there is no imminent risk that, if an extension of the period is granted, the potential respondent will, during the extended period of adjustment, endanger the health or safety of the person seeking to file a family offense petition or any other member of the same family or household, and the facts upon which the opinion is based; and that the matter will not be successfully adjusted unless an extension is granted.

(c) The probation service shall discontinue its efforts at adjustment if, at any time:

(1) the person seeking to file a family offense petition or the potential respondent requests that it do so; or

(2) it appears to the probation service that:

(i) there is no reasonable likelihood that a cessation of the conduct forming the basis of the family offense complaint will result; or

(ii) there is an imminent risk that the potential respondent will inflict or threaten to inflict physical injury upon the person seeking to file a family offense petition or upon any other member of the same family or household; or

(iii) the potential respondent has inflicted or threatened to inflict physical injury on the person seeking to file a family offense petition or any other member of the same family or household since efforts at adjustment began.

(d) If the adjustment process is not successfully concluded, the probation service shall notify in writing all the persons who participated therein:

(1) that the adjustment process has not been successfully concluded, and the reasons therefor; and

(2) that the person seeking to file a family offense petition is entitled to access to the court for that purpose.

(e) If the adjustment process results in an agreement for the cessation of the conduct forming the basis of the family offense complaint:

(1) it shall be reduced to writing by the probation service, shall be signed by both parties to it, and shall be submitted to the court, together with a petition for approval of the agreement and a proposed order incorporating the agreement; and

(2) if the agreement is approved by the court, a copy of the order shall be furnished by the probation service to the person seeking to file a family offense petition and the potential respondent, in person if they are present, and by mail if their presence has been dispensed with by the court.

§205.73   Record and report of unexecuted warrants issued pursuant to section 827 of the Family Court Act (family offenses).

(a) The clerk of court for the Family Court in each county shall obtain and keep a record of unexecuted warrants issued pursuant to section 827 of the Family Court Act.

(b) At the end of each six-month period, on the first of January and on the first of July in each year, a report concerning all unexecuted warrants issued pursuant to section 827 of the Family Court Act shall be made and filed with the Office of Court Administration on a form to be supplied by the Office of Court Administration.

§205.74   Terms and conditions of order in accordance with sections 841(b)-(e), 842 and 843 of the Family Court Act (family offenses).

(a) An order suspending judgment entered pursuant to section 841(b) of the Family Court Act shall contain at least one of the following terms and conditions directing the respondent to:

(1) stay away from the residence of the person against whom the family offense was committed;

(2) stay away from the place of employment or place of education attended by the person against whom the family offense was committed;

(3) abstain from communicating by any means, including, but not limited to, telephone, letter, e-mail or other electronic means with the person against whom the family offense was committed;

(4) abstain from repeating the conduct adjudicated a family offense at the fact-finding hearing;

(5) cooperate in seeking to obtain and in accepting medical or psychiatric diagnosis and treatment, alcoholism or drug abuse treatment, or employment or counseling or child guidance services, or participate in a batterer's educational program designed to help end violent behavior, and permit information to be obtained by the court from any person or agency from whom the respondent is receiving or was directed to receive such services or participate in such program;

(6) allow medical or psychiatric treatment to be furnished to the person against whom the family offense was committed, or any other named family member or household member who is a dependent of the respondent and whose need for medical or psychiatric treatment was occasioned, in whole or in part, by the conduct adjudicated a family offense;

(7) cooperate with the person against whom the family offense was committed, the head of the household or parent, in maintaining the home or household;

(8) pay restitution in an amount not to exceed $10,000; or

(9) comply with such other reasonable terms and conditions as the court shall deem necessary or appropriate to ameliorate the acts or omissions which gave rise to the filing of the petition.

(b) An order placing the respondent on probation in accordance with section 841(c) of the Family Court Act shall contain at least one of the following terms and conditions, directing the respondent to:

(1) observe one or more of the terms and conditions set forth in subdivision (a) of this section;

(2) meet with the assigned probation officer when directed to do so by that officer;

(3) cooperate with the assigned probation officer in arranging for and allowing visitation in the family residence or household; or

(4) cooperate in seeking to obtain and in accepting medical treatment, psychiatric diagnosis and treatment, alcoholism or drug abuse treatment, or employment or counseling services, or participate in a batterer's educational program designed to help end violent behavior, and permit the assigned

probation officer to obtain information from any person or agency from whom the respondent is receiving or was directed to receive such services or participate in such program;

(c) An order of protection entered in accordance with section 841(d) of the Family Court Act may, in addition to the terms and conditions enumerated in sections 842 and 842-a of the Family Court Act, require the petitioner, respondent or both, or, if before the court, any other member of the household, to:

(1) abstain from communicating by any means, including, but not limited to, telephone, letter, e-mail or other electronic means with the person against whom the family offense was committed;

(2) stay away from the place of employment or place of education attended by the person against whom the family offense was committed, of a child or a parent, or of another member of the same family or household;

(3) refrain from engaging in any conduct which interferes with the custody of a child as set forth in the order;

(4) cooperate in seeking to obtain and in accepting medical treatment, psychiatric diagnosis and treatment, alcoholism or drug abuse treatment, or employment or counseling services, or participate in a batterer's educational program designed to help end violent behavior, and permit information to be obtained by the court from any person or agency from whom the respondent is receiving or was directed to receive such services or participate in such program;

(5) pay restitution in an amount not to exceed $10,000; or

(6) comply with such other reasonable terms and conditions as the court may deem necessary and appropriate to ameliorate the acts or omissions which gave rise to the filing of the petition.

(d) A copy of the order setting forth its duration and the terms and conditions imposed shall be furnished to the respondent and to the person or persons against whom the family offense was committed.

(e) Each order issued pursuant to section 828 or 841(b), (c), (d) or (e) of the Family Court Act shall contain a written statement informing the respondent that a failure to obey the order may result in commitment to jail for a term not to exceed six months. Each order issued pursuant to section 828 or 841(d) shall contain a written statement informing the respondent that a failure to obey the order may result in incarceration up to seven years.

§205.75 to 205.79 [Reserved]

§205.80   Procedure when remanded child absconds (child protective proceeding).

(a) When a child absconds from a shelter or holding facility to which the child was remanded pursuant to section 1027(b) or 1051(d) of the Family Court Act, written notice of that fact, signed by an authorized representative of the facility, shall be sent within 48 hours to the clerk of the court from which the remand was made. The notice shall state the name of the child, the docket number of the pending proceeding in which the child was remanded, the date on which the child absconded, and the efforts made to secure the return of the child. Every order of remand pursuant to section 1027(b) or 1051(d) shall include a direction embodying the requirement of this subdivision.

(b) Upon receipt of a written notice of absconding, the clerk of the court shall cause the proceeding to be placed on the calendar for the next court day for such action as the court shall deem appropriate, and shall give notice of such court date to the petitioner and appointed or privately retained counsel for the child.

§205.81 Procedures for compliance with Adoption and Safe Families Act (child protective proceeding).

(a) Temporary removal; required findings. In any case in which removal of the child is ordered by the court pursuant to part 2 of article 10 of the Family Court Act, the court shall set a date certain for a permanency hearing in accordance with section 205.17 of this Part and shall make additional, specific written findings regarding the following issues:

(1) whether the continuation of the child in his or her home would be contrary to his or her best interests; and

(2) whether reasonable efforts, where appropriate, were made, prior to the date of the court hearing that resulted in the removal order, to prevent or eliminate the need for removal of the child from his or her home, and, if the child had been removed from his or her home prior to such court hearing, whether reasonable efforts, where appropriate, were made to make it possible for the child to safely return home. The petitioner shall provide information to the court to aid in its determinations. The court may also consider information provided by respondents, the child's attorney, the non-respondent parent or parents, relatives and other suitable persons.

(b) Motion for an order that reasonable efforts are not required. A motion for a judicial determination, pursuant to section 1039-b of the Family Court Act, that reasonable efforts to prevent or eliminate the need for removal of the child from his or her home or to make it possible to reunify the child with his or her parents are not required shall be governed by section 205.16 of this Part.

(c) Placement; required findings. In any case in which the court is considering ordering placement pursuant to section 1055 of the Family Court Act, the petitioner shall provide information to the court to aid in its required determination of the following issues:

(1) whether continuation in the child's home would be contrary to his or her best interests and, if the child was removed from his or her home prior to or at the time of the dispositional hearing and a judicial determination has not yet been made, whether such removal was in his or her best interests;

(2) whether reasonable efforts, where appropriate, were made, prior to the date of the dispositional hearing, to prevent or eliminate the need for removal of the child from his or her home and, if the child was removed from his or her home prior to the date of such hearing, whether reasonable efforts, where appropriate, were made to make it possible for the child to return safely home. If the court determines that reasonable efforts to prevent or eliminate the need for removal of the child from his or her home were not made, but that the lack of such efforts was appropriate under the circumstances, the court order shall include such a finding;

(3) in the case of a child for whom the permanency plan is adoption, guardianship or some other permanent living arrangement other than reunification with the parent or parents of the child, whether reasonable efforts have been made to make and finalize such other permanency plan;

(4) in the case of a respondent who has attained the age of 14, the services needed, if any, to assist the respondent to make the transition from foster care to independent living; and

(5) in the case of an order of placement specifying a particular authorized agency or foster care provider, the position of the local commissioner of social services regarding such placement.

(d) Permanency hearing. If the child or children is or are placed in foster care or directly placed with a relative or other suitable person, the court shall set a date certain for a permanency hearing under Article 10-A of the Family Court Act. All permanency hearings under Article 10-A shall be governed by section 205.17 of this Part.

§205.82 Record and report of unexecuted warrants issued pursuant to article 10 of the Family Court Act (child protective proceeding).

(a) The clerk of court for the Family Court in each county shall obtain and keep a record of unexecuted warrants issued pursuant to article 10 of the Family Court Act.

(b) At the end of each six-month period, on the first of January and on the first of July in each year, a report concerning all unexecuted warrants issued pursuant to article 10 of the Family Court Act shall be made and filed with the Office of Court Administration on a form to be supplied by the Office of Court Administration.

§205.83 Terms and conditions of order in accordance with sections 1053, 1054 and 1057 of the Family Court Act (child protective proceeding).

(a) An order suspending judgment entered pursuant to section 1052 of the Family Court Act shall, where the child is in foster care, set forth the visitation plan between respondent and the child and between the child and his or her sibling or siblings, if any, and shall require the agency to notify the respondent of case conferences. A copy of the order, along with a current service plan, shall be furnished to the respondent. Any order suspending judgment entered pursuant to section 1052 of the Family Court Act shall contain at least one of the following terms and conditions that relate to the adjudicated acts or omissions of the respondent, directing the respondent to:

(1) refrain from or eliminate specified acts or conditions found at the fact-finding hearing to constitute or to have caused neglect or abuse;

(2) provide adequate and proper food, housing, clothing, medical care, and for the other needs of the child;

(3) provide proper care and supervision to the child and cooperate in obtaining, accepting or allowing medical or psychiatric diagnosis or treatment, alcoholism or drug abuse treatment, counseling or child guidance services for the child;

(4) take proper steps to insure the child's regular attendance at school; and

(5) cooperate in obtaining and accepting medical treatment, psychiatric diagnosis and treatment, alcoholism or drug abuse treatment, employment or counseling services, or child guidance, and permit a child protective agency to obtain information from any person or agency from whom the respondent or the child is receiving or was directed to receive treatment or counseling.

(b) An order pursuant to section 1054 of the Family Court Act placing the person to whose custody the child is released under the supervision of a child protective agency, social services officer or duly authorized agency, or an order pursuant to section 1057 placing the respondent under the supervision of a child protective agency, social services official or authorized agency, shall contain at least one of the following terms and conditions requiring the respondent to:

(1) observe any of the terms and conditions set forth in subdivision (a) of this section;

(2) cooperate with the supervising agency in remedying specified acts or omissions found at the fact-finding hearing to constitute or to have caused the neglect or abuse;

(3) meet with the supervising agency alone and with the child when directed to do so by that agency;

(4) report to the supervising agency when directed to do so by that agency;

(5) cooperate with the supervising agency in arranging for and allowing visitation in the home or other place;

(6) notify the supervising agency immediately of any change of residence or employment of the respondent or of the child; or

(7) do or refrain from doing any other specified act of omission or commission that, in the judgment of the court, is necessary to protect the child from injury or mistreatment and to help safeguard the physical, mental and emotional well-being of the child.

(c) When an order is made pursuant to section 1054 or 1057 of the Family Court Act:

(1) the court shall notify the supervising agency in writing of its designation to act and shall furnish to that agency a copy of the order setting forth the terms and conditions imposed;

(2) the order shall be accompanied by a written statement informing the respondent that a willful failure to obey the terms and conditions imposed may result in commitment to jail for a term not to exceed six months; and

(3) the court may, if it concludes that it is necessary for the protection of the child, direct the supervising agency to furnish a written report to the court at stated intervals not to exceed six months, setting forth whether, and to what extent:

(i) there has been any alteration in the respondent's maintenance of the child that is adversely affecting the child's health or well-being;

(ii) there is compliance with the terms and conditions of the order of supervision; and

(iii) the supervising agency has furnished supporting services to the respondent.

(d) A copy of the order, setting forth its duration and the terms and conditions imposed, shall be furnished to the respondent.

(e) If an order of supervision is issued in conjunction with an order of placement pursuant to section 1055 of the Family Court Act, the order shall, unless otherwise ordered by the court, be coextensive in duration with the order of placement and shall extend until the completion of the permanency hearing. The order of supervision shall be reviewed along with the placement at the permanency hearing.

§205.84 [Repealed]

§205.85   Procedure when a child who has been placed absconds (child protective proceeding).

(a) When a child placed pursuant to section 1055 of the Family Court Act absconds, written notice of that fact shall be sent within 48 hours to the clerk of the court from which the placement was made. The notice shall be signed by the custodial person or by an authorized representative of the place of placement and shall state the name of the child, the docket number of the proceeding in which the child was placed, the date on which the child absconded, and the efforts made to secure the return of the child. Every order of placement pursuant to section 1055 shall include a direction embodying the requirement of this subdivision.

(b) Upon receipt of the written notice of absconding, the clerk of the court shall cause the proceeding to be placed on the calendar no later than the next court day for such action as the court may deem appropriate.

§205.86   Video recording of interviews of children alleged to have been sexually abused.

(a) In any case in which, pursuant to section 1038(c) of the Family Court Act, a video recording is made of an expert's interview with a child alleged to have been sexually abused, the attorney for the party requesting the video recording, or the party, if unrepresented, shall promptly after the video recording has been completed:

(1) cause to be prepared a duplicate video recording, certified by the preparer as a complete and unaltered copy of the original video recording;

(2) deposit the original video recording, certified by the preparer as the original, with the Clerk of the Family Court; and

(3) submit for signature to the judge before whom the case is pending a proposed order authorizing the retention of the duplicate video recording by the attorney, (or the party, if unrepresented) and directing that retention be in conformance with this section.

Both the original video recording and the duplicate thereof shall be labelled with the name of the case, the Family Court docket number, the name of the child, the name of the interviewer, the name and address of the technician who prepared the video recording, the date of the interview, and the total elapsed time of the video recording.

(b) Up receipt, the clerk shall hold the original video recording in a secure place limited to access only by authorized court personnel.

(c) (1) Except as provided in paragraph (2) of this subdivision, the duplicate video recording shall remain in the custody of the attorney for the party who requested it, or the party, if not represented (the "custodian").

(2) The duplicate video recording shall be available for pretrial disclosure pursuant to article 10 of the Family Court Act and any other applicable law. Consistent therewith, the custodian shall permit an attorney for a party, or the party, if not represented by counsel, to borrow the duplicate video recording for a reasonable period of time so that it may be viewed, provided the person to whom it is loaned first certifies, by affidavit filed with the court, that he or she will comply with this subdivision.

(3) A person borrowing the duplicate video recording as provided in paragraph (2) of this subdivision shall not lend it or otherwise surrender custody thereof to any person other than the custodian, and upon returning such video recording to the custodian, such person shall certify, by affidavit filed with the court, that he or she has complied with the provisions of this subdivision.

(4) Subject to court order otherwise, the duplicate video recording may not be viewed by any person other than a party or his or her counsel or prospective expert witnesses. No copy of the duplicate video recording may be made.

(d) Failure to comply with the provisions of this rule shall be punishable by contempt of court.

NEW YORK STATE LAWS

Selected Sections

Part III

43-08 162nd Street
Flushing, NY 11358
www.LooseleafLaw.com   800-647-5547

ARTICLE 1
Short Title; Definitions

Section
1. Short title.
2. Definitions.

§1. Short title.

This chapter shall be known as the "Domestic Relations Law."

§2. Definitions.

A "minor" or "infant", as used in this chapter, is a person under the age of eighteen years.

ARTICLE 2
Marriages

Section
5. Incestuous and void marriages.
6. Void marriages.
7. Voidable marriages.
8. Marriage after divorce.

§5. Incestuous and void marriages.

A marriage is incestuous and void whether the relatives are legitimate or illegitimate between either:

1. An ancestor and a descendant;
2. A brother and sister of either the whole or the half blood;
3. An uncle and niece or an aunt and nephew.

If a marriage prohibited by the foregoing provisions of this section be solemnized it shall be void, and the parties thereto shall each be fined not less than fifty nor more than one hundred dollars and may, in the discretion of the court in addition to said fine, be imprisoned for a term not exceeding six months. Any person who shall knowingly and wilfully solemnize such marriage, or procure or aid in the solemnization of the same, shall be deemed guilty of a misdemeanor and shall be fined or imprisoned in like manner.

§6. Void marriages.

A marriage is absolutely void if contracted by a person whose husband or wife by a former marriage is living, unless either:

1. Such former marriage has been annulled or has been dissolved for a cause other than the adultery of such person; provided, that if such former marriage has been dissolved for the cause of the adultery of such person, he or she may marry again in the cases provided for in section eight of this chapter and such subsequent marriage shall be valid;
3. Such former marriage has been dissolved pursuant to section seven-a of this chapter.

§7. Voidable marriages.

A marriage is void from the time its nullity is declared by a court of competent jurisdiction if either party thereto:

1. Is under the age of legal consent, which is eighteen years, provided that such nonage shall not of itself constitute an absolute right to the annulment of such marriage, but such annulment shall be in the discretion of the court which shall take into consideration all the facts and circumstances surrounding such marriage;

2. Is incapable of consenting to a marriage for want of understanding;
3. Is incapable of entering into the married state from physical cause;
4. Consent to such marriage by reason of force, duress or fraud;
5. Has been incurably mentally ill for a period of five years or more.

§8. Marriage after divorce.

Whenever, and whether prior or subsequent to September first, nineteen hundred sixty-seven, a marriage has been dissolved by divorce, either party may marry again.

ARTICLE 3
Solemnization, Proof and Effect of Marriage

§10. Marriage a civil contract.

Marriage, so far as its validity in law is concerned, continues to be a civil contract, to which the consent of parties capable in law of making a contract is essential.

§10-a. Parties to a marriage.

1. A marriage that is otherwise valid shall be valid regardless of whether the parties to the marriage are of the same or different sex.

2. No government treatment or legal status, effect, right, benefit, privilege, protection or responsibility relating to marriage, whether deriving from statute, administrative or court rule, public policy, common law or any other source of law, shall differ based on the parties to the marriage being or having been of the same sex rather than a different sex. When necessary to implement the

rights and responsibilities of spouses under the law, all gender-specific language or terms shall be construed in a gender-neutral manner in all such sources of law.

§10-b. Religious exception.

1. Notwithstanding any state, local or municipal law, rule, regulation, ordinance, or other provision of law to the contrary, a religious entity as defined under the education law or section two of the religious corporations law, or a corporation incorporated under the benevolent orders law or described in the benevolent orders law but formed under any other law of this state, or a not-for-profit corporation operated, supervised, or controlled by a religious corporation, or any employee thereof, being managed, directed, or supervised by or in conjunction with a religious corporation, benevolent order, or a not-for-profit corporation as described in this subdivision, shall not be required to provide services, accommodations, advantages, facilities, goods, or privileges for the solemnization or celebration of a marriage. Any such refusal to provide services, accommodations, advantages, facilities, goods, or privileges shall not create any civil claim or cause of action or result in any state or local government action to penalize, withhold benefits, or discriminate against such religious corporation, benevolent order, a not-for-profit corporation operated, supervised, or controlled by a religious corporation, or any employee thereof being managed, directed, or supervised by or in conjunction with a religious corporation, benevolent order, or a not-for-profit corporation.

2. Notwithstanding any state, local or municipal law or rule, regulation, ordinance, or other provision of law to the contrary, nothing in this article shall limit or diminish the right, pursuant to subdivision eleven of section two hundred ninety-six of the executive law, of any religious or denominational institution or organization, or any organization operated for charitable or educational purposes, which is operated, supervised or controlled by or in connection with a religious organization, to limit employment or sales or rental of housing accommodations or admission to or give preference to persons of the same religion or denomination or from taking such action as is calculated by such organization to promote the religious principles for which it is established or maintained.

3. Nothing in this section shall be deemed or construed to limit the protections and exemptions otherwise provided to religious organizations under section three of article one of the constitution of the state of New York.

§11. By whom a marriage must be solemnized.

No marriage shall be valid unless solemnized by either:

1. A clergyman or minister of any religion, or by the senior leader, or any of the other leaders, of The Society for Ethical Culture in the city of New York, having its principal office in the borough of Manhattan, or by the leader of The Brooklyn Society for Ethical Culture, having its principal office in the borough of Brooklyn of the city of New York, or of the Westchester Ethical Society, having its principal office in Westchester county, or of the Ethical Culture Society of Long Island, having its principal office in Nassau county, or of the Riverdale-Yonkers Ethical Society having its principal office in Bronx county, or by the leader of any other Ethical Culture Society affiliated with the American Ethical Union; provided that no clergyman or minister as defined in section two of the religious corporations law, or Society for Ethical Culture

leader shall be required to solemnize any marriage when acting in his or her capacity under this subdivision.

1-a. A refusal by a clergyman or minister as defined in section two of the religious corporations law, or Society for Ethical Culture leader to solemnize any marriage under this subdivision shall not create a civil claim or cause of action or result in any state or local government action to penalize, withhold benefits or discriminate against such clergyman or minister.

2. The current or a former governor, a mayor of a village, a county executive of a county, or a mayor, recorder, city magistrate, police justice or police magistrate of a city, a former mayor or the city clerk of a city of the first class of over one million inhabitants or any of his or her deputies or not more than four regular clerks, designated by him or her for such purpose as provided in section eleven-a of this article, except that in cities which contain more than one hundred thousand and less than one million inhabitants, a marriage shall be solemnized by the mayor, or police justice, and by no other officer of such city, except as provided in subdivisions one and three of this section.

3. A judge of the federal circuit court of appeals for the second circuit, a judge of a federal district court for the northern, southern, eastern or western district of New York, a judge of the United States court of international trade, a federal administrative law judge presiding in this state, a justice or judge of a court of the unified court system, a housing judge of the civil court of the city of New York, a retired justice or judge of the unified court system or a retired housing judge of the civil court of the city of New York certified pursuant to paragraph (k) of subdivision two of section two hundred twelve of the judiciary law, the clerk of the appellate division of the supreme court in each judicial department, a retired city clerk who served for more than ten years in such capacity in a city having a population of one million or more or a county clerk of a county wholly within cities having a population of one million or more; or,

3-a. A judge or peacemaker judge of any Indian tribal court, a chief, a headman, or any member of any tribal council or other governing body of any nation, tribe or band of Indians in this state duly designated by such body for the purpose of officiating at marriages, or any other persons duly designated by such body, in keeping with the culture and traditions of any such nation, tribe or band of Indians in this state, to officiate at marriages.

4. A written contract of marriage signed by both parties and at least two witnesses, all of whom shall subscribe the same within this state, stating the place of residence of each of the parties and witnesses and the date and place of marriage, and acknowledged before a judge of a court of record of this state by the parties and witnesses in the manner required for the acknowledgment of a conveyance of real estate to entitle the same to be recorded.

5. Notwithstanding any other provision of this article, where either or both of the parties is under the age of eighteen years a marriage shall be solemnized only by those authorized in subdivision one of this section or by (1) the mayor of a city or village, or county executive of a county, or by (2) a judge of the federal circuit court of appeals for the second circuit, a judge of a federal district court for the northern, southern, eastern or western district of New York, a judge of the United States court of international trade, or a justice or a judge of a court of the unified court system, or by (3) a housing judge of the civil court of the city of New York, or by (4) a former mayor or the clerk of a city of the first class of over one million inhabitants or any of his or her deputies designated by him or her for such purposes as provided in section eleven-a of this chapter.

6. Notwithstanding any other provisions of this article to the contrary no marriage shall be solemnized by a public officer specified in this section, other than a judge of a federal district court for the northern, southern, eastern or western district of New York, a judge of the United States court of international trade, a federal administrative law judge presiding in this state, a judge or justice of the unified court system of this state, a housing judge of the civil court of the city of New York, or a retired judge or justice of the unified court system or a retired housing judge of the civil court certified pursuant to paragraph (k) of subdivision two of section two hundred twelve of the judiciary law, nor by any of the persons specified in subdivision three-a of this section, outside the territorial jurisdiction in which he or she was elected, appointed or duly designated. Such a public officer, however, elected or appointed within the city of New York may solemnize a marriage anywhere within such city.

7. The term "clergyman" or "minister" when used in this article, shall include those defined in section two of the religious corporations law. The word "magistrate," " when so used, includes any person referred to in the second or third subdivision.

§11-a. Duty of city clerk in certain cities of the first class; facsimile signature of said clerk authorized.

1. a. The city clerk of a city of the first class of over one million inhabitants may designate in writing any of his deputies or not more than four from among the permanent members of his staff to perform marriage ceremonies, which designation shall be in writing and be filed in the office of such city clerk. The day of such filing shall be endorsed on the designation. Any such designation shall be and remain in effect for six months from the filing thereof.

b. Whenever persons to whom the city clerk of any such city of the first class shall have issued a marriage license shall request him to solemnize the rites of matrimony between them and present to him such license it shall be the duty of such clerk, either in person or by one of his deputies or the permanent members of his staff so designated by him to solemnize such marriage; provided, however, that nothing contained either in this section or in subdivision two of section eleven of this chapter shall be construed as empowering or requiring either the said city clerk or any of his designated deputies or the permanent members of his staff so designated to solemnize marriages at any place other than at the office of such city clerk.

c. Notwithstanding any other provision of this article upon presentation to said city clerk in person or to any of his deputies of such license by one or both of such persons under the age of eighteen years with a request to solemnize the rites of matrimony between them, it shall be the duty of such city clerk either in person or by one of his deputies to solemnize such marriage provided there is submitted to said city clerk, in addition, the written request therefor by the parents of any such persons under the age of eighteen years and provided further that said parents shall be personally present at such requested solemnization.

d. In all cases in which the city clerk of such city or one of his deputies or the permanent members of his staff so designated shall perform a marriage ceremony such official shall demand and be entitled to collect therefor a fee to be fixed by the council of the city of New York not exceeding twenty-five dollars, which sum shall be paid by the contracting parties before or immediately upon the solemnization of the marriage; and all such fees so received shall be paid over to the commissioner of finance of the city.

2. The signature and seal of said clerk of cities of the first class of over one million inhabitants upon the marriage license, certificate of marriage, registration, and marriage search provided by this article may be a facsimile imprinted, stamped, or engraved thereon.

3. The said clerk of cities of the first class of one million inhabitants or more may designate among the permanent members of his staff one or more individuals who shall be permitted to sign his name and affix his official seal upon the marriage license, certificate of marriage registration, and marriage search provided by this article requiring the signature and seal of the city clerk.

§11-b. Registration of persons performing marriage ceremonies in the city of New York.

Every person authorized by law to perform the marriage ceremony, before performing any such ceremonies in the city of New York, shall register his or her name and address in the office of the city clerk of the city of New York. Every such person, before performing any marriage ceremonies subsequent to a change in his or her address, shall likewise register such change of address. Such city clerk is hereby empowered to cancel the registration of any person so registered upon satisfactory proof that the registration was fraudulent, or upon satisfactory proof that such person is no longer entitled to perform such ceremony.

§11-c. Marriage officers.

1. Notwithstanding the provisions of section eleven of this article or any other law, the governing body of any village, town, or city may appoint one or more marriage officers who shall have the authority to solemnize a marriage which marriage shall be valid if performed in accordance with other provisions of law. Nothing herein contained shall nullify the authority of other persons authorized to solemnize marriages.

2. The number of such marriage officers appointed for a municipality shall be determined by the governing body of the municipality. Such marriage officers shall be eighteen years of age or over, and they shall reside in the municipality by which they are appointed. A marriage officer shall have the authority to solemnize a marriage within the territory of the municipality which makes the appointment.

3. A marriage officer may receive a salary or wage in an amount to be determined by the governing body of the municipality which appoints him or her. In the event that a marriage officer receives a salary or wage, he or she shall not receive any remuneration or consideration from any other source for performing his or her duties. In the event that a marriage officer does not receive a salary or wage, he or she may accept and keep up to seventy-five dollars for each marriage at which he or she officiates, paid by or on behalf of the persons married.

4. The term of office of a marriage officer shall be as determined by the governing body which makes the appointment but shall not exceed four years. A marriage officer shall serve at the pleasure of the appointing authority and may be removed from office with or without cause on ten days written notice filed with the clerk of the municipality and sent by registered mail return receipt requested to the marriage officer.

§12. Marriage, how solemnized.

No particular form or ceremony is required when a marriage is solemnized as herein provided by a clergyman or magistrate, but the parties must solemnly declare in the presence of a clergyman or magistrate and the attending witness or witnesses that they take each other as husband and wife. In every case, at least one witness beside the clergyman or magistrate must be present at the ceremony.

The preceding provisions of this chapter, so far as they relate to the manner of solemnizing marriages, shall not affect marriages among the people called friends or quakers; nor marriages among the people of any other denominations having as such any particular mode of solemnizing marriages; but such marriages must be solemnized in the manner heretofore used and practiced in their respective societies or denominations, and marriages so solemnized shall be as valid as if this article had not been enacted.

§13. Marriage licenses.

It shall be necessary for all persons intended to be married in New York state to obtain a marriage license from a town or city clerk in New York state and to deliver said license, within sixty days, to the clergyman or magistrate who is to officiate before the marriage ceremony may be performed. In case of a marriage contracted pursuant to subdivision four of section eleven of this chapter, such license shall be delivered to the judge of the court of record before whom the acknowledgment is to be taken. If either party to the marriage resides upon an island located not less than twenty-five miles from the office or residence of the town clerk of the town of which such island is a part, and if such office or residence is not on such island such license may be obtained from any justice of the peace residing on such island, and such justice, in respect to powers and duties relating to marriage licenses, shall be subject to the provisions of this article governing town clerks and shall file all statements or affidavits received by him while acting under the provisions of this section with the town clerk of such town. No application for a marriage license shall be denied on the ground that the parties are of the same, or a different, sex.

§13-aa. Test to determine the presence of sickle cell anemia.

1. On and after the effective date of this act, such test as may be necessary shall be given to each applicant for a marriage license who is not of the Caucasian, Indian or Oriental race for the purposes of discovering the existence of sickle cell anemia and notifying the applicant of the results of such test.

2. No application for a marriage license shall be denied solely on the ground that such test proves positive, nor shall the absence of such test invalidate a marriage.

3. The provisions of this section shall not apply to any person who refuses to take such test because of his religious beliefs.

§13-b. Time within which marriage may be solemnized.

A marriage shall not be solemnized within twenty-four hours after the issuance of the marriage license, unless authorized by an order of a court of record as hereinafter provided, nor shall it be solemnized after sixty days from the date of the issuance of the marriage license unless authorized pursuant to section three hundred fifty-four-d of the executive law. Every license to marry hereafter issued by a town or city clerk, in addition to other requirements specified by this chapter, must contain a statement of the day and the hour the license is issued and the period during which the marriage may be solemnized. It shall be the duty of the clergyman or magistrate performing the marriage ceremony, or if the marriage is solemnized by written contract, of the judge before whom the contract is acknowledged, to annex to or endorse upon the marriage license the date and hour the marriage is solemnized. A judge or justice of the supreme court of this state or the county judge of the county in which either party to be married resides, or if such party is under sixteen years of age, the judge of the family court of such county, if it shall appear from an examination of the license and any other proofs submitted by the parties that one of the parties is in danger of imminent death, or by reason of other emergency public interest will be promoted thereby, or that such delay will work irreparable injury or great hardship upon the contracting parties, or one of them, may make an order authorizing the immediate solemnization of the marriage and upon filing such order with the clergyman or magistrate performing the marriage ceremony, or if the marriage is to be solemnized by written contract, with the judge before whom the contract is acknowledged, such clergyman or magistrate may solemnize such marriage, or such judge may take such acknowledgment as the case may be, without waiting for such three day period and twenty-four hour period to elapse. The clergyman, magistrate or judge must file such order with the town or city clerk who issued the license within five days after the marriage is solemnized. Such town or city clerk must record and index the order in the book required to be kept by him for recording affidavits, statements, consents and licenses, and when so recorded the order shall become a public record and available in any prosecution under this section. A person who shall solemnize a marriage in violation of this section shall be guilty of a misdemeanor and upon conviction thereof shall be punished by a fine of fifty dollars for each offense, and in addition thereto, his right to solemnize a marriage shall be suspended for ninety days.

§13-d. Duty of clerk issuing marriage license.

1. It shall be the duty of each town and each city clerk or duly authorized deputy acting in the clerk's stead, upon the issuance of a marriage license to display to the parties a typed or printed statement containing substantially the same following information:

"Rubella, also known as 'German measles', is a common childhood disease. It is usually not serious to children who contract it themselves, but can be a tragic crippler of unborn babies if transmitted to pregnant women.

Rubella infection poses a grave threat to the unborn child, especially during the first four months of pregnancy. It can lead to miscarriage, stillbirth, or one or all of the tragic defects such as deafness, blindness, crippling congenital heart disease, mental retardation and muscular and bone defects.

In order to be immune to rubella, one must either receive the rubella vaccine or actually have had the disease. To see whether you are susceptible to rubella, you can get a blood test from your doctor. Even more important is the availability of a rubella vaccine which will prevent you from ever contracting the disease.

In order to protect yourself, your family, and your friends, please take steps to prevent the tragic effects of rubella. Please contact your family doctor, health care provider, public health facility or clinic for further information."

2. It shall also be the duty of each town and city clerk or duly authorized deputy acting in the clerk's stead to provide to each applicant for a marriage license information regarding the Thalassemia Trait. The department of health shall prepare information, including but not limited to, the blood disorder Thalassemia Trait and other inherited conditions affecting the population of New York state.

3. No cause of action for damages shall arise in favor of any person or person yet to be born by reason of any failure to comply with the provisions of this section.

§14. Town and city clerks to issue marriage licenses; form.

The town or city clerk of each and every town or city in this state is hereby empowered to issue marriage licenses to any parties applying for the same who may be entitled under the laws of this state to apply therefor and to contract matrimony, authorizing the marriage of such parties, which license shall be substantially in the following form:

State of New York
County of . . . .
City or town of . . . .

Know all men by this certificate that any person authorized by law to perform marriage ceremonies within the state of New York to whom this may come, he not knowing any lawful impediment thereto, is hereby authorized and empowered to solemnize the rites of matrimony between . . . . of . . . . in the county of . . . . and state of New York and . . . . of . . . . in the county of . . . . and state of New York and to certify the same to the said parties or either of them under his hand and seal in his ministerial or official capacity and thereupon he is required to return his certificate in the form hereto annexed. The statements endorsed hereon or annexed hereto, by me subscribed, contain a full and true abstract of all of the facts concerning such parties disclosed by their affidavits or verified statements presented to me upon the application for this license. This certificate is to be returned addressed to the undersigned at . . . . , ... , ...
(Street)   (City, Town, Village)   (State)

In testimony whereof, I have hereunto set my hand and affixed the seal of said town or city at . . . . this . . . . day of . . . . nineteen . . . . , at . . . . . m. Seal.

The form of the certificate annexed to said license and therein referred to shall be as follows:

I, ... a . . . . . , residing at . . . . in the county of . . . . and state of New York do hereby certify that I did on this . . . . day of . . . . in the year, nineteen . . . . at . . . . . m, at . . . . in the county of . . . . and the state of New York, solemnize the rites of matrimony between . . . . of . . . . . in the county of . . . . and state of New York, and . . . . of . . . . in the county of . . . . and state of New York in the presence of . . . . . and . . . . . as witness, and the license therefor is hereto annexed.
    Witness my hand . . . . . . in the county of . . . . this . . . . day of . . . . . , nineteen . . . . .
    In the presence of

. . . .
. . . .

There shall be endorsed upon the license or annexed thereto at the end thereof, subscribed by the clerk, an abstract of the facts concerning the parties as disclosed in their affidavits or verified statements at the time of the application for the license made in conformity to the provisions of section fifteen of this chapter.

There shall also be stated upon the license the exact period during which the marriage may be solemnized.

The license issued, including the abstract of facts, and the certificate duly signed by the person who shall have solemnized the marriage therein authorized, shall be returned by him, and where the marriage is solemnized by a written contract, the judge before whom acknowledgment is made shall forward such contract and marriage license to the office of the town or city clerk who issued the license within five days succeeding the date of the solemnizing of the marriage therein authorized and any person or persons who shall wilfully neglect to make such return within the time above required shall be deemed guilty of a misdemeanor and upon conviction thereof shall be punished by a fine of not less than twenty-five dollars or more than fifty dollars for each and every offense.

When a marriage is solemnized by a city, town or village justice outside of the territorial jurisdiction in which such justice was elected or appointed, as provided in subdivision six of section eleven of this chapter, there shall be affixed to such license prior to filing, the official or common seal of the court or of the municipality in which such justice was elected or appointed.

§14-a. Town and city clerks to issue certificates of marriage registration; form.

1. Upon receipt of the return of the marriage license, properly endorsed and completed by the person who shall have solemnized a marriage as provided in this article, the town and city clerks of each and every town or city in the state shall, after abstracting, recording and indexing the statement of performance of solemnization, issue to the couple within fifteen days after such receipt or return of the completed marriage license a certificate of marriage, which certificate shall be substantially in the following form and contain the following facts:

Record No. . . . . of Year . . . .

THIS IS TO CERTIFY

that . . . . ,
        first name, premarriage surname, new surname (if applicable)
residing at . . . .,
who was born on . . . ., at . . . .,
             date
and . . . . ,
        first name, premarriage surname, new surname (if applicable)
residing at . . . .,
who was born . . . ., at . . . .,
             date
. . . . , were married on. . . . . at
                                      date
. . . . as shown by the duly registered license and certificate of marriage of said persons on file in this office.

(SEAL)   . . . .
                                                  Town or City Clerk
Dated at . . . ., N. Y.

No other facts contained in the affidavits, statements, consents or licenses shall be certified by such town and city clerks, unless expressly requested in writing by the man or woman named in such affidavit, license, statement or record.

2. a. Such town and city clerks shall be entitled to a fee for such certificate, payable at the time of issuance of the marriage license, in a sum not exceeding ten dollars, to be fixed in the case of town clerks by the town board, and in the case of city clerks by the common council or governing body of such cities. The town and city clerks shall, upon request of any applicant whose name appears thereon, issue a similar certificate of marriage, as set forth above, and similarly expanded with additional facts upon the express additional request, for all marriages heretofore indexed and recorded in the office of the town or city clerks. For such certificate of marriage, the town and city clerks shall be entitled to a fee not exceeding ten dollars, to be fixed in the case of town clerks by the town board, and in the case of city clerks by the common council or governing body of such city.

b. In addition to the foregoing, upon request of any applicant whose name appears thereon for a certificate of marriage, the town or city clerk may issue a photograph, micro-photograph or photocopy of the marriage record on file in the office of such clerk. Such photograph, micro-photograph or photocopy, when certified by the town or city clerk, shall be deemed an original record for all purposes, including introduction in evidence in all courts or administrative agencies. For such certificate of marriage and the certification thereof, the town or city clerk shall be entitled to a fee not exceeding ten dollars, to be fixed in the case of town clerks by the town board, and in the case of city clerks by the common council or governing body of such city.

3. No fee shall be charged for any certificate when required by the veterans administration or by the division of veterans' affairs of the state of New York to be used in determining the eligibility of any person to participate in the benefits made available by the veterans administration or by the state of New York.

4. A copy of the record of marriage registration when properly certified by the city and town clerks or their duly authorized deputies, as herein provided, shall be prima facie evidence of the facts therein stated and in all actions, proceedings or applications, judicial, administrative or otherwise, and any such certificate of registration of marriage shall be accepted with the same force and effect with respect to the facts therein stated as the original certificate of marriage or certified copy thereof.

5. Upon request of any applicant whose name appears thereon for a certificate of marriage, the town or city clerk shall be authorized to correct any errors on such marriage certificate where:

a. such error was not the result of any intended fraud, deception or attempt to avoid the effect of any valid law, regulation or statute; and

b. either party to the marriage provides proof, satisfactory to the clerk, of the accuracy of the facts presented in support of correcting the error.

To effectuate such correction and provide certified copies of the amended certificate, the town or city clerk shall be entitled to a fee not exceeding ten dollars to be fixed in the case of town clerks by the town board, and in the case of city clerks by the common council or governing body of such city. The clerk shall forward a copy of such amended certificate to the commissioner of health.

§15.   Duty of town and city clerks.

1. (a) It shall be the duty of the town or city clerk when an application for a marriage license is made to him or her to require each of the contracting parties to sign and verify a statement or affidavit before such clerk or one of his or her deputies, containing the following information. From the groom: Full name of husband, place of residence, social security number, age, occupation, place of birth, name of father, country of birth, maiden name of mother, country of birth, number of marriage. From the bride: Full name of bride, place of residence, social security number, age, occupation, place of birth, name of father, country of birth, maiden name of mother, country of birth, number of marriage. The said clerk shall also embody in the statement if either or both of the applicants have been previously married, a statement as to whether the former husband or husbands or the former wife or wives of the respective applicants are living or dead and as to whether either or both of said applicants are divorced persons, if so, when and where and against whom the divorce or divorces were granted and shall also embody therein a statement that no legal impediment exists as to the right of each of the applicants to enter into the marriage state. The town or city clerk is hereby given full power and authority to administer oaths and may require the applicants to produce witnesses to identify them or either of them and may examine under oath or otherwise other witnesses as to any material inquiry pertaining to the issuing of the license, and if the applicant is a divorced person the clerk may also require the production of a certified copy of the decree of the divorce, or proof of an existing marriage of parties who apply for a license to be used for a second or subsequent ceremony; provided, however, that in cities or towns the verified statements and affidavits may be made before any regular clerk or designee of the clerk's office.

(b) Every application for a marriage license shall contain a statement to the following effect:

NOTICE TO APPLICANTS

(1) Every person has the right to adopt any name by which he or she wishes to be known simply by using that name consistently and without intent to defraud.

(2) A person's last name (surname) does not automatically change upon marriage, and neither party to the marriage must change his or her last name. Parties to a marriage need not have the same last name.

(3) One or both parties to a marriage may elect to change the surname by which he or she wishes to be known after the solemnization of the marriage by entering the new name in the space below. Such entry shall consist of one of the following surnames:

(i) the surname of the other spouse; or

(ii) any former surname of either spouse; or

(iii) a name combining into a single surname all or a segment of the premarriage surname or any former surname of each spouse; or

(iv) a combination name separated by a hyphen, provided that each part of such combination surname is the premarriage surname, or any former surname, of each of the spouses.

(4) The use of this option will have the effect of providing a record of the change of name. The marriage certificate, containing the new name, if any, constitutes proof that the use of the new name, or the retention of the former name, is lawful.

(5) Neither the use of, nor the failure to use, this option of selecting a new surname by means of this application abrogates the right of each person to adopt a different name through usage at some future date.

. . . .
(Optional -- Enter new surname above)

2. If it appears from the affidavits and statements so taken, that the persons for whose marriage the license in question is demanded are legally competent to marry, the said clerk shall issue such license except in the following cases. If it shall appear upon an application that the applicant is under eighteen years of age, before the town or city clerk shall issue a license, he shall require documentary proof of age in the form of an original or certified copy of a birth record, a certification of birth issued by the state department of health, a local registrar of vital statistics or other public officer charged with similar duties by the laws of any other state, territory or country, a baptismal record, passport, automobile driver's license, life insurance policy, employment certificate, school record, immigration record, naturalization record or court record, showing the date of birth of such minor. If the town or city clerk shall be in doubt as to whether an applicant claiming to be over eighteen years of age is actually over eighteen years of age, he shall, before issuing such license, require documentary proof as above defined. If it shall appear upon an application of the applicants as provided in this section or upon information required by the clerk that either party is at least sixteen years of age but under eighteen years of age, then the town or city clerk before he shall issue a license shall require the written consent to the marriage from both parents of the minor or minors or such as shall then be living, or if the parents of both are dead, then the written consent of the guardian or guardians of such minor or minors. If one of the parents has been missing and has not been seen or heard from for a period of one year preceding the time of the application for the license, although diligent inquiry has been made to learn the whereabouts of such parent, the town or city clerk may issue a license to such minor upon the sworn statement and consent of the other parent. If the marriage of the parents of such minor has been dissolved by decree of divorce or annulment, the consent of the parent to whom the court which granted the decree has awarded the custody of such minor shall be sufficient. If there is no parent or guardian of the minor or minors living to their knowledge then the town or city clerk shall require the written consent to the marriage of the person under whose care or government the minor or minors may be before a license shall be issued. If a parent of such minor has been adjudicated an incompetent, the town or city clerk may issue a license to such minor upon the production of a certified copy of such judgment so determining and upon the written consent of the other parent. If there is no other parent whose consent is required by this section, then and in such event, the town or city clerk shall require the written consent of the guardian of such minor or of the person under whose care or government the minor may be before a license shall be issued. The parents, guardians, or other persons whose consent it shall be necessary to obtain and file with the town or city clerk before the license shall issue, shall personally appear and acknowledge or execute the same before the town or city clerk, or some other officer authorized to administer oaths and take acknowledgments provided that where such affidavit or acknowledgment is made before an official other than an officer designated in section two hundred ninety-eight of the real property law as authorized to take such affidavit or acknowledgment if a conveyance of real property were being

acknowledged or proved, or if a certificate of authentication would be required by section three hundred ten of the real property law to entitle the instrument to be recorded if it were a conveyance of real property, the consent when filed must have attached thereto a certificate of authentication.

3. If it shall appear upon an application for a marriage license that either party is under the age of sixteen years, the town or city clerk shall require, in addition to any consents provided for in this section, the written approval and consent of a justice of the supreme court or of a judge of the family court, having jurisdiction over the town or city in which the application is made, to be attached to or endorsed upon the application, before the license is issued. The application for such approval and consent shall be heard by the judge at chambers. All papers and records pertaining to any such application shall be sealed by him and withheld from inspection, except by order of a court of competent jurisdiction. Before issuing any licenses herein provided for, the town or city clerk shall be entitled to a fee of thirty dollars, which sum shall be paid by the applicants before or at the time the license is issued. Any town or city clerk who shall issue a license to marry any persons one or both of whom shall not be at the time of the marriage under such license legally competent to marry without first requiring the parties to such marriage to make such affidavits and statements or who shall not require the production of documentary proof of age or the procuring of the approval and consents provided for by this article, which shall show that the parties authorized by said license to be married are legally competent to marry, shall be guilty of a misdemeanor and on conviction thereof shall be fined in the sum of one hundred dollars for each and every offense. On or before the fifteenth day of each month, each town and city clerk, except in the city of New York, shall transmit to the state commissioner of health twenty-two dollars and fifty cents of the amount received for each fee collected, which shall be paid into the vital records management account as provided by section ninety-seven-cccc of the state finance law. In any city the balance of all fees collected for the issuing of a marriage license, or for solemnizing a marriage, so far as collected for services rendered by any officer or employee of such city, shall be paid monthly into the city treasury and may by ordinance be credited to any fund therein designated, and said ordinance, when duly enacted, shall have the force of law in such city. Notwithstanding any other provisions of this article, the clerk of any city with the approval of the governing body of such city is hereby authorized to designate, in writing filed in the city clerk's office, a deputy clerk, if any, and/or other city employees in such office to receive applications for, examine applications, investigate and issue marriage licenses in the absence or inability of the clerk of said city to act, and said deputy and/or employees so designated are hereby vested with all the powers and duties of said city clerk relative thereto. Such deputy and/or employees shall perform said duties without additional compensation.

4. Notwithstanding any other provision of this section, the city clerk of the city of New York, before issuing any licenses herein provided for, shall be entitled to a fee of twenty-five dollars, which sum shall be paid by the applicants before or at the time the license is issued and all such fees so received shall be paid monthly into the city treasury.

§15-a. Marriages of minors under fourteen years of age.

Any marriage in which either party is under the age of fourteen years is hereby prohibited. Any town or city clerk who shall knowingly issue a marriage license to any persons, one or both of whom shall be at the time of their contemplated marriage actually under the age of fourteen years, shall be guilty of a misdemeanor and on conviction thereof shall be fined in the sum of one hundred dollars.

§16. False statements and affidavits.

Any person who shall in any affidavit or statement required or provided for in this article wilfully and falsely swear in regard to any material fact as to the competency of any person for whose marriage the license in question or concerning the procuring or issuing of which such affidavit or statement may be made shall be deemed guilty of perjury and on conviction thereof shall be punished as provided by the statutes of this state.

§17. Clergyman or officer violating article; penalty.

If any clergyman or other person authorized by the laws of this state to perform marriage ceremonies shall solemnize or presume to solemnize any marriage between any parties without a license being presented to him or them as herein provided or with knowledge that either party is legally incompetent to contract matrimony as is provided for in this article he shall be guilty of a misdemeanor and on conviction thereof shall be punished by a fine not less than fifty dollars nor more than five hundred dollars or by imprisonment for a term not exceeding one year.

§18. Clergymen or officer, when protected.

Any such clergymen or officer as aforesaid to whom any such license duly issued may come and not having personal knowledge of the incompetency of either party therein named to contract matrimony, may lawfully solemnize matrimony between them.

§19. Records to be kept by town and city clerks.

1. Each town and city clerk hereby empowered to issue marriage licenses shall keep a book supplied by the state department of health in which such clerk shall record and index such information as is required therein, which book shall be kept and preserved as a part of the public records of his office. Whenever an application is made for a search of such records the city or town clerk, excepting the city clerk of the city of New York, may make such search and furnish a certificate of the result to the applicant upon the payment of a fee of five dollars for a search of one year and a further fee of one dollar for the second year for which such search is requested and fifty cents for each additional year thereafter, which fees shall be paid in advance of such search. Whenever an application is made for a search of such records in the city of New York, the city clerk of the city of New York may make such search and furnish a certificate of the result to the applicant upon the payment of a fee of five dollars for a search of one year and a further fee of one dollar for the second year for which search is requested and fifty cents each additional year thereafter. Notwithstanding any other provision of this article, no fee shall be charged for any search or certificate when required by the veterans administration or by the division of veterans' affairs of the state of New York to be used in determining the eligibility of any person to participate in the benefits made available by the veterans administration or by the state of New York. All such affidavits, statements and consents, immediately upon the taking or receiving of the same by the town or city clerk, shall be recorded and indexed

as provided herein and shall be public records and open to public inspection whenever the same may be necessary or required for judicial or other proper purposes. At such times as the commissioner shall direct, the said town or city clerk, excepting the city clerk of the city of New York, shall file in the office of the state department of health the original of each affidavit, statement, consent, order of a justice or judge authorizing immediate solemnization of marriage, license and certificate, filed with or made before such clerk during the preceding month. Such clerk shall not be required to file any of said documents with the state department of health until the license is returned with the certificate showing that the marriage to which they refer has been actually performed.

The county clerks of the counties comprising the city of New York shall cause all original applications and original licenses with the marriage solemnization statements thereon heretofore filed with each, and all papers and records and binders relating to such original documents pertaining to marriage licenses issued by said city clerk, in their custody and possession to be removed, transferred, and delivered to the borough offices of the city clerk in each of said counties.

2. (a) In lieu of the requirement of maintaining a book supplied by the state department of health pursuant to subdivision one hereof, each town or city clerk may cause all information as is required by law or rule or regulation of the department to be kept in such books to be photocopied, photographed, microphotographed or reproduced on film which shall be kept and preserved as part of the public records of his office together with an index thereto. Such photographic film shall be of durable material and the device used to reproduce such records on such film shall be one which accurately reproduces the original record in all details.

(b) Such photocopy or photographic film shall be deemed to be an original record for all purposes, including introduction in evidence in all courts or administrative agencies. A transcript, exemplification or certified copy thereof shall, for all purposes, be deemed to be a transcript, exemplification or certified copy of the original.

§19-a. Marriages on vessels; reports and records.

The master, chief officer, ship's surgeon, or the company, corporation, charterer, or person having the management and control of any vessel which shall arrive at the port of New York, shall report, in writing, to the city clerk of the city of New York within three days after the arrival of such vessel the marriage of any resident of such city occurring thereon at sea, and shall file with such clerk a transcript of the entry made in the log book of such vessel in respect to any such marriage.

§20. Records to be kept by the state department of health and the city clerk of the city of New York.

All original affidavits, statements, consents and licenses with certificates attached, and also all written contracts of marriages outside of the city of New York shall be kept on file and properly indexed by the state department of health, and such similar evidences of marriage in the city of New York shall be kept on file and properly indexed by the city clerk of the city of New York. They shall be carefully examined, and if any such are incomplete or unsatisfactory the state commissioner of health and in the city of New York the city clerk shall require such further information to be supplied as may be necessary to make the record complete and satisfactory. Whenever it is claimed that a mistake has been made through inadvertence in any of the statements, affidavits or other papers required by this section to be filed with the state department of health, and in the city of New York with the city clerk's office, the state commissioner of health and in the city of New York the city clerk may file with the same, affidavits upon the part of the person claiming to be aggrieved by such mistake, showing the true facts and the reason for the mistake and may make a note upon such original paper, statement or affidavit showing that a mistake is claimed to have been made and the nature thereof.

§20-a. Certified transcripts of records; state commissioner of health may furnish.

The state commissioner of health or person authorized by him shall, upon request, supply to any applicant a certified transcript of any marriage registered under the provisions of this article, unless he is satisfied that the same does not appear to be necessary or required for judicial or other proper purposes. Any transcript of the record of a marriage, when properly certified by the state commissioner of health or person authorized to act for him, shall be prima facie evidence in all courts and places of the facts therein stated. For any search of the files and records conducted for authorized research purposes, the state commissioner of health shall be entitled to a fee of twenty dollars for each hour or fractional part of an hour of time of search, together with a fee of two dollars for each uncertified copy or abstract of such marriage record requested by the applicant, said fees to be paid by the applicant. Each applicant for a certified transcript of a marriage record shall remit to the state commissioner of health a fee of thirty dollars in payment for the search of the files and records and the furnishing of a certified copy if such record is found or for a certification that a search discloses no record of a marriage.

§20-b. Certification of marriage; state commissioner of health may furnish.

1. The state commissioner of health or person authorized by him shall, upon request, issue to any applicant a certification of any marriage registered under the provisions of this article, unless he is satisfied that the same does not appear to be necessary or required for judicial or other proper purposes. Any such certification of marriage made by such commissioner or person authorized to act for him shall be prima facie evidence in all courts and places of the facts therein stated.

2. Such certification shall contain a statement of the respective names, dates and places of birth and places of the then residence of each of the parties to such marriage and the date and place thereof.

3. Each applicant for a certification of marriage shall remit to the commissioner with such application a fee of thirty dollars in payment for the search of the files and records and the furnishing of such certification if a record thereof is found or for a certification that a search discloses no record of a marriage.

4. The federal agency in charge of vital statistics may obtain, at a fee acceptable to the commissioner, information from marriage records for use solely as statistical data.

§21. Forms and books to be furnished.

The proper books for registration, blank forms for marriage licenses, certificates, statements and affidavits and such other blanks as shall be necessary to comply with the provisions of this article, shall be prepared by the state department of health and shall be furnished by said department at the expense of the state to the town and city clerks filing records with the state department of health in such quantities as their necessities shall require.

§22. Penalty for violation.

Any town or city clerk who shall violate any of the provisions of this article or shall fail to comply therewith shall be deemed guilty of a misdemeanor and shall pay a fine not exceeding the sum of one hundred dollars on conviction thereof.

§23. Supervision of and inspection of town and city clerks' records by state commissioner of health.

The registration and recording of all marriages outside the city of New York shall be under the supervision of the state commissioner of health. The commissioner, either personally or by an accredited representative, may at any time inspect the record and index of marriage licenses issued by any town or city clerk and promulgate rules and regulations for insuring complete registration. When he shall deem it necessary, he shall report cases of violation of any of the provisions of this article to the district attorney of the county, with a statement of the facts and circumstances; and when any such case is reported to him by the state commissioner of health, the prosecuting attorney shall forthwith initiate and promptly follow up the necessary court proceedings against the person or persons responsible for the alleged violation of law. Upon request of the state commissioner of health, the attorney-general shall assist in the enforcement of the provisions of this article.

§24. Effect of marriage on legitimacy of children.

1. A child heretofore or hereafter born of parents who prior or subsequent to the birth of such child shall have entered into a civil or religious marriage, or shall have consummated a common-law marriage where such marriage is recognized as valid, in the manner authorized by the law of the place where such marriage takes place, is the legitimate child of both birth parents notwithstanding that such marriage is void or voidable or has been or shall hereafter be annulled or judicially declared void.

2. Nothing herein contained shall be deemed to affect the construction of any will or other instrument executed before the time this act shall take effect or any right or interest in property or right of action vested or accrued before the time this act shall take effect, or to limit the operation of any judicial determination heretofore made containing express provision with respect to the legitimacy, maintenance or custody of any child, or to affect any adoption proceeding heretofore commenced, or limit the effect of any order or orders entered in such adoption proceeding.

§25. License, when to be obtained.

The provisions of this article pertaining to the granting of the licenses before a marriage can be lawfully celebrated apply to all persons who assume the marriage relation in accordance with subdivision four of section eleven of this chapter. Nothing in this article contained shall be construed to render void by reason of a failure to procure a marriage license any marriage solemnized between persons of full age nor to render void any marriage between minors or with a minor under the legal age of consent where the consent of parent or guardian has been given and such marriage shall be for such cause voidable only as to minors or a minor upon complaint of such minors or minor or of the parent or guardian thereof.

ARTICLE 4
Certain Rights and Liabilities
of Husband and Wife

Section
50. Property of married woman.
52. Insurance of married person's life.
58. Pardon not to restore marital rights.
61. Married person's domicile.

§50. Property of married woman.

Property, real or personal, now owned by a married woman, or hereafter owned by a woman at the time of her marriage, or acquired by her as prescribed in this chapter, and the rents, issues, proceeds and profits thereof, shall continue to be her sole and separate property as if she were unmarried, and shall not be subject to her husband's control or disposal nor liable for his debts.

§52. Insurance of married person's life.

The right of a married person to cause the life of his or her spouse or any other person to be insured and to dispose of any interest such married person may have in a policy of insurance on the life of the other spouse or of any other person shall be governed by the insurance law and by statutes and rules of law governing rights of a married person in respect to property and the acquisition, use, enjoyment and disposition thereof.

§58. Pardon not to restore marital rights.

A pardon granted to a person sentenced to imprisonment for life within this state does not restore that person to the rights of a previous marriage or to the guardianship of a child, the issue of such a marriage.

§61. Married person's domicile.

The domicile of a married man or woman shall be established for all purposes without regard to sex.

ARTICLE 5
The Custody and Wages of Children

Section
70. Habeas corpus for child detained by parent.
71. Special proceeding or habeas corpus to obtain visitation rights in respect to certain infant siblings.
72. Special proceeding or habeas corpus to obtain visitation rights or custody in respect to certain infant grandchildren.
73. Legitimacy of children born by artificial insemination.
74. Certain provisions relating to the custody of children by persons who are not the parents of such children.

§70. Habeas corpus for child detained by parent.

(a) Where a minor child is residing within this state, either parent may apply to the supreme court for a writ of habeas corpus to have such minor child brought before such court; and on the return thereof, the court, on due consideration, may award the natural guardianship, charge and custody of such child to either parent for such time, under such regulations and restrictions, and with such provisions and directions, as the case may require, and may at any time thereafter vacate or modify such order. In all cases there shall be no prima facie right to the custody of the child in either parent, but the court shall determine solely what is for the best interest of the child, and what will best promote its welfare and happiness, and make award accordingly.

(b) Any order under this section which applies to rights of visitation with a child remanded or placed in the care of a person, official, agency or institution pursuant to article ten of the family court act or pursuant to an instrument approved under section three hundred fifty-eight-a of the social services law, shall be enforceable pursuant to the provisions of part eight of article ten of such act, sections three hundred fifty-eight-a and three hundred eighty-four-a of the social services law and other applicable provisions of law against any person or official having care and custody, or temporary care and custody, of such child.

§71. Special proceeding or habeas corpus to obtain visitation rights in respect to certain infant siblings.

Where circumstances show that conditions exist which equity would see fit to intervene, a brother or sister or, if he or she be a minor, a proper person on his or her behalf of a child, whether by half or whole blood, may apply to the supreme court by commencing a special proceeding or for a writ of habeas corpus to have such child brought before such court, or may apply to the family court pursuant to subdivision (b) of section six hundred fifty-one of the family court act; and on the return thereof, the court, by order, after due notice to the parent or any other person or party having the care, custody, and control of such child, to be given in such manner as the court shall prescribe, may make such directions as the best interest of the child may require, for visitation rights for such brother or sister in respect to such child.

§72. Special proceeding or habeas corpus to obtain visitation rights or custody in respect to certain infant grandchildren.

1. Where either or both of the parents of a minor child, residing within this state, is or are deceased, or where circumstances show that conditions exist which equity would see fit to intervene, a grandparent or the grandparents of such child may apply to the supreme court by commencing a special proceeding or for a writ of habeas corpus to have such child brought before such court, or may apply to the family court pursuant to subdivision (b) of section six hundred fifty-one of the family court act; and on the return thereof, the court, by order, after due notice to the parent or any other person or party having the care, custody, and control of such child, to be given in such manner as the court shall prescribe, may make such directions as the best interest of the child may require, for visitation rights for such grandparent or grandparents in respect to such child.

2. (a) Where a grandparent or the grandparents of a minor child, residing within this state, can demonstrate to the satisfaction of the court the existence of extraordinary circumstances, such grandparent or grandparents of such child may apply to the supreme court by commencing a special proceeding or for a writ of habeas corpus to have such child brought before such court, or may apply to family court pursuant to subdivision (b) of section six hundred fifty-one of the family court act; and on the return thereof, the court, by order, after due notice to the parent or any other person or party having the care, custody, and control of such child, to be given in such manner as the court shall prescribe, may make such directions as the best interests of the child may

require, for custody rights for such grandparent or grandparents in respect to such child. An extended disruption of custody, as such term is defined in this section, shall constitute an extraordinary circumstance.

(b) For the purposes of this section "extended disruption of custody" shall include, but not be limited to, a prolonged separation of the respondent parent and the child for at least twenty-four continuous months during which the parent voluntarily relinquished care and control of the child and the child resided in the household of the petitioner grandparent or grandparents, provided, however, that the court may find that extraordinary circumstances exist should the prolonged separation have lasted for less than twenty-four months.

(c) Nothing in this section shall limit the ability of parties to enter into consensual custody agreements absent the existence of extraordinary circumstances.

§73. Legitimacy of children born by artificial insemination.

1. Any child born to a married woman by means of artificial insemination performed by persons duly authorized to practice medicine and with the consent in writing of the woman and her husband, shall be deemed the legitimate, birth child of the husband and his wife for all purposes.

2. The aforesaid written consent shall be executed and acknowledged by both the husband and wife and the physician who performs the technique shall certify that he had rendered the service.

§74. Certain provisions relating to the custody of children by persons who are not the parents of such children.

1. Notwithstanding any provision of law to the contrary, a person possessing a lawful order of guardianship or custody of a minor child, who is not the parent of such child, may enroll such child in public school in the applicable school district where he or she and such child reside. Upon application for enrollment of a minor child by a guardian or custodian who is not the parent of such child, a public school shall enroll such child for such time as the child resides with the guardian or custodian in the applicable school district, upon verification that the guardian or custodian possess a lawful order of custody for such child and that the guardian or custodian and the child properly reside in the same household within the school district.

2. Notwithstanding any provision of law to the contrary, persons possessing a lawful order of custody of a child who are not a parent of such child shall have the right to enroll and receive coverage for such child in their employer based health insurance plan and to assert the same legal rights under such employer based health insurance plans as persons who possess lawful orders of guardianship of the person for a child pursuant to rule twelve hundred ten of the civil practice laws and rules, article seventeen of the surrogate's court procedure act, or part four of article six of the family court act.

ARTICLE 5-A
Uniform Child Custody Jurisdiction
and Enforcement Act

Title I
General Provisions

§75. Short title and statement of legislative intent.

1. This article may be cited as the "uniform child custody jurisdiction and enforcement act".

2. It is the intent of the legislature in enacting this article to provide an effective mechanism to obtain and enforce orders of custody and visitation across state lines and to do so in a manner that ensures that the safety of the children is paramount and that victims of domestic violence and child abuse are protected. It is further the intent of the legislature that this article be construed so as to ensure that custody and visitation by perpetrators of domestic violence or homicide of a parent, legal custodian, legal guardian, sibling, half-sibling or step-sibling of a child is restricted pursuant to subdivision one-c of section two hundred forty of this chapter and section one thousand eighty-five of the family court act.

§75-a. Definitions.

In this article:

1. "Abandoned" means left without provision for reasonable and necessary care or supervision.

2. "Child" means an individual who has not attained eighteen years of age.

3. "Child custody determination" means a judgment, decree, or other order of a court providing for the legal custody, physical custody, or visitation with respect to a child. The term includes a permanent, temporary, initial, and modification order. The term does not include an order relating to child support or other monetary obligation of an individual.

4. "Child custody proceeding" means a proceeding in which legal custody, physical custody, or visitation with respect to a child is an issue. The term includes a proceeding for divorce, separation, neglect, abuse, dependency, guardianship, paternity, termination of parental rights, and protection from domestic violence, in which the issue may appear. The term does not include a proceeding involving juvenile delinquency, person in need of supervision, contractual emancipation, or enforcement under title three of this article.

5. "Commencement" means the filing of the first pleading in a proceeding.

6. "Court" means an entity authorized under the law of a state to establish, enforce, or modify a child custody determination.

7. "Home state" means the state in which a child lived with a parent or a person acting as a parent for at least six consecutive months immediately before the commencement of a child custody proceeding. In the case of a child less than six months of age, the term means the state in which the child lived

from birth with any of the persons mentioned. A period of temporary absence of any of the mentioned persons is part of the period.

8. "Initial determination" means the first child custody determination concerning a particular child.

9. "Issuing court" means the court that makes a child custody determination for which enforcement is sought under this article.

10. "Issuing state" means the state in which a child custody determination is made.

11. "Modification" means a child custody determination that changes, replaces, supersedes, or is otherwise made after a previous determination concerning the same child, whether or not it is made by the court that made the previous determination.

12. "Person" means an individual, corporation, business trust, estate, trust, partnership, limited liability company, association, joint venture, government, governmental subdivision, agency or instrumentality, public corporation or any other legal or commercial entity.

13. "Person acting as a parent" means a person, other than a parent, who:

(a) has physical custody of the child or has had physical custody for a period of six consecutive months, including any temporary absence, within one year immediately before the commencement of a child custody proceeding; and

(b) has been awarded legal custody by a court or claims a right to legal custody under the law of this state.

14. "Physical custody" means the physical care and supervision of a child.

15. "State" means a state of the United States, the District of Columbia, Puerto Rico, the United States Virgin Islands, or any territory or insular possession subject to the jurisdiction of the United States.

16. "Tribe" means an Indian tribe or band, or Alaskan Native village, which is recognized by federal law or formally acknowledged by a state.

17. "Warrant" means an order issued by a court authorizing law enforcement officers to take physical custody of a child.

18. "Law enforcement officer" means a police officer as defined in subdivision thirty-four of section 1.20 of the criminal procedure law.

§75-b. Proceedings governed by other laws.

This article does not govern an adoption proceeding or a proceeding pertaining to the authorization of emergency medical care for a child.

§75-c. Application to Indian tribes.

1. A child custody proceeding that pertains to an Indian child as defined in the Indian Child Welfare Act, 25 U.S.C. § 1901 et seq., is not subject to this article to the extent that it is governed by the Indian Child Welfare Act.

2. A court of this state shall treat a tribe as if it were a state of the United States for the purpose of applying this title and title two of this article.

3. A child custody determination made by a tribe under factual circumstances in substantial conformity with the jurisdictional standards of this article must be recognized and enforced under title three of this article.

§75-d. International application of article.

1. A court of this state shall treat a foreign country as if it were a state of the United States for the purpose of applying this title and title two of this article.

2. Except as otherwise provided in subdivision three of this section, a child custody determination made in a foreign country under factual circumstances

in substantial conformity with the jurisdictional standards of this article must be recognized and enforced under title three of this article.

3. A court of this state need not apply this article if the child custody law of a foreign country as written or as applied violates fundamental principles of human rights.

§75-e. Effect of child custody determination.

A child custody determination made by a court of this state that had jurisdiction under this article binds all persons who have been served in accordance with the laws of this state or notified in accordance with section seventy-five-g of this title or who have submitted to the jurisdiction of the court, and who have been given an opportunity to be heard. As to those persons, the determination is conclusive as to all decided issues of law and fact except to the extent the determination is modified or except to the extent that enforcement of an order would violate subdivision one-c of section two hundred forty of this chapter or section one thousand eighty-five of the family court act.

§75-f. Priority.

If a question of existence or exercise of jurisdiction under this article is raised in a child custody proceeding, the question, upon request of a party, child or child's attorney must be given priority on the calendar and handled expeditiously.

§75-g. Notice to persons outside state.

1. Notice required for the exercise of jurisdiction when a person is outside this state shall be given in a manner prescribed by the law of this state for service of process, as provided in paragraph (a), (b) or (c) of this subdivision, or by the law of the state in which the service is made, as provided in paragraph (d) of this subdivision. Notice must be given in a manner reasonably calculated to give actual notice. If a person cannot be served with notice within the state, the court shall require that such person be served in a manner reasonably calculated to give actual notice, as follows:

(a) by personal delivery outside the state in the manner prescribed by section three hundred thirteen of the civil practice law and rules; or

(b) by any form of mail requesting a receipt; or

(c) in such manner as the court, upon motion, directs, including publication, if service is impracticable under paragraph (a) or (b) of this subdivision; or

(d) in such manner as prescribed by the law of the state in which service is made.

2. Proof of service outside the state shall be by affidavit of the individual who made the service, or in the manner prescribed by the order pursuant to which service is made. If service is made by mail, proof may be by a receipt signed by the addressee or other evidence of delivery to the addressee. Proof of service may also be in the manner prescribed by the law of the state in which the service is made.

3. Notice is not required for the exercise of jurisdiction with respect to a person who submits to the jurisdiction of the court.

§75-h. Appearance and limited immunity.

1. A party to a child custody proceeding, including a modification proceeding, or a petitioner or respondent in a proceeding to enforce or register a child custody determination, is not subject to personal jurisdiction in this state

for another proceeding or purpose solely by reason of having participated, or of having been physically present for the purpose of participating, in the proceeding.

2. A person who is subject to personal jurisdiction in this state on a basis other than physical presence is not immune from service of process in this state. A party present in this state who is subject to the jurisdiction of another state is not immune from service of process allowable under the laws of that state.

3. The immunity granted by subdivision one of this section does not extend to civil litigation based on acts unrelated to the participation in a proceeding under this article committed by an individual while present in this state.

§75-i. Communication between courts.

1. A court of this state may communicate and, pursuant to subdivision four of section seventy-six-c, subdivision two of section seventy-six-e and section seventy-seven-f of this article, must communicate, with a court in another state concerning a proceeding arising under this article.

2. The court may allow the parties to participate in the communication. If the parties are not able to participate in the communication, they must be given the opportunity to present facts and legal arguments before a decision on jurisdiction is made.

3. Communication between courts on schedules, calendars, court records, and similar matters may occur without informing the parties. A record need not be made of the communication.

4. Except as otherwise provided in subdivision three of this section, a record must be made of a communication under this section. The parties must be informed promptly of the communication and granted access to the record.

5. For the purposes of this section, "record" means information that is inscribed on a tangible medium or that is stored in an electronic or other medium and is retrievable in perceivable form.

§75-j. Taking testimony in another state.

1. In addition to other procedures available to a party, a party to a child custody proceeding may offer testimony of witnesses who are located in another state, including testimony of the parties and the child, by deposition or other means allowable in this state for testimony taken in another state. The court on its own motion may order that the testimony of a person be taken in another state and may prescribe the manner in which and the terms upon which the testimony is taken.

2. A court of this state may permit an individual residing in another state to be deposed or to testify by telephone, audiovisual means, or other electronic means before a designated court or at another location in that state. A court of this state shall cooperate with courts of other states in designating an appropriate location for the deposition or testimony and the procedures to be followed by the persons taking such deposition or testimony. Any such testimony or deposition shall be recorded and preserved for transcription.

3. Documentary evidence transmitted from another state to a court of this state by technological means that do not produce an original writing may not be excluded from evidence on an objection based on the means of transmission.

§75-k. Cooperation between courts; preservation of records.

1. A court of this state may request the appropriate court of another state to:
(a) hold an evidentiary hearing;

(b) order a person to produce or give evidence pursuant to procedures of that state;

(c) order that an evaluation be made with respect to the custody of a child involved in a pending proceeding;

(d) forward to the court of this state a certified copy of the transcript of the record of the hearing, the evidence otherwise presented, and any evaluation prepared in compliance with the request; and

(e) order a party to a child custody proceeding or any person having physical custody of the child to appear in the proceeding with or without the child.

2. Upon the request of a court of another state, a court of this state may hold a hearing or enter an order described in subdivision one of this section.

3. Travel and other necessary and reasonable expenses incurred under subdivisions one and two of this section may be assessed against the parties according to the law of this state.

4. A court of this state shall preserve the pleadings, orders, decrees, records of hearings, evaluations, and other pertinent records with respect to a child custody proceeding at least until the child attains eighteen years of age. Upon appropriate request by a court or law enforcement official of another state, the court shall forward a certified copy of those records.

§75-*l*. Military service by parent; effect on child custody orders pursuant to this article.

1. During the period of time that a parent is activated, deployed or temporarily assigned to military service, such that the parent's ability to continue as a joint caretaker or the primary caretaker of a minor child is materially affected by such military service, any orders issued pursuant to this article, based on the fact that the parent is activated, deployed or temporarily assigned to military service, which would materially affect or change a previous judgment or order regarding custody of that parent's child or children as such judgment or order existed on the date the parent was activated, deployed, or temporarily assigned to military service shall be subject to review pursuant to subdivision three of this section. Any relevant provisions of the Service Member's Civil Relief Act shall apply to all proceedings governed by this section.

2. During such period the court may enter an order to modify custody if there is clear and convincing evidence that the modification is in the best interests of the child. An attorney for the child shall be appointed in all cases where a modification is sought during such military service. Such order shall be subject to review pursuant to subdivision three of this section. When entering an order under this section, the court shall consider and provide for, if feasible and if in the best interests of the child, contact between the military service member and his or her child including, but not limited to, electronic communication by e-mail, webcam, telephone, or other available means. During the period of the parent's leave from military service, the court shall consider the best interests of the child when establishing a parenting schedule, including visiting and other contact. For such purpose, a "leave from service" shall be a period of not more than three months.

3. Unless the parties have otherwise stipulated or agreed, if an order is issued under this section, the return of the parent from active military service, deployment or temporary assignment shall be considered a substantial change in circumstances. Upon the request of either parent, the court shall determine

on the basis of the child's best interests whether the custody judgment or order previously in effect should be modified.

4. This section shall not apply to assignments to permanent duty stations or permanent changes of station.

Title II
Jurisdiction

§76. Initial child custody jurisdiction.

1. Except as otherwise provided in section seventy-six-c of this title, a court of this state has jurisdiction to make an initial child custody determination only if:

(a) this state is the home state of the child on the date of the commencement of the proceeding, or was the home state of the child within six months before the commencement of the proceeding and the child is absent from this state but a parent or person acting as a parent continues to live in this state;

(b) a court of another state does not have jurisdiction under paragraph (a) of this subdivision, or a court of the home state of the child has declined to exercise jurisdiction on the ground that this state is the more appropriate forum under section seventy-six-f or seventy-six-g of this title, and:

(i) the child and the child's parents, or the child and at least one parent or a person acting as a parent, have a significant connection with this state other than mere physical presence; and

(ii) substantial evidence is available in this state concerning the child's care, protection, training, and personal relationships;

(c) all courts having jurisdiction under paragraph (a) or (b) of this subdivision have declined to exercise jurisdiction on the ground that a court of this state is the more appropriate forum to determine the custody of the child under section seventy-six-f or seventy-six-g of this title; or

(d) no court of any other state would have jurisdiction under the criteria specified in paragraph (a), (b) or (c) of this subdivision.

2. Subdivision one of this section is the exclusive jurisdictional basis for making a child custody determination by a court of this state.

3. Physical presence of, or personal jurisdiction over, a party or a child is not necessary or sufficient to make a child custody determination.

§76-a. Exclusive, continuing jurisdiction.

1. Except as otherwise provided in section seventy-six-c of this title, a court of this state which has made a child custody determination consistent with section seventy-six or seventy-six-b of this title has exclusive, continuing jurisdiction over the determination until:

(a) a court of this state determines that neither the child, the child and one parent, nor the child and a person acting as a parent have a significant connection with this state and that substantial evidence is no longer available in this state concerning the child's care, protection, training, and personal relationships; or

(b) a court of this state or a court of another state determines that the child, the child's parents, and any person acting as a parent do not presently reside in this state.

2. A court of this state which has made a child custody determination and does not have exclusive, continuing jurisdiction under this section may modify that determination only if it has jurisdiction to make an initial determination under section seventy-six of this title.

§76-b. Jurisdiction to modify determination.

Except as otherwise provided in section seventy-six-c of this title, a court of this state may not modify a child custody determination made by a court of another state unless a court of this state has jurisdiction to make an initial determination under paragraph (a) or (b) of subdivision one of section seventy-six of this title and:

1. The court of the other state determines it no longer has exclusive, continuing jurisdiction under section seventy-six-a of this title or that a court of this state would be a more convenient forum under section seventy-six-f of this title; or

2. A court of this state or a court of the other state determines that the child, the child's parents, and any person acting as a parent do not presently reside in the other state.

§76-c. Temporary emergency jurisdiction.

1. A court of this state has temporary emergency jurisdiction if the child is present in this state and the child has been abandoned or it is necessary in an emergency to protect the child, a sibling or parent of the child.

2. If there is no previous child custody determination that is entitled to be enforced under this article and a child custody proceeding has not been commenced in a court of a state having jurisdiction under sections seventy-six through seventy-six-b of this title, a child custody determination made under this section remains in effect until an order is obtained from a court of a state having jurisdiction under sections seventy-six through seventy-six-b of this title. Where the child who is the subject of a child custody determination under this section is in imminent risk of harm, any order issued under this section shall remain in effect until a court of a state having jurisdiction under sections seventy-six through seventy-six-b of this title has taken steps to assure the protection of the child. If a child custody proceeding has not been or is not commenced in a court of a state having jurisdiction under sections seventy-six through seventy-six-b of this title, a child custody determination made under this section becomes a final determination, if it so provides and this state becomes the home state of the child.

3. If there is a previous child custody determination that is entitled to be enforced under this article, or a child custody proceeding has been commenced in a court of a state having jurisdiction under sections seventy-six through seventy-six-b of this title, any order issued by a court of this state under this section must specify in the order a period that the court considers adequate to allow the person seeking an order to obtain an order from the state having jurisdiction under sections seventy-six through seventy-six-b of this title. The order issued in this state remains in effect until an order is obtained from the other state within the period specified or the period expires, provided, however, that where the child who is the subject of a child custody determination under

this section is in imminent risk of harm, any order issued under this section shall remain in effect until a court of a state having jurisdiction under sections seventy-six through seventy-six-b of this title has taken steps to assure the protection of the child.

4. A court of this state which has been asked to make a child custody determination under this section, upon being informed that a child custody proceeding has been commenced in, or a child custody determination has been made by, a court of a state having jurisdiction under sections seventy-six through seventy-six-b of this title, shall immediately communicate with the other court. A court of this state which is exercising jurisdiction pursuant to sections seventy-six through seventy-six-b of this title, upon being informed that a child custody proceeding has been commenced in, or a child custody determination has been made by, a court of another state under a statute similar to this section shall immediately communicate with the court of that state to resolve the emergency, protect the safety of the parties and the child, and determine a period for the duration of the temporary order.

§76-d. Notice; opportunity to be heard; joinder.

1. Before a child custody determination is made under this article, notice and an opportunity to be heard in accordance with the standards of section seventy-five-g of this article must be given to all persons entitled to notice under the law of this state as in child custody proceedings between residents of this state, any parent whose parental rights have not been previously terminated, and any person having physical custody of the child.

2. This article does not govern the enforceability of a child custody determination made without notice or an opportunity to be heard.

3. The obligation to join a party and the right to intervene as a party in a child custody proceeding under this article are governed by the laws of this state as in child custody proceedings between residents of this state.

§76-e. Simultaneous proceedings.

1. Except as otherwise provided in section seventy-six-c of this title, a court of this state may not exercise its jurisdiction under this title if, at the time of the commencement of the proceeding, a proceeding concerning the custody of the child has been commenced in a court of another state having jurisdiction substantially in conformity with this article, unless the proceeding has been terminated or is stayed by the court of the other state because a court of this state is a more convenient forum under section seventy-six-f of this title.

2. Except as otherwise provided in section seventy-six-c of this title, a court of this state, before hearing a child custody proceeding, shall examine the court documents and other information supplied by the parties pursuant to section seventy-six-h of this title. If the court determines that a child custody proceeding has been commenced in a court in another state having jurisdiction substantially in accordance with this article, the court of this state shall stay its proceeding and communicate with the court of the other state. If the court of the state having jurisdiction substantially in accordance with this article does not determine that the court of this state is a more appropriate forum, the court of this state shall dismiss the proceeding.

3. In a proceeding to modify a child custody determination, a court of this state shall determine whether a proceeding to enforce the determination has been commenced in another state. If a proceeding to enforce a child custody determination has been commenced in another state, the court may:

(a) stay the proceeding for modification pending the entry of an order of a court of the other state enforcing, staying, denying, or dismissing the proceeding for enforcement:

(b) enjoin the parties from continuing with the proceeding for enforcement; or

(c) proceed with the modification under conditions it considers appropriate.

§76-f. Inconvenient forum.

1. A court of this state which has jurisdiction under this article to make a child custody determination may decline to exercise its jurisdiction at any time if it determines that it is an inconvenient forum under the circumstances and that a court of another state is a more appropriate forum. The issue of inconvenient forum may be raised upon motion of a party, the child or the child's attorney, or upon the court's own motion, or request of another court.

2. Before determining whether it is an inconvenient forum, a court of this state shall consider whether it is appropriate for a court of another state to exercise jurisdiction. For this purpose, the court shall allow the parties to submit information and shall consider all relevant factors, including:

(a) whether domestic violence or mistreatment or abuse of a child or sibling has occurred and is likely to continue in the future and which state could best protect the parties and the child;

(b) the length of time the child has resided outside this state;

(c) the distance between the court in this state and the court in the state that would assume jurisdiction;

(d) the relative financial circumstances of the parties;

(e) any agreement of the parties as to which state should assume jurisdiction;

(f) the nature and location of the evidence required to resolve the pending litigation, including testimony of the child;

(g) the ability of the court of each state to decide the issue expeditiously and the procedures necessary to present the evidence; and

(h) the familiarity of the court of each state with the facts and issues in the pending litigation.

3. If a court of this state determines that it is an inconvenient forum and that a court of another state is a more appropriate forum, it shall stay the proceedings upon condition that a child custody proceeding be promptly commenced in another designated state and may impose any other condition the court considers just and proper.

4. A court of this state may decline to exercise its jurisdiction under this article if a child custody determination is incidental to an action for divorce or another proceeding while still retaining jurisdiction over the divorce or other proceeding.

§76-g. Jurisdiction declined by reason of conduct.

1. Except as otherwise provided in section seventy-six-c of this title or by other law of this state, if a court of this state has jurisdiction under this article because a person seeking to invoke its jurisdiction has engaged in unjustifiable conduct, the court shall decline to exercise its jurisdiction unless:

(a) the parents and all persons acting as parents have acquiesced in the exercise of jurisdiction;

(b) a court of the state otherwise having jurisdiction under sections seventy-six through seventy-six-b of this title determines that this state is a more appropriate forum under section seventy-six-f of this title; or

(c) no court of any other state would have jurisdiction under the criteria specified in sections seventy-six through seventy-six-b of this title.

2. If a court of this state declines to exercise its jurisdiction pursuant to subdivision one of this section, it may fashion an appropriate remedy to ensure the safety of the child and prevent a repetition of the unjustifiable conduct, including staying the proceeding until a child custody proceeding is commenced in a court having jurisdiction under sections seventy-six through seventy-six-b of this title.

3. If a court dismisses a petition or stays a proceeding because it declines to exercise its jurisdiction pursuant to subdivision one of this section, it shall assess against the party seeking to invoke its jurisdiction necessary and reasonable expenses including costs, communication expenses, attorney's fees, investigative fees, expenses for witnesses, travel expenses, and child care during the course of the proceedings, unless the party from whom fees are sought establishes that the assessment would be inappropriate. No fees, costs or expenses shall be assessed against a party who is fleeing an incident or pattern of domestic violence or mistreatment or abuse of a child or sibling, unless the court is convinced by a preponderance of evidence that such assessment would be clearly appropriate. The court may not assess fees, costs, or expenses against this state unless authorized by law other than this article.

4. In making a determination under this section, a court shall not consider as a factor weighing against the petitioner any taking of the child, or retention of the child after a visit or other temporary relinquishment of physical custody, from the person who has legal custody, if there is evidence that the taking or retention of the child was to protect the petitioner from domestic violence or the child or sibling from mistreatment or abuse.

§76-h. Information to be submitted to court.

1. Subject to subdivision five of this section, in a child custody proceeding, each party, in its first pleading or in an attached affidavit, shall give information, if reasonably ascertainable, under oath as to the child's present address or whereabouts, the places where the child has lived during the last five years, and the names and present addresses of the persons with whom the child has lived during that period. The pleading or affidavit must state whether the party:

(a) has participated, as a party or witness or in any other capacity, in any other proceeding concerning the custody of or visitation with the child and, if so, identify the court, the case number, and the date of the child custody determination, if any;

(b) knows of any proceeding that could affect the current proceeding, including proceedings for enforcement and proceedings relating to domestic violence, protective orders, termination of parental rights, and adoptions and, if so, identify the court, the case number, and the nature of the proceeding; and

(c) knows the names and addresses of any person not a party to the proceeding who has physical custody of the child or claims rights of legal custody or physical custody of, or visitation with, the child and, if so, the names and addresses of those persons.

2. If the information required by subdivision one of this section is not furnished, the court, upon motion of a party or its own motion, may stay the proceeding until the information is furnished.

3. If the declaration as to any of the items described in paragraphs (a) through (c) of subdivision one of this section is in the affirmative, the declarant shall give additional information under oath as required by the court. The court may examine the parties under oath as to details of the information furnished and other matters pertinent to the court's jurisdiction and the disposition of the case.

4. Each party has a continuing duty to inform the court of any proceeding in this or any other state that could affect the current proceeding.

5. Upon a finding, which may be made ex parte, that the health or safety of a party or child would be unreasonably put at risk by the disclosure of identifying information, or if an existing order so provides, a tribunal shall order that the address of the child or party or other identifying information not be disclosed in a pleading or other document filed in a proceeding under this article. Notwithstanding any other provision of law, if the party seeking custody of the child has resided or resides in a residential program for victims of domestic violence as defined in section four hundred fifty-nine-a of the social services law, the present address of the child and the present address of the party seeking custody and the address of the residential program for victims of domestic violence shall not be revealed. Upon making an order that the address of the child or party or other identifying information not be disclosed, the court shall designate the clerk of the court or such other disinterested person as the agent for service of process for the party whose address is to remain confidential and shall notify the adverse party of such designation in writing. The clerk or disinterested person designated by the court shall, when served with process on behalf of the party whose address is to remain confidential, promptly notify such party whose address is to remain confidential and forward such process to him or her. The party whose address is to remain confidential shall inform the clerk of the court or disinterested person designated by the court of any change in address for purposes of receipt of service of process.

§76-i. Appearance of parties and child.

1. In a child custody proceeding in this state, the court may order a party to the proceeding who is in this state to appear before the court in person with or without the child. The court may order any person who is in this state and who has physical custody or control of the child to appear in person with the child.

2. If a party to a child custody proceeding whose presence is desired by the court is outside this state, the court may order that a notice given pursuant to section seventy-five-g of this article include a statement directing the party to appear in person with or without the child and informing the party that failure to appear may result in a decision adverse to the party.

3. The court may enter any orders necessary to ensure the safety of the child and of any person ordered to appear under this section.

4. If a party to a child custody proceeding who is outside this state is directed to appear under subdivision two of this section or desires to appear personally before the court with or without the child, the court may require another party to pay reasonable and necessary travel and other expenses of the party so appearing and of the child.

Title III
Enforcement

§77. Definitions.
As used in this title:

1. "Petitioner" means a person who seeks enforcement of an order for return of a child under the Hague Convention on the Civil Aspects of International Child Abduction or enforcement of a child custody determination.

2. "Respondent" means a person against whom a proceeding has been commenced for enforcement of an order for return of a child under the Hague Convention on the Civil Aspects of International Child Abduction or enforcement of a child custody determination.

§77-a. Enforcement under Hague Convention.
Under this act, a court of this state may enforce an order for the return of the child made under the Hague Convention on the Civil Aspects of International Child Abduction as if it were a child custody determination.

§77-b. Duty to enforce.
1. A court of this state shall recognize and enforce a child custody determination of a court of another state if the latter court exercised jurisdiction in substantial conformity with this article or the determination was made under factual circumstances meeting the jurisdictional standards of this article and the determination has not been modified in accordance with this article; provided, however, that recognition and enforcement of the determination would not violate subdivision one-c of section two hundred forty of this chapter or section one thousand eighty-five of the family court act.

2. A court of this state may utilize any remedy available under other law of this state to enforce a child custody determination made by a court of another state. The remedies provided in this title are cumulative and do not affect the availability of other remedies to enforce a child custody determination.

§77-c. Temporary visitation.
1. A court of this state which does not have jurisdiction to modify a child custody determination, may, if consistent with subdivision one-c of section two hundred forty of this chapter or section one thousand eighty-five of the family court act, issue a temporary order enforcing:

(a) a visitation schedule made by a court of another state; or

(b) the visitation provisions of a child custody determination of another state that does not provide for a specific visitation schedule.

2. If a court of this state makes an order under paragraph (b) of subdivision one of this section, it shall specify in the order a period that it considers adequate to allow the petitioner to obtain an order from a court having jurisdiction under the criteria specified in title two of this article. The order remains in effect until an order is obtained from the other court or the period expires.

§77-d. Registration of child custody determination.

1. A child custody determination issued by a court of another state may be registered in this state, with or without a simultaneous request for enforcement, by sending to the appropriate court in this state;

(a) a letter or other document requesting registration;

(b) two copies, including one certified copy, of the determination sought to be registered, and a statement under penalty of perjury that to the best of the knowledge and belief of the person seeking registration the order has not been modified; and

(c) except as otherwise provided in section seventy-six-h of this article, the name and address of the person seeking registration and any parent or person acting as a parent who has been awarded custody or visitation in the child custody determination sought to be registered.

2. On receipt of the documents required by subdivision one of this section, the registering court shall:

(a) cause the determination to be filed as a foreign judgment, together with one copy of any accompanying documents and information, regardless of their form; and

(b) serve notice upon the persons named pursuant to subdivision one of this section and provide them with an opportunity to contest the registration in accordance with this section.

3. The notice required by paragraph (b) of subdivision two of this section must state that:

(a) a registered determination is enforceable as of the date of the registration in the same manner as a determination issued by a court of this state;

(b) a hearing to contest the validity of the registered determination must be requested within twenty days after service of notice; and

(c) failure to contest the registration will result in confirmation of the child custody determination and preclude further contest of that determination with respect to any matter that could have been asserted.

4. A person seeking to contest the validity of a registered order must request a hearing within twenty days after service of the notice. At that hearing, the court shall confirm the registered order unless the person contesting registration establishes that:

(a) the issuing court did not have jurisdiction under title two of this article;

(b) the child custody determination sought to be registered has been vacated, stayed, or modified by a court having jurisdiction to do so under title two of this article; or

(c) the person contesting registration was entitled to notice, but notice was not given in accordance with the standards of section seventy-five-g of this article, in the proceedings before the court that issued the order for which registration is sought.

5. If a timely request for a hearing to contest the validity of the registration is not made, the registration is confirmed as a matter of law and the person

requesting registration and all persons served must be notified of the confirmation.

6. Confirmation of a registered order, whether by operation of law or after notice and hearing, precludes further contest of the order with respect to any matter that could have been asserted at the time of registration.

§77-e. Enforcement of registered determination.

1. A court of this state may grant any relief normally available under the laws of this state to enforce a registered child custody determination made by a court of another state.

2. A court of this state shall recognize and enforce, but may not modify, except in accordance with title two of this article, a registered child custody determination of a court of another state; provided, however, that recognition and enforcement of the determination would not violate subdivision one-c of section two hundred forty of this chapter or section one thousand eighty-five of the family court act.

§77-f. Simultaneous proceedings.

If a proceeding for enforcement under this title is commenced in a court of this state and the court determines that a proceeding to modify the determination is pending in a court of another state having jurisdiction to modify the determination under title two of this article, the enforcing court shall immediately communicate with the modifying court. The proceeding for enforcement continues unless the enforcing court, after consultation with the modifying court, stays or dismisses the proceeding.

§77-g. Expedited enforcement of child custody determination.

1. A petition under this title must be verified. Certified copies of all orders sought to be enforced and of any order confirming registration must be attached to the petition. A copy of a certified copy of an order may be attached instead of the original.

2. A petition for enforcement of a child custody determination must state:

(a) whether the court that issued the determination identified the jurisdictional basis it relied upon in exercising jurisdiction and, if so, what the basis was;

(b) whether the determination for which enforcement is sought has been vacated, stayed, or modified by a court whose decision must be enforced under this article and, if so, identify the court, the case number, and the nature of the proceeding;

(c) whether any proceeding has been commenced that could affect the current proceeding, including proceedings relating to domestic violence, child abuse or neglect, protective orders, termination of parental rights, and adoptions and, if so, identify the court, the case number, and the nature of the proceeding;

(d) the present physical address of the child and the respondent, if known;

(e) whether relief in addition to the immediate physical custody of the child and attorney's fees is sought, including a request for assistance from law enforcement officials and, if so, the relief sought; and

(f) if the child custody determination has been registered and confirmed under section seventy-seven-d of this title, the date and place of registration.

3. Upon the filing of a petition, the court shall issue an order directing the respondent to appear in person with or without the child at a hearing within

three court days and may enter any order necessary to ensure the safety of the parties and the child. The hearing must be held not more than three court days after the filing of the petition, provided that the petition has been served not less than twenty-four hours prior to the hearing. Service may be by any means directed by the court pursuant to section three hundred eight of the civil practice law and rules. The court may extend the date of the hearing briefly for good cause shown or upon the request of the petitioner.

4. An order issued under subdivision three of this section must state the time and place of the hearing and advise the respondent that at the hearing the court will order that the petitioner may take immediate physical custody of the child and the payment of fees, costs, and expenses under section seventy-seven-k of this title, and may schedule a hearing to determine whether further relief is appropriate, unless the respondent appears and establishes that:

(a) the child custody determination has not been registered and confirmed under section seventy-seven-d of this title and that:

(1) the issuing court did not have jurisdiction under title two of this article;

(2) the child custody determination for which enforcement is sought has been vacated, stayed, or modified by a court having jurisdiction to do so under title two of this article or that enforcement would violate subdivision one-c of section two hundred forty of this chapter or section one thousand eighty-five of the family court act;

(3) the respondent was entitled to notice, but notice was not given in accordance with the standards of section seventy-five-g of this article, in the proceedings before the court that issued the order for which enforcement is sought; or

(b) the child custody determination for which enforcement is sought was registered and confirmed under section seventy-seven-c of this title, but has been vacated, stayed, or modified by a court of a state having jurisdiction to do so under title two of this article.

§77-h. Service of petition and order.

Except as otherwise provided in section seventy-seven-j of this title, the petition and order must be served, by any method authorized by the law of this state, upon respondent and any person who has physical custody of the child. Service may be made outside the state in the manner prescribed by section seventy-five-g of this article.

§77-i. Hearing and order.

1. Unless the court issues a temporary emergency order pursuant to section seventy-six-c of this article, upon a finding that a petitioner is entitled to immediate physical custody of the child, the court shall order that the petitioner may take immediate physical custody of the child unless the respondent establishes that:

(a) the child custody determination has not been registered and confirmed under section seventy-seven-d of this title and that:

(i) the issuing court did not have jurisdiction under title two of this article;

(ii) the child custody determination for which enforcement is sought has been vacated, stayed, or modified by a court of a state having jurisdiction to do so under title two of this article or enforcement of the determination would violate subdivision one-c of section two hundred forty of this chapter or section one thousand eighty-five of the family court act; or

(iii) the respondent was entitled to notice, but notice was not given in accordance with the standards of section seventy-five-g of this article, in the proceedings before the court that issued the order for which enforcement is sought; or

(b) the child custody determination for which enforcement is sought was registered and confirmed under section seventy-seven-d of this title but has been vacated, stayed, or modified by a court of a state having jurisdiction to do so under title two of this article.

2. The court shall award the fees, costs, and expenses authorized under section seventy-seven-k of this title and may grant additional relief, including a request for the assistance of law enforcement officials, and set a further hearing to determine whether additional relief is appropriate.

3. If a party called to testify refuses to answer on the ground that the testimony may be self-incriminating, the court may draw an adverse inference from the refusal.

4. A privilege against disclosure of communications between spouses and a defense of immunity based on the relationship of husband and wife or parent and child may not be invoked in a proceeding under this act.

§77-j. Warrant to take physical custody of child.

1. Upon the filing of a petition seeking enforcement of a child custody determination, the petitioner may file a verified application for the issuance of a warrant to take physical custody of the child if the child is at imminent risk of suffering serious physical harm or of removal from this state.

2. If the court, upon the testimony of the petitioner or other witness, finds that the child is likely to suffer imminent serious physical harm or to be removed from this state, it may issue a warrant to take physical custody of the child. Except in extraordinary circumstances, the petition must be heard on the next court day after the warrant is executed. Any adjournment for extraordinary circumstances shall be for not more than three court days. The application for the warrant must include the statements required by subdivision two of section seventy-seven-g of this title.

3. A warrant to take physical custody of a child must:

(a) recite the facts upon which a conclusion of imminent serious physical harm or removal from the jurisdiction is based;

(b) direct law enforcement officers to take physical custody of the child immediately and deliver the child to the petitioner or, where necessary, to act jointly with the local child protective service to take immediate steps to protect the child; and

(c) provide for the placement of the child pending final relief.

4. The respondent must be served with the petition, warrant, and order immediately after the child is taken into physical custody.

5. A warrant to take physical custody of a child is enforceable throughout this state. If the court finds on the basis of the testimony of the petitioner or other witness that a less intrusive remedy is not effective, it may authorize law enforcement officers to enter private property in order to execute the warrant and take physical custody of the child. If required by exigent circumstances of the case and necessary to the protection of the child, the court may authorize law enforcement officers to make a forcible entry at any hour.

6. The court may impose conditions upon placement of a child to ensure the appearance of the child and the child's custodian.

§77-k. Costs, fees and expenses.
1. The court shall award the prevailing party, including a state, necessary and reasonable expenses incurred by or on behalf of the party, including costs, communication expenses, attorney's fees, investigative fees, expenses for witnesses, travel expenses, and child care during the course of the proceedings, unless the party from whom fees or expenses are sought establishes that the award would be inappropriate. No fees, costs or expenses shall be assessed against a party who is fleeing an incident of domestic violence or mistreatment or abuse of a child or sibling, unless the court is convinced by a preponderance of evidence that such assessment would be clearly appropriate.
2. The court may not assess fees, costs, or expenses against a state unless authorized by law other than this article.

§77-*l*. Recognition and enforcement.
A court of this state shall accord full faith and credit to an order issued by another state and consistent with this article which enforces a child custody determination by a court of another state unless the order has been vacated, stayed, or modified by a court having jurisdiction to do so under title two of this article, unless recognition and enforcement would violate subdivision one-c of section two hundred forty of this chapter or section one thousand eighty-five of the family court act.

§77-m. Appeals.
An appeal may be taken from a final order in a proceeding under this title in accordance with article fifty-five of the civil practice law and rules and article eleven of the family court act and may be granted a preference in the discretion of the court to which the appeal is taken. Unless the court enters a temporary emergency order under section seventy-six-c of this article, the enforcing court may not stay an order enforcing a child custody determination pending appeal.

§77-n. Role of prosecutor or public official.
1. In a case arising under this article or involving the Hague Convention on the Civil Aspects of International Child Abduction, the prosecutor or other appropriate public official may take any lawful action, including resort to a proceeding under this title or any other available civil proceeding to locate a child, obtain the return of a child, or enforce a child custody determination if there is:
(a) an existing child custody determination;
(b) a request to do so from a court in a pending child custody proceeding;
(c) a reasonable belief that a criminal statute has been violated; or
(d) a reasonable belief that the child has been wrongfully removed or retained in violation of the Hague Convention on the Civil Aspects of International Child Abduction.
2. A prosecutor or appropriate public official acting under this section acts on behalf of the state or local government entity and may not represent any private party.

§77-o. Role of law enforcement.
At the request of a prosecutor or other appropriate public official acting under section seventy-seven-n of this title, a law enforcement officer, as defined in subdivision thirty-four of section 1.20 of the criminal procedure law,

may take any lawful action reasonably necessary to locate a child or a party and assist a prosecutor or appropriate public official with responsibilities under section seventy-seven-n of this title.

§77-p. Costs and expenses.

If the respondent is not the prevailing party, the court may assess against the respondent all direct expenses and costs incurred by the prosecutor or other appropriate public official and law enforcement officers under section seventy-seven-n or seventy-seven-o of this title.

Title IV
Miscellaneous Provisions

Section
78.   Application and construction.
78-a. Severability clause.

§78. Application and construction.

In applying and construing this article, consideration must be given to the need to promote uniformity of the law with respect to its subject matter among states that enact it.

§78-a. Severability clause.

If any provision of this article or its application to any person or circumstance is held invalid, the invalidity does not affect other provisions or applications of this article which can be given effect without the invalid provision or application, and to this end the provisions of this article are severable.

ARTICLE 6
Guardians

Section
80.   Guardians in socage.
81.   Appointment of guardians by parent.
82.   Powers and duties of such guardians.
83.   Duties and liabilities of all general guardians.
84.   Guardianship of a married minor.
85.   Investment of trust funds by guardian.

§80. Guardians in socage.

Where a minor for whom a general guardian of the property has not been appointed shall acquire real property, the guardianship of his property with the rights, powers and duties of a guardian in socage belongs: (1) to the parents jointly, or, if they be separated, or divorced, to the parent who has been given the custody of the minor by a decree of court, or in the absence of such a decree, to the parent having the actual custody of the minor; (2) if one of the parents be dead, to the sole surviving parent; (3) if there be no father or mother, to the nearest and eldest relative of full age, not under any legal incapacity.

The rights and authority of every such guardian shall be superseded by a testamentary or other guardian appointed in pursuance of this article or in pursuance of article ten of the surrogates court act.

§81. Appointment of guardians by parent.

A married woman is a joint guardian of her children with her husband, with equal powers, rights and duties in regard to them. Upon the death of either father or mother, the surviving parent, whether of full age or a minor, of a child likely to be born, or of any living child under the age of eighteen years and unmarried, may, by deed or last will, duly executed, dispose of the custody and tuition of such child during its minority or for any less time, to any person or persons. Such surviving parent may appoint a guardian or guardians of the person and of the property of the infant and in making such appointment shall not be limited to the appointment of the same person or persons in both capacities. Either the father or mother may in the life-time of them both, by last will duly executed, appoint the other the guardian of the person and property of such child, during its minority. Either the father or mother may in the life-time of them both by last will duly executed, and with the written consent of the other duly acknowledged, appoint the other and a third person to be the guardians of the person and property of such child during its minority, and in making such appointment shall not be limited to the appointment of the same person or persons in both capacities. Such consent must have as part thereof a sworn statement that the consenting parent in so consenting, is motivated solely by the welfare of the child or children, the guardianship of whom is the subject of such consent, and that such consenting parent has not received and will not receive any consideration for such consent, and such consent may be revoked by such consenting parent at any time prior to the death of the other, by filing in the office of the county clerk of the county in which said other then resides, a written revocation of such consent, subscribed and acknowledged by the person so revoking, with proof of service of a copy thereof on such other parent in the manner provided for service of a summons. An appointment of a guardian of the person and property of an infant made by duly executed last will of his father or mother shall be valid and effective if at the time the will is admitted to probate the other parent shall have died or the surviving parent be an adjudicated incompetent. If both parents die under circumstances which render it difficult or impossible to determine which of them died first and both of them left last wills appointing the same person as guardian, the appointment shall be valid and effective. If both parents die under circumstances which render it difficult or impossible to determine which of them died first, leaving last wills appointing different persons as guardians, the surrogate's court shall determine which of the appointments will best serve the welfare of the child and issue letters of guardianship accordingly. If at any time during the minority of the infant the surviving parent becomes competent to serve as guardian, he may apply to the court which issued letters of guardianship to the guardian appointed by will for a decree revoking such letters and the court shall on such application make such order or decree as justice requires. A person appointed guardian in pursuance of this section shall not exercise the power of authority thereof unless such will is admitted to probate, or such deed executed and recorded as provided by SCPA 1710.

§82. Powers and duties of such guardians.

Every such disposition, from the time it takes effect, shall vest in the person to whom made, if he accepts the appointment, all the rights and powers, and subject him to all the duties and obligations of a guardian of such minor, and shall be valid and effectual against every other person claiming the custody and tuition of such minor, as guardian in socage or otherwise. He may take the custody and charge of the tuition of such minor, and may maintain all proper actions for the wrongful taking or detention of the minor, and shall recover damages in such actions for the benefit of his ward. He shall also take the custody and management of the personal estate of such minor and the profits of his real estate, during the time for which such disposition shall have been made, and may bring such actions in relation thereto as a guardian in socage might by law.

§83. Duties and liabilities of all general guardians.

A general guardian or guardian in socage shall safely keep the property of his ward that shall come into his custody, and shall not make or suffer any waste, sale or destruction of such property or inheritance, but shall keep in repair and maintain the houses, gardens and other appurtenances to the lands of his ward, by and with the issues and profits thereof, or with such other moneys belonging to his ward as shall be in his possession; and shall deliver the same to his ward, when he comes to full age, in at least as good condition as such guardian received the same, inevitable decay and injury only excepted; and shall answer to his ward for the issues and profits of the real estate, received by him, by a lawful account, to be settled before any court, judge or surrogate having authority to settle the accounts of general and testamentary guardians; and any order, judgment or decree in any action or proceeding to settle such accounts may be enforced to the same extent, and in like manner as in the case of general and testamentary guardians. If any guardian shall make or suffer any waste, sale or destruction of the inheritance of his ward, he shall lose the custody of the same, and of such ward, and shall be liable to the ward for any damage caused thereby.

§84. Guardianship of a married minor.

The lawful marriage of a person before he or she attains majority terminates a general guardianship with respect to his or her person, but not with respect to his or her property.

§85. Investment of trust funds by guardian.

A guardian holding funds for investment has the powers provided by section twenty-one of the personal property law and must not invest the funds in any other securities or manner.

ARTICLE VII
Adoption

Title
1. Adoptions generally.
2. Adoption from an authorized agency.
3. Private-placement adoption.
4. Effect of adoption from an authorized agency, of private-placement adoption, and abrogations thereof.

Title 1
Adoptions Generally

§109. Definitions.

When used in this article, unless the context or subject matter manifestly requires a different interpretation:

1. "Adoptive parent" or "adoptor" shall mean a person adopting and "adoptive child" or "adoptee" shall mean a person adopted.

2. "Judge" shall mean a judge of the family court of any county in the state.

3. "Surrogate" shall mean the surrogate of any county in the state and any other judicial officer while acting in the capacity of surrogate.

4. "Authorized agency" shall mean an authorized agency as defined in the social services law and, for the purpose of this article, shall include such corporations incorporated or organized under the laws of this state as may be specifically authorized by their certificates of incorporation to receive children for purposes of adoption.

5. "Private-placement adoption" shall mean any adoption other than that of a minor who has been placed for adoption by an authorized agency.

6. "Lawful custody" shall mean a custody (a) specifically authorized by statute or (b) pursuant to judgment, decree or order of a court or (c) otherwise authorized by law.

7. "A child who has been surrendered to an authorized agency for the purpose of adoption" shall mean a child who has been surrendered to such an agency pursuant to the provisions of section three hundred eighty-three-c or three hundred eighty-four of the social services law.

§110. Who may adopt; effect of article.

An adult unmarried person, an adult married couple together, or any two unmarried adult intimate partners together may adopt another person. An adult married person who is living separate and apart from his or her spouse pursuant to a decree or judgment of separation or pursuant to a written agreement of separation subscribed by the parties thereto and acknowledged or proved in the form required to entitle a deed to be recorded or an adult married person who has been living separate and apart from his or her spouse for at least three years prior to commencing an adoption proceeding may adopt another person; provided, however, that the person so adopted shall not be deemed the child or step-child of the non-adopting spouse for the purposes of inheritance or support rights or obligations or for any other purposes. An adult or minor married couple together may adopt a child of either of them born in or out of wedlock and an adult or minor spouse may adopt such a child of the other spouse. No person shall hereafter be adopted except in pursuance of this article, and in conformity with section three hundred seventy-three of the social services law.

An adult married person who has executed a legally enforceable separation agreement or is a party to a marriage in which a valid decree of separation has been entered or has been living separate and apart from his or her spouse for at least three years prior to commencing an adoption proceeding and who becomes or has been the custodian of a child placed in their care as a result of court ordered foster care may apply to such authorized agency for placement of said child with them for the purpose of adoption. Final determination of the propriety of said adoption of such foster child, however, shall be within the sole discretion of the court, as otherwise provided herein.

Adoption is the legal proceeding whereby a person takes another person into the relation of child and thereby acquires the rights and incurs the responsibilities of parent in respect of such other person.

A proceeding conducted in pursuance of this article shall constitute a judicial proceeding. An order of adoption or abrogation made therein by a surrogate or by a judge shall have the force and effect of and shall be entitled to all the presumptions attaching to a judgment rendered by a court of general jurisdiction in a common law action.

No adoption heretofore lawfully made shall be abrogated by the enactment of this article. All such adoptions shall have the effect of lawful adoptions hereunder.

Nothing in this article in regard to a minor adopted pursuant hereto inheriting from the adoptive parent applies to any will, devise or trust made or created before June twenty-fifth, eighteen hundred seventy-three, nor alters, changes or interferes with such will, devise or trust. As to any such will, devise or trust a minor adopted before that date is not an heir so as to alter estates or trusts or devises in wills so made or created. Nothing in this article in regard to an adult adopted pursuant hereto inheriting from the adoptive parent applies to any will, devise or trust made or created before April twenty-second, nineteen hundred fifteen, nor alters, changes or interferes with such will, devise or trust. As to any such will, devise or trust an adult so adopted is not an heir so as to alter estates or trusts or devises in wills so made or created.

It shall be unlawful to preclude a prospective adoptive parent or parents solely on the basis that the adoptor or adopters has had, or has cancer, or any other disease. Nothing herein shall prevent the rejection of a prospective applicant based upon his or her poor health or limited life expectancy.

§111. Whose consent required.

1. Subject to the limitations hereinafter set forth consent to adoption shall be required as follows:

(a) Of the adoptive child, if over fourteen years of age, unless the judge or surrogate in his discretion dispenses with such consent;

(b) Of the parents or surviving parent, whether adult or infant, of a child conceived or born in wedlock;

(c) Of the mother, whether adult or infant, of a child born out of wedlock;

(d) Of the father, whether adult or infant, of a child born out-of-wedlock and placed with the adoptive parents more than six months after birth, but only if such father shall have maintained substantial and continuous or repeated contact with the child as manifested by: (i) the payment by the father toward the support of the child of a fair and reasonable sum, according to the father's means, and either (ii) the father's visiting the child at least monthly when physically and financially able to do so and not prevented from doing so by the person or authorized agency having lawful custody of the child, or (iii) the father's regular communication with the child or with the person or agency having the care or custody of the child, when physically and financially unable to visit the child or prevented from doing so by the person or authorized agency having lawful custody of the child. The subjective intent of the father, whether expressed or otherwise, unsupported by evidence of acts specified in this paragraph manifesting such intent, shall not preclude a determination that the father failed to maintain substantial and continuous or repeated contact with the child. In making such a determination, the court shall not require a showing of diligent efforts by any person or agency to encourage the father to perform the acts specified in this paragraph. A father, whether adult or infant, of a child born out-of-wedlock, who openly lived with the child for a period of six months within the one year period immediately preceding the placement of the child for adoption and who during such period openly held himself out to be the father of such child shall be deemed to have maintained substantial and continuous contact with the child for the purpose of this subdivision.

(e) Of the father, whether adult or infant, of a child born out-of-wedlock who is under the age of six months at the time he is placed for adoption, but only if: (i) such father openly lived with the child or the child's mother for a continuous period of six months immediately preceding the placement of the child for adoption; and (ii) such father openly held himself out to be the father of such child during such period; and (iii) such father paid a fair and reasonable sum, in accordance with his means, for the medical, hospital and nursing expenses incurred in connection with the mother's pregnancy or with the birth of the child.

(f) Of any person or authorized agency having lawful custody of the adoptive child.

2. The consent shall not be required of a parent or of any other person having custody of the child:

(a) who evinces an intent to forego his or her parental or custodial rights and obligations as manifested by his or her failure for a period of six months to visit the child and communicate with the child or person having legal custody of the child, although able to do so; or

(b) who has surrendered the child to an authorized agency under the provisions of section three hundred eighty-three-c or three hundred eighty-four of the social services law; or

(c) for whose child a guardian has been appointed under the provisions of section three hundred eighty-four-b of the social services law; or

(d) who, by reason of mental illness or intellectual disability, as defined in subdivision six of section three hundred eighty-four-b of the social services law, is presently and for the foreseeable future unable to provide proper care for the child. The determination as to whether a parent is mentally ill or intellectually disabled shall be made in accordance with the criteria and procedures set forth in subdivision six of section three hundred eighty-four-b of the social services law; or *(Eff.5/25/16,Ch.37,L.2016)*

(e) who has executed an instrument, which shall be irrevocable, denying the paternity of the child, such instrument having been executed after conception and acknowledged or proved in the manner required to permit the recording of a deed.

3. (a) Notice of the proposed adoption shall be given to a person whose consent to adoption is required pursuant to subdivision one and who has not already provided such consent.

(b) Notice and an opportunity to be heard upon the proposed adoption may be afforded to a parent whose consent to adoption may not be required pursuant to subdivision two, if the judge or surrogate so orders.

(c) Notice under this subdivision shall be given in such manner as the judge or surrogate may direct.

(d) Notwithstanding any other provision of law, neither the notice of a proposed adoption nor any process in such proceeding shall be required to contain the name of the person or persons seeking to adopt the child.

4. Where the adoptive child is over the age of eighteen years the consents specified in paragraphs (b), (c) and (d) of subdivision one of this section shall not be required, and the judge or surrogate in his discretion may direct that the consent specified in paragraph (f) of subdivision one of this section shall not

be required if in his opinion the best interests of the adoptive child will be promoted by the adoption and such consent cannot for any reason be obtained.

5. An adoptive child who has once been lawfully adopted may be readopted directly from such child's adoptive parents in the same manner as from its birth parents. In such case the consent of such birth parents shall not be required but the judge or surrogate in his discretion may require that notice be given to the birth parents in such manner as he may prescribe.

6. For the purposes of paragraph (a) of subdivision two:

(a) In the absence of evidence to the contrary, the ability to visit and communicate with a child or person having custody of the child shall be presumed.

(b) Evidence of insubstantial or infrequent visits or communication by the parent or other person having custody of the child shall not, of itself, be sufficient as a matter of law to preclude a finding that the consent of such parent or person to the child's adoption shall not be required.

(c) The subjective intent of the parent or other person having custody of the child, whether expressed or otherwise, unsupported by evidence of acts specified in paragraph (a) of subdivision two manifesting such intent, shall not preclude a determination that the consent of such parent or other person to the child's adoption shall not be required.

(d) Payment by a parent toward the support of the child of a fair and reasonable sum, according to the parent's means, shall be deemed a substantial communication by such parent with the child or person having legal custody of the child.

§111-a.   Notice in certain proceedings to fathers of children born out-of-wedlock.

1. Notwithstanding any inconsistent provisions of this or any other law, and in addition to the notice requirements of any law pertaining to persons other than those specified in subdivision two of this section, notice as provided herein shall be given to the persons specified in subdivision two of this section of any adoption proceeding initiated pursuant to this article or of any proceeding initiated pursuant to section one hundred fifteen-b of this article relating to the revocation of an adoption consent, when such proceeding involves a child born out-of-wedlock provided, however, that such notice shall not be required to be given to any person who previously has been given notice of any proceeding involving the child, pursuant to section three hundred eighty-four-c of the social services law, and provided further that notice in an adoption proceeding, pursuant to this section shall not be required to be given to any person who has previously received notice of any proceeding pursuant to section one hundred fifteen-b of this article. In addition to such other requirements as may be applicable to the petition in any proceeding in which notice must be given pursuant to this section, the petition shall set forth the names and last known addresses of all persons required to be given notice of the proceeding, pursuant to this section, and there shall be shown by the petition or by affidavit or other proof satisfactory to the court that there are no persons other than those set forth in the petition who are entitled to notice. For the purpose of determining persons entitled to notice of adoption proceedings initiated pursuant to this article, persons specified in subdivision two of this section shall not include any person who has been convicted of one or more of the following sexual offenses in this state or convicted of one or more offenses in another jurisdiction which, if committed in this state, would constitute one or more of

the following offenses, when the child who is the subject of the proceeding was conceived as a result: (A) rape in first or second degree; (B) course of sexual conduct against a child in the first degree; (C) predatory sexual assault; or (D) predatory sexual assault against a child.

2. Persons entitled to notice, pursuant to subdivision one of this section, shall include:

(a) any person adjudicated by a court in this state to be the father of the child;

(b) any person adjudicated by a court of another state or territory of the United States to be the father of the child, when a certified copy of the court order has been filed with the putative father registry, pursuant to section three hundred seventy-two-c of the social services law;

(c) any person who has timely filed an unrevoked notice of intent to claim paternity of the child, pursuant to section three hundred seventy-two-c of the social services law;

(d) any person who is recorded on the child's birth certificate as the child's father;

(e) any person who is openly living with the child and the child's mother at the time the proceeding is initiated and who is holding himself out to be the child's father;

(f) any person who has been identified as the child's father by the mother in written, sworn statement;

(g) any person who was married to the child's mother within six months subsequent to the birth of the child and prior to the execution of a surrender instrument or the initiation of a proceeding pursuant to section three hundred eighty-four-b of the social services law; and

(h) any person who has filed with the putative father registry an instrument acknowledging paternity of the child, pursuant to section 4-1.2 of the estates, powers and trusts law.

3. The provisions of this section shall not apply to persons entitled to notice pursuant to section one hundred eleven. The sole purpose of notice under this section shall be to enable the person served pursuant to subdivision two to present evidence to the court relevant to the best interests of the child.

4. Notice under this section shall be given at least twenty days prior to the proceeding by delivery of a copy of the petition and notice to the person. Upon a showing to the court, by affidavit or otherwise, on or before the date of the proceeding or within such further time as the court may allow, that personal service cannot be effected at the person's last known address with reasonable effort, notice may be given, without prior court order therefor, at least twenty days prior to the proceeding by registered or certified mail directed to the person's last known address or, where the person has filed a notice of intent to claim paternity pursuant to section three hundred seventy-two-c of the social services law, to the address last entered therein. Notice by publication shall not be required to be given to a person entitled to notice pursuant to the provisions of this section.

5. A person may waive his right to notice under this section by written instrument subscribed by him and acknowledged or proved in the manner required for the execution of a surrender instrument pursuant to section three hundred eighty-four of the social services law.

6. The notice given to persons pursuant to this section shall inform them of the time, date, place and purpose of the proceeding and shall also apprise such persons that their failure to appear shall constitute a denial of their interest in

the child which denial may result, without further notice, in the adoption or other disposition of the custody of the child.

7. No order of adoption and no order of the court pursuant to section one hundred fifteen-b shall be vacated, annulled or reversed upon the application of any person who was properly served with notice in accordance with this section but failed to appear, or who waived notice pursuant to subdivision five. Nor shall any order of adoption be vacated, annulled or reversed upon the application of any person who was properly served with notice in accordance with this section in any previous proceeding pursuant to section one hundred fifteen-b in which the court determined that the best interests of the child would be served by adoption of the child by the adoptive parents.

§111-b.   Determination of issue of paternity by surrogate; limitations.
1. In the course of an adoption proceeding conducted pursuant to this article the surrogate shall have jurisdiction to determine any issue of paternity arising in the course of the same proceeding and to make findings and issue an order thereon.

2. Such determination shall be made substantially in accordance with the relevant and otherwise consistent provisions of the family court act except that the surrogate shall have no power to grant any relief relating to support of the child as an incident thereto.

3. A judge of the family court shall continue to exercise all of the powers relating to adoption and declaration of paternity conferred upon the family court by law.

§111-c.   Adoption order from foreign country or foreign jurisdiction.
1. A final judgment of adoption granted by a judicial, administrative or executive body of a jurisdiction or country other than the United States shall have the same force and effect in this state as that given to a judgment of adoption entered by a court of competent jurisdiction of New York state, without additional proceedings or documentation provided:

(a) either adopting parent is a resident of this state; and

(b) the validity of the foreign adoption has been verified by the granting of an IR-3, IH-3, or a successor immigrant visa, for the child by the United States Citizenship and Immigration Services.

2. Notwithstanding any other provision of law or rule or regulation to the contrary, an adoptive parent referred to in subdivision one of this section shall not be required to petition a court in this state for adoption of the child provided the conditions of paragraphs (a) and (b) of subdivision one of this section are met. The foreign adoption shall be considered "final" under the laws of New York state upon the satisfaction of paragraphs (a) and (b) of subdivision one of this section.

3. Either adoptive parent or a guardian or a guardian ad litem may register the order in this state with the judge or surrogate of the county in which the adoptive parent or parents reside. A petition for registration of a foreign adoption order may be combined with a petition for a name change. If the court finds that the foreign adoption order meets the requirements of subdivision one of this section, the court shall issue a finding as to aspects of the foreign adoption, to wit, the names of the adoptive parents, the name or names and reported birth date of the adoptive child, the country of the adoptive child's birth, the country and the date of the foreign adoption, the state residency of the adoptive parent or parents and adoptive child, and a finding as to the date and

issuance of an IR-3, IH-3, or a successor immigrant visa; and, the court shall issue an order of adoption to the party who has petitioned for such an order.

4. The judge or surrogate is hereby directed to expedite the issuance of an order of adoption pursuant to the provisions of subdivision three of this section in order to ensure minimal expense of time and money to the petitioning parties in attaining such order of adoption.

Title II
Adoption from an Authorized Agency

§112. General provisions relating to adoption from authorized agencies.
In an adoption from an authorized agency the following requirements shall be observed:

1. The adoptive parents or parent and the adoptive child must appear for examination before a judge or surrogate of the county specified in section one hundred thirteen of this title. The judge or surrogate, however, may in his discretion dispense with the personal appearance of the adoptive child or of an adoptive parent who is on active duty in the armed forces of the United States.

2. The adoptive parents or parent and the adoptive child if over eighteen years of age must present to such judge or surrogate (a) a petition stating the names and place of residence of the petitioners; whether they are of full age; whether they are married or unmarried and, if married, whether they are living together as husband and wife; the first name, date and place of birth of the adoptive child as nearly as the same can be ascertained; a statement on information and belief that there will be annexed to the petition a schedule verified by a duly constituted official of the authorized agency as required by this section; the religious faith of the petitioners; the religious faith of the adoptive child and his or her parents as nearly as the same can be ascertained; the manner in which the adoptive parents obtained the adoptive child; whether the child was placed or brought into the state of New York from out of state for the purpose of adoption, whether the placement was subject to the provisions of section three hundred seventy-four-a of the social services law and if the placement was subject to the provisions of such section, whether the provisions of such section were complied with; the period of time during which the adoptive child has resided with the adoptive parents; the occupation and approximate income of the petitioners, including support and maintenance, if any, to be received on behalf of the adoptive child from a commissioner of social services, pursuant to the social services law, and the new name, if any, by which the adoptive child is to be known; whether the adoptive parent or parents has or have knowledge that an adoptive parent is the subject of an indicated report, as such terms are defined in section four hundred twelve of the social services law, filed with the statewide central register of child abuse and maltreatment pursuant to title six of article six of the social services law, or has been the subject of or the respondent in a child protective proceeding commenced under article ten of the family court act, which proceeding resulted in an order finding that the child is an abused or neglected child; that no

previous application has been made to any court or judge for the relief sought or if so made, the disposition of it and a statement as to whether the adoptive child had been previously adopted, all of which statements shall be taken prima facie as true; (b) an agreement on the part of the adoptive parents or parent to adopt and treat the adoptive child as their or his or her own lawful child; (c) the consents required by section one hundred eleven of this article.

2-a. In the petition provided for in subdivision two of this section, the adoptive parents or parent and the adoptive child if over eighteen years of age shall present to the judge or surrogate as nearly as can be ascertained the heritage of the parents, which shall include nationality, ethnic background and race; education, which shall be the number of years of school completed by the parents at the time of the birth of the adoptive child; general physical appearance of the parents at the time of the birth of the adoptive child, which shall include height, weight, color of hair, eyes, skin; occupation of the parents at the time of the birth of the adoptive child; health and medical history of the parents at the time of the birth of the adoptive child, including all available information setting forth conditions or diseases believed to be hereditary, any drugs or medication taken during the pregnancy by the child's mother; and any other information which may be a factor influencing the child's present or future health, talents, hobbies and special interests of parents. The petition shall also include the names and current addresses of the biological parents, if known.

3. The authorized agency must present to such judge or surrogate a schedule to be annexed to the petition which shall be verified by a duly constituted official of the authorized agency having custody of the adoptive child or actually placing the child for adoption and shall contain (1) the full name of the child, (2) the manner in which the authorized agency obtained custody of the adoptive child, (3) the facts, if any, which render unnecessary the consent of either or both of the parents of the adoptive child, (4) a statement whether either parent had ever requested the agency to return the child to the parent, within thirty days of the execution and delivery of an instrument of surrender to an authorized agency and, if so, all facts relating thereto. If a request for return of the child to a parent be made after the presentation to the court of the petition and schedule, the authorized agency shall promptly report to the court in writing the facts relating thereto and (5) all available information comprising the child's medical history. If the child was placed into the state of New York for the purpose of adoption and such placement was subject to the provisions of section three hundred seventy-four-a of the social services law, the authorized agency shall attach to the petition a copy of the document, signed by New York's administrator of the interstate compact for the placement of children or his designee, which informs the agency or person who placed the child into the state that such placement complied with the provisions of the compact.

4. None of the papers in the proceeding shall state the surname of the child in the title and no petition, agreement, consent, affidavit, nor any other document which is required to be signed by the adoptive parents shall contain the surname of the adoptive child.

5. The petition must be verified, the agreement and consents executed and acknowledged and the proof given by the respective persons before such judge or surrogate; but where the verification, agreement or necessary consent is duly acknowledged or proved and certified in form sufficient to entitle a conveyance to be recorded in this state, (except that when executed and acknowledged

within the state of New York, no certificate of the county clerk shall be required), such judge or surrogate may grant the order of adoption without the personal appearance of such persons or parties or any of them for good cause shown, which reason shall be recited in the order of adoption.

6. Where the adoptive child is less than eighteen years of age, no order of adoption shall be made until such child has resided with the adoptive parents for at least three months unless the judge or surrogate in his discretion shall dispense with such period of residence and shall recite in the order the reason for such action. When the adoptive parents are the foster parents in whose home the adoptive child has been placed out or boarded out for a period in excess of three months, such period shall be deemed to constitute the required period of residence.

7. Before making an order of adoption the judge or surrogate shall inquire of the department of social services and the department shall inform the court whether an adoptive parent is the subject of an indicated report, as such terms are defined in section four hundred twelve of the social services law, filed with the statewide central register of child abuse and maltreatment pursuant to title six of article six of the social services law and shall cause to be made an investigation by a disinterested person or by an authorized agency specifically designated by the judge or surrogate to examine into the allegations set forth in the petition and to ascertain such other facts relating to the adoptive child and adoptive parents as will give such judge or surrogate adequate basis for determining the propriety of approving the adoption. A written report of such investigation shall be submitted before the order of adoption is made. As used in this subdivision, "disinterested person" includes the probation service of the family court. Such an inquiry shall not be required if the findings of such an inquiry made within the past twelve months is available to the judge or surrogate.

7-a. Any order subject to the provisions of this section shall include an adoption information registry birth parent registration consent form, stating whether or not such biological parent or parents whose consent is subject to the provisions of this section, consents to the receipt of identifying information by the child to be adopted upon registration with the adoption information registry established by section forty-one hundred thirty-eight-c of the public health law and upon the adoptee reaching the age of eighteen. If such consent is made, it shall be revocable by either of the biological parents at any time. The revocation of the consent by one of the parents shall revoke the consent of both parents. The failure of a biological parent to complete the consent form shall have no effect on the finality of the consent to adoption. A copy of the form required by this subdivision, shall be forwarded to the state adoption information registry for inclusion in the records maintained by such registry. Any fees authorized to be charged by the state adoption registry for filing documentation with such registry shall be waived for the form required by this subdivision.

8. Rules of court shall permit the filing of a petition for adoption of a child whose custody and guardianship has not yet been committed to an authorized agency where a proceeding to terminate parental rights is pending. Such adoption petition shall be filed in the court where the termination of parental rights proceeding is pending. The clerk of such court shall accept the adoption petition for filing and processing and shall request such inquiries of the department of social services as are required by subdivision seven of this section, provided, however, that the petition, supporting documents and the fact

of their filing shall not be provided to the judge before whom the petition for termination of parental rights is pending until such time as fact-finding is concluded under such petition.

§112-a. Expedited calendaring of adoption proceedings.

1. The adoption proceeding shall be deemed filed upon receipt by the clerk of the court of all the documents required in subdivisions two, two-a, three, five and seven of section one hundred twelve of this title, and by rules of the court, together with an affidavit of readiness from the petitioner's attorney. The affidavit of readiness shall attest that the petitioner has prepared a petition for the adoption of the child and has collected documentation as required by such rules and subdivisions two, two-a, three and five of section one hundred twelve of this title.

2. Upon the filing of the documents required by subdivision one of this section, the court, pursuant to rules promulgated by the chief administrator of the court, shall schedule the proceeding for a review, to take place within time frames established by such rules, to determine if there is adequate basis for approving the adoption.

(a) If such basis is found, the appearance of the adoptive parents and child before the court for approval of the adoption shall be calendared pursuant to such rules.

(b) If, upon the court's review, the court finds that there is not an adequate basis for approval of the adoption, the court shall direct such further hearings, submissions or appearances as may be required, and the proceedings shall be adjourned as required for such purposes.

3. The chief administrator of the court shall establish by rule time frames for the calendaring and disposition of adoption proceedings and shall report by the thirty-first day of December of each year to the governor and the temporary president of the senate, speaker of the assembly, and chairpersons of the judiciary and children and families committees on the implementation of such rules and their impact upon adoptions from authorized agencies.

§112-b. Post-adoption contact agreements; judicial approval; enforcement.

1. Nothing in this section shall be construed to prohibit the parties to a proceeding under this chapter from entering into an agreement regarding communication with or contact between an adoptive child, adoptive parent or parents and a birth parent or parents and/or the adoptive child's biological siblings or half-siblings.

2. Agreements regarding communication or contact between an adoptive child, adoptive parent or parents, and a birth parent or parents and/or biological siblings or half-siblings of an adoptive child shall not be legally enforceable unless the terms of the agreement are incorporated into a written court order entered in accordance with the provisions of this section. The court shall not incorporate an agreement regarding communication or contact into an order unless the terms and conditions of the agreement have been set forth in writing and consented to in writing by the parties to the agreement, including the attorney representing the adoptive child. The court shall not enter a proposed order unless the court that approved the surrender of the child determined and stated in its order that the communication with or contact between the adoptive child, the prospective adoptive parent or parents and a birth parent or parents and/or biological siblings or half-siblings, as agreed upon and as set forth in the agreement, would be in the adoptive child's best interests. Notwithstanding any other provision of law, a

copy of the order entered pursuant to this section incorporating the post-adoption contact agreement shall be given to all parties who have agreed to the terms and conditions of such order.

3. Failure to comply with the terms and conditions of an approved order regarding communication or contact that has been entered by the court pursuant to this section shall not be grounds for setting aside an adoption decree or revocation of written consent to an adoption after that consent has been approved by the court as provided in this section.

4. An order incorporating an agreement regarding communication or contact entered under this section may be enforced by any party to the agreement or the attorney for the child by filing a petition in the family court in the county where the adoption was approved. Such petition shall have annexed to it a copy of the order approving the agreement regarding communication or contact. The court shall not enforce an order under this section unless it finds that the enforcement is in the child's best interests.

5. If a birth parent has surrendered a child to an authorized agency pursuant to the provisions of section three hundred eighty-three-c or section three hundred eighty-four of the social services law, and if the court before whom the surrender instrument was presented for approval approved an agreement providing for communication or contact pursuant to paragraph (a) of subdivision two of section three hundred eighty- three-c or paragraph (a) of subdivision two of section three hundred eighty-four of the social services law, a copy of the surrender instrument and of the approved agreement shall be annexed to the petition of adoption. The court shall issue an order incorporating the terms and conditions of the approved agreement into the order of adoption. Notwithstanding any other provision of law, a copy of any order entered pursuant to this subdivision shall be given to the parties who approved such agreement.

6. If a surrender instrument executed by a birth parent pursuant to section three hundred eighty-three-c or three hundred eighty-four of the social services law contains terms and conditions that provide for communication with or contact between a child and a birth parent or parents, such terms and conditions shall not be legally enforceable after any adoption approved by a court pursuant to this article unless the court has entered an order pursuant to this section incorporating those terms and conditions into a court ordered adoption agreement.

§113. Special provisions relating to adoption from authorized agencies.

1. An authorized agency may consent to the adoption of a minor whose custody and guardianship has been transferred to such agency. An authorized agency may also consent to the adoption of a minor whose care and custody has been transferred to such agency pursuant to section one thousand fifty-five of the family court act or section three hundred eighty-four-a of the social services law, where such child's parents are both deceased, or where one parent is deceased and the other parent is not a person entitled to notice pursuant to sections one hundred eleven and one hundred eleven-a of this chapter.

2. In accordance with subparagraph three of paragraph (g) of subdivision six of section three hundred ninety-eight of the social services law, an authorized agency may submit a written request to a social services district with a population of more than two million for approval to consent to the adoption of a child whose custody and guardianship, or of a child where such child's parents are both deceased, or where one parent is deceased and the other parent is not entitled to notice pursuant to sections one hundred eleven and one

hundred eleven-a of this chapter, and whose care and custody, has been transferred to a social services official and who has been placed by the social services official with the authorized agency. If the request is not disapproved by the social services district within sixty days after its submission, it shall be deemed approved, and the authorized agency may give all necessary consent to the adoption of the child. Nothing herein shall result in the transfer of care and custody or custody and guardianship of the child from the social services official to the authorized agency.

3. (a) The agreement of adoption shall be executed by such authorized agency.

(b)(i) If the adoption petition is filed pursuant to subdivision eight of section one hundred twelve of this article or subdivision ten of section three hundred eighty-three-c or subdivision eleven of section three hundred eighty-four-b of the social services law, the petition shall be filed in the county where the termination of parental rights proceeding or judicial surrender proceeding, as applicable, is pending and shall be assigned, wherever practicable, to the same judge.

(ii) In any other agency adoption proceeding, the petition shall be filed in the same court and, wherever practicable, shall be assigned to the same judge of the county in which parental rights had been terminated, a judicial surrender had been approved or the most recent proceeding under article ten or ten-A of the family court act or section three hundred fifty-eight-a of the social services law had been heard, whichever occurred last, or in the county where the adoptive parents reside or, if such adoptive parents do not reside in this state, in the county where such authorized agency has its principal office. The following procedures shall be applicable in cases where the child is under the jurisdiction of a family court, but where the adoption petition has been filed in a court other than the court that presided over the termination of parental rights, surrender or most recent proceeding under article ten or ten-A of the family court act or section three hundred fifty-eight-a of the social services law, whichever occurred last:

(A) Before hearing such an adoption proceeding, the court in which the adoption petition was filed shall ascertain whether the child is under the jurisdiction of a family court as a result of a placement under article ten or ten-A of the family court act or section three hundred fifty-eight-a of the social services law, a surrender under section three hundred eighty-three-c or three hundred eighty-four of the social services law or an order committing guardianship and custody under article six of the family court act or section three hundred eighty-four-b of the social services law, and, if so, which court exercised jurisdiction over the most recent permanency or other proceeding involving the child.

(B) If the court determines that the child is under the jurisdiction of a different family court, the court in which the adoption petition was filed shall stay its proceeding for not more than thirty days and shall communicate with the family court judge who exercised jurisdiction over the most recent permanency or other proceeding involving the child. The communication shall be recorded or summarized on the record by the court in which the adoption petition was filed. Both courts shall notify the parties and the attorney for the child, if any, in their respective proceedings and shall give them an opportunity to present facts and legal argument or to participate in the communication prior to the issuance of a decision on jurisdiction.

(C) The family court judge who exercised jurisdiction over the most recent permanency or other proceeding involving the child shall determine whether he or she should assume or decline jurisdiction over the adoption proceeding. In making its determination, the family court judge shall consider, among other factors: the relative familiarity of each court with the facts and circumstances regarding permanency planning for, and the needs and best interests of, the child; the ability of the attorney for the child to continue such representation in the adoption proceeding, if appropriate; the convenience of each court to the residence of the prospective adoptive parent or parents; and the relative ability of each court to hear and determine the adoption petition expeditiously. The court in which the adoption petition was filed shall issue an order incorporating this determination of jurisdiction within thirty days of the filing of the adoption petition.

(D) If the family court that exercised jurisdiction over the most recent permanency or other proceeding determines that it should exercise jurisdiction over the adoption petition, the order of the court in which the adoption petition was filed shall direct the transfer of the proceeding forthwith but in no event more than thirty-five days after the filing of the petition. The petition shall be assigned, wherever practicable, to the family court judge who heard the most recent permanency or other proceeding involving the child.

(E) If the family court that exercised jurisdiction over the permanency or other proceeding involving the child declines to exercise jurisdiction over the adoption petition, the court in which the adoption petition was filed shall issue an order incorporating that determination and shall proceed forthwith.

(iii) Neither such authorized agency nor any officer or agent thereof need appear before the judge or surrogate. The judge or surrogate in his or her discretion may accept the report of an authorized agency verified by one of its officers or agents as the report of investigation hereinbefore required. In making orders of adoption the judge or surrogate when practicable must give custody only to persons of the same religious faith as that of the adoptive child in accordance with article six of the social services law.

§113-a.   Effect of death of potential adoptive parent.
Notwithstanding any other provision of law to the contrary, when a petition for adoption by two persons has been duly filed, and one of the petitioners dies before the adoption is complete, it shall be treated as a change of circumstance. This change may be reviewed to assure that the adoption is in the best interest of the child. The death of one of the adoptive parents shall not, by itself, invalidate a certification nor shall the death of one of the adoptive parents cause a new petition for adoption to be filed. The deceased adoptive parent shall be considered one of the legal parents, unless the surviving adoptive parent requests otherwise.

§114.   Order of adoption.
1. If satisfied that the best interests of the adoptive child will be promoted thereby the judge or surrogate shall make an order approving the adoption and directing that the adoptive child shall thenceforth be regarded and treated in all respects as the child of the adoptive parents or parent. In determining whether the best interests of the adoptive child will be promoted by the adoption, the judge or surrogate shall give due consideration to any assurance by a commissioner of social services that he will provide necessary support and maintenance for the adoptive child pursuant to the social services law. Such

order shall contain the full name, date and place of birth and reference to the schedule annexed to the petition containing the medical history of the child in the body thereof and shall direct that the child's medical history, heritage of the parents, which shall include nationality, ethnic background and race; education, which shall be the number of years of school completed by the parents at the time of the birth of the adoptive child; general physical appearance of the parents at the time of the birth of the adoptive child, which shall include height, weight, color of hair, eyes, skin; occupation of the parents at the time of the birth of the adoptive child; health and medical history of the parents at the time of the birth of the adoptive child, including all available information setting forth conditions or diseases believed to be hereditary, any drugs or medication taken during the pregnancy by the child's mother; and any other information which may be a factor influencing the child's present or future health, talents, hobbies and special interests of parents as contained in the petition be furnished to the adoptive parents. If the judge or surrogate is also satisfied that there is no reasonable objection to the change of name proposed, the order shall direct that the name of the adoptive child be changed to the name stated in the agreement of adoption and that henceforth he shall be known by that name. All such orders made by a family court judge of Westchester county since September first nineteen hundred sixty-two, and on file in the office of the county clerk of such county shall be transferred to the clerk of the family court of such county. Such order and all the papers in the proceeding shall be filed in the office of the court granting the adoption and the order shall be entered in books which shall be kept under seal and which shall be indexed by the name of the adoptive parents and by the full original name of the child. Such order, including orders heretofore entered, shall be subject to inspection and examination only as hereinafter provided. Notwithstanding the fact that adoption records shall be sealed and secret, they may be microfilmed and processed pursuant to an order of the court, provided that such order provides that the confidentiality of such records be maintained. If the confidentiality is violated, the person or company violating it can be found guilty of contempt of court. The fact that the adoptive child was born out of wedlock shall in no case appear in such order. The written report of the investigation together with all other papers pertaining to the adoption shall be kept by the judge or surrogate as a permanent record of his court and such papers must be sealed by him and withheld from inspection. No certified copy of the order of adoption shall issue unless authorized by court order, except that certified copies may issue to the agency or agencies in the proceeding prior to the sealing of the papers. Before the record is sealed, such order may be granted upon written ex parte application on good cause shown and upon such conditions as the court may impose. After the record is sealed, such order may be granted only upon notice as hereinafter provided for disclosure or access and inspection of records. The clerk upon request of a person or agency entitled thereto shall issue certificates of adoption which shall contain only the new name of the child and the date and place of birth of the child, the name of the adoptive parents and the date when and court where the adoption was granted, which certificate as to the facts recited therein shall have the same force and effect as a certified copy of an order of adoption.

2. No person, including the attorney for the adoptive parents shall disclose the surname of the child directly or indirectly to the adoptive parents except upon order of the court. No person shall be allowed access to such sealed records and order and any index thereof except upon an order of a judge or

surrogate of the court in which the order was made or of a justice of the supreme court. No order for disclosure or access and inspection shall be granted except on good cause shown and on due notice to the adoptive parents and to such additional persons as the court may direct. Nothing contained herein shall be deemed to require the state commissioner of health or his designee to secure a court order authorizing disclosure of information contained in adoption or birth records requested pursuant to the authority of section forty-one hundred thirty-eight-c or section forty-one hundred thirty-eight-d of the public health law; upon the receipt of such request for information, the court shall transmit the information authorized to be released thereunder to the state commissioner of health or his designee.

3. In like manner as a court of general jurisdiction exercises such powers, a judge or surrogate of a court in which the order of adoption was made may open, vacate or set aside such order of adoption for fraud, newly discovered evidence or other sufficient cause.

4. Good cause for disclosure or access to and inspection of sealed adoption records and orders and any index thereof, hereinafter the "adoption records", under this section may be established on medical grounds as provided herein. Certification from a physician licensed to practice medicine in the state of New York that relief under this subdivision is required to address a serious physical or mental illness shall be prima facie evidence of good cause. Such certification shall indentify* the information required to address such illness. Except where there is an immediate medical need for the information sought, in which case the court may grant access to the adoption records directly to the petitioner, the court hearing petition under the subdivision shall appoint a guardian ad litem or other disinterested person, who shall have access to the adoption records for the purpose of obtaining the medical information sought from those records or, where the records are insufficient for such purpose, through contacting the biological parents. The guardian or other disinterested person shall offer a biological parent the option of disclosing the medical information sought by the petitioner pursuant to this subdivision, as well as the option of granting consent to examine the parent's medical records. If the guardian or other disinterested person appointed does not obtain the medical information sought by the petitioner, such guardian or disinterested person shall make a report of his or her efforts to obtain such information to the court. Where further efforts to obtain such information are appropriate, the court may in its discretion authorize direct disclosure or access to and inspection of the adoption records by the petitioner.

Title III
Private-Placement Adoption

*(So in original. Probably should read "identify.")

§115. General provisions relating to private-placement adoptions.

1. (a) Except as otherwise provided in this title, private-placement adoptions shall be effected in the same manner as provided in sections one hundred twelve and one hundred fourteen of title two of this article.

(b) A person or persons seeking to commence a private-placement adoption shall, prior to the submission of a petition for such adoption and prior to any transfer of physical custody of an adoptive child, be certified as a qualified adoptive parent or parents by a court of competent jurisdiction pursuant to section one hundred fifteen-d of this title. The provisions of such section may be waived upon the court's own motion or upon the application of any party for good cause shown.

(c) A non-resident person or persons seeking to commence a private-placement adoption of a child present within the state at the time of placement shall, prior to any transfer of physical custody of an adoptive child, make application for certification as a qualified adoptive parent or parents by a court of competent jurisdiction pursuant to section one hundred fifteen-d of this title. Upon application of such person or persons, the court of the county to which the certification petition is properly filed may take or retain jurisdiction of the adoption proceeding. The provisions of this paragraph may be waived upon the court's own motion or upon the application of any party for good cause shown.

2. The proceeding shall be instituted in the county where the adoptive parents reside or, if such adoptive parents do not reside in this state, in the county where the adoptive child resides.

3. The adoptive parents or parent, the adoptive child and all persons whose consent is required by section one hundred eleven of this article must appear for examination before the judge or surrogate of the court where the adoption proceedings are instituted. The judge or surrogate may dispense with the personal appearance of the adoptive child or of an adoptive parent who is on active duty in the armed forces of the United States.

4. The agreement of adoption shall be executed by the adoptive parents or parent.

5. Where the petition alleges that either or both of the birth parents of the child have been deprived of civil rights or are mentally ill or mentally retarded, proof shall be submitted that such disability exists at the time of the proposed adoption.

6. The adoptive parent or parents shall also present in an affidavit a description of any change of circumstances since their certification as a qualified adoptive parent or parents, pursuant to section one hundred fifteen-d of this title, which may be relevant and material to such certification.

7. Where the adoptive child is to be adopted upon the consent of some person other than his father or mother, there shall also be presented the affidavit of such person showing how he or she obtained lawful custody of the child.

8. The adoptive parent or parents shall also present an affidavit describing all fees, compensation and other remunerations paid by such parent or parents on account of or incidental to the birth or care of the adoptive child, the pregnancy or care of the adoptive child's mother or the placement or adoption of the child and on account of or incidental to assistance in arrangements for such placement or adoption. The attorney representing the adoptive parents shall also present an affidavit describing all fees, compensation and other remuneration received by him on account of or incidental to the placement or adoption of the child or assistance in arrangements for such placement or adoption.

9. The petition must be verified, the agreement and consents executed and acknowledged, the proof given and the affidavit sworn to by the respective persons before such judge or surrogate; but where the verification, agreement or consent of an adoptive parent, birth parent or person whose consent is necessary to the adoption is duly acknowledged or proved and certified in form sufficient to entitle a conveyance to be recorded in this state, (except that when executed and acknowledged within the state of New York, no certificate of the county clerk shall be required), such judge or surrogate may grant the order of adoption without the personal appearance of such adoptive parent, birth parent or person. The judge or surrogate may, in his discretion, dispense with the requirement that the adoptive child appear for examination or join in the petition, where otherwise required. In any adoption proceeding where the judge or surrogate shall dispense with the personal appearance of such adoptive parent, birth parent, person whose consent is necessary to the adoption, or adoptive child, the reason therefor must be for good cause shown, and shall be recited in the order of adoption.

10. In all cases where the consents of the persons mentioned in subdivision two, three and four of section one hundred eleven of this article are not required or where the adoptive child is an adult notice of such application shall be served upon such persons as the judge or surrogate may direct.

11. The provisions of title two prohibiting the surname of the child from appearing in the papers, prohibiting disclosure of the surname of the child to the adoptive parents, and requiring a separate application for issuance of a certified copy of an order of adoption prior to the sealing of the papers, requiring the filing of a verified schedule, shall not apply to private-placement adoptions; provided, however, that the facts required to be stated in the verified schedule in an agency adoption shall be set forth in the petition.

12. (a) If the child who is being adopted was placed or brought into New York for the purpose of adoption from a state which is a party to the interstate compact on the placement of children and the provisions of the compact applied to such placements, the petition must contain a statement that the provisions of section three hundred seventy-four-a of the social services law were complied with and where applicable, that the provisions of section three hundred eighty-two of such law were also complied with.

(b) If the child who is being adopted was placed or brought into New York for the purpose of adoption from a state which is not a party to the interstate compact on the placement of children, the petition, where applicable, must contain a statement that the provisions of section three hundred eighty-two of the social services law were complied with.

13. If the placement of a child into the state of New York is subject to the provisions of sections three hundred seventy-four-a and/or three hundred eighty-two of the social services law, there shall be attached to the petition a copy of the document signed by New York's administrator of the interstate compact on the placement of children or his designee which informs the agency or person who placed the child into the state that such placement complied with the provisions of the compact and/or a copy of the license which is issued pursuant to the provisions of section three hundred eighty-two of the social services law to the person, institution, corporation or agency which placed or brought the child into this state.

§115-a. Special provisions relating to children to be brought into the state for private-placement adoption.
1. In the case of a child whose admission to the United States as an eligible orphan with non-quota immigrant status pursuant to the federal immigration and nationality act is sought for the purpose of adoption in the state of New York, the following pre-adoption requirements shall be observed:

(a) The adoptive parents or parent must present to a judge or surrogate having jurisdiction of adoption proceedings, in the county of residence of such adoptive parents or parent, a verified written application containing the information set forth in subdivision two of this section, in such form as the judge or surrogate may prescribe for an order of pre-adoption investigation, to determine whether the adoption may be in the best interests of the child.

(b) The adoptive parents or parent must appear for examination before the judge or surrogate of the court where the pre-adoption proceedings are instituted.

(c) The application must be accompanied by duly authenticated documentary evidence: (1) that the child is an alien under the age of sixteen and (2) that he is an orphan because of the death or disappearance of both parents, or because of abandonment, or desertion by, or separation or loss from, both parents, or who has only one parent due to the death or disappearance of, abandonment, or desertion by, or separation or loss from the other parent, and the remaining parent is incapable of providing care for such orphan and has in writing irrevocably released him for emigration and adoption, and has consented to the proposed adoption. In all cases where the orphan has no remaining parent under the circumstances set forth above, documentary evidence must be presented that the person, public authority or duly constituted agency having lawful custody of the orphan at the time of the making of the application, hereunder, has in writing irrevocably released him for immigration and adoption and has consented to the proposed adoption and (3) that the adoptive parents agree to adopt and treat the adoptive child as their or his or her own lawful child.

(d) In addition thereto such additional releases and consents as the court may in its sound discretion require.

2. The verified written application shall contain the following information: the names and place of residence of the adoptive parent or parents; whether they are of full age; whether they are married or unmarried and, if married, whether they are living together as husband and wife; the name, date and place of birth of the adoptive child as nearly as the same can be ascertained; the religious faith of the adoptive parent or parents; the religious faith of the adoptive child and his parents as nearly as the same can be ascertained; the medical history of the adoptive child as nearly as the same can be ascertained; the occupation and approximate income of the adoptive parent or parents, and the name by which the adoptive child is to be known; that no previous application has been made to any court or judge for the relief sought or if so made, the disposition of it and a statement as to whether the adoptive child has been previously adopted, if such fact is known to the adoptive parent or parents; the facts which establish that the child is an eligible orphan who would be entitled to enter the United States with non-quota immigrant status for the purpose of adoption in New York state, pursuant to the provisions in the federal immigration and nationality act, in such case made; the circumstances whereby, and names and addresses of the intermediaries, if any, through whom the adoptive parent or parents learned of the existence and eligibility of the

child and the names and addresses of the person or persons, public authority or duly constituted agency in the land of the child's residence executing the written release of the child for emigration and adoption, and the consent to such adoption, the circumstances under which the release and consent were obtained, insofar as they are known to the adoptive parent or parents.

2-a. The verified written application shall contain the following information: the heritage of the parents as nearly as the same can be ascertained, which shall include nationality, ethnic background and race; education, which shall be the number of years of school completed by the parents at the time of the birth of the adoptive child; general physical appearance of the parents at the time of the birth of the adoptive child, which shall include height, weight, color of hair, eyes, skin; occupation of the parents at the time of the birth of the adoptive child; health and medical history of the parents at the time of the birth of the adoptive child, including all available information setting forth conditions or diseases believed to be hereditary, any drugs or medication taken during the pregnancy by the child's mother; and any other information which may be a factor influencing the child's present or future health, talents, hobbies and special interests of parents.

3. Upon receiving the verified written application, required documentary evidence, agreement and consents, the judge or surrogate, upon finding that the applicable provisions of section one hundred fifteen-a have been complied with and that it appears that the proposed adoption may be in the best interests of the child, shall issue an order of pre-adoption investigation hereunder. The order of pre-adoption investigation shall require that the report of such investigation be made by a disinterested person who in the opinion of the judge or surrogate is qualified by training and experience, or by an authorized agency specifically designated by him to examine into the statements set forth in the application. The investigator shall make a written report of his investigation into the truth and accuracy of the statements in the application and where applicable, into the validity of the documentary evidence, submitted with the application, and he shall ascertain as fully as possible, and incorporate in his report the various factors which may bear upon the determination of the application for adoption including, but not limited to, the following information:

(a) the marital and family status, and history, of adoptive parents;

(b) the physical and mental health of the adoptive parents;

(c) the property owned by and the income of the adoptive parents;

(d) the compensation paid or agreed upon with respect to the placement of the child for adoption;

(e) whether either adoptive parent has ever been respondent in any proceeding concerning allegedly neglected, abandoned or delinquent children;

(f) the desirability of bringing the child into New York state for private-placement adoption;

(g) any other facts relating the familial, social, religious, emotional and financial circumstances of the adoptive parents which may be relevant to a determination of suitability of the adoption. The written report of pre-adoption investigation shall be submitted to the judge or surrogate within thirty days after the same is directed to be made, unless for good cause shown the judge or surrogate shall grant a reasonable extension of such period. The report shall be filed with the judge or surrogate, in any event, before the court shall issue its pre-adoption certificate that it appears that the adoption is in the best interests of the child.

4. On the return of the pre-adoption investigation order the judge or surrogate shall examine the written report of the pre-adoption investigation, and shall determine upon the basis of such written report and such further proof, if any, as he may deem necessary, whether to issue a pre-adoption certificate as provided for in this subdivision.

If the court is satisfied that the adoption may be in the best interests of the child, and that there has been compliance with all requirements hereof and is satisfied that the moral and temporal interests of the child will be promoted by the adoption, the judge or surrogate shall issue an original certificate under seal of the court and two certified copies thereof, setting forth the fact that a pre-adoption investigation has been conducted, and reciting the documents and papers submitted therewith and stating that in the opinion of the court there is compliance with all applicable laws and that it appears from such investigation that the moral and temporal interests of the child will be promoted by the proposed adoption. The original certificate shall be filed with the clerk of the court, one certified copy with the state commissioner of social services, and the adoptive parents shall receive the second certified copy. The fact that the adoptive child was born out of wedlock shall in no case appear in such certificate. The written report of pre-adoption investigation together with all other papers pertaining to the pre-adoption investigation and the original certificate shall be kept by the court as a permanent record and such papers must be sealed by the judge and withheld from inspection. No person shall be allowed access to such sealed records and original certificate and any index thereof except upon an order of the court in which the pre-adoption certificate was made or an order of a justice of the supreme court. No order for access and inspection shall be granted except on due notice to the adoptive parents and on good cause shown. In like manner as a court of general jurisdiction exercises such powers, the court in which the pre-adoption certificate was made may open, vacate or set aside such certificate for fraud, newly discovered evidence or other sufficient cause.

5. The private-placement adoption of children who have been brought into the United States and the state for such purpose and placed with the adoptive parent or parents, shall be effected after issuance of the pre-adoption certificate, in the manner provided by this title, excepting that (a) the petition shall also recite the pre-adoption proceedings, and (b) the court may in its discretion for good cause shown, waive a subsequent investigation. In such case the order of adoption shall recite the reason for such action.

6. In any case where there has been a failure to comply with the requirements of this section, if applicable, no order of adoption shall be made until one year after the court shall have received the petition to adopt. The court may shorten such waiting period for good cause shown, and, in such case the order of adoption shall recite the reason for such action.

7. The provisions of this section, shall not be applicable to the adoption of children placed out or to be placed out for adoption by an authorized agency as defined in section three hundred seventy-one of the social services law.

8. Notwithstanding any provision of law to the contrary, where a child is placed with a couple or individual in New York state for the purpose of adoption, and where said adoption has theretofore been finalized in the country of birth, outside the United States, the couple or person may petition the court in their county of residence in New York state, for the readoption of said child in accordance with the provisions of this chapter, providing for adoptions originally commenced in this state. In any proceeding for readoption, proof of

finalization of an adoption outside the United States shall be prima facie evidence of the consent of those parties required to give consent to an adoption pursuant to section one hundred eleven of this article.

§115-b. Special provisions relating to consents in private-placement adoptions.

1. A duly executed and acknowledged consent to a private-placement adoption shall state that no action or proceeding may be maintained by the consenting parent for the custody of the child to be adopted except as provided in this section. Notwithstanding any other section of law, a consent to adoption executed by a person who is in foster care shall only be executed before a judge of the family court.

2. Judicial consents.

(a) A consent to a private placement adoption may be executed or acknowledged before any judge or surrogate in this state having jurisdiction over adoption proceedings. Such consent shall state that it is irrevocable upon such execution or acknowledgment. A consent executed or acknowledged before a court in another state shall satisfy the requirements of this section if it is executed by a resident of the other state before a court of record which has jurisdiction over adoption proceedings in that state, and a certified copy of the transcript of that proceeding, showing compliance with paragraph (b) of this subdivision, is filed as part of the adoption proceeding in this state.

(b) At the time that a parent appears before a judge or surrogate to execute or acknowledge a consent to adoption, the judge or surrogate shall inform such parent of the consequences of such act pursuant to the provisions of this section, including informing such parent of the right to be represented by legal counsel of the parent's own choosing; of the right to obtain supportive counseling and of any rights the parent may have pursuant to section two hundred sixty-two of the family court act, section four hundred seven of the surrogate's court procedure act, or section thirty-five of the judiciary law. The judge or surrogate shall give such parent a copy of such consent upon the execution thereof.

3. Extrajudicial consents.

(a) Whenever a consent is not executed or acknowledged before a judge or surrogate pursuant to subdivision two of this section such consent shall become irrevocable forty-five days after the execution of the consent unless written notice of revocation thereof is received by the court in which the adoption proceeding is to be commenced within said forty-five days.

(b) Notwithstanding that such written notice is received within said forty-five days, the notice of revocation shall be given effect only if the adoptive parents fail to oppose such revocation, as provided in subdivision six of this section, or, if they oppose such revocation and the court as provided in subdivision six of this section has determined that the best interests of the child will be served by giving force and effect to such revocation.

4. (a) In any case where a consent is not executed or acknowledged before a judge or surrogate pursuant to subdivision two of this section, the consent shall state, in conspicuous print of at least eighteen point type:

(i) the name and address of the court in which the adoption proceeding has been or is to be commenced; and

(ii) that the consent may be revoked within forty-five days of the execution of the document and where the consent is not revoked within said forty-five days no proceeding may be maintained by the parent for the return of the custody of the child; and

(iii) that such revocation must be in writing and received by the court where the adoption proceeding is to be commenced within forty-five days of the execution of said consent; and

(iv) that, if the adoptive parents contest the revocation, timely notice of the revocation will not necessarily result in the return of the child to the parent's custody, and that the rights of the parent to custody of the child shall not be superior to those of the adoptive parents but that a hearing will be required before a judge pursuant to the provisions of this section to determine: (1) whether the notice of revocation was timely and properly given; and if necessary, (2) whether the best interests of the child will be served by: (A) returning custody of the child to the parent; or (B) by continuing the adoption proceeding commenced by the adoptive parents; or (C) by disposition other than adoption by the adoptive parents; or (D) by placement of the child with an authorized agency, and if any such determination is made, the court shall make such disposition of the custody of the child as will best serve the interests of the child; and

(v) that the parent has the right to legal representation of the parent's own choosing; the right to obtain supportive counseling and may have the right to have the court appoint an attorney pursuant to section two hundred sixty-two of the family court act, section four hundred seven of the surrogate's court procedure act, or section thirty-five of the judiciary law.

(b) Such consent shall be executed or acknowledged before a notary public or other officer authorized to take proof of deeds.

(c) A copy of such consent shall be given to such parent upon the execution thereof. The consent shall include the following statement:

"I, (name of consenting parent), this ____ day of _____, ____, have received a copy of this consent. (Signature of consenting parent)". Such consenting parent shall so acknowledge the delivery and the date of the delivery in writing on the consent.

(d) The adoptive parent may commence the adoption proceeding in a court of competent jurisdiction other than the court named in the consent provided that such commencement is initiated more than forty-five days after the consent is executed. Such commencement shall not revive, extend or toll the period for revocation of a consent pursuant to this section.

5. For the purposes of commencing an adoption proceeding, the clerk of a court of competent jurisdiction shall accept an adoption petition for filing which is complete on its face and shall not require any supplementary documentation as a condition of filing. Nothing in this section shall compel a court to hear an adoption petition until all documents necessary to the adoption proceeding have been filed to the satisfaction of the court.

6. (a) A parent may revoke his consent to adoption only by giving notice, in writing, of such revocation, no later than forty-five days after the execution of the consent, or twenty days after the receipt of a notice of denial, withdrawal or removal pursuant to paragraph (a) of subdivision four of section seventeen hundred twenty-five of the surrogate's court procedure act, whichever is later, to the court in which the adoption proceeding has been or is to be commenced. Such notice shall set forth the name and address of the court in which the adoption proceeding is to be commenced, the address of the parent and may, in addition, set forth the name and address of the attorney for the parent.

(b) If, within forty-five days of the execution of the consent, the court has received such notice of revocation, the court shall promptly notify the adoptive parents and their attorney, by certified mail, of the receipt by the court of such notice of revocation.

(i) Such notice to the adoptive parents shall set forth that if within fifteen days from the date of such notice the court has not received from the adoptive parents or their attorneys notice, in writing, of their intention to oppose such revocation by the parents, the adoption proceeding will be dismissed and that, in case of such dismissal, the court will send to the parents, the adoptive parents and their respective attorneys the notice of dismissal, as provided in paragraph (c) of this subdivision.

(ii) Such notice to the adoptive parents shall further set forth that if, within fifteen days from the date of such notice, the court shall receive from the adoptive parents notice, in writing, of their intention to oppose such revocation by the parents, the court will, upon notice to the parents, the adoptive parents and their respective attorneys, proceed, as provided in paragraph (d) of this subdivision, to a determination of whether such notice of revocation by the parents shall be given force and effect and to a determination of what disposition shall be made of the custody of the child.

(c) If the adoption proceeding is dismissed pursuant to the provisions of paragraph (b) of this subdivision,

(i) Written notice of such dismissal shall forthwith be sent to the parent, the adoptive parents and their respective attorneys.

(ii) Such notice of dismissal shall set forth the name and address of the parent, the name and address of the attorney for the parent, if any, the name and address of the attorney for the adoptive parents.

(iii) Such notice of dismissal shall further set forth that if the child is not returned to the custody of the parent within ten days from the date of such notice of dismissal, the court will forthwith upon request, in writing, by the parent or by the attorney for the parent, furnish to said parent or attorney so requesting, the names and address of the adoptive parents.

(iv) Such notice of dismissal shall further state that, in the event the custody of the child is not returned to the parent by the adoptive parents upon request therefor, a proceeding to obtain custody may be instituted by the parent in the Supreme Court or the Family Court.

(d) If, pursuant to the provisions of paragraph (b) of this subdivision, the adoptive parents give timely and proper notice of their intention to oppose the revocation of the parent's consent:

(i) The court shall promptly notify, in writing, the parent, the adoptive parents, their respective attorneys, and the attorney for the child appointed pursuant to section two hundred forty-nine of the family court act or a guardian ad litem appointed pursuant to section four hundred three-a of the surrogate's court procedure act, that the court will, upon the date specified in such notice by the court, or as soon thereafter as the parties may be heard pursuant to this paragraph, hear and determine whether revocation of the consent of the parent was timely and properly given and whether the adoptive parent's notice of intent to oppose such revocation was timely and properly given and if necessary, hear and determine what disposition should be made with respect to the custody of the child.

(ii) The court shall, upon the date specified, take proof as to whether the best interests of the child will be served by returning custody of the child to the parents, or by the adoption of the child by the adoptive parents, or by placement of the child with an authorized agency for foster care with or without authority to consent to the adoption of the child, or by other disposition of the custody of the child.

(iii) If the court determines that the best interests of the child will be served by returning custody of the child to the parent or by placement of the child with an authorized agency or by disposition other than adoption by the adoptive parents, the revocation of consent shall be given force and effect and the court shall make such disposition of the custody of the child as will best serve the interests of the child.

(iv) If the court determines that the best interests of the child will be served by adoption of the child by the adoptive parents, the court shall enter an order denying any force or effect to the notice of revocation of consent and shall dispose of the custody of the child as if no such notice of revocation had been given by the parent.

(v) In such proceeding the parent or parents who consented to such adoption shall have no right to the custody of the child superior to that of the adoptive parents, notwithstanding that the parent or parents who consented to the adoption are fit, competent and able to duly maintain, support and educate the child. The custody of such child shall be awarded solely on the basis of the best interests of the child, and there shall be no presumption that such interests will be promoted by any particular custodial disposition.

7. Nothing contained in this section shall limit or affect the power and authority of the court in an adoption proceeding, pursuant to the provisions of section one hundred sixteen of this title, to remove the child from the home of the adoptive parents, upon the ground that the welfare of the child requires such action, and thereupon to return the child to a birth parent or place the child with an authorized agency, or, in the case of a surrogate, transfer the child to the family court; nor shall this section bar actions or proceedings brought on the ground of fraud, duress or coercion in the execution or inducement of an adoption consent.

8. Notwithstanding any other provision of this section, a parent having custody of a child whose adoption is sought by his or her spouse need only consent that his or her child be adopted by a named stepfather or stepmother.

9. Any consent to adoption subject to the provisions of this section shall include an adoption information registry birth parent registration consent form, stating whether or not such biological parent or parents whose consent is subject to the provisions of this section, consents to the receipt of identifying information by the child to be adopted upon registration with the adoption information registry established by section forty-one hundred thirty-eight-c of the public health law and upon the adoptee reaching the age of eighteen. If such consent is made, it shall be revocable by either of the biological parents at any time. The revocation of the consent by one of the parents shall revoke the consent of both parents. The failure of a biological parent to complete the consent form shall have no effect on the finality of the consent to adoption. A copy of the form required by this subdivision, shall be forwarded to the state adoption information registry for inclusion in the records maintained by such registry. Any fees authorized to be charged by the state adoption registry for filing documentation with such registry shall be waived for the form required by this subdivision.

§115-c. Temporary guardianship by adoptive parent.
In any case where physical custody of a child is transferred from the child's parent or guardian to another person or persons for the purposes of adoption and a consent to the adoption of such child has been executed pursuant to section one hundred fifteen-b of this title, the adoptive parent or parents shall, within ten court days of taking physical custody, either file a petition for adoption with a court of competent jurisdiction or file an application for temporary guardianship of the person of the child pursuant to this section with the court in which the adoption will be filed, pursuant to section seventeen hundred twenty-five of the surrogate's court procedure act or section six hundred sixty-one of the family court act except as otherwise provided herein. Such application shall include an affidavit by the adoptive parent or parents describing any change of circumstances since their certification as a qualified adoptive parent or parents, pursuant to section one hundred fifteen-d of this title, which may be material to such certification. Such a petition for adoption shall also be deemed an application for temporary guardianship, where no prior application for an order for temporary guardianship has been filed.

In any case where the adoptive parent or parents take physical custody of an adoptive child and requirements for certification as a qualified adoptive parent or parents have been waived, pursuant to section one hundred fifteen-d of this title, an application for temporary guardianship or petition for adoption for such child shall be filed with the court not later than five court days from obtaining physical custody of such child. Such time period may be extended upon motion of any person or upon the court's own motion for good cause shown.

§115-d. Petition for certification.
1. Except as provided for in subdivision eight of this section, a person or persons petitioning for certification as a qualified adoptive parent or parents shall upon a form, promulgated by the chief administrator of the courts, provide to the court:

(a) the applicant's name or applicants' names, residential address and telephone number;

(b) a statement by the applicant or applicants that they are seeking certification by the court as a person or persons qualified to take physical custody of an infant prior to or contemporaneous with the filing of a private-placement adoption petition;

(c) a statement by the applicant or applicants as to whether such applicant or applicants have been the subject of an indicated report of child abuse or maltreatment, pursuant to title six of article six of the social services law; and

(d) a statement that a pre-placement investigation will be undertaken by a disinterested person, as such term is defined in subdivision four of this section, and that a written report of such investigation will be furnished directly to the court by such disinterested person with a copy of such report to be delivered simultaneously to the applicant or applicants. Such disinterested person shall certify to the court that he or she is a disinterested person and has no interest in the outcome of the party's or parties' application. Such disinterested person shall further disclose to the court any fee paid or to be paid to such person for services rendered in connection with the pre-placement investigation.

Such petition shall also require information regarding:

(i) the marital and family status and history of the adoptive parent or parents;

(ii) the physical and mental health of the adoptive parent or parents;

(iii) the property owned by and the income of adoptive parent or parents;

(iv) whether the adoptive parent or either of the adoptive parents has ever been a respondent in any proceeding concerning allegedly abused, neglected, abandoned or delinquent children; and

(v) whether the applicant or applicants have made any prior application for certification as a qualified adoptive parent or parents and, if so, the disposition of such application for certification.

2. In any case where the applicant or applicants do not intend to cause a pre-placement investigation to be undertaken pursuant to the provisions of paragraph (d) of subdivision one of this section, such applicant or applicants shall request the court to appoint a disinterested person to conduct such pre-placement investigation. The investigative written report shall be submitted to the judge or surrogate within thirty days, unless for good cause shown the judge or surrogate shall grant a reasonable extension of such period.

3. Such applicant or applicants shall be financially responsible for the costs of any pre-placement investigation conducted pursuant to subdivision one or two of this section.

3-a. (a) The court shall submit fingerprint cards and order a report from the division of criminal justice services setting forth any existing criminal history record of the applicant for certification as a qualified adoptive parent.

(b) Notwithstanding any other provision of law to the contrary, a petition for certification as a qualified adoptive parent shall be denied where a criminal history record of the applicant reveals a conviction for (i) a felony conviction at any time involving: (1) child abuse or neglect; (2) spousal abuse; (3) a crime against a child, including child pornography; or (4) a crime involving violence, including rape, sexual assault, or homicide, other than a crime involving physical assault or battery; or (ii) a felony conviction within the past five years for physical assault, battery, or a drug-related offense.

(c) For the purposes of this subdivision, "spousal abuse" is an offense defined in section 120.05, 120.10, 121.12 or 121.13 of the penal law where the victim of such offense was the defendant's spouse; provided, however, spousal abuse shall not include a crime in which the applicant was the defendant, and the court finds in accordance with this subdivision that he or she was the victim of physical, sexual or psychological abuse by the victim of such offense and such abuse was a factor in causing the applicant to commit such offense.

4. A pre-placement investigation conducted pursuant to the provisions of this section shall be made by a disinterested person who in the opinion of the judge or surrogate is qualified by training and experience to examine into the allegations set forth in the application and any other factors which may be relevant to the suitability of the applicant or applicants as a qualified adoptive parent or parents. For the purposes of this section, a disinterested person shall also include a licensed master social worker, licensed clinical social worker, the probation service of the family court or an authorized agency specifically designated by the court to conduct pre-placement investigations.

5. Such disinterested person shall file with the court a written report of his or her investigation into the truth and accuracy of the allegations set forth in the application and his or her investigation of the various factors which may be relevant to the suitability of the applicant or applicants as qualified adoptive parents. Such investigation shall include, but not be limited to, a personal interview and visit at the applicant's or applicants' home and an investigation of any other facts relating to the familial, social, religious, emotional and

financial circumstances of the adoptive parent or parents which may be relevant to certification as a qualified adoptive parent or parents.

6. Certification and provisional certification. If after consideration of the report submitted by the disinterested person, and all other relevant and material factors, the court grants the application, the applicant or applicants may accept physical custody of a child for the purposes of adoption, either prior to or contemporaneous with the filing of an adoption petition. The order granting the petition shall be valid for a period not to exceed eighteen months and shall be accepted as proof of certification by any court of competent jurisdiction within the state. The court may in its discretion grant a conditional order of certification upon satisfactory completion and submission of a petition wherein the prospective adoptive parent or parents indicate no prior criminal convictions or founded findings of child abuse or neglect, and after completion of a disinterested person investigation provided for in this section, pending completion of any further reports, investigations or inquiries ordered by the court or required by any other statute or court rule. A conditional order of certification shall be valid and remain in force and effect until replaced by an order of certification or by an order denying the petition, whichever shall first occur, but in no event shall such provisional certification continue beyond one hundred eighty days from the date of original issuance. If the court denies the petition, the reasons for such denial shall be stated on the record or in the order.

7. Nothing in this section shall be deemed to waive, limit or restrict the provisions of any other law requiring any inquiry, disinterested person investigation or court review of any persons seeking to adopt a child under any provision of law.

8. The provisions of this section shall not apply to petitions brought by a step-parent for the adoption of a step-child where the step-child has resided with the birth parent and the step-parent for a continuous period of at least one year.

9. Extension of certification. When a petition for adoption is filed by a qualified parent or parents previously certified and the balance of the time period remaining under such certification in accordance with subdivision six of this section is less than one year, the court may on its own motion or on the motion of the petitioners extend the time period of the original certification to a date eighteen months from the date of filing of the adoption petition. When a petition for adoption is filed by a qualified parent or parents who have previously been certified by an order which has expired within a year preceding the date of the adoption petition, the court may extend the termination date of the earlier certification until eighteen months from the filing of such petition, provided the petitioner apply for such extension and set forth any change of circumstances of the qualified parent or parents since issuance and expiration of the last certification which may be relevant and material to the extension of such certification and affix thereto written verification of any such changed circumstance or lack thereof by a disinterested person as defined in subdivision four of this section. Except as is provided for by this subdivision, the court shall not extend a previously expired order of certification. Any further certification shall require the filing of a new petition for certification in accordance with subdivision six of this section.

In any instance when the court determines whether to extend a certification under this subdivision, the court, in its discretion, may order each or any of (a) a report from the statewide central registry of child abuse and maltreatment to determine whether the child or the petitioner is or has been the subject of or another person named in an indicated report, as such terms are defined in section four hundred twelve of the social services law, filed with such register, (b) a report from the division of criminal justice services setting forth any criminal record of such petitioner or petitioners, and (c) an additional pre-placement investigation to be undertaken by a disinterested person. Nothing herein shall be deemed to require that the court enter such an order.

§115-e. Effect of death of potential adoptive parent.

Notwithstanding any other provision of law to the contrary, when a petition for adoption by two persons has been duly filed, and one of the petitioners dies before the adoption is complete, it shall be treated as a change of circumstance. This change may be reviewed to assure that the adoption is in the best interest of the child. The death of one of the adoptive parents shall not, by itself, invalidate a certification nor shall the death of one of the adoptive parents cause a new petition for adoption to be filed. The deceased adoptive parent shall be considered one of the legal parents, unless the surviving adoptive parent requests otherwise.

§116. Orders of investigation and order of adoption.

1. When the adoptive child is less than eighteen years of age, no order of adoption shall be made until three months after the court shall have received the petition to adopt, except where the spouse of the adoptive parent is the birth parent of the child and the child has resided with the birth parent and adoptive parent for more than three months, such waiting period shall not be required. The judge or surrogate may shorten such waiting period for good cause shown, and, in such case the order of adoption shall recite the reason for such action. The three months residence period specified in section one hundred twelve of title two of this article and the three months waiting period provided in this subdivision may run concurrently in whole or in part.

2. Stage one of private-placement adoption. At the time of receiving the petition, agreement and consents, the judge or surrogate, upon finding that the applicable provisions of this title have been complied with and that it appears that the adoption may be in the best interests of the child, shall issue an order of investigation hereunder. The order of investigation shall require that the report of such investigation be made in accordance with subdivision three of this section, and may require or authorize further investigations from time to time until the granting of the order of adoption. Such order shall direct that such investigation shall not unnecessarily duplicate any previous investigations which have been made of the petitioner or petitioners pursuant to section one hundred fifteen-d of this title. Should such investigation give apparent cause, the judge or surrogate shall require the petitioner or petitioners to show cause why the child should not be removed from the home, upon due notice to all persons whose consent is required for the adoption, and in any case where the consent of the birth mother would not otherwise be required, the judge or surrogate may in his discretion require that she be given due notice. On the return date the judge or surrogate shall take proof of the facts shown by any such investigation. If the court is satisfied that the welfare of the child requires that it be removed from the home, the judge or surrogate shall by order remove the child from the home of the petitioner or petitioners and return the child to a birth parent or place the child with an appropriate authorized agency, or, in the case of a surrogate, transfer the child to the family court. The judge or

surrogate may also require that notice be given to an appropriate authorized agency.

3. The judge or surrogate shall cause to be made an investigation by a disinterested person who in the opinion of the judge or surrogate is qualified by training and experience, or by an authorized agency specifically designated by him to examine into the allegations set forth in the petition. A post-placement investigation conducted pursuant to the provisions of this section shall be made by a disinterested person who in the opinion of the judge or surrogate is qualified by training and experience to perform post-placement investigations. Such disinterested person shall certify to the court that he or she is a disinterested person and has no interest in the outcome of petitioner's or petitioners' application. Such disinterested person shall further disclose to the court any fee paid or to be paid to such person for services rendered in connection with the post-placement investigation. The investigator shall make a written report of his investigation into the truth and accuracy of the allegations of the petition, and, where applicable, into the statements contained in the affidavit required by section one hundred fifteen of this title, and he shall ascertain as fully as possible, and incorporate in his report the various factors which may bear upon the determination of the application for adoption including, but not limited to, the following information:

(a) the marital and family status, and history, of the adoptive parents and adoptive child;

(b) the physical and mental health of the adoptive parents and adoptive child;

(c) the property owned by and the income of the adoptive parents;

(d) the compensation paid or agreed upon with respect to the placement of the child for adoption;

(e) whether either adoptive parent has ever been respondent in any proceeding concerning allegedly abused, neglected, abandoned or delinquent children;

(f) any other facts relating to the familial, social, religious, emotional and financial circumstances of the adoptive parents which may be relevant to a determination of adoption.

The written report of investigation shall be submitted to the judge or surrogate within thirty days after the same is directed to be made, unless for good cause shown the judge or surrogate shall grant a reasonable extension of such period. The report shall be filed with the judge or surrogate, in any event, before the final order of adoption is granted.

4. Stage two of private-placement adoption. If the judge or surrogate has found that there has been compliance with all the requirements hereof and is satisfied that the best interests of the child will be promoted by granting an order of adoption, the provisions of section one hundred fourteen of title two of this article shall apply.

5. As used in this section, "disinterested person" includes the probation service of the family court, a licensed master social worker, licensed clinical social worker, or an authorized agency specifically designated by the court to conduct pre-placement investigations.

Title IV
Effect of Adoption from an Authorized Agency,
of Private-placement Adoption,
and Abrogations Thereof

Section
117. Effect of adoption.

§117. Effect of adoption.

1. (a) After the making of an order of adoption the birth parents of the adoptive child shall be relieved of all parental duties toward and of all responsibilities for and shall have no rights over such adoptive child or to his property by descent or succession, except as hereinafter stated.

(b) The rights of an adoptive child to inheritance and succession from and through his birth parents shall terminate upon the making of the order of adoption except as hereinafter provided.

(c) The adoptive parents or parent and the adoptive child shall sustain toward each other the legal relation of parent and child and shall have all the rights and be subject to all the duties of that relation including the rights of inheritance from and through each other and the birth and adopted kindred of the adoptive parents or parent.

(d) When a birth or adoptive parent, having lawful custody of a child, marries or remarries and consents that the stepparent may adopt such child, such consent shall not relieve the parent so consenting of any parental duty toward such child nor shall such consent or the order of adoption affect the rights of such consenting spouse and such adoptive child to inherit from and through each other and the birth and adopted kindred of such consenting spouse.

(e) Notwithstanding the provisions of paragraphs (a), (b) and (d) of this subdivision, as to estates of persons dying after the thirty-first day of August, nineteen hundred eighty-seven, if:

(1) the decedent is the adoptive child's birth grandparent or is a descendant of such grandparent, and

(2) an adoptive parent (i) is married to the child's birth parent, (ii) is the child's birth grandparent, or (iii) is descended from such grandparent, the rights of an adoptive child to inheritance and succession from and through either birth parent shall not terminate upon the making of the order of adoption.

However, an adoptive child who is related to the decedent both by birth relationship and by adoption shall be entitled to inherit only under the birth relationship unless the decedent is also the adoptive parent, in which case the adoptive child shall then be entitled to inherit pursuant to the adoptive relationship only.

(f) The right of inheritance of an adoptive child extends to the distributees of such child and such distributees shall be the same as if he were the birth child of the adoptive parent.

(g) Adoptive children and birth children shall have all the rights of fraternal relationship including the right of inheritance from each other. Such right of inheritance extends to the distributees of such adoptive children and birth children and such distributees shall be the same as if each such child were the birth child of the adoptive parents.

(h) The consent of the parent of a child to the adoption of such child by his or her spouse shall operate to vest in the adopting spouse only the rights as distributee of a birth parent and shall leave otherwise unaffected the rights as distributee of the consenting spouse.

(i) This subdivision shall apply only to the intestate descent and distribution of real and personal property.

2. (a) Except as hereinafter stated, after the making of an order of adoption, adopted children and their issue thereafter are strangers to any birth relatives for the purpose of the interpretation or construction of a disposition in any instrument, whether executed before or after the order of adoption, which does not express a contrary intention or does not expressly include the individual by name or by some classification not based on a parent-child or family relationship.

(b) As to the wills of persons executed after the thirty-first day of August, nineteen hundred eighty-six, or to lifetime instruments executed after such date whether executed before or after the order of adoption, a designation of a class of persons described in section 2-1.3 of the estates, powers and trusts law shall, unless the will or instrument expresses a contrary intention, be deemed to include an adoptive child who was a member of such class in his or her birth relationship prior to adoption, and the issue of such child, only if:

(1) an adoptive parent (i) is married to the child's birth parent, (ii) is the child's birth grandparent, or (iii) is a descendant of such grandparent, and

(2) the testator or creator is the child's birth grandparent or a descendant of such grandparent.

(c) A person who, by reason of this subdivision, would be a member of the designated class, or a member of two or more designated classes pursuant to a single instrument, both by birth relationship and by adoption shall be entitled to benefit only under the birth relationship, unless the testator or creator is the adoptive parent, in which case the person shall then be entitled to benefit only under the adoptive relationship.

(d) The provisions of this subdivision shall not impair or defeat any rights which have vested on or before the thirty-first day of August, nineteen hundred eighty-six, or which have vested prior to the adoption regardless of when the adoption occurred.

3. The provisions of law affected by the provisions of this section in force prior to March first, nineteen hundred sixty-four shall apply to the estates or wills of persons dying prior thereto and to lifetime instruments theretofore executed which on said date were not subject to grantor's power to revoke or amend.

ARTICLE 13
Provisions Applicable to More than
One Type of Matrimonial Action

Section
240. Custody and child support; orders of protection.

§240. Custody and child support; orders of protection.

1. (a) In any action or proceeding brought (1) to annul a marriage or to declare the nullity of a void marriage, or (2) for a separation, or (3) for a divorce, or (4) to obtain, by a writ of habeas corpus or by petition and order to show cause, the custody of or right to visitation with any child of a marriage, the court shall require verification of the status of any child of the marriage with respect to such child's custody and support, including any prior orders, and shall enter orders for custody and support as, in the court's discretion, justice requires, having regard to the circumstances of the case and of the respective parties and to the best interests of the child and subject to the provisions of subdivision one-c of this section. Where either party to an action

concerning custody of or a right to visitation with a child alleges in a sworn petition or complaint or sworn answer, cross-petition, counterclaim or other sworn responsive pleading that the other party has committed an act of domestic violence against the party making the allegation or a family or household member of either party, as such family or household member is defined in article eight of the family court act, and such allegations are proven by a preponderance of the evidence, the court must consider the effect of such domestic violence upon the best interests of the child, together with such other facts and circumstances as the court deems relevant in making a direction pursuant to this section and state on the record how such findings, facts and circumstances factored into the direction. If a parent makes a good faith allegation based on a reasonable belief supported by facts that the child is the victim of child abuse, child neglect, or the effects of domestic violence, and if that parent acts lawfully and in good faith in response to that reasonable belief to protect the child or seek treatment for the child, then that parent shall not be deprived of custody, visitation or contact with the child, or restricted in custody, visitation or contact, based solely on that belief or the reasonable actions taken based on that belief. If an allegation that a child is abused is supported by a preponderance of the evidence, then the court shall consider such evidence of abuse in determining the visitation arrangement that is in the best interest of the child, and the court shall not place a child in the custody of a parent who presents a substantial risk of harm to that child, and shall state on the record how such findings were factored into the determination. Where a proceeding filed pursuant to article ten or ten-A of the family court act is pending at the same time as a proceeding brought in the supreme court involving the custody of, or right to visitation with, any child of a marriage, the court presiding over the proceeding under article ten or ten-A of the family court act may jointly hear the dispositional hearing on the petition under article ten or the permanency hearing under article ten-A of the family court act and, upon referral from the supreme court, the hearing to resolve the matter of custody or visitation in the proceeding pending in the supreme court; provided however, the court must determine custody or visitation in accordance with the terms of this section.

An order directing the payment of child support shall contain the social security numbers of the named parties. In all cases there shall be no prima facie right to the custody of the child in either parent. Such direction shall make provision for child support out of the property of either or both parents. The court shall make its award for child support pursuant to subdivision one-b of this section. Such direction may provide for reasonable visitation rights to the maternal and/or paternal grandparents of any child of the parties. Such direction as it applies to rights of visitation with a child remanded or placed in the care of a person, official, agency or institution pursuant to article ten of the family court act, or pursuant to an instrument approved under section three hundred fifty-eight-a of the social services law, shall be enforceable pursuant to part eight of article ten of the family court act and sections three hundred fifty-eight-a and three hundred eighty-four-a of the social services law and other applicable provisions of law against any person having care and custody, or temporary care and custody, of the child. Notwithstanding any other provision of law, any written application or motion to the court for the establishment, modification or enforcement of a child support obligation for persons not in receipt of public assistance and care must contain either a request for child support enforcement services which would authorize the collection of the support obligation by the immediate issuance of an income execution for support enforcement as provided for by this chapter, completed in the manner specified in section one hundred eleven-g of the social services law; or a statement that the applicant has applied for or is in receipt of such services; or a statement that the applicant knows of the availability of such services, has declined them at this time and where support enforcement services pursuant to section one hundred eleven-g of the social services law have been declined that the applicant understands that an income deduction order may be issued pursuant to subdivision (c) of section fifty-two hundred forty-two of the civil practice law and rules without other child support enforcement services and that payment of an administrative fee may be required. The court shall provide a copy of any such request for child support enforcement services to the support collection unit of the appropriate social services district any time it directs payments to be made to such support collection unit. Additionally, the copy of any such request shall be accompanied by the name, address and social security number of the parties; the date and place of the parties' marriage; the name and date of birth of the child or children; and the name and address of the employers and income payors of the party from whom child support is sought or from the party ordered to pay child support to the other party. Such direction may require the payment of a sum or sums of money either directly to the custodial parent or to third persons for goods or services furnished for such child, or for both payments to the custodial parent and to such third persons; provided, however, that unless the party seeking or receiving child support has applied for or is receiving such services, the court shall not direct such payments to be made to the support collection unit, as established in section one hundred eleven-h of the social services law. Every order directing the payment of support shall require that if either parent currently, or at any time in the future, has health insurance benefits available that may be extended or obtained to cover the child, such parent is required to exercise the option of additional coverage in favor of such child and execute and deliver to such person any forms, notices, documents or instruments necessary to assure timely payment of any health insurance claims for such child.

(a-1)(1) Permanent and initial temporary orders of custody or visitation. Prior to the issuance of any permanent or initial temporary order of custody or visitation, the court shall conduct a review of the decisions and reports listed in subparagraph three of this paragraph.

(2) Successive temporary orders of custody or visitation. Prior to the issuance of any successive temporary order of custody or visitation, the court shall conduct a review of the decisions and reports listed in subparagraph three of this paragraph, unless such a review has been conducted within ninety days prior to the issuance of such order.

(3) Decisions and reports for review. The court shall conduct a review of the following:

(i) related decisions in court proceedings initiated pursuant to article ten of the family court act, and all warrants issued under the family court act; and

(ii) reports of the statewide computerized registry of orders of protection established and maintained pursuant to section two hundred twenty-one-a of the executive law, and reports of the sex offender registry established and maintained pursuant to section one hundred sixty-eight-b of the correction law.

(4) Notifying counsel and issuing orders. Upon consideration of decisions pursuant to article ten of the family court act, and registry reports and notifying

counsel involved in the proceeding, or in the event of a self-represented party, notifying such party of the results thereof, including any court appointed attorney for children, the court may issue a temporary, successive temporary or final order of custody or visitation.

(5) Temporary emergency order. Notwithstanding any other provision of the law, upon emergency situations, including computer malfunctions, to serve the best interest of the child, the court may issue a temporary emergency order for custody or visitation in the event that it is not possible to timely review decisions and reports on registries as required pursuant to subparagraph three of this paragraph.

(6) After issuing a temporary emergency order. After issuing a temporary emergency order of custody or visitation, the court shall conduct reviews of the decisions and reports on registries as required pursuant to subparagraph three of this paragraph within twenty-four hours of the issuance of such temporary emergency order. Should such twenty-four hour period fall on a day when court is not in session, then the required reviews shall take place the next day the court is in session. Upon reviewing decisions and reports the court shall notify associated counsel, self-represented parties and attorneys for children pursuant to subparagraph four of this paragraph and may issue temporary or permanent custody or visitation orders.

(7) Feasibility study. The commissioner of the office of children and family services, in conjunction with the office of court administration, is hereby authorized and directed to examine, study, evaluate and make recommendations concerning the feasibility of the utilization of computers in courts which are connected to the statewide central register of child abuse and maltreatment established and maintained pursuant to section four hundred twenty-two of the social services law, as a means of providing courts with information regarding parties requesting orders of custody or visitation. Such commissioner shall make a preliminary report to the governor and the legislature of findings, conclusions and recommendations not later than January first, two thousand nine, and a final report of findings, conclusions and recommendations not later than June first, two thousand nine, and shall submit with the reports such legislative proposals as are deemed necessary to implement the commissioner's recommendations.

(a-2) Military service by parent; effect on child custody orders.

(1) During the period of time that a parent is activated, deployed or temporarily assigned to military service, such that the parent's ability to continue as a joint caretaker or the primary caretaker of a minor child is materially affected by such military service, any orders issued pursuant to this section, based on the fact that the parent is activated, deployed or temporarily assigned to military service, which would materially affect or change a previous judgment or order regarding custody of that parent's child or children as such judgment or order existed on the date the parent was activated, deployed, or temporarily assigned to military service, shall be subject to review pursuant to subparagraph three of this paragraph. Any relevant provisions of the Service Member's Civil Relief Act shall apply to all proceedings governed by this section.

(2) During such period, the court may enter an order to modify custody if there is clear and convincing evidence that the modification is in the best interests of the child. An attorney for the child shall be appointed in all cases where a modification is sought during such military service. Such order shall be subject to review pursuant to subparagraph three of this paragraph. When

entering an order pursuant to this section, the court shall consider and provide for, if feasible and if in the best interests of the child, contact between the military service member and his or her child, including, but not limited to, electronic communication by e-mail, webcam, telephone, or other available means. During the period of the parent's leave from military service, the court shall consider the best interests of the child when establishing a parenting schedule, including visiting and other contact. For such purposes, a "leave from military service" shall be a period of not more than three months.

(3) Unless the parties have otherwise stipulated or agreed, if an order is issued pursuant to this paragraph, the return of the parent from active military service, deployment or temporary assignment shall be considered a substantial change in circumstances. Upon the request of either parent, the court shall determine on the basis of the child's best interests whether the custody judgment or order previously in effect should be modified.

(4) This paragraph shall not apply to assignments to permanent duty stations or permanent changes of station.

(b) As used in this section, the following terms shall have the following meanings:

(1) "Health insurance benefits" means any medical, dental, optical and prescription drugs and health care services or other health care benefits that may be provided for a dependent through an employer or organization, including such employers or organizations which are self insured, or through other available health insurance or health care coverage plans.

(2) "Available health insurance benefits" means any health insurance benefits that are reasonable in cost and that are reasonably accessible to the person on whose behalf the petition is brought. Health insurance benefits that are not reasonable in cost or whose services are not reasonably accessible to such person, shall be considered unavailable.

(3) When the person on whose behalf the petition is brought is a child in accordance with paragraph (c) of this subdivision, health insurance benefits shall be considered "reasonable in cost" if the cost of health insurance benefits does not exceed five percent of the combined parental gross income. The cost of health insurance benefits shall refer to the cost of the premium and deductible attributable to adding the child or children to existing coverage or the difference between such costs for self-only and family coverage. Provided, however, the presumption that the health insurance benefits are reasonable in cost may be rebutted upon a finding that the cost is unjust or inappropriate which finding shall be based on the circumstances of the case, the cost and comprehensiveness of the health insurance benefits for which the child or children may otherwise be eligible, and the best interests of the child or children. In no instance shall health insurance benefits be considered "reasonable in cost" if a parent's share of the cost of extending such coverage would reduce the income of that parent below the self-support reserve. Health insurance benefits are "reasonably accessible" if the child lives within the geographic area covered by the plan or lives within thirty minutes or thirty miles of travel time from the child's residence to the services covered by the health insurance benefits or through benefits provided under a reciprocal agreement; provided, however, this presumption may be rebutted for good cause shown including, but not limited to, the special health needs of the child. The court shall set forth such finding and the reasons therefor in the order of support.

(c) When the person on whose behalf the petition is brought is a child, the court shall consider the availability of health insurance benefits to all parties and shall take the following action to ensure that health insurance benefits are provided for the benefit of the child:

(1) Where the child is presently covered by health insurance benefits, the court shall direct in the order of support that such coverage be maintained, unless either parent requests the court to make a direction for health insurance benefits coverage pursuant to paragraph two of this subdivision.

(2) Where the child is not presently covered by health insurance benefits, the court shall make a determination as follows:

(i) If only one parent has available health insurance benefits, the court shall direct in the order of support that such parent provide health insurance benefits.

(ii) If both parents have available health insurance benefits the court shall direct in the order of support that either parent or both parents provide such health insurance. The court shall make such determination based on the circumstances of the case, including, but not limited to, the cost and comprehensiveness of the respective health insurance benefits and the best interests of the child.

(iii) If neither parent has available health insurance benefits, the court shall direct in the order of support that the custodial parent apply for the state's child health insurance plan pursuant to title one-A of article twenty-five of the public health law and the medical assistance program established pursuant to title eleven of article five of the social services law. A direction issued under this subdivision shall not limit or alter either parent's obligation to obtain health insurance benefits at such time as they become available, as required pursuant to paragraph (a) of this subdivision. Nothing in this subdivision shall alter or limit the authority of the medical assistance program to determine when it is considered cost effective to require a custodial parent to enroll a child in an available group health insurance plan pursuant to paragraphs (b) and (c) of subdivision one of section three hundred sixty-seven-a of the social services law.

(d) The cost of providing health insurance benefits or benefits under the state's child health insurance plan or the medical assistance program, pursuant to paragraph (c) of this subdivision, shall be deemed cash medical support, and the court shall determine the obligation of either or both parents to contribute to the cost thereof pursuant to subparagraph five of paragraph (c) of subdivision one-b of this section.

(e) The court shall provide in the order of support that the legally responsible relative immediately notify the other party, or the other party and the support collection unit when the order is issued on behalf of a child in receipt of public assistance and care or in receipt of services pursuant to section one hundred eleven-g of the social services law, of any change in health insurance benefits, including any termination of benefits, change in the health insurance benefit carrier, premium, or extent and availability of existing or new benefits.

(f) Where the court determines that health insurance benefits are available, the court shall provide in the order of support that the legally responsible relative immediately enroll the eligible dependents named in the order who are otherwise eligible for such benefits without regard to any seasonal enrollment restrictions. Such order shall further direct the legally responsible relative to maintain such benefits as long as they remain available to such relative. Such order shall further direct the legally responsible relative to assign all insurance reimbursement payments for health care expenses incurred for his or her eligible dependents to the provider of such services or the party actually having incurred and satisfied such expenses, as appropriate.

(g) When the court issues an order of child support or combined child and spousal support on behalf of persons in receipt of public assistance and care or in receipt of services pursuant to section one hundred eleven-g of the social services law, such order shall further direct that the provision of health care benefits shall be immediately enforced pursuant to section fifty-two hundred forty-one of the civil practice law and rules.

(h) When the court issues an order of child support or combined child and spousal support on behalf of persons other than those in receipt of public assistance and care or in receipt of services pursuant to section one hundred eleven-g of the social services law, the court shall also issue a separate order which shall include the necessary direction to ensure the order's characterization as a qualified medical child support order as defined by section six hundred nine of the employee retirement income security act of 1974 (29 USC 1169). Such order shall: (i) clearly state that it creates or recognizes the existence of the right of the named dependent to be enrolled and to receive benefits for which the legally responsible relative is eligible under the available group health plans, and shall clearly specify the name, social security number and mailing address of the legally responsible relative, and of each dependent to be covered by the order; (ii) provide a clear description of the type of coverage to be provided by the group health plan to each such dependent or the manner in which the type of coverage is to be determined; and (iii) specify the period of time to which the order applies. The court shall not require the group health plan to provide any type or form of benefit or option not otherwise provided under the group health plan except to the extent necessary to meet the requirements of a law relating to medical child support described in section one thousand three hundred and ninety-six g of title forty-two of the United States code.

(i) Upon a finding that a legally responsible relative wilfully failed to obtain health insurance benefits in violation of a court order, such relative will be presumptively liable for all health care expenses incurred on behalf of such dependents from the first date such dependents were eligible to be enrolled to receive health insurance benefits after the issuance of the order of support directing the acquisition of such coverage.

(j) The order shall be effective as of the date of the application therefor, and any retroactive amount of child support due shall be support arrears/past due support and shall, except as provided for herein, be paid in one lump sum or periodic sums, as the court shall direct, taking into account any amount of temporary support which has been paid. In addition, such retroactive child support shall be enforceable in any manner provided by law including, but not limited to, an execution for support enforcement pursuant to subdivision (b) of section fifty-two hundred forty-one of the civil practice law and rules. When a child receiving support is a public assistance recipient, or the order of support is being enforced or is to be enforced pursuant to section one hundred eleven-g of the social services law, the court shall establish the amount of retroactive child support and notify the parties that such amount shall be enforced by the support collection unit pursuant to an execution for support enforcement as provided for in subdivision (b) of section fifty-two hundred forty-one of the civil practice law and rules, or in such periodic payments as would have been authorized had such an execution been issued. In such case, the courts shall not direct the schedule of repayment of retroactive support. Where such direction is for child support and paternity has been established by a voluntary acknowledgement of paternity as defined in section forty-one hundred thirty-five-b of the public health law, the court shall inquire of the parties whether the acknowledgement has been duly filed, and unless satisfied that it has been so filed shall require the clerk of the court to file such acknowledgement with the appropriate registrar within five business days. Such direction may be made in the final judgment in such action or proceeding, or by one or more orders from time to time before or subsequent to final judgment, or by both such order or orders and the final judgment. Such direction may be made notwithstanding that the court for any reason whatsoever, other than lack of jurisdiction, refuses to grant the relief requested in the action or proceeding. Any order or judgment made as in this section provided may combine in one lump sum any amount payable to the custodial parent under this section with any amount payable to such parent under section two hundred thirty-six of this article. Upon the application of either parent, or of any other person or party having the care, custody and control of such child pursuant to such judgment or order, after such notice to the other party, parties or persons having such care, custody and control and given in such manner as the court shall direct, the court may annul or modify any such direction, whether made by order or final judgment, or in case no such direction shall have been made in the final judgment may, with respect to any judgment of annulment or declaring the nullity of a void marriage rendered on or after September first, nineteen hundred forty, or any judgment of separation or divorce whenever rendered, amend the judgment by inserting such direction. Subject to the provisions of section two hundred forty-four of this article, no such modification or annulment shall reduce or annul arrears accrued prior to the making of such application unless the defaulting party shows good cause for failure to make application for relief from the judgment or order directing such payment prior to the accrual of such arrears. Such modification may increase such child support nunc pro tunc as of the date of application based on newly discovered evidence. Any retroactive amount of child support due shall be support arrears/past due support and shall be paid in one lump sum or periodic sums, as the court shall direct, taking into account any amount of temporary child support which has been paid. In addition, such retroactive child support shall be enforceable in any manner provided by law including, but not limited to, an execution for support enforcement pursuant to subdivision (b) of section fifty-two hundred forty-one of the civil practice law and rules.

1-a. In any proceeding brought pursuant to this section to determine the custody or visitation of minors, a report made to the statewide central register of child abuse and maltreatment, pursuant to title six of article six of the social services law, or a portion thereof, which is otherwise admissible as a business record pursuant to rule forty-five hundred eighteen of the civil practice law and rules shall not be admissible in evidence, notwithstanding such rule, unless an investigation of such report conducted pursuant to title six of article six of the social services law has determined that there is some credible evidence of the alleged abuse or maltreatment and that the subject of the report has been notified that the report is indicated. In addition, if such report has been reviewed by the state commissioner of social services or his designee and has been determined to be unfounded, it shall not be admissible in evidence. If such report has been so reviewed and has been amended to delete any finding, each such deleted finding shall not be admissible. If the state commissioner of social services or his designee has amended the report to add any new finding, each such new finding, together with any portion of the original report not deleted by the commissioner or his designee, shall be admissible if it meets the other requirements of this subdivision and is otherwise admissible as a business record. If such a report, or portion thereof, is admissible in evidence but is uncorroborated, it shall not be sufficient to make a fact finding of abuse or maltreatment in such proceeding. Any other evidence tending to support the reliability of such report shall be sufficient corroboration.

1-b. (a) The court shall make its award for child support pursuant to the provisions of this subdivision. The court may vary from the amount of the basic child support obligation determined pursuant to paragraph (c) of this subdivision only in accordance with paragraph (f) of this subdivision.

(b) For purposes of this subdivision, the following definitions shall be used:

(1) "Basic child support obligation" shall mean the sum derived by adding the amounts determined by the application of subparagraphs two and three of paragraph (c) of this subdivision except as increased pursuant to subparagraphs four, five, six and seven of such paragraph.

(2) "Child support" shall mean a sum to be paid pursuant to court order or decree by either or both parents or pursuant to a valid agreement between the parties for care, maintenance and education of any unemancipated child under the age of twenty-one years.

(3) "Child support percentage" shall mean:

(i) seventeen percent of the combined parental income for one child;

(ii) twenty-five percent of the combined parental income for two children;

(iii) twenty-nine percent of the combined parental income for three children;

(iv) thirty-one percent of the combined parental income for four children; and

(v) no less than thirty-five percent of the combined parental income for five or more children.

(4) "Combined parental income" shall mean the sum of the income of both parents.

(5) "Income" shall mean, but shall not be limited to, the sum of the amounts determined by the application of clauses (i), (ii), (iii), (iv), (v) and (vi) of this subparagraph reduced by the amount determined by the application of clause (vii) of this subparagraph:

(i) gross (total) income as should have been or should be reported in the most recent federal income tax return. If an individual files his/her federal income tax return as a married person filing jointly, such person shall be required to prepare a form, sworn to under penalty of law, disclosing his/her gross income individually;

(ii) to the extent not already included in gross income in clause (i) of this subparagraph, investment income reduced by sums expended in connection with such investment;

(iii) to the extent not already included in gross income in clauses (i) and (ii) of this subparagraph, the amount of income or compensation voluntarily deferred and income received, if any, from the following sources:

(A) workers' compensation,

(B) disability benefits,

(C) unemployment insurance benefits,

(D) social security benefits,

(E) veterans benefits,

(F) pensions and retirement benefits,

(G) fellowships and stipends,

(H) annuity payments, and

(I) alimony or maintenance actually paid or to be paid to a spouse who is a party to the instant action pursuant to an existing court order or contained in the order to be entered by the court, or pursuant to a validly executed written agreement, in which event the order or agreement shall provide for a specific adjustment, in accordance with this subdivision, in the amount of child support payable upon the termination of alimony or maintenance to such spouse; provided, however, that the specific adjustment in the amount of child support is without prejudice to either party's right to seek a modification in accordance with subparagraph two of paragraph b of subdivision nine of part B of section two hundred thirty-six of this article. In an action or proceeding to modify an order of child support, including an order incorporating without merging an agreement, issued prior to the effective date of this subclause, the provisions of this subclause shall not, by themselves, constitute a substantial change of circumstances pursuant to paragraph b of subdivision nine of part B of section two hundred thirty-six of this article.

(iv) at the discretion of the court, the court may attribute or impute income from, such other resources as may be available to the parent, including, but not limited to:

(A) non-income producing assets,

(B) meals, lodging, memberships, automobiles or other perquisites that are provided as part of compensation for employment to the extent that such perquisites constitute expenditures for personal use, or which expenditures directly or indirecly* confer personal economic benefits,

(C) fringe benefits provided as part of compensation for employment, and

(D) money, goods, or services provided by relatives and friends;

(v) an amount imputed as income based upon the parent's former resources or income, if the court determines that a parent has reduced resources or income in order to reduce or avoid the parent's obligation for child support;

(vi) to the extent not already included in gross income in clauses (i) and (ii) of this subparagraph, the following self-employment deductions attributable to self-employment carried on by the taxpayer:

(A) any depreciation deduction greater than depreciation calculated on a straight-line basis for the purpose of determining business income or investment credits, and

(B) entertainment and travel allowances deducted from business income to the extent said allowances reduce personal expenditures;

(vii) the following shall be deducted from income prior to applying the provisions of paragraph (c) of this subdivision:

(A) unreimbursed employee business expenses except to the extent said expenses reduce personal expenditures,

(B) alimony or maintenance actually paid to a spouse not a party to the instant action pursuant to court order or validly executed written agreement,

(C) alimony or maintenance actually paid or to be paid to a spouse who is a party to the instant action pursuant to an existing court order or contained in the order to be entered by the court, or pursuant to a validly executed written agreement, in which event the order or agreement shall provide for a specific adjustment, in accordance with this subdivision, in the amount of child support

---

*(So in original. Probably should be "indirectly.")

payable upon the termination of alimony or maintenance to such spouse; provided, however, that the specific adjustment in the amount of child support is without prejudice to either party's right to seek a modification in accordance with subparagraph two of paragraph b of subdivision nine of part B of section two hundred thirty-six of this article. In an action or proceeding to modify an order of child support, including an order incorporating without merging an agreement, issued prior to the effective date of this subclause, the provisions of this subclause shall not, by themselves, constitute a substantial change of circumstances pursuant to paragraph b of subdivision nine of part B of section two hundred thirty-six of this article.

(D) child support actually paid pursuant to court order or written agreement on behalf of any child for whom the parent has a legal duty of support and who is not subject to the instant action,

(E) public assistance,

(F) supplemental security income,

(G) New York city or Yonkers income or earnings taxes actually paid, and

(H) federal insurance contributions act (FICA) taxes actually paid.

(6) "Self-support reserve" shall mean one hundred thirty-five percent of the poverty income guidelines amount for a single person as reported by the federal department of health and human services. For the calendar year nineteen hundred eighty-nine, the self-support reserve shall be eight thousand sixty-five dollars. On March first of each year, the self-support reserve shall be revised to reflect the annual updating of the poverty income guidelines as reported by the federal department of health and human services for a single person household.

(c) The amount of the basic child support obligation shall be determined in accordance with the provision of this paragraph:

(1) The court shall determine the combined parental income.

(2) The court shall multiply the combined parental income up to the amount set forth in paragraph (b) of subdivision two of section one hundred eleven-i of the social services law by the appropriate child support percentage and such amount shall be prorated in the same proportion as each parent's income is to the combined parental income.

(3) Where the combined parental income exceeds the dollar amount set forth in subparagraph two of this paragraph, the court shall determine the amount of child support for the amount of the combined parental income in excess of such dollar amount through consideration of the factors set forth in paragraph (f) of this subdivision and/or the child support percentage.

(4) Where the custodial parent is working, or receiving elementary or secondary education, or higher education or vocational training which the court determines will lead to employment, and incurs child care expenses as a result thereof, the court shall determine reasonable child care expenses and such child care expenses, where incurred, shall be prorated in the same proportion as each parent's income is to the combined parental income. Each parent's pro rata share of the child care expenses shall be separately stated and added to the sum of subparagraphs two and three of this paragraph.

(5) The court shall determine the parties' obligation to provide health insurance benefits pursuant to this section and to pay cash medical support as provided under this subparagraph.

(i) "Cash medical support" means an amount ordered to be paid toward the cost of health insurance provided by a public entity or by a parent through an employer or organization, including such employers or organizations which are self insured, or through other available health insurance or health care coverage plans, and/or for other health care expenses not covered by insurance.

(ii) Where health insurance benefits pursuant to subparagraph one and clauses (i) and (ii) of subparagraph two of paragraph (c) of subdivision one of this section are determined by the court to be available, the cost of providing health insurance benefits shall be prorated between the parties in the same proportion as each parent's income is to the combined parental income. If the custodial parent is ordered to provide such benefits, the non-custodial parent's pro rata share of such costs shall be added to the basic support obligation. If the non-custodial parent is ordered to provide such benefits, the custodial parent's pro rata share of such costs shall be deducted from the basic support obligation.

(iii) Where health insurance benefits pursuant to subparagraph one and clauses (i) and (ii) of subparagraph two of paragraph (c) of subdivision one of this section are determined by the court to be unavailable, if the child or children are determined eligible for coverage under the medical assistance program established pursuant to title eleven of article five of the social services law, the court shall order the non-custodial parent to pay cash medical support as follows:

(A) In the case of a child or children authorized for managed care coverage under the medical assistance program, the lesser of the amount that would be required as a family contribution under the state's child health insurance plan pursuant to title one-A of article twenty-five of the public health law for the child or children if they were in a two-parent household with income equal to the combined income of the non-custodial and custodial parents or the premium paid by the medical assistance program on behalf of the child or children to the managed care plan. The court shall separately state the non-custodial parent's monthly obligation. The non-custodial parent's cash medical support obligation under this clause shall not exceed five percent of his or her gross income, or the difference between the non-custodial parent's income and the self-support reserve, whichever is less.

(B) In the case of a child or children authorized for fee-for-service coverage under the medical assistance program other than a child or children described in item (A) of this clause, the court shall determine the non-custodial parent's maximum annual cash medical support obligation, which shall be equal to the lesser of the monthly amount that would be required as a family contribution under the state's child health insurance plan pursuant to title one-A of article twenty-five of the public health law for the child or children if they were in a two-parent household with income equal to the combined income of the non-custodial and custodial parents times twelve months or the number of months that the child or children are authorized for fee-for-service coverage during any year. The court shall separately state in the order the non-custodial parent's maximum annual cash medical support obligation and, upon proof to the court that the non-custodial parent, after notice of the amount due, has failed to pay the public entity for incurred health care expenses, the court shall order the non-custodial parent to pay such incurred health care expenses up to the maximum annual cash medical support obligation. Such amounts shall be support arrears/past due support and shall be subject to any remedies as provided by law for the enforcement of support arrears/past due support. The total annual amount that the non-custodial parent is ordered to pay under this clause shall not exceed five percent of his or her gross income or the difference between the non-custodial parent's income and the self-support reserve, whichever is less.

(C) The court shall order cash medical support to be paid by the non-custodial parent for health care expenses of the child or children paid by the medical assistance program prior to the issuance of the court's order. The amount of such support shall be calculated as provided under item (A) or (B) of this clause, provided that the amount that the non-custodial parent is ordered to pay under this item shall not exceed five percent of his or her gross income or the difference between the non-custodial parent's income and the self-support reserve, whichever is less, for the year when the expense was incurred. Such amounts shall be support arrears/past due support and shall be subject to any remedies as provided by law for the enforcement of support arrears/past due support.

(iv) Where health insurance benefits pursuant to subparagraph one and clauses (i) and (ii) of subparagraph two of paragraph (c) of subdivision one of this section are determined by the court to be unavailable, and the child or children are determined eligible for coverage under the state's child health insurance plan pursuant to title one-A of article twenty-five of the public health law, the court shall prorate each parent's share of the cost of the family contribution required under such child health insurance plan in the same proportion as each parent's income is to the combined parental income, and state the amount of the non-custodial parent's share in the order. The total amount of cash medical support that the non-custodial parent is ordered to pay under this clause shall not exceed five percent of his or her gross income, or the difference between the non-custodial parent's income and the self-support reserve, whichever is less.

(v) In addition to the amounts ordered under clause (ii), (iii), or (iv), the court shall pro rate each parent's share of reasonable health care expenses not reimbursed or paid by insurance, the medical assistance program established pursuant to title eleven of article five of the social services law, or the state's child health insurance plan pursuant to title one-A of article twenty-five of the public health law, in the same proportion as each parent's income is to the combined parental income, and state the non-custodial parent's share as a percentage in the order. The non-custodial parent's pro rata share of such health care expenses determined by the court to be due and owing shall be support arrears/past due support and shall be subject to any remedies provided by law for the enforcement of support arrears/past due support. In addition, the court may direct that the non-custodial parent's pro rata share of such health care expenses be paid in one sum or in periodic sums, including direct payment to the health care provider.

(vi) Upon proof by either party that cash medical support pursuant to clause (ii), (iii), (iv), or (v) of this subparagraph would be unjust or inappropriate pursuant to paragraph (f) of this subdivision, the court shall:

(A) order the parties to pay cash medical support as the court finds just and appropriate, considering the best interests of the child; and

(B) set forth in the order the factors it considered, the amount calculated under this subparagraph, the reason or reasons the court did not order such amount, and the basis for the amount awarded.

(6) Where the court determines that the custodial parent is seeking work and incurs child care expenses as a result thereof, the court may determine reasonable child care expenses and may apportion the same between the custodial and non-custodial parent. The non-custodial parent's share of such expenses shall be separately stated and paid in a manner determined by the court.

(7) Where the court determines, having regard for the circumstances of the case and of the respective parties and in the best interests of the child, and as justice requires, that the present or future provision of post-secondary, private, special, or enriched education for the child is appropriate, the court may award educational expenses. The non-custodial parent shall pay educational expenses, as awarded, in a manner determined by the court, including direct payment to the educational provider.

(d) Notwithstanding the provisions of paragraph (c) of this subdivision, where the annual amount of the basic child support obligation would reduce the non-custodial parent's income below the poverty income guidelines amount for a single person as reported by the federal department of health and human services, the basic child support obligation shall be twenty-five dollars per month], provided, however, that if the court finds that such basic child support obligation is unjust or inappropriate, which finding shall be based upon considerations of the factors set forth in paragraph (f) of this subdivision, the court shall order the non-custodial parent to pay such amount of the child support as the court finds just and appropriate. Notwithstanding the provisions of paragraph (c) of this subdivision, where the annual amount of the basic child support obligation would reduce the non-custodial parent's income below the self-support reserve but not below the poverty income guidelines amount for a single person as reported by the federal department of health and human services, the basic child support obligation shall be fifty dollars per month or the difference between the non-custodial parent's income and the self-support reserve, whichever is greater, in addition to any amounts that the court may, in its discretion, order in accordance with subparagraphs four, five, six and/or seven of paragraph (c) of this subdivision.

(e) Where a parent is or may be entitled to receive non-recurring payments from extraordinary sources not otherwise considered as income pursuant to this section, including but not limited to:
(1) Life insurance policies;
(2) Discharges of indebtedness;
(3) Recovery of bad debts and delinquency amounts;
(4) Gifts and inheritances; and
(5) Lottery winnings, the court, in accordance with paragraphs (c), (d) and (f) of this subdivision may allocate a proportion of the same to child support, and such amount shall be paid in a manner determined by the court.

(f) The court shall calculate the basic child support obligation, and the non-custodial parent's pro rata share of the basic child support obligation. Unless the court finds that the non-custodial parents's pro-rata share of the basic child support obligation is unjust or inappropriate, which finding shall be based upon consideration of the following factors:
(1) The financial resources of the custodial and non-custodial parent, and those of the child;
(2) The physical and emotional health of the child and his/her special needs and aptitudes;
(3) The standard of living the child would have enjoyed had the marriage or household not been dissolved;
(4) The tax consequences to the parties;
(5) The non-monetary contributions that the parents will make toward the care and well-being of the child;
(6) The educational needs of either parent;

(7) A determination that the gross income of one parent is substantially less than the other parent's gross income;

(8) The needs of the children of the non-custodial parent for whom the non-custodial parent is providing support who are not subject to the instant action and whose support has not been deducted from income pursuant to subclause (D) of clause (vii) of subparagraph five of paragraph (b) of this subdivision, and the financial resources of any person obligated to support such children, provided, however, that this factor may apply only if the resources available to support such children are less than the resources available to support the children who are subject to the instant action;

(9) Provided that the child is not on public assistance (i) extraordinary expenses incurred by the non-custodial parent in exercising visitation, or (ii) expenses incurred by the non-custodial parent in extended visitation provided that the custodial parent's expenses are substantially reduced as a result thereof; and

(10) Any other factors the court determines are relevant in each case, the court shall order the non-custodial parent to pay his or her pro rata share of the basic child support obligation, and may order the non-custodial parent to pay an amount pursuant to paragraph (e) of this subdivision.

(g) Where the court finds that the non-custodial parent's pro rata share of the basic child support obligation is unjust or inappropriate, the court shall order the non-custodial parent to pay such amount of child support as the court finds just and appropriate, and the court shall set forth, in a written order, the factors it considered; the amount of each party's pro rata share of the basic child support obligation; and the reasons that the court did not order the basic child support obligation. Such written order may not be waived by either party or counsel; provided, however, and notwithstanding any other provision of law, the court shall not find that the non-custodial parent's pro rata share of such obligation is unjust or inappropriate on the basis that such share exceeds the portion of a public assistance grant which is attributable to a child or children. Where the non-custodial parent's income is less than or equal to the poverty income guidelines amount for a single person as reported by the federal department of health and human services, unpaid child support arrears in excess of five hundred dollars shall not accrue.

(h) A validly executed agreement or stipulation voluntarily entered into between the parties after the effective date of this subdivision presented to the court for incorporation in an order or judgment shall include a provision stating that the parties have been advised of the provisions of this subdivision, and that the basic child support obligation provided for therein would presumptively result in the correct amount of child support to be awarded. In the event that such agreement or stipulation deviates from the basic child support obligation, the agreement or stipulation must specify the amount that such basic child support obligation would have been and the reason or reasons that such agreement or stipulation does not provide for payment of that amount. Such provision may not be waived by either party or counsel. Nothing contained in this subdivision shall be construed to alter the rights of the parties to voluntarily enter into validly executed agreements or stipulations which deviate from the basic child support obligation provided such agreements or stipulations comply with the provisions of this paragraph. The court shall, however, retain discretion with respect to child support pursuant to this section. Any court order or judgment incorporating a validly executed agreement or stipulation which deviates from the basic child support obligation shall set forth the court's reasons for such deviation.

(i) Where either or both parties are unrepresented, the court shall not enter an order or judgment other than a temporary order pursuant to section two hundred thirty-seven of this article, that includes a provision for child support unless the unrepresented party or parties have received a copy of the child support standards chart promulgated by the commissioner of the office of temporary and disability assistance pursuant to subdivision two of section one hundred eleven-i of the social services law. Where either party is in receipt of child support enforcement services through the local social services district, the local social services district child support enforcement unit shall advise such party of the amount derived from application of the child support percentage and that such amount serves as a starting point for the determination of the child support award, and shall provide such party with a copy of the child support standards chart.

(j) In addition to financial disclosure required in section two hundred thirty-six of this article, the court may require that the income and/or expenses of either party be verified with documentation including, but not limited to, past and present income tax returns, employer statements, pay stubs, corporate, business, or partnership books and records, corporate and business tax returns, and receipts for expenses or such other means of verification as the court determines appropriate. Nothing herein shall affect any party's right to pursue discovery pursuant to this chapter, the civil practice law and rules, or the family court act.

(k) When a party has defaulted and/or the court is otherwise presented with insufficient evidence to determine gross income, the court shall order child support based upon the needs or standard of living of the child, whichever is greater. Such order may be retroactively modified upward, without a showing of change in circumstances.

(*l*) In any action or proceeding for modification of an order of child support existing prior to the effective date of this paragraph, brought pursuant to this article, the child support standards set forth in this subdivision shall not constitute a change of circumstances warranting modification of such support order; provided, however, that (1) where the circumstances warrant modification of such order, or (2) where any party objects to an adjusted child support order made or proposed at the direction of the support collection unit pursuant to section one hundred eleven-h or one hundred eleven-n of the social services law, and the court is reviewing the current order of child support, such standards shall be applied by the court in its determination with regard to the request for modification, or disposition of an objection to an adjusted child support order made or proposed by a support collection unit. In applying such standards, when the order to be modified incorporates by reference or merges with a validly executed separation agreement or stipulation of settlement, the court may consider, in addition to the factors set forth in paragraph (f) of this subdivision, the provisions of such agreement or stipulation concerning property distribution, distributive award and/or maintenance in determining whether the amount calculated by using the standards would be unjust or inappropriate.

1-c. (a) Notwithstanding any other provision of this chapter to the contrary, no court shall make an order providing for visitation or custody to a person who has been convicted of murder in the first or second degree in this state, or convicted of an offense in another jurisdiction which, if committed in this state, would constitute either murder in the first or second degree, of a parent, legal custodian, legal guardian, sibling , half-sibling or step-sibling of any child who is the subject of the proceeding. Pending determination of a petition for visitation or custody, such child shall not visit and no person shall visit with such child present, such person who has been convicted of murder in the first or second degree in this state, or convicted of and* offense in another jurisdiction which, if committed in this state, would constitute either murder in the first or second degree, of a parent, legal custodian, legal guardian, sibling, half-sibling or step-sibling of a child who is the subject of the proceeding without the consent of such child's custodian or legal guardian.

(b) Notwithstanding any other provision of this chapter to the contrary, there shall be a rebuttable presumption that it is not in the best interests of the child to be placed in the custody of or to visit with a person who has been convicted of one or more of the following sexual offenses in this state or convicted of one or more offenses in another jurisdiction which, if committed in this state, would constitute one or more of the following offenses, when a child who is the subject of the proceeding was conceived as a result: (A) rape in the first or second degree; (B) course of sexual conduct against a child in the first degree; (C) predatory sexual assault; or (D) predatory sexual assault against a child.

(c) Notwithstanding paragraph (a) or (b) of this subdivision a court may order visitation or custody where:

(i) (A) such child is of suitable age to signify assent and such child assents to such visitation or custody; or

(B) if such child is not of suitable age to signify assent, the child's custodian or legal guardian assents to such order; or

(C) the person who has been convicted of murder in the first or second degree, or an offense in another jurisdiction which if committed in this state, would constitute either murder in the first or second degree, can prove by a preponderance of the evidence that:

(1) he or she, or a family or household member of either party, was a victim of domestic violence by the victim of such murder; and

(2) the domestic violence was causally related to the commission of such murder; and

(ii) the court finds that such visitation or custody is in the best interests of the child.

(d) For the purpose of making a determination pursuant to clause (C) of subparagraph (i) of paragraph (b) of this subdivision, the court shall not be bound by the findings of fact, conclusions of law or ultimate conclusion as determined by the proceedings leading to the conviction of murder in the first or second degree in this state or of an offense in another jurisdiction which, if committed in this state, would constitute murder in either the first or second degree, of a parent, legal guardian, legal custodian, sibling, half-sibling or step-sibling of a child who is the subject of the proceeding. In all proceedings under this section, an attorney shall be appointed for the child.

2. (a)** An order directing payment of money for child support shall be enforceable pursuant to section fifty-two hundred forty-one or fifty-two hundred forty-two of the civil practice law and rules or in any other manner provided by law. Such orders or judgments for child support and maintenance shall also be enforceable pursuant to article fifty-two of the civil practice law and rules upon a debtor's default as such term is defined in paragraph seven of subdivision (a) of section fifty-two hundred forty-one of the civil practice law and rules. The establishment of a default shall be subject to the procedures established for the determination of a mistake of fact for income executions pursuant to subdivision (e) of section fifty-two hundred forty-one of the civil practice law and rules. For the purposes of enforcement of child support orders or combined spousal and child support orders pursuant to section five thousand

*(So in original. Probably should read "an.")
**(So in original. Probably should read "a.")

two hundred forty-one of the civil practice law and rules, a "default" shall be deemed to include amounts arising from retroactive support.

b. (1) When a child receiving support is a public assistance recipient, or the order of support is being enforced or is to be enforced pursuant to section one hundred eleven-g of the social services law, the court shall direct that the child support payments be made to the support collection unit. Unless (i) the court finds and sets forth in writing the reasons that there is good cause not to require immediate income withholding; or (ii) when the child is not in receipt of public assistance, a written agreement providing for an alternative arrangement has been reached between the parties, the support collection unit shall issue an income execution immediately for child support or combined maintenance and child support, and may issue an execution for medical support enforcement in accordance with the provisions of the order of support. Such written agreement may include an oral stipulation made on the record resulting in a written order. For purposes of this paragraph, good cause shall mean substantial harm to the debtor. The absence of an arrearage or the mere issuance of an income execution shall not constitute good cause. When an immediate income execution or an execution for medical support enforcement is issued by the support collection unit, such income execution shall be issued pursuant to section five thousand two hundred forty-one of the civil practice law and rules, except that the provisions thereof relating to mistake of fact, default and any other provisions which are not relevant to the issuance of an income execution pursuant to this paragraph shall not apply; provided, however, that if the support collection unit makes an error in the issuance of an income execution pursuant to this paragraph, and such error is to the detriment of the debtor, the support collection unit shall have thirty days after notification by the debtor to correct the error. Where permitted under federal law and where the record of the proceedings contains such information, such order shall include on its face the social security number and the name and address of the employer, if any, of the person chargeable with support; provided, however, that failure to comply with this requirement shall not invalidate such order. When the court determines that there is good cause not to immediately issue an income execution or when the parties agree to an alternative arrangement as provided in this paragraph, the court shall provide expressly in the order of support that the support collection unit shall not issue an immediate income execution. Notwithstanding any such order, the support collection unit shall issue an income execution for support enforcement when the debtor defaults on the support obligation, as defined in section five thousand two hundred forty-one of the civil practice law and rules.

(2) When the court issues an order of child support or combined child and spousal support on behalf of persons other than those in receipt of public assistance or in receipt of services pursuant to section one hundred eleven-g of the social services law, the court shall issue an income deduction order pursuant to subdivision (c) of section five thousand two hundred forty-two of the civil practice law and rules at the same time it issues the order of support. The court shall enter the income deduction order unless the court finds and sets forth in writing (i) the reasons that there is good cause not to require immediate income withholding; or (ii) that an agreement providing for an alternative arrangement has been reached between the parties. Such agreement may include a written agreement or an oral stipulation, made on the record, that results in a written order. For purposes of this paragraph, good cause shall mean substantial harm to the debtor. The absence of an arrearage or the mere issuance of an income deduction order shall not constitute good cause. Where

permitted under federal law and where the record of the proceedings contains such information, such order shall include on its face the social security number and the name and address of the employer, if any, of the person chargeable with support; provided, however, that failure to comply with this requirement shall not invalidate the order. When the court determines that there is good cause not to issue an income deduction order immediately or when the parties agree to an alternative arrangement as provided in this paragraph, the court shall provide expressly in the order of support the basis for its decision and shall not issue an income deduction order.

c. Any order of support issued on behalf of a child in receipt of family assistance or child support enforcement services pursuant to section one hundred eleven-g of the social services law shall be subject to review and adjustment by the support collection unit pursuant to section one hundred eleven-n of the social services law. Such review and adjustment shall be in addition to any other activities undertaken by the support collection unit relating to the establishment, modification, and enforcement of support orders payable to such unit.

3. Order of protection.

a. The court may make an order of protection in assistance or as a condition of any other order made under this section. The order of protection may set forth reasonable conditions of behavior to be observed for a specified time by any party. Such an order may require any party:

(1) to stay away from the home, school, business or place of employment of the child, other parent or any other party, and to stay away from any other specific location designated by the court;

(2) to permit a parent, or a person entitled to visitation by a court order or a separation agreement, to visit the child at stated periods;

(3) to refrain from committing a family offense, as defined in subdivision one of section 530.11 of the criminal procedure law, or any criminal offense against the child or against the other parent or against any person to whom custody of the child is awarded or from harassing, intimidating or threatening such persons;

(4) to permit a designated party to enter the residence during a specified period of time in order to remove personal belongings not in issue in a proceeding or action under this chapter or the family court act;

(5) to refrain from acts of commission or omission that create an unreasonable risk to the health, safety or welfare of a child;

(6) to pay the reasonable counsel fees and disbursements involved in obtaining or enforcing the order of the person who is protected by such order if such order is issued or enforced;

(7) to refrain from intentionally injuring or killing, without justification, any companion animal the respondent knows to be owned, possessed, leased, kept or held by the person protected by the order or a minor child residing in such person's household. "Companion animal," as used in this section, shall have the same meaning as in subdivision five of section three hundred fifty of the agriculture and markets law;

(8) (i) to promptly return specified identification documents to the protected party, in whose favor the order of protection or temporary order of protection is issued; provided, however, that such order may: (A) include any appropriate provision designed to ensure that any such document is available for use as evidence in this proceeding, and available if necessary for legitimate use by the party against whom such order is issued; and (B) specify the manner in which such return shall be accomplished.

(ii) For purposes of this subdivision, "identification document" shall mean any of the following: (A) exclusively in the name of the protected party: birth certificate, passport, social security card, health insurance or other benefits card, a card or document used to access bank, credit or other financial accounts or records, tax returns, any driver's license, and immigration documents including but not limited to a United States permanent resident card and employment authorization document; and (B) upon motion and after notice and an opportunity to be heard, any of the following, including those that may reflect joint use or ownership, that the court determines are necessary and are appropriately transferred to the protected party: any card or document used to access bank, credit or other financial accounts or records, tax returns, and any other identifying cards and documents; and

(9) to observe such other conditions as are necessary to further the purposes of protection.

b. An order of protection entered pursuant to this subdivision shall bear in a conspicuous manner, on the front page of said order, the language "Order of protection issued pursuant to section two hundred forty of the domestic relations law". The order of protection shall also contain the following notice: "This order of protection will remain in effect even if the protected party has, or consents to have, contact or communication with the party against whom the order is issued. This order of protection can only be modified or terminated by the court. The protected party cannot be held to violate this order nor be arrested for violating this order.". The absence of such language shall not affect the validity of such order. The presentation of a copy of such an order to any peace officer acting pursuant to his or her special duties, or police officer, shall constitute authority, for that officer to arrest a person when that person has violated the terms of such an order, and bring such person before the court and, otherwise, so far as lies within the officer's power, to aid in securing the protection such order was intended to afford.

c. An order of protection entered pursuant to this subdivision may be made in the final judgment in any matrimonial action or in a proceeding to obtain custody of or visitation with any child under this section, or by one or more orders from time to time before or subsequent to final judgment, or by both such order or orders and the final judgment. The order of protection may remain in effect after entry of a final matrimonial judgment and during the minority of any child whose custody or visitation is the subject of a provision of a final judgment or any order. An order of protection may be entered notwithstanding that the court for any reason whatsoever, other than lack of jurisdiction, refuses to grant the relief requested in the action or proceeding.

d. The chief administrator of the courts shall promulgate appropriate uniform temporary orders of protection and orders of protection forms, applicable to proceedings under this article, to be used throughout the state. Such forms shall be promulgated and developed in a manner to ensure the compatibility of such forms with the statewide computerized registry established pursuant to section two hundred twenty-one-a of the executive law.

e. No order of protection may direct any party to observe conditions of behavior unless: (i) the party requesting the order of protection has served and filed an action, proceeding, counter-claim or written motion and, (ii) the court has made a finding on the record that such party is entitled to issuance of the order of protection which may result from a judicial finding of fact, judicial acceptance of an admission by the party against whom the order was issued or judicial finding that the party against whom the order is issued has given knowing, intelligent and voluntary consent to its issuance. The provisions of this subdivision shall not preclude the court from issuing a temporary order of protection upon the court's own motion or where a motion for such relief is made to the court, for good cause shown. In any proceeding pursuant to this article, a court shall not deny an order of protection, or dismiss an application for such an order, solely on the basis that the acts or events alleged are not relatively contemporaneous with the date of the application or the conclusion of the action. The duration of any temporary order shall not by itself be a factor in determining the length or issuance of any final order.

f. In addition to the foregoing provisions, the court may issue an order, pursuant to section two hundred twenty-seven-c of the real property law, authorizing the party for whose benefit any order of protection has been issued to terminate a lease or rental agreement pursuant to section two hundred twenty-seven-c of the real property law.

g. Any party moving for a temporary order of protection pursuant to this subdivision during hours when the court is open shall be entitled to file such motion or pleading containing such prayer for emergency relief on the same day that such person first appears at such court, and a hearing on the motion or portion of the pleading requesting such emergency relief shall be held on the same day or the next day that the court is in session following the filing of such motion or pleading.

h. Upon issuance of an order of protection or temporary order of protection or upon a violation of such order, the court shall make a determination regarding the suspension and revocation of a license to carry, possess, repair or dispose of a firearm or firearms, ineligibility for such a license and the surrender of firearms in accordance with sections eight hundred forty-two-a and eight hundred forty-six-a of the family court act, as applicable. Upon issuance of an order of protection pursuant to this section or upon a finding of a violation thereof, the court also may direct payment of restitution in an amount not to exceed ten thousand dollars in accordance with subdivision (e) of section eight hundred forty-one of such act; provided, however, that in no case shall an order of restitution be issued where the court determines that the party against whom the order would be issued has already compensated the injured party or where such compensation is incorporated in a final judgment or settlement of the action.

i. The protected party in whose favor the order of protection or temporary order of protection is issued may not be held to violate such an order nor may such protected party be arrested for violating such order.

*3-a. Service of order of protection. a. If a temporary order of protection has been issued or an order of protection has been issued upon a default, unless the party requesting the order states on the record that she or he will arrange for other means for service or deliver the order to a peace or police officer directly for service, the court shall immediately deliver a copy of the temporary order of protection or order of protection to a peace officer, acting pursuant to his or her special duties and designated by the court, or to a police officer as defined in paragraph (b) or (d) of subdivision thirty-four of section 1.20 of the criminal procedure law, or, in the city of New York, to a designated representative of the police department of the city of New York. Any peace or police officer or designated person receiving a temporary order of protection or an order of protection as provided hereunder shall serve or provide for the service thereof together with any associated papers that may be served simultaneously, at any address designated therewith, including the summons and petition or complaint if not previously served. Service of such temporary order of protection or order of protection and associated papers shall, insofar as practicable, be achieved promptly. An officer or designated person obliged to perform service pursuant to this subdivision, and his or her employer, shall not be liable for damages resulting from failure to achieve service where, having made a reasonable effort, such officer or designated person is unable to locate and serve the temporary order of protection or order of protection at any address provided by the party requesting the order. A statement subscribed by the officer or designated person, and affirmed by him or her to be true under the penalties of perjury, stating the papers served, the date, time, address or in the event there is no address, place, and manner of service, the name and a brief physical description of the party served, shall be proof of service of the summons, petition and temporary order of protection or order of protection. When the temporary order of protection or order of protection and other papers, if any, have been served, such officer or designated person shall provide the court with an affirmation, certificate or affidavit of service and shall provide notification of the date and time of such service to the statewide computer registry established pursuant to section two hundred twenty-one-a of the executive law.

b. Notwithstanding any other provision of law, all orders of protection and temporary orders of protection filed and entered along with any associated papers that may be served simultaneously may be transmitted by facsimile transmission or electronic means for expedited service in accordance with the provisions of this subdivision. For purposes of this subdivision, "facsimile transmission" and "electronic means" shall be as defined in subdivision (f) of rule twenty-one hundred three of the civil practice law and rules.

Separately amended cannot be put together

*3-a. Service of order of protection. (a) If a temporary order of protection has been issued or an order of protection has been issued upon a default, unless the party requesting the order states on the record that she or he will arrange for other means for service or deliver the order to a peace or police officer directly for service, the court shall immediately deliver a copy of the temporary order of protection or order of protection together with any associated papers that may be served simultaneously including the summons and petition, to a peace officer, acting pursuant to his or her special duties and designated by the court, or to a police officer as defined in paragraph (b) or (d) of subdivision thirty-four of section 1.20 of the criminal procedure law, or, in the city of New York, to a designated representative of the police department of the city of New York. Any peace or police officer or designated person receiving a temporary order of protection or an order of protection as provided in this section shall serve or provide for the service thereof together with any associated papers that may be served simultaneously, at any address designated therewith, including the summons and petition or complaint if not previously served. Service of such temporary order of protection or order of protection and associated papers shall, insofar as practicable, be achieved promptly. An officer or designated person obliged to perform service pursuant to this subdivision, and his or her employer, shall not be liable for damages resulting from failure to achieve service where, having made a reasonable effort, such officer or designated person is unable to locate and serve the temporary order of protection or order of protection at any address provided by the party requesting the order. (b) When the temporary order of protection or order of protection and associated papers, if any, have been served, such officer or designated person shall provide the court with an affirmation, certificate or affidavit of service when the temporary order of protection or order of protection has been served, and shall provide notification of the date and time of such service to the statewide computer registry established pursuant to section two hundred twenty-one-a of the executive law. A statement subscribed by the officer or designated person, and affirmed by him or her to be true under the penalties of perjury, stating the papers served, the date, time, address or in the event there is no address, place, and manner of service, the name and a brief physical description of the party served, shall be proof of service of the summons, petition and temporary order of protection or order of protection.

(c) Where an officer or designated person obliged to perform service pursuant to this section is unable to complete service of the temporary order of protection or order of protection, such officer or designated person shall provide the court with proof of attempted service of the temporary order of protection or order of protection with information regarding the dates, times, locations and manner of attempted service. An affirmation, certificate or affidavit of service with a statement subscribed by the officer or designated person, and affirmed by him or her to be true under the penalties of perjury, stating the name of the party and the papers attempted to be served on said person, and for each attempted service, the date, time, address or in the event there is no address, place, and manner of attempted service, shall be proof of attempted service.

(d) Any peace or police officer or designated person performing service under this subdivision shall not charge a fee for such service, including, but not limited to, fees as provided under section eight thousand eleven of the civil practice law and rules.   *Separately amended cannot be put together

3-b. Emergency powers; local criminal court. If the court that issued an order of protection or temporary order of protection under this section or warrant in connection thereto is not in session when an arrest is made for an alleged violation of the order or upon a warrant issued in connection with such violation, the arrested person shall be brought before a local criminal court in the county of arrest or in the county in which such warrant is returnable pursuant to article one hundred twenty of the criminal procedure law and arraigned by such court. Such local criminal court shall order the commitment of the arrested person to the custody of the sheriff, admit to, fix or accept bail, or release the arrested person on his or her recognizance pending appearance in the court that issued the order of protection, temporary order of protection or warrant. In making such order, such local criminal court shall consider the bail recommendation, if any, made by the supreme or family court as indicated on the warrant or certificate of warrant. Unless the petitioner or complainant requests otherwise, the court, in addition to scheduling further criminal proceedings, if any, regarding such alleged family offense or violation allegation, shall make such matter returnable in the supreme or family court, as applicable, on the next day such court is in session.

3-c. Orders of protection; filing and enforcement of out-of-state orders. A valid order of protection or temporary order of protection issued by a court of competent jurisdiction in another state, territorial or tribal jurisdiction shall be accorded full faith and credit and enforced as if it were issued by a court within the state for as long as the order remains in effect in the issuing jurisdiction in accordance with sections two thousand two hundred sixty-five and two thousand two hundred sixty-six of title eighteen of the United States Code.

a. An order issued by a court of competent jurisdiction in another state, territorial or tribal jurisdiction shall be deemed valid if:

(1) the issuing court had personal jurisdiction over the parties and over the subject matter under the law of the issuing jurisdiction;

(2) the person against whom the order was issued had reasonable notice and an opportunity to be heard prior to issuance of the order; provided, however, that if the order was a temporary order of protection issued in the absence of such person, that notice had been given and that an opportunity to be heard had been provided within a reasonable period of time after the issuance of the order; and

(3) in the case of orders of protection or temporary orders of protection issued against both a petitioner and respondent, the order or portion thereof sought to be enforced was supported by: (i) a pleading requesting such order, including, but not limited to, a petition, cross-petition or counterclaim; and (ii) a judicial finding that the requesting party is entitled to the issuance of the order, which may result from a judicial finding of fact, judicial acceptance of an admission by the party against whom the order was issued or judicial finding that the party against whom the order was issued had give* knowing, intelligent and voluntary consent to its issuance.

b. Notwithstanding the provisions of article fifty-four of the civil practice law and rules, an order of protection or temporary order of protection issued by a court of competent jurisdiction in another state, territorial or tribal jurisdiction, accompanied by a sworn affidavit that upon information and belief such order is in effect as written and has not been vacated or modified, may be filed without fee with the clerk of the court, who shall transmit information regarding such order to the statewide registry of orders of protection and warrants established pursuant to section two hundred twenty-one-a of the executive law; provided, however, that such filing and registry entry shall not be required for enforcement of the order.

4. One-time adjustment of child support orders issued prior to September fifteenth, nineteen hundred eighty-nine. Any party to a child support order issued prior to September fifteenth, nineteen hundred eighty-nine on the behalf of a child in receipt of public assistance or child support services pursuant to section one hundred eleven-g of the social services law may request that the support collection unit undertake one review of the order for adjustment purposes pursuant to section one hundred eleven-h of the social services law. A hearing on the adjustment of such order shall be granted upon the objection of either party pursuant to the provisions of this section. An order shall be adjusted if as of the date of the support collection unit's review of the correct amount of child support as calculated pursuant to the provisions of this section would deviate by at least ten percent from the child support ordered in the current order of support. Additionally, a new order shall be issued upon a showing that the current order of support does not provide for the health care needs of the child through insurance or otherwise. Eligibility of the child for medical assistance shall not relieve any obligation the parties otherwise have to provide for the health care needs of the child. The support collection unit's review of a child support order shall be made on notice to all parties to the current support order. Nothing herein shall be deemed in any way to limit, restrict, expand or impair the rights of any party to file for a modification of a child support order as is otherwise provided by law.

(1) Upon mailing of an adjustment finding and where appropriate a proposed order in conformity with such finding filed by either party or by the support collection unit, a party shall have thirty-five days from the date of mailing to submit to the court identified thereon specific written objections to such finding and proposed order.

(So in original. Probably should be "given.")

(a) If specific written objections are submitted by either party or by the support collection unit, a hearing shall be scheduled by the court on notice to the parties and the support collection unit, who then shall have the right to be heard by the court and to offer evidence in support of or in opposition to adjustment of the support order.

(b) The party filing the specific written objections shall bear the burden of going forward and the burden of proof; provided, however, that if the support collection unit has failed to provide the documentation and information required by subdivision fourteen of section one hundred eleven-h of the social services law, the court shall first require the support collection unit to furnish such documents and information to the parties and the court.

(c) If the court finds by a preponderance of the evidence that the specific written objections have been proven, the court shall recalculate or readjust the proposed adjusted order accordingly or, for good cause, shall remand the order to the support collection unit for submission of a new proposed adjusted order. Any readjusted order so issued by the court or resubmitted by the support collection unit after a remand by the court shall be effective as of the date the proposed adjusted order would have been effective had no specific written objections been filed.

(d) If the court finds that the specific written objections have not been proven by a preponderance of the evidence, the court shall immediately issue the adjusted order as submitted by the support collection unit, which shall be effective as of the date the order would have been effective had no specific written exceptions been filed.

(e) If the court receives no specific written objections to the support order within thirty-five days of the mailing of the proposed order the clerk of the court shall immediately enter the order without further review, modification, or other prior action by the court or any judge or support magistrate thereof, and the clerk shall immediately transmit copies of the order of support to the parties and to the support collection unit.

(2) A motion to vacate an order of support adjusted pursuant to this section may be made no later than forty-five days after an adjusted support order is executed by the court where no specific written objections to the proposed order have been timely received by the court. Such motion shall be granted only upon a determination by the court issuing such order that personal jurisdiction was not timely obtained over the moving party.

*5. Provision of child support orders to the state case registry. The court shall direct that a copy of any child support or combined child and spousal support order issued by the court on or after the first day of October, nineteen hundred ninety-eight, in any proceeding under this section be provided promptly to the state case registry established pursuant to subdivision four-a of section one hundred eleven-b of the social services law.

5. On-going cost of living adjustment of child support orders issued prior to September fifteenth, nineteen hundred eighty-nine. Any party to a child support order issued prior to September fifteenth, nineteen hundred eighty-nine on the behalf of a child in receipt of public assistance or child support services pursuant to section one hundred eleven-g of the social services law may request that the support collection unit review the order for a cost of living adjustment in accordance with the provisions of section two hundred forty-c of this article.

---

*There are 2 subdivisions "5."

ARTICLE 19-G
Office of Children and Family Services

Title 1

§500. Office of children and family services; commissioner.

1. There is hereby continued in the department of family assistance an autonomous office of children and family services. The head of such office shall be the commissioner of children and family services, who shall be appointed by the governor, by and with the advice and consent of the senate, and shall serve at the pleasure of the governor. The commissioner may appoint such officers, employees, agents and consultants as he or she may deem necessary, prescribe their duties, fix their compensation and provide for reimbursement of their expenses within the amounts available therefor by appropriation.

2. The commissioner may promulgate, adopt, amend or rescind rules and regulations necessary to carry out the provisions of this article, provided, however, that such rules and regulations shall be strictly limited in their application to the means and methods of compliance with the provisions of this article.

3. Whenever the division for youth or its director is referred to in any provision of this chapter or in any other law, such reference shall be deemed to refer to the office of children and family services or the commissioner of children and family services.

§501. General functions, powers and duties of division.

The division for youth shall have the following functions, powers and duties:

1. To develop policies and plans for improving the administration of division facilities and the delivery of services therein.

2. To establish, operate and maintain treatment programs and other services for youth placed with or committed to the division and programs for the care of conditionally released children.

3. To establish, operate and maintain division facilities and to contract with authorized agencies as defined in section three hundred seventy-one of the social services law for the operation and maintenance of non-secure facilities.

4. To establish, operate and maintain all division facilities and programs and all necessary powers to see that the purposes of each facility or program are carried into effect.

5. To promulgate rules and regulations for the establishment, operation and maintenance of division facilities and programs.

6. To enter into contracts with any person, firm, corporation, not-for-profit corporation, authorized agency as defined by section three hundred seventy-one of the social services law, municipality or governmental agency.

7. To establish, operate and maintain programs and services alternative to division facilities for persons placed with the division pursuant to section five hundred seven-a of this article. The division may contract with political subdivisions of the state, agencies thereof or supported thereby, not-for-profit associations, institutions or agencies concerned with youth, for the operation and maintenance of such programs and services.

8. (a) Subject to the amounts appropriated therefor, to establish, operate and maintain or to contract for the operation and maintenance of programs which may include, but not be limited to work training programs and alternative to placement programs authorized by law, in order to prevent and control juvenile delinquency, and to advance the moral, physical, mental and social well-being of the youth of this state;

(b) To establish and operate or to participate with the federal government in the establishment and operation of job corps camps pursuant to the federal economic opportunity program and any federal laws amendatory or supplemental thereto, and to accept and receive such youths as may be referred by federal agencies pursuant to such law.

9. To cooperate with other departments, divisions and agencies of the state, its political subdivisions and municipalities and cooperate with public and private agencies and departments throughout the state in order to assist in the rehabilitation and training of youth placed with or committed to the division.

10. To encourage and foster an exchange of information and to cooperate with social agencies, both public and private, which may be administering to the needs or assisting any members of the families of youth placed with or committed to the division.

11. To develop a comprehensive five year plan for the provision of services for youths ordered by the court into the custody of the division. Such plan shall include, but not be limited to:

(a) a projection of the numbers of youths to be placed into or committed to the care of the division at secure, limited secure and non-secure levels of care for the five years encompassed by the plan;

(b) an analysis of current and anticipated utilization of division facilities;

(c) a plan for increasing or decreasing residential capacities at all levels as indicated by paragraph (b) of this subdivision;

(d) a comprehensive description of the types of services and programs to be provided to youths in the custody of the division; and

(e) a plan for containing costs at all levels of residential care.

12. To promulgate regulations concerning standards for the protection of children in residential facilities and programs operated or certified by the division, from abuse and maltreatment. Such standards shall include the prevention and remediation of abuse and maltreatment of children in such residential facilities or programs, including procedures for:

(a) consistent with appropriate collective bargaining agreements and applicable provisions of the civil service law, the review and evaluation of the backgrounds of and the information supplied by any person applying to be an employee, a volunteer or consultant which shall include but not be limited to the following requirements: that the applicant set forth his or her employment history, provide personal and employment references and relevant experiential and educational information and sign a sworn statement indicating whether the applicant, to the best of his or her knowledge, has ever been convicted of a crime in this state or any other jurisdiction;

(b) establishing for employees, relevant minimal experiential and educational qualifications, consistent with appropriate collective bargaining agreements and applicable provisions of the civil service law;

(c) assuring adequate and appropriate supervision of employees, volunteers and consultants;

(d) demonstrating by a residential facility or program that appropriate action is taken to assure the safety of the child who is reported to the state central register as well as other children in care, immediately upon notification that a report of child abuse or maltreatment has been made with respect to a child in a residential facility or program;

(e) removing of a child, consistent as applicable with any court order placing the child, when it is determined that there is risk to such child if he or she continues to remain within a residential facility or program; and

(f) appropriate preventive and remedial action to be taken, including legal actions, consistent with appropriate collective bargaining agreements and applicable provisions of the civil service law. Such standards shall also establish as a priority that:

(i) subject to the amounts appropriated therefor, administrators, employees, volunteers and consultants receive training in at least the following: child abuse prevention and identification, safety and security procedures, the principles of child development, the characteristics of children in care and techniques of group and child management including crisis intervention, the laws, regulations and procedures governing the protection of children from abuse and maltreatment, and other appropriate topics; provided however, that the division may exempt administrators and consultants from such requirements upon demonstration of substantially equivalent knowledge or experience;

(ii) subject to the amounts appropriated therefor, children receive instruction, consistent with their age, needs and circumstances as well as the needs and circumstances within the residential facility or program, in techniques and procedures which will enable such children to protect themselves from abuse and maltreatment. The division shall take all reasonable and necessary actions to assure that employees, volunteers and consultants in residential facilities and programs are kept apprised on a current basis of all division policies and procedures relating to the protection of children from abuse and maltreatment, and shall monitor and supervise the provision of training to such administrators, employees, volunteers, children and consultants. Such standards shall, to the extent possible, be consistent with those promulgated by other state agencies for such purposes.

13. To cooperate with the state department of social services and other departments, divisions and agencies of the state when a report is received pursuant to title six of article six of the social services law to protect the health and safety of children in residential facilities or programs. Such cooperation shall include: the making of reports of alleged child abuse and maltreatment, providing necessary assistance to the state department of social services in the department's investigation thereof and considering the recommendations of the state department of social services for appropriate preventive and remedial action, including legal actions, and provide or direct the residential facility to provide such written reports thereon to the department of social services as to

the implementation of plans of prevention and remediation approved by the division pursuant to title six of article six of the social services law.

14. To provide for the development and implementation of a plan of prevention and remediation with respect to an indicated report of child abuse or maltreatment. Such action shall include:

(a) within ten days of receipt of an indicated report of child abuse or maltreatment, development and implementation of a plan of prevention and remediation to be taken with respect to a custodian or the residential facility in order to assure the continued health and safety of children and to provide for the prevention of future acts of abuse or maltreatment; and

(b) development and implementation of a plan of prevention and remediation, in the event an investigation of a report of alleged child abuse or maltreatment determines that some credible evidence of abuse or maltreatment exists and such abuse or maltreatment may be attributed in whole or in part to noncompliance by the residential facility or program with provisions of this chapter or regulations of the division applicable to the operation of such residential facility or program. Any plan of prevention and remediation required to be developed pursuant to paragraph (b) of this subdivision by a facility supervised by the division shall be submitted to and approved by the division in accordance with time limits established by regulations of the division. Implementation of the plan shall be monitored by the division. In reviewing the continued qualifications of a residential facility or program for an operating certificate, the division shall evaluate such facility's compliance with plans of prevention and remediation developed and implemented pursuant to this subdivision.

15. In the event that the office of children and family services determines that significant service reductions, public employee staffing reductions and/or the transfer of operations to a private or not-for-profit entity are anticipated in the office of children and family services long term planning process or for a particular facility in a future year, to take the following actions:

(a) confer with the department of civil service, the governor's office of employee relations and any other state agency to develop strategies which attempt to minimize the impact on the state workforce by providing assistance in obtaining state employment in state-operated community-based services or other employment opportunities, and to develop strategies for the development of necessary retraining and redeployment programs. In planning such strategies, the commissioner of the office of children and family services shall provide for the participation of the representatives of the employee labor organizations and for the participation of managerial and confidential employees to ensure continuity of employment;

(b) consult with the department of economic development and any other appropriate state agencies to develop strategies which attempt to minimize the impact of such significant service reductions, public employee staffing reductions and/or the transfer of operations to a private or not-for-profit entity on the local and regional economies;

(c) provide for a mechanism which may reasonably be expected to provide notice to local governments, community organizations, employee labor organizations, managerial and confidential employees, consumer and advocacy groups of the potential for significant service reductions, public employee staffing reductions and/or the transfer of operations to a private or not-for-profit entity at such state-operated facilities, at least twelve months prior to commencing such service reduction; and

(d) consult with the office of general services and any other appropriate state agency in developing a mechanism for determining alternative uses for land and buildings to be vacated by the office of children and family services. Such a mechanism should include a review of other programs or state agencies that could feasibly expand their operations onto a state-operated campus and are compatible with health, safety and programmatic needs of persons served in such facilities.

16. To perform such acts as are necessary or convenient to carry out the division's functions, powers and duties in furtherance of the best interests of youth, consistent with the provisions of this article.

§501-a. Actions against persons designated foster parents of the division; defense and indemnification.

The provisions of section seventeen of the public officers law shall apply to persons designated foster parents whose duties involve the care, treatment or supervision of persons admitted to institutions operated by the division, whether within such institutions or released therefrom pursuant to section five hundred twenty-three of this article or whose duties involve services to or for applicants while rendering such care, treatment or services.

§501-b. Intervention as of right; notice.

The division for youth, pursuant to paragraph one of subdivision (a) of section ten hundred twelve of the civil practice law and rules, shall be permitted to intervene in any action involving an appeal from a decision of any Court of this State which relates to programs, conditions or services provided by the division for youth. Written notice shall be given to the attorney general and the director of the division for youth by the party taking the appeal.

§501-c. Confidentiality.

1.(a) Records or files of youths kept by the division for youth shall be deemed confidential and shall be safeguarded from coming to the knowledge of and from inspection or examination by any person other than one authorized to receive such knowledge or to make such inspection or examination: (i) by the division pursuant to its regulations; (ii) or by a judge of the court of claims when such records are required for the trial of a claim or other proceeding in such court; or (iii) by a federal court judge or magistrate, a justice of the supreme court, a judge of the county court or family court, or a grand jury when such records are required for a trial or proceeding in such court or grand jury. No person shall divulge the information thus obtained without authorization to do so by the division, or by such justice, judge or grand jury.

(b) The division shall not release information which would reasonably identify such youth as ever being in the custody of the division, except as provided in paragraph (a) of this subdivision.

(c) Nothing in this subdivision shall limit a person's or agency's responsibility or authority to report suspected child abuse or maltreatment pursuant to title six of article six of the social services law.

(d) Nothing in this subdivision shall be deemed to prevent access by a parent or legal guardian of a youth to records or files of such youth where access is otherwise specifically authorized by law.

2. Notwithstanding any other provision of this section, the official case records produced and maintained by the division shall be made available to a probation department, upon written request, where an order of the court has

been issued directing such department to conduct an investigation pursuant to the provisions of sections 390.20 and 720.20 of the criminal procedure law and section 351.1 of the family court act. Any written requests for records shall be accompanied by a copy of the court order and shall request only a copy of the youth's official case record. The division shall be granted a minimum of ten days to produce such records. The division shall be required to forward only records less than three years old in its possession, or copies thereof, relating to a youth less than twenty-one years of age at the time of the request. The division may impose a fee upon a probation department for its costs in photocopying records provided under this subdivision. A probation department shall retain copies of records received or information obtained therein under the same conditions of confidentiality that apply to the investigation and any report on the investigation which was the basis for obtaining such records.

§501-d.   Grants or gifts.
The director of the division for youth, with the approval of the governor, may accept as agent of the state any grant, including federal grants, or any gift for any of the purposes of this article. Any moneys so received may be expended by the division for youth to effectuate any purpose of this article, subject to the same limitations as to approval of expenditures and audit as are prescribed for state moneys appropriated for the purposes of this article.

*§501-e.   Interstate compact for juveniles.
The interstate compact for juveniles is hereby enacted into law and entered into with all other jurisdictions legally joining therein in a form substantially as follows:

THE INTERSTATE COMPACT FOR JUVENILES

ARTICLE I
PURPOSE

The compacting states to this interstate compact recognize that each state is responsible for the proper supervision or return of juveniles, delinquents and status offenders who are on probation or parole and who have absconded, escaped or run away from supervision and control and in so doing have endangered their own safety and the safety of others. The compacting states also recognize that each state is responsible for the safe return of juveniles who have run away from home and in doing so have left their state of residence. The compacting states also recognize that congress, by enacting the Crime Control Act, 4 U.S.C. Section 112 (1965), has authorized and encouraged compacts for cooperative efforts and mutual assistance in the prevention of crime. It is the purpose of this compact, through means of joint and cooperative action among the compacting states to:

A. ensure that the adjudicated juveniles and status offenders subject to this compact are provided adequate supervision and services in the receiving state as ordered by the adjudicating judge or parole authority in the sending state;

B. ensure that the public safety interests of the citizens, including the victims of juvenile offenders, in both the sending and receiving states are adequately protected;

C. return juveniles who have run away, absconded or escaped from supervision or control or have been accused of an offense to the state requesting their return;

D. make contracts for the cooperative institutionalization in public facilities in member states for delinquent youth needing special services;

E. provide for the effective tracking and supervision of juveniles;

F. equitably allocate the costs, benefits and obligations of the compacting states;

G. establish procedures to manage the movement between states of juvenile offenders released to the community under the jurisdiction of courts, juvenile departments, or any other criminal or juvenile justice agency which has jurisdiction over juvenile offenders;

H. insure immediate notice to jurisdictions where defined offenders are authorized to travel or to relocate across state lines;

I. establish procedures to resolve pending charges (detainers) against juvenile offenders prior to transfer or release to the community under the terms of this compact;

J. establish a system of uniform data collection on information pertaining to juveniles subject to this compact that allows access by authorized juvenile justice and criminal justice officials, and regular reporting of compact activities to heads of state executive, judicial, and legislative branches and juvenile and criminal justice administrators;

K. monitor compliance with rules governing interstate movement of juveniles and initiate interventions to address and correct noncompliance;

L. coordinate training and education regarding the regulation of interstate movement of juveniles for officials involved in such activity; and

M. coordinate the implementation and operation of the compact with the interstate compact for the placement of children, the interstate compact for adult offender supervision and other compacts affecting juveniles particularly in those cases where concurrent or overlapping supervision issues arise.

It is the policy of the compacting states that the activities conducted by the interstate commission created herein are the formation of public policies and therefore are public business. Furthermore, the compacting states shall cooperate and observe their individual and collective duties and responsibilities for the prompt return and acceptance of juveniles subject to the provisions of this compact. The provisions of this compact shall be reasonably and liberally construed to accomplish the purposes and policies of the compact.

ARTICLE II
DEFINITIONS

As used in this compact, unless the context clearly requires a different construction:

A. "Bylaws" means those bylaws established by the interstate commission for its governance, or for directing or controlling its actions or conduct;

B. "Compact administrator" means the individual in each compacting state appointed pursuant to the terms of this compact, responsible for the administration and management of the state's supervision and transfer of juveniles subject to the terms of this compact, the rules adopted by the interstate commission and policies adopted by the state council under this compact;

C. "Compacting state" means any state which has enacted the enabling legislation for this compact;

D. "Commissioner" means the voting representative of each compacting state appointed pursuant to article III of this compact;

E. "Court" means any court having jurisdiction over delinquent, neglected, or dependent children;

F. "Deputy compact administrator" means the individual, if any, in each compacting state appointed to act on behalf of a compact administrator pursuant to the terms of this compact responsible for the administration and management of the state's supervision and transfer of juveniles subject to the terms of this compact, the rules adopted by the interstate commission and policies adopted by the state council under this compact;

G. "Interstate commission" means the interstate commission for juveniles created by article III of this compact;

H. "Juvenile" means any person defined as a juvenile in any member state or by the rules of the interstate commission, including any:

1. "accused delinquent" which means a person charged with an offense that, if committed by an adult, would be a criminal offense;

2. "adjudicated delinquent" which means a person found to have committed an offense that, if committed by an adult, would be a criminal offense;

3. "accused status offender" which means a person charged with an offense that would not be a criminal offense if committed by an adult;

4. "adjudicated status offender" which means a person found to have committed an offense that would not be a criminal offense if committed by an adult; and

5. "non-offender" which means a person in need of supervision who has not been accused or adjudicated a status offender or delinquent;

I. "Non-compacting state" means any state which has not enacted the enabling legislation for this compact;

J. "Probation" or "parole" means any kind of supervision or conditional release of juveniles authorized under the laws of the compacting states;

K. "Rule" means a written statement by the interstate commission promulgated pursuant to article VI of this compact that is of general applicability, implements, interprets or prescribes a policy or provision of the compact, or an organizational, procedural, or practical requirement of the commission, and has the force and effect of statutory law in a compacting state, and includes the amendment, repeal, or suspension of an existing rule; and

L. "State" means a state of the United States, the District of Columbia (or its designee), the Commonwealth of Puerto Rico, the U.S. Virgin Islands, Guam, American Samoa, and the Northern Marianas Islands.

ARTICLE III
INTERSTATE COMMISSION FOR JUVENILES

A. The compacting states hereby create the "interstate commission for juveniles." The commission shall be a body corporate and joint agency of the compacting states. The commission shall have all the responsibilities, powers and duties set forth herein, and such additional powers as may be conferred upon it by subsequent action of the respective legislatures of the compacting states in accordance with the terms of this compact.

B. The interstate commission shall consist of commissioners appointed by the appropriate appointing authority in each state pursuant to the rules and requirements of each compacting state and in consultation with the state council for interstate juvenile supervision created hereunder. The commissioner shall be the compact administrator, deputy compact administrator or designee from that state who shall serve on the interstate commission in such capacity under or pursuant to the applicable law of the compacting state.

C. In addition to the commissioners who are the voting representatives of each state, the interstate commission shall include individuals who are not commissioners, but who are members of interested organizations. Such non-commissioner members must include a member of the national organizations of governors, legislators, state chief justices, attorneys general, interstate compact for adult offender supervision, interstate compact for the placement of children, juvenile justice and juvenile corrections officials, and crime victims. All non-commissioner members of the interstate commission shall be ex-officio (non-voting) members. The interstate commission may provide in its bylaws for such additional ex-officio (non-voting) members, including members of other national organizations, in such numbers as shall be determined by the commission.

D. Each compacting state represented at any meeting of the commission is entitled to one vote. A majority of the compacting states shall constitute a quorum for the transaction of business, unless a larger quorum is required by the bylaws of the interstate commission.

E. The commission shall meet at least once each calendar year. The chairperson may call additional meetings and, upon the request of a simple majority of the compacting states, shall call additional meetings. Public notice shall be given of all meetings and meetings shall be open to the public.

F. The interstate commission shall establish an executive committee, which shall include commission officers, members, and others as determined by the bylaws. The executive committee shall have the power to act on behalf of the interstate commission during periods when the interstate commission is not in session, with the exception of rulemaking and/or amendment to the compact. The executive committee shall oversee the day-to-day activities of the administration of the compact managed by an executive director and interstate commission staff; administer enforcement and compliance with the provisions of the compact, its bylaws and rules, and perform such other duties as directed by the interstate commission or set forth in the bylaws.

G. Each member of the interstate commission shall have the right and power to cast a vote to which that compacting state is entitled and to participate in the business and affairs of the interstate commission. A member shall vote in person and shall not delegate a vote to another compacting state. However, a commissioner, in consultation with the state council, shall appoint another authorized representative, in the absence of the commissioner from that state, to cast a vote on behalf of the compacting state at a specified meeting. The bylaws may provide for members' participation in meetings by telephone or other means of telecommunication or electronic communication.

H. The interstate commission's bylaws shall establish conditions and procedures under which the interstate commission shall make its information and official records available to the public for inspection or copying. The interstate commission may exempt from disclosure any information or official records to the extent they would adversely affect personal privacy rights or proprietary interests.

I. Public notice shall be given of all meetings and all meetings shall be open to the public, except as set forth in the rules or as otherwise provided in the compact. The interstate commission and any of its committees may close a meeting to the public where it determines by two-thirds vote that an open meeting would be likely to:

1. relate solely to the interstate commission's internal personnel practices and procedures;

2. disclose matters specifically exempted from disclosure by statute;

3. disclose trade secrets or commercial or financial information which is privileged or confidential;

4. involve accusing any person of a crime, or formally censuring any person;

5. disclose information of a personal nature where disclosure would constitute a clearly unwarranted invasion of personal privacy;

6. disclose investigative records compiled for law enforcement purposes;

7. disclose information contained in or related to examination, operating or condition reports prepared by, or on behalf of or for the use of, the interstate commission with respect to a regulated person or entity for the purpose of regulation or supervision of such person or entity;

8. disclose information, the premature disclosure of which would significantly endanger the stability of a regulated person or entity; or

9. specifically relate to the interstate commission's issuance of a subpoena, or its participation in a civil action or other legal proceeding.

J. For every meeting closed pursuant to this provision, the interstate commission's legal counsel shall publicly certify that, in the legal counsel's opinion, the meeting may be closed to the public, and shall reference each relevant exemptive provision. The interstate commission shall keep minutes which shall fully and clearly describe all matters discussed in any meeting and shall provide a full and accurate summary of any actions taken, and the reasons therefor, including a description of each of the views expressed on any item and the record of any roll call vote (reflected in the vote of each member on the question). All documents considered in connection with any action shall be identified in such minutes.

K. The interstate commission shall collect standardized data concerning the interstate movement of juveniles as directed through its rules which shall specify the data to be collected, the means of collection and data exchange and reporting requirements. Such methods of data collection, exchange and reporting shall insofar as is reasonably possible conform to up-to-date technology and coordinate its information functions with the appropriate repository of records.

ARTICLE IV
POWERS AND DUTIES OF THE INTERSTATE COMMISSION

The commission shall have the following powers and duties:

A. To provide for dispute resolution among compacting states;

B. To promulgate rules to effect the purposes and obligations as enumerated in this compact, which shall have the force and effect of statutory law and shall be binding in the compacting states to the extent and in the manner provided in this compact;

C. To oversee, supervise and coordinate the interstate movement of juveniles subject to the terms of this compact and any bylaws adopted and rules promulgated by the interstate commission;

D. To enforce compliance with the compact provisions, the rules promulgated by the interstate commission, and the bylaws, using all necessary and proper means, including but not limited to the use of judicial process;

E. To establish and maintain offices which shall be located within one or more of the compacting states;

F. To purchase and maintain insurance and bonds;

G. To borrow, accept, hire or contract for services of personnel;

H. To establish and appoint committees and hire staff which it deems necessary for the carrying out of its functions including, but not limited to, an executive committee as required by article III of this compact which shall have the power to act on behalf of the interstate commission in carrying out its powers and duties hereunder;

I. To elect or appoint such officers, attorneys, employees, agents, or consultants, and to fix their compensation, define their duties and determine their qualifications; and to establish the interstate commission's personnel policies and programs relating to, inter alia, conflicts of interest, rates of compensation, and qualifications of personnel;

J. To accept any and all donations and grants of money, equipment, supplies, materials, and services, and to receive, utilize, and dispose of it;

K. To lease, purchase, accept contributions or donations of, or otherwise to own, hold, improve or use any property, real, personal, or mixed;

L. To sell, convey, mortgage, pledge, lease, exchange, abandon, or otherwise dispose of any property, real, personal, or mixed;

M. To establish a budget and make expenditures and levy dues as provided in article VIII of this compact;

N. To sue and be sued;

O. To adopt a seal and bylaws governing the management and operation of the interstate commission;

P. To perform such functions as may be necessary or appropriate to achieve the purposes of this compact;

Q. To report annually to the legislatures, governors, judiciary, and state councils of the compacting states concerning the activities of the interstate commission during the preceding year. Such reports shall also include any recommendations that may have been adopted by the interstate commission;

R. To coordinate education, training and public awareness regarding the interstate movement of juveniles for officials involved in such activity;

S. To establish uniform standards of the reporting, collecting and exchanging of data; and

T. The interstate commission shall maintain its corporate books and records in accordance with the bylaws.

ARTICLE V
ORGANIZATION AND OPERATION
OF THE INTERSTATE COMMISSION

A. Bylaws.

The interstate commission shall, by a majority of the members present and voting, within twelve months after the first interstate commission meeting, adopt bylaws to govern its conduct as may be necessary or appropriate to carry out the purposes of the compact, including, but not limited to:

a. establishing the fiscal year of the interstate commission;

b. establishing an executive committee and such other committees as may be necessary;

c. providing for the establishment of committees governing any general or specific delegation of any authority or function of the interstate commission;

d. providing reasonable procedures for calling and conducting meetings of the interstate commission, and ensuring reasonable notice of each such meeting;

e. establishing the titles and responsibilities of the officers of the interstate commission;

f. providing a mechanism for concluding the operations of the interstate commission and the return of any surplus funds that may exist upon the termination of the compact after the payment and/or reserving of all of its debts and obligations;

g. providing "start-up" rules for initial administration of the compact; and

h. establishing standards and procedures for compliance and technical assistance in carrying out the compact.

B. Officers and staff.

1. The interstate commission shall, by a majority of the members, elect annually from among its members a chairperson and a vice-chairperson, each of whom shall have such authority and duties as may be specified in the bylaws. The chairperson or, in the chairperson's absence or disability, the vice-chairperson shall preside at all meetings of the interstate commission. The officers so elected shall serve without compensation or remuneration from the interstate commission; provided that, subject to the availability of budgeted funds, the officers shall be reimbursed for any ordinary and necessary costs and expenses incurred by them in the performance of their duties and responsibilities as officers of the interstate commission.

2. The interstate commission shall, through its executive committee, appoint or retain an executive director for such period, upon such terms and conditions and for such compensation as the interstate commission may deem appropriate. The executive director shall serve as secretary to the interstate commission, but shall not be a member and shall hire and supervise such other staff as may be authorized by the interstate commission.

C. Qualified immunity, defense and indemnification.

1. The interstate commission's executive director and employees shall be immune from suit and liability, either personally or in their official capacity, for any claim for damage to or loss of property or personal injury or other civil liability caused or arising out of or relating to any actual or alleged act, error, or omission that occurred, or that such person had a reasonable basis for believing occurred within the scope of interstate commission employment, duties, or responsibilities; provided, that any such person shall not be protected from suit or liability for any damage, loss, injury, or liability caused by the intentional or willful and wanton misconduct of any such person.

2. The liability of any commissioner, or the employee or agent of a commissioner, acting within the scope of such person's employment or duties for acts, errors, or omissions occurring within such person's state may not exceed the limits of liability set forth under the constitution and laws of that state for state officials, employees, and agents. Nothing in this subdivision shall be construed to protect any such person from suit or liability for any damage, loss, injury, or liability caused by the intentional or willful and wanton misconduct of any such person.

3. The interstate commission shall defend the executive director or the employees or representatives of the interstate commission and, subject to the approval of the attorney general of the state represented by any commissioner of a compacting state, shall defend such commissioner or the commissioner's representatives or employees in any civil action seeking to impose liability arising out of any actual or alleged act, error, or omission that occurred within the scope of interstate commission employment, duties, or responsibilities, or that the defendant had a reasonable basis for believing occurred within the scope of interstate commission employment, duties, or responsibilities, provided that the actual or alleged act, error, or omission did not result from intentional or willful and wanton misconduct on the part of such person.

4. The interstate commission shall indemnify and hold the commissioner of a compacting state, or the commissioner's representatives or employees, or the interstate commission's representatives or employees, harmless in the amount of any settlement or judgment obtained against such persons arising out of any actual or alleged act, error, or omission that occurred within the scope of interstate commission employment, duties, or responsibilities, or that such persons had a reasonable basis for believing occurred within the scope of interstate commission employment, duties, or responsibilities, provided that the actual or alleged act, error, or omission did not result from intentional or willful and wanton misconduct on the part of such persons.

ARTICLE VI
RULEMAKING FUNCTIONS OF
THE INTERSTATE COMMISSION

A. The interstate commission shall promulgate and publish rules in order to effectively and efficiently achieve the purposes of the compact.

B. Rulemaking shall occur pursuant to the criteria set forth in this article and the bylaws and rules adopted pursuant thereto. Such rulemaking shall substantially conform to the principles of the "Model State Administrative Procedures Act," 1981 act, uniform laws annotated, vol. 15, p.1 (2000), or such other administrative procedures acts, as the interstate commission deems appropriate, consistent with due process requirements under the United States Constitution as now or hereafter interpreted by the United States supreme court. All rules and amendments shall become binding as of the date specified, as published with the final version of the rules as approved by the interstate commission.

C. When promulgating a rule, the interstate commission shall, at a minimum:

1. publish the proposed rule's entire text stating the reason or reasons for that proposed rule;

2. allow and invite any and all persons to submit written data, facts, opinions and arguments, which information shall be added to the record, and be made publicly available;

3. provide an opportunity for an informal hearing if petitioned by ten or more persons;

4. promulgate a final rule and its effective date, if appropriate, based on input from state or local officials, or interested parties; and

5. allow, not later than sixty days after a rule is promulgated, any interested person to file a petition in the United States district court for the District of Columbia or in the federal district court where the interstate commission's principal office is located for judicial review of such rule. If the court finds that

the interstate commission's action is not supported by substantial evidence in the rulemaking record, the court shall hold the rule unlawful and set it aside. For purposes of this subdivision, evidence is substantial if it would be considered substantial evidence under the model state administrative procedures act.

D. If a majority of the legislatures of the compacting states rejects a rule, those states may, by enactment of a statute or resolution in the same manner used to adopt the compact, cause such rule to have no further force and effect in any compacting state.

E. The existing rules governing the operation of the interstate compact on juveniles superseded by this act shall be null and void twelve months after the first meeting of the interstate commission created hereunder.

F. Upon determination by the interstate commission that a state of emergency exists, it may promulgate an emergency rule which shall become effective immediately upon adoption, provided that the usual rulemaking procedures provided hereunder shall be retroactively applied to said rule as soon as reasonably possible, but no later than ninety days after the effective date of the emergency rule.

ARTICLE VII
OVERSIGHT, ENFORCEMENT AND DISPUTE RESOLUTION
BY THE INTERSTATE COMMISSION

A. Oversight.

1. The interstate commission shall oversee the administration and operations of the interstate movement of juveniles subject to this compact in the compacting states and shall monitor such activities being administered in non-compacting states which may significantly affect compacting states.

2. The courts and executive agencies in each compacting state shall enforce this compact and shall take all actions necessary and appropriate to effectuate the compact's purposes and intent. The provisions of this compact and the rules promulgated hereunder shall be received by all the judges, public officers, commissions, and departments of the state government as evidence of the authorized statute and administrative rules. All courts shall take judicial notice of the compact and the rules. In any judicial or administrative proceeding in a compacting state pertaining to the subject matter of this compact which may affect the powers, responsibilities, or actions of the interstate commission, it shall be entitled to receive all service of process in any such proceeding, and shall have standing to intervene in the proceeding for all purposes.

B. Dispute resolution.

1. The compacting states shall report to the interstate commission on all issues and activities necessary for the administration of the compact as well as issues and activities pertaining to compliance with the provisions of the compact and its bylaws and rules.

2. The interstate commission shall attempt, upon the request of a compacting state, to resolve any disputes or other issues which are subject to the compact and which may arise among compacting states and between compacting and non-compacting states. The commission shall promulgate a rule providing for both mediation and binding dispute resolution for disputes among the compacting states.

3. The interstate commission, in the reasonable exercise of its discretion, shall enforce the provisions and rules of this compact using any or all means set forth in article XI of this compact.

ARTICLE VIII
FINANCE

A. The interstate commission shall pay or provide for the payment of the reasonable expenses of its establishment, organization and ongoing activities.

B. The interstate commission shall levy on and collect an annual assessment from each compacting state to cover the cost of the internal operations and activities of the interstate commission and its staff which must be in a total amount sufficient to cover the interstate commission's annual budget as approved each year. The aggregate annual assessment amount shall be allocated based upon a formula to be determined by the interstate commission, taking into consideration the population of each compacting state and the volume of interstate movement of juveniles in each compacting state and shall promulgate a rule binding upon all compacting states which governs said assessment.

C. The interstate commission shall not incur any obligations of any kind prior to securing the funds adequate to meet the same; nor shall the interstate commission pledge the credit of any of the compacting states, except by and with the authority of the compacting state.

D. The interstate commission shall keep accurate accounts of all receipts and disbursements. The receipts and disbursements of the interstate commission shall be subject to the audit and accounting procedures established under its bylaws. However, all receipts and disbursements of funds handled by the interstate commission shall be audited yearly by a certified or licensed public accountant and the report of the audit shall be included in and become part of the annual report of the interstate commission.

ARTICLE IX
THE STATE COUNCIL

Each member state shall create a state council for interstate juvenile supervision. While each state may determine the membership of its own state council, its membership must include at least one representative from the legislative, judicial, and executive branches of government, victims groups, and the compact administrator, deputy compact administrator or designee. Each compacting state retains the right to determine the qualifications of the compact administrator or deputy compact administrator. Each state council will advise and may exercise oversight and advocacy concerning that state's participation in interstate commission activities and other duties as may be determined by that state, including but not limited to, development of policy concerning operations and procedures of the compact within that state.

ARTICLE X
COMPACTING STATES, EFFECTIVE DATE AND AMENDMENT

A. Any state, the District of Columbia (or its designee), the Commonwealth of Puerto Rico, the U.S. Virgin Islands, Guam, American Samoa, and the Northern Marianas Islands as defined in article II of this compact is eligible to become a compacting state.

B. The compact shall become effective and binding upon legislative enactment of the compact into law by no less than thirty-five of the states. The initial effective date shall be the later of July first, two thousand four or upon enactment into law by the thirty-fifth jurisdiction. Thereafter it shall become effective and binding as to any other compacting state upon enactment of the compact into law by that state. The governors of non-member states or their designees shall be invited to participate in the activities of the interstate commission on a nonvoting basis prior to adoption of the compact by all states and territories of the United States.

C. The interstate commission may propose amendments to the compact for enactment by the compacting states. No amendment shall become effective and binding upon the interstate commission and the compacting states unless and until it is enacted into law by unanimous consent of the compacting states.

ARTICLE XI
WITHDRAWAL, DEFAULT, TERMINATION
AND JUDICIAL ENFORCEMENT

A. Withdrawal.

1. Once effective, the compact shall continue in force and remain binding upon each and every compacting state; provided that a compacting state may withdraw from the compact by specifically repealing the statute which enacted the compact into law.

2. The effective date of withdrawal is the effective date of the repeal.

3. The withdrawing state shall immediately notify the chairperson of the interstate commission in writing upon the introduction of legislation repealing this compact in the withdrawing state. The interstate commission shall notify the other compacting states of the withdrawing state's intent to withdraw within sixty days of its receipt thereof.

4. The withdrawing state is responsible for all assessments, obligations and liabilities incurred through the effective date of withdrawal, including any obligations, the performance of which extend beyond the effective date of withdrawal.

5. Reinstatement following withdrawal of any compacting state shall occur upon the withdrawing state reenacting the compact or upon such later date as determined by the interstate commission.

B. Technical assistance, fines, suspension, termination and default.

1. If the interstate commission determines that any compacting state has at any time defaulted in the performance of any of its obligations or responsibilities under this compact, or the bylaws or duly promulgated rules, the interstate commission may impose any or all of the following penalties:

a. Remedial training and technical assistance as directed by the interstate commission;

b. Alternative dispute resolution;

c. Fines, fees, and costs in such amounts as are deemed to be reasonable as fixed by the interstate commission; and

d. Suspension or termination of membership in the compact, which shall be imposed only after all other reasonable means of securing compliance under the bylaws and rules have been exhausted and the interstate commission has therefore determined that the offending state is in default. Immediate notice of suspension shall be given by the interstate commission to the governor, the chief justice or the chief judicial officer of the state, the majority and minority leaders of the defaulting state's legislature, and the state council. The grounds for default include, but are not limited to, failure of a compacting state to perform such obligations or responsibilities imposed upon it by this compact, the bylaws, or duly promulgated rules and any other grounds designated in commission bylaws and rules. The interstate commission shall immediately notify the defaulting state in writing of the penalty imposed by the interstate commission and of the default pending a cure of the default. The commission shall stipulate the conditions and the time period within which the defaulting state must cure its default. If the defaulting state fails to cure the default within the time period specified by the commission, the defaulting state shall be terminated from the compact upon an affirmative vote of a majority of the compacting states and all rights, privileges and benefits conferred by this compact shall be terminated from the effective date of termination.

2. Within sixty days of the effective date of termination of a defaulting state, the commission shall notify the governor, the chief justice or chief judicial officer, the majority and minority leaders of the defaulting state's legislature, and the state council of such termination.

3. The defaulting state is responsible for all assessments, obligations and liabilities incurred through the effective date of termination including any obligations, the performance of which extends beyond the effective date of termination.

4. The interstate commission shall not bear any costs relating to the defaulting state unless otherwise mutually agreed upon in writing between the interstate commission and the defaulting state.

5. Reinstatement following termination of any compacting state requires both a reenactment of the compact by the defaulting state and the approval of the interstate commission pursuant to the rules.

C. Judicial enforcement.

The interstate commission may, by majority vote of the members, initiate legal action in the United States district court for the District of Columbia or, at the discretion of the interstate commission, in the federal district where the interstate commission has its offices, to enforce compliance with the provisions of the compact, its duly promulgated rules and bylaws, against any compacting state in default. In the event judicial enforcement is necessary the prevailing party shall be awarded all costs of such litigation including reasonable attorney's fees.

D. Dissolution of compact.

1. The compact dissolves effective upon the date of the withdrawal or default of any compacting state, which reduces membership in the compact to one compacting state.

2. Upon the dissolution of this compact, the compact becomes null and void and shall be of no further force or effect, and the business and affairs of the interstate commission shall be concluded and any surplus funds shall be distributed in accordance with the bylaws.

ARTICLE XII
SEVERABILITY AND CONSTRUCTION

A. The provisions of this compact shall be severable, and if any phrase, clause, sentence or provision is deemed unenforceable, the remaining provisions of the compact shall be enforceable.

B. The provisions of this compact shall be liberally construed to effectuate its purposes.

ARTICLE XIII
BINDING EFFECT OF COMPACT AND OTHER LAWS

A. Other laws.

1. Nothing herein prevents the enforcement of any other law of a compacting state that is not inconsistent with this compact.

2. All compacting states' laws other than state constitutions and other interstate compacts conflicting with this compact are superseded to the extent of the conflict.

B. Binding effect of the compact.

1. All lawful actions of the interstate commission, including all rules and bylaws promulgated by the interstate commission, are binding upon the compacting states.

2. All agreements between the interstate commission and the compacting states are binding in accordance with their terms.

3. Upon the request of a party to a conflict over meaning or interpretation of interstate commission actions, and upon a majority vote of the compacting states, the interstate commission may issue advisory opinions regarding such meaning or interpretation.

4. In the event any provision of this compact exceeds the constitutional limits imposed on the legislature of any compacting state, the obligations, duties, powers or jurisdiction sought to be conferred by such provision upon the interstate commission shall be ineffective and such obligations, duties, powers or jurisdiction shall remain in the compacting state and shall be exercised by the agency thereof to which such obligations, duties, powers or jurisdiction are delegated by law in effect at the time this compact becomes effective. *Repealed September 1, 2020*

*§501-f. Commissioner for the interstate compact for juveniles.

Pursuant to subdivision B of article III of section five hundred one-e of this article, the commissioner shall be appointed by the governor in consultation with the state council established pursuant to article IX of section five hundred one-e and section five hundred one-g of this article. *Repealed September 1, 2020*

*§501-g. State council for interstate juvenile supervision.

1. Pursuant to article IX of section five hundred one-e of this article, there is hereby created within the office of children and family services a state council for interstate juvenile supervision. The council shall consist of the compact administrator, who shall be the commissioner of the office of children and family services, and ten other members to be appointed as follows:

(a) one legislative representative to be appointed by the governor upon recommendation of the speaker of the assembly;

(b) one legislative representative to be appointed by the governor upon recommendation of the temporary president of the senate;

(c) a judicial representative to be appointed by the governor upon recommendation of the chief judge of the court of appeals;

(d) the commissioner of the division of criminal justice services or his or her designee;

(e) the executive director of the council on children and families or his or her designee;

(f) the director of the office of probation and correctional alternatives or his or her designee;

(g) the director of the office of victim services or his or her designee;

(h) the commissioner of the New York city administration for children's services or his or her designee;

(i) a member of the New York juvenile justice advisory group as appointed by the governor; and

(j) an attorney appointed upon the recommendation of the New York state bar association who has represented juveniles in family court in this state for a total of at least five years.

2. The council shall advise and exercise oversight and advocacy concerning the state's participation in interstate commission activities and other duties as the council may determine, including but not limited to, development of policy concerning the operations and procedures of the compact within the state. The appointments provided for in this section shall be made within ninety days of the effective date of this section. Each appointed member of the council shall serve a term of five years. Any member chosen to fill a vacancy created other than by expiration of term shall be appointed for the unexpired term of the member whom he or she is to succeed. Vacancies caused by the expiration of term shall be filled in the same manner as original appointments and for a term of five years. The council members shall serve without salary but shall be entitled to receive reimbursement for travel and other related expenses associated with participation in the work of the council.

3. The state council for interstate juvenile supervision shall provide an annual report on or before the first day of January, two thousand twelve, and the first day of January each year thereafter, to the governor, the speaker of the assembly, the temporary president of the senate, the minority leader in the assembly, the minority leader in the senate and the chief judge of the court of appeals on the operations of the council pertaining to juveniles subject to the interstate compact for juveniles. Such report shall include an evaluation of the implementation and operation of the interstate compact for juveniles and the rules adopted by the interstate commission; a description of the policies adopted by the state council under the compact; the data collected by the interstate commission and the council; the status of and interstate movement of juveniles subject to the compact, including the number of juveniles subject to the compact and the supervision status of such juveniles, and, where available, statistical information on the age, ethnic and racial background, education, and institutional or criminal history of the juveniles subject to the compact. The report shall further include the council's evaluation of the efficiency and effectiveness of the interstate compact for juveniles and shall make recommendations concerning the operations, procedures and this state's continued inclusion in the interstate compact for juveniles.

Repealed September 1, 2020

*§501-h. Detention and appointment of an attorney for the child in proceedings involving youth governed by the interstate compact for juveniles.

1. If a youth is detained under the interstate compact for juveniles established pursuant to section five hundred one-e of this article, he or she shall be brought before the appropriate court within seventy-two hours or the next day the court is in session, whichever is sooner, and shall be advised by the judge of his or her right to remain silent, his or her right to be represented by counsel of his or her own choosing, and of the right to have an attorney assigned in accord with, as applicable, section two hundred forty-nine of the family court act or article eighteen-B of the county law. The youth shall be allowed a reasonable time to

retain counsel, contact his or her parents or other person or persons legally responsible for his or her care or an adult with whom the youth has a significant connection, and the judge may adjourn the proceedings for such purposes. Provided, however, that nothing in this section shall be deemed to require a youth to contact his or her parents or other person or persons legally responsible for his or her care. Provided further, however, that counsel shall be assigned immediately, and continue to represent the youth until any retained counsel appears. The court shall schedule a court appearance for the youth no later than ten days after the initial court appearance, and every ten days thereafter, while the youth is detained pursuant to the interstate compact for juveniles unless any such appearance is waived by the attorney for the child.

2. All youth subject to proceedings governed by the interstate compact for juveniles established pursuant to section five hundred one-e of this article shall be appointed an attorney pursuant to, as applicable, section two hundred forty-nine of the family court act or article eighteen-B of the county law if independent legal representation is not available to such youth.

Repealed September 1, 2020

Title 2
Facilities

§502. Definitions.

Unless otherwise specified in this article:

1. "Director" means the director of the division for youth.

2. "Division" means the division for youth.

3. "Detention" means the temporary care and maintenance of youth held away from their homes pursuant to article three or seven of the family court act, or held pending a hearing for alleged violation of the conditions of release from an office of children and family services facility or authorized agency, or held pending a hearing for alleged violation of the condition of parole as a juvenile offender, or held pending return to a jurisdiction other than the one in which the youth is held, or held pursuant to a securing order of a criminal court if the youth named therein as principal is charged as a juvenile offender or held pending a hearing on an extension of placement or held pending transfer to a facility upon commitment or placement by a court. Only alleged or convicted juvenile offenders who have not attained their eighteenth birthday shall be subject to detention in a detention facility.

4. For purposes of this article, the term "youth" shall be synonymous with the term "child" and means a person not less than seven years of age and not more than twenty years of age.

5. "Placement" means the transfer of a youth to the custody of the division pursuant to the family court act.

6. "Commitment" means the transfer of a youth to the custody of the division pursuant to the penal law.

7. "Conditional release" means the transfer of a youth from facility status to aftercare supervision under the continued custody of the division.

8. "Discharge" means the termination of division custody of a youth.

9. "Aftercare" means supervision of a youth on conditional release status under the continued custody of the division.

§502-a. Day placement.

1. Definition. "Day placement" shall mean a program for youth placed with the division which is an alternative to or includes a period of residential placement. Such program shall require the youth to adhere to conditions of participation and to attend programs on certain days or during certain periods of days, or both, as specified by the director.

2. Authorization for day placement. The director is authorized to establish day placement programs for eligible youth as defined by the director, pursuant to the rules and regulations of the division. The director's decision to allow a youth to participate in the day placement program shall be discretionary. As a part of day placement, the director shall impose conditions of participation upon the youth. Such conditions may include but shall not be limited to community, educational, vocational, recreational and treatment services; evening and weekend reporting programs; alternative educational programs; and periods of residential placement.

3. Use of day placement. The director, pursuant to the rules and regulations of the division, may approve a day placement in any case where the court has ordered placement with the division pursuant to section 353.3 of the family court act.

4. Duration of day placement. The duration of a day placement may be for the same period of placement imposed by the court pursuant to section 353.3 of the family court act. The term of the placement shall commence on the day it is imposed and shall be calculated upon the basis of the duration of its term, rather than upon the basis of the days spent in residential placement, so that no youth shall be subject to placement for a period that is longer than the initial period of placement, unless an extension is granted pursuant to section 355.3 of the family court act.

5. Interruption of placement. Consistent with the rule and regulation of the division, in any case where a youth fails to report to the facility or program specified by the director, the term of placement shall be interrupted and such interruption shall continue until the youth reports to such facility or program or is otherwise returned to the custody of the division.

6. Modification or termination of day placement. It shall be within the discretion of the director to modify or terminate a youth's participation in day placement at any time. If the day placement is terminated the youth shall be immediately placed in a residential facility consistent with the court order.

7. Release and discharge. Decisions of the director regarding day placement pursuant to this section or any conditional release or discharge pursuant to sections five hundred ten-a and five hundred ten-c of this article shall be

deemed a judicial function and shall not be reviewable if done in accordance with law.

§503. Detention.
1. The division shall establish regulations for the operation of secure and non-secure detention facilities pursuant to this article and section two hundred eighteen-a of the county law.

2. To assure that adequate, suitable and conveniently accessible accommodations and proper care will be available when required for detention, the division may contract for or establish, operate, maintain and certify secure and non-secure detention facilities if funds shall have been made available for the lease or purchase and maintenance and operation of appropriate facilities.

3. Each social services district may establish, operate and maintain secure and non-secure detention facilities for the purposes defined in section five hundred two of this article. Each such detention facility shall be established, operated and maintained in compliance with this article and the regulations of the division for youth.

4. The office of children and family services shall visit and inspect all facilities used for detention and make periodic reports of the operation and adequacy of such facilities, and the need for provision of such facilities to the county executive, if there be one, the county legislature and the family court judges of the county in which such facilities are located, and the office of court administration.

5. No detention facility shall receive or care for children detained pursuant to the family court act or the criminal procedure law unless certified by the division, which certification shall include a maximum-capacity which shall not be exceeded. No certification shall be issued or renewed unless such a facility has developed and implemented a procedure, consistent with appropriate collective bargaining agreements and applicable provisions of the civil service law, for reviewing and evaluating the backgrounds of and the information supplied by any person applying to be an employee, volunteer or consultant, which shall include but not be limited to the following requirements: that the applicant set forth his or her employment history, provide personal and employment references and sign a sworn statement indicating whether the applicant, to the best of his or her knowledge, has ever been convicted of a crime in this state or any other jurisdiction.

(a) The division shall promulgate regulations governing procedures for certification of detention facilities and for renewal, suspension and revocation of such certifications. Such regulations shall provide for a hearing prior to the suspension or revocation of a certification.

(b) The office of children and family services may suspend a certification for good cause shown. Suspension shall mean that no persons coming within the provisions of article three or seven of the family court act and no alleged or convicted juvenile offender may be received for care in a detention facility, but persons already in care may remain in care. The office may impose such conditions in the event of a suspension as it shall deem necessary and proper.

(c) Such office may revoke a certification for good cause shown. Revocation shall mean that no persons coming within the provisions of article three or seven of the family court act and no alleged or convicted juvenile offender may be received for care nor remain at the detention facility.

6. The division shall be responsible for bringing violations of law pertaining to detention of juveniles to the attention of each appropriate attorney for the

child or counsel for the defendant who may petition for habeas corpus for persons aggrieved thereby.

7. The person in charge of each detention facility shall keep a record of all time spent in such facility for each youth in care. The detention facility shall deliver a certified transcript of such record to the office, social services district, or other agency taking custody of the youth pursuant to article three or seven of the family court act, before, or at the same time as the youth is delivered to the office, district or other agency, as is appropriate.

8. The division shall list all facilities certified for the detention of children and shall file a copy of that list periodically with the clerk of the family court in each county, the clerk of the criminal court of the city of New York, the clerk of the supreme court in each county within the city of New York and the clerk of the county court in each county outside the city of New York.

§503-a. Temporary hold over units.

1. The division may establish secure temporary hold over units at its facilities for the accommodation of youth placed with the division pursuant to article three of the family court act, who are being transported to a division facility or program, a court appearance or a home visit, where travel arrangements or the distance to be travelled requires such a holdover. No youth shall be held in these units in excess of twenty-four hours unless emergency conditions, including illness of the youth or severe weather, prevent travel.

2. Temporary hold over units may be established on a regional basis. Contact between youth who are housed in a hold over unit and residents of the facility shall be minimal. Youth staying in a temporary hold over unit shall be under supervision at all times. At least one staff on duty shall be of the same gender as the youth.

3. The temporary hold over units shall contain individual sleeping rooms, dining facilities and an area for recreation.

4. Juvenile offenders committed to the custody of the division shall not be housed in temporary hold over units at any time. Notwithstanding any other law, the division shall have the authority to house any adjudicated youth placed with the division pursuant to article three of the family court act, in a secure temporary hold over unit, subject to the provisions of this section.

§504. Division facilities.

1. The division shall operate and maintain secure, limited secure and non-secure facilities for the care, custody, treatment, housing, education, rehabilitation and guidance of youth placed with or committed to the division.

2. Each separate facility may bear the name, designated by the division, of an individual known for outstanding service to youth.

3. A youth attending a local public school while in residence at a division facility shall be deemed a resident of the school district where the youth's parent or guardian resides at the commencement of each school year for the purpose of determining which school district shall be responsible for the youth's tuition.

4. The division shall determine the particular division facility or program in which a child placed with the division shall be cared for, based upon an evaluation of such child. The division shall also have authority to discharge or conditionally release children placed with it and to transfer such children from a limited secure or non-secure facility to any other limited secure or non-secure facility, when the interest of such children requires such action; provided that

a child transferred to a non-secure facility from a limited secure facility may be returned to a limited secure facility upon a determination by the division that, for any reason, care and treatment at the non-secure facility is no longer suitable.

§504-a.   Secure facilities.

1. As used in this article, "secure facility" means a residential facility in which a juvenile delinquent may be placed under this article, which is characterized by physically restricting construction, hardware and procedures, and is designated as a secure facility by the division under this section.

2. Secure facilities shall provide appropriate services to the residents, including but not limited to: residential care, educational and vocational training, physical and mental health services, and employment counseling.

3. A youth shall be placed in or transferred to a secure facility only:

(a) by order of the family court pursuant to section 353.5 of the family court act; or

(b) after a hearing pursuant to regulations of the division, with the written approval of the director of the division or his or her designee.

4. The division shall promulgate regulations governing secure facilities of the division, including but not limited to:

(a) limitations as to capacity;

(b) services to be provided and conditions to be maintained;

(c) a grievance procedure for residents to be run by the division, with the use of personnel separate from that of the facility;

(d) procedures for admission to and release or transfer from the facility;

(e) periodic inspection by the division, not to be conducted by personnel of the facility.

5. A juvenile delinquent residing in a facility operated pursuant to this title may be maintained in group confinement if he constitutes a serious and evident danger to himself or other persons, if such confinement is clearly necessary to prevent escape, if the child demonstrates by his behavior that he is in need of special care and attention in a living unit separate from his normal surroundings, or if such confinement is necessary for purposes of the child's own protection. The division shall promulgate regulations providing for a procedure governing transfers to group confinement and periodic review of such confinement.

§504-b.   Transport and warrant units.

The division is authorized to establish transport and warrant units and designate employees to be assigned to such units. Such units shall have the powers and responsibilities specified in regulations promulgated by the division, including but not limited to the conveyance of youth placed with or committed to the custody of the division to and from its facilities. Employees of such unit who are specifically designated by the director in writing, shall have the power and authority of peace officers in respect thereto.

§505.   Directors of facilities.

1. There shall be a facility director of each office of children and family services operated facility. Such facility director shall be appointed by the commissioner of the office of children and family services and the position shall be in the noncompetitive class and designated as confidential as defined by subdivision two-a of section forty-two of the civil service law. The facility director shall have such experience and other qualifications as may be

prescribed by the director of classification and compensation within the department of civil service in consultation with the commissioner of the office of children and family services, based on differences in duties, levels of responsibility, size and character of the facility, knowledge, skills and abilities required, and other factors affecting the position. Such facility director shall serve at the pleasure of the commissioner of the office of children and family services.

2. Subject to regulations of the division, the facility director of a state facility in the division shall:

(a) operate and manage the facility,

(b) submit a monthly report on such matters as the division may specify.

3. Subject to the regulations of the division, the facility director may authorize the use of the buildings and grounds of the facility by a municipality, special district or non-profit association, corporation or organization for educational, recreational, social and civic purposes whenever such use may promote better relationships with the community in which the facility is located, provided, however, that such use does not interfere with the purposes and program of the facility.

§506. Claims for damage to employees' personal property.

Claims for damages to personal property of employees of the division for youth caused by youths in program may be examined, audited and certified for payment by the state comptroller. Such claims must be approved by the director of the division for youth prior to submission to the office of the state comptroller. The payment of any such claim shall not exceed the sum of three hundred fifty dollars.

§507-a. Placement and commitment; procedures.

1. Youth may be placed in or committed to the custody of the division:

(a) for placement, as a juvenile delinquent pursuant to the family court act; or

(b) for commitment pursuant to the penal law.

2. (a) Consistent with other provisions of law, only those youth who have reached the age of seven but who have not reached the age of twenty-one may be placed in, committed to or remain in the division's custody. Whenever it shall appear to the satisfaction of the division that any youth placed therewith is not of proper age to be so placed or is not properly placed, or is mentally or physically incapable of being materially benefited by the program of the division, the division shall cause the return of such youth to the county from which placement was made.

(b) The division shall deliver such youth to the custody of the placing court, along with the records provided to the division pursuant to section five hundred seven-b of this article, there to be dealt with by the court in all respects as though no placement had been made.

(c) The cost and expense of the care and return of such youth incurred by the division shall be reimbursed to the state by the social services district from which such youth was placed in the manner provided by section five hundred twenty-nine of this article.

3. The division may photograph any youth in its custody. Such photograph may be used only for the purpose of assisting in the return of conditionally released children and runaways pursuant to section five hundred ten-b of this article. Such photograph shall be destroyed immediately upon the discharge of the youth from division custody.

4. (a) A youth placed with or committed to the division may, immediately following placement or commitment, be remanded to an appropriate detention facility.

(b) The division shall admit a child placed with the division to a facility of the division within fifteen days of the date of the order of placement with the division and shall admit a juvenile offender committed to the division to a facility of the division within ten days of the date of the order of commitment to the division, except as provided in section five hundred seven-b of this article.

5. Consistent with other provisions of law, in the discretion of the director, youth who attain the age of eighteen while in division custody may reside in a non-secure facility until the age of twenty-one, provided that such youth attend a full-time vocational or educational program and are likely to benefit from such program.

§507-b. Placement and commitment; papers to be furnished.

1. No placement or commitment order to the division which recites the facts upon which it was based shall be deemed or held to be invalid by reason of any imperfection or defect in form.

2. The court shall immediately notify the division of the placement or commitment of any youth therewith. The orders of the court and copies of the probation report and all other relevant evaluative records in the possession of the court, detention facility, and probation department related to such youth, including but not limited to any diagnostic, educational, medical, psychological and psychiatric records, fingerprints, photographs, a certified copy of the sentence and any pre-sentence memoranda filed with the court, where applicable, and reports relating to assaults or other violent acts, attempts at suicide or escape by the youth shall be delivered together with the youth or earlier to a person authorized by the director to receive the child, notwithstanding any contrary provision of law.

3. The court shall, before placing or committing any such youth, inquire into and determine the age of the youth at the time of placement or commitment, and the youth's age as so determined shall be stated in the order. The statement of the age of such youth in such order shall be conclusive evidence as to such age in any action to recover damages for allegedly unlawful detention under such order, and shall be presumptive evidence thereof in any other inquiry, action or proceeding relating to such detention.

4. Notwithstanding the time frames provided in paragraph (b) of subdivision four of section five hundred seven-a of this article, the division may delay acceptance of a youth placed or committed to the division in accordance with division regulations promulgated prior to the effective date of this subdivision.

§507-c. Restrictive placements.

1. The division shall promulgate regulations governing restrictive placements of juveniles under section 353.5 of the family court act, not inconsistent with such act.

2. The regulations shall establish within the division a restrictive placement committee. The division shall make and revise as needed a plan for the care, treatment, services and supervision of each youth under restrictive placement, which plan shall be reviewed and may be revised by the committee. The youth may not be released or transferred from a facility without the approval of the committee, except by written order of the director.

3. For youths placed with the division pursuant to a restrictive placement under section 353.5 of the family court act, the division shall (a) report in writing to the court not less than once every six months during the placement on the status, adjustment and progress of the respondent, unless otherwise provided in the order of disposition; and (b) provide intensive supervision of the youth whenever he or she is not in a secure or residential facility of the division.

§507-d. Confinement of juvenile delinquents under sentence of the courts of the United States.

The directors of secure and limited secure facilities shall receive and safely keep in such facilities, subject to the provisions of this article, any person not over the age of sixteen years convicted of any offense against the United States, and sentenced to imprisonment by any court of the United States, sitting within this state, until such sentences be executed, or until such delinquent shall be discharged by due course of law, conditioned upon the United States supporting such delinquent and paying the expenses attendant upon the execution of such sentence.

§508. Juvenile offender facilities.

1. The office of children and family services shall maintain secure facilities for the care and confinement of juvenile offenders committed for an indeterminate, determinate or definite sentence pursuant to the sentencing provisions of the penal law. Such facilities shall provide appropriate services to juvenile offenders including but not limited to residential care, educational and vocational training, physical and mental health services, and employment counseling.

2. Juvenile offenders shall be confined in such facilities until the age of twenty-one and shall not be released, discharged or permitted home visits except pursuant to the provisions of this section.

*(a) The director of the division for youth may authorize the transfer of a juvenile offender in his custody, who has been convicted of burglary or robbery, to a school or center established and operated pursuant to title three of this article at any time after the juvenile offender has been confined in a division for youth secure facility for one year or one-half of his minimum sentence, whichever is greater. *Expired September 1, 1992*

*(b) The director of the division for youth may authorize the transfer of a juvenile offender in his custody, who has been convicted of burglary or robbery, and who is within ninety days of release as established by the board of parole, to any facility established and operated pursuant to this article. *Expired September 1, 1992*

*(c) A juvenile offender may be transferred as provided in paragraphs (a) and (b) herein, only after the director determines that there is no danger to public safety and that the offender shall substantially benefit from the programs and services of another division facility. In determining whether there is a danger to public safety the director shall consider: (i) the nature and circumstances of the offense including whether any physical injury involved was inflicted by the offender or another participant; (ii) the record and background of the offender; and (iii) the adjustment of the offender at division facilities. *Expired September 1, 1992*

*(d) For a period of six months after a juvenile offender has been transferred pursuant to paragraph (a) or (b) herein, the juvenile offender may have only

accompanied home visits. After completing six months of confinement following transfer from a secure facility, a juvenile offender may not have an unaccompanied home visit unless two accompanied home visits have already occurred. An "accompanied home visit" shall mean a home visit during which the juvenile offender shall be accompanied at all times while outside the facility by appropriate personnel of the division for youth designated pursuant to regulations of the director of the division.   *Expired September 1, 1992*

* (e) The director of the division for youth shall promulgate rules and regulations including uniform standards and procedures governing the transfer of juvenile offenders from secure facilities to other facilities and the return of such offenders to secure facilities. The rules and regulations shall provide a procedure for the referral of proposed transfer cases by the secure facility director, and shall require a determination by the facility director that transfer of a juvenile offender to another facility is in the best interests of the division for youth and the juvenile offender and that there is no danger to public safety.

The rules and regulations shall further provide for the establishment of a division central office transfer committee to review transfer cases referred by the secure facility directors. The committee shall recommend approval of a transfer request to the director of the division only upon a clear showing by the secure facility director that the transfer is in the best interests of the division for youth and the juvenile offender and that there is no danger to public safety. In the case of the denial of the transfer request by the transfer committee, the juvenile offender shall remain at a secure facility. Notwithstanding the recommendation for approval of transfer by the transfer committee, the director of the division may deny the request for transfer if there is a danger to public safety or if the transfer is not in the best interests of the division for youth or the juvenile offender.

The rules and regulations shall further provide a procedure for the immediate return to a secure facility, without a hearing, of a juvenile offender transferred to another facility upon a determination by that facility director that there is a danger to public safety.   *Expired September 1, 1992*

3. The division shall report in writing to the sentencing court and district attorney, not less than once every six months during the period of confinement, on the status, adjustment, programs and progress of the offender.

4. The office of children and family services may apply to the sentencing court for permission to transfer a youth not less than sixteen nor more than eighteen years of age to the department of corrections and community supervision. Such application shall be made upon notice to the youth, who shall be entitled to be heard upon the application and to be represented by counsel. The court shall grant the application if it is satisfied that there is no substantial likelihood that the youth will benefit from the programs offered by the office facilities.

5. The office of children and family services may transfer an offender not less than eighteen nor more than twenty-one years of age to the department of corrections and community supervision if the commissioner of the office certifies to the commissioner of corrections and community supervision that there is no substantial likelihood that the youth will benefit from the programs offered by office facilities.

6. At age twenty-one, all juvenile offenders shall be transferred to the custody of the department of correction and community supervision for confinement pursuant to the correction law.

7. While in the custody of the office of children and family services, an offender shall be subject to the rules and regulations of the office, except that his parole, temporary release and discharge shall be governed by the laws applicable to inmates of state correctional facilities and his transfer to state hospitals in the office of mental health shall be governed by section five hundred nine of this chapter. The commissioner of the office of children and family services shall, however, establish and operate temporary release programs at office of children and family services facilities for eligible juvenile offenders and contract with the department of corrections and community supervision for the provision of parole supervision services for temporary releasees. The rules and regulations for these programs shall not be inconsistent with the laws for temporary release applicable to inmates of state correctional facilities. For the purposes of temporary release programs for juvenile offenders only, when referred to or defined in article twenty-six of the correction law, "institution" shall mean any facility designated by the commissioner of the office of children and family services, "department" shall mean the office of children and family services, "inmate" shall mean a juvenile offender residing in an office of children and family services facility, and "commissioner" shall mean the director of the office of children and family services. Time spent in office of children and family services facilities and in juvenile detention facilities shall be credited towards the sentence imposed in the same manner and to the same extent applicable to inmates of state correctional facilities.

8. Whenever a juvenile offender or a juvenile offender adjudicated a youthful offender shall be delivered to the director of a division for youth facility pursuant to a commitment to the director of the division for youth, the officer so delivering such person shall deliver to such facility director a certified copy of the sentence received by such officer from the clerk of the court by which such person shall have been sentenced, a copy of the report of the probation officer's investigation and report, any other pre-sentence memoranda filed with the court, a copy of the person's fingerprint records, a detailed summary of available medical records, psychiatric records and reports relating to assaults, or other violent acts, attempts at suicide or escape by the person while in the custody of a local detention facility.

9. Notwithstanding any provision of law, including section five hundred one-c of this article, the office of children and family services shall make records pertaining to a person convicted of a sex offense as defined in subdivision (p) of section 10.03 of the mental hygiene law available upon request to the commissioner of mental health or the commissioner of developmental disabilities, as appropriate; a case review panel; and the attorney general; in accordance with the provisions of article ten of the mental hygiene law. *(Eff.5/25/16,Ch.37,L.2016)*

§509. Transfers to state hospitals and schools in the department of mental hygiene.

1. (a) The director of the division for youth may apply for the transfer of any child in the care of the division to the department of mental hygiene for care and treatment in a state hospital or school under the jurisdiction of said department whenever it appears to the satisfaction of the director of the division:

(i) that such child is mentally ill or mentally retarded and will substantially benefit from care and treatment in such a state school or hospital; and

(ii) that the interests of the state will be best served thereby.

(b) The office for people with developmental disabilities may receive, treat and otherwise care for such a child pursuant to article nine or fifteen of the mental hygiene law if suitable for admission thereunder. *(Eff.5/25/16,Ch.37,L.2016)*

2. (a) Except in the case of an emergency requiring immediate admission to a state hospital pursuant to the mental hygiene law, a child in the care of the division may be transferred:

(i) after notice thereof has been given to the child to be transferred, his parents or legal guardian, and his attorney of record, if any; and

(ii) after he has been afforded an opportunity to be heard with respect thereto at a hearing conducted by an impartial hearing officer and to be represented at such hearing by counsel. If in the judgment of the division such child is financially unable to obtain counsel, the division shall pay such counsel's fees as shall be necessary to assure adequate representation for such child.

(b) The hearing officer may accept the written waiver by a child of his right to a hearing, provided the child knowingly and voluntarily executed such waiver with the advice of counsel.

3. A child transferred pursuant to this section:

(a) shall continue to be under the general care and supervision of the division for youth except that he shall be temporarily cared for and treated by the institution to which the transfer is made.

(b) shall be subject to the laws and rules pertaining to the institution to which he is admitted; and

(c) shall be entitled to the same rights and procedures under the mental hygiene law as any other person admitted or converted in status thereunder.

4. Whenever the commissioner of mental health or the director of a residential treatment facility for children and youth, or the commissioner of developmental disabilities finds that care and treatment of a child transferred pursuant to this section or section 353.4 of the family court act is no longer suitable under the mental hygiene law, he or she shall forthwith so certify and discharge the child to the custody of the child himself or herself, his or her parents, his or her legal guardian, the local department of social services or the office of children and family services, as appropriate, except that so long as there is a valid order of the family court placing the child with the office of children and family services, or a valid order of a criminal court sentencing a child to the office of children and family services, the child shall be returned to the care and custody of the office of children and family services. The duration of the placement or sentence with the such office of a child transferred pursuant to this section shall not be extended or increased by reason of any such transfer. *(Eff.5/25/16,Ch.37,L.2016)*

5. All expenses incident to a transfer under this section shall be borne by the division, subject to the provisions of title four of this article. All expenses for the care and treatment of a child transferred to the department of mental hygiene pursuant to this section shall be borne by the department of mental hygiene.

6. An application by the director for admission of a child to a state hospital shall be considered an application for voluntary admission in accordance with section 9.13 of the mental hygiene law if such child is under the age of sixteen or if the child is sixteen years of age or older and has waived his right to a hearing in accordance with subdivision two of this section. An application by the director for admission to a state hospital of a child sixteen years of age or older who has not knowingly and voluntarily consented to such application in accordance with paragraph (b) of subdivision two of this section shall be

considered an application for involuntary admission in accordance with section 9.27 of the mental hygiene law.

7. The director may, following the procedures outlined in this section and subject to the requirements of section 9.51 of the mental hygiene law, apply for the transfer of any child in the care of the division who has not been sentenced as a juvenile offender pursuant to section 70.05 of the penal law, and who is not subject to a restrictive placement pursuant to section 353.5 of the family court act, to a residential treatment facility for children and youth.

8. Notwithstanding any other provision of law to the contrary, juvenile offenders shall be transferred only to a facility under the jurisdiction of the office of mental health specially designed for the care and treatment of juvenile offenders which is characterized by physically restricting construction, hardware and procedures.

Title 3
Programs and Services for Youth

Subtitle
A Additional Services for Youth (§§ 510-a – 522)

Subtitle A
Additional Services for Youth

§510-a. Conditional release.

1. The division may conditionally release any youth placed with the division to aftercare whenever it deems such conditional release to be in the best interest of the youth, that suitable care and supervision can be provided and that there is a reasonable probability that the youth can be conditionally released without endangering the public safety; provided, however, that no youth while absent from a facility or program without the consent of the director of such facility or program shall be conditionally released by the division solely by reason of the absence. The division may establish regulations in connection with such conditional release.

2. It shall be a condition of such release that the youth so released shall continue to be the responsibility of the division for the period provided in the order of placement, notwithstanding the youth's conditional release therefrom, and that the division, pursuant to its regulations, may cause such youth to be returned to a division facility or authorized agency at any time within the period of placement, where there is a violation of the conditions of release or a change of circumstances.

3. Youth conditionally released by the division may be provided for as follows:

(a)If, in the opinion of the office of children and family services, there is no suitable parent, relative or guardian to whom a youth can be conditionally released, and suitable care cannot otherwise be secured, the division may conditionally release such youth to the care of an authorized agency established pursuant to section three hundred seventy-one of the social services law or any other suitable person; provided that where such suitable person has no legal relationship with the juvenile, the office shall advise such person of the procedures for obtaining custody or guardianship of the juvenile.

(b) The division may provide clothing, other necessities and services for any conditionally released youth, as may be required, including medical care and services not provided to such youth as medical assistance for needy persons pursuant to title eleven of article five of the social services law.

(c) If the youth so released is subject to article sixty-five of the education law or elects to participate in an educational program leading to a high school diploma, the youth shall be enrolled in a school or educational program leading to a high school diploma following release, or, if such release occurs during the summer recess, upon the commencement of the next school term. If the youth so released is not subject to article sixty-five of the education law and does not elect to participate in an educational program leading to a high school diploma, steps shall be taken to the extent possible to facilitate the youth's gainful employment or enrollment in a vocational program following release.

4. In addition to the other requirements of this section, no youth placed with the division pursuant to a restrictive placement under the family court act shall be released except pursuant to section 353.5 of the family court act.

§510-b. Return of conditionally released children or runaways.

1. If a child under the jurisdiction of the division runs away from a division facility or an authorized agency or violates any condition of release therefrom, or if there is a change of circumstances, the division shall cause said child to be apprehended and returned to a division facility or authorized agency pursuant to the regulations of the division.

2. The facility director shall, with respect to any person placed with the division by order of the family court, give immediate written notice to said family court when any such person is absent from such facility without consent. In cases involving persons placed with the division who are cared for by authorized agencies pursuant to court direction or authorization, the authorized agency shall give written notice to the division and the appropriate family court when any such division placement is absent from such authorized agency without consent.

3. An employee designated by the division may, without a warrant, apprehend a runaway or conditionally released child in any county in this state whose return has been ordered by the division, and return said child to any appropriate division facility, detention facility, authorized agency or program.

4. The division, pursuant to its regulations, shall issue a warrant directed generally to any peace officer, acting pursuant to such officer's special duties, or police officer in the state for the apprehension and return of any runaway or conditionally released child under the jurisdiction of the division and such warrant shall be executed by any peace officer, acting pursuant to such officer's special duties, or police officer to whom it may be delivered. The division also shall provide relevant law enforcement agencies within forty-eight hours with any photographs of any runaway or conditionally released child for whom a warrant is issued together with any pertinent information relative to such child.

Such photographs shall remain the property of the division and shall be kept confidential for use solely in the apprehension of such child. Such photographs shall be returned promptly to the division upon apprehension of such child, or upon the demand of the division.

5. A magistrate may cause a runaway or released child to be held in custody until returned to the division.

6. In a city with a population of one million or more, the commissioner of juvenile justice, or the designee of such commissioner, may issue a warrant directed generally to any peace officer, acting pursuant to such officer's special duties, or police officer in the state for the apprehension and return of any youth who has run away or escaped from a secure detention facility, as defined in the family court act, operated by such commissioner. Such warrant shall be executed by any peace officer, acting pursuant to such officer's special duties, or police officer to whom it may be delivered.

7. When a child who is placed with the division pursuant to article three of the family court act or committed pursuant to the penal law is absent from a division facility or an authorized agency without the consent of the director of such facility or authorized agency, the absence shall interrupt the calculation of the time of such placement or commitment and such interruption shall continue until the return of the child to the facility or authorized agency in which the child was placed or committed. Any time spent by such child in custody from the date of absence to the date the placement pursuant to article three of the family court act or commitment pursuant to the penal law resumes shall be credited against the time of such placement or commitment provided:

(a) That such custody was due to an arrest or surrender based upon the absence; or

(b) That such custody arose from an arrest or surrender on another charge which did not culminate in a conviction, adjudication or adjustment.

8. When a youth who is absent without consent from division custody is apprehended outside of the state of New York, the terms of the interstate compact on juveniles, set forth in chapter one hundred fifty-five of the laws of nineteen hundred fifty-five, as amended, shall govern the return of such youth to division custody.

§510-c. Discharge from custody.

1. The division may discharge from its custody any child placed with the division whenever it deems such discharge to be in the best interest of the child and there is reasonable probability that the child can be discharged without endangering the public safety; provided, however, that no child while absent from a division facility without the consent of the director of such facility shall be discharged by the division solely by reason of the absence, and provided further that no child in the custody of the division and transferred to the department of mental hygiene, while absent from a department of mental hygiene facility without the consent of the superintendent or director of such facility, shall be discharged by the division.

2. Except as provided in subdivision three of this section, any child who has been placed with the office of children and family services shall be deemed to have been discharged therefrom if, during the period provided in the order of placement or extension thereof, the child is convicted of a crime or adjudicated a youthful offender, and is committed to an institution in the department of corrections and community supervision or department of mental hygiene, or receives a one year sentence in a local correctional facility.

3. A child placed with the division pursuant to a restrictive placement under the family court act shall not be discharged solely by reason of conviction for a crime or adjudication as a juvenile delinquent or youthful offender, nor shall any such child be discharged except pursuant to section 353.5 of the family court act.

4. Upon the placement of any child eighteen years of age or over, or upon the eighteenth birthday of any child placed in the custody of the division for an adjudication of juvenile delinquency for having committed an act which if committed by an adult would constitute a felony, and still in the custody of the division, the division shall notify the division of criminal justice services of such placement or birthday provided, however, in the case of a child eleven or twelve years of age, at the time the act or acts were committed, the division of criminal justice services shall not be provided with the child's name, unless the acts committed by such child would constitute a class A or B felony. Upon the subsequent discharge of said child it shall be the duty of the division to notify the division of criminal justice services of that fact and the date of discharge. For the purposes of this subdivision, a child's age shall be determined to be the age stated in the placement order.

§512. Weekly allowances; work experience.

1. Every child being cared for in a division facility may receive a weekly allowance approved by the director of the budget, in accordance with regulations of the division, as compensation for work or services performed in a division facility. Such weekly allowance shall be paid from moneys appropriated to the division for maintenance and operation.

2. A child who is being cared for in a division facility may, with the permission of the facility director, work outside of such facility when attendance upon instruction is not required pursuant to the education law. No such child may be permitted to work unless the conditions of work, including wages, meet the standards therefor prescribed pursuant to the labor law. The facility director may require that a part of the wages of such child, not to exceed twenty-five per centum thereof, be deposited in a general welfare fund to be utilized for the benefit of all children in such facility.

§512-a. Earnings of youth.

The division for youth may grant compensation to youth for work performed in division facility programs, or pursuant to work programs in accordance with rules and regulations established by the division for youth and approved by the director of the budget. Such rules and regulations need not be uniform as to each program and may establish, on the basis of work performed, the amount of compensation to be paid and the manner in which it is to be paid to each youth, or paid to the youth's dependents, or credited to the youth's account until his or her discharge from such program. Such compensation may be paid from moneys appropriated to the division for youth for maintenance and operation.

§513. Career education.

1. Purpose. The purpose of this section is to provide for career education opportunities for youth in the division's care as a part of general curricula and specialized programs to allow youth to gain actual business experiences relating to the production and marketing of products. The emphasis of business experiences provided to youth shall be on education and rehabilitation.

2. Career education program. The director may establish career education programs for residents of division facilities. These programs may include a comprehensive career education program within division facilities whereby eligible division youth participate in a special program designed to develop practical and theoretical understanding from the production through the marketing of goods. No youth may be employed by private persons or entities pursuant to this section.

3. Sale of products. The director of the division for youth or his designees are authorized to sell the products resulting from the career education of the residents of division facilities. The sale of such products shall be governed by the rules and regulations of the director of the division.

4. Career education; definition. For purposes of this section, career education is defined as any activity in the nature of vocational instruction, prescribed, guided or supervised for the purpose of contributing to the welfare or rehabilitation of residents of division facilities.

5. Sales to state agencies, political subdivisions and public benefit corporations. The director of the division for youth or his designee is authorized to enter into contracts with state agencies, political subdivisions and public benefit corporations for the sale of the products resulting from the vocational education of the residents provided that such products are not available to the purchasing entity under a centralized contract and the sale does not exceed monetary limits established by statute or by any such entity which would mandate competitive bidding for the purchase of such product.

6. Vocational education fund. A career education fund may be established for the receipt of proceeds from products sold, as authorized by subdivisions three and five of this section, incident to an avocational or career project.

7. Distribution of proceeds. Pursuant to rules, regulations, policies or procedures of the director of the division, moneys of the fund shall be disbursed as follows: (i) an amount equal to the proceeds from the sale of the product produced by one resident may be deposited to the account of such resident or paid directly to such resident; or (ii) an amount equal to the proceeds from the sale of a product produced by two or more residents may be divided equally among such residents and deposited to their respective accounts or paid directly to them. In determining the amount of the proceeds from a sale of a product that may be deposited to the account of a resident, or paid directly to a resident, the director of the division for youth shall provide for a deduction from the sum of the proceeds of the reasonable expenses of the division for youth incident to the sale, including but not limited to, the value of materials and supplies for the production of the product supplied without financial charge to the resident and the expense of transporting the product for sale, display or otherwise. The amount deducted for such expenses shall be deposited in the career education fund and expended to pay for services and expenses of operating career education programs at division for youth facilities pursuant to this chapter.

§515. Freedom of worship.

It shall be the duty of the division to afford a child placed with it freedom of worship as provided for in the state constitution.

§516. Care of infants by division for youth.

The division for youth is authorized to provide residential care in division facilities subject to the regulations of the division, for infants born to or being nursed by female residents placed with the division. Residential care for such an infant may be provided for such period of time as is deemed desirable for the welfare of the mother or infant.

§517. Commissaries.

The director of the division for youth may authorize the director of any facility operated by the division to establish a commissary in such facility for the use of residents and employees. The moneys received by the director of the division from the sales of the commissary shall be deposited in a special fund to be known as the commissary fund and such funds shall be used for the general purposes of the facilities subject to the provisions of section fifty-three of the state finance law.

§518. Restitution; services for public good.

The division shall develop and operate programs for youths placed or referred to the division or in conjunction with an order provided in section 353.6 of the family court act. The division shall promulgate regulations as required in such section.

§519. Persons authorized to visit division facilities.

1. The following persons shall be authorized to visit at pleasure all facilities operated by the division: the governor, lieutenant governor, commissioner of general services, secretary of state, comptroller, attorney general, members of the legislature, judges of the court of appeals, supreme court, family court, and county courts, district attorneys, county attorneys, and any person or agency otherwise authorized by statute.

2. The director of the division shall promulgate rules and regulations setting forth the policy of the division regarding visitation of division facilities and residents therein by persons other than those listed in subdivision one of this section. The overall security and uninterrupted operation of such facilities and the safety and well being of the staff and residents therein shall be given due consideration in the formulation of these rules and regulations for visitation as necessary to ensure such security, safety and facility operation. Such regulations shall include provisions regarding reasonable and appropriate visitation by family members and consultation by the youth's legal representative.

§522. Actions against persons rendering health care services at the request of the division; defense and indemnification.

The provisions of section seventeen of the public officers law shall apply to any person holding a license to practice a profession pursuant to article one hundred thirty-one, one hundred thirty-one-B, one hundred thirty-two, one hundred thirty-three, one hundred thirty-six, one hundred thirty-seven, one hundred thirty-nine, one hundred forty-one, one hundred forty-three, one hundred fifty-six or one hundred fifty-nine of the education law, who is rendering or has rendered professional services authorized under such license while acting at the request of the division or a facility of the division in providing health care and treatment or professional consultation to residents of division facilities, or to infants of residents while such infants are cared for in division facilities pursuant to section five hundred sixteen of this article, without regard to whether such health care and treatment or professional consultation is provided within or without a division facility.

ARTICLE 19
Contempts

§750.   Power of courts to punish for criminal contempts.

A. A court of record has power to punish for a criminal contempt, a person guilty of any of the following acts, and no others:

1. Disorderly, contemptuous, or insolent behavior, committed during its sitting, in its immediate view and presence, and directly tending to interrupt its proceedings, or to impair the respect due to its authority.

2. Breach of the peace, noise, or other disturbance, directly tending to interrupt its proceedings.

3. Wilful disobedience to its lawful mandate.

4. Resistance wilfully offered to its lawful mandate.

5. Contumacious and unlawful refusal to be sworn as a witness; or, after being sworn, to answer any legal and proper interrogatory.

6. Publication of a false, or grossly inaccurate report of its proceedings. But a court can not punish as a contempt, the publication of a true, full, and fair report of a trial, argument, decision, or other proceeding therein.

7. Wilful failure to obey any mandate, process or notice issued pursuant to articles sixteen, seventeen, eighteen, eighteen-a or eighteen-b of the judiciary law, or to rules adopted pursuant thereto, or to any other statute relating thereto, or refusal to be sworn as provided therein, or subjection of an employee to discharge or penalty on account of his absence from employment by reason of jury or subpoenaed witness service in violation of this chapter or section 215.11 of the penal law. Applications to punish the accused for a contempt specified in this subdivision may be made by notice of motion or by order to show cause, and shall be made returnable at the term of the supreme court at which contested motions are heard, or of the county court if the supreme court is not in session.

B. In addition to the power to punish for a criminal contempt as set forth in subdivision A, the supreme court has power under this section to punish for a criminal contempt any person who unlawfully practices or assumes to practice law; and a proceeding under this subdivision may be instituted on the court's own motion or on the motion of any officer charged with the duty of investigating or prosecuting unlawful practice of law, or by any bar association incorporated under the laws of this state.

C. A court not of record has only such power to punish for a criminal contempt as is specifically granted to it by statute and no other.

§751.   Punishment for criminal contempts.

1. Except as provided in subdivisions (2), (3) and (4), punishment for a contempt, specified in section seven hundred fifty, may be by fine, not exceeding one thousand dollars, or by imprisonment, not exceeding thirty days,

in the jail of the county where the court is sitting, or both, in the discretion of the court. Where the punishment for contempt is based on a violation of an order of protection issued under section 530.12 or 530.13 of the criminal procedure law, imprisonment may be for a term not exceeding three months. Where a person is committed to jail, for the nonpayment of a fine, imposed under this section, he must be discharged at the expiration of thirty days; but where he is also committed for a definite time, the thirty days must be computed from the expiration of the definite time.

Such a contempt, committed in the immediate view and presence of the court, may be punished summarily; when not so committed, the party charged must be notified of the accusation, and have a reasonable time to make a defense.

2. (a) Where an employee organization, as defined in section two hundred one of the civil service law, wilfully disobeys a lawful mandate of a court of record, or wilfully offers resistance to such lawful mandate, in a case involving or growing out of a strike in violation of subdivision one of section two hundred ten of the civil service law, the punishment for each day that such contempt persists may be by a fine fixed in the discretion of the court. In the case of a government exempt from certain provisions of article fourteen of the civil service law, pursuant to section two hundred twelve of such law, the court may, as an additional punishment for such contempt, order forfeiture of the rights granted pursuant to the provisions of paragraph (b) of subdivision one, and subdivision three of section two hundred eight of such law, for such specified period of time, as the court shall determine or, in the discretion of the court, for an indefinite period of time subject to restoration upon application, with notice to all interested parties, supported by proof of good faith compliance with the requirements of subdivision one of section two hundred ten of the civil service law since the date of such violation, such proof to include, for example, the successful negotiation, without a violation of subdivision one of section two hundred ten of the civil service law, of a contract covering the employees in the unit affected by such violation; provided, however, that where a fine imposed pursuant to this subdivision remains wholly or partly unpaid, after the exhaustion of the cash and securities of the employee organization, such forfeiture shall be suspended to the extent necessary for the unpaid portion of such fine to be accumulated by the public employer and transmitted to the court. In fixing the amount of the fine and/or duration of the forfeiture, the court shall consider all the facts and circumstances directly related to the contempt, including, but not limited to: (i) the extent of the wilful defiance of or a resistance to the court's mandate (ii) the impact of the strike on the public health, safety, and welfare of the community and (iii) the ability of the employee organization to pay the fine imposed; and the court may consider (i) the refusal of the employee organization or the appropriate public employer, as defined in section two hundred one of the civil service law, or the representatives thereof, to submit to the mediation and fact-finding procedures provided in section two hundred nine of the civil service law and (ii) whether, if so alleged by the employee organization, the appropriate public employer or its representatives engaged in such acts of extreme provocation as to detract from the responsibility of the employee organization for the strike. In determining the ability of the employee organization to pay the fine imposed, the court shall consider both the income and the assets of such employee organization.

(b) In the event membership dues and sums equivalent to dues are collected by the public employer as provided respectively in paragraph (b) of subdivision one and subdivision three of section two hundred eight of the civil service law, the books and records of such public employer shall be prima facie evidence of the amount so collected.

(c) (i) An employee organization appealing an adjudication and fine for criminal contempt imposed pursuant to subdivision two of this section, shall not be required to pay such fine until such appeal is finally determined.

(ii) The court to which such an appeal is taken shall, on motion of any party thereto, grant a preference in the hearing thereof.

3. (a) Where a union or hospital wilfully disobeys a lawful mandate of a court of record, or wilfully offers resistance to such lawful mandate, in a case involving or growing out of a violation of section seven hundred thirteen of the labor law, the punishment for each day that such contempt persists may be by a fine fixed in the discretion of the court. In fixing the amount of such fine, the court shall consider all the facts and circumstances directly related to the contempt, including, but not limited to: (i) the extent of the wilful defiance of, or resistance to, the court's mandate (ii) the impact of the strike or lockout on the public health, safety and welfare of the community and (iii) the ability of the union or hospital to pay the fine imposed; and the court may consider (i) the refusal of the union or hospital, or the representatives thereof, to submit to or comply with, the fact-finding and arbitration procedures provided in section seven hundred sixteen of the labor law. In determining the ability of the union or hospital to pay the fine imposed, the court shall consider both the income and the assets of such union or hospital.

(b) A union or hospital appealing an adjudication and fine for criminal contempt imposed pursuant to this subdivision, shall not be required to pay such fine until such appeal is finally determined. The court to which such an appeal is taken shall, on motion of any party thereto, grant a preference in the hearing thereof.

(c) As used in this subdivision, "union" shall mean any labor organization or company union as defined in section seven hundred one of the labor law, and "hospital" shall mean any non-profit-making hospital or residential care center as defined in that section.

4. Where any person wilfully disobeys a lawful mandate of the supreme court issued pursuant to subdivision twelve of section sixty-three of the executive law, the punishment for each day that such contempt persists may be by a fine fixed in the discretion of the court, but not to exceed five thousand dollars per day. In fixing the amount of the fine, the court shall consider all the facts and circumstances directly related to the contempt, including, but not limited to: (i) the extent of the wilful defiance of or resistance to the court's mandate, (ii) the amount of gain obtained by the wilful disobedience of the mandate, and (iii) the effect upon the public of the wilful disobedience.

5. Where any member of the news media as defined in subdivision two of section two hundred eighteen of this chapter, willfully disobeys a lawful mandate of a court issued pursuant to such section, the punishment for each day that such contempt persists may be by a fine fixed in the discretion of the court, but not to exceed five thousand dollars per day or imprisonment, not exceeding thirty days, in the jail of the county where the court is sitting or both, in the discretion of the court. In fixing the amount of the fine, the court shall consider all the facts and circumstances directly related to the contempt, including, but not limited to: (i) the extent of the willful defiance of or resistance to the

court's mandate, (ii) the amount of gain obtained by the willful disobedience of the mandate, and (iii) the effect upon the public and the parties to the proceeding of the willful disobedience.

§752. Requisites of commitment for criminal contempt; review of certain mandates.

Where a person is committed for contempt, as prescribed in section seven hundred fifty-one, the particular circumstances of his offense must be set forth in the mandate of commitment. Such mandate, punishing a person summarily for a contempt committed in the immediate view and presence of the court, is reviewable by a proceeding under article seventy-eight of the civil practice law and rules.

§753. Power of courts to punish for civil contempts.

A. A court of record has power to punish, by fine and imprisonment, or either, a neglect or violation of duty, or other misconduct, by which a right or remedy of a party to a civil action or special proceeding, pending in the court may be defeated, impaired, impeded, or prejudiced, in any of the following cases:

1. An attorney, counsellor, clerk, sheriff, coroner, or other person, in any manner duly selected or appointed to perform a judicial or ministerial service, for a misbehavior in his office or trust, or for a wilful neglect or violation of duty therein; or for disobedience to a lawful mandate of the court, or of a judge thereof, or of an officer authorized to perform the duties of such a judge.

2. A party to the action or special proceeding, for putting in fictitious bail or a fictitious surety, or for any deceit or abuse of a mandate or proceeding of the court.

3. A party to the action or special proceeding, an attorney, counsellor, or other person, for the non-payment of a sum of money, ordered or adjudged by the court to be paid, in a case where by law execution can not be awarded for the collection of such sum except as otherwise specifically provided by the civil practice law and rules; or for any other disobedience to a lawful mandate of the court.

4. A person, for assuming to be an attorney or counsellor, or other officer of the court, and acting as such without authority; for rescuing any property or person in the custody of an officer, by virtue of a mandate of the court; for unlawfully detaining, or fraudulently and wilfully preventing, or disabling from attending or testifying, a witness, or a party to the action or special proceeding, while going to, remaining at, or returning from, the sitting where it is noticed for trial or hearing; and for any other unlawful interference with the proceedings therein.

5. A person subpoenaed as a witness, for refusing or neglecting to obey the subpoena, or to attend, or to be sworn, or to answer as a witness.

6. A person duly notified to attend as a juror, at a term of the court, for improperly conversing with a party to an action or special proceeding, to be tried at that term, or with any other person, in relation to the merits of that action or special proceeding; or for receiving a communication from any person, in relation to the merits of such an action or special proceeding, without immediately disclosing the same to the court; or a person who attends and acts or attempts to act as a juror in the place and stead of a person who has been duly notified to attend.

7. An inferior magistrate, or a judge or other officer of an inferior court, for proceeding, contrary to law, in a cause or matter, which has been removed from his jurisdiction to the court inflicting the punishment; or for disobedience to a lawful order or other mandate of the latter court.

8. In any other case, where an attachment or any other proceeding to punish for a contempt, has been usually adopted and practiced in a court of record, to enforce a civil remedy of a party to an action or special proceeding in that court, or to protect the right of a party.

B. A court not of record has such power to punish for a civil contempt as is specifically granted to it by statute.

§753-a. Contempts in cases involving or growing out of labor disputes.

1. Notwithstanding any inconsistent provision of law, where the alleged contempt is punishable under section seven hundred fifty and/or section seven hundred fifty-three and arises out of any failure or refusal to obey any mandate of a court contained in or incidental to an injunction order granted by such court in any case involving or growing out of a labor dispute, no punishment, prescribed by either of such sections, shall be meted out except after a trial by jury to which the defendant shall be entitled as a matter of right; provided, however, that this section shall not apply to any alleged contempt of such an injunction order committed in the presence of the court.

2. As used in this section and in subdivision three of section 215.50 of the penal law:

(a) A case shall be held to involve or to grow out of a labor dispute when the case involves persons who are engaged in the same industry, trade, craft or occupation; or who are employees of one employer; or who are members of the same or an affiliated organization of employers or employees; whether such dispute is between one or more employers or associations of employers and one or more employees or associations of employees; between one or more employers or associations of employers and one or more employers or associations of employers; or between one or more employees or associations of employees and one or more employees or associations of employees; or when the case involves any conflicting or competing interests in a "labor dispute" (as hereinafter defined) of "persons participating or interested" therein (as hereinafter defined).

(b) The term "labor dispute" includes any controversy concerning terms or conditions of employment, or concerning the association or representation of persons in negotiating, fixing, maintaining, changing or seeking to arrange terms or conditions of employment, or concerning employment relations, or any other controversy arising out of the respective interests of employer and employee, regardless of whether or not the disputants stand in the relation of employer and employee.

(c) A person or association shall be held to be a person participating or interested in a labor dispute if relief is sought against him or it and if he or it is engaged in the industry, trade, craft or occupation in which such dispute occurs, or is a member, officer or agent of any association of employers or employees engaged in such industry, trade, craft or occupation.

§754. Special proceeding to punish for contempt punishable civilly.

Sections seven hundred and fifty, seven hundred and fifty-one, and seven hundred and fifty-two, do not extend to a special proceeding to punish a person in a case specified in section seven hundred and fifty-three. In a case specified in section seven hundred and fifty-three, or in any other case where it is specially prescribed by law, that a court of record, or a judge thereof, or a referee appointed by the court, has power to punish, by fine and imprisonment, or either, or generally as a contempt, a neglect or violation of duty, or other misconduct; and a right or remedy of a party to a civil action or special proceeding pending in the court, or before the judge or the referee, may be defeated, impaired, impeded, or prejudiced thereby, the offense must be punished as prescribed in the following sections of this article.

§755. When punishment may be summary.

Where the offense is committed in the immediate view and presence of the court, or of the judge or referee, upon a trial or hearing, it may be punished summarily. For that purpose, an order must be made by the court, judge, or referee, stating the facts which constitute the offense and which bring the case within the provisions of this section, and plainly and specifically prescribing the punishment to be inflicted therefor. Such order is reviewable by a proceeding under article seventy-eight of the civil practice law and rules.

§756. Application to punish for contempt; procedure.

An application to punish for a contempt punishable civilly may be commenced by notice of motion returnable before the court or judge authorized to punish for the offense, or by an order of such court or judge requiring the accused to show cause before it, or him, at a time and place therein specified, why the accused should not be punished for the alleged offense. The application shall be noticed, heard and determined in accordance with the procedure for a motion on notice in an action in such court, provided, however, that, except as provided in section fifty-two hundred fifty of the civil practice law and rules or unless otherwise ordered by the court, the moving papers shall be served no less than ten and no more than thirty days before the time at which the application is noticed to be heard. The application shall contain on its face a notice that the purpose of the hearing is to punish the accused for a contempt of court, and that such punishment may consist of fine or imprisonment, or both, according to law together with the following legend printed or type written in a size equal to at least eight point bold type:

WARNING:
YOUR FAILURE TO APPEAR
IN COURT MAY RESULT IN
YOUR IMMEDIATE ARREST
AND IMPRISONMENT FOR
CONTEMPT OF COURT.

§757. Application to punish for contempt committed before referee.

Where the offense is committed upon the trial of an issue referred to a referee appointed by the court, or consists of a witness's non-attendance, or refusal to be sworn or testify, before him, the application prescribed in this section may be made returnable before him or before the court. The application shall contain on its face a notice that the purpose of the hearing is to punish the accused for a contempt of court, and that such punishment may consist of fine or imprisonment, or both, according to law.

§758. Notice to delinquent officer to show cause.

Where it is prescribed by law, or by the rules of civil practice, that a notice may be served in behalf of a party, upon a sheriff or other person, requiring him to return a mandate, delivered to him, or to show cause, at a term of a court, why he should not be punished, or why an attachment should not be issued against him, for a contempt of the court; the party, in whose behalf the notice is served, may, at the time specified therein, file with the clerk, proof, by affidavit or other written evidence, of the delivery of the mandate to the accused; of the default or other act, upon the occurrence of which, he was entitled to serve the notice; of the service of the notice; and of the failure to comply therewith. Thereupon the proceedings are the same, as where an order to show cause is made, and it, and a copy of the affidavits upon which it is granted, are served upon the accused.

§773.   Amount of fine.

If an actual loss or injury has been caused to a party to an action or special proceeding, by reason of the misconduct proved against the offender, and the case is not one where it is specially prescribed by law, that an action may be maintained to recover damages for the loss or injury, a fine, sufficient to indemnify the aggrieved party, must be imposed upon the offender, and collected, and paid over to the aggrieved party, under the direction of the court. The payment and acceptance of such a fine constitute a bar to an action by the aggrieved party, to recover damages for the loss or injury.

Where it is not shown that such an actual loss or injury has been caused, a fine may be imposed, not exceeding the amount of the complainant's costs and expenses, and two hundred and fifty dollars in addition thereto, and must be collected and paid, in like manner. A corporation may be fined as prescribed in this section.

If a fine is imposed to punish an offense committed with respect to an enforcement procedure under the civil practice law and rules or pursuant to section two hundred forty-five of the domestic relations law, and it has not been shown that such an actual loss or injury has been caused and the defendant has not appeared upon the return of the application, the order imposing fine, if any, shall include a provision granting the offender leave to purge himself of the contempt within ten days after personal service of the order by appearing and satisfying the court that he is unable to pay the fine or, in the discretion of the court, by giving an undertaking in a sum to be fixed by the court conditioned upon payment of the fine plus costs and expenses and his appearance and performance of the act or duty, the omission of which constitutes the misconduct for which he is to be punished. The order may also include a provision committing the offender to prison until the fine plus costs and expenses are paid, or until he is discharged according to law. Upon a certified copy of the order imposing fine, together with proof by affidavit that more than ten days have elapsed since personal service thereof upon the offender, and that the fine plus costs and expenses has not been paid, the court may issue without notice a warrant directed to the sheriff or other enforcement officer of any jurisdiction in which the offender may be found. The warrant shall command such officer to arrest the offender forthwith and bring him before the court, or a judge thereof, to be committed or for such other disposition as the court in its discretion shall direct.

This page intentionally left blank.

ARTICLE 9
Hospitalization of the Mentally Ill

§9.01 Definitions.

As used in this article:

"in need of care and treatment" means that a person has a mental illness for which in-patient care and treatment in a hospital is appropriate.

"in need of involuntary care and treatment" means that a person has a mental illness for which care and treatment as a patient in a hospital is essential to such person's welfare and whose judgment is so impaired that he is unable to understand the need for such care and treatment.

"likelihood to result in serious harm" or "likely to result in serious harm" means (a) a substantial risk of physical harm to the person as manifested by threats of or attempts at suicide or serious bodily harm or other conduct demonstrating that the person is dangerous to himself or herself, or (b) a substantial risk of physical harm to other persons as manifested by homicidal or other violent behavior by which others are placed in reasonable fear of serious physical harm.

"need for retention" means that a person who has been admitted to a hospital pursuant to this article is in need of involuntary care and treatment in a hospital for a further period.

"record" of a patient shall consist of admission, transfer or retention papers and orders, and accompanying data required by this article and by the regulations of the commissioner.

"director of community services" means the director of community services for the mentally disabled appointed pursuant to article forty-one of this chapter.

"qualified psychiatrist" means a physician licensed to practice medicine in New York state who: (a) is a diplomate of the American board of psychiatry and neurology or is eligible to be certified by that board; or (b) is certified by the American osteopathic board of neurology and psychiatry or is eligible to be certified by that board.

§9.03   Admission to a hospital.

Unless otherwise specifically provided for by statute, a mentally ill person shall be admitted to a hospital as an in-patient only pursuant to the provisions of this article, except that chemically dependent patients may be admitted to chemical dependence facilities operated by such hospitals under contract or agreement with the office of alcoholism and substance abuse services in accordance with the provisions of article twenty-two of this chapter. The section of the mental hygiene law under which a patient is admitted or under which any change of legal status is subsequently effected shall be stated in the patient's record.

§9.05   Examining physicians and medical certificates.

(a) A person is disqualified from acting as an examining physician in the following cases:

1. if he is a relative of the person applying for the admission or of the person alleged to be mentally ill.

2. if he is a manager, trustee, visitor, proprietor, officer, director, or stockholder of the hospital in which the patient is hospitalized or to which it is proposed to admit such person, except as otherwise provided in this chapter, or if he has any pecuniary interest, directly or indirectly, in such hospital, provided that receipt of fees, privileges, or compensation for treating or examining patients in such hospital shall not be deemed to be a pecuniary interest.

3. if he is on the staff of a proprietary facility to which it is proposed to admit such person.

(b) A certificate, as required by this article, must show that the person is mentally ill and shall be based on an examination of the person alleged to be mentally ill made within ten days prior to the date of admission. The date of the certificate shall be the date of such examination. All certificates shall contain the facts and circumstances upon which the judgment of the physicians is based and shall show that the condition of the person examined is such that he needs involuntary care and treatment in a hospital and such other information as the commissioner may by regulation require.

§9.07   Notice to all patients of their rights and of the availability of the mental hygiene legal service.

(a) Immediately upon the admission of any patient to a hospital or upon his conversion to a different status, the director shall inform the patient in writing of his status, including the section of this chapter under which he is hospitalized, and of his rights under this article, including the availability of the mental hygiene legal service. At any time thereafter, upon the request of the patient or of anyone on the patient's behalf, the patient shall be permitted to communicate with the mental hygiene legal service and avail himself of the facilities thereof.

(b) The director of every hospital shall post copies of a notice, in a form and manner to be determined by the commissioner, at places throughout the hospital where such notice will be conspicuous and visible to all patients, stating the following:

1. the availability of the mental hygiene legal service.

2. a general statement of the rights of patients under the various admission or retention provisions of this article.

3. the right of the patient to communicate with the director, the board of visitors, the commissioner of mental health, and the mental hygiene legal service.

§9.09   Notices to mental hygiene legal service concerning minors.

When any person under the age of eighteen years is admitted to or is converted from one admission status to another in any hospital, written notice of such admission or conversion shall be given to the mental hygiene legal service within three days thereof and such notice shall specify the age of and admission procedure applicable to such person. No such person shall be transferred to any other hospital without the prior consent of such person and the prior written consent of his parent or legal guardian unless three days prior written notice of such proposed transfer is given to the mental hygiene legal service and an opportunity is afforded to the service to see such person and to review the proposed transfer. Immediately upon release or transfer of any such person, the director of the hospital shall give the mental hygiene legal service written notice thereof.

*§9.11   Patients' records.

Except as to informal patients and patients admitted pursuant to section 9.39 or 9.40, the director of a hospital shall within five days, excluding Sunday and holidays, after the admission of any patient forward to the mental hygiene legal service a record of such patient and shall simultaneously forward to the department such information from the record as the commissioner by regulation shall require. Such information from the record in the department shall be accessible only in the manner set forth in section 33.13.

Effective until July 1, 2020

*§9.11   Patients' records.

Except as to informal patients and patients admitted pursuant to section 9.39, the director of a hospital shall within five days, excluding Sunday and holidays, after the admission of any patient forward to the mental hygiene legal service a record of such patient and shall simultaneously forward to the department such information from the record as the commissioner by regulation shall require. Such information from the record in the department shall be accessible only in the manner set forth in section 33.13.   *Effective July 1, 2020*

§9.13   Voluntary admissions.

(a) The director of any hospital may receive as a voluntary patient any suitable person in need of care and treatment, who voluntarily makes written application therefor. If the person is under sixteen years of age, the person may be received as a voluntary patient only on the application of the parent, legal guardian, or next-of-kin of such person, or, subject to the terms of any court order or any instrument executed pursuant to section three hundred eighty-four-a of the social services law, a social services official or authorized agency with care and custody of such person pursuant to the social services law, the director of the division for youth, acting in accordance with section five hundred nine of the executive law, or a person or entity having custody of the person pursuant to an order issued pursuant to section seven hundred fifty-six or one thousand fifty-five of the family court act. If the person is over sixteen and under eighteen years of age, the director may, in his discretion, admit such person either as a voluntary patient on his own application or on the application of the person's parent, legal guardian, next-of-kin, or, subject to the terms of any court order or any instrument executed pursuant to section three hundred eighty-four-a of the social services law, a social services official or authorized agency with care and custody of such person pursuant to the social services law, the director of the division for youth, acting in accordance with section five hundred nine of the executive law, provided that such person knowingly and voluntarily consented to such application in accordance with such section, or a person or entity having custody of the person pursuant to an order issued pursuant to section seven hundred fifty-six or one thousand fifty-five of the family court act.

(b) If such voluntary patient gives notice in writing to the director of the patient's desire to leave the hospital, the director shall promptly release the patient; provided, however, that if there are reasonable grounds for belief that the patient may be in need of involuntary care and treatment, the director may retain the patient for a period not to exceed seventy-two hours from receipt of such notice. Before the expiration of such seventy-two hour period, the director shall either release the patient or apply to the supreme court or the county court in the county where the hospital is located for an order authorizing the involuntary retention of such patient. The application and proceedings in connection therewith shall be in the manner prescribed in this article for a court authorization to retain an involuntary patient, except that notice of such application shall be served forthwith and, if a hearing be demanded, the date for hearing to be fixed by the court shall be at a time not later than three days from the date such notice has been received by the court. If it be determined by the court that the patient is mentally ill and in need of retention for involuntary care and treatment in the hospital, the court shall forthwith issue an order authorizing the retention of such patient for care and treatment in the hospital, or, if requested by the patient, his guardian, or committee, in such other non-public hospital as may be within the financial means of the patient, for a period not exceeding sixty days from the date of such order. Further application for retention of the patient for periods not exceeding six months, one year, and two year periods thereafter, respectively, may thereafter be made in accordance with the provisions of this article. In the case of a patient under eighteen years of age, such notice requesting release of the patient may be given by the patient, by the person who made application for his admission, by a person of equal or closer relationship, or by the mental hygiene legal service. If such notice be given by any other person, the director may in his discretion refuse to discharge the patient and in the event of such refusal, such other person or the mental hygiene legal service may apply to the supreme court or to a county court for the release of the patient.

§9.15 Informal admissions.

The director of any hospital approved by the commissioner for such purpose may receive therein as an informal patient any suitable person in need of care and treatment requesting admission thereto. Such person may be admitted as a patient without making formal or written application therefor and any such patient shall be free to leave such hospital at any time after such admission.

§9.17 Voluntary and informal admissions; suitability.

(a) In order for a person to be suitable for admission to a hospital as a voluntary or informal patient, or for conversion to such status he must be notified of and have the ability to understand the following:

1. that the hospital to which he is requesting admission is a hospital for the mentally ill.

2. that he is making an application for admission.

3. the nature of the voluntary or informal status, as the case may be and the provisions governing release or conversion to involuntary status.

(b) The department shall have the power to examine the patients admitted pursuant to this section and determine if they belong to the voluntary or informal class. If it be determined that any such patient does not belong to the voluntary or informal class, the department shall determine whether the patient shall be discharged or whether procedures shall be commenced for the admission of such patient to a hospital pursuant to other sections of this article. The decision of the department shall be forthwith complied with by the director or person in charge of any such hospital. Any failure to conform to the requirements of this section shall be considered a sufficient cause for revocation of an operating certificate theretofore issued to a hospital.

§9.19 Voluntary and informal admissions; notices.

The director shall cause all patients admitted as voluntary or informal patients to be informed once during each one hundred twenty days of hospitalization of their status and rights, including their right to avail themselves of the facilities of the mental hygiene legal service. At the time of such periodic notification, the written consent of a patient to his continued stay as a voluntary or informal patient shall be obtained and a copy thereof shall be given to the mental hygiene legal service.

§9.21 Voluntary and informal admissions; encouragement of.

(a) It shall be the duty of all state and local officers having duties to perform relating to the mentally ill to encourage any person suitable therefor and in need of care and treatment for mental illness to apply for admission as a voluntary or informal patient.

(b) No requirement shall be made by rule, regulation, or otherwise as a condition to admission or retention that any person applying for admission shall have the legal capacity to contract.

(c) A person requesting admission to a hospital, who is suitable for admission on a voluntary or informal status, shall be admitted only on such a voluntary or informal status. The hospital shall, in such case, have the discretion to admit the person on either such status, except that, if the person specifically requests admission on an informal status and is suitable therefor, he shall be admitted only on such informal status.

§9.23 Voluntary and informal admissions; conversion to.

(a) Nothing contained in this article shall be construed to prohibit any director from converting, and it shall be his duty to convert, the admission of any involuntary patient suitable and willing to apply therefor to a voluntary status. The mental hygiene legal service shall be given notice of every conversion from an involuntary status to a voluntary status.

(b) Any patient converted from an involuntary status to a voluntary status shall have the right to a judicial hearing before the supreme court or a county court on the questions of his suitability for such conversion and on his willingness to be so converted. The procedure for requesting such a hearing, except as to time limitations and questions to be determined, shall be pursuant to subdivisions (a) and (b) of section 9.31 of this article.

§9.25 Voluntary and informal admissions; review of status.

(a) No voluntary or informal patient, whether admitted on such status or converted thereto, shall be continued in such status for a period beyond twelve months from the date of commencement of such status or beyond twelve months from the effective date of this statute, whichever is later, unless the suitability of such patient to remain in such status and his willingness to so remain have been reviewed. The director shall review the suitability of such patient to remain in such status, and the mental hygiene legal service shall review the willingness of such patient to remain in such status. Notice of the determination of the patient's suitability made by the director shall be given to the mental hygiene legal service. If the mental hygiene legal service finds that there is any ground to doubt the director's determination of the suitability of such patient to remain in a voluntary or informal status or the willingness of the patient to so remain, it shall make an application upon notice to the patient and the director of the hospital, for a court order determining those questions. In any such proceeding, the patient or someone on his behalf or the mental hygiene legal service may request a hearing. If the mental hygiene legal service finds no grounds to doubt the determination of the director as to the suitability, or the willingness of the patient to continue in a voluntary or informal status, it shall so certify and the patient may be continued in the hospital in such status. A copy of such certification of review shall be filed in the patient's record.

(b) If an application for a court order has been made and a hearing is requested, the provisions governing hearings contained in section 9.31 of this article shall be applicable.

(c) If an application for a court order has been made, the court, in determining the proceeding, may approve the continued hospitalization of the patient as a voluntary or informal patient or, if the court finds that the patient is not suitable or willing to continue as a voluntary or informal patient, it may order the discharge of the patient or make such other order as it may deem appropriate in the circumstances.

(d) Prior to the termination of twelve months from the date of the certification on such first review by the mental hygiene legal service or, if an application for a court order has been made, from the date of the first order and, thereafter, prior to the termination of twelve months from any subsequent certification or subsequent order, as the case may be, the director and the mental hygiene legal service shall conduct another review of the patient's suitability and willingness to remain as a voluntary or informal patient as set forth in the foregoing subdivisions.

§9.27 Involuntary admission on medical certification.

(a) The director of a hospital may receive and retain therein as a patient any person alleged to be mentally ill and in need of involuntary care and treatment upon the certificates of two examining physicians, accompanied by an application for the admission of such person. The examination may be conducted jointly but each examining physician shall execute a separate certificate.

(b) Such application must have been executed within ten days prior to such admission. It may be executed by any one of the following:

1. any person with whom the person alleged to be mentally ill resides.

2. the father or mother, husband or wife, brother or sister, or the child of any such person or the nearest available relative.

3. the committee of such person.

4. an officer of any public or well recognized charitable institution or agency or home, including but not limited to the superintendent of a correctional facility, as such term is defined in paragraph (a) of subdivision four of section two of the correction law, in whose institution the person alleged to be mentally ill resides and the designee authorized by the commissioner of the department of corrections and community supervision responsible for community supervision in the region where such person alleged to be mentally ill has been released to any form of supervision following incarceration.

5. the director of community services or social services official, as defined in the social services law, of the city or county in which any such person may be.

6. the director of the hospital or of a general hospital, as defined in article twenty-eight of the public health law, in which the patient is hospitalized.

7. the director or person in charge of a facility providing care to alcoholics, or substance abusers or substance dependent persons.

8. the director of the division for youth, acting in accordance with the provisions of section five hundred nine of the executive law.

9. subject to the terms of any court order or any instrument executed pursuant to section three hundred eighty-four-a of the social services law, a social services official or authorized agency which has, pursuant to the social services law, care and custody or guardianship and custody of a child over the age of sixteen.

10. subject to the terms of any court order a person or entity having custody of a child pursuant to an order issued pursuant to section seven hundred fifty-six or one thousand fifty-five of the family court act.

11. a qualified psychiatrist who is either supervising the treatment of or treating such person for a mental illness in a facility licensed or operated by the office of mental health.

(c) Such application shall contain a statement of the facts upon which the allegation of mental illness and need for care and treatment are based and shall be executed under penalty of perjury but shall not require the signature of a notary public thereon.

(d) Before an examining physician completes the certificate of examination of a person for involuntary care and treatment, he shall consider alternative forms of care and treatment that might be adequate to provide for the person's needs without requiring involuntary hospitalization. If the examining physician knows that the person he is examining for involuntary care and treatment has been under prior treatment, he shall, insofar as possible, consult with the physician or psychologist furnishing such prior treatment prior to completing his certificate. Nothing in this section shall prohibit or invalidate any involuntary admission made in accordance with the provisions of this chapter.

(e) The director of the hospital where such person is brought shall cause such person to be examined forthwith by a physician who shall be a member of the psychiatric staff of such hospital other than the original examining physicians whose certificate or certificates accompanied the application and, if such person is found to be in need of involuntary care and treatment, he may be admitted thereto as a patient as herein provided.

(f) Following admission to a hospital, no patient may be sent to another hospital by any form of involuntary admission unless the mental hygiene legal service has been given notice thereof.

(g) Applications for involuntary admission of patients to residential treatment facilities for children and youth or transfer of involuntarily admitted patients to such facilities shall be reviewed by the pre-admission certification committee serving such facility in accordance with section 9.51 of this article.

(h) If a person is examined and determined to be mentally ill, the fact that such person suffers from alcohol or substance abuse shall not preclude commitment under this section.

(i) After an application for the admission of a person has been completed and both physicians have examined such person and separately certified that he or she is mentally ill and in need of involuntary care and treatment in a hospital, either physician is authorized to request peace officers, when acting pursuant to their special duties, or police officers, who are members of an authorized police department or force or of a sheriff's department, to take into custody and transport such person to a hospital for determination by the director whether such person qualifies for admission pursuant to this section. Upon the request of either physician an ambulance service, as defined by subdivision two of section three thousand one of the public health law, is authorized to transport such person to a hospital for determination by the director whether such person qualifies for admission pursuant to this section.

§9.29   Involuntary admission on medical certification; notice of admission to patients and others.

(a) The director shall cause written notice of a person's involuntary admission on an application supported by medical certification to be given forthwith to the mental hygiene legal service.

(b) The director shall cause written notice of the admission of such person, including such person's rights under this article, to be given personally or by mail not later than five days, excluding Sunday and holidays, after such admission to the following:

1. the nearest relative of the person alleged to be mentally ill, other than the applicant, if there be any such person known to the director.

2. as many as three additional persons, if designated in writing to receive such notice by the person so admitted.

§9.31 Involuntary admission on medical certification; patient's right to a hearing.

(a) If, at any time prior to the expiration of sixty days from the date of involuntary admission of a patient on an application supported by medical certification, he or any relative or friend or the mental hygiene legal service gives notice in writing to the director of request for hearing on the question of need for involuntary care and treatment, a hearing shall be held as herein provided. The patient or person requesting a hearing on behalf of the patient may designate the county where the hearing shall be held, which shall be either in the county where the hospital is located, the county of the patient's residence, or the county in which the hospital to which the patient was first admitted is located. Such hearing shall be held in the county so designated, subject to application by any interested party, including the director, for change of venue to any other county because of the convenience of parties or witnesses or the condition of the patient upon notice to the persons required to be served with notice of the patient's initial admission.

(b) It shall be the duty of the director upon receiving notice of such request for hearing to forward forthwith a copy of such notice with a record of the patient to the supreme court or the county court in the county designated by the applicant, if one be designated, or if no designation be made, then to the supreme court or the county court in the county where such hospital is located. A copy of such notice and record shall also be given the mental hygiene legal service.

(c) The court which receives such notice shall fix the date of such hearing at a time not later than five days from the date such notice is received by the court and cause the patient, any other person requesting the hearing, the director, the mental hygiene legal service, and such other persons as the court may determine to be advised of such date. Upon such date, or upon such other date to which the proceeding may be adjourned, the court shall hear testimony and examine the person alleged to be mentally ill, if it be deemed advisable in or out of court. If it be determined that the patient is in need of retention, the court shall deny the application for the patient's release. If the patient is in a psychiatric hospital maintained by a political subdivision of the state or in a general hospital the court, upon notice to the patient and the mental hygiene legal service and an opportunity to be heard, may order the patient transferred to the jurisdiction of the department for retention in a hospital operated by the state designated by the commissioner or to a private facility having an appropriate operating certificate for retention therein for the balance of the period for which the hospital is authorized to retain the patient. If it appears, however, that the relatives of the patient or a committee of his person are willing and able properly to care for him at some place other than a hospital, then, upon their written consent, the court may order the transfer of the patient to the care and custody of such relatives or such committee. If it be determined that the patient is not mentally ill or not in need of retention, the court shall order the release of the patient.

(d) If the court shall order the release of the patient, such patient shall forthwith be released.

(e) The department or the director of the hospital authorized to retain or receive and retain such patient, as the case may be, shall be immediately furnished with a copy of the order of the court and, if a transfer is ordered, shall immediately make provisions for the transfer of such patient.

(f) The papers in any proceeding under this article which are filed with the county clerk shall be sealed and shall be exhibited only to the parties to the proceeding or someone properly interested, upon order of the court.

§9.33　Court authorization to retain an involuntary patient.

(a) If the director shall determine that a patient admitted upon an application supported by medical certification, for whom there is no court order authorizing retention for a specified period, is in need of retention and if such patient does not agree to remain in such hospital as a voluntary patient, the director shall apply to the supreme court or the county court in the county where the hospital is located for an order authorizing continued retention. Such application shall be made no later than sixty days from the date of involuntary admission on application supported by medical certification or thirty days from the date of an order denying an application for patient's release pursuant to section 9.31, whichever is later; and the hospital is authorized to retain the patient for such further period during which the hospital is authorized to make such application or during which the application may be pending. The director shall cause written notice of such application to be given the patient and a copy thereof shall be given personally or by mail to the persons required by this article to be served with notice of such patient's initial admission and to the mental hygiene legal service. Such notice shall state that a hearing may be requested and that failure to make such a request within five days, excluding Sunday and holidays, from the date that the notice was given to the patient will permit the entry without a hearing of an order authorizing retention.

(b) If no request is made for a hearing on behalf of the patient within five days, excluding Sunday and holidays, from the date such notice of such application was given such patient, and if the mental hygiene legal service has not requested a hearing, the court receiving the application may, if satisfied that the patient requires continued retention for care and treatment or transfer and continued retention, immediately issue an order authorizing continued retention of such patient in such hospital for a period not to exceed six months from the date of the order or, if such patient is in a psychiatric hospital operated by a political subdivision of the state or in a general hospital, such order may direct the transfer of such patient to the jurisdiction of the department for retention in a hospital operated by the state or to a private facility having an appropriate operating certificate, to be retained therein for a period not to exceed six months from the date of such order.

(c) Upon the demand of the patient or of anyone on his behalf or upon request of the mental hygiene legal service, the court shall, or may on its own motion, fix a date for the hearing of the application, in like manner as is provided for hearings in section 9.31. The provisions of such section shall apply to the procedure for obtaining and holding a hearing and to the granting or refusal to grant an order of retention by the court, except that if the patient has already had a hearing, he shall not have the right to designate initially the county in which the hearing shall be held.

(d) If the director of a hospital, in which a patient is retained pursuant to the foregoing subdivisions of this section, shall determine that the condition of such patient requires his further retention in a hospital, he shall, if such patient does not agree to remain in such hospital as a voluntary patient, apply during the period of retention authorized by the last order of the court to the supreme court or the county court in the county where the hospital is located for an order authorizing further continued retention of such patient. The procedures for obtaining any order pursuant to this subdivision shall be in accordance with the provisions of the foregoing subdivisions of this section; provided that the patient or anyone on his behalf or the mental hygiene legal service may request that the patient be brought personally before the court, in which case the court shall not grant an order for periods of one year or longer unless such patient shall have appeared personally before the court. The period for continued retention pursuant to the first order obtained under this subdivision shall authorize further continued retention of the patient for not more than one year from the date of the order. The period for the further continued retention of the patient authorized by any subsequent order under this subdivision shall be for periods not to exceed two years each from the date of the order.

§9.35   Review of court authorization to retain an involuntary patient.

If a person who has been denied release or whose retention, continued retention, or transfer and continued retention has been authorized pursuant to this article, or any relative or friend in his behalf, be dissatisfied with any such order he may, within thirty days after the making of any such order, obtain a rehearing and a review of the proceedings already had and of such order upon a petition to a justice of the supreme court other than the judge or justice presiding over the court making such order. Such justice shall cause a jury to be summoned and shall try the question of the mental illness and the need for retention of the patient so authorized to be retained. Any such patient or the person applying on his behalf for such review may waive the trial of the fact by a jury and consent in writing to trial of such fact by the court. No such petition for rehearing and review shall be made by anyone other than the person so authorized to be retained or the father, mother, husband, wife, or child of such person, unless the petitioner shall have first obtained the leave of the court upon good cause shown. If the verdict of the jury, or the decision of the court when jury trial has been waived, be that such person is not mentally ill or is not in need of retention the justice shall forthwith discharge him, but if the verdict of the jury, or the decision of the court where a jury trial has been waived, be that such person is mentally ill and in need of retention the justice shall certify that fact and make an order authorizing continued retention under the original order. Such order shall be presented, at the time of authorization of continued retention of such mentally ill person, to, and filed with, the director of the hospital in which the mentally ill person is authorized to be retained, and a copy thereof shall be forwarded to the department by such director and filed in the office thereof. Proceedings under the order shall not be stayed pending an appeal therefrom, except upon an order of a justice of the supreme court, made upon a notice and after a hearing, with provisions made therein for such temporary care or confinement of the alleged mentally ill person as may be deemed necessary.

§9.37   Involuntary admission on certificate of a director of community services or his designee.

*(a) The director of a hospital, upon application by a director of community services or an examining physician duly designated by him or her, may receive and care for in such hospital as a patient any person who, in the opinion of the director of community services or the director's designee, has a mental illness for which immediate inpatient care and treatment in a hospital is appropriate and which is likely to result in serious harm to himself or herself or others.

The need for immediate hospitalization shall be confirmed by a staff physician of the hospital prior to admission. Within seventy-two hours, excluding Sunday and holidays, after such admission, if such patient is to be retained for care and treatment beyond such time and he or she does not agree to remain in such hospital as a voluntary patient, the certificate of another examining physician who is a member of the psychiatric staff of the hospital that the patient is in need of involuntary care and treatment shall be filed with the hospital. From the time of his or her admission under this section the retention of such patient for care and treatment shall be subject to the provisions for notice, hearing, review, and judicial approval of continued retention or transfer and continued retention provided by this article for the admission and retention of involuntary patients, provided that, for the purposes of such provisions, the date of admission of the patient shall be deemed to be the date when the patient was first received in the hospital under this section.

Effective until July 1, 2020

*(a) The director of a hospital, upon application by a director of community services or an examining physician duly designated by him, may receive and care for in such hospital as a patient any person who, in the opinion of the director of community services or his designee, has a mental illness for which immediate inpatient care and treatment in a hospital is appropriate and which is likely to result in serious harm to himself or others; "likelihood of serious harm" shall mean:

1. substantial risk of physical harm to himself as manifested by threats of or attempts at suicide or serious bodily harm or other conduct demonstrating that he is dangerous to himself, or

2. a substantial risk of physical harm to other persons as manifested by homicidal or other violent behavior by which others are placed in reasonable fear or serious physical harm.

The need for immediate hospitalization shall be confirmed by a staff physician of the hospital prior to admission. Within seventy-two hours, excluding Sunday and holidays, after such admission, if such patient is to be retained for care and treatment beyond such time and he does not agree to remain in such hospital as a voluntary patient, the certificate of another examining physician who is a member of the psychiatric staff of the hospital that the patient is in need of involuntary care and treatment shall be filed with the hospital. From the time of his admission under this section the retention of such patient for care and treatment shall be subject to the provisions for notice, hearing, review, and judicial approval of continued retention or transfer and continued retention provided by this article for the admission and retention of involuntary patients, provided that, for the purposes of such provisions, the date of admission of the patient shall be deemed to be the date when the patient was first received in the hospital under this section.   *Effective July 1, 2020*

(b) The application for admission of a patient pursuant to this section shall be based upon a personal examination by a director of community services or his designee. It shall be in writing and shall be filed with the director of such hospital at the time of the patient's reception, together with a statement in a form prescribed by the commissioner giving such information as he may deem appropriate.

(c) Notwithstanding the provisions of subdivision (b) of this section, in counties with a population of less than two hundred thousand, a director of community services who is a licensed psychologist pursuant to article one hundred fifty-three of the education law or a licensed clinical social worker pursuant to article one hundred fifty-four of the education law but who is not a physician may apply for the admission of a patient pursuant to this section without a medical examination by a designated physician, if a hospital approved by the commissioner pursuant to section 9.39 of this article is not located within thirty miles of the patient, and the director of community services has made a reasonable effort to locate a designated examining physician but such a designee is not immediately available and the director of community services, after personal observation of the person, reasonably believes that he may have a mental illness which is likely to result in serious harm to himself or others and inpatient care and treatment of such person in a hospital may be appropriate. In the event of an application pursuant to this subdivision, a physician of the receiving hospital shall examine the patient and shall not admit the patient unless he or she determines that the patient has a mental illness for which immediate inpatient care and treatment in a hospital is appropriate and which is likely to result in serious harm to himself or others. If the patient is admitted, the need for hospitalization shall be confirmed by another staff physician within twenty-four hours. An application pursuant to this subdivision shall be in writing and shall be filed with the director of such hospital at the time of the patient's reception, together with a statement in a form prescribed by the commissioner giving such information as he may deem appropriate, including a statement of the efforts made by the director of community services to locate a designated examining physician prior to making an application pursuant to this subdivision.

(d) After signing the application, the director of community services or the director's designee shall be authorized and empowered to take into custody, detain, transport, and provide temporary care for any such person. Upon the written request of such director or the director's designee it shall be the duty of peace officers, when acting pursuant to their special duties, or police officers who are members of the state police or of an authorized police department or force or of a sheriff's department to take into custody and transport any such person as requested and directed by such director or designee. Upon the written request of such director or designee, an ambulance service, as defined in subdivision two of section three thousand one of the public health law, is authorized to transport any such person.

(e) Reasonable expenses incurred by the director of community mental hygiene services or his designee for the examination and temporary care of the patient and his transportation to and from the hospital shall be a charge upon the county from which the patient was admitted and shall be paid from any funds available for such purposes.

(f) The provisions of this section shall not be applicable to continue any patient in a hospital who has already been admitted to the hospital under this or any other section of this article.

(g) If a person is examined and determined to be mentally ill the fact that such person suffers from alcohol or substance abuse shall not preclude commitment under this section.

§9.39 Emergency admissions for immediate observation, care, and treatment.

(a) The director of any hospital maintaining adequate staff and facilities for the observation, examination, care, and treatment of persons alleged to be mentally ill and approved by the commissioner to receive and retain patients pursuant to this section may receive and retain therein as a patient for a period of fifteen days any person alleged to have a mental illness for which immediate observation, care, and treatment in a hospital is appropriate and which is likely to result in serious harm to himself or others. "Likelihood to result in serious harm" as used in this article shall mean:

1. substantial risk of physical harm to himself as manifested by threats of or attempts at suicide or serious bodily harm or other conduct demonstrating that he is dangerous to himself, or

2. a substantial risk of physical harm to other persons as manifested by homicidal or other violent behavior by which others are placed in reasonable fear of serious physical harm.

The director shall cause to be entered upon the hospital records the name of the person or persons, if any, who have brought such person to the hospital and the details of the circumstances leading to the hospitalization of such person.

The director shall admit such person pursuant to the provisions of this section only if a staff physician of the hospital upon examination of such person finds that such person qualifies under the requirements of this section. Such person shall not be retained for a period of more than forty-eight hours unless within such period such finding is confirmed after examination by another physician who shall be a member of the psychiatric staff of the hospital. Such person shall be served, at the time of admission, with written notice of his status and rights as a patient under this section. Such notice shall contain the patient's name. At the same time, such notice shall also be given to the mental hygiene legal service and personally or by mail to such person or persons, not to exceed three in number, as may be designated in writing to receive such notice by the person alleged to be mentally ill. If at any time after admission, the patient, any relative, friend, or the mental hygiene legal service gives notice to the director in writing of request for court hearing on the question of need for immediate observation, care, and treatment, a hearing shall be held as herein provided as soon as practicable but in any event not more than five days after such request is received, except that the commencement of such hearing may be adjourned at the request of the patient. It shall be the duty of the director upon receiving notice of such request for hearing to forward forthwith a copy of such notice with a record of the patient to the supreme court or county court in the county where such hospital is located. A copy of such notice and record shall also be given the mental hygiene legal service. The court which receives such notice shall fix the date of such hearing and cause the patient or other person requesting the hearing, the director, the mental hygiene legal service and such other persons as the court may determine to be advised of such date. Upon such date, or upon such other date to which the proceeding may be adjourned, the court shall hear testimony and examine the person alleged to be mentally ill, if it be deemed advisable in or out of court, and shall render a decision in writing that there is reasonable cause to believe that the patient has a mental illness for which immediate inpatient care and treatment in a hospital is appropriate and which is likely to result in serious harm to himself or others. If it be determined that there is such reasonable cause, the court shall forthwith issue an order authorizing the retention of such patient for any such purpose or purposes in the hospital for a period not to exceed fifteen days from the date of admission. Any such order entered by the court shall not be deemed to be an adjudication that the patient is mentally ill, but only a determination that there is reasonable cause to retain the patient for the purposes of this section.

(b) Within fifteen days of arrival at the hospital, if a determination is made that the person is not in need of involuntary care and treatment, he shall be discharged unless he agrees to remain as a voluntary or informal patient. If he is in need of involuntary care and treatment and does not agree to remain as a voluntary or informal patient, he may be retained beyond such fifteen day period only by admission to such hospital or another appropriate hospital pursuant to the provisions governing involuntary admission on application supported by medical certification and subject to the provisions for notice, hearing, review, and judicial approval of retention or transfer and retention governing such admissions, provided that, for the purposes of such provisions, the date of admission of the patient shall be deemed to be the date when the patient was first received under this section. If a hearing has been requested pursuant to the provisions of subdivision (a), the filing of an application for involuntary admission on medical certification shall not delay or prevent the holding of the hearing.

(c) If a person is examined and determined to be mentally ill the fact that such person suffers from alcohol or substance abuse shall not preclude commitment under this section.

*§9.40 Emergency observation, care and treatment in comprehensive psychiatric emergency programs.

(a) The director of any comprehensive psychiatric emergency program may receive and retain therein for a period not to exceed seventy-two hours, any person alleged to have a mental illness for which immediate observation, care and treatment in such program is appropriate and which is likely to result in serious harm to the person or others. The director shall cause to be entered upon the program records the name of the person or persons, if any, who have brought the person alleged to have a mental illness to the program and the details of the circumstances leading the person or persons to bring the person alleged to have a mental illness to the program.

(b) The director shall cause examination of such persons to be initiated by a staff physician of the program as soon as practicable and in any event within six hours after the person is received into the program's emergency room. Such person may be retained for observation, care and treatment and further examination for up to twenty-four hours if, at the conclusion of such examination, such physician determines that such person may have a mental illness for which immediate observation, care and treatment in a comprehensive psychiatric emergency program is appropriate, and which is likely to result in serious harm to the person or others.

(c) No person shall be involuntarily retained in accordance with this section for more than twenty-four hours, unless (i) within that time the determination of the examining staff physician has been confirmed after examination by another physician who is a member of the psychiatric staff of the program and (ii) the person is admitted to an extended observation bed, as such term is defined in section 31.27 of this chapter. At the time of admission to an extended observation bed, such person shall be served with written notice of his status and rights as a patient under this section. Such notice shall contain the patient's name. The notice shall be provided to the same persons and in the manner as if provided pursuant to subdivision (a) of section 9.39 of this article. Written requests for court hearings on the question of need for immediate observation, care and treatment shall be made, and court hearings shall be scheduled and held, in the manner provided pursuant to subdivision (a) of section 9.39 of this article, provided however, if a person is removed or admitted to a hospital pursuant to subdivision (e) or (f) of this section the director of such hospital shall be substituted for the director of the comprehensive psychiatric emergency program in all legal proceedings regarding the continued retention of the person.

(d) If at any time it is determined that the person is no longer in need of immediate observation, care and treatment in accordance with this section and is not in need of involuntary care and treatment in a hospital, such person shall be released without regard to the provisions of section 29.15 of this chapter, unless such person agrees to be admitted to another appropriate hospital as a voluntary or informal patient.

(e) If at any time within the seventy-two hour period it is determined that such person continues to require immediate observation, care and treatment in accordance with this section and such requirement is likely to continue beyond the seventy-two hour period, such person shall be removed within a reasonable period of time to an appropriate hospital authorized to receive and retain patients pursuant to section 9.39 of this article and such person shall be evaluated for admission and, if appropriate, shall be admitted to such hospital in accordance with section 9.39 of this article, except that if the person is admitted, the fifteen day retention period of subdivision (b) of section 9.39 of this article shall be calculated from the time such person was initially registered into the emergency room of the comprehensive psychiatric emergency program. Any person removed to a hospital pursuant to this paragraph shall be removed without regard to the provisions of section 29.11 or 29.15 of this chapter and shall not be considered to have been transferred or discharged to another hospital.

(f) Nothing in this section shall preclude the involuntary admission of a person to an appropriate hospital pursuant to the provisions of this article if at any time during the seventy-two hour period it is determined that the person is in need of involuntary care and treatment in a hospital and the person does not agree to be admitted to a hospital as a voluntary or informal patient. Efforts shall be made to assure that any arrangements for such involuntary admissions in an appropriate hospital shall be made within a reasonable period of time.

(g) If a person is examined and determined to be mentally ill the fact that such person suffers from alcohol or substance abuse shall not preclude receipt or retention under this section.

(h) All time periods referenced in this section shall be calculated from the time such person is initially registered into the emergency room of the comprehensive psychiatric emergency program. *Repealed July 1, 2020*

*§9.41 Emergency admissions for immediate observation, care, and treatment; powers of certain peace officers and police officers.

Any peace officer, when acting pursuant to his or her special duties, or police officer who is a member of the state police or of an authorized police department or force or of a sheriff's department may take into custody any person who appears to be mentally ill and is conducting himself or herself in a manner which is likely to result in serious harm to the person or others. Such officer may direct the removal of such person or remove him or her to any hospital specified in subdivision (a) of section 9.39 or any comprehensive psychiatric emergency program specified in subdivision (a) of section 9.40, or, pending his or her examination or admission to any such hospital or program, temporarily detain any such person in another safe and comfortable place, in which event, such officer shall immediately notify the director of community services or, if there be none, the health officer of the city or county of such action.   *_Effective until July 1, 2020_

*§9.41 Emergency admissions for immediate observation, care, and treatment; powers of certain peace officers and police officers.
Any peace officer, when acting pursuant to his special duties, or police officer who is a member of the state police or of an authorized police department or force or of a sheriff's department may take into custody any person who appears to be mentally ill and is conducting himself in a manner which is likely to result in serious harm to himself or others. "Likelihood to result in serious harm" shall mean (1) substantial risk of physical harm to himself as manifested by threats of or attempts at suicide or serious bodily harm or other conduct demonstrating that he is dangerous to himself, or (2) a substantial risk of physical harm to other persons as manifested by homicidal or other violent behavior by which others are placed in reasonable fear of serious physical harm. Such officer may direct the removal of such person or remove him to any hospital specified in subdivision (a) of section 9.39 or, pending his examination or admission to any such hospital, temporarily detain any such person in another safe and comfortable place, in which event, such officer shall immediately notify the director of community services or, if there be none, the health officer of the city or county of such action.
                                                                *_Effective July 1, 2020_

*§9.43 Emergency admissions for immediate observation, care, and treatment; powers of courts.
(a) Whenever any court of inferior or general jurisdiction is informed by verified statement that a person is apparently mentally ill and is conducting himself or herself in a manner which in a person who is not mentally ill would be deemed disorderly conduct or which is likely to result in serious harm to himself or herself, such court shall issue a warrant directing that such person be brought before it. If, when said person is brought before the court, it appears to the court, on the basis of evidence presented to it, that such person has or may have a mental illness which is likely to result in serious harm to himself or herself or others, the court shall issue a civil order directing his or her removal to any hospital specified in subdivision (a) of section 9.39 or any comprehensive psychiatric emergency program specified in subdivision (a) of section 9.40, willing to receive such person for a determination by the director of such hospital or program whether such person should be retained therein pursuant to such section.
(b) Whenever a person before a court in a criminal action appears to have a mental illness which is likely to result in serious harm to himself or herself or others and the court determines either that the crime has not been committed or that there is not sufficient cause to believe that such person is guilty thereof, the court may issue a civil order as above provided, and in such cases the criminal action shall terminate.   *_Effective until July 1, 2020_

*§9.43 Emergency admissions for immediate observation, care, and treatment; powers of courts.
(a) Whenever any court of inferior or general jurisdiction is informed by verified statement that a person is apparently mentally ill and is conducting himself in a manner which in a person who is not mentally ill would be deemed

disorderly conduct or which is likely to result in serious harm to himself or others as defined in section 31.39, such court shall issue a warrant directing that such person be brought before it. If, when said person is brought before the court, it appears to the court, on the basis of evidence presented to it, that such person has or may have a mental illness which is likely to result in serious harm to himself or others, the court shall issue a civil order directing his removal to any hospital specified in subdivision (a) of section 31.39 willing to receive such person for a determination by the director of such hospital whether such person should be retained therein pursuant to such section.

(b) Whenever a person before a court in a criminal action appears to have a mental illness which is likely to result in serious harm to himself or others and the court determines either that the crime has not been committed or that there is not sufficient cause to believe that such person is guilty thereof, the court may issue a civil order as above provided, and in such cases the criminal action shall terminate.   *Effective July 1, 2020*

*§9.45 Emergency admissions for immediate observation, care, and treatment; powers of directors of community services.

The director of community services or the director's designee shall have the power to direct the removal of any person, within his or her jurisdiction, to a hospital approved by the commissioner pursuant to subdivision (a) of section 9.39 of this article, or to a comprehensive psychiatric emergency program pursuant to subdivision (a) of section 9.40 of this article, if the parent, adult sibling, spouse or child of the person, the committee or legal guardian of the person, a licensed psychologist, registered professional nurse or certified social worker currently responsible for providing treatment services to the person, a supportive or intensive case manager currently assigned to the person by a case management program which program is approved by the office of mental health for the purpose of reporting under this section, a licensed physician, health officer, peace officer or police officer reports to him or her that such person has a mental illness for which immediate care and treatment in a hospital is appropriate and which is likely to result in serious harm to himself or herself or others. It shall be the duty of peace officers, when acting pursuant to their special duties, or police officers, who are members of an authorized police department or force or of a sheriff's department to assist representatives of such director to take into custody and transport any such person. Upon the request of a director of community services or the director's designee an ambulance service, as defined in subdivision two of section three thousand one of the public health law, is authorized to transport any such person. Such person may then be retained in a hospital pursuant to the provisions of section 9.39 of this article or in a comprehensive psychiatric emergency program pursuant to the provisions of section 9.40 of this article *Effective July 1, 2020*

*§9.45 Emergency admissions for immediate observation, care, and treatment; powers of directors of community services.

The director of community services or his designee shall have the power to direct the removal of any person, within his jurisdiction, to a hospital approved by the commissioner pursuant to subdivision (a) of section 9.39 of this article if the parent, spouse, or child of the person, a licensed physician, health officer, peace officer or police officer reports to him that such person has a mental illness for which immediate care and treatment in a hospital is appropriate and which is likely to result in serious harm to himself or others, as defined in section 9.39 of this article. It shall be the duty of peace officers, when acting pursuant to their special duties, or police officers, who are members of an authorized police department or force or of a sheriff's department to assist representatives of such director to take into custody and transport any such person. Upon the request of a director of community services or his designee an ambulance service, as defined in subdivision two of section three thousand one of the public health law, is authorized to transport any such person. Such person may then be retained pursuant to the provisions of section 9.39 of this article.   *Effective July 1, 2020*

§9.46   Reports of substantial risk or threat of harm by mental health professionals.

(a) For purposes of this section, the term "mental health professional" shall include a physician, psychologist, registered nurse or licensed clinical social worker.

(b) Notwithstanding any other law to the contrary, when a mental health professional currently providing treatment services to a person determines, in the exercise of reasonable professional judgment, that such person is likely to engage in conduct that would result in serious harm to self or others, he or she shall be required to report, as soon as practicable, to the director of community services, or the director's designee, who shall report to the division of criminal justice services whenever he or she agrees that the person is likely to engage in such conduct. Information transmitted to the division of criminal justice services shall be limited to names and other non-clinical identifying information, which may only be used for determining whether a license issued pursuant to section 400.00 of the penal law should be suspended or revoked, or for determining whether a person is ineligible for a license issued pursuant to section 400.00 of the penal law, or is no longer permitted under state or federal law to possess a firearm.

(c) Nothing in this section shall be construed to require a mental health professional to take any action which, in the exercise of reasonable professional judgment, would endanger such mental health professional or increase the danger to a potential victim or victims.

(d) The decision of a mental health professional to disclose or not to disclose in accordance with this section, when made reasonably and in good faith, shall not be the basis for any civil or criminal liability of such mental health professional.

§9.47   Duties of local officers in regard to their mentally ill.

*(a) All directors of community services, health officers, and social services officials, as defined by the social services law, are charged with the duty of seeing that all mentally ill persons within their respective communities who are in need of care and treatment at a hospital are admitted to a hospital pursuant to the provisions of this article. Social services officials and health officers shall notify the director of community services of any such person coming to their attention. Pending the determination of the condition of an alleged mentally ill person, it shall be the duty of the director of community services and, if there be no such director, of the local health officer to provide for the proper care of such person in a suitable facility.   *Effective until June 30, 2017*

*All directors of community services, health officers, and social services officials, as defined by the social services law, are charged with the duty of seeing that all mentally ill persons within their respective communities who are in need of care and treatment at a hospital are admitted to a hospital pursuant to the provisions of this article. Social services officials and health officers shall notify the director of community services of any such person coming to their attention. Pending the determination of the condition of an alleged mentally ill person, it shall be the duty of the director of community services and, if there be no such director, of the local health officer to provide for the proper care of such person in a suitable facility.   *Effective June 30, 2017*

*(b) All directors of community services shall be responsible for:

(1) receiving reports of persons who may be in need of assisted outpatient treatment and documenting the receipt date of such reports;

(2) conducting timely investigations of such reports and providing written notice upon the completion of investigations to reporting persons and program coordinators, appointed by the commissioner of mental health pursuant to subdivision (f) of section 7.17 of this title, and documenting the initiation and completion dates of such investigations and the dispositions;

(3) filing of petitions for assisted outpatient treatment pursuant to paragraph (vii) of subdivision (e) of section 9.60 of this article, and documenting the petition filing date and the date of the court order;

(4) coordinating the timely delivery of court ordered services with program coordinators and documenting the date assisted outpatients begin to receive the services mandated in the court order; and

(5) ensuring evaluation of the need for ongoing assisted outpatient treatment pursuant to subdivision (k) of section 9.60 of this article prior to the expiration of any assisted outpatient treatment order;

(6) if he or she has been ordered to provide for or arrange for assisted outpatient treatment pursuant to paragraph five of subdivision (j) of section 9.60 of this article or became the appropriate director pursuant to this paragraph or subdivision (c) of section 9.48 of this article, notifying the director of community services of the new county of residence when he or she has reason to believe that an assisted outpatient has or will change his or her county of residence during the pendency of an assisted outpatient treatment order. Upon such change of residence, the director of the new county of residence shall become the appropriate director, as such term is defined in section 9.60 of this article; and

(7) reporting on a quarterly basis to program coordinators the information collected pursuant to this subdivision.   *Repealed June 30, 2017*

*(c) In discharge of the duties imposed by subdivision (b) of section 9.60 of this article, directors of community services may provide services directly, or may coordinate services with the offices of the department or may contract with any public or private provider to provide services for such programs as may be necessary to carry out the duties imposed pursuant to this subdivision.

    Repealed June 30, 2017

*§9.48 Duties of directors of assisted outpatient treatment programs.

(a)(1) Directors of assisted outpatient treatment programs established pursuant to section 9.60 of this article shall provide a written report to the program coordinators, appointed by the commissioner of mental health pursuant to subdivision (f) of section 7.17 of this chapter, within three days of the issuance of a court order. The report shall demonstrate that mechanisms are in place to ensure the delivery of services and medications as required by the court order and shall include, but not be limited to the following:

(i) a copy of the court order;

(ii) a copy of the written treatment plan;

(iii) the identity of the case manager or assertive community treatment team, including the name and contact data of the organization which the case manager or assertive community treatment team member represents;

(iv) the identity of providers of services; and

(v) the date on which services have commenced or will commence.

(2) The directors of assisted outpatient treatment programs shall ensure the timely delivery of services described in paragraph one of subdivision (a) of section 9.60 of this article pursuant to any court order issued under such section. Directors of assisted outpatient treatment programs shall immediately commence corrective action upon receiving notice from program coordinators, that services are not being provided in a timely manner. Such directors shall inform the program coordinator of such corrective action.

(b) Directors of assisted outpatient treatment programs shall submit quarterly reports to the program coordinators regarding the assisted outpatient treatment program operated or administered by such director. The report shall include the following information:

(i) the names of individuals served by the program;

(ii) the percentage of petitions for assisted outpatient treatment that are granted by the court;

(iii) any change in status of assisted outpatients, including but not limited to the number of individuals who have failed to comply with court ordered assisted outpatient treatment;

(iv) a description of material changes in written treatment plans of assisted outpatients;

(v) any change in case managers;

(vi) a description of the categories of services which have been ordered by the court;

(vii) living arrangements of individuals served by the program including the number, if any, who are homeless;

(viii) any other information as required by the commissioner of mental health; and

(ix) any recommendations to improve the program locally or statewide.

(c) Directors of assisted outpatient treatment programs providing services described in paragraph one of subdivision (a) of section 9.60 of this article pursuant to any court order issued under such section shall evaluate the need for ongoing assisted outpatient treatment pursuant to subdivision (k) of section 9.60 of this article prior to the expiration of any assisted outpatient treatment order; and shall notify the director of community services of the new county of residence when he or she has reason to believe that an assisted outpatient has or will change his or her county of residence during the pendency of an assisted outpatient treatment order. Upon such change of residence, the director of the new county of residence shall become the appropriate director, as such term is defined in section 9.60 of this article.   **Repealed June 30, 2017*

§9.49   Transfer of juvenile delinquents.

(a) The commissioner shall receive and arrange the admission to the appropriate office facility of juvenile delinquents temporarily transferred to his custody pursuant to section 353.4 of the family court act.

(b) Immediately upon the admission of a juvenile to an office facility pursuant to this section, the director shall comply with the provisions of section 9.07 of this chapter, and the mental hygiene legal service shall contact such juvenile and explain and make available the facilities thereof. Any juvenile placed pursuant to this section shall be subject to the provisions of article nine of this chapter.

§9.51 Residential treatment facilities for children and youth; admissions.
(a) The director of a residential treatment facility for children and youth may receive as a patient a person in need of care and treatment in such a facility who has been certified as needing such care by the pre-admission certification committee serving the facility and in accordance with priorities for admission established by such committee, as provided by this section. Subject to the provisions of this section, the provisions of this article shall apply to admission and retention of patients to residential treatment facilities for children and youth.

(b) Persons admitted as in-patients to hospitals operated by the office of mental health upon the application of the director of the division for youth pursuant to section five hundred nine of the executive law or 353.4 of the family court act who are not subject to a restrictive placement pursuant to section 353.5 of the family court act, may, if appropriate, and subject to the provisions of subdivision (d) of this section, be transferred to a residential treatment facility for children and youth. The director of the division for youth shall be notified of any such transfer. When appropriate, the director of the residential treatment facility may arrange the return of a patient so transferred to the hospital or the transfer of a patient to another hospital or, in accordance with subdivision four of section five hundred nine of the executive law, to the division for youth.

(c) The commissioner shall designate pre-admission certification committees for defined geographic areas to evaluate each person proposed for admission or transfer to a residential treatment facility for children and youth. When designating persons to serve on pre-admission certification committees, the commissioners shall assure that the interests of the people residing in the area to be served by each committee are represented. Such committees shall include a person designated by the office of mental health, a person designated by the state commissioner of social services and a person designated by the state commissioner of education. The commissioner of mental health shall consult with the conference of local mental hygiene directors and the commissioner of social services shall consult with county commissioners of social services in the area to be served by a committee prior to designating persons to serve on a committee. The commissioners may designate persons who are not state employees to serve on pre-admission certification committees. Membership of pre-admission certification committees shall be limited to persons licensed in accordance with the education law to practice medicine, nursing, psychology, or licensed clinical social work. In the event the persons originally designated to a committee by the commissioners do not include a physician, the commissioner shall designate a physician to serve as an additional member of the committee. Each pre-admission certification committee shall designate five persons representing local governments, voluntary agencies, parents and other interested persons who shall serve as an advisory board to the committee. Such board shall have the right to visit residential treatment facilities for children and youth served by the committee and shall have the right to review clinical records obtained by the pre-admission certification committee and shall be bound by the confidentiality requirements of section 33.13 of this chapter.

(d) All applications for admission or transfer of an individual to a residential treatment facility for children and youth shall be referred to a pre-admission certification committee for evaluation of the needs of the individual and certification of the individual's need for treatment in a residential treatment facility for children and youth. Applications shall include an assessment of the individual's psychiatric, medical and social needs prepared in accordance with a uniform assessment method specified by the regulations of the commissioner. The committee may at its discretion refer an applicant to a hospital or other facility operated or licensed by the office for an additional assessment. In the event of such an additional assessment of the individual's needs, the facility conducting the assessment shall attempt to receive all third party insurance or federal reimbursement available as payment for the assessment. The state shall pay the balance of the fees which may be charged by the provider in accordance with applicable provisions of law. In addition, if necessary, in accordance with section four thousand five of the education law, the pre-admission certification committee shall obtain an evaluation of the educational needs of the child by the committee on special education of the school district of residence. The pre-admission certification committee shall review all requests for evaluation and certification within thirty days of receipt of a complete application and any additional assessments it may require and, using a uniform assessment method specified by regulation of the commissioner, evaluate the psychiatric, medical and social needs of the proposed admittee and certify: (i) the individual's need for services in a residential treatment facility for children and youth and (ii) the immediacy of that need, given the availability of such services in the area and the needs of other children evaluated by the committee and certified as eligible for admission to a residential treatment facility for children and youth who have not yet been admitted to such a facility. A pre-admission certification committee shall not certify an individual for admission unless it finds that:

(1) Available ambulatory care resources and other residential placements do not meet the treatment needs of the individual;

(2) Proper treatment of the individual's psychiatric condition requires in-patient care and treatment under the direction of a physician; and

(3) Care and treatment in a residential treatment facility for children and youth can reasonably be expected to improve the individual's condition or prevent further regression so that services will no longer be needed, provided that a poor prognosis shall not in itself constitute grounds for a denial of certification if treatment can be expected to effect a change in prognosis. All decisions of the committee to recommend admission or priority of admission shall be based on the unanimous vote of those present. The decision of the committee shall be reported to the applicant. In the event a committee evaluates a child who is the subject of a proceeding currently pending in the family court, the committee shall report its decision to the family court.

No residential treatment facility for children and youth shall admit a person who has not been certified as suitable for such admission by the appropriate pre-admission certification committee. Residential treatment facilities shall admit children in accordance with priorities for admission of children most immediately in need of such services established by the pre-admission certification committee serving the facility in accordance with standards established by the commissioner.

(e) Notwithstanding any inconsistent provision of law, no government agency shall make payments pursuant to title nineteen of the federal social security act or articles five and six of the social services law to a residential treatment facility for children and youth for service to a person whose need for care and treatment in such a facility was not certified pursuant to this section.

(f) No person shall be admitted to a residential treatment facility for children and youth who has a mental illness which presents a likelihood of serious harm to others; "likelihood of serious harm" shall mean a substantial risk of physical harm to other persons as manifested by recent homicidal or other violent behavior by which others are placed in reasonable fear of serious physical harm.

(g) Notwithstanding any other provision of law, pre-admission certification committees shall be entitled to review clinical records maintained by any person or entity which pertain to an individual on whose behalf an application is made for admission to a residential treatment facility for children and youth. Any clinical records received by a pre-admission certification committee and all assessments submitted to the committee shall be kept confidential in accordance with the provisions of section 33.13 of the mental hygiene law, provided, however, that the commissioner may have access to and receive copies of such records for the purpose of evaluating the operation and effectiveness of the committee.

Confidentiality of clinical records of treatment of a person in a residential treatment facility for children and youth shall be maintained as required in section 33.13 of this chapter. That portion of the clinical record maintained by a residential treatment facility for children and youth operated by an authorized agency specifically related to medical care and treatment shall not be considered part of the record required to be maintained by such authorized agency pursuant to section three hundred seventy-two of the social services law and shall not be discoverable in a proceeding under section three hundred fifty-eight-a of the social services law or article ten-A of the family court act except upon order of the family court; provided, however, that all other information required by a local social services district or the office of children and family services for purposes of sections three hundred fifty-eight-a, four hundred nine-e and four hundred nine-f of the social services law and article ten-A of the family court act shall be furnished on request, and the confidentiality of such information shall be safeguarded as provided in section four hundred sixty-e of the social services law.

§9.53   Children in the custody of social services officials or the division for youth.

(a) Admission of a child in the care and custody of a social services official or authorized agency, the director of the division for youth or a person or entity granted such custody pursuant to section seven hundred fifty-six or one thousand fifty-five of the family court act to a hospital or residential treatment facility for children and youth shall not be considered to effect a change in custody of such child and the responsibilities of such person or entity having custody of the child shall continue as described in the social services law, the executive law, the family court act and in any court order granting such custody.

(b) Persons in the custody of a social services official, authorized agency, the division for youth or another person or entity pursuant to an outstanding and valid court order shall only be released to the custody of that person or entity.

(c) Prior to the discharge or release of a child who at the time of such release remains in the custody of a social services official, authorized agency, the division for youth, or a person or entity granted such custody pursuant to section seven hundred fifty-six or one thousand fifty-five of the family court act, the facility in which the child is receiving treatment shall plan the discharge of the child as required in section 29.15 of this chapter. The facility shall prepare the plan in collaboration with the person or entity having custody of the child and it shall be the duty of such person or entity to cooperate with the facility in that effort. Notwithstanding any inconsistent provision of law, and subject to separate interagency agreements to be negotiated by the commissioner of mental health and the commissioner of social services and the commissioner of mental health and the director of the division for youth, information derived from the clinical record as required by this section may be revealed to the person or entity having custody of the child, to the extent release of such information is necessary to assure adequate discharge planning.

*§9.55 Emergency admissions for immediate observation, care and treatment; powers of qualified psychiatrists.
 A qualified psychiatrist shall have the power to direct the removal of any person, whose treatment for a mental illness he or she is either supervising or providing in a facility licensed or operated by the office of mental health which does not have an inpatient psychiatric service, to a hospital approved by the commissioner pursuant to subdivision (a) of section 9.39 of this article or to a comprehensive psychiatric emergency program, if he or she determines upon examination of such person that such person appears to have a mental illness for which immediate observation, care and treatment in a hospital is appropriate and which is likely to result in serious harm to himself or herself or others. Upon the request of such qualified psychiatrist, peace officers, when acting pursuant to their special duties, or police officers, who are members of an authorized police department or force or of a sheriff's department shall take into custody and transport any such person. Upon the request of a qualified psychiatrist an ambulance service, as defined by subdivision two of section three thousand one of the public health law, is authorized to transport any such person. Such person may then be admitted to a hospital in accordance with the provisions of section 9.39 of this article or to a comprehensive psychiatric emergency program in accordance with the provisions of section 9.40 of this article.   **Effective until July 1, 2020*

*§9.55 Emergency admissions for immediate observation, care and treatment; powers of qualified psychiatrists.
 A qualified psychiatrist shall have the power to direct the removal of any person, whose treatment for a mental illness he is either supervising or providing in a facility licensed or operated by the office of mental health which does not have an inpatient psychiatric service, to a hospital approved by the commissioner pursuant to subdivision (a) of section 9.39 of this article, if he determines upon examination of such person that such person appears to have a mental illness for which immediate observation, care and treatment in a hospital is appropriate and which is likely to result in serious harm to himself or others, as defined in section 9.39 of this article. Upon the request of such qualified psychiatrist, peace officers, when acting pursuant to their special duties, or police officers, who are members of an authorized police department or force or of a sheriff's department shall take into custody and transport any such person. Upon the request of a qualified psychiatrist an ambulance service, as defined by subdivision two of section three thousand one of the public health law, is authorized to transport any such person. Such person may then be admitted in accordance with the provisions of section 9.39 of this article.
                  *Effective July 1, 2020

*§9.57 **Emergency admissions for immediate observation, care and treatment; powers of emergency room physicians.**

A physician who has examined a person in an emergency room or provided emergency medical services at a general hospital, as defined in article twenty-eight of the public health law, which does not have an inpatient psychiatric service, or a physician who has examined a person in a comprehensive psychiatric emergency program shall be authorized to request that the director of the program or hospital, or the director's designee, direct the removal of such person to a hospital approved by the commissioner pursuant to subdivision (a) of section 9.39 of this article or to a comprehensive psychiatric emergency program, if the physician determines upon examination of such person that such person appears to have a mental illness for which immediate care and treatment in a hospital is appropriate and which is likely to result in serious harm to himself or others. Upon the request of the physician, the director of the program or hospital or the director's designee, is authorized to direct peace officers, when acting pursuant to their special duties, or police officers, who are members of an authorized police department or force or of a sheriff's department to take into custody and transport any such person. Upon the request of an emergency room physician or the director of the program or hospital, or the director's designee, an ambulance service, as defined by subdivision two of section three thousand one of the public health law, is authorized to take into custody and transport any such person. Such person may then be admitted to a hospital in accordance with the provisions of section 9.39 of this article or to a comprehensive psychiatric emergency program in accordance with the provisions of section 9.40 of this article.   **Effective until July 1, 2020*

*§9.57 **Emergency admissions for immediate observation, care and treatment; powers of emergency room physicians.**

A physician who has examined a person in an emergency room or provided emergency medical services at a general hospital, as defined in article twenty-eight of the public health law, which does not have an inpatient psychiatric service, shall be authorized to request that the director of the hospital, or his designee, direct the removal of such person to a hospital approved by the commissioner pursuant to subdivision (a) of section 9.39 of this article, if the physician determines upon examination of such person that such person appears to have a mental illness for which immediate care and treatment in a hospital is appropriate and which is likely to result in serious harm to himself or others, as defined in section 9.39 of this article. Upon the request of the physician, the director of the hospital or his designee, is authorized to direct peace officers, when acting pursuant to their special duties, or police officers, who are members of an authorized police department or force or of a sheriff's department to take into custody and transport any such person. Upon the request of an emergency room physician or the director of the hospital, or his designee, an ambulance service, as defined by subdivision two of section three thousand one of the public health law, is authorized to take into custody and transport any such person. Such person may then be admitted in accordance with the provisions of section 9.39 of this article.   **Effective July 1, 2020*

§9.58 **Transport for evaluation; powers of approved mobile crisis outreach teams.**

(a) A physician or qualified mental health professional who is a member of an approved mobile crisis outreach team shall have the power to remove, or pursuant to subdivision (b) of this section, to direct the removal of any person to a hospital approved by the commissioner pursuant to subdivision (a) of section 9.39 or section 31.27 of this chapter for the purpose of evaluation for admission if such person appears to be mentally ill and is conducting himself or herself in a manner which is likely to result in serious harm to the person or others.

(b) If the team physician or qualified mental health professional determines that it is necessary to effectuate transport, he or she shall direct peace officers, when acting pursuant to their special duties, or police officers, who are members of an authorized police department or force or of a sheriff's department, to take into custody and transport any persons identified in subdivision (a) of this section. Upon the request of such physician or qualified mental health professional, an ambulance service, as defined in subdivision two of section three thousand one of the public health law, is authorized to transport any such persons. Such persons may then be evaluated for admission in accordance with the provisions of section 9.27, 9.39, 9.40 or other sections of this article, provided that such admission decisions shall be made independent of the fact that the person was transported pursuant to the provisions of this section and, provided further, such transport shall not create a presumption that the person should be involuntarily admitted to a hospital.

(c) The commissioner shall be authorized to develop standards, in consultation with the commissioner of the division of criminal justice services, relating to the training requirements of teams established pursuant to this section. Such training shall, at a minimum, help to ensure that the provision of crisis and emergency services are provided in a manner which protects the health and safety and respects the individual needs and rights of persons being evaluated or transported pursuant to this section.

(d) As used in this section:

(1) "Approved mobile crisis outreach team" shall mean a team of persons operating as part of a mobile crisis outreach program approved by the commissioner of mental health, which may include mobile crisis outreach teams funded pursuant to section 41.55 of this chapter.

(2) "Qualified mental health professional" shall mean a licensed psychologist, registered professional nurse, licensed clinical social worker or a licensed master social worker under the supervision of a physician, psychologist or licensed clinical social worker.

*§9.59 Immunity from liability.

(a) Notwithstanding any inconsistent provision of any general, special or local law, an ambulance service as defined by subdivision two of section three thousand one of the public health law and any member thereof who is an emergency medical technician or an advanced emergency medical technician transporting a person to a hospital as authorized by this article, any peace officers, when acting pursuant to their special duties, any police officers, who are members of an authorized police department or force or of a sheriff's department, and any members of mobile crisis outreach teams approved by the commissioner pursuant to section 9.58 of this article, who are taking into custody and transporting a person to a hospital as authorized by this article, or to a hospital or other facility as authorized by section 22.09 of this chapter, and any employee of a licensed comprehensive psychiatric emergency program, specially trained in accordance with standards developed by the commissioner, who transports a person to a hospital, shall not be liable for damages for injuries alleged to have been sustained by such person or for the death of such person alleged to have occurred by reason of an act or omission unless it is established that such injuries or such death was caused by gross negligence on the part of such emergency medical technician, advanced emergency medical technician, peace officer, police officer, mobile crisis outreach team member, or specially trained employee of a licensed comprehensive psychiatric emergency program.

(b) Nothing in this section shall be deemed to relieve or alter the liability of any such ambulance service or members thereof, peace officers, police officers or specially trained employees of a licensed comprehensive psychiatric emergency program for damages or injuries or death arising out of the operation of motor vehicles.   *Effective until July 1, 2020

*§9.59 Immunity from liability.

(a) Notwithstanding any inconsistent provision of any general, special or local law, an ambulance service as defined by subdivision two of section three thousand one of the public health law and any member thereof who is an emergency medical technician or an advanced emergency medical technician transporting a person to a hospital as authorized by this article, any peace officers, when acting pursuant to their special duties, and any police officers, who are members of an authorized police department or force or of a sheriff's department, who are taking into custody and transporting a person to a hospital as authorized by this article, shall not be liable for damages for injuries alleged to have been sustained by such person or for the death of such person alleged to have occurred by reason of an act or omission unless it is established that such injuries or such death was caused by gross negligence on the part of such emergency medical technician, advanced emergency medical technician, peace officer or police officer.

(b) Nothing in this section shall be deemed to relieve or alter the liability of any such ambulance service or members thereof, peace officers, or police officers for damages or injuries or death arising out of the operation of motor vehicles.   *Effective July 1, 2020

*§9.60 Assisted outpatient treatment.

(a) Definitions. For purposes of this section, the following definitions shall apply:

(1) "assisted outpatient treatment" shall mean categories of outpatient services which have been ordered by the court pursuant to this section. Such treatment shall include case management services or assertive community treatment team services to provide care coordination, and may also include any of the following categories of services: medication; periodic blood tests or urinalysis to determine compliance with prescribed medications; individual or group therapy; day or partial day programming activities; educational and vocational training or activities; alcohol or substance abuse treatment and counseling and periodic tests for the presence of alcohol or illegal drugs for persons with a history of alcohol or substance abuse; supervision of living arrangements; and any other services within a local services plan developed pursuant to article forty-one of this chapter, prescribed to treat the person's mental illness and to assist the person in living and functioning in the community, or to attempt to prevent a relapse or deterioration that may reasonably be predicted to result in suicide or the need for hospitalization.

(2) "director" shall mean the director of community services of a local governmental unit, or the director of a hospital licensed or operated by the office of mental health which operates, directs and supervises an assisted outpatient treatment program.

(3) "director of community services" and "local governmental unit" shall have the same meanings as provided in article forty-one of this chapter. The "appropriate director" shall mean the director of community services of the county where the assisted outpatient resides, even if it is a different county than the county where the assisted outpatient treatment order was originally issued.

(4) "assisted outpatient treatment program" shall mean a system to arrange for and coordinate the provision of assisted outpatient treatment, to monitor treatment compliance by assisted outpatients, to evaluate the condition or needs of assisted outpatients, to take appropriate steps to address the needs of such individuals, and to ensure compliance with court orders.

(5) "assisted outpatient" shall mean the person under a court order to receive assisted outpatient treatment.

(6) "subject of the petition" or "subject" shall mean the person who is alleged in a petition, filed pursuant to the provisions of this section, to meet the criteria for assisted outpatient treatment.

(7) "correctional facility" and "local correctional facility" shall have the same meanings as provided in section two of the correction law.

(8) "health care proxy" and "health care agent" shall have the same meanings as provided in article twenty-nine-C of the public health law.

(9) "program coordinator" shall mean an individual appointed by the commissioner of mental health, pursuant to subdivision (f) of section 7.17 of this chapter, who is responsible for the oversight and monitoring of assisted outpatient treatment programs.

(b) Programs. The director of community services of each local governmental unit shall operate, direct and supervise an assisted outpatient treatment program. The director of a hospital licensed or operated by the office of mental health may operate, direct and supervise an assisted outpatient treatment program, upon approval by the commissioner. Directors of community services shall be permitted to satisfy the provisions of this subdivision through the operation of joint assisted outpatient treatment programs. Nothing in this subdivision shall be interpreted to preclude the combination or coordination of efforts between and among local governmental units and hospitals in providing and coordinating assisted outpatient treatment.

(c) Criteria. A person may be ordered to receive assisted outpatient treatment if the court finds that such person:

(1) is eighteen years of age or older; and

(2) is suffering from a mental illness; and

(3) is unlikely to survive safely in the community without supervision, based on a clinical determination; and

(4) has a history of lack of compliance with treatment for mental illness that has:

(i) prior to the filing of the petition, at least twice within the last thirty-six months been a significant factor in necessitating hospitalization in a hospital, or receipt of services in a forensic or other mental health unit of a correctional facility or a local correctional facility, not including any current period, or period ending within the last six months, during which the person was or is hospitalized or incarcerated; or

(ii) prior to the filing of the petition, resulted in one or more acts of serious violent behavior toward self or others or threats of, or attempts at, serious physical harm to self or others within the last forty-eight months, not including any current period, or period ending within the last six months, in which the person was or is hospitalized or incarcerated; and

(5) is, as a result of his or her mental illness, unlikely to voluntarily participate in outpatient treatment that would enable him or her to live safely in the community; and

(6) in view of his or her treatment history and current behavior, is in need of assisted outpatient treatment in order to prevent a relapse or deterioration which would be likely to result in serious harm to the person or others as defined in section 9.01 of this article; and

(7) is likely to benefit from assisted outpatient treatment.

(d) Health care proxy. Nothing in this section shall preclude a person with a health care proxy from being subject to a petition pursuant to this chapter and consistent with article twenty-nine-C of the public health law.

(e) Petition to the court. (1) A petition for an order authorizing assisted outpatient treatment may be filed in the supreme or county court in the county in which the subject of the petition is present or reasonably believed to be present. Such petition may be initiated only by the following persons:

(i) any person eighteen years of age or older with whom the subject of the petition resides; or

(ii) the parent, spouse, sibling eighteen years of age or older, or child eighteen years of age or older of the subject of the petition; or (iii) the director of a hospital in which the subject of the petition is hospitalized; or

(iv) the director of any public or charitable organization, agency or home providing mental health services to the subject of the petition or in whose institution the subject of the petition resides; or

(v) a qualified psychiatrist who is either supervising the treatment of or treating the subject of the petition for a mental illness; or

(vi) a psychologist, licensed pursuant to article one hundred fifty-three of the education law, or a social worker, licensed pursuant to article one hundred fifty-four of the education law, who is treating the subject of the petition for a mental illness; or

(vii) the director of community services, or his or her designee, or the social services official, as defined in the social services law, of the city or county in which the subject of the petition is present or reasonably believed to be present; or

(viii) a parole officer or probation officer assigned to supervise the subject of the petition.

(2) The petition shall state:

(i) each of the criteria for assisted outpatient treatment as set forth in subdivision (c) of this section;

(ii) facts which support the petitioner's belief that the subject of the petition meets each criterion, provided that the hearing on the petition need not be limited to the stated facts; and

(iii) that the subject of the petition is present, or is reasonably believed to be present, within the county where such petition is filed.

(3) The petition shall be accompanied by an affirmation or affidavit of a physician, who shall not be the petitioner, stating either that:

(i) such physician has personally examined the subject of the petition no more than ten days prior to the submission of the petition, recommends assisted outpatient treatment for the subject of the petition, and is willing and able to testify at the hearing on the petition; or

(ii) no more than ten days prior to the filing of the petition, such physician or his or her designee has made appropriate attempts but has not been successful in eliciting the cooperation of the subject of the petition to submit to an examination, such physician has reason to suspect that the subject of the petition meets the criteria for assisted outpatient treatment, and such physician is willing and able to examine the subject of the petition and testify at the hearing on the petition.

(4) In counties with a population of less than eighty thousand, the affirmation or affidavit required by paragraph three of this subdivision may be made by a physician who is an employee of the office. The office is authorized to make available, at no cost to the county, a qualified physician for the purpose of making such affirmation or affidavit consistent with the provisions of such paragraph.

(f) Service. The petitioner shall cause written notice of the petition to be given to the subject of the petition and a copy thereof to be given personally or by mail to the persons listed in section 9.29 of this article, the mental hygiene legal service, the health care agent if any such agent is known to the petitioner, the appropriate program coordinator, and the appropriate director of community services, if such director is not the petitioner.

(g) Right to counsel. The subject of the petition shall have the right to be represented by the mental hygiene legal service, or privately financed counsel, at all stages of a proceeding commenced under this section.

(h) Hearing.

(1) Upon receipt of the petition, the court shall fix the date for a hearing. Such date shall be no later than three days from the date such petition is received by the court, excluding Saturdays, Sundays and holidays. Adjournments shall be permitted only for good cause shown. In granting adjournments, the court shall consider the need for further examination by a physician or the potential need to provide assisted outpatient treatment expeditiously. The court shall cause the subject of the petition, any other person receiving notice pursuant to subdivision (f) of this section, the petitioner, the physician whose affirmation or affidavit accompanied the petition, and such other persons as the court may determine to be advised of such date. Upon such date, or upon such other date to which the proceeding may be adjourned, the court shall hear testimony and, if it be deemed advisable and the subject of the petition is available, examine the subject of the petition in or out of court. If the subject of the petition does not appear at the hearing, and appropriate attempts to elicit the attendance of the subject have failed, the court may conduct the hearing in the subject's absence. In such case, the court shall set forth the factual basis for conducting the hearing without the presence of the subject of the petition.

(2) The court shall not order assisted outpatient treatment unless an examining physician, who recommends assisted outpatient treatment and has personally examined the subject of the petition no more than ten days before the filing of the petition, testifies in person at the hearing. Such physician shall state the facts and clinical determinations which support the allegation that the subject of the petition meets each of the criteria for assisted outpatient treatment.

(3) If the subject of the petition has refused to be examined by a physician, the court may request the subject to consent to an examination by a physician

appointed by the court. If the subject of the petition does not consent and the court finds reasonable cause to believe that the allegations in the petition are true, the court may order peace officers, acting pursuant to their special duties, or police officers who are members of an authorized police department or force, or of a sheriff's department to take the subject of the petition into custody and transport him or her to a hospital for examination by a physician. Retention of the subject of the petition under such order shall not exceed twenty-four hours. The examination of the subject of the petition may be performed by the physician whose affirmation or affidavit accompanied the petition pursuant to paragraph three of subdivision (e) of this section, if such physician is privileged by such hospital or otherwise authorized by such hospital to do so. If such examination is performed by another physician, the examining physician may consult with the physician whose affirmation or affidavit accompanied the petition as to whether the subject meets the criteria for assisted outpatient treatment.

(4) A physician who testifies pursuant to paragraph two of this subdivision shall state: (i) the facts which support the allegation that the subject meets each of the criteria for assisted outpatient treatment, (ii) that the treatment is the least restrictive alternative, (iii) the recommended assisted outpatient treatment, and (iv) the rationale for the recommended assisted outpatient treatment. If the recommended assisted outpatient treatment includes medication, such physician's testimony shall describe the types or classes of medication which should be authorized, shall describe the beneficial and detrimental physical and mental effects of such medication, and shall recommend whether such medication should be self-administered or administered by authorized personnel.

(5) The subject of the petition shall be afforded an opportunity to present evidence, to call witnesses on his or her behalf, and to cross-examine adverse witnesses.

(i) Written treatment plan.

(1) The court shall not order assisted outpatient treatment unless a physician appointed by the appropriate director, in consultation with such director, develops and provides to the court a proposed written treatment plan. The written treatment plan shall include case management services or assertive community treatment team services to provide care coordination. The written treatment plan also shall include all categories of services, as set forth in paragraph one of subdivision (a) of this section, which such physician recommends that the subject of the petition receive. All service providers shall be notified regarding their inclusion in the written treatment plan. If the written treatment plan includes medication, it shall state whether such medication should be self-administered or administered by authorized personnel, and shall specify type and dosage range of medication most likely to provide maximum benefit for the subject. If the written treatment plan includes alcohol or substance abuse counseling and treatment, such plan may include a provision requiring relevant testing for either alcohol or illegal substances provided the physician's clinical basis for recommending such plan provides sufficient facts for the court to find (i) that such person has a history of alcohol or substance abuse that is clinically related to the mental illness; and (ii) that such testing is necessary to prevent a relapse or deterioration which would be likely to result in serious harm to the person or others. If a director is the petitioner, the written treatment plan shall be provided to the court no later than the date of the hearing on the petition. If a person other than a director is the petitioner, such

plan shall be provided to the court no later than the date set by the court pursuant to paragraph three of subdivision (j) of this section.

(2) The physician appointed to develop the written treatment plan shall provide the following persons with an opportunity to actively participate in the development of such plan: the subject of the petition; the treating physician, if any; and upon the request of the subject of the petition, an individual significant to the subject including any relative, close friend or individual otherwise concerned with the welfare of the subject. If the subject of the petition has executed a health care proxy, the appointed physician shall consider any directions included in such proxy in developing the written treatment plan.

(3) The court shall not order assisted outpatient treatment unless a physician appearing on behalf of a director testifies to explain the written proposed treatment plan. Such physician shall state the categories of assisted outpatient treatment recommended, the rationale for each such category, facts which establish that such treatment is the least restrictive alternative, and, if the recommended assisted outpatient treatment plan includes medication, such physician shall state the types or classes of medication recommended, the beneficial and detrimental physical and mental effects of such medication, and whether such medication should be self-administered or administered by an authorized professional. If the subject of the petition has executed a health care proxy, such physician shall state the consideration given to any directions included in such proxy in developing the written treatment plan. If a director is the petitioner, testimony pursuant to this paragraph shall be given at the hearing on the petition. If a person other than a director is the petitioner, such testimony shall be given on the date set by the court pursuant to paragraph three of subdivision (j) of this section.

(j) Disposition.

(1) If after hearing all relevant evidence, the court does not find by clear and convincing evidence that the subject of the petition meets the criteria for assisted outpatient treatment, the court shall dismiss the petition.

(2) If after hearing all relevant evidence, the court finds by clear and convincing evidence that the subject of the petition meets the criteria for assisted outpatient treatment, and there is no appropriate and feasible less restrictive alternative, the court may order the subject to receive assisted outpatient treatment for an initial period not to exceed one year. In fashioning the order, the court shall specifically make findings by clear and convincing evidence that the proposed treatment is the least restrictive treatment appropriate and feasible for the subject. The order shall state an assisted outpatient treatment plan, which shall include all categories of assisted outpatient treatment, as set forth in paragraph one of subdivision (a) of this section, which the assisted outpatient is to receive, but shall not include any such category that has not been recommended in both the proposed written treatment plan and the testimony provided to the court pursuant to subdivision (i) of this section.

(3) If after hearing all relevant evidence presented by a petitioner who is not a director, the court finds by clear and convincing evidence that the subject of the petition meets the criteria for assisted outpatient treatment, and the court has yet to be provided with a written proposed treatment plan and testimony pursuant to subdivision (i) of this section, the court shall order the appropriate director to provide the court with such plan and testimony no later than the third day, excluding Saturdays, Sundays and holidays, immediately following

the date of such order. Upon receiving such plan and testimony, the court may order assisted outpatient treatment as provided in paragraph two of this subdivision.

(4) A court may order the patient to self-administer psychotropic drugs or accept the administration of such drugs by authorized personnel as part of an assisted outpatient treatment program. Such order may specify the type and dosage range of such psychotropic drugs and such order shall be effective for the duration of such assisted outpatient treatment.

(5) If the petitioner is the director of a hospital that operates an assisted outpatient treatment program, the court order shall direct the hospital director to provide or arrange for all categories of assisted outpatient treatment for the assisted outpatient throughout the period of the order. In all other instances, the order shall require the appropriate director, as that term is defined in this section, to provide or arrange for all categories of assisted outpatient treatment for the assisted outpatient throughout the period of the order.

(6) The director shall cause a copy of any court order issued pursuant to this section to be served personally, or by mail, facsimile or electronic means, upon the assisted outpatient, the mental hygiene legal service or anyone acting on the assisted outpatient's behalf, the original petitioner, identified service providers, and all others entitled to notice under subdivision (f) of this section.

(k) Petition for additional periods of treatment.

(1) Prior to the expiration of an order pursuant to this section, the appropriate director shall review whether the assisted outpatient continues to meet the criteria for assisted outpatient treatment. If, as documented in the petition, the director determines that such criteria continue to be met or has made appropriate attempts to, but has not been successful in eliciting, the cooperation of the subject to submit to an examination, within thirty days prior to the expiration of an order of assisted outpatient treatment, such director may petition the court to order continued assisted outpatient treatment pursuant to paragraph two of this subdivision. Upon determining whether such criteria continue to be met, such director shall notify the program coordinator in writing as to whether a petition for continued assisted outpatient treatment is warranted and whether such a petition was or will be filed.

(2) Within thirty days prior to the expiration of an order of assisted outpatient treatment, the appropriate director or the current petitioner, if the current petition was filed pursuant to subparagraph (i) or (ii) of paragraph one of subdivision (e) of this section, and the current petitioner retains his or her original status pursuant to the applicable subparagraph, may petition the court to order continued assisted outpatient treatment for a period not to exceed one year from the expiration date of the current order. If the court's disposition of such petition does not occur prior to the expiration date of the current order, the current order shall remain in effect until such disposition. The procedures for obtaining any order pursuant to this subdivision shall be in accordance with the provisions of the foregoing subdivisions of this section; provided that the time restrictions included in paragraph four of subdivision (c) of this section shall not be applicable. The notice provisions set forth in paragraph six of subdivision (j) of this section shall be applicable. Any court order requiring periodic blood tests or urinalysis for the presence of alcohol or illegal drugs shall be subject to review after six months by the physician who developed the written treatment plan or another physician designated by the director, and such physician shall be authorized to terminate such blood tests or urinalysis without further action by the court.

(*l*) Petition for an order to stay, vacate or modify.

(1) In addition to any other right or remedy available by law with respect to the order for assisted outpatient treatment, the assisted outpatient, the mental hygiene legal service, or anyone acting on the assisted outpatient's behalf may petition the court on notice to the director, the original petitioner, and all others entitled to notice under subdivision (f) of this section to stay, vacate or modify the order.

(2) The appropriate director shall petition the court for approval before instituting a proposed material change in the assisted outpatient treatment plan, unless such change is authorized by the order of the court. Such petition shall be filed on notice to all parties entitled to notice under subdivision (f) of this section. Not later than five days after receiving such petition, excluding Saturdays, Sundays and holidays, the court shall hold a hearing on the petition; provided that if the assisted outpatient informs the court that he or she agrees to the proposed material change, the court may approve such change without a hearing. Non-material changes may be instituted by the director without court approval. For the purposes of this paragraph, a material change is an addition or deletion of a category of services to or from a current assisted outpatient treatment plan, or any deviation without the assisted outpatient's consent from the terms of a current order relating to the administration of psychotropic drugs.

(m) Appeals. Review of an order issued pursuant to this section shall be had in like manner as specified in section 9.35 of this article.

(n) Failure to comply with assisted outpatient treatment. Where in the clinical judgment of a physician, (i) the assisted outpatient, has failed or refused to comply with the assisted outpatient treatment, (ii) efforts were made to solicit compliance, and (iii) such assisted outpatient may be in need of involuntary admission to a hospital pursuant to section 9.27 of this article or immediate observation, care and treatment pursuant to section 9.39 or 9.40 of this article, such physician may request the appropriate director of community services, the director's designee, or any physician designated by the director of community services pursuant to section 9.37 of this article, to direct the removal of such assisted outpatient to an appropriate hospital for an examination to determine if such person has a mental illness for which hospitalization is necessary pursuant to section 9.27, 9.39 or 9.40 of this article. Furthermore, if such assisted outpatient refuses to take medications as required by the court order, or he or she refuses to take, or fails a blood test, urinalysis, or alcohol or drug test as required by the court order, such physician may consider such refusal or failure when determining whether the assisted outpatient is in need of an examination to determine whether he or she has a mental illness for which hospitalization is necessary. Upon the request of such physician, the appropriate director, the director's designee, or any physician designated pursuant to section 9.37 of this article, may direct peace officers, acting pursuant to their special duties, or police officers who are members of an authorized police department or force or of a sheriff's department to take the assisted outpatient into custody and transport him or her to the hospital operating the assisted outpatient treatment program or to any hospital authorized by the appropriate director of community services to receive such persons. Such law enforcement officials shall carry out such directive. Upon the request of such physician, the director, the director's designee, or any physician designated pursuant to section 9.37 of this article, an ambulance service, as defined by subdivision two of section three thousand one of the public health law, or an approved mobile crisis outreach team as defined in section 9.58 of this article shall be authorized to take into custody and transport any such person to the hospital operating the assisted outpatient treatment program, or to any other hospital authorized by the director of community services to receive such persons. Any director of community services, or designee, shall be authorized to direct the removal of an assisted outpatient who is present in his or her county to an appropriate hospital, in accordance with the provisions of this subdivision, based upon a determination of the appropriate director of community services directing the removal of such assisted outpatient pursuant to this subdivision. Such person may be retained for observation, care and treatment and further examination in the hospital for up to seventy-two hours to permit a physician to determine whether such person has a mental illness and is in need of involuntary care and treatment in a hospital pursuant to the provisions of this article. Any continued involuntary retention in such hospital beyond the initial seventy-two hour period shall be in accordance with the provisions of this article relating to the involuntary admission and retention of a person. If at any time during the seventy-two hour period the person is determined not to meet the involuntary admission and retention provisions of this article, and does not agree to stay in the hospital as a voluntary or informal patient, he or she must be released. Failure to comply with an order of assisted outpatient treatment shall not be grounds for involuntary civil commitment or a finding of contempt of court.

(o) Effect of determination that a person is in need of assisted outpatient treatment. The determination by a court that a person is in need of assisted outpatient treatment shall not be construed as or deemed to be a determination that such person is incapacitated pursuant to article eighty-one of this chapter.

(p) False petition. A person making a false statement or providing false information or false testimony in a petition or hearing under this section shall be subject to criminal prosecution pursuant to article one hundred seventy-five or article two hundred ten of the penal law.

(q) Exception. Nothing in this section shall be construed to affect the ability of the director of a hospital to receive, admit, or retain patients who otherwise meet the provisions of this article regarding receipt, retention or admission.

(r) Education and training.

(1) The office of mental health, in consultation with the office of court administration, shall prepare educational and training materials on the use of this section, which shall be made available to local governmental units, providers of services, judges, court personnel, law enforcement officials and the general public.

(2) The office, in consultation with the office of court administration, shall establish a mental health training program for supreme and county court judges and court personnel. Such training shall focus on the use of this section and generally address issues relating to mental illness and mental health treatment.

Repealed June 30, 2017

*§9.61 Transportation of persons to or between hospitals.

In carrying out the transportation of any person to or between a hospital, including a comprehensive psychiatric emergency program, pursuant to the provisions of this article appropriate attempts shall be made to elicit the cooperation of the person to be transported, prior to resorting to compulsory means of transportation.   *(Eff. June 30, 2017)*

*§9.63 Transportation of persons to or between hospitals.

In carrying out the transportation of any person to or between a hospital, including a comprehensive psychiatric emergency program, pursuant to the provisions of this article appropriate attempts shall be made to elicit the cooperation of the person to be transported, prior to resorting to compulsory means of transportation.

**Reverts to § 9.61 on June 30, 2017 per ch 408/99-Ext. per Ch.139/10*

ARTICLE 29
General Provisions Relating to
In-patient Facilities

Section

29.15 Discharge and conditional release of patients to the community.

§29.15 Discharge and conditional release of patients to the community.

(a) A patient may be discharged or conditionally released to the community by the director of a department facility, if, in the opinion of staff familiar with the patient's case history, such patient does not require active in-patient care and treatment.

(b) A patient may be conditionally released, rather than discharged, when in the opinion of staff familiar with the patient's case history, the clinical needs of such patient warrant this more restrictive placement, provided, however, that

1. an involuntary patient may be conditionally released only for the remainder of the authorized retention period; and

2. except as provided in subdivision (d) of this section, a voluntary patient may be conditionally released only for a twelve month period, provided however that (i) a voluntary patient under sixteen years of age may be conditionally released only after consultation with the parent, legal guardian, or next-of-kin of such patient; (ii) a voluntary patient over sixteen and under eighteen years of age may be conditionally released only with his consent or with the consent of the parent, legal guardian, or next-of-kin of such patient; (iii) a voluntary patient eighteen years of age or older may be conditionally released only with his consent.

(c) The director of a department facility from which any patient is conditionally released shall cause all such patients to be informed once during each one hundred twenty days of conditional release of their status and rights, including their right to avail themselves of the facilities of the mental hygiene legal service. At the time of such periodic notification, the written consent of a patient to his continued stay on conditional release status shall be obtained and a copy thereof shall be given to the mental hygiene legal service.

(d) 1. No voluntary patient who has been conditionally released shall be continued on such status for a period beyond twelve months from the date of commencement of such status or beyond twelve months from the effective date of this statute, whichever is later, unless the suitability of such patient to remain on such status and his willingness to so remain have been reviewed. The director shall review the suitability of such patient to remain in such status, and the mental hygiene legal service shall review the willingness of such patient to remain in such status. Notice of the determination of the patient's suitability made by the director shall be given to the mental hygiene legal service. If the mental hygiene legal service finds that there is any ground to doubt the director's determination of the suitability of such patient to remain on such status, or the willingness of the patient to so remain, it shall make an application, upon notice to the patient and the director of the facility for a court order determining those questions. In any such proceeding, the patient or someone on his behalf or the mental hygiene legal service may request a hearing. If the mental hygiene legal service finds no grounds to doubt the determination of the director as to the suitability or the willingness of the patient to continue on conditional release status, it shall so certify and the patient may be continued on such status. A copy of such certification of review shall be filed in the patient's record.

2. If an application for a court order has been made, the court, in determining the proceeding, may approve the continued conditional release of the patient or, if the court finds that the patient is not suitable or willing to continue on conditional release status, it may order the discharge of such patient.

3. Prior to the termination of twelve months from the date of the certification by the mental hygiene legal service of such first review or, if an application for a court order has been made, from the date of the first order and, thereafter, prior to the termination of twelve months from any subsequent certification or subsequent order, as the case may be, the director and the mental hygiene legal service shall conduct another review of the patient's suitability and willingness to remain on conditional release status, as set forth in the foregoing subdivisions.

(e) *1. In the case of an involuntary patient on conditional release, the director may terminate the conditional release and order the patient to return to the facility at any time during the period for which retention was authorized, if, in the director's judgment, the patient needs in-patient care and treatment and the conditional release is no longer appropriate; provided, however, that in any such case, the director shall cause written notice of such patient's return to be given to the mental hygiene legal service. The director shall cause the patient to be retained for observation, care and treatment and further examination in a hospital for up to seventy-two hours if a physician on the staff of the hospital determines that such person may have a mental illness and may be in need of involuntary care and treatment in a hospital pursuant to the provisions of article nine of this chapter. Any continued retention in such hospital beyond the initial seventy-two hour period shall be in accordance with the provisions of this chapter relating to the involuntary admission and retention of a person. If at any time during the seventy-two hour period the person is determined not to meet the involuntary admission and retention provisions of this chapter, and does not agree to stay in the hospital as a voluntary or informal patient, he or she must be released, either conditionally or unconditionally.   *Effective until June 30, 2017*

*1. In the case of an involuntary patient on conditional release, the director may terminate the conditional release and order the patient to return to the facility at any time during the period for which retention was authorized, if, in the director's judgment, the patient needs in-patient care and treatment and the conditional release is no longer appropriate provided, however, that in any such case, the director shall cause written notice of such patient's return to be given to the mental hygiene legal service. If, at any time prior to the expiration of thirty days from the date of return to the facility, he or any relative or friend or the mental hygiene legal service gives notice in writing to the director of request for hearing on the question of the suitability of such patient's return to the facility, a hearing shall be held pursuant to the provisions of this chapter relating to the involuntary admission of a person.   *Effective June 30, 2017*

2. In the case of a voluntary patient on conditional release, the director may terminate the conditional release and order the patient to return to the facility at any time, if, in the judgment of the director, the patient needs in-patient care and treatment and the conditional release is no longer appropriate, provided, however, that if such patient does not consent to return to the facility, he shall not be returned to the facility, except in accordance with the provisions of this chapter and the regulations of the commissioner for the involuntary admission of a person.

(f) The discharge or conditional release of all clients at developmental centers, patients at psychiatric centers or patients at psychiatric inpatient services subject to licensure by the office of mental health shall be in accordance with a written service plan prepared by staff familiar with the case history of the client or patient to be discharged or conditionally released and in cooperation with appropriate social services officials and directors of local governmental units. In causing such plan to be prepared, the director of the facility shall take steps to assure that the following persons are interviewed, provided an opportunity to actively participate in the development of such plan and advised of whatever services might be available to the patient through the mental hygiene legal service: the patient to be discharged or conditionally released; an authorized representative of the patient, to include the parent or parents if the patient is a minor, unless such minor sixteen years of age or older objects to the participation of the parent or parents and there has been a clinical determination by a physician that the involvement of the parent or parents is not clinically appropriate and such determination is documented in the clinical record and there is no plan to discharge or release the minor to the home of such parent or parents; and upon the request of the patient sixteen years of age or older, a significant individual to the patient including any relative, close friend or individual otherwise concerned with the welfare of the patient, other than an employee of the facility.

(g) A written service plan prepared pursuant to this section shall include, but shall not be limited to, the following:

1. a statement of the patient's need, if any, for supervision, medication, aftercare services, and assistance in finding employment following discharge or conditional release, and

2. a specific recommendation of the type of residence in which the patient is to live and a listing of the services available to the patient in such residence.

3. A listing of organizations, facilities, including those of the department, and individuals who are available to provide services in accordance with the identified needs of the patient.

4. The notification of the appropriate school district and the committee on special education regarding the proposed discharge or release of a patient under twenty-one years of age, consistent with all applicable federal and state laws relating to confidentiality of such information.

5. An evaluation of the patient's need and potential eligibility for public benefits following discharge or conditional release, including public assistance, medicaid, and supplemental security income. An inpatient facility operated or licensed by the office of mental health shall provide reasonable and appropriate assistance to the patient, in cooperation with local social services districts, in applying for benefits identified in the written service plan pursuant to paragraph five of this subdivision, prior to discharge or conditional release.

(h) It shall also be the responsibility of the director of any department facility from which a client or patient has been discharged or conditionally released, in collaboration, when appropriate, with appropriate social services officials and directors of local governmental units, to prepare, to cause to be implemented, and to monitor a comprehensive program designed:

1. to determine whether the residence in which such client or patient is living, is adequate and appropriate for the needs of such patient or client;

2. to verify that such patient or client is receiving the services specified in such patient's or client's written service plan; and

3. to recommend, and to take steps to assure the provision of, any additional services.

(i) 1. No patient about to be discharged or conditionally released from a department facility or an inpatient facility operated or licensed by the office of mental health shall be directly referred to any facility subject to licensure, certification or approval by any state agency or department, unless it has been determined that such facility has a current and valid license, certificate or approval. In addition, no patient about to be discharged or conditionally released from a department facility shall be directly referred to any residential accommodation not subject to licensure, certification or approval by any state agency or department unless it has been determined, after consultation with appropriate local agencies, that such residential accommodation complies with all appropriate local zoning, building, fire and safety codes, ordinances and regulations.

2. (I) A patient about to be discharged or conditionally released from a department facility licensed or operated by the office for people with developmental disabilities or from an inpatient facility operated or licensed by the office of alcoholism and substance abuse services or the office of mental health to an adult home or residence for adults, as defined in section two of the social services law, shall be referred only to such home or residence that is consistent with that patient's needs and that operates pursuant to section four hundred sixty of the social services law, provided further that: (A) for a department facility licensed or operated by the office for people with developmental disabilities or for an inpatient facility operated by the office of alcoholism and substance abuse services or the office of mental health, the facility director retains authority to determine whether the home, program or residence is consistent with that patient's needs and (B) such referral shall be made to the patient's home county whenever possible or appropriate.

(II) No patient about to be discharged or conditionally released from a department facility licensed or operated by the office for people with developmental disabilities or from an inpatient facility operated or licensed by the office of alcoholism and substance abuse services or the office of mental health shall be referred to any adult home or residence for adults, as defined in section two of the social services law, which has received an official written notice from the department of health of: (A) the proposed revocation, suspension or denial of its operating certificate; (B) the limitation of its operating certificate with respect to new admissions; (C) the issuance of a department of health order or commissioner of health's order or the seeking of equitable relief pursuant to section four hundred sixty-d of the social services law; (D) the proposed assessment of civil penalties for violations of the provisions of subparagraph two of paragraph (b) of subdivision seven of section four hundred sixty-d of the social services law; or placement on the "do not refer list" pursuant to subdivision fifteen of section four hundred sixty-d of the social services law. Referrals may resume when such enforcement actions are resolved.

(III) A community provider of mental hygiene services, including a provider of case management services, which serves residents of any home or residence in which the department of social services has acted pursuant to subdivision nine of section four hundred sixty-one-c of the social services law, shall assist the operator of such home or residence or the department of social services in efforts to secure an appropriate alternate placement of a resident.

(IV) The commissioner shall promptly refer to the department of social services any serious complaint received about the care provided or health and safety conditions in an adult home or residence for adults. The commissioner may as appropriate assist the department of social services in the investigation and resolution of such complaints as well as in the investigation and resolution of any such complaint which is initially received by the department of social services.

(j) The department shall submit to the legislature and the governor by the first day of January, nineteen hundred seventy-eight, a comprehensive plan describing those reasonable steps taken or to be taken by the department to locate former patients who had been in a department facility for a continuous period for two or more years prior to their discharge or conditional release and who had been discharged or conditionally released on or after the thirty-first day of December, nineteen hundred seventy without the benefit of a written service plan. In each case in which the person has been located, the department, in cooperation with appropriate social services officials and directors of community services, shall make every effort to develop a written service plan for such person and shall assume the same responsibilities with respect to such person as the department is required to assume with respect to a person who was discharged or conditionally released from a department facility pursuant to a written service plan.

(k) No patient shall be required, as a condition precedent to his discharge, to agree to the terms of a written service plan. If after the advisability of following the program proposed in the written service plan has been explained to the patient who has been discharged or who is to be discharged, such patient expresses his objection to such program or any part thereof, a notation of such objection shall be made in the patient's records.

(*l*) Nothing in this section shall be construed to prohibit, limit, or restrict the obligation of the director of a department facility to make necessary expenditures for the board and family care of patients subject to the approval of the commissioner, provided that no such expenditure shall be made with respect to any patient who is receiving public assistance and care under the social services law.

(m) It shall be the responsibility of the chief administrator of any facility providing inpatient services subject to licensure by the office of mental health to notify, when appropriate, the local social services commissioner and appropriate state and local mental health representatives when an inpatient is about to be discharged or conditionally released and to provide to such officials the written service plan developed for such inpatient as required under subdivision (f) of this section.

(n) It shall be the duty of directors of local social services districts and local governmental units to cooperate with facilities licensed or operated by an office of the department in the preparation and implementation of comprehensive written services plans as required by this section.

ARTICLE 33
Rights of Patients

§33.13 Clinical records; confidentiality.

(a) A clinical record for each patient or client shall be maintained at each facility licensed or operated by the office of mental health or the office for people with developmental disabilities, hereinafter referred to as the offices. For the purposes of this section, the term "facility" shall mean "facility" as such term is defined in section 1.03 of this chapter, provided, however, such term shall also include any provider of services for individuals with mental illness or developmental disabilities which is operated by, under contract with, receives funding from, or is otherwise approved to render services by, a director of community services pursuant to article forty-one of this chapter or one or both of the offices, including any such provider which is exempt from the requirement for an operating certificate under article sixteen or article thirty-one of this chapter. The record shall contain information on all matters relating to the admission, legal status, care, and treatment of the patient or client and shall include all pertinent documents relating to the patient or client. The commissioners of such offices, by regulation, each shall determine the scope and method of recording information, including data pertaining to admission, legal matters affecting the patient or client, records and notation of course of care and treatment, therapies, restrictions on patient's or client's rights, periodic examinations, and such other information as he or she may require.

*(b) The commissioners may require that statistical information about patients or clients be reported to the offices.   *Effective until June 30, 2017

*(b) The commissioners may require that statistical information about patients or clients be reported to the offices. Names of patients treated at out-patient or non-residential facilities shall not be required as part of any such reports. Hospitals licensed by the office of mental health and general hospitals shall provide to the office of mental health, upon request, records relating to persons described in subdivision (j) of section 7.09 of this chapter who may be disqualified from possessing a firearm pursuant to 18 USC 422(4)(d).

*Effective June 30, 2017

(c) Such information about patients or clients reported to the offices, including the identification of patients or clients, clinical records or clinical information tending to identify patients or clients, and records and information concerning persons under consideration for proceedings pursuant to article ten of this chapter, at office facilities shall not be a public record and shall not be released by the offices or its facilities to any person or agency outside of the offices except as follows:

1. pursuant to an order of a court of record requiring disclosure upon a finding by the court that the interests of justice significantly outweigh the need for confidentiality, provided, however, that nothing herein shall be construed to affect existing rights of employees in disciplinary proceedings.

2. to the mental hygiene legal service.

3. to attorneys representing patients or clients in proceedings in which the patients' or clients' involuntary hospitalization or assisted outpatient treatment is at issue.

4. to the justice center for the protection of people with special needs.

5. to the medical review board of the state commission of correction when such board has requested such information with respect to the death of a named person, or, with the consent of a patient or client when such board has requested information about the patient or client providing that such board requires such information in the exercise of its statutory functions, powers and duties. Information, books, records or data which are confidential as provided by law shall be kept confidential by the commission and any limitation on the release thereof imposed by law upon the party furnishing the information, books, records or data shall apply to the medical review board.

6. to an endangered individual and a law enforcement agency when a treating psychiatrist or psychologist has determined that a patient or client presents a serious and imminent danger to that individual. The reasons for any such disclosures shall be fully documented in the clinical record. Nothing in this paragraph shall be construed to impose an obligation upon a treating psychiatrist or psychologist to release information pursuant to this paragraph.

7. with the consent of the patient or client or of someone authorized to act on the patient's or client's behalf, to persons and entities who have a demonstrable need for such information and who have obtained such consent, provided that disclosure will not reasonably be expected to be detrimental to the patient, client or another provided, however, that release of such information to a patient or client shall not be governed by this subdivision.

8. to the state board for professional medical conduct or the office of professional discipline or their respective representatives when such persons or entities request such information in the exercise of their statutory function, power and duties provided, however, that no such information shall be released when it concerns the subject of an inquiry who is also a patient or client, except pursuant to paragraph one of this subdivision.

9. with the consent of the appropriate commissioner, to:

(i) governmental agencies, insurance companies licensed pursuant to the insurance law and other third parties requiring information necessary for payments to be made to or on behalf of patients or clients pursuant to contract or in accordance with law, such information to be kept confidential and limited to the information required.

(ii) persons and agencies needing information to locate missing persons or to governmental agencies in connection with criminal investigations, such information to be limited to identifying data concerning hospitalization.

(iii) qualified researchers upon the approval of the institutional review board or other committee specially constituted for the approval of research projects at the facility, provided that the researcher shall in no event disclose information tending to identify a patient or client.

(iv) a coroner, a county medical examiner, or the chief medical examiner for New York city upon the request of a facility director that an investigation be conducted into the death of a patient or client for whom such record is maintained.

(v) appropriate persons and entities when necessary to prevent imminent serious harm to the patient or client or another person, provided, however, nothing in this subparagraph shall be construed to impose an obligation to release information pursuant to this subparagraph.

(vi) a district attorney when such request for information is in connection with and necessary to the furtherance of a criminal investigation of patient or client abuse.

(vii) appropriate persons and entities when necessary to protect the public concerning a specific sex offender requiring civil management under article ten of this chapter.

(viii) to the attorney general, case review panel, or psychiatric examiners described in article ten of this chapter, when such persons or entities request such information in the exercise of their statutory functions, powers and duties under article ten of this chapter.

10. to a correctional facility, when the chief administrative officer has requested such information with respect to a named inmate of such correctional facility as defined by subdivision three of section forty of the correction law or to the department of corrections and community supervision, when the department has requested such information with respect to a person under its jurisdiction or an inmate of a state correctional facility, when such inmate is within four weeks of release from such institution to community supervision. Information released pursuant to this paragraph may be limited to a summary of the record, including but not limited to: the basis for referral to the facility; the diagnosis upon admission and discharge; a diagnosis and description of the patient's or client's current mental condition; the current course of treatment, medication and therapies; and the facility's recommendation for future mental hygiene services, if any. Such information may be forwarded to the department of corrections and community supervision staff in need of such information for the purpose of making a determination regarding an inmate's health care, security, safety or ability to participate in programs. In the event an inmate is transferred, the sending correctional facility shall forward, upon request, such summaries to the chief administrative officer of any correctional facility to which the inmate is subsequently incarcerated. The office of mental health and the office for people with developmental disabilities, in consultation with the commission of correction and the department of corrections and community supervision, shall promulgate rules and regulations to implement the provisions of this paragraph.

11. to a qualified person pursuant to section 33.16 of this chapter.

12. to a director of community services as defined in article nine of this chapter or his or her designee, provided that such director or his or her designee (i) requests such information in the exercise of his or her statutory functions, powers and duties pursuant to section 9.37, 9.45, 9.47, 9.48, 9.60 or 41.13 of this chapter; or (ii) the disclosure of information is required pursuant to section 9.46 of this chapter.

13. to the state division of criminal justice services for the sole purposes of:

(i) providing, facilitating, evaluating or auditing access by the commissioner of mental health to criminal history information pursuant to subdivision (i) of section 7.09 of this chapter; or

(ii) providing information to the criminal justice information services division of the federal bureau of investigation by the commissioner of mental health or the commissioner of developmental disabilities, for the purposes of responding to queries to the national instant criminal background check system regarding attempts to purchase or otherwise take possession of firearms, in accordance with applicable federal laws or regulations.

14. to the criminal justice information services division of the federal bureau of investigation, for the purposes of responding to queries to the national

instant criminal background check system, regarding attempts to purchase or otherwise take possession of firearms, in accordance with applicable federal laws or regulations.

15. to the division of criminal justice services, names and other non-clinical identifying information for the sole purpose of implementing the division's responsibilities and duties under sections 400.00 and 400.02 of the penal law.

16. to a mental health incident review panel, or members thereof, established by the commissioner pursuant to section 31.37 of this title, in connection with incident reviews conducted by such panel.

*(d) Nothing in this section shall prevent the electronic or other exchange of information concerning patients or clients, including identification, between and among (i) facilities or others providing services for such patients or clients pursuant to an approved local services plan, as defined in article forty-one of this chapter, or pursuant to agreement with the department, and (ii) the department or any of its licensed or operated facilities. Furthermore, subject to the prior approval of the commissioner of mental health, hospital emergency services licensed pursuant to article twenty-eight of the public health law shall be authorized to exchange information concerning patients or clients electronically or otherwise with other hospital emergency services licensed pursuant to article twenty-eight of the public health law and/or hospitals licensed or operated by the office of mental health; provided that such exchange of information is consistent with standards, developed by the commissioner of mental health, which are designed to ensure confidentiality of such information. Additionally, information so exchanged shall be kept confidential and any limitations on the release of such information imposed on the party giving the information shall apply to the party receiving the information.   *Effective until June 30, 2017*

*(d) Nothing in this section shall prevent the exchange of information concerning patients or clients, including identification, between (i) facilities or others providing services for such patients or clients pursuant to an approved local services plan, as defined in article forty-one, or pursuant to agreement with the department and (ii) the department or any of its facilities. Information so exchanged shall be kept confidential and any limitations on the release of such information imposed on the party giving the information shall apply to the party receiving the information.   *Effective June 30, 2017*

(e) Clinical information tending to identify patients or clients and clinical records maintained at a facility not operated by the offices, shall not be a public record and shall not be released to any person or agency outside such facility except pursuant to subdivisions (b), (c) and (d) of this section. The director of such a facility may consent to the release of such information and records, subject to regulation by the commissioner, pursuant to the exceptions stated in subdivision (c) of this section; provided that, for the purpose of this subdivision, such consent shall be deemed to be the consent otherwise required of the commissioner pursuant to subdivision (c) of this section. Nothing in this subdivision shall be construed to limit, restrict or otherwise affect access to such clinical information or records by the mental hygiene legal service, the commission on quality of care for the mentally disabled or the offices when such access is authorized elsewhere in law.

(f) Any disclosure made pursuant to this section shall be limited to that information necessary in light of the reason for disclosure. Information so disclosed shall be kept confidential by the party receiving such information and the limitations on disclosure in this section shall apply to such party. Except for disclosures made to the mental hygiene legal service, to persons reviewing information or records in the ordinary course of insuring that a facility is in compliance with applicable quality of care standards, or to governmental agents requiring information necessary for payments to be made to or on behalf of patients or clients pursuant to contract or in accordance with law, a notation of all such disclosures shall be placed in the clinical record of that individual who shall be informed of all such disclosures upon request; provided, however, that for disclosures made to insurance companies licensed pursuant to the insurance law, such a notation need only be entered at the time the disclosure is first made.

17. to the agency designated by the governor pursuant to subdivision (b) of section 558 of the executive law to provide protection and advocacy services and administer the protection and advocacy system as provided for by federal law.

§33.16 Access to clinical records.
(a) Definitions. For the purposes of this section:
1. "Clinical record" means any information concerning or relating to the examination or treatment of an identifiable patient or client maintained or possessed by a facility which has treated or is treating such patient or client, except data disclosed to a practitioner in confidence by other persons on the basis of an express condition that such data would never be disclosed to the patient or client or other persons, provided that such data has never been disclosed by the practitioner or a facility to any other person. If at any time such data is disclosed, it shall be considered clinical records for the purposes of this section. For purposes of this subdivision, "disclosure to any other person" shall not include disclosures made pursuant to section 33.13 of this article, to practitioners as part of a consultation or referral during the treatment of the patient or client, to the statewide planning and research cooperative system, or to the committee or a court pursuant to the provisions of this section or to an insurance carrier insuring, or an attorney consulted by, a facility.
2. "Committee" means a clinical record access review committee appointed pursuant to this section.
3. "Facility" means a facility as defined in section 1.03 of this chapter, a program requiring approval for operation pursuant to article thirty-two of this chapter, institutions offering training in psychotherapy, psychoanalysis and related areas chartered pursuant to section two hundred sixteen of the education law, or, notwithstanding section 1.03 of this chapter, any provider of services for persons with mental illness or developmental disabilities which is operated by, under contract with, receives funding from, or is otherwise approved to render services by, a director of community services pursuant to article forty-one of this chapter or one or both of the offices, including any such provider which is exempt from the requirement for an operating certificate under article sixteen or article thirty-one of this chapter.
4. "Mental health practitioner" or "practitioner" means a person employed by or rendering a service at a facility maintaining the clinical record licensed under article one hundred thirty-one of the education law who practices psychiatry or a person licensed under article one hundred thirty-nine, one hundred fifty-three or one hundred fifty-four of the education law or any other person not prohibited by law from providing mental health or developmental disabilities services.

5. "Patient or client" means an individual concerning whom a clinical record is maintained or possessed by a facility as defined in paragraph three of this subdivision.

6. "Qualified person" means any properly identified patient or client, guardian of a person with a developmental disability appointed pursuant to article seventeen-A of the surrogate's court procedure act, or committee for an incompetent appointed pursuant to this chapter or a parent of an infant, or a guardian of an infant appointed pursuant to article seventeen of the surrogate's court procedure act or other legally appointed guardian of an infant who may be entitled to request access to a clinical record pursuant to paragraph three of subdivision (b) of this section, or a parent, spouse or adult child of an adult patient or client who may be entitled to request access to a clinical record pursuant to paragraph four of subdivision (b) of this section.

7. "Treating practitioner" means the practitioner, who has or had primary responsibility for the care of the patient or client within the facility or if such practitioner is unavailable, a practitioner designated by such facility.

(b) Access by qualified persons.

1. Subject to the provisions of subdivision (c) of this section, upon the written request of any patient or client, a facility shall provide an opportunity, within ten days, for such individual to inspect any clinical record concerning or relating to the examination or treatment of such individual in the possession of such facility.

2. Subject to the provisions of subdivision (c) of this section, upon the written request of a committee for an incompetent appointed pursuant to this chapter or a guardian of the person of a person with a developmental disability appointed pursuant to article seventeen-A of the surrogate's court procedure act, a facility shall provide an opportunity, within ten days, for the committee or such guardian to inspect any clinical record concerning the patient or client in the possession of such facility. Provided, however, in the case of any such request by such a guardian to inspect the clinical record concerning a client eighteen years of age or older, the facility shall notify such client of such request.

3. Subject to the provisions of subdivision (c) of this section and except as otherwise provided by law, upon the written request of a parent of an infant or guardian of an infant appointed pursuant to article seventeen of the surrogate's court procedure act, or any other legally appointed guardian of an infant, a facility shall provide an opportunity, within ten days, for such parent or guardian to inspect any clinical record maintained or possessed by such facility concerning care and treatment of the infant for which the consent of a parent or guardian was obtained or has been requested; provided, however, that such parent or guardian shall not be entitled to inspect or make copies of any clinical record concerning the care and treatment of an infant where the treating practitioner determines that access to the information requested by such parent or guardian would have a detrimental effect on the practitioner's professional relationship with the infant, or on the care and treatment of the infant or on the infant's relationship with his or her parents or guardians.

4. Subject to the provisions of subdivision (c) of this section and except as otherwise required by law, upon the written request of a parent of an adult patient or client, spouse or adult child of a patient or client, a facility shall provide an opportunity, within ten days, for such parent, spouse or adult child to inspect any clinical record maintained or possessed by such facility concerning the care and treatment of such patient or client for which the parent,

spouse or adult child is authorized pursuant to law, rule or regulation to provide consent and has consented or is being requested to provide such consent; provided, however, that such parent, spouse or adult child shall not be entitled to inspect or make copies of any clinical record concerning the care and treatment of the patient or client where the treating practitioner determines that access to the information requested by such parent, spouse or adult child would have a detrimental effect on the practitioner's professional relationship with the patient or client, or on the care and treatment of the patient or client or on the relationship of the patient or client with his or her parents, spouse or adult child. Any inspection of a clinical record made pursuant to this paragraph shall be limited to that information which is relevant in light of the reason for such inspection.

5. Subject to the provisions of this subdivision and subdivision (c) of this section, upon the written request of any qualified person, a facility shall furnish to such person, within a reasonable time, a copy of any clinical record requested which the person is authorized to inspect pursuant to this subdivision.

6. The facility may impose a reasonable charge for all inspections and copies, not exceeding the costs incurred by such provider. However, the reasonable charge for paper copies shall not exceed seventy-five cents per page. A qualified person shall not be denied access to the clinical record solely because of inability to pay.

7. A facility may place reasonable limitations on the time, place, and frequency of any inspection of clinical records.

8. A treating practitioner may request the opportunity to review the patient information with the qualified person requesting such information, but such review shall not be a prerequisite for furnishing the record.

9. A facility may make available for inspection either the original or a copy of clinical records.

(c) Limitations on access.

1. Upon receipt of a written request by a qualified person to inspect or copy the clinical record maintained by a facility, the facility shall inform the treating practitioner of the request. The treating practitioner may review the information requested. Unless the treating practitioner determines pursuant to paragraph three of this subdivision that the requested review of the clinical record can reasonably be expected to cause substantial and identifiable harm to the patient or client or others which would outweigh the qualified person's right of access to the record, review of such record shall be permitted or copies provided.

2. A patient or client over the age of twelve may be notified of any request by a qualified person to review his/her record and if the patient or client objects to disclosure, the facility, in consultation with the treating practitioner may deny the request.

3. If, after consideration of all the attendant facts and circumstances, the practitioner or treating practitioner determines that the requested review of all or part of the clinical record can reasonably be expected to cause substantial and identifiable harm to the patient or client or others, or would have a detrimental effect as defined in subdivision (b) of this section, the facility may accordingly deny access to all or a part of the record and may grant access to a prepared summary of the record. In determining whether the review can reasonably be expected to cause substantial and identifiable harm to the patient or client or others which would outweigh the qualified person's right of access to the record or whether review of the record would have a detrimental effect

as defined in subdivision (b) of this section, the practitioner or treating practitioner may consider, among other things, the following: (i) the need for, and the fact of, continuing care and treatment; (ii) the extent to which the knowledge of the information contained in the clinical record may be harmful to the health or safety of the patient or client or others; (iii) the extent to which the clinical record contains sensitive information disclosed in confidence to the practitioner or treating practitioner by family members, friends and other persons; (iv) the extent to which the clinical record contains sensitive information disclosed to the practitioner or the treating practitioner by the patient or client which would be injurious to the patient's or client's relationships with other persons except where the patient or client is requesting information concerning himself or herself; and (v) in the case of a minor making a request for access pursuant to paragraph one of subdivision (b), the age of the patient or client.

4. In the event of a denial of access, the qualified person shall be informed by the facility of such denial, and of the qualified person's right to obtain, without cost, a review of the denial by the appropriate clinical record access review committee. If the qualified person requests such review, the facility shall, within ten days of receipt of such request, transmit the record to the chairman of the appropriate committee with a statement setting forth the specific reasons access was denied. After an in camera review of the materials provided and after providing all parties a reasonable opportunity to be heard, the committee shall promptly make a determination whether the requested reviews of the record can reasonably be expected to cause substantial and identifiable harm to the patient or client or others which outweighs the qualified person's right of access to the record pursuant to paragraph three of this subdivision or whether the requested review would have a detrimental effect as defined in subdivision (b) of this section, and shall accordingly determine whether access to all or part of such record shall be granted. In the event that the committee determines that the request for access shall be granted in whole or in part, the committee shall notify all parties and the facility shall grant access pursuant to such determination.

5. In the event that access is denied in whole or in part the committee shall notify the qualified person of his or her right to seek judicial review of the facility's determination pursuant to this section. Within thirty days of receiving notification of the decision, the qualified person may commence, upon notice, a special proceeding in supreme court for a judgment requiring the provider to make available the record for inspection or copying. The court upon such application and after an in camera review of the materials provided, including the determination and record of the committee, and after providing all parties an opportunity to be heard, shall determine whether there exists a reasonable basis for the denial of access. The relief available pursuant to this section shall be limited to a judgment requiring the facility to make available to the qualified person the requested record for inspection or copying.

(d) Clinical records access review committees. The commissioner of mental health, the commissioner of developmental disabilities and the commissioner of alcoholism and substance abuse services shall appoint clinical record access review committees to hear appeals of the denial of access to patient or client records as provided in paragraph four of subdivision (c) of this section. Members of such committees shall be appointed by the respective commissioners. Such clinical record access review committees shall consist of no less than three nor more than five persons. The commissioners shall promulgate rules and regulations necessary to effectuate the provisions of this subdivision.

(f) Applicability of federal law. Whenever federal law or applicable federal regulations restrict, or as a condition for the receipt of federal aid require, that the release of clinical records or information be more restrictive than is provided under this section, the provisions of federal law or federal regulation shall be controlling.

(g) Challenges to accuracy. A qualified person may challenge the accuracy of information maintained in the clinical record and may require that a brief written statement prepared by him/her concerning the challenged information be inserted into the clinical record. This statement shall become a permanent part of the record and shall be released whenever the clinical record at issue is released. This subdivision shall apply only to factual statements and shall not include a provider's observations, inferences or conclusions. A facility may place reasonable restrictions on the time and frequency of any challenges to accuracy.

(h) Waivers void. Any agreement by an individual to waive any right to inspect, copy or seek correction of the clinical record as provided for in this section shall be deemed to be void as against public policy and wholly unenforceable.

(i) Disclosure. Nothing contained in this section shall restrict, expand or in any way limit the disclosure of any information pursuant to articles twenty-three, thirty-one and forty-five of the civil practice law and rules or section six hundred seventy-seven of the county law.

(j) Proceedings. No proceeding shall be brought or penalty assessed, except as provided for in this section, against a facility, which in good faith, denies access to a clinical record.

(k) Immunity from liability. No facility, practitioner, treating practitioner, mental health practitioner or clinical records access review committee member shall be subjected to civil liability arising solely from granting or providing access to any clinical record in accordance with this section.

§33.21 Consent for mental health treatment of minors.

(a) For the purposes of this section:

(1) "minor" shall mean a person under eighteen years of age, but shall not include a person who is the parent of a child, emancipated, has married or is on voluntary status on his or her own application pursuant to section 9.13 of this chapter;

(2) "mental health practitioner" shall mean a physician, a licensed psychologist, or persons providing services under the supervision of a physician in a facility operated or licensed by the office of mental health;

(3) "outpatient mental health services" shall mean those services provided in an outpatient program licensed or operated pursuant to the regulations of the commissioner of mental health;

(4) "reasonably available" shall mean a parent or guardian can be contacted with diligent efforts by a mental health practitioner; and

(5) "capacity" shall mean the minor's ability to understand and appreciate the nature and consequences of the proposed treatment, including the benefits and risks of, and alternatives to, such proposed treatment, and to reach an informed decision.

(b) In providing outpatient mental health services to a minor, or psychotropic medications to a minor residing in a hospital, the important role of the parents or guardians shall be recognized. As clinically appropriate, steps shall be taken to actively involve the parents or guardians, and the consent of such persons shall be required for such treatment in non-emergency situations, except as provided in subdivisions (c), (d) and (e) of this section or section two thousand five hundred four of the public health law.

(c) A mental health practitioner may provide outpatient mental health services, other than those treatments and procedures for which consent is specifically required by section 33.03 of this article, to a minor voluntarily seeking such services without parental or guardian consent if the mental health practitioner determines that:

(1) the minor is knowingly and voluntarily seeking such services; and

(2) provision of such services is clinically indicated and necessary to the minor's well-being; and

(3) (i) a parent or guardian is not reasonably available; or

(ii) requiring parental or guardian consent or involvement would have a detrimental effect on the course of outpatient treatment; or

(iii) a parent or guardian has refused to give such consent and a physician determines that treatment is necessary and in the best interests of the minor. The mental health practitioner shall fully document the reasons for his or her determinations. Such documentation shall be included in the minor's clinical record, along with a written statement signed by the minor indicating that he or she is voluntarily seeking services. As clinically appropriate, notice of a determination made pursuant to subparagraph (iii) of paragraph three of this subdivision shall be provided to the parent or guardian.

(d) A mental health practitioner may provide a minor voluntarily seeking outpatient services an initial interview without parental or guardian consent or involvement to determine whether the criteria of subdivision (c) of this section are present.

(e) (1) Subject to the regulations of the commissioner of mental health governing the patient's right to object to treatment, subdivision (b) of this section and paragraph two of this subdivision, the consent of a parent or guardian or the authorization of a court shall be required for the non-emergency administration of psychotropic medications to a minor residing in a hospital.

(2) A minor sixteen years of age or older who consents may be administered psychotropic medications without the consent of a parent or guardian or the authorization of a court where:

(i) a parent or guardian is not reasonably available, provided the treating physician determines that (A) the minor has capacity; and (B) such medications are in the minor's best interests; or

(ii) requiring consent of a parent or guardian would have a detrimental effect on the minor, provided the treating physician and a second physician who specializes in psychiatry and is not an employee of the hospital determine that (A) such detrimental effect would occur; (B) the minor has capacity; and (C) such medications are in the minor's best interests; or

(iii) the parent or guardian has refused to give such consent, provided the treating physician and a second physician who specializes in psychiatry and is not an employee of the hospital determine that (A) the minor has capacity; and (B) such medications are in the minor's best interests. Notice of the decision to administer psychotropic medications pursuant to this subparagraph shall be provided to the parent or guardian.

(3) The reasons for an exception authorized pursuant to paragraph two of this subdivision shall be fully documented and such documentation shall be included in the minor's clinical record.

§33.25 Release of records pertaining to allegations and investigations of abuse and mistreatment.

(a) Records and documents pertaining to allegations and investigations into reportable incidents at a facility, as defined in subdivision six of section 1.03 of this chapter, including but not limited to all complaints and reports made pursuant to article eleven of the social services law, shall be released to a qualified person, as defined in paragraph six of subdivision (a) of section 33.16 of this article, upon a written request by such qualified person. Such records and documents shall be made available by the appropriate office within twenty-one days of the conclusion of its investigation, provided that the names and other personally identifying information of other patients and employees shall not be included unless such patients and employees authorize disclosure.

(b) Records and reports released in accordance with this section shall be released pursuant to subdivision (b) of section 33.23 of this article and shall not be further disseminated by the recipient, provided that a recipient may share any records and reports with: (i) a health care provider; (ii) a behavioral health care provider; (iii) law enforcement if the recipient believes a crime has been committed; or (iv) the recipient's attorney.

(c) A cover letter shall accompany records and reports released in accordance with this section and shall state: PURSUANT TO SECTION 33.25 OF THE MENTAL HYGIENE LAW, THE ATTACHED RECORDS AND REPORTS SHALL NOT BE FURTHER DISSEMINATED, EXCEPT THAT YOU MAY SHARE THE REPORT WITH: (i) A HEALTH CARE PROVIDER; (ii) A BEHAVIORAL HEALTH CARE PROVIDER; (iii) LAW ENFORCEMENT, IF YOU BELIEVE A CRIME HAS BEEN COMMITTED; OR (iv) YOUR ATTORNEY.

(d) Nothing in this section shall prohibit the receipt, use or dissemination of any such records, reports, information or results of investigations or inquiry by any patient, former patient, or qualified person or person or official specified in paragraph (i), (ii), (iii) or (iv) of subdivision (b) of this section acting on behalf of any patient, former patient or patient's estate, in any legal action or proceeding brought by or on behalf of such patient, former patient or patient's estate.

ARTICLE 27-F
HIV and AIDS Related Information

§2780. Definitions.

As used in this article, the following terms shall have the following meanings:

1. "AIDS" means acquired immune deficiency syndrome, as may be defined from time to time by the centers for disease control of the United States public health service.

2. "HIV infection" means infection with the human immunodeficiency virus or any other related virus identified as a probable causative agent of AIDS.

3. "HIV related illness" means any illness that may result from or may be associated with HIV infection.

4. "HIV related test or HIV related testing" means any laboratory test, tests or series of tests approved for the diagnosis of HIV.

4-a. "Rapid HIV test or testing" means any laboratory screening test or tests approved for detecting antibodies to HIV, that produce results in sixty minutes or less, and encompasses a confirmatory HIV related test if the screening test is reactive.

5. "Capacity to consent" means an individual's ability, determined without regard to the individual's age, to understand and appreciate the nature and consequences of a proposed health care service, treatment, or procedure, or of a proposed disclosure of confidential HIV related information, as the case may be, and to make an informed decision concerning the service, treatment, procedure or disclosure.

6. "Protected individual" means a person who is the subject of an HIV related test or who has been diagnosed as having HIV infection, AIDS or HIV related illness.

7. "Confidential HIV related information" means any information, in the possession of a person who provides one or more health or social services or who obtains the information pursuant to a release of confidential HIV related information, concerning whether an individual has been the subject of an HIV related test, or has HIV infection, HIV related illness or AIDS, or information which identifies or reasonably could identify an individual as having one or more of such conditions, including information pertaining to such individual's contacts.

8. "Health or social service" means any public or private care, treatment, clinical laboratory test, counseling or educational service for adults or children, and acute, chronic, custodial, residential, outpatient, home or other health care provided pursuant to this chapter or the social services law; public assistance or care as defined in article one of the social services law; employment-related services, housing services, foster care, shelter, protective services, day care, or preventive services provided pursuant to the social services law; services for the mentally disabled as defined in article one of the mental hygiene law; probation services, provided pursuant to articles twelve and twelve-A of the

executive law; parole services, provided pursuant to article eight of the correction law; corrections and community supervision, provided pursuant to the correction law; detention and rehabilitative services provided pursuant to article nineteen-G of the executive law; and the activities of the health care worker HIV/HBV advisory panel pursuant to article twenty-seven-DD of this chapter.

9. "Release of confidential HIV related information" means a written authorization for disclosure of confidential HIV related information which is signed by the protected individual, or if the protected individual lacks capacity to consent, a person authorized pursuant to law to consent to health care for the individual. Such release shall be dated and shall specify to whom disclosure is authorized, the purpose for such disclosure and the time period during which the release is to be effective. A general authorization for the release of medical or other information shall not be construed as a release of confidential HIV related information, unless such authorization specifically indicates its dual purpose as a general authorization and an authorization for the release of confidential HIV related information and complies with the requirements of this subdivision.

10. "Contact" means an identified spouse or sex partner of the protected individual, a person identified as having shared hypodermic needles or syringes with the protected individual or a person who the protected individual may have exposed to HIV under circumstances that present a risk of transmission of HIV, as determined by the commissioner.

11. "Person" includes any natural person, partnership, association, joint venture, trust, public or private corporation, or state or local government agency.

12. "Health facility" means a hospital as defined in section two thousand eight hundred one of this chapter, blood bank, blood center, sperm bank, organ or tissue bank, clinical laboratory, or facility providing care or treatment to persons with a mental disability as defined in article one of the mental hygiene law.

13. "Health care provider" means any physician, nurse, provider of services for the mentally disabled as defined in article one of the mental hygiene law, or other person involved in providing medical, nursing, counseling, or other health care or mental health service, including those associated with, or under contract to, a health maintenance organization or medical services plan.

14. "Child" means any protected individual actually or apparently under eighteen years of age.

15. "Authorized agency" means any agency defined by section three hundred seventy-one of the social services law and, for the purposes of this article, shall include such corporations incorporated or organized under the laws of the state as may be specifically authorized by their certificates of incorporation to receive children for the purposes of adoption or foster care.

16. "Insurance institution" means any corporation, association, partnership, reciprocal exchange, interinsurer, fraternal benefits society, agent, broker or other entity including, but not limited to, any health maintenance organization, medical service plan, or hospital plan which: (a) is engaged in the business of insurance; (b) provides health services coverage plans; or (c) provides benefits under, administers, or provides services for, an employee welfare benefit plan as defined in 29 U.S.C. 1002(1).

17. "Insurance support organization" means any person who regularly engages, in whole or in part, in the practice of assembling or collecting information about natural persons for the primary purpose of providing the information to an insurance institution for insurance transactions, including: (a) the furnishing of consumer reports or investigative consumer reports to an insurance insti-

tution for use in connection with an insurance transaction; or (b) the collection of personal information from insurance institutions or other insurance support organizations for the purpose of detecting or preventing fraud, material misrepresentation, or material non-disclosure in connection with insurance underwriting or insurance claim activity. The following persons shall not be considered "insurance-support organizations" for the purposes of this article: government institutions, insurance institutions, health facilities and health care providers.

§2781. HIV related testing.

1. Except as provided in section three thousand one hundred twenty-one of the civil practice law and rules, or unless otherwise specifically authorized or required by a state or federal law, no person shall order the performance of an HIV related test without first having received informed consent of the subject of the test who has capacity to consent or, when the subject lacks capacity to consent, of a person authorized pursuant to law to consent to health care for such individual. In order for there to be informed consent, the person ordering the test shall, prior to obtaining informed consent, at a minimum advise the protected individual that an HIV-related test is being performed.

2. Informed consent for HIV related testing pursuant to this section shall be valid for such testing until such consent is revoked. Each time that an HIV related test is ordered pursuant to informed consent in accordance with this section, the physician or other person authorized pursuant to law to order the performance of the HIV related test, or such person's representative, shall orally notify the subject of the test or, when the subject lacks capacity to consent, a person authorized pursuant to law to consent to health care for such individual, that an HIV related test will be conducted at such time, and shall note the notification in the patient's record.

3. A person ordering the performance of an HIV related test shall provide either directly or through a representative to the subject of an HIV related test or, if the subject lacks capacity to consent, to a person authorized pursuant to law to consent to health care for the subject, an explanation that:

(a) HIV causes AIDS and can be transmitted through sexual activities and needle-sharing, by pregnant women to their fetuses, and through breastfeeding infants;

(b) there is treatment for HIV that can help an individual stay healthy;

(c) individuals with HIV or AIDS can adopt safe practices to protect uninfected and infected people in their lives from becoming infected or multiply infected with HIV;

(d) testing is voluntary and can be done anonymously at a public testing center;

(e) the law protects the confidentiality of HIV related test results;

(f) the law prohibits discrimination based on an individual's HIV status and services are available to help with such consequences; and

(g) the law allows an individual's informed consent for HIV related testing to be valid for such testing until such consent is revoked by the subject of the HIV related test.

Protocols shall be in place to ensure compliance with this section.

4. A person authorized pursuant to law to order the performance of an HIV related test shall provide directly or through a representative to the person seeking such test an opportunity to remain anonymous through use of a coded system with no linking of individual identity to the test request or results. A health care provider who is not authorized by the commissioner to provide HIV

related tests on an anonymous basis shall refer a person who requests an anonymous test to a test site which does provide anonymous testing. The provisions of this subdivision shall not apply to a health care provider ordering the performance of an HIV related test on an individual proposed for insurance coverage.

5. At the time of communicating the test result to the subject of the test, a person ordering the performance of an HIV related test shall, directly or through a representative:

(a) in the case of a test indicating evidence of HIV infection, provide the subject of the test or, if the subject lacks capacity to consent, the person authorized pursuant to law to consent to health care for the subject with counseling or referrals for counseling: (i) for coping with the emotional consequences of learning the result; (ii) regarding the discrimination problems that disclosure of the result could cause; (iii) for behavior change to prevent transmission or contraction of HIV infection; (iv) to inform such person of available medical treatments; and (v) regarding the need to notify his or her contacts; and

(b) in the case of a test not indicating evidence of HIV infection, provide (in a manner which may consist of oral or written reference to information previously provided) the subject of the test, or if the subject lacks capacity to consent, the person authorized pursuant to law to consent to health care for the subject, with information concerning the risks of participating in high risk sexual or needle-sharing behavior.

5-a. With the consent of the subject of a test indicating evidence of HIV infection or, if the subject lacks capacity to consent, with the consent of the person authorized pursuant to law to consent to health care for the subject, the person who ordered the performance of the HIV related test, or such person's representative, shall provide or arrange with a health care provider for an appointment for follow-up medical care for HIV for such subject.

6. The provisions of this section shall not apply to the performance of an HIV related test:

(a) by a health care provider or health facility in relation to the procuring, processing, distributing or use of a human body or a human body part, including organs, tissues, eyes, bones, arteries, blood, semen, or other body fluids, for use in medical research or therapy, or for transplantation to individuals provided, however, that where the test results are communicated to the subject, post-test counseling, as described in subdivision five of this section, shall nonetheless be required; or

(b) for the purpose of research if the testing is performed in a manner by which the identity of the test subject is not known and may not be retrieved by the researcher; or

(c) on a deceased person, when such test is conducted to determine the cause of death or for epidemiological purposes; or

(d) conducted pursuant to section twenty-five hundred-f of this chapter; or

(e) in situations involving occupational exposures which create a significant risk of contracting or transmitting HIV infection, as defined in regulations of the department and pursuant to protocols adopted by the department,

(i) provided that:

(A) the person who is the source of the occupational exposure is deceased, comatose or is determined by his or her attending health care professional to lack mental capacity to consent to an HIV related test and is not reasonably expected to recover in time for the exposed person to receive appropriate medical treatment, as determined by the exposed person's attending health care professional who would order or provide such treatment;

(B) there is no person available or reasonably likely to become available who has the legal authority to consent to the HIV related test on behalf of the source person in time for the exposed person to receive appropriate medical treatment; and

(C) the exposed person will benefit medically by knowing the source person's HIV test results, as determined by the exposed person's health care professional and documented in the exposed person's medical record;

(ii) in which case

(A) a provider shall order an anonymous HIV test of the source person; and

(B) the results of such anonymous test, but not the identity of the source person, shall be disclosed only to the attending health care professional of the exposed person solely for the purpose of assisting the exposed person in making appropriate decisions regarding post-exposure medical treatment; and

(C) the results of the test shall not be disclosed to the source person or placed in the source person's medical record.

7. In the event that an HIV related test is ordered by a physician or certified nurse practitioner pursuant to the provisions of the education law providing for non-patient specific regimens, then for the purposes of this section the individual administering the test shall be deemed to be the individual ordering the test.

§2781-a. Required offering of HIV related testing.

1. Every individual between the ages of thirteen and sixty-four years (or younger or older if there is evidence or indication of risk activity) who receives health services as an inpatient or in the emergency department of a general hospital defined in subdivision ten of section twenty-eight hundred one of this chapter or who receives primary care services in an outpatient department of such hospital or in a diagnostic and treatment center licensed under article twenty-eight of this chapter or from a physician, physician assistant, nurse practitioner, or midwife providing primary care shall be offered an HIV related test unless the health care practitioner providing such services reasonably believes that (a) the individual is being treated for a life threatening emergency; or (b) the individual has previously been offered or has been the subject of an HIV related test (except that a test shall be offered if otherwise indicated); or (c) the individual lacks capacity to consent to an HIV related test.

2. As used in this section, "primary care" means the medical fields of family medicine, general pediatrics, primary care, internal medicine, primary care obstetrics, or primary care gynecology, without regard to board certification.

3. The offering of HIV related testing under this section shall be culturally and linguistically appropriate in accordance with rules and regulations promulgated by the commissioner.

4. This section shall not affect the scope of practice of any health care practitioner or diminish any authority or legal or professional obligation of any health care practitioner to offer an HIV related test or to provide services or care for the subject of an HIV related test.

§2782. Confidentiality and disclosure.

1. No person who obtains confidential HIV related information in the course of providing any health or social service or pursuant to a release of confidential HIV related information may disclose or be compelled to disclose such information, except to the following:

(a) the protected individual or, when the protected individual lacks capacity to consent, a person authorized pursuant to law to consent to health care for the individual;

(b) any person to whom disclosure is authorized pursuant to a release of confidential HIV related information;

(c) an agent or employee of a health facility or health care provider if (1) the agent or employee is permitted to access medical records, (2) the health facility or health care provider itself is authorized to obtain the HIV related information, and (3) the agent or employee provides health care to the protected individual, or maintains or processes medical records for billing or reimbursement;

(d) a health care provider or health facility when knowledge of the HIV related information is necessary to provide appropriate care or treatment to the protected individual, a child of the individual, a contact of the protected individual or a person authorized to consent to health care for such a contact;

(e) a health facility or health care provider, in relation to the procurement, processing, distributing or use of a human body or a human body part, including organs, tissues, eyes, bones, arteries, blood, semen, or other body fluids, for use in medical education, research, therapy, or for transplantation to individuals;

(f) health facility staff committees or accreditation or oversight review organizations authorized to access medical records; provided that such committees or organizations may only disclose confidential HIV related information: (1) back to the facility or provider of a health or social service; (2) to carry out the monitoring, evaluation, or service review for which it was obtained; or (3) to a federal, state or local government agency for the purposes of and subject to the conditions provided in subdivision six of this section;

(g) a federal, state, county or local health officer when such disclosure is mandated by federal or state law;

(h) an authorized agency in connection with foster care or adoption of a child. Such agency shall be authorized to redisclose such information only pursuant to this article or in accordance with the provisions of subdivision eight of section three hundred seventy-two and section three hundred seventy-three-a of the social services law;

(i) third party reimbursers or their agents to the extent necessary to reimburse health care providers for health services; provided that, where necessary, an otherwise appropriate authorization for such disclosure has been secured by the provider;

(j) an insurance institution, for other than the purpose set forth in paragraph (i) of this subdivision, provided the insurance institution secures a dated and written authorization that indicates that health care providers, health facilities, insurance institutions, and other persons are authorized to disclose information about the protected individual, the nature of the information to be disclosed, the purposes for which the information is to be disclosed and which is signed by: (1) the protected individual; (2) if the protected individual lacks the capacity to consent, such other person authorized pursuant to law to consent for such individual; or (3) if the protected individual is deceased, the beneficiary or claimant for benefits under an insurance policy, a health services plan, or an employee welfare benefit plan as defined in 29 U.S.C. 1002(1), covering such protected individual;

(k) any person to whom disclosure is ordered by a court of competent jurisdiction pursuant to section twenty-seven hundred eighty-five of this article;

(*l*) an employee or agent of the department of corrections and community supervision, in accordance with paragraph (a) of subdivision two of section twenty-seven hundred eighty-six of this article, to the extent the employee or agent is authorized to access records containing such information in order to carry out the department's functions, powers and duties with respect to the protected individual, pursuant to section two hundred fifty-nine-a of the executive law;

(m) an employee or agent of the office of probation and correctional alternatives or any local probation department, in accordance with paragraph (a) of subdivision two of section twenty-seven hundred eighty-six of this article, to the extent the employee or agent is authorized to access records containing such information in order to carry out the office's or department's functions, powers and duties with respect to the protected individual, pursuant to articles twelve and twelve-A of the executive law;

(n) a medical director of a local correctional facility as defined in section forty of the correction law, in accordance with paragraph (a) of subdivision two of section twenty-seven hundred eighty-six of this article, to the extent the medical director is authorized to access records containing such information in order to carry out his or her functions, powers and duties with respect to the protected individual; or

(o) an employee or agent of the commission of correction, in accordance with paragraph (a) of subdivision two of section twenty-seven hundred eighty-six of this article, to the extent the employee or agent is authorized to access records containing such information in order to carry out the commission's functions, powers and duties with respect to the protected individual, pursuant to article three of the correction law.

(p) an attorney appointed to represent a minor pursuant to the social services law or the family court act, with respect to confidential HIV related information relating to the minor and for the purpose of representing the minor. If the minor has the capacity to consent, the minor's attorney may not redisclose confidential HIV related information without the minor's permission. If the minor lacks capacity to consent, the minor's attorney may redisclose confidential HIV related information for the sole purpose of representing the minor. This paragraph shall not limit the ability of the minor's attorney to seek relief under section twenty-seven hundred eighty-five of this chapter.

(q) an executor or an administrator of an estate shall have access to the confidential HIV information of a deceased person as needed to fulfill his or her responsibilities/duties as an executor or administrator.

2. A state, county or local health officer may disclose confidential HIV related information when:

(a) disclosure is specifically authorized or required by federal or state law; or

(b) disclosure is made pursuant to a release of confidential HIV related information; or

(c) disclosure is requested by a physician pursuant to subdivision four of this section; or

(d) disclosure is authorized by court order pursuant to the provisions of section twenty-seven hundred eighty-five of this article.

3. No person to whom confidential HIV related information has been disclosed pursuant to this article shall disclose the information to another person except as authorized by this article, provided, however, that the provisions of this subdivision shall not apply:

(a) to the protected individual; or

(b) to a natural person who is authorized pursuant to law to consent to health care for the protected individual; or

(c) to a protected individual's foster parent as defined in section three hundred seventy-one of the social services law and subject to regulations promulgated pursuant to paragraph (a) of subdivision two of section twenty-seven hundred eighty-six of this article, for the purpose of providing care, treatment or supervision of the protected individual; or

(d) a prospective adoptive parent as specified in section three hundred seventy-three-a of the social services law and subject to regulations promulgated pursuant to paragraph (a) of subdivision two of section twenty-seven hundred eighty-six of this article with whom a child who is the protected individual has been placed for adoption; or

(e) to a relative or other person legally responsible to whom a child who is the protected individual is to be placed or discharged pursuant to section ten hundred seventeen or ten hundred fifty-five of the family court act and subject to regulations promulgated pursuant to paragraph (a) of subdivision two of section twenty-seven hundred eighty-six of this article, for the purpose of providing care, treatment or supervision of the protected individual.

4. (a) A physician may disclose confidential HIV related information under the following conditions:

(1) disclosure is made to a contact, to a public health officer for the purpose of making the disclosure to said contact and pursuant to section twenty-one hundred thirty of this chapter; or

(2) the physician believes disclosure is medically appropriate and there is a significant risk of infection to the contact; and

(3) the physician has counseled the protected individual regarding the need to notify the contact; and

(4) the physician has informed the protected individual of his or her intent to make such disclosure to a contact, the physician's responsibility to report the infected individual's case pursuant to section twenty-one hundred thirty of this chapter and has given the protected individual the opportunity to express a preference as to whether disclosure should be made by the physician directly or to a public health officer for the purpose of said disclosure. If the protected individual expresses a preference for disclosure by a public health officer, the physician shall honor such preference.

(5) If a physician chooses to make a notification pursuant to this section, he or she shall report to the municipal health commissioner of district health officer on his or her efforts to notify the contacts of the protected individual. Such report shall be in a manner and on forms prescribed by the commissioner and shall include the identity of the protected individual and any contacts as well as information as to whether the contacts were successfully notified.

(6) Within a reasonable time of receiving a report that a physician or his or her designated agent did not notify or verify notification of contacts provided by the protected individual, the health commissioner or district health officer of the municipality from which the report originates shall take reasonable measures to notify such contacts and otherwise comply with the provisions of this chapter.

(b) When making such disclosures to the contact, the physician or public health officer shall provide or make referrals for the provision of the appropriate medical advice and counseling for coping with the emotional consequences of learning the information and for changing behavior to prevent transmission or contraction of HIV infection. The physician or public health officer shall not disclose the identity of the protected individual or the identity of any other contact. A physician or public health officer making a notification pursuant to this subdivision shall make such disclosure in person, except where circumstances reasonably prevent doing so.

(c) A physician or public health officer shall have no obligation to identify or locate any contact except as provided pursuant to title three of article twenty-one of this chapter.

(d) A physician may, upon the consent of a parent or guardian, disclose confidential HIV related information to a state, county, or local health officer for the purpose of reviewing the medical history of a child to determine the fitness of the child to attend school.

(e) A physician may disclose confidential HIV related information pertaining to a protected individual to a person (known to the physician) authorized pursuant to law to consent to health care for a protected individual when the physician reasonably believes that: (1) disclosure is medically necessary in order to provide timely care and treatment for the protected individual; and (2) after appropriate counseling as to the need for such disclosure, the protected individual will not inform a person authorized by law to consent to health care; provided, however, that the physician shall not make such disclosure if, in the judgment of the physician: (A) the disclosure would not be in the best interest of the protected individual; or (B) the protected individual is authorized pursuant to law to consent to such care and treatment. Any decision or action by a physician under this paragraph, and the basis therefor, shall be recorded in the protected individual's medical record.

5. (a) Whenever disclosure of confidential HIV related information is made pursuant to this article, except for disclosures made pursuant to paragraphs (a), (d) and (i) of subdivision one of this section or paragraph (a) or (e) of subdivision four of this section, such disclosure shall be accompanied or followed by a statement in writing which includes the following or substantially similar language: "This information has been disclosed to you from confidential records which are protected by state law. State law prohibits you from making any further disclosure of this information without the specific written consent of the person to whom it pertains, or as otherwise permitted by law. Any unauthorized further disclosure in violation of state law may result in a fine or jail sentence or both. A general authorization for the release of medical or other information is NOT sufficient authorization for further disclosure." An oral disclosure shall be accompanied or followed by such a notice within ten days.

(b) Except for disclosures made pursuant to paragraph (c) of subdivision one of this section, or to persons reviewing information or records in the ordinary course of ensuring that a health facility is in compliance with applicable quality of care standards or any other authorized program evaluation, program monitoring or service review, or to governmental agents requiring information necessary for payments to be made on behalf of patients or clients pursuant to contract or in accordance to law, a notation of all such disclosures shall be placed in the medical record of a protected individual, who shall be informed of such disclosures upon request; provided, however, that for disclosures made to insurance institutions such a notation need only be entered at the time the disclosure is first made.

6. (a) The provisions of this subdivision shall apply where a provider of a health or social service possesses confidential HIV related information relating to individuals who are recipients of the service, and a federal, state or local government agency supervises or monitors the provider or administers the program under which the service is provided.

(b) Confidential HIV related information relating to a recipient of such service may be disclosed in accordance with regulations promulgated pursuant to paragraph (a) of subdivision two of section twenty-seven hundred eighty-six of this article to an authorized employee or agent of such provider or government agency, when reasonably necessary for such supervision, monitoring, administration, or provision of such service. The term "authorized employee or agent", as used in this subdivision shall only include any employee or agent who would, in the ordinary course of business of the provider or government agency, have access to records relating to the care of, treatment of, or provision of a health or social service to the protected individual.

7. Nothing in this section shall limit a person's or agency's responsibility or authority to report, investigate, or redisclose, child protective and adult protective services information in accordance with title six of article six and titles one and two of article nine-B of the social services law, or to provide or monitor the provision of child and adult protective or preventive services.

8. Confidential HIV related information shall be recorded in the medical record of the protected individual. The provisions of this section shall not prohibit the listing of acquired immune deficiency syndrome, HIV related illness or HIV infection in a certificate of death, autopsy report or related documents prepared pursuant to article forty-one of this chapter or other applicable laws, ordinances, rules or regulations relating to the documentation of cause of death, nor shall this section be construed to modify any laws, ordinances, rules or regulations relative to access to death certificates, autopsy reports or such other related documents. Under no circumstances shall confidential HIV related information be disclosable pursuant to article six of the public officers law. Notwithstanding the foregoing, confidential HIV information obtained pursuant to section 390.15 of the criminal procedure law or section 347.1 of the family court act by either court order or consent of the protected individual shall not be recorded in the medical record of the protected individual unless he or she consents to the recording of such information in a written statement containing the relevant information specified in subdivision two of section two thousand seven hundred eighty-one of this article.

9. Confidential HIV related information shall be disclosed upon the request of the health care worker HIV/HBV advisory panel, established pursuant to article twenty-seven-DD of this chapter, to the panel or its designee only when reasonably necessary for the evaluation of a worker who has voluntarily sought the panel's review.

§2783. Penalties; immunities.

1. Any person who shall:

(a) perform, or permit or procure the performance of, an HIV related test in violation of section twenty-seven hundred eighty-one of this article; or

(b) disclose, or compel another person to disclose, or procure the disclosure of, confidential HIV related information in violation of section twenty-seven hundred eighty-two of this article; shall be subject to a civil penalty not to exceed five thousand dollars for each occurrence. Such penalty may be recovered in the same manner as the penalty provided in section twelve of this chapter.

2. Any person who willfully commits an act enumerated in subdivision one of this section shall be guilty of a misdemeanor and subject to the penalties provided in section twelve-b of this chapter.

3. There shall be no criminal sanction or civil liability on the part of, and no cause of action for damages shall arise against any physician, his or her employer, or a physician's designated agent, or health facility or health care provider with which the physician is associated, or public health officer, on account of:

(a) the failure to disclose confidential HIV related information to a contact or person authorized pursuant to law to consent to health care for a protected individual; or

(b) the disclosure of confidential HIV related information to a contact or person authorized pursuant to law to consent to health care for a protected individual, when carried out in compliance with this article; or

(c) the disclosure of confidential HIV related information to any person, agency, or officer authorized to receive such information, when carried out in good faith and without malice, and in compliance with the provisions of this article; or

(d) the municipal health commissioner or district health officer's failure to notify contacts pursuant to this chapter.

4. Any cause of action to recover damages based on a failure to provide information, explanations, or counseling prior to the execution of a written informed consent, or based on a lack of informed consent in the ordering or performance of an HIV related test in violation of this article shall be governed by the provisions of section two thousand eight hundred five-d of this chapter.

§2784. Applicability to insurance institutions and insurance support organizations.

Except for disclosure to third party reimbursers and insurance institutions pursuant to paragraphs (i) and (j) of subdivision one of section twenty-seven hundred eighty-two of this article and except for disclosures pursuant to section twenty-seven hundred eighty-five of this article, the provisions of this article shall not apply to insurance institutions and insurance support organizations, except that health care providers associated with or under contract to a health maintenance organization or other medical services plan shall be subject to the provisions of this article.

§2785. Court authorization for disclosure of confidential HIV related information.

1. Notwithstanding any other provision of law, no court shall issue an order for the disclosure of confidential HIV related information, except a court of record of competent jurisdiction in accordance with the provisions of this section.

2. A court may grant an order for disclosure of confidential HIV related information upon an application showing: (a) a compelling need for disclosure of the information for the adjudication of a criminal or civil proceeding; (b) a clear and imminent danger to an individual whose life or health may unknowingly be at significant risk as a result of contact with the individual to whom the information pertains; (c) upon application of a state, county or local health officer, a clear and imminent danger to the public health; or (d) that the applicant is lawfully entitled to the disclosure and the disclosure is consistent with the provisions of this article.

3. Upon receiving an application for an order authorizing disclosure pursuant to this section, the court shall enter an order directing that all pleadings, papers, affidavits, judgments, orders of the court, briefs and memoranda of law which are part of the application or the decision thereon, be

sealed and not made available to any person, except to the extent necessary to conduct any proceedings in connection with the determination of whether to grant or deny the application, including any appeal. Such an order shall further direct that all subsequent proceedings in connection with the application shall be conducted in camera, and, where appropriate to prevent the unauthorized disclosure of confidential HIV related information, that any pleadings, papers, affidavits, judgments, orders of the court, briefs and memoranda of law which are part of the application or the decision thereon not state the name of the individual concerning whom confidential HIV related information is sought.

4. (a) The individual concerning whom confidential HIV related information is sought and any person holding records concerning confidential HIV related information from whom disclosure is sought shall be given adequate notice of such application in a manner which will not disclose to any other person the identity of the individual, and shall be afforded an opportunity to file a written response to the application, or to appear in person for the limited purpose of providing evidence on the statutory criteria for the issuance of an order pursuant to this section.

(b) The court may grant an order without such notice and opportunity to be heard, where an ex parte application by a public health officer shows that a clear and imminent danger to an individual whose life or health may unknowingly be at risk requires an immediate order. (c) Service of a subpoena shall not be subject to this subdivision.

5. In assessing compelling need and clear and imminent danger, the court shall provide written findings of fact, including scientific or medical findings, citing specific evidence in the record which supports each finding, and shall weigh the need for disclosure against the privacy interest of the protected individual and the public interest which may be disserved by disclosure which deters future testing or treatment or which may lead to discrimination.

6. An order authorizing disclosure of confidential HIV related information shall:

(a) limit disclosure to that information which is necessary to fulfill the purpose for which the order is granted; and

(b) limit disclosure to those persons whose need for the information is the basis for the order, and specifically prohibit redisclosure by such persons to any other persons, whether or not they are parties to the action; and

(c) to the extent possible consistent with this section, conform to the provisions of this article; and

(d) include such other measures as the court deems necessary to limit any disclosures not authorized by its order.

§2785-a.   Court order for HIV related testing in certain cases.

1. Notwithstanding any contrary provision of law or regulation, a state, county or local public health officer to whom an order or a consent for an HIV test is addressed or sent, in accordance with section 390.15 of the criminal procedure law or section 347.1 of the family court act, must cause HIV related testing to be administered to the subject named therein and, if the test is pursuant to court order, must immediately provide to the court that issued the order a written report specifying the date on which such test was completed. Such report to the court shall not, however, disclose the results of such test. Such officer must disclose the results of the testing to the victim indicated in the order or consent and must also disclose the results to the person tested, unless the person tested has been asked to but declines to authorize such disclosure to himself or herself.

2. At the time of communicating the test results to the subject or the victim, such public health officer shall directly provide the victim and person tested with (a) counseling or referrals for counseling for the purposes specified in subdivision five of section two thousand seven hundred eighty-one of this article; (b) counseling with regard to HIV disease and HIV testing in accordance with law and consistent with subdivision five of section two thousand seven hundred eighty-one of this article; and (c) appropriate health care and support services, or referrals to such available services. If at the time of communicating the test results, the person tested is in the custody of the department of corrections and community supervision, office of children and family services, office of mental health or a local correctional institution, the counseling and services required by this subdivision may be provided by a public health officer associated with the county or facility within which the person tested is confined.

3. Unless inconsistent with this section, the provisions of this article regarding the confidentiality and disclosure of HIV related information shall apply to proceedings conducted pursuant to section 390.15 of the criminal procedure law or section 347.1 of the family court act.

§2786. Rules and regulations; forms; report.

1. The commissioner shall promulgate rules and regulations concerning implementation of this article for health facilities, health care providers and other persons to whom this article is applicable. The commissioner shall also develop standardized model forms to be used for informed consent for HIV related testing and for the release of confidential HIV related information and materials for pre-test counseling as required by subdivision three of section twenty-seven hundred eighty-one of this article, and for post-test counseling as required by subdivision five of section twenty-seven hundred eighty-one of this article. Persons, health facilities and health care providers may use forms for informed consent for HIV related testing, and for the release of confidential HIV related information other than those forms developed pursuant to this section, provided they contain information consistent with the standardized model forms developed by the commissioner. All forms developed or used pursuant to this section shall be written in a clear and coherent manner using words with common, everyday meanings. The commissioner, in consultation with the AIDS institute advisory council, shall promulgate regulations to identify those circumstances which create a significant risk of contracting or transmitting HIV infection; provided, however, that such regulations shall not be determinative of any significant risk determined pursuant to paragraph (a) of subdivision four of section twenty-seven hundred eighty-two or section twenty-seven hundred eighty-five of this article.

2. (a) Each state agency authorized pursuant to this article to obtain confidential HIV related information shall, in consultation with the department of health, promulgate regulations: (1) to provide safequards to prevent discrimination, abuse or other adverse actions directed toward protected individuals; (2) to prohibit the disclosure of such information except in accordance with this article; (3) to seek to protect individuals in contact with the protected individual when such contact creates a significant risk of contracting or transmitting HIV infection through the exchange of body fluids, and (4) to establish criteria for determining when it is reasonably necessary for a provider of a health or social service or the state agency or a local government agency to have or to use confidential HIV related information for supervision, monitoring, investigation, or administration and for determining

which employees and agents may, in the ordinary course of business of the agency or provider, be authorized to access confidential HIV related information pursuant to the provisions of paragraphs (l) and (m) of subdivision one and subdivision six of section twenty-seven hundred eighty-two of this article; and provided further that such regulations shall be promulgated by the chairperson of the commission of correction where disclosure is made pursuant to paragraphs (n) and (o) of subdivision one of section twenty-seven hundred eighty-two of this article.

(b) The department of health, in consultation with agencies referred to in paragraph (a) of this subdivision, shall submit a report to the legislature by December first, nineteen hundred eighty-nine, outlining the status and content of such regulations, their effect on the regulated facilities and the protected individuals served by them, the extent to which they conform with current medical and scientific knowledge on the transmissibility of HIV infection, and any recommendations for changes in said regulations.

§2787. Separability.

If any section, clause or provision of this article shall be deemed by any court of competent jurisdiction to be unconstitutional or ineffective in whole or in part, to the extent that it is not unconstitutional or ineffective, it shall be valid and effective and no other section, clause or provision shall on account thereof be deemed invalid or ineffective.

ARTICLE 3
Local Public Welfare Organization;
Powers and Duties

Title 6-A
Establishment of Paternity and
Enforcement of Support

§111-a.   Federal aid; state plan.

1. The department is hereby designated as the single state agency to supervise the administration of the state's child support program provided for by this title, and a single organizational unit shall be established within the department for such purposes.

2. The department shall develop and submit a state child support program plan as required by part D of title IV of the federal social security act to the federal department of health, education and welfare for approval pursuant to such part in order to qualify the state for federal aid under such part. The department shall act for the state in any negotiations relative to the submission and approval of such plan and shall make such arrangements as may be necessary to obtain and retain such approval and to secure for the state the benefits of the provisions of such federal act relating to child support programs. The department shall promulgate regulations not inconsistent with law as may be necessary to assure that such plan conforms to the provisions of such part and any federal regulations adopted pursuant thereto. The department shall make all reports required by law to be made to such federal department in the form and manner required by federal regulations.

§111-b.   Functions, powers and duties of the department.

1. The single organizational unit within the department shall be responsible for the supervision of the activities of state and local officials relating to establishment of paternity of children born out-of-wedlock, location of absent parents and enforcement of support obligations of legally responsible relatives to contribute for the support of their dependents.

2. The department is hereby authorized to accept, on behalf of the state and the social services districts concerned, assignments of support rights owed to persons receiving (i) aid to dependent children pursuant to title ten of article five of this chapter or, (ii) where appropriate, foster care maintenance payments made pursuant to title IV-E of the federal social security act; provided however, that it will not be appropriate where such requirement will have a negative impact upon the health, safety or welfare of such child or other individuals in the household or impair the likelihood of the child returning to his or her family when discharged from foster care or, (iii) home relief pursuant to title three of article five of this chapter. Notwithstanding any inconsistent provisions of title six of this article or any other provisions of law, the department may enforce such assigned support rights either directly, through social services officials or, if there is in effect an approved agreement between the social services official and another governmental agency, through such other agency. In any proceeding to enforce such assignment, the official bringing such proceeding shall have the same rights as if the proceeding were being brought to enforce section four hundred fifteen of the family court act.

2-a. The department shall prepare a notice which shall be distributed by social services officials to persons who may be required to assign support rights which notice shall explain the rights and obligations that may result from the establishment of paternity and the right of the assignor to be kept informed, upon request, of the time, date and place of any proceedings involving the assignor and such other information as the department believes is pertinent. The notice shall state that the attorney initiating the proceeding represents the department.

3. In appropriate cases, the department is authorized to utilize support enforcement and collection and location services made available through the secretary of health and human services, including the services of federal courts, the federal parent locator service, the federal case registry of child support orders, the national directory of new hires, and the treasury department, if and so long as authorized and required by federal law.

4. The department shall maintain and operate a parent locator service with respect to cases being provided services pursuant to this title.

To effectuate the purposes of this subdivision, the commissioner shall request and receive from the departments, authorities, boards, bureaus, commissions, corporations, councils, funds, offices, or other agencies of the state, or any of its political subdivisions, and all such organizational entities of the state and social services districts are hereby directed, to provide and the political subdivisions are hereby authorized to provide, such assistance and data as will enable the department and social services districts to properly carry out their powers and duties to locate such parents and to enforce their liability for the support of their children. Any records established pursuant to the provisions of this section shall be available only to the secretary of health and human services, office of the inspector general, social services districts, district attorneys, county attorneys, corporation counsels, and courts having jurisdiction in any proceeding under article four, five, five-A, or five-B of the family court act; provided, however, no organizational entity of the state need make available any data or information which is otherwise required by statute to be maintained in a confidential manner.

4-a. (a) The department shall maintain and operate a state case registry that contains records with respect to:

(1) each case receiving services pursuant to this title; and

(2) each support order established or modified in the state on or after the first day of October, nineteen hundred ninety-eight.

(b) For the purpose of subparagraph two of paragraph (a) of this subdivision, the term support order means a judgment, decree, or order, whether temporary, final, or subject to modification, issued by a court or an administrative agency of competent jurisdiction, including any adjusted order issued by a support collection unit, for the support and maintenance of a child, including a child who has attained the age of majority under the law of the issuing state, or a child and the parent with whom the child is living, which provides for monetary support, health care, arrearages, or reimbursement, and which may include related costs and fees, interest and penalties, income withholding, attorney's fees, and other relief.

(c) Each case record in the state case registry with respect to cases described in subparagraph one of paragraph (a) of this subdivision for which a support order has been established shall include a record of:

(1) the amount of monthly (or other periodic) support owed under the order, and other amounts (including arrearages, interest or late payment penalties, and fees) due or overdue under the order;

(2) any amount described in subparagraph one of this paragraph that has been collected;

(3) the distribution of such collected amounts;

(4) the birth date of any child for whom the order requires the provision of support; and

(5) the amount of any lien imposed with respect to the order pursuant to section one hundred eleven-u of this article.

(d) The department shall update and monitor each case record in the state registry described in subparagraph one of paragraph (a) of this subdivision on the basis of:

(1) information on administrative actions and administrative and judicial proceedings and orders relating to paternity and support;

(2) information obtained from comparison with federal, state or local sources of information;

(3) information on support collections and distributions; and

(4) any other relevant information.

(e) Information maintained as part of the state case registry shall be made available to other state and federal agencies as provided for in federal statutes and regulations promulgated by the federal secretary of health and human services.

5. (a) There shall be established for each state fiscal year a statewide child support collections goal for amounts of collections of support obligations pursuant to this title, which goal shall be set forth in that portion of the state's local assistance budget intended for the appropriation of reimbursement to social services districts pursuant to this chapter. The commissioner shall, subject to the approval of the director of the budget, annually allocate a portion of the statewide goal to each social services district, which portion shall be based upon the district's portion of the statewide aid to dependent children program and other relevant factors.

(b) Notwithstanding any inconsistent provision of section one hundred fifty-three of this chapter, for each social services district which fails to meet its portion of the collection goal established by this section, the commissioner shall deny state reimbursement for such district's expenditures for aid to dependent children, in an amount equal to the difference between the amount of non-federal funds such district is required to repay to the state out of collections actually made and the amount of non-federal funds such district would have been required to repay to the state had it met its collection goal.

(c) Any social services district which has been determined to have failed to meet its portion of the collection goal may request a redetermination by the commissioner or his designee in a manner to be established by department regulations. Upon a showing by such district that such failure was due in whole or in part to factors other than those administrative and processing functions or organizations which are subject to the jurisdiction of such district's local legislative body, the commissioner shall waive such failure in whole or in part and shall restore all or a corresponding portion of any state reimbursement previously denied pursuant to this section.

(d) For purposes of determining the amount of child support collections which are attributable toward meeting a district's portion of the statewide collections goal, any amounts collected by one social services district on behalf of another shall be credited to the district to which support payments have been assigned. Support payments collected on behalf of another state or on behalf of persons not in receipt of aid to dependent children shall not be taken into consideration in determining whether such district has met its goal.

(e) The department may for purposes of administrative convenience set monthly or quarterly goals based upon each district's annual goal and may deny reimbursement on a monthly or quarterly basis, subject to a final adjustment at the end of each year reflecting the extent to which each such district has met its portion of the statewide annual goal.

6. When the commissioner has determined that a social services district has failed to meet its portion of the statewide child support collections goal, as determined in accordance with the provisions of subdivision five of this section, or has failed to comply with the applicable provisions of federal law and regulations, he shall notify such district and the appropriate local legislative body of such determination and may promulgate any regulations he determines are necessary to improve such district's organization, administration, management or program. Such regulations shall be fully complied with by the effective date of such regulations.

7. The department, through the commissioner, shall enter into the agreement provided for in section one hundred seventy-one-c of the tax law and is authorized to furnish to the commissioner of taxation and finance and the state tax commission such information and to take such other actions as may be necessary to carry out the agreement provided for in such section, for the crediting of overpayments of tax to past-due support which is owed to persons receiving services pursuant to this title and title six-B of this article. A person receiving services under this title shall receive a pro rata share of the overpayment of tax, based on the amount of past-due support owed to such person as certified to the tax commission by the department pursuant to section one hundred seventy-one-c of the tax law, in cases where the individual, estate or trust owing past-due support to such person owes past-due support to other persons or entities so certified to the tax commission by the department. Amounts certified to the state tax commission under such agreement may include amounts specified in subdivision eight of this section. The amount paid by the state comptroller to the department pursuant to subdivision one of section one hundred seventy-one-c of the tax law shall be distributed in accordance with applicable provisions of this chapter and the department's regulations. To the extent permitted by federal law, the department may also

certify amounts to the federal department of health and human services for tax interception to the same extent as it certifies amounts pursuant to such section of the tax law. The department shall by regulation establish procedures by which any individual, estate or trust which is the subject of a certification to the state tax commission in accordance with such agreement may contest such certification based on defenses that are not subject to family court jurisdiction. Such regulations and the notice required by subdivision four of section one hundred seventy-one-c of the tax law shall set forth defenses which may be available to the individual, estate or trust to contest such certification, and the manner in which a review of the certification based on such defenses may be obtained.

8. (a) Amounts certified to the state tax commission under the agreement described in subdivision seven of this section for persons who are receiving services pursuant to this title may include:

(i) amounts representing delinquencies which have accrued under a court order of support;

(ii) with respect to any court order of support made before September first, nineteen hundred eighty-four which provided for periodic payments toward an established arrears amount, the entire amount of such arrears where the respondent is, at any time after September first, nineteen hundred eighty-four, delinquent in making such periodic payments; and

(iii) with respect to any court order of support made on or after September first, nineteen hundred eighty-four which establishes an arrears amount, the entire amount of such arrears, unless such order includes a finding that anticipated tax refunds pursuant to the most recently filed state and federal tax returns have been considered by the court and taken into account in determining the amount of periodic payments to be made toward the arrears amount, or in determining the amount of the current support order, and expressly provides that such arrears are not to be so certified.

(b) For the purpose of the state child support program any payment made by a respondent which is insufficient to fully satisfy both a current court order of support and a periodic payment toward the balance of any arrears amount established by court order shall be first applied toward the current order of support or any delinquency thereon and then toward the periodic payment on any arrears amount established by court order unless otherwise required by federal regulation.

*10. (a) The department, through the commissioner, shall enter into the agreement provided for in section sixteen hundred thirteen-a of the tax law and is authorized to furnish to the director of the lottery and the division of the lottery such information and to take such other actions as may be necessary to carry out the provisions of the agreement provided for in such section, for the crediting of lottery prizes of six hundred dollars or more to past-due support which is owed to persons receiving services pursuant to this title. A person receiving services under this title shall receive a pro rata share of the prize winning based on the amount of past-due support owed to such person as provided to the division of the lottery by the department pursuant to section sixteen hundred thirteen-a of the tax law, in cases where the individual, estate or trust owing past-due support to such person owes past-due support to other persons or entities so provided to the division of the lottery by the department. Amounts provided to the division of the lottery under such agreement may include amounts specified in this subdivision. The amount paid by the state comptroller to the department pursuant to subdivision one of section sixteen hundred thirteen-a of the tax law shall be distributed in accordance with applicable provisions of this chapter and the department's regulations.

(b) The department shall by regulation establish procedures by which any individual, estate or trust which is the subject of crediting of any lottery prize of six hundred dollars or more to the state division of the lottery in accordance with such agreement may contest such crediting based on defenses that are not subject to family court jurisdiction. Such regulations shall require that notice be given to the individual, estate or trust which shall set forth:

(i) defenses which may be available to the individual, estate or trust to contest such crediting;

(ii) the manner in which a review of the crediting of lottery prizes of six hundred dollars or more based on such defenses may be obtained;

(iii) the address and telephone number of the local department of social services' support collection unit which may be contacted with respect to correction of any error in such crediting concerning such individual's, estate's or trust's liability for past-due support or with respect to payment of such liability; and

(iv) the time frame by which such a defense must be made.

*10. The commissioner must review the child support standards act at least once every four years to ensure that its application results in the determination of appropriate child support amounts. As part of such review, the commissioner must consider economic data on the cost of raising children and analyze case data, gathered through sampling or other methods, on the application of, and deviations from the basic child support obligation. The analysis of the data must be used to ensure that such deviations are limited and, if appropriate, necessary revisions to the child support standards act must be submitted to the legislature to accomplish such purpose.

11. (a) Amounts certified to the division of the lottery under the agreement described in subdivision ten of this section for persons who are receiving services pursuant to this title may include:

(i) amounts representing delinquencies which have accrued under a court order of support;

(ii) with respect to any court order of support made which establishes an arrears amount, the entire amount of such arrears.

(b) For the purpose of the state child support program any payment made by a respondent which is insufficient to fully satisfy both a current court order of support and a periodic payment toward the balance of any arrears amount established by court order shall be first applied toward the current order of support or any delinquency thereon and then toward the periodic payment on any arrears amount established by court order unless otherwise required by federal regulation.

**12. (a) The department, through the commissioner, shall enter into the agreement provided for in section five hundred ten of the vehicle and traffic law and is authorized to furnish to the commissioner of motor vehicles such information and to take such actions as may be necessary to carry out the agreement provided for in such section, for the enforcement of child support orders through the suspension of delinquent obligors' driving privileges.

(b) (1) When a support obligor who is or was under a court order to pay child support or combined child and spousal support to a support collection unit on behalf of persons receiving services under this title has accumulated

*There are 2 subdivisions "10"
**Expires & Repealed 8/31/17,Ch.29,L.2015)

support arrears equivalent to or greater than the amount of support due pursuant to such order for a period of four months, the office of temporary and disability assistance shall notify the support obligor in writing that his or her continued failure to pay the support arrears shall result in notification to the department of motor vehicles to suspend the support obligor's driving privileges unless the support obligor complies with the requirements set forth in paragraph (e) of this subdivision. For purposes of determining whether a support obligor has accumulated support arrears equivalent to or greater than the amount of support due for a period of four months, the amount of any retroactive support, other than periodic payments of retroactive support which are past due, shall not be included in the calculation of support arrears pursuant to this section; however, if at least four months of support arrears have accumulated subsequent to the date of the court order, the entire amount of any retroactive support may be collected pursuant to the provisions of this subdivision or as otherwise authorized by law.

(2) The department shall provide the notice required by subparagraph one of this paragraph by first class mail to the support obligor's last known address or such other place where the support obligor is likely to receive notice, or in the same manner as a summons may be served. Forty-five days after the date of such notice, if the support obligor has not challenged the determination of the support collection unit pursuant to subparagraph one of paragraph (d) of this subdivision or if the support obligor has failed to satisfy the arrears/past due support or to otherwise comply with the requirements set forth in paragraph (e) of this subdivision, the department shall notify the department of motor vehicles that the support obligor's driving privileges are to be suspended pursuant to section five hundred ten of the vehicle and traffic law. Upon the support obligor's compliance with the provisions of paragraph (e) of this subdivision, the department shall advise the department of motor vehicles within five business days that the suspension of the support obligor's driving privileges shall be terminated. If the support obligor appears in person at the support collection unit to satisfy the requirements of paragraph (e) of this subdivision, the support collection unit shall immediately provide a notice of compliance to the support obligor, in addition to the notice sent directly to the department of motor vehicles.

(3) Notwithstanding the requirements of this subdivision, no notice shall be issued by the department pursuant to subparagraph one of this paragraph to a support obligor from whom support payments are being received by the support collection unit as a result of an income execution or an income deduction order issued pursuant to section five thousand two hundred forty-one or five thousand two hundred forty-two of the civil practice law and rules.

(c) The notice provided to a support obligor by the department pursuant to paragraph (b) of this subdivision shall contain the caption of the order of support, the date the order of support was entered, the court in which it was entered, the amount of the periodic payments directed, and the amount of arrears/past due support. In addition, the notice shall include:

(1) an explanation of the action required pursuant to paragraph (e) of this subdivision to be taken by the support obligor to avoid the suspension of his or her driving privileges;

(2) a statement that forty-five days after the date of the notice, the department of motor vehicles will be notified to suspend the support obligor's driving privileges unless the support obligor may challenge the support collection unit's determination as set forth in paragraph (d) of this subdivision

within forty-five days of the date of such notice; a statement of the manner in which the support obligor may challenge the determination, and a statement that if the support obligor challenges the determination, a review will be completed by the support collection unit within seventy-five days of the date of the notice;

(3) a statement that if the support obligor does not challenge the support collection unit's determination then the department of motor vehicles shall be notified to suspend the support obligor's driving privileges unless the support obligor contacts the support collection unit to arrange for full payment or commencement of satisfactory payment arrangements on the arrears/past due support, or to comply otherwise with the requirements set forth in paragraph (e) of this subdivision, within forty-five days of the date of the notice;

(4) the address and telephone number of the support collection unit that the support obligor may contact to request information about a challenge or to comply with the requirements set forth in paragraph (e) of this subdivision;

(5) a statement that the suspension of driving privileges will continue until the support obligor pays the support arrears or complies otherwise with the requirements set forth in paragraph (e) of this subdivision; and

(6) a statement printed in boldface type that the support obligor's intentional submission of false written statements to the support collection unit for the purpose of frustrating or defeating the lawful enforcement of support obligations is punishable pursuant to section 175.35 of the penal law.

(d) (1) A support obligor may challenge in writing the correctness of the determination of the support collection unit that the obligor's driving privileges should be suspended, and in support of the challenge may submit documentation demonstrating mistaken identity, error in calculation of arrears, financial exemption from license suspension pursuant to the conditions enumerated in paragraph (e) of this subdivision, the absence of an underlying court order to support such determination, or other reason that the person is not subject to such determination. Such documents may include but are not limited to a copy of the order of support pursuant to which the obligor claims to have made payment, other relevant court orders, copies of cancelled checks, receipts for support payments, pay stubs or other documents identifying wage withholding, and proof of identity. The support collection unit shall review the documentation submitted by the support obligor, shall adjust the support obligor's account if appropriate, and shall notify the support obligor of the results of the review initiated in response to the challenge within seventy-five days from the date of the notice required by paragraph (b) of this subdivision. If the support collection unit's review indicates that the determination to suspend driving privileges was correct, the support collection unit shall notify the support obligor of the results of the review and that the support obligor has thirty-five days from the date of mailing of such notice to satisfy the full amount of the arrears or commence payment of the arrears/past due support as specified in paragraph (e) of this subdivision and if the support obligor fails to do so, the support collection unit shall notify the department of motor vehicles to suspend the support obligor's driving privileges pursuant to section five hundred ten of the vehicle and traffic law. The support obligor shall be further notified that if the support obligor files objections with the family court and serves these objections on the support collection unit within thirty-five days from the date of mailing of the notice denying the challenge pursuant to subdivision five of section four hundred fifty-four of the family court act, the support collection unit shall not notify the department of motor vehicles to suspend the support obligor's driving privileges until fifteen days after entry of judgement by the family court denying the objections.

(2) A support obligor may within thirty-five days of mailing of the notice denying his or her challenge by the support collection unit request that the family court review the support collection unit's determination pursuant to subdivision five of section four hundred fifty-four of the family court act. If the support obligor requests the family court to review the determination of the support collection unit, the support collection unit shall not notify the department of motor vehicles to suspend the support obligor's driving privileges until fifteen days after mailing of a copy of the judgment by the family court to the support obligor denying the objections.

(e) A support obligor who has received a notice that his or her driving privileges shall be suspended may avoid the suspension by:

(1) making full payment of all arrears/past due support to the support collection unit; or

(2) making satisfactory payment arrangements with the support collection unit for payment of the arrears/past due support and the current support obligation. "Satisfactory payment arrangements" shall mean:

(i) execution of a confession of judgment for the total balance of the arrears/past due support; and

(ii) execution of a verified statement of net worth on a form prescribed by the commissioner setting forth the obligor's income from all sources, liquid assets and holdings, copies of the obligor's drivers license, most recent federal and state tax return, and a representative pay stub, and an eighteen month employment history; and

(iii) execution and verification of a stipulation that the obligor will notify the support collection unit of all future changes of address until such time as the obligation to pay support is terminated; and

(iv) payment of support to the support collection unit by income execution pursuant to section five thousand two hundred forty-one of the civil practice law and rules, which shall include deductions sufficient to ensure compliance with the direction in the order of support and shall include an additional amount to be applied to the reduction of arrears as required by subdivision (b) of such section, or by execution of an agreement for payment of the arrears/past due support and any current support directly to the support collection unit in an amount which is consistent with that which would have been made under such an income execution; provided however, that where the support obligor fails to comply with the agreement, he/she may avoid or terminate the suspension of driving privileges only by making at least fifty percent payment of all arrears/past due support to the support collection unit and in addition, entering into a payment plan pursuant to this subdivision with the support collection unit within fifteen days. However, in any case when the support obligor fails to comply with a payment plan as described herein more than once within twelve months, the obligor must pay the balance of all arrears/past due support to avoid or terminate license suspension. "Failure to comply" for these purposes shall mean missing payments in an amount equivalent to four months of support under the payment plan, unless the support obligor demonstrates that he or she has filed a petition for modification that is pending; or

(3) providing documentation that shows the support obligor is receiving public assistance or supplemental security income; or

(4) providing to the support collection unit the documentation required by clauses (i) through (iii) of subparagraph two of this paragraph, where such documentation is sufficient for the support collection unit to determine:

(i) that the support obligor's income, as defined by subparagraph five of paragraph (b) of subdivision one of section four hundred thirteen of the family court act, falls below the self-support reserve as defined by subparagraph six of paragraph (b) of subdivision one of section four hundred thirteen of the family court act; or

(ii) that the amount of the support obligor's income, as defined by subparagraph five of paragraph (b) of subdivision one of section four hundred thirteen of the family court act, remaining after the payment of the current support obligation would fall below the self-support reserve as defined by subparagraph six of paragraph (b) of subdivision one of section four hundred thirteen of the family court act.

(f) A support obligor who alleges that he or she has not received actual notice pursuant to paragraph one of subdivision (b) of this section and whose driving privileges were suspended may at any time request a review pursuant to subdivision (d) of this section or comply with the requirements of subdivision (e) of this section, and upon a determination that he or she has not accumulated support arrears equivalent to or greater than the amount of support due for a period of four months or that he or she meets the requirements of subdivision (e) of this section, the department shall notify the department of motor vehicles that the suspension of driving privileges shall be terminated.

**Repealed 8/31/17,Ch.29,L.2015)

13. (a) The commissioner shall enter into the agreement provided for in section one hundred seventy-one-g of the tax law and is authorized to furnish to the commissioner of taxation and finance any information, and to take such other actions, as may be necessary to carry out the agreement provided for in such section, for the purpose of reviewing support orders pursuant to subdivision twelve of section one hundred eleven-h of this title.

(b) Information obtained under paragraph (a) of this subdivision shall be confidential and shall not be disclosed to persons or agencies other than those entitled to such information when such disclosure is necessary for the proper administration of the child support enforcement program pursuant to this title.

14. For purposes of this subdivision, the department or, pursuant to contract, a fiscal agent is authorized to collect and disburse any support paid pursuant to any order of child support or combined child and spousal support issued on or after the first day of January, nineteen hundred ninety-four under the provisions of section two hundred thirty-six or two hundred forty of the domestic relations law, or article four, five, five-A or five-B of the family court act, and which the court has ordered to be paid pursuant to an income execution issued by the sheriff, the clerk of the court, or the attorney for the creditor pursuant to subdivision (c) of section five thousand two hundred forty-one of the civil practice law and rules or an income deduction order issued by the court pursuant to subdivision (c) of section five thousand two hundred forty-two of the civil practice law and rules. Such support received shall be disbursed within two business days of receipt. The department shall maintain records of its collection and disbursement of such support and furnish such records to the parties to the order upon request. The department shall be entitled to collect an annual service fee not to exceed the maximum fee permitted pursuant to federal law for its provision of such services. Funds received in satisfaction of such fee shall be deposited in an account and shall

be made available to the department for costs incurred in the implementation of this section. The department shall not furnish any additional services to the parties; however, a party seeking child support services may apply for such services pursuant to section one hundred eleven-g of this title. The department shall not be responsible for the collection and disbursement of any support until after it has received a copy of the income execution from the sheriff, the clerk of the court, or the attorney for the creditor or a copy of the income deduction order issued by the court and the person entitled to the payment of support pursuant to the order of support has submitted payment of the annual service fee if any, and unless its records show that it has received such support on behalf of the parties to the order, and that the party to whom the funds are to be disbursed has provided the department with any address changes.

15. (a) The department, through the commissioner, shall enter into the agreement provided for in section one hundred seventy-one-i of the tax law and is authorized to furnish to the commissioner of taxation and finance such information and to take such other actions as may be necessary to carry out such agreement.

(b) (1) When a support obligor who is or was under a court order to pay child support or combined child and spousal support to a support collection unit on behalf of persons receiving services under this title has accumulated support arrears equivalent to or greater than the amount of support due pursuant to such order for a period of four months, the office of temporary and disability assistance shall notify the support obligor in writing that his or her continued failure to fully pay the support arrears shall result in notification to the department of taxation and finance that they are authorized to collect such arrearage. For purposes of determining whether a support obligor has accumulated support arrears equivalent to or greater than the amount of support due for a period of four months, the amount of any retroactive support, other than periodic payments of retroactive support which are past due, shall not be included in the calculation of support arrears pursuant to this section; however, if at least four months of support arrears have accumulated subsequent to the date of the court order, the entire amount of any retroactive support may be collected pursuant to the provisions of this subdivision or as otherwise authorized by law.

(2) The department shall provide the notice required by subparagraph one of this paragraph by first class mail to the support obligor's last known address or such other place where the support obligor is likely to receive notice by first class mail. Forty-five days after the date of such notice, if the support obligor has not challenged the determination of the support collection unit pursuant to subparagraph one of paragraph (d) of this subdivision or if the support obligor has failed to satisfy the arrears, the department shall notify the department of taxation and finance that the support obligor's support arrearage are authorized to be collected as prescribed in subparagraph one of this paragraph.

(3) Notwithstanding the requirements of this subdivision, no notice shall be issued by the department pursuant to subparagraph one of this paragraph to a support obligor from whom support payments are being received by the support collection unit as a result of an income execution or an income deduction order issued pursuant to section five thousand two hundred forty-one or five thousand two hundred forty-two of the civil practice law and rules.

(c) The notice provided to a support obligor by the department pursuant to paragraph (b) of this subdivision shall contain the caption of the order of support, the date the order of support was entered, the court in which it was entered, the amount of the periodic payments directed, and the amount of arrears. In addition, the notice shall include:

(1) a statement that unless the support arrears are satisfied within forty-five days after the date of the notice, the department of taxation and finance will be notified that they are authorized to commence collection action unless the support obligor challenges the support collection unit's determination as set forth in paragraph (d) of this subdivision within forty-five days of the date of such notice; a statement of the manner in which the support obligor may challenge the determination, and a statement that if the support obligor challenges the determination, a review will be completed by the support collection unit within seventy-five days of the date of the notice;

(2) a statement that if the support obligor does not challenge the support collection unit's determination then the department of taxation and finance shall be notified that they are authorized to commence collection action unless the support obligor contacts the support collection unit to arrange for full payment of the arrears;

(3) the address and telephone number of the support collection unit that the support obligor may contact to request information about a challenge to the determination of the support collection unit;

(4) a statement that the collection actions by the department of taxation and finance is authorized to continue until the support obligor pays the support arrears; and

(5) a statement printed in boldface type that the support obligor's intentional submission of false written statements to the support collection unit for the purpose of frustrating or defeating the lawful enforcement of support obligations is punishable pursuant to section 175.35 of the penal law.

(d) A support obligor who has received a notice that his or her support arrearage shall be referred to the department of taxation and finance for collection action may avoid such action by making payment of all arrears to the support collection unit; providing documentation that shows the support obligor is receiving public assistance, medical assistance, food stamps or supplemental security income; or providing to the support collection unit the documentation sufficient for the support collection unit to determine:

(1) an error in the calculation of the obligor's support arrears which would render the obligor ineligible for collection by the department of taxation and finance; or

(2) a mistake in the identity of the obligor showing that the individual making the challenge is not the obligor identified by the department; or

(3) the absence of an underlying court order for support pursuant to which the obligor's arrears gave rise to eligibility for collection action on such arrears by the department of taxation and finance.

16. Bureaus of special hearings; child support unit. (a) The department is authorized to establish a bureau of special hearings; child support unit solely for the purposes of providing administrative law judges to decide objections to the determination of a support collection unit to refer an obligor's arrears to the department of taxation and finance for collection pursuant to subdivision nineteen of section one hundred eleven-h of this title. The administrative law judges employed by the unit shall serve exclusively within the unit and shall not be utilized for any purpose other than those described in this subdivision and shall be salaried employees of the department and shall not be removed from such unit except for cause.

(b) The unit shall review a support collection unit's denial of a challenge made by a support obligor pursuant to paragraph two of subdivision nineteen of section one hundred eleven-h of this title if objections thereto are filed by a support obligor who has received notice that the department intends to notify the department of taxation and finance to collect such support obligor's support arrears. Specific written objections to a support collection unit's denial must be submitted by the support obligor to the unit within thirty days of the date of the notice of the support collection unit's denial. A support obligor who files such objections shall serve a copy of the objections upon the support collection unit, which shall have ten days from such service to file a written rebuttal to such objections and a copy of the record upon which the support collection unit's denial was made, including all documentation submitted by the support obligor. Proof of service shall be filed with the unit at the time of filing of objections and any rebuttal. The unit's review shall be based solely upon the record and submissions of the support obligor and the support collection unit upon which the support collection unit's denial was made. Within fifteen days after the rebuttal, if any, is filed, an administrative law judge of the unit shall (i) deny the objections and remand to the support collection unit or (ii) affirm the objections if the administrative law judge finds the determination of the support collection unit is based upon an erroneous determination of fact by the support collection unit. Such decision shall pertain solely to the mistaken identity of the obligor, a prejudicial error in the calculation of the obligor's arrears, the obligor's financial exemption from collection of support arrears by the department of taxation and finance or the absence of an underlying court order establishing arrears to support eligibility for such enforcement. Upon an affirmation of the objections the administrative law judge shall direct the support collection unit not to notify the department of taxation and finance of their authority to collect the support obligor's arrears. Provisions set forth in this subdivision relating to procedures for hearing objections by the unit shall apply solely to such cases and not affect or modify any other procedure for review or appeal of administrative enforcement of child support requirements. The decision of the administrative law judge pursuant to this section shall be final and not reviewable by the commissioner, and shall be reviewable only pursuant to article seventy-eight of the civil practice law and rules.

17. Special services for review and adjustment. The department shall develop procedures for and require local social services districts to dedicate special staff to the review and adjustment of child support orders entered prior to September fifteenth, nineteen hundred eighty-nine on behalf of children in receipt of public assistance or child support services pursuant to section one hundred eleven-g of this title. Such review and adjustment shall be performed pursuant to subdivisions twelve, thirteen, fourteen, fifteen and sixteen of section one hundred eleven-h of this title. All such cases shall be reviewed and if necessary adjusted no later than December thirty-first, two thousand.

§111-c. Functions, powers and duties of social services officials.

1. Each social services district shall establish a single organizational unit which shall be responsible for such district's activities in assisting the state in the location of absent parents, establishment of paternity and enforcement and collection of support in accordance with the regulations of the department.

2. Each social services district shall:

a. obtain assignments to the state and to such district of support rights of each applicant for or recipient of public assistance required to execute such an assignment as a condition of receiving assistance;

b. report to the state all recipients of public assistance with respect to whom a parent has been reported absent from the household;

c. obtain information regarding the income and resources of absent parents whose whereabouts are known, and shall have access to the statement of net worth filed pursuant to section four hundred twenty-four-a of the family court act and supporting documentation in any case where support collection services are being provided as may be necessary to ascertain their ability to support or contribute to the support of their dependents;

d. enforce support obligations owed to the state and to the social services district pursuant to subdivision two of section one hundred eleven-b of this title; and disburse amounts collected as support payments in accordance with the provisions of this chapter and the regulations of the department, including the disbursement to the family in receipt of public assistance of up to the first one hundred dollars for one child, and up to the first two hundred dollars for two or more children, collected as current support;

e. make periodic reports and perform such other functions in accordance with the regulations of the department as may be necessary to assure compliance with federal child support program requirements.

f. confer with a potential respondent, respondent or other interested person in a proceeding under article four, five, five-A or five-B of the family court act in an attempt to obtain support payments from such potential respondent or respondent;

g. obtain from respondent, when appropriate and in accordance with the procedures established by section one hundred eleven-k of this chapter, an acknowledgement of paternity or an agreement to make support payments, or both;

h. report periodically to consumer reporting agencies (as defined in section 603(f) of the Fair Credit Reporting Act (15 U.S.C. 1681a(f)) information regarding past-due support owed by the parent owing support. Such information must be made available whenever a parent who owes past-due support, and shall indicate the name of the parent and the amount of the delinquency. However, such information shall not be made available to (i) a consumer reporting agency that the office determines does not have sufficient capability to systematically and timely make accurate use of such information, or (ii) an entity that has not furnished evidence satisfactory to the office that the entity is a consumer reporting agency. In determining whether a consumer reporting agency lacks sufficient capability to systematically and timely make accurate use of such information, the office may require such agency to demonstrate its ability to comply with the provisions of section three hundred eighty-j of the general business law and any other requirements the office may prescribe by regulation. A social services official, at least ten days prior to making the information available to a consumer reporting agency, must provide notice to the parent who owes the support informing such parent of the proposed release of the information to the consumer reporting agency and informing such parent of the opportunity to be heard and the methods available for contesting the accuracy of the information.

3. Notwithstanding the foregoing, the social services official shall not be required to establish the paternity of any child born out-of-wedlock, or to secure support for any child, with respect to whom such official has determined

that such actions would be detrimental to the best interests of the child, in accordance with procedures and criteria established by regulations of the department consistent with federal law.

4. a. A social services district represents the interests of the district in performing its functions and duties as provided in this title and not the interests of any party. The interests of a district shall include, but are not limited to, establishing paternity, and establishing, modifying and enforcing child support orders.

b. Notwithstanding any other provision of law, the provision of child support services pursuant to this title does not constitute nor create an attorney-client relationship between the individual receiving services and any attorney representing or appearing for the district. A social services district shall provide notice to any individual requesting or receiving services that the attorney representing or appearing for the district does not represent the individual and that the individual has a right to retain his or her own legal counsel.

c. A social services district may appear in any action to establish paternity, or to establish, modify, or enforce an order of support when an individual is receiving services under this title.

§111-d.   **State reimbursement.**

1. The provisions of section one hundred fifty-three of this chapter shall be applicable to expenditures by social services districts for activities related to the establishment of paternity of children born out-of-wedlock, the location of deserting parents and the enforcement and collection of support obligations owed to recipients of aid to dependent children and persons receiving services pursuant to section one hundred eleven-g of this title.

2. The local share of expenditures incurred by the department for the provision of centralized collection and disbursement services pursuant to section one hundred eleven-h of this title shall be charged back to social services districts. The local share shall be fifty per centum of the amount expended by the department after first deducting therefrom any federal funds properly received or to be received on account thereof; provided, however, that a social services district's share of the costs related to the centralized collection and disbursement functions shall not exceed those incurred for the year immediately preceding implementation of such functions, except to the extent to which those costs would have increased had centralization of collection and disbursement functions not occurred.

§111-e.   **Reimbursement to the state.**

1. A share of any support payments collected by the social services official, less any amount disbursed to the family receiving family assistance, shall, subject to section one hundred eleven-f, be paid to the state as reimbursement toward the amount contributed by the state and federal governments to assistance furnished to such family. Such share shall bear the same ratio to the amounts collected as the state and federal funds bear to assistance granted.

2. Whenever one social services district makes collections on behalf of a person or family for whom another social services district or another state is responsible for providing assistance, the amount collected shall be paid to the district or such other state responsible for providing such assistance, in accordance with the regulations of the department.

§111-f.   Federal incentives.
The department is authorized to distribute to local districts the full amount of federal incentive payments received under title IV-D of the federal social security act.

§111-g.   Availability of paternity and support services.
1. The office of temporary and disability assistance and the social services districts, in accordance with the regulations of the office of temporary and disability assistance, shall make services relating to the establishment of paternity and the establishment and enforcement of support obligations available to persons not receiving family assistance upon application by such persons. Such persons must apply by (i) completing and signing a form as prescribed by the office of temporary and disability assistance, or (ii) filing a petition with the court or applying to the court in a proceeding for the establishment of paternity and/or establishment and/or enforcement of a support obligation, which includes a statement signed by the person requesting services clearly indicating that such person is applying for child support enforcement services pursuant to this title.
2. The office of temporary and disability assistance may, by regulation, require payment of an application fee for such services and the deduction of costs in excess of such fee from amounts collected on behalf of such persons.
3. (a) A person who is receiving child support services pursuant to this section who has never received assistance pursuant to title IV-A of the federal social security act shall be subject to an annual service fee of twenty-five dollars for each child support case if at least five hundred dollars of support has been collected in the federal fiscal year. Where a custodial parent has children with different noncustodial parents, the order payable by each noncustodial parent shall be a separate child support case for the purpose of imposing an annual service fee. The fee shall be deducted from child support payments received on behalf of the individual receiving services.
(b) In international cases under section 454(32) of the federal social security act which meet the criteria for imposition of the annual service fee under paragraph (a) of this subdivision, the annual service fee shall be imposed but may not be collected from the country requesting services or a person living in another country unless permitted by federal law or regulation.

§111-h.   Support collection unit.
1. Each social services district shall establish a support collection unit in accordance with regulations of the department to collect, account for and disburse funds paid pursuant to any order of child support or child and spousal support issued under the provisions of section two hundred thirty-six or two hundred forty of the domestic relations law, or article four, five, five-A or five-B of the family court act; provided however, that the department, subject to availability of funds, shall furnish centralized collection and disbursement services for and on behalf of each social services district. Until such time as the department performs collection and disbursement functions for a particular social services district, that social services district shall continue to perform those functions.
2. The support collection unit shall inform the petitioner and respondent of any case in which a required payment has not been made within two weeks after it was due and shall assist in securing voluntary compliance with such orders or in preparation and submission of a petition for a violation of a

support order. Upon the written request of the debtor, the support collection unit shall issue an income execution as provided in section fifty-two hundred forty-one of the civil practice law and rules, except that the provisions of subdivisions (d) and (e) thereof shall not apply. Upon receipt of written revocation of such request, the support collection unit shall notify the employer or income payor that the levy is no longer effective, and the execution shall be returned.

3. The support collection unit shall require that a person applying for child support enforcement services provide his or her name, address and social security number and disclose whether he or she is in receipt of safety net assistance or family assistance; provided, however, that a social security number may be required only where permitted under federal law.

4. Any and all moneys paid into the support collection unit pursuant to an order of support made under the family court act or the domestic relations law, where the petitioner is not a recipient of public assistance, shall upon payment into such support collection unit be deemed for all purposes to be the property of the person for whom such money is to be paid.

5. With respect to any funds paid to the support collection unit established by a social services district pursuant to an order of support under the provisions of article four, five, five-A or five-B of the family court act and which have remained unclaimed for not less than two years after diligent effort to locate the person entitled to such funds, the family court may enter an order decreeing

(a) that the funds be returned to the person who paid the funds pursuant to the order of support, or

(b) that the funds be deposited with the county treasurer or commissioner of finance of the city of New York, whose duty it shall be to receive such funds and invest them for a period of five years in such securities as are specified by law for investment by savings banks, the interest on such securities to accrue and become part of such funds.

6. If a claimant proves to the satisfaction of the family court within five years after the deposit of funds under paragraph (b) of subdivision five of this section his just and legal claim to any part of the funds, the court may require that repayment shall be made to the claimant as provided by order of the court. The clerk of the court shall issue a certificate under the official seal of the court embodying the terms and provisions of the order and transmit the certificate to the office of the county treasurer or commissioner of finance of the city of New York with whom the funds were deposited. The certificate shall constitute the authority of the county treasurer or commissioner of finance of the city of New York for making such repayment.

7. Upon the expiration of five years from the date of deposit with the county treasurer or commissioner of finance of the city of New York under paragraph (b) of subdivision five of this section, all such funds remaining in the custody of the county treasurer or commissioner of finance of the city of New York shall be paid to the state comptroller pursuant to the provisions of section six hundred two of the abandoned property law and such payment shall be accomplished by the report required by section six hundred three of the abandoned property law.

8. Banks and other fiduciary institutions are authorized and required to report to the support collection unit, when so requested, full information relative to any fund therein deposited by a petitioner or respondent in a proceeding under section two hundred thirty-six or two hundred forty of the domestic relations law or article five-B of the family court act, where there is

an order of support payable through the support collection unit or article four, five or five-A of the family court act.

9. Employers are authorized and required to report to the support collection unit, when so requested, full information as to the earnings of a petitioner or respondent in a proceeding under section two hundred thirty-six or two hundred forty of the domestic relations law or article five-B of the family court act, where there is an order of support payable through the support collection unit or article four, five, five-A or five-B of the family court act. Employers also are authorized and required to report to the support collection unit, when so requested, information relating to any group health plans available for the provision of care or other medical benefits by insurance or otherwise for the benefit of the employee and/or the child or children for whom such parties are legally responsible for support.

10. The support collection unit is authorized and required to report to the family court, when so requested, full information relative to amounts paid or any arrearages by a respondent in a proceeding under articles four, five, five-A or article five-B of the family court act.

11. The department may provide for the performance of the collection and disbursement functions of the support collection units by contract with a fiscal agent. For purposes of any reference to support collection unit in this chapter or any other law, the fiscal agent under contract with the department shall be deemed to be part of all support collection units for which the fiscal agent performs collection and disbursement functions.

12. In any case where the child support order was issued prior to September fifteenth, nineteen hundred eighty-nine in which there is an assignment of support rights or in which a request for an adjustment review is made, the support collection unit shall initiate a one-time review of the order for adjustment purposes unless: (i) the child is in receipt of public assistance, and the support collection unit determines that such review would not be in the best interest of the child or the custodial parent, and neither parent has requested review; or (ii) the child is not in receipt of public assistance and neither parent has requested such review. The support collection unit shall conduct such review in a manner consistent with section four hundred thirteen of the family court act and subdivision one-b of section two hundred forty of the domestic relations law, commonly referred to as the child support guidelines, and the definition of adjustment as set forth in subdivision three of section four hundred thirteen of the family court act and paragraph b of subdivision one of section two hundred forty of the domestic relations law.

13. Upon the conclusion of the adjustment review, the support collection unit shall send the findings of such review by first class mail to the parties, together with a notice describing the rights of the parties to seek adjustment pursuant to applicable provisions of law.

14. Where the support collection unit determines that there is a basis for an upward adjustment, it shall also file a proposed order together with an affidavit in support thereof with the clerk of the appropriate court, and send a copy of such proposed order and affidavit by first class mail to the parties.

15. Where the support collection unit has determined that an adjustment review is appropriate, and the child or children are in receipt of public assistance, the unit shall, at least thirty days before the commencement of such review, notify the parties that the support collection unit will commence review, and provide notice of their obligations pursuant to subdivision sixteen

of this section. Such notice shall also be provided, whether or not a child is in receipt of public assistance, upon a request by any party for adjustment review.

16. Such notice shall include a statement that the party must, within thirty-five days of the date of mailing of the notice, send to the support collection unit:

(i) a current and representative paycheck stub with respect to each source of employment income;

(ii) copies of the most recently filed state and federal income tax returns; and

(iii) a sworn statement of net worth which shall also identify the carrier and policy number of all health insurance currently in place, for the benefit of the obligor and eligible dependents, and whether such coverage has been in place for the previous year.

The notice shall also include a statement that the party may schedule a conference with the support collection unit and submit a written explanation of his or her present tax and financial information to determine the appropriate modification, and thereby may avoid further administrative and judicial proceedings.

The notice shall also state that in the event the party fails to provide such information within thirty-five days of the date of the mailing of the notice, the department of social services shall be entitled to make use of certain tax data from the commissioner of taxation and finance pursuant to section one hundred seventy-one-g of the tax law and section one hundred eleven-c of the social services law to initiate proceedings to adjust the child support order.

17. The department shall develop and disseminate a notice informing both parties to child support orders issued prior to September fifteenth, nineteen hundred eighty-nine, of the availability of the one-time adjustment of child support orders pursuant to the provisions of subdivision three of section four hundred thirteen of the family court act and subdivision four of section two hundred forty of the domestic relations law. The department shall also develop a notice that shall set out the options for adjustment of child support orders issued prior to September fifteenth, nineteen hundred eighty-nine, and the methods for exercising those options. Said notice shall be sent by first class mail to persons in receipt of services pursuant to this title, and shall contain a reply form and envelope with postage pre-paid.

18. The support collection unit shall undertake a public service campaign as soon as practicable to inform citizens of the possibility of driver, business and professional license suspension for support enforcement.

19. (1) A support obligor may challenge in writing the correctness of the determination of the support collection unit pursuant to this section and section one hundred seventy-one-i of the tax law that the obligor's arrearage should be collected through the department of taxation and finance, and in support of the challenge may submit documentation demonstrating mistaken identity, error in calculation of arrears, financial exemption from such collection, the absence of an underlying court order establishing arrears to support such determination. Such documents may include a copy of the order of support pursuant to which the obligor claims to have made payment, other relevant court orders, copies of cancelled checks, receipts for support payments, pay stubs or other documents identifying wage withholding, proof of identity, and like documents. The support collection unit shall review the documentation submitted by the support obligor, shall adjust the support obligor's account if appropriate, and shall notify the support obligor of the results of the review initiated in response to the challenge within seventy-five days from the date of the notice required.

If the support collection unit's review indicates that the determination to refer to the department of taxation and finance for collection was correct, the support collection unit shall notify the support obligor of the results of the review and that the support obligor has thirty days from the date of such notice to satisfy the full amount of the arrears. If the support obligor fails to do so, the support collection unit shall notify the department of taxation and finance that they are authorized to commence collection of the arrears. The support obligor shall be further notified that if the support obligor files objections to the review determination of the support collection unit with the bureau of special hearings; child support unit of the department pursuant to subdivision sixteen of section one hundred eleven-b of this title, and serves these objections on the support collection unit within thirty days from the date of notice denying the challenge, the support collection unit shall not notify the department of taxation and finance of their authority to collect the arrearages until fifteen days after receipt of a decision by the administrative law judge pursuant to such section.

(2) A support obligor may within thirty days of the date of notice denying his or her challenge by the support collection unit file objections to such denial with the bureau of special hearings; child support unit of the department which shall review the support collection unit's determination to refer the obligor's case to the department of taxation and finance for collection pursuant to subdivision sixteen of section one hundred eleven-b of this title. If the support obligor timely files such objections with such bureau the support collection unit shall not notify the department of taxation and finance of their authority to collect the arrearages until fifteen days after entry of an order by the administrative law judge denying the objections.

20. If the support obligor is required to participate in work programs pursuant to section four hundred thirty-seven-a of the family court act, and the court enters an order of support on behalf of the persons in receipt of public assistance, the support collection unit shall not file a petition to increase the support obligation for twelve months from the date of entry of the order of support if the support obligor's income is derived from participation in such programs.

§111-i. Child support standards.
1. Each social services district shall ascertain the ability of an absent parent to support or contribute to the support of his or her children, in accordance with the statewide child support standards as set forth in subdivision one of section four hundred thirteen of the family court act.

2. (a) The commissioner shall publish annually a child support standards chart. The child support standards chart shall include: (i) the revised poverty income guideline for a single person as reported by the federal department of health and human services; (ii) the revised self-support reserved as defined in section two hundred forty of the domestic relations law; (iii) the dollar amounts yielded through application of the child support percentage as defined in section two hundred forty of the domestic relations law and section four hundred thirteen of the family court act; and (iv) the combined parental income amount.

(b) The combined parental income amount to be reported in the child support standards chart and utilized in calculating orders of child support in accordance with subparagraph two of paragraph (c) of subdivision one of section four hundred thirteen of the family court act and subparagraph two of paragraph (c) of subdivision one-b of section two hundred forty of the domestic relations law as of January thirty-first, two thousand fourteen shall be one hundred forty-one thousand dollars; provided, however, beginning March first, two thousand sixteen and every two years thereafter, the combined parental income amount shall increase by the sum of the average annual percentage changes in the consumer price index for all urban consumers (CPI-U) as published by the United States department of labor bureau of labor statistics for the prior two years multiplied by the current combined parental income amount and then rounded to the nearest one thousand dollars.

(c) The commissioner shall publish the child support standards chart on an annual basis by April first of each year and in no event later than forty-five days following publication of the annual poverty income guideline for a single person as reported by the federal department of health and human services.

§111-j. Interception of unemployment insurance benefits.

1. (a) The department shall determine on a periodic basis whether any individual receiving unemployment insurance benefits pursuant to article eighteen of the state's labor law owes child support obligations which are being enforced by the department or the child support enforcement unit of a social services district and shall enforce any child support obligations which are owed by such individual but are not being met through an agreement with such individual to have specific amounts withheld from such benefits otherwise payable to such individual and by submitting a copy of such agreement to the New York state department of labor.

(b) In the absence of such an agreement, the department shall enforce any such child support obligations as authorized by the court in any order establishing such obligations and as otherwise provided by law.

2. Any amounts of unemployment insurance benefits deducted, withheld and paid over by the department of labor pursuant to section five hundred ninety-six of the labor law shall be treated as if it were paid to the person entitled to such compensation and paid by such person to the department or appropriate child support collection unit toward satisfaction of such person's child support obligations. Each agency or district receiving payments deducted by the department of labor shall reimburse that department for the administrative costs attributable thereto.

§111-k. Procedures relating to acknowledgments of paternity, agree-ments to support, and genetic tests.

1. A social services official or his or her designated representative who confers with a potential respondent or respondent, hereinafter referred to in this section as the "respondent", the mother of a child born out of wedlock and any other interested persons, pursuant to section one hundred eleven-c of this title, may obtain:

(a) an acknowledgment of paternity of a child, as provided for in article five-B or section five hundred sixteen-a of the family court act, by a written statement, witnessed by two people not related to the signator or as provided for in section four thousand one hundred thirty-five-b of the public health law. Prior to the execution of such acknowledgment by the child's mother and the respondent, they shall be advised, orally, which may be through the use of audio or video equipment, and in writing, of the consequences of making such an acknowledgment. Upon the signing of an acknowledgment of paternity pursuant to this section, the social services official or his or her representative shall file the original acknowledgment with the registrar.

(b) an agreement to make support payments as provided in section four hundred twenty-five of the family court act. Prior to the execution of such agreement, the respondent shall be advised, orally, which may be through the use of audio or video equipment, and in writing, of the consequences of such agreement, that the respondent can be held liable for support only if the family court, after a hearing, makes an order of support; that respondent has a right to consult with an attorney and that the agreement will be submitted to the family court for approval pursuant to section four hundred twenty-five of the family court act; and that by executing the agreement, the respondent waives any right to a hearing regarding any matter contained in such agreement.

2. (a) When the paternity of a child is contested, a social services official or designated representative may order the mother, the child, and the alleged father to submit to one or more genetic marker or DNA tests of a type generally acknowledged as reliable by an accreditation body designated by the secretary of the federal department of health and human services and performed by a laboratory approved by such an accreditation body and by the commissioner of health or by a duly qualified physician to aid in the determination of whether or not the alleged father is the father of the child. The order may be issued prior or subsequent to the filing of a petition with the court to establish paternity, shall be served on the parties by certified mail, and shall include a sworn statement which either (i) alleges paternity and sets forth facts establishing a reasonable possibility of the requisite sexual contact between the parties, or (ii) denies paternity and sets forth facts establishing a reasonable possibility that the party is not the father. The parties shall not be required to submit to the administration and analysis of such tests if they sign a voluntary acknowledgment of paternity in accordance with paragraph (a) of subdivision one of this section, or if there has been a written finding by the court that it is not in the best interests of the child on the basis of res judicata, equitable estoppel or the presumption of legitimacy of a child born to a married woman.

(b) The record or report of the results of any such genetic marker or DNA test may be submitted to the family court as evidence pursuant to subdivision (e) of rule forty-five hundred eighteen of the civil practice law and rules where no timely objection in writing has been made thereto.

(c) The cost of any test ordered pursuant to this section shall be paid by the social services district provided however, that the alleged father shall reimburse the district for the cost of such test at such time as the alleged father's paternity is established by a voluntary acknowledgment of paternity or an order of filiation. If either party contests the results of genetic marker or DNA tests, an additional test may be ordered upon written request to the social services district and advance payment by the requesting party.

(d) The parties shall be required to submit to such tests and appear at any conference scheduled by the social services official or designee to discuss the notice of the allegation of paternity or to discuss the results of such tests. If the alleged father fails to appear at any such conference or fails to submit to such genetic marker or DNA tests, the social services official or designee shall petition the court to establish paternity, provide the court with a copy of the records or reports of such tests if any, and request the court to issue an order for temporary support pursuant to section five hundred forty-two of the family court act.

§111-m. Agreement relating to information obtained by the state directory of new hires.
The department, through the commissioner, shall enter into the agreement provided for in section one hundred seventy-one-h of the tax law, and shall take such other actions as may be necessary to carry out the agreement provided for in such section for matching recipient records of public assistance and of the child support enforcement program with information provided by employers to the state directory of new hires for the purposes of verifying eligibility for such public assistance programs and for the administration of the child support enforcement program.

§111-n. Review and cost of living adjustment of support orders.
1. Orders subject to review. In accordance with the timeframes set forth in subdivision three of this section, the support collection unit shall conduct a review for adjustment purposes of:

(a) all orders of support being enforced pursuant to this title on behalf of persons in receipt of family assistance; and

(b) those orders of support being enforced pursuant to this title on behalf of persons not in receipt of family assistance, for which a request for a cost of living adjustment review has been received from either party to the order.

2. Definitions. For purposes of this section, the following definitions shall be used:

(a) "Adjusted child support obligation amount" shall mean the sum of the cost of living adjustment and the support obligation amount contained in the order under review.

(b) "Adjusted order" shall mean an order issued by the support collection unit reflecting a change to the obligation amount of the most recently issued order of support made on behalf of a child in receipt of family assistance or child support enforcement services pursuant to section one hundred eleven-g of this title.

(c) "Cost of living adjustment" shall mean the amount by which the support obligation is changed as the result of a review, and shall be determined based upon annual average changes to the consumer price index for all urban consumers (CPI-U), as published by the United States department of labor bureau of labor statistics, for the years preceding the year of the review, as follows:

(1) Identify the CPI-U "percent change from the previous annual average" for each year preceding the year of the review, beginning with and including the later of the year in which the most recent order was issued or nineteen hundred ninety-four, and calculate the sum of the percentages for those years.

(2) Where the sum as calculated pursuant to subparagraph one of this paragraph equals or exceeds ten percent, multiply the support obligation in the order under review by such percentage. The product is the cost of living adjustment.

(d) "Order" shall mean an original, modified, or adjusted order of support; or, after a hearing in response to objections to a cost of living adjustment as set forth in an adjusted order of support, the order of support reflecting the application of the child support standards pursuant to section two hundred forty of the domestic relations law or section four hundred thirteen of the family court act, or an order of no adjustment.

(e) "Review" shall mean the calculation of the cost of living adjustment and the adjusted child support obligation amount by the support collection unit for the most recently issued order of support made on behalf of a child in receipt of family assistance, or child support enforcement services pursuant to section one hundred eleven-g of this title.

3. Timeframes. The review of support orders for cost of living adjustment purposes shall be conducted by the support collection unit in accordance with the following timeframes:

(a) For all orders of support on behalf of persons in receipt of family assistance, a review shall be conducted during the second calendar year following the year in which the order was issued, or the current year, whichever is later. Any cost of living adjustment resulting from a review shall be effective sixty days following the date of the adjusted order, or twenty-four months after the date of the order under review, whichever is later.

(b) For all orders of support on behalf of persons not in receipt of family assistance, a review shall be conducted during the second calendar year following the year in which the order was issued, or the current year, whichever is later; provided, however, that no such review shall occur unless a request for such review has been received from a party to the order. Any cost of living adjustment resulting from a review shall be effective sixty days following the date of the adjusted order, or twenty-four months after the date of the order under review, whichever is later.

4. Adjustment process. (a) A cost of living adjustment shall be made by the support collection unit with respect to each order of support under review, if the sum of the annual average changes of the consumer price index for all urban consumers (CPI-U), as published by the United States department of labor bureau of labor statistics, is ten percent or greater. The child support obligation amount, as increased by the cost of living adjustment calculated during the review, shall be rounded to the nearest dollar. In the event that the sum of the annual average changes of the CPI-U is less than ten percent, no cost of living adjustment shall occur.

(b) Upon the conclusion of the adjustment review, the support collection unit shall issue and send an adjusted order by first class mail to the parties. The cost of living adjustment and the adjusted child support obligation amount as calculated by the review shall be reflected in the adjusted order. The child support obligation amount contained in the adjusted order shall be due and owing on the date the first payment is due under the terms of the order of support which was reviewed and adjusted occurring on or after the effective date of the adjusted order.

(c) The support collection unit shall provide a copy of the adjusted order to the court which issued the most recent order of support, which shall append it to the order.

5. Objections. (a) Where there is an objection to a cost of living adjustment, either party or the support collection unit shall have thirty-five days from the date of mailing of the adjusted order by the support collection unit to submit to the court identified thereon written objections, requesting a hearing on the adjustment of the order of support.

(b) If objections are submitted timely to the court, the cost of living adjustment shall not take effect, and a hearing shall be scheduled by the court. The hearing shall be conducted and a determination made by the court pursuant to section two hundred forty-c of the domestic relations law or section four hundred thirteen-a of the family court act.

(c) Where no objection has been timely raised to a cost of living adjustment as reflected in an adjusted order, such adjusted order shall become final without further review by the court or any judge or support magistrate thereof.

6. Adjusted order - form. The adjusted order shall contain the following information:

(a) the caption of the order of support subject to the review, the date of such order, and the court in which it was entered;

(b) the identification, telephone number, and address of the support collection unit which conducted the review;

(c) the cost of living adjustment and the adjusted child support obligation amount as calculated during the review of the order, and a statement that such amount shall be due and owing on the date the first payment is due under the term of the order of support which was reviewed and adjusted, occurring on or after the effective date of the adjusted order;

(d) the definition of cost of living adjustment;

(e) a statement that the child support obligation amount, as increased by the cost of living adjustment, has been rounded to the nearest dollar;

(f) a statement that all other provisions of the order of support which was reviewed and adjusted remain in full force and effect;

(g) a statement that the application of a cost of living adjustment in no way limits, restricts, expands, or impairs the rights of any party to file for a modification of a child support order as otherwise provided by law;

(h) a statement that where either party objects to the cost of living adjustment, the party has the right to be heard by the court and to present evidence to the court which the court will consider in adjusting the child support order in compliance with section four hundred thirteen of the family court act or section two hundred forty of the domestic relations law, known as the child support standards act; provided, however, that written objections are filed with the court within thirty-five days from the date the adjusted order was mailed by the support collection unit; that when filing objections the objecting party should attach a copy of the adjusted order, if available; and

(i) a statement that where any party fails to provide, and update upon any change, the support collection unit with a current address to which an adjusted order can be sent, the support obligation amount contained therein shall become due and owing on the date the first payment is due under the order of support which was reviewed and adjusted occurring on or after the effective date of the adjusted order, regardless of whether or not the party has received a copy of the adjusted order.

7. Notice of right to review. On or after the first day of January, nineteen hundred ninety-eight, any order of support twenty-four or more months old which was issued on behalf of a child in receipt of family assistance or child support enforcement services pursuant to section one hundred eleven-g of this title, is eligible for a cost of living adjustment every two years. The support collection unit shall notify the parties to the order of their right to make a written request to the support collection unit for a cost of living adjustment of such support order. Such notice shall contain the amount of the cost of living adjustment, the amount of the adjusted child support obligation, the applicable CPI-U used in the calculation of that amount, the address and telephone number of the support collection unit where assistance can be obtained in commencing an adjustment review, and other information deemed necessary and relevant by the department, and shall be sent to the parties by first class mail at their last known address, and shall contain a reply form and envelope

with postage pre-paid. The support collection unit shall provide the notice described herein not less than once every two years.

§111-o.   Data matches with financial institutions.

The department or a social services district, through the commissioner, is authorized to enter into agreements with financial institutions as provided for in subdivision two of section four of the banking law and subsection (e) of section three hundred twenty of the insurance law, and is authorized to furnish to and receive from those and any other financial institutions, as defined in paragraph one of subdivision (d) of section four hundred sixty-nine A of the federal social security act, such information as may be necessary to carry out the agreements provided for in section four of the banking law and section three hundred twenty of the insurance law, for the enforcement of child support orders.

§111-p.   Authority to issue subpoenas.

The department or the child support enforcement unit coordinator or support collection unit supervisor of a social services district, or his or her designee, or another state's child support enforcement agency governed by title IV-D of the social security act, shall be authorized, whether or not a proceeding is currently pending, to subpoena from any person, public or private entity or governmental agency, and such person, entity or agency shall provide any financial or other information needed to establish paternity and to establish, modify or enforce any support order. If a subpoena is served when a petition is not currently pending, the supreme court or a judge of the family court may hear and decide all motions relating to the subpoena. If the subpoena is served after a petition has been served, the court in which the petition is returnable shall hear and decide all motions relating to the subpoena. Any such person, entity, or agency shall provide the subpoenaed information by the date as specified in the subpoena. Such subpoena shall be subject to the provisions of article twenty-three of the civil practice law and rules. The department or district may impose a penalty for failure to respond to such information subpoenas pursuant to section twenty-three hundred eight of the civil practice law and rules.

§111-q.   Voiding of fraudulent transfers of income or property.

The department or a social services district, or its authorized representative, after obtaining information that a debtor has transferred income, property or other assets to avoid payment to a child support creditor shall, pursuant to article ten of the debtor and creditor law (1) commence a proceeding to void such transfer; or (2) obtain a settlement that is in the best interests of the child support creditor. Provided, however, that no settlement shall reduce or annul any arrears of child support which have accrued prior to the date of settlement.

§111-r.   Requirement to respond to requests for information.

All employers, as defined in section one hundred eleven-m of this article (including for-profit, not-for-profit and governmental employers), are required to provide information promptly on the employment, compensation and benefits of any individual employed by such employer as an employee or contractor, when the department or a social services district or its authorized representative, or another state's child support enforcement agency governed by title IV-D of the social security act, requests such information for the purpose of establishing paternity, or establishing, modifying or enforcing an order of support. To the extent feasible, such information shall be requested and provided using automated systems, and shall include, but is not limited to, information regarding the individual's last known address, date of birth, social security number, plans providing health care or other medical benefits by insurance or otherwise, wages, salaries, earnings or other income of such individual. Notwithstanding any other provision of law to the contrary, such officials are not required to obtain an order from any judicial or administrative tribunal in order to request or receive such information. The department shall be authorized to impose a penalty for failure to respond to such requests of five hundred dollars for an initial failure and seven hundred dollars for the second and subsequent failure.

§111-s. Access to information contained in government and private records.
1. For the purpose of establishing paternity, or establishing, modifying or enforcing an order of support, the department or a social services district or its authorized representative, and child support enforcement agencies of other states established pursuant to title IV-D of the social security act, without the necessity of obtaining an order from any other judicial or administrative tribunal and subject to safeguards on privacy and information security, shall have access to information contained in the following records:

(a) records of other state and local government agencies including:

(i) vital statistics (including records of marriage, birth and divorce);

(ii) state and local tax and revenue records (including information on residence address, employer, income and assets);

(iii) records concerning real and titled personal property;

(iv) records of occupational and professional licenses, and records concerning the ownership and control of corporations, partnerships and other business entities;

(v) employment security records;

(vi) records of agencies administering public assistance programs;

(vii) records of the department of motor vehicles; and

(viii) corrections records; and

(b) certain records held by private corporations, companies, or other entities with respect to individuals who owe or are owed support (or against or with respect to whom a support obligation is being sought), consisting of:

(i) pursuant to an administrative subpoena authorized by section one hundred eleven-p of this title, the names, addresses, telephone numbers and dates of birth of such individuals, and the names and addresses of the employers of such individuals, as appearing in customer records of public utilities companies and corporations, including, but not limited to, cable television, gas, electric, steam, and telephone companies and corporations, as defined in section two of the public service law, doing business within the state of New York; and

(ii) information on such individuals held by financial institutions, including information regarding assets and liabilities.

2. Notwithstanding any other provision of law to the contrary, any government or private entity to which a request for access to information is directed pursuant to subdivision one of this section, is authorized and required to comply with such request. To the extent feasible, access to such information shall be requested and provided using automated systems. Any government or private entity which discloses information pursuant to this section shall not be liable under any federal or state law to any person for such disclosure, or for any other action taken in good faith to comply with this subdivision.

§111-t. Authority to secure assets.
The department or a social services district or its authorized representative, or another state's child support enforcement agency governed by title IV-D of the social security act, for the purpose of collecting overdue support, shall be authorized in accordance with all applicable provisions of law, to secure assets otherwise due a support obligor by:

1. intercepting or seizing periodic or lump sum payments due such obligor from:

(a) a state or local agency, including unemployment compensation, workers' compensation, and other benefits; and

(b) judgments, settlements and lottery winnings;

2. attaching and seizing assets of such obligors which are held in financial institutions;

3. attaching public and private retirement funds of such obligors; and

4. imposing liens against real and personal property owned by such obligors; and where appropriate, forcing the sale of property owned by such obligors and distributing proceeds from the sale of such properties.

§111-u.   Liens.
1. The office of temporary and disability assistance, or a social services district, or its authorized representative shall have a lien against real and personal property owned by a support obligor when such support obligor is or was under a court order to pay child support or combined child and spousal support to a support collection unit on behalf of persons receiving services under this title, and such obligor has accumulated support arrears/past due in an amount equal to or greater than the amount of support due pursuant to such order for a period of four months. Such lien shall incorporate unpaid support which accrues in the future.

2. For the purposes of determining whether a support obligor has accumulated support arrears/past due support for a period of four months, the amount of any retroactive support, other than periodic payments of retroactive support which are past due, shall not be included in the calculation of arrears/past due support pursuant to this section; however, if at least four months of support arrears/past due support have accumulated subsequent to the date of the court order, the entire amount of any retroactive support may be collected pursuant to the provisions of this subdivision or as otherwise authorized by law.

3. When the office of temporary and disability assistance, or a social services district, or its authorized representative on behalf of a person receiving services pursuant to this title determines that the requisite amount of child support is past due, it shall send, by first class mail, a notice of intent to file a lien to the support obligor. The obligor may assert a mistake of fact and shall have an opportunity to make a submission in support of the assertion. The assertion and any supporting papers shall be submitted within thirty-five days from the date a notice was mailed. Thereafter, the social services district shall determine the merits of the assertion, and shall notify the obligor of its determination within ninety days after notice to the obligor was mailed.

4. If the social services district finds no mistake of fact exists or, the obligor fails to assert a mistake of fact within the thirty-five days, the social services district may file a notice of lien, which shall contain the caption of the support order and a statement of arrears and which shall constitute a lien on the property. The social services district shall not enforce its lien until after

expiration of any applicable period for review of an administrative action or, if the obligor has initiated a proceeding pursuant to article seventy-eight of the civil practice law and rules, until completion of such review.

5. Filing of the notice of the lien shall be as provided in sections sixty-five and two hundred eleven of the lien law, article forty-six of the vehicle and traffic law, or as otherwise authorized by law.

6. Within five days before or thirty days after filing the notice of the lien, the social services district shall send by first class mail a copy of such notice upon the owner of the property.

§111-v. Confidentiality, integrity, and security of information.
1. The department, in consultation with appropriate agencies including but not limited to the New York state office for the prevention of domestic violence, shall by regulation prescribe and implement safeguards on the confidentiality, integrity, accuracy, access, and the use of all confidential information and other data handled or maintained, including data obtained pursuant to section one hundred eleven-o of this article and including such information and data maintained in the automated child support enforcement system. Such information and data shall be maintained in a confidential manner designed to protect the privacy rights of the parties and shall not be disclosed except for the purpose of, and to the extent necessary to, establish paternity, or establish, modify or enforce an order of support.

2. These safeguards shall include provisions for the following:
(a) Policies restricting access to and sharing of information and data, including:
(1) safeguards against unauthorized use or disclosure of information relating to procedures or actions to establish paternity or to establish or enforce support;
(2) prohibitions against the release of information on the whereabouts of one party to another party against whom an order of protection with respect to the former party has been entered; and
(3) prohibitions against the release of information on the whereabouts of one party to another party if the department has reason to believe that the release of the information may result in the physical or emotional harm to the former party.
(b) Systems controls to ensure strict adherence to policies.
(c) Monitoring of access to and use of the automated system to prevent unauthorized access or use.
(d) Training in security procedures for all staff with access, and provisions of information regarding these requirements and penalties.
(e) Administrative penalties for unauthorized access, disclosure, or use of confidential data.

3. If any person discloses confidential information in violation of this section, any individual who incurs damages due to the disclosure may recover such damages in a civil action.

4. Any person who willfully releases or permits the release of any confidential information obtained pursuant to this title to persons or agencies not authorized by this title or regulations promulgated thereunder to receive it shall be guilty of a class A misdemeanor.

5. The safeguards established pursuant to this section shall apply to staff of the department, local social services districts, and any contractor.

Title 6-B
Services for Enforcement of Support Provided by
the Department of Social Services

§111-y.   Spousal support; crediting of overpayments of tax to past-due support.

1. The department shall provide services for the crediting of overpayments of tax to past-due support, pursuant to section one hundred seventy-one-c of the tax law, which is owed to any current or former spouse entitled to enforce an order of support, who applies to the department for such services, if such spouse is not eligible to receive services pursuant to title six-A of this article. For purposes of this section, "order of support" means any final order, decree or judgment in a matrimonial action or family court proceeding, or any foreign support order, decree or judgment which is registered pursuant to article 5-B of the family court act which requires the payment of alimony, maintenance or support.

2. (a) An applicant for services under this section shall provide the department with the following:

(i) a certified transcript of a money judgment for a sum certain for arrears accrued under an order of support;

(ii) a sworn statement that the order of support is no longer subject to appellate judicial review and that the sum set forth as uncollected on the judgment is accurate;

(iii) the name and address of the applicant; and

(iv) the name, last known address and social security number of the person or entity owning past-due support against whom a judgment has been obtained.

(b) If an application for services is rejected by the department, the department shall inform the applicant in writing of the reason for such rejection.

3. An applicant for services under this section shall receive a pro rata share of the overpayment of tax, based on the amount of past-due support owed to such applicant as certified to the tax commission by the department pursuant to section one hundred seventy-one-c of the tax law, in cases where the individual, estate or trust owing past-due support to such applicant owes past-due support to other persons or entities so certified to the tax commission by the department.

4. The department shall promulgate such regulations as are necessary to carry out the provisions of this section, including regulations as to the date by which an applicant for services under this section shall provide the department with the information and documentation required in subdivision two of this section.

§111-z.   Spousal and child support; crediting of overpayments of tax to past-due support.

1. The department shall provide services for the crediting of overpayments of tax to past-due support, pursuant to section one hundred seventy-one-c of the tax law, which is owed to persons entitled to enforce an order of support, for persons not receiving public assistance who are eligible to receive services pursuant to title six-A of this article, but who do not receive such services. For

purposes of this section, "order of support" shall mean any final order, decree or judgment in a matrimonial action or family court proceeding, or any foreign support order, decree or judgment which is registered pursuant to article five-B of the family court act which requires the payment of alimony, maintenance, support or child support.

2. (a) An applicant for services under this section shall provide the department with the following:

(i) a certified transcript of a money judgment for a sum certain for arrears accrued under an order of support;

(ii) a sworn statement that the order of support is no longer subject to appellate judicial review and that the sum set forth as uncollected on the judgment is accurate;

(iii) the name and address of the applicant; and

(iv) the name, last known address and social security number of the person or entity owing past-due support against whom a judgment has been obtained.

(b) If an application for services is rejected by the department, the department shall inform the applicant in writing of the reason for such rejection.

(c) The department shall inform applicants for services under this section of the support collection and enforcement services available through the support collection units pursuant to title six-A of this article.

3. An applicant for services under this section shall receive a pro rata share of the overpayment of tax, based on the amount of past-due support owed to such applicant as certified to the tax commission by the department pursuant to section one hundred seventy-one-c of the tax law, in cases where the individual, estate or trust owing past-due support to such applicant owes past-due support to other persons or entities so certified to the tax commission by the department.

4. The department may charge an applicant for services under this section a fee based on cost, but not to exceed the lesser of twenty-five dollars or the amount of overpayment of tax received by the department. The department shall recover such fee from such overpayment and pay any balance to the applicant. The fee provided for herein shall not be a charge against the individual, estate or trust owing past-due support.

5. The department shall promulgate such regulations as are necessary to carry out the provisions of this section, including regulations as to the date by which an applicant for services under this section shall provide the department with the information and documentation required in subdivision two of this section.

ARTICLE 5 - Assistance and Care

Title 10 - Aid to Dependent Children

Section
358-a.   Dependent children in foster care.
358-b.   Limitations on state reimbursement for foster care.

§358-a.   Dependent children in foster care.

(1) Initiation of judicial proceeding. (a) A social services official who accepts or proposes to accept the custody and guardianship of a child by means of an instrument executed pursuant to the provisions of section three hundred eighty-four of this chapter, or the care and custody of a child as a public charge by means of an instrument executed pursuant to the provisions of section three hundred eighty-four-a of this chapter, shall determine whether such child is likely to remain in the care of such official for a period in excess of thirty consecutive days. If such official determines that the child is likely to remain in care for a period in excess of thirty consecutive days, such official shall petition the family court judge of the county or city in which the social services official has his or her office, to approve such instrument upon a determination that the placement of the child is in the best interest of the child, that it would be contrary to the welfare of the child to continue in his or her own home and, that where appropriate, reasonable efforts were made prior to the placement of the child into foster care to prevent or eliminate the need for removal of the child from his or her home and that prior to the initiation of the court proceeding required to be held by this subdivision, reasonable efforts were made to make it possible for the child to return safely home. In the case of a child whose care and custody have been transferred to a social services official by means of an instrument executed pursuant to the provisions of section three hundred eighty-four-a of this chapter, approval of the instrument shall only be made upon an additional determination that all of the requirements of such section have been satisfied.

*(b) The social services official shall initiate the proceeding by filing the petition as soon as practicable, but in no event later than thirty days following removal of the child from the home provided, however, that the court shall receive, hear and determine petitions filed later than thirty days following removal of the child from his or her home, but state reimbursement shall not be available to the social services district for care and maintenance provided to such child. The social services official shall diligently pursue such proceeding. Where the care and custody of a child as a public charge has been transferred to a social services official by means of an instrument executed pursuant to the provisions of section three hundred eighty-four-a of this chapter for a period of thirty days or less for an indeterminate period which such official deems unlikely to exceed thirty days, and thereafter such official determines that such child will remain in his or her care and custody for a period in excess of thirty days, such official shall, as soon as practicable but in no event later than thirty days following such determination, execute with the child's parent, parents or guardian a new instrument pursuant to the provision of section three hundred eighty-four or three hundred eighty-four-a of this chapter and shall file a petition in family court, pursuant to this section, for approval of such instrument. In such cases involving a social services official, expenditures for the care and maintenance of such child from the date of the initial transfer of his care and custody to the social services official shall be subject to state reimbursement.   *Effective until June 30, 2017

*(b) The social services official shall initiate the proceeding by filing the petition as soon as practicable, but in no event later than thirty days following removal of the child from the home provided, however, that the court shall receive, hear and determine petitions filed later than thirty days following removal of the child from his or her home, but state reimbursement to the social services district for care and maintenance provided to such child shall be denied pursuant to section one hundred fifty-three-d of this chapter. The social services official shall diligently pursue such proceeding. Where the care and custody of a child as a public charge has been transferred to a social services official by means of an instrument executed pursuant to the provisions of section three hundred eighty-four-a of this chapter for a period of thirty days or less for an indeterminate period which such official deems unlikely to exceed thirty days, and thereafter such official determines that such child will remain in his or her care and custody for a period in excess of thirty days, such official shall, as soon as practicable but in no event later than thirty days following such determination, execute with the child's parent, parents or guardian a new instrument pursuant to the provision of section three hundred eighty-four or three hundred eighty-four-a of this chapter and shall file a petition in family court, pursuant to this section, for approval of such instrument. In such cases involving a social services official, expenditures for the care and maintenance of such child from the date of the initial transfer of his care and custody to the social services official shall be subject to state reimbursement, notwithstanding the provisions of section one hundred fifty-three-d of this chapter.   *Effective June 30, 2017*

(2) Contents of petition. (a) Any petition required or authorized pursuant to subdivision one of this section shall allege whether the parent, parents or guardian executed the instrument because the parent, parents or guardian would be unable to make adequate provision for the care, maintenance and supervision of such child in his or their own home, and shall include facts supporting the petition. The petition shall contain a notice in conspicuous print providing that if the child remains in foster care for fifteen of the most recent twenty-two months, the agency may be required by law to file a petition to terminate parental rights. The petition shall also set forth the names and last known addresses of all persons required to be given notice of the proceeding, pursuant to this section and section three hundred eighty-four-c of this chapter, and there shall be shown by the petition or by affidavit or other proof satisfactory to the court that there are no persons other than those set forth in the petition who are entitled to notice pursuant to the provisions of this section or of section three hundred eighty-four-c of this chapter. The petition shall also set forth the efforts which were made, prior to the placement of the child into foster care, to prevent or eliminate the need for removal of the child from his or her home and the efforts which were made prior to the filing of the petition to make it possible for the child to return safely home. If such efforts were not made, the petition shall set forth the reasons why these efforts were not made. The petition shall request that, pending any hearing which may be required by the family court judge, a temporary order be made transferring the care and custody of the child to the social services official in accordance with the provisions of subdivision three of this section. In the case of a child whose care and custody have been transferred to a social services official by means of an instrument executed pursuant to section three hundred eighty-four-a of this chapter, the petition shall also allege and there shall be shown by affidavit or other proof satisfactory to the court that all the requirements of such section

have been satisfied, including the results of the investigation to locate relatives of the child, including any non-respondent parent and all of the child's grandparents. Such results shall include whether any relative who has been located expressed an interest in becoming a foster parent for the child or in seeking custody or care of the child.

(b) The social services official who initiated the proceeding shall file supplemental information with the clerk of the court not later than ten days prior to the date on which the proceeding is first heard by the court. Such information shall include relevant portions, as determined by the department, of the assessment of the child and his family circumstances performed and maintained, and the family's service plan if available, pursuant to sections four hundred nine-e and four hundred nine-f of this chapter. Copies of such supplemental information need not be served upon those persons entitled to notice of the proceeding and a copy of the petition pursuant to subdivision four of this section.

(2-a) Continuing jurisdiction. (a) The court shall possess continuing jurisdiction over the parties until the child is discharged from placement and all orders regarding supervision, protection or services have expired.

(b)The court, upon approving an instrument under this section, shall schedule a permanency hearing pursuant to article ten-A of the family court act for a date certain not more than eight months after the placement of the child into foster care. Such date certain shall be included in the order approving the instrument.

(3) Disposition of petition. (a) If the court is satisfied that the parent, parents or guardian executed such instrument knowingly and voluntarily and because he or she would be unable to make adequate provision for the care, maintenance and supervision of such child in his or her home, and that the requirements of section three hundred eighty-four-a of this chapter, if applicable, have been satisfied and that where appropriate, reasonable efforts were made prior to the placement of the child into foster care to prevent or eliminate the need for removal of the child from his or her home and that prior to the initiation of the court proceeding required to be held by subdivision one of this section, reasonable efforts were made to make it possible for the child to return safely to his or her home, the court may find and determine that the best interests and welfare of the child would be promoted by removal of the child from such home, and that it would be contrary to the welfare of such child for the child to continue in such home, and the court shall thereupon grant the petition and approve such instrument and the transfer of the custody and guardianship or care and custody of such child to such social services official in accordance therewith. If the court determines that, where appropriate, reasonable efforts were made prior to the placement of the child into foster care to prevent or eliminate the need for removal of the child from his or her home, that prior to the initiation of the court proceeding reasonable efforts were made to make it possible for the child to return safely to his or her home, or that it would be contrary to the best interests of the child to continue in the home, or that reasonable efforts to prevent or eliminate the need for removal of the child from the home were not made but that the lack of such efforts was appropriate under the circumstances, the court order shall include such findings. Approval of such instrument in a proceeding pursuant to this section shall not constitute a remand or commitment pursuant to this chapter and shall not preclude challenge in any other proceeding to the validity of the instrument. If the permanency plan for the child is adoption, guardianship, permanent placement

with a fit and willing relative or another planned permanent living arrangement other than reunification with the parent or parents of the child, the court must consider and determine in its order whether reasonable efforts are being made to make and finalize such alternate permanent placement.

(b) For the purpose of this section, reasonable efforts to prevent or eliminate the need for removing the child from the home of the child or to make it possible for the child to return safely to the home of the child shall not be required where the court determines that:

(1) the parent of such child has subjected the child to aggravated circumstances, as defined in subdivision twelve of this section;

(2) the parent of such child has been convicted of (i) murder in the first degree as defined in section 125.27 or murder in the second degree as defined in section 125.25 of the penal law and the victim was another child of the parent; or (ii) manslaughter in the first degree as defined in section 125.20 or manslaughter in the second degree as defined in section 125.15 of the penal law and the victim was another child of the parent, provided, however, that the parent must have acted voluntarily in committing such crime;

(3) the parent of such child has been convicted of an attempt to commit any of the foregoing crimes, and the victim or intended victim was the child or another child of the parent; or has been convicted of criminal solicitation as defined in article one hundred, conspiracy as defined in article one hundred five or criminal facilitation as defined in article one hundred fifteen of the penal law for conspiring, soliciting or facilitating any of the foregoing crimes, and the victim or intended victim was the child or another child of the parent;

(4) the parent of such child has been convicted of assault in the second degree as defined in section 120.05, assault in the first degree as defined in section 120.10 or aggravated assault upon a person less than eleven years old as defined in section 120.12 of the penal law, and the commission of one of the foregoing crimes resulted in serious physical injury to the child or another child of the parent;

(5) the parent of such child has been convicted in any other jurisdiction of an offense which includes all of the essential elements of any crime specified in subparagraph two, three or four of this paragraph, and the victim of such offense was the child or another child of the parent; or

(6) the parental rights of the parent to a sibling of such child have been involuntarily terminated; unless the court determines that providing reasonable efforts would be in the best interests of the child, not contrary to the health and safety of the child, and would likely result in the reunification of the parent and the child in the foreseeable future. The court shall state such findings in its order.

If the court determines that reasonable efforts are not required because of one of the grounds set forth above, a permanency hearing shall be held within thirty days of the finding of the court that such efforts are not required. Such hearing shall be conducted pursuant to section one thousand eighty-nine of the family court act. The local social services official shall thereafter make reasonable efforts to place the child in a timely manner and to complete whatever steps are necessary to finalize the permanent placement of the child as set forth in the permanency plan approved by the court. If reasonable efforts are determined by the court not to be required because of one of the grounds set forth in this paragraph, the local social services official may file a petition for termination of parental rights of the parent in accordance with section three hundred eighty-four-b of this chapter.

(c) For the purpose of this section, in determining reasonable efforts to be made with respect to a child, and in making such reasonable efforts, the child's health and safety shall be the paramount concern.

(d) For the purpose of this section, a sibling shall include a half-sibling.

(e) The order granting the petition of a social services official and approving an instrument executed pursuant to section three hundred eighty-four-a of this chapter may include conditions, where appropriate and specified by the judge, requiring the implementation of a specific plan of action by the social services official to exercise diligent efforts toward the discharge of the child from care, either to his own family or to an adoptive home; provided, however, that such plan shall not include the provision of any service or assistance to the child and his or her family which is not authorized or required to be made available pursuant to the comprehensive annual services program plan then in effect. An order of placement shall include, at the least:

(i) a description of the visitation plan;

(ii) a direction that the respondent or respondents shall be notified of the planning conference or conferences to be held pursuant to subdivision three of section four hundred nine-e of this chapter, of their right to attend the conference, and of their right to have counsel or other representative or companion with them;

A copy of the court's order and the service plan shall be given to the respondent. The order shall also contain a notice that if the child remains in foster care for more than fifteen of the most recent twenty-two months, the agency may be required by law to file a petition to terminate parental rights.

Nothing in such order shall preclude either party to the instrument from exercising its rights under this section or under any other provision of law relating to the return of the care and custody of the child by the social services official to the parent, parents or guardian. Violation of such on order shall be subject to punishment pursuant to section seven hundred fifty-three of the judiciary law.

(f) For a child who has attained the age of fourteen, if the court grants the petition and approves an instrument executed pursuant to section three hundred eighty-four or three hundred eighty-four-a of this chapter and the transfer of custody and guardianship or care and custody of the child to a local social services official the court shall determine in its order the services and assistance needed to assist the child in learning independent living skills.

(4) Notice. (a) Upon the filing of a petition pursuant to this section, the family court judge shall direct that service of a notice of the proceeding and a copy of the petition shall be made upon such persons and in such manner as the judge may direct. If the instrument executed by the parent, parents or guardian of a child consents to the jurisdiction of the family court over such proceeding, and waives service of the petition and notice of proceeding, then the family court judge may, in his discretion, dispense with service upon the consenting parent, parents or guardian, provided, however, that a waiver of service of process and notice of the proceeding by a parent or guardian who has transferred the care and custody of a child to an authorized agency, pursuant to section three hundred eighty-four-a of this chapter, shall be null and void and shall not be given effect by the court. Notice to any parent, parents or guardian who has not executed the instrument shall be required.

(b) In the event the family court judge determines that service by publication is necessary and orders service by publication, service shall be made in accordance with the provisions of rule three hundred sixteen of the civil practice law and rules, provided, however, that a single publication of the summons or other process with a notice as specified herein in only one newspaper designated in the order shall be sufficient. In no event shall the whole petition be published. The petition shall be delivered to the person summoned at the first court appearance pursuant to section one hundred fifty-four-a of the family court act. The notice to be published with the summons or other process shall state the date, time, place and purpose of the proceeding.

(i) If the petition is initiated to transfer custody and guardianship of a child by an instrument executed pursuant to the provisions of section three hundred eighty-four of this chapter, the notice to be published shall also state that failure to appear may result, without further notice, in the transfer of custody and guardianship of the child to a social services official in this proceeding.

(ii) If the petition is initiated to transfer care and custody of a child by an instrument executed pursuant to the provisions of section three hundred eighty-four-a of this chapter, the notice to be published shall also state that failure to appear may result, without further notice, in the transfer of care and custody of the child to a social services official in this proceeding.

(5) Hearing and waiver. The instrument may include a consent by the parent, parents or guardian to waiver of any hearing and that a determination may be made by the family court judge based solely upon the petition, and other papers and affidavits, if any, submitted to the family court judge, provided, however, that a waiver of hearing by a parent or guardian who has transferred the care and custody of a child to an authorized agency, pursuant to section three hundred eighty-four-a of this chapter, shall be effective only if such waiver was executed in an instrument separate from that transferring the child's care and custody. In any case where an effective waiver has been executed, the family court judge may dispense with a hearing, approve the instrument and the transfer of the custody and guardianship or care and custody of the child to the social services official and make the requisite findings and determinations provided for in subdivision three of this section, if it appears to the satisfaction of the family court judge that the allegations in the petition are established sufficiently to warrant the family court judge to grant such petition, to make such findings and determination, and to issue such order.

In any case where a hearing is required, the family court judge, if the holding of an immediate hearing on notice is impractical, may forthwith, upon the basis of the instrument and the allegations of the petition, make a temporary finding that the parent, parents, or guardian of the child are unable to make adequate provision for the care, maintenance and supervision of such child in the child's own home and that the best interest and welfare of the child will be promoted by the removal of such child from such home and thereupon, the family court judge shall make a temporary order transferring the care and custody of such child to the social services official, and shall set the matter down for hearing on the first feasible date.

(6) Representation. In any case where a hearing is directed by the family court judge, he or she shall, pursuant to section two hundred forty-nine of the family court act, appoint an attorney to represent the child, who shall be admitted to practice law in the state of New York.

(7) Return of child. If an instrument provides for the return of the care and custody of a child by the local social services official to the parent, parents or guardian upon any terms and conditions or at any time, the local social services

official shall comply with such terms of such instrument without further court order. Every order approving an instrument providing for the transfer of the care and custody of a child to a local social services official shall be served upon the parent, parents or guardian who executed such instrument in such manner as the family court judge may provide in such order, together with a notice of the terms and conditions under which the care and custody of such child may be returned to the parent, parents or guardian. If an instrument provides for the return of the care and custody of a child by the local social services official to the parent, parents or guardian without fixing a definite date for such return, or if the local social services official shall fail to return a child to the care and custody of the child's parent, parents or guardian in accordance with the terms of the instrument, the parent, parents or guardian may seek such care and custody by motion for return of such child and order to show cause in such proceeding or by writ of habeas corpus in the supreme court. Nothing in this subdivision shall limit the requirement for a permanency hearing pursuant to article ten-A of the family court act.

(8) Appealable orders. Any order of a family court denying any petition of a local social services official filed pursuant to this section, or any order of a family court granting or denying any motion filed by a parent, parents or guardian for return of a child pursuant to this section, shall be deemed an order of disposition appealable pursuant to article eleven of the family court act.

(9) Duty of social services official. In the event that a family court judge denies a petition of a social services official for approval of an instrument, upon a finding that the welfare of the child would not be promoted by foster care, such social services official shall not accept or retain the care and custody as a public charge or custody and guardianship of such child, provided, however, that the denial by a family court judge of a petition of a social services official filed pursuant to this section shall not limit or affect the duty of such social services official to take such other action or offer such services as are authorized by law to promote the welfare and best interests of the child.

(10) Visitation rights; non-custodial parents and grandparents. (a) Where a social services official incorporates in an instrument visitation rights set forth in an order, judgment or agreement as described in paragraph (d) of subdivision two of section three hundred eighty-four-a of this chapter, such official shall make inquiry of the state central register of child abuse and maltreatment to determine whether or not the person having such visitation rights is a subject or another person named in an indicated report of child abuse or maltreatment, as such terms are defined in section four hundred twelve of this chapter, and shall further ascertain, to the extent practicable, whether or not such person is a respondent in a proceeding under article ten of the family court act whereby the respondent has been alleged or adjudicated to have abused or neglected such child.

(b) Where a social services official or the attorney for the child opposes incorporation of an order, judgment or agreement conferring visitation rights as provided for in paragraph (e) of subdivision two of section three hundred eighty-four-a of this chapter, the social services official or attorney for the child shall apply for an order determining that the provisions of such order, judgment or agreement should not be incorporated into the instrument executed pursuant to such section. Such order shall be granted upon a finding, based on competent, relevant and material evidence, that the child's life or health would be endangered by incorporation and enforcement of visitation rights as described in such order, judgment or agreement. Otherwise, the court shall deny such application.

(c) Where visitation rights pursuant to an order, judgment or agreement are incorporated in an instrument, the parties may agree to an alternative schedule of visitation equivalent to and consistent with the original or modified visitation order, judgment, or agreement where such alternative schedule reflects changed circumstances of the parties and is consistent with the best interests of the child. In the absence of such an agreement between the parties, the court may, in its discretion, upon application of any party or the child's attorney, order an alternative schedule of visitation, as described herein, where it determines that such schedule is necessary to facilitate visitation and to protect the best interests of the child.

(d) The order providing an alternative schedule of visitation shall remain in effect for the length of the placement of the child as provided for in such instrument unless such order is subsequently modified by the court for good cause shown. Whenever the court makes an order denying or modifying visitation rights pursuant to this subdivision, the instrument described in section three hundred eighty-four-a of this chapter shall be deemed amended accordingly.

(11) Siblings, placement and visitation. (a) In reviewing any petition brought under this section, the court shall inquire if the social services official has arranged for the placement of the child who is the subject of the petition with any minor siblings or half-siblings who are placed in care or, if such children have not been placed together, whether such official has arranged for regular visitation and other forms of regular communication between such child and such siblings.

(b) If the court determines that the subject child has not been placed with his or her minor siblings or half-siblings who are in care, or that regular visitation and other forms of regular communication between the subject child and his or her minor siblings or half-siblings has not been provided or arranged for, the court may direct such official to provide or arrange for such placement or regular visitation and communication where the court finds that such placement or visitation and communication is in the child's best interests. Placement or regular visitation and communication with siblings or half-siblings shall be presumptively in the child's best interests unless such placement or visitation and communication would be contrary to the child's health, safety or welfare, or the lack of geographic proximity precludes or prevents visitation.

(12) For the purposes of this section, aggravated circumstances means where a child has been either severely or repeatedly abused, as defined in subdivision eight of section three hundred eighty-four-b of this chapter; or where a child has subsequently been found to be an abused child, as defined in paragraph (i) or (iii) of subdivision (e) of section one thousand twelve of the family court act, within five years after return home following placement in foster care as a result of being found to be a neglected child, as defined in subdivision (f) of section one thousand twelve of the family court act, provided that the respondent or respondents in each of the foregoing proceedings was the same; or where the court finds by clear and convincing evidence that the parent of a child in foster care has refused and has failed completely, over a period of at least six months from the date of removal, to engage in services necessary to eliminate the risk of abuse or neglect if returned to the parent, and has failed to secure services on his or her own or otherwise adequately prepare for the return home and, after being informed by the court that such an admission

could eliminate the requirement that the local department of social services provide reunification services to the parent, the parent has stated in court under oath that he or she intends to continue to refuse such necessary services and is unwilling to secure such services independently or otherwise prepare for the child's return home; provided, however, that if the court finds that adequate justification exists for the failure to engage in or secure such services, including but not limited to a lack of child care, a lack of transportation, and an inability to attend services that conflict with the parent's work schedule, such failure shall not constitute an aggravated circumstance; or where a court has determined a child five days old or younger was abandoned by a parent with an intent to wholly abandon such child and with the intent that the child be safe from physical injury and cared for in an appropriate manner.

*§358-b. Limitations on state reimbursement for foster care.

In the event that a petition for approval of an instrument and the transfer of the custody and guardianship or care and custody of a child is filed within thirty days following removal of the child from his home and diligently pursued pursuant to section three hundred fifty-eight-a of this title, state reimbursement shall not be denied for expenditures made by a social services district for the care and maintenance of such a child away from his home prior to denial of such petition by a family court judge solely by reason of such denial.

(Effective until June 30, 2017)

*§358-b. Limitations on state reimbursement for foster care.

In the event that a petition for approval of an instrument and the transfer of the custody and guardianship or care and custody of a child is filed within thirty days following removal of the child from his home and diligently pursued pursuant to section three hundred fifty-eight-a of this chapter, state reimbursement shall not be denied pursuant to section one hundred fifty-three-d of this chapter, for expenditures made by a social services district for the care and maintenance of such a child away from his home prior to denial of such petition by a family court judge solely by reason of such denial.

(Effective June 30, 2017)

ARTICLE 6
Children

Title 1
Care and Protection of Children

§371. Definitions.

Unless the context or the subject matter manifestly requires a different interpretation, when used in this article or in any special act relating to children,

1. "Child" means a person actually or apparently under the age of eighteen years;

2. "Abandoned child" means a child under the age of eighteen years who is abandoned by both parents, or by the parent having its custody, or by any other person or persons lawfully charged with its care or custody, in accordance with the definition and other criteria set forth in subdivision five of section three hundred eighty-four-b;

3. "Destitute child" means:

(a) a child under the age of eighteen who is in a state of want or suffering due to lack of sufficient food, clothing, shelter, or medical or surgical care; and:

(i) does not fit within the definition of an "abused child" or a "neglected child" as such terms are defined in section one thousand twelve of the family court act; and

(ii) is without any parent or caretaker as such term is defined in section one thousand ninety-two of the family court act, available to sufficiently care for him or her, due to:

(A) the death of a parent or caretaker; or

(B) the incapacity or debilitation of a parent or caretaker, where such incapacity or debilitation would prevent such parent or caretaker from being able to knowingly and voluntarily enter into a written agreement to transfer the care and custody of said child pursuant to section three hundred fifty-eight-a or three hundred eighty-four-a of the social services law; or

(C) the inability of the local social services district to locate any parent or caretaker, after making reasonable efforts to do so; or

(D) the parent or caretaker being physically located outside of the state of New York and the local social services district is or has been unable to return said child to such parent or caretaker while or after making reasonable efforts to do so, unless the lack of such efforts is or was appropriate under the circumstances;

(b) a child who is under the age of eighteen years and absent from his or her legal residence without the consent of his or her parent, legal guardian or custodian; or

(c) a child under the age of eighteen who is without a place of shelter where supervision and care are available who is not otherwise covered under paragraph (a) of this subdivision; or

(d) a person who is a former foster care youth under the age of twenty-one who was previously placed in the care and custody or custody and guardianship of the local commissioner of social services or other officer, board or department authorized to receive children as public charges, and who was discharged from foster care due to a failure to consent to continuation in placement, who has returned to foster care pursuant to section one thousand ninety-one of the family court act.

4-a. "Neglected child" means a child less than eighteen years of age

(i) whose physical, mental or emotional condition has been impaired or is in imminent danger of becoming impaired as a result of the failure of his parent or other person legally responsible for his care to exercise a minimum degree of care

(A) in supplying the child with adequate food, clothing, shelter, education, medical or surgical care, though financially able to do so or offered financial or other reasonable means to do so; or

(B) in providing the child with proper supervision or guardianship, by unreasonably inflicting or allowing to be inflicted harm, or a substantial risk thereof, including the infliction of excessive corporal punishment; or by misusing a drug or drugs; or by misusing alcoholic beverages to the extent that he loses self-control of his actions; or by any other acts of a similarly serious nature requiring the aid of the court; provided, however, that where the respondent is voluntarily and regularly participating in a rehabilitative program, evidence that the respondent has repeatedly misused a drug or drugs or alcoholic beverages to the extent that he loses self-control of his actions shall not establish that the child is a neglected child in the absence of evidence establishing that the child's physical, mental or emotional condition has been impaired or is in imminent danger of becoming impaired as set forth in paragraph (i) of this subdivision; or

(ii) who has been abandoned by his parents or other person legally responsible for his care.

4-b. "Abused child" means a child less than eighteen years of age whose parent or other person legally responsible for his care

(i) inflicts or allows to be inflicted upon such child physical injury by other than accidental means which causes or creates a substantial risk of death, or serious or protracted disfigurement, or protracted impairment of physical or emotional health or protracted loss or impairment of the function of any bodily organ, or

(ii) creates or allows to be created a substantial risk of physical injury to such child by other than accidental means which would be likely to cause death or serious or protracted disfigurement, or protracted impairment of physical or emotional health or protracted loss or impairment of the function of any bodily organ, or

(iii) commits, or allows to be committed, an act of sexual abuse against such child as defined in the penal law.

5. "Juvenile delinquent" means a person over seven and less than sixteen years of age who does any act which, if done by an adult, would constitute a crime.

6. "Person in need of supervision" means a person less than eighteen years of age who is habitually truant or who is incorrigible, ungovernable or habitually disobedient and beyond the lawful control of a parent or other person legally responsible for such child's care, or other lawful authority.

7. "Dependent child" means a child who is in the custody of, or wholly or partly maintained by an authorized agency or an institution, society or other organization of charitable, eleemosynary, correctional, or reformatory character;

8. "Mentally disabled child" means a child who has a mental disability as defined in section 1.03 of the mental hygiene law;

9. "Physically handicapped child" means a child who, by reason of a physical disability or infirmity, whether congenital or acquired by accident, injury or disease, is or may be expected to be totally or partially incapacitated for education or for remunerative occupation, as provided in the education law, or is or may be expected to be handicapped, as provided in the public health law;

10. "Authorized agency" means

(a) Any agency, association, corporation, institution, society or other organization which is incorporated or organized under the laws of this state with corporate power or empowered by law to care for, to place out or to board out children, which actually has its place of business or plant in this state and which is approved, visited, inspected and supervised by the office of children and family services or which shall submit and consent to the approval, visitation, inspection and supervision of such office as to any and all acts in relation to the welfare of children performed or to be performed under this title; provided, however, that on and after June first, two thousand seven, such term shall not include any for-profit corporation or other for-profit entity or organization for the purposes of the operation, management, supervision or ownership of agency boarding homes, group homes, homes including family boarding homes of family free homes, or institutions which are located within this state;

(b) Any court or any social services official of this state authorized by law to place out or to board out children or any Indian tribe that has entered into an agreement with the department pursuant to section thirty-nine of this chapter;

(c) Any agency, association, corporation, institution, society or other organization which is not incorporated or organized under the laws of this state, placing out a child for adoption whose admission to the United States as an eligible orphan with non-quota immigrant status pursuant to the federal immigration and nationality act is sought for the purpose of adoption in the State of New York or who has been brought into the United States with such status and for such purpose, provided, however, that such agency, association, corporation, institution, society or other organization is licensed or otherwise authorized by another state to place out children for adoption, that such agency, association, corporation, institution, society or other organization is approved by the department to place out such children with non-quota immigrant status for adoption in the State of New York, and provided further, that such agency, association, corporation, institution, society or other organization complies with the regulations of the department pertaining to such placements. Notwithstanding any other provision of law to the contrary, such agency shall be limited in its functioning as an authorized agency to the placing out and adoption of such children. This paragraph shall not require the department to approve any such agency, association, corporation, institution, society or other organization which is located in a state which is a party to the interstate compact on the placement of children.

11. "Custody" means custody in pursuance of or in compliance with expressed provisions of law;

12. "Place out" means to arrange for the free care of a child in a family other than that of the child's parent, step-parent, grandparent, brother, sister, uncle, or aunt or legal guardian, for the purpose of adoption or for the purpose of providing care;

13. "Place" or "commit" includes replace and recommit;

14. "Board out" means to arrange for the care of a child in a family, other than that of the child's parent, step-parent or legal guardian, to whom payment is made or agreed to be made for care and maintenance.

15. "Home" includes a family boarding home or a family free home.

16. agency boarding home shall mean a family-type home for children and/or for minors operated by an authorized agency, in quarters or premises owned, leased or otherwise under the control of such agency, for the purpose of providing care and maintenance therein for children or minors under the care of such agency.

17. "Group home" shall mean a facility for the care and maintenance of not less than seven, nor more than twelve children, who are at least five years of

age, operated by an authorized agency except that such minimum age shall not be applicable to siblings placed in the same facility nor to children whose mother is placed in the same facility.

18. "Public institution for children" shall mean an institution which is established and maintained by a public welfare district for the purpose of providing care and maintenance therein for children and minors for whose care such district is responsible and who require care away from their own homes.

19. "Foster parent" shall mean any person with whom a child, in the care, custody or guardianship of an authorized agency, is placed for temporary or long-term care, and "foster child" shall mean any person, in the care, custody or guardianship of an authorized agency, who is placed for temporary or long-term care.

20. "Therapeutic foster parent" means a foster parent who is certified or licensed pursuant to section three hundred seventy-five or section three hundred seventy-six of this article, or otherwise approved and who has successfully completed a training program developed by professionals experienced in treating children who exhibit high levels of disturbed behavior, emotional disturbance or physical or health needs. For any such child placed in their care, such parent shall assist in the implementation of the therapeutic treatment portion of the family service plan required by section four hundred nine-e of this article.

21. "Supervised independent living program" shall mean one or more of a type of agency boarding home operated and certified by an authorized agency in accordance with the regulations of the office of children and family services to provide a transitional experience for older youth who, based upon their circumstances, are appropriate for transition to the level of care and supervision provided in the program. Each supervised independent living unit shall be located in the community separate from any of the agency's other congregate dwellings.

§371-a. Procedure.

In any proceeding commenced pursuant to this chapter in which the family court has exercised jurisdiction, the provisions of articles one, two and eleven of the family court act shall apply to the extent that they do not conflict with the specific provisions of the social services law.

§371-b. Citizen review panels.

1. There shall be established at least three citizen review panels. At least one panel shall be established for the city of New York and at least two panels shall be established for social services districts or combinations of districts outside of the city of New York. The panel in the city of New York shall create one subcommittee for each borough for the purposes of evaluating the extent to which the state and the social services district are discharging their child protection responsibilities within that particular borough, in accordance with subsection three of this section. The office of children and family services shall make available resources to support the needs of each citizen review panel.

2. Each citizen review panel shall consist of thirteen members, seven of whom shall be appointed by the governor, three of whom shall be appointed by the temporary president of the senate, and three of whom shall be appointed by the speaker of the assembly. Each panel shall duly elect a chairperson of such panel. Each panel shall be composed of volunteer members who are broadly representative of the community in which such panel is established, including

members who have expertise in the prevention and treatment of child abuse and neglect. No person employed by federal, state, county or municipal agencies which directly deliver child welfare services may be appointed to a panel.

3. Each citizen review panel shall, by examining the policies and procedures of the state and social services districts and, where appropriate, specific cases, evaluate the extent to which the agencies are effectively discharging their child protection responsibilities in accordance with: (a) the state plan established pursuant to 42 U.S.C. §5106a(b); (b) the child protection standards set forth in 42 U.S.C. §5106a(b); and (c) any other criteria that the panel considers important to ensure the protection of children. Each panel shall meet not less than once every three months. Each panel may hold public hearings on issues within the panel's jurisdiction.

4. Each citizen review panel shall have access to information on specific cases in accordance with paragraph (A) of subdivision four of section four hundred twenty-two of this chapter. Each panel shall also have reasonable access to public and private facilities which are in receipt of public funds and are providing child welfare services within the panel's jurisdiction. Where necessary, the office shall assist a panel in obtaining access to information or facilities as authorized in accordance with this section. Each panel shall also have access to the report prepared by the state pursuant to 42 U.S.C. §5106a(d).

5. Each citizen review panel shall prepare and make available to the public, on an annual basis, a report containing: (a) a summary of the activities of the panel; and (b) the findings and recommendations of the panel. Each report shall be submitted by February first and shall omit all confidential information used to prepare the report.

6. The members of each citizen review panel shall not disclose to any person or government official any identifying information about any specific child protection case. A member who knowingly violates this duty of confidentiality may be subject to a civil penalty not to exceed one thousand dollars and removal from the panel.

7. The legal defense of a member of a citizen review panel shall be governed by the terms of section seventeen of the public officers law.

§372. Records and reports.

1. Every court, and every public board, commission, institution, or officer having powers or charged with duties in relation to abandoned, delinquent, destitute, neglected or dependent children who shall receive, accept or commit any child shall provide and keep a record showing:

(a) the full and true name of the child,

(b) his sex and date and place of birth, if ascertainable, or his apparent age,

(c) the full and true names and places of birth of his parents, and their actual residence if living, or their latest known residence, if deceased or whereabouts unknown and the name and actual residence of any other person having custody of the child, as nearly as the same can reasonably be ascertained,

(d) the religious faith of the parents and of the child,

(e) the name and address of any person, agency, institution or other organization to which the child is committed, placed out, boarded out, or otherwise given into care, custody or control,

(f) the religious faith and occupation of the head or heads of the family with whom the child is placed out or boarded out and their relationship, if any, to the child,

(g) if any such child shall die, the date and cause of death and place of burial,

(h) any further disposition or change in care, custody or control of the child,

(i) the date or dates of reception and of any subsequent disposition or change in care, custody or control and, in case of adoption, the name and title of the judge or surrogate making the order of adoption, the date of such order and the date and place of filing of such order,

(j) the reasons for any act performed in reference to such child herein required to be recorded, together with such further information as the department may require; and shall make to the department upon blanks provided by the department reports of each such child placed out, or boarded out, containing the information herein required to be kept; and shall furnish such information to any authorized agency to which any such child shall be committed or otherwise given into custody.

2. Every charitable, eleemosynary, reformatory, or correctional institution, public or private, incorporated or unincorporated, and every agency, association, corporation, institution, society or other organization which shall receive, accept, or admit any child whether or not in receipt of payments from public funds for the support of such child shall provide and keep a record as described in subdivision one, and also showing how, by whom and for what reason such child shall have been given into its custody or committed to it and shall make reports of each such child to the department upon blanks provided by the department giving all the information required by subdivision one to be recorded together with such further information as the department may require. Except as to children placed out, boarded out or surrendered or for whom guardianship is accepted or adoption provided, the requirement of this section shall not apply to hospitals, day nurseries, eleemosynary day schools, and summer and vacation homes and camps, or to institutions for the care of convalescent, anaemic, under-nourished or cardiac children, preventoria, working boys' homes, emergency shelters and schools for the blind and for the deaf, but all such hospitals, homes and institutions shall keep such records and make to the department such reports as the department may require.

3. Such records maintained by the department or an authorized agency, including a local social services district, regarding such children are confidential, provided, however, that such records are subject to the provisions of article thirty-one of the civil practice law and rules. When either the subject foster child, or such child's parent, or such child's guardian if any, is not a party to the action, a copy of the notice or motion for discovery shall be served upon such parent, guardian, and child and, if the child is still a minor, the child's attorney. Such persons may thereafter appear in the action with regard to such discovery. Where no action is pending, upon application by a parent, relative or legal guardian of such child or by an authorized agency, after due notice to the institution or authorized agency affected and hearing had thereon, the supreme court may by order direct the officers of such institution or authorized agency to furnish to such parent, relative, legal guardian or authorized agency such extracts from the record relating to such child as the court may deem proper. The department through its authorized agents and employees may examine at all reasonable times the records required by this section to be kept.

4. (a) All such records relating to such children shall be open to the inspection of the board and the department at any reasonable time, and the information called for under this section and such other data as may be required

by the department shall be reported to the department, in accordance with the regulations of the department. Such records kept by the department shall be deemed confidential and shall be safeguarded from coming to the knowledge of and from inspection or examination by any person other than one authorized, by the department, by a judge of the court of claims when such records are required for the trial of a claim or other proceeding in such court or by a justice of the supreme court, or by a judge of the family court when such records are required for the trial of a proceeding in such court, after a notice to all interested persons and a hearing, to receive such knowledge or to make such inspection or examination. No person shall divulge the information thus obtained without authorization so to do by the department, or by such judge or justice.

(b)(i) Notwithstanding any inconsistent provision of law to the contrary, records relating to children kept pursuant to this section shall be made available to officers and employees of the state comptroller or of the city comptroller of the city of New York, or of the county officer designated by law or charter to perform the auditing function in any county not wholly contained within a city, for the purposes of a duly authorized performance audit, provided that such comptroller shall have certified to the keeper of such records that he or she has instituted procedures developed in consultation with the department to limit access to client-identifiable information to persons requiring such information for purposes of the audit, that such persons shall not use such information in any way except for purposes of the audit and that appropriate controls and prohibitions are imposed on the dissemination of client-identifiable information obtained in the conduct of the audit. Information pertaining to the substance or content of any psychological, psychiatric, therapeutic, clinical or medical reports, evaluations or like materials or information pertaining to such child or the child's family shall not be made available to such officers and employees unless disclosure of such information is absolutely essential to the specific audit activity and the department gives prior written approval.

(ii) Any failure to maintain the confidentiality of client-identifiable information shall subject such comptroller or officer to denial of any further access to records until such time as the audit agency has reviewed its procedures concerning controls and prohibitions imposed on the dissemination of such information and has taken all reasonable and appropriate steps to eliminate such lapses in maintaining confidentiality to the satisfaction of the department. The department shall establish the grounds for denial of access to records contained under this section and shall recommend, as necessary, a plan of remediation to the audit agency. Except as provided in this section, nothing in this paragraph shall be construed as limiting the powers of such comptroller or officer to access records which he is otherwise authorized to audit or obtain under any other applicable provision of law. Any person given access to information pursuant to this paragraph who releases data or information to persons or agencies not authorized to receive such information shall be guilty of a class A misdemeanor.

4-a. Notwithstanding any provisions of law to the contrary, social services districts shall provide a written summary of services rendered to a child upon the request of a probation service conducting an investigation pursuant to the provisions of section 351.1 of the family court act. Information provided to a probation service pursuant to the provisions of this subdivision shall be maintained by such service according to the provisions of subdivision five of section 351.1 of the family court act.

4-b. Notwithstanding any other provision of law, foster care information governed by this section may be released by the department or an authorized agency to a person, agency or organization for purposes of a bona fide research project. Identifying information shall not be made available, however, unless it is absolutely essential to the research purpose and the department gives prior approval. Information released pursuant to this subdivision shall not be re-disclosed except as otherwise permitted by law and upon the approval of the department.

5. The requirements of this section to keep records and make reports shall not apply to the birth parent or parents, or relatives within the second degree of such parents.

6. The provisions of this section as to records and reports to the department shall apply also to the placing out, adoption or boarding out of a child and the acceptance of guardianship or of surrender of a child.

7. An authorized agency as defined in paragraphs (a) and (b) of subdivision ten of section three hundred seventy-one of this chapter or any primary or secondary school or an office of the division for youth, except agencies operating pursuant to article nineteen-H of the executive law, who shall receive, accept, enroll or commit any child under such circumstances as shall reasonably indicate that such child may be a missing person shall make inquiries of each such child to the division of criminal justice services in a manner prescribed by such division; provided that as used in this subdivision a court shall not be included within the definition of an authorized agency. If such child appears to match a child registered with the statewide central register for missing children as described in section eight hundred thirty-seven-e of the executive law, or one registered with the national crime information center register, such agency shall immediately contact the local law enforcement agency.

8. In any case where a child is to be placed with or discharged to a relative or other person legally responsible pursuant to section ten hundred seventeen or ten hundred fifty-five of the family court act, such relative or other person shall be provided with such information by an authorized agency as is provided to foster parents pursuant to this section and applicable regulations of the department.

§372-b. Adoption services.

1. a. A prospective adoptive parent shall have a right to a fair hearing pursuant to section twenty-two of this chapter concerning the failure of a social services official to provide adoption services authorized to be provided pursuant to this section and the state's consolidated services plan. At the time a child is placed in a prospective adoptive home, the prospective adoptive parent shall be notified in writing of his or her right to such fair hearing.

b. Each social services official shall provide, either directly or through purchase of service, adoption services for each child in their care who is freed for adoption. Such adoption services shall include the evaluation of a child's placement needs and pre-placement planning, recruitment of and homestudy for prospective adoptive parents, training of adoptive parents, placement planning, supervision and post adoption services.

2. The department shall promulgate regulations which shall require that adoption services be made available to all children who are listed with the New York state adoption service. Such regulations shall also provide for coopera-tion between local social services commissioners, and for apportioning

reimbursement for adoption services where more than one agency or social services district has provided such services for a child.

2-a. The department shall promulgate regulations requiring all adoption agencies to forward names and addresses of all persons who have applied for adoption of a hard-to-place or handicapped child, as defined in section four hundred fifty-one of this chapter. A list of such names and addresses shall be maintained by the department and made available, without charge, to every agency in the state to assist them in placing such children for adoption.

3. The department shall promulgate regulations to maintain enlightened adoption policies and to establish standards and criteria for adoption practices.

§372-c. Putative father registry.

1. The department shall establish a putative father registry which shall record the names and addresses of: (a) any person adjudicated by a court of this state to be the father of a child born out-of-wedlock; (b) any person who has filed with the registry before or after the birth of a child out-of-wedlock, a notice of intent to claim paternity of the child; (c) any person adjudicated by a court of another state or territory of the United States to be the father of an out-of-wedlock child, where a certified copy of the court order has been filed with the registry by such person or any other person; (d) any person who has filed with the registry an instrument acknowledging paternity pursuant to section 4-1.2 of the estates, powers and trusts law.

2. A person filing a notice of intent to claim paternity of a child or an acknowledgement of paternity shall include therein his current address and shall notify the registry of any change of address pursuant to procedures prescribed by regulations of the department.

3. A person who has filed a notice of intent to claim paternity may at any time revoke a notice of intent to claim paternity previously filed therewith and, upon receipt of such notification by the registry, the revoked notice of intent to claim paternity shall be deemed a nullity nunc pro tunc.

4. An unrevoked notice of intent to claim paternity of a child may be introduced in evidence by any party, other than the person who filed such notice, in any proceeding in which such fact may be relevant.

5. The department shall, upon request, provide the names and addresses of persons listed with the registry to any court or authorized agency, and such information shall not be divulged to any other person, except upon order of a court for good cause shown.

§372-d. Adoption services; purchase by department.

1. The department may provide, through purchase of services from authorized agencies, adoption services for any child who has been referred to the statewide adoption service pursuant to section three hundred seventy-two-c and who has not been placed for adoption within three months after the date of such referral.

2. As used in this section "adoption services" shall mean those services and activities set forth in subdivision one of section three hundred seventy-two-b of this chapter.

3. In accordance with regulations of the department, expenditures made by the department for the provision, through purchase, of adoption services for a child pursuant to this section shall be subject to reimbursement to the state by the social services district charged with the guardianship and custody of the child, as follows: fifty percent of the amount expended for the provision of

such adoption services after first deducting from such amount any federal funds properly received or to be received on account thereof.

§372-e. Adoption applications; appeals.

1. An authorized agency shall keep a record of applications received from persons seeking to become adoptive parents, including all actions taken on such applications.

2. The department shall promulgate regulations setting forth standards and procedures to be followed by authorized agencies in evaluating persons who have applied to such agencies for the adoption of a child. Such regulations shall also restrict the evaluation process so as not to unnecessarily duplicate previous investigations which may have been made of the adoptive applicant in the context of a prior adoption application or an application for licensure or certification to board children.

3. (a) Upon an authorized agency's denial of an application, the authorized agency shall furnish the applicant with a written statement setting forth its reason for the denial of the application. Such written statement shall include a notice to the applicant, in bold face type, of such applicant's right to request and be granted a hearing in accordance with the provisions of subdivision four of this section.

(b) Upon an authorized agency's failure to act on an application within six months of its submission, the authorized agency shall, on such applicant's request, furnish the applicant with a written statement setting forth its reason for its failure to act on the application. Such written statement shall include a notice to the applicant, in bold face type, of such applicant's right to request and be granted a hearing in accordance with the provisions of subdivision four of this section.

4. Any person whose application has been denied or whose application has not been acted upon by an authorized agency within six months of its submission may request and shall be granted a hearing in accordance with the provisions of section twenty-two of this chapter relating to fair hearings.

§372-f. Statewide adoption service.

1. There shall be established by the department either directly or through purchase a statewide adoption service which shall serve all authorized agencies in the state as a means of recruiting adoptive families for children who have been legally freed for adoption but have remained in foster care for a period of three months or more. Such period in foster care shall include any period of foster care immediately preceding the date on which the child was legally freed for adoption. The service shall provide descriptions and photographs of such children, and shall also provide any other information deemed useful in the recruitment of adoptive families for each such child. The service shall be updated monthly.

2. The service may be organized on a regional basis, but shall be provided to all authorized child caring agencies and in accordance with the regulations of the department, to all appropriate citizen groups and other organizations and associations interested in children's services.

3. The department shall promulgate regulations governing the operations of the adoption service.

4. (a) Except as set forth in paragraph (b) of this subdivision, each authorized agency shall refer to the adoption service, accompanied by a photograph and description, as shall be required by departmental regulations,

each child in its care who has been legally freed for adoption and who has been in foster care for the period specified in subdivision one of this section and for whom no adoptive home has been found. If the child is fourteen years or older and will not consent to his or her adoption, such child need not be listed on the service. Such children's names shall be forwarded to the department by the authorized agency, with reference to the specific reason by which the child was not placed on the service. The department shall establish procedures for periodic review of the status of such children. If the department determines that adoption would be appropriate for a child not listed with the service, the agency shall forthwith list the child. Each authorized agency may voluntarily refer any child who has been legally freed for adoption. In addition, upon referral of a child by an authorized agency, the department may determine that the listing of a child with the service is not in the child's best interest where: the child has been placed with a relative within the third degree of consanguinity of the parents of the child and the child does not have a permanency goal of adoption, or the child is not emotionally prepared for an adoptive placement. Any child who is not listed based on one of these factors and who is not placed in an adoptive placement within six months of referral to the department must be listed with the service at the end of the six month period in accordance with regulations of the department except where the child is placed with a relative within the third degree of consanguinity of the parents of the child, in which case the department may determine that the listing continues to be contrary to the child's best interests. The department shall establish procedures for the periodic review of the status of such children.

(b) An authorized agency shall not refer to the adoption service a child in its care who has been legally freed for adoption when the child has been placed with a foster parent who has expressed, in writing, an interest in adopting the child; provided, however, that such child shall be referred to the adoption service in accordance with paragraph (a) of this subdivision where the foster parent has withdrawn interest in adopting the child or has been disapproved as an adoptive resource for the child. An authorized agency shall not refer to the adoption service a child in its care who has been legally freed for adoption where the agency has identified two or more potential placements for the child; provided, however, that such child shall be referred to the adoption service in accordance with paragraph (a) of this subdivision when such child has not been placed into an adoptive home within nine months of having been freed for adoption.

§372-g.   Abandoned infant protection program.
The office of children and family services shall develop and implement a public information program to inform the general public of the provisions of the abandoned infant protection act. The program may include but not be limited to the following elements:
1. educational and informational materials in print, audio, video, electronic, or other media;
2. public service announcements and advertisements; and
3. establishment of toll-free telephone hotlines to provide information.

§ 372-h.   Reporting on post adoption services.
1. The office of children and family services shall place information on its website regarding post adoption services funded by the office. The office shall work with social services districts to place information, to the extent that it is

available, on each social services district website regarding post adoption services funded by the social services district.

2. The office of children and family services shall collect and compile, by social services district:

(a) the following information on post adoption services funded by the office:

(i) the number of children and families served; and

(ii) the type of services provided; and

(b) the number of families receiving preventive services where post adoption services was identified as a necessary and appropriate service as part of the family assessment service plan held pursuant to section four hundred nine-e of this article and the status of such services.

3. The office of children and family services shall compile, to the extent that such information is available electronically through the state automated child welfare information system, the following non-identifying information by social services district:

(a) the number of children entering foster care that had previously been adopted;

(b) the number of families receiving preventive services where at least one child in the household had previously been adopted; and

(c) for the children and families identified in paragraphs (a) and (b) of this subdivision, the types of services, including post adoption services, identified as necessary and appropriate for the child or the members of the child's family as part of the family assessment service plan held pursuant to section four hundred nine-e of this article and the status of such services.

4. (a) The office of children and family services shall submit an annual report to the speaker of the assembly, the temporary president of the senate and the chairpersons of the senate and assembly children and families committees starting no later than September first, two thousand fifteen. Such report shall include data and information required by subdivision two of this section for the preceding year, to the extent that such information is available, and any other information the office of children and family services deems appropriate. The office of children and family services shall indicate the extent to which the information collected reflects the total population described in subdivision two of this section, and identify any impediments to collecting such information.

(b) Beginning September first, two thousand seventeen, the annual report required by paragraph (a) of this subdivision shall be expanded to include data and information required by subdivision three of this section for the preceding year, to the extent that such information is available, and any other information the office of children and family services deems appropriate.

§373. Religious faith.

1. Whenever a child is committed to any agency, association, corporation, institution or society, other than an institution supported and controlled by the state or a subdivision thereof, such commitment shall be made, when practicable, to an authorized agency under the control of persons of the same religious faith as that of the child.

2. Whenever any child is surrendered, released, placed out, or boarded out, in a family, a home or an institution, or in an agency boarding home, or in a group home, or to an authorized agency, or in the custody of any person other than that of a relative within the second degree, such surrender, release, placement or boarding out shall when practicable, be to, with or in the custody of a person or persons of the same religious faith as that of the child or to an

authorized agency under the control of persons of the same religious faith as that of the child.

3. In appointing guardians of children, and in granting orders of adoption of children, the court shall, when practicable, appoint as such guardians, and give custody through adoption, only to a person or persons of the same religious faith as that of the child.

4. The provisions of subdivision one, two and three of this section shall be so interpreted as to assure that in the care, protection, adoption, guardianship, discipline and control of any child, its religious faith shall be preserved and protected.

5. Whenever a child is placed out or boarded out in the custody, or under the supervision or control, of a person or of persons of a religious faith different from that of the child, or if a guardian of a child is appointed whose religious faith is different from that of the child, or if letters of adoption of a child are granted to a person or persons whose religious faith is different from that of the child or if a child is committed to an agency, association, corporation, society or institution, which is under the control of persons of a religious faith different from that of the child, the court, public board, commission or official shall state or recite the facts which impelled such disposition to be made contrary to the religious faith of the child or to any person whose religious faith is different from that of the child and such statement shall be a part of the minutes of the proceeding, and subject to inspection by the department or an authorized agency. This subdivision shall not apply to institutions supported and controlled by the state or a subdivision thereof.

6. The provisions of this section in relation to the protection of the religious faith of children shall also apply to minors between sixteen and eighteen years of age.

7. The provisions of subdivisions one, two, three, four, five and six of this section shall, so far as consistent with the best interests of the child, and where practicable, be applied so as to give effect to the religious wishes of the birth mother, and of the birth father whose consent would be required for the child's adoption pursuant to section one hundred eleven of the domestic relations law, if the child is born out-of-wedlock, or if born in-wedlock, the religious wishes of the birth parents of the child, or if only one of the birth parents of an in-wedlock child is then living, the religious wishes of the birth parent then living. Religious wishes of a parent shall include wishes that the child be placed in the same religion as the birth parent or in a different religion from the birth parent or with indifference to religion or with religion a subordinate consideration. Expressed religious wishes of a birth parent shall mean those which have been set forth in a writing signed by the birth parent, except that, in a non-agency adoption, such writing shall be an affidavit of the birth parent. In the absence of expressed religious wishes, as defined in this subdivision, determination of the religious wishes, if any, of the birth parent, shall be made upon the other facts of the particular case, and, if there is no evidence to the contrary, it shall be presumed that the birth parent wishes the child to be reared in the religion of the birth parent.

§373-a.   Medical histories.

Notwithstanding any other provision of law to the contrary, to the extent they are available, the medical histories of a child legally freed for adoption or of a child to be placed in foster care and of his or her birth parents, with information identifying such birth parents eliminated, shall be provided by an authorized agency to such child's prospective adoptive parent or foster parent and upon request to the adoptive parent or foster parent when such child has been adopted or placed in foster care. To the extent they are available, the medical histories of a child in foster care and of his or her birth parents shall be provided by an authorized agency to such child when discharged to his or her own care and upon request to any adopted former foster child; provided, however, medical histories of birth parents shall be provided to an adoptee with information identifying such birth parents eliminated. Such medical histories shall include all available information setting forth conditions or diseases believed to be hereditary, any drugs or medication taken during pregnancy by the child's birth mother and any other information, including any psychological information in the case of a child legally freed for adoption or when such child has been adopted, or in the case of a child to be placed in foster care or placed in foster care which may be a factor influencing the child's present or future health. The department shall promulgate and may alter or amend regulations governing the release of medical histories pursuant to this section.

§374. Authority to place out or board out children.

1. An authorized agency is hereby empowered and permitted to place out and board out children.

1-a. In any agreement between an authorized agency and foster parents with whom a child or children are to be placed or boarded, there shall be contained therein the following language: "It is duly acknowledged by the parties hereto that pursuant to the law of the state of New York, a foster parent shall have preference in any proceedings to adopt the child subject to this agreement upon such child having been in the custody of such foster parent for a period in excess of twelve months".

2. No person, agency, association, corporation, institution, society or other organization except an authorized agency shall place out or board out any child but the provisions of this section shall not restrict or limit the right of a parent, legal guardian or relative within the second degree to place out or board out a child.

3. Except as hereinafter provided no court, public board, commission or official shall place out or board out a child in a family not residing within this state.

(a) A commissioner of public welfare or a city public welfare officer authorized, pursuant to the provisions of section three hundred ninety-eight of the social welfare law, to accept the surrender of a child, may place out a child for the purpose of adoption in a family not residing within this state. No placement of a child in a family not residing within this state shall be made unless an agreement for such placement shall have been reached between the public welfare official making such placement and the appropriate welfare or other public official on a state or local level in the state where the family resides who is authorized by law to supervise children in institutional or foster care homes. Such agreement shall include provision for the supervision of the family and the child during the period preceding a final adoption.

(b) A commissioner of public welfare or a city public welfare officer authorized, pursuant to the provisions of section three hundred ninety-eight of the social welfare law, to place children in family homes, may board out a child in a family not residing within this state. No child may be boarded out in a family not residing within this state unless an agreement for such placement shall have been reached between the public welfare official making such placement and the appropriate welfare or other public official on a state or local level in the state where the family resides who is authorized by law to supervise children in institutional or foster care homes. Such agreement shall include provision for the supervision of the family and the child during the period while the child is boarded out.

4. (a) No hospital or lying-in asylum whether incorporated or unincorporated where women or girls may be received, cared for or treated during pregnancy or during or after delivery except as hereinafter provided and no person licensed to carry on like work under the provisions of article twenty-eight of the public health law shall be an authorized agency for placing out or boarding out children or place out any child in a foster home whether for adoption or otherwise either directly or indirectly or as agent or representative of the mother or parents of such child.

(b) Every such hospital and licensed person shall forthwith report to the county or city officer or board charged by law with the care of destitute children away from their homes where such hospital is located or where such child is cared for by such licensed person any child abandoned or left in the care or custody of such hospital or licensed person provided, however, that no such report except as provided in section three hundred seventy-two shall be required to be made by a hospital which is also an authorized agency.

(c) Such officer or board shall receive and care for such child as a destitute or abandoned child and may bring the case of such child before the family court in the county or city for adjudication.

(d) The expense of caring for such child as a public charge shall be paid as provided by this chapter.

5. Nothing contained in this section shall deprive any hospital of any right or power conferred upon it by its charter or act of incorporation or specified in its certificate of incorporation.

6. An authorized agency, as defined in paragraphs (a) and (c) of subdivision ten of section three hundred seventy-one of this title, may charge or accept a fee or other compensation to or from a person or persons with whom it has placed out a child, for the reasonable and necessary expenses of such placement; and no agency, association, corporation, institution, society or organization, except such an authorized agency, and no person may or shall request, accept or receive any compensation or thing of value, directly or indirectly, in connection with the placing out or adoption of a child or for assisting a birth parent, relative or guardian of a child in arranging for the placement of the child for the purpose of adoption; and no person may or shall pay or give to any person or to any agency, association, corporation, institution, society or organization, except such an authorized agency, any compensation or thing of value in connection with the placing out or adoption of a child or for assisting a birth parent, relative or guardian of a child in arranging for the placement of the child for the purpose of adoption. The prohibition set forth in this section applies to any adoptive placement activity involving a child born in New York state or brought into this state or involving a New York resident seeking to bring a child into New York state for the purpose of adoption.

This subdivision shall not be construed to prevent the payment of salaries or other compensation by an authorized agency to the officers or employees thereof; nor shall it be construed to prevent the payment by a person with whom a child has been placed out of reasonable and actual medical fees or hospital charges for services rendered in connection with the birth of such child or of other necessary expenses incurred by the birth mother in connection with or as a result of her pregnancy or the birth of the child, or of reasonable and actual nursing, medical or hospital fees for the care of such child, if such payment is made to the physician, nurse or hospital who or which rendered the services or to the birth mother of the child, or to prevent the receipt of such payment by such physician, nurse, hospital or birth mother. This subdivision shall not be construed to prevent the payment by an adoptive parent, as defined in section one hundred nine of the domestic relations law, of the birth mother's reasonable and actual expenses for housing, maternity clothing, clothing for the child and transportation for a reasonable period not to exceed sixty days prior to the birth and the later of thirty days after the birth or thirty days after the parental consent to the adoption, unless a court determines, in writing, that exceptional circumstances exist which require the payment of the birth mother's expenses beyond the time periods stated in this sentence. This subdivision shall not be construed to prevent the payment by an adoptive parent, as defined in section one hundred nine of the domestic relations law, of reasonable and actual legal fees charged for consultation and legal advice, preparation of papers and representation and other legal services rendered in connection with an adoption proceeding or of necessary disbursements incurred for or in an adoption proceeding. No attorney or law firm shall serve as the attorney for, or provide any legal services to both the birth parent and adoptive parent in regard to the placing out of a child for adoption or in an adoption proceeding. No attorney or law firm shall serve as the attorney for, or provide any legal services to, both an authorized agency and adoptive parent or both an authorized agency and birth parent where the authorized agency provides adoption services to such birth parent or adoptive parent, where the authorized agency provides foster care for the child, or where the authorized agency is directly or indirectly involved in the placing out of such child for adoption.

7. After receipt of notice from the state commissioner of health or the department of health of the city of New York, as the case may be, that an application has been received by such commissioner or department for a license or for the renewal of a license to conduct a maternity hospital or lying-in asylum, pursuant to the provisions of article twenty-eight of the public health law, the department shall, after notice to the applicant and opportunity for him to be heard, certify in writing to such commissioner or city department that the department has reasonable cause to believe that the applicant is violating or has violated the provisions of this section, if such be the case. The department shall so certify within thirty days of the date it received notice, or within such additional period, not to exceed thirty days, as the department may request in writing addressed to the commissioner or administration giving notice.

§374-a. **Interstate compact on the placement of children.**
1. The interstate compact on the placement of children is hereby enacted into law and entered into with all other jurisdictions legally joining therein in form substantially as follows:

INTERSTATE COMPACT ON THE PLACEMENT OF CHILDREN

ARTICLE I. PURPOSE AND POLICY

It is the purpose and policy of the party states to cooperate with each other in the interstate placement of children to the end that:
(a) Each child requiring placement shall receive the maximum opportunity to be placed in a suitable environment and with persons or institutions having

appropriate qualifications and facilities to provide a necessary and desirable degree and type of care.

(b) The appropriate authorities in a state where a child is to be placed may have full opportunity to ascertain the circumstances of the proposed placement, thereby promoting full compliance with applicable requirements for the protection of the child.

(c) The proper authorities of the state from which the placement is made may obtain the most complete information on the basis of which to evaluate a projected placement before it is made.

(d) Appropriate jurisdictional arrangements for the care of children will be promoted.

ARTICLE II. DEFINITIONS

As used in this compact:

(a) "Child" means a person who, by reason of minority, is legally subject to parental, guardianship or similar control.

(b) "Sending agency" means a party state, officer or employee thereof; a subdivision of a party state, or officer or employee thereof; a court of a party state; a person, corporation, association, charitable agency or other entity which sends, brings, or causes to be sent or brought any child to another party state.

(c) "Receiving state" means the state to which a child is sent, brought, or caused to be sent or brought, whether by public authorities or private persons or agencies, and whether for placement with state or local public authorities or for placement with private agencies or persons.

(d) "Placement" means the arrangement for the care of a child in a family free or boarding home or in a child-caring agency or institution but does not include any institution caring for the mentally ill, mentally defective or epileptic or any institution primarily educational in character, and any hospital or other medical facility.

ARTICLE III. CONDITIONS FOR PLACEMENT

(a) No sending agency shall send, bring, or cause to be sent or brought into any other party state any child for placement in foster care or as a preliminary to a possible adoption unless the sending agency shall comply with each and every requirement set forth in this article and with the applicable laws of the receiving state governing the placement of children therein.

(b) Prior to sending, bringing or causing any child to be sent or brought into a receiving state for placement in foster care or as a preliminary to a possible adoption, the sending agency shall furnish the appropriate public authorities in the receiving state written notice of the intention to send, bring, or place the child in the receiving state. The notice shall contain:

(1) The name, date and place of birth of the child.

(2) The identity and address or addresses of the parents or legal guardian.

(3) The name and address of the person, agency or institution to or with which the sending agency proposes to send, bring, or place the child.

(4) A full statement of the reasons for such proposed action and evidence of the authority pursuant to which the placement is proposed to be made.

(c) Any public officer or agency in a receiving state which is in receipt of a notice pursuant to paragraph (b) of this article may request of the sending agency, or any other appropriate officer or agency of or in the sending agency's state, and shall be entitled to receive therefrom, such supporting or additional information as it may deem necessary under the circumstances to carry out the purpose and policy of this compact.

(d) The child shall not be sent, brought, or caused to be sent or brought into the receiving state until the appropriate public authorities in the receiving state shall notify the sending agency, in writing, to the effect that the proposed placement does not appear to be contrary to the interests of the child.

ARTICLE IV. PENALTY FOR ILLEGAL PLACEMENT

The sending, bringing, or causing to be sent or brought into any receiving state of a child in violation of the terms of this compact shall constitute a violation of the laws respecting the placement of children of both the state in which the sending agency is located or from which it sends or brings the child and of the receiving state. Such violation may be punished or subjected to penalty in either jurisdiction in accordance with its laws. In addition to liability for any such punishment or penalty, any such violation shall constitute full and sufficient grounds for the suspension or revocation of any license, permit, or other legal authorization held by the sending agency which empowers or allows it to place, or care for children.

ARTICLE V. RETENTION OF JURISDICTION

(a) The sending agency shall retain jurisdiction over the child sufficient to determine all matters in relation to the custody, supervision, care, treatment and disposition of the child which it would have had if the child had remained in the sending agency's state, until the child is adopted, reaches majority, becomes self-supporting or is discharged with the concurrence of the appropriate authority in the receiving state. Such jurisdiction shall also include the power to effect or cause the return of the child or its transfer to another location and custody pursuant to law. The sending agency shall continue to have financial responsibility for support and maintenance of the child during the period of the placement. Nothing contained herein shall defeat a claim of jurisdiction by a receiving state sufficient to deal with an act of delinquency or crime committed therein.

(b) When the sending agency is a public agency, it may enter into an agreement with an authorized public or private agency in the receiving state providing for the performance of one or more services in respect of such case by the latter as agent for the sending agency.

(c) Nothing in this compact shall be construed to prevent a private charitable agency authorized to place children in the receiving state from performing services or acting as agent in that state for a private charitable agency of the sending state; nor to prevent the agency in the receiving state from discharging financial responsibility for the support and maintenance of a child who has been placed on behalf of the sending agency without relieving the responsibility set forth in paragraph (a) hereof.

ARTICLE VI. INSTITUTIONAL CARE OF DELINQUENT CHILDREN

A child adjudicated delinquent may be placed in an institution in another party jurisdiction pursuant to this compact, but no such placement shall be made unless the child is given a court hearing on notice to the parent or guardian with opportunity to be heard, prior to his being sent to such other party jurisdiction for institutional care and the court finds that:

1. Equivalent facilities for the child are not available in the sending agency's jurisdiction; and

2. Institutional care in the other jurisdiction is in the best interest of the child and will not produce undue hardship.

ARTICLE VII. COMPACT ADMINISTRATOR

The executive head of each jurisdiction party to this compact shall designate an officer who shall be general coordinator of activities under this compact in his jurisdiction and who, acting jointly with like officers of other party jurisdictions, shall have power to promulgate rules and regulations to carry out more effectively the terms and provisions of this compact.

ARTICLE VIII. LIMITATIONS

This compact shall not apply to:

(a) The sending or bringing of a child into a receiving state by his parent, step-parent, grandparent, adult brother or sister, adult uncle or aunt, or his guardian and leaving the child with any such relative or non-agency guardian in the receiving state.

(b) Any placement, sending or bringing of a child into a receiving state pursuant to any other interstate compact to which both the state from which the child is sent or brought and the receiving state are party, or to any other agreement between said states which has the force of law.

ARTICLE IX. ENACTMENT AND WITHDRAWAL

This compact shall be open to joinder by any state, territory or possession of the United States, the district of Columbia, the commonwealth of Puerto Rico, and, with the consent of congress, the government of Canada or any province thereof. It shall become effective with respect to any such jurisdiction when such jurisdiction has enacted the same into law. Withdrawal from this compact shall be by the enactment of a statute repealing the same, but shall not take effect until two years after the effective date of such statute and until written notice of the withdrawal has been given by the withdrawing state to the governor of each other party jurisdiction. Withdrawal of a party state shall not affect the rights, duties and obligations under this compact of any sending agency therein with respect to a placement made prior to the effective date of withdrawal.

ARTICLE X. CONSTRUCTION AND SEVERABILITY

The provisions of this compact shall be liberally construed to effectuate the purposes thereof. The provisions of this compact shall be severable and if any phrase, clause, sentence or provision of this compact is declared to be contrary to the constitution of any party state or of the United States or the applicability thereof to any government, agency, person or circumstance is held invalid, the validity of the remainder of this compact and the applicability thereof to any other government, agency, person or circumstance shall not be affected thereby. If this compact shall be held contrary to the constitution of any state party thereto, the compact shall remain in full force and effect as to the remaining states and in full force and effect as to the state affected as to all severable matters.

2. Any requirement of this state for a license, permit, or the posting of a bond to entitle an agency to place children shall not apply to a public sending agency (within the meaning of the interstate compact on the placement of children) of or in another state party to said compact.

3. Financial responsibility for any child placed pursuant to the provisions of the interstate compact for the placement of children shall be determined in accordance with the provisions of article five thereof in the first instance. However, in the event of partial or complete default of performance thereunder, the provisions of section three hundred eighty-two of this chapter with respect to such responsibility also may be invoked.

4. The "appropriate public authorities" as used in article three of the interstate compact on the placement of children shall, with reference to New York, mean the department of social services, except that, with respect to the placement of children "adjudicated delinquent", as that phrase is used in article six thereof, who are to be placed in a facility operated or supervised by the division for youth, shall mean the division for youth, and said department and division shall receive and act with reference to notices required by said article three.

5. As used in paragraph (a) of article five of the interstate compact on the placement of children the phrase "appropriate authority in the receiving state" with reference to New York state shall mean the commissioner of social services of the social services district in which the child may be at the time of discharge, and, with respect to children "adjudicated delinquent", as that phrase is used in article six thereof, who are to be discharged from a facility operated or supervised by the division for youth, shall mean the division for youth.

6. The officers and agencies of this state and its subdivisions having authority to place children are hereby empowered to enter into agreements with appropriate officers or agencies of or in other party states pursuant to paragraph (b) of article five of the interstate compact on the placement of children. Any such agreement which contains a financial commitment or imposes a financial obligation on this state or subdivision or agency thereof shall not be binding unless it has the approval in writing of the comptroller in the case of the state and of the chief local fiscal officer in the case of a subdivision of the state.

7. Any requirements for visitation, inspection or supervision of children, homes, institutions or other agencies in another party state which may apply under sections three hundred eighty-two, three hundred eighty-six or three hundred ninety-eight of this chapter shall be deemed to be met if performed pursuant to an agreement entered into by appropriate officers or agencies of this state or a subdivision thereof as contemplated by paragraph (b) of article five of the interstate compact on the placement of children.

8. Neither the prohibition of, nor the limitations on out of state placement of children contained in sections three hundred seventy-four and three hundred ninety-eight of this chapter shall apply to placements made pursuant to the interstate compact on the placement of children.

9. Any court having jurisdiction to place delinquent children may place such a child in an institution of or in another state pursuant to article six of the interstate compact on the placement of children and shall retain jurisdiction as provided in article five thereof.

10. As used in article seven of the interstate compact on the placement of children, the term "executive head" means the governor. The governor is hereby authorized to appoint a compact administrator in accordance with the terms of said article seven.

11. (a) In addition to the conditions for placement set forth in subdivision one of this section, the sending agency shall, in the case of a placement preliminary to a possible adoption, submit to the compact administrator a full statement setting forth all fees, including the categories of such fees, paid and to be paid by the adoptive parent to any agency or person in exchange for the adoptive placement.

(b) The compact administrator shall not approve a proposed placement where such placement violates subdivision six of section three hundred seventy-four of this chapter.

12. Placement of a child in this state in violation of subdivision one of this section by an out of state sending agency shall, in addition to any other remedy or sanction imposed by law, subject the agency violating such provision to a civil action for money damages including fees, compensation and other remuneration paid by any person on account of or incident to the placement of a child in violation of such provision.

Placement of a child by an out of state sending agency in violation of such provision shall subject such agency to the exercise of personal jurisdiction over such agency by a court pursuant to subparagraph (i) of paragraph three of subdivision (a) of section three hundred two of the civil practice law and rules.

§374-b.   Authority to operate agency boarding home.
1. An authorized agency which is not a court, public board, commission, or official, is hereby empowered and permitted to operate agency boarding homes in compliance with regulations of the department; and a social services official who is authorized to place children in family homes and institutions, pursuant to section three hundred ninety-eight, may be authorized by the department to operate agency boarding homes, in compliance with such regulations, if such official applies for such authority and demonstrates to the department his need therefor and that suitable care is not otherwise available for children and/or minors under the care of such official through an authorized agency under the control of persons of the same religious faith as such children. No agency boarding home shall care for more than six children or minors except that such a home may provide care for more than six brothers and sisters of the same family. Such homes shall be subject to supervision, visitation and inspection by the department and shall also be subject to visitation and inspection by the board.

2. (a) If an authorized agency plans to establish one or more boarding homes within a municipality, it shall notify the chief executive officer of the municipality in writing of its intentions and include in such notice a description of the nature, size and the community support requirements of the program.

(b) For purposes of this subdivision, "municipality" means an incorporated village, if a facility is to be located therein; a town, if the facility is to be located therein, and not simultaneously within an incorporated village; or a city, except that in the city of New York, the community board with jurisdiction over the area in which such a facility is to be located shall be considered the municipality.

3. An authorized agency that has received approval from the office of children and family services may operate a supervised independent living program, as

defined in section three hundred seventy-one of this title. The office of children and family services shall promulgate regulations establishing the standards for approval and operation of supervised independent living programs.

§374-c.   Authority to operate group homes.

1. An authorized agency which is not a court, public board, commission or official is hereby empowered and permitted to operate group homes in compliance with regulations of the department. A social services official who is authorized to place children in family homes and institutions, pursuant to section three hundred ninety-eight, may be authorized by the department to operate group homes in compliance with such regulations, provided that such official demonstrates to the satisfaction of the department the need therefor and that suitable care is not otherwise available for children under the care of such official through an authorized agency under the control of persons of the same religious faith as such children. Such homes shall be subject to supervision, visitation and inspection by the department and shall also be subject to visitation and inspection by the board.

2. (a) If an authorized agency plans to establish one or more group homes within a municipality, it shall notify the chief executive officer of the municipality in writing of its intentions and include in such notice a description of the nature, size and the community support requirements of the program.

(b) For purposes of this subdivision, "municipality" means an incorporated village, if a facility is to be located therein; a town, if the facility is to be located therein, and not simultaneously within an incorporated village; or a city, except that in the city of New York, the community board with jurisdiction over the area in which such a facility is to be located shall be considered the municipality.

§374-d.   Authority to operate public institutions for children.

A social services official who is authorized to place children in family homes and institutions, pursuant to section three hundred ninety-eight, may be authorized by the department to operate public institutions for children in compliance with regulations of the department, provided that such official demonstrates to the satisfaction of the department the need therefor and that suitable care is not otherwise available for children under the care of such official. Such institutions shall be subject to supervision, visitation and inspection by the department and shall also be subject to visitation and inspection by the board.

§374-e.   Authority to place out or board out children with therapeutic foster parents.

A social services official or agency who is authorized to place out or board out children pursuant to section three hundred ninety-eight or three hundred seventy-four of this article, is authorized by the department to place out or board out children having special needs with therapeutic foster parents pursuant to subdivision fifteen of section three hundred ninety-eight of this article and in compliance with regulations of the department. Such placement shall only be made, however, when the official or agency demonstrates to the satisfaction of the department that state expenditures incurred in placing a child with a therapeutic foster parent are less than those that would be incurred if the children were placed in an institution.

§374-f.   Authority to enter into leases for dwelling units.

Any inconsistent provisions of this chapter or any other law notwithstanding, a public welfare official authorized to operate agency boarding homes or group homes is hereby empowered to rent or lease dwelling units in his capacity as a public welfare official, as lessee, in any federal project, state project or municipal project, as defined in the public housing law, or in any municipally-aided project or state-aided project, or other project, as defined in the private housing finance law, or elsewhere, for the purpose of operating therein such agency boarding homes or group homes, and is hereby empowered to contract, in his capacity as a public welfare official, as contractor, with individuals for their services in conducting such homes and caring for children or minors placed in such homes.

§375.   Requirement of certificate or license to board children.

Except for relatives within the second degree or third degree of the parents of a child or children, relatives within the second degree or third degree of the step-parent of a child or children, legally appointed guardians, schools and academies meeting the requirements of the education law as to compulsory education, camps operated for profit for the accommodation of school age children during school vacation periods under permits issued by health officers pursuant to chapter seven of the state sanitary code, and persons with whom a child or children are placed out, no person shall receive, board or keep any child under the age of eighteen years unless certified or licensed to do so as provided in this title.

§376.   Certificate to board children and/or minors under age of eighteen years.

1. An authorized agency which shall board out any child and/or minor under the age of eighteen years shall issue to the person receiving such child and/or minor for board a certificate to receive, board or keep a child and/or minor under the age of eighteen years. Prior to issuing such certificate, the agency shall require that an applicant set forth: his or her employment history, provide personal and employment references and sign a sworn statement indicating whether the applicant, to the best of his or her knowledge, has ever been convicted of a crime in this state or any other jurisdiction. In accordance with the regulations of the office of children and family services, in addition to the requirements set forth in subdivision two of section three hundred seventy-eight-a of this title and paragraph (a) of subdivision one of section four hundred twenty-four-a of this article, the agency shall review information available in the statewide automated child welfare information system to determine whether the applicant previously held such a certificate, or a license or approval as a foster parent and, if so, whether such certificate, license or approval was revoked, not renewed, or a foster child was removed from his or her home for health or safety reasons and shall consider such information in determining whether a certificate should be issued to such applicant. Not until all inquiries are completed and evaluated shall the agency cause such certificate to be issued.

2. The agency issuing or renewing any such certificate shall forthwith transmit a copy or report thereof to the board.

3. No person shall be certified by more than one authorized agency but any person so certified may receive for care at board or otherwise a child and/or minor under the age of eighteen years from other sources upon the written

consent and approval of the certifying agency as to each such child and/or minor.

§377. License to board children.

1. Application for a license to receive, board or keep any child shall be made in writing to the commissioner of social services in and for the social services district wherein the premises to be licensed are located, in the form and manner prescribed by the office of children and family services. The office shall require that an applicant set forth: his or her employment history, provide personal and employment references and sign a sworn statement indicating whether, to the best of his or her knowledge, he or she has ever been convicted of a crime in this state or any other jurisdiction. In accordance with the regulations of the office of children and family services, in addition to the requirements set forth in subdivision two of section three hundred seventy-eight-a of this title and paragraph (a) of subdivision one of section four hundred twenty-four-a of this article, such commissioner of social services shall review information available in the statewide automated child welfare information system to determine whether the applicant previously held such a license, or a certificate or approval as a foster parent, and, if so, whether such license, certificate or approval was revoked, not renewed, or a foster child was removed from his or her home for health or safety reasons and shall consider such information in determining whether a license should be issued to such applicant. Not until all inquiries are completed and evaluated shall the commissioner of social services cause such license to be issued.

2. Before any such license shall be issued an authorized agent or employee of the social services district shall visit and inspect the premises for which such license is requested, make such further inquiry and investigation as may be required to ascertain compliance with applicable requirements.

3. If it appears from such inquiry and investigation that the applicant maintains a home suitable for the care of children in accordance with the regulations of the department, the commissioner of social services shall cause such license to be issued in such manner as the department may provide.

4. The commissioner of social services, issuing or renewing any such license, shall in accordance with the directions of the department, transmit a copy or report thereof to the department.

§378. Form, duration and limitation of certificates and licenses.

1. Certificates or licenses to receive, board or keep any child and/or minor shall be in the form prescribed and provided by the department to the effect that such person is regarded by the issuing authorized agency or social services department, as the case may be, as maintaining a home suitable for the care of children and/or minors and specifying the name, address, and religious faith of the person to whom issued, the number of children and/or minors for whom such person is certified or licensed to care and such other information as the department may require.

2. Such certificates and licenses shall be valid for not more than two years after date of issue but may be renewed or extended subject to regulations established by the office of children and family services.

3. No such license shall permit the reception for board of more than six children and if there are children not received for board living in the home of a person to whom such license is issued, whether children of such person or otherwise, the sum of the number of such children and of the number of

children permitted to be received for board by such license shall not exceed six, excepting, however, that such license may permit the reception for board of additional children if such children (a) are siblings or half-siblings, or are siblings or half-siblings of a child living in the home, (b) are children freed for adoption as defined in subdivision (b) of section one thousand eighty-seven of the family court act, and have been placed for adoption with the person to whom such license is issued, or (c) are minor parents who are foster children and the minor parents' children.

4. No such certificate shall permit the reception for board of more than six children and/or minors and if there are children under thirteen years of age not received for board living in the home of the person to whom such certificate is issued, whether children of such person or otherwise, the total number of such children and of the number of children and/or minors permitted to be received for board by such certificate shall not exceed six, excepting, however, that such certificate may permit the reception for board of up to two additional children if such children (a) are siblings or half-siblings, or are siblings or half-siblings of a child living in the home, (b) are children freed for adoption as defined in subdivision (b) of section one thousand eighty-seven of the family court act, and have been placed for adoption with the person to whom such certificate is issued, or (c) are minor parents who are foster children and the minor parents' children.

5. The department shall establish and may alter or amend regulations governing the issuing and revocation of such licenses and certificates and prescribing standards, records, accommodations and equipment for the care of children and/or minors received under such licenses and certificates.

§378-a.   Access to conviction records by authorized agencies.

1. Every authorized agency which operates a residential program for children licensed or certified by the office of children and family services, and the office of children and family services in relation to any juvenile justice program it operates, shall request that the justice center for the protection of people with special needs check, and upon such request, such justice center shall request and shall be authorized to receive from the division of criminal justice services and the federal bureau of investigation criminal history information, as such phrase is defined in paragraph (c) of subdivision one of section eight hundred forty-five-b of the executive law concerning each prospective operator, employee or volunteer of such residential program who will have regular and substantial unsupervised or unrestricted physical contact with children in such program. For the purposes of this section, "operator" shall include any natural person with an ownership interest in the authorized agency. Access to and the use of such information shall be governed by the provisions of section eight hundred forty-five-b of the executive law.

1-a. Excluding the authorized agencies authorized to request and receive criminal history information pursuant to subdivision one of this section, and subject to the rules and regulations of the division of criminal justice services, an authorized agency defined in subdivision ten of section three hundred seventy-one of this title shall have access to criminal history information, as such phrase is defined in paragraph (c) of subdivision one of section eight hundred forty-five-b of the executive law, pertaining to persons who have applied for and are under active consideration for employment by such authorized agency in positions where such persons will have the potential for regular and substantial unsupervised and unrestricted physical contact with children in the program. Upon receipt of such criminal history information, the authorized agency shall provide the prospective employee with a copy of such criminal history information and a copy of article twenty-three-A of the correction law and inform such prospective employee of his or her right to seek correction of any incorrect information contained in such criminal history information pursuant to the regulations and procedures established by the division of criminal justice services. The authorized agency shall designate one or two persons in its employ who shall be authorized to request, receive and review the criminal history information pursuant to this subdivision, and only such persons and the prospective employee to which the criminal history information relates shall have access to such information; provided, however, that such criminal history information may be disclosed to other personnel empowered by the agency to make decisions concerning prospective employees. The authorized agency shall notify the division of criminal justice services of each person authorized to have access to such criminal history information pursuant to this subdivision. Except as otherwise provided in this subdivision, such criminal history information shall be confidential and any person who willfully permits the release of such confidential criminal history information to persons not permitted by this subdivision to receive such information shall be guilty of a misdemeanor.

2. (a) Notwithstanding any other provision of law to the contrary, and subject to rules and regulations of the division of criminal justice services, an authorized agency, as defined in subdivision ten of section three hundred seventy-one of this title, shall perform a criminal history record check with the division of criminal justice services regarding any prospective foster parent or prospective adoptive parent or, a prospective successor guardian in accordance with paragraph (d) of subdivision two of section four hundred fifty-eight-b of this article, and any person over the age of eighteen who is currently residing in the home of such prospective foster parent, prospective adoptive parent or prospective successor guardian. Provided, however, that for prospective foster parents and prospective adoptive parents and other persons over the age of eighteen in their homes, the checks required by this paragraph shall be conducted before the foster parent or adoptive parent is finally certified or approved for the placement of a child. Persons who are over the age of eighteen residing in the home of a certified or approved foster parent and who previously did not have a criminal history record check performed in accordance with this subdivision shall have such a criminal history record check performed when the foster parent applies for renewal of his or her certification or approval as a foster parent. The division of criminal justice services is authorized to submit fingerprints to the federal bureau of investigation for the purpose of a nationwide criminal history record check pursuant to and consistent with public law 92-544 to determine whether such prospective foster parent, prospective adoptive parent, prospective successor guardian or person over the age of eighteen currently residing in the home of such prospective parent or guardian has a criminal history in any state or federal jurisdiction. The provisions and procedures of this section, including the criminal history record check of persons over the age of eighteen who are currently residing in the home of the foster parent, also shall apply to prospective foster parents certified by the office of children and family services and to family homes certified by any other state agency where such family homes care for foster children in accordance with a memorandum of understanding with the office of children and family services.

(b) Every authorized agency shall obtain a set of the prospective foster parent, prospective adoptive parent or prospective successor guardian's fingerprints and those of any person over the age of eighteen who currently resides in the home of such prospective foster parent, prospective adoptive parent or prospective successor guardian, and such other information as is required by the office of children and family services and the division of criminal justice services. The authorized agency shall provide to the applicant blank fingerprint cards and a description of how the completed fingerprint cards will be used upon submission to the authorized agency. The authorized agency shall promptly transmit such fingerprint cards to the office of children and family services. The office of children and family services shall promptly submit such fingerprint cards and the processing fee imposed pursuant to subdivision eight-a of section eight hundred thirty-seven of the executive law to the division of criminal justice services for its full search and retain processing. Notwithstanding any other provision of law to the contrary, the processing fee shall be submitted by the office of children and family services and no part thereof shall be charged to the prospective foster parent, prospective adoptive parent, prospective successor guardian or any person over the age of eighteen who currently resides in the home of such prospective foster parent, prospective adoptive parent or prospective successor guardian who submitted a fingerprint card pursuant to this subdivision.

(c) The division of criminal justice services shall promptly provide to the office of children and family services a criminal history record, if any, with respect to the prospective foster parent, prospective adoptive parent or prospective successor guardian and any other person over the age of eighteen who resides in the home of the prospective foster parent, prospective adoptive parent or prospective successor guardian, or a statement that the individual has no criminal history record.

(d) Notwithstanding any other provision of law to the contrary, the office of children and family services, upon receipt of a criminal history record from the division of criminal justice services, may request, and is entitled to receive, information pertaining to any offense contained in such criminal history record from any state or local law enforcement agency or court for the purposes of determining whether any ground relating to such criminal conviction or pending criminal charge exists for denying an application.

(e) Except as set forth in paragraph (m) of this section, after reviewing any criminal history record information provided by the division of criminal justice services, the office of children and family services shall promptly notify the authorized agency or other state agency that: *(Eff.12/30/16,Ch.54,L.2016)*

(1) Notwithstanding any other provision of law to the contrary, an application for certification or approval of a prospective foster parent or prospective adoptive parent shall be denied and, in the event of death or incapacity of a relative guardian, an agreement to provide payments to a prospective successor guardian pursuant to title ten of this article shall not be approved pursuant to subparagraph (ii) of paragraph (b) of subdivision five of section four hundred fifty-eight-b of this article, as applicable, where a criminal history record of the prospective foster parent, prospective adoptive parent or prospective successor guardian, as applicable, reveals a conviction for:

(A) a felony conviction at any time involving: (i) child abuse or neglect; (ii) spousal abuse; (iii) a crime against a child, including child pornography; or (iv) a crime involving violence, including rape, sexual assault, or homicide, other than a crime involving physical assault or battery; or

(B) a felony conviction within the past five years for physical assault, battery, or a drug-related offense; or

(2) Notwithstanding any other provision of law to the contrary, a final determination of an application for certification or approval of a prospective foster parent or prospective adoptive parent and, in relation to prospective successor guardians, approval pursuant to subparagraph (ii) of paragraph (b) of subdivision five of section four hundred fifty-eight-b of this article shall be held in abeyance whenever the criminal history record of the prospective foster parent, prospective adoptive parent or prospective successor guardian, as applicable, reveals:

(A) a charge for a crime set forth in subparagraph one of this paragraph which has not been finally resolved; or

(B) a felony conviction that may be for a crime set forth in subparagraph one of this paragraph. An authorized agency may proceed with a determination of such application, in a manner consistent with this subdivision, only upon receiving subsequent notification from the office of children and family services regarding the status of such charge or the nature of such conviction; or

(3) consistent with the provisions of article twenty-three-A of the correction law, an application for certification or approval of a prospective foster parent or prospective adoptive parent may be denied, an agreement to provide payments to a prospective successor guardian pursuant to title ten of this article may not be approved pursuant to subparagraph (ii) of paragraph (b) of subdivision five of section four hundred fifty-eight-b of this article, as applicable, where:

(A) a criminal history record of the prospective foster parent, prospective adoptive parent or prospective successor guardian reveals a charge or a conviction of a crime other than one set forth in subparagraph one of this paragraph; or

(B) a criminal history record of any other person over the age of eighteen who resides in the home of the prospective foster parent, prospective adoptive parent or prospective successor guardian reveals a charge or a conviction of any crime; or

(4) Notwithstanding any other provision of law to the contrary, an application for renewal of the certification or approval of a foster parent submitted on or after October first, two thousand eight shall be denied based on the conviction of the foster parent of a crime set forth in subparagraph one of this paragraph where such conviction occurred on or after October first, two thousand eight; or

(5) Notwithstanding any other provision of law to the contrary, the certification or approval of a foster parent, or the approval of an adoptive parent who has not completed the adoption process, shall be revoked based on the conviction of the foster parent or the adoptive parent of a crime set forth in subparagraph one of this paragraph; or

(6) the prospective foster parent, prospective adoptive parent or prospective successor guardian and any person over the age of eighteen who is residing in the home of the prospective foster parent, prospective adoptive parent or prospective successor guardian has no criminal history record.

(f) Except as otherwise set forth in this paragraph, any notification by the office of children and family services pursuant to paragraph (e) of this subdivision shall include a summary of the criminal history record provided by the division of criminal justice services, including, but not limited to, the specific crime or crimes for which the prospective foster parent or parents, or adoptive parent or parents, prospective successor guardian or guardians or any adults over the age of eighteen living in the home have been charged or convicted, as applicable. When responding to an inquiry from a voluntary authorized agency or other non-public agency with respect to the results of a national criminal history check performed by the federal bureau of investigation, the office of children and family services shall advise the voluntary authorized agency or other non-public agency of the category or categories of crime or crimes and shall not provide the voluntary authorized agency or other non-public agency with the specific crime or crimes absent the written consent of the person for whom the national criminal history check was performed.

(g) When an authorized agency has denied an application or approval in accordance with the provisions of paragraph (e) of this subdivision, the authorized agency shall provide to the applicant a written statement setting forth the reasons for such denial, including, as authorized by paragraph (f) of this subdivision, the summary of the criminal history record provided to the authorized agency by the office of children and family services. The authorized agency shall also provide a description of the division of criminal justice services' record review process and any remedial processes provided by the office of children and family services to any prospective foster parent, prospective adoptive parent or prospective successor guardian. If the applicant is disqualified under item (ii) of clause (A) of subparagraph one of paragraph (e) of this subdivision, then the applicant may apply for relief from the mandatory disqualification based on the grounds that the offense was not spousal abuse as that term is defined in paragraph (j) of this subdivision.

(h) Where a criminal history record of the certified or approved foster parent, prospective adoptive parent or of any other person over the age of eighteen who resides in the home of the certified or approved foster parent or prospective adoptive parent reveals a charge or conviction of any crime, the authorized agency shall perform a safety assessment of the conditions in the household. Such assessment shall include: whether the subject of the charge or conviction resides in the household; the extent to which such person may have contact with foster children or other children residing in the household; and the status, date and nature of the criminal charge or conviction. The authorized agency shall thereafter take all appropriate steps to protect the health and safety of such child or children, including, when appropriate, the removal of any foster child or children from the home. Where the authorized agency denies the application or revokes the approval or certification of the foster parent or the prospective adoptive parent in accordance with the standards set forth in paragraph (e) of this subdivision, such authorized agency shall remove any foster child or children from the home of the foster parent or the prospective adoptive parent.

(i) Any criminal history record provided by the division of criminal justice services, and any summary of the criminal history record provided by the office of children and family services to an authorized agency pursuant to this subdivision, is confidential and shall not be available for public inspection; provided, however, nothing herein shall prevent an authorized agency, the office of children and family services or other state agency referenced in paragraph (a) of this subdivision from disclosing criminal history information to any administrative or judicial proceeding relating to the denial or revocation of a certification or approval of a foster parent or an adoptive parent or the removal of the foster child from the home or the failure to approve a prospective successor guardian pursuant to subparagraph (ii) of paragraph (b) of subdivision five of section four hundred fifty-eight-b of this article or the termination of an agreement for payments pursuant to title ten of this article that is made in accordance with paragraph (h) of subdivision four of section four hundred fifty-eight-b of this article. Where there is a pending court case, the authorized agency which received the criminal history record summary from the office of children and family services, shall provide a copy of such summary to the family court or surrogate's court.

(j) For the purposes of this subdivision "spousal abuse" is an offense defined in section 120.05, 120.10, 121.12 or 121.13 of the penal law where the victim of such offense was the defendant's spouse; provided, however, spousal abuse shall not include a crime in which the prospective foster parent, prospective adoptive parent or prospective successor guardian, who was the defendant, has received notice pursuant to paragraph (g) of this subdivision and the office of children and family services finds after a fair hearing held pursuant to section twenty-two of this chapter, that he or she was the victim of physical, sexual or psychological abuse by the victim of such offense and such abuse was a factor in causing the prospective foster parent, prospective adoptive parent or prospective successor guardian to commit such offense.

(k) The office of children and family services shall inform the division of criminal justice services when a person is no longer certified or approved as a foster parent or is no longer a prospective adoptive parent so that the division of criminal justice services may terminate its retain processing with regard to such person and any person over the age of eighteen who is residing in the home of the foster parent or prospective adoptive parent. At least once a year, the office of children and family services will be required to conduct a validation of the records maintained by the division of criminal justice services.

(l) The office of children and family services, in consultation with the division of criminal justice services, shall promulgate regulations for the purpose of implementing the provisions of this subdivision relating to the standards for the certification or approval of foster parents or adoptive parents.

(m)(1) The office of children and family services shall not release the content of the results of the nationwide criminal history record check conducted by the federal bureau of investigation in accordance with this subdivision to an authorized agency, as defined in paragraphs (a) or (c) of subdivision ten of section three hundred seventy-one of this title.

(2) For any application made to such an authorized agency under this subdivision, the office of children and family services shall:

(A) review and evaluate the results of the nationwide criminal history record check of the prospective foster parent, prospective adoptive parent and any other person over the age of eighteen who resides in the home of such applicant in accordance with the standards set forth in paragraph (e) of this subdivision relating to mandatory disqualifying convictions, hold in abeyance charges or convictions, and discretionary charges and convictions; and

(B) based on the results of the nationwide criminal history record check, inform such authorized agency that the application for certification or approval of the prospective foster parent or the prospective adoptive parent either: (i) must be denied; (ii) must be held in abeyance pending subsequent notification from the office of children and family services; or (iii) that the office of children and family services has no objection, solely based on the nationwide criminal history record check, for the authorized agency to proceed with a determination on such application based on the standards for certification or approval of a prospective foster parent or prospective adoptive parent, as set forth in the regulations of the office of children and family services.

(3) Where the office of children and family services directs the authorized agency to deny the application of a prospective foster parent or a prospective adoptive parent in accordance with this paragraph, the office of children and family services shall also notify the prospective foster parent, prospective adoptive parent or other person over the age of eighteen who resided in the home of the applicant whose criminal history was the basis for the denial and shall provide such prospective foster parent, prospective adoptive parent or other person a copy of the results of the nationwide criminal history record check upon which such denial was based and a written statement setting forth the reasons for such denial. If the applicant is disqualified under item (ii) of clause (A) of subparagraph one of paragraph (e) of this subdivision, then the applicant may apply for relief from the mandatory disqualification based on the grounds that the offense was not spousal abuse as that term is defined in paragraph (j) of this subdivision.

(4) This paragraph does not apply to nationwide criminal history record checks conducted by the federal bureau of investigation on behalf of state agencies or authorized agencies, as defined in paragraph (b) of subdivision ten of section three hundred seventy-one of this title, or to the results of statewide criminal history record checks conducted by the division of criminal justice services.   *(Eff.12/30/16,Ch.54,L.2016)*

§379.   Revocation of certificates and licenses.

1. A certificate or license to receive, board or keep any child and/or minor under the age of eighteen years may be revoked for cause by the authorized agency or the commissioner of social services by which it was issued and any such certificate or license to receive, board or keep any child may be revoked for cause by the commissioner.

2. An agency revoking any such certificate and a commissioner of social services revoking any such license shall notify the department of such revocation at once.

§380.   Boarding and free homes; records.

Every person who receives, boards or keeps a child and/or minor under a license or certificate shall keep a record in a register to be provided by the department showing the name, date of birth and religious faith of each child and/or minor received, the names and addresses of his parents or guardian or of the authorized agency from whom received and of the person by whom placed and by whom removed, the dates of reception and removal and such other information as may be required by the department.

§381.   Maternity homes; records and reports.

Every hospital or lying-in asylum whether incorporated or unincorporated where women or girls may be received, cared for or treated during pregnancy or during or after delivery and every person licensed to carry on like work under the provisions of article twenty-eight of the public health law shall keep a record showing the full and true name and address including street and number, if any, of every such woman or girl and of each child of such woman or girl received, admitted or born on the premises, the full and true names and addresses and the religious faith of the parents of every such child, the dates of reception, admission or birth and of discharge or departure of each such woman, girl or child, the full and true names and addresses of the person or persons by whom any such child is removed or taken away, the amount paid for the care of any such woman, girl or child and the full and true names and addresses of the person or persons making such payment or payments; and shall keep such further record as may be required by regulations of the department. The department may, through its authorized agents and employees, at all reasonable times, inspect and examine such records and may require from such licensed person or from such hospital and its directors, officers, trustees, employees, manager, superintendent, owner or other person responsible for its operation, all information in their possession with reference to any such child not taken away or removed from such hospital by his parents or parent.

§382. **Responsibility for children without state residence; license and board.**

1. Any person, institution, corporation or agency which shall bring, or cause to be brought, into the state of New York any child not having a state residence, or which shall receive or accept any child from outside of the state of New York, not having state residence, shall be responsible for the care and maintenance of such child whether placed out, boarded out or otherwise cared for unless adopted by foster parents. Such responsibility shall continue during the minority of such child and thereafter until he is self-supporting.

2. (a) It shall be unlawful for any person, agency, association, corporation, society, institution or other organization, except an authorized agency, to bring, send or cause to be brought or sent into the state of New York any child for the purpose of placing or boarding such child or procuring the placing of such child, by adoption, guardianship, or otherwise, in a family, a home or institution, except with an authorized agency, in this state, without first obtaining a license from the department.

(b) This subdivision shall not apply to a sending agency, as defined in article two of section three hundred seventy-four-a of this title, which is located in a state which is a party to the interstate compact on the placement of children, provided, however, that all persons who reside in such a state, except officers or employees of the state or a subdivision thereof who are acting in their official capacity, shall comply with the provisions of this section.

(c) This section shall not apply to and shall not restrict or limit the right of a parent, legal guardian, or relative within the second degree of a child from bringing or sending the child or causing the child to be brought or sent, into the state of New York for the purpose of placing out or boarding out the child.

3. Application for a license shall be submitted on a form approved and provided by the department and be accompanied by proof that the applicant holds a license, or is approved by the department or similar body in the state where the applicant resides, or where its chief office is located, or where it has its place of business.

4. Before bringing, sending, or causing to be brought or sent into this state any child, the person, agency, association, corporation, society, institution or other organization, duly licensed as provided in this section must furnish the department a blanket indemnity bond of a reputable surety company in favor of the state in the penal sum of not less than ten thousand dollars. Such bond must be approved as to form and sufficiency by the department and conditioned as follows:

That such licensee (a) will report to the department immediately the name of each such child, its age, the name of the state, and city, town, borough or village, or the name of the country from which such child came, the religious faith of the parents of the child, the full name and last residence of its parent or parents, the name of the custodian from whom it is taken, and the name and residence of the person or authorized agency with whom it is placed or boarded, released or surrendered, or to whom adoption or guardianship is granted, and the death of such child or any reboarding, replacement or other disposition;

(b) will remove from the state within thirty days after written notice is given any such child becoming a public charge during his minority;

(c) will remove from the state immediately upon its release any such child who within three years from the time of its arrival within the state is committed to an institution or prison as a result of conviction for juvenile delinquency or crime;

(d) will place or cause to be placed or board or cause to be boarded such child under agreement which will secure to such child a proper home, and will make the person so receiving such child responsible for its proper care, education and training;

(e) will comply with section three hundred seventy-three;

(f) will supervise the care and training of such child and cause it to be visited at least annually by a responsible agent of the licensee; and

(g) will make to the department such reports as it from time to time may require.

5. In the event of the failure of such licensee to comply with the second and third conditions of the bond hereinbefore mentioned, and to remove, after thirty days' notice so to do, a child becoming a public charge, such portion of the bond shall be forfeited to the state or the county or municipality thereof as shall equal the sum which shall have been expended by the state or such county or municipality thereof for the care or maintenance or in the prosecution of such child or for its return to the licensee.

§383.   Care and custody of children.

1. The parent of a child remanded or committed to an authorized agency shall not be entitled to the custody thereof, except upon consent of the court, public board, commission, or official responsible for the commitment of such child, or in pursuance of an order of a court or judicial officer of competent jurisdiction, determining that the interest of such child will be promoted thereby and that such parent is fit, competent and able to duly maintain, support and educate such child. The name of such child shall not be changed while in the custody of an authorized agency.

2. The custody of a child placed out or boarded out and not legally adopted or for whom legal guardianship has not been granted shall be vested during his minority, or until discharged by such authorized agency from its care and supervision, in the authorized agency placing out or boarding out such child and any such authorized agency may in its discretion remove such child from the home where placed or boarded.

3. Any adult husband and his adult wife and any adult unmarried person, who, as foster parent or parents, have cared for a child continuously for a period of twelve months or more, may apply to such authorized agency for the placement of said child with them for the purpose of adoption, and if said child is eligible for adoption, the agency shall give preference and first consideration to their application over all other applications for adoption placements. However, final determination of the propriety of said adoption of such foster child shall be within the sole discretion of the court, as otherwise provided herein.

Foster parents having had continuous care of a child, for more than twelve months, through an authorized agency, shall be permitted as a matter of right, as an interested party to intervene in any proceeding involving the custody of the child. Such intervention may be made anonymously or in the true name of said foster parents.

4. An adult married person who has executed a legally enforceable separation agreement or is a party to a marriage in which a valid decree of separation has been entered and who becomes or has been the custodian of a child placed in their care as a result of court ordered foster care may apply to such authorized agency for placement of said child with them for the purpose of adoption. Applications filed pursuant to this subdivision by persons who, as foster parents, have cared for a child continuously for a period of twelve months or more shall be entitled to the same consideration and preference as are given to applications filed pursuant to subdivision three of this section. Final determination of the propriety of said adoption of such foster child, however, shall be within the sole discretion of the court, as otherwise provided herein.

5. Any proceeding brought in connection with the provisions of this section shall have preference over all other causes in all courts.

§383-a.   **Immunity from liability for application of the reasonable and prudent parent standard.**

1. Legislative intent. It is the intent of the legislature to promote a safe and nurturing environment for children in foster care that, among other things, allows them to engage in age and developmentally appropriate activities with their peers. It is also the intent of the legislature to encourage caregivers to allow foster children to participate in such activities by providing training, guidance, and appropriate liability protections when caregivers make reasonable and prudent decisions with regard to such activities. It is not the intent of the legislature to relieve caregivers or any other person of any duty or responsibility owed to a foster child.

2. Definitions. As used in this section, the following terms shall have the following meanings:

(a) "Caregiver" shall mean the following person or entity at the time that such person or entity was responsible for the care of the foster child or children:

(i) a foster parent who has been trained in the reasonable and prudent parent standard in accordance with 42 U.S.C. 671 as amended by P.L.113-183 and the regulations of the office of children and family services; or

(ii) the employee of a child care facility operated by an authorized agency that is designated to apply the reasonable and prudent parent standard who has been trained in the reasonable and prudent parent standard in accordance with 42 U.S.C. 671 as amended by P.L. 113-183 and the regulations of the office of children and family services.

(b) "Child" shall mean a child who is in foster care or who was in foster care at the time the reasonable and prudent parent standard was applied.

(c) "Child care facility" shall mean an institution, group residence, group home, agency operated boarding home, or supervised independent living program.

(d) "Reasonable and prudent parent standard" shall mean, in accordance with 42 U.S.C. 675 as amended by P.L. 113-183, the standard characterized by careful and sensible parental decisions that maintain the health, safety, and best interests of a child while at the same time encouraging the emotional and developmental growth of the child that a caregiver shall use when determining whether to allow a child in foster care to participate in extracurricular, enrichment, cultural or social activities.

(e) "Age or developmentally-appropriate" shall mean:

(i) activities or items that are generally accepted as suitable for children of the same chronological age or level of maturity or that are determined to be developmentally-appropriate for a child, based on the development of cognitive, emotional, physical, and behavioral capacities that are typical for an age or age group; and

(ii) in the case of a specific child, activities or items that are suitable for the child based on the developmental stage attained by the child with respect to the cognitive, emotional, physical, and behavioral capacities of the child.

3. Caregivers shall apply the reasonable and prudent parent standard when deciding whether or not to allow a child in foster care to participate in age or developmentally appropriate extracurricular, enrichment, cultural, or social activities. Where such decisions require the input or permission of a local department of social services or a voluntary authorized agency, such department or agency shall also apply the reasonable and prudent parent standard in making a decision about participation in such activities.

4. Whether or not a caregiver is liable for injuries to the child that occur as a result of participation in age or developmentally appropriate extracurricular, enrichment, cultural, or social activities shall be determined based upon whether such decision to allow participation was made in compliance with the standard defined in paragraph (d) of subdivision two of this section and any other factors as required by law. Where such child is injured as a result of the decision to allow participation in such activities, a caregiver shall not be liable for such injuries if the decision to allow such participation was made in compliance with the reasonable and prudent parent standard as set forth herein. Provided however nothing in this section shall otherwise limit the ability of a child to bring an action against a caregiver or any other party whose acts or omissions result in injury to such child. Where a local department of social services or voluntary authorized agency has made or been involved in the decisions under subdivision three of this section, the liability standards for caregivers shall apply to such district or agency. *(Eff.4/4/16,Ch.54,L.2016)*

§383-b. Medical treatment for abused, neglected and destitute children; consent of commissioners.

The local commissioner of social services or the local commissioner of health may give effective consent for medical, dental, health and hospital services for any child who has been found by the family court to be an abused, neglected or destitute child, or who has been taken into or kept in protective custody or removed from the place where he or she is residing, or who has been placed in the custody of such commissioner, pursuant to section four hundred seventeen of this article or section one thousand twenty-two, section one thousand twenty-four, section one thousand twenty-seven, section one thousand ninety-four or section one thousand ninety-five of the family court act.

§383-c. Guardianship and custody of children in foster care.

1. Method. For the purposes of this section, a child in foster care shall mean a child in the care and custody of an authorized agency pursuant to section three hundred eighty-four-a of this title or article three, seven or ten of the family court act. The guardianship of the person and the custody of a child in

foster care under the age of eighteen years may be committed to an authorized agency by a written instrument which shall be known as a surrender, and signed:

(a) if both parents shall then be living, by the parents of such child, or by the surviving parent, if either parent of such child be dead;

(b) if either one of such parents shall have for a period of six months then next preceding abandoned such child as set forth in section three hundred eighty-four-b of this title, by the other of such parents;

(c) if such child is born out of wedlock, by the mother of such child, and by the father of such child, if such father's consent would be required for the child's adoption, pursuant to section one hundred eleven of the domestic relations law;

(d) if both parents of such child are dead, or if such child is born out of wedlock and the mother of such child is dead, by the guardian of the person of such child lawfully appointed, with the approval of the court or officer which appointed such guardian to be entered of record.

2. Terms.

(a) Such guardianship shall be in accordance with the provisions of this article and the instrument shall be upon such terms and subject to such conditions as may be agreed upon by the parties thereto and shall comply with subdivision five of this section; provided, however, that an authorized agency shall not accept a surrender instrument conditioned upon adoption by a particular person, unless such person is a certified or approved foster parent, where the permanency plan for the child is for the child to be adopted by that person or the agency has fully investigated and approved such person as an adoptive parent in accordance with applicable statute and regulations. No such agency shall draw or receive money from public funds for the support of any such child except upon the written order or permit of the social services official of the county or city sought to be charged with the support of such child.

(b) If a surrender instrument designates a particular person or persons who will adopt a child, such person or persons, the child's birth parent or parents, the authorized agency having care and custody of the child and the child's attorney may enter into a written agreement providing for communication or contact between the child and the child's parent or parents on such terms and conditions as may be agreed to by the parties. If a surrender instrument does not designate a particular person or persons who will adopt the child, then the child's birth parent or parents, the authorized agency having care and custody of the child and the child's attorney may enter into a written agreement providing for communication or contact, on such terms and conditions as may be agreed to by the parties. Such agreement also may provide terms and conditions for communication with or contact between the child and the child's biological siblings or half-siblings, if any. If any such sibling or half-sibling is fourteen years of age or older, such terms and conditions shall not be enforceable unless such sibling or half-sibling consents to the agreement in writing. If the court before which the surrender instrument is presented for approval determines that the agreement concerning communication and contact is in the child's best interests, the court shall approve the agreement. If the court does not approve the agreement, the court may nonetheless approve the surrender; provided, however, that the birth parent or parents executing the surrender instrument shall be given the opportunity at that time to withdraw such instrument. Enforcement of any agreement prior to the adoption of the child shall be in accordance with subdivision (b) of section one thousand fifty-five-a of the family court act. Subsequent to the adoption of the child, enforcement of any agreement shall be in accordance with section one hundred twelve-b of the domestic relations law.

3. Judicial surrenders.

(a) A surrender of a child to an authorized agency for the purpose of adoption may be executed and acknowledged before a judge of the family court or a surrogate in this state. If the child being surrendered is in foster care as a result of a proceeding before the family court pursuant to article ten or ten-A of the family court act or section three hundred fifty-eight-a of this chapter, the surrender shall be executed and acknowledged before the family court that exercised jurisdiction over such proceeding and, shall be assigned, wherever practicable, to the judge who last presided over such proceeding. A surrender executed and acknowledged before a court in another state shall satisfy the requirements of this section if it is executed by a resident of the other state before a court of record which has jurisdiction over adoption proceedings in that state, and a certified copy of the transcript of that proceeding, showing compliance with paragraph (b) of this subdivision, is filed as part of the adoption proceeding in this state.

(b) Before a judge or surrogate approves a judicial surrender, the judge or surrogate shall order that notice of the surrender proceeding be given to persons identified in subdivision two of section three hundred eighty-four-c of this title and to such other persons as the judge or surrogate may, in his or her discretion, prescribe. At the time that a parent appears before a judge or surrogate to execute and acknowledge a surrender, the judge or surrogate shall inform such parent of the right to be represented by legal counsel of the parent's own choosing and of the right to obtain supportive counseling and of any right to have counsel assigned pursuant to section two hundred sixty-two of the family court act, section four hundred seven of the surrogate's court procedure act, or section thirty-five of the judiciary law. The judge or surrogate also shall inform the parent of the consequences of such surrender, including informing such parent that the parent is giving up all rights to have custody, visit with, speak with, write to or learn about the child, forever, unless the parties have agreed to different terms pursuant to subdivision two of this section, or, if the parent registers with the adoption information register, as specified in section forty-one hundred thirty-eight-d of the public health law, that the parent may be contacted at any time after the child reaches the age of eighteen years, but only if both the parent and the adult child so choose. The court shall determine whether the terms and conditions agreed to by the parties pursuant to subdivision two of this section are in the child's best interests before approving the surrender. The judge or surrogate shall inform the parent that where a surrender containing conditions has been executed, the parent is obligated to provide the authorized agency with a designated mailing address, as well as any subsequent changes in such address, at which the parent may receive notices regarding any substantial failure of a material condition, unless such notification is expressly waived by a statement written by the parent and appended to or included in such instrument. The judge or surrogate also shall inform the parent that the surrender shall become final and irrevocable immediately upon its execution and acknowledgment. The judge or surrogate shall give the parent a copy of such surrender upon the execution thereof.

4. Extra-judicial surrenders.

(a) In any case where a surrender is not executed and acknowledged before a judge or surrogate pursuant to subdivision three of this section, such surrender shall be executed and acknowledged by the parent, in the presence of at least two witnesses, before a notary public or other officer authorized to take proof of deeds. At least one witness shall be an employee of an authorized agency trained, in accordance with the regulations of the department of children and family services, to receive surrenders. At least one witness shall be a person who is either a licensed master social worker, licensed clinical social worker or an attorney and who is not an employee, volunteer, consultant or agent of or attorney for the authorized agency to which the child is being surrendered. The commissioner of the office of children and family services, after consultation with the chief administrator of the courts, shall promulgate standards to help ensure the impartial selection and independence of such witnesses. Any witness may, if so commissioned, serve as notary under this subdivision.

(b) The authorized agency to which the child was surrendered shall file an application for approval of the extra-judicial surrender with the court in which the adoption proceeding is expected to be filed or, if not known, the family or surrogate's court in the county in which the agency has its principal office. If the child being surrendered is in foster care as a result of a proceeding before the family court pursuant to article ten or ten-A of the family court act or section three hundred fifty-eight-a of this chapter, the application shall be filed in the family court that exercised jurisdiction over such proceeding and, shall be assigned, wherever practicable, to the judge who last presided over such proceeding. The application shall be filed no later than fifteen days after execution of such surrender. The application shall be accompanied by affidavits from all the witnesses before whom the surrender was executed and acknowledged as provided for in paragraph (a) of this subdivision, stating:

(i) the date, time and place where the surrender was executed and acknowledged;

(ii) that the parent was provided with a copy of the surrender;

(iii) that the surrender was read in full to the parent in his or her principal language and the parent was given an opportunity to ask questions and obtain answers regarding the nature and consequences of the surrender, including the consequences of, and procedures to be followed in, cases of a substantial failure of a material condition, if any, contained in the surrender instrument and the obligation to provide the authorized agency with a designated mailing address, as well as any subsequent changes in such address, at which the parent may receive notices regarding any substantial failure of a material condition, unless such notification is expressly waived by a statement written by the parent and appended to or included in such instrument; and

(iv) that the parent executed and acknowledged the surrender.

(c) The authorized agency to which a child is surrendered pursuant to this subdivision must affix an affidavit to the application, by an employee responsible for providing or arranging supportive counseling, which specifies:

(i) when supportive counseling was offered to the parent by the authorized agency;

(ii) whether the parent accepted the offer of supportive counseling; and

(iii) if accepted, when supportive counseling was provided and the nature of such supportive counseling.

(d) Before a judge or surrogate approves an extra-judicial surrender, the judge or surrogate shall order notice to be given to the person who executed the surrender, to persons identified in subdivision two of section three hundred eighty-four-c of this title and to such other persons as the judge or surrogate may, in his or her discretion, prescribe. The petition shall set forth the names and last known addresses of all persons required to be given notice of the proceeding, pursuant to section three hundred eighty-four-c, and there shall be shown by the petition or by affidavit or other proof satisfactory to the court that there are no persons other than those set forth in the petition who are entitled to notice pursuant to such section. No person who has received such notice and been afforded an opportunity to be heard may challenge the validity of a surrender approved pursuant to this subdivision in any other proceeding. Nothing in this section shall be deemed to dispense with the consent to adopt if otherwise required of any person who has not executed the surrender.

(e) The agency to which the child is surrendered promptly shall notify such court of any correspondence or communication received from the parent or a person on the parent's behalf subsequent to the execution of the surrender and prior to a final order of adoption of the child, if such correspondence or communication could reasonably indicate the parent's wish to revoke the surrender.

(f) The court shall enter an order either approving or disapproving the surrender. If the court disapproves the surrender, the surrender shall be deemed a nullity and without force or effect, and the court may direct that any subsequent surrender shall be executed only before the court in accordance with subdivision three of this section.

5. Instrument.

(a) There shall be a form of instrument for a judicial surrender and a form of instrument for an extra-judicial surrender.

(b) The instrument for a judicial surrender and the instrument for an extra-judicial surrender shall be in a form prescribed by the commissioner after consultation with the chief administrator of the courts and shall state in plain language in conspicuous bold print on the first page:

(i) that the parent has the right, before signing the surrender, to speak to a lawyer of her or his own choosing and any other person she or he wishes; to have that lawyer and any other person present with her or him at the time of the signing of the surrender; and has the right to ask the court to appoint a lawyer free of charge if the parent cannot afford to hire one; and has the right to have supportive counseling;

(ii) that the parent is giving up all rights to have custody, visit with, speak with, write to or learn about the child, forever, unless the parties have agreed to different terms pursuant to subdivision two of this section, and unless such terms are written in the surrender, or, if the parent registers with the adoption information register, as specified in section forty-one hundred thirty-eight-d of the public health law, that the parent may be contacted at anytime after the child reaches the age of eighteen years, but only if both the parent and the adult child so choose;

(iii) that the child will be adopted without the parent's consent and without further notice to the parent, and will be adopted by any person that the agency chooses, unless the surrender paper contains the name of the person or persons who will be adopting the child; and

(iv) that the parent cannot be forced to sign the surrender paper, and cannot be punished if he or she does not sign the paper; and would not be subject to any penalty for refusing to sign the surrender.

(c) A surrender instrument for a judicial surrender also shall state in plain language in conspicuous bold print at the beginning thereof that the surrender becomes final and irrevocable immediately upon execution and acknowledgement, and that the parent cannot bring a case in court to revoke the surrender or to regain custody of the child. Where the parties have agreed that the surrender shall be subject to conditions pursuant to subdivision two of this section, the instrument shall further state in plain language that:

(i) the authorized agency shall notify the parent, unless such notice is expressly waived by a statement written by the parent and appended to or included in such instrument, the attorney for the child and the court that approved the surrender within twenty days of any substantial failure of a material condition of the surrender prior to the finalization of the adoption of the child; and

(ii) except for good cause shown, the authorized agency shall file a petition on notice to the parent unless notice is expressly waived by a statement written by the parent and appended to or included in such instrument and the child's attorney in accordance with section one thousand fifty-five-a of the family court act within thirty days of such failure, in order for the court to review such failure and, where necessary, to hold a hearing; provided, however, that, in the absence of such filing, the parent and/or attorney for the child may file such a petition at any time up to sixty days after notification of the failure. Such petition filed by a parent or attorney for the child must be filed prior to the child's adoption; and

(iii) the parent is obligated to provide the authorized agency with a designated mailing address, as well as any subsequent changes in such address, at which the parent may receive notices regarding any substantial failure of a material condition, unless such notification is expressly waived by a statement written by the parent and appended to or included in such instrument. Nothing in this paragraph shall limit the notice on the instrument with respect to a failure to comply with a material condition of a surrender subsequent to the finalization of the adoption of the child.

(d) An extra-judicial surrender instrument also shall state in plain language in conspicuous bold print at the beginning thereof that:

(i) the name and address of the court in which the application for approval of the extra-judicial surrender will be filed;

(ii) that a revocation of the surrender will be effective if it is in writing and postmarked or received by the court named in the surrender within forty-five days of the signing of the surrender; and

(iii) that a revocation of the surrender more than forty-five days after its signing will not be effective if the child has been placed in an adoptive home, and the surrender shall be final and irrevocable and the parent cannot revoke the surrender or bring a case in court to revoke the surrender or regain custody of the child, and that the agency will not notify the parent when the child is placed in an adoptive home, and the parent may lose all rights at the end of the forty-five day period without further notice. Where the parties have agreed that the surrender shall be subject to conditions pursuant to subdivision two of this section, the instrument shall further state in plain language that:

(A) the authorized agency shall notify the parent, unless such notice is expressly waived by a statement written by the parent and appended to or included in such instrument, the law guardian for the child and the court that approved the surrender within twenty days of any substantial failure of a material condition of the surrender prior to the finalization of the adoption of the child; and

(B) except for good cause shown, the authorized agency shall file a petition on notice to the parent unless notice is expressly waived by a statement written by the parent and appended to or included in such instrument and law guardian in accordance with section one thousand fifty-five-a of the family court act within thirty days of such failure in order for the court to review such failure and, where necessary, to hold a hearing; provided, however, that, in the absence of such filing, the parent and/or law guardian for the child may file such a petition at any time up to sixty days after notification of the failure. Such petition filed by a parent or law guardian must be filed prior to the adoption of the child; and

(C) the parent is obligated to provide the authorized agency with a designated mailing address, as well as any subsequent changes in such address, at which the parent may receive notices regarding any substantial failure of a material condition, unless such notice is expressly waived by a statement written by the parent and appended to or included in such instrument. Nothing in this subparagraph shall limit the notice on the instrument with respect to a failure to comply with a material condition of a surrender subsequent to the finalization of the adoption of the child.

(e) Any surrender instrument subject to the provisions of this section shall include an adoption information registry birth parent registration consent form, stating whether or not such biological parent or parents whose consent is subject to the provisions of this section, consents to the receipt of identifying information by the child to be adopted upon registration with the adoption information registry established by section forty-one hundred thirty-eight-c of the public health law and upon the adoptee reaching the age of eighteen. If such consent is made, it shall be revocable by either of the biological parents at any time. The revocation of the consent by one of the parents shall revoke the consent of both parents. The failure of a biological parent to complete the consent form shall have no effect on the finality of the consent to adoption. A copy of the form required by this subdivision, shall be forwarded to the state adoption information registry for inclusion in the records maintained by such registry. Any fees authorized to be charged by the state adoption registry for filing documentation with such registry shall be waived for the form required by this subdivision.

(f) A surrender shall be recorded in the office of the county clerk in the county where the surrender is executed, or where the principal office of such authorized agency is located, in a book which such county clerk shall provide and shall keep under seal. Such record shall be subject to inspection and examination only as provided in subdivisions three and four of section three hundred seventy-two of this title.

(g) Whenever the term surrender, surrender paper or surrender instrument is used in any law relating to the adoption of children in foster care, it shall mean and refer exclusively to the instrument described herein for the commitment of the guardianship of the person and the custody of a child to an authorized agency by the child's parent, parents or guardian, and in no case shall it be deemed to apply to any instrument purporting to commit the guardianship of the person and the custody of a child to any person other than an authorized agency, nor shall such term or the provisions of this section be deemed to apply to any instrument transferring the care and custody of a child to an authorized agency pursuant to section three hundred eighty-four-a of this title.

(h) Upon execution of a surrender instrument, the parent executing the surrender shall provide information to the extent known regarding the other parent, any person to whom the surrendering parent had been married at the time of the conception or birth of the child and any other person who would be entitled to notice of a proceeding to terminate parental rights pursuant to section three hundred eighty-four-c of this title. Such information shall include, but not be limited to, such parent's or person's name, last-known address, social security number, employer's address and any other identifying information. Any information provided pursuant to this paragraph shall be recorded in the uniform case record maintained pursuant to section four hundred nine-f of this article; provided, however, that the failure to provide such information shall not invalidate the surrender.

6. Effect of surrender and revocation.

(a) If the court disapproves the surrender pursuant to subdivision four of this section, or if a revocation of an extra-judicial surrender is mailed and postmarked or otherwise delivered to the court named in the surrender within forty-five days of the execution of the surrender, such surrender shall be deemed a nullity, and the child shall be returned to the care and custody of the authorized agency.

(b) If a revocation of an extra-judicial surrender is mailed and postmarked or otherwise delivered to the court named in the surrender more than forty-five days after its execution and the child has not been placed in an adoptive home, such surrender shall be deemed a nullity, and the child shall be returned to the care and custody of the authorized agency. For the purposes of this subdivision, no child shall be deemed to have been placed in the home of adoptive parents unless the fact of such placement, the date thereof, the date of the agreement pertaining thereto and the names and addresses of the adoptive parents shall have been recorded in a bound volume maintained by the agency for the purpose of recording such information in chronological order. The absence of judicial approval of an extra-judicial surrender shall not revive, extend or toll the period for revocation of such surrender.

(c) In any case in which the authorized agency determines that the persons specified in the surrender will not adopt the child or in any other case of a substantial failure of a material condition prior to the finalization of the adoption of the child, the agency promptly shall notify the parent thereof, unless such notice is expressly waived by a statement written by the parent and appended to or included in such instrument, and shall notify the court and the law guardian for the child within twenty days. In any such case, the authorized agency shall file a petition on notice to the parent unless notice is expressly waived by a statement written by the parent and appended to or included in such instrument and law guardian in accordance with section one thousand fifty-five-a of the family court act, as applicable, within thirty days, except for good cause shown, in order for the court to review such failure and, where necessary, to hold a hearing; provided, however, that, in the absence of such a filing, the parent and/or law guardian for the child may file such a petition at any time up to sixty days after the notification of the failure. Such petition filed by a parent or law guardian must be filed prior to the adoption. Nothing in this paragraph shall limit the rights and remedies, if any, available to the parties and the law guardian with respect to a failure to comply with a material condition of a surrender subsequent to the finalization of the adoption of the child.

(d) Nothing contained in this section shall bar actions or proceedings brought on the ground of fraud, duress or coercion in the execution or inducement of a surrender. No action or proceeding may be maintained by the surrendering parent or guardian for the custody of the surrendered child or to revoke or annul such surrender except as provided herein.

7. Surrenders by persons in foster care. Notwithstanding any other provision of law, a surrender for adoption executed by a parent, parents or guardian who is in foster care shall be executed only before a judge of the family court.

8. Adoption proceeding. (a) Upon the court's order approving the surrender, the attorney for the petitioning authorized agency shall promptly serve upon persons who have been approved by such agency as the child's adoptive parents, notice of entry of the order approving the surrender and advising such persons that they may commence an adoption proceeding. In accordance with the regulations of the department, the authorized agency shall advise such persons of the procedures necessary for adoption of the child. The authorized agency shall cooperate with such persons in the provision of necessary documentation.

(b) The adoptive parent may commence the adoption proceeding in a court of competent jurisdiction in accordance with subdivision three of section one hundred thirteen or subdivision two of section one hundred fifteen of the domestic relations law, as applicable; provided, however, that in the case of an extra-judicial surrender, such proceeding shall be initiated more than forty-five days after the surrender is executed. Commencement of such a proceeding shall not revive, extend or toll the period for revocation of an extra-judicial surrender pursuant to this section.

9. Intervention.

(a) Any person or persons having custody of a child for the purpose of adoption through an authorized agency shall be permitted as a matter of right, as an interested party, to intervene in any proceeding commenced to set aside a surrender purporting to commit a guardianship of the person or custody of a child executed under the provisions of this section. Such intervention may be made anonymously or in the true name of such person.

(b) Any person or persons having custody for more than twelve months through an authorized agency for the purpose of foster care shall be permitted as a matter of right, as an interested party, to intervene in any proceeding commenced to set aside a surrender purporting to commit the guardianship of the person and custody of a child executed under the provisions of this section. Such intervention may be made anonymously or in the true name of such person or persons having custody of the child for the purpose of foster care.

10. Adoption and permanency hearing.

a. Upon acceptance of a judicial surrender or approval of an extra-judicial surrender pursuant to subdivision three or four of this section, the court shall inquire whether any foster parent or parents with whom the child resides, or any relative of the child, or other person, seeks to adopt such child. If such person or persons do seek to adopt such child, such person or persons may submit, and the court shall accept, all such petitions for the adoption of the child, together with an adoption home study, if any, completed by an authorized agency, or disinterested person as such term is defined in subdivision three of section one hundred sixteen of the domestic relations law. The court shall thereafter establish a schedule for completion of other inquiries and investigations necessary to complete review of the adoption of the child and shall immediately set a schedule for completion of the adoption.

b. Upon acceptance of a judicial surrender or approval of an extra-judicial surrender pursuant to subdivision three or four of this section, the court shall schedule an initial freed child permanency hearing pursuant to section one thousand eighty-nine of the family court act. Subsequent permanency hearings shall be held pursuant to section one thousand eighty-nine of the family court act.

§384.   Guardianship and custody of children not in foster care.
1. Method. The guardianship of the person and the custody of a child who
is not in foster care under the age of eighteen years may be committed to an
authorized agency by a written instrument which shall be known as a surrender,
and signed:
(a) if both parents shall then be living, by the parents of such child, or by the
surviving parent, if either parent of such child be dead;
(b) if either one of such parents shall have for a period of six months then
next preceding abandoned such child, by the other of such parents;
(c) if such child is born out of wedlock, by the mother of such child, and by
the father of such child, if such father's consent would be required for the
child's adoption, pursuant to section one hundred eleven of the domestic
relations law;
(d) if both parents of such child are dead, or if such child is born out of
wedlock and the mother of such child is dead by the guardian of the person of
such child lawfully appointed, with the approval of the court or officer which
appointed such guardian to be entered of record.
2. Terms.
(a) Such guardianship shall be in accordance with the provisions of this article
and the instrument shall be upon such terms and subject to such conditions as may
be agreed upon by the parties thereto. The instrument shall recite that the
authorized agency is thereby authorized and empowered to consent to the
adoption of such child in the place and stead of the person signing the instrument,
and may recite that the person signing the instrument waives any notice of such
adoption; provided, however, that an authorized agency shall not accept a
surrender instrument conditioned upon adoption by a particular person, unless the
agency has fully investigated and certified or approved such person as a qualified
adoptive parent. Any surrender instrument subject to the provisions of this section
shall include an adoption information registry birth parent registration consent
form, stating whether or not such biological parent or parents whose consent is
subject to the provisions of this section, consents to the receipt of identifying
information by the child to be adopted, upon registration with the adoption
information registry established by section forty-one hundred thirty-eight-c of the
public health law and upon the adoptee reaching the age of eighteen. If such
consent is made, it shall be revocable by either of the biological parents at any
time. The revocation of the consent by one of the parents shall revoke the consent
of both parents. The failure of a biological parent to complete the consent form
shall have no effect on the finality of the consent to adoption. A copy of the form
required by this subdivision, shall be forwarded to the state adoption information
registry for inclusion in the records maintained by such registry. Any fees
authorized to be charged by the state adoption registry for filing documentation
with such registry shall be waived for the form required by this subdivision. No
such agency shall draw or receive money from public funds for the support of any
such child except upon the written order or permit of the local social services
official of the county or city sought to be charged with the support of such child.
(b) If a surrender instrument designates a particular person or persons who
will adopt a child, such person or persons, the child's birth parent or parents,
the authorized agency having care and custody of the child and the child's
attorney, may enter into a written agreement providing for communication or
contact between the child and the child's parent or parents on such terms and
conditions as may be agreed to by the parties.

If a surrender instrument does not designate a particular person or persons who will adopt the child, then the child's birth parent or parents, the authorized agency having care and custody of the child and the child's attorney, may enter into a written agreement providing for communication or contact, on such terms and conditions as may be agreed to by the parties. Such agreement also may provide terms and conditions for communication with or contact between the child and the child's biological sibling or half-sibling, if any. If any such sibling or half-sibling is fourteen years of age or older, such terms and conditions shall not be enforceable unless such sibling or half-sibling consents to the agreement in writing. If the court before which the surrender instrument is presented for approval determines that the agreement concerning communication and contact is in the child's best interests, the court shall approve the agreement. If the court does not approve the agreement, the court may nonetheless approve the surrender; provided, however, that the birth parent or parents executing the surrender instrument shall be given the opportunity at that time to withdraw such instrument. Enforcement of any agreement prior to the adoption of the child shall be in accordance with subdivision (b) of section one thousand fifty-five-a of the family court act. Subsequent to the adoption of the child, enforcement of any agreement shall be in accordance with section one hundred twelve-b of the domestic relations law.

3. Instrument. The instrument herein provided shall be executed and acknowledged (a) before any judge or surrogate in this state having jurisdiction over adoption proceedings, except that if the child is being surrendered as a result of, or in connection with, a proceeding before the family court pursuant to article ten or ten-A of the family court act, the instrument shall be executed and acknowledged in the family court that exercised jurisdiction over such proceeding and shall be assigned, wherever practicable, to the judge who last presided over such proceeding; or (b) in the presence of one or more witnesses and acknowledged by such witness or witnesses, in the latter case before a notary public or other officer authorized to take proof of deeds, and shall be recorded in the office of the county clerk in the county where such instrument is executed, or where the principal office of such authorized agency is located, in a book which such county clerk shall provide and shall keep under seal. Such record shall be subject to inspection and examination only as provided in subdivisions three and four of section three hundred seventy-two of this title. Notwithstanding any other provision of law, if the parent surrendering the child for adoption is in foster care the instrument shall be executed before a judge of the family court.

Whenever the term surrender or surrender instrument is used in any law relating to the adoption of children who are not in foster care, it shall mean and refer exclusively to the instrument hereinabove described for the commitment of the guardianship of the person and the custody of a child to an authorized agency by his parents, parent or guardian; and in no case shall it be deemed to apply to any instrument purporting to commit the guardianship of the person and the custody of a child to any person other than an authorized agency, nor shall such term or the provisions of this section be deemed to apply to any instrument transferring the care and custody of a child to an authorized agency pursuant to section three hundred eighty-four-a of this chapter.

Any person or persons having custody of a child for the purpose of adoption through an authorized agency shall be permitted as a matter of right, as an interested party, to intervene in any proceeding commenced to set aside a surrender purporting to commit a guardianship of the person or custody of a child executed under the provisions of this section. Such intervention may be made anonymously or in the true name of said person.

Any person or persons having custody for more than twelve months through an authorized agency for the purpose of foster care shall be permitted as a matter of right, as an interested party, to intervene in any proceeding commenced to set aside a surrender purporting to commit the guardianship of the person and custody of a child executed under the provisions of this section. Such intervention may be made anonymously or in the true name of said person or persons having custody of the child for the purpose of foster care.

A copy of such surrender shall be given to such surrendering parent upon the execution thereof. The surrender shall include the following statement: "I, (name of surrendering parent), this ___ day of _____, _____, have received a copy of this surrender. (Signature of surrendering parent)". Such surrendering parent shall so acknowledge the delivery and the date of the delivery in writing on the surrender.

Where the parties have agreed that the surrender shall be subject to conditions pursuant to subdivision two of this section, the instrument shall further state in plain language that:

(i) the authorized agency shall notify the parent, unless such notice is expressly waived by a statement written by the parent and appended to or included in such instrument, the attorney for the child and the court that approved the surrender within twenty days of any substantial failure of a material condition of the surrender prior to the finalization of the adoption of the child; and

(ii) except for good cause shown, the authorized agency shall file a petition on notice to the parent unless notice is expressly waived by a statement written by the parent and appended to or included in such instrument and the child's attorney in accordance with section one thousand fifty-five-a of the family court act within thirty days of such failure, in order for the court to review such failure and, where necessary, to hold a hearing; provided, however, that, in the absence of such filing, the parent and/or attorney for the child may file such a petition at any time up to sixty days after notification of such failure. Such petition filed by a parent or attorney for the child must be filed prior to the child's adoption; and

(iii) the parent is obligated to provide the authorized agency with a designated mailing address, as well as any subsequent changes in such address, at which the parent may receive notices regarding any substantial failure of a material condition, unless such notification is expressly waived by a statement written by the parent and appended to or included in such instrument.

Nothing in this paragraph shall limit the notice on the instrument with respect to a failure to comply with a material condition of a surrender subsequent to the finalization of the adoption of the child.

4. Upon petition by an authorized agency, a judge of the family court, or a surrogate, may approve such surrender, on such notice to such persons as the surrogate or judge may in his or her discretion prescribe. If the child is being surrendered as a result of, or in connection with, a proceeding before the family court pursuant to article ten or ten-A of the family court act, the petition shall be filed in the family court that exercised jurisdiction over such proceeding and shall be assigned, wherever practicable, to the judge who last presided over such proceeding. The petition shall set forth the names and last known addresses of all persons required to be given notice of the proceeding, pursuant to section three hundred eighty-four-c of this title, and there shall be shown by

the petition or by affidavit or other proof satisfactory to the court that there are no persons other than those set forth in the petition who are entitled to notice pursuant to such section. No person who has received such notice and been afforded an opportunity to be heard may challenge the validity of a surrender approved pursuant to this subdivision in any other proceeding. However, this subdivision shall not be deemed to require approval of a surrender by a surrogate or judge for such surrender to be valid.

5. If a duly executed and acknowledged adoption surrender shall so recite, no action or proceeding may be maintained by the surrendering parent or guardian for the custody of the surrendered child or to revoke or annul such surrender where the child has been placed in the home of adoptive parents and more than thirty days have elapsed since the execution of the surrender or where the purpose of such action or proceeding is to return the child to or vest the child's custody in any person other than the parent or guardian who originally executed such surrender. This subdivision shall not bar actions or proceedings brought on the ground of fraud, duress or coercion in the execution or inducement of a surrender.

For the purposes of this subdivision, no child shall be deemed to have been placed in the home of adoptive parents unless the fact of such placement, the date thereof, the date of the agreement pertaining thereto and the names and addresses of the adoptive parents shall have been recorded in a bound volume maintained by the agency for the purpose of recording such information in chronological order.

Where the parties have agreed that the surrender shall be subject to conditions pursuant to subdivision two of this section and where there has been a substantial failure of a material condition prior to the finalization of the adoption of the child, the agency shall notify the parent thereof, unless such notice is expressly waived by a statement written by the parent and appended to or included in such instrument, and shall notify the court and the law guardian for the child within twenty days of such failure. In any such case, the authorized agency shall file a petition on notice to the parent unless notice is expressly waived by a statement written by the parent and appended to or included in such instrument and law guardian in accordance with section one thousand fifty-five-a of the family court act within thirty days of such failure, except for good cause shown, in order for the court to review such failure and, where necessary, to hold a hearing; provided, however, that, in the absence of such a filing, the parent and/or law guardian for the child may file such a petition at any time up to sixty days after notification of the failure. Such a petition filed by a parent or law guardian must be filed prior to the adoption. Nothing in this paragraph shall limit the rights and remedies available to the parties and the law guardian pursuant to section one hundred twelve-b of the domestic relations law with respect to a failure to comply with a material condition of a surrender subsequent to the finalization of the adoption of a child.

6. In an action or proceeding to determine the custody of a child not in foster care surrendered for adoption and placed in an adoptive home or to revoke or annul a surrender instrument in the case of such child placed in an adoptive home, the parent or parents who surrendered such child shall have no right to the custody of such child superior to that of the adoptive parents, notwithstanding that the parent or parents who surrendered the child are fit, competent and able to duly maintain, support and educate the child. The custody of such child shall be awarded solely on the basis of the best interests of the child, and

there shall be no presumption that such interests will be promoted by any particular custodial disposition.

7. Upon acceptance of a judicial surrender or approval of an extra-judicial surrender pursuant to this section, the court shall schedule an initial freed child permanency hearing pursuant to section one thousand eighty-nine of the family court act.

8. Upon execution of a surrender instrument, the parent executing the surrender shall provide information to the extent known regarding the other parent, any person to whom the surrendering parent had been married at the time of the conception or birth of the child and any other person who would be entitled to notice of a proceeding to terminate parental rights pursuant to section three hundred eighty-four-c of this title. Such information shall include, but not be limited to, such parent's or person's name, last-known address, social security number, employer's address and any other identifying information. Any information provided pursuant to this subdivision shall be recorded in the uniform case record maintained pursuant to section four hundred nine-f of this article; provided, however, that the failure to provide such information shall not invalidate the surrender.

§384-a. Transfer of care and custody of children.

1. Method. The care and custody of a child may be transferred by a parent or guardian, and the care of a child may be transferred by any person to whom a parent has entrusted the care of the child, to an authorized agency by a written instrument in accordance with the provisions of this section. Such transfer by a person who is not the child's parent or guardian shall not affect the rights or obligations of the parents or guardian, and such transfer shall be deemed a transfer of the care and custody of the child for the purposes of section three hundred fifty-eight-a of this chapter.

1-a. Prior to accepting a transfer of care and custody, a local social services official shall commence a search to locate any non-respondent parent of the child and shall conduct an immediate investigation to (a) locate relatives of the child, including all of the child's grandparents, all suitable relatives identified by either and any relative identified by a child over the age of five as a relative who plays or has played a significant positive role in his or her life, and to inform them of the opportunity for becoming foster parents or for seeking custody or care of the child, and that the child may be adopted by foster parents if attempts at reunification with the birth parent are not required or are unsuccessful; and to determine whether the child may appropriately be placed with a suitable person related to the child and whether such relative seeks approval as a foster parent pursuant to this chapter for the purposes of providing care for such child, or wishes to provide care and custody for the child until the parent or other person responsible for the care of the child is able to resume custody; and (b) identify minor siblings or half-siblings of the child and to determine whether such siblings or half-siblings have been or are being transferred to the care and custody of such official. Such official shall provide or arrange for the provision of care so as to permit the child and his or her minor siblings or half-siblings to be placed together unless, in the judgment of such official, such placement would be contrary to the best interests of the children; whereupon, such official shall provide or arrange for regular visitation and other forms of regular communication between such children unless, in the judgment of such official, such visitation and communication would be contrary to the best interests of such children. Placement or regular visitation and communication with siblings or half-siblings shall be presumptively in the child's best interests unless such placement or visitation and communication would be contrary to the child's health, safety or welfare, or the lack of geographic proximity precludes or prevents visitation.

1-b. Upon accepting the transfer of care and custody of a child from the parent, guardian or other person to whom care of the child has been entrusted, a local social services official shall obtain information to the extent known from such person regarding the other parent, any person to whom the parent transferring care and custody had been married at the time of the conception or birth of the child and any other person who would be entitled to notice of a proceeding to terminate parental rights pursuant to section three hundred eighty-four-c of this title. Such information shall include, but not be limited to, such parent's or person's name, last-known address, social security number, employer's address and any other identifying information. Any information provided pursuant to this subdivision shall be recorded in the uniform case record maintained pursuant to section four hundred nine-f of this article; provided, however, that the failure to provide such information shall not invalidate the transfer of care and custody.

2. Terms. (a) The instrument shall be upon such terms, for such time and subject to such conditions as may be agreed upon by the parties thereto. The office of children and family services may promulgate suggested terms and conditions for inclusion in such instruments, but shall not require that any particular terms and conditions be included. If the instrument provides that the child is to be returned by the authorized agency on a date certain or upon the occurrence of an identifiable event, such agency shall return such child at such time unless such action would be contrary to court order entered at any time prior to such date or event or within ten days thereafter pursuant to section three hundred eighty-four-b of this title or article six, ten, or ten-A of the family court act or unless and so long as the parent or guardian is unavailable or incapacitated to receive the child. The parent or guardian may, upon written notice to such agency, request return of the child at any time prior to the identified date or event, whereupon such agency may, without court order, return the child or, within ten days after such request, may notify the parent or guardian that such request is denied. If such agency denies or fails to act upon such request, the parent or guardian may seek return of the care and custody of the child by motion in family court for return of such child and order to show cause, or by writ of habeas corpus in the supreme court or family court. If the instrument fails to specify a date or identifiable event upon which such agency shall return such child, such agency shall return the child within twenty days after having received notice that the parent or guardian wishes the child returned, unless such action would be contrary to court order entered at any time prior to the expiration of such twenty day period pursuant to section three hundred eighty-four-b of this title or article six, ten, or ten-A of the family court act. Expenditures by a local social services district for the care and maintenance of a child who has been continued in the care of an authorized agency in violation of the provisions of this subdivision shall not be subject to state reimbursement.

(b) No provisions set forth in any such instrument regarding the right of the parent or guardian to visit the child or to have services provided to the child and to the parent or guardian to strengthen the parental relationship may be terminated or limited by the authorized agency having the care and custody of the child unless: (i) the instrument shall have been amended to so limit or terminate such right, pursuant to subdivision three of this section; or (ii) the right of visitation or to such services would be contrary to or inconsistent with a court order obtained in any proceeding in which the parent or guardian was a party.

(c) The instrument shall state, in lay terms, in conspicuous print of at least eighteen point type:

(i) that the parent or guardian has the right, prior to signing the instrument transferring the care and custody of the child to an authorized agency, to legal representation of the parent's own choosing. The agency shall provide the parent or guardian with a list of attorneys or legal services organizations, if any, which provide free legal services to persons unable to otherwise obtain such services;

(ii) that the parent or guardian has no legal obligation to transfer the care and custody of the child to such official, and will incur no legal sanction for failing to do so;

(iii) that the law permits the instrument to specify a date certain or an identifiable event upon which the child is to be returned, and if no date or event is specified, that the parent or guardian has a right to the return of the child within twenty days of a request for return, unless otherwise ordered by the court; and to otherwise have the child returned in accordance with the terms of the instrument and the provisions of this section;

(iv) that the parent or guardian has a right to supportive services, which shall include preventive and other supportive services authorized to be provided pursuant to the state's consolidated services plan, to visit the child, and to determine jointly with the agency the terms and frequency of visitation;

(v) that the parent or guardian, subject to the terms of the instrument, has an obligation

(A) to visit the child,

(B) to plan for the future of the child,

(C) to meet with and consult with the agency about such plan,

(D) to contribute to the support of the child to the extent of his or her financial ability to do so, and

(E) to inform the agency of any change of name and address;

(vi) that the failure of the parent or guardian to meet the obligations listed in subparagraph (v) could be the basis for a court proceeding for the commitment of the guardianship and custody of the child to an authorized agency thereby terminating parental rights;

(vii) that the parent or guardian has a right to a fair hearing pursuant to section twenty-two of this chapter concerning the agency's failure to permit the parent or guardian to visit the child or to provide supportive services, which shall include preventive and other supportive services authorized to be provided pursuant to the state's consolidated services plan, to the child and to the parent or guardian;

(viii) the amount of money which the parent will periodically contribute to the support of the child and the schedule for such payments, if known.

(ix) that if the child remains in foster care for fifteen of the most recent twenty-two months, the agency may be required by law to file a petition to terminate parental rights.

(d) In any case where a parent who has transferred care and custody of a child to a social services official pursuant to this section informs the social services official that an order or judgment conferring visitation rights relating to the child has been entered by the family court or supreme court or that a written agreement as described in section two hundred thirty-six of the domestic relations law between the parents confers such rights, any instrument executed pursuant to this section shall incorporate the provisions of such order, judgment or agreement to the extent that visitation rights are affected and shall provide for visitation or other rights as required by such order, judgment or agreement. Such incorporation shall not preclude a social services official from exercising his authority pursuant to paragraph (e) or (f) of this subdivision.

(e) Where a social services official opposes incorporation of an order, judgment or agreement described in paragraph (d) of this subdivision, such official may, upon execution of the instrument described in this section and upon notice to the non-custodial parent or grandparent named in such order, judgment or agreement, be heard thereon in a proceeding pursuant to section three hundred fifty-eight-a of this chapter.

(f) Nothing in this section shall be deemed to prohibit a social services official or an attorney for the child, if any, from making an application to modify the terms of a visitation order, incorporated pursuant to this section, for good cause shown, upon notice to all interested parties, or to limit the right of a non-custodial parent or grandparent to seek visitation pursuant to applicable provisions of law.

(g) In the event a child whose care and custody is transferred pursuant to this section is admitted to a hospital operated or licensed by the office of mental health and cannot be returned to the physical custody of his or her parent or guardian upon request because, pursuant to section four hundred of this chapter, the medical director of the facility has not authorized the removal of the child, the child shall nonetheless be deemed to have been returned to the legal care and custody of his or her parent or guardian. Expenditures by a social services district for the care and maintenance of such a child shall be subject to state reimbursement notwithstanding the provisions of section one hundred fifty-three-b of this chapter.

(h) (i) Where a local social services official determines that a child is at significant risk of placement in the care and custody of the local commissioner of social services during the eighteen months immediately following review by such official because the custodial parent or legal guardian of such child is suffering from a progressively chronic or irreversibly fatal illness and it is determined that there is neither a relative nor a close friend identified by the custodial parent or the legal guardian able to assume legal guardianship of the child, the custodial parent or legal guardian shall be assisted by the local social services district in transferring the care and custody of the child to an authorized agency by a written instrument in accordance with the provisions for this section which provides the transfer shall not take effect until the parent or legal guardian dies, becomes debilitated or incapacitated as defined in subdivision one of section seventeen hundred twenty-six of the surrogate's court procedure act.

(ii) Where a local social services official determines that a child is at significant risk of placement in the care and custody of the local commissioner of social services during the eighteen months immediately following a review of such official because the custodial parent or legal guardian is suffering from a progressively chronic or irreversibly fatal illness and there is a relative or close friend identified by the custodial parent or legal guardian who is able and willing to assume care and custody of the child, but who requires foster care services and financial support thereof pursuant to section three hundred ninety-eight-a of this article, the custodial parent or legal guardian shall be assisted by the local social services district in transferring the care and custody of the child to an authorized agency by a written instrument in accordance with the provisions of this section. Such instrument shall provide that the transfer of custody shall not take effect until the parent or legal guardian dies, becomes debilitated or incapacitated as defined in subdivision one of section seventeen hundred twenty-six of the surrogate's court procedure act. If otherwise qualified, the social services official shall assist the person identified to accept care and custody of the child to become certified as a foster parent.

(iii) A local social services official who accepts or proposes to accept the care and custody of a child by means of a written instrument executed pursuant to this paragraph, shall, pursuant to section three hundred fifty-eight-a of this chapter, petition the family court of the county or city in which the local social services official has his or her office to approve such written instrument. A written instrument executed pursuant to this paragraph and approved pursuant to section three hundred fifty-eight-a of this chapter shall be in effect until the court reviews the child's placement pursuant to article ten-A of the family court act. The status of a child subject to such an instrument shall be reviewed by the court pursuant to article ten-A of the family court act.

(iv) Upon receiving a notice from the custodial parent or the legal guardian that the parent or legal guardian is no longer debilitated or incapacitated and that the parent or legal guardian requests the immediate return of the child, the social services district shall return such child to the parent or legal guardian within ten days of receiving notice, except where a contrary court order has been issued pursuant to part two, five or seven of article ten of the family court act.

3. Amendment. (a) The parties to the instrument or anyone acting on their behalf with their consent may amend it by mutual consent but only by a supplemental instrument executed in the same manner as the original instrument. The supplemental instrument shall be attached to, and become part of, the original instrument. The supplemental instrument shall contain the recitation required in paragraph (c) of subdivision two of this section.

(b) The instrument shall also be deemed amended where ordered by the family court pursuant to the provisions of paragraph (d) of subdivision ten of section three hundred fifty-eight-a of this chapter.

4. Execution. The instrument shall be executed in the presence of one or more witnesses and shall include only the provisions, terms and conditions agreed upon by the parties thereto.

5. Records. The instrument shall be kept in a file maintained for that purpose by the agency accepting the care and custody of the child. A copy of the instrument shall be given to the parent or guardian at the time of the execution of the instrument.

6. An instrument executed pursuant to the provisions of this section shall not constitute a remand or commitment pursuant to this chapter.

§384-b. **Guardianship and custody of destitute or dependent children; commitment by court order; modification of commitment and restoration of parental rights.**

1. Statement of legislative findings and intent.

(a) The legislature recognizes that the health and safety of children is of paramount importance. To the extent it is consistent with the health and safety of the child, the legislature further hereby finds that:

(i) it is desirable for children to grow up with a normal family life in a permanent home and that such circumstance offers the best opportunity for children to develop and thrive;

(ii) it is generally desirable for the child to remain with or be returned to the birth parent because the child's need for a normal family life will usually best be met in the home of its birth parent, and that parents are entitled to bring up their own children unless the best interests of the child would be thereby endangered;

(iii) the state's first obligation is to help the family with services to prevent its break-up or to reunite it if the child has already left home; and

(iv) when it is clear that the birth parent cannot or will not provide a normal family home for the child and when continued foster care is not an appropriate plan for the child, then a permanent alternative home should be sought for the child.

(b) The legislature further finds that many children who have been placed in foster care experience unnecessarily protracted stays in such care without being adopted or returned to their parents or other custodians. Such unnecessary stays may deprive these children of positive, nurturing family relationships and have deleterious effects on their development into responsible, productive citizens. The legislature further finds that provision of a timely procedure for the termination, in appropriate cases, of the rights of the birth parents could reduce such unnecessary stays.

It is the intent of the legislature in enacting this section to provide procedures not only assuring that the rights of the birth parent are protected, but also, where positive, nurturing parent-child relationships no longer exist, furthering the best interests, needs, and rights of the child by terminating parental rights and freeing the child for adoption.

2. For the purposes of this section, (a) "child" shall mean a person under the age of eighteen years; and, (b) "parent" shall include an incarcerated parent unless otherwise qualified.

3. (a) The guardianship of the person and the custody of a destitute or dependent child may be committed to an authorized agency, or to a foster parent authorized pursuant to section one thousand eighty-nine of the family court act to institute a proceeding under this section, or to a relative with care and custody of the child, by order of a surrogate or judge of the family court, as hereinafter provided. Where such guardianship and custody is committed to a foster parent or to a relative with care and custody of the child, the family court or surrogate's court shall retain continuing jurisdiction over the parties and the child and may, upon its own motion or the motion of any party, revoke, modify or extend its order, if the foster parent or relative fails to institute a proceeding for the adoption of the child within six months after the entry of the order committing the guardianship and custody of the child to such foster parent or relative. Where the foster parent or relative institutes a proceeding for the adoption of the child and the adoption petition is finally denied or dismissed, the court which committed the guardianship and custody of the child to the foster parent or relative shall revoke the order of commitment. Where the court revokes an order committing the guardianship and custody of a child to a foster parent or relative, it shall commit the guardianship and custody of the child to an authorized agency.

(b) A proceeding under this section may be originated by an authorized agency or by a foster parent authorized to do so pursuant to section one thousand eighty-nine of the family court act or by a relative with care and custody of the child or, if an authorized agency ordered by the court to originate a proceeding under this section fails to do so within the time fixed by the court, by the child's attorney or guardian ad litem on the court's direction.

(c) Where a child was placed or continued in foster care pursuant to article ten, ten-A or ten-C of the family court act or section three hundred fifty-eight-a of this chapter, a proceeding under this section shall be originated in the family court in the county in which the proceeding pursuant to article ten, ten-A or ten-C of the family court act or section three hundred fifty-eight-a of this chapter was last heard and shall be assigned, wherever practicable, to the judge who last heard such proceeding. Where multiple proceedings are commenced under this section concerning a child and one or more siblings or half-siblings of such child, placed or continued in foster care with the same commissioner pursuant to section one thousand fifty-five, one thousand eighty-nine or one thousand ninety-five of the family court act, all of such proceedings may be commenced jointly in the family court in any county which last heard a proceeding under article ten, ten-A or ten-C of the family court act regarding any of the children who are the subjects of the proceedings under this section. In such instances, the case shall be assigned, wherever practicable, to the judge who last presided over such proceeding. In any other case, a proceeding under this section, including a proceeding brought in the surrogate's court, shall be originated in the county where either of the parents of the child reside at the time of the filing of the petition, if known, or, if such residence is not known, in the county in which the authorized agency has an office for the regular conduct of business or in which the child resides at the time of the initiation of the proceeding. To the extent possible, the court shall, when appointing an attorney for the child, appoint an attorney who has previously represented the child.

(c-1) Before hearing a petition under this section, the court in which the termination of parental rights petition has been filed shall ascertain whether the child is under the jurisdiction of a family court pursuant to a placement in a child protective or foster care proceeding or continuation in out-of-home care pursuant to a permanency hearing and, if so, which court exercised jurisdiction over the most recent proceeding. If the court determines that the child is under the jurisdiction of a different family court, the court in which the termination of parental rights petition was filed shall stay its proceeding for not more than thirty days and shall communicate with the court that exercised jurisdiction over the most recent proceeding. The communication shall be recorded or summarized on the record by the court in which the termination of parental rights petition was filed. Both courts shall notify the parties and child's attorney, if any, in their respective proceedings and shall give them an opportunity to present facts and legal argument or to participate in the communication prior to the issuance of a decision on jurisdiction. The court that exercised jurisdiction over the most recent proceeding shall determine whether it will accept or decline jurisdiction over the termination of parental rights petition. This determination of jurisdiction shall be incorporated into an order regarding jurisdiction that shall be issued by the court in which the termination of parental rights petition was filed within thirty days of such filing. If the court that exercised jurisdiction over the most recent proceeding determines that it should exercise jurisdiction over the termination of parental rights petition, the order shall require that the petition shall be transferred to that court forthwith but in no event more than thirty-five days after the filing of the petition. The petition shall be assigned, wherever practicable, to the judge who heard the most recent proceeding. If the court that exercised jurisdiction over the most recent proceeding declines to exercise jurisdiction over the adoption petition, the court in which the termination of parental rights petition was filed shall issue an order incorporating that determination and shall proceed forthwith.

(d) The family court shall have exclusive, original jurisdiction over any proceeding brought upon grounds specified in paragraph (c), (d) or (e) of subdivision four of this section, and the family court and surrogate's court shall have concurrent, original jurisdiction over any proceeding brought upon grounds specified in paragraph (a) or (b) of subdivision four of this section, except as provided in paragraphs (c) and (c-1) of this subdivision.

(e) A proceeding under this section is originated by a petition on notice served upon the child's parent or parents, the attorney for the child's parent or parents and upon such other persons as the court may in its discretion prescribe. Such notice shall inform the parents and such other persons that the proceeding may result in an order freeing the child for adoption without the consent of or notice to the parents or such other persons. Such notice also shall inform the parents and such other persons of their right to the assistance of counsel, including any right they may have to have counsel assigned by the court in any case where they are financially unable to obtain counsel. The petition shall set forth the names and last known addresses of all persons required to be given notice of the proceeding, pursuant to this section and section three hundred eighty-four-c of this title, and there shall be shown by the petition or by affidavit or other proof satisfactory to the court that there are no persons other than those set forth in the petition who are entitled to notice pursuant to the provisions of this section or of section three hundred eighty-four-c of this title. When the proceeding is initiated in family court service of the petition and other process shall be made in accordance with the provisions of section six hundred seventeen of the family court act, and when the proceeding is initiated in surrogate's court, service shall be made in accordance with the provisions of section three hundred seven of the surrogate's court procedure act. When the proceeding is initiated on the grounds of abandonment of a child less than one year of age at the time of the transfer of the care and custody of such child to a local social services official, the court shall take judicial notice of efforts to locate the child's parents or other known relatives or other persons legally responsible pursuant to paragraph (ii) of subdivision (b) of section one thousand fifty-five of the family court act.

(f) In any proceeding under this section in which the surrogate's court has exercised jurisdiction, the provisions of the surrogate's court procedure act shall apply to the extent that they do not conflict with the specific provisions of this section. In any proceeding under this section in which the family court has exercised jurisdiction, the provisions of articles one, two and eleven of the family court act shall apply to the extent that they do not conflict with the specific provisions of this section. In any proceeding under this section, the provisions and limitations of article thirty-one of the civil practice law and rules shall apply to the extent that they do not conflict with the specific provisions of this section. In determining any motion for a protective order, the court shall consider the need of the party for the discovery to assist in the preparation of the case and any potential harm to the child from the discovery. The court shall set a schedule for discovery to avoid unnecessary delay. Any proceeding originated in family court upon the ground specified in paragraph (d) of subdivision four of this section shall be conducted in accordance with the provisions of part one of article six of the family court act.

(g) (i) An order committing the guardianship and custody of a child pursuant to this section shall be granted only upon a finding that one or more of the grounds specified in subdivision four of this section are based upon clear and convincing proof.

(ii) Where a proceeding has been properly commenced under this section by the filing of a petition before the eighteenth birthday of a child, an order committing the guardianship and custody of a child pursuant to this section upon a finding under subdivision four of this section shall be granted after the eighteenth birthday of a child where the child consents to such disposition.

(h) In any proceeding brought upon a ground set forth in paragraph (c) of subdivision four, neither the privilege attaching to confidential communications between husband and wife, as set forth in section forty-five hundred two of the civil practice law and rules, nor the physician-patient and related privileges, as set forth in section forty-five hundred four of the civil practice law and rules, nor the psychologist-client privilege, as set forth in section forty-five hundred seven of the civil practice law and rules, nor the social worker-client privilege, as set forth in section forty-five hundred eight of the civil practice law and rules, shall be a ground for excluding evidence which otherwise would be admissible.

(i) In a proceeding instituted by an authorized agency pursuant to the provisions of this section, proof of the likelihood that the child will be placed for adoption shall not be required in determining whether the best interests of the child would be promoted by the commitment of the guardianship and custody of the child to an authorized agency.

(j) The order and the papers upon which it was granted in a proceeding under this section shall be filed in the court, and a certified copy of such order shall also be filed in the office of the county clerk of the county in which such court is located, there to be recorded and to be inspected or examined in the same manner as a surrender instrument, pursuant to the provisions of section three hundred eighty-four of this chapter.

(k) Where the child is over fourteen years of age, the court may, in its discretion, consider the wishes of the child in determining whether the best interests of the child would be promoted by the commitment of the guardianship and custody of the child.

(*l*) (i) Notwithstanding any other law to the contrary, whenever: the child shall have been in foster care for fifteen months of the most recent twenty-two months; or a court of competent jurisdiction has determined the child to be an abandoned child; or the parent has been convicted of a crime as set forth in subdivision eight of this section, the authorized agency having care of the child shall file a petition pursuant to this section unless based on a case by case determination: (A) the child is being cared for by a relative or relatives; or (B) the agency has documented in the most recent case plan, a copy of which has been made available to the court, a compelling reason for determining that the filing of a petition would not be in the best interest of the child; or (C) the agency has not provided to the parent or parents of the child such services as it deems necessary for the safe return of the child to the parent or parents, unless such services are not legally required; or (D) the parent or parents are incarcerated, or participating in a residential substance abuse treatment program, or the prior incarceration or participation of a parent or parents in a residential substance abuse treatment program is a significant factor in why the child has been in foster care for fifteen of the last twenty-two months, provided that the parent maintains a meaningful role in the child's life based on the criteria set forth in subparagraph (v) of this paragraph and the agency has not documented a reason why it would otherwise be appropriate to file a petition pursuant to this section.

(ii) For the purposes of this section, a compelling reason whereby a social services official is not required to file a petition for termination of parental rights in accordance with subparagraph (i) of this paragraph includes, but is not limited to, where:

(A) the child was placed into foster care pursuant to article three or seven of the family court act and a review of the specific facts and circumstances of the child's placement demonstrate that the appropriate permanency goal for the child is either (1) return to his or her parent or guardian or (2) discharge to independent living;

(B) the child has a permanency goal other than adoption;

(C) the child is fourteen years of age or older and will not consent to his or her adoption;

(D) there are insufficient grounds for filing a petition to terminate parental rights; or

(E) the child is the subject of a pending disposition under article ten of the family court act, except where such child is already in the custody of the commissioner of social services as a result of a proceeding other than the pending article ten proceeding, and a review of the specific facts and circumstances of the child's placement demonstrate that the appropriate permanency goal for the child is discharge to his or her parent or guardian.

(iii) For the purposes of this paragraph, the date of the child's entry into foster care is the earlier of sixty days after the date on which the child was removed from the home or the date the child was found by a court to be an abused or neglected child pursuant to article ten of the family court act.

(iv) In the event that the social services official or authorized agency having care and custody of the child fails to file a petition to terminate parental rights within sixty days of the time required by this section, or within ninety days of a court direction to file a proceeding not otherwise required by this section, such proceeding may be filed by the foster parent of the child without further court order or by the attorney for the child on the direction of the court. In the event of such filing the social services official or authorized agency having care and custody of the child shall be served with notice of the proceeding and shall join the petition.

(v) For the purposes of clause (D) of subparagraph (i) of this paragraph, an assessment of whether a parent maintains a meaningful role in his or her child's life shall be based on evidence, which may include the following: a parent's expressions or acts manifesting concern for the child, such as letters, telephone calls, visits, and other forms of communication with the child; efforts by the parent to communicate and work with the authorized agency, attorney for the child, foster parent, the court, and the parent's attorney or other individuals providing services to the parent, including correctional, mental health and substance abuse treatment program personnel for the purpose of complying with the service plan and repairing, maintaining or building the parent-child relationship; a positive response by the parent to the authorized agency's diligent efforts as defined in paragraph (f) of subdivision seven of this section; and whether the continued involvement of the parent in the child's life is in the child's best interest. In assessing whether a parent maintains a meaningful role in his or her child's life, the authorized agency shall gather input from individuals and agencies in a reasonable position to help make this assessment, including but not limited to, the authorized agency, attorney for the child, parent, child, foster parent or other individuals of importance in the child's life, and parent's attorney or other individuals providing services to the parent, including correctional, mental health and substance abuse treatment program personnel. The court may make an order directing the authorized agency to undertake further steps to aid in completing its assessment.

(Eff.11/16/16,Ch.242,L.2016)

4. An order committing the guardianship and custody of a child pursuant to this section shall be granted only upon one or more of the following grounds:

(a) Both parents of the child are dead, and no guardian of the person of such child has been lawfully appointed; or

(b) The parent or parents, whose consent to the adoption of the child would otherwise be required in accordance with section one hundred eleven of the domestic relations law, abandoned such child for the period of six months immediately prior to the date on which the petition is filed in the court; or

(c) The parent or parents, whose consent to the adoption of the child would otherwise be required in accordance with section one hundred eleven of the domestic relations law, are presently and for the foreseeable future unable, by reason of mental illness or intellectual disability, to provide proper and adequate care for a child who has been in the care of an authorized agency for the period of one year immediately prior to the date on which the petition is filed in the court; or *(Eff.5/25/16,Ch.37,L.2016)*

(d) The child is a permanently neglected child; or

(e) The parent or parents, whose consent to the adoption of the child would otherwise be required in accordance with section one hundred eleven of the domestic relations law, severely or repeatedly abused such child. Where a court has determined that reasonable efforts to reunite the child with his or her parent are not required, pursuant to the family court act or this chapter, a petition to terminate parental rights on the ground of severe abuse as set forth in subparagraph (iii) of paragraph (a) of subdivision eight of this section may be filed immediately upon such determination.

5. (a) For the purposes of this section, a child is "abandoned" by his parent if such parent evinces an intent to forego his or her parental rights and obligations as manifested by his or her failure to visit the child and communicate with the child or agency, although able to do so and not prevented or discouraged from doing so by the agency. In the absence of evidence to the contrary, such ability to visit and communicate shall be presumed.

(b) The subjective intent of the parent, whether expressed or otherwise, unsupported by evidence of the foregoing parental acts manifesting such intent, shall not preclude a determination that such parent has abandoned his or her child. In making such determination, the court shall not require a showing of diligent efforts, if any, by an authorized agency to encourage the parent to perform the acts specified in paragraph (a) of this subdivision.

6. (a) For the purposes of this section, "mental illness" means an affliction with a mental disease or mental condition which is manifested by a disorder or disturbance in behavior, feeling, thinking or judgment to such an extent that if such child were placed in or returned to the custody of the parent, the child would be in danger of becoming a neglected child as defined in the family court act.

(b) For the purposes of this section, "intellectual disability" means subaverage intellectual functioning which originates during the developmental period and is associated with impairment in adaptive behavior to such an extent that if such child were placed in or returned to the custody of the parent, the child would be in danger of becoming a neglected child as defined in the family court act; provided, however, that case law regarding use of the phrase "mental retardation" under this section shall be applicable to the term "intellectual disability". *(Eff.5/25/16,Ch.37,L.2016)*

(c) The legal sufficiency of the proof in a proceeding upon the ground set forth in paragraph (c) of subdivision four of this section shall not be determined until the judge has taken the testimony of a psychologist, or psychiatrist, in accordance with paragraph (e) of this subdivision.

(d) A determination or order upon a ground set forth in paragraph (c) of subdivision four shall in no way affect any other right, or constitute an adjudication of the legal status of the parent.

(e) In every proceeding upon a ground set forth in paragraph (c) of subdivision four the judge shall order the parent to be examined by, and shall take the testimony of, a qualified psychiatrist or a psychologist licensed pursuant to article one hundred fifty-three of the education law as defined in section 730.10 of the criminal procedure law in the case of a parent alleged to be mentally ill or retarded, such psychologist or psychiatrist to be appointed by the court pursuant to section thirty-five of the judiciary law. The parent and the authorized agency shall have the right to submit other psychiatric, psychological or medical evidence. If the parent refuses to submit to such court-ordered examination, or if the parent renders himself unavailable therefor whether before or after the initiation of a proceeding under this section, by departing from the state or by concealing himself therein, the appointed psychologist or psychiatrist, upon the basis of other available information, including, but not limited to, agency, hospital or clinic records, may testify without an examination of such parent, provided that such other information affords a reasonable basis for his opinion.

7. (a) For the purposes of this section, "permanently neglected child" shall mean a child who is in the care of an authorized agency and whose parent or custodian has failed for a period of either at least one year or fifteen out of the most recent twenty-two months following the date such child came into the care of an authorized agency substantially and continuously or repeatedly to maintain contact with or plan for the future of the child, although physically and financially able to do so, notwithstanding the agency's diligent efforts to encourage and strengthen the parental relationship when such efforts will not be detrimental to the best interests of the child. The court shall consider the special circumstances of an incarcerated parent or parents, or of a parent or parents participating in a residential substance abuse treatment program, when determining whether a child is a "permanently neglected child" as defined in this paragraph. In such cases, the court also shall consider the particular constraints, including but not limited to, limitations placed on family contact and the unavailability of social or rehabilitative services to aid in the development of a meaningful relationship between the parent and his or her child, that may impact the parent's ability to substantially and continuously or repeatedly maintain contact with his or her child and to plan for the future of his or her child as defined in paragraph (c) of this subdivision. Where a court has previously determined in accordance with paragraph (b) of subdivision three of section three hundred fifty-eight-a of this chapter or section one thousand thirty-nine-b, subparagraph (A) of paragraph (i) of subdivision (b) of section one thousand fifty-two, paragraph (b) of subdivision two of section seven hundred fifty-four or paragraph (c) of subdivision two of section 352.2 of the family court act that reasonable efforts to make it possible for the child to return safely to his or her home are not required, the agency shall not be required to demonstrate diligent efforts as defined in this section. In the event

that the parent defaults after due notice of a proceeding to determine such neglect, such physical and financial ability of such parent may be presumed by the court.

(b) For the purposes of paragraph (a) of this subdivision, evidence of insubstantial or infrequent contacts by a parent with his or her child shall not, of itself, be sufficient as a matter of law to preclude a determination that such child is a permanently neglected child. A visit or communication by a parent with the child which is of such character as to overtly demonstrate a lack of affectionate and concerned parenthood shall not be deemed a substantial contact.

(c) As used in paragraph (a) of this subdivision, "to plan for the future of the child" shall mean to take such steps as may be necessary to provide an adequate, stable home and parental care for the child within a period of time which is reasonable under the financial circumstances available to the parent. The plan must be realistic and feasible, and good faith effort shall not, of itself, be determinative. In determining whether a parent has planned for the future of the child, the court may consider the failure of the parent to utilize medical, psychiatric, psychological and other social and rehabilitative services and material resources made available to such parent.

(d) For the purposes of this subdivision:

(i) A parent shall not be deemed unable to maintain contact with or plan for the future of the child by reason of such parent's use of drugs or alcohol, except while the parent is actually hospitalized or institutionalized therefor; and

(ii) The time during which a parent is actually hospitalized or institutionalized shall not interrupt, but shall not be part of, a period of failure to maintain contact with or plan for the future of a child.

(e) Notwithstanding the provisions of paragraph (a) of this subdivision, evidence of diligent efforts by an agency to encourage and strengthen the parental relationship shall not be required when:

(i) The parent has failed for a period of six months to keep the agency apprised of his or her location, provided that the court may consider the particular delays or barriers an incarcerated parent or parents, or a parent or parents participating in a residential substance abuse treatment program, may experience in keeping the agency apprised of his or her location; or

(ii) An incarcerated parent has failed on more than one occasion while incarcerated to cooperate with an authorized agency in its efforts to assist such parent to plan for the future of the child, as such phrase is defined in paragraph (c) of this subdivision, or in such agency's efforts to plan and arrange visits with the child as described in subparagraph five of paragraph (f) of this subdivision.

(f) As used in this subdivision, "diligent efforts" shall mean reasonable attempts by an authorized agency to assist, develop and encourage a meaningful relationship between the parent and child, including but not limited to:

(1) consultation and cooperation with the parents in developing a plan for appropriate services to the child and his family;

(2) making suitable arrangements for the parents to visit the child except that with respect to an incarcerated parent, arrangements for the incarcerated parent to visit the child outside the correctional facility shall not be required unless reasonably feasible and in the best interest of the child;

(3) provision of services and other assistance to the parents, except incarcerated parents, so that problems preventing the discharge of the child from care may be resolved or ameliorated;

(4) informing the parents at appropriate intervals of the child's progress, development and health;

(5) making suitable arrangements with a correctional facility and other appropriate persons for an incarcerated parent to visit the child within the correctional facility, if such visiting is in the best interests of the child. When no visitation between child and incarcerated parent has been arranged for or permitted by the authorized agency because such visitation is determined not to be in the best interest of the child, then no permanent neglect proceeding under this subdivision shall be initiated on the basis of the lack of such visitation. Such arrangements shall include, but shall not be limited to, the transportation of the child to the correctional facility, and providing or suggesting social or rehabilitative services to resolve or correct the problems other than incarceration itself which impair the incarcerated parent's ability to maintain contact with the child. When the parent is incarcerated in a correctional facility located outside the state, the provisions of this subparagraph shall be construed to require that an authorized agency make such arrangements with the correctional facility only if reasonably feasible and permissible in accordance with the laws and regulations applicable to such facility; and

(6) providing information which the authorized agency shall obtain from the office of children and family services, outlining the legal rights and obligations of a parent who is incarcerated or in a residential substance abuse treatment program whose child is in custody of an authorized agency, and on social or rehabilitative services available in the community, including family visiting services, to aid in the development of a meaningful relationship between the parent and child. Wherever possible, such information shall include transitional and family support services located in the community to which an incarcerated parent or parent participating in a residential substance abuse treatment program shall return.

8. (a) For the purposes of this section a child is "severely abused" by his or her parent if

(i) the child has been found to be an abused child as a result of reckless or intentional acts of the parent committed under circumstances evincing a depraved indifference to human life, which result in serious physical injury to the child as defined in subdivision ten of section 10.00 of the penal law; or

(ii) the child has been found to be an abused child, as defined in paragraph (iii) of subdivision (e) of section ten hundred twelve of the family court act, as a result of such parent's acts; provided, however, the respondent must have committed or knowingly allowed to be committed a felony sex offense as defined in sections 130.25, 130.30, 130.35, 130.40, 130.45, 130.50, 130.65, 130.67, 130.70, 130.75, 130.80, 130.95 and 130.96 of the penal law and, for the purposes of this section the corroboration requirements contained in the penal law shall not apply to proceedings under this section; or

(iii) (A) the parent of such child has been convicted of murder in the first degree as defined in section 125.27, murder in the second degree as defined in section 125.25, manslaughter in the first degree as defined in section 125.20, or manslaughter in the second degree as defined in section 125.15, and the victim of any such crime was another child of the parent or another child for whose care such parent is or has been legally responsible as defined in subdivision (g) of section one thousand twelve of the family court act, or another parent of the child, unless the convicted parent was a victim of physical, sexual or psychological abuse by the decedent parent and such abuse was a factor in causing the homicide; or has been convicted of an attempt to commit any of the foregoing crimes, and the victim or intended victim was the child or another child of the parent or another child for whose care such parent is or has been legally responsible as defined in subdivision (g) of section one thousand twelve of the family court act, or another parent of the child, unless the convicted parent was a victim of physical, sexual or psychological abuse by the decedent parent and such abuse was a factor in causing the attempted homicide; (B) the parent of such child has been convicted of criminal solicitation as defined in article one hundred, conspiracy as defined in article one hundred five or criminal facilitation as defined in article one hundred fifteen of the penal law for conspiring, soliciting or facilitating any of the foregoing crimes, and the victim or intended victim was the child or another child of the parent or another child for whose care such parent is or has been legally responsible; (C) the parent of such child has been convicted of assault in the second degree as defined in section 120.05, assault in the first degree as defined in section 120.10 or aggravated assault upon a person less than eleven years old as defined in section 120.12 of the penal law, and the victim of any such crime was the child or another child of the parent or another child for whose care such parent is or has been legally responsible; or has been convicted of an attempt to commit any of the foregoing crimes, and the victim or intended victim was the child or another child of the parent or another child for whose care such parent is or has been legally responsible; or (D) the parent of such child has been convicted under the law in any other jurisdiction of an offense which includes all of the essential elements of any crime specified in clause (A), (B) or (C) of this subparagraph; and

(iv) the agency has made diligent efforts to encourage and strengthen the parental relationship, including efforts to rehabilitate the respondent, when such efforts will not be detrimental to the best interests of the child, and such efforts have been unsuccessful and are unlikely to be successful in the foreseeable future. Where a court has previously determined in accordance with this chapter or the family court act that reasonable efforts to make it possible for the child to return safely to his or her home are not required, the agency shall not be required to demonstrate diligent efforts as set forth in this section.

(b) For the purposes of this section a child is "repeatedly abused" by his or her parent if:

(i) the child has been found to be an abused child, (A) as defined in paragraph (i) of subdivision (e) of section ten hundred twelve of the family court act, as a result of such parent's acts; or (B) as defined in paragraph (iii) of subdivision (e) of section ten hundred twelve of the family court act, as a result of such parent's acts; provided, however, the respondent must have committed or knowingly allowed to be committed a felony sex offense as defined in sections 130.25, 130.30, 130.35, 130.40, 130.45, 130.50, 130.65, 130.67, 130.70, 130.75, 130.80, 130.95 and 130.96 of the penal law; and

(ii) (A) the child or another child for whose care such parent is or has been legally responsible has been previously found, within the five years immediately preceding the initiation of the proceeding in which such abuse is found, to be an abused child, as defined in paragraph (i) or (iii) of subdivision (e) of section ten hundred twelve of the family court act, as a result of such parent's acts; provided, however, in the case of a finding of abuse as defined in paragraph (iii) of subdivision (e) of section ten hundred twelve of the family court act the respondent must have committed or knowingly allowed to be committed a felony sex offense as defined in sections 130.25, 130.30, 130.35, 130.40, 130.45, 130.50, 130.65, 130.67, 130.70, 130.75 and 130.80 of the penal law, or (B) the parent has been convicted of a crime under section 130.25, 130.30, 130.35, 130.40, 130.45, 130.50, 130.65, 130.67, 130.70, 130.75 or 130.80 of the penal law against the child, a sibling of the child or another child for whose care such parent is or has been legally responsible, within the five year period immediately preceding the initiation of the proceeding in which abuse is found; and

(iii) the agency has made diligent efforts, to encourage and strengthen the parental relationship, including efforts to rehabilitate the respondent, when such efforts will not be detrimental to the best interests of the child, and such efforts have been unsuccessful and are unlikely to be successful in the foreseeable future. Where a court has previously determined in accordance with this chapter or the family court act that reasonable efforts to make it possible for the child to return safely to his or her home are not required, the agency shall not be required to demonstrate diligent efforts as set forth in this section.

(c) Notwithstanding any other provision of law, the requirements of paragraph (g) of subdivision three of this section shall be satisfied if one of the findings of abuse pursuant to subparagraph (i) or (ii) of paragraph (b) of this subdivision is found to be based on clear and convincing evidence.

(d) A determination by the court in accordance with article ten of the family court act based upon clear and convincing evidence that the child was a severely abused child as defined in subparagraphs (i) and (ii) of paragraph (a) of this subdivision shall establish that the child was a severely abused child in accordance with this section. Such a determination by the court in accordance with article ten of the family court act based upon a fair preponderance of evidence shall be admissible in any proceeding commenced in accordance with this section.

(e) A determination by the court in accordance with article ten of the family court act based upon clear and convincing evidence that a child was abused as defined in paragraph (i) of subdivision (e) of section ten hundred twelve of the family court act, as a result of such parent's acts; or (B) as defined in paragraph (iii) of subdivision (e) of section ten hundred twelve of the family court act, as a result of such parent's acts; provided, however, the respondent must have committed or knowingly allowed to be committed a felony sex offense as defined in sections 130.25, 130.30, 130.35, 130.40, 130.45, 130.50, 130.65, 130.67, 130.70, 130.75 and 130.80 of the penal law shall establish that the child was an abused child for the purpose of a determination as required by subparagraph (i) or (ii) of paragraph (b) of this subdivision. Such a determination by the court in accordance with article ten of the family court act based upon a fair preponderance of evidence shall be admissible in any proceeding commenced in accordance with this section.

(f) Upon a finding pursuant to paragraph (a) or (b) of this subdivision that the child has been severely or repeatedly abused by his or her parent, the court shall enter an order of disposition either (i) committing the guardianship and custody of the child, pursuant to this section, or (ii) suspending judgment in accordance with section six hundred thirty-three of the family court act, upon a further finding, based on clear and convincing, competent, material and relevant evidence introduced in a dispositional hearing, that the best interests of the child require such commitment or suspension of judgment. Where the disposition ordered is the commitment of guardianship and custody pursuant to this section, an initial freed child permanency hearing shall be completed pursuant to section one thousand eighty-nine of the family court act.

9. Nothing in this section shall be construed to terminate, upon commitment of the guardianship and custody of a child to an authorized agency or foster parent, any rights and benefits, including but not limited to rights relating to contact with siblings, inheritance, succession, social security, insurance and wrongful death action claims, possessed by or available to the child pursuant to any other provision of law. For purposes of this section, "siblings" shall include half-siblings and those who would be deemed siblings or half-siblings but for the termination of parental rights or death of a parent. Notwithstanding any other provision of law, a child committed to the custody and guardianship of an authorized agency pursuant to this section shall be deemed to continue in foster care until such time as an adoption or another planned permanent living arrangement is finalized. Where the disposition ordered is the commitment of guardianship and custody pursuant to this section, an initial freed child permanency hearing shall be held pursuant to section one thousand eighty-nine of the family court act. *(Eff.11/16/16,Ch.242,L.2016)*

10. Upon the court's order transferring custody and guardianship to the commissioner, the attorney for the petitioning authorized agency shall promptly serve upon the persons who have been approved by such agency as the child's adoptive parents, notice of entry of such order and advise such persons that an adoption proceeding may be commenced. In accordance with the regulations of the department, the authorized agency shall advise such persons of the procedures necessary for adoption of the child. The authorized agency shall cooperate with such persons in the provision of necessary documentation.

11. Upon the entry of an order committing the guardianship and custody of a child pursuant to this section, the court shall inquire whether any foster parent or parents with whom the child resides, or any relative of the child, or other person, seeks to adopt such child. If such person or persons do seek to adopt such child, such person or persons may submit, and the court shall accept, all such petitions for the adoption of the child, together with an adoption home study, if any, completed by an authorized agency or disinterested person as such term is defined in subdivision three of section one hundred sixteen of the domestic relations law. The court shall thereafter establish a schedule for completion of other inquiries and investigations necessary to complete review of the adoption of the child and shall immediately set a schedule for completion of the adoption.

12. If the court determines to commit the custody and guardianship of the child pursuant to this section, or if the court determines to suspend judgement pursuant to section six hundred thirty-three of the family court act, the court in its order shall determine if there is any parent to whom notice of an adoption would be required pursuant to section one hundred eleven-a of the domestic relations law. In its order the court shall indicate whether such person or persons were given notice of the proceeding and whether such person or persons appeared. Such determinations shall be conclusive in all subsequent proceedings relating to the custody, guardianship or adoption of the child.

13. A petition to modify a disposition of commitment of guardianship and custody in order to restore parental rights may be brought in accordance with part one-A of article six of the family court act where the conditions enumerated in section six hundred thirty-five of such part have been met.

§384-c.   Notice in certain proceedings to fathers of children born out-of-wedlock.

1. Notwithstanding any inconsistent provision of this or any other law, and in addition to the notice requirements of any law pertaining to persons other than those specified in subdivision two of this section, notice as provided herein shall be given to the persons specified in subdivision two of this section of any proceeding initiated pursuant to sections three hundred fifty-eight-a, three hundred eighty-four, and three hundred eighty-four-b of this chapter, involving a child born out-of-wedlock. Persons specified in subdivision two of this section shall not include any person who has been convicted of one or more of the following sexual offenses in this state or convicted of one or more offenses in another jurisdiction which, if committed in this state, would constitute one or more of the following offenses, when the child who is the subject of the proceeding was conceived as a result: (A) rape in first or second degree; (B) course of sexual conduct against a child in the first degree; (C) predatory sexual assault; or (D) predatory sexual assault against a child.

2. Persons entitled to notice, pursuant to subdivision one of this section, shall include:

(a) any person adjudicated by a court in this state to be the father of the child;

(b) any person adjudicated by a court of another state or territory of the United States to be the father of the child, when a certified copy of the court order has been filed with the putative father registry, pursuant to section three hundred seventy-two-c of this chapter;

(c) any person who has timely filed an unrevoked notice of intent to claim paternity of the child, pursuant to section three hundred seventy-two-c of this chapter;

(d) any person who is recorded on the child's birth certificate as the child's father;

(e) any person who is openly living with the child and the child's mother at the time the proceeding is initiated or at the time the child was placed in the care of an authorized agency, and who is holding himself out to be the child's father;

(f) any person who has been identified as the child's father by the mother in written, sworn statement;

(g) any person who was married to the child's mother within six months subsequent to the birth of the child and prior to the execution of a surrender instrument or the initiation of a proceeding pursuant to section three hundred eighty-four-b; and

(h) any person who has filed with the putative father registry an instrument acknowledging paternity of the child, pursuant to section 4-1.2 of the estates, powers and trusts law.

3. The provisions of this section shall not apply to persons entitled to notice pursuant to section one hundred eleven of the domestic relations law. The sole purpose of notice under this section shall be to enable the person served pursuant to subdivision two to present evidence to the court relevant to the best interests of the child. In any proceeding brought upon the ground specified in paragraph (d) of subdivision four of section three hundred eighty-four-b, a person served pursuant to this section may appear and present evidence only in the dispositional hearing.

4. Notice under this section shall be given at least twenty days prior to the proceeding by delivery of a copy of the petition and notice to the person. Upon

a showing to the court, by affidavit or otherwise, on or before the date of the proceeding or within such further time as the court may allow, that personal service cannot be effected at the person's last known address with reasonable effort, notice may be given, without prior court order therefor, at least twenty days prior to the proceeding by registered or certified mail directed to the person's last known address or, where the person has filed a notice of intent to claim paternity pursuant to section three hundred seventy-two-c, to the address last entered therein. Notice by publication shall not be required to be given to a person entitled to notice pursuant to the provisions of this section.

5. A person may waive his right to notice under this section by written instrument subscribed by him and acknowledged or proved in the manner required for the execution of a surrender instrument pursuant to section three hundred eighty-four of this chapter.

6. The notice given to persons pursuant to this section shall inform them of the time, date, place and purpose of the proceeding and shall also apprise such persons that their failure to appear shall constitute a denial of their interest in the child which denial may result, without further notice, in the transfer or commitment of the child's care, custody or guardianship or in the child's adoption in this or any subsequent proceeding in which such care, custody or guardianship or adoption may be at issue.

7. No order of the court in any proceeding pursuant to section three hundred fifty-eight-a, three hundred eighty-four or three hundred eighty-four-b of this chapter or in any subsequent proceeding involving the child's custody, guardianship or adoption shall be vacated, annulled or reversed upon the application of any person who was properly served with notice in accordance with this section but failed to appear, or who waived notice pursuant to subdivision five. Nor shall any order of the court in any proceeding involving the child's custody, guardianship or adoption be vacated, annulled or reversed upon the application of any person who was properly served with notice in accordance with this section in any previous proceeding in which the court determined that the transfer or commitment of the child's care, custody or guardianship to an authorized agency was in the child's best interests.

§385. Orders; prohibiting placing out or boarding out; removal.

1. Prohibiting placing out or boarding out. Whenever the commissioner shall decide that any disposition of a child under this title has been made for purposes of gain, or without due inquiry as to the character and reputation of the person with whom such child is placed, or in such manner that such child is subjected to cruel or improper treatment or neglect or immoral surroundings, or in such manner that the religious faith of the child is not preserved and protected as provided by this title, the commissioner may issue an order prohibiting such an authorized agency, association, corporation, institution, society or other organization from thereafter placing out or boarding out any child. No such order shall be issued until after an opportunity to be heard before the commissioner or his designee and after reasonable notice has been given, with a copy of the charge. A full record of the proceedings and decision on such hearing shall be kept by the department. Any such order issued by the commissioner may be revoked by the commissioner.

2. Whenever the commissioner shall find a minor

(a) placed out or boarded out in a home which is unsuitable or has no license or certificate, or

(b) cared for under a certificate or license but neglected or without suitable care or protection, he may order its removal within thirty days by the agency which placed it and if such order cannot be served upon such agency, it may be addressed to the public board, commission, or officer of the county charged with the care of such child. If such child is not removed within the specified time, the matter may be brought before the children's court or other court having jurisdiction, for adjudication and disposition.

3. Review of orders. Any person, agency, association, corporation, institution, society or other organization, aggrieved by the decision of the commissioner in making any order pursuant to the provisions of this title, may institute, in the judicial district in which the applicant resides or has its chief office, a proceeding under article seventy-eight of the civil practice law and rules in which the reasonableness of such decision shall be subject to review.

§386. Visitation; inspection and supervision.

1. The board or the department is authorized to visit, in its discretion, any minor under the age of twenty-one years committed, placed out or boarded out and not legally adopted or in the custody of a legal guardian.

2. The board or the department is authorized to visit, in its discretion, any home or place where a child or children are received, boarded or kept under a license or certificate whether or not such children are maintained as public charges. Every licensed home shall, if practicable, be visited by the department at least four times in each year.

§387. *Ineligibility for public foster care funds; fiscal penalties.

1. The office of children and family services shall, by regulation, promulgate standards to determine that an authorized agency, or one or more of its programs or facilities, is ineligible to receive public foster care funds or should be assessed a fiscal penalty. Such standards shall include the following:

(a) lack of public need, including but not limited to geographic or programmatic need, for the agency or one or more of its programs or facilities;

(b) failure of the agency to promote the placement of children in permanent, safe family homes through return to the children's own families or through adoption, or other appropriate objectives for children, as measured by such factors as length of stay in foster care for children with similar personal and family characteristics; and

(c) a pattern or practice of repeated violation of the provisions of this chapter or of the regulations of the office of children and family services promulgated thereunder.

2. A determination of ineligibility to receive public foster care funds or the assessment of a fiscal penalty shall be made upon a finding of substantial noncompliance with one or more of the standards developed and adopted pursuant to subdivision one of this section. Such findings and determination shall be made in accordance with the hearing procedures set forth in section four hundred sixty-d of this chapter relating to the revocation, suspension or limiting of operating certificates. Such determination shall be subject to judicial review in accordance with article seventy-eight of the civil practice law and rules.   *Effective until June 30, 2017*

*Public foster care funds; ineligibility. 1. The department shall, by regulation, promulgate standards to determine that an authorized agency, or one or more of its programs or facilities, is ineligible to receive public foster care funds. Such standards shall include the following:

(a) lack of public need, including but not limited to geographic or programmatic need, for the agency or one or more of its programs or facilities;

(b) failure of the agency to promote the placement of children in permanent family homes through return to the children's own families or through adoption, or other appropriate objectives for children, as measured by such factors as length of stay in foster care for children with similar personal and family characteristics; and

(c) a pattern or practice of repeated violation of the provisions of this chapter or of the regulations of the department promulgated thereunder which have occasioned the denial of reimbursement pursuant to section one hundred fifty-three-d or three hundred ninety-eight-b of this chapter.

Such standards shall be developed with the participation of the child welfare standards advisory council established pursuant to section four hundred nine-h of this chapter and in consultation with public and voluntary authorized agencies, citizens' groups and concerned individuals and organizations including the state council on children and families.

2. A determination of ineligibility to receive public foster care funds shall be made upon a finding of substantial noncompliance with one or more of the standards developed and adopted pursuant to subdivision one of this section. Such findings and determination shall be made in accordance with the hearing procedures set forth in section four hundred sixty-d of this chapter relating to the revocation, suspension or limiting of operating certificates. Such determination shall be subject to judicial review in accordance with article seventy-eight of the civil practice law and rules.   *(Effective June 30, 2017)

3. A determination of ineligibility to receive public foster care funds shall specify whether it applies to the agency generally or to a particular program or facility of the agency.

4. A social services official shall not purchase foster care from any authorized agency, or program or facility thereof, which has been determined to be ineligible to receive public foster care funds in accordance with the provisions of this section. Any contract between a social services district and an authorized agency shall be deemed null and void to the extent that it is inconsistent with the provisions of this subdivision.

5. The commissioner shall report forthwith in writing, to the governor, the temporary president of the senate and the speaker of the assembly with respect to each case in which a determination of ineligibility to receive public foster care funds has been made pursuan to this section. Such report shall contain the name of the agency and the reason or reasons for the determination of ineligibility.

*6. Any fiscal penalty received by the office of children and family services pursuant to this section shall be deposited to the credit of the children and family services quality enhancement fund established pursuant to section ninety-seven-yyy of the state finance law.   *(Repealed June 30, 2017)

§388. Special charters.

The power and authority given to agencies, associations, corporations, institutions and societies in their charters shall not be abrogated or nullified, except as the same are in conflict with this title.

§389. Penalty for violations.

1. Except as hereinafter provided, any person, corporation, agency, society, institution or other organization, wilfully violating this title, other than section

three hundred ninety-g of this title, or failing to comply with any order which the department is authorized under this title to make, shall be guilty of a misdemeanor.

2. (a) Any person, corporation, society, institution or other organization who or which violates the provisions of subdivision six of section three hundred seventy-four of this chapter shall be guilty of a misdemeanor, for the first such offense. Any person, corporation, society, institution or other organization who or which violates the provisions of subdivision six of section three hundred seventy-four of this chapter, after having been once convicted of violating such provisions, shall be guilty of a felony.

(b) Notwithstanding the provisions of paragraph (a) of this subdivision, any person, corporation, society, institution or other organization who or which violates subdivision six of section three hundred seventy-four of this title, where such unlawful compensation or thing of value accepted or received exceeds five thousand dollars in value, shall be guilty of a class E felony as defined in the penal law. Any person, corporation, society, institution, or other organization who or which violates subdivision six of section three hundred seventy-four of this title, where such unlawful compensation or thing of value accepted or received exceeds five thousand dollars in value, after having been previously convicted of violating subdivision six of section three hundred seventy-four of this title, shall be guilty of a class D felony as defined in the penal law.

§390. Child day care; license or registration required.
1. Definitions. (a) (i) "Child day care" shall mean care for a child on a regular basis provided away from the child's residence for less than twenty-four hours per day by someone other than the parent, step-parent, guardian, or relative within the third degree of consanguinity of the parents or step-parents of such child.

(ii) Child day care shall not refer to care provided in:

(A) a day camp, as defined in the state sanitary code;

(B) an after-school program operated for the purpose of religious education, sports, or recreation;

(C) a facility:

(1) providing day services under an operating certificate issued by the department;

(2) providing day treatment under an operating certificate issued by the office of mental health or office of mental retardation and developmental disabilities; or

(D) a kindergarten, pre-kindergarten, or nursery school for children three years of age or older, or after-school program for children operated by a public school district or by a private school or academy which is providing elementary or secondary education or both, in accordance with the compulsory education requirements of the education law, provided that the kindergarten, pre-kinder-garten, nursery school, or after school program is located on the premises or campus where the elementary or secondary education is provided.

(b) "Child day care provider" shall mean any individual, association, corporation, partnership, institution or agency whose activities include providing child day care or operating a home or facility where child day care is provided.

(c) "Child day care center" shall mean any program or facility caring for children for more than three hours per day per child in which child day care is provided by a child day care provider except those programs operating as a group family day care home as such term is defined in paragraph (d) of this subdivision, a family day care home, as such term is defined in paragraph (e) of this subdivision, and a school-age child care program, as such term is defined in paragraph (f) of this subdivision.

(d) "Group family day care home" shall mean a program caring for children for more than three hours per day per child in which child day care is provided in a family home for seven to twelve children of all ages, except for those programs operating as a family day care home, as such term is defined in paragraph (e) of this subdivision, which care for seven or eight children. A group family day care provider may provide child day care services to four additional children if such additional children are of school age and such children receive services only before or after the period such children are ordinarily in school or during school lunch periods, or school holidays, or during those periods of the year in which school is not in session. There shall be one caregiver for every two children under two years of age in the group family home. A group family day care home must have at least one assistant to the operator present when child day care is being provided to seven or more children when none of the children are school age, or nine or more children when at least two of the children are school age and such children receive services only before or after the period such children are ordinarily in school or during school lunch periods, or school holidays, or during those periods of the year in which school is not in session. This assistant shall be selected by the group family day care operator and shall meet the qualifications established for such position by the regulations of the office of children and family services.

(e) "Family day care home" shall mean a program caring for children for more than three hours per day per child in which child day care is provided in a family home for three to six children. There shall be one caregiver for every two children under two years of age in the family day care home. A family day care provider may, however, care for seven or eight children at any one time if no more than six of the children are less than school age and the school-aged children receive care primarily before or after the period such children are ordinarily in school, during school lunch periods, on school holidays, or during those periods of the year in which school is not in session in accordance with the regulations of the office of children and family services and the office inspects such home to determine whether the provider can care adequately for seven or eight children.

(f) "School age child care" shall mean a program caring for more than six school-aged children who are under thirteen years of age or who are incapable of caring for themselves. Such programs shall be in operation consistent with the local school calendar. School age child care programs shall offer care during the school year to an enrolled group of children at a permanent site before or after the period children enrolled in such program are ordinarily in school or during school lunch periods and may also provide such care on school holidays and those periods of the year in which school is not in session.

2. (a) Child day care centers caring for seven or more children and group family day care programs, as defined in subdivision one of this section, shall obtain a license from the office of children and family services and shall operate in accordance with the terms of such license and the regulations of such office. Initial licenses shall be valid for a period of up to two years; subsequent licenses shall be valid for a period of up to four years so long as the provider

remains substantially in compliance with applicable law and regulations during such period.

(b) Family day care homes, child day care centers caring for at least three but fewer than seven children, and school-age child care programs shall register with the department and shall operate in compliance with the regulations of the department.

(c) Any child day care provider not required to obtain a license pursuant to paragraph (a) of this subdivision or to register with the department pursuant to paragraph (b) of this subdivision may register with the department.

(d) (i) The office of children and family services shall promulgate regulations for licensure and for registration of child day care pursuant to this section. Procedures for obtaining a license or registration or renewing a license shall include a satisfactory inspection of the facility by the office of children and family services prior to issuance of the license or registration or renewal of the license.

(ii) (A) Initial registrations shall be valid for a period of up to two years, subsequent registrations shall be valid for a period of up to four years so long as the provider remains substantially in compliance with applicable law and regulations during such period.

(B) After initial registration by the child day care provider, the office of children and family services shall not accept any subsequent registration by such provider, unless:

(1) such provider has met the training requirements set forth in section three hundred ninety-a of this title;

(2) such provider has met the requirements of section three hundred ninety-b of this title relating to criminal history screening;

(3) such provider has complied with the requirements of section four hundred twenty-four-a of this article; and

(4) the office of children and family services has received no complaints about the home, center, or program alleging statutory or regulatory violations, or, having received such complaints, the office of children and family services has determined, after inspection pursuant to paragraph (a) of subdivision three of this section, that the home, center, or program is operated in compliance with applicable statutory and regulatory requirements.

(C) Where the office of children and family services has determined that a registration should not be continued because the requirements of clause (B) of this subparagraph have not been satisfied, the office of children and family services may terminate the registration. If the office of children and family services does not terminate the registration, the office of children and family services shall inspect the home or program before acknowledging any subsequent registration. Where the home or program has failed to meet the requirements of this section, the office of children and family services may reject any subsequent registration of a provider. Nothing herein shall prohibit the office of children and family services from terminating or suspending registration pursuant to subdivision ten of this section where the office of children and family services determines that termination or suspension is necessary.

(iv) Child day care providers who have been issued a license shall openly display such license in the facility or home for which the license is issued. Child day care providers who have registered with the department shall provide proof of registration upon request.

(e) Notwithstanding any other provision of this section, where a child is cared for by a parent, guardian or relative within the third degree of consanguinity of the parent of such child and such person simultaneously provides child day care for other children, only the other children shall be considered in determining whether such person must be registered or licensed, provided that such person is not caring, in total, for more than eight children.

2-a. (a) The office of children and family services shall promulgate regulations which establish minimum quality program requirements for licensed and registered child day care homes, programs and facilities. Such requirements shall include but not be limited to (i) the need for age appropriate activities, materials and equipment to promote cognitive, educational, social, cultural, physical, emotional, language and recreational development of children in care in a safe, healthy and caring environment (ii) principles of childhood development (iii) appropriate staff/child ratios for family day care homes, group family day care homes, school age day care programs and day care centers, provided however that such staff/child ratios shall not be les stringent than applicable staff/child ratios as set forth in part four hundred fourteen, four hundred sixteen, four hundred seventeen or four hundred eighteen of title eighteen of the New York code of rules and regulations as of January first, two thousand (iv) appropriate levels of supervision of children in care (v) minimum standards for sanitation, health, infection control, nutrition, buildings and equipment, safety, security procedures, first aid, fire prevention, fire safety, evacuation plans and drills, prevention of child abuse and maltreatment, staff qualifications and training, record keeping, and child behavior management.

(b) The use of electronic monitors as a sole means of supervision of children in day care shall be prohibited, except that electronic monitors may be used in family day care homes and group family day care homes as an indirect means of supervision where the parents of any child to be supervised have agreed in advance to the use of such monitors as an indirect means of supervision and the use of such monitors is restricted to situations where the children so supervised are sleeping.

(c) No child less than six weeks of age may be cared for by a licensed or registered day care provider, except in extenuating circumstances where prior approval for care of such children has been given by the office of children and family services. Extenuating circumstances for the purposes of this section shall include but not be limited to the medical or health needs of the parent or child, or the economic hardship of the parent.

3. (a) The office of children and family services may make announced or unannounced inspections of the records and premises of any child day care provider, whether or not such provider has a license from, or is registered with, the office of children and family services. The office of children and family services shall make unannounced inspections of the records and premises of any child day care provider within fifteen days after the office of children and family services receives a complaint that, if true, would indicate such provider does not comply with the regulations of the office of children and family services or with statutory requirements. If the complaint indicates that there may be imminent danger to the children, the office of children and family services shall investigate the complaint no later than the next day of operation of the provider. The office of children and family services may provide for inspections through the purchase of services.

(b) Where inspections have been made and violations of applicable statutes or regulations have been found, the office of children and family services shall within ten days advise the child day care provider in writing of the violations and require the provider to correct such violations. The office of children and family services may act pursuant to subdivisions ten and eleven of this section.

(c) (i) The office of children and family services shall establish a toll-free statewide telephone number to receive inquiries about child day care homes, programs and facilities and complaints of violations of the requirements of this section or regulations promulgated under this section. The office of children and family services shall develop a system for investigation, which shall include inspection, of such complaints. The office of children and family services may provide for such investigations through purchase of services. The office of children and family services shall develop a process for publicizing such toll-free telephone number to the public for making inquiries or complaints about child day care homes, programs or facilities.

(ii) Information to be maintained and available to the public through such toll-free telephone number shall include, but not be limited to:

(A) current license and registration status of child day care homes, programs and facilities including whether a license or registration is in effect or has been revoked or suspended; and

(B) child care resource and referral programs providing services pursuant to title five-B of this article and other resources known to the office of children and family services which relate to child day care homes, programs and facilities in the state.

(iii) Upon written request identifying a particular child day care home, program or facility, the office of children and family services shall provide the information set forth below. The office of children and family services may charge reasonable fees for copies of documents provided, consistent with the provisions of article six of the public officers law. The information available pursuant to this clause shall be:

(A) the results of the most recent inspection for licensure or registration and any subsequent inspections by the office of children and family services;

(B) complaints filed against child day care homes, programs or facilities which describes the nature of the complaint and states how the complaint was resolved, including the status of the office of children and family services investigation, the steps taken to rectify the complaint, and the penalty, if any, imposed; and

(C) child day care homes, programs or facilities which have requested or received a waiver from any applicable rule or regulation, and the regulatory requirement which was waived.

(iv) Nothing in this paragraph shall be construed to require or permit the disclosure either orally or in writing of any information that is confidential pursuant to law.

(d) Where investigation or inspection reveals that a child day care provider which must be licensed or registered is not, the office of children and family services shall advise the child day care provider in writing that the provider is in violation of the licensing or registration requirements and shall take such further action as is necessary to cause the provider to comply with the law, including directing an unlicensed or unregistered provider to cease operation. In addition, the office of children and family services shall require the provider to notify the parents or guardians of children receiving care from the provider that the provider is in violation of the licensing or registration requirements and shall require the provider to notify the office of children and family services that the provider has done so. Any provider who is directed to cease operations pursuant to this paragraph shall be entitled to a hearing before the office of children and family services. If the provider requests a hearing to contest the directive to cease operations, such hearing must be scheduled to commence as soon as possible but in no event later than thirty days after the receipt of the request by the office of children and family services. The provider may not operate the center, home or program after being directed to cease operations, regardless of whether a hearing is requested. If the provider does not cease operations, the office of children and family services may impose a civil penalty pursuant to subdivision eleven of this section, seek an injunction pursuant to section three hundred ninety-one of this title, or both.

(e) (i) Where an authorized agency is subsidizing child day care pursuant to any provision of this chapter, the authorized agency may submit to the department justification for a need to impose additional requirements upon child day care providers and a plan to monitor compliance with such additional requirements. No such additional requirements or monitoring may be imposed without the written approval of the department.

(ii) An authorized agency may refuse to allow a child day care provider who is not in compliance with this section and regulations issued hereunder or any approved additional requirements of the authorized agency to provide child day care to the child. In accordance with the plan approved by the department, an authorized agency shall have the right to make announced or unannounced inspections of the records and premises of any provider who provides care for such children, including the right to make inspections prior to subsidized children receiving care in a home where the inspection is for the purpose of determining whether the child day care provider is in compliance with applicable law and regulations and any additiona requirements imposed upon such provider by the authorized agency. Where an authorized agency makes such inspections, the authorized agency shall notify the department immediately of any violations of this section or regulations promulgated hereunder, and shall provide the department with an inspection report whether or not violations were found, documenting the results of such inspection.

(iii) Nothing contained in this paragraph shall diminish the authority of the department to conduct inspections or provide for inspections through purchase of services as otherwise provided for in this section. Nothing contained in this paragraph shall obligate the department to take any action to enforce any additional requirements imposed on child day care providers by an authorized agency.

(f) Individual local social services districts may alter their participation in activities related to arranging for, subsidizing, delivering and monitoring the provision of subsidized child day care provided, however, that the total participation of an individual district in all activities related to the provision of subsidized child day care shall be no less than the participation level engaged in by such individual district on the effective date of this section.

4. (a) The office of children and family services on an annual basis shall inspect at least twenty percent of all registered family day care homes, registered child day care centers and registered school age child care programs to determine whether such homes, centers and programs are operating in compliance with applicable statutes and regulations. The office of children and family services shall increase the percentage of family day care homes, child day care centers and school age child care programs which are inspected pursuant to this subdivision as follows: to at least thirty percent by the

thirty-first of December two thousand; and to at least fifty percent by the thirty-first of December two thousand one. The office of children and family services may provide for such inspections through purchase of services. Priority shall be given to family day care homes which have never been licensed or certified prior to initial registration.

(b) Any family day care home or school-age child care program licensed, registered, or certified by the department or by any authorized agency on the effective date of this section shall be deemed registered until the expiration of its then-current license or certificate unless such license or certificate is suspended or revoked pursuant to subdivision ten of this section. Family day care homes and school-age child care programs not licensed, registered, or certified on the effective date of this section shall register pursuant to subdivision two of this section.

5. Child day care providers required to have a license from the department or to be registered with the department pursuant to this section shall not be exempt from such requirement through registration with another state agency, or certification, registration, or licensure by any local governmental agency or any authorized agency.

6. Unless otherwise limited by law, a parent with legal custody or a legal guardian of any child in a child day care program shall have unlimited and on demand access to such child or ward. Such parent or guardian unless otherwise limited by law, also shall have the right to inspect on demand during its hours of operation any area of a child day care center, group family day care home, school-age child care program, or family day care home to which the child or ward of such parent or guardian has access or which could present a hazard to the health and safety of the child or ward.

7. (a) The department shall implement on a statewide basis programs to educate parents and other potential consumers of child day care programs about their selection and use. The department may provide for such implementation through the purchase of services. Such education shall include, but not be limited to, the following topics:

(i) types of child day care programs;

(ii) factors to be considered in selecting and evaluating child day care programs;

(iii) regulations of the department governing the operation of different types of programs;

(iv) rights of parents or guardians in relation to access to children and inspection of child day care programs;

(v) information concerning the availability of child day care subsidies;

(vi) information about licensing and registration requirements;

(vii) prevention of child abuse and maltreatment in child day care programs, including screening of child day care providers and employees;

(viii) tax information; and

(ix) factors to be considered in selecting and evaluating child day care programs when a child needs administration of medications during the time enrolled.

(b) The department shall implement a statewide campaign to educate the public as to the legal requirements for registration of family day care and school-age child care, and the benefits of such registration. The department may provide for such implementation through the purchase of services. The campaign shall:

(i) use various types of media;

(ii) include the development of public educational materials for families, family day care providers, employers and community agencies;

(iii) explain the role and functions of child care resource and referral programs, as such term is used in title five-B of this article;

(iv) explain the role and functions of the department in regard to registered programs; and

(v) publicize the department's toll-free telephone number for making complaints of violations of child day care requirements related to programs which are required to be licensed or registered.

8. The department shall establish and maintain a list of all current registered and licensed child day care programs and a list of all programs whose license or registration has been revoked, rejected, terminated, or suspended. Such information shall be available to the public, pursuant to procedures developed by the department.

8-a. The office of children and family services shall not make available to the public online any group family day care home provider's or family day care provider's home street address or map showing the location of such provider's home where such provider has requested to opt out of the online availability of this information. The office shall provide a written form informing a provider of their right to opt out of providing information online, and shall also permit a provider to request to opt out through the office's website.

9. The department shall make available, directly or through purchase of services, to registered child day care providers information concerning:

(a) liability insurance;

(b) start-up grants;

(c) United States department of agriculture food programs;

(d) subsidies available for child day care;

(e) tax information; and

(f) support services required to be provided by child care resource and referral programs as set forth in subdivision three of section four hundred ten-r of this article.

10. Any home or facility providing child day care shall be operated in accordance with applicable statutes and regulations. Any violation of applicable statutes or regulations shall be a basis to deny, limit, suspend, revoke, or terminate a license or registration. Consistent with articles twenty-three and twenty-three-A of the correction law, and guidelines referenced in subdivision two of section four hundred twenty-five of this article, if the office of children and family services is made aware of the existence of a criminal conviction or pending criminal charge concerning an operator of a family day care home, group family day care home, school-age child care program, or child day care center or concerning any assistant, employee or volunteer in such homes, programs or centers, or any persons age eighteen or over who reside in such homes, such conviction or charge may be a basis to deny, limit, suspend, revoke, reject, or terminate a license or registration. Before any license issued pursuant to the provisions of this section is suspended or revoked, before registration pursuant to this section is suspended or terminated, or when an application for such license is denied or registration rejected, the applicant for or holder of such registration or license is entitled, pursuant to section twenty-two of this chapter and the regulations of the office of children and family services, to a hearing before the office of children and family services. However, a license or registration shall be temporarily suspended or limited without a hearing upon written notice to the

operator of the facility following a finding that the public health, or an individual's safety or welfare, are in imminent danger. The holder of a license or registrant is entitled to a hearing before the office of children and family services to contest the temporary suspension or limitation. If the holder of a license or registrant requests a hearing to contest the temporary suspension or limitation, such hearing must be scheduled to commence as soon as possible but in no event later than thirty days after the receipt of the request by the office of children and family services. Suspension shall continue until the condition requiring suspension or limitation is corrected or until a hearing decision has been issued. If the office of children and family services determines after a hearing that the temporary suspension or limitation was proper, such suspension or limitation shall be extended until the condition requiring suspension or limitation has been corrected or until the license or registration has been revoked.

11. (a) (i) The office of children and family services shall adopt regulations establishing civil penalties of no more than five hundred dollars per day to be assessed against child day care centers, school age child care programs, group family day care homes or family day care homes for violations of this section, sections three hundred ninety-a and three hundred ninety-b of this title and any regulations promulgated thereunder. The regulations establishing civil penalties shall specify the violations subject to penalty.

(ii) The office of children and family services shall adopt regulations establishing civil penalties of no more than five hundred dollars per day to be assessed against child day care providers who operate child day care centers or group family day care homes without a license or who operate family day care homes, school-age child care programs, or child day care centers required to be registered without obtaining such registration.

(iii) In addition to any other civil or criminal penalty provided by law, the office of children and family services shall have the power to assess civil penalties in accordance with its regulations adopted pursuant to this subdivision after a hearing conducted in accordance with procedures established by regulations of the office of children and family services. Such procedures shall require that notice of the time and place of the hearing, together with a statement of charges of violations, shall be served in person or by certified mail addressed to the school age child care program, group family day care home, family day care home, or child day care center at least thirty days prior to the date of the hearing. The statement of charges shall set forth the existence of the violation or violations, the amount of penalty for which the program may become liable, the steps which must be taken to rectify the violation, and where applicable, a statement that a penalty may be imposed regardless of rectification. A written answer to the charges of violations shall be filed with the office of children and family services not less than ten days prior to the date of hearing with respect to each of the charges and shall include all material and relevant matters which, if not disclosed in the answer, would not likely be known to the office of children and family services.

(iv) The hearing shall be held by the commissioner of the office of children and family services or the commissioner's designee. The burden of proof at such hearing shall be on the office of children and family services to show that the charges are supported by a preponderance of the evidence. The commissioner of the office of children and family services or the commissioner's designee, in his or her discretion, may allow the child day care center operator or provider to attempt to prove by a preponderance of the evidence any matter not included in the answer. Where the child day care provider satisfactorily demonstrates that it has rectified the violations in accordance with the requirements of paragraph (c) of this subdivision, no penalty shall be imposed except as provided in paragraph (c) of this subdivision.

(b)(i) In assessing penalties pursuant to this subdivision, the office of children and family services may consider the completeness of any rectification made and the specific circumstances of such violations as mitigating factors.

(ii) Upon the request of the office of children and family services, the attorney general shall commence an action in any court of competent jurisdiction against any child day care program subject to the provisions of this subdivision and against any person, entity or corporation operating such center or school age child care program, group family day care home or family day care home for the recovery of any penalty assessed by the office of children and family services in accordance with the provisions of this subdivision.

(iii) Any such penalty assessed by the office of children and family services may be released or compromised by the office of children and family services before the matter has been referred to the attorney general; when such matter has been referred to the attorney general, such penalty may be released or compromised and any action commenced to recover the same may be settled and discontinued by the attorney general with the consent of the office of children and family services.

(c)(i) Except as provided for in this paragraph, a child day care provider shall avoid payment of a penalty imposed pursuant to this subdivision where the provider has rectified the condition which resulted in the imposition of the penalty within thirty days of notification of the existence of the violation of statute or regulation.

(ii) Clause (i) of this paragraph notwithstanding, rectification shall not preclude the imposition of a penalty pursuant to this subdivision where:

(A) the child day care provider has operated a child day care center or group family day care home without a license, has refused to seek a license for the operation of such a center or home, or has continued to operate such a center or home after denial of a license application, revocation of an existing license or suspension of an existing license;

(B) the child day care provider has operated a family day care home, school-age child care program or child day care center required to be registered without being registered, has refused to seek registration for the operation of such home, program or center or has continued to operate such a home, program or center after denial of a registration application, revocation of an existing registration or suspension of an existing registration;

(C) there has been a total or substantial failure of the facility's fire detection or prevention systems or emergency evacuation procedures;

(D) the child day care provider or an assistant, employee or volunteer has failed to provide adequate and competent supervision;

(E) the child day care provider or an assistant, employee or volunteer has failed to provide adequate sanitation;

(F) the child day care provider or an assistant, employee, volunteer or, for a family day care home or group family day care home, a member of the provider's household, has injured a child in care, unreasonably failed to obtain medical attention for a child in care requiring such attention, used corporal punishment against a child in care or abused or maltreated a child in care;

(G) the child day care provider has violated the same statutory or regulatory standard more than once within a six month period;

(H) the child day care provider or an assistant, employee or volunteer has failed to make a report of suspected child abuse or maltreatment when required to do so pursuant to section four hundred thirteen of this article; or

(I) the child day care provider or an assistant, employee or volunteer has submitted to the office of children and family services a forged document as defined in section 170.00 of the penal law.

(d) Any civil penalty received by the office of children and family services pursuant to this subdivision shall be deposited to the credit of the "quality child care and protection fund" established pursuant to section ninety-seven-www of the state finance law.

(e)(i) The office of children and family services shall deny a new application for licensure or registration made by a day care provider whose license or registration was previously revoked or terminated based on a violation of statute or regulation for a period of two years from the date that the revocation or termination of the license or registration became finally effective, unless such office determines, in its discretion, that approval of the application will not in any way jeopardize the health, safety or welfare of children in the center, program or home. For the purposes of this paragraph, the date that the revocation or termination became finally effective shall be, as applicable:

(A) the date that the revocation or termination became effective based on the notice of revocation or termination;

(B) the date that the hearing decision was issued upholding the revocation or termination;

(C) the date of issuance of a final court order affirming the revocation or termination or affirming a hearing decision that upheld the revocation or termination; or

(D) another date mutually agreed upon by the office of children and family services and the provider.

(ii)(A) Such office shall deny a new application for licensure or registration made by a day care provider who is enjoined or otherwise prohibited by a court order from operation of a day care center, group family day care home, family day care home or school-age child care program without a license or registration for a period of two years from the date of the court order unless the court order specifically enjoins the provider from providing day care for a period longer than two years, in which case the office shall deny any new application made by the provider while the provider is so enjoined.

(B) Such office shall deny a new application for licensure or registration made by a day care provider who is assessed a second civil penalty by such office for having operated a day care center, group family day care home, family day care home or school-age child care program without a license or registration for a period of two years from the date of the second fine. For the purposes of this paragraph, the date of the second fine shall be either the date upon which the day care provider signs a stipulation agreement to pay the second fine or the date upon which a hearing decision is issued affirming the determination of such office to impose the second fine, as applicable.

(iii) A day care provider who surrenders the provider's license or registration while such office is engaged in enforcement seeking suspension, revocation or termination of such provider's license or registration pursuant to the regulations of such office, shall be deemed to have had their license or registration revoked or terminated and shall be subject to the prohibitions against licensing or registration pursuant to subparagraph (i) of this paragraph for a period of two years from the date of surrender of the license or registration.

12. (a) Notwithstanding any other provision of law, except as may be required as a condition of licensure or registration by regulations promulgated pursuant to this section, no village, town (outside the area of any incorporated village), city or county shall adopt or enact any law, ordinance, rule or regulation which would impose, mandate or otherwise enforce standards for sanitation, health, fire safety or building construction on a one or two family dwelling or multiple dwelling used to provide group family day care or family day care than would be applicable were such child day care not provided on the premises. No village, town (outside the area of any incorporated village), city or county shall prohibit or restrict use of a one or two family dwelling, or multiple dwelling for family or group family day care where a license or registration for such use has been issued in accordance with regulations issued pursuant to this section. Nothing in this paragraph shall preclude local authorities with enforcement jurisdiction of the applicable sanitation, health, fire safety or building construction code from making appropriate inspections to assure compliance with such standards.

(b) Notwithstanding any other provision of law, but pursuant to section five hundred eighty-one-b of the real property tax law, no assessing unit, as defined in subdivision one of section one hundred two of the real property tax law, in the assessment of the value of any parcel used for residential purposes and registered as a family day care home pursuant to this section, shall consider the use or registration of such parcel as a family day care home.

13. Notwithstanding any other provision of law, this section, except for paragraph (a-1) of subdivision two-a of this section, shall not apply to child day care centers in the city of New York.

§390-a. Standards and training for child day care.

1. All office of children and family services and municipal staff employed to accept registrations, issue licenses or conduct inspections of child day care homes, programs or facilities, subject to the amounts appropriated therefor, shall receive training in at least the following: regulations promulgated by the office of children and family services pursuant to section three hundred ninety of this title; child abuse prevention and identification; safety and security procedures in child day care settings; the principles of childhood development, and the laws, regulations and procedures governing the protection of children from abuse or maltreatment.

2. No license or registration shall be issued to a family day care home, group family day care home, school age child care program or child day care center and no such registration or license shall be renewed until it can be demonstrated by the employer or licensing agency that there is a procedure developed and implemented, in accordance with section three hundred ninety-b of this title and pursuant to regulations of the office of children and family services, to:

(a) review and evaluate the backgrounds of and information supplied by any person applying to be a child day care center or school-age child care program employee or volunteer or group family day care assistant, a provider of family day care or group family day care, or a director of a child day care center, head start day care center or school-age child care program. Such procedures shall include but not be limited to the following requirements: that the applicant set forth his or her employment history, provide personal and employment references; submit such information as is required for screening with the statewide central register of child abuse and maltreatment in accordance with the provisions of section four hundred twenty-four-a of this article; sign a sworn statement indicating whether, to the best of his or her knowledge, he or she has ever been convicted of a crime in this state or any other jurisdiction; and provide his or her fingerprints for submission to the division of criminal justice services in accordance with the provisions of section three hundred ninety-b of this title;

(b) establish relevant minimal experiential and educational qualifications for employees and directors of child day care centers or head start day care center programs;

(c) assure adequate and appropriate supervision of employees and volunteers of group family day care homes, family day care homes, child day care centers and school-age child care programs; and

(d) demonstrate, in the case of child day care centers, group family day care homes, family day care homes and school-age child care programs the existence of specific procedures which will assure the safety of a child who is reported to the state central register of child abuse and maltreatment as well as other children provided care by such homes, centers or programs, immediately upon notification that a report has been made with respect to a child named in such report while the child was in attendance at such homes, centers or programs.

(e) establish necessary rules to provide for uniform visitor control procedures, including visitor identification.

3. (a) The office of children and family services shall promulgate regulations requiring operators, program directors, employees and assistants of family day care homes, group family day care homes, school-age child care programs and child day care centers to receive thirty hours of training every two years; provided, however, that fifteen hours of such training must be received within the first six months of the initial licensure, registration or employment. Such training requirements shall also apply to any volunteer in such day care homes, programs or centers who has the potential for regular and substantial contact with children. The thirty hours of training required during the first biennial cycle after initial licensure or registration shall include training received while an application for licensure or registration pursuant to section three hundred ninety of this title is pending. The office of children and family services may provide this training through purchase of services.

(b) The training required in paragraph (a) of this subdivision shall address the following topics:

(i) principles of childhood development, focusing on the developmental stages of the age groups for which the program provides care;

(ii) nutrition and health needs of infants and children;

(iii) child day care program development;

(iv) safety and security procedures;

(v) business record maintenance and management;

(vi) child abuse and maltreatment identification and prevention;

(vii) statutes and regulations pertaining to child day care;

(viii) statutes and regulations pertaining to child abuse and maltreatment; and

(ix) for operators, program directors, employees and assistants of family day care homes, group family day care homes and child day care centers, education and information on the identification, diagnosis and prevention of shaken baby syndrome.

(c) For the thirty hours of biennial training required after the initial period of licensure or registration, each provider who can demonstrate basic competency shall determine in which of the specified topics he or she needs further study, based on the provider's experience and the needs of the children in the provider's care.

(d) Family day care home and group family day care home operators shall obtain training pertaining to protection of the health and safety of children, as required by regulation, prior to the issuance of a license or registration by the office of children and family services.

(e) Upon request by the office of children and family services, the child day care applicant or provider shall submit documentation demonstrating compliance with the training requirements of this section.

4. No license or registration shall be issued to a family day care home or group family day care home and no such registration shall be renewed if barriers, as defined in paragraph (d) of subdivision one of section three hundred ninety-d of this title, are not present around any swimming pool or body of water, as defined in paragraphs (b) and (c) of subdivision one of section three hundred ninety-d of this title, located on its grounds, pursuant to section three hundred ninety-d of this title.

5. a. The site provider of a family day care home or group family day care home shall provide that at least one employee who holds a valid certification in a course of study in first aid knowledge and skills and cardiopulmonary resuscitation, with an emphasis on providing that aid to children, as approved by the commissioner of the office of children and family services, be on premises during the operating hours of such family day care home or group family day care home.

b. The site supervisor of a school-age child care program shall provide that at least one employee who holds a valid certification in a course of study in first aid knowledge and skills and cardiopulmonary resuscitation, with an emphasis on providing that aid to children, as approved by the commissioner of the office of children and family services, be on premises during the operating hours of such school-age child care program.

c. The director of a child day care center shall provide that at least one employee who holds a valid certification in a course of study in first aid knowledge and skills and cardiopulmonary resuscitation, with an emphasis on providing that aid to children, as approved by the commissioner of the office of children and family services, be on premises during the operating hours of such child day care center.

§390-b.   Criminal history review of child care providers, generally.

1. (a) Notwithstanding any other provision of law to the contrary, and subject to rules and regulations of the division of criminal justice services, the office of children and family services shall perform a criminal history record check with the division of criminal justice services regarding any operator, employee or volunteer of a child day care center or school age child care provider, as defined in paragraphs (c) and (f) of subdivision one of section three hundred ninety of this title. Child day care center operators, school age child care operators and any employees or volunteers, who previously did not have a criminal history record check performed in accordance with this subdivision shall have such a criminal history record check performed when the child day care center or school age child care provider applies for license or registration renewal. Child day care centers which are not subject to the

provisions of section three hundred ninety of this title, shall not be subject to the provisions of this section. The provisions of this section shall apply to a volunteer only where the volunteer has the potential for regular and substantial contact with children enrolled in the program.

(b) Notwithstanding any other provision of law to the contrary, and subject to rules and regulations of the division of criminal justice services, the office of children and family services shall perform a criminal history record check with the division of criminal justice services regarding the operator, any assistants, employees or volunteers of a group family day care home or family day care home, as defined in paragraphs (d) and (e) of subdivision one of section three hundred ninety of this title, and any person age eighteen or over residing on the premises of the group family day care home or family day care home which is to be licensed or registered in accordance with section three hundred ninety of this title. Group family day care home operators, family day care home operators, any assistants, employees or volunteers, and persons who are age eighteen or over residing on the premises of a licensed group family day care home or registered family day care home who previously did not have a criminal history record check performed in accordance with this subdivision shall have such a criminal history record check performed when the group family day care home or family day care home applies for renewal of the home's license or registration. The provisions of this section shall apply to a volunteer only where the volunteer has the potential for regular and substantial contact with children enrolled in the program.

2. (a) As part of the provider's application for, or renewal of, a child day care center or school age child care license or registration, the provider shall furnish the office of children and family services with fingerprint cards of any operator of a child day care center or school age child care program, and any employee or volunteer, who previously did not have a criminal history record check performed in accordance with this section, together with such other information as is required by the office of children and family services and the division of criminal justice services.

(b) Every child day care center or school age child care provider shall obtain a set of fingerprints for each prospective employee or volunteer and such other information as is required by the office of children and family services and the division of criminal justice services. The child day care center or school age child care program shall furnish to the applicant blank fingerprint cards and a description of how the completed fingerprint cards will be used. The child day care center or school age child care program shall promptly transmit such fingerprint cards to the office of children and family services.

(c) As part of the provider's application for, or renewal of, a group family day care home license or family day care home registration, the provider shall furnish the office of children and family services with fingerprint cards of any operator of a group family day care home or family day care home, and any assistant, employee or volunteer, and any person age eighteen or over residing on the premises of the group family day care home or family day care home, who previously did not have a criminal history record check performed in accordance with this section, together with such other information as is required by the office of children and family services and the division of criminal justice services.

(d) Every group family day care home or family day care home provider shall obtain a set of fingerprints for each prospective assistant, employee, volunteer and any person age eighteen or over who will be residing on the premises of the group family day care home or family day care home, and such other information as is required by the office of children and family services and the division of criminal justice services. The group family day care home or family day care home provider shall furnish to the applicant blank fingerprint cards and a description of how the completed fingerprint cards will be used. The group family day care home or family day care home provider shall promptly transmit such fingerprint cards to the office of children and family services.

(e) The office of children and family services shall pay the processing fee imposed pursuant to subdivision eight-a of section eight hundred thirty-seven of the executive law. The office of children and family services shall promptly submit the fingerprint cards and the processing fee to the division of criminal justice services for its full search and retain processing.

(f) A licensed or registered child day care center, school-age child care program, group family day care home or family day care home may temporarily approve an applicant to be an employee, assistant or volunteer for such provider while the results of the criminal history record check are pending, but shall not allow such person to have unsupervised contact with children during such time.

3. Notwithstanding any other provision of law to the contrary, after reviewing any criminal history record information provided by the division of criminal justice services, of an individual who is subject to a criminal history record check pursuant to this section, the office of children and family services and the provider shall take the following actions:

(a) (i) Where the criminal history record of an applicant to be an operator of a child day care center, school age child care program, group family day care home, family day care home, or any person over the age of eighteen residing in such a home, reveals a felony conviction at any time for a sex offense, crime against a child, or a crime involving violence, or a felony conviction within the past five years for a drug-related offense, the office of children and family services shall deny the application unless the office determines, in its discretion, that approval of the application will not in any way jeopardize the health, safety or welfare of the children in the center, program or home; or

(ii) Where the criminal history record of an applicant to be an operator of a child day care center, school age child care program, group family day care home, family day care home, or any person over the age of eighteen residing in such a home, reveals a conviction for a crime other than one set forth in subparagraph (i) of this paragraph, the office of children and family services may deny the application, consistent with article twenty-three-A of the correction law; or

(iii) Where the criminal history record of an applicant to be an operator of a child day care center, school age child care program, group family day care home, family day care home, or any other person over the age of eighteen residing in such a home, reveals a charge for any crime, the office of children and family services shall hold the application in abeyance until the charge is finally resolved.

(b) (i) Where the criminal history record of a current operator of a child day care center, school age child care program, group family day care home, family day care home, or any other person over the age of eighteen residing in such a home, reveals a conviction for a crime set forth in subparagraph (i) of paragraph (a) of this subdivision, the office of children and family services shall conduct a safety assessment of the program and take all appropriate steps to protect the health and safety of the children in the program. The office of children and family services shall deny, limit, suspend, revoke, reject or terminate a license or registration based on such a conviction, unless the office determines, in its discretion, that continued operation of the center, program or home will not in any way jeopardize the health, safety or welfare of the children in the center, program or home;

 (ii) Where the criminal history record of a current operator of a child day care center, school age child care program, group family day care home, family day care home, or any other person over the age of eighteen residing in such a home, reveals a conviction for a crime other than one set forth in subparagraph (i) of paragraph (a) of this subdivision, the office of children and family services shall conduct a safety assessment of the program and take all appropriate steps to protect the health and safety of the children in the program. The office may deny, limit, suspend, revoke, reject or terminate a license or registration based on such a conviction, consistent with article twenty-three-A of the correction law;

 (iii) Where the criminal history record of a current operator of a child day care center, school age child care program, group family day care home, family day care home, or any other person over the age of eighteen residing in such a home, reveals a charge for any crime, the office of children and family services shall conduct a safety assessment of the program and take all appropriate steps to protect the health and safety of the children in the program. The office may suspend a license or registration based on such a charge where necessary to protect the health and safety of the children in the program.

 (c) (i) Where the criminal history record of an applicant to be an employee or volunteer at a child day care center or school age child care program reveals a conviction for a crime set forth in subparagraph (i) of paragraph (a) of this subdivision, the office of children and family services shall direct the provider to deny the application unless the office determines, in its discretion, that approval of the application will not in any way jeopardize the health, safety or welfare of the children in the center or program;

 (ii) Where the criminal history record of an applicant to be an employee or volunteer at a child day care center or school age child care program reveals a conviction for a crime other than one set forth in subparagraph (i) of paragraph (a) of this subdivision, the office of children and family services may, consistent with article twenty-three-A of the correction law, direct the provider to deny the application;

 (iii) Where the criminal history record of an applicant to be an employee or volunteer at a child day care center or school age child care program reveals a charge for any crime, the office of children and family services shall hold the application in abeyance until the charge is finally resolved.

 (d) (i) Where the criminal history record of a current employee or volunteer at a child day care center or school age child care program reveals a conviction for a crime set forth in subparagraph (i) of paragraph (a) of this subdivision, the office of children and family services shall conduct a safety assessment of the program and take all appropriate steps to protect the health and safety of the children in the program. The office shall direct the provider to terminate the employee or volunteer based on such a conviction, unless the office determines, in its discretion, that the continued presence of the employee or volunteer in the center or program will not in any way jeopardize the health, safety or welfare of the children in the center or program;

(ii) Where the criminal history record of a current employee or volunteer at a child day care center or school age child care program reveals a conviction for a crime other than one set forth in subparagraph (i) of paragraph (a) of this subdivision, the office of children and family services shall conduct a safety assessment of the program and take all appropriate steps to protect the health and safety of the children in the program. The office may direct the provider to terminate the employee or volunteer based on such a conviction, consistent with article twenty-three-A of the correction law;

(iii) Where the criminal history record of a current employee or volunteer at a child day care center or school age child care program reveals a charge for any crime, the office of children and family services shall conduct a safety assessment of the program and take all appropriate steps to protect the health and safety of the children in the program.

(e) (i) Where the criminal history record of an applicant to be an employee, assistant or volunteer at a group family day care home or family day care home reveals a conviction for a crime set forth in subparagraph (i) of paragraph (a) of this subdivision, the office of children and family services shall direct the provider to deny the application unless the office determines, in its discretion, that approval of the application will not in any way jeopardize the health, safety or welfare of the children in the home;

(ii) Where the criminal history record of an applicant to be an employee, assistant or volunteer at a group family day care home or family day care home reveals a conviction for a crime other than one set forth in subparagraph (i) of paragraph (a) of this subdivision, the office of children and family services may, consistent with article twenty-three-A of the correction law, direct the provider to deny the application;

(iii) Where the criminal history record of an applicant to be an employee, assistant or volunteer at a group family day care home or family day care home reveals a charge for any crime, the office of children and family services shall hold the application in abeyance until the charge is finally resolved.

(f) (i) Where the criminal history record of a current employee, assistant or volunteer at a group family day care home or family day care home reveals a conviction for a crime set forth in subparagraph (i) of paragraph (a) of this subdivision, the office of children and family services shall conduct a safety assessment of the program and take all appropriate steps to protect the health and safety of the children in the home. The office of children and family services shall direct the provider to terminate the employee, assistant or volunteer based on such a conviction, unless the office determines, in its discretion, that the continued presence of the employee, assistant or volunteer in the home will not in any way jeopardize the health, safety or welfare of the children in the home;

(ii) Where the criminal history record of a current employee, assistant or volunteer at a group family day care home or family day care home reveals a conviction for a crime other than one set forth in subparagraph (i) of paragraph (a) of this subdivision, the office of children and family services shall conduct a safety assessment of the home and take all appropriate steps to protect the health and safety of the children in the home. The office may direct the provider to terminate the employee, assistant or volunteer based on such a conviction, consistent with article twenty-three-A of the correction law;

(iii) Where the criminal history record of a current employee, assistant or volunteer at a group family day care home or family day care home reveals a charge for any crime, the office of children and family services shall conduct a safety assessment of the home and take all appropriate steps to protect the health and safety of the children in the home.

(g) Advise the provider that the individual has no criminal history record.

4. Prior to making a determination to deny an application pursuant to subdivision three of this section, the office of children and family services shall afford the applicant an opportunity to explain, in writing, why the application should not be denied.

5. Notwithstanding any other provision of law to the contrary, the office of children and family services, upon receipt of a criminal history record from the division of criminal justice services, may request, and is entitled to receive, information pertaining to any crime contained in such criminal history record from any state or local law enforcement agency, district attorney, parole officer, probation officer or court for the purposes of determining whether any ground relating to such criminal conviction or pending criminal charge exists for denying a license, registration, application or employment.

6. The notification by the office of children and family services to the child day care provider pursuant to this section shall include a summary of the criminal history record, if any, provided by the division of criminal justice services.

7. Where the office of children and family services directs a child day care provider to deny an application based on the criminal history record, the provider must notify the applicant that such record is the basis of the denial.

8. Any safety assessment required pursuant to this section shall include a review of the duties of the individual, the extent to which such individual may have contact with children in the program or household and the status and nature of the criminal charge or conviction. Where the office of children and family services performs the safety assessment, it shall thereafter take all appropriate steps to protect the health and safety of children receiving care in the child day care center, school age child care program, family day care home or group family day care home.

9. Any criminal history record provided by the division of criminal justice services, and any summary of the criminal history record provided by the office of children and family services to a child day care provider pursuant to this section, is confidential and shall not be available for public inspection; provided, however, nothing herein shall prevent a child day care provider or the office of children and family services from disclosing criminal history information at any administrative or judicial proceeding relating to the denial or revocation of an application, employment, license or registration. The subject of a criminal history review conducted pursuant to this section shall be entitled to receive, upon written request, a copy of the summary of the criminal history record provided by the office of children and family services to the child day care provider. Unauthorized disclosure of such records or reports shall subject the provider to civil penalties in accordance with the provisions of subdivision eleven of section three hundred ninety of this title.

10. A child day care provider shall advise the office of children and family services when an individual who is subject to criminal history record review in accordance with subdivision one or two of this section is no longer subject to such review. The office of children and family services shall inform the division of criminal justice services when an individual who is subject to criminal history review is no longer subject to such review so that the division of criminal justice services may terminate its retain processing with regard to such person. At least once a year, the office of children and family services will

be required to conduct a validation of the records maintained by the division of criminal justice services.

*§390-c. Notice of pesticide applications.
1. For the purposes of this section the following terms shall have the meanings set forth below:
(a) "Pesticide" shall have the same meaning as in subdivision thirty-five of section 33-0101 of the environmental conservation law.
(b) "Daycare facility" shall mean licensed and registered child daycare homes, programs and facilities.
2. Each daycare facility shall be subject to the following notice requirements when pesticides are used at such facility:
(a) A notice of each pesticide application shall be posted in a common area of the facility which is conspicuously visible to persons dropping off or picking up children from the facility. Such notice shall be posted not less than forty-eight hours prior to the pesticide application.
(b) The notice required to be posted pursuant to paragraph (a) of this subdivision shall include at a minimum:
(i) the location and specific date of the application at the daycare facility. In case of outdoor applications the notice must provide a specific date, and may include two alternative dates in case the application cannot be made due to weather conditions.
(ii) the product name and pesticide registration number assigned by the United States Environmental Protection Agency.
(iii) the following statement "This notice is to inform you of a pending pesticide application at this facility. You may wish to discuss with a representative of the daycare facility what precautions are being taken to protect your child from exposure to these pesticides. Further information about the product or products being applied, including any warnings that appear on the label of the pesticide or pesticides that are pertinent to the protection of humans, animals or the environment, can be obtained by calling the National Pesticide Telecommunications Network Information at 1-800-858-7378 or the New York State Department of Health Center for Environmental Health Info line at 1-800-458-1158".
(iv) the name of a representative of the daycare facility and contact number for additional information.
(c) For purposes of this section the following pesticide applications shall not be subject to the notification posting requirements:
(i) the application of anti microbial pesticides and anti microbial products as defined by FIFRA in 7 U.S.C. §136 (mm) and 136q (h) (2);
(ii) the use of an aerosol product with a directed spray, in containers of eighteen fluid ounces, or less, when used to protect individuals from an imminent threat from stinging and biting insects including venomous spiders, bees, wasps and hornets. This section shall not exempt from notification the use of any fogger product or aerosol product that discharges to a wide area;
(iii) any application where the daycare facility remains unoccupied for a continuous seventy-two hour period following the application of the pesticide;
(iv) nonvolatile rodenticides in tamper resistant bait stations or in areas inaccessible to children;
(v) silica gels and other nonvolatile ready-to-use, paste, foam or gel formulations of insecticides in areas inaccessible to children;

*There are 2 § 390-c's

(vi) nonvolatile insecticidal baits in tamper resistant bait stations or in areas inaccessible to children;

(vii) application of a pesticide classified by the United States Environmental Protection Agency as an exempt material under section 40 CFR Part 152.25;

(viii) boric acid and disodium octaborate tetrahydrate;

(ix) the application of a pesticide which the United States Environmental Protection Agency has determined satisfies its reduced risk criteria, including a biopesticide; or

(x) any emergency application of a pesticide when necessary to protect against an imminent threat to human health, provided however, that prior to any such emergency application, the person making such application shall make a good faith effort to supply the written notice required pursuant to this section. Upon making such an emergency application, the person making such application shall notify the commissioner of health, using a form developed by such commissioner for such purposes that shall include minimally the name of the person making the application, the pesticide business registration number or certified applicator number of the person making such application, the location and date of such application, the product name and USEPA registration number of the pesticide applied and the reason for such application. The commissioner of health shall review such form to ensure that the circumstance did warrant such emergency application. Such forms shall be kept on file at the department of health for three years from the date of application and shall be available to any individual upon request.

3. Any person, other than a daycare facility, who contracts for the application of a pesticide at a daycare facility shall provide to such facility operator information required to be contained in the posting pursuant to subdivision two of this section at least forty-eight hours prior to such application.

4. (a) Any daycare facility that violates the provisions of subdivision two of this section shall, for a first such violation of this section, in lieu of penalty, be issued a written warning and shall also be issued educational materials pursuant to subdivision two of section 33-1005 of the environmental conservation law. Such facility shall, however, for a second violation, be liable to the people of the state for a civil penalty not to exceed one hundred dollars, and not to exceed two hundred fifty dollars for any subsequent violation, such penalties to be assessed by the commissioner after a hearing or opportunity to be heard.

(b) Any person who violates subdivision three of this section shall, for a first such violation of this section, in lieu of penalty, be issued a written warning, and shall also be issued educational materials pursuant to subdivision two of section 33-1005 of the environmental conservation law. Such person shall, however, for a second violation, be liable to the people of the state for a civil penalty not to exceed one hundred dollars, and not to exceed two hundred fifty dollars for any subsequent violation, such penalties to be assessed by the commissioner of environmental conservation after a hearing or opportunity to be heard.

*§390-c. Additional powers and duties of the office of children and family services.

1. The commissioner of children and family services is authorized and directed to promulgate necessary rules and regulations to ensure that, whenever a child day care provider is licensed or registered pursuant to section three hundred ninety of this article, the police department and fire department of the

*There are 2 § 390-c's

municipality wherein such licensee or registrant is authorized to operate and the state police shall be notified of the existence of the child day care center, its location and the fact that children are likely to be at that location in the event of an emergency. In those cases where the local municipality does not have a police department or a fire department, the sheriff of the appropriate county shall be notified in lieu thereof.

2. The commissioner of children and family services is authorized and directed to conduct a study to determine the best method of compiling an accurate and accessible central record of information regarding the safe operation of each day care center licensed or registered within the state. Such record should include but not be limited to complaints by parents or guardians, internal incident reports, reports by police or fire departments, local or state building code violations, any relevant information gathered from utility providers or other visitors to the day care center and any additional information held by another state or local agency regarding a day care provider or a day care center location which could affect safe operation of a day care center.

3. On or before the thirtieth day of June in the year next succeeding the year in which this section takes effect, the commissioner of children and family services shall report to the governor, the temporary president of the senate and the speaker of the assembly regarding the results of the study undertaken pursuant to subdivision two of this section.

§390-d.   **Requiring barriers to be placed around swimming pools and bodies of water on the grounds of family day care homes or group family day care homes.**

1. For the purposes of this section the following terms shall have the meanings set forth below:

(a) "Grounds of a family day care home or group family day care home" shall mean in, on or within any building, structure or land contained within the real property boundary line of a family day care home or a group family day care home.

(b) "Swimming pool" shall mean any outdoor pool or tub intended for swimming, bathing or wading purposes.

(c) "Bodies of water" shall include, but not limited to, ponds, springs, streams, creeks, lakes, rivers and oceans.

(d) "Barriers" shall mean all fences, enclosures or other materials sufficient to form an obstruction to the free passage of persons through such materials.

2. (a) Any swimming pool or body of water located on the grounds of a family day care home or group family day care home shall be surrounded by a barrier sufficient to form an obstruction to the free passage of children through such barrier into such swimming pool or body of water. Such barrier shall be adequate to make such swimming pool or body of water inaccessible to children which, including gates thereto, shall be at least four feet high from the adjacent ground. All such gates shall include a locked barrier which shall be located at least four feet high above the adjacent ground or otherwise made inaccessible to children from the outside.

(b) Where a body of water is present and not wholly contained within the grounds of family day care home or group family day care home, the grounds of such home must be surrounded and enclosed by a barrier sufficient to make such body of water inaccessible to children.

(c) All pathways, walkways, decks or any other connecting entrance to such swimming pool or body of water shall be obstructed by a barrier sufficient to impede the free passage of children into or around the area immediately adjacent to such swimming pool or body of water.

(d) Swimming pools or bodies of water that are entirely covered by a solid object which is secured by sufficient weight, locking apparatus, and/or other device that would prevent a child in care from removing the solid object and accessing the swimming pool or body of water, shall be considered a sufficient barrier for the purposes of this section.

(e) As an alternative to surrounding the pool or other body of water located on the grounds of a family day care home or group family day care home with a barrier as described in paragraph (a) of this subdivision, the day care provider may use the property for day care if the provider bars access to such pool or other body of water by surrounding a part of the grounds not including such pool or other body of water with a barrier as described in paragraph (a) of this subdivision provided that:

(i) There is no unsecured means of egress from the home by which children could gain access to the pool or other body of water. For purposes of this paragraph, the day care provider may secure a door or other means of egress that is remotely located from the pool or other body of water by use of an alarm device or system that will alert the day care provider if the door or other means of egress is opened;

(ii) All children in care are directly and closely supervised by the provider or an assistant at all times the children are outside the home or other dwelling where the day care is provided; and

(iii) The parents or guardians of each child in care have submitted to the provider a written acknowledgment that the pool or other body of water exists, that a barrier as otherwise required by this section has not been provided, and that the children will have the potential for access to the pool or other body of water.

(f) Where a natural barrier or other obstacle located on the property lies between the pool or body of water and the building in which the family or group family day care is provided such that the natural barrier or other obstacle prevents access by children in care to the pool or body of water, a fence or additional barrier as otherwise required by this section shall not be required and the day care provider may use the property for day care provided that:

(i) There is no unsecured means of egress from the home by which children could gain access to the pool or other body of water. For purposes of this paragraph, the day care provider may secure a door or other means of egress that is remotely located from the pool or other body of water by use of an alarm device or system that will alert the day care provider if the door or other means of egress is opened;

(ii) All children in care are directly and closely supervised by the provider or an assistant at all times the children are outside the home or other dwelling where the day care is provided; and

(iii) The parents or guardians of each child in care have submitted to the provider a written acknowledgment that the pool or other body of water exists, that a barrier as otherwise required by this section has not been provided, and that the children will have the potential for access to the body of water.

In determining what constitutes a natural barrier or other obstacle for purposes of this paragraph, the presence of natural and artificial terrain features or constructs may be considered along with the distance between the building in which the family or group family day care is provided and the pool or body of water.

3. Where a swimming pool or body of water is located on a property adjacent to a family or group family day home, the child day care provider must take suitable precautions to prevent the children in care from having access to the adjacent swimming pool or body of water, including taking any precautions specifically required by the office of children and family services to protect the safety of children receiving day care.

4. Nothing in this section shall preclude local authorities with enforcement jurisdiction of the applicable sanitation, health, fire safety or building construction code from making appropriate inspections to assure compliance with such standards.

§390-e. Criminal history review; mentoring programs.

1. For the purposes of this section, the following words shall have the following meanings:

(a) "Prospective employee" shall mean a person being considered for employment by a mentoring program.

(b) "Prospective mentor" shall mean an individual who is currently applying to volunteer to help a child or a group of children in a mentoring program for a period of time. Such help shall include, but not be limited to, being a positive role model for youth, building relationships with youth, and providing youth with academic assistance and exposure to new experiences and examples of opportunity that enhance the ability of children to become responsible adults.

(c) "Mentoring program" shall mean a formalized program, operated by a corporation which has been incorporated pursuant to subparagraph five of paragraph (a) of section one hundred two of the not-for-profit corporation law or pursuant to subparagraph four of paragraph (a) of section one hundred two of the business corporation law, or operated by an educational institution or school district, that matches youth with adult volunteers with the purpose of providing such youth with positive role models to enhance their development.

(d) "Office" shall mean the office of children and family services.

2. Mentoring programs may perform a criminal history record check on all prospective employees and mentors.

3. Notwithstanding any other provision of law to the contrary, subject to the rules and regulations of the division of criminal justice services, mentoring programs may apply for a criminal history record check with the division of criminal justice services regarding any prospective employee or any prospective mentor who may engage in unsupervised activities with youth or in activities with youth in a setting without constant agency or parental oversight. Each mentoring program that chooses to complete such criminal background checks on prospective employees or on prospective mentors shall establish a policy for completing criminal background checks on such prospective employees or mentors. Such policy shall apply one uniform standard for the completion of criminal background checks for all prospective employees and one uniform standard for the completion of criminal background checks for all prospective mentors. Any mentoring program that chooses to complete criminal background checks on both prospective employees and prospective mentors may utilize the same uniform process for the completion of the criminal background checks on prospective employees and prospective mentors or they may choose one uniform process for prospective employees and another uniform process for prospective mentors.

4. Every mentoring program that chooses to apply for a criminal history background check with the division of criminal justice services shall obtain a

set of fingerprints from each individual for whom a criminal background check is to be completed and such other information as is required by the office and the division of criminal justice services. For each prospective employee or mentor for whom the mentoring program completes a criminal background check, the mentoring program shall provide the applicant with blank fingerprint cards and a description of how the completed fingerprint card will be used upon submission to the mentoring program. The mentoring program shall promptly transmit such fingerprint card and the processing fee to the office. The office shall promptly submit the fingerprint card and the processing fee, imposed pursuant to subdivision eight-a of section eight hundred thirty-seven of the executive law, to the division of criminal justice services for its full search and retain processing.

5. Upon receipt of a criminal history record from the division of criminal justice services, the office shall promptly provide to the mentoring program the criminal history record, if any, with respect to the prospective employee or mentor, or a statement that the individual has no criminal history record.

6. Upon receipt of the results of a criminal background check pursuant to this section, the mentoring program shall determine whether or not the prospective employee or mentor shall be offered employment or the opportunity to volunteer with the program. Such determination shall be made in accordance with the criteria established in section seven hundred fifty-two of the correction law.

7. Upon the request of any person previously convicted of one or more criminal offenses who has been denied employment pursuant to subdivision six of this section, the mentoring program shall provide, within thirty days of such request, a written statement setting forth the reasons for such denial. Any such person denied employment pursuant to subdivision six of this section shall be afforded the opportunities for enforcement available pursuant to section seven hundred fifty-five of the correction law.

8. Notwithstanding the provisions of this section, with the exception of a sex offense or a crime against a child, a custodial parent or guardian may sign a waiver authorizing a mentor to work with his or her child regardless of a criminal charge or crime related to a mentor. Such process shall only be initiated upon the consent of the prospective mentor, and be on a form and of a content to be developed by the office. Where applicable, a mentoring program may notify a custodial parent or guardian of his or her waiver right, but a waiver shall only be authorized by a custodial parent or guardian.

9. Any criminal history record provided to a mentoring program pursuant to this section shall be confidential pursuant to the applicable federal and state laws, rules and regulations, and shall not be published or in any way disclosed to persons other than authorized personnel, unless otherwise authorized by law.

10. Every mentoring program shall provide each custodial parent or guardian of every child participating in its mentoring program with a description of the kind of criminal background checks conducted by the mentoring program on its prospective employees and mentors. Such description shall include identification of the source utilized to obtain criminal background histories on prospective employees and mentors, a list of crimes that would lead the program to deny employment or the opportunity to volunteer as a prospective employee or mentor, and any other process utilized to determine whether or not a prospective employee or mentor with a conviction record shall be offered employment or the opportunity to volunteer. Such description shall clearly state whether or not

prospective employees or mentors may be hired or offered the opportunity to volunteer despite the existence of a conviction history.

§390-f. Report on child care insurance.
The commissioner of the office of children and family services in consultation with the superintendent of financial services, shall undertake a study of the availability, accessibility, and affordability of insurance policies to child care providers. The study shall include, but not be limited to, a review of homeowner insurance policies and health insurance policies. The study shall be completed and a report submitted no later than January first, two thousand nine, to the governor, the commissioner of the office of children and family services, the temporary president of the senate and the speaker of the assembly.

§390-g. Pesticide alternatives.
1. For purposes of this section the following terms shall have the meanings set forth below:
(a) "Day care" shall apply to all child day care centers or head start day care centers, as defined in section three hundred ninety of this title.
(b) "Pesticide" shall have the same meaning as set forth in subdivision thirty-five of section 33-0101 of the environmental conservation law, provided however that it shall not include:
(i) the application of anti-microbial pesticides and anti-microbial products as defined by FIFRA in 7 U.S.C. Section 136(mm) and 136q(h)(2);
(ii) the use of an aerosol product with a directed spray, in containers of eighteen fluid ounces or less, when used to protect individuals from an imminent threat from stinging and biting insects, including venomous spiders, bees, wasps and hornets;
(iii) the use of non-volatile insect or rodent bait in a tamper resistant container;
(iv) the application of a pesticide classified by the United States Environmental Protection Agency as an exempt material under 40 CFR Part 152.25;
(v) the use of boric acid and disodium octaborate tetrahydrate; or
(vi) the use of horticultural soap and oils that do not contain synthetic pesticides or synergists.
2. No day care shall apply pesticide to any playgrounds, turf, athletic or playing fields, except that an emergency application of a pesticide may be made as determined by the county health department or for a county not having a health department such authority as the county legislature shall designate, the commissioner of health or his or her designee, the commissioner of environmental conservation or his or her designee, or, in the case of a public school, the school board.

§390-h. Notice requirement before closing certain day care centers.
1. For the purposes of this section, the following terms shall have the following meanings:
(a) "Child day care center" shall mean a child day care center as defined in paragraph (c) of subdivision one of section three hundred ninety of this title.
(b) "Person legally responsible" shall mean a person legally responsible as defined in subdivision (g) of section one thousand twelve of the family court act.
2. (a) Notwithstanding any other provision of law to the contrary, in a city having a population of one million or more, if the social services district seeks

to close a child day care center under contract with such district, it shall provide at least six months written notice to the child day care center and the parents or persons legally responsible for children enrolled in such centers, prior to the closing.

(b) Paragraph (a) of this subdivision shall not apply in cases where a local social services district seeks to close a child day care center for violating the regulations of the office of children and family services, or for health and safety reasons.

(c) Paragraph (a) of this subdivision shall not apply in cases where a local social services district seeks to close a child day care center on an expedited basis for reasons of public safety, criminal behavior by the center, breach of contract with the local social services district, suspension or revocation of the center's license for non-economic reasons.

§390-i. Notice of inspection report.

In every child day care program that is licensed or registered pursuant to section three hundred ninety of this title, the child day care provider shall post and maintain in a prominent place, a notice, to be provided by the office of children and family services, that shall state the date the most recent child care inspection occurred and provide information for parents and caregivers regarding how to obtain information from such office regarding the results of the inspection. If possible, the child day care provider shall also post such information on the child day care program's website. Such child day care programs shall post and maintain, in a prominent place, such program's most recent compliance history as shown on the office of children and family services website.

§390-j. Performance summary card in a city having a population of one million or more.

1. Definitions. For the purposes of this section, the following terms shall have the following meanings:

(a) "Child care service" shall mean any person who provides child day care in a city having a population of one million or more that is required to obtain a permit to operate pursuant to the health code of such city.

(b) "Performance summary card" shall mean an individualized placard that summarizes the health and safety inspections of a child care service to reflect its compliance with applicable laws. The performance summary card shall summarize recent inspection violations and suspensions as required by rules promulgated by the department issuing such card. A performance summary card may also include additional information such as the capacity of the child care service, the length of time for which such child care service has operated, a comparison of the child care service to other child care services in the same social services district, and other information required by such department's rules.

2. Performance summary card. The department of health and mental hygiene of a city having a population of one million or more shall issue a performance summary card to each child care service that is required to be permitted by the board of health of such city. Such performance card shall be updated and reissued by such department at least once every twelve months. The child care service shall conspicuously post its most recently issued performance summary card at or near its entrance in accordance with rules promulgated by such department. *(Eff.12/31/17,Ch.513,L.2016)*

§391. Violation; injunction.

Violations of any provision of this title may be prohibited by injunction. Whenever the commissioner has reason to believe that any provision of this title is being violated, or is about to be violated, he may maintain and prosecute, in the name of the people of this state, an action in the supreme court for the purpose of obtaining an injunction restraining such violation. Notwithstanding any limitation of the civil practice law and rules, such court may, on motion and affidavit, and upon proof that such violation is one which reasonably may result in injury to any person, whether or not such person is a party to such action, grant a preliminary injunction or interlocutory injunction upon such terms as may be just. No security on the part of the people of this state shall be required.

§392. Services for relative caregivers.

Notwithstanding any other provision of law to the contrary, local social services districts shall make available through the district's website or by other means information for relatives caring for children outside of the foster care system. Such information shall include but not necessarily be limited to:

1. information relating to child only grants, including but not limited to, how to apply for child only grants; and

2. information on department of family assistance or local department of social services funded resources for relative caregivers, including those that provide supportive services for relative caregivers.

Title 2
Powers and Duties of Public Welfare Officials

§395. Responsibility of public welfare districts for the welfare of children.

A public welfare district shall be responsible for the welfare of children who are in need of public assistance and care, support and protection, residing or found in its territory, insofar as not inconsistent with the jurisdiction of a family court. Such assistance and care shall be administered either directly by the public welfare official charged therewith, or by another public welfare official acting on his behalf by and pursuant to the provisions of this chapter, or through an authorized agency as defined by this chapter.

§396. Health and welfare services to all children.

All public welfare districts and towns, shall provide children who attend schools other than public with all or any of the health and welfare services and facilities, including but not limited to health, surgical, medical, dental and therapeutic care and treatment, and corrective aids and appliances, authorized by law and now granted or hereafter made available by the public welfare district or districts and/or towns for or to children in the public schools in so far as these services and facilities may be requested by the authorities of the schools other than public. Any such services or facilities shall be so provided notwithstanding any provision of any charter or other provision of law inconsistent herewith.

§397. Powers and duties of social services officials in relation to children.

All social services officials responsible for the administration of safety net assistance to families shall, in relation to all children in such families other than delinquent children, persons in need of supervision, mentally disabled children, physically handicapped children and children born out of wedlock who shall be cared for under the provisions of the following section, have powers and perform duties as follows:

1. As to destitute children:

(a) Investigate the family circumstances of each child reported as destitute in order to determine what care, supervision or treatment, if any, such child requires.

(b) Administer and supervise relief to families with destitute children when such families are unable to care for such children and relief is necessary to prevent the separation of children from their parents.

(c) Furnish children, whose parents or guardians are unable to do so, with suitable clothing, shoes, books, food and other necessaries to enable them to attend upon instruction as required by law.

2. As to neglected and abused children:

(a) Investigate complaints of neglect and abuse of children and offer protective social services to prevent injury to the child, to safeguard his welfare, and to preserve and stabilize family life wherever possible.

(b) Bring such case when necessary before the family court for adjudication.

(c) Institute proceedings in a court of competent jurisdiction against a parent or adult for neglect or abuse of a child.

3. Provide any necessary medical or hospital care for such children when responsible for the provision of such care under section sixty-nine.

4. The provisions of this section shall not be deemed to confer on social services officials responsible only for the authorization of safety net assistance or of safety net assistance and hospital care, any powers and duties in relation to destitute and neglected children except as follows:

(a) As to destitute children:

(1) Authorize relief to families with destitute children when such families are unable to care for such children and relief is necessary to prevent the separation of children from their parents.

(2) Furnish children, whose parents or guardians are unable to do so, with suitable clothing, shoes, books, food and other necessaries to enable them to attend upon instruction as required by law.

(b) As to neglected and abused children:
Report to the county commissioner any complaint they may receive of neglect and abuse of children.

(c) Provide any necessary medical care or hospital care for such children when responsible for the provision of such care under section sixty-nine.

§398. Additional powers and duties of commissioners of public welfare and certain city public welfare officers in relation to children.
Commissioners of public welfare and city public welfare officers responsible under the provisions of a special or local law for the children hereinafter specified shall have powers and perform duties as follows:

1. As to destitute children:
(a) offer preventive services in accordance with section four hundred nine-a of this article when necessary to avert an impairment or disruption of a family which could result in the placement of the child in foster care;

(b) report to the local criminal justice agency and to the statewide central register for missing children as described in section eight hundred thirty-seven-e of the executive law such relevant information as required on a form prescribed by the commissioner of the division of criminal justice services, in appropriate instances; and

(c) assume charge of and provide care and support for any child who is a destitute child pursuant to paragraph (a) of subdivision three of section three hundred seventy-one of this article who cannot be properly cared for in his or her home, and if required, petition the family court to obtain custody of the child in accordance with article ten-C of the family court act.

2. As to neglected, abused or abandoned children:
(a) Investigate the alleged neglect, abuse or abandonment of a child, offer protective social services to prevent injury to the child, to safeguard his welfare, and to preserve and stabilize family life wherever possible and, if necessary, bring the case before the family court for adjudication and care for the child until the court acts in the matter and, in the case of an abandoned child, shall promptly petition the family court to obtain custody of such child.

(b) Receive and care for any child alleged to be neglected, abused or abandoned who is temporarily placed in his care by the family court pending adjudication by such court of the alleged neglect, abuse or abandonment including the authority to establish, operate, maintain and approve facilities for such purpose in accordance with the regulations of the department; and receive and care for any neglected, abused or abandoned child placed or discharged to his care by the family court.

(c) Any facility designated as of the effective date of this act shall not be disapproved except after consultation with the designating appellate division.

(d) The local social services department shall list all facilities approved under this article for the temporary custody and care of children remanded by the family court and shall file a copy of that list periodically with the clerk of the family court in each county in the judicial district in which the facility is located.

(e) Report to the local registrar of vital statistics of the district in which the child was found the sex, color, approximate date of birth, place of finding, and the name assigned to any child who may be found whose parents are unknown, within ten days whenever possible after the child is found, on a form prescribed therefor by the state commissioner of health, and report the subsequent identification of any such child to the state commissioner of health; provided, however, that in the city of New York such form shall be prescribed by, and such report shall be made to, the department of health.

(f) Report to the local criminal justice agency and to the statewide central register for missing children as described in section eight hundred thirty-seven-e of the executive law such information as required on a form prescribed by the commissioner of the division of criminal justice services within forty-eight hours after an abandoned child is found.

3. As to delinquent children and persons in need of supervision:

(a) Investigate complaints as to alleged delinquency of a child.

(b) Bring such case of alleged delinquency when necessary before the family court.

(c) Receive within fifteen days from the order of placement as a public charge any delinquent child committed or placed or person in need of supervision placed in his or her care by the family court provided, however, that the commissioner of the social services district with whom the child is placed may apply to the state commissioner or his or her designee for approval of an additional fifteen days, upon written documentation to the office of children and family services that the youth is in need of specialized treatment or placement and the diligent efforts by the commissioner of social services to locate an appropriate placement.

3-a. As to delinquent children:

(a)(1) Conditionally release any juvenile delinquent placed with the district to aftercare whenever the district determines conditional release to be consistent with the needs and best interests of such juvenile delinquent, that suitable care and supervision can be provided, and that there is a reasonable probability that such juvenile delinquent can be conditionally released without endangering public safety; provided, however, that such conditional release shall be made in accordance with the regulations of the office of children and family services, and provided further that no juvenile delinquent while absent from a facility or program without the consent of the director of such facility or program shall be conditionally released by the district solely by reason of the absence.

(2) It shall be a condition of such release that a juvenile delinquent so released shall continue to be the responsibility of the social services district for the period provided in the order of placement.

(3) The social services district may provide clothing, services and other necessities for any conditionally released juvenile delinquent, as may be required, including medical care and services not provided to such juvenile delinquent as medical assistance for needy persons pursuant to title eleven of article five of this chapter.

(4) The social services district, pursuant to the regulations of the office of children and family services, may cause a juvenile delinquent to be returned to a facility operated and maintained by the district, or an authorized agency under contract with the district, at any time within the period of placement, where there is a violation of the conditions of release or a change of circumstances.

(5) Juvenile delinquents conditionally released by a social services district may be provided for as follows:

(i) If, in the opinion of the social services district, there is no suitable parent, relative or guardian to whom a juvenile delinquent can be conditionally released, and suitable care cannot otherwise be secured, the district may conditionally release such juvenile delinquent to the care of any other suitable person; provided that where such suitable person has no legal relationship with the juvenile, the district shall advise such person of the procedures for obtaining custody or guardianship of the juvenile.

(ii) If a conditionally released juvenile delinquent is subject to article sixty-five of the education law or elects to participate in an educational program leading to a high school diploma, he or she shall be enrolled in a school or educational program leading to a high school diploma following release, or, if such release occurs during the summer recess, upon the commencement of the next school term. If a conditionally released juvenile delinquent is not subject to article sixty-five of the education law, and does not elect to participate in an educational program leading to a high school diploma, steps shall be taken, to the extent possible, to facilitate his or her gainful employment or enrollment in a vocational program following release.

(b) When a juvenile delinquent placed with the social services district is absent from placement without consent, such absence shall interrupt the calculation of time for his or her placement. Such interruption shall continue until such juvenile delinquent returns to the facility or authorized agency in which he or she was placed. Provided, however, that any time spent by a juvenile delinquent in custody from the date of absence to the date placement resumes shall be credited against the time of such placement provided that such custody:

(1) was due to an arrest or surrender based upon the absence; or

(2) arose from an arrest or surrender on another charge which did not culminate in a conviction, adjudication or adjustment.

(c) In addition to the other requirements of this section, no juvenile delinquent placed with a social services district operating an approved juvenile justice services close to home initiative pursuant to section four hundred four of this chapter pursuant to a restrictive placement under the family court act shall be released except pursuant to section 353.5 of the family court act.

4. As to mentally disabled and physically handicapped children:

(a) Obtain admission to state and other suitable schools, hospitals, other institutions, or care in their own homes or in family free or boarding homes or in agency boarding homes or group homes for such children in accordance with the provisions of the mental hygiene law, education law and acts relating to the family court.

(b) Maintain supervision over such disabled or physically handicapped children as are not in institutions, hospitals or schools or under the jurisdiction of the family court.

5. As to children born out of wedlock:

(a) Provide care in a family free or boarding home, in an agency boarding home or group home or in an institution for any child born out of wedlock and for his mother as for any other person in need of public assistance and care during pregnancy and during and after delivery, when in the judgment of such social services official needed care cannot be provided in the mother's own home. However, nothing in this section or elsewhere in this chapter contained shall be construed to make any such child or his mother ineligible for such care away from home, regardless of ability or liability to pay therefor; provided, however, that except as hereinafter provided, it shall rest in the discretion of the social services official, in view of all the facts and circumstances present in each case, to determine whether or not to require such mother, or any other person or persons liable by law to contribute to the support thereof, to pay all or any part of such cost, pursuant to the provisions of this section or any other section of this chapter. Any inconsistent provision of law notwithstanding, the acceptance by a private authorized adoption agency of an absolute surrender of a child born out of wedlock from the mother of such child shall relieve her from any and all liability for the support of such child. When in the judgment of a social services official needed care cannot be provided in the home of a minor pregnant with an out of wedlock child, and he has made a determination pursuant to subdivision one of section one hundred thirty-two of this chapter not to make an investigation of the circumstances of such minor and not to require support from persons liable therefor, the authorization of such social services official of necessary medical care for such minor shall have the same force and effect as a consent executed by a parent or guardian of such minor.

(b) Institute proceedings to establish paternity and secure the support and education of any child born out of wedlock or make a compromise with the father of such child, in accordance with the provisions of law, relating to children born out of wedlock.

(c) Hold and disburse the money received from such a compromise or pay it to the mother if she gives security for the support of the child.

(d) When practicable, require the mother to contribute to the support of the child.

6. As to all foregoing classes of children:

(a) Investigate the family circumstances of each child reported to him as destitute, neglected, abused, delinquent, disabled or physically handicapped in order to determine what assistance and care, supervision or treatment, if any, such child requires.

(b) Provide for expert mental and physical examination of any child whom he has reason to suspect of mental or physical disability or disease and pay for such examination from public funds, if necessary.

(c) Provide necessary medical or surgical care in a suitable hospital, sanatorium, preventorium or other institution or in his own home for any child needing such care and pay for such care from public funds, if necessary. However, in the case of a child or minor who is eligible to receive care as medical assistance for needy persons pursuant to title eleven of article five of this chapter, such care shall be provided pursuant to the provisions of that title.

(d) Ascertain the financial ability of the parents of children who become public charges and collect toward the expense of such child's care such sum as the parents are able to pay.

(e) Collect from parents whose children have been discharged to his care by the family court such sums as they are ordered to pay for the maintenance of such children and report any failure to comply with such order to such court.

(f) When in his judgment it is advisable for the welfare of the child, accept the surrender of a child by an instrument in writing in accordance with the provisions of this chapter. Any inconsistent provision of law notwithstanding, the acceptance by the social services official of a surrender of a child born out of wedlock from the mother or father of such child shall relieve the parent executing such surrender from any and all liability for the support of such child.

(g) (1) Place children in its care and custody or its custody and guardianship, in suitable instances, in family homes, agency boarding homes, group homes or institutions under the proper safeguards. Such placements can be made either directly, or through an authorized agency, except that, direct placements in agency boarding homes or group homes may be made by the social services district only if the office of children and family services has authorized the district to operate such homes in accordance with the provisions of section three hundred seventy-four-b of this chapter and only if suitable care is not otherwise available through an authorized agency under the control of persons of the same religious faith as the child. Where such district places a child in an agency boarding home, group home or institution, either directly, or through an authorized agency, the district shall certify in writing to the office of children and family services, that such placement was made because it offers the most appropriate and least restrictive level of care for the child, and, is more appropriate than a family foster home placement, or, that such placement is necessary because there are no qualified foster families available within the district who can care for the child. If placements in agency boarding homes, group homes or institutions are the result of a lack of foster parents within a particular district, the office of children and family services shall assist such district to recruit and train foster parents. Placements shall be made only in institutions visited, inspected and supervised in accordance with title three of article seven of this chapter and conducted in conformity with the applicable regulations of the supervising state agency in accordance with title three of article seven of this chapter. With the approval of the office of children and family services, a social services district may place a child in its care and custody or its custody and guardianship in a federally funded job corps program and may receive reimbursement for the approved costs of appropriate program administration and supervision pursuant to a plan developed by the department and approved by the director of the budget.

(2) A social services district may place a child in its care and custody or its custody and guardianship in a home or facility operated or licensed by any office of the department of mental hygiene, subject to the relevant provisions of the mental hygiene law and the admission criteria of the facility. The director of the budget may authorize such transfers of appropriations under the provisions of section fifty of the state finance law as may be necessary to secure federal reimbursement for such placements.

(3) (i) Effective sixty days after the enactment of this subparagraph, there is hereby established within a social services district with a population in excess of two million a two-year demonstration project which affords authorized agencies with which foster children are placed enhanced administrative flexibility. Pursuant to such demonstration project, an authorized agency with which the social services district has placed a child shall have the authority to:

(A) give all necessary consents to the discharge of the child from foster care when such authorized agency has submitted a written request for approval of such discharge to the social services official and the social services official has not disapproved such discharge within thirty days of receiving such request;

(B) change a goal for the child when such authorized agency has submitted a written request for approval of such change of goal to the social services official and the social services official has not disapproved such goal within thirty days of receiving such request;

(C) commence a proceeding to free the child for adoption when such authorized agency has submitted a written request for approval of the commencement of such proceeding to the social services official, if the social services official has not disapproved such commencement within thirty days of receiving such request, in which case such a request shall be deemed approved; and

(D) consent to the adoption of a child whose custody and guardianship, or of a child where such child's parents are both deceased, or where one parent is deceased and the other parent is not entitled to notice pursuant to sections one hundred eleven and one hundred eleven-a of the domestic relations law, and whose care and custody, has been transferred to a social services district and who has been placed by the social services official with the authorized agency when the authorized agency has submitted a written request for approval to consent to the adoption, if the social services district has not disapproved the request to consent to adoption within sixty days after its submission, in which case such request shall be deemed approved and the authorized agency may give all necessary consent to the adoption of the child.

(ii) Nothing herein shall result in the transfer of care and custody or custody and guardianship of a child from the social services official to the authorized agency.

(iii) Within three months of the conclusion of the demonstration project, such social services district shall issue a report to the department regarding the effectiveness of the demonstration project. Such report shall include recommendations for possible statutory and regulatory amendments in relation to the administration of foster care.

(4) A social services district may place a child in its care and custody or its custody and guardianship in a family home certified by the division for youth, which shall not include a group home. Such placements shall be subject to the relevant provisions of this chapter, the executive law and the admission criteria of the home.

(h) Supervise children who have been cared for away from their families until such children become twenty-one years of age or until they are discharged to their own parents, relatives within the third degree or guardians, or adopted, provided, however, that in the case of a child who is developmentally disabled as such term is defined in section 1.03 of the mental hygiene law, emotionally disturbed or physically handicapped, and who is receiving care in a group home, agency boarding home or any child care facility operated by an authorized agency with a capacity of thirteen or more children, and who is in receipt of educational services and under the care and custody of a local department of social services, the commissioner of the office of children and family services shall allow such child who reaches the age of twenty-one during the period commencing on the first day of September and ending on the thirtieth day of June to be entitled to continue in such program until the thirtieth day of June or until the termination of the school year, whichever shall first occur.

(i) *(REPEALED, Eff. 9/18/12, Ch.3, L.2012)*

(j) Permit children and minors who are being cared for away from their own homes as public charges to retain the maximum amount of their monthly earned income for future identifiable needs in accordance with the regulations of the department and consistent with the federal law applicable to the treatment of income and resources under the aid to families with dependent children program.

(k) In accordance with regulations of the department, provide suitable vocational training through any institution licensed or approved by the state education department, for any minor in his care who demonstrates to his satisfaction the possession of talent, aptitude and ability necessary to benefit therefrom, provided such minor could not otherwise obtain such training. Expenditures may be made for tuition, books, supplies, and all other necessary items to enable such minor to obtain such training.

(*l*) In accordance with regulations of the department, provide maintenance in a summer camp for children and minors who are being cared for away from their own homes as public charges, when in his judgment it is advisable for the welfare of such children and minors.

(n) When it is in the best interest of the child, place a child who is being returned to foster care, following an interruption in care, or a child who is being returned to a family boarding home following placement in a foster care facility with the foster care parents with whom that child was last placed, notwithstanding the provisions of subdivisions three and four of section three hundred seventy-eight of this chapter. When it is in the best interests of the minor parent and the minor parent's child or children, place the minor parent who is being returned to foster care following an interruption in care, and the minor parent's child or children or the minor parent who is being returned to a family boarding home following placement in a foster care facility and the minor parent's child or children with the foster care parents with whom the minor parent was last placed, notwithstanding the provisions of subdivisions three and four of section three hundred seventy-eight of this chapter.

(o) Compliance with a court order enforcing visitation rights of a non-custodial parent or grandparent pursuant to part eight of article ten of the family court act, subdivision ten of section three hundred fifty-eight-a or paragraph (d) of subdivision two of section three hundred eighty-four-a of this chapter, and responsibility for the return of such child after visitation so ordered.

*(p) Provide respite care for children who have special needs as described in subdivision fifteen of this section including, but not limited to, those children who are diagnosed as having AIDS or HIV related disease. For the purposes of this paragraph, respite care shall mean the provision of temporary care and supervision of children on behalf of a foster parent of a child with such special needs. Such care may be provided by a foster family boarding home, an agency operated boarding home, a group home, an institution or by an authorized staff member of such programs or other provider approved by the local district based on the individual circumstances of the caregiver and the needs of the child, for up to three consecutive weeks but no more than seven weeks in a calendar year. The department shall, by regulation, establish standards for respite care and training for the providers of such care.

*(p) Consistent with the provisions of this chapter, provide necessary care, services and supervision including medical care, to a child placed in foster care pursuant to subparagraph (ii) of paragraph (a) of subdivision two of section ten hundred seventeen of the family court act, and reimbursement therefor to relatives of such child as approved foster parents with whom such child is residing.

7. Notwithstanding any inconsistent provisions of law, no city forming part of a county public welfare district may hereafter assume any of the powers, duties and responsibilities mentioned in this section. However, this subdivision shall not be deemed or construed to prohibit a public welfare officer of a city forming part of a county public welfare district from exercising and performing on behalf of the county commissioner of public welfare, pursuant to the provisions of title three-a of article three, any of the powers and duties mentioned in this section. A city forming part of a county public welfare district which heretofore assumed or upon which was heretofore imposed the responsibility for providing any or all of the assistance, care and service mentioned in this section, shall hereafter continue to have such responsibility, provided, however, that the continuance of such responsibility shall be

*There are 2 paragraphs "(p)"

consistent with the powers, duties and responsibilities of such city under and pursuant to the provisions of title three-a of article three.

8. A public welfare official who is authorized to place children or minors in homes or institutions pursuant to provisions of this section shall have the power to place children or minors in a public institution for children.

9. A social services official shall have the same authority as a peace officer to remove a child from his home without an order of the family court and without the consent of the parent or person responsible for such child's care if the child is in such condition that his continuing in the home presents an imminent danger to the child's life or health. When a child is removed from his home pursuant to the provisions of this subdivision, the social services official shall promptly inform the parent or person responsible for such child's care and the family court of his action.

10. Any provision of this chapter or any other law notwithstanding, where a foster child for whom a social services official has been making foster care payments is in attendance at a college or university away from his foster family boarding home, group home, agency boarding home or institution, a social services official may make foster payments, not to exceed the amount which would have been paid to a foster parent on behalf of said child had the child been cared for in a foster family boarding home, to such college or university in lieu of payment to the foster parents or authorized agency, for the purpose of room and board, if not otherwise provided.

11. In the case of a child who is adjudicated a person in need of supervision or a juvenile delinquent and is placed by the family court with the division for youth and who is placed by the division for youth with an authorized agency pursuant to court order, the social services official shall make expenditures in accordance with the regulations of the department for the care and maintenance of such child during the term of such placement subject to state reimbursement pursuant to this title, or article nineteen-G of the executive law in applicable cases.

12. A social services official shall be permitted to place persons adjudicated in need of supervision or delinquent, and alleged persons to be in need of supervision in detention pending transfer to a placement, in the same foster care facilities as are providing care to destitute, neglected, abused or abandoned children. Such foster care facilities shall not provide care to a youth in the care of a social services official as a convicted juvenile offender.

13. (a) In the case of a child with a handicapping condition who is placed, pursuant to this chapter, in a foster care agency or institution located outside the state, and who attains the age of eighteen, the social services official shall:

(i) determine whether such child will need services after the age of twenty-one, and, if such need exists;

(ii) assess the nature of the services required;

(iii) notify the parent or guardian of such child's need for services; and

(iv) upon the written consent of the parent or guardian, and notwithstanding section three hundred seventy-two of this article, submit a report on the child's need for services after age twenty-one to the department for planning purposes.

(b) Upon the written consent of the parent or guardian, the department shall submit the report received pursuant to paragraph (a) of this subdivision to the council on children and families.

(c) When a child's report is submitted to the council on children and families pursuant to this subdivision, the council shall cooperate with adult service providers, such as the department of social services, the office of mental retardation and developmental disabilities, the office of mental health and the office of vocational rehabilitation of the education department in planning and coordinating such child's return to New York state for adult services. The council shall arrange with the appropriate state agency for the development of a recommendation of all appropriate in-state programs operated, licensed, certified or authorized by such agency and which may be available when such child attains the age of twenty-one. Such recommendation of all programs shall be made available to the parent or guardian of such child at least six months before such child attains the age of twenty-one. All records, reports and information received, compiled or maintained by the council pursuant to this subdivision shall be subject to the confidentiality requirements of the department.

14. (a) In the case of a child who is developmentally disabled as such term is defined in section 1.03 of the mental hygiene law, emotionally disturbed or physically handicapped and who is receiving care in a group home, agency boarding home, or any child care facility operated by an authorized agency with a capacity of thirteen or more children, who attains the age of eighteen and who will continue in such care after the age of eighteen, or who is placed in such care after the age of eighteen, the social services official shall notify the parent or guardian of such child that such care will terminate when such child attains the age of twenty-one provided, however, that any such child in receipt of educational services and under the care and custody of a local department of social services who reaches the age of twenty-one during the period commencing on the first day of September and ending on the thirtieth day of June shall be entitled to continue in such program until the thirtieth day of June or until the termination of the school year, whichever shall first occur. Such notice shall be in writing and shall describe in detail the parent's or guardian's opportunity to consent to having such child's name and other information forwarded in a report to the commissioner of mental health, commissioner of mental retardation and developmental disabilities, commissioner of education or commissioner of the office of children and family services or their designees for the purpose of determining whether such child will likely need services after the age of twenty-one and, if so, recommending possible adult services.

(b) Upon the written consent of the parent or guardian, and notwithstanding section three hundred seventy-two of this article, the social services official shall submit a report on such child's possible need for services after age twenty-one to the commissioner of mental health, commissioner of mental retardation and developmental disabilities, commissioner of social services or commissioner of education or their designees for the development of a recommendation pursuant to section 7.37 or 13.37 of the mental hygiene law, section three hundred ninety-eight-c of this article or subdivision ten of section four thousand four hundred three of the education law. The social services official shall determine which commissioner shall receive the report by considering the child's handicapping condition. If the social services official determines that the child will need adult services from the department and such social services official is the commissioner's designee pursuant to this subdivision and section three hundred ninety-eight-c of this article, such social services official shall perform the services described in section three hundred ninety-eight-c of this article.

(c) A copy of such report shall also be submitted to the department at the same time that such report is submitted to the commissioner of mental health, commissioner of mental retardation and developmental disabilities or commissioner of education or their designees.

(d) When the social services official is notified by the commissioner who received the report that such state agency is not responsible for determining and recommending adult services for the child, the social services official shall forward the report to another commissioner; or, if the social services official determines that there exists a dispute between state agencies as to which state agency has the responsibility for determining and recommending adult services, the social services official may forward the report to the council on children and families for a resolution of such dispute.

(e) The social services official shall prepare and submit an annual report to the department on October first, nineteen hundred eighty-four and thereafter on or before October first of each year. Such annual report shall contain the number of cases submitted to each commissioner pursuant to paragraph (b) of this subdivision, the type and severity of the handicapping condition of each such case, the number of notices received which deny responsibility for determining and recommending adult services, and other information necessary for the department and the council on children and families to monitor the need for adult services, but shall not contain personally identifying information. The department shall forward copies of such annual reports to the council on children and families. All information received by the council on children and families pursuant to this paragraph shall be subject to the confidentiality requirements of the department.

15. (a) In the case of a child who has special needs due to a high level of disturbed behavior, emotional disturbance or physical or health needs as determined by the district in accordance with the rules and regulations of the department and who has been placed with a therapeutic foster parent, the social services official shall make available periodic respite care services for such parent, necessary consultation services between the therapeutic foster care parent and professionals familiar with the special needs of the child and such other support services as are reasonably necessary to prevent placement of the child in a group home, an agency operated boarding home or an institution.

(b) Prior to placement of a child who has been determined to have special needs with a therapeutic foster parent, the social services official shall require such foster parent to complete an approved training program. The department shall not provide enhanced reimbursement for such placement unless the social services official certifies that the foster parent has successfully completed an approved training program.

(c) A social services official shall require that the family services plan developed pursuant to section four hundred nine-e of this article for a child placed with a therapeutic foster parent include a treatment plan prepared in consultation with the therapeutic foster parent and approved by the social services official.

16. Notwithstanding any provision of law to the contrary, with regard to the placement of all categories of foster children, the social services official or the voluntary authorized agency under contract with such official must consider giving preference to placement of a child with an adult relative over a non-related caregiver, provided that the relative caregiver meets relevant child welfare standards.

§398-a.   Standards of payment for foster care.

(1) For purposes of this section, notwithstanding any other provisions of law, the term foster child shall mean a person who is cared for away from his or her home under conditions prescribed by regulations of the department and who is: (a) under the age of eighteen years, (b) under the age of twenty-one years if a student attending a school, college or university or regularly attending a course of vocational or technical training designed to fit him or her for gainful employment or (c) between the ages of eighteen and twenty-one who lacks the skills or ability to live independently and consents to continue in care.

*(2) The office of children and family services shall promulgate, subject to consultation with appropriate state agencies, the approval of the director of the budget and certification to the chairmen of the senate finance and assembly ways and means committees, regulations establishing standards of payment for care provided foster children when the care of such children is subject to public financial support, when such care is provided by relatives, authorized agencies, family boarding homes, or state agencies. Such standards of payment shall include the care required to be provided for foster children and the cost of such care. When the office of children and family services has established such standards, reimbursement under subdivision two of section one hundred fifty-three-k of this chapter, for the care of foster children shall be limited in accordance with such standards.   *Effective until June 30, 2017*

*(2) The department shall promulgate, subject to consultation with appropriate state agencies, the approval of the director of the budget and certification to the chairmen of the senate finance and assembly ways and means committees, regulations establishing standards of payment for care provided foster children when the care of such children is subject to public financial support, when such care is provided by relatives, authorized agencies, family boarding homes, or state agencies. Such standards of payment shall include the care required to be provided for the foster child and the cost of such care. When the department has established such standards, reimbursement under section one hundred fifty-three of this chapter, for the care of foster children shall be limited in accordance with such standards.   *Effective June 30, 2017*

(2-a) Those social services districts that as of January first, two thousand five were paying at least one hundred percent of the applicable rates published by the office of children and family services for the two thousand four--two thousand five rate year for care provided to foster children in institutions, group residences, group homes and agency boarding homes and/or the applicable administrative/services rates published by the office for the operations of authorized agencies for care provided to foster children in therapeutic, special needs and emergency foster boarding homes must pay for the two thousand five--two thousand six rate year and for each subsequent rate year thereafter at least one hundred percent of the applicable rates published by the office for that rate year. Those social services districts that as of January first, two thousand five were paying less than the applicable rates published by the office for the two thousand four--two thousand five rate year for care provided to foster children in institutions, group residences, group homes and agency boarding homes and/or the applicable administrative/services rates published by the office for the operations of authorized agencies for care provided to foster children in therapeutic, special needs and emergency foster boarding homes must increase their rates of payment so that: effective July first, two thousand five, the difference between the percentage of the applicable rates published by the office for the two thousand five--two thousand six rate year and the rates such districts are paying is at least two-thirds less than the difference between the percentage of the applicable rates published by the office for the two thousand four--two thousand five rate year and the rates that such districts were paying for such programs on January first, two thousand five; and effective July first, two thousand six for the two thousand six--two thousand seven rate year and for each subsequent year thereafter all social services districts shall pay at least one hundred percent of the applicable rates published by the office for the applicable rate year.

(2-b) Payments made directly by social services districts to foster boarding homes for foster care pursuant to this section may be made by direct deposit or debit card, as elected by the recipient, and administered electronically, and in accordance with such guidelines as may be set forth by regulation of the office of children and family services. The office of children and family services may enter into contracts on behalf of social services districts for such direct deposit or debit card services in accordance with section twenty-one-a of this chapter.

(3) If the commissioner finds that a social services district or a city containing a social services district has adopted regulations establishing standards of payment for care provided foster children by relatives, authorized agencies or family boarding homes, when the care of such children is subject to public financial support, which standards are substantially equivalent to those promulgated by the department, such department standards shall not be applicable in such district or city.

(4) If and so long as federal aid is available therefor and subject to the approval of the director of the budget, the department is authorized to conduct a three year demonstration project to test the effectiveness of establishing capitated rates for foster care. The demonstration project shall be entitled the homerebuilders demonstration project. The goal of the project shall be to demonstrate how innovative methods to fund foster care programs may result in the discharge of children from foster care to suitable, permanent homes in a more timely manner, at no additional costs to state and local governments, through service continuity, intensified discharge planning, pre-adoption services, after-care services and/or post-adoption services. Notwithstanding any inconsistent provision of law, in order to implement a demonstration project relating to the effectiveness of establishing capitated rates for foster care, the department may waive provisions set forth in: (a) section one hundred fifty-three and this section, with regard to limitations on capitated reimbursement to a social services district for after-care or post-adoption services to children and families participating in the homerebuilders demonstration project, where the child is no longer in the care and custody or custody and guardianship of the local commissioner of social services; and (b) subparagraph (ii) of paragraph (e) of subdivision five of section four hundred nine-a of this title, with regard to limitations on reimbursement for intensive home based family preservation services to children participating in the homerebuilders demonstration project who are in the care and custody or custody and guardianship of a local commissioner of social services; and (c) the regulations promulgated implementing such provisions of law. The authority of the department to waive such provisions shall be limited to the purpose of implementing such demonstration project and shall expire with the completion of the demonstration project, unless otherwise authorized by law. The department shall report to the governor and the legislature on the status of the homerebuilders demonstration project at least annually after its commencement and shall submit a final report thereon to the governor and the legislature no

later than July first, nineteen hundred ninety-seven. Such final report shall set forth the findings of the homebuilders demonstration project and any recommendations for statutory or regulatory changes.

(5) (a) The office of children and family services shall establish, subject to consultation with appropriate state agencies, the approval of the director of the budget and federal approval, standards of payment for the capital costs of approved projects for residential institutions for children which enter into a lease, sublease or other agreement with the dormitory authority pursuant to subdivision forty of section sixteen hundred eighty of the public authorities law. The maintenance rate established by the commissioner of the office of children and family services for such residential institutions for children shall be established in two parts, one part of which will be the capital financing add on rate, which shall be the cost per child of the annual payment pursuant to such lease, sublease or other agreement. The applicable social services district or school district responsible for the maintenance cost of a child placed in such residential institution for children, must agree to pay and is responsible for paying the residential institution for children one hundred percent of the capital financing add-on rate for each such child placed in such institution. To the extent permissible under federal law and regulation, the capital financing add-on rate shall not be subject to any cost screens, caps or parameters limiting or reducing the amount of such cost required by this subdivision.

(b) The expenditures made by a social services district or school district for the capital financing add on rate for children placed by a committee on special education of a school district in a residential institution for children which has a lease, sublease or other agreement with the dormitory authority pursuant to subdivision forty of section sixteen hundred eighty of the public authorities law, shall be subject to state reimbursement in accordance with subdivision ten of section one hundred fifty-three of this chapter or article eighty-nine of the education law, as applicable.

(c) The expenditures of a social services district for the capital financing add-on rate for foster children placed in a residential institution for children which has a lease, sublease or other agreement with the dormitory authority pursuant to subdivision forty of section sixteen hundred eighty of the public authorities law shall be subject to fifty percent state reimbursement from the office of children and family services, net of any available federal funds, for the portion of the costs that exceed the district's foster care block grant allocation.

§398-b.   Transition to managed care.
1. Notwithstanding any inconsistent provision of law to the contrary and subject to the availability of federal financial participation, the commissioner is authorized to make grants up to a gross amount of five million dollars for state fiscal year two thousand fourteen--fifteen and up to a gross amount of fifteen million dollars for state fiscal year two thousand fifteen--sixteen to facilitate the transition of foster care children placed with voluntary foster care agencies to managed care. The use of such funds may include providing training and consulting services to voluntary agencies to assess readiness and make necessary infrastructure and organizational modifications, collecting service utilization and other data from voluntary agencies and other entities, and making investments in health information technology, including the infrastructure necessary to establish and maintain electronic health records. Such funds shall be distributed pursuant to a formula to be developed by the commissioner of health, in consultation with the commissioner of the office of children and

family services. In developing such formula the commissioners may take into account size and scope of provider operations as a factor relevant to eligibility for such funds. Each recipient of such funds shall be required to document and demonstrate the effective use of funds distributed herein. If federal financial participation is unavailable, then the nonfederal share of payments pursuant to this subdivision may be made as state grants.

2. Data provided by voluntary foster care agencies shall be compliant with the health insurance portability and accountability act, and shall be transmitted securely using eMEDS or other mechanism to be determined by the department of health. Such data may be used by the department of health to establish rates of payment for managed care organizations for services provided to children in foster care. In establishing such rates the commissioner of health shall also take into account care coordination services that will continue to be provided by the voluntary foster care agencies.

3. The commissioner of health shall issue a report to be made public on the department of health's website. Such report shall conform to the requirements of subdivision five of section ninety-two of part H of chapter fifty-nine of the laws of two thousand eleven.

§398-c. **Powers and duties of the commissioner in relation to children.**
1. The commissioner shall determine whether a child, whose report is submitted to the department pursuant to subparagraph five of paragraph b of subdivision one of section forty-four hundred two of the education law or subdivision thirteen of section three hundred ninety-eight of this article, will likely need adult services and, if such need will likely exist, develop a recommendation of all appropriate programs authorized or operated by the department which may be available when the child attains the age of twenty-one. If necessary and appropriate, the commissioner may conduct an evaluation of the child to determine if adult services will be necessary. Such recommendation of all programs shall be made available to the parent or guardian of such child as soon as practicable but no later than six months before such child attains the age of twenty-one.

2. If the commissioner determines pursuant to subdivision one of this section, that such child will not require adult services, the commissioner shall notify the child's parent or guardian in writing of such determination. Such notice shall be given as soon as practicable but no later than six months before the child attains the age of twenty-one.

3. Notwithstanding subdivisions one and two of this section, the commissioner may determine that the department is not responsible for determining and recommending adult services for such child. When such a determination is made it shall be made as soon as practicable after receiving the report and the commissioner shall promptly notify in writing the committee on special education, multidisciplinary team or social services official who sent the report that such determination has been made. Such notice shall state the reasons for the determination and may recommend a state agency which may be responsible for determining and recommending adult services.

4. Nothing in this section shall be construed to create an entitlement to adult services.

5. A designee of the commissioner may carry out the functions of the commissioner described in this section.

§398-d.   Child welfare services community demonstration projects.

1. The legislature finds that the centralized delivery of child protective services, preventive services, adoption services and foster care services in a social service district with a population of more than two million hinders their effective delivery and adds unnecessary costs. Numerous studies have recommended that such services serve small areas, be located in such areas, and be integrated. Such relocation will: give caseworkers greater knowledge of their assigned community, the residents of that community and the availability of community-based services; increase the availability of caseworkers; reduce travel time for caseworkers; enable children in foster care to remain in their own communities and schools and maintain their friendships; enable children in foster care to have greater visitation with their parents; provide for more effective delivery of preventive services; and expedite adoptions and otherwise reduce the amount of time children spend in foster care.

The relocation of child welfare service delivery to the community sites will strengthen efforts to provide a wide range of community-based early intervention programs including, but not limited to, school-based health clinics and community schools, thereby ensuring the continued development of a critical mass of community services.

2. No later than March first, nineteen hundred ninety-six, a social service district with a population in excess of two million shall implement at least three demonstration projects for a period of at least two years to provide child welfare services on a community level to improve the delivery of child welfare services, increase adoptions and reduce the rate of foster care placements. These projects shall be located in and serve community school districts which have high rates of: children at risk of becoming a part of the foster care system, poverty, households on public assistance, juvenile delinquency, and unemployment. Such projects shall provide foster care, preventive, adoption and child protective services as required by this article.

3. In proposed demonstration areas, child welfare services must be coordinated with community schools, school health clinics, and other relevant programs to provide and administer the most efficient services. In one demonstration area, the district shall use a caseworker to client ratio equal to the preferred national average of one to fourteen.

4. A report evaluating such projects shall be presented no later than June first, nineteen hundred ninety-eight, to the governor, the department and the respective chairpersons of the assembly children and families committee, the senate children and families committee, the assembly ways and means committee, and the senate finance committee. Such report shall include: (a) the number of children and families who received preventive services, child protective services and foster care, (b) the number of delinquent and incarcerated youth in the demonstration projects, (c) the length of an average foster care placement, (d) the number of completed adoptions for youth residing within the demonstration area, including their age, gender, race, ethnicity and religion, (e) the gross expenditures for foster care, compared to the gross expenditures for child protective, preventive and adoption services, (f) changes in the quality and quantity of time spent by caseworkers with clients, (g) staffing ratios of foster care, preventive and child protective services, (h) the perspective (attitude, viewpoint, outlook) of caseworkers serving and clients served in the demonstration project, and (i) recommendations for expansion of community-based provisions for child welfare services. For purposes of the report, the data described above should be compared to the extent possible with non-demonstration areas.

§398-e.   Eligibility for protective services, foster care services, and residential services for victims of domestic violence.
An alien, including a non-qualified alien, as determined by applicable federal statute and regulation, is eligible for protective services for adults and children, foster care services, and residential services for victims of domestic violence, to the extent such person is otherwise eligible pursuant to this chapter and the regulations of the office of children and family services and the office of temporary and disability assistance.

§399.   Children discharged from state institutions.
The commissioner of social services shall co-operate with the state institutions for delinquent, mentally disabled and physically handicapped children to ascertain the conditions of the home and the character and habits of the parents of a child before his discharge from a state institution, and make recommendations as to the advisability of returning said child to his home. In case the commissioner of social services shall deem it unwise to have any such child returned to his former home, such state institution may, with the consent of the commissioner, place such child into the care of said commissioner of social services.

§400.   Removal of children.
1. When any child shall have been placed in an institution or in a family home by a social services official, the social services official may remove such child from such institution or family home and make such disposition of such child as is provided by law, provided however, that in the case of a child who is a patient in a hospital licensed or operated by the office of mental health, such social services official may remove such child only upon the written authorization of the medical director of the facility in which the child is a patient. A medical director may only refuse to authorize the removal of a child if involuntary care and treatment of the child is warranted. In such case the director shall institute necessary civil commitment proceedings in accordance with article nine of the mental hygiene law.
2. Any person aggrieved by such decision of a social services official may appeal to the department pursuant to the provisions of section twenty-two of this chapter.

§401.   Births to inmates of public homes.
No commissioner of public welfare shall provide care in a public home for any pregnant woman during confinement unless such public home has adequate hospital or infirmary facilities, is equipped to give the necessary medical and nursing care and has a certificate from the department authorizing such public home to care for maternity cases. Certificates authorizing a public home to care for maternity cases may be issued by the department for a one-year period, subject to renewal, but may be revoked at any time by the department. If the public home is not so certified, a commissioner of public welfare shall, a reasonable time before the expected confinement of any pregnant woman inmate, provide suitable maintenance and medical care for her in a hospital or some other place equipped to give adequate care.

§402.   Children forbidden in public homes.
No public welfare official shall send a child to be cared for in a public home, and no commissioner of public welfare and no superintendent of a public home

shall receive a child in a public home, except that a child under the age of two years may be cared for with his mother in a public home. Such child shall not remain in the public home after he becomes two years of age. Provided, however, that when so authorized by the department a child may be sent to a general hospital connected with a public home or to a separate institution located in the grounds of a public home used only for special or temporary care of children. Provided, further, that the provisions of this section shall not be deemed to prohibit the placement of a child or minor in a public institution for children, as defined in section three hundred seventy-one of this chapter.

§403. The religious faith of children and minors.
The religious faith of children and minors between sixteen and eighteen years of age coming under the jurisdiction of public welfare officials shall be preserved and protected in accordance with section three hundred seventy-three.

§404. Juvenile justice services close to home initiative.
1. A social services district in a city with a population in excess of one million may implement a close to home initiative to provide juvenile justice services to all adjudicated juvenile delinquents determined by a family court in such district as needing placement other than in a secure facility and to enter into contracts with any authorized agency, as defined by section three hundred seventy-one of this chapter, to operate and maintain non-secure and limited secure facilities. Such a social services district shall have sufficient capacity to serve all adjudicated juvenile delinquents needing residential placements within the district within twenty-four months of approval of a plan for each setting level except for those juvenile delinquents who need specialized services that are not available within the district.

2. A social services district shall obtain prior approval from the office of children and family services of its plan for establishing and implementing such an initiative in accordance with guidelines established and in the format, and including the information required, by such office. Such district shall submit separate plans for how the district will implement initiatives for juvenile delinquents placed in non-secure settings and in limited secure settings. Any such plan shall specify, in detail, as applicable:

(a) how the district will provide a continuum of evidence informed, high-quality community-based and residential programming that will protect community safety and provide appropriate services to youth, including the operation of non-secure and limited secure facilities, in sufficient capacity and in a manner designed to meet the needs of juvenile delinquents cared for under the initiative. Such programming shall be based on an analysis of recent placement trends of youth from within such district, including the number of youth who have been placed in the custody of the office of children and family services for placement in other than a secure facility;

(b) the anticipated start-up and on-going services and administrative costs of the initiative;

(c) the readiness of the district to establish the initiative and the availability of all needed resources, including the location of services and availability of the providers that will provide all necessary services under the initiative including, but not limited to, residential, non-residential, educational, medical, substance abuse, mental health and after care services and community supervision;

(d) the proposed effective date of the plan and documentation of the district's readiness to begin accepting and appropriately serving juvenile delinquents under the plan;

(e) how the district will provide necessary and appropriate staffing to implement the initiative;

(f) how the district will monitor the quality of services provided to youth, including how the district will provide case management services;

(g) how, throughout the initiative, the district will seek and receive on-going community and stakeholder input relating to the implementation and effectiveness of the initiative;

(h) how the district will ensure that all staff working directly with youth served under the initiative have received necessary and appropriate training;

(i) how the district will monitor the use of restraints on youth, including, but not limited to, the use of mechanical restraints;

(j) how the district will develop and implement programs and policies to ensure program safety and that youth receive appropriate services based on their needs, including, but not limited to, educational, behavioral, mental health and substance abuse services in accordance with individualized treatment plans developed for each youth;

(k) how the district will develop and implement gender specific programming and policies to meet the specialized needs of lesbian, gay, bisexual and transgender youth;

(*l*) how the district will develop and implement programming that is culturally competent to meet the diverse needs of the youth;

(m) how the district will develop and implement local programs that will seek to reduce the disproportionate placement of minority youth in residential programs in the juvenile justice system;

(n) how the district will develop and implement a plan to reduce the number of youth absent without leave from placement;

(o) how the district will develop and implement policies to serve youth in the least restrictive setting consistent with the needs of youth and public safety, and to avoid modifications of placements to the office of children and family services;

(p) how the district will engage in permanency and discharge planning for juvenile delinquents placed in its custody including, but not limited to, securing adequate housing and health insurance and education and employment, as appropriate;

(q) how the district will develop and implement a comprehensive after care program to provide services and supports for youth who have re-entered the community following a juvenile justice placement with the district;

(r) how the district will develop and implement policies focused on reducing recidivism of youth who leave the program;

(s) how the local probation department will implement a comprehensive predisposition investigation process that includes, at least, the use of appropriate assessments to determine the cognitive, educational/vocational, and substance abuse needs of the youth and the use of a validated risk assessment instrument, approved by the office of children and family services; and how the district will implement an intake process for youth placed in residential care that includes the use of appropriate assessments to determine the medical, dental, mental and behavioral health needs of the youth; and

(t) how the district will provide for the restrictive setting and programs necessary to serve youth who need placement in a limited secure setting consistent with the necessity for the protection of the health and safety of the juvenile delinquents in the facility and the surrounding community.

3. (a) Prior to submitting any plan pursuant to subdivision two of this section to implement a juvenile justice services close to home initiative for juvenile delinquents placed in non-secure settings, the social services district shall conduct at least one public hearing on the proposed plan. Any such public hearings shall only be held after thirty days notice has been provided in a newspaper of general circulation within the jurisdiction for which the social services district is located. The notice shall specify the times of the public hearing and provide information on how written comments on the plan may be submitted to the district for consideration. Additionally, for a period of at least thirty days prior to a hearing, the district shall post on its website a notice of the hearing, a copy of the proposed plan, and information on how written comments on the plan may be submitted to the district for consideration.

(b) Prior to submitting a plan pursuant to subdivision two of this section to implement a juvenile justice services close to home initiative for juvenile delinquents placed in limited secure settings, the social services district shall:

(i) hold at least one forum in each of the five boroughs within the district for community members and relevant stakeholders including potential provider agencies to discuss, in general, the manner in which the district intends to provide the residential and aftercare services to youth who need placement in limited secure settings in a manner to protect community safety and provide appropriate services to such youth, and to respond to concerns and receive suggested alternatives;

(ii) conduct at least one public hearing in each of the five boroughs within the district on the proposed plan. Such public hearings shall only be held after thirty days notice has been provided in a newspaper of general circulation in the respective borough. The notice shall specify the time of the hearing in the respective borough and provide information on how written comments on the plan may be submitted to the district for consideration. Additionally, for a period of at least thirty days prior to each such hearing, the district shall post on its website a notice of the hearing, a copy of the proposed plan, and information on how written comments on the plan may be submitted to the district for consideration.

4. The social services district shall submit, with any such plan, an assessment of any written comments received, and any comments presented at the public hearing. At a minimum, such assessment shall contain:

(a) a summary and analysis of the issues raised and significant alternatives suggested;

(b) a statement of the reasons why any significant alternatives were not incorporated into the plan; and

(c) a description of any changes made to the plan as a result of such comments.

At the time of, or prior to, the submission of each such plan to the office, the social services district shall post on its website the plan and the assessment of comments. At the time it submits its plan to the office, the social services district shall provide a copy of the plan and assessment of comments to the temporary president of the senate and the speaker of the assembly.

5. The office of children and family services, in consultation with the office of mental health and the office of alcoholism and substance abuse services, shall be authorized to request amendments to any plan prior to approval. For any plan that only covers juvenile delinquents placed in non-secure settings, the

office shall, within thirty days of receiving the plan, either approve or disapprove the plan or request amendments to the plan. If any amendments are requested to the plan, the office shall approve or disapprove the plan within fifteen days of its resubmission with the requested amendments. For any plan that covers juvenile delinquents placed in limited secure settings, the office shall, within sixty days of receiving the plan, either approve or disapprove the plan or request amendments to the plan. If any amendments are requested to the plan, the office shall approve or disapprove the plan within fifteen days of its resubmission with the requested amendments. In no event shall the office approve such a plan for limited secure settings prior to April first, two thousand thirteen.

6. (a) Notwithstanding any other provision of law to the contrary, if the office of children and family services approves a social services district's plan to implement a juvenile justice services close to home initiative for juvenile delinquents placed in non-secure settings, such office shall work with such district to identify those juvenile delinquents in the office's custody residing in non-secure placements and those conditionally released from a facility who were placed by a family court within the jurisdiction of said social services district. The office shall evaluate the placement length and the needs of such juvenile delinquents and, where appropriate, file a petition pursuant to section 355.1 of the family court act to transfer custody of such youth to said social services district on the effective date of the plan, or as soon as appropriate thereafter, but in no event later than ninety days after such effective date; provided, however, if the office determines, on a case-by-case basis, for reasons documented in writing submitted to the social services district, that a transfer within ninety days of the effective date of the plan would be detrimental to the education or the emotional, mental or physical health of a youth, or would seriously interfere with the youth's interstate transfer or imminent discharge, the office shall provide an estimated time by which the office expects to be able to petition for the transfer of such youth or to release such youth from its care, and shall notify the district and the attorney for the respondent of any delay of that expected date and the reasons for such a delay.

(b) Notwithstanding any other provision of law to the contrary, if the office approves a social services district's plan to implement a juvenile justice services close to home initiative for juvenile delinquents placed in limited-secure settings, such office shall work with such district to identify juvenile delinquents in the office's custody residing in limited secure placements who were placed by a family court in the social services district. The office of children and family services shall evaluate the placement length and needs of such juvenile delinquents and, where appropriate, file a petition pursuant to section 355.1 of the family court act to transfer custody of such youth to said social services district on the effective date of the plan or as soon as appropriate thereafter, but in no event later than ninety days after such effective date; provided, however, if the office determines, on a case-by-case basis, for reasons documented in writing submitted to the social services district, that a transfer within ninety days of the effective date of the plan would be detrimental to the education or the emotional, mental or physical health of a youth, or would seriously interfere with the youth's interstate transfer or imminent discharge, the office shall provide an estimated time by which the office expects to be able to petition for the transfer of such youth or to release such youth from its care, and shall notify the district and the attorney for the respondent of any delay of that expected date and the reasons for such a delay.

7. (a) Notwithstanding the provisions of paragraph (c) of subdivision fifteen of section five hundred one of the executive law, or any other law to the contrary, if the office of children and family services approves a social services district's plan for a juvenile justice services close to home initiative to implement services for juvenile delinquents placed in non-secure or limited secure settings, such office shall be authorized, for up to a year after the effective date of the first of any such approved plan for a district to implement services for each setting level, but in no event later than September first, two thousand fourteen: (1) to close any of its facilities in the corresponding setting levels covered by the approved plan and to make significant associated service reductions and public employee staffing reductions and transfer operations for those setting levels to a private or not-for-profit entity, as determined by the commissioner of the office of children and family services solely to reflect the decrease in the number of juvenile delinquents placed with such office from such social services district; (2) to reduce costs to the state and other social services districts resulting from such decrease; and (3) to adjust services to provide regionally-based care to juvenile delinquents from other parts of the state needing services in those levels of residential services. At least sixty days prior to taking any such action, the commissioner of the office shall provide notice of such action to the speaker of the assembly and the temporary president of the senate and shall post such notice upon its public website. Such notice may be provided at any time on or after the date the office approves a plan authorizing a social services district to implement programs for juvenile delinquents placed in the applicable setting level. Such commissioner shall be authorized to conduct any and all preparatory actions which may be required to effectuate such closures or significant service or staffing reductions and transfer of operations during such sixty day period. In assessing which of such facilities to close, or at which to implement any significant service reductions, public employee staffing reductions and/or transfer of operations to a private or not-for-profit entity, the commissioner shall consider the following factors: (1) ability to provide a safe, humane and therapeutic environment for placed youth; (2) ability to meet the educational, mental health, substance abuse and behavioral health treatment needs of placed youth; (3) community networks and partnerships that promote the social, mental, economic and behavioral development of placed youth; (4) future capacity requirements for the effective operation of youth facilities; (5) the physical characteristics, conditions and costs of operation of the facility; and (6) the location of the facility in regards to costs and ease of transportation of placed youth and their families.

(b) Any transfers of capacity or any resulting transfer of functions shall be authorized to be made by the commissioner of the office of children and family services and any transfer of personnel upon such transfer of capacity or transfer of functions shall be accomplished in accordance with the provisions of section seventy of the civil service law.

8. (a) Notwithstanding any other provision of law to the contrary, eligible expenditures during the applicable time periods made by a social services district for an approved juvenile justice services close to home initiative shall, if approved by the department of family assistance, be subject to reimbursement with state funds only up to the extent of an annual appropriation made specifically therefor, after first deducting therefrom any federal funds properly received or to be received on account thereof; provided, however, that when such funds have been exhausted, a social services district may receive state reimbursement from other available state appropriations for that state

fiscal year for eligible expenditures for services that otherwise would be reimbursable under such funding streams. Any claims submitted by a social services district for reimbursement for a particular state fiscal year for which the social services district does not receive state reimbursement from the annual appropriation for the approved close to home initiative may not be claimed against that district's appropriation for the initiative for the next or any subsequent state fiscal year.

(i) State funding for reimbursement shall be, subject to appropriation, in the following amounts: for state fiscal year 2013-14, $35,200,000 adjusted by any changes in such amount required by subparagraphs (ii) and (iii) of this paragraph; for state fiscal year 2014-15, $41,400,000 adjusted to include the amount of any changes made to the state fiscal year 2013-14 appropriation under subparagraphs (ii) and (iii) of this paragraph plus any additional changes required by such subparagraphs; and, such reimbursement shall be, subject to appropriation, for all subsequent state fiscal years in the amount of the prior year's actual appropriation adjusted by any changes required by subparagraphs (ii) and (iii) of this paragraph.

(ii) The reimbursement amounts set forth in subparagraph (i) of this paragraph shall be increased or decreased by the percentage that the average of the most recently approved maximum state aid rates for group residential foster care programs is higher or lower than the average of the approved maximum state aid rates for group residential foster care programs in existence immediately prior to the most recently approved rates.

(iii) The reimbursement amounts set forth in subparagraph (i) of this paragraph shall be increased if either the population of alleged juvenile delinquents who receive a probation intake or the total population of adjudicated juvenile delinquents placed on probation combined with the population of adjudicated juvenile delinquents placed out of their homes in a setting other than a secure facility pursuant to section 352.2 of the family court act, increases by at least ten percent over the respective population in the annual baseline year. The baseline year shall be the period from July first, two thousand ten through June thirtieth, two thousand eleven or the most recent twelve month period for which there is complete data, whichever is later. In each successive year, the population of the previous July first through June thirtieth period shall be compared to the baseline year for determining any adjustments to a state fiscal year appropriation. When either population increases by ten percent or more, the reimbursement will be adjusted by a percentage equal to the larger of the percentage increase in either the number of probation intakes for alleged juvenile delinquents or the total population of adjudicated juvenile delinquents placed on probation combined with the population of adjudicated juvenile delinquents placed out of their homes in a setting other than a secure facility pursuant to section 352.2 of the family court act.

(iv) The social services district and/or the New York city department of probation shall provide an annual report including the data required to calculate the population adjustment to the New York city office of management and budget, the division of criminal justice services and the state division of the budget no later than the first day of September following the close of the previous July first through June thirtieth period.

(b) The department of family assistance is authorized, in its discretion, to make advances to a social services district in anticipation of the state reimbursement provided for in this section.

(c) A social services district shall conduct eligibility determinations for federal and state funding and submit claims for reimbursement in such form and manner and at such times and for such periods as the department of family assistance shall determine.

(d) Notwithstanding any inconsistent provision of law or regulation of the department of family assistance, state reimbursement shall not be made for any expenditure made for the duplication of any grant or allowance for any period.

(e) Claims submitted by a social services district for reimbursement shall be paid after deducting any expenditures defrayed by fees, third party reimbursement, and any non-tax levy funds including any donated funds.

(f) The office of children and family services shall not reimburse any claims for expenditures for residential services that are submitted more than twenty-two months after the calendar quarter in which the expenditures were made.

(g) Notwithstanding any other provision of law, the state shall not be responsible for reimbursing a social services district and a district shall not seek state reimbursement for any portion of any state disallowance or sanction taken against the social services district, or any federal disallowance attributable to final federal agency decisions or to settlements made, when such disallowance or sanction results from the failure of the social services district to comply with federal or state requirements, including, but not limited to, failure to document eligibility for the federal or state funds in the case record. To the extent that the social services district has sufficient claims other than those that are subject to disallowance or sanction to draw down the full annual appropriation, such disallowance or sanction shall not result in a reduction in payment of state funds to the district unless the district requests that the department use a portion of the appropriation toward meeting the district's responsibility to repay the federal government for the disallowance or sanction and any related interest payments.

(h) Rates for residential services. (i) The office shall establish the rates, in accordance with section three hundred ninety-eight-a of this chapter, for any non-secure facilities established under an approved juvenile justice services close to home initiative. For any such non-secure facility that will be used primarily by the social services district with an approved close to home initiative, final authority for establishment of such rates and any adjustments thereto shall reside with the office, but such rates and any adjustments thereto shall be established only upon the request of, and in consultation with, such social services district.

(ii) A social services district with an approved juvenile justice services close to home initiative for juvenile delinquents placed in limited secure settings shall have the authority to establish and adjust, on an annual or regular basis, maintenance rates for limited secure facilities providing residential services under such initiative. Such rates shall not be subject to the provisions of section three hundred ninety-eight-a of this chapter but shall be subject to maximum cost limits established by the office of children and family services.

9. Upon approval of a social services district's plan, the office of children and family services shall notify the supervising family court judge responsible for the family courts serving such district of the effective date and placement settings covered by the plan.

(a) Beginning on the effective date of a district's approved plan that only covers juvenile delinquents placed in non-secure settings, a family court judge serving in a county where such social services district is located shall only be authorized to place an adjudicated juvenile delinquent in the custody of the commissioner of the office of children and family services for placement in a secure or limited secure facility pursuant to section 353.3 or 353.5 of the family court act.

(b) Beginning on the effective date of a district's approved plan to implement programs for juvenile delinquents placed in limited secure settings, a family court judge serving in a county where such social services district is located shall only be authorized to place an adjudicated juvenile delinquent in the custody of the commissioner of the office of children and family services for placement in a secure facility pursuant to section 353.3 or 353.5 of the family court act.

10. If the social services district receives the necessary approval to implement a close to home initiative, the district shall implement the initiative in accordance with all applicable federal and state laws and regulations. If the social services district receives the necessary approval of a plan for juvenile delinquents placed in limited secure settings, the office shall promulgate regulations governing the operation of such limited secure facilities. If such regulations are not adopted prior to the date that an authorized agency applies for a license to operate such a facility, the facility shall be subject to the existing regulations of the office that would apply to the operation of a foster care facility of the same size; provided, however, that the office shall be authorized to grant an exception to the authorized agency, until such limited secure regulations are adopted, to any such existing regulation that the office determines would impede the ability of the authorized agency to provide the restrictive setting and programs necessary to serve youth who need placement in a limited secure setting in accordance with the approved plan. Any limited secure facility that is granted such a waiver shall comply with any alternate requirements the office may consider necessary for the protection of the health or safety of the juvenile delinquents in the facility or the surrounding community. The office shall take all reasonable steps available to finalize the adoption of regulations governing the operation of such limited secure facilities no later than six months after it issues the first license for a program to provide services to juvenile delinquents placed in limited secure settings but in no event shall such regulations be adopted on an emergency basis.

(a) The initiative shall be subject to the office of children and family services' ongoing oversight and monitoring including, but not limited to: case record reviews; staff, family, and client interviews; on-site inspections; review of data regarding provider performance, youth and staff safety, and quality of care, which must be provided to the office in order to carry out its responsibilities, in the form and manner and at such times as required by the office; and continued licensing and monitoring of the authorized agencies providing services under the plan pursuant to this chapter.

(b) The social services district shall provide each juvenile delinquent with an appropriate level of services designed to meet his or her individual needs and to enhance public safety and shall provide the office of children and family services with specific information as required by the office, in the format and at such times as required by such office, on the youth participating in the initiative and the programs serving such youth. Such information shall be provided to the office of children and family services on a monthly basis for the first twelve months immediately following the implementation of the programs for each level of care and shall be provided to such office on a quarterly basis thereafter.

11. The social services district shall submit an annual report to the office of children and family services, the temporary president of the senate and the speaker of the assembly, in the format required by such office, detailing overall initiative performance. Such report shall include, but not be limited to:

(a) number of juvenile delinquents placed with the local social services district;

(b) number of juvenile delinquents placed in a non-secure facility with the social services district;

(c) number of juvenile delinquents placed in a limited secure facility with the social services district, as applicable;

(d) demographic information about juvenile delinquents in care;

(e) number of specialized beds in each category of specialized program;

(f) number and nature of incident reports;

(g) number of juvenile delinquents absent without leave per facility;

(h) average length of stay;

(i) number of conditionally released juvenile delinquents;

(j) number of discharged juvenile delinquents who are subsequently placed with the district;

(k) number and nature of corrective action plans and resolutions;

(l) number of juvenile delinquents transferred between facilities, including the number of juvenile delinquents transferred between non-secure and limited-secure facilities, as applicable; and

(m) number of petitions filed to transfer juvenile delinquents between the custody of the office and the social services district.

12. If the office of children and family services determines that the social services district is failing to adequately provide for the juvenile delinquents placed under an approved plan, such office may require the social services district to submit a corrective action plan, for such office's approval, demonstrating how it will rectify the inadequacies in the time specified by the office, but no later than thirty days from such request. If the office determines that the social services district is failing to make sufficient progress towards implementing the corrective action plan in the time and manner approved by the office but no later than sixty days from the date of submission of the corrective action plan, the office shall provide the district written notice of such determination and the basis therefor, and mandate that the district take all necessary actions to implement the plan. If a district has failed, within a reasonable time thereafter as specified by the office based on the nature of the failure, which shall in no event exceed sixty days, to make progress implementing any regulation, or any other portion of such plan that is intended to prevent imminent danger to the health, safety or welfare of the youth being served under the plan, the office may withhold or set aside a portion of the funding due under subdivision eight of this section until the district demonstrates that sufficient progress is being made; or terminate the district's authority to operate all or a portion of the juvenile justice services close to home initiative, take all necessary steps to assume custody for, and provide services to, the applicable juvenile delinquents being served under the initiative, and discontinue funds provided to the district for such services. The office shall not withhold, set aside or discontinue state aid to a district until written notice is given to the commissioner of the district, and in the event funding is withheld, set aside or discontinued, the district may appeal to the office, which shall hold a fair hearing thereon in accordance with the provisions of section twenty-two of this chapter relating to fair hearings. The

district may institute a proceeding for a review of the determination of the office following the fair hearing pursuant to article seventy-eight of the civil practice law and rules. Any funds withheld, set aside or discontinued pursuant to this provision shall be applied to address the problem which was the basis for such sanction. If the office terminates a district's authority to operate any portion of a juvenile justice services close to home initiative in accordance with this subdivision, the office shall notify the supervising family court judge responsible for the family courts serving such district of such termination and the effective date of such termination.

13. Once a plan becomes operative pursuant to this section, the social services district shall carry out the following functions, powers and duties with respect to placements of juvenile delinquents in accordance with the provisions of such plan and all applicable federal and state laws and regulations:

(a) to enter into contracts with authorized agencies, as defined in section three hundred seventy-one of this chapter, to operate and maintain facilities authorized under such plan; such contracts may include such program requirements as deemed necessary by the district;

(b) to determine the particular facility or program in which a juvenile delinquent placed with the district shall be cared for, based upon any applicable court order, pursuant to subdivision two of section 353.3 of the family court act, and an evaluation of such juvenile delinquent;

(c) to transfer a juvenile delinquent from one facility to any other facility, when the interests of such juvenile delinquent require such action, upon prior notice to the respondent, the attorney for the respondent and the respondent's parent or legal guardian, unless an immediate change of placement is necessary, in which case such notice shall be transmitted on the next business day; provided that, if the district has an approved plan to implement services for juvenile delinquents placed in limited secure settings, a juvenile delinquent transferred to a non-secure facility from a limited secure facility may be returned to a limited secure facility upon a determination by the district that, for any reason, care and treatment at the non-secure facility is no longer suitable;

(d) to cause a juvenile delinquent under the jurisdiction of the district who has run away from a facility run by the district or an authorized agency; or is conditionally released and has violated a condition of release therefrom, or if there is a change in circumstances and the district determines that it would be consistent with the needs and best interests of said juvenile delinquent and the need to protect the community; to be apprehended and returned to the district, detention facility, authorized agency, or program pursuant to regulations of the office of children and family services; provided further that:

(i) a social services official shall give immediate written notice to both the office and the family court when any juvenile delinquent placed with the social services district is absent from such placement without consent;

(ii) an authorized agency shall give immediate written notice to the office, the district and the family court when any juvenile delinquent placed by the district for care in such authorized agency is absent from such placement without consent;

(iii) a magistrate may cause a runaway or conditionally released juvenile delinquent to be held in custody until returned to the district;

(e) to issue a warrant for the apprehension and return of a juvenile delinquent under the jurisdiction of the district who has run away from a facility run by the district or an authorized agency; or is conditionally released and has violated a condition of release therefrom, or if there is a change in circumstances and the district determines that it would be consistent with the needs and best interest of said juvenile delinquent and the need to protect the community; pursuant to regulations of the office of children and family services; provided that:

(i) a social services official, pursuant to the regulations of the office of children and family services, shall issue a warrant directed generally to any peace officer, acting pursuant to such officer's special duties, or police officer in the state for the apprehension and return of any runaway or conditionally released juvenile delinquent under the jurisdiction of the district and such warrant shall be executed by any peace officer, acting pursuant to such officer's special duties, or police officer to whom it may be delivered; the social services district also shall provide relevant law enforcement agencies within forty-eight hours with any photographs of any runaway or conditionally released juvenile delinquent for whom a warrant is issued, together with any pertinent information relative to such juvenile delinquent; such photographs shall remain the property of the social services district and shall be kept confidential for use solely in the apprehension of such juvenile delinquent and shall be returned promptly to the district upon apprehension of such juvenile delinquent, or upon the demand of the district;

(f) to authorize an employee designated by the social services district, without a warrant, to apprehend a runaway or conditionally released juvenile delinquent under the jurisdiction of the district who has run away from a facility run by the district or an authorized agency; or is conditionally released and has violated a condition of release therefrom, or if there is a change in circumstances and the district determines that it would be consistent with the needs and best interests of said juvenile delinquent and the need to protect the community; in any county in this state whose return has been ordered by the district pursuant to the regulations of the office, and return said juvenile delinquent to any appropriate social services district, detention facility, authorized agency or program;

(g) pursuant to the regulations of the office of children and family services, to develop and operate programs for youth placed or referred to the district or in conjunction with an order provided in accordance with section 353.6 of the family court act;

(h) upon the placement of any juvenile delinquent eighteen years of age or older, or upon the eighteenth birthday of any youth placed in the custody of the social services district for an adjudication of juvenile delinquency for having committed an act which if committed by an adult would constitute a felony, and still in the custody of the social services district, to notify the division of criminal justice services of such placement or birthday. Provided, however, in the case of a youth eleven or twelve years of age at the time the act or acts were committed, the division of criminal justice services shall not be provided with the youth's name, unless the acts committed by such youth would constitute a class A or B felony. Upon the subsequent discharge it shall be the duty of the social services district to notify the division of criminal justice services of that fact and the date of discharge. For the purposes of this paragraph, a youth's age shall be determined to be the age stated in the placement order;

(i) to provide juvenile delinquents in residential placements with reasonable and appropriate visitation by family members and consultation with their legal representative in accordance with the regulations of the office of children and family services; and

(j) to provide residential care in programs subject to the regulations of the office of children and family services, for infants born to or being nursed by female juvenile delinquents placed with the district; residential care for such an infant may be provided for such period of time as is deemed desirable for the welfare of the mother or infant.

14. The following persons shall be authorized to visit, at their pleasure, all programs operated by a social services district pursuant to, or in accordance with this section: the governor; lieutenant governor; comptroller; attorney general; members of the legislature; judges of the court of appeals; judges from supreme court, family court and county courts and district attorneys, county attorneys and attorneys employed in the office of the corporation counsel having jurisdiction within the applicable social services district or county where a program is located; and any person or agency otherwise authorized by statute.

15. A juvenile delinquent in the care of the social services district who attends public school while in residence at a facility shall be deemed a resident of the school district where the youth's parent or guardian resides at the commencement of each school year for the purpose of determining which school district shall be responsible for the youth's tuition.

16. The social services district shall be permitted to appear as amicus in any action involving an appeal from a decision of any court of this state that relates to programs, conditions or services provided by such district or any authorized agency with which the district has placed a juvenile delinquent pursuant to this section. Written notice shall be given by the corporation counsel of the city of New York, or county attorney, as applicable, to the parties to the appeal when such amicus status is requested.

17. Notwithstanding any provision of law to the contrary, the social services district may delay acceptance of a juvenile delinquent in detention who is placed in the district's custody in accordance with the regulations of the office of children and family services; provided, however, that where the juvenile delinquent is in detention, such delay may not exceed fifteen days from the date the placement was made except as provided for in subdivision three of section three hundred ninety-eight of this article.

18. No order that places a juvenile delinquent in the custody of the social services district that recites the facts upon which it is based shall be deemed or held to be invalid by reason of any imperfection or defect in form.

Title 3
Child Welfare Services

Section
406.   Department of social welfare designated as state agency.
407.   Powers of department of social welfare.
408.   Custodian of funds.

§406.   Department of social welfare designated as state agency.

The department is hereby designated as the agency of the state to administer and expend any and all grants of moneys allocated or made available to the state under the provisions of the federal social security act for child welfare services as defined in such act, subject to the provisions of such act and rules and regulations established thereunder and to the laws of the state and rules and regulations established by the state comptroller.

§407. Powers of department of social welfare.

The department is hereby authorized and required:

1. to prepare a plan or plans for such child welfare services and upon their approval by such federal authority to execute the same. Such plans shall make provision for coordination between the services provided under such plans and the services provided as family assistance under title ten of article five with the view of providing welfare and related services which will best promote the welfare of children and their families.

2. to allocate and disburse to districts, counties or other local subdivisions of the state such amounts from moneys received by the state under the provisions of this title as are available for payment of part of the cost of district, county or other local child welfare services in accordance with such approved plans. Such district, county and other local subdivisions of the state are hereby authorized to receive and expend such allotments but only for the purposes of such plans and subject to the supervision and general direction of the department. Such district, county and other local subdivisions shall, when required by the department to comply with the provisions of such approved plan, perform the functions required.

3. to develop within the department services for the encouragement and assistance of adequate methods of community child welfare organization in accordance with such approved plans.

4. to establish and to alter and amend such regulations as may be necessary for the administration of such plans and the provisions of this title.

5. to prepare for inclusion in the annual report required by subdivision (d) of section seventeen of this chapter to be filed with the governor and the legislature prior to the fifteenth day of December of each year, a written evaluation report of the delivery of child welfare services in the state. Such evaluation report shall include, but need not be limited to, supervision of foster care and the agencies providing such care, information on the types of problems creating the need for foster care placements, preventive and protective services, the transfer of children in care and the reasons therefor, identification of target groups not receiving adequate services, and projected plans for providing services to such groups. Such report shall include progress made and problems encountered in the implementation of "the child welfare reform act of 1979", and amendments thereto. Such report shall also include aggregate expenditures; persons receiving services; cost comparisons among social services districts, among types of services and services programs, and among fiscal periods; unit costs; and cost-effectiveness of the provision of preventive services pursuant to title four of this chapter. In developing such evaluation, the department shall consult and coordinate with the board of social welfare, the division for youth, and the departments of mental hygiene, health and education.

§408. Custodian of funds.

The department of taxation and finance is hereby authorized to accept and receive on behalf of the state any and all grants or allotments of money made available to the state by or pursuant to the federal social security act for such child welfare services. All moneys so accepted and received shall be deposited by the department of taxation and finance to the credit of a special fund for use exclusively for the purposes for which such grants or allotments were made. The department shall certify to the comptroller all expenditures to be made from such special fund for payment of the part of the cost of district, county or other local child welfare services and for developing state services for the encouragement and assistance of adequate methods of community child welfare organization. Such expenditures may be made for personal service and for administrative and other costs of operation.

Title 4
Preventive Services for Children
and Their Families

Section
409.   Preventive services; definition.
409-a.   Preventive services; provision by social services officials.

§409. Preventive services; definition.

As used in this title, "preventive services" shall mean supportive and rehabilitative services provided, in accordance with the provisions of this title and regulations of the department, to children and their families for the purpose of: averting an impairment or disruption of a family which will or could result in the placement of a child in foster care; enabling a child who has been placed in foster care to return to his family at an earlier time than would otherwise be possible; or reducing the likelihood that a child who has been discharged from foster care would return to such care.

§409-a. Preventive services; provision by social services officials.

1. (a) A social services official shall provide preventive services to a child and his or her family, in accordance with the family's service plan as required by section four hundred nine-e of this chapter and the social services district's child welfare services plan submitted and approved pursuant to section four hundred nine-d of this chapter, upon a finding by such official that (i) the child will be placed, returned to or continued in foster care unless such services are provided and that it is reasonable to believe that by providing such services the child will be able to remain with or be returned to his or her family, and for a former foster care youth under the age of twenty-one who was previously placed in the care and custody or custody and guardianship of the local commissioner of social services or other officer, board or department authorized to receive children as public charges where it is reasonable to believe that by providing such services the former foster care youth will avoid a return to foster care or

*(ii) the child is the subject of a petition under article seven of the family court act, or has been determined by the assessment service established pursuant to section two hundred forty-three-a of the executive law, or by the probation service where no such assessment service has been designated, to be at risk of being the subject of such a petition, and the social services official determines that the child is at risk of placement into foster care. Such finding shall be entered in the child's uniform case record established and maintained pursuant to section four hundred nine-f of this chapter. The commissioner shall promulgate regulations to assist social services officials in making determinations of eligibility for mandated preventive services pursuant to this subparagraph.   *Effective until June 30, 2017*

*(ii) the child is the subject of a petition under article seven of the family court act, or has been determined by the assessment service established pursuant to section two hundred forty-three-a of the executive law, or by the probation service where no such assessment service has been designated, to be at risk of being the subject of such a petition, and the social services official determines

according to standards promulgated pursuant to section three hundred ninety-eight-b of this chapter that the child is at risk of placement into foster care. Such finding shall be entered in the child's uniform case record established and maintained pursuant to section four hundred nine-f of this chapter. The commissioner shall promulgate regulations to assist social services officials in making determinations of eligibility for mandated preventive services pursuant to clause (ii) of this paragraph.   *Effective June 30, 2017*

(b) When a child and his family have received preventive services for a period of six months pursuant to this subdivision, the social services official shall continue to provide such services only upon making a new finding that the child will be placed or continued in foster care unless such services are provided and that it is reasonable to believe that by providing such services, the child will be able to remain with or be returned to his family. Such new finding shall be entered in the child's uniform case record established and maintained pursuant to section four hundred nine-f of this chapter.

2. A social services official is authorized to provide preventive services to a child and his family to accomplish the purposes set forth in section four hundred nine of this chapter, when such services are not required to be provided pursuant to subdivision one of this section.

3. *(a) A social services official is authorized to provide community preventive services to communities likely to benefit from such services to accomplish the purposes set forth in section four hundred nine of this chapter. Social services officials may apply to the office of children and family services for waiver of eligibility and administrative requirements for preventive services to be provided pursuant to this subdivision. Such application shall include a plan setting forth the services to be provided, the persons or community that will receive the services and the estimated cost of such services. Upon approval of the application by the office of children and family services, eligibility requirements established in statute or regulation may be waived for those persons and communities identified in the plan as recipients of the services set forth in the plan. Where services are administered pursuant to a plan approved by the office of children and family services, the office of children and family services may waive the requirements of section four hundred nine-f or four hundred forty-two of this article.   *Effective until June 30, 2017*

*(a) A social services official is authorized to provide community preventive services to communities likely to benefit from such services to accomplish the purposes set forth in section four hundred nine of this chapter. Social services officials may apply to the department for waiver of eligibility and administrative requirements for preventive services to be provided pursuant to this subdivision. Such application shall include a plan setting forth the services to be provided, the persons or community that will receive the services and the estimated cost of such services. Upon approval of the application by the department, eligibility requirements established in statute or regulation may be waived for those persons and communities identified in the plan as recipients of the services set forth in the plan. Where services are administered pursuant to a plan approved by the department, the department may waive the requirements of sections one hundred fifty-three-d and three hundred ninety-eight-b of this chapter pertaining to denial or reimbursement. Where such a waiver is approved, the department approval must specify standards whereby services provided will be subject to denial of reimbursement. Where services are administered pursuant to a plan approved by the department, the

department may waive the requirements of section four hundred nine-f or four hundred forty-two of this article.   *Effective June 30, 2017

(b) The department must inform social services districts of procedures governing application for waivers of eligibility and administrative requirements and approval of waivers of eligibility and administrative requirements. Where such waivers are granted, the department shall have the authority to establish alternative standards to be followed by social services officials who are granted waivers by the department. Upon approval of an application for such waivers, the department approval must specify the requirements being waived and any alternative standards established.

(c) Community preventive services may be provided pursuant to this subdivision through demonstration projects to the extent the department makes funds available for such projects.

(d) The department shall develop an evaluation plan no later than April first, nineteen hundred eighty-eight, for community service demonstration projects and, subject to the approval of the director of the budget, may use up to five percent of the amount annually appropriated for project grants to conduct such evaluation which shall include but need not be limited to: an assessment of the effectiveness of various service delivery models in creating or enhancing linkages among school, housing, health, and income support services available in the community; the effectiveness of various preventive services in averting family disruption; the cost effectiveness of providing community focused preventive services; the impact of this service provision on requirements for more intensive mandated preventive services; and, the feasibility of replicating successful service models in other communities throughout the state.

4. Preventive services may be provided directly by the social services official or through purchase of service, in accordance with regulations of the department.

5. (a) Regulations of the department, promulgated pursuant to and not inconsistent with this section, shall contain program standards including, but not limited to: specification of services to be classified as preventive services; appropriate circumstances and conditions for the provision of particular services; appropriate providers and recipients of such services; and time limits, as may be appropriate, for the provision of particular services. The department shall, subject to the approval of the director of the budget, establish reimbursement or charge limitations for particular services or groups of services to be provided. The department shall also promulgate regulations to prevent social services districts from overutilizing particular forms or types of preventive services and to encourage districts to provide balanced preventive services programs based on the identified needs of children and families residing in such districts.

(b) The program standards promulgated pursuant to this subdivision shall be developed with the participation of the child welfare standards advisory council established pursuant to section four hundred nine-h of this chapter and in consultation with public and voluntary authorized agencies, citizens' groups and concerned individuals and organizations, including the state council on children and families.

(c) Notwithstanding any other provision of this section, where a social services official determines that a lack of adequate housing is the primary factor preventing the discharge of a child or children from foster care including, but not limited to, children with the goal of discharge to independent living, preventive services shall include, in addition to any other payments or benefits received by the family, special cash grants in the form of rent subsidies, including rent arrears, or any other assistance, sufficient to obtain adequate housing. Such rent subsidies or assistance shall not exceed the sum of three hundred dollars per month, shall not be provided for a period of more than three years, and shall be considered a special grant. The provisions of this paragraph shall not be construed to limit such official's authority to provide other preventive services.

(e) (i) A social services official is authorized to establish and operate, or contract for the establishment and operation of, intensive, homebased, family preservation programs.

(ii) Notwithstanding any other provision of law, reimbursement for intensive, homebased family preservation services shall be limited to those programs that reduce or avoid the need for foster care of children who are in imminent danger of placement. Such programs shall employ caseworkers trained in family preservation techniques and who provide at least half of their direct services in the client's residence or temporary home, work with no more than four families at any given time, provide direct therapeutic services for up to thirty days which may be extended up to an additional thirty days per family and are available twenty-four hours a day. No program described herein shall receive reimbursement unless such program agrees to collect and provide to the department information necessary to evaluate and assess the degree to which such program results in lower costs to the state and to social services districts than those of foster care placement. Such information shall be compiled in a manner that permits comparisons between families served by such programs and those families who meet eligibility criteria but who were not able to be served within available resources.

(f) Notwithstanding any other provision of law, where a social services official authorizes the provision of respite care, such care shall mean the temporary care and supervision of a child to relieve parents or other persons legally responsible for the care of such child where immediate relief is needed to maintain or restore family functioning.

6. In accordance with regulations of the department, where the child's family is able to pay all or part of the cost of such services, payments of such fees as may be reasonable or other third party reimbursement as may be available in the light of such ability shall be required. Expenditures subject to reimbursement pursuant to section four hundred nine-b of this title shall be reduced by the sum of all fees received or to be received pursuant to this subdivision.

*7. Notwithstanding any other provision of this section, if a social services official determines that a lack of adequate housing is a factor that may cause the entry of a child or children into foster care and the family has at least one service need other than lack of adequate housing, preventive services may include, in addition to any other payments or benefits received by the family, special cash grants in the form of rent subsidies, including rent arrears, or any other assistance, sufficient to obtain adequate housing. Such rent subsidies or assistance shall not exceed the sum of three hundred dollars per month, shall not be provided for a period of more than three years, and shall be considered a special grant. The provisions of this paragraph shall not be construed to limit such official's authority to provide other preventive services.

**7. Notwithstanding any other provision of law, preventive services information governed by this section may be released by the department, social services district or other provider of preventive services to a person, agency or

*There are two subdivisions "7"
**There are two subdivisions "7"

organization for purposes of a bona fide research project. Identifying information shall not be made available, however, unless it is absolutely essential to the research purpose and the department gives prior approval. Information released pursuant to this subdivision shall not be re-disclosed except as otherwise permitted by law and upon the approval of the department.

8. In contracting for the provision of preventive services, social services districts shall, to the extent feasible, place such services in areas with a high rate of child abuse and neglect and foster care placements. Social services districts shall, to the extent feasible, consider as a priority community-based organizations with a record of providing quality services to children and families in such communities.

9. (a) Notwithstanding any provision of law to the contrary, records relating to children pursuant to this section shall be made available to officers and employees of the state comptroller, or of the city comptroller of the city of New York, or of the county officer designated by law or charter to perform the auditing function in any county not wholly contained within a city, for purposes of a duly authorized performance audit, provided, however that such comptroller or officer shall have certified to the keeper of such records that he or she has instituted procedures developed in consultation with the department to limit access to client-identifiable information to persons requiring such information for purposes of the audit, that such persons shall not use such information in any way except for purposes of the audit and that appropriate controls and prohibitions are imposed on the dissemination of client-identifiable information obtained in the conduct of the audit. Information pertaining to the substance or content of any psychological, psychiatric, therapeutic, clinical or medical reports, evaluations or like materials or information pertaining to such child or the child's family shall not be made available to such officers and employees unless disclosure of such information is absolutely essential to the specific audit activity and the department gives prior written approval.

(b) Any failure to maintain the confidentiality of client-identifiable information shall subject such comptroller or officer to denial of any further access to records until such time as the audit agency has reviewed its procedures concerning controls and prohibitions imposed on the dissemination of such information and has taken all reasonable and appropriate steps to eliminate such lapses in maintaining confidentiality to the satisfaction of the department. The department shall establish the grounds for denial of access to records contained under this section and shall recommend as necessary a plan of remediation to the audit agency, except as provided in this section, nothing in this subdivision shall be construed as limiting the powers of such comptroller or officer to records which he is otherwise authorized to audit or obtain under any other applicable provision of law, any person given access to information pursuant to this subdivision who released data or information to persons or agencies not authorized to receive such information shall be guilty of a class A misdemeanor.

10. All sums received by the state under section 201 of Federal Public Law 105-89 shall be paid to the districts in proportion to the amount earned by the district for federal adoption incentives and shall only be used to provide preventive services to a child and his or her family as defined in paragraph (a) of subdivision five of this section, in addition to those required by the maintenance of effort requirement contained in subdivision six of section one hundred fifty-three-i of this chapter, except that up to thirty percent of such sums may be used to provide post-adoption services to children or families.

Preventive services shall include substance abuse treatment services provided to pregnant women or a caretaker person in an outpatient, residential or in-patient setting. Amounts expended by the state in accordance with this section shall be disregarded in determining the state's expenditures for purposes of federal matching payments under sections four hundred twenty-three, four hundred thirty-four and four hundred seventy-four of this chapter.

Title 4-A
Child Welfare Services Planning
and Administration

§409-d.   District-wide child welfare services plan.
1. Each social services district shall prepare and submit to the department, in such form and manner and times as the department shall by regulation require, a district-wide child welfare services plan which shall be a component of the district's multi-year consolidated services plan setting forth: the child welfare services needs of children and families for whom the social services district is or may be responsible; historic program and fiscal trends of the district in the level of care, maintenance and services provided to children and their families, including but not limited to expenditure trends, children and families served and costs of services provided; an assessment of projected program and fiscal requirements of the district in meeting identified needs in the next state fiscal year; and a description of the resources known to be available or likely to become available to meet those needs. Commencing the year following preparation of a multi-year consolidated services plan, each social services district shall prepare an annual implementation report related to its child welfare services plan. As used in this section "services" shall mean and include preventive services, foster care maintenance and services, and adoption services. Such regulations shall include but need not be limited to criteria and methodology for determining child welfare services needs and the adequacy of the resources known to be available or likely to become available to meet those needs.
2. The child welfare services plan and annual implementation reports shall be developed by the district in consultation with other government agencies concerned with the welfare of children residing in the district, authorized agencies, and other concerned individuals and organizations. The plan as submitted to the department for approval and as approved by the department shall be made available to such agencies, individuals and organizations upon request.
3. (a) Each social services district shall submit its child welfare services plan and annual implementation reports pertaining to this plan to the department as a component of the multi-year consolidated services plan and subsequent annual implementation reports and the department shall review and approve or disapprove the proposed plan in accordance with the procedures set forth in section thirty-four-a of this chapter.
(b) Such plan shall not be approved unless:
(i) it complies with the provisions of this section;

(ii) it demonstrates that child welfare services included in the plan are appropriate to meet the assessed needs of the children and families for whom the social services district is or may be responsible;

(iii) it is consistent with applicable provisions of this chapter and regulations of the department promulgated thereunder; and

(iv) it is in the format and includes such standardized information and data as may be required by the department to effectively evaluate such plans.

§409-e. Family service plan.

1. With respect to each child who is identified by a local social services district as being considered for placement in foster care as defined in section one thousand eighty-seven of the family court act by a social services district, such district, within thirty days from the date of such identification, shall perform an assessment of the child and his or her family circumstances. Where a child has been removed from his or her home, within thirty days of such removal the local social services district shall perform an assessment of the child and his or her family circumstances, or update any assessment performed when the child was considered for placement. Any assessment shall be in accordance with such uniform procedures and criteria as the office of children and family services shall by regulation prescribe. Such assessment shall include the following:

(a) a statement of the specific immediate problems which appear to require some intervention by the social services officials;

(b) a description of the long term family relationships, an assessment of trends in the stability of the family unit, and of the likelihood that specific preventive services will increase family stabilization sufficiently to prevent placement or to reduce the duration of a necessary placement;

(c) an estimate of the time period necessary to ameliorate the conditions leading to a need for placement, and a description of any immediate actions that have been taken or must be taken during or immediately after the conclusion of the assessment; and

(d) where placement in foster care is determined necessary, the reasonable efforts made to prevent or eliminate the need for placement or the reason such efforts were not made, the kind and level of placement and the reasons therefor, whether the child will be placed with the child's siblings and half-siblings and, if not, the reasons therefor and the arrangements made for contact between the siblings and half-siblings, identification of all available placement alternatives and the specific reasons why they were rejected, an estimate of the anticipated duration of placement, and plan for termination of services under appropriate circumstances, with specific explanation of the reasons for such termination plan.

2. Upon completion of any assessment provided for in subdivision one of this section, and not later than thirty days after placement of a child in foster care pursuant to article three or seven of the family court act or not later than thirty days after a child is removed from his or her home, the local social services district shall establish or update and maintain a family service plan based on the assessment required by subdivision one of this section. The plan shall be prepared in consultation with the child's parent or guardian, unless such person is unavailable or unwilling to participate, or such participation would be harmful to the child, and with the child if the child is ten years of age or older, and, where appropriate, with the child's siblings. Such consultation shall be done in person, unless such a meeting is impracticable or would be

harmful to the child. If it is impracticable to hold such consultation in person, such consultation may be done through the use of technology, including but not limited to, videoconferencing and teleconference technology. If the parent is incarcerated or residing in a residential drug treatment facility, the plan shall reflect the special circumstances and needs of the child and the family. The plan shall include at least the following:

(a) time frames for periodic reassessment of the care and maintenance needs of each child and the manner in which such reassessments are to be accomplished;

(b) short term, intermediate and long range goals for the child and family and actions planned to meet the need of the child and family and each goal;

(c) identification of necessary and appropriate services and assistance to the child and members of the child's family. The services so identified shall, before being included in the family service plan, be assessed to determine the projected effectiveness of such plan including but not limited to the following considerations:

(i) the family's concurrence with the plan;

(ii) the ability and motivation of the family to access services, including geographic accessibility;

(iii) the relatedness of the services to the family's needs and its socio-economic and cultural circumstances; and

(iv) other factors which may impact upon the effectiveness of such plan. The service plan shall also describe the availability of such services and the manner in which they are to be provided;

(d) any alternative plans for services where specific services are not available, and any viable options for services considered during the planning process;

(e) where placement in foster care is determined necessary, specification of the reasons for such determination, the kind and level of placement, any available placement alternatives, an estimate of the anticipated duration of placement, and plan for termination of services under appropriate circumstances.

3. The plan shall be reviewed and revised, in accordance with the procedures and standards in subdivision two of this section, at least within the first ninety days following the date the child was first considered for placement in foster care, and, if the child has been placed in foster care pursuant to article three or seven of the family court act or removed from his or her home, within the first ninety days following the date of placement or removal. The plan shall be further reviewed and revised not later than one hundred twenty days from this initial review and at least every six months thereafter; provided, however, that if a sibling or half-sibling of the child has previously been considered for placement or removed from the home, the plan shall be further reviewed and revised on the schedule established for the family based on the earliest of those events. Such revisions shall indicate the types, dates and sources of services that have actually been provided and an evaluation of the efficacy of such services, and any necessary or desirable revisions in goals or planned services. The review and revision of the plan shall be prepared in consultation with the child's parent or guardian, unless such person is unavailable or unwilling to participate, or such participation would be harmful to the child, and with the child if the child is ten years of age or older, and, where appropriate, with the child's siblings. Such consultation shall be done in person, unless such a meeting is impracticable or would be harmful to the child. If it is impracticable to hold such consultation in person, such consultation may be done through the

use of technology, including but not limited to, videoconferencing and tele-conference technology.

4. In accordance with regulations of the department, relevant portions of the assessment of the child and family circumstances, including but not limited to the material described in paragraph (d) of subdivision one of this section, and a complete copy of the family service plan, established pursuant to subdivisions one and two, respectively, of this section shall be given to the child's parent or guardian, counsel for such parent or guardian, and the child's attorney, if any, within ten days of preparation of any such plan.

5. The family service plan developed in regard to a child in foster care pursuant to this section shall include the permanency plan provided to the court in accordance with the family court act and this chapter.

6. Nothing in this section shall require a social services district to complete an assessment or service plan for a child who is in the custody of the office of children and family services, unless the child is also in the care and custody or custody and guardianship of the commissioner of the social services district.

§409-f. Uniform case recording.

1. With respect to each child described in subdivision one of section four hundred nine-e of this title, the social services district shall establish and maintain a uniform case record, consisting of the assessment, the family service plan, descriptions of care, maintenance or services provided to such child and family and the dates provided, essential data relating to the identification and history of such child and family, all official documents and records of any judicial or administrative proceedings relating to the district's contact with the child and family, and such other records as the department may by regulation require to adequately review case management by the districts. The department shall by regulation specify the format and contents of the uniform case record. Such regulation shall be developed in consultation with public and voluntary authorized agencies, citizens' groups and concerned individuals and organizations, including the state council on children and families. The uniform case record shall be maintained by the district in a manner consistent with the confidential nature of such records and shall be made available in accordance with applicable provisions of law. When a hearing has been requested in accordance with section twenty-two of this chapter, a copy of the portions of the record relevant to the hearing shall also be made available to the child's parent or guardian, counsel for the parent or guardian, and, if participating in the hearing, the child's attorney.

2. Notwithstanding any other provision of law, uniform case record information governed by this section may be released by the department, social services district or other provider of child welfare services to a person, agency or organization for purposes of a bona fide research project. Identifying information shall not be made available, however, unless it is absolutely essential to the research purpose and the department gives prior approval. Information released pursuant to this subdivision shall not be re-disclosed except as otherwise permitted by law and upon the approval of the department.

3. (a) Notwithstanding any inconsistent provision of law to the contrary, records relating to children pursuant to this section shall be made available to officers and employees of the state comptroller or of the city comptroller of the city of New York, or of the county officer designated bylaw or charter to perform the auditing function in any county not wholly contained within a city, for purposes of a duly authorized performance audit; provided, however, that

such comptroller or officer shall have certified to the keeper of such records that he or she has instituted procedures developed in consultation with the department to limit access to client-identifiable information to persons requiring such information for purposes of the audit, that such persons shall not use such information in any way except for purposes of the audit and that appropriate controls and prohibitions are imposed on the dissemination of client-identifiable information obtained in the conduct of the audit. Information pertaining to the substance or content of any psychological, psychiatric, therapeutic, clinical or medical reports, evaluations or like materials or information pertaining to such child or the child's family shall not be made available to such officers and employees unless disclosure of such information is absolutely essential to the specific audit activity and the department gives prior written approval.

(b) Any failure to maintain the confidentiality of client-identifiable information shall subject such comptroller or officer to denial of any further access to records until such time as the audit agency has reviewed its procedures concerning controls and prohibitions imposed on the dissemination of such information and has taken all reasonable and appropriate steps to eliminate such lapses in maintaining confidentiality to the satisfaction of the department. The department shall establish the grounds for denial of access to records contained under this section and shall recommend as necessary a plan of remediation to the audit agency. Except as provided in this section, nothing in this subdivision shall be construed as limiting the powers of such comptroller or officer to access records which he is otherwise authorized to audit or obtain under any other applicable provision of law. Any person given access to information pursuant to this subdivision who releases data or information to persons or agencies not authorized to receive such information shall be guilty of a class A misdemeanor.

§409-g. Training of child welfare personnel.
Within the amounts appropriated therefor, including all federal reimbursement received or to be received on account thereof, the department shall develop and implement a plan for the training of social services district and other authorized agency personnel, including caseworkers involved in the provision or supervision of preventive services, foster care services and adoption services. Such training shall include but need not be limited to:

1. Permanence casework: casework methodologies focused on activities designed to prevent placement in foster care or to shorten the length of stay in care for those children who can be returned home or freed for adoption;

2. Development of skills to facilitate rehabilitation or restoration of the family unit;

3. Development of knowledge and skills in legally freeing children for adoption and providing adoption services;

4. Development of knowledge and skills to prepare for court processes necessary in foster care and adoption; and

5. Development of case management skills including planning for permanence for each child.

Title 4-B
Services; Pregnant Adolescents

§409-i. Short title; legislative findings; purpose.

1. This title shall be known and may be cited and referred to as the "teenage services act".

2. The legislature finds that the rising incidence of adolescent pregnancy and teenage parenthood is the subject of a widespread and growing concern. As a result of early pregnancy, the attainment of needed education and job skills is often curtailed. Coupled with the added responsibilities accompanying parenthood, these young families are often locked into long term public dependency. Studies have confirmed that up to sixty percent of the current aid to families with dependent children cases in New York state are headed by mothers who were teenagers when they gave birth to their first child. In fact, the predominant cause of welfare dependency in New York state may well be due to the result of teenage pregnancy and adolescent motherhood. The objective of this title is to increase the potential of these youths to become financially independent by helping the teenager to complete her education, and receive sufficient manpower skills for participation in the labor market.

The department of social services is not only statutorily required to provide financial support to these dependent teenagers and their children, but also has equal responsibility to provide personal counselling and support services needed to strengthen family life and provide opportunities for economic independence. In order to facilitate accessibility to the full range of needed services, case management responsibilities should be assigned to appropriate local social services staff or to authorized agencies outside of the department. Any reluctance or refusal on the part of the teenager to participate in a program of services shall not carry any threat of fiscal sanctions as regards public assistance benefits. In the event that a teenager refuses to participate, it shall be the responsibility of the local social services district to make continued and repeated efforts to engage the teenager in a counselling relationship which has as its result a mutually agreed upon service plan which meets the objectives of this title.

Therefore, this title provides for the establishment of a service case management system in order to strengthen the service role of the department of social services. Local social services districts shall be required to separate public assistance cases involving pregnant adolescents and teenage mothers under eighteen years of age, and assign ongoing case management services for such caseloads to appropriate staff responsible for service delivery. By defining such specialized caseloads, personal counselling and provision of needed community-based support services will be facilitated. Such case management activities shall also include the follow-up and evaluation of services rendered.

The enactment of the provisions of this title shall maximize the effectiveness, efficiency and accountability of support services provided on behalf of pregnant adolescents and teenage parents under eighteen years of age, thereby reducing the long-term dependency needs of this youthful population.

§409-j. Case management.
1. As used in this title, "case management" shall refer to a method of providing necessary prevention and support services, directly or by purchase of services, to recipients of public assistance and shall require the facilitating of such services for the purpose of insuring family stability and assistance in achieving the greatest degree of economic independence.

2. Appropriate local social services staff shall be designated as responsible on a case by case basis, for the assessment of services needed by the adolescent or teenage recipient to achieve defined service goals, and for the planning and referral of services and follow-up activities, including the monitoring and evaluation of services provided. Designated case management staff shall be responsible for performing such activities for a specified period prescribed pursuant to department regulations dependent on such factors as age, education and job skills attainment of the individual, household size and stability of the family unit.

3. When referrals to services are provided under other state-funded programs or are directly purchased by the social services district, the district may request that the provider obtain and transmit to the district the information necessary to perform the case management function.

4. The provisions of this title shall apply to those cases involving pregnant adolescents and teen parents in receipt of public assistance, including any males and females under eighteen years of age who are designated payees of their own cases, payees of their children's cases or those public assistance recipients under eighteen years of age identified pursuant to rules and regulations as at-risk youth needing prevention services, where appropriate. At local option, case management services may be provided to those cases headed by persons eighteen years of age or older but under twenty-one years of age.

5. In the event that an adolescent or teenage recipient refuses to accept services identified by social services district staff as needed by the adolescent or teenager, such refusal shall not carry any threat of fiscal sanctions.

6. Case records developed by social services districts and other agencies for persons eligible for or receiving services pursuant to the provisions of this section shall be confidential and maintained in accordance with the provisions of section one hundred thirty-six of this chapter and the regulations of the department.

§409-k. Case plan and service record.
1. With respect to each individual who is identified as requiring case management services pursuant to this title, the social services district shall, within thirty days of such identification, perform or have performed an initial joint assessment with the individual, and other persons where appropriate, for the purpose of identifying those problems that have an impact on family stability and hinder the potential for economic independence. A social services district shall prior to implementing the provisions of this title submit a plan for a service case management system to the commissioner for approval.

2. Upon completion of the assessment provided in subdivision one of this section, the social services district shall, in consultation with the individual, establish and maintain or have established and maintained a case plan and service record prescribed pursuant to regulations of the department which shall include at least the following:

(a) identification of short term and long range goals which will ameliorate the problems indicated in subdivision one of this section. Such identification shall also include an estimate of the time period necessary to meet these goals;

(b) identification of services needed by the client, and a description of the available resources in the community to meet identified needs; if services are not available the record should reflect such;

(c) documentation of the arrangements made for the referral of the client to service providers;

(d) listing of all services rendered, both direct and those provided by other public and private agencies in the community;

(e) follow-up action taken to assure clients are in receipt of services, and any actions taken to remove any existing barriers which impede the maximum efficiency of service delivery; and

(f) recordation of the types, cost and auspices of services provided.

3. The case plan and service record shall be reviewed and may be revised, in consultation with the individual, at least once every six months after the plan and record have been prepared. Such review shall include an evaluation of the effectiveness of services rendered and any necessary revisions in goals or planned services as they meet the objectives indicated in paragraph (a) of subdivision two of this section.

4. The case plan and service record shall include information for the purpose of obtaining information regarding services rendered and the cost of such services based on assessed values or the value of services rendered, where no fees are charged as in other publicly financed programs together with such other information as may be required by rules and regulations of the department.

5. The department is authorized and directed to make such rules and regulations as are necessary to carry out the provisions of this title.

§409-*l*. Advisory board.

An advisory board shall be established by the commissioner to assist in the development and implementation of the case management provisions. It will be the responsibility of this board to assist in the development of various service models that local social services districts shall employ, assist in the formulation of appropriate procedures for evaluating such case management services, and determine the fiscal impact of such services as defined in section four hundred nine-j of this title. Appointments to the advisory board shall be obtained from public and private organizations providing teenage and child welfare services.

§409-m. Reports.

1. The commissioner shall prepare, for inclusion in the annual report required by subdivision (d) of section seventeen of this chapter to be filed with the governor and the legislature prior to December fifteenth of each year, a progress report on the planning and implementation of the provisions of this title.

2. The report shall contain, but not be limited to, information reported statewide and by districts, the number of individuals certified as eligible for services under this title, and those for whom services were rendered and expenditures made for services identified by type, provider, and funding source. Such report shall also include progress made in implementing the provisions of this title with particular reference to efforts made to insure the effectiveness of the case management provisions.

§409-n. Implementation.
1. The department shall plan for the implementation of the services case management system during the period from the first day of July, nineteen hundred eighty-four to the thirty-first day of March, nineteen hundred eighty-five.
2. Subject to the appropriation of funds, the provisions of this title shall be implemented from the first day of October, nineteen hundred eighty-five in a select number of representative pilot social services districts which shall be designated by the commissioner in consultation with the advisory board established pursuant to this title, in communities with a higher than state average teen population applying for or receiving public assistance.
3. Subject to the appropriation of funds, social services districts which had not implemented the provisions of this title by the thirty-first day of March, nineteen hundred eighty-seven shall be required to implement the provisions of this title during the period April first, nineteen hundred eighty-seven through March thirty-first, nineteen hundred ninety. The social services districts subject to the provisions of this subdivision shall implement this title in accordance with a schedule to be developed by the department which will ensure statewide implementation by the thirty-first day of March, nineteen hundred eighty-eight.

Title 5
Day Care for Certain Children

§410. Day care; when public welfare official to furnish.
1. A public welfare official of a county, city or town is authorized, provided funds have been made available therefor, to provide day care at public expense for children residing in his territory who are eligible therefor pursuant to provisions of this title. Such care may be provided only in cases where it is determined, under criteria established by the department, that there is a need therefor because of inability of the parents to provide care and supervision for a substantial part of the day and that such care is in the best interest of the child and parent. Where the family is able to pay part or all of the costs of such care, payment of such fees as may be reasonable in the light of such ability shall be required.
2. The furnishing of such care is hereby declared to be a proper municipal purpose for which the monies of a county, city or town may be raised and expended. A county, city or town may receive and expend monies from the state, the federal government or private individuals, corporations or associations for furnishing such care.
3. (a) Day care under this title shall mean care in a group facility, in a family home, in a group family day care home or in a day care center project as defined in title five-a of this article for part of the day. Day care may be provided by a social services official either directly or through purchase. Purchase of such care may be made only from a private non-profit corporation or association except when the commissioner shall have approved the purchase of such care from private proprietary facilities by a social services official who

has demonstrated that conveniently accessible non-profit facilities are inadequate to provide required care. Purchase of such care may also be made from a school district in accordance with state and federal requirements pursuant to a contract between the social services district and the school district.

(b) Care under this title may be provided only in group facilities, family homes, group family day care homes or in a day care center project as defined in title five-a which are operated in compliance with applicable regulations of the department. A group facility shall include a public school which provides day care pursuant to this subdivision.

(c) Except as hereinafter provided, care under this title shall not include care, supervision, training or participation in kindergartens, nursery schools or other schools, classes or activities operated or conducted by public or private schools. However such care shall include day care provided by a school district pursuant to the provisions of this subdivision and subdivision thirty-three of section sixteen hundred four of the education law in accordance with a contract entered into between such school district and a social services district.

(d) The commissioner shall encourage social services districts and day care providers to offer flexible hours of day care. Each provider may provide a flexible schedule in accordance with the rules and regulations of the commissioner and an application for day care services shall not be denied solely by reason of the time of day or days that care will be required provided that an available day care provider can accommodate such hours or days of care in accordance with such regulations.

4. The provisions of this title shall not apply to child care assistance provided under title five-C of this article.

§410-a.   Day care; when department to furnish.

Any inconsistent provision of law notwithstanding, if and so long as federal funds are available for the care provided pursuant to the provisions of this section, and to the extent of such funds and state funds appropriated or made available therefor, the department shall be authorized to provide day care, through appropriate arrangements and cooperative agreements with the state departments of education and agriculture and markets, approved by the director of the budget, in public schools operated by school districts and in facilities operated by or for the state department of agriculture and markets for children who are receiving family assistance or who are former or potential recipients of such aid in accordance with the regulations of the department, including only such children who are in pre-kindergarten programs of such schools or who are children of migrant workers.

§410-b. Federal grants.

1. The department of taxation and finance is authorized to accept and receive from the federal government any moneys which the federal government shall offer to the state for or with respect to the construction, maintenance or operation of facilities for day care for children, under or pursuant to any federal law heretofore or hereafter enacted authorizing grants to the state for such purpose or similar purposes, including payments to political subdivisions of, and any public agencies in the state.

2. The department of social welfare is hereby designated and empowered to act as the agent of the state in carrying out the provisions of any such federal law with respect to such day care facilities in this state.

3. Any and all such grants and moneys awarded for assistance to this state under or pursuant to any federal law shall be accepted and received by the department of taxation and finance as custodian thereof and such moneys, so received, shall be deposited by such department of taxation and finance in a special fund or funds and shall be used exclusively for the purposes of any such federal law. Such moneys shall be paid from such fund or funds on the audit and warrant of the comptroller upon vouchers certified or approved by the commissioner of welfare.

4. Any federal funds made available to the state for day care facilities shall be retained by the state.

§410-bb. Grants to not-for-profit facilities providing day care for children for employee salary and benefit enhancements.
1. The legislature finds and declares that a crisis exists in the availability and quality of child day care in New York state and that this crisis poses a danger both to the welfare and safety of the children and to the productivity of this state's workforce; that inadequate salaries and in many cases nonexistent benefit packages have substantially contributed to the existing crisis by precluding day care centers from recruiting and retaining necessary teaching and supervisory staff; that an extremely high turnover rate has interfered in many instances with the ability of day care centers to comply with regulatory requirements and to properly serve the children in their care; and that because of these extraordinary circumstances New York state must intervene and provide assistance for recruitment and retention of child care workers. The legislature recognizes that a long-term solution to this crisis will require cooperative efforts among the business community, local and state governments and families.

2. Within amounts appropriated specifically therefor, and after deducting funds as specified in subdivision three of this section the commissioner shall allocate funds to local social services districts for grants to eligible not-for-profit day care centers for retention and recruitment of teaching and supervisory staff, as follows:

(a) a city social services district with a population in excess of one million shall be allocated a portion of such funds based on an equal weighting of:

(i) its proportion of the state population of children aged five and under, and

(ii) its proportion of total claims for reimbursement received by the department by May thirty-first, nineteen hundred eighty-eight for the low income, transitional and teen parent day care programs authorized by chapter fifty-three of the laws of nineteen hundred eighty-seven.

(b) all other eligible local social services districts shall be allocated the remaining portion of funds based on each district's proportionate share of licensed not-for-profit day care capacity relative to the total capacity of all such other eligible districts.

3. Five percent of the funds appropriated for such recruitment and retention purposes shall be reserved for administration of the program and allocated as follows:

(a) each local social services district shall be allocated an amount equivalent to five percent of the funds it receives under paragraphs (a) and (b) of subdivision two of this section, provided that no district shall receive an amount less than twenty-five hundred dollars nor greater than one hundred fifty thousand dollars, and

(b) remaining funds shall be allocated to the department. In the event that a not-for-profit child care resource and referral agency or the department distributes funds in an eligible district, as provided herein, such agency or department may retain the amount that otherwise would be available to the eligible district.

4. Not later than thirty days following the effective date of this section, the commissioner shall notify local social services districts of the amounts allocated to each district and provide forms for the collecting of information pursuant to this section.

5. For the purposes of this section, an eligible district shall mean a local social services district that is providing, as of the effective date of this section, or which shall agree to provide in such written form and by such date as shall be acceptable to the department, subsidized day care services under the special day care services program authorized by chapter fifty-three of the laws of nineteen hundred eighty-eight.

6. Eligible districts may apply on or before the ninetieth day following the effective date of this section to receive such allocated funds by submitting to the department a plan on forms provided by the department. Such plan shall be developed by the local social services commissioner in consultation with directors of participating eligible day care centers, as such term is defined herein. Such plan shall include: methods to increase the amount of day care provided for families having an income at or below two hundred percent of the federal poverty level in such district; proposed steps to be taken to sustain gains in recruitment and retention of staff achieved by funds provided herein; information specified in paragraph (c) of subdivision seven of this section; and a proposed allocation of funds to eligible day care centers based on the following factors:

(a) forty percent of the funds allocated to such district shall be distributed to each eligible center based on such center's share of the total full time equivalent teaching and supervisory staff of such centers in the district as a whole;

(b) forty percent of the funds allocated to such district shall be distributed to each eligible center based on such center's share of the number of children from families having an income at or below two hundred percent of the federal poverty level receiving day care services in all such centers in the district, regardless of whether such children are receiving subsidized care; and

(c) notwithstanding any other provision of this subdivision, twenty percent of the funds allocated to such district shall be distributed to some or all eligible centers in a manner to further improve recruitment and retention of qualified staff. Distributions under this paragraph shall be based on factors including, but not be limited to seniority; educational qualifications; worker income; benefit levels, vacancy and turnover rates; or enhancement of distributions pursuant to paragraph (a) or (b) of this subdivision. The commissioner shall make copies of proposals available to the public upon request.

7. For the purposes of this section, an eligible day care center means a not-for-profit center which provides services for children in single or double sessions for six or more hours per day for five or more days per week and holds a permit or certificate issued pursuant to (i) the provisions of section three hundred ninety of this article, or (ii) the New York city health code as authorized by section five hundred fifty-eight of the New York city charter; provided, however, that:

(a) a center whose permit has been denied, suspended or revoked, or which is found in any twelve month period preceding or following the date of the allocation of funds made pursuant to subdivision two of this section to be in violation of section three hundred ninety of this article after a hearing conducted as provided therein or after decision by any court of competent jurisdiction, shall not be eligible to receive funds pursuant to this section;

(b) the existence of a current contract for purchase of day care services between an eligible district and a center may not be required as a precondition to receive such funds, but such center shall agree to accept children subsidized by the district in the next available space after receipt of a request from the district to place a child in such center;

(c) each such center must provide to the local social services district the following information on forms provided by the department:

(i) child care capacity, by ages of children;

(ii) the number of children in such center, by ages, whose families have incomes at or below two hundred percent of the federal poverty level, regardless of whether such children are receiving subsidized care;

(iii) the number of children specified in subparagraph (ii) of this paragraph receiving subsidies and the type of subsidy;

(iv) a schedule of fees charged for services;

(v) the total annual revenue from all sources, including fees, donations, grants, revenue from local governments and revenue from state agencies;

(vi) the total annual expenditures for rent or mortgage payments; equipment, property, liability and other insurance; utilities; food; supplies and materials; and

(vii) total annual expenditures for salaries and benefits, including the number, title, qualifications and salary levels of existing staff and types and amounts of benefits; and

(d) each eligible day care center must agree, to the maximum extent feasible, to enhance its future revenues to sustain the level of staff salary and benefits as provided herein.

8. Should an eligible district not apply for such funds, the commissioner may contract with a not-for-profit child care resource and referral agency as such term is defined in title five-B of this article which is serving such district to distribute such funds allocated to the district in the same manner as is required of an eligible district in accordance with the other provisions of this section. If two or more not-for-profit child care resource and referral agencies are serving such district, preference shall be given to the agency or agencies with existing contracts with the commissioner. If such agency does not exist or declines to participate, the department shall disburse funds in the manner as is required of an eligible district pursuant to this section.

9. A plan developed and submitted to the department pursuant to the provisions of this section shall be considered approved unless, within thirty days of the receipt of such plan, the department notifies the eligible district or agency that the plan is not approved and specifies in writing the basis for such disapproval. The commissioner shall make allocated funds and administrative funds available as advances to eligible districts whose plans have been approved pursuant to this section.

10. Eligible districts shall make allocated funds available as advances to eligible day care centers in accordance with the plan approved by the department. Such districts shall notify the department when all such funds have

been disbursed but all such funds must be disbursed not later than October first, nineteen hundred eighty-nine.

11. Any funds allocated to eligible districts or day care centers which cannot be used in the manner as provided herein shall be reallocated among other eligible districts as provided in paragraph (b) of subdivision two of this section.

12. Funds received by eligible day care centers shall be used solely for employee benefits and salary enhancements for teaching and supervisory staff, and shall not be used to supplant or substitute for any other funding available for day care services, or to provide services which eligible day care centers are required to provide pursuant to contracts with the state, local social services districts, authorized agencies, individuals or other organizations.

13. Nothing contained herein shall prevent an eligible district, or any other person or entity, at its discretion, from contributing funds, including administrative funds received pursuant to subdivision three of this section, to the program established pursuant to this section.

14. The department shall: (a) provide or cause to be provided, to the maximum extent feasible, technical assistance to eligible day care centers and districts concerning employee benefit options, long-term planning, management of funds, responsibilities required pursuant to this section, maximization of the use of available subsidy funds including Title XX and Title IV-A of the Federal Social Security Act and such other matters as may be helpful to sustain the level of staff salary and benefits as provided herein;

(b) annually examine cost data concerning rates of payment for day care and establish appropriate recommended fee schedules as guidelines for use by local social services districts in developing comprehensive annual social services program plans;

(c) promulgate regulations not later than July first, nineteen hundred eighty-nine, to establish a maximum rate of payment for day care centers which shall reflect adjustments in the cost of care since the establishment of the maximum rate in effect on January first, nineteen hundred eighty-six. Such maximum rate shall be calculated by applying thereto increases in the cost of living since January first, nineteen hundred eighty-six, updated by the department through December thirty-first, nineteen hundred eighty-nine, and also to the extent possible and based on the availability of such information, factors such as changes in the costs of insurance, rent, utilities and labor and benefits and such other factors the department shall deem appropriate, which exceed such increases in the cost of living, as updated through December thirty-first, nineteen hundred eighty-nine; provided, however, that:

(i) actual payment for day care services rendered shall not exceed the actual cost of such care;

(ii) nothing contained herein shall prevent the department from establishing a rate of payment for day care centers greater than that required pursuant to this subdivision;

(iii) approved rates of payment in excess of the rate established pursuant to this paragraph in effect prior to July first, nineteen hundred eighty-nine shall be continued;

(iv) nothing contained herein shall prevent the department from approving exceptions to the rate of payment established herein to meet specific identified needs of a local social services district;

(v) such regulations may include a higher maximum rate of payment for infant care, or care of children with special needs.

(d) Notwithstanding any other section of law to the contrary, by April first, nineteen hundred eighty-nine, the department shall develop guidelines and may, with the approval of the director of the division of the budget grant to local districts for one year waivers to income eligibility standards established pursuant to law for subsidized day care under the special day care services program. Such waivers shall be granted to increase eligibility standards up to twenty-five percent of the federal poverty level above the income eligibility standard established by law as a percentage of the federal poverty level. Waivers shall be granted only upon the submission of documentation establishing that:

(i) the local social services district is serving substantially all eligible families with incomes at or below the established income eligibility standard. A district shall be deemed to be serving substantially all eligible families if it meets the following two criteria: (a) the percentage of eligible children served in the district meets or exceeds the percentage of eligible children served statewide under the special day care services program and (b) the district has provided day care services to any additional children whose families have been identified in such district's outreach program as described in subparagraph (ii) of this paragraph as eligible for and desiring subsidized day care services;

(ii) the local district has established a district-wide outreach program which identifies eligible families who are not receiving subsidized child day care under the special day care services program, and informs all such families of their availability, and assists such families desiring subsidized services to obtain them;

(iii) a family receiving a subsidy under the district's waiver provisions shall be required to contribute a greater amount towards the cost of care than a family eligible under the established income eligibility standard;

(iv) the local district has included an estimate of the number of children who will be served under the waiver provisions;

(v) the local district has submitted claims to income eligible day care expenses under Title XX of the federal Social Security Act;

(vi) the district has available to it a higher allocation in the current fiscal year than the amount of reimbursement received by such district in the previous fiscal year for subsidized care under the special day care services program.

(e) submit a report to the governor and to the chairmen of the senate finance committee and the assembly ways and means committee not later than December thirty-first, nineteen hundred eighty-nine on the program established pursuant to this section, including the number, amount and recipients of grants in each eligible district; the purposes and uses of such grants; an evaluation of any resulting improvements in recruitment and retention of qualified staff, current local eligibility standards, any use of the waiver process, state cost of increasing the eligibility standards established by law up to twenty-five percent and fifty percent of the federal poverty level on a county by county basis for subsidized day care under the special day care services program and recommendations for long-term solutions to the problems of recruitment and retention of teaching and supervisory staff.

§410-c.   State reimbursement.
1. (a) Expenditures made by counties, cities, and towns for day care and its administration, and day care center projects, pursuant to the provisions of this title, shall, if approved by the department, be subject to reimbursement by the state, in accordance with the regulations of the department, as follows: There

shall be paid to each county, city or town (1) the amount of federal funds, if any, properly received or to be received on account of such expenditures; (2) fifty per centum of its expenditures for day care and its administration and day care center projects, after first deducting therefrom any federal funds received or to be received on account thereof, and any expenditures defrayed by fees paid by parents or by other private contributions.

(b) For the purpose of this title, expenditures for administration of day care shall include expenditures for compensation of employees in connection with the furnishing of day care, including but not limited to costs incurred for pensions, federal old age and survivors insurance and health insurance for such employees; training programs for personnel, operation, maintenance and service costs; and such other expenditures such as equipment costs, depreciation and charges and rental values as may be approved by the department. It shall not include expenditures for capital costs. In the case of day care purchased from a non-profit corporation constituting an eligible borrower pursuant to title five-a of this article, expenditures shall include an allocable proportion of all operating costs of such facility as may be approved by the department including but not limited to the expenditures enumerated in this paragraph (b) and expenditures for amortization, interest and other financing costs of any mortgage loan made to such non-profit corporation.

2. (a) Claims for state reimbursement shall be made in such form and manner and at such times and for such periods as the department shall determine.

(b) When certified by the department, state reimbursement shall be paid from the state treasury upon the audit and warrant of the comptroller out of funds made available therefor.

3. The department is authorized in its discretion to approve and certify to the comptroller for payment, advances to counties, cities or towns in anticipation of the state reimbursement provided for in this section.

4. Payment of state reimbursement and advances shall be made to local fiscal officers as in the case of state reimbursement for public assistance and care under other provisions of this chapter.

5. (a) As used in this subdivision "school age child day care programs" shall mean programs which offer care to school age children under the age of fourteen before or after the period when these children are in school. Such programs may include, but are not limited to, programs provided in school buildings in accordance with paragraph (i) of subdivision one of section four hundred fourteen of the education law.

(b) The commissioner shall, within appropriations made available therefor, select proposed school age child day care programs which shall be eligible to receive an award of no more than twenty-five thousand dollars for start up or expansion costs, including planning, rental, operational and equipment costs, or minor renovations identified as being necessary in order for the program to comply with applicable state or local building, fire safety or licensing standards, based on plans submitted to him. The commissioner shall give preference to those areas of the state which are significantly underserved by existing school age child day care programs and to those programs which involve parents in the development and implementation of programs. The commissioner shall publicize this availability of funds to be used for purposes of this subdivision in awarding grants. Plans may be submitted by private not-for-profit corporations, organizations or governmental subdivisions.

(c) Notwithstanding any other provisions of law, social services districts shall be authorized to purchase services which are to be provided pursuant to this subdivision from programs which have been approved by the commissioner to receive funds pursuant to this subdivision.

6. Any other provision of law notwithstanding, and within amounts appropriated therefor, the department shall have authority to make start-up grants to prospective programs that will provide child day care, as such term is defined in section three hundred ninety of this article, from any funds available for such purpose.

§410-cc. Start up grants for child day care.

The commissioner shall provide funds to start up grants to not-for-profit organizations or corporations for the development of new or expanded all day child day care programs including costs related to planning, renting, renovating, operating, and purchasing equipment. The commissioner shall establish guidelines including, but not limited to, allowable costs, and criteria for eligibility for grants giving preference to those child day care providers who will, to the maximum extent feasible, target services to households having incomes up to two hundred percent of the federal poverty standard. The commissioner shall publicize the availability of funds. No awards shall be granted which exceed twenty-five hundred dollars for a new family day care provider or new group family day care provider, and one hundred thousand dollars for a new child day care center. Child care resource and referral agencies may receive family day care start up grants not to exceed two thousand five hundred dollars per new provider if the agency trains such new family provider and thereby expands the supply of family day care programs in the community. The commissioner shall give preference to those communities which are significantly underserved by existing programs and to those programs which and those providers who will serve infants under two years of age.

§410-ccc. Child day care facility development.

1. Notwithstanding any other provision of law, of the moneys appropriated to the department in section one of chapter fifty-four of the laws of nineteen hundred ninety-four, enacting the capital projects budget, four million seven hundred fifty thousand dollars shall be available as follows: seven hundred fifty thousand dollars for child care project development grants and related administrative expenses; the remaining four million dollars shall be available for the child care facilities construction program as defined in section sixteen-g of the urban development corporation act; of this amount, no less than three million dollars shall be available for child care construction grants and related administrative expenses and any remaining funds may be available for child care construction revolving loans and loan guarantees, and related administrative expenses. The amounts available for the child care facilities construction program, as defined in section sixteen-g of the urban development corporation act, shall be suballocated to the urban development corporation pursuant to this section.

Up to five percent of the moneys available pursuant to this subdivision may be used for payments to the department or other state agencies or authorities, and the urban development corporation for administrative expenses required to develop requests for proposals and to approve contracts for child care construction projects pursuant to this section and/or section sixteen-g of the urban development corporation act. The director of the division of the budget shall approve such payments.

2. Child care project development grants. The department shall develop a request for proposals to provide grants to not-for-profit organizations, including, but not limited to, child care resource and referral programs, local development corporations, neighborhood preservation companies and rural preservation companies as defined in section nine hundred two of the private housing finance law, to support pre-development planning, management, and coordination of activities, leading to the development of child day care centers in under-served areas meeting the needs of low-income working families. Such activities may include: (a) design studies and services and other development or redevelopment work in connection with the design and development of child day care centers; and (b) studies, surveys or reports, including preliminary planning studies to assess a particular site or sites or facility or facilities for the development of child day care centers.

(c) In determining grants to be awarded, the department shall consider the following: (i) that a not-for-profit organization applying for a grant under this subdivision is a bonafide organization which shall have demonstrated by its immediate past and current activities its ability to lead or to assist in the development of projects, such as child day care centers meeting the needs of low-income families; (ii) the need for day care centers in the area; (iii) the potential viability for a child day care center to succeed in the area; and (iv) such other matters as the department determines necessary.

(d) Grants shall be awarded to eligible entities where the department identifies an insufficient supply of child day care programs. Grants awarded pursuant to the request for proposals shall not exceed seventy-five thousand dollars per project.

3. Child care construction grants. (a) The child care construction grants awarded pursuant to this section and section sixteen-g of the urban development corporation act shall be available for not-for-profit child care facilities construction projects owned or to be owned by not-for-profit corporations for use as child day care centers that will be duly approved, licensed, inspected, supervised, and regulated as may be determined to be necessary and appropriate by the department, except that with respect to child day care centers located in the city of New York, such child day care centers will be duly approved, licensed, inspected, supervised, and regulated as may be determined to be necessary and appropriate by the commissioner of the department of health of the city of New York.

(b) Grants shall be made through contracts to not-for-profit corporations for child care facilities construction projects pursuant to a request for proposal process jointly developed by the department and the urban development corporation in consultation with the department of economic development. The department shall receive, initially review, and assess applications to determine which projects should be referred to the urban development corporation and to rank by groups, the referred projects according to the capacity of such projects to meet identified needs for child day care. In assessing such applications, the department shall consider: (i) the need for day care services in the area; (ii) the potential viability for a child day care center to succeed in the area; (iii) the qualifications of the proposed provider to operate a child care center; (iv) the potential for meeting applicable regulatory requirements; (v) the appropriateness of the site for licensing as a day care center and (vi) such other matters as the department determines necessary.

(c) Upon the timely completion of the department's initial review and selection of applications meeting criteria, the department shall immediately submit such selected applications and the group rankings of such applications to the urban development corporation which, in consultation with the department of economic development, shall select award recipients. No later than upon submission of the selected applications, the department shall also suballocate all moneys appropriated for such purposes to such corporation.

4. Programs conducted pursuant to this section of law are limited to the amounts appropriated therefor.

Title 5-A
Youth Facilities Improvement Act

§410-d.   Short title: policy and purposes of title.

This title shall be known, and may be cited and referred to, as the "Youth Facilities Improvement Act".

There is a serious shortage throughout the state of facilities suitable for use for the care of children especially those of pre-school age and primary school age whose parents are unable to provide such care for all or a substantial part of the day or post-school day. A similar shortage of residential child care facilities also exists. Existing day care and residential child care facilities are overcrowded with long waiting lists. Many such facilities are so located that they are not accessible to families in need of such services. The absence of adequate day care and residential child care facilities is contrary to the interest of the people of the state, is detrimental to the health and welfare of the child and his parents and prevents the gainful employment of persons, who are otherwise qualified, because of the need to provide such care in their home.

It is the purpose of this article to encourage the timely construction and equipment of such facilities with mortgage loan participation by the New York state housing finance agency. The provision of such facilities is hereby declared to be a public purpose which it is the policy of the state to encourage.

§410-e.   Definitions.

As used in this title the following words and phrases shall have the following meanings unless a different meaning is plainly required by the context:

1. "Board". The state board of social welfare.

2. "Commissioner". The commissioner of social services of the state of New York.

3. "Department". The state department of social services.

4. "Eligible borrower". A non-profit corporation organized under the laws of the state of New York which is authorized to care for children and which has entered into a regulatory agreement in accordance with the provisions of section four hundred ten-f of this title.

5. "Project." "Youth facilities project." A specific work or improvement, including lands, buildings, improvements, fixtures and articles of personal property acquired, constructed, rehabilitated, managed, owned and operated by an eligible borrower to provide day care in the manner prescribed by the department for children of pre-school and primary school age or to provide residential child care in the manner prescribed by the rules of the board for children of pre-school, primary school or secondary school age, or to provide any combination of the foregoing, and for facilities incidental or appurtenant thereto.

6. "Project cost". "Youth facilities project cost". The sum total of all costs incurred by an eligible borrower as approved by the commissioner as reasonable and necessary for carrying out all works and undertakings and providing all necessary equipment for the development of a project exclusive of any private or federal, state or local financial assistance available for and received by an eligible borrower for the payment of such project cost. These shall include but are not necessarily limited to the carrying charges during construction or rehabilitation up to and including the occupancy date, working capital not exceeding three percentum of the estimated total cost or three percentum of the actual total final cost, whichever is larger, the cost of all necessary studies, surveys, plans and specifications, architectural, engineering, legal or other special services, the cost of acquisition of land and any buildings and improvements thereon, site preparation and development, construction, reconstruction and equipment, including fixtures, equipment, and articles of personal property required for the operation of the project, the reasonable cost of financing incurred by the eligible borrower in the course of the development of the project, up to and including the occupancy date, the fees imposed by the commissioner and by the New York state housing finance agency; other fees charged, including any premium payments to the youth facilities project guarantee fund created by the youth facilities project guarantee fund act, and necessary expenses incurred in connection with the initial occupancy of the project, and the cost of such other items as the commissioner may determine to be reasonable and necessary for the development of a project, less any and all rents and other net revenues from the operation of the real property, improvements or personal property on the project site, or any part thereof, by the eligible borrower on and after the date on which the contract between the eligible borrower and the New York state housing finance agency was entered into and prior to the occupancy date.

7. "Occupancy date". The date defined in the documents providing for a mortgage loan between an eligible borrower and the New York state housing finance agency.

8. "Youth facilities development fund company". A company incorporated and organized pursuant to subdivision two of section four hundred ten-n of this title.

9. "Youth Facilities Center" means a facility suitable to provide day care for children of pre-school age and primary school age or to provide residential child care for children of pre-school, primary school or secondary school age or to provide any combination of the foregoing, which has been approved by the state department of social services.

§410-f. Regulation of eligible borrowers.

1. Every eligible borrower, as a condition precedent to borrowing funds from the agency, shall enter into a regulatory agreement with the commissioner which shall provide:

(a) that the real property or other assets mortgaged or otherwise pledged to the agency shall not be sold, transferred, encumbered or assigned until the eligible borrower shall have repaid in full all obligations under the mortgage of the agency and has paid such other obligations as may be required by the commissioner provided, however, the provisions of this paragraph (a) shall not apply to any actions taken pursuant to section four hundred ten-l of this article;

(b) that the eligible borrower will maintain books and records and a system of accounts satisfactory to the commissioner and the agency including but not limited to separate books, records and accounts for (i) all monies advanced to the eligible borrower by the agency or from any other source or sources, public or private, for the construction, reconstruction, rehabilitation, improvement or equipment of the project and (ii) all monies repaid in satisfaction of any indebtedness to the agency or other indebtedness as required by the commissioner; and the eligible borrower agrees that all of its books, records and accounts shall be open to examination by the commissioner and the agency at any time;

(c) that the eligible borrower shall file with the commissioner and the agency such financial statements including an annual report setting forth such information as the commissioner may require;

(d) that the eligible borrower shall not acquire any real property or interest therein for the purpose of constructing, reconstructing, rehabilitating or improving a project without first having obtained from the commissioner a certificate that such acquisition is consistent with the purposes of this article;

(e) that the eligible borrower shall not issue notes, bonds, debentures or other obligations other than for money or property actually received for the use and lawful purposes of the eligible borrower and no such note, bond, debenture or other obligation shall constitute a lien or encumbrance against the project, or any real property or other asset mortgaged or otherwise pledged to the agency;

(f) that the eligible borrower shall not without first having obtained the written consent of the commissioner:

(i) construct, reconstruct, rehabilitate, improve, alter or repair the project or enter into a contract therefor;

(ii) enter into contracts relating to the management or operation of the project;

(iii) make a guaranty of payment out of monies pledged to the agency or pledge any or all of its assets, income or revenue pledged to the agency to secure payment of its obligations;

(iv) lease a project or a portion thereof to a third party for the purposes of operation;

(v) voluntarily dissolve;

(g) that no member, officer or employee of the corporation which is an eligible borrower shall acquire any interest, direct or indirect, in any property then or thereafter included or planned to be included in a project, nor retain any interest direct or indirect in any property acquired subsequent to his appointment or employment which is later included or planned to be included in a project. If any member, officer or employee of a corporation which is an eligible borrower owns or controls an interest, direct or indirect, in any property included in a project which was acquired prior to his appointment or employment, he shall disclose such interest and the date of acquisition to the corporation and such disclosure shall be entered upon the minutes of such corporation and a copy of such minutes shall be forwarded to the commissioner;

(h) that all income and earnings of the eligible borrower shall be used exclusively for its corporate purposes;

(i) that no part of the net income or earnings of the corporation shall inure to the benefit or profit of any private individual, firm or corporation;

j. That the eligible borrower, in the case of a residential child care center project, will be subject to the visitation, inspection and supervision of the department, and that the eligible borrower, in the case of a day care center project will be subject to the visitation, inspection and supervision of the department, as to any and all acts in relation to the welfare of children to be performed pursuant to this title;

(k) such other matters as the commissioner or the agency may require;

2. This regulatory agreement shall terminate at any time after the expiration of ten years after the occupancy date upon the consent of the commissioner and upon the repayment in full of all obligations under the mortgage of the agency and of such other obligations as the commissioner may require.

§410-g. Mortgage loans.

1. Any eligible borrower may, subject to the approval of the commissioner, borrow funds from the agency and secure the repayment thereof by bond or note and mortgage which shall contain such terms and conditions as may be deemed necessary or desirable by the agency or required by any agreement between the agency and the holders of its notes and bonds, including the right to assignment of rates and charges and entry into possession in case of default, but the operation of such project, in the event of such entry, shall be subject to the regulations of the commissioner.

2. The agency may make contracts to make loans to an eligible borrower in an amount not to exceed the total project cost. Any such loan shall be secured by a first mortgage lien upon all the real property and improvements of which the project consists and may be secured by such a lien upon other real property owned by the eligible borrower, and upon all fixtures and articles of personal property attached to or used in connection with the operation of the project.

3. Any inconsistent provision of law to the contrary notwithstanding, mortgages of an eligible borrower shall be exempt from the mortgage recording taxes imposed by article eleven of the tax law.

§410-h. Conditions and security for loans.

No loan shall be made by the agency to an eligible borrower until the commissioner has approved the project and finds that:

1. The eligible borrower has been approved by the commissioner and complied with all the provisions of this title;

2. The plans and specifications conform to the requirements of all laws and regulations applicable thereto and assure adequate light, air, sanitation and fire protection and are satisfactory to him;

3. The estimated revenue of the project or from other funds of the eligible borrower pledged, assigned or otherwise to be made available to the agency will be sufficient to cover all probable costs of operation and maintenance, of fixed charges and such reserves as may be authorized by the commissioner or required by the agency;

4. Provision has been made for the purpose of providing for the payment of the difference between the estimated project cost and the mortgage loan; and in the event the final project cost shall exceed the estimated project cost, the difference between such final project cost and the mortgage loan;

5. The eligible borrower has entered into a regulatory agreement pursuant to section four hundred ten-f of this title.

§410-i. Rates and admission of children.

1. An eligible borrower shall, with the approval of the commissioner, fix a schedule of rates to be charged parents, guardians or other persons having legal custody of the child and to social services officials or other authorized agencies for the facilities and services provided by the eligible borrower pursuant to this title. The commissioner upon his own motion, or upon application by the eligible borrower or lienholder may vary the amount of such charge from time to time so as to secure, together with all other income of the eligible borrower pledged, assigned or otherwise made available to the agency, sufficient income to meet, within reasonable limits, all necessary payments by the said eligible borrower of all expenses, including fixed charges, sinking funds and reserves.

2. The facilities and services to be provided by the eligible borrower pursuant to this title shall be available to all children in need thereof.

§410-j. Transfer of real property.

Notwithstanding any requirement of law to the contrary or any provision of any general, special or local law, charter or ordinance, every executor, administrator, trustee, guardian or other person holding trust funds or acting in a fiduciary capacity, unless the instrument under which such fiduciary is acting expressly forbids, and the state, its subdivisions, municipalities, all other public bodies, all public officers, persons, partnerships and corporations owning or holding any real property, may grant, sell, lease or otherwise transfer any such real property or interest therein to an eligible borrower and receive and hold any cash, exchange therefor by such an eligible borrower and may execute such instruments and do such acts as may be deemed necessary or desirable by them or it and by the eligible borrower in connection with a project or projects and such sale, lease or transfer may be made without public auction or bidding; providing, however, that where such real property is within an urban renewal area the disposition thereof shall be in accordance with the provisions of paragraph (d) of subdivision two of section five hundred seven of the general municipal law.

§410-k. Supervision.

1. The commissioner may from time to time make, alter, amend and repeal rules and regulations for the supervision, examination, regulation and audit of an eligible borrower and for carrying into effect this title, and each eligible borrower shall submit an annual report of its operations to the commissioner and the agency who may examine and audit the books and records of the eligible borrower at any time.

2. The commissioner and the department shall have power to act for and in behalf of the agency in servicing the project mortgage loans of the agency, and to perform such functions and services in connection with the making, servicing and collection of such loans as shall be requested by the agency.

3. (a) The commissioner and the department may, with respect to any project of which the agency has acquired the fee or otherwise, enter into an agreement with said agency subject to the approval of the director of the budget, for the department, as provided in paragraph (b) hereof, to operate the said project in a manner consistent with the purposes of this title. In such event, the commissioner, on behalf of the department, shall have the power to use any

available funds to pay all operating expenses and to comply with all the terms and provisions of the mortgage, as though the mortgage had not been foreclosed, and to comply with the provisions of this title.

(b) Subject to the provisions of the agreement with said agency, the commissioner may contract with any person, firm or corporation which he deems qualified to operate and manage such project and to perform such duties and functions as he may deem necessary.

4. Whenever the commissioner shall be of the opinion that an eligible borrower is failing or omitting, or is about to fail or omit to do anything required of it by law or by order of the commissioner and is doing or is about to do anything, or permitting anything, or is about to permit anything to be done, contrary to or in violation of law or of any order of the commissioner, or which is improvident or prejudicial to the interest of the public, the lienholders, the shareholders, or the occupants, the commissioner may, in addition to such other remedies as may be available, commence an action or proceeding in the supreme court of the state of New York in the name of the commissioner, for the purpose of having such violations or threatened violations stopped and prevented, and in such action or proceeding, the court may appoint a temporary or permanent receiver or both. Such action or proceeding shall be commenced by a petition to the supreme court, alleging the violation complained of and praying for appropriate relief. It shall thereupon be the duty of the court to specify the time, not exceeding twenty days after service of a copy of the petition, within which the eligible borrowers complained of must answer the petition. In case of any default or after answer the court shall immediately inquire into the facts and circumstances in such manner as the court shall direct in the interest of substantial justice without other or formal pleading. Such other persons or corporations as it shall seem to the court necessary or proper to join as parties in order to make its order or judgment effective, may be joined as parties. The final judgment in any such action or proceeding shall either dismiss the action or proceeding or direct that an order or an injunction, or both, issue, or provide for the appointment of a receiver as prayed for in the petition, or grant such other relief as the court may deem appropriate.

§410-*l*.   Foreclosures and judgments.

1. In any foreclosure action the commissioner shall be made a party defendant. He shall take all steps necessary to protect the interests of the public therein and no costs shall be awarded against him. Foreclosures shall not be decreed unless the court to which application is made shall be satisfied that the interests of the lienholder or holders cannot be adequately assured except by the sale of the property. In any such proceeding, the court shall be authorized to appoint the commissioner as receiver of the property, or to grant such other and further relief as may be reasonable and proper.

2. Notwithstanding the foregoing provisions of this section, wherever it shall appear that the agency shall have loaned on a mortgage which is a first lien upon any such property, such agency shall have all the remedies available to a mortgagee under the laws of the state of New York, free from any restrictions contained in this section, except that the commissioner shall be made a party defendant and that the commissioner shall take all steps necessary to protect the interests of the public and no costs shall be awarded against him.

3. In the event of a judgment against an eligible borrower in any action not pertaining to the collection of a mortgage indebtedness, there shall be no sale of any of the real property of such eligible borrower except upon sixty days'

written notice to the commissioner and the agency. Upon receipt of such notice the commissioner and the agency shall take such steps as in their judgment may be necessary to protect the rights of all parties.

§410-m. Fees and charges.
The commissioner may, by regulation, establish and charge to eligible borrowers such fees and charges for inspection, regulation, supervision and audit as to the commissioner may appear just and reasonable in order to recover the departmental costs in performing these functions.

§410-o. Separability.
If any clause, sentence, paragraph or part of this article shall be adjudged by any court of competent jurisdiction to be invalid, such judgment shall not affect, impair or invalidate the remainder thereof, but shall be confined in its operation to the clause, sentence, paragraph, section or part thereof directly involved in the controversy in which such judgment shall have been rendered.

Title 5-B
Child Care Resource and Referral Program

§410-p. Definitions.
As used in this title, the term:
1. "Agency" shall mean a not-for-profit corporation or group of not-for-profit corporations. With respect to any county for which no appropriate not-for-profit corporation or group of corporations has submitted a proposal, such term shall mean a statewide or regional not-for-profit corporation which establishes such a corporation or shall mean a local governmental entity which provides the services authorized by this title;
2. "Resource and referral program" shall mean an agency funded pursuant to this title to provide services specified in section four hundred ten-r of this title within a defined geographic area;
3. "Early childhood services" shall mean services which include, but are not limited to, registered, certified or licensed care in family day care homes, group family day care homes, school-age child care programs; head start programs, day care centers; child care which may be provided without a permit, certificate or registration in accordance with this statute; early childhood education programs approved by the state education department; and care provided in a children's camp as defined in section one thousand four hundred of the public health law;
4. "Required resource and referral services" shall mean those services listed in subdivision one of section four hundred ten-q of this title which must be provided by each child care resource and referral program to parents and other guardians, child care and early childhood services providers, employers and communities within the geographic area served by the program, to the extent funds are available for such services;
5. "Enhanced services" shall mean additional or more intensive levels of services as listed in subdivision two of section four hundred ten-q of this title,

which an agency agrees to provide in order to receive additional funding pursuant to this title;

6. "Parent" or "Parents" shall mean and include biological and adoptive parents, guardians or other persons in parental relationship to a child.

§410-q. Child care resource and referral program services.

1. Each agency approved to receive funding pursuant to this title shall, to the extent funds are available for such purposes, provide the following:

(a) Information and referral services directed at educating parents who contact the agency regarding early childhood services options and methods of selecting the best option for his or her child; referring parents or guardians to early childhood services providers; informing parents about the availability of financial assistance and tax credits; referral for parents in coordinating part-day early childhood services providers and programs to meet the full-day care needs of parents; referrals for parents of preschool children with handicapping conditions pursuant to section forty-four hundred ten of the education law and section twenty-five hundred forty-two of the public health law; providing written information to those who contact the agency seeking information about early childhood services; maintaining a provider resource file and a file of parents currently seeking early childhood services; and publicizing child care resource and referral services as necessary to assure that the availability of those services are known to the community;

(b) Services directed at expanding the number of available family day care providers and recruiting potential providers; providing information on licensing and registration requirements and available funding sources to potential early childhood services providers and programs; and assisting individuals or organizations to qualify as legal early childhood services providers or programs by providing information on applicable laws and regulations relating to zoning, taxes, insurance, government licensing or registration, and other matters of concern to new providers;

(c) Services directed at maintaining and providing information and resources on early childhood training and other relevant programs for prospective and current providers, including educating child care providers not requiring a license or registration pursuant to section three hundred ninety of this article with information on available training opportunities at the time of enrollment and re-enrollment;

(d) Services directed at developing and maintaining provider data bases to determine service utilization and unmet needs for additional early childhood services;

(e) Assuring access to the United States department of agriculture child care food program for providers in the service area;

(f) Services directed at providing written materials and conducting outreach to employers to encourage their support of child care resource and referral services and other early childhood services; and

(g) Each agency funded herein shall provide services in a manner responsive to the cultural, linguistic and economic characteristics of the community served.

2. Enhanced services which an agency agrees to provide pursuant to a contract may include one or more of the following:

(a) Services directed at expanding the supply of regulated care in areas where such care is not readily available;

(b) Services directed at enhancing the availability and quality of early childhood services which serve families with particular language, ethnic and cultural backgrounds;

(c) Services directed at meeting the early childhood services needs of children with special needs;

(d) Training or technical assistance services targeted to meet specific local early childhood services needs; and

(e) Services directed at promoting, coordinating and assisting collaborative efforts between early childhood services providers and programs to meet the local need for full-day early childhood services.

§410-r. Child care resource and referral programs.

1. The commissioner shall solicit applications for available funds from agencies pursuant to this title in a manner to ensure that agencies in every area of the state will have an opportunity to apply for funds. The commissioner shall designate areas to be served by child care resource and referral services to ensure that services are accessible statewide to the maximum extent feasible.

2. (a) In reviewing the applications, the commissioner shall consider the ability of each applicant to provide the services delineated in section four hundred ten-q of this title. Each agency shall demonstrate that it has a viable plan to offer the required services to families in the area without regard to income, and to attract local support for additions to the required and enhanced services delineated in section four hundred ten-q of this title.

(b) In connection with the review of an application for funds pursuant to this title, the commissioner shall consider requests from agencies for additional funding for the provision of enhanced services.

3. In accordance with the provisions of this title and subject to funds appropriated specifically therefor, the commissioner is authorized to award contracts for the operation of child care resource and referral programs.

§410-s. State reimbursement.

1. The commissioner shall allocate annually any state funds, including any available federal funds, appropriated for such purposes among the agencies approved for funding pursuant to this title. The commissioner shall allocate such funds pursuant to a statewide formula developed by the department, which shall be based upon the relative numbers of children, children in working families, and children in low income families in each county, as defined by the department for this purpose. The commissioner shall notify the legislature prior to the implementation of any change or adjustment in the formula.

2. As a condition of receiving funds pursuant to this section, the child care resource and referral program shall demonstrate that it is receiving or has an agreement to receive funds, from sources other than the department pursuant to this title. Funds other than those paid by the department pursuant to this title may come from any other source, including but not limited to the department or other state agencies, federal programs such as the United States department of agriculture child care food program, local agencies, employers or community organizations, so long as such funds are for reasonably related services. To continue to receive funds pursuant to this section, such resource and referral program must demonstrate to the commissioner that it has secured funds or commitments from other sources or that extraordinary circumstances exist which preclude the securing of such funds.

3. All applications approved by the commissioner shall include a commitment to use appropriate accounting and fiscal control procedures which shall include the filing of an annual financial statement which has been audited as required by the department so as to ensure: (a) the proper disbursement and accounting for funds received; and (b) appropriate written records regarding the population served and type and extent of services rendered.

§410-t. Responsibilities of the commissioner.

1. The commissioner shall monitor the performance of agencies to assure that the terms of the contract are met, that the services are provided in accordance with the intent of this title and that funds are used as required by this title.

2. The commissioner may contract for technical support, planning, coordination and data collection services to assist agencies in offering child care resource services in unserved areas.

3. Beginning July first, nineteen hundred ninety-four and biennially thereafter, the commissioner shall submit a report to the governor and the legislature on the implementation of this title which shall include but not be limited to:

(a) the names of the agencies serving the counties and the counties served by a child care resources and referral agency;

(b) the awards made to each agency;

(c) the characteristics and number of children and families who have received services;

(d) the improvements in the accessibility of early childhood services, the improvement in quality and the expanded supply;

(e) the nature of services contracted for and additional services the agency is able to provide with other funding sources;

(f) the amount of state and federal funding available for services provided under this title; and

(g) the cost to the state to administer the programs funded under this title.

Title 5-C
Block Grant for Child Care

Section
410-u.   Establishment of block grant for child care.
410-v.   Allocation of block grant funds.
410-w.   Eligible families.
410-x.   Use of funds.
410-y.   Maintenance of effort.
410-z.   Reporting requirements.

§410-u.   Establishment of block grant for child care.

1. The department shall establish a state block grant for child care comprised of all of the federal funds appropriated for child care under title IV-A of the federal social security act and under the federal child care and development block grant act and any additional federal funds that the state chooses to transfer from the federal family assistance to needy families block grant to the child care and development block grant plus any state funds appropriated for the provision by social services districts of child care assistance to families in receipt of family assistance and other low income families and for activities to increase the availability and/or quality of child care programs.

2. The state block grant for child care shall be divided into two parts pursuant to a plan developed by the department and approved by the director

of the budget. One part shall be retained by the state to provide child care on a statewide basis to special groups and for activities to increase the availability and/or quality of child care programs, including, but not limited to, the start-up of child care programs, the operation of child care resource and referral programs, training activities, the regulation and monitoring of child care programs, the development of computerized data systems, and consumer education, provided however, that child care resource and referral programs funded under title five-B of article six of this chapter shall meet additional performance standards developed by the department of social services including but not limited to: increasing the number of child care placements for persons who are at or below two hundred percent of the state income standard with emphasis on placements supporting local efforts in meeting federal and state work participation requirements, increasing technical assistance to all modalities of legal child care to persons who are at or below two hundred percent of the state income standard, including the provision of training to assist providers in meeting child care standards or regulatory requirements, and creating new child care opportunities, and assisting social services districts in assessing and responding to child care needs for persons at or below two hundred percent of the state income standard. The department shall have the authority to withhold funds from those agencies which do not meet performance standards. Agencies whose funds are withheld may have funds restored upon achieving performance standards. The other part shall be allocated to social services districts to provide child care assistance to families receiving family assistance and to other low income families.

3. Notwithstanding any other provision of law, expenditures of funds from the block grant shall be governed by this title.

§410-v.   Allocation of block grant funds.
1. The part of the block that is determined to be available to social services districts for child care assistance shall be apportioned among the social services districts by the department according to an allocation plan developed by the department and approved by the director of the budget. The allocation plan shall be based, at least in part, on historical costs and on the availability and cost of, and the need for, child care assistance in each social services district. Annual allocations shall be made on a federal fiscal year basis.

2. Reimbursement under the block grant to a social services district for its expenditures for child care assistance shall be available for seventy-five percent of the district's expenditures for child care assistance provided to those families in receipt of public assistance which are eligible for child care assistance under this title and for one hundred percent of the social services district's expenditures for other eligible families; provided, however, that such reimbursement shall be limited to the social services district's annual state block grant allocation.

3. Any portion of a social services district's block grant allocation for a particular federal fiscal year that is not claimed by such district during that federal fiscal year shall be added to that social services district's block grant allocation for the next federal fiscal year.

4. Any claims for child care assistance made by a social services district for services that occurred from October first, nineteen hundred ninety-six through September thirtieth, nineteen hundred ninety-seven, other than claims made under title XX of the federal social security act, shall be counted against the social services district's first block grant allocation.

§410-w. Eligible families.

1. A social services district may use the funds allocated to it from the block grant to provide child care assistance to:

(a) families receiving public assistance when such child care assistance is necessary: to enable a parent or caretaker relative to engage in work, participate in work activities or perform a community service pursuant to title nine-B of article five of this chapter; to enable a teenage parent to attend high school or other equivalent training program; because the parent or caretaker relative is physically or mentally incapacitated; or because family duties away from home necessitate the parent or caretaker relative's absence; child day care shall be provided during breaks in activities, for a period of up to two weeks. Such child day care may be authorized for a period of up to one month if child care arrangements shall be lost if not continued, and the program or employment is scheduled to begin within such period;

(b) families with incomes up to two hundred percent of the state income standard who are attempting through work activities to transition off of public assistance when such child care is necessary in order to enable a parent or caretaker relative to engage in work provided such families' public assistance has been terminated as a result of increased hours of or income from employment or increased income from child support payments or the family voluntarily ended assistance; and, provided that the family received public assistance at least three of the six months preceding the month in which eligibility for such assistance terminated or ended or provided that such family has received child care assistance under subdivision four of this section;

(c) families with incomes up to two hundred percent of the state income standard which are determined in accordance with the regulations of the department to be at risk of becoming dependent on family assistance;

(d) families with incomes up to two hundred percent of the state income standard who are attending a post secondary educational program and working at least seventeen and one-half hours per week; and

(e) other families with incomes up to two hundred percent of the state income standard which the social services district designates in its consolidated services plan as eligible for child care assistance in accordance with criteria established by the department.

2. For the purposes of this title, the term "state income standard" means the most recent federal income official poverty line (as defined and annually revised by the federal office of management and budget) updated by the department for a family size of four and adjusted by the department for family size.

3. A social services district shall guarantee child care assistance to families in receipt of public assistance with children under thirteen years of age when such child care assistance is necessary for a parent or caretaker relative to engage in work or participate in work activities pursuant to the provisions of title nine-B of article five of this chapter. Child care assistance shall continue to be guaranteed for such a family for a period of twelve months after the month in which the family's eligibility for public assistance has terminated or ended when such child care is necessary in order to enable the parent or caretaker relative to engage in work, provided that the family's public assistance has been terminated as a result of an increase in the hours of or income from employment or increased income from child support payments or because the family voluntarily ended assistance; that the family received public assistance in at least three of the six months preceding the month in which

eligibility for such assistance terminated or ended or provided that such family has received child care assistance under subdivision four of this section; and that the family's income does not exceed two hundred percent of the state income standard. Such child day care shall recognize the need for continuity of care for the child and a district shall not move a child from an existing provider unless the participant consents to such move.

4. (a) Local social services districts shall guarantee applicants who would otherwise be eligible for, or are recipients of, public assistance benefits and who are employed, the option to choose to receive continuing child day care subsidies in lieu of public assistance benefits, for such period of time as the recipient continues to be eligible for public assistance. For the purposes of this subdivision, an eligible applicant for, or recipient of, public assistance benefits and who is employed includes a person whose gross earnings equal, or are greater than, the required number of work hours times the state minimum wage. Recipients of child care subsidies under this subdivision who are no longer eligible for public assistance benefits, shall be eligible for transitional child care described in paragraph (b) of subdivision one of this section as if they had been recipients of public assistance.

(b) Nothing herein shall be construed to waive the right of an applicant who chooses to receive continuing child day care subsidies pursuant to this section from applying for ongoing public assistance.

5. A family eligible for child care assistance under paragraph (a) of subdivision one of this section shall suffer no break in child care services and shall not be required to reapply for such assistance so long as eligibility under subdivision three of this section continues.

6. Notwithstanding any other provision of law, rule or regulation to the contrary, applicants for child care subsidy assistance shall be encouraged to obtain a child support order and shall be advised of the benefits of obtaining such orders. Provided however, no applicant for, or recipient of, child care assistance under this title shall be required to pursue, or to obtain, a court order for child support as a condition of eligibility for child care assistance.

7. For purposes of determining financial eligibility under this title, the earned income of a dependent child under the age of eighteen, who is not legally responsible for the child or children for which child care assistance is sought, shall be disregarded when determining the eligibility of a household for a child care subsidy.

8. Notwithstanding any other provision of law, rule or regulations to the contrary, a social services district that implements a plan amendment to the child care portion of its child and family services plan, either as part of an annual plan update, or through a separate plan amendment process, where such amendment reduces eligibility for, or increases the family share percentage of, families receiving child care services, or that implements the process for closing child care cases as set forth in the district's approved child and family services plan, due to the district determining that it cannot maintain its current caseload because all of the available funds are projected to be needed for open cases, shall provide all families whose eligibility for child care assistance or family share percentage will be impacted by such action with at least thirty days prior written notice of the action.

§410-x. Use of funds.

1. A social services district shall expend its allocation from the block grant in a manner that provides for equitable access to child care assistance funds to eligible families, and in accordance with the applicable provisions in federal law regarding the portion of the funds which must be spent on families in receipt of family assistance, families who are attempting through work activities to transition off of family assistance and families at-risk of becoming dependent on family assistance and the portion which must be spent on other working low-income families. Each social services district may spend no more than five percent of its block grant allocation for administrative activities. The term "administrative activities" shall not include the costs of providing direct services.

2. (a) A social services district may establish priorities for the families which will be eligible to receive funding; provided that the priorities provide that eligible families will receive equitable access to child care assistance funds to the extent that these funds are available.

(b) A social services district shall set forth its priorities for child care assistance in the district's consolidated services plan. The commissioner of the office of children and family services shall not approve any plan that does not provide for equitable access to child care assistance funds.

(c) A social services district shall be authorized to set aside portions of its block grant allocation to serve one or more of its priority groups and/or to discontinue funding to families with lower priorities in order to serve families with higher priorities; provided that the method of disbursement to priority groups provides that eligible families within a priority group will receive equitable access to child care assistance funds to the extent that these funds are available.

(d) Each social services district shall collect and submit to the commissioner of the office of children and family services in a manner to be specified by the commissioner of the office of children and family services information concerning the disbursement of child care assistance funds showing geographic distribution of children receiving assistance within the district.

(e) The commissioner of the office of children and family services shall submit a report to the governor, temporary president of the senate and the speaker of the assembly on or before August thirty-first, two thousand one concerning the implementation of this section. This report shall include information concerning the disbursement of child care assistance funds showing geographic distribution of children receiving assistance within the state.

3. Child care assistance funded under the block grant must meet all applicable standards set forth in section three hundred ninety of this article or the administrative code of the city of New York, including child day care in a child day care center, family day care home, group family day care home, school age child care program, or in home care which is not subject to licensure, certification or registration, or any other lawful form of care for less than twenty-four hours per day. The department also is required to establish, in regulation, minimum health and safety requirements that must be met by those providers providing child care assistance funded under the block grant which are not required to be licensed or registered under section three hundred ninety of this article or to be licensed under the administrative code of the city of New York and to those public assistance recipients who are providing child care assistance as part of their work activities or as community service under title nine-B of article five of this chapter. A social services district may submit to the department justification for a need to impose additional minimum health

and safety requirements on such providers and a plan to monitor compliance with such additional requirements. No such additional requirements or monitoring may be imposed without the written approval of the department. Social services districts shall provide, directly or through referral, technical assistance and relevant health and safety information to all public assistance recipients who voluntarily choose to provide child care assistance as part of their work activities under title nine-B of article five of this chapter.

4. The amount to be paid or allowed for child care assistance funded under the block grant shall be the actual cost of care but no more than the applicable market-related payment rate established by the department in regulations. The payment rates established by the department shall be sufficient to ensure equal access for eligible children to comparable child care assistance in the substate area that are provided to children whose parents are not eligible to receive assistance under any federal or state programs. Such payment rates shall take into account the variations in the costs of providing child care in different settings and to children of different age groups, and the additional costs of providing child care for children with special needs.

5. The department shall promulgate regulations under which provision for child care assistance may be made by providing child care directly; through purchase of services contracts; by providing cash, vouchers or reimbursement to the providers of child care or to the parents or caretaker relatives; or through such other arrangement as the department finds appropriate. Such regulations shall require the use of at least one method by which child care arranged by the parent or caretaker relative can be paid.

6. Pursuant to department regulations, child care assistance shall be provided on a sliding fee basis based upon the family's ability to pay.

7. A social services district may suspend the eligibility of a provider who is not required to be licensed or registered under section three hundred ninety of this article to provide child care assistance funded under the block grant, where the provider is the subject of a report of child abuse or maltreatment that is under investigation by child protective services.

8. Notwithstanding any provision of law to the contrary, child care assistance payments made pursuant to this section may be made by direct deposit or debit card, as elected by the recipient, and administered electronically, and in accordance with such guidelines, as may be set forth by regulation of the office of children and family services. The office of children and family services may enter into contracts on behalf of local social services districts for such direct deposit or debit card services in accordance with section twenty-one-a of this chapter.

§410-y. Maintenance of effort.

Each social services district shall maintain the amount of local funds spent for child care assistance under the child care block grant at a level equal to or greater than the amount the district spent for child care assistance during federal fiscal year nineteen hundred ninety-five under title IV-A of the federal social security act, the federal child care development block grant program and the state low income child care program. If the state fails to meet the level of state and local child care funding necessary to maintain the federal matching funds for child care assistance available under title IV-a of the federal social security act, the state shall withhold funding from those social services districts which spent a lower amount of local funds for child care assistance than the amount they spent during federal fiscal year nineteen hundred ninety-five, based on a formula established in department regulations, equal to the amount of the matching funds which have been lost.

§410-z. Reporting requirements.

Each social services district shall collect and submit to the department, in such form and at such times as specified by the department, such data and information regarding child care assistance provided under the block grant as the department may need to comply with federal reporting requirements.

Title 6
Child Protective Services

§411. Findings and purpose.

Abused and maltreated children in this state are in urgent need of an effective child protective service to prevent them from suffering further injury and impairment. It is the purpose of this title to encourage more complete reporting of suspected child abuse and maltreatment and to establish in each county of the state a child protective service capable of investigating such reports swiftly and competently and capable of providing protection for the child or children from further abuse or maltreatment and rehabilitative services for the child or children and parents involved.

§412. General Definitions.

When used in this title and unless the specific context indicates otherwise:

1. An "abused child" means a child under eighteen years of age and who is defined as an abused child by the family court act;

2. A "maltreated child" includes a child under eighteen years of age
    (a) defined as a neglected child by the family court act, or

(b) who has had serious physical injury inflicted upon him or her by other than accidental means;

3. "Person legally responsible" for a child means a person legally responsible as defined by the family court act;

4. "Subject of the report" means any parent of, guardian of, or other person eighteen years of age or older legally responsible for, as defined in subdivision (g) of section one thousand twelve of the family court act, a child reported to the statewide central register of child abuse and maltreatment who is allegedly responsible for causing injury, abuse or maltreatment to such child or who allegedly allows such injury, abuse or maltreatment to be inflicted on such child; or a director or an operator of, or employee or volunteer in, a home operated or supervised by an authorized agency, the office of children and family services, or in a family day-care home, a day-care center, a group family day care home, a school-age child care program or a day-services program who is allegedly responsible for causing injury, abuse or maltreatment to a child who is reported to the statewide central register of child abuse or maltreatment or who allegedly allows such injury, abuse or maltreatment to be inflicted on such child;

5. "Other persons named in the report" shall mean and be limited to the following persons who are named in a report of child abuse or maltreatment other than the subject of the report: the child who is reported to the statewide central register of child abuse and maltreatment; and such child's parent, guardian, or other person legally responsible for the child who has not been named in the report as allegedly responsible for causing injury, abuse or maltreatment to the child or as allegedly allowing such injury, abuse or maltreatment to be inflicted on such child; or

6. An "unfounded report" means any report made pursuant to this title unless an investigation determines that some credible evidence of the alleged abuse or maltreatment exists;

7. An "indicated report" means a report made pursuant to this title if an investigation determines that some credible evidence of the alleged abuse or maltreatment exists.

8. "Substance abuse counselor" or "alcoholism counselor" means any person who has been issued a credential therefor by the office of alcoholism and substance abuse services, pursuant to paragraphs one and two of subdivision (d) of section 19.07 of the mental hygiene law.

9. *(REPEALED, Eff.1/19/16, Ch.13, L.2016)*

§413. Persons and officials required to report cases of suspected child abuse or maltreatment.

1. (a) The following persons and officials are required to report or cause a report to be made in accordance with this title when they have reasonable cause to suspect that a child coming before them in their professional or official capacity is an abused or maltreated child, or when they have reasonable cause to suspect that a child is an abused or maltreated child where the parent, guardian, custodian or other person legally responsible for such child comes before them in their professional or official capacity and states from personal knowledge facts, conditions or circumstances which, if correct, would render the child an abused or maltreated child: any physician; registered physician assistant; surgeon; medical examiner; coroner; dentist; dental hygienist; osteopath; optometrist; chiropractor; podiatrist; resident; intern; psychologist; registered nurse; social worker; emergency medical technician; licensed

creative arts therapist; licensed marriage and family therapist; licensed mental health counselor; licensed psychoanalyst; licensed behavior analyst; certified behavior analyst assistant; hospital personnel engaged in the admission, examination, care or treatment of persons; a Christian Science practitioner; school official, which includes but is not limited to school teacher, school guidance counselor, school psychologist, school social worker, school nurse, school administrator or other school personnel required to hold a teaching or administrative license or certificate; full or part-time compensated school employee required to hold a temporary coaching license or professional coaching certificate; social services worker; director of a children's overnight camp, summer day camp or traveling summer day camp, as such camps are defined in section thirteen hundred ninety-two of the public health law; day care center worker; school-age child care worker; provider of family or group family day care; employee or volunteer in a residential care facility for children that is licensed, certified or operated by the office of children and family services; or any other child care or foster care worker; mental health professional; substance abuse counselor; alcoholism counselor; all persons credentialed by the office of alcoholism and substance abuse services; peace officer; police officer; district attorney or assistant district attorney; investigator employed in the office of a district attorney; or other law enforcement official.

(b) Whenever such person is required to report under this title in his or her capacity as a member of the staff of a medical or other public or private institution, school, facility or agency, he or she shall make the report as required by this title and immediately notify the person in charge of such institution, school, facility or agency, or his or her designated agent. Such person in charge, or the designated agent of such person, shall be responsible for all subsequent administration necessitated by the report. Any report shall include the name, title and contact information for every staff person of the institution who is believed to have direct knowledge of the allegations in the report. Nothing in this section or title is intended to require more than one report from any such institution, school or agency.

(c) A medical or other public or private institution, school, facility or agency shall not take any retaliatory personnel action, as such term is defined in paragraph (e) of subdivision one of section seven hundred forty of the labor law, against an employee because such employee believes that he or she has reasonable cause to suspect that a child is an abused or maltreated child and that employee therefore makes a report in accordance with this title. No school, school official, child care provider, foster care provider, residential care facility provider, hospital, medical institution provider or mental health facility provider shall impose any conditions, including prior approval or prior notification, upon a member of their staff specifically required to report under this title. At the time of the making of a report, or at any time thereafter, such person or official may exercise the right to request, pursuant to paragraph (A) of subdivision four of section four hundred twenty-two of this title, the findings of an investigation made pursuant to this title.

(d) Social services workers are required to report or cause a report to be made in accordance with this title when they have reasonable cause to suspect that a child is an abused or maltreated child where a person comes before them in their professional or official capacity and states from personal knowledge facts, conditions or circumstances which, if correct, would render the child an abused or maltreated child.

2. Any person, institution, school, facility, agency, organization, partnership or corporation which employs persons mandated to report suspected incidents of child abuse or maltreatment pursuant to subdivision one of this section shall provide consistent with section four hundred twenty-one of this chapter, all such current and new employees with written information explaining the reporting requirements set out in subdivision one of this section and in sections four hundred fifteen through four hundred twenty of this title. The employers shall be responsible for the costs associated with printing and distributing the written information.

3. Any state or local governmental agency or authorized agency which issues a license, certificate or permit to an individual to operate a family day care home or group family day care home shall provide each person currently holding or seeking such a license, certificate or permit with written information explaining the reporting requirements set out in subdivision one of this section and in sections four hundred fifteen through four hundred twenty of this title.

4. Any person, institution, school, facility, agency, organization, partnership or corporation, which employs persons who are mandated to report suspected incidents of child abuse or maltreatment pursuant to subdivision one of this section and whose employees, in the normal course of their employment, travel to locations where children reside, shall provide, consistent with section four hundred twenty-one of this title, all such current and new employees with information on recognizing the signs of an unlawful methamphetamine laboratory. Pursuant to section 19.27 of the mental hygiene law, the office of alcoholism and substance abuse services shall make available to such employers information on recognizing the signs of unlawful methamphetamine laboratories.

§414. Any person permitted to report.

In addition to those persons and officials required to report suspected child abuse or maltreatment, any person may make such a report if such person has reasonable cause to suspect that a child is an abused or maltreated child.

§415. Reporting procedure.

Reports of suspected child abuse or maltreatment made pursuant to this title shall be made immediately by telephone or by telephone facsimile machine on a form supplied by the commissioner of the office of children and family services. Oral reports shall be followed by a report in writing within forty-eight hours after such oral report. Oral reports shall be made to the statewide central register of child abuse and maltreatment unless the appropriate local plan for the provision of child protective services provides that oral reports should be made to the local child protective service. In those localities in which oral reports are made initially to the local child protective service, the child protective service shall immediately make an oral or electronic report to the statewide central register. Written reports shall be made to the appropriate local child protective service except that written reports involving children being cared for in a home operated or supervised by an authorized agency or the office of children and family services shall be made to the statewide central register of child abuse and maltreatment which shall transmit the reports to the agency responsible for investigating the report, in accordance with section four hundred twenty-four-b of this title. Written reports shall be made in a manner prescribed and on forms supplied by the commissioner of the office of children and family services and shall include the following information: the names and addresses of the child and his or her parents or other person responsible for his or her care, if known, and, as the case may be, the name and address of the program in which the child is receiving care; the child's age, sex and race; the nature and extent of the child's injuries, abuse or maltreatment, including any evidence of prior injuries, abuse or maltreatment to the child or, as the case may be, his or her siblings; the name of the person or persons alleged to be responsible for causing the injury, abuse or maltreatment, if known; family composition, where appropriate; the source of the report; the person making the report and where he or she can be reached; the actions taken by the reporting source, including the taking of photographs and x-rays, removal or keeping of the child or notifying the medical examiner or coroner; and any other information which the commissioner of the office of children and family services may, by regulation, require, or the person making the report believes might be helpful, in the furtherance of the purposes of this title. Notwithstanding the privileges set forth in article forty-five of the civil practice law and rules, and any other provision of law to the contrary, mandated reporters who make a report which initiates an investigation of an allegation of child abuse or maltreatment are required to comply with all requests for records made by a child protective service relating to such report, including records relating to diagnosis, prognosis or treatment, and clinical records, of any patient or client that are essential for a full investigation of allegations of child abuse or maltreatment pursuant to this title; provided, however, that disclosure of substance abuse treatment records shall be made pursuant to the standards and procedures for disclosure of such records delineated in federal law. Written reports from persons or officials required by this title to report shall be admissible in evidence in any proceedings relating to child abuse or maltreatment.

§416. Obligations of persons required to report.

Any person or official required to report cases of suspected child abuse and maltreatment may take or cause to be taken at public expense photographs of the areas of trauma visible on a child who is subject to a report and, if medically indicated, cause to be performed a radiological examination on the child. Any photographs or x-rays taken shall be sent to the child protective service at the time the written report is sent, or as soon thereafter as possible. Whenever such person is required to report under this title in his capacity as a member of the staff of a medical or other public or private institution, school, facility, or agency, he shall immediately notify the person in charge of such institution, school, facility or agency, or his designated agent, who shall then take or cause to be taken at public expense color photographs of visible trauma and shall, if medically indicated, cause to be performed a radiological examination on the child.

§417. Taking a child into protective custody.

1. (a) Pursuant to the requirements and provisions of the family court act, a peace officer, acting pursuant to his or her special duties, a police officer, a law enforcement official, or an agent of a duly incorporated society for the prevention of cruelty to children, or a designated employee of a city or county department of social services, or an agent or employee of an Indian tribe that has entered into an agreement with the department pursuant to section thirty-nine of this chapter to provide child protective services shall take all appropriate measures to protect a child's life and health including, when appropriate, taking or keeping a child in protective custody without the consent of a parent or guardian if such person has reasonable cause to believe that the

circumstances or condition of the child are such that continuing in his or her place of residence or in the care and custody of the parent, guardian, custodian or other person responsible for the child's care presents an imminent danger to the child's life or health.

(b) Any physician shall notify the appropriate police authorities or the local child protective service to take custody of any child such physician is treating whether or not additional medical treatment is required, if such physician has reasonable cause to believe that the circumstances or condition of the child are such that continuing in his place of residence or in the care and custody of the parent, guardian, custodian or other person responsible for the child's care presents an imminent danger to the child's life or health.

2. Notwithstanding any other provision of law, the person in charge of any hospital or similar institution shall, where he has reasonable cause to believe that the circumstances or conditions of the child are such that continuing in his place of residence or in the care and custody of the parent, guardian, custodian or other person responsible for the child's care presents an imminent danger to the child's life or health, take all necessary measures to protect the child including, where appropriate, retaining custody of an abused or maltreated child, until the next regular week day session of the family court in which a child protection proceeding pursuant to article ten of the family court act may be commenced whether or not additional medical treatment is required during that period and whether or not a request is made by a parent or guardian for the return of the child during that period. In all cases where the person in charge of a hospital or similar institution has retained custody of a child pursuant to this section, he shall immediately notify the appropriate local child protective service which immediately shall commence an investigation. In the case of a child in residential care, the child protective service shall notify the appropriate state agency which shall immediately commence an investigation. If no further medical treatment is necessary, the child protective service shall take all necessary measures to protect a child's life and health, including when appropriate, taking custody of a child. Such child protective service shall commence a child protective proceeding in the family court at the next regular week day session of the appropriate family court or recommend to the court at that time that the child be returned to his parents or guardian.

3. Whenever a child protective service takes a child into protective custody and the parent, guardian or custodian of the child is not present, the service shall immediately notify the local police station closest to the child's home of such removal, and shall provide them with a copy of the notice required pursuant to paragraph (iii) of subdivision (b) of section one thousand twenty-four of the family court act. Upon request by the parent, guardian or custodian of the child, the police shall provide such person with a copy of the notice.

§418. Mandatory reporting to and post-mortem investigation of deaths by medical examiner or coroner.

Any person or official required to report cases of suspected child abuse or maltreatment, including workers of the local child protective service who has reasonable cause to suspect that a child died as a result of child abuse or maltreatment shall report that fact to the appropriate medical examiner or coroner. The medical examiner or coroner shall accept the report for investigation and shall issue a preliminary written report of his or her finding within sixty days of the date of death, absent extraordinary circumstances, and his or her final written report promptly, absent extraordinary circumstances, to the police, the appropriate district attorney, the local child protective service, the office of children and family services, and, if the institution making the report is a hospital, the hospital. The office of children and family services shall promptly provide a copy of the preliminary and final reports to the statewide central register of child abuse and maltreatment.

§419. Immunity from liability.

Any person, official, or institution participating in good faith in the providing of a service pursuant to section four hundred twenty-four of this title, the making of a report, the taking of photographs, the removal or keeping of a child pursuant to this title, or the disclosure of child protective services information in compliance with sections twenty, four hundred twenty-two and four hundred twenty-two-a of this chapter shall have immunity from any liability, civil or criminal, that might otherwise result by reason of such actions. For the purpose of any proceeding, civil or criminal, the good faith of any such person, official, or institution required to report cases of child abuse or maltreatment or providing a service pursuant to section four hundred twenty-four or the disclosure of child protective services information in compliance with sections twenty, four hundred twenty-two and four hundred twenty-two-a of this chapter shall be presumed, provided such person, official or institution was acting in discharge of their duties and within the scope of their employment, and that such liability did not result from the willful misconduct or gross negligence of such person, official or institution.

§420. Penalties for failure to report.

1. Any person, official or institution required by this title to report a case of suspected child abuse or maltreatment who willfully fails to do so shall be guilty of a class A misdemeanor.

2. Any person, official or institution required by this title to report a case of suspected child abuse or maltreatment who knowingly and willfully fails to do so shall be civilly liable for the damages proximately caused by such failure.

§421. Responsibility of the office.

The office shall: 1. in conjunction with local departments, both jointly and individually, within the appropriation available, conduct a continuing publicity and education program for local department staff, persons and officials required to report including district attorneys, assistant district attorneys, police officers, peace officers, investigators employed in the office of a district attorney, and any other appropriate persons to encourage the fullest degree of reporting of suspected child abuse or maltreatment. Such program shall be developed and implemented in coordination with those established pursuant to section 31.06 of the mental hygiene law, section twenty-eight hundred five-n of the public health law, section thirty-two hundred nine-a of the education law, sections two hundred fourteen-a and eight hundred forty of the executive law and article eleven of this chapter. The program shall include but not be limited to responsibilities, obligations and powers under this title and chapter as well as the diagnosis of child abuse and maltreatment, the procedures of the child protective service, the family court and other duly authorized agencies and the prevention, treatment and remediation of abuse and maltreatment of children in residential care.

2. (a) provide technical assistance to local social services departments regarding case planning and provision of services and performance of other

responsibilities pursuant to this title. Such assistance shall be provided on a regular, ongoing basis and shall also be made available as needed, upon request of any such local department.

(b) issue guidelines to assist local social services departments in evaluating and establishing investigative priorities for reports describing situations or events which may pose a clear and present danger to the life, health or safety of a child and which require immediate, personal contact between the local child protective service and the subject of the report, the subject's family, or any other persons named in the report.

(c) issue guidelines to assist local child protective services in the interpretation and assessment of reports of abuse and maltreatment made to the statewide central register described in section four hundred twenty-two of this article. Such guidelines shall include information, standards and criteria for the identification of credible evidence of alleged abuse and maltreatment required to determine whether a report may be indicated.

3. promulgate regulations setting forth requirements for the performance by local social services departments of the duties and powers imposed and conferred upon them by the provisions of this title and of article ten of the family court act. Such regulations shall establish uniform requirements for the investigation of reports of child abuse or maltreatment under this title. The department shall also issue guidelines which shall set forth the circumstances or conditions under which:

(a) personal contact shall be made with the child named in the report and any other children in the same household, including interviewing such child or children absent the subject of the report whenever possible and appropriate;

(b) photographs of visible physical injuries or trauma of children who may be the victims of abuse or maltreatment shall be taken or arranged for;

(c) medical examination of a child who may be a victim of abuse or maltreatment and documentation of findings of such examination, shall be required.

The department shall promulgate regulations to establish standards for intervention, criteria for case closings, criteria for determining whether or not to initiate a child protective proceeding, and criteria for the formulation of treatment plans and for the delivery of child protective services including specification of the services to be classified as child protective services, which shall also apply to any society for the prevention of cruelty to children which has entered into a currently valid contract with a local department of social services to investigate child abuse or maltreatment reports. The department shall promulgate regulations establishing minimum standards and practices for the delivery of child protective services in connection with monitoring and supervising respondents and their families as ordered by a family court pursuant to section ten hundred thirty-nine and paragraphs (i), (iii), (iv) and (v) of subdivision (a) of section ten hundred fifty-two of the family court act. Such regulations shall also require local child protective services to comply with notification requirements of the family court act in connection with such monitoring and supervisory responsibilities.

4. (a) after consultation with the local child protective services, promulgate regulations relating to staff qualifications for non-supervisory child protective services workers, prescribing any baccalaureate or equivalent college degree and/or relevant human service experience as requirements. Such requirements shall not apply to persons currently employed by such child protective services who were hired before January first, nineteen hundred eighty-six.

(b) after consultation with the local child protective services, promulgate regulations relating to staff qualifications for those assigned to be supervisors of child protective services, prescribing any baccalaureate or equivalent college degree and/or relevant human services experience as requirements. Provided, however, that such regulations shall at a minimum provide that those assigned to be supervisors of child protective services have either a baccalaureate degree or three years of relevant work experience in a human services field. Such requirements shall not apply to persons currently assigned to be a child protective services supervisor who were hired before December first, two thousand six.

5. (a) directly or through the purchase of services, implement, subject to the amounts appropriated therefor, an ongoing, statewide training program for employees of the department and of each local department of social services employed in the provision and supervision of child protective services or in other activities required in accordance with the provisions of this title.

(b) promulgate regulations setting forth training requirements which shall specify, among other things, that all persons hired by a child protective service on or after April first, nineteen hundred eighty-six shall have satisfactorily completed a course approved by the department within the first three months of employment, in the fundamentals of child protection. Such course shall include at least basic training in the principles and techniques of investigations, including relationships with other investigative bodies, legal issues in child protection, and methods of remediation, diagnosis, treatment and prevention. Such regulations shall also specify that all persons employed by a child protective service on or after December first, two thousand six shall satisfactorily complete six hours of annual in service training, beginning in their second year of employment. Such annual in service training shall include, but is not limited to, review of the protocols for identification and investigation of child abuse and maltreatment, any developments in legal, treatment and prevention issues in child protection, and review and analysis of field experiences of child protective services workers.

(c) require all persons assigned to be a supervisor by a child protective service on or after April first, nineteen hundred eighty-six, shall have satisfactorily completed, within the first three months of employment as a supervisor or within three months of the effective date of this paragraph, whichever shall occur first, a course in the fundamentals of child protection developed by the office of children and family services. Such training course shall, among other things, strengthen and expand current training procedures for child protective service supervisors; provide the skills, knowledge and standards to practice effective case planning and case management; provide comprehensive assessment tools needed in critical decision making; require participation in the existing common core training required by child protective service caseworkers; strengthen recognition and response to safety and risk indicators; improve skills to promote consistent implementation of training and practice; provide the necessary tools and assistance to build the ability to coach and monitor child protective service caseworkers and model effective investigation practice; increase cultural competency and sensitivity; and establish an annual in service training program specifically focused on child protective service supervisors.

(d) withhold reimbursement, otherwise payable to social services districts, for the salaries of employees of child protective services who do not comply with the background review, educational, experience or training requirements of this title.

6. promulgate regulations which require social services districts to make local procedural manuals and service directories available to employees of a child protective service, service providers and other professionals involved in the prevention of child abuse and maltreatment.

7. take all reasonable and necessary actions to assure that the local departments of social services are kept apprised on a current basis of the laws, regulations and policies of the department concerning child abuse and maltreatment.

8. monitor and supervise the performance of the local departments of social services.

§422. Statewide central register of child abuse and maltreatment.

1. There shall be established in the office of children and family services a statewide central register of child abuse and maltreatment reports made pursuant to this title.

2. (a) The central register shall be capable of receiving telephone calls alleging child abuse or maltreatment and of immediately identifying prior reports of child abuse or maltreatment and capable of monitoring the provision of child protective service twenty-four hours a day, seven days a week. To effectuate this purpose, but subject to the provisions of the appropriate local plan for the provision of child protective services, there shall be a single statewide telephone number that all persons, whether mandated by the law or not, may use to make telephone calls alleging child abuse or maltreatment and that all persons so authorized by this title may use for determining the existence of prior reports in order to evaluate the condition or circumstances of a child. In addition to the single statewide telephone number, there shall be a special unlisted express telephone number and a telephone facsimile number for use only by persons mandated by law to make telephone calls, or to transmit telephone facsimile information on a form provided by the commissioner of children and family services, alleging child abuse or maltreatment, and for use by all persons so authorized by this title for determining the existence of prior reports in order to evaluate the condition or circumstances of a child. When any allegations contained in such telephone calls could reasonably constitute a report of child abuse or maltreatment, such allegations and any previous reports to the central registry involving the subject of such report or children named in such report, including any previous report containing allegations of child abuse and maltreatment alleged to have occurred in other counties and districts in New York state shall be immediately transmitted orally or electronically by the office of children and family services to the appropriate local child protective service for investigation. The inability of the person calling the register to identify the alleged perpetrator shall, in no circumstance, constitute the sole cause for the register to reject such allegation or fail to transmit such allegation for investigation. If the records indicate a previous report concerning a subject of the report, the child alleged to be abused or maltreated, a sibling, other children in the household, other persons named in the report or other pertinent information, the appropriate local child protective service shall be immediately notified of the fact. If the report involves either (i) an allegation of an abused child described in paragraph (i), (ii) or (iii) of subdivision (e) of section one thousand twelve of the family court act or sexual abuse of a child or the death of a child or (ii) suspected maltreatment which alleges any physical harm when the report is made by a person required to report pursuant to section four hundred thirteen of this title within six months of any other two reports that were indicated, or may still be pending, involving the same child, sibling,

or other children in the household or the subject of the report, the office of children and family services shall identify the report as such and note any prior reports when transmitting the report to the local child protective services for investigation.

(b) Any telephone call made by a person required to report cases of suspected child abuse or maltreatment pursuant to section four hundred thirteen of this chapter containing allegations, which if true would constitute child abuse or maltreatment shall constitute a report and shall be immediately transmitted orally or electronically by the department to the appropriate local child protective service for investigation.

(c) Whenever a telephone call to the statewide central register described in this section is received by the department, and the department finds that the person allegedly responsible for abuse or maltreatment of a child cannot be a subject of a report as defined in subdivision four of section four hundred twelve of this chapter, but believes that the alleged acts or circumstances against a child described in the telephone call may constitute a crime or an immediate threat to the child's health or safety, the department shall convey by the most expedient means available the information contained in such telephone call to the appropriate law enforcement agency, district attorney or other public official empowered to provide necessary aid or assistance.

3. The central register shall include but not be limited to the following information: all the information in the written report; a record of the final disposition of the report, including services offered and services accepted; the plan for rehabilitative treatment; the names and identifying data, dates and circumstances of any person requesting or receiving information from the register; and any other information which the commissioner believes might be helpful in the furtherance of the purposes of this chapter.

4. (A) Reports made pursuant to this title as well as any other information obtained, reports written or photographs taken concerning such reports in the possession of the office or local departments shall be confidential and shall only be made available to:

(a) a physician who has before him or her a child whom he or she reasonably suspects may be abused or maltreated;

(b) a person authorized to place a child in protective custody when such person has before him or her a child whom he or she reasonably suspects may be abused or maltreated and such person requires the information in the record to determine whether to place the child in protective custody;

(c) a duly authorized agency having the responsibility for the care or supervision of a child who is reported to the central register of abuse and maltreatment;

(d) any person who is the subject of the report or other persons named in the report;

(e) a court, upon a finding that the information in the record is necessary for the determination of an issue before the court;

(f) a grand jury, upon a finding that the information in the record is necessary for the determination of charges before the grand jury;

(g) any appropriate state legislative committee responsible for child protective legislation;

(h) any person engaged in a bona fide research purpose provided, however, that no information identifying the subjects of the report or other persons named in the report shall be made available to the researcher unless it is absolutely essential to the research purpose and the department gives prior approval;

(i) a provider agency as defined by subdivision three of section four hundred twenty-four-a of this chapter, or a licensing agency as defined by subdivision four of section four hundred twenty-four-a of this chapter, subject to the provisions of such section;

(j) the justice center for the protection of people with special needs or a delegate investigatory entity in connection with an investigation being conducted under article eleven of this chapter;

(k) a probation service conducting an investigation pursuant to article three or seven or section six hundred fifty-three of the family court act where there is reason to suspect the child or the child's sibling may have been abused or maltreated and such child or sibling, parent, guardian or other person legally responsible for the child is a person named in an indicated report of child abuse or maltreatment and that such information is necessary for the making of a determination or recommendation to the court; or a probation service regarding a person about whom it is conducting an investigation pursuant to article three hundred ninety of the criminal procedure law, or a probation service or the department of corrections and community supervision regarding a person to whom the service or department is providing supervision pursuant to article sixty of the penal law or article eight of the correction law, where the subject of investigation or supervision has been convicted of a felony under article one hundred twenty, one hundred twenty-five or one hundred thirty-five of the penal law or any felony or misdemeanor under article one hundred thirty, two hundred thirty-five, two hundred forty-five, two hundred sixty or two hundred sixty-three of the penal law, or has been indicted for any such felony and, as a result, has been convicted of a crime under the penal law, where the service or department requests the information upon a certification that such information is necessary to conduct its investigation, that there is reasonable cause to believe that the subject of an investigation is the subject of an indicated report and that there is reasonable cause to believe that such records are necessary to the investigation by the probation service or the department, provided, however, that only indicated reports shall be furnished pursuant to this subdivision;

(*l*) a criminal justice agency, which for the purposes of this subdivision shall mean a district attorney, an assistant district attorney or an investigator employed in the office of a district attorney; a sworn officer of the division of state police, of the regional state park police, of a county department of parks, of a city police department, or of a county, town or village police department or county sheriff's office or department; or an Indian police officer, when:

(i) such criminal justice agency requests such information stating that such information is necessary to conduct a criminal investigation or criminal prosecution of a person, that there is reasonable cause to believe that such person is the subject of a report, and that it is reasonable to believe that due to the nature of the crime under investigation or prosecution, such person is the subject of a report, and that it is reasonable to believe that due to that nature of the crime under investigation or prosecution, such records may be related to the criminal investigation or prosecution; or

(ii) such criminal justice agency requests such information stating that: such agency is conducting an investigation of a missing child; such agency has reason to suspect such child's parent, guardian or other person legally responsible for such child is or may be the subject of a report, or, such child or such child's sibling is or may be another person named in a report of child abuse or maltreatment and that any such information is or may be needed to further such investigation;   *(Eff.1/19/16,Ch.13,L.2016)*

(m) the New York city department of investigation provided however, that no information identifying the subjects of the report or other persons named in the report shall be made available to the department of investigation unless such information is essential to an investigation within the legal authority of the department of investigation and the state department of social services gives prior approval;

(n) chief executive officers of authorized agencies, directors of day care centers and directors of facilities operated or supervised by the department of education, the office of children and family services, the office of mental health or the office for people with developmental disabilities, in connection with a disciplinary investigation, action, or administrative or judicial proceeding instituted by any of such officers or directors against an employee of any such agency, center or facility who is the subject of an indicated report when the incident of abuse or maltreatment contained in the report occurred in the agency, center, facility or program, and the purpose of such proceeding is to determine whether the employee should be retained or discharged; provided, however, a person given access to information pursuant to this subparagraph shall, notwithstanding any inconsistent provision of law, be authorized to redisclose such information only if the purpose of such redisclosure is to initiate or present evidence in a disciplinary, administrative or judicial proceeding concerning the continued employment or the terms of employment of an employee of such agency, center or facility who has been named as a subject of an indicated report and, in addition, a person or agency given access to information pursuant to this subparagraph shall also be given information not otherwise provided concerning the subject of an indicated report where the commission of an act or acts by such subject has been determined in proceedings pursuant to article ten of the family court act to constitute abuse or neglect;   *(Eff.5/25/16,Ch.37,L.2016)*

(o) a provider or coordinator of services to which a child protective service or social services district has referred a child or a child's family or to whom the child or the child's family have referred themselves at the request of the child protective service or social services district, where said child is reported to the register when the records, reports or other information are necessary to enable the provider or coordinator to establish and implement a plan of service for the child or the child's family, or to monitor the provision and coordination of services and the circumstances of the child and the child's family, or to directly provide services; provided, however, that a provider of services may include appropriate health care or school district personnel, as such terms shall be defined by the department; provided however, a provider or coordinator of services given access to information concerning a child pursuant to this subparagraph (o) shall, notwithstanding any inconsistent provision of law, be authorized to redisclose such information to other persons or agencies which also provide services to the child or the child's family only if the consolidated services plan prepared and approved pursuant to section thirty-four-a of this chapter describes the agreement that has been or will be reached between the provider or coordinator of service and the local district. An agreement entered into pursuant to this subparagraph shall include the specific agencies and categories of individuals to whom redisclosure by the provider or coordinator of services is authorized. Persons or agencies given access to information pursuant to this subparagraph may exchange such information in order to facilitate the provision or coordination of services to the child or the child's family;

(p) a disinterested person making an investigation pursuant to section one hundred sixteen of the domestic relations law, provided that such disinterested person shall only make this information available to the judge before whom the adoption proceeding is pending;

(q) *(REPEALED,Eff.1/19/16,Ch.436,L.2015)*

(r) *(REPEALED,Eff.6/30/13,Ch.501,L.2012)*

(s) a child protective service of another state when such service certifies that the records and reports are necessary in order to conduct a child abuse or maltreatment investigation within its jurisdiction of the subject of the report and shall be used only for purposes of conducting such investigation and will not be redisclosed to any other person or agency;

(t) an attorney for a child, appointed pursuant to the provisions of section one thousand sixteen of the family court act, at any time such appointment is in effect, in relation to any report in which the respondent in the proceeding in which the attorney for a child has been appointed is the subject or another person named in the report, pursuant to sections one thousand thirty-nine-a and one thousand fifty-two-a of the family court act;

(u) a child care resource and referral program subject to the provisions of subdivision six of section four hundred twenty-four-a of this title;

(v)(i) officers and employees of the state comptroller or of the city comptroller of the city of New York, or of the county officer designated by law or charter to perform the auditing function in any county not wholly contained within a city, for purposes of a duly authorized performance audit, provided that such comptroller shall have certified to the keeper of such records that he or she has instituted procedures developed in consultation with the department to limit access to client-identifiable information to persons requiring such information for purposes of the audit and that appropriate controls and prohibitions are imposed on the dissemination of client-identifiable information contained in the conduct of the audit. Information pertaining to the substance or content of any psychological, psychiatric, therapeutic, clinical or medical reports, evaluations or like materials or information pertaining to such child or the child's family shall not be made available to such officers and employees unless disclosure of such information is absolutely essential to the specific audit activity and the department gives prior written approval.

(ii) any failure to maintain the confidentiality of client-identifiable information shall subject such comptroller or officer to denial of any further access to records until such time as the audit agency has reviewed its procedures concerning controls and prohibitions imposed on the dissemination of such information and has taken all reasonable and appropriate steps to eliminate such lapses in maintaining confidentiality to the satisfaction of the office of children and family services. The office of children and family services shall establish the grounds for denial of access to records contained under this section and shall recommend as necessary a plan of remediation to the audit agency. Except as provided in this section, nothing in this subparagraph shall be construed as limiting the powers of such comptroller or officer to access records which he or she is otherwise authorized to audit or obtain under any other applicable provision of law. Any person given access to information pursuant to this subparagraph who releases data or information to persons or agencies not authorized to receive such information shall be guilty of a class A misdemeanor;

(w) members of a local or regional fatality review team approved by the office of children and family services in accordance with section four hundred twenty-two-b of this title;

(x) members of a local or regional multidisciplinary investigative team as established pursuant to subdivision six of section four hundred twenty-three of this title;

(y) members of a citizen review panel as established pursuant to section three hundred seventy-one-b of this article; provided, however, members of a citizen review panel shall not disclose to any person or government official any identifying information which the panel has been provided and shall not make public other information unless otherwise authorized by statute;

(z) an entity with appropriate legal authority in another state to license, certify or otherwise approve prospective foster parents, prospective adoptive parents, prospective relative guardians or prospective successor guardians where disclosure of information regarding such prospective foster or prospective adoptive parents or prospective relative or prospective successor guardians and other persons over the age of eighteen residing in the home of such persons is required under title IV-E of the federal social security act; and

(aa) a social services official who is investigating whether an adult is in need of protective services in accordance with the provisions of section four hundred seventy-three of this chapter, when such official has reasonable cause to believe such adult may be in need of protective services due to the conduct of an individual or individuals who had access to such adult when such adult was a child and that such reports and information are needed to further the present investigation.

After a child, other than a child in residential care, who is reported to the central register of abuse or maltreatment reaches the age of eighteen years, access to a child's record under subparagraphs (a) and (b) of this paragraph shall be permitted only if a sibling or off-spring of such child is before such person and is a suspected victim of child abuse or maltreatment. In addition, a person or official required to make a report of suspected child abuse or maltreatment pursuant to section four hundred thirteen of this chapter shall receive, upon request, the findings of an investigation made pursuant to this title. However, no information may be released unless the person or official's identity is confirmed by the office. If the request for such information is made prior to the completion of an investigation of a report, the released information shall be limited to whether the report is "indicated", "unfounded" or "under investigation", whichever the case may be. If the request for such information is made after the completion of an investigation of a report, the released information shall be limited to whether the report is "indicated" or "unfounded", whichever the case may be. A person given access to the names or other information identifying the subjects of the report, or other persons named in the report, except the subject of the report or other persons named in the report, shall not divulge or make public such identifying information unless he or she is a district attorney or other law enforcement official and the purpose is to initiate court action or the disclosure is necessary in connection with the investigation or prosecution of the subject of the report for a crime alleged to have been committed by the subject against another person named in the report. Nothing in this section shall be construed to permit any release, disclosure or identification of the names or identifying descriptions of persons who have reported suspected child abuse or maltreatment to the statewide central register or the agency, institution, organization, program or other entity where such persons are employed or the agency, institution, organization or program with which they are associated without such persons' written permission except to persons, officials, and agencies enumerated in subparagraphs (e), (f), (h), (j), (l), (m) and (v) of this paragraph.

To the extent that persons or agencies are given access to information pursuant to subparagraphs (a), (b), (c), (j), (k), (l), (m), (o) and (q) of this paragraph, such persons or agencies may give and receive such information to each other in order to facilitate an investigation conducted by such persons or agencies.

(B) Notwithstanding any inconsistent provision of law to the contrary, a city or county social services commissioner may withhold, in whole or in part, the release of any information which he or she is authorized to make available to persons or agencies identified in subparagraphs (a), (k), (l), (m), (n), (o), (p) and (q) of paragraph (A) of this subdivision if such commissioner determines that such information is not related to the purposes for which such information is requested or when such disclosure will be detrimental to the child named in the report.

(C) A city or county social services commissioner who denies access by persons or agencies identified in subparagraphs (a), (k), (l), (m), (n), (o), (p) and (q) of paragraph (A) of this subdivision to records, reports or other information or parts thereof maintained by such commissioner in accordance with this title shall, within ten days from the date of receipt of the request fully explain in writing to the person requesting the records, reports or other information the reasons for the denial.

(D) A person or agency identified in subparagraphs (a), (k), (l), (m), (n), (o), (p) and (q) of paragraph (A) of this subdivision who is denied access to records, reports or other information or parts thereof maintained by a local department pursuant to this title may bring a proceeding for review of such denial pursuant to article seventy-eight of the civil practice law and rules.

(E) *(REPEALED, Eff. 1/19/16, Ch. 13, L. 2016)*

5. (a) Unless an investigation of a report conducted pursuant to this title determines that there is some credible evidence of the alleged abuse or maltreatment, all information identifying the subjects of the report and other persons named in the report shall be legally sealed forthwith by the central register and any local child protective services or the state agency which investigated the report. Such unfounded reports may only be unsealed and made available:

(i) to the office of children and family services for the purpose of supervising a social services district;

(ii) to the office of children and family services and local or regional fatality review team members for the purpose of preparing a fatality report pursuant to section twenty or four hundred twenty-two-b of this chapter;

(iii) to a local child protective service, the office of children and family services, or all members of a local or regional multidisciplinary investigative team or the justice center for the protection of people with special needs when investigating a subsequent report of suspected abuse, neglect or maltreatment involving a subject of the unfounded report, a child named in the unfounded report, or a child's sibling named in the unfounded report pursuant to this article or article eleven of this chapter;

(iv) to the subject of the report; and

(v) to a district attorney, an assistant district attorney, an investigator employed in the office of a district attorney, or to a sworn officer of the division of state police, of a city, county, town or village police department or of a county sheriff's office when such official verifies that the report is necessary to conduct an active investigation or prosecution of a violation of subdivision four of section 240.50 of the penal law.

(b) Persons given access to unfounded reports pursuant to subparagraph (v) of paragraph (a) of this subdivision shall not redisclose such reports except as necessary to conduct such appropriate investigation or prosecution and shall request of the court that any copies of such reports produced in any court proceeding be redacted to remove the names of the subjects and other persons named in the reports or that the court issue an order protecting the names of the subjects and other persons named in the reports from public disclosure. The local child protective service or state agency shall not indicate the subsequent report solely based upon the existence of the prior unfounded report or reports. Notwithstanding section four hundred fifteen of this title, section one thousand forty-six of the family court act, or, except as set forth herein, any other provision of law to the contrary, an unfounded report shall not be admissible in any judicial or administrative proceeding or action; provided, however, an unfounded report may be introduced into evidence: (i) by the subject of the report where such subject is a respondent in a proceeding under article ten of the family court act or is a plaintiff or petitioner in a civil action or proceeding alleging the false reporting of child abuse or maltreatment; or (ii) in a criminal court for the purpose of prosecuting a violation of subdivision four of section 240.50 of the penal law. Legally sealed unfounded reports shall be expunged ten years after the receipt of the report.

(c) Notwithstanding any other provision of law, the office of children and family services may, in its discretion, grant a request to expunge an unfounded report where: (i) the source of the report was convicted of a violation of subdivision three of section 240.55 of the penal law in regard to such report; or (ii) the subject of the report presents clear and convincing evidence that affirmatively refutes the allegation of abuse or maltreatment; provided however, that the absence of credible evidence supporting the allegation of abuse or maltreatment shall not be the sole basis to expunge the report. Nothing in this paragraph shall require the office of children and family services to hold an administrative hearing in deciding whether to expunge a report. Such office shall make its determination upon reviewing the written evidence submitted by the subject of the report and any records or information obtained from the state or local agency which investigated the allegations of abuse or maltreatment.

5-a. Upon notification from a local social services district, that a report is part of the family assessment and services track pursuant to subparagraph (i) of paragraph (c) of subdivision four of section four hundred twenty-seven-a of this title, the central register shall forthwith identify the report as an assessment track case and legally seal such report. Access to reports assigned to, and records created under the family assessment and services track and information concerning such reports and records is governed by paragraph (d) of subdivision five of section four hundred twenty-seven-a of this title.

6. In all other cases, the record of the report to the statewide central register shall be expunged ten years after the eighteenth birthday of the youngest child named in the report. In the case of a child in residential care the record of the report to the central register shall be expunged ten years after the reported child's eighteenth birthday. In any case and at any time, the commissioner of the office of children and family services may amend any record upon good

cause shown and notice to the subjects of the report and other persons named in the report.

7. At any time, a subject of a report and other persons named in the report may receive, upon request, a copy of all information contained in the central register; provided, however, that the commissioner is authorized to prohibit the release of data that would identify the person who made the report or who cooperated in a subsequent investigation or the agency, institution, organization, program or other entity where such person is employed or with which he is associated, which he reasonably finds will be detrimental to the safety or interests of such person.

8. (a) (i) At any time subsequent to the completion of the investigation but in no event later than ninety days after the subject of the report is notified that the report is indicated the subject may request the commissioner to amend the record of the report. If the commissioner does not amend the report in accordance with such request within ninety days of receiving the request, the subject shall have the right to a fair hearing, held in accordance with paragraph (b) of this subdivision, to determine whether the record of the report in the central register should be amended on the grounds that it is inaccurate or it is being maintained in a manner inconsistent with this title.

(ii) Upon receipt of a request to amend the record of a child abuse and maltreatment report the office of children and family services shall immediately send a written request to the child protective service or the state agency which was responsible for investigating the allegations of abuse or maltreatment for all records, reports and other information maintained by the service or state agency pertaining to such indicated report. The service or state agency shall as expeditiously as possible but within no more than twenty working days of receiving such request, forward all records, reports and other information it maintains on such indicated report to the office of children and family services. The office of children and family services shall as expeditiously as possible but within no more than fifteen working days of receiving such materials from the child protective service or state agency, review all such materials in its possession concerning the indicated report and determine, after affording such service or state agency a reasonable opportunity to present its views, whether there is a fair preponderance of the evidence to find that the subject committed the act or acts of child abuse or maltreatment giving rise to the indicated report and whether, based on guidelines developed by the office of children and family services pursuant to subdivision five of section four hundred twenty-four-a of this title, such act or acts could be relevant and reasonably related to employment of the subject of the report by a provider agency, as defined by subdivision three of section four hundred twenty-four-a of this title, or relevant and reasonably related to the subject of the report being allowed to have regular and substantial contact with children who are cared for by a provider agency, or relevant and reasonably related to the approval or disapproval of an application submitted by the subject of the report to a licensing agency, as defined by subdivision four of section four hundred twenty-four-a of this title.

(iii) If it is determined at the review held pursuant to this paragraph (a) that there is no credible evidence in the record to find that the subject committed an act or acts of child abuse or maltreatment, the department shall amend the record to indicate that the report is "unfounded" and notify the subject forthwith.

(iv) If it is determined at the review held pursuant to this paragraph (a) that there is some credible evidence in the record to find that the subject committed such act or acts but that such act or acts could not be relevant and reasonably related to the employment of the subject by a provider agency or to the subject being allowed to have regular and substantial contact with children who are cared for by a provider agency or the approval or disapproval of an application which could be submitted by the subject to a licensing agency, the department shall be precluded from informing a provider or licensing agency which makes an inquiry to the department pursuant to the provisions of section four hundred twenty-four-a of this title concerning the subject that the person about whom the inquiry is made is the subject of an indicated report of child abuse or maltreatment. The department shall notify forthwith the subject of the report of such determinations and that a fair hearing has been scheduled pursuant to paragraph (b) of this subdivision. The sole issue at such hearing shall be whether the subject has been shown by some credible evidence to have committed the act or acts of child abuse or maltreatment giving rise to the indicated report.

(v) If it is determined at the review held pursuant to this paragraph (a) that there is some credible evidence in the record to prove that the subject committed an act or acts of child abuse or maltreatment and that such act or acts could be relevant and reasonably related to the employment of the subject by a provider agency or to the subject being allowed to have regular and substantial contact with children cared for by a provider agency or the approval or disapproval of an application which could be submitted by the subject to a licensing agency, the department shall notify forthwith the subject of the report of such determinations and that a fair hearing has been scheduled pursuant to paragraph (b) of this subdivision.

(b) (i) If the department, within ninety days of receiving a request from the subject that the record of a report be amended, does not amend the record in accordance with such request, the department shall schedule a fair hearing and shall provide notice of the scheduled hearing date to the subject, the statewide central register and, as appropriate, to the child protective service or the state agency which investigated the report.

(ii) The burden of proof in such a hearing shall be on the child protective service or the state agency which investigated the report, as the case may be. In such a hearing, the fact that there is a family court finding of abuse or neglect against the subject in regard to an allegation contained in the report shall create an irrebuttable presumption that said allegation is substantiated by some credible evidence.

(c) (i) If it is determined at the fair hearing that there is no credible evidence in the record to find that the subject committed an act or acts of child abuse or maltreatment, the department shall amend the record to reflect that such a finding was made at the administrative hearing, order any child protective service or state agency which investigated the report to similarly amend its records of the report, and shall notify the subject forthwith of the determination.

(ii) Upon a determination made at a fair hearing held on or after January first, nineteen hundred eighty-six scheduled pursuant to the provisions of subparagraph (v) of paragraph (a) of this subdivision that the subject has been shown by a fair preponderance of the evidence to have committed the act or acts of child abuse or maltreatment giving rise to the indicated report, the hearing officer shall determine, based on guidelines developed by the office of children and family services pursuant to subdivision five of section four hundred twenty-four-a of this title, whether such act or acts are relevant and reasonably related to employment of the subject by a provider agency, as defined by subdivision three of section four hundred twenty-four-a of this title, or relevant and reasonably related to the subject being allowed to have regular and substantial contact with children who are cared for by a provider agency or relevant and reasonably related to the approval or disapproval of an application submitted by the subject to a licensing agency, as defined by subdivision four of section four hundred twenty-four-a of this title.

Upon a determination made at a fair hearing that the act or acts of abuse or maltreatment are relevant and reasonably related to employment of the subject by a provider agency or the subject being allowed to have regular and substantial contact with children who are cared for by a provider agency or the approval or denial of an application submitted by the subject to a licensing agency, the department shall notify the subject forthwith. The department shall inform a provider or licensing agency which makes an inquiry to the department pursuant to the provisions of section four hundred twenty-four-a of this title concerning the subject that the person about whom the inquiry is made is the subject of an indicated child abuse or maltreatment report.

The failure to determine at the fair hearing that the act or acts of abuse and maltreatment are relevant and reasonably related to the employment of the subject by a provider agency or to the subject being allowed to have regular and substantial contact with children who are cared for by a provider agency or the approval or denial of an application submitted by the subject to a licensing agency shall preclude the department from informing a provider or licensing agency which makes an inquiry to the department pursuant to the provisions of section four hundred twenty-four-a of this title concerning the subject that the person about whom the inquiry is made is the subject of an indicated child abuse or maltreatment report.

(d) The commissioner or his or her designated agent is hereby authorized and empowered to make any appropriate order respecting the amendment of a record to make it accurate or consistent with the requirements of this title.

(e) Should the department grant the request of the subject of the report pursuant to this subdivision either through an administrative review or fair hearing to amend an indicated report to an unfounded report. Such report shall be legally sealed and shall be released and expunged in accordance with the standards set forth in subdivision five of this section.

9. Written notice of any expungement or amendment of any record, made pursuant to the provisions of this title, shall be served forthwith upon each subject of such record, other persons named in the report, the commissioner, and, as appropriate, the applicable local child protective service, the justice center for the protection of people with special needs, department of education, office of mental health, for people with developmental disabilities, the local social services commissioner or school district placing the child, any attorney for the child appointed to represent the child whose appointment has been continued by a family court judge during the term of a child's placement, and the director or operator of a residential care facility or program. The local child protective service or the state agency which investigated the report, upon receipt of such notice, shall take the appropriate similar action in regard to its child abuse and maltreatment register and records and inform, for the same purpose, any other agency which received such record.

10. *(REPEALED, Eff. 6/30/13, Ch. 501, L. 2012)*

11. *(REPEALED, Eff. 6/30/13, Ch. 501, L. 2012)*

12. Any person who willfully permits and any person who encourages the release of any data and information contained in the central register to persons or agencies not permitted by this title shall be guilty of a class A misdemeanor.

13. There shall be a single statewide telephone number for use by all persons seeking general information about child abuse, maltreatment or welfare other than for the purpose of making a report of child abuse or maltreatment.

14. The office shall refer suspected cases of falsely reporting child abuse and maltreatment in violation of subdivision four of section 240.50 of the penal law to the appropriate law enforcement agency or district attorney.

§422-a. Child abuse and neglect investigations; disclosure.

1. Notwithstanding any inconsistent provision of law to the contrary, the commissioner or a city or county social services commissioner may disclose information regarding the abuse or maltreatment of a child as set forth in this section, and the investigation thereof and any services related thereto if he or she determines that such disclosure shall not be contrary to the best interests of the child, the child's siblings or other children in the household and any one of the following factors are present:

(a) the subject of the report has been charged in an accusatory instrument with committing a crime related to a report maintained in the statewide central register; or

(b) the investigation of the abuse or maltreatment of the child by the local child protective service or the provision of services by such service has been publicly disclosed in a report required to be disclosed in the course of their official duties, by a law enforcement agency or official, a district attorney, any other state or local investigative agency or official or by judge of the unified court system; or

(c) there has been a prior knowing, voluntary, public disclosure by an individual concerning a report of child abuse or maltreatment in which such individual is named as the subject of the report as defined by subdivision four of section four hundred twelve of this title; or

(d) the child named in the report has died or the report involves the near fatality of a child. For the purposes of this section, "near fatality" means an act that results in the child being placed, as certified by a physician, in serious or critical condition.

2. For the purposes of this section, the following information may be disclosed:

(a) the name of the abused or maltreated child;

(b) the determination by the local child protective service or the state agency which investigated the report and the findings of the applicable investigating agency upon which such determination was based;

(c) identification of child protective or other services provided or actions, if any, taken regarding the child named in the report and his or her family as a result of any such report or reports;

(d) whether any report of abuse or maltreatment regarding such child has been "indicated" as maintained by the statewide central register;

(e) any actions taken by the local child protective service and the local social services district in response to reports of abuse or maltreatment of the child to the statewide central register including but not limited to actions taken after each and every report of abuse or maltreatment of such child and the dates of such reports;

(f) whether the child or the child's family has received care or services from the local social services district prior to each and every report of abuse or maltreatment of such child;

(g) any extraordinary or pertinent information concerning the circumstances of the abuse or maltreatment of the child and the investigation thereof, where the commissioner or the local commissioner determines such disclosure is consistent with the public interest.

3. Information may be disclosed pursuant to this section as follows:

(a) information released prior to the completion of the investigation of a report shall be limited to a statement that a report is "under investigation";

(b) when there has been a prior disclosure pursuant to paragraph (a) of this subdivision, information released in a case in which the report has been unfounded shall be limited to the statement that "the investigation has been completed, and the report has been unfounded";

(c) if the report has been "indicated" then information may be released pursuant to subdivision two of this section.

4. Any disclosure of information pursuant to this section shall be consistent with the provisions of subdivision two of this section. Such disclosure shall not identify or provide an identifying description of the source of the report, and shall not identify the name of the abused or maltreated child's siblings, the parent or other person legally responsible for the child or any other members of the child's household, other than the subject of the report.

5. In determining pursuant to subdivision one of this section whether disclosure will be contrary to the best interests of the child, the child's siblings or other children in the household, the commissioner or a city or county social services commissioner shall consider the interest in privacy of the child and the child's family and the effects which disclosure may have on efforts to reunite and provide services to the family.

6. Whenever a disclosure of information is made pursuant to this section, the city or county social services commissioner shall make a written statement prior to disclosing such information to the chief county executive officer where the incident occurred setting forth the paragraph in subdivision one of this section upon which he or she is basing such disclosure.

7. Except as it applies directly to the cause of the abuse or maltreatment of the child, nothing in this section shall be deemed to authorize the release or disclosure of the substance or content of any psychological, psychiatric, therapeutic, clinical or medical reports, evaluations or like materials or information pertaining to such child or the child's family. Prior to the release or disclosure of any psychological, psychiatric or therapeutic reports, evaluations or like materials or information pursuant to this subdivision, the city or county social services commissioner shall consult with the local mental hygiene director.

§422-b. Local and regional fatality review teams.

1. A fatality review team may be established at a local or regional level, with the approval of the office of children and family services, for the purpose of investigating the death of any child whose care and custody or custody and guardianship has been transferred to an authorized agency, other than a vulnerable child as defined in article eleven of this chapter, any child for whom child protective services has an open case, any child for whom the local department of social services has an open preventive services case, and in the case of a report made to the statewide central register of child abuse and maltreatment involving the death of a child. A fatality review team may also

investigate any unexplained or unexpected death of any child under the age of eighteen.

2. A local or regional fatality review team may exercise the same authority as the office of children and family services with regard to the preparation of a fatality report as set forth in paragraphs (b) and (c) of subdivision five of section twenty of this chapter. Notwithstanding any other provision of law to the contrary and to the extent consistent with federal law, such local or regional fatality review team shall have access to those client-identifiable records necessary for the preparation of the report, as authorized in accordance with paragraph (d) of subdivision five of section twenty of this chapter. A fatality report prepared by a local or regional fatality review team and approved by the office of children and family services satisfies the obligation to prepare a fatality report as set forth in subdivision five of section twenty of this chapter. Such report shall be subject to the same redisclosure provisions applicable to fatality reports prepared by the office of children and family services.

3. For the purposes of this section, a local or regional fatality review team must include, but need not be limited to, representatives from the child protective service, office of children and family services, county department of health, or, should the locality not have a county department of health, the local health commissioner or his or her designee or the local public health director or his or her designee, office of the medical examiner, or, should the locality not have a medical examiner, office of the coroner, office of the district attorney, office of the county attorney, local and state law enforcement, emergency medical services and a pediatrician or comparable medical professional, preferably with expertise in the area of child abuse and maltreatment or forensic pediatrics. A local or regional fatality review team may also include representatives from local departments of social services, mental health agencies, domestic violence agencies, substance abuse programs, hospitals, local schools, and family court.

4. A local or regional fatality review team established pursuant to this section shall have access to all records, except those protected by statutory privilege, within twenty-one days of receipt of a request.

5. Members of a local or regional fatality review team, persons attending a meeting of a local or regional fatality review team, and persons who present information to a local or regional fatality review team shall have immunity from civil and criminal liability for all reasonable and good faith actions taken pursuant to this section, and shall not be questioned in any civil or criminal proceeding regarding any opinions formed as a result of a meeting of a local or regional fatality review team. Nothing in this section shall be construed to prevent a person from testifying as to information obtained independently of a local or regional fatality review team or which is public information.

6. All meetings conducted and all reports and records made and maintained, and books and papers obtained, by a local or regional fatality review team shall be confidential and not open to the general public except by court order and except for an annual report or a fatality report, if the fatality review team chooses to complete such an annual report or fatality report. The release of any fatality report prepared by a local or regional fatality review team shall be governed by the provisions of subdivision five of section twenty of this chapter. Any such annual report or fatality report shall not contain any individually identifiable information and shall be provided to the office of children and family services upon completion. The office of children and family services shall forward copies of any such report to all other local or regional fatality

review teams established pursuant to this section, to all citizen review panels established pursuant to section three hundred seventy-one-b of this chapter, and to the governor, the temporary president of the senate and the speaker of the assembly.

§422-c. Establishment of the child abuse medical provider program (CHAMP).

1. The child abuse medical provider program shall be established by the office of children and family services and operated by the child abuse referral and evaluation (CARE) program of the SUNY Upstate medical university, provided other similarly qualified organizations may also operate a CHAMP program, to improve access to quality medical care for suspected child abuse victims by providing training in the assessment and diagnostic skills for medical providers to identify and treat child abuse victims and by developing and providing continuing education and mentoring to certain persons mandated to report suspected child abuse or maltreatment pursuant to section four hundred thirteen of this title. CHAMP shall be a network of expert child abuse medical professionals, that provides a comprehensive source of child abuse information that offers resources and educational tools created to assist and educate mandated reporters in the identification of child abuse and maltreatment.

2. The CHAMP program shall provide information, training and mentoring on child abuse or neglect to certain persons mandated to report suspected child abuse or maltreatment pursuant to section four hundred thirteen of this title, and may include, but not be limited to:

(a) distant learning;

(b) a web based curriculum;

(c) video conferencing;

(d) workshops;

(e) mailings;

(f) self-study courses;

(g) continued learning through case conferences and peer review; and

(h) direct training of medical providers.

§423. Child protective service responsibilities and organization; purchase of service and reimbursement of cost; local plan.

1. (a) Every local department of social services shall establish a "child protective service" within such department. The child protective service shall perform those functions assigned by this title to it and only such others that would further the purposes of this title. Local social services departments shall distribute the laws, regulations and policies of the department pursuant to section four hundred twenty- one of this article to any society for the prevention of cruelty to children which has entered into a currently valid contract with a local department of social services.

(b) Every local department of social services shall provide to the child protective service information available to the local department which is relevant to the investigation of a report of child abuse or maltreatment or to the provision of protective services, where the confidentiality of such information is not expressly protected by law.

(c) The child protective service shall have a sufficient staff of sufficient qualifications to fulfill the purposes of this title and be organized in such a way as to maximize the continuity of responsibility, care and service of individual workers toward individual children and families. A social services district shall have flexibility in assigning staff to the child protective service provided that each staff assigned to such service has the staff qualifications and has received the training required by the department regulations promulgated pursuant to subdivisions four and five of section four hundred twenty- one of this title.

(d) Consistent with appropriate collective bargaining agreements and applicable provisions of the civil service law, every child protective service shall establish a procedure to review and evaluate the backgrounds of and information supplied by all applicants for employment. Such procedures shall include but not be limited to the following requirements: that the applicant set forth his or her employment history, provide personal and employment references and relevant experiential and educational information, and sign a sworn statement indicating whether the applicant, to the best of his or her knowledge, has ever been convicted of a crime in this state or any other jurisdiction.

(e) For purposes of this title, a child protective service shall include an Indian tribe that has entered into an agreement with the department pursuant to section thirty- nine of this chapter to provide child protective services to Indians residing upon the tribe's reservation in the state. Notwithstanding any other provision of law, for the purposes of this title, a social services district or a local department of social services shall include an Indian tribe that has entered into an agreement with the department pursuant to section thirty- nine of this chapter to provide child protective services. Such Indian tribe shall only be considered a child protective service while such an agreement is in effect.

2. Any other provision of law notwithstanding, but consistent with subdivision (1) of this section, the child protective service, based upon the local plan of services as provided in subdivision (3) of this section, may purchase and utilize the services of any appropriate public or voluntary agency including a society for the prevention of cruelty to children. When services are purchased by the local department pursuant to this section and title, they shall be reimbursed by the state to the locality in the same manner and to the same extent as if the services were provided directly by the local department.

3. (a) Each social services district shall prepare and submit to the com-missioner, after consultation with local law enforcement agencies, the family court and appropriate public or voluntary agencies including societies for the prevention of cruelty to children and after a public hearing, a district- wide plan, as prescribed by the commissioner, for the provision of child protective services which shall be a component of the district's multi-year consolidated services plan. This plan shall describe the district's implementation of this title including the organization, staffing, mode of operations and financing of the child protective service as well as the provisions made for purchase of service and inter- agency relations. Commencing the year following preparation of a multi-year consolidated services plan, each local district shall prepare annual implementation reports including information related to its child protective services plan. The social services district shall submit the child protective services plan to the department as a component of its multi- year consolidated services plan and subsequent thereto as a component of its annual implementa-tion reports and the department shall review and approve or disapprove the proposed plan and reports in accordance with the procedures set forth in section thirty-four-a of this chapter.

4. As used in this section, "service" or "services" shall include the coordinating and monitoring of the activities of appropriate public or voluntary agencies utilized in the local plan.

5. In accordance with the provisions of subdivisions one and two of this section, a local department of social services may submit to the department a plan for a special program for the purpose of (a) ensuring the delivery of services to children and their families by arranging for the purchase and utilization of the service of any appropriate public or voluntary agency to provide rehabilitative services to at least the majority of children and families assisted by the child protective service; and (b) strengthening the monitoring role of the child protective service.

Such program shall also include provisions for the training of employees of public and private agencies assigned functions of the child protective service, in the duties and responsibilities of the child protective service and in the provision of services to children and families, pursuant to this title. The department shall approve such a plan in not more than six social services districts upon satisfactory demonstration that a local department of social services will effectively discharge all responsibilities required by this title. Any such plan must be submitted to the department as part of the multi-year services plan required pursuant to section thirty- four- a of this chapter and, if approved, shall be operative for a period not to exceed three years. The department shall contract with an individual, partnership, corporation, institution or other organization for the performance of a comprehensive evaluation of the effectiveness of the implementation of such plans. A report of such evaluations shall be submitted by the department to the governor and the legislature by January first, nineteen hundred ninety. Nothing in this subdivision shall be deemed to relieve a child protective service from any responsibilities assigned to it by this title.

6. A social services district may establish a multidisciplinary investigative team or teams and may establish or work as part of a child advocacy center established pursuant to section four hundred twenty-three-a of this title, at a local or regional level, for the purpose of investigating reports of suspected child abuse or maltreatment. The social services district shall have discretion with regard to the category or categories of suspected child abuse or maltreatment such team or teams may investigate, provided, however, the social services district shall place particular emphasis on cases involving the abuse of a child as described in paragraph (i), (ii) or (iii) of subdivision (e) of section one thousand twelve of the family court act, sexual abuse of a child or the death of a child. Members of multidisciplinary teams shall include but not be limited to representatives from the following agencies: child protective services, law enforcement, district attorney's office, physician or medical provider trained in forensic pediatrics, mental health professionals, victim advocacy personnel and, if one exists, a child advocacy center. Members of the multidisciplinary team primarily responsible for the investigation of child abuse reports, including child protective services, law enforcement and district attorney's office, shall participate in joint interviews and conduct investigative functions consistent with the mission of the particular agency member involved. It shall not be required that members of a multidisciplinary team not responsible for the investigation of reports participate in every investigation. Such other members shall provide victim advocacy, emotional support, and access to medical and mental health care, where applicable. All members, consistent with their respective agency missions, shall facilitate efficient

delivery of services to victims and appropriate disposition of cases through the criminal justice system and/or the family court system in a collaborative manner, however, non-investigative team members shall note their specific role in the team for reports covered under this title.

Notwithstanding any other provision of law to the contrary, members of a multidisciplinary investigative team or a child advocacy center may share with other team members client-identifiable information concerning the child or the child's family to facilitate the investigation of suspected child abuse or maltreatment. Nothing in this subdivision shall preclude the creation of multidisciplinary teams or child advocacy centers which include more than one social services district. Each team shall develop a written protocol for investigation of child abuse and maltreatment cases and for interviewing child abuse and maltreatment victims. The social services district is encouraged to train each team member in risk assessment, indicators of child abuse and maltreatment, and appropriate interview techniques.

§423-a.   Child advocacy centers established.
1. The office of children and family services shall to the greatest extent practicable facilitate the establishment of child advocacy centers in every region of the state so that child victims of sexual abuse or serious physical abuse have reasonable access to such a center and so that their cases are handled in an expert and timely manner, by a coordinated and cooperative effort that minimizes trauma to the children and their non-offending family members. Child advocacy centers shall be established by either a governmental entity or a private, nonprofit incorporated agency and shall meet the state office of children and family services program standards for child advocacy centers approval and strive to co-locate members of the local multidisciplinary team at the child advocacy center.
2. Child advocacy centers may assist in the investigation of child abuse and maltreatment cases and shall provide at a minimum for the following:
(a) a comfortable, private setting that is both physically and psychologically safe for children;
(b) sound program, fiscal and administrative practices;
(c) policies, practices and procedures that are culturally competent; for the purpose of this paragraph "culturally competent" is defined as the capacity to function in more than one culture, requiring the ability to appreciate, understand and interact with members of diverse populations within the local community;
(d) a multidisciplinary investigative team established pursuant to subdivision six of section four hundred twenty-three of this article;
(e) a written set of interagency protocols for an interdisciplinary and coordinated approach to the investigation of child abuse;
(f) forensic interviews to be conducted in a manner which is neutral and fact-finding and coordinated to avoid duplicative interviewing;
(g) specialized medical evaluation and treatment as part of the multi-disciplinary investigative team response, either at the center or through coordination with and referral to other appropriate treatment providers;
(h) specialized mental health services as part of the multidisciplinary investigative team response, either at the center or through coordination with and referral to other appropriate treatment providers;

(i) victim support and advocacy as part of the multidisciplinary team investigative team response, either at the center or through coordination with and referral to other appropriate treatment providers;

(j) a routine interdisciplinary case review process for purposes of decision making, problem solving, systems coordination and information sharing concerning case status and services needed by the child and family;

(k) a comprehensive tracking system for monitoring case process and tracking case outcomes for team members; and

(l) a process for evaluating its effectiveness and its operation.

3. Child advocacy centers may also provide space for medical evaluation, therapeutic intervention, support services for child abuse victims and their families, community education about child abuse, and any other services the center deems critical to the provision of service to child victims and their families and the multidisciplinary investigation of abuse allegations.

4. Any child advocacy center established prior to the effective date of this section shall, within six months of the effective date of this section, revise its policies and practices to comply with subdivision two of this section. No organization shall refer to itself as a child advocacy center unless it complies with this section.

5.(a) The files, reports, records, communications, working papers or videotaped interviews used or developed in providing services under this section are confidential. Provided, however, that disclosure may be made to members of a multidisciplinary investigative team who are engaged in the investigation of a particular case and who need access to the information in order to perform their duties for purposes consistent with this section and to other employees of a child advocacy center who are involved in tracking cases for the child advocacy center. Disclosure shall also be made for the purpose of investigation, prosecution and/or adjudication in any relevant court proceeding or, upon written release by any non-offending parent, for the purpose of counseling for the child victim.

(b) Any public or private department, agency or organization may share with a child advocacy center information that is made confidential by law when it is needed to provide or secure services pursuant to this section. Confidential information shared with or provided to a center remains the property of the providing organization.

(c) The office of children and family services shall have access to all records created or maintained by a child advocacy center in order to carry out the responsibilities of that office pursuant to this title.

§424. Duties of the child protective service concerning reports of abuse or maltreatment.

Each child protective service shall:

1. receive on a twenty-four hour, seven day a week basis all reports of suspected child abuse or maltreatment in accordance with this title, the local plan for the provision of child protective services and the regulations of the commissioner;

2. maintain and keep up-to-date a local child abuse and maltreatment register of all cases reported under this title together with any additional information obtained and a record of the final disposition of the report, including services offered and accepted;

3. upon the receipt of each written report made pursuant to this title, transmit, forthwith, a copy thereof to the state central register of child abuse

and maltreatment. In addition, not later than seven days after receipt of the initial report, the child protective service shall send a preliminary written report of the initial investigation, including evaluation and actions taken or contemplated, to the state central register. Follow-up reports shall be made at regular intervals thereafter in a manner and form prescribed by the commissioner by regulation to the end that the state central register is kept fully informed and up-to-date concerning the handling of reports;

4. give telephone notice and forward immediately a copy of reports made pursuant to this title which involve the death of a child to the appropriate district attorney. In addition, telephone notice shall be given and a copy of any or all reports made pursuant to this title shall be forwarded immediately by the child protective service to the appropriate district attorney if a prior request in writing for such notice and copies has been made to the service by the district attorney. Such request shall specify the kinds of allegations concerning which the district attorney requires such notice and copies and shall provide a copy of the relevant provisions of law;

5. forward an additional copy of each report to the appropriate duly incorporated society for the prevention of cruelty to children or other duly authorized child protective agency if a prior request for such copies has been made to the service in writing by the society or agency;

5-a. give telephone notice and forward immediately a copy of reports made pursuant to this title which involve suspected physical injury as described in paragraph (i) of subdivision (e) of section ten hundred twelve of the family court act or sexual abuse of a child or the death of a child to the appropriate local law enforcement. Investigations shall be conducted by an approved multidisciplinary investigative team, established pursuant to subdivision six of section four hundred twenty-three of this title provided that in counties without a multidisciplinary investigative team investigations shall be conducted jointly by local child protective services and local law enforcement. Provided however, that co-reporting in these instances shall not be required when the local social services district has an approved protocol on joint investigations of child abuse and maltreatment between the local district and law enforcement. Such protocol shall be submitted to the office of children and family services for approval and the office shall approve or disapprove of such protocols within thirty days of submission. Nothing in this subdivision shall prohibit local child protective services from consulting with local law enforcement on any child abuse or maltreatment report.

5-b. shall make an assessment in a timely manner of each report made pursuant to this title which involves suspected maltreatment which alleges any physical harm when the report is made by a person required to report pursuant to section four hundred thirteen of this title within six months of any other two reports that were indicated or may still be pending involving the same child, sibling, or other children in the household or the subject of the report to determine whether it is necessary to give notice of the report to the appropriate local law enforcement entity. If the local child protective services determines that local law enforcement shall be given notice, they shall give telephone notice and immediately forward a copy of the reports to local law enforcement. If the report is shared with local law enforcement, investigations shall be conducted by an approved multidisciplinary investigative team, established pursuant to subdivision six of section four hundred twenty-three of this title provided that in counties without a multidisciplinary investigative team investigations shall be conducted jointly by local child protective services and local law enforcement. Provided however, that co-reporting in these instances shall not be required when the local social services district has an approved protocol on joint investigations of child abuse and maltreatment between the local district and law enforcement. Such protocol shall be submitted to the office of children and family services for approval and the office shall approve or disapprove of such protocols within thirty days of submission. Nothing in this subdivision shall modify the requirements of this section. Nothing in this subdivision shall prohibit local child protective services from consulting with local law enforcement on any child abuse or maltreatment report and nothing in this subdivision shall prohibit local child protective services and local law enforcement or a multidisciplinary team from agreeing to co-investigate any child abuse or maltreatment report.

6. (a) upon receipt of such report, commence or cause the appropriate society for the prevention of cruelty to children to commence, within twenty-four hours, an appropriate investigation which shall include an evaluation of the environment of the child named in the report and any other children in the same home and a determination of the risk to such children if they continue to remain in the existing home environment, as well as a determination of the nature, extent and cause of any condition enumerated in such report and the name, age and condition of other children in the home, and, after seeing to the safety of the child or children, forthwith notify the subjects of the report and other persons named in the report in writing of the existence of the report and their respective rights pursuant to this title in regard to amendment.

(b) subject to rules and regulations of the division of criminal justice services, a manager of the child protective services unit, or a person with law enforcement background who is specifically designated by the commissioner of the local social services district for this purpose, shall have access to conviction records maintained by state law enforcement agencies pertaining to persons of or over the age of eighteen years who (1) are currently residing in the residence of any child who is alleged to be or suspected of being abused, maltreated, or neglected or (2) are named in any report of suspected or alleged child abuse, maltreatment, or neglect; provided that nothing in this subdivision shall be construed to contradict or modify section one thousand forty-six of the family court act. Any criminal history record provided by the division of criminal justice services, and any summary of the criminal history record provided by the office of children and family services to the child protective services unit of a local social services district pursuant to this subdivision, shall be kept confidential and shall not be made available for public inspection. Child protective services units shall not indicate a report solely based upon the existence of a conviction record;

6-a. upon receipt of such report and commencement of the appropriate investigation, where the child protective service is not able to locate the child or has been denied access to the home or denied access to the child named in the report or to any children in the household, and where the child protective investigator has cause to believe a child or children's life or health may be in danger immediately advise the parent or person legally responsible for the child's care or with whom the child is residing that, when denied sufficient access to the child or other children in the home, the child protective investigator may contact the family court to seek an immediate court order to gain access to the home and/or the child named in the report or any children in the household without further notice and that while such request is being made to such court, law enforcement may be contacted and if contacted shall respond and shall remain where the child or children are or are believed to be present;

6-b. should the parent or persons legally responsible for the child's care or with whom the child is residing continue to deny access to the child, children and/or home sufficient to allow the child protective investigator to determine their safety and if a child protective investigator seeks an immediate family court order to gain access to the child, children and/or home, law enforcement may be contacted and if contacted shall respond and shall remain where the child or children are or are believed to be present while the request is being made;

7. determine, within sixty days, whether the report is "indicated" or "unfounded";

8. refer suspected cases of falsely reporting child abuse and maltreatment in violation of subdivision four of section 240.50 of the penal law to the appropriate law enforcement agency or district attorney;

9. take a child into protective custody to protect him from further abuse or maltreatment when appropriate and in accordance with the provisions of the family court act;

10. based on the investigation and evaluation conducted pursuant to this title, offer to the family of any child believed to be suffering from abuse or maltreatment such services for its acceptance or refusal, as appear appropriate for either the child or the family or both; provided, however, that prior to offering such services to a family, explain that it has no legal authority to compel such family to receive said services, but may inform the family of the obligations and authority of the child protective service to petition the family court for a determination that a child is in need of care and protection;

11. in those cases in which an appropriate offer of service is refused and the child protective service determines or if the service for any other appropriate reason determines that the best interests of the child require family court or criminal court action, initiate the appropriate family court proceeding or make a referral to the appropriate district attorney, or both;

12. assist the family court or criminal court during all stages of the court proceeding in accordance with the purposes of this title and the family court act;

13. coordinate, provide or arrange for and monitor, as authorized by the social services law, the family court act and by this title, rehabilitative services for children and their families on a voluntary basis or under a final or intermediate order of the family court.

14. comply with provisions of sections ten hundred thirty-nine-a and ten hundred fifty-two-a of the family court act.

The provisions of this section shall not apply to a child protective service with respect to reports involving children in homes operated or supervised by the office of children and family services, the office of mental health, or the office of people with developmental disabilities subject to the provisions of section four hundred twenty-four-b of this title.   *(Eff.5/25/16,Ch.37,L.2016)*

§424-a. Access to information contained in the statewide central register of child abuse and maltreatment.

1. (a) A licensing agency shall inquire of the department and the department shall, subject to the provisions of paragraph (e) of this subdivision, inform such agency and the subject of the inquiry whether an applicant for a certificate, license or permit, assistants to group family day care providers, the director of a camp subject to the provisions of article thirteen-B of the public health law,

a prospective successor guardian when a clearance is conducted pursuant to paragraph (d) of subdivision two of section four hundred fifty-eight-b of this article, and any person over the age of eighteen who resides in the home of a person who has applied to become an adoptive parent or a foster parent or to operate a family day care home or group family day care home or any person over the age of eighteen residing in the home of a prospective successor guardian when a clearance is conducted of a prospective successor guardian pursuant to this paragraph, has been or is currently the subject of an indicated child abuse and maltreatment report on file with the statewide central register of child abuse and maltreatment.

(b) (i) Subject to the provisions of subdivision seven of this section, a provider agency shall inquire of the office and the office shall, subject to the provisions of paragraph (e) of this subdivision, inform such agency and the subject of the inquiry whether any person who is actively being considered for employment and who will have the potential for regular and substantial contact with individuals who are cared for by the agency, is the subject of an indicated child abuse and maltreatment report on file with the statewide central register of child abuse and maltreatment prior to permitting such person to have unsupervised contact with such individuals. Such agency may inquire of the office and the office shall inform such agency and the subject of the inquiry whether any person who is currently employed and who has the potential for regular and substantial contact with individuals who are cared for by such agency is the subject of an indicated child abuse and maltreatment report on file with the statewide central register of child abuse and maltreatment. A provider agency shall also inquire of the office and the office shall inform such agency and the subject of the inquiry whether any person who is employed by an individual, corporation, partnership or association which provides goods or services to such agency who has the potential for regular and substantial contact with individuals who are cared for by the agency, is the subject of an indicated child abuse and maltreatment report on file with the statewide central register of child abuse and maltreatment prior to permitting such person to have unsupervised contact with such individuals. Inquiries made to the office pursuant to this subparagraph by a provider agency on current employees shall be made no more often than once in any six month period.

(ii) A provider agency may inquire of the office and the office shall, upon receipt of such inquiry and subject to the provisions of paragraph (e) of this subdivision, inform such agency and the subject of the inquiry whether any person who is to be hired as a consultant by such agency who has the potential for regular and substantial contact with individuals who are cared for by the agency is the subject of an indicated child abuse and maltreatment report on file with the statewide central register of child abuse and maltreatment.

(iii) A provider agency may inquire of the office and the office shall, upon receipt of such inquiry and subject to the provisions of paragraph (e) of this subdivision, inform such agency and the subject of the inquiry whether any person who has volunteered his or her services to such agency and who will have the potential for regular and substantial contact with individuals who are cared for by the agency, is the subject of an indicated child abuse and maltreatment report on file with the statewide central register of child abuse and maltreatment.

(iv) The office shall promulgate regulations which effectuate the provisions of this paragraph.

(c) An authorized agency shall inquire of the department and the department shall inform such agency and the subject of the inquiry, whether any person who has applied to adopt a child is the subject of an indicated child abuse and maltreatment report on file with the statewide central register of child abuse and maltreatment.

(d) Any person who has applied to a licensing agency for a certificate, license or permit or who has applied to be an employee of a provider agency or who has applied to an authorized agency to adopt a child, or who may be hired as a consultant or used as a volunteer by a provider agency and any other person about whom an inquiry is made to the department pursuant to the provisions of this section shall be notified by such agency at the time of application or prior to the time that a person may be hired as a consultant or used as a volunteer that the agency will or may inquire of the department whether such person is the subject of an indicated child abuse and maltreatment report. All employees of a provider agency shall be notified by their employers that an inquiry may be made to the department pursuant to this section and no such inquiry shall be made regarding any employee until such notice has been made.

(d-1) A law enforcement agency pursuant to section eight hundred thirty-seven-k of the executive law may inquire of the department and the department may inform such agency and the subject of the inquiry, whether any person who has applied for a symbol provided for in section eight hundred thirty-seven-k of the executive law or persons residing or regularly visiting said location are the subject of an indicated child abuse and maltreatment report on file with the statewide central register of child abuse and maltreatment.

(e) (i) Subject to the provisions of subparagraph (ii) of this paragraph, the department shall inform the provider or licensing agency, or child care resource and referral programs pursuant to subdivision six of this section whether or not the person is the subject of an indicated child abuse and maltreatment report only if: (a) the time for the subject of the report to request an amendment of the record of the report pursuant to subdivision eight of section four hundred twenty-two has expired without any such request having been made; or (b) such request was made within such time and a fair hearing regarding the request has been finally determined by the commissioner and the record of the report has not been amended to unfound the report or delete the person as a subject of the report.

(ii) If the subject of an indicated report of child abuse or maltreatment has not requested an amendment of the record of the report within the time specified in subdivision eight of section four hundred twenty-two of this title or if the subject had a fair hearing pursuant to such section prior to January first, nineteen hundred eighty-six and an inquiry is made to the department pursuant to this subdivision concerning the subject of the report, the department shall, as expeditiously as possible but within no more than ten working days of receipt of the inquiry, determine whether, in fact, the person about whom an inquiry is made is the subject of an indicated report. Upon making a determination that the person about whom the inquiry is made is the subject of an indicated report of child abuse and maltreatment, the department shall immediately send a written request to the child protective service or state agency which was responsible for investigating the allegations of abuse or maltreatment for all records, reports and other information maintained by the service or state agency on the subject. The service or state agency shall, as expeditiously as possible but within no more than twenty working days of receiving such request, forward all records, reports and other information it maintains on the indicated report to the department. The department shall, within fifteen working days of receiving such records, reports and other information from the child protective service or state agency, review all records, reports and other information in its possession concerning the subject and determine whether there is some credible evidence to find that the subject had committed the act or acts of child abuse or maltreatment giving rise to the indicated report.

(iii) If it is determined, after affording such service or state agency a reasonable opportunity to present its views, that there is no credible evidence in the record to find that the subject committed such act or acts, the department shall amend the record to indicate that the report was unfounded and notify the inquiring party that the person about whom the inquiry is made is not the subject of an indicated report. If the subject of the report had a fair hearing pursuant to subdivision eight of section four hundred twenty-two of this title prior to January first, nineteen hundred eighty-six and the fair hearing had been finally determined by the commissioner and the record of the report had not been amended to unfound the report or delete the person as a subject of the report, then the department shall determine that there is some credible evidence to find that the subject had committed the act or acts of child abuse or maltreatment giving rise to the indicated report.

(iv) If it is determined after a review by the office of all records, reports and information in its possession concerning the subject of the report that there is a preponderance of the evidence to find that the subject committed the act or acts of child abuse or maltreatment giving rise to the indicated report, the office shall also determine whether such act or acts are relevant and reasonably related to issues concerning the employment of the subject by a provider agency or the subject being allowed to have regular and substantial contact with individuals cared for by a provider agency or the approval or disapproval of an application which has been submitted by the subject to a licensing agency, based on guidelines developed pursuant to subdivision five of this section. If it is determined that such act or acts are not relevant and related to such issues, the office shall be precluded from informing the provider or licensing agency which made the inquiry to the office pursuant to this section that the person about whom the inquiry is made is the subject of an indicated report of child abuse or maltreatment.

(v) If it is determined after a review by the department of all records, reports and information in its possession concerning the subject of the report that there is some credible evidence to prove that the subject committed the act or acts of abuse or maltreatment giving rise to the indicated report and that such act or acts are relevant and reasonably related to issues concerning the employment of the subject by a provider agency or to the subject being allowed to have regular and substantial contact with children cared for by a provider agency or the approval or disapproval of an application which has been submitted by the subject to a licensing agency, the department shall inform the inquiring party that the person about whom the inquiry is made is the subject of an indicated report of child abuse and maltreatment; the department shall also notify the subject of the inquiry of his or her fair hearing rights granted pursuant to paragraph (c) of subdivision two of this section.

(f) The office of children and family services shall charge a fee of twenty-five dollars when it conducts a search of its records within the statewide central register for child abuse or maltreatment in accordance with this section or regulations of the office to determine whether an applicant for employment is the subject of an indicated child abuse or maltreatment report including an applicant to be a child day care provider and a request made pursuant to subdivision six of this section. Such fees shall be deposited in a special revenue - other account and shall be made available to the office for costs incurred in the implementation of this section.

(g) The office shall determine actions necessary to develop an automated search, available for the use of the office, of records at the statewide central registry of child abuse and maltreatment.

2. (a) Upon notification by the office or by a child care resource and referral program in accordance with subdivision six of this section that any person who has applied to a licensing agency for a license, certificate or permit or who seeks to become an employee of a provider agency, or to accept a child for adoptive placement or who will be hired as a consultant or used as a volunteer by a provider agency, or that any other person about whom an inquiry is made to the office pursuant to the provisions of this section is the subject of an indicated report the licensing or provider agency shall determine on the basis of information it has available whether to approve such application or retain the employee or hire the consultant or use the volunteer or permit an employee of another person, corporation, partnership or association to have access to the individuals cared for by the provider agency, provided, however, that if such application is approved, or such employee is retained or consultant hired or volunteer used or person permitted to have access to the children cared for by such agency the licensing or provider agency shall maintain a written record, as part of the application file or employment record, of the specific reasons why such person was determined to be appropriate to receive a foster care or adoption placement or to provide day care services, to be the director of a camp subject to the provisions of article thirteen-B of the public health law, to be approved as a successor guardian in accordance with subparagraph (ii) of paragraph (b) of subdivision five of section four hundred fifty-eight-b of this article, to be employed, to be retained as an employee, to be hired as a consultant, used as a volunteer or to have access to the individuals cared for by the agency.

(b) (i) Upon denial of such application by a licensing or a provider agency or failure to hire the consultant or use the volunteer, or denial of access by a person to the children cared for by the agency, or failure to approve a successor guardian in accordance with subparagraph (ii) of paragraph (b) of subdivision five of section four hundred fifty-eight-b of this article, such agency shall furnish the applicant, prospective consultant, volunteer or person who is denied access to the children cared for by the agency with a written statement setting forth whether its denial, failure to hire or failure to use was based, in whole or in part, on such indicated report, and if so, its reasons for the denial or failure to hire or failure to use.

(ii) Upon the termination of employment of an employee of a provider agency, who is the subject of an indicated report of child abuse or maltreatment on file with the statewide central register of child abuse and maltreatment, the agency shall furnish the employee with a written statement setting forth whether such termination was based, in whole or in part, on such indicated report and, if so, the reasons for the termination of employment.

(c) If the reasons for such denial or termination or failure to hire a consultant or use a volunteer or failure to approve a successor guardian in accordance with subparagraph (ii) of paragraph (b) of subdivision five of section four hundred fifty-eight-b of this article include the fact that the person is the subject of an indicated child abuse or maltreatment report, such person may request from the department within ninety days of receipt of notice of such denial, termination, failure to hire a consultant or use a volunteer and shall be granted a hearing in accordance with the procedures set forth in section twenty-two of this chapter relating to fair hearings. All hearings held pursuant to the provisions of this subdivision shall be held within thirty days of a request for the hearing unless the hearing is adjourned for good cause shown. Any subsequent adjournment for good cause shown shall be granted only upon consent of the person who requested the hearing. The hearing decision shall be rendered not later than sixty days after the conclusion of the hearing.

(d) At any such hearing, the sole question before the department shall be whether the applicant, employee, prospective consultant, volunteer, prospective successor guardian or person who was denied access to the children cared for by a provider agency has been shown by a fair preponderance of the evidence to have committed the act or acts of child abuse or maltreatment giving rise to the indicated report. In such hearing, the burden of proof on the issue of whether an act of child abuse or maltreatment was committed shall be upon the local child protective service or the state agency which investigated the report, as the case may be. The failure to sustain the burden of proof at a hearing held pursuant to this section shall not result in the expungement or unfounding of an indicated report but shall be noted on the report maintained by the state central register and shall preclude the department from notifying a party which subsequently makes an inquiry to the department pursuant to this section that the person about whom the inquiry is made is the subject of an indicated report.

(e) Upon the failure, at the fair hearing held pursuant to this section, to prove by a fair preponderance of the evidence that the applicant committed the act or acts of child abuse or maltreatment giving rise to the indicated report, the department shall notify the provider or licensing agency which made the inquiry pursuant to this section that it should reconsider any decision to discharge an employee, or to deny the subject's application for employment, or to become an adoptive parent, or to become a successor guardian, or for a certificate, license or permit; or not to hire a consultant, use a volunteer, or allow access to children cared for by the agency.

3. For purposes of this section, the term "provider" or "provider agency" shall mean an authorized agency, the office of children and family services, juvenile detention facilities subject to the certification of such office, programs established pursuant to article nineteen-H of the executive law, non-residential or residential programs or facilities licensed or operated by the office of mental health or the office for people with developmental disabilities except family care homes, licensed child day care centers, including head start programs which are funded pursuant to title V of the federal economic opportunity act of nineteen hundred sixty-four, as amended, early intervention service established pursuant to section twenty-five hundred forty of the public health law, preschool services established pursuant to section forty-four hundred ten of the education law, school-age child care programs, special act school districts as enumerated in chapter five hundred sixty-six of the laws of nineteen hundred sixty-seven, as amended, programs and facilities licensed by the office of alcoholism and substance abuse services, residential schools which are operated, supervised or approved by the education department, and any other facility or provider agency, as defined in subdivision four of section four hundred eighty-eight of this chapter, in regard to the employment of staff, or

use of providers of goods and services and staff of such providers, consultants, interns and volunteers.

4. For purposes of this section, the term "licensing agency" shall mean an authorized agency which has received an application to become an adoptive parent or an authorized agency which has received an application for a certificate or license to receive, board or keep any child pursuant to the provisions of section three hundred seventy-six or three hundred seventy-seven of this article or an authorized agency which has received an application from a relative within the second degree or third degree of consanguinity of the parent of a child or a relative within the second degree or third degree of consanguinity of the step-parent of a child or children, or the child's legal guardian for approval to receive, board or keep such child, or an authorized agency that conducts a clearance pursuant to paragraph (d) of subdivision two of section four hundred fifty-eight-b of this article, or a state or local governmental agency which receives an application to provide child day care services in a child day care center, school-age child care program, family day care home or group family day care home pursuant to the provisions of section three hundred ninety of this article, or the department of health and mental hygiene of the city of New York, when such department receives an application for a certificate of approval to provide child day care services in a child day care center pursuant to the provisions of the health code of the city of New York, or the office of mental health or the office for people with developmental disabilities when such office receives an application for an operating certificate pursuant to the provisions of the mental hygiene law to operate a family care home, or a state or local governmental official who receives an application for a permit to operate a camp which is subject to the provisions of article thirteen-B of the public health law or the office of children and family services which has received an application for a certificate to receive, board or keep any child at a foster family home pursuant to articles nineteen-G and nineteen-H of the executive law or any other facility or provider agency, as defined in subdivision four of section four hundred eighty-eight of this chapter, in regard to any licensing or certification function carried out by such facility or agency.

5. (a) The office of children and family services, after consultation with the justice center for the protection of people with special needs, the office of mental health, the office for people with developmental disabilities, the office of alcoholism and substance abuse services, the department of health, and the state education department shall develop guidelines to be utilized by a provider agency, as defined by subdivision three of this section, and a licensing agency, as defined by subdivision four of this section, in evaluating persons about whom inquiries are made to the office pursuant to this section who are the subjects of indicated reports of child abuse and maltreatment, as defined by subdivision four of section four hundred twelve of this chapter.

(b) The guidelines developed pursuant to subdivision one of this section shall not supersede similar guidelines developed by local governmental agencies prior to January first, nineteen hundred eighty-six.

6. A child care resource and referral program as defined in subdivision two of section four hundred ten-p of this article may inquire of the office of children and family services and the office shall, upon receipt of such inquiry and subject to the provisions of paragraph (e) of subdivision one of this section, inform such program and the subject of such inquiry whether any person who has requested and agreed to be included in a list of substitute child day care caregivers for employment by registered or licensed day care

providers maintained by such program in accordance with regulations promulgated by the office, is the subject of an indicated child abuse and maltreatment report on file with the statewide central register of child abuse and maltreatment. Inquiries made to the office by such programs pursuant to this subdivision shall be made no more often than once in any six month period and no less often than once in any twelve month period. Notwithstanding any provision of law to the contrary, a child care resource and referral program may redisclose such information only if the purpose of such redisclosure is to respond to a request for such information by a registered or licensed provider and only if after an individual included in the list of substitute child day care caregivers for employment by registered or licensed day care providers has consented to be referred for employment to such inquiring agency. Upon such referral, the provisions related to notice and fair hearing rights of this section shall otherwise apply. Inquiries made pursuant to this subdivision shall be in lieu of the inquiry requirements set forth in paragraph (b) of subdivision one of this section.

7. Any facility, provider agency, or program that is required to conduct an inquiry pursuant to section four hundred ninety-five of this chapter shall first conduct the inquiry required under such section. If the result of the inquiry under section four hundred ninety-five of this chapter is that the person about whom the inquiry is made is on the register of substantiated category one cases of abuse or neglect and the facility or provider agency is required to deny the application in accordance with article eleven of this chapter, the facility or provider agency shall not be required to make an inquiry of the office under this section.

§424-b. Children in the care of certain public and private agencies.

Notwithstanding any inconsistent provisions of law, when a report of child abuse or maltreatment involves a child being cared for in a home operated or supervised by an authorized agency or the office of children and family services, such report shall be accepted and maintained by the office of children and family services and shall be referred for the purposes of conducting an investigation to the appropriate staff within the office of children and family services where the child is in the care of such agency; and where the child is in a home operated or supervised by an authorized agency, to the social services district wherein such home is located. The office or social services district receiving such referral shall undertake an appropriate investigation of the report, in accordance with the terms and conditions set forth in this title. Any person who is alleged to have abused or maltreated a child in a report accepted and referred pursuant to this section shall be accorded the procedural rights set forth in section four hundred twenty-two and in subdivision six of section four hundred twenty-four of this title. Nothing in this section shall impose any duty or responsibility on any child protective service pursuant to section four hundred twenty-two, four hundred twenty-four or any other provision of this article.

§425. Cooperation of other agencies.

1. To effectuate the purposes of this title, the commissioner may request and shall receive from departments, boards, bureaus, or other agencies of the state, or any of its political subdivisions, or any duly authorized agency, or any other agency providing services under the local child protective services plan such assistance and data as will enable the department and local child protective

services to fulfill their responsibilities properly. Nothing contained in this subdivision shall limit the department's authority under sections three hundred seventy-two, four hundred sixty-c and four hundred sixty-e of this chapter to access the records of authorized agencies.

2. The department, after consultation with the division for youth, the division of criminal justice services, the department of mental hygiene, the commission on quality of care for the mentally disabled and the state education department shall develop guidelines to be utilized by appropriate state and local governmental agencies and authorized agencies as defined by subdivision ten of section three hundred seventy-one of this article which have responsibility for the care and protection of children, in evaluating persons who have a criminal conviction record and who have applied to such agencies or provider agencies, as defined in subdivision three of section four hundred twenty-four-a of this title for employment or who have applied to such state agencies or licensing agency as defined in subdivision four of section four hundred twenty-four-a of this title, for a license, certificate, permit or approval to be an adoptive parent, provider of day care services in a day care center, family day care home or group family day care home, an operator of a camp subject to the provisions of article thirteen-B of the public health law, or an operator of a foster family home subject to the provisions of subdivision seven of section five hundred one, section five hundred two or subdivision three of section five hundred thirty-two-a of the executive law or section three hundred seventy-six and three hundred seventy-seven of this article.

3. The guidelines developed pursuant to subdivision two of this section shall not supercede any similar guidelines developed by local governmental agencies prior to January first, nineteen hundred eighty-six.

§426. Annual reports.

The commissioner shall prepare for inclusion in the annual report required by subdivision (d) of section seventeen of this chapter to be filed with the governor and the legislature prior to December fifteenth of each year, a report on the operations of the state central register of child abuse and maltreatment and the various local child protective services. The report shall include a full statistical analysis of the reports made to the central register together with a report on the implementation of this title, his or her evaluation of services offered under this chapter and his or her recommendations for additional legislation to fulfill the purposes of this title. Such report shall indicate the number of child abuse and maltreatment reports and cases received by the statewide central register of child abuse and maltreatment by each district in the preceding year, the number of such cases determined to have been indicated and the number of such cases determined to be unfounded by each district in the preceding year, the number of such cases which have not been indicated or unfounded within the time period required by subdivision seven of section four hundred twenty-four of this article by each district in the preceding year and the number of workers assigned to the child protective service in each district in the preceding year. Such report shall include, among other information, available demographic information and available information concerning the racial and ethnic characteristics of the family members and persons served by the differential response program pursuant to section four hundred twenty-seven-a of the social services law, as well as available information concerning the racial and ethnic characteristics of the family members and persons serviced under the traditional child protective services program, in each local social services district in the state.

§427.   Regulations of the commissioner.
    1. The commissioner shall adopt regulations necessary to implement this title.
    2. The commissioner shall establish, by regulation, standards and criteria under which the child protective service of the appropriate local department of social services as petitioner in abuse and neglect proceedings pursuant to article ten of the family court act shall not consent to an order pursuant to section one thousand thirty-nine of the family court act.

§427-a.   Differential response programs for child protection assessments or investigations.
    1. Any social services district may, upon the authorization of the office of children and family services, establish a program that implements differential responses to reports of child abuse and maltreatment. Such programs shall create a family assessment and services track as an alternative means of addressing certain matters otherwise investigated as allegations of child abuse or maltreatment pursuant to this title. Notwithstanding any other provision of law to the contrary, the provisions of this section shall apply only to those cases involving allegations of abuse or maltreatment in family settings expressly included in the family assessment and services track of the differential response program, and only in those social services districts authorized by the office of children and family services to implement a differential response program. Such cases shall not be subject to the requirements otherwise applicable to cases reported to the statewide central register of child abuse and maltreatment pursuant to this title, except as set forth in this section.
    2. Any social services district interested in implementing a differential response program shall apply to the office of children and family services for permission to participate. The criteria for a social services district to participate will be determined by the office of children and family services after consultation with the office for the prevention of domestic violence, however the social services district's application must include a plan setting forth the following:
        (a) in conjunction with any additional requirements imposed by the office of children and family services and the provisions of this subdivision, the factors to be considered by the social services district in determining which cases will be addressed through the family assessment and services track and the size of the population to be the subject of the differential response program;
        (b) the types of services and interventions to be provided to families included in the family assessment and services track and a description of how the services will be offered;
        (c) a description of the process to be followed for planning and monitoring the services provided under the family assessment and services track;
        (d) a description of how the principles of family involvement and support consistent with maintaining the safety of the child will be implemented in the family assessment and services track;
        (e) a description of how the differential response program will enhance the ability of the district to protect children, maintain the safety of children and preserve families;

(f) a description of how the district will reduce the involvement of government agencies with families and maintain the safety of children through the use of community resources;

(g) a description of the staff resources proposed to be used in the family assessment and services track, including the proposed staff workloads and qualifications;

(h) a description of the training that will be provided to district and any non-district staff to be used in the differential response program including, but not limited to, a description of the training involving maintaining the safety and well-being of children and any cross training planned for family assessment and investigative staff;

(i) a description of the community resources that are proposed to be used in the family assessment and services track;

(j) a description of any additional funding that may be utilized to enhance the differential response program; and

(k) a description of the protocol to be followed for handling cases where domestic violence is present in order to maintain the safety of the child through the family assessment and services track.

3. The criteria for determining which cases may be placed in the assessment track shall be determined by the local department of social services, in conjunction with the office of children and family services and after consultation with the office for the prevention of domestic violence. Provided, however, that reports including any of the following allegations shall not be included in the assessment track of a differential response program:

(a) reports alleging that the subject committed or allowed to be committed an offense defined in article one hundred thirty of the penal law;

(b) reports alleging that the subject allowed, permitted or encouraged a child to engage in any act described in sections 230.25, 230.30 and 230.32 of the penal law;

(c) reports alleging that the subject committed any of the acts described in section 255.25, 255.26 or 255.27 of the penal law;

(d) reports alleging that the subject allowed a child to engage in acts or conduct described in article two hundred sixty-three of the penal law;

(e) reports alleging that the subject committed assault in the first, second or third degree against a child;

(f) reports alleging that the subject committed or attempted to commit murder or manslaughter in the first or second degree;

(g) reports alleging that the subject abandoned a child pursuant to subdivision five of section three hundred eighty-four-b of this article;

(h) reports alleging that the subject has subjected a child to severe or repeated abuse as those terms are defined in paragraphs (a) and (b) of subdivision eight of section three hundred eighty-four-b of this article; and

(i) reports alleging that the subject has neglected a child so as to substantially endanger the child's physical or mental health, including a growth delay, which may be referred to as failure to thrive, that has been diagnosed by a physician and is due to parental neglect.

4. The following procedures shall be followed for all cases included in the family assessment and services track:

(a) Reports taken at the statewide central register of child abuse and maltreatment shall be transmitted to the appropriate local child protective service.

(b) A social services district permitted by the office of children and family services to participate in the implementation of a differential response program shall, consistent with the criteria developed pursuant to subdivision three of this section, identify those reports which are initially eligible to be included in the family assessment and services track.

(c) For those reports which are included in the family assessment and services track, the social services district shall not be subject to the requirements of this title concerning initial investigation of reports of suspected abuse and maltreatment of children, including notification requirements. For reports assigned to the family assessment and services track, the social services district shall be responsible for ensuring that the children are safe in their homes. Such safety assessment shall be commenced within twenty-four hours of receipt of the report and completed within seven days. Based on the initial safety assessment, the district shall determine if the report shall continue under the family assessment and services track. This safety assessment must be documented in the manner specified by the office of children and family services. Should the children be found to be safe in the home, the social services district shall then identify service needs and family issues, if any, that should be addressed.

(i) Where the social services district determines, based on the initial safety assessment, that the report is appropriate to be included in the family assessment and services track, the social services district shall document the reason for that determination in the initial safety assessment and inform the statewide central register of child abuse and maltreatment that the report is part of the family assessment and services track and request that the records of the statewide central register of child abuse and maltreatment of such report be classified as an assessment track case and be legally sealed. Such sealed reports shall be maintained at the statewide central register of child abuse and maltreatment for ten years after the report was made. Access to reports assigned to, and records created under the family assessment and services track and information concerning such reports and records is governed by paragraph (d) of subdivision five of this section.

(ii) Where the social services district determines, based on the initial safety assessment, to investigate the report as a report of suspected child abuse or maltreatment, the social services district shall document the reason for that decision in the initial safety assessment. Where the social services district makes the determination to investigate the report, all of the requirements of this title concerning investigations of reports of suspected child abuse and maltreatment shall apply, including the notification requirements. The report shall no longer be eligible to be included in the family assessment and services track.

(d) Where the social services district has determined that a case is appropriate to be included in the family assessment and services track, the district's activities shall include, at a minimum, the following:

(i) the provision of written notice to each parent, guardian or other person legally responsible for the child or children participating in the family assessment and services track explaining that it is the intent of the social services district to meet the needs of the family without engaging in a traditional child protective services investigation. The notice shall also explain that the workers assisting the family in the family assessment and services track are mandated reporters who are required to report suspected child abuse or maltreatment and that those workers are required to report new information that they receive in their work with the family if that information gives them reasonable cause to suspect that a child in the family is an abused or maltreated child;

(ii) an examination, with the family, of the family's strengths, concerns and needs;

(iii) where appropriate, an offer of assistance which shall include case management that is supportive of family stabilization;

(iv) the planning and provision of services responsive to the service needs of the family; and

(v) an on-going joint evaluation and assessment of the family's progress including ongoing, periodic assessments of risk to the child.

(e) After the social services district has received a report of suspected maltreatment and determined that the report is initially eligible to be included in the family assessment and services track, pursuant to paragraph (b) of this subdivision, the activities described in paragraphs (c) and (d) of this subdivision may be performed by the social services district directly or through any other method currently utilized by social services districts to obtain preventive services for children and families. If a community-based agency determines, pursuant to subparagraph (ii) of paragraph (c) of this subdivision, that a report must be investigated as a case of suspected child abuse or maltreatment, the community-based agency shall so inform the social services district, which shall then become responsible for conducting the child protective services investigation in accordance with the requirements of this title.

(f) A report selected for inclusion in the demonstration project shall cease to be eligible for inclusion in the demonstration project if at any time in the course of providing services the district or community-based agency finds that:

(i) there is evidence of child abuse, including sexual abuse; or

(ii) the parent or parents refuse to cooperate with the district or community-based agency in developing or implementing a plan to address the family problems or issues and there is evidence of maltreatment of a child.

(g) Where the district finds or is advised by a community-based agency, subsequent to the completion of the initial safety assessment and after the report is legally sealed, that the report is no longer eligible for inclusion in the demonstration project pursuant to paragraph (f) of this subdivision, the district shall contact the statewide central register of child abuse and maltreatment and make a new report of suspected child abuse or maltreatment pursuant to section four hundred thirteen of this title.

(h) Where a report has been included in the family assessment and services track and a subsequent report involving the family is made to the statewide central register of child abuse and maltreatment, and such subsequent report is not eligible for inclusion in the family assessment and services track, the local child protective services, in conducting its investigation, shall work cooperatively with any district or community-based agency staff that are already working with the family to minimize to the extent practicable the chance that existing services being provided to the family will be disrupted and to maximize to the extent practicable the coordination of the existing services being provided to the family with any new services to be provided to the family.

5. (a) Cases included in the family assessment and services track shall not be subject to the requirements of section four hundred nine-e or four hundred nine-f of this article.

(b) All records created as part of the family assessment and services track shall include, but not be limited to, documentation of the initial safety assessment, the examination of the family's strengths, concerns and needs, all services offered and accepted by the family, the plan for supportive services for the family, all evaluations and assessments of the family's progress, and all periodic risk assessments.

(c) Records created under the family assessment and services track shall be maintained for ten years after the report initiating the case at the statewide central register was made.

(d) All reports assigned to, and records created under, the family assessment and services track, including but not limited to reports made or written as well as any other information obtained or photographs taken concerning such reports or records shall be confidential and shall be made available only to:

(i) staff of the office of children and family services and persons designated by the office of children and family services;

(ii) the social services district responsible for the family assessment and services track case;

(iii) community-based agencies that have contracts with the social services district to carry out activities for the district under the family assessment and services track;

(iv) providers of services under the family assessment and services track;

(v) any social services district investigating a subsequent report of abuse or maltreatment involving the same subject or the same child or children named in the report;

(vi) a court, but only while the family is receiving services provided under the family assessment and services track and only pursuant to a court order or judicial subpoena, issued after notice and an opportunity for the subject of the report and all parties to the present proceeding to be heard, based on a judicial finding that such reports, records, and any information concerning such reports and records, are necessary for the determination of an issue before the court. Such reports, records and information to be disclosed pursuant to a judicial subpoena shall be submitted to the court for inspection and for such directions as may be necessary to protect confidentiality, including but not limited to redaction of portions of the reports, records, and information and to determine any further limits on redisclosure in addition to the limitations provided for in this title. A court shall not have access to the sealed family assessment and services reports, records, and any information concerning such reports and records, after the conclusion of services provided under the family assessment and services track; and

(vii) the subject of the report included in the records of the family assessment and services track.

(e) Persons given access to sealed reports, records, and any information concerning such reports and records, pursuant to paragraph (d) of this subdivision shall not redisclose such reports, records and information except as follows:

(i) the office of children and family services and social services districts may disclose aggregate, non-client identifiable information;

(ii) social services districts, community-based agencies that have contracts with a social services district to carry out activities for the district under the family assessment and services track, and providers of services under the family assessment and services track, may exchange such reports, records and information concerning such reports and records as necessary to carry out activities and services related to the same person or persons addressed in the records of a family assessment and services track case;

(iii) the child protective service of a social services district may unseal a report, record and information concerning such report and record of a case under the family assessment and services track in the event such report, record or information is relevant to a subsequent report of suspected child abuse or maltreatment. Information from such an unsealed report or record that is relevant to the subsequent report of suspected child abuse and maltreatment may be used by the child protective service for purposes of investigation and family court action concerning the subsequent report and may be included in the record of the investigation of the subsequent report. If the social services district initiates a proceeding under article ten of the family court act in connection with such a subsequent report of suspected child abuse and maltreatment and there is information in the report or record of a previous case under the family assessment and services track that is relevant to the proceeding, the social services district shall include such information in the record of the investigation of the subsequent report of suspected child abuse or maltreatment and shall make that information available to the family court and the other parties for use in such proceeding provided, however, that the information included from the previous case under the family assessment and services track shall then be subject to all laws and regulations regarding confidentiality that apply to the record of the investigation of such subsequent report of suspected child abuse or maltreatment. The family court may consider the information from the previous case under the family assessment and services track that is relevant to such proceeding in making any determinations in the proceeding; and

(iv) a subject of the report may, at his or her discretion, present a report, records and information concerning such report and records from the family assessment and services track case, in whole or in part, in any proceeding under article ten of the family court act in which the subject is a respondent. A subject of the report also may, at his or her discretion, present a report, records and information concerning such report and records from the family assessment and services track, in whole or in part, in any proceeding involving the custody of, or visitation with the subject's children, or in any other relevant proceeding. In making any determination in such a proceeding, the court may consider any portion of the family assessment and service track report, records and any information concerning such report and records presented by the subject of the report that is relevant to the proceeding. Nothing in this subparagraph, however, shall be interpreted to authorize a court to order the subject to produce such report, records or information concerning such report and records, in whole or in part.

6. Expenditures by a social services district pursuant to this section shall be reimbursable from the annual appropriations available for social services district expenditures for child welfare services which shall include, but not be limited to, preventive services provided pursuant to section four hundred nine-a of this article, child protective services, independent living services and any other appropriation made specifically to support these differential response programs. Nothing shall preclude a social services district from seeking private funds for support of their differential response programs.

7. The office of children and family services shall post the plan contained in any application approved for implementation of a differential response program on the office of children and family services website within sixty days of such approval.

8. The office of children and family services shall report on the differential response programs established pursuant to this section as part of the annual report required pursuant to section four hundred twenty-six of this title.

§428. Separability.
If any provision of this title or the application thereof to any person or circumstances is held to be invalid, the remainder of the act and the application of such provision to other persons or circumstances shall not be affected thereby.

Title 6-A
Home Visiting

Section
429. Home visiting.

§429. Home visiting.
1. In accordance with a plan developed by the office of children and family services and approved by the director of the budget and within the amounts which the director of the budget determines should be made available therefor, such office, in conjunction with the department of health, is authorized to issue grants for home visiting programs to prevent child abuse and maltreatment, enhance positive parent child interactions, increase healthy outcomes for families and empower families to develop and achieve their self-sufficiency goals. To the extent that federal funds are used to support home visiting programs, such programs must be operated in accordance with all applicable federal laws and regulations. To the extent possible and appropriate, funding for the home visiting program shall be coordinated with other available funding to maximize the effective use of federal, state and local moneys and to promote the program's purposes.
2. Each home visiting program funded under this section shall include, but not be limited to, the following activities:
(a) providing screening of families in the targeted geographical area upon the birth of a child and prenatally, if possible;
(b) engaging those expectant parents and families with an infant determined to be at risk of child abuse or maltreatment and/or poor health outcomes to participate in the home visiting program;
(c) providing home visits by nurses or by community workers under the supervision of a health or social services professional to those at risk expectant parents and families who choose to participate in the program;
(d) requiring the home visitors to:
(i) assist parents in learning about child development principles;
(ii) assist parents in accessing appropriate preventive health care for their children and themselves; and
(iii) link the families to other supports and activities in the community;
(e) determining the frequency of the home visiting services provided to each participating family based on the family's needs;
(f) continuing home visits for a particular family until the child enters school or a head start program, when necessary; and
(g) assisting families to develop and obtain the necessary supports to achieve their self-sufficiency goals.
3. A request for proposals shall be issued to solicit applications for home visiting programs. Priority for funding shall be given to applicants from communities identified as high need by such factors as poverty rates, rates of adolescent pregnancy, rates of child abuse and maltreatment, immunization rates and infant mortality rates.
4. Not-for-profit organizations and local public agencies such as community-based organizations, family resource centers, local health departments, local

social services departments, schools, hospitals and other health agencies shall be eligible to apply for the grants available pursuant to this section.

5. Each applicant shall demonstrate among other things:

(a) a working relationship with the applicable local departments of health and social services and key services providers in the community;

(b) the commitment of local hospitals, prenatal clinics and early intervention programs servicing families in the targeted geographical area to promote the effective screening of families so that the program can be offered to the maximum number of at-risk expectant parents and families possible;

(c) its administrative and fiscal viability and the community's support for the home visiting program; and

(d) how the home visiting program would be integrated with other available services, programs and funding streams.

6. The commissioner of the office of children and family services shall establish policies governing enrollees' rights and confidentiality, and each home visiting program shall, in accordance with such policies, inform enrollees of their rights, and of such policies governing confidentiality.

7. The office of children and family services shall submit to the governor and the legislature by December first, two thousand, and every three years thereafter, a report which shall include a review of all the home visiting programs funded under this section; and comments and recommendations based on a comprehensive evaluation regarding the most effective models for providing home visiting services and statutory changes which could improve the state's ability to prevent child abuse and maltreatment, improve healthy outcomes for families and empower families to develop and obtain their self-sufficiency goals.

Title 7
Day Services for Children and Families

Section
430. Day services; when social services official may furnish.
431. Licensure.
432. State reimbursement; standards of payment.
433. Other state funding sources.
434. Funding limitations.

§430. Day services; when social services official may furnish.

1. In order to preserve and stabilize family life, to prevent the need for placement of children outside their homes, and to enable children in foster care to return to their families as expeditiously as possible, a social services official is authorized to provide day services at public expense to children and their families residing in his territory, pursuant to the provisions of this title.

2. Day services may be provided in cases where the social services official has determined that such services would promote or accomplish one or more of the following objectives:

(a) to avert a risk of serious impairment or disruption of a family unit which would result in the placement of a child outside his own home;

(b) to enable a child who has been placed in a child care institution or other group care facility to be placed in a foster care setting more closely oriented to community or family life;

(c) to enable a child who has been placed in foster care to return to his family at an earlier time than would otherwise be possible.

3. If the child's family is able to pay part or all of the costs of day services, such family shall be required to pay such fees therefor as may be reasonable in the light of such ability pursuant to regulations of the department.

4. Day services may be provided by a social services official either directly or through purchase. Purchase of such services may be made only from a private non-profit corporation or association, except when the commissioner shall have approved the purchase of such services from a private proprietary facility by a social services official who has demonstrated a lack of conveniently accessible non-profit facilities that are adequate to provide the required services.

5. As used in this title, "day services" shall mean care and treatment for part of the day of one or more children under eighteen years of age and their families in a program which provides to such children and families in accordance with their needs various services such as psychiatric, psychological, social casework, educational, vocational, health, transportation and such other services as may be appropriate. Such services shall be provided in accordance with program standards promulgated by the department. Day services may be continued after the eighteenth birthday of a child in the care of an authorized agency and until he becomes twenty-one years of age. Day services shall not be provided to any children and their families for periods in excess of one year, without the approval of the department.

§431. Licensure.

1. No place, person, association, corporation, institution or agency shall operate a day services program without first obtaining a permit issued therefor by the department, or otherwise than in accordance with the terms of such permit and with the regulations of the department.

2. The department shall promulgate regulations specifying the procedures for obtaining a permit required pursuant to this section and enumerating the documentation needed for such a permit. The regulations shall also include program standards which the department shall develop with the advice of the board of social welfare, the department of mental hygiene and the department of education. An application for a permit pursuant to this section shall include full information regarding the applicant's efforts to secure funding for its day services program. The department shall advise and otherwise assist the applicant in obtaining funds where such funds may be available under the provisions of this and any other law.

3. The department shall not issue a permit for the operation of a day services program which includes the provision of care, treatment or services requiring licensure or any other form of approval from or by another state agency or official, unless such license or approval has been obtained. There shall be such co-operative and coordinated arrangements between and among the department and the state departments of mental hygiene and education and other appropriate state departments and agencies as shall be necessary to assure that applications for required licenses or other forms of approval will be processed expeditiously.

4. Before any permit issued pursuant to this section is suspended or revoked, or when an application for such permit is denied, the applicant or holder of the permit shall be entitled, pursuant to the regulations of the department, to a hearing before the department. However, a permit may be temporarily suspended or limited without a hearing for a period not in excess of thirty days upon written notice to the holder of the permit following a finding that the public health, or any individual's health, safety or welfare, is in imminent danger.

§432. State reimbursement; standards of payment.

1. (a) Expenditures made by social services officials for day services programs and their administration pursuant to the provisions of this title shall, if approved by the department, be subject to reimbursement by the state, in accordance with the regulations of the department as follows: there shall be paid to each social services district (1) the amount of federal funds, if any, properly received or to be received on account of such expenditures; (2) fifty per centum of allowable expenditures for day services and its administration, after first deducting therefrom any federal funds properly received or to be received on account thereof and the amount of any fees paid to the social services official for day services. The local government share of the cost of day services may be met in whole or in part by donated private funds, exclusive of in-kind services.

(b) For purposes of this title, expenditures for administration of day services shall include expenditures for compensation of employees in connection with the furnishing of day services, including but not limited to costs incurred for pensions, federal old age and survivors insurance and health insurance for such employees; training programs for personnel, operation, maintenance and service costs; and such other expenditures as equipment costs, depreciation and charges and rental values as may be approved by the department. It shall not include expenditures for capital costs.

2. The department shall, after consultation with appropriate state agencies and with the approval of the director of the budget, promulgate regulations establishing standards of payment for day services provided children with public financial support. Such standards of payment shall include the services required to be provided to the child and his family and the cost of such services. When the department has established such standards, reimbursement under this section shall be limited in accordance with such standards.

3. (a) Claims for state reimbursement shall be made in such form and manner and at such times and for such periods as the department shall determine.

(b) When certified by the department, state reimbursement shall be paid from the state treasury upon the audit and warrant of the comptroller out of funds made available therefor.

4. Payment of state reimbursement shall be made to local fiscal officers as in the case of state reimbursement for public assistance and care under other provisions of this chapter.

§433. Other state funding sources.

1. Prior to purchasing day services pursuant to section four hundred thirty, a social services official shall inquire of the department, and the department shall inform him, as to the available funding sources, if any, of which the day services facility was advised pursuant to subdivision two of section four hundred thirty-one. The social services official shall not purchase services from the day services facility until he has determined that the facility has cooperated with the department in efforts to obtain funding from all available sources.

2. No state agency or official with authority, pursuant to this or any other law, to provide financial assistance for care, treatment or services which may be included in a day services program shall deny or reduce such assistance on the ground that such assistance is available under this title.

§434. Funding limitations.

Notwithstanding any other provisions of this chapter the total amount of reimbursement to social services districts pursuant to this title shall be limited to the amount of the annual appropriation made by the legislature for preventive services.

Title 8
State Child Care Review Service

§440. Findings; purpose.

1. The legislature finds that children who are in care away from their own homes on a full time basis, whether temporarily or for a prolonged period, require effective supervision and review of their status in care and of the plans for them. It is the policy of the state of New York to assure that such children are appropriately placed, that needed services are provided to them and their families, and that unnecessary and prolonged placements are avoided. The legislature further finds that this policy is often frustrated, and fiscal and program accountability have not been promoted because of divergent and overlapping jurisdictions of various government and private agencies; the lack of coordination among programs of these agencies; and the excessive workloads of judicial personnel, social services workers, and others responsible for reviewing the status in care of these children.

2. To assist in overcoming these difficulties, it is the intent of the legislature to establish a statewide management assistance system to be called the child care review service. The service shall be designed and operated to effectuate the following purposes:

(a) identification and assessment of the needs and problems of children in care and their families, to effectuate meaningful case planning;

(b) case management and supervision by child care agencies of children in full-time care away from their homes;

(c) supervision and evaluation by state agencies of local and voluntary child care agency performance;

(d) planning and policy making by state agencies, the governor and the legislature;

(e) meeting in a timely manner all judicial review requirements of this chapter, the family court act and any other applicable provisions of law;

(f) reduction of the need for manual form preparation; and

(g) meeting federal reporting requirements so as to qualify for federal funds under the federal social security act.

§441. Definitions.

As used in this title, the following terms shall have the following meanings:

1. "Service" shall mean the child care review service created by this title.

2. "Advisory committee" shall mean the committee established by section four hundred forty-three of this title.

§442. Child care review service; establishment, operations and procedure.
1. The department, in consultation with the advisory committee, shall establish and operate a child care review service to accomplish the purposes of this title, for all children who are in the care of an authorized agency and shall make such regulations as are appropriate to implement this title.

2. The service shall be implemented with respect to all children under the age of twenty-one years for whom an authorized agency is providing foster care as defined in subdivision (c) of section one thousand eighty-seven of the family court act and for whom an application is pending to an authorized agency for foster care.

3. The department is authorized to enter into agreements with any person, firm, organization or association for the whole or any part of the design or operation of the service as described in this title. Any such agreements shall specify that such person, firm, corporation or association shall safeguard the confidentiality of information received or maintained by the service, in the same manner, and will remain subject to the same confidentiality requirements, as the department. In addition, any such agreement shall require such person, firm, corporation or association to comply with other applicable federal and state laws protecting the confidentiality of the information received or maintained by the service.

4. The service shall collect, maintain, update, and distribute, as provided in this title, information from each authorized agency to further the purpose of this title.

5. The service may request from any authorized agency, and such agency shall submit to the service all information, including updating of information, in the form and manner and at such times as the department may require that is appropriate to the purposes and operation of the service.

6. Information to be submitted to or collected by the service, pursuant to subdivisions four and five, shall, to the extent possible, be in compatible form so as to facilitate the making of public policy decisions relating to child care programs supported by public funds and administered by various state, local and voluntary agencies.

7. In designing the service, the department, in consultation with the advisory committee, shall review all information reporting forms and financial claims forms, and shall make every effort to consolidate and, where appropriate, eliminate duplicative claiming and information reporting forms in order to develop uniform statewide claiming forms and information reporting forms.

8. Subject to regulations of the department the service shall:

(a) prepare and make available on a regular basis to each authorized agency such data as they may require to meet the purposes of this title;

(b) issue regular reports setting forth aggregate statewide and local statistical data with appropriate analyses, but not including individual identifying information; and

(c) issue reports as to the capabilities of the service and the types of information maintained by the service.

9. The department in consultation with the advisory committee shall prepare and submit an annual report to the governor and the legislature as part of the annual report required to be filed prior to the fifteenth day of December of each year by subdivision (d) of section seventeen of this chapter on its progress in the development and operation of the service, including any significant problems encountered or anticipated in the design and operation of the service

and any recommendations for administrative or legislative changes that would further the purposes of this title.

10. The state child care review service established pursuant to this title shall design and implement a system to:

(a) monitor all financial claims made by social services districts for each child in foster care and child and family in receipt of preventive services pursuant to title four of this chapter;

(b) compile and maintain a cumulative record of information with respect to actions taken on behalf of each individual child throughout his or her length of stay in foster care;

(c) compile and maintain information on actions taken by local social services districts to initiate judicial proceedings as provided by section three hundred fifty-eight-a of this chapter and to comply with judicial orders made pursuant to section one thousand eighty-nine of the family court act, to refer legally free children to the state adoption service pursuant to section three hundred seventy-two-c of this chapter, and to comply with the provisions of section four hundred nine-e of this article and the regulations of the office of children and family services promulgated thereunder; and

(e) compile and maintain comparative data for authorized agencies including, but not limited to, characteristics and numbers of children entering care and their families, admissions practices, delineated reasons for initial and continued placement or provision of preventive or child protective services, length of stay in care, length of time in receipt of preventive services or child protective services, foster care reentry rates, number of children discharged to parents and relatives, the characteristics, numbers and rates of children leaving foster care through adoption, costs of care and preventive services and other information indicative of authorized agency performance.

§443. Advisory committee.

1. The department shall establish and meet regularly with an advisory committee of not more than twenty members to consider policy and planning issues relating to the service and to assist in the design, development, establishment and on-going operation of the service, including assisting in the resolution of issues concerning the safeguarding of the confidentiality of information. The advisory committee may in its discretion submit reports to the governor and the legislature.

2. The advisory committee shall be appointed by the commissioner, who shall appoint one of the committee's members to be its chairman. The members of the committee shall be appointed from the following categories, one or more from each category:

(a) designees of the commissioner;

(b) designees of the administrative judge of the state of New York;

(c) designees of the director of the division of the budget;

(d) commissioners of local social services districts or their designees;

(e) representatives of voluntary child care agencies;

(f) persons active in organizations involved in the protection of civil liberties;

(g) persons active in organizations involved in promoting the interests of children.

§444. Confidentiality of records; related matters.

1. The department in consultation with the advisory committee shall make regulations;

(a) protecting the confidentiality of individual identifying information submitted to or provided by the service, and preventing access thereto, by, or the distribution thereof to, persons not authorized by law;

(b) setting forth procedures for informing any child or his representative of the nature of the system and its uses;

(c) allowing any child or his representative or any member of his family, an opportunity to review any information pertaining to such child or family and to request that any part of such information be amended or expunged; and

(d) providing that the service shall remove from its records and expunge the individual identifying information, excluding non-identifying child or family data to be used for historical purposes, concerning any child who has been discharged from care.

2. Prior to final promulgation of any regulations as described in subdivision one of this section, the department shall, in addition to complying with all other advance notice requirements make proposed regulations available to all state agencies charged with the administration or supervision of child care programs and to local government agencies and persons that have expressed an interest in safeguarding information maintained by the service, and shall provide such agencies with an opportunity to comment on the proposed regulations. In promulgating final regulations the department shall consider any comments received.

3. Any persons wilfully violating or failing to comply with the provisions of subdivision one of this section or wilfully violating or failing to comply with any regulation which the department is authorized under such subdivision to make, shall be guilty of a misdemeanor.

4. The regulations promulgated pursuant to subdivision one of this section, shall provide that the information compiled and maintained by the service pursuant to paragraph (d) of subdivision ten of section four hundred forty-two of this title shall be subject to the confidentiality provisions of title six of this article.

§445. Funding.

The department shall explore the possibility of, and is authorized to take steps necessary to qualify for any available funding from any private source or from the federal government, and is authorized to use any funds for which the state qualifies for the purposes of the design, establishment or operation of the service.

§446. Statewide automated child welfare information system.

(1) The department shall promulgate regulations required to implement federal requirements for the establishment and administration of a statewide automated child welfare information system as required by applicable federal statute and regulation. The regulations shall set forth standards for the timely submission of data elements relating to child welfare services, including foster care, adoption assistance, preventive services, child protective services and other family preservation and family support services.

(2) The statewide automated child welfare information system shall be designed to improve convenience to consumers of services and reduce the administrative burden of child welfare workers of social services districts and their contracted agencies which provide direct services. The statewide automated child welfare information system shall be designed to provide computers to the majority of individual child welfare workers of social services districts and their contracted agencies which provide direct child welfare

services, allow such workers and agencies to communicate with and enter information directly into the statewide automated child welfare information system while preparing required documents and eliminate duplicate entry of information and preparation of documents, and allow for direct determination of claims and sanctions. The department shall immediately expand the existing advisory group of consumers, social services districts and their contracted agencies and other persons with expertise in child welfare. The statewide automated child welfare information system shall be designed to permit communication with the family courts and to protect the confidentiality of individuals as prescribed by this chapter.

Title 8-A
Safe Harbour for Exploited Children Act
Section
447-a. Definitions.
447-b. Services for exploited children.

§447-a. Definitions.
As used in this title:

1. The term "sexually exploited child" means any person under the age of eighteen who has been subject to sexual exploitation because he or she:

(a) is the victim of the crime of sex trafficking as defined in section 230.34 of the penal law;

(b) engages in any act as defined in section 230.00 of the penal law;

(c) is a victim of the crime of compelling prostitution as defined in section 230.33 of the penal law;

(d) engages in acts or conduct described in article two hundred sixty-three or section 240.37 of the penal law.

2. The term "short-term safe house" means a residential facility operated by an authorized agency as defined in subdivision ten of section three hundred seventy-one of this article including a residential facility operating as part of an approved runaway program as defined in subdivision four of section five hundred thirty-two-a of the executive law or a not-for-profit agency with experience in providing services to sexually exploited youth and approved in accordance with the regulations of the office of children and family services that provides emergency shelter, services and care to sexually exploited children including food, shelter, clothing, medical care, counseling and appropriate crisis intervention services at the time they are taken into custody by law enforcement and for the duration of any legal proceeding or proceedings in which they are either the complaining witness or the subject child. The short-term safe house shall also be available at the point in time that a child under the age of eighteen has first come into the custody of juvenile detention officials, law enforcement, local jails or the local commissioner of social services or is residing with the local runaway and homeless youth authority.

3. The term "advocate" means an employee of the short-term safe house defined in subdivision two of this section that has been trained to work with and advocate for the needs of sexually exploited children. The advocate shall accompany the child to all court appearances and will serve as a liaison between the short-term safe house and the court.

4. The term "safe house" means a residential facility operated by an authorized agency as defined in subdivision ten of section three hundred seventy-one of this article including a residential facility operating as part of an approved runaway program as defined in subdivision four of section five

hundred thirty-two-a of the executive law or a not-for-profit agency with experience in providing services to sexually exploited youth and approved in accordance with the regulations of the office of children and family services that provides shelter for sexually exploited children. In addition, a long-term safe house may be operated by a transitional independent living support program as defined in subdivision six of section five hundred thirty-two-a of the executive law. A safe house serving sexually exploited children as defined in this title shall provide or assist in securing necessary services for such sexually exploited children either through direct provision of services, or through written agreements with other community and public agencies for the provision of services including but not limited to housing, assessment, case management, medical care, legal, mental health and substance and alcohol abuse services. Where appropriate such safe house in accordance with a service plan for such sexually exploited child may also provide counseling and therapeutic services, educational services including life skills services and planning services to successfully transition residents back to the community. Nothing in the provisions of this title or article nineteen-H of the executive law shall prevent a child who is the subject of a proceeding which has not reached final disposition from residing at the safe house for the duration of that proceeding nor shall it prevent any sexually exploited child who is not the subject of a proceeding from residing at the safe house. An advocate employed by a short-term safe house or other appropriate staff of a short-term safe house shall, to the maximum extent possible, preferably within twenty-four hours but within no more than seventy-two hours following a sexually exploited child's admission into the program other than pursuant to a court order, notify such child's parent, guardian or custodian of his or her physical and emotional condition and the circumstances surrounding the child's presence at the program, unless there are compelling circumstances why the parent, guardian or custodian should not be so notified. Where such circumstances exist, the advocate or other appropriate staff member shall either file an appropriate petition in the family court, refer the youth to the local social services district, or in instances where abuse or neglect is suspected, report such case pursuant to title six of this article.

5. The term "community-based program" means a program operated by a not-for-profit organization that provides services such as street outreach, voluntary drop-in services, peer counseling, individual counseling, family-therapy and referrals for services such as educational and vocational training and health care. Any such community-based program may also work with the safe house serving sexually exploited children as defined in this title to provide transitional services to such children returning to the community.

§447-b.   Services for exploited children.

1. Notwithstanding any inconsistent provision of law, pursuant to regulations of the office of children and family services, every local social services district shall as a component of the district's multi-year consolidated services child welfare services plan address the child welfare services needs of sexually exploited children and to the extent that funds are available specifically therefor ensure that a short-term safe house or another short-term safe placement such as an approved runaway and homeless youth program, approved respite or crisis program providing crisis intervention or respite services or community-based program to serve sexually exploited children is available to children residing in such district. Nothing in this section shall prohibit a local social

services district from utilizing existing respite or crisis intervention services already operated by such social services district or homeless youth programs or services for victims of human trafficking pursuant to article ten-D of this chapter so long as the staff members have received appropriate training approved by the office of children and family services regarding sexually exploited children and the existing programs and facilities provide a safe, secure and appropriate environment for sexually exploited children. Crisis intervention services, short-term safe house care and community-based programming may, where appropriate, be provided by the same not-for-profit agency. Local social services districts may work cooperatively to provide such short-term safe house or other short-term safe placement, services and programming and access to such placement, services and programming may be provided on a regional basis, provided, however, that every local social services district shall to the extent that funds are available ensure that such placement, services and programs shall be readily accessible to sexually exploited children residing within the district.

2. All of the services created under this title may, to the extent possible provided by law, be available to all sexually exploited children whether they are accessed voluntarily, as a condition of an adjournment in contemplation of dismissal issued in criminal court, through the diversion services created under section seven hundred thirty-five of the family court act, through a proceeding under article three of the family court act, a proceeding under article ten of the family court act or through a referral from a local social services agency.

3. The capacity of the crisis intervention services and community-based programs in subdivision one of this section shall be based on the number of sexually exploited children in each district who are in need of such services. A determination of such need shall be made in two thousand ten and every five years thereafter in every social services district by the local commissioner of social services and be included in the integrated county plan. Such determination shall be made in consultation with local law enforcement, runaway and homeless youth program providers, local probation departments, local social services commissioners, the runaway and homeless youth coordinator for the local social services district, local law guardians, presentment agencies, public defenders and district attorney's offices and child advocates and services providers who work directly with sexually exploited youth.

4. In determining the need for and capacity of the services created under this section, each local social services district shall recognize that sexually exploited youth have separate and distinct service needs according to gender and, where a local social services district determines that the need exists, to the extent that funds are available, appropriate programming shall be made available.

5. To the extent funds are specifically appropriated therefor, the office of children and family services shall contract with an appropriate not-for-profit agency with experience working with sexually exploited children to operate at least one long-term safe house in a geographically appropriate area of the state which shall provide safe and secure long term housing and specialized services for sexually exploited children throughout the state. The appropriateness of the geographic location shall be determined taking into account the areas of the state with high numbers of sexually exploited children and the need for sexually exploited children to find shelter and long term placement in a region that cannot be readily accessed by the perpetrators of sexual exploitation. The need for more than one long-term safe house shall be determined by the office of children and family services based on the numbers and geographical location

of sexually exploited children within the state. Nothing herein shall be construed to preclude an agency from applying for and accepting grants, gifts and bequests of funds from private individuals, foundations and the federal government for the purpose of creating or carrying out the duties of a long-term safe house.

6. The local social services commissioner may, to the extent that funds are available, in conjunction with the division of criminal justice services and local law enforcement officials, contract with an appropriate not-for-profit agency with experience working with sexually exploited children to train law enforcement officials who are likely to encounter sexually exploited children in the course of their law enforcement duties on the provisions of this section and how to identify and obtain appropriate services for sexually exploited children. Local social services districts may work cooperatively to provide such training and such training may be provided on a regional basis. The division of criminal justice services shall assist local social services districts in obtaining any available funds for the purposes of conducting law enforcement training from the federal justice department and the office of juvenile justice and delinquency prevention.

Title 9
Subsidies for the Adoption of Children

§450. Statement of legislative intent.

The legislature intends, by the enactment of this title, to promote permanency of family status through adoption for children who might not otherwise derive the benefits of that status. By providing for an adoption subsidy program which will be applied uniformly on a statewide basis, the legislature also intends to eliminate, or at the very least substantially reduce, unnecessary and inappropriate long-term foster care situations which have proven financially burdensome to the state and, more importantly, inimical to the best interests of many children who have not been placed for adoption because of emotional or physical handicaps, age or other factors, in accordance with regulations of the department.

§451. Definitions.

As used in this title:

1. "Child" shall mean a person under the age of twenty-one years whose guardianship and custody have been committed to a social services official or a voluntary authorized agency, or whose guardianship and custody have been committed to a certified or approved foster parent pursuant to a court order prior to such person's eighteenth birthday, except as provided in paragraph (g) of subdivision three of section three hundred eighty-four-b of this article and section six hundred thirty-one of the family court act. A "child" shall also mean a person under the age of twenty-one years whose care and custody have been

transferred prior to such person's eighteenth birthday to a social services official or a voluntary authorized agency pursuant to section one thousand fifty-five of the family court act or section three hundred eighty-four-a of this article, whose parents are deceased or where one parent is deceased and the other parent is not a person entitled to notice pursuant to section one hundred eleven-a of the domestic relations law, and where such official or agency consents to the adoption of such person in accordance with section one hundred thirteen of the domestic relations law.

2. "Handicapped child" shall mean a child who possesses a specific physical, mental or emotional condition or disability of such severity or kind which, in accordance with regulations of the department, would constitute a significant obstacle to the child's adoption.

3. "Hard to place child" shall mean a child, other than a handicapped child, (a) who has not been placed for adoption within six months from the date his guardianship and custody were committed to the social services official or a voluntary authorized agency, or (b) who has not been placed for adoption within six months from the date a previous adoption placement terminated and the child was returned to the care of the social services official or a voluntary authorized agency, or (c) who possesses or presents any personal or familial attribute, condition, problem or characteristic which, in accordance with regulations of the department, would be an obstacle to the child's adoption, notwithstanding the child has been in the guardianship and custody of the social services official or a voluntary authorized agency for less than six months.

4. (a) "Board rate" shall mean an amount equal to the monthly payment which has been or would have been made by a social services official, in accordance with section three hundred ninety-eight-a and other provisions of this chapter, for the care and maintenance of the child, if such child had been boarded out in a foster family boarding home. Such rate shall reflect annual increases in room and board rates and clothing replacement allowances.

(b) When a child is placed for adoption by a social services official or a voluntary authorized agency with adoptive parents residing in another social services district, the "board rate" shall mean the board rate of the social services district placing the child for adoption or the social services district in which the adoptive parents reside.

5. "Persons" shall include a single person eligible to adopt a child as well as a couple eligible therefor.

6. "Voluntary authorized agency" shall mean an authorized agency as defined in paragraphs (a) and (c) of subdivision ten of section three hundred seventy-one of this article.

7. "Social services official" shall mean a county commissioner of social services, a city commissioner of social services, or an Indian tribe with which the department has entered into an agreement to provide adoption services in accordance with subdivision two of section thirty-nine of this chapter.

§453.   Maintenance subsidy; handicapped or hard to place child.

1. (a) A social services official shall make monthly payments for the care and maintenance of a handicapped or hard to place child whom a social services official has placed for adoption or who has been adopted and for the care and maintenance of a handicapped or hard to place child placed for adoption by a voluntary authorized agency who is residing in such social services district. Where a handicapped or hard to place child is placed in an adoptive placement outside the state, monthly payments for the care and

maintenance of the child shall be made by the social services official placing the child or in whose district the voluntary authorized agency maintains its principal office. Such payments shall be made until the child's twenty-first birthday to persons with whom the child has been placed, or to persons who have adopted the child and who applied for such payments prior to the adoption, pursuant to a written agreement therefor between such official or agency and such persons; provided, however, that an application may be made subsequent to the adoption if the adoptive parents first become aware of the child's physical or emotional condition or disability subsequent to the adoption and a physician certifies that the condition or disability existed prior to the child's adoption. The social services official shall consider the financial status of such persons only for the purpose of determining the amount of the payments to be made, pursuant to subdivision three of this section. Upon the death of persons who have adopted the child prior to the twenty-first birthday of the child, such payments shall continue to the legal guardian or custodian of the child under the age of eighteen upon issuance of letters of guardianship or order of custody and shall continue until the child shall attain the age of twenty-one. If the guardian or custodian was the caretaker of the child under the age of eighteen prior to the issuance of letters of guardianship or order of custody, such payments shall be made retroactively from the death of the adoptive parent or parents.

(a-1) Payments pursuant to this section may be made by direct deposit or debit card, as elected by the recipient, and administered electronically, and in accordance with such guidelines as may be set forth by regulation of the office of children and family services. The office of children and family services may enter into contracts on behalf of local social services districts for such direct deposit or debit card services in accordance with section twenty-one-a of this chapter.

(b) Any child with respect to whom federally reimbursable maintenance subsidy payments are made under this subdivision shall be deemed to be a recipient of aid to families with dependent children for purposes of determining eligibility for medical assistance.

(c) No payments may be made pursuant to this subdivision if the social services official determines that the adoptive parents are no longer legally responsible for the support of the child or the child is no longer receiving any support from such parents. The social services official on a biennial basis shall remind the adoptive parents of their obligation to support the child and to notify the social services official if the adoptive parents are no longer providing any support of the child or are no longer legally responsible for the support of the child.

(d) Applications for such subsidies shall be accepted prior to the commitment of the guardianship and custody of the child to an authorized agency pursuant to the provisions of this chapter, and approval thereof may be granted contingent upon such commitment.

(e) Upon the death of the sole or surviving adoptive parent or both adoptive parents after the eighteenth birthday and before the twenty-first birthday of the adopted child, where such adoptive parent or parents were receiving adoption subsidy payments at the time of death, such subsidy payments shall continue but shall be made to the guardian of the child on behalf of such child, where the child consents to the appointment of a guardian. Such subsidy payments shall be made retroactively from the death of the adoptive parent or parents to the appointment of a guardian, and shall continue until the twenty-first birthday of the child. If, however, there is no willing or suitable person to be appointed as guardian, or the child does not consent to the appointment of a guardian, such subsidy payments shall be made retroactively from the death of the adoptive parent or parents and shall continue to be made until the twenty-first birthday of the child: (i) through direct payments to the child, if the social services official determines that the child demonstrates the ability to manage such direct payments; or (ii) to a representative payee certified by the social services official.

(f) Upon receipt of notification of the death of the sole or surviving adoptive parent or both adoptive parents after the eighteenth birthday and before the twenty-first birthday of the adopted child, where such adoptive parent or parents were receiving adoption subsidy payments at the time of death, the social services official shall notify the child of: (i) the processes available to continue subsidy payments until the twenty-first birthday of the child including appointment of a guardian under the surrogate's court procedure act, application to be approved for direct subsidy payments, or the appointment of a representative payee; and (ii) the right of the child to be involved in all such processes.

(g) Where the social services official has determined that the child does not demonstrate the ability to manage direct subsidy payments, the social services official shall certify payment to a representative payee on behalf of the child. Subsidy payments received by the representative payee shall be held and used strictly for the use and benefit of the child. Designation of the appropriate entity or individual and investigation of an individual for certification as a representative payee shall be conducted by the social services official responsible for payment of the adoption subsidy pursuant to this section.

(i) The social services official may designate an employee of the social services district to be the representative payee responsible for receipt of the adoption subsidy on behalf of the child only where the official determines that such employee has no conflict of interest in performing the duties and obligations as representative payee. If the child resides in a social services district other than the district responsible for payment of the adoption subsidy, the social services district in which the child resides may be designated the representative payee and a social services official of such district shall select an employee of such social services district to be responsible for receipt of the adoption subsidy as the representative payee, only where the official determines that such employee has no conflict of interest in performing the duties and obligations as a payee. Where a voluntary authorized agency has a prior relationship with a child, or where the social services district does not have sufficient or appropriate staff available to perform the functions of the representative payee, the social services district may contract with a voluntary authorized agency as the representative payee on behalf of the child where the social services district determines it would be in the best interests of the child to do so.

(ii) The social services official may designate an individual for certification as a representative payee who shall perform the functions and duties of a representative payee in accordance with the best interests of the child. In determining whether an individual is appropriate to be certified as the representative payee, the social services official shall first consult with the child and shall give the child's preferences significant weight. The child's preference shall be determinative of the representative payee only where such preference does not conflict with the best interests of the child. Prior to designation of an individual by the social services official for certification as a representative payee, the social services official shall:

(A) collect proof of identity and a verifiable social security number of the nominated representative payee;

(B) conduct an in-person interview of the individual;

(C) investigate any potential conflicts of interest that may ensue if such individual is certified; and

(D) determine the capabilities and qualifications of the individual to manage the subsidy payment for the child.

(iii) (A) If, after completion of the investigation, the social services official is satisfied that the individual is qualified, appropriate and will serve the best interests of the child, the social services official shall certify the selected individual as the representative payee for the child.

(B) If the twenty-first birthday of the child occurs while awaiting the certification of a representative payee, the child shall be entitled to retroactive direct payment of subsidy payments since the death of the adoptive parent or parents after the eighteenth birthday of the child.

(iv) The representative payee shall submit reports to the social services official no less than once a year describing the use of the payments in the preceding year. Such reports shall be submitted by December thirty-first of each year. The social services official may also request reports from time to time from the representative payee. If a representative payee fails to submit a report, the social services official may require that the representative payee appear in person to collect payments. The social services official shall keep a centralized file and update it periodically with information including the addresses and social security or tax-payer identification numbers of the representative payee and the child.

(v) The social services official shall revoke the certification of a representative payee upon:

(A) determining that the representative payee has misused the payments intended for the benefit of the child;

(B) the failure of the representative payee to submit timely reports or appear in person as required by the social services official after such failure; or

(C) the request of the child upon good cause shown.

(vi) The social services official shall notify the child of the contact information of the representative payee within five days of making a designation.

(vii) A child may appeal the refusal of the social services official to certify the individual preferred by the child for certification as the representative payee or revoke the certification of a representative payee upon request of the child pursuant to section four hundred fifty-five of this title.

2. The agreement provided for in subdivision one of this section shall be subject to the approval of the department upon the application of the social services official; provided, however, that in accordance with the regulations of the department, the department may authorize the social services official to approve or disapprove the agreement on behalf of the department. In either situation, if the agreement is not approved or disapproved by the social services official within thirty days of submission, the voluntary authorized agency may submit the agreement directly to the department for approval or disapproval. If the agreement is not disapproved in writing by the department within thirty days after its submission to the department, it shall be deemed approved. Any such disapproval shall be accompanied by a written statement of the reasons therefor.

3. The amount of the monthly payment made pursuant to this section shall be determined pursuant to regulations of the department and based upon the financial need of such persons. The department shall review such regulations annually. The amount of the monthly payment shall not be less than seventy-five per centum of the board rate nor more than one hundred per centum of such rate.

4. Except as may be required by federal law as a condition for federal reimbursement of public assistance expenditures, payments under this section shall not be considered for the purpose of determining eligibility for public assistance or medical assistance for needy persons.

§453-a.   Payments for non-recurring adoption expenses.

1. A social services official shall make payments for non-recurring adoption expenses incurred by or on behalf of the adoptive parents of a child with special needs, when such expenses are incurred in connection with the adoption of a child with special needs through an authorized agency. In accordance with subdivision two of this section, the payments shall be made by the social services official either to the adoptive parents directly, to the authorized agency on behalf of the adoptive parents or to an attorney on behalf of the adoptive parents for the allowable amount of attorney's fees or court costs incurred in connection with such completed adoption.

2. The amount of the payment made pursuant to this section shall be determined pursuant to the regulations of the department. Nothing herein shall obligate a social services official to make payments for the full amount of non-recurring adoption expenses incurred by or on behalf of the adoptive parents of a child with special needs.

3. Payments for non-recurring adoption expenses made by a social services official pursuant to this section shall be treated as administrative expenditures under title IV-E of the social security act and shall be reimbursed by the state accordingly.

4. Payments under this section shall be made pursuant to a written agreement between the social services official, other relevant authorized agencies and the adoptive parents of a child with special needs. The written agreement shall specify the nature and amount of any payments, services and assistance to be provided, shall stipulate that the agreement remain in effect regardless of the state of residence of the adoptive parents at any time and shall contain provisions for the protection of the interests of the child where the adoptive parents and the child move to another state while the agreement is effective. Applications for such subsidies shall be accepted prior to the commitment of the guardianship and custody of the child to an authorized agency pursuant to the provisions of this chapter, and approval thereof may be granted contingent upon such commitment.

5. When the parental rights of a child with special needs have been terminated in this state and the child's guardianship has been committed to an authorized agency, the child is adopted in another state and the adoptive parents are not eligible for payments of non-recurring adoption expenses in the other state, a social services official shall make payments of the non-recurring adoption expenses incurred by or on behalf of the adoptive parents, if such parents are otherwise eligible for payments under subdivision one of this section.

6. As used in this section, non-recurring adoption expenses shall mean reasonable and necessary adoption fees, court costs, attorney fees and other expenses which are directly related to the legal adoption of a child with special

needs and which are not incurred in violation of federal law or the laws of this state or any other state.

7. As used in this section, a child with special needs shall mean a child who:

(a) the state has determined cannot or shall not be returned to the home of his or her parents; and

(b) the state has first determined:

(i) is a handicapped child as defined in subdivision two of section four hundred fifty-one of this title, or is a hard-to-place child as defined in paragraph (c) of subdivision three of section four hundred fifty-one of this title; and

(ii) a reasonable, but unsuccessful effort has been made to place the child with appropriate adoptive parents without adoption assistance. Such an effort need not be made where such efforts would not be in the best interests of the child because of such factors as the existence of significant emotional ties with prospective adoptive parents while in the care of such parents as a foster child.

§454. Medical subsidy.

1. A social services official shall make payments for the cost of care, services and supplies payable under the state's program of medical assistance for needy persons, provided to a handicapped child whom he or a voluntary authorized agency has placed out for adoption or who has been adopted. Such payments shall not be restricted to care, services and supplies required for the treatment of the specific condition or disability for which a child was determined to be a handicapped child. For the purposes of this section, a handicapped child shall include, but not be limited to, a child with special needs where a social services official has determined the child cannot be placed with an adoptive parent or parents without medical subsidy because such child has special needs for medical, mental health or rehabilitative care. Such payments also shall be made with respect to a hard to place child who has been placed out for adoption with a person or persons who is or are sixty-two years old or over or who will be subject to mandatory retirement from his or their present employment within five years from the date of the adoption placement.

2. Payments pursuant to subdivision one of this section shall be made to or on behalf of the person or persons with whom the child has been placed or who have adopted the child and shall be made without regard to the financial need of such person or persons.

3. Payments pursuant to subdivision one of this section shall be made only with respect to the cost of care, services and supplies which are not otherwise covered or subject to payment or reimbursement by insurance, medical assistance or other sources.

4. An application for payment under this section shall be made prior to the child's adoption; provided, however, that an application may be made subsequent to a handicapped child's adoption if the adoptive parents first become aware of the child's physical or emotional condition or disability subsequent to the adoption and a physician certifies that the condition or disability existed prior to the child's adoption. An approval of an application for payments under this section shall not be subject to annual review by the social services official, and such approval shall remain in effect until the child's twenty-first birthday. Applications for such subsidies shall be accepted prior to the commitment of the guardianship and custody of the child to an authorized agency pursuant to the provisions of this chapter, and approval thereof may be granted contingent upon such commitment.

5. Upon the death of persons who have adopted the child prior to the twenty-first birthday of the child, payments pursuant to subdivision one of this section shall continue to the legal guardian of the child until the child shall attain the age of twenty-one.

§455.   Fair hearings.

1. Any person aggrieved by the decision of a social services official or an official of the office of children and family services not to make a payment or payments pursuant to this title or to make such payment or payments in an inadequate or inappropriate amount or the failure of a social services official or an official of the office of children and family services to determine an application under this title within thirty days after filing, may appeal to the office of children and family services which shall review the case, give such person an opportunity for a fair hearing thereon, and render its decision within thirty days. The office of children and family services may also, on its own motion, review any such decision made by a social services official or any case in which a decision has not been made within the time specified. All decisions of the office of children and family services shall be binding upon the social services district involved and shall be complied with by the social services official thereof.

2. The only issues which may be raised in a fair hearing under this section are (a) whether the social services official or an official of the office of children and family services has improperly denied an application for payments under this title, or (b) whether the social services official or an official of the office of children and family services has improperly discontinued payments under this title, or (c) whether the social services official or an official of the office of children and family services has determined the amount of the payments made or to be made in violation of the provisions of this title or the regulations of the office of children and family services promulgated hereunder, or (d) whether the social services official improperly refused to certify the individual preferred by a child for certification as the representative payee or improperly denied a request by a child to revoke the certification of a representative payee pursuant to section four hundred fifty-three of this title.

3. When an issue is raised as to whether a social services official or an official of the department has improperly denied an application for payments under this title, the department shall affirm such denial if: (a) the child is not a hard to place child or a handicapped child or (b) there is another approved adoptive parent or parents who is or are willing to accept the placement of the child in his or their home without payment under this title within sixty days of such denial and placement of the child with such other parent or parents would not be contrary to the best interests of the child.

4. The provisions of subdivisions two and four of section twenty-two of this chapter shall apply to fair hearings held and appeals taken pursuant to this section.

§456.   State reimbursement and payments.

1. Payments made by social services officials pursuant to the provisions of this title shall, if approved by the department, be subject to reimbursement by the state, in accordance with the regulations of the department as follows: there shall be paid to each social services district (a) the amount of federal funds, if any, properly received or to be received on account of such payments; and (b) except as set forth below, seventy-five per centum of such payments after first deducting

therefrom any federal funds properly received or to be received on account thereof; provided, however, that when payments under section four hundred fifty-three of this title are made to a person or persons residing in a social services district whose board rate exceeds that of the district making such payments, that portion of the payments which exceeds the board rate of the district making the payments shall be subject to reimbursement by the state in the amount of one hundred per centum thereof, or (c) one hundred per centum of such payments after first deducting therefrom any federal funds properly to be received on account of such payments, for children placed out for adoption or being adopted after being placed out for adoption by an Indian tribe as referenced in subdivision seven of section four hundred fifty-one of this title.

2. (a) Claims for state reimbursement shall be made in such form and manner and at such times and for such periods as the department shall determine.

(b) When certified by the department, state reimbursement shall be paid from the state treasury upon the audit and warrant of the comptroller out of funds made available therefor.

3. Notwithstanding any other provision of law to the contrary, for a child who has been placed for adoption by a voluntary authorized agency with guardianship and custody or care and custody of such child, as referenced in subdivision one of section four hundred fifty-one of this title, payments available under section four hundred fifty-three, four hundred fifty-three-a or four hundred fifty-four of this title shall be made by the state pursuant to a written agreement between an official of the office of children and family services and the persons who applied for such payments prior to adoption. Notwithstanding any other provision of law to the contrary, the office of children and family services shall not enter into written agreements for, or issue, any such payments in instances where the person or persons applying for such payments reside outside of the state of New York at the time the application for such payments is made.

§457. Out-of-state adoptive parents.

With respect to a child who has been adopted within this state but who has been removed from this state by his adoptive parents, or a child who has been adopted by residents of another state or of the commonwealth of Puerto Rico and who is, or who is likely to become, a public charge within this state, payments under section four hundred fifty-three or four hundred fifty-four of this title may be made pursuant to an agreement between the district and the adoptive parents, provided that such agreement is in accordance with the regulations of the department promulgated to achieve the objective of increasing the number of adoptions of potential public charges, with particular emphasis upon handicapped and hard to place children. Any such agreement shall become void at such time as it is determined by the social services official that a child on whose behalf payments are being received pursuant to such agreement was brought into this state for the sole purpose of qualifying prospective out-of-state adoptive parents for such payments. Such determination may be appealed to the department which, upon receipt of the appeal, shall conduct a fair hearing in accordance with the provisions of section four hundred fifty-five of this title.

§458. Availability of subsidy; publicity.

The department shall promulgate regulations providing for the publicizing of the availability of payments under this title. Such regulations shall provide for the dissemination of literature and other means in each social services district of informing persons, at the time of any inquiry, application or other expression of interest in adoption, of the provisions of the adoption subsidy program. Additionally, each social services district and authorized agency shall provide information on the adoption subsidy program to all foster care parents who are caring for a child who is eligible for adoption.

Title 10
Kinship Guardianship Assistance Program

§458-a.   Definitions.

As used in this title:

1. "Child" shall mean a person under the age of twenty-one years whose custody, care and custody, or custody and guardianship have been committed to a social services official prior to such person's eighteenth birthday pursuant to section three hundred fifty-eight-a, three hundred eighty-four, three hundred eighty-four-a or three hundred eighty-four-b of this chapter or article three, seven, ten or 10-C of the family court act.

2. "Applicable board rate" shall mean an amount equal to the monthly payment that has been made by a social services official, in accordance with section three hundred ninety-eight-a of this article and other provisions of this chapter, for the care and maintenance of the child, while such child was boarded out in the approved or certified foster family boarding home with the prospective relative guardian. Such rate shall reflect annual changes in room and board rates and clothing replacement allowances.

3. "Prospective relative guardian" shall mean a person or persons who is related to the child through blood, marriage, or adoption who has been caring for the child as a fully certified or approved foster parent for at least six consecutive months prior to applying for kinship guardianship assistance payments.

4. "Relative guardian" shall mean a person or persons who was appointed, as a guardian or permanent guardian for a child after entering into an agreement with a social services official for the receipt of payments and services in accordance with this title.

5. "Social services official" shall mean a county commissioner of social services, a city commissioner of social services, or an Indian tribe with which the office of children and family services has entered into an agreement to provide foster care services in accordance with subdivision two of section thirty-nine of this chapter.

6. "Successor guardian" shall mean a person or persons that is approved by a local social services district to receive payments pursuant to this title in accordance with subparagraph (ii) of paragraph (b) of subdivision five of section four hundred fifty-eight-b of this title and that has been named in the agreement in effect between the relative guardian and social services official for kinship guardianship assistance payments pursuant to this title who shall provide care and guardianship for a child in the event of death or incapacity of the relative guardian, as set forth in section four hundred fifty-eight-b of this title, who has assumed care for and is the guardian or permanent guardian of

such child, provided that such person was appointed guardian or permanent guardian of such child by the court following, or due to, the death or incapacity of the relative guardian. Once approved in accordance with subparagraph (ii) of paragraph (b) of section four hundred fifty-eight-b of this title, a successor guardian shall be deemed to have the same rights and responsibilities as a relative guardian in relation to any provisions of this title and any agreement entered into under this title.

7. "Prospective successor guardian" shall mean a person or persons whom a prospective relative guardian or a relative guardian seeks to name or names in the original kinship guardianship assistance agreement, or any amendment thereto, as set forth in section four hundred fifty-eight-b of this title, as the person or persons to provide care and guardianship for a child in the event of the death or incapacity of a relative guardian, who has not been approved in accordance with subparagraph (ii) of paragraph (b) of subdivision five of section four hundred fifty-eight-b of this title.

8. "Incapacity" shall mean a substantial inability to care for a child as a result of: (a) a physically debilitating illness, disease or injury; or (b) a mental impairment that results in a substantial inability to understand the nature and consequences of decisions concerning the care of a child.

§458-b. Kinship guardianship assistance payments.

1. A child is eligible for kinship guardianship assistance payments under this title if the social services official determines the following:

(a) The child has been in foster care for at least six consecutive months in the home of the prospective relative guardian; and

(b) The child being returned home or adopted are not appropriate permanency options for the child; and

(c) The child demonstrates a strong attachment to the prospective relative guardian and the prospective relative guardian has a strong commitment to caring permanently for the child; and

(d) That age appropriate consultation has been held with the child, provided however with respect to a child who has attained fourteen years of age, that the child has been consulted regarding the kinship guardianship arrangement, and with respect to a child who has attained eighteen years of age, that the child has consented to the kinship guardianship arrangement.

(e) (i) If the child has been placed into foster care pursuant to article ten or ten-C of the family court act, that both the fact finding hearing pursuant to section one thousand fifty-one of the family court act or section one thousand ninety-five of the family court act, respectively, and the first permanency hearing pursuant to paragraph two of subdivision (a) of section one thousand eighty-nine of the family court act have been completed; or

(ii) for all the other children, that the first permanency hearing has been completed.

(f) The financial status of the prospective relative guardian shall not be considered in determining eligibility for kinship guardianship assistance payments.

1-a. A child shall remain eligible for kinship guardianship assistance payments under this title when a successor guardian as defined in subdivision six of section four hundred fifty-eight-a of this title assumes care and guardianship of the child.

2. (a) A prospective relative guardian who has been caring for an eligible foster child for at least six consecutive months and who intends to seek

guardianship or permanent guardianship of the child may apply to the social services official who has custody, care and custody, or guardianship and custody of the child to receive kinship guardianship assistance payments, non-recurring guardianship payments, and other applicable services and payments available under this title on behalf of the child.

(b) Applications shall only be accepted prior to issuance of letters of guardianship of the child to the relative guardian pursuant to the provisions of the family court act or the surrogate's court procedure act.

(c) Notwithstanding any other provision of law to the contrary, a prospective relative guardian and any person over the age of eighteen living in the home of the prospective relative guardian who has not already been subject to a national and state criminal history record check pursuant to section three hundred seventy-eight-a of this article as part of the process of the prospective relative guardian becoming a certified or approved foster parent must complete such a record check in accordance with the procedures and standards set forth in such section prior to the social services official acting upon the application. The social services official must inquire of the office of children and family services whether each prospective relative guardian and each person over the age of eighteen living in the home of the prospective relative guardian has been or is currently the subject of an indicated report of child abuse or maltreatment on file with the statewide central register of child abuse and maltreatment and, if the prospective relative guardian or any other person over the age of eighteen residing in the home of the prospective relative guardian resided in another state in the five years preceding the application, request child abuse and maltreatment information maintained by the child abuse and maltreatment registry from the applicable child welfare agency in each such state of previous residence, if such a request has not been made as part of the process of the prospective relative guardian becoming a certified or approved foster parent.

(d) (i) Notwithstanding any other provision of law to the contrary, prior to the social services official approving a prospective successor guardian to receive payments pursuant to this title in accordance with subparagraph (ii) of paragraph (b) of subdivision five of this section: (1) the social services official must complete a national and state criminal history record check pursuant to subdivision two of section three hundred seventy-eight-a of this article for the prospective successor guardian and any person over the age of eighteen living in the home of the prospective successor guardian, in accordance with the procedures and standards set forth in such subdivision; and (2) the social services official must inquire of the office of children and family services, in accordance with section four hundred twenty-four-a of this article, whether each prospective successor guardian and each person over the age of eighteen living in the home of the prospective successor guardian has been or is currently the subject of an indicated report of child abuse or maltreatment on file with the statewide central register of child abuse and maltreatment and, if the prospective successor guardian or any other person over the age of eighteen residing in the home of the prospective successor guardian resided in another state in the five years preceding the inquiry, request child abuse and maltreatment information maintained by the child abuse and maltreatment registry from the applicable child welfare agency in each such state of previous residence.

(ii) It shall be the duty of the prospective successor guardian to inform the social services official that has entered into an agreement with the relative guardian for payments under this title in writing of the death or incapacity of the relative guardian and of the prospective successor guardian's desire to enforce the provisions in the agreement that authorize payment to him or her in the event of the death or incapacity of the relative guardian.

(iii) The clearances requires by subparagraph (i) of this paragraph shall be conducted following receipt by the social services official of the written communication required by subparagraph (ii) of this paragraph.

3. If the social services official determines that the child is eligible for kinship guardianship assistance payments and it is in the best interests of the child for the relative to become the legal guardian of the child, the social services official shall enter into an agreement with the prospective relative guardian authorizing the provision of kinship guardianship assistance payments, non-recurring guardianship payments, and other services and payments available under this title subject to the issuance by the court of letters of guardianship of the child to the prospective relative guardian and the child being finally discharged from foster care to such relative. In determining whether it is in the best interests of the child for the relative to become the relative guardian of the child, the social services official must determine and document that compelling reasons exist for determining that the return home of the child and the adoption of the child are not in the best interests of the child and are, therefore, not appropriate permanency options. A copy of the fully executed agreement must be provided by the social services official to the prospective relative guardian.

4. (a) Payments and eligibility for services under this title shall be made pursuant to a written agreement between the social services official and the prospective relative guardian.

(b) The written agreement shall specify, at a minimum: the amount of, and manner in which, each kinship guardianship assistance payment will be provided under the agreement; the manner in which the payments may be adjusted periodically, in consultation with the relative guardian, based on the circumstances of the relative guardian and the needs of the child; the additional services and assistance that the child and the relative guardian will be eligible for under the agreement, which shall be limited to the additional services and assistance set forth in this title; the procedures by which the relative guardian may apply for additional services, as needed; that the social services official will pay the total cost of nonrecurring expenses associated with obtaining legal guardianship of the child, to the extent the total cost does not exceed two thousand dollars in accordance with section four hundred fifty- eight-c of this title; and, that the agreement will remain in effect regardless of the state of residence of the relative guardian at any time.

(c) The agreement must be fully executed prior to the issuance of letters of guardianship of the child to the relative guardian in order for the child to be eligible for payments and services under this title.

(d) Payments pursuant to this section may be made by direct deposit or debit card, as elected by the recipient, and administered electronically, and in accordance with section twenty-one-a of this chapter and with such guidelines as may be set forth by regulation of the office of children and family services. The office of children and family services may enter into contracts on behalf of local social services districts for such direct deposit or debit card services in accordance with section twenty-one-a of this chapter.

(e) The original kinship guardianship assistance agreement executed in accordance with this section and any amendments thereto may name an appropriate person to act as a successor guardian for the purpose of providing care and guardianship for a child in the event of death or incapacity of the relative guardian. Nothing herein shall be deemed to require the relative guardian to name a prospective successor guardian as a condition for the approval of a kinship guardianship assistance agreement.

(f) A fully executed agreement between a relative guardian and a social services official may be amended to add or modify terms and conditions mutually agreeable to the relative guardian and the social services official, including the naming of an appropriate person to provide care and guardianship for a child in the event of death or incapacity of the relative guardian.

(g) The social services official shall inform the relative guardian of the right to name an appropriate person to act as a successor guardian in the original kinship guardianship assistance agreement or through an amendment to such agreement.

(h) A fully executed agreement between a relative guardian or a successor guardian and a social services official may be terminated if:

(i) in accordance with paragraph (b) of subdivision seven of this section, a social services official has determined that a relative guardian or a successor guardian is no longer legally responsible for the support of the child; or

(ii) following the death or permanent incapacity of a relative guardian, all prospective successor guardians named in such agreement were not approved by the social services district pursuant to subparagraph (ii) of paragraph (b) of subdivision five of this section.

5. (a) Once the prospective relative guardian with whom a social services official has entered into an agreement under subdivision four of this section has been issued letters of guardianship for the child and the child has been finally discharged from foster care to such relative, a social services official shall make monthly kinship guardianship assistance payments for the care and maintenance of the child.

(b) (i) In the event of death or incapacity of a relative guardian, a social services district shall make monthly kinship guardianship assistance payments for the care and maintenance of a child to a successor guardian that has been approved pursuant to subparagraph (ii) of this paragraph.

(ii) Following the death or incapacity of the relative guardian, a social services official shall approve a prospective successor guardian that is named in the agreement between the relative guardian and a social services official for payments under this title and that has been awarded guardianship or permanent guardianship of the child by the court unless, based on the results of the clearances required by paragraph (d) of subdivision two of this section, the social services official has determined that approval of the prospective successor guardian is not authorized or appropriate. Provided however, that no approval can be issued pursuant to this paragraph unless the prospective successor guardian has been awarded guardianship or permanent guardianship of the child by the court and the clearances required by paragraph (d) of subdivision two of this section have been conducted.

(iii) Notwithstanding any other provision of law to the contrary, if a prospective successor guardian assumes care of the child prior to being approved pursuant to subparagraph (ii) of this paragraph, payments under this title shall be made once a prospective guardian is approved pursuant to such subparagraph retroactively from: (1) in the event of death of the relative guardian, the date the successor guardian assumed care of the child or the date of death of the relative guardian, whichever is later; or (2) in the event of incapacity of the relative guardian, the date the successor guardian assumed care of the child or the date of incapacity of the relative guardian, whichever is later.

(c) In the event that a successor guardian assumed care and was awarded guardianship or permanent guardianship of a child due to the incapacity of a relative guardian and the relative guardian is subsequently awarded or resumes guardianship or permanent guardianship of such child and assumes care of such child after the incapacity ends, a social services official shall make monthly kinship guardianship assistance payments for the care and maintenance of the child to the relative guardian, in accordance with the terms of the fully executed written agreement.

6. The amount of the monthly kinship guardianship assistance payment made pursuant to this section shall be determined pursuant to regulations of the office. The amount of the monthly payment shall not be less than seventy-five per centum of the applicable board rate nor more than one hundred per centum of such rate as determined by the social services district in accordance with the regulations of the office; provided, however, that the rate chosen by the social services district shall be equal to the rate used by the district for adoption subsidy payments under section four hundred fifty-three of this article. The social services official shall consider the financial status of the prospective relative guardian or relative guardian only for the purpose of determining the amount of the payments to be made.

7. (a) Kinship guardianship assistance payments shall be made to the relative guardian or guardians until the child's eighteenth birthday or, if the child had attained sixteen years of age before the agreement became effective, until the child attains twenty-one years of age provided the child is: (i) completing secondary education or a program leading to an equivalent credential; (ii) enrolled in an institution which provides post-secondary or vocational education; (iii) employed for at least eighty hours per month; (iv) participating in a program or activity designed to promote, or remove barriers to, employment; or (v) incapable of any of such activities due to a medical condition, which incapability is supported by regularly updated information in the case plan of the child.

(b) (i) Notwithstanding paragraph (a) of this subdivision, and except as provided for in paragraph (b) of subdivision five of this section, no kinship guardianship assistance payments may be made pursuant to this title if the social services official determines that the relative guardian is no longer legally responsible for the support of the child, including if the status of the legal guardian is terminated or the child is no longer receiving any support from such guardian. In accordance with the regulations of the office, a relative guardian who has been receiving kinship guardianship assistance payments on behalf of a child under this title must keep the social services official informed, on an annual basis, of any circumstances that would make the relative guardian ineligible for such payments or eligible for payments in a different amount.

(ii) Notwithstanding paragraph (a) of this subdivision, and except as provided for in paragraph (c) of subdivision five of this section, no kinship guardianship assistance payments may be made pursuant to this title to a successor guardian if the social services official determines that the successor guardian is no longer legally responsible for the support of the child, including if the status of the successor guardian is terminated or the child is no longer receiving any support from such guardian. A successor guardian who has been receiving kinship guardianship assistance payments on behalf of a child under this title must keep the social services official informed, on an annual basis, of any circumstances that would make the successor guardian ineligible for such payments or eligible for payments in a different amount.

8. The placement of the child with the relative guardian or successor guardian and any kinship guardianship assistance payments made on behalf of the child under this section shall be considered never to have been made when determining the eligibility for adoption subsidy payments under title nine of this article of a child in such legal guardianship arrangement.

§458-c. Payments for non-recurring guardianship expenses.

1. A social services official shall make payments for non-recurring guardianship expenses incurred by or on behalf of the relatives or successor guardians who have been approved by the social services official to receive kinship guardianship assistance payments, when such expenses are incurred in connection with assuming the guardianship of a foster child or a former foster child in regard to successor guardians. The agreement for the payment of non-recurring guardianship expenses must be reflected in the written agreement set forth in subdivision four of section four hundred fifty-eight-b of this title. In accordance with subdivision two of this section, the payments shall be made by the social services official either to the relative or successor guardian or guardians directly or to an attorney on behalf of the relative or successor guardian or guardians, as applicable, for the allowable amount of non-recurring guardianship expenses incurred in connection with obtaining such guardianship. *(Eff.4/4/16,Ch.54,L.2016)*

2. The amount of the payment made pursuant to this section shall not exceed two thousand dollars for each foster child for whom the relatives, or each former foster child for whom the successor guardians, seek guardianship or permanent guardianship and shall be available only for those expenses that are determined to be eligible for reimbursement by the social services official in accordance with the regulations of the office of children and family services. *(Eff.4/4/16,Ch.54,L.2016)*

3. Payments for non-recurring guardianship expenses made by a social services official pursuant to this section shall be treated as administrative expenditures under title IV-E of the federal social security act and shall be reimbursed by the state accordingly.

4. As used in this section, non-recurring guardianship expenses shall mean reasonable and necessary fees, court costs, attorney fees, and other expenses which are directly related to obtaining legal guardianship of an eligible child and which are not incurred in violation of federal law or the laws of this state or any other state.

§458-d. Medical subsidy.

1. Any child with respect to whom federally reimbursable kinship guardianship assistance payments are made under this title is eligible for medical assistance under title XIX of the federal social security act.

2. In addition, a social services official shall make payments for the cost of care, services and supplies payable under the state's program of medical assistance for needy persons provided to any child for whom kinship guardianship assistance payments are being made under this title who is not eligible for medical assistance under subdivision one of this section and for whom the relative or successor guardian is unable to obtain appropriate and affordable medical

coverage through any other available means, regardless of whether the child otherwise qualifies for medical assistance for needy persons. Payments pursuant to this subdivision shall be made only with respect to the cost of care, services, and supplies which are not otherwise covered or subject to payment or reimbursement by insurance, medical assistance or other sources. Payments made pursuant to this subdivision shall only be made if the relative or successor guardian applies to obtain such medical coverage for the child from all available sources, unless the social services official determines that the relative guardian has good cause for not applying for such coverage; which shall include that appropriate coverage is not available or affordable.

3. An application for payments under this section shall be made prior to the issuance of letters of guardianship for the child. An approval of an application for payments under this section shall not be subject to annual review by the social services official, and such approval shall remain in effect for as long as kinship guardianship assistance payments are being made under this title for the child. Applications for such payments shall be accepted prior to the issuance of letters of guardianship of the child, and approval thereof may be granted contingent upon such issuance.

§458-e. Independent living services.

In accordance with regulations of the office of children and family services, any child who leaves foster care for guardianship with a relative after attaining sixteen years of age for whom kinship guardianship assistance payments are being made under this title shall be eligible:

1. to receive those independent living services that are made available by the social services district to foster children pursuant to section 477 of the federal social security act; and

2. to apply for educational and training vouchers made available pursuant to such section, which will be awarded based on the priorities established by the office of children and family services and the amount of funds made available therefor.

§458-f. Fair hearings.

1. Any person aggrieved by the decision of a social services official not to make a payment or payments pursuant to this title or to make such payment or payments in an inadequate or inappropriate amount or the failure of a social services official to determine an application under this title within thirty days after filing, or the failure of a social services district to agree to a prospective successor guardian being named in an agreement or to approve a prospective successor guardian pursuant to subparagraph (ii) of paragraph (b) of subdivision five of section four hundred fifty-eight-b of this title, or the decision of a social services district to terminate an agreement pursuant to paragraph (h) of subdivision four of section four hundred fifty-eight-b of this title, may appeal to the office of children and family services, which shall review the case and give such person an opportunity for a fair hearing thereon and render its decision within thirty days. All decisions of the office of children and family services shall be binding upon the social services district involved and shall be complied with by the social services official thereof.

2. The only issues which may be raised in a fair hearing under this section are: (a) whether the social services official has improperly denied an application for payments under this title; (b) whether the social services official has improperly discontinued payments under this title; (c) whether the social

services official has determined the amount of the payments made or to be made in violation of the provisions of this title or the regulations of the office of children and family services promulgated hereunder; (d) whether the social services official has failed to determine an application under this title within thirty days; (e) whether the social services official has improperly denied an application to name a prospective successor guardian in the original kinship guardianship assistance agreement for payments pursuant to this title or any amendments thereto; (f) whether a social services official has inappropriately failed to approve a prospective successor guardian; or (g) whether a social services official has inappropriately terminated an agreement for payments under this title.

3. The provisions of subdivisions two and four of section twenty-two of this chapter shall apply to fair hearings held and appeals taken pursuant to this section.

Title 11
Education Reform Program
Section
458-*l*. Education reform program.

§458-*l*. Education reform program.
1. As used in this section:

(a) "eligible person" means an individual who (i) is, or is at the risk of being, the subject of a person in need of supervision petition in family court where elements of an eligible offense have been indicated; or (ii) has been arrested for or charged with an eligible offense, or it is otherwise alleged that such person has committed an eligible offense, as that term is defined in paragraph (b) of this subdivision. In determining whether to order an eligible person who has been arrested for or charged with an eligible offense as an adult to participate in the education reform program under this section, a judge must consider, among other factors, prior participation in the program as an adult.

(b) "eligible offense" means a crime or offense committed, or, in the case of a person who is, or is at risk of being the subject of a person in need of supervision petition, conduct engaged in, by an eligible person that involved cyberbullying or the sending or receipt through electronic means of obscenity, as defined in subdivision one of section 235.00 of the penal law, or nudity, as defined in subdivision two of section 235.20 of the penal law, when the sender and the receiver thereof were both under the age of twenty at the time of such communication, but not more than five years apart in age.

(c) "program" means the education reform program developed pursuant to subdivision two of this section.

2. The office of children and family services, hereinafter the "office," shall develop and implement, in consultation with the division of criminal justice services and the state education department, an education reform program to be provided to eligible persons as a diversion program in accordance with section seven hundred thirty-five of the family court act, as a condition of adjustment pursuant to section 308.1 of the family court act, or as a condition of an order of adjournment in contemplation of dismissal, suspended judgment, discharge with warning, conditional discharge or probation pursuant to article three or seven of the family court act, as a condition of probation or a conditional discharge pursuant to or section 60.37 of the penal law or as a condition of an adjournment in contemplation of dismissal pursuant to section 170.55 of the criminal procedure law, as applicable.

3. The program shall be available in every judicial department in the state; provided that if the office determines that there is not a sufficient number of eligible offenses in a judicial department to mandate the implementation of a program, provisions shall be made for the residents of such judicial department to participate in a program in another judicial department where a program exists if practicable with regard to travel and cost, or to complete the education course online.

4. Such program shall be provided in an age-appropriate manner which focuses on the crime, offense or conduct, shall involve up to eight hours of instruction and shall provide, at a minimum, information concerning:

(a) the legal consequences of and potential penalties for sharing sexually suggestive materials, explicit materials or abusive materials, including sanctions imposed under applicable federal and state statutes;

(b) the non-legal consequences of sharing sexually suggestive materials, explicit materials or abusive materials, including, but not limited to, the possible effect on relationships, loss of educational and employment opportunities, and the potential for being barred or removed from school programs and extracurricular activities;

(c) how the unique characteristics of cyberspace and the internet, including the potential ability of an infinite audience to utilize the internet to search for and replicate materials, can produce long-term and unforeseen consequences for sharing sexually suggestive materials, explicit materials or abusive materials; and

(d) the potential connection between bullying and cyber-bullying and juveniles sharing sexually suggestive materials, explicit materials or abusive materials.

5. The office, in conjunction with the office of court administration, the office of probation and correctional alternatives and the division of criminal justice services, shall provide annual notice regarding the program to local probation departments, applicable court personnel, county defender offices, organizations or groups assigned to act as attorneys for children, district attorneys, presentment agencies and county attorneys, for the purpose of such information being provided to each eligible person, his or her attorney and his or her parent or guardian where necessary, upon an order that they complete such program. The notice shall include, at a minimum, a short description of the program, when use of the program is authorized by statute, and the means of accessing and completing the program. The office shall maintain information on its website regarding the program, including directions for accessing the program.

6. Within twenty days of the date upon which the eligible person completes the program, the office shall provide such person with a certification that he or she has successfully completed the program and the date the program was completed. The eligible person shall be responsible for completing the program, and providing any necessary proof of completion.

NEW YORK CODE OF RULES & REGULATIONS

Selected Sections

Part IV

Looseleaf
Law Publications, Inc.

43-08 162nd Street
Flushing, NY 11358
www.LooseleafLaw.com   800-647-5547

TITLE 4
Department of Civil Service

Part 83
Confidentiality of HIV and
Aids Related Information

§83.1   Purpose.

It is the responsibility and the intent of the State Department of Civil Service to adopt regulations pursuant to the HIV and AIDS Related Information Act (Public Health Law, article 27-F). All officers, employees and agents of the department shall at all times maintain the confidentiality of any HIV related information in their possession, in accordance with the requirements of the statute and these regulations.

§83.2   Definitions.

For the purposes of this Part:

(a) The term department or Department of Civil Service means the New York State Department of Civil Service.

(b) The term AIDS means acquired immune deficiency syndrome, as may be defined from time to time by the centers for disease control of the United States Public Health Service.

(c) The term HIV infection means infection with the human immunodeficiency virus or any other related virus identified as a probable causative agent of AIDS.

(d) The term HIV related illness means any illness that may result from or may be associated with HIV infection.

(e) The term HIV related test means any laboratory test or series of tests for any virus, antibody, antigen or etiologic agent whatsoever thought to cause or to indicate the presence of HIV/AIDS.

(f) The term confidential HIV related information means any information concerning whether an individual has been the subject of an HIV related test, or has HIV infection, HIV related illness or AIDS, or information which identifies or reasonably could identify an individual as having one or more of such conditions, including information pertaining to such individual's contacts.

(g) The term contact means an identified spouse or sex partner of the protected individual or a person identified as having shared hypodermic needles or syringes with the protected individual.

(h) The term significant risk of transmitting or contracting HIV infection or significant risk includes the following circumstances:

(1) sexual contact which exposes a mucous membrane or broken skin of a noninfected individual to blood, semen or vaginal secretions of an infected individual;

(2) sharing of needles or other paraphernalia used for preparing and injecting drugs between infected and noninfected individuals;

(3) the gestation, birthing or breast feeding of an infant when the mother is infected with HIV;

(4) transfusion or transplantation of blood, organs, or other tissues obtained from an infected individual to an uninfected individual, provided that such products have not tested negatively for antibody or antigen and have not been rendered noninfective by heat or chemical treatment;

(5) other circumstances, not identified in paragraphs (1) through (4) of this subdivision, during which a significant risk body substance (other than breast milk) of an infected person contacts mucous membranes (e.g., eyes, nose, mouth) or nonintact skin (e.g., open wound, dermatitis, abraded areas) or the vascular system of a non-infected person;

(6) circumstances that constitute significant risk shall not include:

(i) exposure to urine, feces, sputum, nasal secretions, saliva, sweat, tears or vomitus that does not contain visible blood;

(ii) human bites where there is no direct blood to blood, or blood to mucous membrane contact;

(iii) exposure of intact skin to blood or any other body substance; and

(iv) occupational settings where individuals use scientifically accepted barrier techniques and preventing practices in circumstances which would otherwise pose a significant risk.

§83.3 Antidiscrimination.

(a) It is the policy of the department that the department and its officers, employees and agents shall not discriminate against any individual by virtue of his or her being identified as, or suspected of, having AIDS, HIV infection, or HIV related illness.

(b) The department will take appropriate steps to make its officers, employees and agents aware of the department's policy as set forth in this section. All officers, employees and agents of the department shall act in a manner consistent with this policy when performing their official duties for the department.

§83.4 Access to confidential HIV related information.

(a) Employees or agents of the department are not to have access to confidential HIV related information maintained by the department except as part of their official duties.

(b) Agents of the department may be authorized to have access to confidential HIV related information maintained by the department only when reasonably necessary to perform the specific activities for which they have been designated as agents of the department.

§83.5 Confidentiality.

(a) No person who obtains confidential HIV related information in the course of performing his or her duties as an employee or agent of the department may disclose such information except in accordance with the provisions of the HIV and AIDS Related Information Act (Public Health Law, article 27-F) and the provisions of this Part.

(b) Any disclosure, except disclosures to employees or agents of the department where reasonably necessary to carry out their official duties and to any person to whom disclosure is mandated by a court of competent jurisdiction, must be accompanied by the following written statement prohibiting further disclosure: "This information has been disclosed to you from confidential records which are protected by State law. State law prohibits you from making any further disclosure of this information without the specific written consent of the person to whom it pertains, or as otherwise permitted by law. Any unauthorized further disclosure in violation of State law may result in a fine or jail sentence or both. A general authorization for the release of medical or other information is not sufficient authorization to further disclosure."

(c) All disclosures, except disclosures to employees and agents as reasonably necessary to perform their official duties, are to be appropriately documented in the case folder of the protected individual, who shall be informed of such disclosures upon request.

(d) No flags on case folders, lists on walls, or other similar displays shall be used to indicate clients with HIV infection. This shall not be construed to prevent the existence of specialized caseloads.

(e) Confidential HIV related information shall not be disclosed in response to a request under the Freedom of Information Law (Public Officers Law, article 6) or in response to a subpoena. A court order issued pursuant to Public Health Law, section 2785 is required.

(f) The department will take appropriate steps to make all employees and agents aware of the provisions of the HIV and AIDS Related Information Act (PHL, article 27-F) concerning confidentiality of HIV related information and the department's rules regarding confidentiality of records. All authorized employees and agents of the department shall at all times maintain the confidentiality of any confidential HIV related information in their possession.

§83.6   Records control.

(a) The department will ensure the security of files which may contain confidential HIV related information. All officers, employees and agents of the department in possession of, or having access to, confidential HIV related information shall at all times maintain the security of all records that contain confidential HIV related information.

§83.7   Protection of others at significant risk of infection.

(a) The department shall implement and enforce a plan for the prevention of circumstances which could result in an employee or individual becoming exposed to blood or body fluids. Such a plan shall include:

(1) training for appropriate persons on the use of protective equipment, preventive practices, and circumstances that constitute significant risk exposure;

(2) appropriate training, counseling and supervision of persons regarding behaviors which pose a risk for HIV transmission at the work site. Contact notification, when appropriate, shall be conducted in accordance with Public Health Law, section 2782(4) and 10 NYCRR 63.7;

(3) use of accepted protective practices to prevent skin and mucous membrane exposure to blood, other body fluids, or other significant risk body substances, as defined in 10 NYCRR 63.9(b);

(4) the use of accepted preventive practices while handling instruments or equipment that may cause puncture injuries; and

(5) the provision, as appropriate, of personal protective equipment which is of appropriate quality and quantity.

(b) The department shall implement and enforce a plan for responding to incidents of exposure at the employee's work site to blood, other body fluids or other significant risk body substances. Such program shall include:

(1) a system for receiving voluntary reports of all exposures thought to represent a circumstance for significant risk;

(2) availability of services for evaluating the circumstances of such a reported exposure and providing appropriate follow-up of anyone who has been exposed, which includes:

(i) medical and epidemiological assessment of an employee or individual who is the source of the exposure, where that source is known, available and agrees to be tested;

(ii) if epidemiologically indicated, HIV counseling and testing of the source as permitted under article 27-F of the Public Health Law. Where the HIV status is not known to anyone who has been exposed, disclosure of the HIV status of a living person can be made only with the express written consent of the source or pursuant to court order; and

(iii) appropriate medical follow-up of employees and individuals who have been exposed; and

(3) assurances for protection of confidentiality for those involved in reported exposures.

§83.8　Severability.

If any provision of this Part or the application thereof to any person or circumstance is judged invalid by a court of competent jurisdiction, such judgment shall not affect or impair the validity of the other provisions of this Part or the application thereof to other persons and circumstances.

TITLE 9
Executive Department

Part 168
State Schools and Centers

§168.1　Discipline of children.

(a) Abuse of children in any form, including corporal punishment, is prohibited.

(b) Deprivation of meals, mail and family visits, as methods of punishment, is prohibited.

(c) A child may not be punished for failing or refusing to eat.

(d) Punishment, control and discipline of children shall be an adult responsibility and shall not be prescribed or administered by children.

(e) Every school and center shall submit its discipline policies and any amendments thereto in writing to the deputy director of rehabilitation services or his designee for approval prior to implementation.

(f) Notice in writing of any violations of subdivisions (a)-(d) of this section shall be immediately reported by the facility superintendent or director to the deputy director of rehabilitation services or his designee.

§168.2 Standards relating to the use of room confinement.

(a) Definition of room confinement. For the purpose of this Part, the term room confinement shall mean confinement of a child in a room, including the child's own room, when locked or when the child is authoritatively told not to leave.

(b) Room confinement shall not be used as punishment. It shall be used only in cases where a child constitutes a serious and evident danger to himself or others. It is not to be considered, in itself, as a method or technique of treatment.

(c) Place of confinement-environmental needs. Places of confinement within the institution shall be designated by the institution superintendent (or director) and approved by the deputy director of rehabilitation services or his designee. The place of confinement shall be lighted, heated and ventilated the same as other comparable living areas in the institution.

(d) Required furniture and furnishings within the place of confinement. The place of confinement shall be furnished with the items necessary for the health and comfort of the occupant, including, but not limited to, a bed, chair, desk or chest, mattress, pillow, sheet and blanket. If the possession of any of these items would be detrimental to the safety of the occupant or others, they may be removed during that period upon authorization by the superintendent (or director) or the acting superintendent (or director).

(e) Authorization of room confinement. Room confinement shall be authorized only by the superintendent (or director) or the acting superintendent (or director). Authorization should be obtained prior to actual placement in room confinement. In instances where immediate physical restraint is clearly necessary, authorization must be obtained within 15 minutes of lock-up.

(f) Maximum period of confinement. The maximum period of confinement shall not exceed 24 consecutive hours without the approval of the deputy director of rehabilitation services or designee within the bureau.

(g) Visitation. For the purpose of this Part, a visit shall mean actual entry into the room of confinement with the child or removal of the child from the room of confinement for the purpose of discussion or counseling. A visit shall not include routine visual checks or discussion through the door or window of the confinement room. Children in room confinement shall be visited at least once each day by the following institutional personnel:

(1) Administrative staff--a person at least at the level of senior youth, division counselor assistant director of cottage program or higher.

(2) Clinical staff--psychiatrist, psychologist, social worker.

(3) Medical staff--a nurse or physician shall examine the child in room confinement on a daily basis. A record of visits shall be maintained by the school (or center) on forms designated by the division and shall be posted on the door of the confinement room during the entire period of confinement.

(h) Reading materials. Educational and recreational reading materials shall be provided within the first 24 hours unless the superintendent (or director) or acting superintendent (or director) shall determine that such materials shall be detrimental to the child's rehabilitation. These materials shall be provided on a daily basis thereafter.

(i) Recreation and exercise. For the purpose of this Part, recreation and exercise shall be defined as an activity taking place outside the room of confinement and shall mean to include, sports, athletics, games, light physical exercise and like activities. It shall not include hard labor, unduly arduous exercise and other activities of a generally unpleasant or punishing nature. Recreation and exercise shall be provided on a daily basis for at least one prescribed period of not less than 30 minutes unless the superintendent (or director) or acting superintendent (or director) shall authorize its deletion upon determination that such a liberty would present a serious and evident danger to the child or others.

(j) Reports of room confinement. Schools and centers must report each instance of room confinement, lasting more than one hour, on forms designated by the division. Every instance where physical or medical restraints are used shall be reported on these forms, regardless of the length of time of the subsequent confinement. Reports are to be submitted on a weekly basis to the director of the bureau of children's institutional services. For the purpose of this Part, a week begins on a Monday and ends on a Sunday. Reports are to be submitted on or before Tuesday of the following week. A copy of each report shall be sent to the ombudsman assigned to that institution.

(k) Consecutive periods of room confinement.

(1) Any student who is returned to room confinement within six hours of his release shall be considered to have been in continuous room confinement for purposes of reporting and seeking central office approval; however, a notation as to unsuccessful efforts to return the student to program should be made so that an accurate description of the confinement is available.

(2) Return to room confinement after a lapse of six hours from the time of release shall be considered as commencing a new period of room confinement for the purpose of reporting and seeking central office approval.

(3) Manipulation of consecutive periods of room confinement to evade reporting and approval requirements, or to evade the spirit of the division's regulations, is prohibited.

(*l*) Review and request for extension of room confinement. A review of the necessity for continued room confinement shall be made prior to the beginning of each new 24 hour period by the superintendent (or director) or acting superintendent (or director). Room confinement may be extended beyond the 24 hours only with the approval of the deputy director of rehabilitation services or designee. Approval shall be obtained prior to the beginning of each 24 hour period. Initially, such requests may be made orally (by telephone). The request must then be submitted in writing on forms designated by the division. This written request must be forwarded to the deputy director of rehabilitation services or his designee within 24 hours of the oral request.

(m) Every effort shall be made to return the child to the regular program of care as quickly as possible.

§168.3 Use of physical and medical restraints.

(a) Physical restraints. Permissible physical restraints, consisting solely of handcuffs and footcuffs, shall be used only in cases where a child is uncontrollable and constitutes a serious and evident danger to himself or others. They shall be removed as soon as the child is controllable. Use of physical restraints shall be prohibited beyond one-half hour unless a child is being transported by vehicle and physical restraint is necessary for public safety. If restraints are placed on a child's hands and feet, the hand and foot restraints are not to be joined, as for example, in hog tying. When in restraints, a child may not be attached to any furniture or fixture in a room nor to any object in a vehicle.

(1) The division shall prohibit the utilization of foot manacles.

(2) Physical restraints may be utilized beyond one-half hour only in the case of vehicular transportation where such utilization of physical restraints is necessary for public safety.

(b) Medical restraint. For the purposes of this Part, medical restraint shall mean medication administered either by injection or orally for the purposes of quieting an uncontrollable child.

(1) Medical restraint shall be administered only in situations where a child is so uncontrollable that no other means of restraint can prevent the child from harming himself.

(2) Medical restraint shall be authorized only by a physician and be administered only by a registered nurse or a medical doctor.

(c) Prn orders of psychiatric medication. A pro re nata order, authorizing a registered nurse to administer prescribed psychiatric medication, for purposes of crisis intervention, may be used by the Division for Youth pursuant to the following guidelines:

(1) Prescription by medical doctor. Before any Prn order may be prescribed, a medical doctor must examine the child and determine the need for such an order in terms of the individual child's ongoing treatment needs at the facility. These Prn orders shall be prescribed on an individual basis and shall not be prescribed pro forma to all children at the time of their arrival at a facility, as follows:

(i) The medical doctor must sign the order and the medical doctor must provide specific instructions and guidelines for the nurse.

(ii) Periodic review of all Prn orders must be made by a medical doctor, monthly, including physically examining the child.

(iii) At the time of the periodic review, the medical doctor must indicate, in writing, reasons for his continuing the Prn order.

(2) Administration by registered nurse. A registered nurse may administer a Prn order when the actions of the child clearly present a danger to himself or other residents, as follows:

(i) She must physically examine the child and refer to the child's medical record including the specific instructions left by the medical doctor for utilization of the Prn order.

(ii) The pulse and blood pressure of children receiving such medication must be taken during the first half hour by the nurse and periodically thereafter until his release.

(iii) The nurse must keep a record indicating the results of those examinations and shall prepare a medication report indicating reasons giving rise to her dispensing the medication.

(iv) If the initial or subsequent examination by the nurse reveals the development of any symptoms indicating an adverse reaction to the medication, she shall immediately notify the medical doctor.

(d) Reporting requirements. Use of physical and medical restraints shall be reported, pursuant to subdivision (j) of section 168.2 of this Part.

§168.4 Group confinement.

(a) Group confinement shall be construed to include situations where a child is separated from the general population and normal daily program by confinement in a locked cottage or living unit.

(b) Group confinement shall not be used as punishment. It shall be used only in cases where a child constitutes a serious and evident danger to himself or others, is himself in serious and evident danger, or demonstrates by his own behavior or by his own expressed desire, that he is in need of special care and attention in a living unit separate from his normal surroundings.

(c) Each institution wishing to institute a group confinement program must submit a detailed description of the program, including regulations governing its administration to the deputy director of rehabilitation services for approval.

(d) Each institution administering an approved group confinement program shall maintain a daily log indicating the number of children in group confinement and their period of stay in the program. This information shall be forwarded to the director or his designee monthly.

(e) The ombudsman for each institution administering an approved group confinement program shall have access to the daily log and the confinement area. It shall be his responsibility to report any deviation from the approved program to the institution's superintendent or director and, in an appropriate case, he may include documented deviations in his ombudsman's reports.

(f) Where institutions instituted group confinement programs prior to the adoption of this section, they shall submit detailed written program description and regulations to the deputy director of rehabilitation services within 30 days from receipt of notice of adoption of this section. Any institution failing to have an approved program within 60 days of the adoption of this Part, shall terminate the use of group confinement.

(g) Program description, regulations and amendments governing each approved group confinement program shall be kept on file at the institution and in the Albany central office.

(h) Changes in group confinement programs and regulations shall be approved in the same manner as the initial program was approved.

§168.5 Powers and duties of the boards of visitors.

(a) Members of the boards of visitors shall be selected from a cross-section of lay people in the community, including but not limited to individuals in the fields of law, judiciary, education, sociology, psychology and other related fields who shall serve in an advisory capacity to the superintendent of the institution to which they are appointed. The boards may report to the Governor, directly, when they deem it appropriate in the performance of their duties. Members of the boards of visitors, because of their deep concern for the welfare of the youths in care within their respective institutions, are in a position to offer pertinent and valuable assistance, comments and advice to the superintendent and to the director of the Division for Youth, in order to improve the facility's treatment and training program.

(b) The boards of visitors shall hold at least six meetings per annum with the superintendent and cause a copy of the minutes and proceedings thereof to be sent forthwith to each member of the boards of visitors, to the superintendent of the institution and to the director of the Division for Youth.

(c) The boards of visitors, subject to the approval of the superintendent, have the authority to seek ways of establishing cooperation, understanding and mutual respect between the institution and the local community.

(d) The boards of visitors shall submit, by the 31st day of July each year, a detailed annual report of their visits and meetings and suggestions to the superintendent of the institution for the year ending on the 30th day of June preceding the day of such report, and such report shall be forwarded by the superintendent of the institution, together with the superintendent's response and commentary, to the director of the Division for Youth by the 31st day of August of each year.

(e) The boards of visitors, subject to the approval of the superintendent, have the authority to act as liaison with services within the institution, such as recreational, educational, cultural and therapeutic services which have not been provided in the regular institutional program.

(f) The boards of visitors, subject to the approval of the superintendent, have the authority to aid their respective institutions in the establishment of programs within the local community which will assist youths residing in the institution to secure local employment, educational, recreational, cultural and therapeutic services.

(g) Members of the boards of visitors shall have access to residents and shall have the right to inspect all physical areas, facilities and programs conducted under the auspices of their respective institutions. They may request of the superintendent the appearance of any staff member to attend regular meetings in order to remain fully briefed and knowledgeable as to institutional operations.

(h) The boards of visitors, as agents of the division, and with its approval, may receive and accept any grant, gift, devise or bequest of money or land to it, the State, board, division or institution, subject to the provisions of the State Finance Law. Any such acquisitions, including income therefrom, shall be applied or expended subject to the regulations of the division.

(i) Members of the boards of visitors, shall not receive any compensation for their services, but shall receive actual and necessary traveling and other expenses, to be paid after audit as other current expenditures of the institutions.

§168.6 Reporting to counsel's office.

(a) All incidents which could give rise to claims against the State shall be reported in writing to the deputy director of rehabilitation services and to the office of general counsel within 48 hours. Incidents to be reported shall include, but not be limited to, the following: damage to property by students, death of any student in program, commission of criminal acts by staff or students, use of physical force by staff, and injury of staff in line of duty.

(b) General counsel shall review the incident reports and supporting material to determine those incidents which have a substantial likelihood of giving rise to a claim or proceeding against the State. He shall then give notice of these claims to the Attorney General as required pursuant to section 72 of the Public Officers Law.

§168.7 Confidentiality of Division for Youth records.

(a) Records or files of children who are or have been under the care or supervision of the Division for Youth may not be disclosed in whole or part to any person, agency or institution, other than the Division for Youth and New York State family courts, with the following exceptions:

(1) Records or pertinent parts thereof must be disclosed pursuant to Supreme Court order as authorized by Social Services Law article 6, section 372.

(2) Educational records may be disclosed to the extent that, when a child is attending or has attended a school located on the premises of a Division for Youth facility:

(i) all school records may be visually displayed to a child's parent, in person only;

(ii) the child's name, date of birth, a list of subjects studied, grades received, credits earned through academic/vocational courses, work experience or cooperative educational experience, record of attendance, last grade level achieved, previous school attended, standardized test scores, academic/vocational assessment results, Regents examination and Regents competency test results, general educational development test results, recommended educational program and grade placement, whether a committee on the handicapped has determined that the child has a handicapping condition, and immunization records only may be forwarded to the principal or guidance counselor of a school to which a child may be sent or desires to attend.

(3) Medical records may be disclosed to a physician at the written request of the physician and with the written approval of the child's parent or guardian; however, if the child is over the age of 18 years at the time of the request, only his or her approval shall be necessary, in addition to the physician's request.

(4) Records, or summaries of records, may be disclosed to the probation department of a Family Court of the State of New York, on request for use in accord with The Family Court Act, article 1, section 166, and article 7, sections 746(b), 783.

(5) The division is prohibited from making records available to a county probation department, pursuant to section 372.3 of the Social Services Law.

(6) Information concerning a child's date of admission, release, revocation of release, and discharge only may be forwarded to the director of a New York social welfare district or State or Federal agency on request, when such information is necessary to enable said district or agency to determine that the child is under its jurisdiction, thereby enabling it to provide for a child's welfare and the necessities of life.

(7) Records pertaining to the vital statistics of children may be disclosed to law enforcement authorities when a child is absent from an institution without proper authorization or has violated a condition of release.

(8) Records may be made available to authorized child caring agencies, within and without the State, which have actual custody of the youth and request specific information in writing for the purpose of developing a program to meet his needs. However, when the request is made by an out-of-state child caring agency, the division shall request written confirmation, from the juvenile compact administrator for the state in which the requesting agency is located, that the agency is authorized to provide child care within that state and is in good standing. No record shall be made available until such information is received by the division in writing.

(9) Division records shall be made available to the Attorney General or his designee in furtherance of the duties of that office.

(10) Records pertaining to youths referred to the division as a condition of probation or pursuant to a continuance authorized by section 502 of the Executive Law shall be made available to the referring court or its probation department upon written request during the period of referral.

(b) When requests for records or other information concerning a child is received by any agent of the Division for Youth, and when such information is not included in the exceptions listed in paragraphs (1) through (10) of subdivision (a) of this section, the correct response shall be: "We are not authorized by law to disclose whether or not any individual was ever under our jurisdiction."

(c) No part of this section shall be construed to prohibit the free exchange of information within the Division for Youth, or between the division and New York family courts, when the best interest and treatment of the child is at issue, nor shall it serve to prohibit a bona fide study of information, with the approval of the executive deputy director and the deputy director for research of the Division for Youth and when guided by the superintendent or director of the institution, agency or facility at which the study is being conducted, with the stipulation that the name of no child shall be disclosed by the study group. In addition all such study groups shall sign an agreement to this effect before approval for such study shall be granted.

(d) When any child who has been under the care of the Division for Youth, according to title II, article 19-G of the Executive Law, reaches the age of 20 years, and a child cared for by the Division for Youth, according to title III, article 19-G of the Executive Law, reaches the age of 21, all records possessed by said division shall be sealed and shall only be revealed by the division, pursuant to an order by the Supreme Court of the State of New York, except such records may be made available to the Attorney General of the State of New York in furtherance of the duties of that office.

§168.8 Group punishment.

Children in residential care at division facilities shall not be disciplined, sanctioned, deprived of any right or privilege or otherwise punished solely on account of the behavior or acts of other children at the facility.

Part 169
Release and Return

§169.1 Revocation of release, grounds.

Release pursuant to section 523 of the Executive Law may be revoked by the division upon a violation of aone* or more of the following conditions of release including, but not limited to:

(a) adhere to a reasonable curfew set by the youth service team worker;

(b) not associate with persons whose influence would have a detrimental effect, including but not limited to persons previously convicted of crime or having a known criminal background;

(c) attend school in accordance with the provisions of part I of article 65 of the Education Law and/or cooperate with the assigned youth service team worker in seeking to obtain and in accepting employment and employment counseling services;

*So in original. "aone" sb "one"

(d) abstain from the use of alcoholic beverages, hallucinogenic drugs, habit forming drugs not lawfully prescribed, or any other harmful or dangerous substance;

(e) report to the youth service team worker as directed;

(f) not commit an act which would be a crime if committed by an adult;

(g) not operate a motor vehicle without a license;

(h) obey all reasonable commands of parents or other persons legally responsible for care and treatment;

(i) not run away from the lawful custody of parents or other lawful authorities; and

(j) any other reasonable condition of which the releasee is informed.

§169.2 Notice of grounds for revocation of release.

Each child released from a school or center of the division, pursuant to section 523 of the Executive Law, shall receive, prior to his release, an orientation session at which he shall be informed orally and receive in writing the terms of his release, including notification of the grounds upon which release may be revoked. A copy of the terms of release shall be mailed to the releasee's parent or guardian at the time of release.

§169.3 Initiation of release revocation proceeding.

(a) The youth worker who has reasonable knowledge of the child's behavior shall prepare a report documenting reasons why return to a school or center is the best interest of the child and/or the community, including specific violations of prescribed conditions of release.

(b) Said report, if endorsed by the immediate supervisor of the youth worker shall be submitted to the director of the community services bureau.

(c) The director of community services bureau or his designee shall review the report and make a determination which may be:

(1) continuation of the child's present release program;

(2) modification of the child's release program;

(3) referral to either Family Court or a court of other jurisdiction for other disposition where it is the opinion of the director of Children's Services Bureau that a new placement is required;

(4) return to a State training school is in the best interest of the child and/or the community.

§169.4 Notice of hearing, statement of allegations and return to custody.

When the director of community services bureau determines that it is in the best interest of the child and/or the community that the child should be returned to the division's facility program for further treatment, the following procedure should be followed:

(a) Documentation of the grounds upon which the recommendation that release be revoked shall be forwarded to the office of the counsel of the division with a request that a revocation hearing be held.

(b) Counsel's office shall prepare a notice of hearing which shall include a statement describing the allegations upon which the hearing will be based and a warrant for apprehension of the released child to be used at the discretion of the director of community services.

(c) The notice of hearing shall state in writing the rights of the releasee to a hearing, including the right of each party to be represented, to testify, to produce witnesses, to present documentary evidence, to examine opposing witnesses to the extent necessary to assure that the hearing officer is accurately informed of the facts and to examine evidence.

(d) The notice of hearing shall be forwarded to the director of community services who shall arrange for an employee, designated by the division, to apprehend the releasee named in the notice of hearing and have said releasee returned to the custody of the division. However, where it is the opinion of the director of community services that there are reasonable grounds to believe the child would appear at the time and place of hearing without being taken into custody, the child shall be left in the community.

(e) Copies of the notice of hearing shall be served by mail upon releasee, parents of the releasee, the releasee's legal counsel as soon as he is identified, and the hearing officer who shall conduct the revocation hearing.

§169.5 Rights of parties.

(a) The revocation hearing shall be held within 20 days from the date that the releasee is taken into custody and within 20 days of mailing the notice of hearing to the releasee where the releasee is not taken into custody, subject to the authority of the hearing officer to grant reasonable adjournments.

(b) The hearing shall be presided over by a hearing officer who shall be an attorney employed by the division exclusively to conduct hearings for the division.

(c) The releasee shall have the right to legal counsel at the hearing.

(d) The office of counsel of the Division for Youth shall act as agency representative at the hearing.

(e) Notification of hearing date. At least five days prior to the date of hearing, notice shall be given to the parties and representatives by the hearing officer, including: the releasee, the releasee's attorney, and the parents of the releasee. The notice to the parties shall inform them:

(1) of the date and place of hearing

(2) of the name and address of the hearing officer who will conduct the hearing

(f) Opportunity shall be afforded the releasee or his attorney, upon request, to examine copies of documentary evidence in the possession of the division which the division plans to introduce at the hearing.

(g) The following persons may be present at the hearing: the releasee, his parents or lawful guardian, his legal counsel, counsel for the division, witnesses of both parties and any who may be called by the hearing officers, representatives of the division and other persons may be admitted by the hearing officer in his discretion.

§169.6 Conduct of hearing.

(a) The hearing officer shall preside. He shall make an opening statement describing the nature of the proceeding, the issues and the manner in which the hearing will be conducted.

(b) The hearing officer shall have all the powers conferred by law and regulations of the division to acquire attendance of witnesses and the production of books and records and to administer oaths and to take testimony.

(c) The hearing officers shall conduct an impartial hearing.

(d) Technical rules and evidence followed in a court of law shall not apply, but evidence must be relevant and material.

(e) Each party has a right to be represented by counsel, or other representative, to testify, to produce witnesses to testify, to offer documentary evidence, to examine opposing witnesses to the extent necessary to assure that the hearing officer is accurately informed of the fact, to offer evidence in rebuttal and to examine any documentary evidence offered by the other party.

(f) The hearing officer may, in his discretion, order the removal of any person present at a hearing when the presence of that person interferes with the orderly conduct of the hearing.

(g) The hearing may be adjourned by the hearing officer for good cause on his own motion or at the request of either party.

(h) A verbatim record of the hearings shall be made.

§169.7 Examination of record after hearing.

The record of the hearing shall be confidential, but it may be examined by either party, including the releasee, his parent or his designated legal representative.

§169.8 The decision.

(a) The hearing officers shall issue a decision determining whether the releasee has knowingly violated any of the conditions of his release as alleged. The hearing officer's decision shall be based upon substantial evidence presented at the hearing. Where substantial evidence is found to exist, the hearing officer shall order revocation of release. Where the hearing officer finds that there is no substantial evidence upon which the allegation is based, the hearing officer shall order the return of the releasee to the community under continued aftercare supervision.

(b) The hearing officer, on motion of the releasee or his representative, or on his own motion, may order a releasee returned to the community under continued aftercare supervision at the time of the hearing where there is no evidence to support the allegations presented at the hearing.

(c) In all cases, a written decision shall be served upon the parties to the proceedings within four days following the hearing.

(d) Notice of revocation of release shall also be sent to the Family Court which placed the releasee.

§169.9 Judicial review.

In the letter transmitting the decision, the hearing officer shall make clear references to the availability of judicial review, pursuant to article 78 of the Civil Practice Law and Rules.

§169.10 Voluntary return.

A child on release status may volunteer to return to the custody of the division for youth without a revocation hearing. In such cases, release shall be revoked without a hearing, provided that a waiver of hearing is signed by the youth while represented by an attorney, who shall determine that the youth is aware of the significance of his act.

Part 180
Juvenile Detention Facilities Regulations

§180.1 Introduction.

The regulations in this Part are established pursuant to section 510-a of article 19-G of the Executive Law, section 462 of the Social Services Law and section 712 of the Family Court Act. They shall be known as the juvenile detention facilities regulations. The purpose of these regulations is to provide uniform standards and procedures for the establishment and operation of secure and nonsecure juvenile detention facilities in the State of New York.

§180.2 Application.

These regulations shall apply to all juvenile detention facilities as defined in Social Services Law, section 371; the Family Court Act, section 712; Executive Law, article 19-G, section 510-a; and established and operated pursuant to County Law, section 218-a. Nothing contained herein shall be construed as grounds for contravening court order or statute.

§180.3 Definitions.

(a) Detention, as defined in these regulations, shall mean the temporary care and maintenance, away from their homes, of children held pursuant to article 3 or 7 of the Family Court Act, or held pending a hearing for alleged violation of the conditions of release from a school, center or youth center of the division, or held pending return to a jurisdiction other than the one in which the child is held, or held pending return from AWOL, or held pursuant to a securing order of a criminal court if the person named therein as principal is under 16 or held pending transfer pursuant to sentence.

(b) Juvenile detention facility shall mean a facility, certified by the division, for the care of children detained in accordance with provisions of the Family Court Act, regulations of the division, and the Criminal Procedure Law.

(1) No juvenile detention facility shall be located in a building which is also used as an adult detention or jail facility.

(2) If a juvenile detention facility is located on premises adjacent to an adult detention or jail facility, there must be total sight and sound separation between the facilities.

(3) A juvenile detention facility shall not share program space with any other type of program or facility without the prior written consent of the division.

(c) Secure detention facility shall mean a juvenile detention facility characterized by physically restricting construction, hardware and procedures.

(d) Nonsecure detention facility shall mean a juvenile detention facility characterized by the absence of physically restricting construction, hardware and procedures. Nonsecure detention facilities may be family boarding homes, agency-operated boarding homes, group care or institutional facilities and nonresidential programs and services as defined herein.

(1) Nonsecure detention family boarding care facility shall mean a family boarding home, certified by the division, to provide care for one to six children, and operated in accordance with this Part.

(2) Nonsecure detention agency-operated boarding care facility shall mean a family-type home, certified by the division, to provide care for one through six children, and operated in accordance with this Part.

(3) Nonsecure detention group care facility shall mean a facility, certified by the division, to provide detention care for 7 through 12 children, and operated in accordance with this Part.

(4) Nonsecure detention institutional facility shall mean a facility, certified by the division, to provide care for 13 or more children, operated in accordance with this Part.

(e) Holdover facility shall mean a juvenile detention facility with physically restricting features within which care may be provided for not more than 48 hours.

(f) Capacity shall mean the maximum number of children for whom care may be provided in any one facility. Any change of capacity must have the prior written approval of the division.

(g) Temporary care shall mean a period of not more than 45 days.

(h) "Division" shall mean the New York State Office of Children and Family Services, which has succeeded the New York State Division for Youth.

(i) "Board" shall mean the New York State Office of Children and Family Services, which has succeeded the New York State Board of Social Welfare.

(j) "Department" shall mean the New York State Office of Children and Family Services, which has succeeded the New York State Department of Social Services.

(k) Administrative agency shall mean the agency of county government responsible for the administration of the county detention program.

(*l*) Operating agency shall mean the authorized agency selected by the administrative agency to operate detention programs in a county.

(m) "Office" shall mean the New York State Office of Children and Family Services.

§180.4 Certification.

(a) No juvenile detention facility subject to inspection and supervision by the Division for Youth shall be operated unless it shall possess a valid operating certificate issued by the division pursuant to section 510-a(6) of the Executive Law and regulations of the division.

(b) (1) Application for an operating certificate pursuant to these regulations shall be made upon forms prescribed by the division. An application for an operating certificate shall contain:

(i) the name of the facility and its location;

(ii) the name and address of the authorized agency, corporation, association, organization, proprietary operator or public agency, who or which operates such facility;

(iii) the type of facility;

(iv) the kind or kinds of care and services to be provided;

(v) a physical description of the facility, including land, buildings and equipment;

(vi) resident capacity;

(vii) a plan and description of staff positions, including duties and qualifications;

(viii) if applicant is a corporation, the names, addresses and occupations of the members of the board of directors;

(ix) the ownership or control of the land and premises, if other than the operator;

(x) the financial resources and sources of future revenue of the facility; and

(xi) such other information as may be required.

(2) Approval of application. The application shall be approved and an operating certificate shall be issued when it is established that the facility meets, and will be operated in accordance with, the requirements of this Part.

(c) Certification shall be granted in writing for a period of not more than two years and may be suspended or revoked by the division when there is noncompliance with any of these regulations, except that the division may waive any regulation where there is substantial compliance and a determination is made that the well-being of the youth in care is not endangered.

(d) Renewals. At least 60 days prior to the termination of the period of validity of an operating certificate, the facility shall refile an application for the renewed issuance of such operating certificate.

§180.5 Administration and operation of detention.

(a) Administrations of detention. (1) Each county, and the City of New York, shall designate the agency responsible for administering detention on behalf of that jurisdiction, and shall so advise the New York State Division for Youth of such designation.

(2) Governmental agencies appointed as in subdivision (a) of this section may establish and operate detention facilities, pursuant to applicable statutes and regulations, and upon certification by the division.

(3) Agencies responsible for administering detention may contract with public or nonprofit child caring agencies to operate detention facilities, pursuant to applicable statutes and regulations, and upon certification by the division.

(i) Nonpublic agencies shall assure that their corporate purposes authorize operation of detention for PINS and JD's. Organizations seeking to incorporate for the purpose of operating detention facilities must comply with section 460-a of the Social Services Law.

(ii) Written contracts or agreements shall be required between agencies administering detention and persons or agencies operating detention facilities.

(iii) Contracts between agencies administering detention and persons or agencies operating detention facilities, shall be approved by the division for both programmatic and fiscal provisions.

(iv) Each county, and the City of New York, should take reasonable steps to provide conveniently accessible and adequate nonsecure detention care. Where a county does not have conveniently accessible and adequate nonsecure detention care in conformance with the requirements of section 218-a of the County Law, or where the City of New York does not have such nonsecure detention care, a formalized arrangement may be made with another county. The fiscal and programmatic provisions of this arrangement must be approved by the division.

(4) Agencies responsible for administering detention shall assure the availability of conveniently accessible adequate detention care for each day of the year. The administrative agency shall provide for adequate available detention care during periods of vacation, sickness or other emergencies, upon approval by the division.

(5) Where a county provides regional detention care, it shall be authorized to designate a maximum number of beds that shall be available to a county.

(6) Staff and volunteers of detention providers shall not engage in or condone discrimination or harassment of youth on the basis of race, creed, color, national origin, age, sex, sexual orientation, gender identity or expression, marital status, religion, or disability. Detention providers shall promote and maintain a safe environment, take reasonable steps to prevent discrimination and harassment against youth by other youth, promptly investigate incidents of discrimination and harassment by staff, volunteers and youth, and take reasonable and appropriate corrective or disciplinary action when such incidents occur. For the purposes of this section, "gender identity or expression" shall mean having or being perceived as having a gender identity, self-image, appearance, behavior or expression whether or not that gender, identity, self-image, appearance, behavior or expression is different from that traditionally associated with the sex assigned to that person at birth. "Gender identity" refers to a person's internal sense of self as male, female, no gender, or another gender, and "gender expression" refers to the manner in which a person expresses his or her gender through clothing, appearance, behavior, speech, or other like.

(b) Prevention and remediation of child abuse. (1) Each detention facility shall establish, subject to and consistent with any applicable collective bargaining agreement(s) and provisions of the Civil Service Law, a written procedure to review, evaluate and verify the backgrounds of and information supplied by all applicants for employment or voluntary work. This procedure shall include provisions for receiving, at a minimum, the following information from each applicant:

(i) a statement or summary of the applicant's employment history, including but not limited to any relevant child-caring experience;

(ii) the names, addresses, and where available, telephone numbers of references who can verify the applicant's employment history, work record and qualifications;

(iii) a statement or summary of the applicant's or volunteer's educational experience showing elementary school(s), if the applicant or volunteer does not have a secondary school diploma or high school equivalency diploma, secondary school(s) or college(s) attended, highest grade level or degree attained, and any additional credits earned;

(iv) the names and addresses of educational institutions that can verify the applicant's or volunteer's educational information;

(v) a listing of special skills or completed training courses which might aid in the performance of duties of the position for which he or she is applying;

(vi) the names, addresses and telephone numbers of at least two personal references, other than relatives, who can attest to the applicant's character, reputation and personal qualifications; and

(vii) a sworn statement by the applicant, indicating whether, to the best of his or her knowledge, he or she has ever been convicted of a crime in New York State or any jurisdiction and that all statements in the application are true, to the best of his or her knowledge.

(2) Each detention facility shall develop a plan for adequate supervision of staff and volunteers, taking into consideration the population served and the type, size and physical layout of the facility, to assure appropriate care of youth and the prevention of child abuse and maltreatment. The plan shall be submitted to the division for review and approval. The plan shall include, but not be limited to, the following:

(i) staffing patterns and the rationale for such patterns;

(ii) identification of all supervisors of staff and volunteers, including the designation of onsite supervisors;

(iii) a list of the qualifications and responsibilities of the supervisors;

(iv) procedures for periodic observations by supervisors of staff and volunteer interactions with youth in program;

(v) procedures for periodic supervisory conferences for staff and volunteers;

(vi) procedures, consistent with any applicable collective bargaining agreement(s) and provisions of the Civil Service Law, for periodic written performance evaluations of staff conducted by supervisors; and

(vii) methods for distributing written supervisory procedures to employees and volunteers.

(3) Each detention facility shall develop written procedures, available onsite, for the protection of program participants when there is reason to believe an incident has occurred which would render a program participant abused or neglected as defined in section 488 of the Social Services Law. Such procedures shall include, but not be limited to, the following:

(i) Notifications. Immediate notification of suspected incidents of abuse or neglect shall be made to:

(a) the Vulnerable Persons' Central Register;

(b) local law enforcement officials, if it appears likely that a crime has been committed against a child, or confirm that such notification has already been made; and

(c) the office and the facility's administrative agency.

(ii) Investigation procedures. Immediately upon notification that a report of abuse or neglect has been made to the Vulnerable Persons' Central Register and/or local law enforcement officials, the director of the facility or his or her designee shall:

(a) preserve any relevant audio and/or visual recording;

(b) preserve any other potential evidence;

(c) obtain proper medical evaluation and/or treatment for the program participants, as needed, with documentation of any evidence of abuse or neglect; and

(d) provide necessary assistance to the Justice Center for the Protection of People with Special Needs, office and, if applicable, local law enforcement officials in their investigation thereof.

(iii) Safety procedures. Upon notification that a report of abuse or neglect has been made to the Vulnerable Persons' Central Register and/or local law enforcement officials with respect to a program participant in the detention facility, the director or his or her designee shall evaluate the situation and immediately take appropriate action to protect the health and safety of the program participant involved in the report and of any other program participants similarly situated in the facility. Additional action shall be taken whenever necessary to prevent future incidents of abuse or neglect . Any action taken should cause as little disruption as possible to the daily routines of the program participants. The following alternatives shall be considered in determining the course of action that will be taken with regard to a specific incident of alleged abuse or neglect:

(a) removal or transfer of the subject of the report, consistent with appropriate collective bargaining agreement(s) and applicable provisions of the Civil Service Law;

(b) initiation of disciplinary action against the subject of the report, consistent with appropriate collective bargaining agreement(s) and provisions of the Civil Service Law;

(c) increasing the degree of supervision of the subject of the report;

(d) provision of counseling to the subject of the report;

(e) provision of increased training to staff and volunteers pertinent to the prevention and remediation of abuse and maltreatment;

(f) removal or transfer of the program participant consistent with applicable placement procedures if it is determined that there is a risk to such program participant in remaining in that facility. The office shall be notified of any such removal or transfer; and

(g) provision of counseling to the program participant involved in the report and any other program participant, as appropriate.

(iv) Corrective action plans. Upon receipt from the Justice Center for the Protection of Persons with Special Needs (Justice Center) or the office of a substantiated report of abuse or neglect or an unsubstantiated report of abuse or neglect where the Justice Center or the office has determined that there has been a violation of the statutory, regulatory or other requirements related to the care and treatment of individuals receiving services, the director of the facility, with consideration of any appropriate recommendations received from the Justice Center or the office for preventative and remedial action, including legal action, shall:

(a) within 10 calendar days of receipt of a substantiated report of abuse or neglect, develop and implement a written plan of action to be taken with respect to an individual employee or volunteer to protect the continued health and safety of the program participant and to provide for the prevention of future acts of abuse or neglect, which plan shall include, at a minimum, those actions taken pursuant to subparagraph (iii) of this paragraph. Such plan will also describe the actions taken to address the investigation's findings. The plan shall be submitted to and approved by the office; and

(b) in the event an investigation of such a report indicates that such abuse or neglect may be attributed in whole or in part to noncompliance by the facility with provisions of article 7, article 11, or title 6 of article 6 of the Social Services Law, article 19-G of the Executive Law or the regulations of the office, develop and implement a plan of prevention and remediation which, at a minimum, shall address each area of noncompliance and indicate how the facility will come into compliance with article 7, article 11, or title 6 of article

6 of the Social Services Law, article 19-G of the Executive Law and the applicable regulations. Such plan will also describe the actions taken to address the office's findings. Such plan shall be submitted to and approved by the office and, upon approval, implemented.

(4) Training. (i) Staff training. Subject to the amounts appropriated therefor, abuse and neglect prevention training shall be provided to all administrators, employees and volunteers of the facility on a regular basis, but at least annually. Priority shall be given to the training of administrators, employees, consultants, and volunteers who have the potential for regular and substantial contact with the program participant in residential care.

(a) The purpose of such training shall be to increase participant's level of awareness, encourage positive attitudes and enhance knowledge and skill development in at least the following areas:

(1) abuse, neglect and significant incident prevention and identification.

(2) safety and security procedures;

(3) principles of child development;

(4) characteristics of youth in care;

(5) techniques of group and child management, including crisis intervention;

(6) laws, regulations and procedures governing the protection of children from abuse, neglect, and significant incidents, including reporting responsibilities; and

(7) relevant information which shall be provided on a regular basis by the division.

(b) Administrators may be exempted by the Office from such training requirements upon demonstration of substantially equivalent knowledge or experience.

(ii) Instruction of program participants. Subject to the amounts appropriated therefor, instruction shall be provided to all program participants in techniques and procedures which will enable such program participants to protect themselves from abuse and neglect.

(a) Such instruction shall be:

(1) appropriate for the age, individual needs and particular circumstances of the program participants, including the existence of mental, physical, emotional or sensory disabilities, as well as the needs and circumstances within the residential facility;

(2) provided at the time of admission in a manner which will ensure that all program participants receive such instruction; and

(3) provided by individuals who possess appropriate knowledge and training, documentation of which must be retained by the facility.

(c) (1) AIDS testing and confidentiality of HIV-related information. Requirements regarding testing, confidentiality and precautions concerning the human immunodeficiency virus (HIV) and acquired immune deficiency syndrome (AIDS).

(i) Background and intent.

(a) The purpose of this section is to establish standards for the proper disclosure of HIV-related information within detention facilities certified or operated by the Division for Youth, including family boarding homes.

(b) The purpose of this section is to establish standards which limit the risk of discrimination and harm to a child's privacy which unauthorized disclosure of HIV information can cause.

(c) The purpose of this section is to establish standards which seek to enhance the safety of employees and children at detention facilities or detention programs certified or operated by the Division for Youth.

(ii) Legal basis.

(a) Sections 500 and 510-a of the Executive Law grant the director of the Division for Youth (director) the power and responsibility to adopt regulations that are necessary and proper to implement matters under his or her jurisdiction, and to set standards of quality and adequacy of facilities, equipment, personnel, services, records and programs for the rendition of services for youth.

(b) Section 2786 of the Public Health Law requires the director to promulgate regulations which provide safeguards against discrimination, abuse and other adverse actions directed toward protected individuals; provide for the proper disclosure of HIV-related information; protect individuals in contact with protected individuals when such contact creates a significant risk of contracting or transmitting HIV infection and establish criteria for determining when it is reasonably necessary for a provider of a health or social service or a State agency or a local government agency to have or use confidential HIV-related information for supervision, monitoring, investigation or administration.

(iii) Applicability. This section applies to any Division for Youth operated or certified detention facility, including family boarding homes.

(iv) Definitions pertaining to this section.

(a) HIV infection means infection with the human immuno-deficiency virus or any other related virus identified as a probable causative agent of AIDS.

(b) HIV-related illness means any illness that may result from or be associated with HIV infection.

(c) HIV-related test means any laboratory test or series of tests for any virus, antibody, antigen or etiologic agent whatsoever thought to cause or to indicate the presence of HIV infection.

(d) Capacity to consent means an individual's ability, determined without regard to such individual's age, to understand and appreciate the nature and consequences of a proposed health care service, treatment or procedure, and to make an informed decision concerning such service, treatment or procedure.

(e) Protected individual means a person who is the subject of an HIV-related test or who has been diagnosed as having HIV infection, AIDS or HIV-related illness.

(f) Confidential HIV-related information means any information, in the possession of a person who provides one or more health or social services or who obtains the information pursuant to a release of confidential HIV-related information, concerning whether an individual has been the subject of an HIV-related test, or has HIV infection, HIV-related illness or AIDS, or information which identifies or reasonably could identify an individual as having one or more of such conditions, including information pertaining to such individual contact;

(g) Health or social service means any public or private care; treatment, clinical laboratory test, counseling or educational service for children, and acute, chronic, custodial, residential, outpatient, home or other health care; public assistance; employment-related services, housing services, foster care, shelter, protective services, day care or preventive services; services for the mentally disabled; probation services; parole services;

correctional services; and detention and rehabilitative services, all as defined in section 2780(8) of the Public Health Law.

(h) Health facility means a hospital as defined in section 2801 of the Public Health Law, blood bank, blood center, sperm bank, organ or tissue bank, clinical laboratory, or facility providing care or treatment to persons with a mental disability.

(i) Health care provider means any physician, nurse, provider of services for the mentally disabled or other person involved in providing medical, nursing, counseling, or other health care or mental health service including those associated with, or under contract to, a health maintenance organization or medical services plan.

(j) Contact means an identified spouse or sex partner of the protected individual or a person identified as having shared hypodermic needles or syringes with the protected individual.

(k) Person includes any natural person, partnership, association, joint venture, trust, public or private corporation or State or local government agency.

(*l*) Division means the New York State Division for Youth.

(m) Child means any person between the ages of 7 and 18 years (inclusive) who has been remanded to any detention facility certified by the Division for Youth, including family boarding homes.

(n) AIDS means acquired immune deficiency syndrome, as may be defined from time to time by the centers for disease control of the United States Public Health Service.

(v) Prevention of discrimination and abuse.

(a) No child or staff will be subjected to discrimination because that child is or is thought to be HIV infected. All children shall be appropriately served by detention programs certified by the division according to the needs of the child.

(b) All detention facilities shall provide for training to all direct care personnel which shall include, at a minimum:

(1) initial employee and annual in-service training regarding the symptoms, causes and transmission of AIDS or AIDS-related complex, and universal infection control procedures; and

(2) initial employee training and annual in-service training regarding legal prohibitions against unauthorized disclosure of confidential HIV-related information.

(c) A list of all employees who have had such training shall be maintained by the detention facility together with a list of those employees authorized to access confidential HIV-related information. Such lists shall be updated annually.

(d) Each facility certified by the division shall establish and promulgate policies ensuring:

(1) maintenance of records containing confidential HIV-related information in a secure manner, limiting access to only those individuals permitted access pursuant to this subparagraph (iv) of this paragraph; and

(2) procedures for handling requests by other parties for confidential HIV-related information.

(vi) HIV-related testing.

(a) Except as noted in subclause (b)(2) of this subparagraph, no physician or other person authorized pursuant to law may order an HIV-related test without obtaining written informed consent.

(1) Informed consent shall consist of providing to the child to be tested or, if such child lacks capacity to consent, as defined in subparagraph (iv) of this paragraph to the person lawfully authorized to consent to health care for such person, pre-testing counseling that includes:

(i) explanations regarding the nature of HIV infection and HIV-related illness, benefits of the test and its results, an explanation of the HIV-related test results, the accuracy of the HIV-related test, the significance and benefits of the test and its result; and the benefits of taking the test, including early diagnosis and medical intervention;

(ii) information regarding discrimination problems which might occur as a result of unauthorized disclosure of HIV-related information and legal protections prohibiting such disclosures;

(iii) information on preventing exposure or transmission of HIV infection, including behavior which poses a risk of HIV transmissions; and

(iv) an explanation that the test is voluntary and that consent may be withdrawn at any time; information on the availability of anonymous HIV testing, including the location and telephone numbers of anonymous test sites.

(b) (1) Written informed consent must be executed on a form developed or approved by the Department of Health, pursuant to that department's regulations found at 10 NYCRR section 63.4(a).

(2) Informed consent is not required in the following situations:

(i) for court ordered testing pursuant to Civil Practice Law and Rules section 3121;

(ii) if otherwise authorized or required by State or Federal law;

(iii) for testing related to procuring, processing, distributing or use of human body or human body part, including organs, tissue, eyes, bones, arteries, blood, semen or other body fluids for use in medical research or therapy, or for transplantation to persons, provided that if the test results are communicated to the tested person, post-test counseling is required;

(iv) for research if the testing is performed in a manner by which the identity of the test subject is not known and may not be retrieved by the researcher; and

(v) for testing of a deceased to determine cause of death or for epidemiological purposes.

(c) Post-testing counseling, and referrals with respect to a positive or negative test result, shall be provided to the person who consented to the test. Such post-test counseling and referrals must address:

(1) coping emotionally with the test results;

(2) discrimination issues;

(3) information on the ability to release or revoke the release of confidential HIV-related information;

(4) information on preventing exposure to or transmission of HIV infection and the availability of medical treatment; and

(5) the need to notify contacts; to prevent transmission, including information on State or county assistance in voluntary contact notification, if appropriate.

(d) A physician or other person authorized pursuant to law to order an HIV-related test shall certify on a laboratory requisition form that informed consent has been obtained.

(vii) Confidentiality and disclosure.

(a) Access to a child's confidential HIV-related information shall be strictly limited. No flags or other markings on charts, lists on walls, or similar public displays shall be used to indicate child's HIV status. Nothing in these regulations shall be construed to limit or enlarge access to that portion of a child's file not containing confidential HIV-related information.

(b) No person who obtains confidential HIV-related information in the course of providing any health or social service or pursuant to a release of confidential HIV-related information may disclose or be compelled to disclose such information, except to the following:

(1) the protected individual or, when the protected individual lacks capacity to consent, a person authorized pursuant to law to consent to health care for the individual;

(2) any person to whom disclosure is authorized pursuant to a release of confidential HIV-related information in accordance with the regulations of the Department of Health set forth at 10 NYCRR section 63.4(a);

(3) an agent or employee of a health facility or health care provider if:

(i) the agent or employee is authorized to access medical records;

(ii) the health facility or health care provider itself is authorized to obtain the HIV-related information; and

(iii) the agent or employee provides health care to the protected individual, or maintains or processes medical records for billing or reimbursement;

(4) a health care provider or health facility when knowledge of the HIV-related information is necessary to provide appropriate care or treatment to the protected child or offspring of that child;

(5) a health facility or health care provider, in relation to the procurement, processing, distributing or use of a human body or a human body part, including organs, tissues, eyes, bones, arteries, blood, semen, or other body fluids, for use in medical education, research, therapy, or for transplantation to individuals;

(6) health facility staff committees, or accreditation or oversight review organizations authorized to access medical records, provided that such committees or organizations may only disclose confidential HIV-related information;

(i) back to the facility or provider of a health or social services;

(ii) to carry out the monitoring, evaluation, or service review for which it was obtained; or

(iii) to a Federal, State or local government agency for the purposes of and subject to the conditions provided in subclause (19) of this clause;

(7) a Federal, State, county or local health officer when such disclosure is mandated by Federal or State law;

(8) authorized agencies certified as detention facilities by the Division for Youth. Such agency shall be authorized to redisclosure such information only pursuant tot he provisions of article 27-F of the Public Health Law or in accordance with the provisions of section 373-A of the Social Services Law;

(9) third-party reimbursers or their agents to the extent necessary to reimburse health care providers, including health facilities, for health services, provided that, where necessary, an otherwise appropriate authorization for such disclosure has been secured by the provider;

(10) an insurance institution, for other than the purpose set forth in subclause (9) of this clause, provided the insurance institution secures a dated

and written authorization that indicates that health care providers, health facilities, insurance institutions, and other persons are authorized to disclose information about the protected individual, the nature of the information to be disclosed, the purposes for which the information is to be disclosed and which is signed by:

(i) the protected individual;

(ii) if the protected individual lacks the capacity to consent, such other person authorized pursuant to law to consent for such individual; or

(iii) if the protected individual is deceased, the beneficiary or claimant for benefits under an insurance policy, a health services plan, or an employee welfare benefit plan as authorized in article 27-F of the Public Health Law;

(11) any person to whom disclosure is ordered by a court of competent jurisdiction pursuant to section 2785 of the Public Health Law;

(12) an employee or agent of the Division of Parole, Division of Probation or Commission of Correction, in accordance with regulations promulgated by those agencies;

(13) a medical director of a local correctional facility in accordance with regulations promulgated by the facility operator. Redisclosure by the medical director is prohibited except as permitted under Public Health Law, article 27-F and its implementing regulations;

(14) a physician may disclose the confidential HIV-related information during contact notification pursuant to Public Health Law, article 27-F;

(15) a physician may, upon the informed consent of a child or, if the child lacks the capacity to consent, other person qualified to give consent on behalf of the child, disclose confidential HIV-related information to a State, county, or local health officer for the purpose of reviewing the medical history of a child to determine the fitness of the child to attend school;

(16) confidential HIV-related information may be disclosed to a governmental agency or to authorized employers or agents of a governmental agency when the person providing health services is regulated by the governmental agency or when the governmental agency administers a health or social services program and when such employees or agents have access to records in the ordinary course of business and when access is reasonably necessary for supervision, monitoring, administration or provision of services. Such authorized employees or agents may include attorneys authorized by a government agency when access occurs in the ordinary course of providing legal services and is reasonably necessary for supervision, monitoring, administration or provision of services;

(17) confidential HIV-related information may be disclosed to authorized employees or agents of a person providing health services when such person is either regulated by a governmental agency or when a governmental agency administers a health or social services program, and when such employees or agents have access to records in the ordinary course of business and when access is reasonably necessary for supervision, monitoring, administration or provision of services and when such employee or agent has been authorized by the detention facility or program pursuant to these regulations. Such authorized employees or agents may include attorneys authorized by persons providing health services when access occurs in the ordinary course of providing legal services and is reasonably necessary for supervision, monitoring, administration or provision of services;

(18) no person to whom confidential HIV-related information has been disclosed shall disclose the information to another person except as authorized by this section; provided, however, that the provisions of this section shall not apply to the protected child or a natural person who is authorized pursuant to law to consent to health care for the protected individual;

(19) nothing in this section shall limit a person's or agency's responsibility or authority to report, investigate, or redisclose, child protective and adult protective services information in accordance with title 6 of article 6 and title 1 and 2 of article 9-B of the Social Services Law, or to provide or monitor the provision of child and adult protective or preventive services;

(20) confidential HIV-related information shall not be disclosed to a health care provider or health care facility if the sole purpose of disclosure is infection control when such provider or facility is regulated under the Public Health Law and required to implement infection control procedures pursuant to Department of Health regulations;

(21) confidential HIV information shall not be released pursuant to a subpoena. A court order pursuant to Public Health Law, section 2785 is required;

(22) where confidential HIV-related information has been obtained from an alternate anonymous testing site, sexually transmitted disease clinic or the child's private physician, the child may choose not to disclose any information to detention staff. The test results will not be disclosed to any other person unless the child, or other person authorized to give consent, gives prior written consent, pursuant to this subdivision or unless disclosed pursuant to subclause (23) of this clause. Children must also be informed that once a positive test result is disclosed, it will be shared confidentially with a limited number of people directly involved with the child's care and planning for care, as set forth below. These people will be limited to the following:

(i) the facility's medical staff caring for the child (i.e., physician's assistant, nurse and the supervising physician of the physician's assistant or primary care physician serving the child where the facility lacks other medical staff);

(ii) the facility director or, as applicable, the family boarding home parents and the family boarding home supervisor responsible for the child's case;

(iii) the chief administrative officers of the county administering agency;

(iv) for division-operated detention facilities, the division's Office of Counsel and the New York State Attorney General's office, where such access is necessary in furtherance of that office's duties;

(23) if, in the judgment of the facility health staff and facility director or, as applicable, the family boarding home supervisor responsible for the child's case, the results must be disclosed to additional party(ies) including the child's parent(s) or guardian(s), the facility director or family boarding home supervisor shall consult with the chief administrative officer of the county administrative agency. The chief administrative officer of the county administrative agency must concur with the facility director or family boarding home supervisor, if the information is to be disclosed to others not approved by the child. In such cases the criterion used for overriding the child's objections shall be that further disclosure of the information is critically important for the child's physical or mental well-being, and that such benefit may not otherwise be obtained. At no time will confidential HIV-related

information be disclosed in violation of Public Health Law, article 27-F. Any decision or action taken pursuant to this paragraph and the basis for such decision or action shall be recorded in the child's medical record; and

(24) where a child who has acquired HIV-related information through a detention employed physician or physician's assistant or through a physician maintained to serve detention children, either on a contract or fee-for-service basis, the child must be advised that such information will be disclosed as set forth in subclauses (22) and (23) of this clause.

(viii) Disclosure and release.

(a) No confidential HIV-related information shall be disclosed pursuant to a general release or subpoena without a court order, pursuant to Public Health Law, section 2785, unless such release is to another health care provider. Disclosure is permitted for HIV-related information pursuant to a specific release form which has been developed or approved by the Department of Health. The release must be signed by the protected individual, or if the protected individual lacks capacity to consent pursuant to clause (vi)(d) of this paragraph, by a person authorized pursuant to law to consent to health care for the individual.

(b) All written disclosures of confidential HIV information must be accompanied by a statement prohibiting redisclosure. The statement shall include the following language or substantially similar language: "This information has been disclosed to you from confidential records which are protected by state law. State law prohibits you from making any further disclosure of this information without the specific written content * of the person to whom it pertains, or as otherwise permitted by law. Any unauthorized further disclosure in violation of State law may result in a fine or jail sentence or both. A general authorization for the release of medical or other information is not sufficient authorization for further disclosure. Disclosure of confidential HIV information that occurs as the result of a general authorization for the release of medical or other information will be in violation of the State law and may result in a fine or jail sentence or both."

(c) If oral disclosures are necessary, they must be accompanied or followed as soon as possible, but no later than 10 days, by the statement required in clause (b) of this subparagraph. All disclosures, oral or written, shall be recorded in the child's official record.

(d) The statement required by clauses (a) and (b) of this subparagraph is not required for release to the protected person or to his or her legal representative, for releases made by a physician or public health officer to a contact, or for releases made by a physician to a person authorized pursuant to law to consent to the health care of the protected person when the person has been counseled and the disclosure is medically necessary pursuant to Public Health Law, section 2782(4)(e). For disclosure of confidential HIV-related information from the youth's medical files to persons who are permitted access pursuant to subclauses (vii)(b)(3)-(4), (6)-(7), (9)-(10) and (16)-(17) of this paragraph, it shall be sufficient for the statement required by clauses (b) and (c) of this subparagraph to appear in the child's medical record.

(ix) Protection of others at significant risk of infection.

(a) Staff and child protection. Since medical history and examination cannot reliably identify all children infected with HIV or other blood-borne pathogens, blood and body fluid precautions shall be consistently used for all children. This approach, referred to as "universal blood and body-fluid precautions" or "universal precautions," or "universal infection control procedures" shall be used during job-related activities which involve or may involve exposure to significant risk body substances as defined in Department of Health regulations at 10 NYCRR, section 63.9.

(b) Facilities and programs shall abide by any additional regulations regarding protective barriers or procedures as may be promulgated by the division.

(c) Staff will educate children regarding behaviors which pose a risk for HIV transmission.

(d) Each detention facility shall:

(1) implement and enforce a plan for the prevention of circumstances which could result in another employee or individual becoming exposed to blood or body fluids which could put them at risk for HIV infection, during the provision of services. Such a plan shall include:

(i) use of generally accepted protective barriers during the job-related activities which involve, or may involve, exposure to blood or body fluids. Such preventive action shall be taken by the employee with each youth and shall constitute an essential element for the prevention of bi-directional spread of HIV;

(ii) use of generally accepted preventive practices during job-related activities which involve the use of contaminated instruments or equipment which may cause puncture injuries;

(iii) training at the time of employment and yearly staff development programs on the use of protective equipment, preventive practices, and circumstances which represent a risk for all employees whose job-related tasks involve, or may involve, exposure to blood or body fluids;

(iv) provision of personal protective equipment for employees which is appropriate to the tasks being performed; and

(v) a system for monitoring preventive programs to assure compliance and safety; and

(2) implement and enforce a plan for the management of individuals who are exposed to blood or body fluids. The plan shall include:

(i) a system for voluntary reporting of all exposures thought to represent a circumstance for significant risk;

(ii) availability of services for evaluating the circumstance of a reported exposure and providing appropriate follow-up of the exposed individual which includes:

(A) medical and epidemiological assessment of the individual who is the source of the exposure, where that individual is known and available;

(B) If epidemiologically indicated, HIV counseling and testing of the source individual as permitted under Public Health Law, article 27-F. Where the HIV status is not known to the exposed individual, disclosure can be made only with the express written consent of the protected individual or pursuant to a Supreme Court order; and

(C) appropriate medical follow-up of the exposed individual; and

(iii) assurances for protection of confidentiality for those involved in reported exposures.

(x) Monitoring. Employees and agents of the division responsible for monitoring, inspecting, supervising, and investigating programs certified by the division shall have access to confidential HIV information to the extent necessary to discharge those responsibilities.

§180.6 Length of stay.

(a) No youth shall be kept in continuous detention care beyond 45 days from admission; except that such youth may remain beyond 45 days pursuant to court order or where the detention facility has obtained prior written approval by the division.

(b) A youth shall be considered absent without leave when absent from a facility where his or her whereabouts are unknown and where the youth's assigned bed is relinquished. A secure detention facility shall relinquish a youth's assigned bed on the day following a runaway when a child is not returned within 24 hours. Such absences shall be considered an interruption of continuous detention care. Reimbursement shall terminate upon AWOL and shall continue only upon the return of the youth to the facility.

(c) The agency administering detention shall be responsible for terminating detention care no later than the 45th continuous day of care, except where such termination would be contrary to court order or when prior division written approval for extension of detention has been granted. Notification of removal of the youth shall be given by the agency to the appropriate Family Court and other appropriate agencies.

(d) It shall be the responsibility of the agency administering detention to notify appropriate agencies, including the Family Court, no later than the 35th day of continuous care, and to notify the Family Court and such agencies of the granting or denial of approval for extension of detention.

(1) The agency administering detention shall assure the submission to the division, in such form and in such manner as the division may require, of requests for extension of detention beyond 45 continuous days of care, to be received not later than the 35th day.

(2) The agency administering detention shall be responsible for securing all information required by the division for review of requests for extension of detention.

(3) No approval of requests for extension of detention shall be made by the division where complete and adequate information is not provided in the request, including but not limited to:

(i) reason youth may not appear at court hearing or presents a serious risk to commit what would be a crime if the youth were an adult;

(ii) statement of major offense with which youth is charged (label of "Delinquency" or "Person in Need of Supervision" is not adequate);

(iii) reason for extension request, including dates for referrals, replies, study reports or dispositional placement;

(iv) status of placement efforts, if the final placement order has been handed down by the Family Court.

§180.7 Intake and admission.

(a) Admission to a detention facility shall be limited to:

(1) youth referred pursuant to article 7 of The Family Court Act;

(2) children held pending a hearing for alleged violation of the conditions of release from a school, or center or youth center, of the division in compliance with Part 169 of this Subtitle;

(3) youth on whom a warrant has been issued by the division, in compliance with Part 181 of this Subtitle;

(4) youth held pending return to a jurisdiction other than the one in which the youth is held; or

(5) alleged juvenile offenders held pursuant to a securing order of a criminal court or pending transfer pursuant to sentence.

(b) Youth shall be admitted to a detention facility only when accompanied by police, sheriff, or a private or public agency official, or peace officer, who shall provide the legal basis for custody and detention referral in writing, and who shall provide, or certify that they will provide, documentation as to the true identity of the youth. Documentation shall include, but not be limited to, the youth's name, age and address of parents or legal guardian.

(c) A youth may be admitted to a detention facility for detention care without a warrant when referred by a peace officer who has taken the child into custody pursuant to section 718, 721 or 723 of The Family Court Act when such officer certifies, in writing, that he has complied with section 724 of The Family Court Act. Such certification shall include the fact that efforts have been made to notify the parent or other person legally responsible for care, and state the reasons such person or persons will not, or cannot, produce the youth before the Family Court as ordered. Said officer shall further certify that he will cause a petition to be filed against the youth on the next day Family Court is in session.

(1) When placement is from a county other than the operating county, contact information for a public official authorized to make emergency decisions regarding the youth, and the telephone numbers where such official may be reached on a 24-hour basis, shall be provided at the time of admission.

(2) Visitors shall be authorized as follows:

(i) Family Court judges, criminal court judges, or their designees, may visit detention facilities, interview youth and review records as they may deem appropriate.

(ii) Law guardians, probation workers and other agency officials, actively working with the youngster, may visit the youth through prior appointment at the facility. The facility director may authorize a tour of the facility for such visitors.

(iii) Parents and other visitors shall be permitted to visit the youth at least once a week, except when the facility director determines that such visits are detrimental to the youth or that the visitors refuse to comply with rules governing visitation. Where a parent cannot visit during established visiting hours, arrangements shall be made by the facility director to establish special visiting periods. The facility director shall publish written rules governing visiting hours and conditions for visitation. Where a visitor is excluded for any reason, the facility director shall specify, in writing, the reason for such exclusion. A copy of such statement shall be provided to the rejected visitor.

(d) When a youth is brought to a detention facility, pursuant to section 724(b) (iii) of The Family Court Act, the probation service or the administrator responsible for operating the detention facility is authorized, before the filing of a petition, to release the youth to the custody of a parent or other relative, guardian or legal custodian when the events that occasioned the taking into custody:

(1) appear to involve a petition to determine whether the youth is a person in need of supervision, rather than a petition to determine whether the youth is a juvenile delinquent;

(2) do not appear to involve any act which, if done by an adult, would constitute a crime; or

(3) appear to involve a petition to determine whether the youth is a juvenile delinquent unless:

(i) there is a substantial probability that the youth will not appear or be produced before the Family Court at a specified time and place;

(ii) there is a serious risk that, before the petition is filed, the child may do an act which, if committed by an adult, would be a crime;

(iii) the conduct involved the use or threatened use of violence; or

(iv) there is a reason to believe that a proceeding to determine whether the youth is a juvenile delinquent is currently pending.

(e) Youth referred for detention by the division shall be placed in a non-secure detention facility, unless a determination is made by the division that secure detention is needed. Requirements to be met for secure detention are:

(1) the offense or history of offenses is of such a serious nature as to be a threat to the community;

(2) the youth's behavior indicates need for intense supervision; and

(3) the youth's admission will be in compliance with Federal statutes and regulations pertaining to the detention of juveniles.

(f) No youth shall be fingerprinted or be photographed or otherwise identified for security purposes while a resident of a detention facility.

(g) When a youth absconds from a facility to which he or she was remanded pursuant to section 739 of The Family Court Act, or to which he or she has been delivered pursuant to section 510.15 of the Criminal Procedure Law, notice shall be given forthwith by an authorized representative of the facility to the clerk of the court from which the remand was made. An oral notice shall be confirmed in writing within 48 hours. The notice shall state the name of the youth, the docket number of the pending proceeding in which the youth was remanded, and the date on which the youth absconded.

(h) Intake official(s) shall be designated by the agency responsible for administering detention. Such intake official(s) shall be available on a 24-hour basis. Except when detention is pursuant to court order, prior to authorizing detention, the official(s) shall determine that the referral meets statutory criteria for detention admission and conforms to division regulations and pertinent local procedures.

§180.8 Personnel requirements.

The following requirements shall be applicable to all detention facilities except for family boarding care facilities and agency-operated boarding care facilities.

(a) Staff and complementary services. As approved by the office of children and family services, each facility shall provide the staff and complementary services necessary for the health and safety and the proper care and treatment of the children under care of the facility.

(b) Qualifications of staff. Personnel employed in a detention facility shall meet the qualifications required by this section. Professional staff also shall meet all New York State licensing requirements for that profession.

(c) Administrative staff.

(1) Chief executive officer. The chief executive officer or supervisor of major detention programs shall be a college graduate with appropriate training and experience in the care or education of children.

(2) Supervisor of child care workers. The supervisor of child care workers shall have a high school or equivalency diploma and be further qualified by appropriate training, and have experience with children in a group living facility.

(d) Case management staff.

(1) Personnel providing case management services shall be graduates of an accredited college and have two years' experience working with children.

(2) Personnel who supervise case management services shall meet the requirements for a licensed master social worker.

(e) Recreation supervisor. A recreation supervisor shall be a graduate of an accredited college with experience in recreation or related fields.

(f) Medical staff.

(1) Attending physician or medical director. An attending physician or medical director shall be licensed and currently registered to practice medicine in accordance with the laws of New York State.

(2) Dentist. A dentist shall be currently licensed to practice dentistry.

(3) Nurse. A nurse shall be either a registered professional or a practical nurse licensed in accordance with the laws of New York State.

(4) Psychiatrist. A psychiatrist shall be qualified by training in psychiatry and licensed to practice medicine in accordance with the laws of New York State.

(g) Education staff. Teacher. A teacher shall be eligible for certification by the New York State Education Department.

(h) Dietary staff.

(1) Dietitian or dietary consultant. A dietitian or dietary consultant shall be a graduate of an accredited college with a major in dietetics and nutrition and shall be a Certified Dietitian Nutritionist.

(i) Personnel practices.

(1) Each detention facility shall observe the following:

(i) Health examination. A physical examination, including a tuberculin skin test with a chest X-ray where such test is positive, and serological tests as indicated, shall be required of all staff as a condition of employment.

(ii) Annual reexaminations, including a tuberculin skin test with a chest X-ray where such test is positive, shall be required of all food handlers and other staff having frequent and regular contact with children.

(iii) A record of the results of examinations shall be kept on file at the facility.

(2) Time off with pay. All staff shall have adequate time off with pay.

(3) Staff development. A plan for staff orientation, integration with the total agency services, and education through in-service training shall be a permanent part of the institution's program.

(4) At the time of commencement of employment each staff member shall be apprised of the institution's personnel practices and policies and shall thereafter be apprised of any changes made therein.

§180.9 Program requirements–secure and non-secure institutional detention facilities.

(a) Education program. The purpose of educational programming in an institutional detention facility is to provide success-oriented, short-term educational activity.

(1) Children under care shall receive suitable educational instruction in accordance with the New York State Education Law for such short-term programs.

(2) A minimum of three hours of educational activity instruction each weekday shall be provided each child.

(3) Educational instruction shall be provided by a teacher qualified by, or eligible for certification by, the New York State Education Department, as provided in 8 NYCRR 80.32.

(b) Medical program. The purpose of the health program of an institutional detention facility should be the provision of adequate and appropriate health services to assure that both public and individual health care needs of the children are met. The health care rendered should be of good quality, efficient, accessible and continuous. Provisions should be made for basic primary health care which would also include, but not be restricted to, dental, obstetrical, gynecological, mental health, and public and preventive health services. The extent that these services can be reasonably delivered will depend on the health needs of the youngsters, the length of stay at the facility and the health resources of both the detention facility and the surrounding community. The highest priorities in providing health services for youngsters in detention are the identification and treatment of emergency and/or serious acute health conditions, and the responsible interim management and treatment of chronic serious health conditions.

(1) Administration. As a minimum, detention facilities should have a health program which includes, but is not restricted to, the following:

(i) A specific administrative structure with designated director or administrative head with open access and reporting responsibilities to the chief administrator of the facility.

(ii) There should be the identification and documentation of all licensed physicians and medical personnel who supervise health personnel, directly render service, devise and review medical procedures.

(2) (i) Procedures. A set of written procedures disseminated to and understood by all relevant detention staff, established to assure that basic health services are met. These procedures should include but not be limited to the health assessments.

(ii) Health assessments. All youngsters upon entering detention shall have a prompt health assessment conducted by a licensed physician or a health professional, trained specifically to perform health assessments under the supervision of a physician. This health assessment should be conducted within at least 72 hours after the youngster is admitted to the facility on routine cases. In circumstances where there exist conditions, indications or circumstances, either reported by the youngster, the youngster's family, those transporting and/or referring youngsters or other members of the detention facility, that indicate a physician's assessment is required sooner than 72 hours, the facility should make provisions to perform an immediate health assessment on an emergency basis. The health assessment should include the following:

(a) The health history--including but not restricted to pertinent data, family and social history, history of hospitalizations and/or past medical illness, review of body systems, current medical illness or complaints, any allergies or drug reactions and current use of prescribed medications, history of alcohol or substance abuse.

(b) Physical examination--should include measurement of height, weight, body temperature, blood pressure, pulse, respiration rate; and include the physical inspection of those parts of the body pertinent for the assessment of the status of growth and development, psychoneurologic, cardio-respiratory, gastrointestinal, genitourinary, integement, musculosketal, metabolic, endocrine, and immunohematologic systems.

(c) Laboratory testing (where appropriate)--should include and not be restricted to hemoglobin and hematocrit, urinalysis, tuberculosis skin test, serology test for syphilis, Pap test and culture for gonorrhea for sexually active persons; other laboratory testing as appropriate or medically indicated to assure the proper diagnosis and/or treatment of any serious individual or public health disorder.

(3) Service plans for all identified health problems. The records should reflect service plans for all identified health problems. For those health problems in which the physician has deemed it appropriate to defer further diagnostic inquiry and/or treatment, the records should reflect this deferment as part of the treatment plan. Appropriate immunization services should be provided.

(4) Health policies and admission into the detention facility.

(i) The life or the health of a child should not be jeopardized by admitting into detention any child with serious health problems that exceed the capacity for the detention facility to provide necessary health services. Unconscious or frankly suicidal children should not be admitted or maintained at a detention facility. Children in these categories should receive at the detention site those emergency health services that should assure the safe and immediate transportation to the appropriate local health facility.

(ii) Children with obvious signs of injury, altered state of consciousness, inexplicable bizarre behavior, obviously intoxicated states or other indications of serious health problems should be immediately assessed by the detention physician or health personnel as to the extent of the problem. A clinical decision should be made as to whether there exists a serious health problem that exceeds the capacity of the detention facility to provide the necessary health services. In the event that a physician or other health personnel are not onsite, the highest administrative detention official at a detention center must act immediately to secure such a decision by telephone consultation with the detention health personnel or other health care professionals. In the event that a clinical decision is made that there is any likelihood that the necessary health care cannot be rendered at the detention site, then immediate steps should be taken to transport such youngsters to the appropriate health facility.

(5) Prescription medications. (i) The detention facility should have the facilities, equipment, records and personnel to assure the provisions for the prescription, storage, dispensation, administration of prescribed medication and/or controlled medication in compliance with Federal, State and local laws.

(ii) The services of a licensed pharmacist should be enlisted to oversee and supervise the storage and dispensation of prescribed medication. The administration of prescribed medication can only be performed by a physician or licensed, registered, professional or practical nurse.

(6) Health professional staffing. Health professional staffing is largely indicated by the health needs of the institution, and may vary from institution to institution. However, staffing should include no less than the following:

(i) Physician. A primary care physician should be readily available on a 24-hour basis for telephone consultation. Physician should make onsite visits as required to assure appropriate medical service, but shall visit at least twice a week. The length of stay for the visits and the timing of the stay should be designated by the health needs of the children and the health program needs of the facility. The physician shall be responsible for the referral to appropriate and required medical specialty services for youngsters with health problems falling into the scope of the responsibility of the detention facility.

(ii) Psychiatric consultative services. The services of a licensed MD Board Certified or Board Eligible in Psychiatry should be available on an on-call basis for the examination and treatment of minor and/or acute mental disorders which can be appropriately handled in a detention facility. The psychiatrist should take major responsibilities in referring, when a youngster is brought into a detention facility requiring the services of mental hygiene.

(iii) Nursing service. The coverage of the nursing staff should also be determined by the individual health needs of the youngster and program health needs of the facility. Facilities for 13 or more children shall have on staff a full-time nurse for every 25 children. All facilities should have the capabilities to provide 24-hour nursing coverage on an on-call basis. Facilities with a capacity exceeding 60 require 24-hour nursing coverage. Such 24-hour coverage may be provided through child care staff who are qualified nurses.

(7) Formal arrangements for obtaining services of backup general and mental hospital and other essential specialty health services. The administration of detention facilities should develop, when at all possible, formal arrangements, through contracts or letters of understanding, that would assure that local hospitals and other community health care providers deliver needed health services for the detained youngsters.

(8) Provisions for the transfer of health information. The detention health services shall be responsible for the efficient communication of health information to those health providers responsible for the health care of the child after detention. The consent of the child, parent and/or guardian should be obtained for the transfer of this information.

(c) Child care and treatment.

(1) There shall be only one child per bedroom.

(2) Children shall be humanely treated and provided with whatever is necessary for their safety, comfort and well-being.

(3) Staff supervision, awake and on duty, shall be provided at all times.

(4) Each facility shall provide for the proper isolation of children with communicable or infectious disease.

(5) Children in care shall not be permitted overnight home visits except for emergencies.

(6) Personal care. Each facility shall provide the program, facilities and training necessary for the children's daily needs and development of sound habits and practices in regard to personal hygiene and general appearance.

(7) Clothing. Each institution shall assure that each child has appropriate clothing, individually selected and properly fitted. Clothing shall be adequate in amount, attractive and of good quality, and properly maintained for comfort and health.

(8) Recreation and leisure time. Each facility shall provide for leisure time activities and planned recreation for the children to include active and quiet games, both indoors and outdoors, appropriate to the children's needs.

(9) Work for children. No child shall be used as a substitute for staff. Work performed by children shall be only that which clearly has a constructive value for their training.

(10) Discipline of children.

(i) abuse of children in any form is prohibited;

(ii) deprivation of meals, mail and family visits as methods of punishment of children is prohibited;

(iii) solitary confinement is prohibited;

(iv) punishment, control and discipline of children shall be an adult responsibility and shall not be prescribed or administered by children; and

(v) institutions shall maintain their discipline policies in writing.

(11) Room confinement.

(i) Room confinement shall only be authorized for secure detention facilities and shall mean confinement of a child in a room, including the child's own room, when locked or when the child is authoritatively told not to leave.

(ii) Room confinement of children shall not be used for punishment. It shall be authorized only in cases where a child constitutes a serious and evident danger to himself/herself or others.

(iii) Room confinement may be authorized, in writing, by the head of the institution or designee, and shall include a statement of the reasons and grounds for the confinement.

(iv) The place of confinement shall be furnished with the items necessary for the health and comfort of the occupant, including but not limited to a bed, chair, desk or chest, mattress, pillow, sheet and blanket. If the presence of any of these items would be detrimental to the safety of the occupant or others, they may be removed during the period of confinement upon authorization of the head of the institution or designee.

(v) The designated place of confinement shall be lighted, heated and ventilated in parity with the other comparable living areas in the institution.

(vi) Auditory and/or visual adult supervision of the child shall be maintained throughout the period of room confinement.

(vii) Each child in confinement shall be visited at least once within each 24 hours by administrative or social work staff, and shall be examined at least once within 24 hours by a registered nurse, licensed practical nurse or duly licensed physician.

(viii) A review of the necessity for continued confinement of each child shall be made at least one time in each 24-hour period, by the head of the institution or designee, to effectuate the return of the child to the regular program as soon as the child is no longer a danger to himself/herself or others.

(ix) Each secure detention facility shall submit reports to the division, on such forms as required by the division, on a monthly basis. Such reports shall include:

(a) the number of children who have been placed in confinement; and

(b) the name of each child placed in confinement, with a report of the length of confinement, the official authorizing the confinement, and the names of administrative or social work staff and medical staff visiting each such child, and the times and dates of such visits.

(12) Protection of religious faith. The religious faith of each child shall be preserved and protected.

(13) Treatment services.

(i) Casework service shall be made available to all children under the care of the facility as soon after admission as practicable, and personnel providing casework service shall visit each child daily at least during the first week of each child's placement. Casework service shall be provided by personnel with qualifications described in this Part.

(ii) Psychiatric and psychological services, including tests and examination, shall be made available for children under care.

(14) There shall be a recreation supervisor, responsible for coordinating recreational activities, in each facility.

(15) Minimum staff ratios shall be as follows:

(i) one child care worker per eight children per shift; and

(ii) one social worker per 15 children.

(16) Minimum staff shall be determined by the division, in consultation with the administering agency, to insure an adequate program standard. Maximum

staffing shall be determined by the division, in consultation with the administering agency, for reimbursement purposes. All staffing patterns shall be determined annually, based on the annual detention plan as submitted to the division for approval.

(17) Nutrition and food services.

(i) Food served shall be of good quality and of sufficient quantity.

(ii) Children's diet shall meet the nutritional standards recommended by the National Research Council.

(iii) All milk and milk products shall be pasteurized.

(iv) Food preparation and services.

(a) Food shall be prepared and served under the direct supervision of, or in scheduled consultation with a qualified dietitian or dietary consultant.

(b) Menus, as served, shall be retained on file for one year after date of use.

(18) Sleeping accommodations.

(i) Single rooms. Single sleeping rooms for children shall contain not less than 70 square feet of floor area and shall have a minimum horizontal dimension of seven feet. Walls shall be at least seven feet in height.

(ii) Children's sleeping accommodations shall not be permitted in spaces where the floor is located below ground level or where natural light and ventilation is lacking.

(iii) Each agency shall provide each child with a bed suitably equipped, and clothing storage space for his own private use, conveniently located.

(iv) Sheets and pillowcases shall be changed once a week and more often when necessary. Children's beds shall be equipped with waterproof materials when necessary.

(19) Bathing and toilet facilities.

(i) Number of bathrooms, toilets and lavatories for multiple use. Bathrooms, toilets and lavatories shall be convenient to children's sleeping quarters which are not individually equipped with these facilities. There shall be a minimum of one toilet (water closet) to serve every six children, and one tub or shower to serve every eight children. All toilets and urinals, and all girls' showers, shall be separated by screening or partitions for at least minimal privacy.

(ii) Number of bathrooms, toilets and lavatories for single use. Bedrooms equipped with toilets and lavatories shall have appropriately located floor drains and shall have shutoff valves, exterior to the rooms and conveniently accessible, for supply and drainage pipelines. Bedrooms so equipped may be used for medical isolation, for children needing separation from the group or for general purposes.

(iii) Toilet facilities and sanitary drinking fountains shall be provided convenient to all indoor and outdoor program areas.

(iv) Children's toilet articles. Each child shall be provided with his own toothbrush, comb, towel and washcloth. Each child's towel and washcloth shall be kept in a separate space and shall be changed at least twice a week and more often when necessary.

(v) Staff facilities. Bathrooms, toilets and coat closets for staff shall be separate from those of the children and shall be appropriately located.

(20) Recreation facilities.

(i) Indoor recreation and living facilities. The detention facility shall provide resources for a balanced program of indoor recreation and for lounge facilities to accommodate its full capacity of children at any given time. Such resources shall permit a range of activities from vigorous, organized games through quiet informal play and shall include appropriate equipment, furnishings, storage, toilets and similar service features.

(ii) Outdoor recreation. The detention facility shall provide resources for a balanced program of outdoor recreation to adequately accommodate its full capacity of children at any given time. Outdoor play areas shall provide a minimum of one acre of securely fenced, properly drained, play space for 20-bed and smaller detention facilities and proportionally larger areas for higher capacity facilities to meet the requirements of this section. Such facilities shall permit a range of activities from vigorous organized games through informal play and shall include supportive equipment, pavings, shaded areas, storage, lighting, access to toilets and similar service features.

(21) School facilities.

(i) Academic and industrial arts or homemaking classrooms shall be provided to permit formal instruction for the full capacity of children. Classrooms shall provide a minimum of 40 square feet per pupil in new construction. Classroom equipment shall be sturdy and in keeping with the requirements of the local school authorities.

(ii) The maximum group size for school classes shall be one teacher per 12 students.

(22) Health facilities.

(i) Rooms for medical examinations. A room or rooms shall be provided for medical examinations, nurse's office, first aid and other treatment. The room or rooms shall be adequately furnished and equipped to fulfill these functions, and shall be used for no other purposes.

(ii) Rooms for care of children with minor illnesses. Children with minor illnesses, not requiring hospital care, shall be cared for in a room or rooms not occupied by children who are not ill.

(iii) Isolation facilities. Facilities for the isolation of children with communicable disease are required and shall be equipped for the efficient care of such children. Such facilities shall be maintained in a manner to prevent the spread of disease. Separate toilet facilities shall be utilized by children with communicable disease.

(iv) First aid supplies, as recommended by the staff physician, shall be readily available for use.

(v) All drugs, medicines and instruments shall be kept in a suitable locked cabinet and accessible only to the physician or nurse in charge.

(d) Physical plant requirements.

(1) Office and reception facilities. Each detention facility shall provide:

(i) onsite office space adequate to permit the efficient, businesslike operation of the program and related services, and for private interviews, consultations or conferences. Space and equipment shall be provided for the safekeeping and privacy of essential records and the temporary storage of the children's personal belongings;

(ii) reception space for the orderly intake and release of children and for visiting with the children.

(2) Dining rooms. Dining rooms in all facilities shall be adequate to serve the children under care. A minimum of 15 square feet of floor space per person, to accommodate the planned seating capacity, shall be provided.

(3) Kitchens.

(i) Equipment. All kitchens shall be well-lighted, properly ventilated, provided with essential and proper equipment for the preparation and serving of food, storage, refrigeration and freezer facilities, for the number of persons to be served.

(ii) Defective utensils. Dishes, glassware and other utensils with chips, cracks or other defects shall be discarded.

(iii) Protection from rodents and insects. Food and dishes shall be protected from rodents and insects.

(iv) Cleanliness. All kitchen equipment and surroundings shall be kept clean.

(v) Food handlers. Employees engaged in the handling and preparation of food shall meet all State and local health requirements and shall wear proper and clean apparel and give special attention to personal cleanliness.

(vi) Compliance with health and safety regulations. Each institution shall comply with the regulations relating to kitchen operations for fire protection, safety, sanitation and health, as set forth by the State, and county and local health and fire departments.

(4) Food storage.

(i) Storerooms and pantries. Storerooms and pantries shall be dry, well-lighted and ventilated. All proper measures shall be taken to keep them free from vermin and rodents.

(ii) Cleaning supplies shall be kept separate from food supplies.

(iii) Refrigeration of perishable foods. In the refrigeration of all perishable foods, the temperature shall be at or below 45° F.

(iv) Freezers. Freezers and frozen food compartments shall be maintained at minus 10° to 0° F.

(v) Thermometers. Accurate thermometers shall be attached to all refrigerated areas in the warmest zones.

(5) Sanitation.

(i) Compliance with State and local requirements. Each institution shall comply with the requirements of State and local departments of health.

(ii) Water supply and sewage facilities. Adequate and safe water supply and sewage facilities shall be provided and shall comply with State and local laws.

(iii) Washing of food containers and utensils. Dishes, glassware, eating and cooking utensils, and food containers (including those used in transporting food) shall be properly washed, rinsed, disinfected and dried in a sanitary manner to conform to the following standards:

(a) scraping to remove food particles;

(b) prerinsing and proper stacking;

(c) mechanical dishwashing:

(1) washing in clear water, maintained at 140° F to 160° F, containing recommended amount of effective detergent or washing compound;

(2) rinsing in water maintained at 180° Fahrenheit;

(3) drying by air;

(d) hand dishwashing:

(1) washing in clear water, maintained at 100° Fahrenheit to 120° F, containing recommended amount of effective detergent or washing compound;

(2) rinsing in clear, hot water;

(3) sanitizing by use of a sanitizing agent recommended by the Department of Health or immersing in water at temperature of 170° to 180° F;

(4) drying by air.

(6) Compliance with regulations; washing of hands by food handlers. The food preparation and service area shall conform to State and local

regulations. Soap and single-service towels shall be provided as part of the handwashing facilities. Handwashing signs shall be posted in each toilet facility used by employees.

(7) Screens. Insect screens shall be used where food is stored, prepared or served, and wherever else necessary.

(8) Cleaning of equipment. Adequate provision shall be made for the effective cleaning of all equipment and surroundings.

(9) Trash and garbage. All trash and garbage shall be kept in suitable covered containers, stored away from the food preparation areas, and shall be removed from premises at regular intervals.

(10) Storage rooms and closets. Housekeeping service closets shall be provided within, or convenient to, each children's living unit, program areas and food service spaces.

(11) Screening and fencing. (i) Proper screening and fencing shall be provided throughout the building where and when needed. Such screening and fencing shall effectively and humanely detain the children within the program and living areas, shall provide privacy as needed and shall discourage unauthorized or objectionable communications with the outside community.

(ii) Screening and pesticides shall be used to control insects and other vermin to maintain a safe and sanitary environment for staff and children.

(12) Communications.

(i) Telephones. Each separate living unit shall have 24-hour telephone service, or an intercom system connected with an outside telephone service.

(ii) There shall be an electrical signal system between the child care workers' station and rooms in children's sleeping areas which would permit a child to call for assistance from within a locked room.

(iii) There shall be an intercommunications or emergency signal system readily available and operable to permit staff members to summon aid immediately to supervisory areas, teaching stations, interview rooms and similar spaces wherever supervisory assistance may not be readily available.

§180.10   Program requirements–noninstitutional, non-secure detention facilities.

(a) Family boarding care facilities and agency-operated boarding care facilities.

(1) General requirements.

(i) All members of the household must be of good character and reputation. Fitness shall be attested by satisfactory references.

(ii) The operators and relief shall be in good health and have no disqualifying physical or mental handicap.

(iii) The operators and relief operators shall have the ability to relate positively to the children in care and shall have an understanding of their needs. At least one of the operators shall be present in the home and available for supervision at all times.

(iv) The home must be in an appropriate neighborhood, as determined by the division.

(v) The home must be readily accessible to community resources and activities.

(vi) The home and premises must be kept in clean and sanitary condition and in good repair, and provide for the reasonable comfort and well-being of the household.

(vii) The home must provide reasonable (as determined by the division) security against fire hazards.

(viii) There must be adequate and accessible supply of water of satisfactory sanitary quality for drinking and household use. There must be provision for hot water for washing and bathing.

(ix) The dwelling must be effectively screened against flies and other insects where appropriate.

(x) The temperature in the home shall be maintained at a comfortable level as determined by the division.

(xi) Adequate bathing, toilet and lavatory facilities (as determined by the division) shall be kept in sanitary condition.

(xii) Sleeping arrangements shall be as follows:

(a) Each child in care shall have a separate bed. Sleeping rooms shall provide at least 30 square feet of floor space for each bed and two feet of space between beds, with walls at least seven feet high, and shall have a minimum horizontal dimension of seven feet. No more than three children shall occupy any bedroom.

(b) Every sleeping room occupied by children in care shall have good natural light and ventilation, and shall have one or more windows opening directly to the outside.

(c) No bed shall be located in any unfinished attic, basement, or in any stair, hall, or room commonly used for other than bedroom purposes.

(d) Children of different sex shall not sleep in the same room.

(e) Separate and accessible drawer space for personal belongings and closet space for clothing shall be available for individual children in care.

(xiii) There shall be outdoor play space available, other than in a street. It shall be readily accessible either on the premises or elsewhere.

(xiv) The following conditions shall be observed:

(a) Children in care shall mingle freely and on equal footing with other children in the household.

(b) The religious faith of the child shall be preserved and protected.

(c) Provisions shall be made to meet the educational needs of children in care.

(d) Food supplied to the children in care shall be of good quality, properly prepared, and served at regular hours in sufficient quantity.

(e) Clothing shall be kept in proper condition of repair and cleanliness, and shall be adapted to seasonal conditions and be of such style and quality so as not to distinguish the children in care from other children in the community.

(f) Individual toilet articles such as comb and toothbrush shall be provided.

(g) Health supervision, medical and dental care shall be provided each child in accordance with his needs. Each child continued in care for more than three days shall have a physical examination which shall be recorded.

(h) Records of admission and discharges shall be maintained as described in these regulations.

(i) No home shall care for more than six children. This shall include any children under 13 years of age who live with supervisory personnel in the facility.

(2) Other requirements--family boarding care facilities.

(i) Operators of family boarding care detention facilities shall meet the following requirements:

(a) They shall be free from communicable disease. There shall be a recent physical examination of the operators. Additional reports shall be provided upon request by the division.

(b) They shall be in reasonably secure economic position and self-supporting aside from payments to be made for the children in care. One of the operators may work.

(c) The authorized agency must be able to communicate successfully with operators in the best interest of the children in care where there is a language barrier.

(d) No operator shall operate a commercial lodging or boarding house, seasonal or otherwise, or conduct maternity or convalescent business or other business which might adversely affect the welfare of the children in care.

(ii) Couples who operate a facility and are living together shall be legally married.

(3) Additional requirements for agency-operated boarding care detention facilities.

(i) At least two adults shall be responsible for the care of the children in care. In the case of a married couple, it is permissible for the man to work outside of the detention program operation.

(ii) There shall be provision for relief persons on a regular basis.

(iii) There shall be provision for emergency coverage.

(b) Nonsecure group care facilities. Nonsecure group care facilities for the care of at least 7 but not more than 12 children shall be operated only when the following conditions are met:

(1) A professionally qualified social worker, as required herein, with experience in child welfare, who may be in the employ of the local department of social services or Family Court probation service, shall provide casework service as soon after admission as practicable, and visit each child daily at least during the first week of each child's placement.

(2) Adequate supervision shall be provided for the children. Persons caring for children shall be sufficient in number for the children under care and shall be selected on the basis of good moral character, interest in and ability to care for children. There shall be:

(i) at least two adults responsible for the care of children on duty in each detention facility;

(ii) appropriate housekeeping staff;

(iii) provision for relief personnel on a regular basis; and

(iv) provision for coverage in the case of any emergency.

(3) Physical facility.

(i) Location. The nonsecure group care facility shall be in an appropriate neighborhood and so located that it is accessible to religious, school and recreational facilities and other community resources. Suitable outdoor play areas shall be readily available to the children.

(ii) Building and grounds. Buildings used in whole or in part as a detention facility shall be in compliance with all applicable local building and fire regulations.

(iii) General requirements.

(a) The facility shall be of sufficient size to provide adequate living accommodations for the residents and shall be suitably furnished and equipped.

(b) The facility shall be kept in sanitary condition and good repair.

(c) The facility shall be effectively screened against flies and other insects.

(d) Adequate and safe water supply and sewage facilities shall be provided and shall comply with State and local laws.

(iv) Heating, electrical, ventilating and other mechanical systems shall be designed and maintained so that, under normal conditions of use, danger to the health and welfare of the residents from such equipment will be held to a minimum.

(v) Temperature in the facility shall be maintained at a comfortable level.

(vi) Rooms shall be adequately lighted and ventilated.

(vii) All floors used by children shall have alternate exits, remotely located from each other and readily accessible to the occupants, except that a two-story detached dwelling shall have a minimum of one exit stair from the second floor and at least one additional alternate, safe means of emergency egress from the second floor to ground level outside of the building, with access to a street or other suitable open space.

(viii) Occupancy by children shall not be permitted above the second floor in a building of wood-frame construction.

(ix) Sleeping rooms.

(a) Every sleeping room occupied by children shall have good natural light and ventilation and shall have one or more windows opening directly to the exterior.

(b) Separate and accessible drawer or shelf space for personal belongings, and sufficient closet space for indoor and outdoor clothing, shall be available for each child.

(c) No sleeping accommodations shall be located in any unfinished attic, basement, stair, hall, or room commonly used for other than bedroom purposes.

(d) Children of different sex shall not sleep in the same room.

(e) All single sleeping rooms for children shall contain not less than 70 square feet of floor area in a minimum horizontal and vertical dimension of seven feet.

(f) All sleeping rooms for the accommodation of more than one child shall contain not less than 60 square feet of floor area per child and a minimum horizontal dimension of eight feet with walls seven feet high.

(1) No more than three children shall occupy a bedroom.

(2) Each child shall have a separate bed, spaced at least three feet apart from other beds.

(g) Staff members who sleep at the facility shall be provided with sleeping quarters separate from those for children.

(x) Bathing and toilet facilities. Bathing and toilet facilities shall be provided as follows:

(a) Minimum requirements as to lavatories, tubs or showers:

Children	Lavatories	Tubs or Showers
7–8	2	1
9–12	3	2

(b) A minimum of two toilets shall be provided and available for the children.

(xi) Living rooms. Living rooms or rooms of sufficient size shall be provided to serve the needs of the residents.

(xii) Dining facilities. Dining facilities shall be provided with sufficient space and equipment to serve all the residents.

(xiii) Kitchen. The kitchen shall be equipped to provide adequate food preparation, storage and service.

(xiv) Facilities for storage and laundry. Facilities for storage and laundry shall be provided and shall include:

(a) space for storage of household supplies, larger personal items, seasonal clothing and outside sports and gardening equipment; and

(b) linen closet.

(xv) Sanitation.

(a) Compliance with State and local requirements. Each facility shall comply with the requirements of State and local departments of health.

(b) Water supply and sewage facilities. Adequate and safe water supply and sewage facilities shall be provided and shall comply with State and local laws.

(c) Washing of food containers and utensils. Dishes, glassware, eating utensils, and food containers (including those used in transportating food) shall be properly washed, rinsed, disinfected and dried in a sanitary manner to conform to the following standards:

(1) scraping to remove food particles;

(2) prerinsing and proper stacking;

(3) mechanical dishwashing:

(i) washing in clear water, maintained at 140° to 160° F Fahrenheit, containing recommended amount of effective detergent or washing compound;

(ii) rinsing in water maintained at 180° F;

(iii) drying by air;

(4) hand dishwashing:

(i) washing in clear water, maintained at 100° to 120° F, containing recommended amount of effective detergent or washing compound;

(ii) rinsing in clear, hot water;

(iii) sanitizing by use of a sanitizing agent recommended by the Department of Health or immersing in water at temperature of 170° to 180° F;

(iv) drying by air.

(d) Washing of hands by food handlers. The food preparation and service area shall conform to State and local regulations. Soap and single-service towels shall be provided as part of the handwashing facilities. Handwashing signs shall be posted in each toilet facility used by employees.

(e) Closets and lockers for dietary personnel. Either closets or lockers shall be provided for dietary personnel to hang their clothing.

(f) Screens. Window and door screens shall be used where food is stored, prepared or served, and wherever else necessary.

(g) Cleaning of equipment. Adequate provision shall be made for effective cleaning of all equipment and surroundings.

(h) Trash and garbage. All trash and garbage shall be kept in suitable covered containers, stored away from the food preparation areas, and shall be removed from premises at regular intervals.

(xvi) Medical policies and procedures.

(a) The medical policies and procedures shall be described in writing and interpreted to all the personnel of the facility. They shall be subject to frequent and regular review.

(b) Health supervision, medical and dental care shall be provided each child in accordance with his needs, and shall follow the written medical policies and procedures.

(c) Examinations. Each child continued in care for more than three days shall have a complete physical examination, including an appraisal of his health, which shall be properly recorded.

(d) A continuing individual medical record shall be maintained for each child in care.

(xvii) Child care.

(a) Food supplied to the children shall be of good quality, properly prepared, served at regular hours and sufficient in quantity. The diet shall meet the nutritional standards recommended by the National Research Council. All milk and milk products shall be pasteurized.

(b) Menus, as served, shall be retained on file for one year after date of use.

(c) Each child shall be provided with appropriate clothing, individually selected and properly fitted. Clothing shall be adequate in amount, attractive and of good quality, and properly maintained for comfort and health.

(d) Treatment services shall be provided children in accordance with their individual needs, and shall include psychiatric and psychological services, including tests and examinations.

(e) Appropriate educational and recreational programs shall be provided for the children in care.

(f) Protection of religious faith. The religious faith of each child shall be preserved and protected.

§180.11   Secure detention holdover programs.

(a) A holdover facility shall be established only when an approved available secure detention facility is located more than 1½ hours distant from the Family Court under normal travel conditions.

(b) Children shall not be detained in a holdover facility in excess of 48 hours, except that a youth may be detained in such facility for up to 72 hours in the case of holidays or court recess.

(c) Capacity of a holdover facility shall not exceed three children.

(d) A holdover facility shall be located in a fire resistant building, have at least one individual sleeping room, a separate area for recreation, waiting, interviewing or visiting, a bathroom (to include a toilet, sink and shower) with hot and cold running water. Outside communications, such as 24-hour telephone service, shall be available.

(e) Each facility shall provide for dining and make provisions to serve snacks or meals to newly admitted children, and for regular meals.

(f) When a holdover facility is located in an institution caring for other people, detained children shall be kept in separate quarters out of sight and hearing of such other people.

(g) Provision shall be made for 24-hour awake, on-duty supervision when children are detained in a holdover facility. A woman shall be on duty whenever a female child is detained. Personnel shall be drawn from a panel of persons who have personal characteristics and experience appropriate for work with children who may be disturbed or angry after apprehension for violation of law and removal from home.

(h) Only children of the same sex may sleep in the same room.

(i) There may be no more than two children sleeping in each bedroom.

§180.12   Records, reports and notification.

(a) Reports shall be submitted to the division on forms prescribed by the division. Such reports shall include but not be limited to:

(1) reimbursement claims;

(2) statistical reports;

(3) population reports;

(4) report of room confinement;

(5) report of fire in facility;

(6) report of death of child in facility; and

(7) other reports as may be required and needed.

(b) The division shall be notified in writing of any request for change in program, capacity or plans to subsequently change or modify physical plant. The division shall also be notified of any unusual or serious events such as, but not limited to, riots, assaults, or birth by residents. Such notification shall be submitted in writing within five days of the occurrence of the incident, after verbal notification within 24 hours.

(c) Records and reports.

(1) Each facility shall maintain a current case record for each child, which shall include intake information, observation and treatment reports and transfer or discharge summary.

(2) Other records relating to children.

(i) Each facility shall keep records of individual children required by section 372 of the Social Services Law.

(ii) Records shall include information concerning date and time of admission, reasons for admission (pertinent section of law), place to which child is discharged, specific offense alleged, length of stay prior to petition, length of stay from adjudication to final disposition, and total length of stay.

(iii) Records shall be conveniently indexed and provision shall be made, either by means of a card index or otherwise, so that an accurate roll call of the children present or under care at any time may be readily made.

(iv) Records shall be retained by the administrative agency until the child becomes 18 years of age.

(v) Records and reports maintained by the facility related to children under the jurisdiction of the division shall be confidential, pursuant to section 372 of the Social Services Law and section 168.7 of this Subtitle.

(3) Visitors. Each facility shall keep a book in which shall be entered the name, address, date of visit, and relationship of every person visiting each child, which name and address shall be secured by each such visit.

(i) Each facility shall report all deaths of children to the division within 24 hours of the occurrence of such deaths, on forms and in the manner prescribed by the division.

(ii) Each facility shall report to the division all injuries to children which require the services of physician and which, in his opinion, have caused or may cause death, serious disability or disfigurement of the body.

(iii) Report of fires. All institutional fires, or incidents involving the use of fire fighting or fire safety equipment, shall be orally reported to the division within 48 hours of the time of occurrence. A written report shall be submitted to the division within 10 days.

(d) Examination by State Division for Youth. Representatives of the State Division for Youth shall, at all reasonable times, be allowed to observe and interview children with relation to any matter pertaining to their health, safety, treatment and training.

(e) The division shall list all facilities certified for the detention of children and shall file a copy of that list semiannually with the clerk of the Family Court in each county, the clerk of the Criminal Court of the City of New York, the clerk of the Supreme Court in each county within the City of New York, and the clerk of the County Court in each county outside the City of New York.

§180.13 Division for Youth visitation and inspection.

(a) Officials, agents or representatives of the division shall visit and inspect all facilities used for the detention of children, pursuant to The Family Court Act and the Criminal Procedure Law, and subject to certification by the division. Such officials, agents or representatives are empowered to inspect and review all areas, physical plants, programs, records, reports, files, memoranda and other pertinent material and locations relating to the establishment and operation of such facilities, programs and services.

(b) Officials, agents or representatives of the division shall have access to contact, visit and interview all children received for detention care, and all staff employed to provide services in detention facilities.

(c) Reports, data and other material relating to establishment and operation of detention facilities, programs or services shall be made available to officials, agents or representatives of the division on such forms, at such time and in such manner as may be prescribed by the division.

(d) The division shall make periodic reports of the operation and adequacy of such facilities, and the need for provision of such facilities, to the county executive, if there be one, the county legislature and the Family Court judges of the county in which such facilities are located, and the Office of Court Administration.

§180.14 Fire safety and accident prevention.

(a) General requirements.

(1) Each facility shall comply with all applicable State and local laws, ordinances, rules and regulations relative to fire protection, applying any which are more restrictive than the requirements in this Part.

(2) Each non-secure and secure detention institutional facility shall arrange an annual inspection of each building and its fire protection equipment, (which shall be installed according to recommendations by the National Fire Protection Association) by a qualified fire inspection official, who shall give the facility a written report of his findings which shall be kept on file on the premises until the next annual report of inspection has been received and filed. The facility shall be responsible for correcting any fire hazards called to its attention through such inspection, and for keeping a written record on file of the action taken with date. Copies of the inspection report and report on repairs made must be forwarded to the division.

(3) Each detention facility staff member and facility operator shall be familiar with the fire safety prevention program, which shall be in writing, appropriate to their facility program and approved by local fire officials.

(4) No hazardous condition shall be permitted to exist in any detention facility.

(5) Children shall not operate any power equipment, except under the close supervision of a responsible adult and only when such children are of legal age to do so.

(6) For each non-secure and secure detention, institutional and group care facility, fire drills shall be held at different times during the day and night and as often as is needed to familiarize and instruct children and staff with routine, but not less often than once in each 60-day period. A fire drill census taken at each drill shall be checked against the daily or bedtime census. A written record of all fire drills, to include at least the date, the time of day and the amount of time taken to evacuate, shall be kept on file for one year.

(7) Combustible or highly flammable materials shall not be used by children, except under the personal supervision of an adult. Such materials, if required, shall be stored in a fire-restrictive receptacle or room in a separate building.

(8) All exit doors, halls and stairs shall be well-lighted and kept clean, free of obstruction.

(b) Non-secure detention group care facility.

(1) An automatic fire protection system shall be provided throughout buildings containing sleeping quarters. Such systems may utilize smoke-detecting or automatic sprinkler systems or may be an appropriate combination of these systems. A procedure for action to be taken when the system is activated must be provided and all residents and local fire districts shall be familiar with the procedures.

(2) Emergency instructions shall be posted in all areas, clearly showing alternate means of egress and means of securing fire, police and medical assistance.

(3) Children (and staff) shall be instructed, at time of intake (or employment) and at regular intervals, in emergency procedures.

(c) Secure and non-secure institutional detention facilities.

(1) An automatic fire detection system or an automatic sprinkler system, or appropriate combinations of these systems, shall be located throughout each building occupied by children. These systems shall include appropriately located manual fire alarm pull stations and smoke detector protection of required paths of exit. Fire protection equipment may be omitted from children's bedrooms where the possibility of tampering exists.

(2) All areas of high fire hazard in all buildings used by children shall be protected by an automatic sprinkler system.

(3) Fire extinguishers shall be provided and maintained. Soda-acid type extinguishers shall not be permitted in areas accessible to the children.

(4) All floors used by children shall have suitable remotely located alternate exits which shall be properly marked with exit signs.

(5) Interior finish trim and decorative materials shall be either noncombustible or shall have low flame-spread ratings and characteristics as specified by the New York State Building Construction Code.

(6) The night staff shall be provided with emergency lights, such as flashlight or battery-operated lanterns, in good working order.

(7) A written plan of evacuation of buildings with printed procedures to be followed in case of fire shall be posted in conspicuous places throughout the institution.

(8) Each employee shall be instructed in the use of fire fighting equipment and procedures, and shall be assigned specific responsibilities which shall include knowledge of the location and proper use of fire extinguishers in the part of the building for which he is responsible.

§180.15 Secure and non-secure institutional facilities–new construction and alteration.

(a) Plans for construction of secure detention facilities. On and after the date this rule becomes effective, no building to be used as a detention facility for children shall be constructed or remodeled, in whole or in part, except on plans and designs approved in writing by the division. Plans shall be submitted for approval in accordance with the procedure prescribed by the division. No child shall be detained in any new or remodeled building where plans and designs have not been approved by the division or have not been submitted to the division for its approval.

(b) Definitions. As used in this section, the following definitions apply:

(1) Building means a structure.

(2) Construction means the erection of a new structure.

(3) Addition means extension or increase in area or height of an existing structure.

(4) Substantial modification means any alteration, change, rearrangement or reconstruction to an existing structure, except for ordinary repairs and maintenance.

(5) Equipment means fixtures or articles affixed to the structure.

(6) Occupancy means use or purpose of a building, structure or premises or any room located therein.

(c) Construction, addition, substantial modification and change in occupancy.

(1) There shall be no construction, addition, substantial modification or change in occupancy of buildings or parts of buildings used or to be used in the operation of a secure detention facility except on plans and designs approved in writing by the New York State Division for Youth. Plans shall be submitted for approval in accordance with the procedures prescribed by the division. To qualify for approval by the division, plans and specifications must be in substantial compliance with the appropriate provisions of the State Building Construction Code relating to institutions, the regulations of the division and all other applicable provisions of State and local laws, ordinances, rules and regulations.

(2) No changes or modifications shall be made in approved plans or specifications without the approval of the division.

(3) The approval of the division shall become void one year after given, unless a contract for the approved construction or reconstruction shall have been entered into prior thereto.

(d) Site design. Site design considerations shall include at least the following: security, privacy, ease of group movement and supervision, outdoor play features, parking, service access, lighting, and convenient accessibility to public transportation. Planning shall tend to discourage unauthorized or objectionable communication with the outside community.

(e) Design for supervision. The design of new detention facilities shall encompass good planning for the movement of supervised groups and individual children throughout. Glazing in doors and partitions, using shatter-resistant safety glass, shall be utilized to promote effective supervision, security and safety of the children. Steel bars, exposed toilet fixtures, and similar equipment exhibiting a jail-like character are to be avoided wherever possible.

§180.16   Jail placement.

(a) Authorization. Section 304.1(2) of the Family Court Act requires Division for Youth approval prior to the jail placement of alleged or adjudicated juvenile delinquents remanded to detention and requires the division to promulgate regulations which it will apply in determining whether approval for such jail placement will be granted. Section 510.15 of the Criminal Procedure Law prohibits jail placement of an alleged or convicted juvenile offender under the age of 16 without the approval of the division. Approval for a jail placement may be requested by calling the Division for Youth Detention Services Unit at (518) 473-4630. This line is available 24 hours a day.

(b) Definition. Jail placement shall mean the detention of a youth in a prison, jail, lockup or other place used for the incarceration of adults convicted of a crime or under arrest and charged with a crime.

(c) Circumstances under which jail placement may be approved:

(1) The youth is alleged to have committed or has been found to have committed an act or acts which if committed by an adult would constitute a crime or crimes as defined in the following provisions of the Penal Law: section 125.25(1)-(2) (murder in the second degree) and subdivision (3) of such section provided that the underlying crime for the murder charge is one for which such person is criminally responsible; section 135.25 (kidnapping in the first degree); 150.20 (arson in the first degree); section 120.10(1)-(2) (assault in the first degree); 125.20 (manslaughter in the first degree); section 130.35(1)-(2) (rape in the first degree); section 130.50(1)-(2) (sodomy in the first degree); 130.70 (aggravated sexual abuse); 140.30 (burglary in the first degree); section 140.25(1) (burglary in the second degree); 150.15 (arson in the second degree); 160.15 (robbery in the first degree); or section 160.10(2) (robbery in the second degree); or defined in the Penal Law as an attempt to commit murder in the second degree or kidnapping in the first degree.

(2) No secure juvenile detention facility, including a 48-hour hold-over facility, has a bed available to provide secure detention care. A bed may be deemed unavailable in the following emergency conditions: when road conditions have been defined by The National Weather Service as hazardous; or when the time in transporting to and from that facility would make it impractical (considering the health and welfare of the youth) to assure a timely court appearance; or when a child needs secure care in a hospital and no children's ward is available.

(d) Circumstances under which jail placement will not be approved. Jail placement will not be approved for a juvenile under the age of 14 years, with the exception of a 13 year-old alleged or convicted juvenile offender.

(e) Conditions of jail placement.

(1) Authorization shall be for a 12-hour period and may be renewed for additional 12-hour periods only so long as the emergency conditions as defined above continue to exist.

(2) Youth shall be housed in quarters separate from incarcerated adults.

(3) There shall be complete audio and visual separation of youth from incarcerated adults.

(4) There shall be continuous direct staff supervision of youth in jail placement. Audio and visual monitoring devices may not be substituted for direct staff supervision.

(5) Each youth shall be provided with a bed, mattress, blanket and pillow.

(6) Each facility shall assure that a youth is provided meals at established mealtimes. A meal must be provided to any youth detained more than five hours.

(7) Youth may be visited by parents, legal guardian or attorney at any time during the time of incarceration.

(8) Persons requesting jail placement of a youth shall be obligated to notify the youth's parent, or legal guardian of the youth's location.

(9) Youth shall be held only in jails or lockups which are monitored by the New York State Commission of Correction.

§180.17 Reimbursement.

(a) A county legislature or its designee shall submit to the director of the division an annual plan for the detention care for youth. A detention plan shall be included in the program for comprehensive youth services planning where such a comprehensive plan exists, and shall be submitted by the county youth board, bureau, department or agency. Such plan shall be submitted on forms as required by the division and shall conform with appropriate State law, rules and regulations governing the temporary care of children and shall include provision or arrangement for adequate secure and nonsecure detention care.

(b) A county detention plan, upon approval by the division, shall be the basis for reimbursement of county expenditures for detention care.

(1) Care provided for alleged or adjudicated persons in need of supervision in a secure detention facility shall be reimbursed only as determined by State standards for the care of status offenders.

(2) Counties which do not have nonsecure detention care available shall be charged 100 percent of cost of care for youth in State-operated detention facilities.

(3) Counties which do not have adequate nonsecure detention care conveniently available, as determined by the division, will not be eligible for reimbursement for detention care.

(c) Quarterly claims for actual expenditures shall be submitted to the division, on forms as required by the division, at the end of each quarter ending in March, June, September and December. The division may, at its discretion, permit submission of such accountings for periods greater than three months, but not exceeding one year.

(d) Annual allocations for depreciation of county-owned buildings certified and used for detention programs may be reimbursed, in accordance with the rules and regulations of the division, as expenditures for care, maintenance and supervision.

(e) The Division for Youth shall reimburse a social services district for the full amount for approved expenditures, where such program is provided, at the request of the division, for a child under the jurisdiction of the division who is a nonresident of the district. The division will charge the county of residence 50 percent of the cost of care of such youth.

(f) Rates of expenditures for detention care by the county shall be approved (and established) by the Division for Youth annually.

(g) Changes in rates of expenditure for detention care shall be made by the county only after prior written approval of the division.

(h) Approved family boarding home expenditures by the county shall be subject to reimbursement through established per diem rates approved by the division. Approved expenditures for reserved accommodations by the county may be reimbursed by the division. These rates shall have prior approval of the division annually.

(i) Reimbursement for approved expenditures by the county for detention care in certified facilities (family boarding homes, as above may be) shall be accomplished according to contract with the division. Such contracts shall include operational and other costs, as well as specified operating conditions as agreed to by the county and the division.

(j) Expenditures made by the Division for Youth for the care, maintenance and supervision of children in a regional secure detention facility who are local charges, within the meaning ascribed to such term by the Social Services Law, shall be subject to reimbursement to the State by the social services district from which the youth was referred, at the rate of 50 percent of the per diem amount expended by the division to provide care, maintenance and supervision in the secure detention facility. The Division for Youth, subject to the approval of the Director of the Budget and certification to the chairmen of the Senate Finance and Assembly Ways and Means Committees, shall annually compute and determine the per diem rate, and shall assess the social services district on such forms and in such manner as it may deem appropriate. Billing shall be discontinued on the day following a runaway, when a child is not returned within 24 hours. If a runaway child from a Division for Youth facility is apprehended pursuant to a Division for Youth warrant, the aforesaid reimbursement to the division shall be made by the social services district which originally placed the child with the division.

(k) For purposes of this section, reimbursement for administrative-related expenditures shall not exceed:

(1) 17 percent of the total approved expenditures for facilities of 25 beds or more; and

(2) 21 percent of the total approved expenditures for facilities with less than 25 beds.

(*l*) For purposes of this section, administrative-related expenditures shall mean:

(1) costs associated with persons whose primary function is the policy direction, general management and support of the operation of the detention program in accordance with applicable rules and regulations of the division, State Education Department and all other applicable requirements of law. Such expenditures shall include, but shall not be limited to costs associated with persons primarily performing the following functions:

Commissioner	Assistant to Commissioners
Deputy Commissioner	Assistant Commissioner
Chief Executive	Assistant Executive
Executive Director	Assistant Director
Superintendent	Assistant Superintendent
Principal of On-Grounds School	Assistant Principal
Associate Director	Assistant to Director
Co-Administrator	Assistant to Co-Administrator
Director of Division	
Assistant to Executive	Executive Assistant
Facility Director	
Counsel and All Legal Staff	Planners
Ombudsmen	Researchers
Administrative Manager	Chauffeur
Administrative Associate	Administrative Analyst
Budget Director and Staff	Office Associate
College Aide	Federal Resource Specialist
Policy Information	Architect
Affirmative Action	Telephone Operator
Staff Analyst	Messenger
Internal Auditors	Secretaries - all
Investigators	
Disciplinary Specialist	
Community Service Managers, Workers	
Director of Electronic Data Processing Staff	
Department Heads (School)	
Director of Personnel and Staff	
Director of Purchasing and Staff	

Financial Director, Controller
Accountant
Business Manager
Office Manager, Clerical Supervisor
Bookkeeper
Statistician, Statistical Analyst
Business Machine Operator
Clerk, Office Worker
Receptionist, Transcriber
Stenographer, Typist

(2) Include but not be limited to all costs associated with the following:

Fringe benefits on Administrative Salaries	Data Processing
Telephone/Communications	Accounting
Postage	Audit
Office Services	Legal
Office Supplies	Insurance
All Conferences	Research
Travel of Administrative Personnel	
Parent Organization Charges	
Office Equipment	
Consultants	

§180.18 Revocation and suspension of operating certificates.

(a) General. No operating certificate shall be revoked or suspended, nor shall an application for renewal of an operating certificate be denied, without a hearing held in accordance with procedures established in this Part; except that an operating certificate may, nevertheless, be temporarily suspended or limited without a hearing for a period not in excess of 30 days upon a finding by the division that the public health, or an individual's health, safety or welfare are in imminent danger.

(b) Notice of hearing. A notice of hearing shall be served, in person or by registered mail addressed to the facility, at least 21 days prior to the date of hearing. The hearing shall be held within 30 days of mailing the notice of hearing. The notice shall specify the time and place of hearing, the proposed action, and the charges which are the basis for the proposed action. The charges shall specify the statutes, regulations of the division, or other applicable requirements of law with which the facility failed to comply, and a brief statement of the facts pertaining to such noncompliance.

(c) Answer. An answer to the charges, in writing, may be filed with the division not less than eight days prior to the date of hearing.

(d) Hearing officer. The hearing shall be conducted by a hearing officer, appointed by the division for such purpose, who has not been previously involved in the case. He shall have authority to administer oaths, issue subpoenas, require the attendance of witnesses and the production of records, rule upon requests for adjournment, rule upon offers of evidence, and to otherwise regulate the hearing, preserve requirements of due process and effectuate the purposes and provisions of applicable law, in accordance with the State Administrative Procedure Act.

(e) Hearing procedures.

(1) The hearing officer shall preside and shall make all procedural rulings.

(2) The rules of evidence as applied in courts of law shall not apply, except that all evidence shall be relevant and material.

(3) All testimony shall be given under oath.

(4) The hearing shall be recorded verbatim.

(5) The facility shall be entitled to be represented by an attorney-at-law or other representative of its choice at its own expense, to have witnesses give testimony and to otherwise present relevant and material evidence on its behalf, to cross-examine witnesses, and to examine any document or item offered into evidence.

(f) The decision.

(1) Upon conclusion of the hearing, the hearing officer shall make recommended findings of fact and conclusions of law, and shall make a recommended decision. He shall transmit such recommendations to the division, as expeditiously as possible, in a written report which shall be made part of the record, together with the notice of hearing, the answer, the verbatim transcript of the hearing, all documents marked into evidence at the hearing or otherwise designated as part of the record by the hearing officer.

(2) The decision of the division shall be based exclusively upon consideration of the record. The division shall not, however, be bound by the hearing officer's recommendations, but may adopt, reject or modify such recommendations, in whole or in part, as may be appropriate to its considered judgment of the record.

(3) The division shall expeditiously render a decision, in writing, which shall include findings of fact and conclusions of law, and a copy of such decision shall be mailed to the facility and to its attorney or other designated hearing representative.

(4) In the event the decision is adverse to the facility, the copy of the decision shall be sent together with a notice of the right to judicial review in accordance with the provisions of article 78 of the Civil Practice Law and Rules.

(g) Denial of an application for initial operating certificate. Upon the denial of an application for an initial operating certificate, the applicant may request a hearing. The division is required to grant a hearing upon such request in accordance with the procedures in this Part. The hearing shall be held within 30 days of the division's receipt of the request, subject to the authority of the hearing officer to grant reasonable adjournments. In the event that the request is denied, the applicant shall be notified in writing, together with a notice of the right to judicial review in accordance with the provisions of article 78 of the Civil Practice Law and Rules.

(h) Termination of operating certificate; temporary extension; retroactive issuance.

(1) The division shall extend the duration of an operating certificate for a temporary period, as may be appropriate, when the period of validity of an operating certificate terminates during the course of a hearing, and pending the hearing decision.

(2) In the event that an operating certificate terminates without the issuance of a renewal certificate, as a result of administrative error or delay by the division, the renewal certificate, when issued, shall be made effective as of the date of termination of the prior certificate; and the facility shall be considered as

having been operated under a valid operating certificate during the interval between termination of the prior certificate and issuance of the current certificates.

(3) The division may extend the duration of the period of validity of an operating certificate for a temporary period, under such terms and conditions as may be appropriate, whenever such extension may be required to adequately protect the health, safety or welfare of the residents of a facility.

§180.19 Enforcement.

(a) Division for Youth officials, as assigned by the director of the division or his representative, shall be responsible for assuring conformity for all statutes, rules and regulations which apply to detention care.

(b) The Director of the Division for Youth or his representative shall be responsible for originating, or referring to other appropriate enforcement officials, sanctions for serious violation of statutes, rules or regulations relating to the detention care of children as described in this Part.

(c) The Division for Youth shall be responsible for bringing violations of law pertaining to detention of juveniles to the attention of each appropriate law guardian or counsel for the defendant, who may petition for habeas corpus for persons aggrieved thereby.

(d) These regulations shall become effective immediately, except where otherwise noted herein, upon being filed with and recorded by the Secretary of State.

§180.20 State aid for construction or improvement of locally operated secure detention facilities.

(a) General conditions.

(1) Notwithstanding any other provision of regulation, State aid, subject to the limits of appropriations made by the Legislature and the regulations set forth in this section, is available to counties and the City of New York in an amount not to exceed 50 percent of approved expenditures incurred for construction or improvement of locally operated secure detention facilities.

(2) Counties and the City of New York may request State aid in the form of lump sum reimbursement for the aggregate of approved capital costs of construction or improvement of county-owned or New York City-owned buildings certified by the Division for Youth pursuant to Executive Law, section 510-a and in use, or to be used, as secure detention facilities.

(3) State aid is limited to 60 percent of division-approved capital costs or, when applicable, the amount appropriated for the county or the city, whichever is less.

(4) Eligible projects and costs, as defined below, are qualified for reimbursement only if the expenses therefor were incurred on or after January 1, 1970.

(b) Eligibility. In order to receive State aid under this section, a project must be eligible for reimbursement, the costs must be eligible, and the county or the city must meet the programmatic criteria set forth herein. The division shall have sole discretion to determine if eligibility and programmatic criteria have been met.

(1) Eligible projects shall include the following:

(i) new construction project, which shall mean the construction of an entirely new physical facility; and

(ii) alteration/rehabilitation/improvement project, which shall mean modification of an existing facility in order to allow it to be used for secure detention, or which will appreciably extend the useful life of the facility or which will upgrade a facility to provide for more efficient utilization.

(2) Ineligible projects shall include the following:

(i) repairs/maintenance projects which have as their purpose maintaining a secure detention facility in an ordinary efficient operating condition and which do not significantly add to the value of the facility or appreciably prolong its useful life.

(3) Eligible costs must be part of the costs of an eligible project and shall include costs associated with the following:

(i) planning and design, including preliminary surveys or studies, preparation of plans and specifications, and related architect or engineering fees;

(ii) site acquisition, including appraisals, abstracts, demolition and other costs necessary to acquire property;

(iii) construction, including all work necessary to prepare project for operation, also inspection and supervision;

(iv) equipment, including purchase and installation of original furnishings and built-in equipment necessary for the project operation; and

(v) interest on bonds, notes or other type of indebtedness necessarily undertaken to finance construction costs.

(4) Ineligible costs include the following:

(i) any costs financed by any Federal funds (except revenue sharing funds), other State aid or other noncounty funds;

(ii) administrative overhead costs associated with the capital project such as, but not limited to, centralized services costs, indirect cost rates, costs associated with bid lettings, etc.;

(iii) management fees related to marketing of bonds, notes or any other type of indebtedness;

(iv) any other cost which the division deems inappropriate.

(5) Programmatic criteria.

(i) The county or the city, when requesting reimbursement, shall provide or assure the availability of conveniently accessible and adequate nonsecure detention facilities, certified by the State Division for Youth, as resources for the Family Court, to be operated in compliance with the regulations of the Division for Youth for the temporary care and maintenance of alleged juvenile delinquents and persons in need of supervision held for or at the discretion of the Family Court.

(ii) Adequate nonsecure detention facilities for the purpose of this reimbursement shall mean that there shall be a sufficient range of nonsecure detention programs to meet the needs of all youth in need of nonsecure detention care, in the county or in the city. The county or the city shall, in consultation with the Division for Youth, establish facilities or programs sufficient to meet such needs.

(iii) The county or the city shall meet Federal detention requirements which relate to the removal of status offenders (PINS) from secure detention facilities.

(iv) The county or the city shall provide secure detention care, pursuant to law, to other counties through contract between the county or city and the division.

(6) Claiming/documentation. All claims shall be made by the county or city agency operating the secure detention facility or its authorized designee on forms provided by the division. Claims shall be made in accordance with procedures of the division and shall include all documentation necessary to allow the division or its designees to properly audit the claim. The division or

its designees shall have the right to inspect, at reasonable times and after written notification, any and all records and documents relating to such claim and the right to inspect the facilities for which reimbursement is requested. No reimbursement will be made until a certificate of allocation has been approved by the Division of the Budget and copies thereof filed with the State Comptroller, the Chairman of the Senate Finance Committee and the Chairman of the Assembly Ways and Means Committee.

§180.21   Abuse, neglect and significant incidents.

All juvenile detention facilities shall be subject to and must comply with the requirements as set forth in Part 433 of Title 18 of the New York Code, Rules, and Regulations.

TITLE 14
Department of Mental Hygiene

Part 583
Pre-admission Certification Committees for
Residential Treatment Facilities for
Children and Youth

§583.1 Background and intent.

(a) Chapter 947 of the Laws of 1981 authorized the establishment of residential treatment facility for children and youth. The legislation established procedures for admission to residential treatment facility for children and youth, designated pre-admission certification committees to carry out these procedures, and provided for advisory boards to the pre-admission certification committees.

(b) The purpose of the pre-admission certification committees and their advisory boards is to assure uniform access to residential treatment facilities for children and youth regardless of the current placement or source of referral of an individual child.

(c) The purpose of these regulations is to provide for the establishment and operation of the pre-admission certification committees and their advisory boards; to articulate the criteria for determining the eligibility of an individual for admission or transfer to a residential treatment facility for children and youth; and to specify the procedure to be used in determining eligibility and certifying individuals as the pre-admission certification committee's priority for admission or transfer to a residential treatment facility for children and youth.

§583.2 Legal Base.

(a) Sections 7.09 and 31.04 of the Mental Hygiene Law grant the Commissioner of Mental Health the power and responsibility to adopt regulations that are necessary and proper to implement matters under his or her jurisdiction and to set standards of quality and adequacy of facilities, equipment, personnel, services, records and programs for the rendition of services for the mentally ill pursuant to an operating certificate.

(b) Section 9.51 of the Mental Hygiene Law provides for the designation of pre-admission certification committees for defined geographic areas to evaluate each child proposed for admission or transfer to a residential treatment facility and for the establishment of an advisory board to serve each pre-admission certification committee.

(c) Section 31.26(c) of the Mental Hygiene Law provides for the adoption by the Commissioner of Mental Health and the Commissioner of Social Services, in consultation with the Commissioner of Education and the Director of the Division for Youth, of rules and regulations governing the operation of the pre-admission certification committees.

§583.3 Applicability.

(a) These regulations apply to the establishment and operation of the pre-admission certification committee. The pre-admission certification committee is responsible for reviewing each application made by or on behalf of a child or youth for admission to a residential treatment facility; for determining eligibility of such children; and for certifying children as the priority of the pre-admission certification committee for admission to a residential treatment facility.

(b) These regulations apply to the establishment and operation of the advisory boards to the pre-admission certification committees.

§583.4 Definitions.

(a) Child is an individual who has passed at least his/her 5th birthday, and who has not yet reached his/her 22nd birthday.

(b) Committee on the handicapped is a multidisciplinary team established in accordance with the provisions of the New York State Education Law to evaluate each handicapped child who resides within a school district.

(c) Likelihood of serious harm is a substantial risk of physical harm to other persons as manifested by recent homicidal or other violent behavior by which others are placed in reasonable fear of serious physical harm.

(d) Mental illness means an affliction with a mental disease or mental condition which is manifested by a disorder or disturbance in behavior, feeling, thinking, or judgment to such an extent that the person afflicted requires care, treatment and rehabilitation

(e) Nurse is an individual who is currently licensed as a registered professional nurse by the New York State Education Department.

(f) Physician is an individual who is currently licensed to practice medicine by the New York State Education Department.

(g) Psychiatrist is an individual who is currently licensed as a physician by the New York State Education Department and who is certified by, or is eligible to be certified by, the American Board of Psychiatry and Neurology as a psychiatrist or a child psychiatrist.

(h) Psychologist is an individual who is currently licensed as a psychologist by the New York State Education Department.

(i) Region is a geographically defined area within the State established by the Commissioner of Mental Health. Such regions are established for the purpose of administering those matters under the jurisdiction of the commissioner.

(j) Residential treatment facility is a residential treatment facility for children and youth as defined in Part 584 of this Chapter.

(k) Social worker is an individual who is currently licensed as a certified social worker by the New York State Education Department.

§583.5 Establishment of Pre-admission Certification Committees.

(a) A pre-admission certification committee shall be established for geographic areas which are coterminous with the regions of the Office of Mental Health.

(b) The Commissioner of Mental Health, the Commissioner of Social Services and the Commissioner of Education shall each designate a specific person as a member of the pre-admission certification committee in each region. In designating such persons, the commissioners shall assure that the interests of the people residing in the region are represented such committee shall be an independent team.

(c) Prior to designating pre-admission certification committee members, the Commissioner of Mental Health shall consult with the Conference of Local Mental Hygiene Directors and the Commissioner of Social Services shall consult with county commissioners of social services within the region.

(d) Pre-admission certification committee members shall be psychiatrists, physicians, nurses, psychologists or social workers as defined in this Part, and shall have experience in the assessment and treatment of mental illness, preferably in the area of children and youth.

(e) If the persons designated to the pre-admission certification committee do not include a psychiatrist or physician, the Commissioner of Mental Health shall designate a psychiatrist or physician to serve as an additional member.

(f) Pre-admission certification committee members shall not have an affiliation with a residential treatment facility as member of the governing body, an employee or a consultant.

(g) Pre-admission certification committee members may be employees of the State of New York but this is not a requirement.

§583.6 Responsibilities of the pre-admission certification committee.

(a) The pre-admission certification committee for each region shall be responsible for reviewing the applications of children within the region referred for admission to a residential treatment facility. The pre-admission certification committee shall review each child and determine whether or not such child is eligible for admission in accordance with the criteria specified in section 583.8 of this Part and the immediacy of the need of the individual child given the availability of services and the needs of the other children determined to be eligible who have not yet been admitted.

(b) The pre-admission certification committee for each region shall be responsible for referring children for admission to those residential treatment facility beds designated for that region by the Office of Mental Health.

(c) The pre-admission certification committee in any region may refer a child determined to be eligible to a pre-admission certification committee in another region when appropriate services are not available in a residential treatment facility within the region and placement outside the region is determined to be appropriate.

(d) For each available bed, the pre-admission certification committee shall consider all children that have been determined to be eligible that meet the admission criteria of the individual residential treatment facility as approved pursuant to section 584.7 of this Chapter and certify children as the priority of the pre-admission certification committee for admission. The children considered shall include those children determined to be eligible by the pre-admission certification committee and those referred by another pre-admission certification committee pursuant to section 583.9 of this Part. The pre-admission certification committee shall consider, among other factors, the immediacy of the need of the individual child as determined pursuant to subdivision (a) of this section.

§583.7 Organization and administration.

(a) The pre-admission certification committee shall meet on a regularly scheduled basis and shall hold such additional meetings as may be required.

(b) The pre-admission certification committee may meet in executive session to consider individual applications for admission to residential treatment facilities or other confidential matters as authorized in the Open Meetings Law.

(c) The pre-admission certification committee shall maintain written minutes of all meetings.

(d) The pre-admission certification committee shall prepare a written annual work plan for the 12 months commencing April first. Such work plan shall be subject to the approval of the appropriate regional director of the Office of Mental Health. The plan shall identify specific responsibilities of each member of the pre-admission certification committee; procedures for scheduling, conducting and providing public notice of meetings; procedures for reviewing applications for eligibility determinations and certifications as priority for admission, and procedures for storing and maintaining confidentiality of records.

(e) The pre-admission certification committee shall submit a monthly report to the appropriate regional director of the Office of Mental Health. The report shall, at a minimum, address the number of children referred to the pre-admission certification committee for an eligibility determination; the actions taken with respect to such referrals; the characteristics of the children determined to be eligible; and the availability of residential treatment facility beds in the region.

(f) The work plan and monthly reports shall be made available to the Commissioner of Education, the Commissioner of Social Services, the Director of the Division for Youth, and to local governmental officials in the region, including representatives of mental health, social services and education agencies.

(g) The pre-admission certification committee shall maintain the confidentiality of information pertaining to individual children. Such information shall not be a public record and shall not be released to any person or agency outside the Office of Mental Health and the advisory board except as follows:

(1) pursuant to an order of a court of record;

(2) to the mental health information service;

(3) to attorneys representing the child in proceedings in which the residents' involuntary admission to a residential treatment facility is at issue;

(4) with the consent of the child or of someone legally authorized to act on the child's behalf, to physicians and providers of health, mental health, and social or welfare services involved in caring for, treating, or rehabilitating the child. Such information shall be kept confidential and used solely for the benefit of the child; and

(5) to agencies requiring information to make payments to or on behalf of residents. Such information shall be kept confidential and limited to the information required.

§583.8 Eligibility criteria.

(a) The pre-admission certification committee shall make a determination that a child is eligible for admission only if the child is mentally ill and meets each of the following criteria:

(1) current diagnosis of a mental disorder as specified in the American Psychiatric Association's Diagnostic and Statistical Manual, Third Edition (DSM-III) or the International Classification of Diseases, Ninth Revision, Clinical Modification (ICD-9-CM);

(2) Identification of a serious and persistent psychopathology as evidenced by:

(i) severe thought disorder;

(ii) severe affective disorder;

(iii) moderate thought disorder in conjunction with an impulse control disorder or a deficit in activities of daily living skills;

(iv) moderate affective disorder in conjunction with an impulse control disorder or a deficit in activities of daily living skills;

(v) severe conduct disorder in conjunction with an impulse control disorder or a deficit in activities of daily living skills;

(vi) severe personality disorder in conjunction with as impulse control disorder or a deficit in activities of daily living skills; or

(vii) any combination of the above.

(3) intelligence quotient equal to or greater than 51;

(4) attainment of at least the 5th birthday but not the 21st birthday; and

(5) presentation of no likelihood of serious harm to others as defined in section 583.4(c) of this Part.

(b) The pre-admission certification committee shall not make an eligibility determination unless it finds that:

(1) available ambulatory care resources and other residential placements, other than a hospital, do not meet the treatment needs of the individual child;

(2) proper treatment of the child's psychiatric condition requires care and treatment under the direction of a physician within a residential treatment facility; and

(3) care and treatment in a residential treatment facility can reasonably be expected to improve the child's condition or prevent further regression so that services will no longer be needed, provided that a poor prognosis shall not in itself constitute grounds for a denial of determination of eligibility if treatment can be expected to effect a change in prognosis.

§583.9 Pre-admission process; expiration of eligibility.

(a) Applications for admission to residential treatment facilities may be made by a parent or guardian, directors of facilities licensed or operated by the Office of Mental Health; the committee of such person; social services officials or authorized agencies with care and custody of a child pursuant to the Social Services Law; the Director of the Division for Youth or a person or organization having custody of a child pursuant to an order issued under section 756 or 1055 of The Family Court Act; or the child himself/herself pursuant to section 9.13 of the Mental Hygiene Law. Such application shall include parental consent unless otherwise permitted by law.

(b) All applications shall be made directly to the pre-admission certification committee serving the region that includes the county in which the child's family resides or the county in which the child resided immediately prior to his/her most recent entry into the care or custody of social services officials, authorized agencies pursuant to the Social Services Law; the Director of the Division for Youth; or the Commissioner of Mental Health.

(c) The pre-admission certification committee shall obtain whatever information is necessary to make an eligibility determination.

(1) Application shall include, at a minimum, assessments of the child's psychiatric, medical, educational and social needs.

(2) When additional information is necessary, the pre-admission certification committee is legally authorized to request and receive clinical information regarding the child maintained by any person or entity.

(3) When additional information is necessary, the pre-admission certification committee may refer a child for additional assessment to a hospital or other facility licensed or operated by the Office of Mental Health.

(4) When an assessment is not available from a committee on the handicapped, the pre-admission certification committee shall request such assessment from the appropriate committee on the handicapped, to be provided within 30 days. For the purposes of this Part, the appropriate committee on the handicapped shall be the committee on the handicapped of the school district of residence at the time of the application for admission.

(e) The pre-admission certification committee shall base its determination of eligibility and immediacy of need of the individual child on a unanimous decision of those present. Such determinations shall be made in writing and shall include the physician's signature and the recommendation of each member of the pre-admission certification committee.

(f) The pre-admission certification committee in any region may refer a child determined to be eligible to a pre-admission certification committee in another region for consideration for certification as a priority for admission when appropriate services are not available in a residential treatment facility within their region and placement outside the region is determined to be appropriate.

(g) For each available bed, the pre-admission certification committee shall consider all children that have been determined to be eligible that meet the admission criteria of the individual residential treatment facility as approved pursuant to section 584.7 of this Chapter and shall certify children as the priority of the pre-admission certification committee for admission. The children considered shall include those children determined to be eligible by the pre-admission certification committee and those referred by another pre-admission certification committee pursuant to this section. The pre-admission certification committee shall consider, among other factors, the immediacy of the need of the individual child as determined pursuant to section 583.6(a) of this Part.

(h) The pre-admission certification committee shall base certification of children as the priority of the pre-admission certification committee on a unanimous decision of those present. Such determination shall be made in writing.

(i) The pre-admission certification committee shall reconfirm its determination of eligibility of a child when admission to a residential treatment facility does not occur within 60 days of the determination of eligibility pursuant to subdivisions (b) and (d) of section 583.6 and section 583.8 of this Part by requesting an update of the child's status, including the child's clinical status, current placement, and willingness and ability to be admitted if offered a placement. The committee shall base its reconfirmation of eligibility on a review of the documentation provided. Such reconfirmation shall be based on a unanimous decision, made in writing and shall include the physician's signature. If a child found eligible is expected to be unavailable for admission for a period of less than 30 days, the child's eligibility shall be considered to be suspended. The child may be put back on eligibility status as of the date that the temporary suspension ends.

(j) The pre-admission certification committee shall decertify the child from eligibility and shall provide written notice of the decertification to the referral agency contact and child and/or family if:

(1) the committee is notified or independently determines that the child has been placed in another appropriate setting and care in a residential treatment facility is no longer needed;

(2) the child is receiving appropriate services that meet the child's clinical needs;

(3) the parent(s) or guardian(s) state that the child's admission into a residential treatment facility is no longer desired;

(4) the child's clinical condition has deteriorated such that admission to a residential treatment facility as set forth in Section 583.8 of this Part would no longer be appropriate for a period of more than 30 days; or,

(5) that the child no longer meets criteria for admission. The committee may consider the sufficiency and accuracy of documentation it has received, and may request clarification and/or additional documentation, in determining whether to certify the child as eligible or decertify the child from eligibility.

(k) The pre-admission certification committee shall provide written notification to the referral agency contact and child and/or child's parent or legal guardian, as appropriate, or to the Family Court, if the child is the subject of a proceeding currently pending in the Family Court:

(1) that additional information or assessments have been requested prior to making an eligibility determination;

(2) that an eligibility determination has been made and whether or not the child has been determined to be eligible;

(3) that a referral has been made to another pre-admission certification committee for consideration for certification as priority for admission to a residential treatment facility bed designated in that region; or

(4) that a certification for admission to a residential treatment facility has been made.

(*l*) The pre-admission certification committee shall act in a timely manner.

(1) All applications shall be reviewed for completeness within seven calendar days of receipt.

(2) Once all necessary information has been obtained, an eligibility determination shall be made within 30 calendar days.

(3) Once an eligibility determination has been made, written notification shall be made within seven calendar days.

(4) Eligibility shall be reviewed every 60 days as required by Section 583.9(i).

§583.10 Advisory board.

(a) It is the purpose of the advisory board to the pre-admission certification committee to represent the interests of children in the region relating to the need for services provided in residential treatment facilities.

(b) The advisory board shall be designated as follows:

(1) The Commissioner of the Office of Mental Health shall consult with the Conference of Local Mental Hygiene Directors and other State and local government officials to develop a list of recommendations for membership on the advisory board to the pre-admission certification committee.

(2) The commissioner shall recommend at least five persons.

(3) The pre-admission certification committee shall designate the members of the advisory board from the recommendations.

(c) The advisory board shall consist of five members, with at least one person representing local government, one person representing voluntary agencies, and one person representing parents of children with mental illness.

(d) The membership of the advisory board shall be designated for staggered terms of three years.

(e) The advisory board shall have the following responsibilities:

(1) to meet at least quarterly with the pre-admission certification committee;

(2) to review the monthly reports of the pre-admission certification committee;

(3) to identify, in consultation with the pre-admission certification committee, information that will be of assistance to the pre-admission certification committee in determining the priorities for admission to residential treatment facilities in the region; and

(4) to visit residential treatment facilities at the request of the pre-admission certification committee. Such visits shall be relevant to the function of the pre-admission certification committee regarding the maintenance of current data on the residential treatment facilities within the region. Reasonable notice shall be provided to the residential treatment facility regarding visits of the advisory board.

(f) The advisory board shall maintain the confidentiality of information relating to individual children in accordance with the requirements of section 583.7(g) of this Part. The advisory board shall have access to information obtained by the pre-admission certification committee but shall not be provided with duplicate copies of such information.

Part 584
Operation of Residential Treatment Facilities
for Children and Youth

§584.1   Background and Intent.

(a) Chapter 947 of the Laws of 1981 authorized the establishment of residential treatment facilities for children and youth.

(b) The purpose of residential treatment facilities for children and youth is to provide comprehensive mental health services under the supervision of a physician for children and youth who have attained their 5th birthday and have not, in most cases, attained their 21st birthday and who are in need of long-term active treatment in a residential setting.

(c) Residential treatment facilities for children and youth are not intended for children and youth who:

(1) present a likelihood of serious harm to others; or

(2) have a primary diagnosis of mental retardation or developmental disability.

(d) The purpose of these regulations is to describe requirements for the establishment and operation of residential treatment facilities for children and youth; outline the requirements for admissions, transfers and discharge; and specify the requirements for staffing, services, treatment planning, quality assurance and recordkeeping.

(e) These regulations provide for the active involvement, to the extent possible, of the family or guardian of a child in all aspects of the care and treatment of that child.

§584.2 Legal base.

(a) Sections 7.09 and 31.04 of the Mental Hygiene Law grant the Commissioner of Mental Health the power and responsibility to adopt regulations that are necessary and proper to implement matters under his/her jurisdiction and to set standards of quality and adequacy of facilities, equipment, personnel, services, records and programs for the rendition of services for persons with mental illness, pursuant to an operating certificate.

(b) Section 31.26 of the Mental Hygiene Law provides for the establishment of the subclass of hospitals known as residential treatment facilities for children and youth which provide active treatment under the direction of a physician for individuals who are under 21 years of age.

(c) Section 31.02 of the Mental Hygiene Law prohibits any individual, association, corporation or public or private agency from operating a residential facility, hospital or institution for the examination, diagnosis, care, treatment, rehabilitation or training of persons with mental illness unless an operating certificate has been obtained from the commissioner of the Office of Mental Health.

(d) Sections 31.05, 31.07, 31.09, 31.11 and 31.19 of the Mental Hygiene Law authorize the commissioner or his or her representative to examine and inspect such facilities to determine their suitability and operation. Sections 31.16 and 31.17 authorize the commissioner to suspend, revoke or limit any operating certificate.

§584.3 Applicability.

(a) These regulations apply to any provider of services which operates or proposes to operate a residential treatment facility for children and youth. Such facilities are a subclass of hospitals pursuant to section 1.03 of the Mental Hygiene Law.

(b) These regulations do not apply to hospitals operated by the Office of Mental Health, or to hospitals issued an operating certificate by the Office of Mental Health pursuant to Part 582 of this Title.

§584.4 Definitions pertaining to this part.

(a) General.

(1) Abused child in residential care means:

(i) a child whose custodian inflicts or allows to be inflicted upon such child physical injury by other than accidental means, which causes or creates a substantial risk of death, serious protracted disfigurement, protracted impairment of physical or emotional health or protracted loss or impairment of the function of any organ;

(ii) a child whose custodian creates or allows to be created a substantial risk of physical injury to such child, by other than accidental means, which would be likely to cause death or serious or protracted disfigurement, protracted impairment of physical or emotional health or protracted loss or impairment of the function of any organ; or

(iii) a child whose custodian commits or allows to be committed a sexual offense against such a child, as described in the Penal Law.

(2) Admission criteria are those factors of psychopathology, activities of daily living skills, age and intelligence quotient which are identified for use in determining a child's eligibility for admission or transfer to a residential treatment facility.

(3) Alternate care determination is a utilization review committee decision that another specifically identified method of care or no care is more appropriate than the method being provided. This decision is the result of a utilization review committee evaluation of a resident, in person or through review of the resident's case record, against criteria for continued stay in the residential treatment facility program.

(4) Case records are those reports which contain information on all matters relating to the admission, legal status, assessment, treatment planning, treatment and discharge of the resident, and shall include all pertinent documents relating to the resident.

(5) Child is an individual who has passed at least his/her 5th birthday, and who has not yet reached his/her 22nd birthday.

(6) Clinical staff are all staff members who provide services directly to residents and their families or legal guardian. Clinical staff shall include professional staff, paraprofessional staff and other nonprofessional staff.

(7) Continued stay criteria are those factors of psychopathology, activities of daily living skills and age which are identified for use in determining the necessity and appropriateness of the resident's continued placement in the residential treatment facility. These factors shall provide the basis for determining that the resident continues to meet the admission criteria of the residential treatment facility. Such evidence shall be directly observed and documented by staff of the residential treatment facility or be documented in reports of trial visits to the home or to less restrictive settings.

(8) Custodian means the director, operator, employee or volunteer of a residential care facility or program.

(9) Education records means those reports which contain information on all matters relating to the education of the resident, and shall include all pertinent documents. For children determined to have a handicapping condition by a committee on the handicapped, the education record shall contain the individualized education program. Education records shall be separate and distinct from the case record.

(10) Likelihood of serious harm is a substantial risk of physical harm to other persons as manifested by recent homicidal or other violent behavior by which others are placed in reasonable fear of serious physical harm.

(11) Maltreated child means a child under the age of 18 years who is in residential care and identified as a neglected child.

(12) dental illness means an affliction with a mental disease or mental condition which is manifested by a disorder or disturbance in behavior, feeling, thinking or judgment to such an extent that the person afflicted requires care, treatment and rehabilitation.

(13) Neglected child in residential care means a child whose custodian impairs, or places in imminent danger of becoming impaired, the child's physical, mental or emotional condition:

(i) by intentionally administering to the child any prescription drug other than in accordance with a physician's or physician's assistant's prescription;

(ii) by failing to adhere to standards for the provision of food, clothing, shelter, education, medical, dental, optometrical or surgical care, or for the use of restraint or seclusion;

(iii) by failing to adhere to standards for the supervision of children by inflicting or allowing to be inflicted physical harm, or a substantial risk thereof; or

(iv) by failing to conform to applicable State regulations for appropriate custodial conduct.

(14) Pre-admission certification committee is a committee, established and operated pursuant to the provisions of Part 583 of this Title, whose purpose is to determine the eligibility of children for placement in a residential treatment facility and to certify children as priority for admission to a residential treatment facility.

(15) Provider of services means the organization which is legally responsible for the operation of a program. The organization may be an individual, partnership, association, corporation, public agency, or a psychiatric center or institute operated by the Office of Mental Health.

(16) Restraint is the use of an apparatus, except for a mechanical support such as a splint, that interferes with the free movement of the resident's arms and/or legs, or which immobilizes a resident and which the resident is unable to remove easily.

(17) Seclusion is the placement of a resident alone in a room with a closed door which the resident cannot open from the inside.

(18) Residential treatment facility is an inpatient psychiatric facility which provides active treatment under the direction of a physician for children who are under 21 years of age and is issued an operating certificate pursuant to this Part.

(19) Time-out is the placement of a child alone in an unlocked room in which the child is expected to remain for a period of time which is dependent upon specified changes in the child's problem behavior.

(b) Services.

(1) Case coordination services are activities to assure the full integration of all services provided to each resident. Case coordination activities include, but are not limited to, monitoring the resident's daily functioning to assure the continuity of service in accordance with the resident's treatment plan and insuring that all clinical staff responsible for the care and delivery of services actively participate in the development and implementation of the resident's treatment plan.

(2) Dietetic services are services designed to meet the nutritional needs of all residents. Dietetic services include, but are not limited to: assuring that each resident on a special diet receives the prescribed diet; insuring food storage and preparation in a safe and sanitary manner; directing the nutritional aspects of resident care; and providing planned menus that reflect the food acceptance of the residents.

(3) Educational and vocational services are those activities the purpose of which is to assist the resident in the acquisition or development of academic and occupational skills.

(4) Medication therapy is the process of determining the medication to be utilized during the course of treatment; reviewing the appropriateness of the resident's existing medication regimen through review of the resident's

medication record and consultation with the resident and, as appropriate, his/her family or guardian; prescribing and/or administering medication; and monitoring the effects and side effects of the medication on the resident's mental and physical health.

(5) Physical health services is a comprehensive program of preventive, routine and emergency medical and dental care, and an age-appropriate program of health education.

(6) Task and skill training is a nonvocational activity whose purpose is to enhance a resident's age-appropriate skills necessary to facilitate the resident's ability to care for himself/herself and to function effectively in community settings. Task and skill training activities include, but are not limited to: homemaking; personal hygiene; budgeting; shopping; and the use of community resources.

(7) Therapeutic recreation services are planned therapeutic activities whose purposes are: the acquisition or development of social and interpersonal skills; the improvement of the psychomotor and cardiovascular abilities of the residents; the enhancement of the self concept of the residents; the of healthy, lifelong activities toward participation in recreation and physical activity; and the improvement or maintenance of a resident's capacity for social and/or recreational involvement by providing opportunities for the application of social and/or recreational skills.

(8) Verbal therapies are planned activities whose purpose is to provide formal individual, family, and group therapies. These therapies include, but are not limited to, psychotherapy and other face-to-face verbal contacts between staff and the resident which are planned to enhance the resident's psychological and social functioning as well as to facilitate the resident's integration into a family unit. Verbal contacts that are incidental to other activities are excluded from this service. Verbal therapy shall include play therapy and other forms of expressive therapy.

(c) Staff qualifications.

(1) Dentist is an individual who is currently licensed as a dentist by the New York State Education Department.

(2) Dietitian is an individual who is either currently registered or eligible for registration by the Commission on Dietetic Registration; or has the documented equivalent in education, training and experience, with evidence of relevant continuing education.

(3) Limited permit physician is an individual who has received from the New York State Education Department a current permit to practice medicine which is limited as to eligibility, practice and duration.

(4) Nurse is an individual who is currently licensed as a registered professional nurse by the New York State Education Department.

(5) Occupational therapist is an individual who is currently licensed as an occupational therapist by the New York State Education Department.

(6) Physician is an individual who is currently licensed to practice medicine by the New York State Education Department.

(7) Psychiatrist is an individual who is currently licensed as a physician by the New York State Education Department and who is certified by, or eligible to be certified by, the American Board of Psychiatry and Neurology as a psychiatrist or a child psychiatrist.

(8) Psychologist is an individual who is currently licensed as a psychologist by the New York State Education Department.

(9) Rehabilitation counselor is an individual who either has a master's degree in rehabilitation counseling from a program approved by the New York State Education Department, or is currently certified by the Commission on Rehabilitation Counselor Certification.

(10) Social worker is an individual who is either currently licensed as a licensed master social worker or as a licensed clinical social worker by the New York State Education Department, or has a master's degree in social work from a program approved by the New York State Education Department.

(11) Speech pathologist is an individual who either has a master's degree in speech pathology or speech and/or language therapy, or who is currently licensed as a speech pathologist by the New York State Education Department.

(12) Therapeutic recreation specialist is an individual who either has a master's degree in therapeutic recreation or in recreation with emphasis in therapeutic recreation from a program approved by the New York State Education Department, or is currently registered as a therapeutic recreation specialist by the National Therapeutic Recreation Society.

(13) Teacher is an individual who is currently licensed as a teacher by the New York State Education Department.

§584.5 Certification.

(a) Each provider of services that intends to operate a residential treatment facility must be issued an operating certificate by the Office of Mental Health prior to the operation of the facility.

(b) Residential treatment facilities may only be operated by not-for-profit corporations.

(c) An operating certificate may be issued to a residential treatment facility which complies with the requirements of these regulations.

(d) The term of the operating certificate shall be determined by the Office of Mental Health, but in no event shall the term exceed three years.

(e) An operating certificate shall be issued for a residential treatment facility for a resident capacity of no fewer than 14 and no more than 56 residents; provided, however, that for the period commencing April 1, 2000 through September 30, 2016, bed capacity for facilities primarily serving New York City residents may be temporarily increased up to an additional ten beds over the maximum certified capacity with the prior approval of the Commissioner. In order to receive such approval, the residential treatment facility must demonstrate that the additional capacity will be used to serve those children and youth deemed most in need of RTF services by the New York City Preadmission Certification Committee as set forth in Section 583.8 of this Title.

(f) A residential treatment facility must provide the full range of services required by section 584.11 of this Part at a single location.

(g) An operating certificate may be limited, suspended, invalidated or revoked by the Office of Mental Health in accordance with the provisions of Part 573 of this Title. Certificates shall remain the property of the Office of Mental Health and invalidated or revoked certificates shall be returned to the Office of Mental Health.

(h) Each operating certificate will specify:

(1) the location of the residential treatment facility;

(2) the term of the operating certificate;

(3) any changes to be made in the operation of the residential treatment facility in order to retain the operating certificate; and

(4) the resident capacity of the residential treatment facility.

(i) In order to receive and retain an operating certificate, a provider of services shall:

(1) submit an application on such forms and such supporting documents as shall be required by the Office of Mental Health;

(2) frame and display the operating certificate within the residential treatment facility in a conspicuous place which is readily accessible to the public;

(3) cooperate with the Office of Mental Health during any review or inspection of the facility or program;

(4) make available to the Office of Mental Health or its designee upon request all documentation, files, reports, case records, or other materials required by this Part or requested by the Office of Mental Health in the course of visitation and inspection;

(5) undertake changes in the operation of the facility or program as required by the operating certificate;

(6) obtain prior approval of the Office of Mental Health in accordance with the procedures specified in Part 51 of this Title, to:

(i) change the physical location of the residential treatment facility or utilize additional physical locations;

(ii) initiate major changes in the program;

(iii) terminate the program or services in the program; or

(iv) change the powers or purposes set forth in the certificate of incorporation;

(7) comply with site selection requirements of section 41.34 of the Mental Hygiene Law if the residential treatment facility will have a resident capacity of 14 or fewer; and:

(i) is not located on the grounds of a residential facility licensed by the Department of Social Services or another State agency; or

(ii) is not a residential facility licensed by the Department of Social Services or another State agency at the time an application is submitted to the Office of Mental Health.

§584.6 Organization and administration.

(a) The provider of services shall identify the individuals who have overall responsibility for the operation of the residential treatment facility. These individuals shall be known as the governing body. No individual shall serve as both a member of the governing body and of the paid staff of the residential treatment facility without the prior approval of the Office of Mental Health.

(b) The provider of services shall assure that the residential treatment facility has space, programs, staff and policies and procedures that are separately identifiable from any other programs which may be operated by the provider of services.

(c) The governing body shall meet on a regular basis, in no event less often than quarterly, and shall maintain written minutes of all meetings as a permanent record of the decisions made in relation to the operation of the residential treatment facility. The minutes shall be reviewed and approved by the governing body.

(d) The governing body shall approve a written plan or plans that, at a minimum, address the following aspects of the operation of the residential treatment facility:

(1) the goals and objectives of the residential treatment facility, including the admission and discharge criteria and a statement of the involvement of the family;

(2) the plan of organization that clearly indicates lines of responsibility;

(3) a written plan for services and staff composition which:

(i) includes the qualifications and duties of each staff position by title, and addresses all essential aspects of the operation of the residential treatment facility including clinical, administration, fiscal, clerical, housekeeping, maintenance, dietetic, and recordkeeping and reporting functions; and

(ii) specifies all services available through the residential treatment facility including the treatment program and environment;

(4) the written quality assurance plan; and

(5) the written utilization review plan.

(e) The governing body shall approve written policies and procedures of the residential treatment facility, including but not limited to:

(1) Admission, transfer and discharge policies and procedures.

(2) The governing body shall develop, and revise as necessary, written policies for the quantity, quality, scope, goals, objectives and evaluation of all programs, policies for the accomplishment of stated purposes, and personnel policies. Personnel policies shall prohibit discrimination on the basis of race, color, creed, disability, sex, marital status, age or national origin. Personnel policies and procedures shall provide for verification of employment history, personal references, work record and qualifications. Such policies shall also provide for securing a signed sworn statement whether, to the best of his/her knowledge, the applicant has ever been convicted of a crime in this State or any other jurisdiction.

(3) Staff training and development policies and procedures. Such policies and procedures shall address preemployment orientation, ongoing staff development and training which shall include child abuse prevention and identification, safety and security procedures, the principles of child development, use of physical intervention, techniques of group and child management, the laws and regulations governing the protection of children from child abuse and maltreatment.

(4) The governing body shall establish written volunteer policies and procedures. Such policies and procedures shall provide for screening of volunteers and verification of employment history, personal references and work history; supervision of volunteers; training in accordance with paragraph (3) of this subdivision. Such policies shall also provide for securing a signed sworn statement whether, to the best of his/her knowledge, the volunteer has been convicted of a crime in this State or any other jurisdiction.

(5) Prescription and administration of medication policies and procedures. Such policies and procedures shall be consistent with applicable Federal and State laws and regulations.

(6) Case record policies and procedures. Such policies and procedures shall ensure confidentiality of patient records in accordance with the Mental Hygiene Law and shall ensure appropriate retention of case records.

(f) The governing body shall review the written plan or plans and policies and procedures required pursuant to subdivisions (d) and (e) of this section at least annually and shall make appropriate amendments or revisions.

(g) The governing body may delegate responsibility for the day-to-day management of the residential treatment facility in accordance with the written plan of organization provided for in paragraph (d)(2) of this section.

(1) Ongoing direction may be delegated to an individual who shall be known as the director and who shall meet the qualifications specified in section 584.10(d) of this Part.

(2) The director shall be employed by the residential treatment facility at least one half of the hours of a full-time employee.

(3) Administrative direction may be the responsibility of the director or may be delegated by the governing body to an individual who shall meet qualifications that are acceptable to the Office of Mental Health.

(h) The residential treatment facility shall participate with the local governmental unit in local planning processes. At a minimum, participation shall include:

(1) provision of budgeting and planning data as requested by the local governmental unit;

(2) identification of the population being served by the residential treatment facility;

(3) identification of the geographic area being served;

(4) description of the relationship to other providers of services which serve the same geographic area, including but not limited to written agreements to ensure expeditious access to programs by persons who need them. At a minimum, these agreements shall provide for prompt referral, evaluation and, as necessary, admission to cooperating programs, and for sharing information about residents being served; and

(5) attendance at planning meetings as may reasonably be required by the local governmental unit.

(i) The residential treatment facility shall provide for the following:

(1) an annual written evaluation of the residential treatment facility's attainment of its stated goals and objectives which indicates any required changes in policies and procedures;

(2) an annual audit of the financial condition and accounts of the residential treatment facility performed by a certified public accountant who is not a member of the governing body or an employee of the residential treatment facility;

(3) emergency evacuation plans for the building in which the residential treatment facility is located. Evacuation plans shall address emergencies resulting from fire as well as potential hazards in the geographic area in which the residential treatment facility is located; and

(4) up-to-date copies of any regulations, guidelines, manuals, or other information required by the Office of Mental Health.

§584.7 Admission and discharge criteria.

(a) Each residential treatment facility shall maintain written admission and discharge criteria which are consistent with its goals and objectives and which are subject to the approval of the Office of Mental Health.

(b) The admission criteria must, at a minimum, provide that the child meet each of the following criteria:

(1) identification of a serious and persistent psychopathology as evidenced by:

(i) severe thought disorder;

(ii) severe affective disorder;

(iii) moderate thought disorder in conjunction with an impulse control disorder or a deficit in activities of daily living skills;

(iv) moderate affective disorder in conjunction with an impulse control disorder or a deficit in activities of daily living skills;

(v) severe conduct disorder in conjunction with an impulse control disorder or a deficit in activities of daily living skills;

(vi) severe personality disorder in conjunction with an impulse control disorder or a deficit in activities of daily living skills; or

(vii) any combination of the above;

(2) intelligence quotient equal to or greater than 51;

(3) attainment of at least the 5th birthday but not the 21st birthday; and

(4) presentation of no likelihood of serious harm to others as defined in section 584.4(a)(8) of this Part.

(c) Any additional admission criteria must relate to observable characteristics of the child. Such criteria may include age and gender.

(d) The discharge criteria must relate to the necessity and appropriateness of the individual child's continued stay in a residential treatment facility. Age in and of itself is not an appropriate basis for discharge from a residential treatment facility, except that no resident may remain in a residential treatment facility after attaining the age of 22.

§584.8 Admission, transfer and discharge policies and procedures.

(a) A residential treatment facility may only admit children who have been certified to the residential treatment facility by a preadmission certification committee established pursuant to Part 583 of this Chapter. This requirement applies to admissions and transfers.

(b) A residential treatment facility may only admit children who meet the written admission criteria maintained pursuant to section 584.7 of this Part and for whom the residential treatment facility finds:

(1) proper treatment of the child's psychiatric condition requires care and treatment under the direction of a physician within a residential treatment facility; and

(2) care and treatment in a residential treatment facility can reasonably be expected to improve the child's condition or prevent further regression so that services will no longer be needed, provided that a poor prognosis shall not in itself constitute grounds for a denial of determination of eligibility if treatment can be expected to effect a change in prognosis.

(c) A residential treatment facility shall provide written notice to the preadmission certification committee and families or legal guardian as follows:

(1) Upon referral of a child as a priority for admission or transfer, notice shall be provided within 30 calendar days. The notice shall indicate the anticipated date of admission or transfer or, if the child is determined to be not appropriate for admission, the specific reason for such determination.

(2) When a resident is ready for discharge or transfer, notice shall be provided, if possible, 30 calendar days in advance of the anticipated date of discharge or transfer.

(3) When a resident attains the age of 21, notice shall be provided within 30 calendar days.

(d) Admissions, transfers and discharges shall be in accordance with the applicable requirements of articles 9 and 29 of the Mental Hygiene Law and Parts 15, 17 and 36 of this Title.

(e) Written admission, transfer and discharge policies and procedures shall be maintained as required in section 584.7 of this Part and shall be subject to approval by the Office of Mental Health. Such policies and procedures shall:

(1) specify that admission, transfer and discharge shall be based on the written criteria established pursuant to section 584.7 of this Part;

(2) delineate special requirements for admission, transfer and discharge of children in the custody of a social services official, the Director of the Division for Youth, or another person granted custody by the Family Court;

(3) prohibit discrimination solely on the basis of race, color, creed, handicap, national origin, sex or age;

(4) provide for notification of the mental health information service of each admission in accordance with the requirements of Part 15 of this Title;

(5) require that the necessity and appropriateness of each resident's continued stay in the residential treatment facility be regularly evaluated;

(6) be available to the staff, residents and their families, cooperating agencies and the general public; and

(7) require that discharge planning for each resident begin upon admission or transfer. Discharge planning shall be in accordance with section 29.15 of the Mental Hygiene Law and shall include, at a minimum, identification of the discharge goals and the criteria for determining the necessity and appropriateness of the resident's continued stay.

§584.9 Written plan for services and staff composition.

(a) Each residential treatment facility shall develop and specify in a written plan for services and staff composition its goals and objectives and the manner in which it intends to achieve them. The written plan for services and staff composition shall be subject to approval by the Office of Mental Health.

(b) The written plan for services and staff composition shall address:

(1) the comprehensive treatment needs of the residents;

(2) the physical health needs of the residents;

(3) the vocational and educational needs of the residents; and

(4) the residential needs, including dietary, on a 24-hour basis.

(c) The written plan for services and staff composition shall encompass the following written plans and rationales required under this Part:

(1) services required to be available through the residential treatment facility;

(2) treatment program and environment addressing the day-to-day activities of the residents; and

(3) staffing required to provide services and day-to-day management and monitoring of the treatment program and environment.

(d) The written plan for services and staff composition shall address the manner in which the treatment team will integrate the services available through the residential treatment facility and the treatment program and environment into an individual treatment plan designed to meet the needs of each individual resident, and will involve the family or legal guardian.

§584.10 Staffing.

(a) A residential treatment facility shall continuously employ an adequate number of staff and an appropriate mix of staff to carry out its goals and objectives as well as to ensure the continuous provision of sufficient regular and emergency supervision of all residents 24 hours a day. As a component of the written plan for services and staff composition, the residential treatment facility shall submit a staffing plan which includes the qualifications and duties of each staff position, by title. The residential treatment facility shall submit a written staffing rationale which justifies the staff to be utilized, the mix of staff and the plan for appropriate supervision of staff. The staffing plan shall include procedures for periodic supervisory conferences with staff and procedures for written performance evaluation consistent with any collective bargaining requirements. This staffing plan shall be based on the population to be served and the services to be provided. The staffing plan and its rationale shall be submitted for approval by the Office of Mental Health.

(b) All clinical staff shall have at least a high school diploma or its equivalent.

(c) At least 50 percent of the clinical staff hours shall be provided by full-time employees.

(d) For purposes of this Part, professional staff are individuals who are qualified by training and experience to provide direct treatment services under minimal supervision.

(1) Professional staff shall include the following as defined in section 584.4(c) of this Part:

    (i) nurse;
    (ii) occupational therapist;
    (iii) physician;
    (iv) psychiatrist;
    (v) psychologist;
    (vi) rehabilitation counselor;
    (vii) social worker;
    (viii) teacher;
    (ix) therapeutic recreation specialist; and
    (x) speech pathologist.

(2) Other professional disciplines may be included as professional staff, provided that the discipline is acceptable to the Office of Mental Health and is approved as part of the staffing plan by the Office of Mental Health. The discipline shall either be from a field related to the treatment of mental illness. The individual shall be licensed in such discipline by the New York State Education Department, or have a master's degree in such discipline from a program approved by the New York State Education Department, and shall have specialized training or experience in treating the mentally ill.

(e) In order to assure that the residential treatment facility employ an adequate number and mix of professional staff who meet the qualifications provided in section 584.4(c) of this Part, the staffing plan shall meet each of the following requirements. A single staff member may be counted against more than one requirement.

(1) At least two persons representing different professional staff categories as delineated in subdivision (f) of this section shall be employed on a full-time basis.

(2) Persons representing each of the following professional staff categories shall be employed at least one fifth of the hours of a full-time employee: nurse, psychiatrist, psychologist, social worker, and recreation therapist.

(3) One full-time equivalent professional staff member shall be employed for each seven residents.

(f) In order to assure that an adequate number of professional staff are qualified by training and experience to provide clinical supervision of other staff and to provide programmatic direction, at least 25 percent of the professional staff required to comply with paragraph (e)(3) of this section in each residential treatment facility shall meet the following qualifications:

(1) a nurse who has a bachelor's degree and at least three years' post-licensure experience in treating mentally ill children;

(2) a physician who has at least one year of post-medical degree experience in treating mentally ill children;

(3) a psychiatrist who has at least one year of post-medical degree experience in treating mentally ill children;

(4) a psychologist who has specialized training in clinical psychology or counseling psychology and at least two years of post-licensure experience in treating mentally ill children;

(5) a rehabilitation counselor who has a master's degree in rehabilitation counseling from a program approved by the New York State Education Department, current certification by the Commission on Rehabilitation Counselor Certification and three years of post-certification experience in treating mentally ill children;

(6) a social worker who has specialized training in clinical practice and two years post-graduate experience in treating mentally ill children; and/or

(7) a therapeutic recreation specialist who has a master's degree in therapeutic recreation from a program approved by the New York State Education Department, current registration as a therapeutic recreation specialist by the National Therapeutic Recreation Society and three years of post-registration experience in treating mentally ill children.

(g) In order to assure that the residents are adequately supervised and are cared for in a safe and therapeutic manner, the staffing plan shall meet each of the following requirements:

(1) At least two clinical staff members shall be assigned to direct care responsibilities for each living unit during all hours the residents are awake and not in school.

(2) At least one clinical staff member shall be assigned to direct care responsibilities for each living unit for each five residents during all hours the residents are awake and not in school.

(3) At least one clinical staff member shall be assigned direct care responsibility, be awake, and be continuously available to the children on each living unit during all hours the residents are asleep. A minimum of one additional clinical staff member for each 14 children shall be immediately available onsite to assist with emergencies or problems which might arise.

(4) Appropriate professional staff shall be available to assist in emergencies on at least an on-call basis at all times.

(5) A physician shall be available on at least an on-call basis at all times.

(h) In order to assure the appropriate supervision of the nutritional aspects of dietetic services, a qualified dietitian shall be available on at least a consultation basis.

(1) The amount of time a qualified dietitian is available shall be sufficient to permit the dietitian to direct nutritional aspects of patient care, assure that dietetic instructions are carried out and assist in the evaluation of the dietetic service.

(2) When a qualified dietitian is only available on a consultation basis, regular written reports shall be submitted to the director regarding the implementation and evaluation of dietetic services.

(i) All staff shall have qualifications appropriate to assigned responsibilities as set forth in the staffing plan and shall practice within the scope of their professional discipline.

(1) All staff shall submit documentation of their training and experience to the provider of services. Such documentation shall be retained on file by the residential treatment facility.

(2) Clinical psychological testing and evaluation procedures may only be provided by or under the supervision of a licensed psychologist.

(j) Students or trainees may qualify as clinical staff under the following conditions:

(1) The students and trainees are actively participating in a program leading to attainment of a recognized degree or certificate in a field related to mental health at an institution chartered or approved by the New York State Education Department. Limited permit physicians are considered students or trainees.

(2) The students or trainees are supervised and trained by professional staff meeting the qualifications specified in subdivision (f) of this section and limited permit physicians are trained by physicians.

(3) The students or trainees receive at least one hour of supervision for every five hours of treatment services provided. Limited permit physicians must work under the direct supervision of physicians.

(4) The students or trainees use titles that clearly indicate their status.

(5) Written policies and procedures pertaining to the integration of students and trainees within the overall operation of the residential treatment facility receive prior approval by the Office of Mental Health.

§584.11 Service requirements.

(a) The services available through a residential treatment facility must address the treatment needs of the resident and must include mental health services, educational and vocational services, physical health services and dietetic services.

(b) As a component of the written plan for services and staff composition, the residential treatment facility shall provide a written plan and rationale for the services available which shall be subject to approval by the Office of Mental Health. The written plan shall indicate what services will be available and whether the residential treatment facility will provide the services directly or through a written agreement with the provider of services. The written plan shall indicate what services will be available for involvement by the families or legal guardians of the residents.

(c) The mental health services available through the residential treatment facility shall include, but are not limited to, the services listed below. These mental health services must be provided directly by the residential treatment facility:

(1) case coordination services;

(2) verbal therapies;

(3) medication therapy;

(4) therapeutic recreation services; and

(5) task and skill training.

(d) The physical health services available through the residential treatment facility shall include, but are not limited to, the services listed below. Physical health services may be provided directly by the residential treatment facility or may be provided by written agreement as provided for in subdivision (e) of this section.

(1) a physical examination upon admission, periodic assessment of physical condition, and treatment as needed;

(2) a dental examination within six months of admission, periodic assessment, and treatment as needed;

(3) an assessment of immunization upon admission, and an ongoing immunization program;

(4) health education and sex education; and

(5) emergency care on a 24-hour basis.

(e) When physical health services are not provided directly by the residential treatment facility, there shall be a written agreement between the provider of services and the residential treatment facility. When physical health services are provided by the same provider of services, written policies and procedures will be an acceptable alternative to a written agreement. The written agreement or written policies and procedures shall, at a minimum, address:

(1) referral of residents;

(2) qualifications of staff providing services;

(3) exchange of clinical information; and

(4) financial arrangements.

(f) Educational and vocational services available through the residential treatment facility shall include, but are not limited to, the minimum requirements of the State Education Law regarding regular education, vocational education and special education, as appropriate to meet the needs of the residents. Education services may be provided directly by the residential treatment facility or may be provided by written agreement as provided for in subdivision (g) of this section. In any case, education services approved by the Education Department must be available either on the same site or in close physical proximity to the residential treatment facility.

(g) When the education services are not provided directly by the residential treatment facility, there shall be a written agreement between the provider of services and the residential treatment facility. The provider of education services shall be a State Education Department-approved program. When education services are provided by the same provider of services, written policies and procedures will be an acceptable alternative to a written agreement. The written agreement or written policies and procedures shall, at a minimum, address:

(1) qualifications of staff providing services;

(2) participation of educational and vocational staff in the treatment planning process;

(3) access by staff of the residential treatment facility to educational and vocational programs and records; and

(4) financial arrangements.

(h) The dietetic services available through the residential treatment facility shall include, but are not limited to, the services listed below. Dietetic services may be provided directly by the residential treatment facility or may be provided by written agreement as provided for in subdivision (i) of this section.

(1) safe and sanitary storage and serving of foods;

(2) planned menus that provide for a nutritionally adequate diet for all residents; and

(3) provisions to meet special dietary needs.

(i) When dietetic services are not provided directly by the residential treatment facility, there shall be a written agreement between the provider of services and the residential treatment facility. When dietetic services are provided by the same provider of services, written policies and procedures will be an acceptable alternative to a written agreement. The written agreement or written policies and procedures shall, at a minimum, address:

(1) qualifications of staff providing services;

(2) planned menus that provide for a nutritionally adequate diet served in an appetizing manner to all residents;

(3) provisions to meet special dietary needs; and

(4) financial arrangements.

(j) The residential treatment facility must have a written agreement for the provision of emergency psychiatric services with a provider of inpatient psychiatric services operated or certified by the Office of Mental Health.

§584.12   Treatment program and environment.

(a) The treatment program and environment shall be designed to provide appropriate care on a 24-hour basis and to enhance treatment for all residents. The treatment program and environment shall ensure:

(1) a planned and predictable day-to-day routine for all residents;

(2) the provision of a balance of privileges, expectations and responsibilities as appropriate to the ages and levels of functioning of the residents; and

(3) the safety, comfort and well-being of all residents.

(b) As a component of the written plan for services and staff composition, the residential treatment facility shall provide a written plan and rationale for the treatment program and environment which shall be subject to approval by the Office of Mental Health, and addresses, at a minimum, the following:

(1) the manner in which the treatment program and environment will be implemented. Implementation must be consistent for all residents, yet must be sufficiently flexible to accommodate the needs of individual residents;

(2) the manner in which the treatment program and environment will be explained to the residents and their families or legal guardians upon admission;

(3) the day-to-day routines that the residents and staff will follow;

(4) the behavioral expectations for all residents, including identification of behaviors that are acceptable and unacceptable. This must address time both in the residential treatment facility and away from it;

(5) the means for providing instruction to residents, consistent with their age, needs and clinical condition as well as the needs and circumstances within the facility or program, in techniques and procedures which will enable such residents to protect themselves from abuse and maltreatment;

(6) the house rules and the response the resident can expect if he/she either complies or fails to comply with them. This can include staff response, limitations on privileges or other actions specified by the residential treatment facility;

(7) the mechanism for enabling residents, where appropriate, to participate in the decisionmaking process within the residential treatment facility relating to the treatment program and environment;

(8) the means of observing holidays and personal milestones in keeping with the cultural and religious background of the residents;

(9) the procedure for communications and/or visitations with family, legal guardians, friends, and significant others; and

(10) the means of providing restitution or reimbursement for damages to property of the resident, other residents, and the residential treatment facility.

§584.13 Special treatment procedures.

(a) There shall be a written plan for the use of restraint and seclusion, as defined in section 584.4 of this Part, that is in accordance with Part 27 of this Title.

(b) There shall be a written plan for the use of time-out, as defined in section 584.4 of this Part. This plan shall, at a minimum, specify the criteria and procedures for the use of time-out, the rooms to be used, the procedures for monitoring that shall provide for visual observation of the child at intervals of no more than 15 minutes, and the requirements for documentation in the case record. Time-out shall be limited to 30 minutes at one time, 45 minutes in any hour and two hours in any 24-hour period.

(c) No residential treatment facility shall use extraordinary risk procedures without prior approval by the Office of Mental Health of a written plan for the use of such procedures. The plan shall demonstrate compliance with all applicable Federal and State requirements. Extraordinary risk procedures include, but are not limited to, experimental treatment modalities, psychosurgery, aversive conditioning and electroconvulsive therapies.

§584.14 Treatment team.

(a) Treatment shall be the responsibility of an inter-disciplinary treatment team. A treatment team shall be responsible for developing and implementing a treatment plan for each resident as required by section 584.15 of this Part.

(b) In order to address all aspects of the resident's needs, a treatment team shall be established for each resident and shall be comprised of clinical staff who are involved in the treatment of the individual resident on a regular basis, and where appropriate, of the family or legal guardian.

(1) The treatment team shall include all staff having significant participation in the treatment of the resident. The team shall, at a minimum, include a psychiatrist, at least one member of the clinical staff who is assigned to the living unit on a daily basis, and at least one member of the professional staff responsible for providing each of the following services to the resident:

(i) verbal therapies;

(ii) therapeutic recreation services; and

(iii) education and vocational services.

(2) One member of the treatment team must be designated as case coordinator for the resident.

(c) The residential treatment facility must develop written policies and procedures for the operation of its treatment teams which shall be subject to approval by the Office of Mental Health. At a minimum, the policies and procedures must address the following:

(1) the composition of treatment teams;

(2) the criteria for changing treatment team members;

(3) the representation required for the development of initial and comprehensive treatment plans and for treatment plan reviews;

(4) the responsibilities of the case coordinator;

(5) the manner in which the treatment team will coordinate with the appropriate committee on the handicapped; and

(6) the manner in which the treatment team will involve the family or legal guardian in the treatment process.

§584.15 Individual treatment plan.

(a) An individual treatment plan shall be developed and implemented for each resident by the resident's treatment team.

(b) The individual treatment plan shall be based on a complete assessment of each resident.

(1) The assessment shall include, but shall not necessarily be limited to, physical, emotional, behavioral, social, educational, recreational and, when appropriate, vocational and nutritional needs. Special consideration shall be given to the role of the resident's family in each area of assessment.

(2) Clinical consideration of each resident's needs shall include a determination of the type and extent of special clinical examinations, tests and evaluations necessary for a complete assessment.

(3) The complete assessment shall be updated and documented at least annually as required in section 584.16 of this Part.

(c) The individual treatment plan shall address the needs of the resident.

(1) The individual treatment plan shall identify all service needs of the resident, whether or not the services are provided directly by the residential treatment facility.

(2) The individual treatment plan shall address the manner in which the family or legal guardian will be involved in the treatment process.

(3) The individual treatment plan shall address the manner in which the resident and his/her family or legal guardian will participate in the overall treatment program and environment of the residential treatment facility as provided for in section 584.12 of this Part.

(4) For those children that have been determined to be educationally handicapped and in need of special educational services and programs, the individual treatment plan shall address the special educational needs identified in the individualized education program. However, the individualized education program shall be maintained as a separate and distinct record.

(d) The resident and, as appropriate, the resident's family shall participate in the development and implementation of the individual treatment plan.

(e) The individual treatment plan shall be developed and revised as follows:

(1) an initial treatment plan which complies with the requirements of section 584.16(e) of this Part shall be developed within 72 hours of the resident's admission or transfer;

(2) a comprehensive treatment plan which complies with the requirements of section 584.16(f) of this Part shall be developed within 14 days of the resident's admission or transfer; and

(3) the comprehensive treatment plan shall be reviewed and revised if necessary at least every 30 days.

§584.16 Case record.

(a) There shall be a complete case record maintained at one location for each resident admitted to the residential treatment facility. For those children that have been determined to be educationally handicapped and in need of special educational services and programs, there may also be an individualized education program, but such individualized education program shall be separate and distinct from the case record.

(b) The case record shall be confidential and access shall be governed by the requirements of section 33.13 of the Mental Hygiene Law. Case records shall not be released to any person or agency except as follows:

(1) pursuant to an order of a court of record;

(2) to the mental health information service;

(3) to attorneys representing the child in proceedings in which the resident's involuntary admission to a residential treatment facility is at issue;

(4) with the consent of the child or of someone legally authorized to act on the child's behalf, to physicians and providers of health, mental health, and social or welfare services involved in caring for, treating or rehabilitating the child, such information to be kept confidential and used solely for the benefit of the child; or

(5) to agencies requiring information to make payments to or on behalf of residents; such information shall be kept confidential and limited to the information required.

(c) The case record shall be available to all clinical staff involved in the care and treatment of the resident.

(d) Each case record shall include:

(1) identifying information about the resident served and the resident's family;

(2) a note upon admission, indicating source of referral, date of admission, rationale for admission, the date service commenced, presenting problem and immediate treatment needs of the resident;

(3) the application for admission to a residential treatment facility or any other information obtained from the pre-admission certification committee, including an assessment from the committee on the handicapped, when available;

(4) assessments of psychiatric, medical, educational, emotional, social and recreational needs. Where appropriate, assessments of vocational and nutritional needs shall be included. Special consideration shall be given to the role of the resident's family in each area of assessment;

(5) reports of all mental and physical diagnostic examinations and assessments, including findings and conclusions;

(6) reports of all special studies performed, including, but not limited to, X-rays, clinical laboratory tests, psychological tests, or electroencephalograms;

(7) initial and comprehensive treatment plans;

(8) progress notes which relate to the goals and objectives of the initial or comprehensive treatment plans, which shall be signed by the staff member who provided the service or by one participating staff member when several staff members have had significant interaction with the resident.

(i) Progress notes shall be written at least weekly and additionally whenever a significant event occurs that affects, or potentially affects, the resident's condition or course of treatment.

(ii) Progress notes shall be written regarding the educational program as determined in the resident's individualized education program.

(iii) Progress notes shall be written regarding the involvement of the family or legal guardian in treatment as determined in the resident's treatment plan;

(9) summaries of treatment plan reviews and special consultations regarding all aspects of the resident's complete daily program;

(10) dated and signed orders which indicate commencement and termination dates for all medications;

(11) a discharge summary, prepared within 15 days of discharge or transfer, which includes a summary of the clinical treatment, or reasons for discharge or transfer and, if appropriate, the provision for alternative treatment services which the resident may require; and

(12) information as may be required for the effective implementation of the utilization review plan provided for in section 584.18 of this Part.

(e) initial treatment plan shall include:

(1) admission diagnosis or diagnostic impression;

(2) a brief description of the resident's and the resident's family problems, strengths, conditions, disabilities or needs;

(3) objectives relating to the resident's problems, conditions, disabilities and needs, and the treatments, therapies and staff actions which will be implemented to accomplish these objectives; and

(4) initial discharge goals and criteria for determining the necessity and appropriateness of the resident's continued stay.

(f) The comprehensive treatment plan shall include:

(1) diagnosis;

(2) a brief description of the resident's and the resident's family problems, strengths, conditions, disabilities, functional deficits or needs;

(3) a brief description of the treatment and treatment planning which demonstrates that the program is addressing the functional deficits of the resident which substantiated the resident's eligibility for admission to the residential treatment facility;

(4) goals to address the resident's problems, conditions, disabilities and needs which indicate the expected duration of the resident's need for services in the residential treatment facility;

(5) objectives relating to the resident's goals. Objectives must be written to reflect the expected progress of the resident. Projections for accomplishing these objectives should be specific;

(6) the specific treatments, therapies and staff actions which will be implemented to accomplish each of the objectives and goals. These must be stated clearly to enable all staff members participating in the treatment program to implement the goals and objectives;

(7) discharge goals and criteria for determining the necessity and appropriateness of the resident's continued stay;

(8) the name of the clinical staff member, designated as case coordinator, exercising primary responsibility for the resident;

(9) identification of the staff members who will provide the specified services, experiences and therapies;

(10) documentation of participation by the patient in the development of the treatment plan whenever possible and by representatives of the resident's school district, parent or legal guardian and referring agent, where appropriate;

(11) date for the next scheduled review of the treatment plan; and

(12) a copy of the individualized education program as defined in accordance with requirements of the Commissioner of Education.

§584.17   Quality assurance.

(a) Each residential treatment facility shall have an organized quality assurance program designed to enhance resident care through the ongoing objective assessment of important aspects of resident care and the correction of identified problems. The quality assurance program shall provide for the following:

(1) identification of problems or concerns related to the care of residents;

(2) objective assessment of the cause and scope of the problems or concerns, including the determination of priorities for both investigating and resolving

problems. Priorities shall be related to the degree of adverse impact on the care provided to residents that can be expected if the problems remain unresolved; (3) implementation of decisions or actions that are designed to eliminate, insofar as possible, identified problems; and

(4) monitoring to assess whether or not the desired result has been achieved and sustained.

(b) Each residential treatment facility shall prepare a written quality assurance plan designed to ensure that there is an ongoing quality assurance program that includes effective mechanisms for reviewing and evaluating resident care and provides for appropriate response to findings. This quality assurance plan shall be subject to approval by the Office of Mental Health. The written quality assurance plan shall address at a minimum:

(1) the individual or group with the overall responsibility to administer or coordinate the quality assurance program;

(2) the activities or mechanisms for reviewing and evaluating resident care;

(3) the individuals or organizational entities to whom responsibility will be delegated for specific activities or mechanisms;

(4) the activities or mechanisms for assuring the accountability of the clinical staff for the care they provide;

(5) the individuals or organizational entities to whom responsibility will be delegated for responding to findings or implementing corrective actions designed to eliminate insofar as possible identified problems; and

(6) the activities or mechanisms for monitoring whether or not the corrective actions have been implemented, and whether or not the desired result has been achieved and sustained.

(c) As a component of the quality assurance program, each residential treatment facility shall establish a written plan for reviewing untoward incidents. Untoward incidents include, but are not limited to, serious drug reactions, suicide attempts, suicides and sudden deaths, assaults, alleged abuse and maltreatment of residents, accidents, and terminations of service against professional advice when such termination presents a risk of hospitalization or danger to the resident or others. This plan shall be subject to approval by the Office of Mental Health. The written plan for reviewing untoward incidents shall address, at a minimum:

(1) the establishment of a special review committee that shall include at least three members of the clinical staff who meet the qualifications provided in section 584.10(d) of this Part. The special review committee shall include a physician on a regular membership basis or by special arrangement;

(2) the review of all untoward incidents by the special review committee to determine the facts in any untoward incident reported, and to review ongoing practices and procedures in relation to such untoward incidents;

(3) the operating procedures of the special review committee, including convening meetings as often as necessary to execute its functions, but in no event less often than quarterly; maintaining written minutes of meetings; and submitting reports to the director. Special review committee members who are directly involved in the untoward incident shall be excluded from the committee's final deliberations;

(4) the establishment of procedures to assure the health and safety of the resident and of other residents in the facility and preventive and remedial actions to be taken as necessary to prevent incidents of child abuse or maltreatment;

(5) the establishment of a procedure for notification of the resident's parent or guardian of an untoward incident involving the resident;

(6) the procedures for the proper reporting of all incidents of alleged child abuse or maltreatment as follows, in accordance with the Mental Hygiene Law and Part 24 of this Title:

(i) to the New York State Central Child Abuse and Maltreatment Register immediately;

(ii) to the appropriate Office of Mental Health regional office, within two weeks, using forms designated by the Office of Mental Health;

(iii) to the Commission on Quality of Care for the Mentally Disabled within 72 hours; and

(iv) to the Mental Hygiene Legal Service within the next working day; and

(7) the integration of the plan for reviewing untoward incidents into the overall quality assurance program.

§584.18   Utilization review.

(a) Each residential treatment facility shall have an organized utilization review program designed to monitor the appropriateness of continued stay and to identify the overutilization or underutilization of services.

(b) Each residential treatment facility shall prepare a written utilization review plan designed to ensure that there will be an ongoing utilization review program. This utilization review plan shall be subject to approval by the Office of Mental Health. The written utilization review plan shall address at a minimum:

(1) the establishment of a utilization review committee that shall be composed of at least three members of the clinical staff who meet the qualifications provided in section 584.10(d) of this Part, at least two of whom shall be physicians. The utilization review committee shall include at least one physician who is knowledgeable in the diagnosis and treatment of mental illness;

(2) the operating procedures of the utilization review committee, including convening meetings as often as necessary to execute its functions, but in no event less often than quarterly; maintaining written minutes of meetings; and submitting reports to the director. Utilization review committee members who are directly involved in the care of a resident whose care is being reviewed shall be excluded from the committee's deliberations;

(3) the review of continued stays in accordance with section 584.18(c) of this Part; and

(4) the integration of the utilization review program into the quality assurance program provided for in section 584.17 of this Part.

(c) The utilization review committee shall review each resident's continued stay in accordance with the following requirements:

(1) An initial continued stay review shall be completed by the utilization review committee or its designee no later than 30 days after admission.

(2) Subsequent continued stay reviews shall be completed by the utilization review committee or its designee 90 days after the initial continued stay review and every 90 days thereafter.

(3) Review of each alternate care determination by the utilization review committee or a subcommittee of the utilization review committee which includes at least one physician.

(4) Notification of the physician on the resident's interdisciplinary treatment team of an alternative determination. Additional information provided by such

physician shall be considered by the utilization review committee that includes at least two physicians.

(5) Notification of the director of final adverse decisions.

§584.19 Premises.

The following standards shall apply to the physical plant or physical facilities of a residential treatment facility:

(a) Construction standards.

(1) Facilities shall be and remain in compliance with applicable sections of the 2010 edition of the Guidelines for Design and Construction of Health Care Facilities published by the Facility Guidelines Institute with assistance from the United States Department of Health and Human Services, provided, however, that this provision shall apply only to facilities which undertake construction or major renovations on or after the effective date of this paragraph. Facilities which have been constructed or have completed major renovations prior to that date in accordance with Part 77 of this Title shall be deemed to be in compliance with this paragraph.

(2) The design of the facility shall meet the requirements of the applicable sections of the Americans with Disabilities Act and the ADA Standards for Accessible Design and implementing regulations found at 28 CFR Parts 35 and 36.

(3) Waivers of up to 10 percent of the square footage for bedroom space will be considered by the Office of Mental Health upon application from the agency.

(b) Fire safety.

(1) All buildings containing sleeping quarters for children shall be protected by a fire detection system or a sprinkler system installed throughout. All buildings used by children, but not containing sleeping quarters for them shall be protected throughout by a sprinkler system, fire detection system, or manually operated fire alarm system. All areas of high fire hazard in all buildings used by children, whether or not they contain sleeping quarters for them, shall be protected by a sprinkler system and be separated from other areas by substantial, fire-resistant construction.

(2) All fire protection systems and equipment shall be installed according to recommendations of the National Fire Protection Association, and shall be inspected at least quarterly by a person who is expert in the installation, operation and inspection of such systems and equipment. A record of these inspections shall be kept by the facility. Facilities shall immediately correct any deficiency noted during inspection and testing.

(3) Each residential treatment facility shall request an annual inspection of each building used by children and its fire protection equipment by local fire authorities and/or the residential treatment facility's fire and casualty insurance carrier, who shall be requested to give the facility a written report of their findings. This report shall be kept on file on the premises until replaced by the next annual report of inspection. The residential treatment facility shall be responsible for correcting any fire hazards called to its attention throughout such inspection, and for keeping a written record on file of the action taken and when.

(4) Fire safety training. Facilities shall provide fire safety training to all staff. Newly hired staff shall be trained upon hiring and existing staff trained at least annually. Fire safety training shall include, but not be limited to:

(i) fire prevention;

(ii) discovering a fire;

(iii) operating the fire alarm system;

(iv) use of firefighting equipment; and

(v) building evacuation including fire drill protocols which identify staff roles.

(5) Fire drills. On a quarterly basis, facilities shall conduct fire drills in each building that houses patients. At least 50 percent of such drills must be unannounced.

(i) For each quarter, each such building must have a minimum of one practice fire drill per shift.

(ii) Facilities must direct all staff members on all shifts to participate in fire drills.

(iii) Drills shall be scheduled at varying times during a shift.

(iv) Use of alternative exits shall be practiced during fire drills.

(v) Whenever practicable, drills shall involve the actual evacuation of patients to an assembly point as specified in the evacuation plan. Consistent with the Life Safety Code standards, in larger facilities that are subdivided into separate smoke compartments to limit the spread of fire and smoke and move patients without leaving the building or changing floors, evacuation may include the relocation of patients to such compartments.

(vi) Properly documented actual or false alarms may be used for up to 50 percent of required drills for each shift, if all elements of the facility's fire plan were implemented.

(vii) Facilities must document and maintain records regarding fire drill performance which include an evaluation of the results of each fire drill, any corrective action that may be required, and completion of steps taken to achieve such corrective action.

(c) Prohibited items.

(1) The following items are prohibited from use within the structure:

(i) devices for heating, cooking, or lighting which use kerosene, gasoline, wood, or alcohol;

(ii) portable electric hot plates; and

(iii) barbeque grills. The use of barbeque grills is permissible when used outside of buildings but not within 30 feet of any structure including overhangs, canopies or awnings.

(2) The use of portable space heating devices is prohibited in patient sleeping and treatment areas of the facility, as well as in the facility administration offices. Use of a portable space heating device in any other building on the grounds of a facility shall be in accordance with guidelines of the office, provided that:

(i) the unit has an Underwriters Laboratories (UL) certification mark;

(ii) the unit is thermostat-controlled and has a tip-over cutoff device;

(iii) the unit is plugged directly into a wall receptacle (no extension cords);

(iv) combustible materials are not stored around or near the unit;

(v) at least a three-foot clearance around the unit is maintained; and

(vi) the unit is not placed underneath a desk, furniture or other combustible items.

(d) Smoking. Facilities must not permit smoking within any buildings on the grounds of the facility. If smoking is permitted on the grounds of the facility, it shall be contained to a specific location(s) equipped with an approved non-combustible ash receptacle. Smoking shall not be permitted within 30 feet of any building structure, including overhangs, canopies or awnings.

(e) Medication storage. If medications are stored on the premises of the residential treatment facility, the residential treatment facility shall provide for controlled access maintenance of supplies in accordance with all applicable Federal and State laws and regulations.

(1) There shall be a single medication storage area within a single unit of the residential treatment facility.

(2) Medication shall be stored in a sturdy metal or sturdy wooden cabinet without glazing which shall be locked except when medication is needed. Controlled substances shall be stored in double-locked cabinets as follows:

(i) Schedule I, II, III and IV controlled substances shall be kept in stationary, double-locked cabinets. Both inner and outer cabinets shall have key-locked doors with separate keys. Spring locks or combination dial locks are not acceptable.

(ii) Schedule V controlled substances shall be stored in a stationary, secure, locked cabinet of substantial construction.

(3) Refrigerators used for storage of medication shall not be used for the storage of food or beverages unless the medication is stored in separate locked compartment within the refrigerator.

(f) Each living unit shall provide for the comfort and privacy of the residents and shall be limited in size to 14 residents. The premises shall be reasonably maintained to ensure access to services by all residents.

§584.20 Statistical records and reports.

(a) Such statistical information shall be prepared and maintained as may be necessary for the effective operation of the facility and as may be required by the Office of Mental Health.

(b) Statistical information shall be reported to Office of Mental Health in a manner and within time limits specified by the Office of Mental Health.

(c) Statistical reporting shall be the responsibility of an individual whose name and title shall be made known to the Office of Mental Health.

(d) Summaries of statistical information shall be reviewed at least annually as part of the annual evaluation process.

§584.21 Waiver provisions.

In order to be eligible for the waiver provisions of this section, a residential treatment facility must meet one of the three following requirements:

(a) The residential treatment facility is located in a rural area and can demonstrate to the satisfaction of the Office of Mental Health the need for a waiver. For purposes of this Part, a rural area shall be a county where the population density is less than one hundred persons per square mile based upon current available data. The following sections of this Part are eligible for waiver:

(1) Section 584.5(d). The Office of Mental Health may approve a resident capacity of less than 14 where the residential treatment facility can demonstrate that this limitation would adversely affect the services provided. Consideration will be given to factors such as, but not limited to, geographic distance and transportation problems of residents' families and availability of staff.

(2) Section 584.10(e). The Office of Mental Health may approve the use of a physician in lieu of a psychiatrist where the residential treatment facility can demonstrate that a psychiatrist is unavailable to meet the requirement. The physician must have specialized training or experience in treating mentally ill children and youth.

(3) Section 584.10(e). The Office of Mental Health may approve the use of a person who has received a bachelor's degree in one of the following areas, art education, drama, early childhood education, music education, physical education, psychology, rehabilitation, sociology or special education in lieu of a therapeutic recreation specialist in circumstances where the residential treatment facility can demonstrate that a therapeutic recreation specialist is unavailable to meet the requirement. The person holding such a degree must also have specialized training or experience in treating mentally ill children and youth. This provision is extended to residential treatment facilities in other than rural areas.

(4) Section 584.11(f). Educational and vocational services may be provided at a location different than the residential treatment facility when the residential treatment facility can demonstrate that such arrangements would benefit the residents and that such services will be fully integrated through the treatment planning process.

(b) The residential treatment facility serves a specialized target population and can demonstrate to the satisfaction of the Office of Mental Health the needs for a waiver based upon the specialized needs of the target population. Section 584.5(d) of this Part is eligible for a waiver if the residential treatment facility can demonstrate that the need for such a program would not justify a program serving 14 or more residents.

(c) The residential treatment facility has a physical plant with living units designed for more than 14 residents and the residential treatment facility can demonstrate to the satisfaction of the Office of Mental Health the need for a waiver. Section 584.19(c) of this Part is eligible for a waiver if the residential treatment facility can demonstrate that such arrangements would be consistent with its goals and objectives and it would not be detrimental to the residents.

This page intentionally left blank.

§357.1 Nature of information to be safeguarded.

(a) Information to be safeguarded includes names and addresses of applicants, recipients, and their relatives, including lists thereof; information contained in applications and correspondence; reports of investigations; reports of medical examination, diagnostic tests and treatment, including reports on whether an applicant or recipient has had an HIV related test or has been diagnosed as having AIDS, HIV infection or an HIV related illness; resource information; financial statements; and record of agency evaluation of such information. This applies to all information secured by the agency whether or not it is contained in the written record.

(b) For purposes of this Part:

(1) AIDS means acquired immune deficiency syndrome, as may be defined from time to time by the Centers for Disease Control of the United States Public Health Service.

(2) HIV infection means infection with the human immunodeficiency virus or any other related virus identified as a probable causative agent of AIDS.

(3) HIV related illness means any illness that may result from or may be associated with HIV infection.

(4) HIV related test means any laboratory test or series of tests for any virus, antibody, antigen or etiologic agent whatsoever thought to cause or to indicate the presence of AIDS.

§357.2 Prohibition against disclosure of information.

(a) Officers and employees of social services districts shall not reveal information obtained in the course of administering public assistance for purposes other than those directly connected with the administration of public assistance, except for the name, address and the amount received by or expended for a recipient of public assistance when the appropriating body or social services official has authorized their disclosure to an agency or person deemed entitled to it pursuant to section 136 of the Social Services Law.

(b) Any release of information pursuant to this section which would reveal that a person has been the subject of an HIV related test, or has HIV infection, HIV related illness or AIDS, is subject to the provisions of section 2782 of the Public Health Law. In accordance with such section, confidential HIV related information relating to a recipient of a health or social service as defined in section 2780 of the Public Health Law, may be disclosed to authorized employees of the department or of social services districts when reasonably necessary for such employees to supervise, monitor, administer or provide such service and such employees would, in the ordinary course of business, have access to records relating to the care of, treatment of or provision of a health or social service to such recipient.

(c) Each social services official shall designate the person, or persons, within the agency with authority to disclose information.

§357.3 Basis for disclosure of information.

(a) Safeguards in disclosing information. Information shall be released to another agency or person only when the public welfare official providing such data is assured that:

(1) the confidential character of the information will be maintained;

(2) the information will be used for the purposes for which it is made available, such purposes to be reasonably related to the purposes of the public welfare program and the function of the inquiring agency; and

(3) the information will not be used for commercial or political purposes.

(b) Disclosure of medical information. (1) Upon the transfer of a foster child to the care of another authorized agency, the former agency must provide to the receiving agency the child's comprehensive health history, both physical and mental, to the extent it is available.

(2) To the extent they are available, the comprehensive health history of the child and of his or her biological parents and the health care needs of the child must be provided by an authorized agency to foster parents at the time of the child's placement in foster care. In all cases, information identifying the biological parents must be removed from the comprehensive medical history.

(3) To the extent it is available, the comprehensive health history, both physical and mental, of a child legally freed for adoption and of his or her biological parents must be provided by an authorized agency to the child's prospective adoptive parent(s). Prospective adoptive parent means an individual who meets criteria as defined in section 421.16 of this Title and who has indicated an interest in adopting a particular child, and for whom the authorized agency has begun the placement agreement process in accordance with section 421.18 of this Title. In the case of finalized adoptions, such information must be provided upon request to the child's adoptive parents. In all cases, information identifying the biological parents must be removed from the comprehensive health history.

(4) To the extent it is available, the comprehensive health history, including both physical and mental, of the child in foster care and of his or her biological parents must be provided by an authorized agency at no cost to such child when discharged to his or her own care. Such information must include the names and addresses of the child's health care providers.

(5) To the extent it is available, the comprehensive health history of a child in foster care must be provided to the child's parents or guardian when the child is discharged to their care, except that confidential HIV-related information must not be disclosed without a written release from the child if the child has the capacity to consent as defined in section 360-8.1(a)(8) of this Title and in article 27-F of the Public Health Law. The conditions for the written release authorizing such disclosure are described in section 360-8.1(a)(8) of this Title and in article 27-F of the Public Health Law. The term confidential HIV-related information is defined in section 360-8.1(a)(5) of this Title and in article 27-F of the Public Health Law.

(6) To the extent it is available, the comprehensive health history, both physical and mental, of any adopted former foster child and of his or her biological parents must be provided by an authorized agency to the adopted former foster child upon request. In all cases, information identifying the biological parents must be removed from the comprehensive health history.

(7) For the purposes of this subdivision, the comprehensive health history must include, but is not limited to, conditions or diseases believed to be hereditary, where known; drugs or medication taken during pregnancy by the child's biological mother, where known; immunizations received by the child while in foster care and prior to placement in care, where known; medications dispensed to the child while in care and prior to placement in care, where known; allergies the child is known to have exhibited while in care and prior to placement in care, where known; diagnostic tests, including developmental or psychological tests and evaluations given to the child while in care and prior to placement in care, where known, and their results, laboratory tests for HIV, where known, and their results; and any follow-up treatment provided to the child prior to placement in care, where known, or provided to the child while in care, or still needed by the child.

(c) Disclosure to applicant, recipient, or person acting in his behalf. (1) The case record shall be available for examination at any reasonable time by the applicant or recipient or his authorized representative upon reasonable notice to the local district. The only exceptions to access are:

(i) those materials to which access is governed by separate statutes, such as child welfare, foster care, adoption or child abuse or neglect or any records maintained for the purposes of the Child Care Review Service;

(ii) those materials being maintained separate from public assistance files for purposes of criminal prosecution and referral to the district attorney's office; and

(iii) the county attorney or welfare attorney's files.

(2) Information may be released to a person, a public official, or another social agency from whom the applicant or recipient has requested a particular service when it may properly be assumed that the client has requested the inquirer to act in his behalf and when such information is related to the particular service requested.

(d) Disclosure to relatives and other legally responsible persons.

(1) To the extent available and upon request, an authorized agency must provide a relative or other legally responsible person with whom a child is placed, or to whom a child is discharged or released, by the family court pursuant to section 1017 or 1054 of the Family Court Act, but who is not a foster parent for the child, with the same background information regarding the child as is provided to a foster parent with whom a child is placed. Such information, as available, must include the child's medical history and any other information which is provided to a foster parent as necessary for the child's health, safety and welfare pursuant to this section, section 443.2 of this Title, and any other applicable regulations of the Office of Children and Family Services. However, if the child's medical history includes confidential HIV-related information, such information must not be provided to the relative or other legally responsible person without a written release from:

(i) the child, if the child has capacity to consent as defined in section 360-8.1(a)(8) of this Title and in article 27-F of the Public Health Law; or

(ii) a person authorized to consent to health care for the child, if the child lacks capacity to consent.

(2) A social services district is required, under section 132 of the Social Services Law, to investigate the ability and willingness of relatives, and the liability of legally responsible relatives, to contribute to the support of an applicant for or recipient of public assistance or care. In regard to these investigations, such a relative is a person considered entitled, under section 136 of the Social Services Law, to necessary and appropriate information regarding the applicant or recipient. Information concerning the applicant's or recipient's needs and basic circumstances may be disclosed to such a relative to the extent necessary to discuss contributions of support from that relative. However, confidential HIV-related information may not be disclosed to such a relative without a written release from:

(i) the applicant or recipient, if the applicant or recipient has capacity to consent as defined in section 360-8.1(a)(8) of this Title and in article 27-F of the Public Health Law; or

(ii) from a person authorized to consent to health care for the applicant or recipient, if the applicant or recipient lacks capacity to consent.

(3) The social services district or other authorized agency must, in writing, inform the relative or other legally responsible person receiving information under this subdivision, of the confidential nature of the information and of any restrictions against redisclosure of such information. In the case of confidential HIV-related information, the warning statement against redisclosure set forth in section 360-8.1(h) of this Title and in article 27-F of the Public Health Law must be provided to the person receiving confidential HIV-related information.

(4) The term confidential HIV-related information is defined in section 360-8.1(a)(5) of this Title and in article 27-F of the Public Health Law. The conditions for the written release authorizing disclosure of such information are set forth in section 360-8.1(g) of this Title and in article 27-F of the Public Health Law.

(e) Disclosure to Federal, State or local official. (1) Information may be disclosed to any properly constituted authority. This includes a legislative body or committee upon proper legislative order, an administrative board charged with investigating or appraising the operation of public welfare, law enforcement officers, grand juries, probation and parole officers, government auditors, and members of public welfare boards, as well as the administrative staff of public welfare agencies.

(2) Information may be released to a selective service board when such information is necessary in order that the board may arrive at a valid and consistent decision regarding dependency.

(3) A social services official must disclose to a Federal, State or local law enforcement officer, upon request of the officer, the current address of any recipient of family assistance, or safety net assistance if the duties of the officer include the location or apprehension of the recipient and the officer furnishes the social services official with the name of the recipient and notifies the agency that such recipient is fleeing to avoid prosecution, custody or confinement after conviction, under the laws of the place from which the recipient is fleeing for a crime or an attempt to commit a crime which is a felony under the laws of the place from which the recipient is fleeing, or which, in the case of the state of New Jersey, is a high misdemeanor under the laws of that state, or is violating a condition of probation or parole imposed under a Federal or State law or has information that is necessary for the officer to conduct his or her official duties. In a request for disclosure pursuant to this paragraph, such law

enforcement officer must endeavor to include identifying information to help ensure that the social services official discloses only the address of the person sought and not the address of a person with the same or similar name.

(4) Nothing in this Part precludes a social services official from reporting to an appropriate agency or official, including law enforcement agencies or officials, known or suspected instances of physical or mental injury, sexual abuse or exploitation, sexual contact with a minor or negligent treatment or maltreatment of a child of which the social services official becomes aware of in the administration of public assistance and care.

(5) Nothing in this Part precludes a social services official from communicating with the Federal Immigration and Naturalization Service regarding the immigration status of any individual.

(f) Disclosure upon subpoena by court. (1) When a public assistance record is subpoenaed by court, the public welfare agency shall immediately consult its legal counsel before producing any record or revealing any information or giving any testimony.

(2) When the subpoena is for a purpose directly related to the administration of public assistance or protection of the child, the agency before complying with the subpoena shall endeavor to get in touch with the client whose record is involved or his attorney and secure permission to reveal the contents of the record which relate to the administration of public assistance.

(3) In the event that the subpoena is for a purpose not directly related to the administration of public assistance or the protection of a child, the agency shall plead, in support of its request to withhold information, that the Social Security Act, the Social Services Law and the regulations of the State Department of Social Services prohibit disclosure of confidential information contained in records and files, including names of clients. The agency will be governed by the final order of the court after this plea is made.

(g) Disclosure to bona fide news disseminating firm. The written assurance required by section 136 of the Social Services Law that the names and addresses of applicants and recipients of assistance shall not be published, shall be obtained by the public welfare official before allowing examination of records of disbursements by that bona fide news disseminating firm.

(h) Disclosure of confidential HIV-related information. (1) Notwithstanding any other provision of any law or regulation, confidential HIV-related information concerning persons claiming disability benefits under the provisions of titles II and XVI of the Social Security Act may be disclosed to persons employed by or acting on behalf of the department's office of disability determinations engaged in the conduct of processing such claims on the basis of a general medical release in the form approved by the Social Security Administration of the United States Department of Health and Human Services. The employees and agents of the office of disability determinations, including providers of clinical laboratory services, consultative medical examinations or claimant-related medical information, to the extent they have acted in accordance with department procedures and instructions, will be held harmless and indemnified by the department for any liability for the disclosure or redisclosure of any HIV-related information when such information is solicited by or provided to the office of disability determination.

(2) All medical information, including confidential HIV-related information, solicited by or provided to the office of disability determinations for the purpose of determining a person's disability will be treated as confidential and this information must not be disclosed except as prescribed by

the regulations of the Secretary of the United States Department of Health and Human Services.

(3) The term confidential HIV-related information is defined in section 360-8.1 of this Title.

(i) Disclosure of domestic violence related information. (1) Information with respect to victims of domestic violence collected as a result of procedures for domestic violence screening, assessment, referrals and waivers pursuant to Part 351 of this Title shall not be released to any outside party or parties or other government agencies unless the information is required to be disclosed by law, or unless authorized in writing by the public assistance applicant or recipient.

(2) Employees of the office, social services district or any agency providing domestic violence liaison services, consistent with applicable statute and regulation, may have access to client identifiable information maintained by a domestic violence liaison or by the welfare management system only when the employees' specific job responsibilities cannot be accomplished without access to client identifiable information.

(3) Each social service district and agency providing domestic violence liaison services, with access to the welfare management system, must develop and implement policies and practices to ensure the maintenance of confidential individual information.

(j) Disclosure of education information. To the extent available, an authorized agency must provide a copy of a foster child's education record at no cost to the child when such foster child is discharged to his or her own care. For the purposes of this subdivision, the education record of a foster child includes the names and addresses of the child's educational providers; the child's grade level performance; assurances that the child's placement in foster care took into account proximity to the school in which the child was enrolled at the time of placement; and any other relevant education information concerning the child.

§357.4　Prohibition against improper use of lists of applicants and recipients.

(Additional statutory authority: Social Services Law, §§136, 258, 320) All material sent to applicants and recipients of public assistance, including material enclosed in envelopes containing checks, must be directly related to the administration of the public assistance programs and shall not have political implications.

§357.5　Procedures for safeguarding information maintained by the New York State Department of Social Services, local social services districts and other authorized agencies.

(a) Records containing individually identifiable information shall be marked "confidential" and kept in locked files or in rooms that are locked when the records are not in use.

(b) When in use, records shall be maintained in such a manner as to prevent exposure of individual identifiable information to anyone other than the authorized party directly utilizing the case record.

(c) No records shall be taken from the place of business without prior authorization by appropriate supervisory staff of the New York State Department of Social Services, the local social services district or other authorized agency.

(d) No records shall be taken home by agency staff except upon prior authorization by appropriate supervisory staff in order to perform a function which requires the possession of the records outside of the agency and where return of the records to the agency at the close of business would result in an undue burden to the staff. In those cases where records are taken home by staff, the records are to be maintained in a secure location and are not to be disclosed to anyone other than those expressly authorized by statute or regulation. The records are to be returned to the agency by staff on the following business day.

(e) Records shall be transmitted from one location to another in sealed envelopes stamped "confidential," and a receipt shall be obtained documenting delivery of said records.

(f) Interviews with clients shall be conducted at a location and in a manner which maximizes privacy.

(g) Employees of the New York State Department of Social Services, the local social services district or the other authorized agency, consistent with applicable statute and regulation, shall have access to individual identifiable information only where the employee's specific job responsibilities cannot be accomplished without access to individual identifiable information.

§357.6 Confidentiality policy and procedures manual.

The New York State Department of Social Services, local social services districts, and other authorized agencies shall disseminate to staff a policy and procedures manual establishing and describing:

(a) responsibilities of staff to safeguard information pursuant to regulation and policy;

(b) procedures for properly informing clients of records collection, access, utilization and dissemination;

(c) policies and practices relating to the safeguarding of confidential information by the agency;

(d) procedures relating to employee access to information; and

(e) disciplinary actions for violations of confidentiality statutes, regulations and policies.

Part 407
Consolidated Services Plan
(In its Entirety)

§407.1 General statement.

(a) All references to the Comprehensive Annual Social Services Plan in this Title are deemed to be references to the Consolidated Services Plan.

(b) Each social services district must prepare and submit to the department a multi-year Consolidated Services Plan, hereinafter referred to as the "plan," setting forth its plan for four years of service for adults and for family and children's services.

(c) Commencing with the year following initial preparation of the plan and for each succeeding year of the plan, local social services district must prepare and submit to the department for approval, in a format and at a time specified by the department, an annual implementation report.

(d) A common planning process will be implemented integrating the separate plans required for family and children's services, protective services for adults, child protective services and title XX services into the plan. The plan requirements supersede the following:

(1) Family and Children's Services Plan as specified in Part 429 of this Subchapter;

(2) Protective Services for Adults Plan as specified in section 457.8 of this Subchapter;

(3) Child Protective Services Plan as specified in subdivision (e) of section 432.2 of this Subchapter; and

(4) Comprehensive Annual Social Services Program Plan as specified in Part 401 of this Subchapter.

§407.2 Services program year.

(a) The plan becomes effective on the date so designated by the commissioner once the plan is approved by the commissioner, and remains in effect until such time as the commissioner approves a plan for the next three-year period.

(b) Any plan submitted to the department must be modified by the approved annual implementation report. Amendments to the plan may be made in accordance with section 407.10 of this Part.

§407.3 Submission of the plan and annual implementation reports.

(a) In accordance with a schedule to be determined by the commissioner, each social services district must develop and submit a plan and annual implementation reports in such format as prescribed by the department.

(b) Once the plan or annual implementation report is submitted to the department, the district must make it available to the public upon request.

§407.4 Services.

The plan must provide information on services provided directly or purchased by the social services district which include but are not limited to:

(a) foster care for children;
(b) residential placement services for adults;
(c) preventive services for children;
(d) preventive services for adults;
(e) child protective services;
(f) protective services for adults;
(g) adoption services;
(h) employment services;
(i) housing improvement services;
(j) day care;
(k) domestic violence services;
(*l*) unmarried parent services;
(m) family planning services;
(n) health-related services;
(o) home management services;
(p) homemaker services;
(q) housekeeper/chore services;
(r) educational services;
(s) social group services to senior citizens;

(t) transportation; and

(u) information and referral.

The district may include information on other services at its discretion.

§407.5 Content of the plan.

Each plan must contain the following components:

(a) Needs assessment. (1) For the services specified in section 407.4 of this Part, the needs of families, children and adults for whom the social services district is or may be responsible must be assessed.

(2) The assessment must be based on but not limited to:

(i) previous years' needs assessments;

(ii) previous years' success or failure to achieve State objectives as specified in a department release;

(iii) manner of current service delivery;

(iv) statistical measure of the number of persons requiring services and care;

(v) characteristics of persons currently receiving service and care;

(vi) data obtained through the district's public participation process as required in subdivision (g) of this section; and

(vii) indicators of general social and economic conditions in the district.

(3) The needs assessment must include a numerical estimate of families, children and adults requiring each service listed in section 407.4 of this Part.

(4) Each social services district must provide a narrative description of how the numerical estimates were derived.

(b) Resource inventory. (1) The plan must reflect the existing resources in the county and surrounding region which are available to provide services and care to children and their families, and to adults. Social services districts must review information which is provided by the department on the number and capacity of service providers and note any addition, deletions, changes or corrections to the resources listed.

(2) Each social services district must describe its organizational structure for family and children's services and for adult services, including the operational relationship of those units both to the commissioner and to other components of the department, and the number of full-time equivalent staff. For protective services for adults, the total number of professional staff involved in the provision of such services must also be indicated.

(c) District goals, objectives and activities. (1) Each social services district must indicate in the plan, its goals, objectives and activities. These goals, objectives and activities must be established for foster care, child protective services, child preventive services, adoption services, protective services for adults and for at least two other services.

(2) Such goals, objectives and activities must be based on the needs assessments and resource inventory, and must be intended to ensure that:

(i) families are able to stay together and develop supportive relationships and maintain or achieve independence;

(ii) families with children in foster care are able to reunite and develop supportive relationships and maintain or achieve independence;

(iii) children whose families are unable to care adequately for them receive appropriate, stable, substitute care;

(iv) children in foster care who are unable to return to their families are provided permanent homes to develop the capacity to live independently upon achieving adulthood;

(v) elderly and disabled people are able to participate to the fullest possible extent in the life of their communities, particularly through the availability of a full range of in-home and community-based services; and

(vi) residential care for adults and the elderly is provided in a manner that reflects the full range of their social and medical needs, and that affords them the fullest possible opportunity for continued participation in community life.

(3) Objectives shall be stated in terms of outcomes for the client, and be expressed in measurable quantifiable terms. The majority of objectives will be for three years.

(4) For each service for which goals and objectives have been established, the district must describe the explicit activities which will be undertaken to meet the indicated objectives. The activities must be measurable, time limited and contain a defined target for achievement. Activities may include the development of new resources, expansion of existing resources, utilization of available resources, and modification of the district's organizational structure.

(5) Each social services district must, in a manner to be specified by the department, address issues identified by the department in its analysis of economic and social indicators.

(6) For those program procedures/functions which are required by Federal or State law or regulation and for which the social services district notes it is not in compliance with the legal assurance and program information section of the plan, the district must develop ways to achieve compliance and describe activities to be undertaken to achieve compliance.

(7) For those program areas which are noted as not current practice in the legal assurance and program information section of the plan, each social services district must describe activities to address at least two of these items.

(d) Program and fiscal requirements. For each service for which a needs assessment is completed, each social services district must identify in the plan projected program and fiscal requirements including:

(1) numbers of persons to receive each service;

(2) estimated expenditures for each service and identification of expected reimbursement from all sources; and

(3) method of provision for each service.

(e) Unmet needs. Each social services district must describe the major areas and issues of need which are not able to be addressed by its plan.

(f) Each social services district must include in the plan income eligibility standards for those services for which such standards are at a local district's option.

(g) Public participation. Each social services district must include in its plan a description of how public participation was achieved, and the mechanisms used to obtain public comment in accordance with the following:

(1) At least one public hearing on the plan must be held during the development and prior to the submission of the plan. Such public hearing(s) shall be held only after 15 days notice is provided in a newspaper of general circulation in the district. Such notice must specifically identify the times during the public hearing when the child protective services, adult services and family and children's services components of the plan are to be considered. The plan must include the date(s) of such hearing(s); how the hearing(s) was publicized; the number of persons who attended and a general description of their interests and affiliations; and the major issues raised at the hearing(s) and how these comments were used in the planning process.

(2) Local advisory councils established pursuant to Part 341 of this Subchapter must participate in the development of the plan. At a minimum, prior to submission of the plan, the local commissioner must present the plan to the council for review. The plan must contain the role and activities of the council in the development of the plan, the date(s) of the meeting(s) at which the plan is discussed, the issues discussed at each such meeting and their impact, if any, on the plan.

(3) As required by sections 423.3 (a) and 473.2 (b) of the Social Services Law, discussions and meetings with public, private and voluntary organizations which are involved in adult and family and children's services must be held to acquire their advice and consultation in the development of the plan. The plan must include the dates of such meetings, the organizations represented, the issues discussed and the degree to which such comments were incorporated into the planning process. At a minimum, such organizations must include: health and mental health agencies; aging, legal and law enforcement agencies; societies for the prevention of cruelty to children; family court judges; youth bureaus or boards; and departments of probation.

(h) Legal assurances and program information. Each social services district must include in its plan, legal assurances and program information which it is prepared to document on request of the department. These assurances and information must describe the district's operations of services programs required by Federal and State law and regulation.

(1) Each social services district must provide the following general legal assurances:

(i) All providers of services under the plan will operate fully in conformance with all applicable Federal, State and local fire, health, safety and sanitation and other standards prescribed in law or regulations. Where a social services district is required to provide licensure for the provision of services, agencies providing such services must be licensed.

(ii) All providers of services under the plan are required to operate each program or activity so that, when viewed in its entirety, the program or activity is readily accessible to and usable by handicapped persons.

(iii) Benefits and services available under the plan are provided in a nondiscriminatory manner as required by title VI of the Civil Rights Act of 1964 as amended.

(iv) The activities covered by the plan serve only those individuals and groups eligible under the provision of applicable State and Federal statutes.

(v) No requirements as to duration of residence or citizenship will be imposed as a condition of participation in the State's program for the provision of services.

(2) Each social services district must provide the following legally required program assurances:

(i) The district provides applicants for or recipients of services and care adequate and timely notice regarding denial, discontinuation, suspension, reduction or restriction of services, consistent with applicable statutes and regulations.

(ii) In accordance with Part 358 of this Chapter, applicants for or recipients of services and care have a right to a fair hearing to review the denial, discontinuation, suspension, reduction, restriction or adequacy of service/care or the failure to take timely action upon an application for service/care.

(iii) Title XX funded services are available to eligible individuals in every geographic area within the district. Where different services are made available to a specific category or individuals in different geographic areas, services are available to all eligible individuals in that category who reside in that area.

(3) Each social services district must assure implementation of each responsibility contained in Part 432 of this Subchapter concerning child protective services.

(4) Each social services district must assure implementation of each responsibility contained in Part 457 of this Subchapter concerning adult protective services.

(5) Each social services district must include in its plan a statement whether the following have been established for its protective services for adults program:

(i) a financial management system with written procedures;

(ii) the roles and responsibilities have been defined and written for the delivery of protective services for adults for the various divisions and offices of the social services district, including accounting, income maintenance, medical assistance, protective services for adults and all relevant services;

(iii) an interagency service delivery network has been developed with other appropriate agencies including, but not limited to, the Office for the Aging, the Department of Health, community mental health services, psychiatric center(s), legal services and appropriate law enforcement agencies, which at a minimum will:

(a) designate contact persons;

(b) establish referral procedures and follow-up mechanisms;

(c) indicate the locus of responsibility for cases with multi-agency needs; and

(d) include written policies and procedures and interagency agreements; and

(iv) a mechanism to ensure coordination between the protective services for adults and the post institutional services planning (PISP) programs.

(i) Summary of actions to address change in funds. According to the format provided by the department, each social services district must show how a change in the amount of funds available to the district for services provided under the plan would be addressed in that district.

§407.6 Annual implementation report.

According to a schedule to be determined by the commissioner, each social services district must submit an annual implementation report of the plan to the department. The report must include but not be limited to:

(a) a chart describing the organizational structure and staffing of the district as required in section 407.5(b) of this Part, if there have been any changes since the submittal of the plan;

(b) goals, objectives and activities as described in section 407.5 (c) of this Part, including:

(1) Objectives and activities for child protective services, foster care, adoption, child preventive services, protective services for adults and two other services;

(2) Activities for those program procedures/functions which are required by Federal or State law or regulation for which the district has stated in the plan it is not in compliance and continues to be in noncompliance;

(3) Activities addressing at least two of the program information items noted as not current practice in the plan and which continue to be not current practice;

(c) in a manner to be specified by the department, each social services district must address issues identified by the department in its analysis of economic and social indicators;

(d) if goals and objectives approved for the plan must be changed, an explanation of the reason(s) for this change;

(e) persons to be served and resources required to meet objectives as required by section 407.5(d) of this Part;

(f) income eligibility standards for services as required by section 407.5(f) of this Part;

(g) information on public participation in the planning process as required by section 407.5(g) of this Part;

(h) the signature of approval by the chief executive officer or the chairperson of the legislative body in those districts without a chief executive officer; and

(i) summary information on how the district will address changes in the amount of funds available to the district for services, if such changes occur, as required by section 407.5(i) of this Part.

§407.7 Criteria for approval of plan and annual implementation reports.
The plan and the annual implementation reports must be approved or disapproved by the commissioner of the State Department of Social Services. The criteria for approval are that the plan or report:

(a) complies with requirements of the planning process, including but not limited to those concerning public participation and submission dates;

(b) contains all required information including all required charts; and for the annual implementation reports, the signature of the chief executive officer or the chairperson of the legislative body in those districts without a chief executive officer;

(c) is internally consistent so that objectives and activities and projected expenditures are clearly related to district needs, and client and expenditure estimates are consistent with objectives and activities; and

(d) addresses those issues identified by the department pursuant to sections 407.5(c)(5) and 407.6 (c) of this Part.

§407.8 Procedures for review and approval of the plan and annual implementation reports.

(a) Upon receipt of the plan or the annual implementation report, the department has 45 days to transmit a letter to the local commissioner which indicates approval or disapproval of all or certain components of the plan or annual implementation report. A letter of disapproval must indicate the criteria set forth in section 407.7 of this Part which the plan or annual implementation report did not meet, and the action necessary to qualify for approval. The letter must also notify the district that it must submit a revised plan or annual implementation report or parts thereof within 30 days of receipt of a notice of disapproval of the whole or part of the plan or annual implementation report.

(b) Within 30 days of receipt of a notice of disapproval, the district must submit to the department a revised plan or annual implementation report or parts thereof.

(c) The department shall approve or disapprove the initial revision of the disapproved plan or annual implementation report within 15 days of receipt of such initial revision.

(d) The commissioner may grant extensions of time for resubmittal of plans or annual implementation reports, or permit additional revisions and resubmittals.

(e) No portion of the plan or annual implementation report can be finally disapproved until the district has had at least one opportunity to resubmit the plan or report.

(f) State reimbursement may be withheld for all or any portion of a district's activities if the plan, the annual implementation report or portions of either are disapproved.

(g) Any social services district aggrieved by a final disapproval of a plan or annual implementation report is entitled to a hearing in accordance with the applicable provisions of the Social Services Law and this Title. In the event of an adverse hearing decision, a social services district is entitled to judicial review pursuant to Article 78 of the Civil Practice law and Rules. The withholding of reimbursement for expenditures incurred pursuant to disapproved portions of a district's plan or annual implementation report begins on the date of the final disapproval or a later date set by the department, and continues until the date on which the corrective action by the district is completed.

§407.9 Monitoring of the plan and annual implementation reports.

(a) On an ongoing basis, the department shall monitor and review local plan implementation, and where it finds substantive noncompliance with the plan, the department may withhold reimbursement for claims submitted for services that are not in compliance with the plan. Such monitoring must focus on: achievement of activities and objectives as defined in the plan and annual implementation reports of each social services district, and compliance with applicable laws and regulations. Written monitoring reports shall be prepared by the department on a regular basis.

(b) Any social services district aggrieved by a determination of the department to withhold reimbursement pursuant to this section is entitled to a hearing in accordance with the provisions of section 407.8(g) of this Part.

§407.10 Amendments to the plan.

A social services district may propose amendments to the plan at any time. If a reduction in services, a change in eligibility, or a change in fees is proposed, the amendment must be published for public comment and be presented to the local advisory council for review, prior to submission to the department. If an amendment is approved by the department, it becomes effective on the date so designated by the commissioner.

§407.11 Waivers.

(a) Upon receipt of a written request from a social services district, the department may issue a written waiver of any provision of this Part. Any request for a waiver must include:

(1) the specific regulation(s) for which a waiver is sought;

(2) a statement indicating how granting the waiver will enhance or simplify the planning process;

(3) a proposal describing, to the satisfaction of the department, what the social services district intends to do to achieve or maintain the intended purpose of the regulations(s) if a waiver is granted; and

(4) any other information the department may deem necessary to determine whether a waiver should be granted.

(b) Waivers granted pursuant to this section will be based upon the department's review of the information submitted pursuant to this section, and may be limited in duration and scope at the discretion of the department.

(c) Failure to adhere to the terms of the waiver will result in the recision of the waiver.

(d) The department will maintain a record of any waiver issued under this section, a list of any regulations waived, and the reasons why each such waiver was issued.

Part 421
Standards of Practice for Adoption Services

§421.1 Definitions.

For the purpose of this Part, the following definitions shall apply:

(a) Adoptive applicant means a married couple, an adult unmarried person, an adult married person living separate and apart from his or her spouse pursuant to a legally recognizable separation agreement or a decree of separation, or an adult married person living separate and apart from his or her spouse for a period of three years or more prior to the commencement of the adoption proceeding who has applied to adopt or who has received agency approval for the placement of a child in his or her home for the purpose of adoption.

(b) Adoption services means assisting a child to secure an adoptive home through: counseling with biological parent or legal guardian concerning surrender of, or legal termination of parental rights with regard to a child; the evaluation of child's placement needs; preplacement planning; the recruitment, study and evaluation of interested prospective adoptive parents; counseling for families after placement; supervision of children in adoptive homes until legal adoption; and counseling of adoptive families after legal adoption.

(c) Adoptive parent means a person with whom a child has been placed for adoption or who has adopted a child with agency approval.

(d) Adoptive placement means the child has been placed into a home for the purpose of adoption and the agency and adoptive parent or the child's foster parent have signed an adoption agreement and the facts of such placement have been recorded in accordance with paragraph (e) of subdivision (5) of section 383-c or subdivision 5 of section 384 of the Social Services Law.

(e) Authorized agency means an organization covered by section 371.10(a) and (b) of the Social Services Law.

(f) Biological parent means a parent who has conceived or given birth to the child, or from whom the child was conceived, either in or out of wedlock.

(g) Foster parent means any person certified or approved pursuant to section 375 of the Social Services Law, and Part 443 of this Title with whom a child, in the care, custody or guardianship of an authorized agency, is placed for temporary or long-term care.

(h) Legal guardian means a person to whom or an agency to which the guardianship of a child has been committed by surrender in accordance with the terms of a surrender instrument or pursuant to a court order under section 383-c, 384 or 384-b of the Social Services Law. A legal guardian may also be a person appointed as guardian of the person of a child pursuant to a duly executed will or deed as provided by section 81 of the Domestic Relations Law.

(i) Legally freed child means a person under the age of 18 years:

(1) whose custody and guardianship have been transferred to an authorized agency as a result of either a surrender instrument executed pursuant to section 383-c or 384 of the Social Services Law or an order of the Family Court or the Surrogate's Court made pursuant to section 384-b of the Social Services Law; or

(2) whose care and custody have been transferred to an authorized agency pursuant to article 3, 7 or 10-C of the Family Court Act, section 1055 of the Family Court Act or section 384-a of the Social Services Law and where such child's parents are both deceased, or where one parent is deceased and the other parent is not a person entitled to notice pursuant to sections 111 and 111-a of the Domestic Relations Law.

(j) Photo-listed means having placed a legally freed child's picture and description in New York State's Waiting Children books which are organized, prepared, and distributed to authorized agencies and to appropriate citizen groups by the department.

(k) Prospective adoptive parent means an individual who meets criteria as defined in section 421.16 of this Title, and who has indicated an interest in adopting a particular child, and for whom the authorized agency has begun the placement process in accordance with section 421.18 of this Title.

(*l*) Registered child means a child who has been included in the listing of legally freed children maintained by the Statewide Adoption Service (State Photo Listing Service) pursuant to the requirements of section 420.2 of this Title.

§421.5 Services to fathers of out-of-wedlock children.

With regard to the rights and interests of the biological father of an out-of-wedlock child, an agency shall comply with the following procedures:

(a) In all cases:

(1) take steps to identify the father and determine the extent of relationship between father and mother and between father and child;

(2) make efforts to involve the father in planning for the child;

(3) give the alleged father an opportunity to recognize or deny paternity;

(4) if father admits paternity but is unwilling or unable to plan for the child, attempt to obtain a voluntary surrender of father's rights in child when such action would be in the best interests of the child; and

(5) if the father is unwilling or unable to plan, and is also unwilling to voluntarily surrender rights, take such steps to obtain termination of the father's parental rights as are appropriate to the best interests of the child.

(b) The child shall not be placed for adoption without the father's consent or the surrender or termination of his parental rights in cases where the child being placed is not yet six months old and the unwed mother's parental rights have been surrendered or terminated, and the father has:

(1) paid or offered to pay, a fair and reasonable sum, according to his means, for medical, hospital and nursing expenses incurred in connection with the mother's pregnancy or with the birth of the child;

(2) openly lived with the child or child's mother for a continuous period of six months immediately prior to the placement of the child for adoption; and

(3) openly held himself out to be the father of the child during a continuous period of six months prior to the placement of the child for adoption.

(c) The child shall not be placed for adoption without the father's consent or the surrender or termination of his parental rights in cases where the child is over six months old and the unwed mother's parental rights have been surrendered or terminated, and the father has maintained substantial and continuous or repeated contact with the child as manifested by paragraphs (1) and (2) of this subdivision:

(1) by payment of a fair and reasonable sum toward support for the child, according to the father's means, and either:

(i) monthly visitations to the child when financially and physically able to do so and not prevented from doing so by actions of the agency having custody of the child;

(ii) by regular communication with the child or the person or agency having care or custody of the child, when visitation is either not financially or physically possible or has been prevented by the agency having custody of the child; or

(2) a father who has openly lived with the child for a period of six months in the one-year period immediately preceding the child's placement for adoption and who had openly held himself out to be the father of the child during such period shall be deemed to have maintained substantial and continuous contact with the child for the purpose of this subdivision.

(d) A written instrument executed by the biological father denying paternity or consenting to the mother's surrender of the child for adoption or consenting to the adoption of the child shall be completed in accordance with section 111 of the Domestic Relations Law.

§421.15 Adoption study process.

Authorized agencies operating an adoption program shall:

(a) Conduct an adoption study process in groups, individually, or in any combination thereof. Such adoption study shall include at least one visit to the applicant's home.

(b) In at least one session in any study process containing two or more group sessions, include the participation of parents who have adopted a child.

(c) Inform applicants at the first appointment or meeting that the following will be required prior to the conclusion of the adoption study:

(1) report from a physician about the health of each member of the household;

(2) references from at least three persons, only one of which may be related to the applicant(s) who can attest to the character, habits, reputation and personal qualifications of the applicant(s) and their suitability for caring for a child;

(3) if married, proof of marriage;

(4) if married and living separate and apart from their spouse:

(i) proof that the separation is based upon a legally recognizable separation agreement or decree of separation; or

(ii) an affidavit executed by the prospective adoptive parent attesting that he or she has been or will be living separate and apart from his or her spouse for a period of three years or more prior to the commencement of the adoption proceeding;

(5) if previously married, proof of dissolution of marriage by death or divorce;

(6) evidence of employment and salary, such as W-2 form or pay stub for each employed applicant;

(7) (i) a response to an agency inquiry to the Statewide Central Registry of Child Abuse and Maltreatment indicating whether the applicant(s) and/or any other person over the age of 18 who resides in the home of the applicant(s) are the subject(s) of an indicated child abuse or maltreatment report and, if the applicant(s) or any other person over the age of eighteen who resides in the home of the applicant(s) resided in another state at any time during the five years preceding the application for approval as adoptive parent(s) made in accordance with this Part, the response from the child abuse and maltreatment registry of the applicable child welfare agency in each such state of previous residence; and

(ii) a response to an agency inquiry to the Justice Center for the Protection of People with Special Needs whether the applicant(s) and/or any other person over the age of 18 who resides in the home of the applicant(s) are listed on the register of substantiated category one cases of abuse or neglect maintained by the Justice Center for the Protection of People with Special Needs.

(8) a response from the Office of Children and Family Services to the federal and state criminal history record checks of the applicant and any other person over the age of 18 currently residing in the home of such applicant in accordance with section 421.27 of this Part. If a prospective adoptive parent is approved or if the approval of an approved adoptive parent is not revoked, notwithstanding that the agency is notified by the Office of Children and Family Services that the prospective or approved adoptive parent or any other person over the age of 18 who is currently residing in the home of the prospective or approved adoptive parent has a criminal history record, a record of the reasons why the prospective or approved adoptive parent was determined to be appropriate and acceptable to be approved as an adoptive parent provided, however, the agency may not grant or continue approval where the prospective or approved adoptive parent has been convicted of a mandatory disqualifying crime or where an authorized agency, as defined in section 371(10)(a) or (c) of the Social Services Law, has been directed by the Office of Children and Family Services to deny such application or to hold such application in abeyance because of the results of the Federal Bureau of Investigation criminal history record check conducted in accordance with section 421.27 of this Part; and   *(Eff. 1/25/17)*

(9) a sworn statement from each applicant, indicating whether to the best of such applicant's knowledge, such applicant or any person over the age of 18 currently residing in the home has ever been convicted of a crime in New York State or any other jurisdiction. If an applicant discloses in the sworn statement furnished in accordance with this paragraph that he/she or any other person over the age of 18 currently residing in the home has been convicted of a crime, the agency must determine, in accordance with guidelines developed and disseminated by the office of children and family services to the extent consistent with section 421.27 of this Part, whether to approve the applicant to

be an adoptive parent. If the agency determines it will approve the applicant, the agency must maintain a written record, as part of the application file or home study, of the reason(s) why the applicant was determined to be appropriate and acceptable to receive an adoptive placement.

(d) Determine compliance with all of the criteria set forth in section 421.16 of this Part, explore each applicant's ability to be an adoptive parent, and discuss the following topics:

(1) characteristics and needs of children available for adoption;

(2) the principles and requirements for adopting a child who is a member of a sibling group in accordance with sections 421.2(e) and 421.18(b) of this Part;

(3) principles related to the development of children;

(4) reasons a person seeks to become an adoptive parent;

(5) the understanding of the adoptive parent role;

(6) the person's concerns and questions about adoption;

(7) the person's psychological readiness to assume responsibility for a child;

(8) the attitudes that each person in the applicant's home has about adoption and their concept of an adopted child's role in the family;

(9) the awareness of the impact that adoptive responsibilities have upon family life, relationships and current life style;

(10) a person's self-assessment of his/her capacity to provide a child with a stable and meaningful relationship; and

(11) the role of the agency in supervising and supporting the adoptive placement.

(e) When an adoption study has been completed and an authorized agency intends to approve an applicant, it shall:

(1) prepare a written summary of the study findings and activities, including significant characteristics of their family members, the family interaction, the family's relationship to other persons and the community, the family's child rearing practices and experiences, and any other material needed to describe the family for adoption purposes, to be submitted to workers in the agency or other agencies responsible for making placement decisions about children;

(2) arrange for the applicant(s) to review this written summary with the exception of any comments by references which have sought confidentiality;

(3) encourage the applicant(s) to express their views on the substance of any significant aspect of the written summary;

(4) give applicant(s) the opportunity to enter their reaction as an addendum to the written summary;

(5) arrange for the applicant(s) and the caseworker to sign the summary after it has been reviewed and any addendum has been attached; and

(6) provide a dated written notice of approval to applicant.

(f) Discontinue a study process and by mutual consent:

(1) the applicant's record shall reflect the discussion leading to such mutual agreement to discontinue; and

(2) the applicant shall be informed in writing of the discontinuation of the adoption study.

(g) Reject an applicant:

(1) during a study if his lack of cooperation does not permit the study to be carried out; or

(2) if it is determined after a thorough adoption study based on casework principles that he is:

(i) physically incapable of caring for an adopted child;

(ii) emotionally incapable of caring for an adopted child; or

(iii) that his approval would not be in the best interests of children awaiting adoptions.

(3) A decision to reject an applicant shall be made by at least two staff members in conference, one of whom shall be at a supervisory level.

(4) The record shall reflect the names of the participants in the decision and the reason for the decision.

(5) The agency must inform the applicant in writing that he has not been accepted, stating its reason(s) for rejection. If the rejection is based in whole or in part on the existence of an indicated report of child abuse or maltreatment, that fact and the reasons therefor must be included in the notice.

(6) The notification shall offer the applicant the opportunity to discuss this decision in person with the worker's supervisor.

(7) The notification must inform the applicant that he may apply for a hearing before the department pursuant to section 372-e of the Social Services Law regarding the rejection of the application and must state the procedure to be used for this purpose.

(8) If the reason for the rejection is based in whole or in part on the existence of an indicated report of child abuse or maltreatment, the agency must comply with the provisions of section 421.16(o) of this Part pertaining to notice of right to a hearing pursuant to section 424-a of the Social Services Law.

(h) Conclude an adoption study process in either discontinuation, rejection, or approval within four months of initiation:

(1) except where illness or geographic absence of the applicant makes him/her unavailable for a substantial part of said four-month period. In such a case, the record shall clearly show such unavailability and what efforts were made to contact the applicant; or

(2) provided, however, where an adoption study has been interrupted by unavailability of agency staff, the period of four months may be extended, but to not more than six months, if the applicant agrees to such extension in writing. If the applicant agrees to delay in order to avoid caseworker change, the record must show when this agreement was obtained. If the applicant does not accept such delay, the study must be concluded within the four months through the utilization of substitute staff or purchase of service.

(i) At the conclusion of the adoption study process, the registering agency shall update the adoptive parent registry required by section 424.3(a) of this Title, either by noting that an applicant has had the study approved or, in the case of a study resulting in either discontinuation or rejection, removing the applicant from the registry.

§421.16 Adoption study criteria.

(a) An adoption study shall explore the following characteristics of applicants:

(1) capacity to give and receive affection;

(2) ability to provide for a child's physical and emotional needs;

(3) ability to accept the intrinsic worth of a child, to respect and share his past, to understand the meaning of separation he has experienced, and to have realistic expectations and goals;

(4) flexibility and ability to change;

(5) ability to cope with problems, stress and frustration;

(6) feelings about parenting an adopted child and the ability to make a commitment to a child placed in the home; and

(7) ability to use community resources to strengthen and enrich family functioning.

(b) Age. Applicants accepted for adoption study shall be at least 18 years old. The agency shall not establish any other minimum or maximum age for study or acceptance.

(c) Health.

(1) An approved applicant shall be in such physical condition that it is reasonable to expect him/her to live to the child's majority and to have the energy and other abilities needed to fulfill the parental responsibilities.

(2) A report of a physical examination conducted not more than one year preceding the date of the adoption application and a written statement from a physician, physician assistant, nurse practitioner or other licensed and qualified health care practitioner as appropriate, regarding the family's general health, the absence of communicable disease, infection, or illness or any physical condition(s) which might affect the proper care of an adopted child, must be filed with the agency. This examination must include a tuberculosis screening and additional related tests as deemed necessary within the last 12 months; an additional report of chest X-rays is required where a physician determines that such X-rays are necessary to rule out the presence of current diseases. If the adoptive applicant is or has been a foster parent, and the agency which certified, licensed or approved the foster parent has a completed medical report on the foster family in its records, the foster family medical report will satisfy this requirement, if the medical report was completed within the past year.

(3) Upon a finding of physical condition(s) which are likely to have negative effects upon an applicant's ability to carry out the parental role, an adoption study may be discontinued with the agreement of the applicant. If the applicant does not agree about the likelihood of such negative effects, he shall be given the opportunity to seek another medical opinion, and file another medical report, before a final decision is made.

(4) The record of a study discontinued or resulting in rejection because of present or expected effects of a medical condition, must identify the condition found and effects found or expected.

(d) Marital status. Agencies must not consider marital status in their acceptance or rejection of applicants. However, one married partner may not adopt without the other unless one partner is living separate and apart from his or her spouse pursuant to a legally recognizable separation agreement or decree of separation, or one partner has been or will be living separate and apart from his or her spouse for a period of three years or more prior to the commencement of the adoption proceeding. Agencies must not establish policies which place single or divorced applicants, applicants who are separated from their spouses pursuant to a legally recognizable separation agreement or decree of separation, applicants who have been or will be living separate and apart from their spouses for a period of three or more years, or widowed applicants, at a disadvantage.

(e) Fertility. An adoptive applicant may not be rejected for adoption because of his, her or their fertility (capacity to have biological children). The significance of fertility and/or infertility as it relates to the desire to adopt shall always be explored in the adoption process, but applicants shall not be required to provide proof of infertility.

(f) Family composition.

(1) The agency may study family size as it relates to the ability of a family to care for another child and the quality of life which will be offered to an

adoptive child. Policies shall not be established which require rejection of an applicant based on family composition without determining its effect on the ability to care for a child and the quality of life which will be offered.

(2) Presence or absence of children in applicant's home regardless of their age and sex shall not be a basis for rejecting applicants.

(3) Adoptive placement which will result in there being more than two infants under the age of two in the home at the same time shall be made only after a study specifically focusing on the family's ability to care successfully for such a number of infants.

(4) If any children in an approved home are there as foster children, placement of an adoptive child shall be delayed if it would result in a family composition which violates section 378(4) of the Social Services Law.

(5) An adoptive placement shall not be made where a child previously placed for adoption has not yet been adopted, except:

(i) where the child to be placed is a sibling of one already in the home;

(ii) where the delay in adoption is due primarily to court delays; or

(iii) where the child to be placed is unusually hard to place and other placement resources are not available.

(6) Any exceptions pursuant to paragraph (5) of this subdivision shall be fully documented in the records.

(g) Sex preference and matching.

(1) Single applicants shall not be rejected because they seek children of only the same sex (or only the opposite sex).

(2) Exploration of a preference to adopt a child of a particular gender, where found necessary and appropriate, shall be carried out openly with a clear explanation to the applicant of the basis for, and relevance of, the inquiry.

(h) Employment and education of parents. Employment, education, or volunteer activities of applicants may not be a basis for rejection.

(i) Religion and race. Race, ethnic group, and religion shall not be a basis for rejecting an adoption applicant.

(j) Income. No applicant shall be rejected on the basis of low income, or because of receipt of income maintenance payments. The adoption study process shall evaluate an applicant's ability to budget his resources in such a way that a child placed with him can be reasonably assured of minimum standards of nutrition, health, shelter, clothing and other essentials. An applicant whose budgeting and money management skills appear deficient to assure such minimum standards shall be referred to any available resources which might help improve these skills.

(k) Employment and geographical stability. Changes in employment and residences may be examined to determine the significance of such changes for the functioning and well-being of the family and any child to be placed in the home. Frequent changes in employment and residences shall not be a basis for rejection unless it is determined that such changes reflect an inability to provide for the well-being of any child to be placed in the home.

(*l*) Child care experience. An adoption study shall inquire into an applicant's experience with children and offer him and/or her, if feasible, the opportunity to increase his/her experience, knowledge and skills in this area. However, no applicant should be rejected solely on the basis of a lack of such experience.

(m) Socialization and community support. The adoption study process shall include inquiry into the applicant's ability to locate and take advantage of human and organizational resources to strengthen their own capacity as parents. There shall not be any requirement for particular levels of educational achievement or kinds of organizational involvement or community recognition.

(n) Inquiry of State Central Register of Child Abuse and Maltreatment. An adoption study must include an inquiry of the department regarding whether the applicant is the subject of an indicated child abuse and maltreatment report on file with the State Central Register of Child Abuse and Maltreatment.

(1) If the applicant is the subject of such a report, the agency must determine on the basis of the information it has available and in accordance with guidelines developed and disseminated by the department whether to approve the application, except that any agency operated by a local social services district which had guidelines for the review of persons who are the subjects of indicated reports of child abuse or maltreatment in use prior to January 1, 1986 may continue to use such agency guidelines in making the required determination.

(2) If the application is approved, the agency must indicate in writing in the adoption study record the specific reason(s) why the person who is the subject of an indicated report was determined to be appropriate to receive an adoption placement.

(3) If the agency rejects the applicant, giving the indicated report as a reason, the applicant must be informed in writing of the reasons for such decision and that:

(i) he/she has a right to a hearing under section 424-a of the Social Services Law, regarding the record maintained in the State Central Register of Child Abuse and Maltreatment;

(ii) a request for such a hearing must be made within 90 days of the receipt of the written notice of rejection which indicates that the rejection is based in whole or in part on the existence of the indicated report; and

(iii) the sole issue at any such hearing will be whether the applicant has been shown by a fair preponderance of the evidence to have committed the act or acts of child abuse or maltreatment giving rise to the indicated report.

(4) If in a hearing under section 424-a of the Social Services Law the department fails to show by a preponderance of the evidence that the applicant committed the act or acts upon which the indicated report is based, the department will notify the agency which made the inquiry that, pursuant to the hearing decision, any decision to deny the applicant based on the indicated report should be reconsidered, upon receiving such notification from the department, the agency should reopen the adoption study and review its decision without considering the indicated report.

(5) Notwithstanding any other provision of this part, the requirements of this section relating to an inquiry to the Statewide Central Register of Child Abuse and Maltreatment apply to a person applying to be an approved adoptive parent to an authorized agency as defined by section 371(10)(a), (b) or (c) of the social services law or an agency approved by the office of children and family services to place out children for the purpose of adoption in accordance with article 13 of the not-for-profit corporation law.

(o) Inquiry of Out-of-State Child Abuse and Maltreatment Registry.

(1) This subdivision applies where an applicant or other person over the age of eighteen who resides in the home of the applicant resided in another state at any time during the five years preceding the application for approval as an adoptive parent made in accordance with this Part.

(2) If the applicant or other person who resides in the home of the applicant has a history of child abuse or maltreatment in another state, the agency must

determine on the basis of the information provided by the applicable child welfare agency in the other state and by the applicant and the guidelines developed by the Office of Children and Family Services, as referenced in subdivision (o) of this section, whether to approve or deny the application.

(3) If the application is approved, the agency must indicate in the adoption study record the specific reason(s) why the application was approved where an applicant or other person who resides in the home of the applicant has a history of child abuse or maltreatment.

(4) The agency must safeguard the confidentiality of the information received from the applicable child welfare agency in the other state to prevent unauthorized disclosure and such agency is prohibited from using such information for any purpose other than conducting background checks pursuant to this Part.

(p) Additional factors.

(1) Current abuse of alcohol or other drugs requires the rejection of an application. The record must clearly show how the finding of such abuse was made.

(2) An applicant may not be rejected for past drug or alcohol abuse, or past psychiatric illness or treatment, unless the record shows how these factors would contribute to the applicant's inability to care for an adopted child.

(q) Inquiry of Vulnerable Persons' Central Register. An adoption study must include inquiry of the Justice Center for the Protection of People with Special Needs regarding whether the applicant or other person over the age of 18 who resides in the home of the applicant is listed on the Vulnerable Persons' Central Register.

(1) If the applicant or other person over the age of 18 who resides in the home of the applicant is listed on the Vulnerable Persons' Central Register, the agency must determine on the basis of the information it has available and in accordance with guidelines developed and disseminated by the Office of Children and Family Services whether to approve the application.

(2) If the application is approved, the agency must indicate in writing in the adoption study record the specific reason(s) why the person who was listed in the above referenced Register was determined to be appropriate to receive an adoption placement.

(r) Inquiry of Vulnerable Persons' Central Register. An adoption study must include inquiry of the Justice Center for the Protection of People with Special Needs regarding whether the applicant or other person over the age of 18 who resides in the home of the applicant is listed on the Vulnerable Person's Central Register.

(1) If the applicant or other person over the age of 18 who resides in the home of the applicant is listed on the register of substantiated category one cases of abuse or neglect maintained by the Justice Center for the Protection of People with Special Needs, the agency must determine on the basis of the information it has available and in accordance with guidelines developed and disseminated by the Office of Children and Family Services whether to approve the application.

(2) If the application is approved, the agency must indicate in writing in the adoption study record the specific reason(s) why the person who was listed in the above referenced Register was determined to be appropriate to receive an adoption placement.

§421.24   Adoption with subsidy.
(a) Definitions.

(1) Child means a person under the age of 21 years whose guardianship and custody have been committed to a social services official or a voluntary authorized agency, or whose guardianship and custody have been committed to a certified or approved foster parent pursuant to a court order prior to such person's 18th birthday, except as provided in section 384-b(3)(g) of the Social Services Law and section 631 of the Family Court Act, or a person under the age of 21 whose care and custody have been transferred prior to such person's 18th birthday to a social services official or a voluntary authorized agency pursuant to section 1055 of the Family Court Act or section 384-a of the Social Services Law, whose parents are deceased or where one parent is deceased and the other parent is not a person entitled to notice of an adoption pursuant to sections 111 and 111-a of the Domestic Relations Law, and where such official or agency consents to the adoption of such person in accordance with section 113 of the Domestic Relations Law.

(2) Handicapped child means a child who possesses a specific physical, mental or emotional condition or disability of such severity or kind which, in the opinion of the department, would constitute a significant obstacle to the child's adoption. Such conditions include, but are not limited to:

(i) any medical or dental condition which will require repeated or frequent hospitalization, treatment or follow-up care;

(ii) any physical handicap, by reason of physical defect or deformity, whether congenital or acquired by accident, injury or disease, which makes or may be expected to make a child totally or partially incapacitated for education or for remunerative occupation, as described in sections 1002 and 4001 of the Education Law; or makes or may be expected to make a child handicapped, as described in section 2581 of the Public Health Law;

(iii) any substantial disfigurement, such as the loss or deformation of facial features, torso or extremities; or

(iv) a diagnosed personality or behavioral problem, psychiatric disorder, serious intellectual incapacity or brain damage which seriously affects the child's ability to relate to his peers and/or authority figures, including mental retardation or developmental disability.

(3) Hard-to-place child means a child, other than a handicapped child:

(i) who has not been placed for adoption within six months from the date his or her guardianship and custody were committed to the social services official or the voluntary authorized agency; or

(ii) who has not been placed for adoption within six months from the date a previous adoption placement terminated and the child was returned to the care of the social services official or the voluntary authorized agency; or

(iii) who meets any of the conditions listed in clauses (a) through (f) of this subparagraph, which the Office of Children and Family Services has identified as constituting a significant obstacle to a child's adoption, notwithstanding that the child has been in the guardianship and custody of the social services official or the voluntary authorized agency for less than six months;

(a) the child is one of a group of two siblings (including half-siblings) who are free for adoption and it is considered necessary that the group be placed together pursuant to sections 421.12(e) and 421.18(d) of this Part; and

(1) at least one of the children is five years old or older; or

(2) at least one of the children is a member of a minority group which is substantially overrepresented in New York State foster care in relation to the percentage of that group to the State's total population; or

(3) at least one of the children is otherwise eligible for subsidy in accordance with the provisions of this subdivision;

(b) the child is the sibling or half-sibling of a child already adopted and it is considered necessary that such children be placed together pursuant to sections 421.2(e) and 421.18(d) of this Part; and

(1) the child to be adopted is five years old or older; or

(2) the child is a member of a minority group which is substantially overrepresented in New York State foster care in relation to the percentage of that group to the State's total population; or

(3) the sibling or half-sibling already adopted is eligible for subsidy or would have been eligible for subsidy if application had been made at the time of or prior to the adoption;

(c) the child is one of a group of three or more siblings (including half-siblings) who are free for adoption and it is considered necessary that the group be placed together pursuant to sections 421.2(e) and 421.18(d) of this Part; or

(d) the child is eight years old or older and is a member of a minority group which is substantially overrepresented in New York State foster care in relation to the percentage of that group to the State's total population; or

(e) the child is 10 years old or older; or

(f) the child is hard to place with parent(s) other than his/her present foster parent(s) because he/she has been in care with the same foster parent(s) for 12 months or more prior to the signing of the adoption placement agreement by such foster parent(s) and has developed a strong attachment to his/her foster parent(s) while in such care and separation from the foster parent(s) would adversely affect the child's development.

(4) Board rate means the board rate paid to the boarding family including any rate increases in room and board rates and clothing replacement allowances as a result of, but not limited to cost of living adjustments and a change in the age of the child. Such rate includes board, clothing replacement allowance, child's allowance, and any other routine cash payments made to the boarding family for this child, or that would have been made for this child if boarded out, which rate was established pursuant to section 398-a of the Social Services Law as implemented by Part 427 of this Title. In the case of a minor parent who is adopted, such rate also includes amounts as may be necessary to cover the costs associated with the care and maintenance of the child or children of such minor parent who remain(s) with the minor parent following adoption.

(5) Applicable board rate means:

(i) in the case of a child in the guardianship and custody of a social services official and placed out for adoption, the board rate of the social services district placing the child for adoption or of the social services district in which the adoptive parent(s) reside(s), at the discretion of the placing district; or

(ii) in the case of a child in the guardianship and custody of a social services official and adopted by the parent(s) residing outside the State, the board rate governing the social services district which had custody of the child; or

(iii) in the case of a child in the guardianship and custody of a voluntary authorized agency and placed out for adoption with adoptive parent(s) residing in the same district, the board rate of such district; or

(iv) in the case of a child in the guardianship and custody of a voluntary authorized agency placed out for adoption with adoptive parent(s) residing in another district, the board rate of such other district; or

(v) in the case of a child in the guardianship and custody of a voluntary authorized agency and adopted by parent(s) residing outside the State, the board rate of the district where the voluntary authorized agency has its principal office or business.

(6) Maximum rate of reimbursement for applicable board rates means the maximum rate of payment for care provided in a foster boarding home, as determined by the department pursuant to section 398-a of the Social Services Law, as implemented by Part 427 of this Title and the annual appropriation set forth in the State's aid to localities budget. State reimbursement may not exceed the maximum rates set forth below. Social services districts may set an amount less than the maximum rate. For the period July 1, 1991 through June 30, 1992, the maximum rate of reimbursement for applicable board rates are as follows:

(i) Maximum rates for board and care:

(a) For adoptions finalized prior to July 1, 1987:

Region	Age 0-5	Age 6-11	Age 12 and over
New York City and Nassau , Suffolk, Rockland and Westchester Counties	$310	$365	$423
All other counties	$284	$340	$395

For children who require special foster care services
    -up to $681 per month

For children who require exceptional foster care services
    -up to $1,033 per month

(b) For adoptions finalized on or after July 1, 1987:

Region	Age 0-5	Age 6-11	Age 12 and over
New York City and Nassau , Suffolk, Rockland and Westchester Counties	$386	$455	$526
All other counties	$353	$424	$490

For children who require special foster care services
    -up to $845 per month

For children who require exceptional foster care services
    -up to $1,281 per month

(ii) The maximum rates for clothing replacement:

Age	Yearly Rate for Replacement
0-5	$292
6-11	409
12-15	634
16 and over	775

(iii) The maximum rates for diaper allowance:

Age	Monthly Allowance
0-3	$45

(7) Voluntary authorized agency means an authorized agency as defined in paragraphs (a) and (c) of section 371(10) of the Social Services Law.

(8) State income standard means the most recent federal income official poverty line (as defined and annually revised by the federal Office of Management and Budget) updated by the department for a family size of four and adjusted by the department for family size.

(9) Applicable State income standard means 275 percent of the State income standard.

(10) Social services official means a county commissioner of social services, a city commissioner of social services, or an Indian tribe with which the department has entered into an agreement to provide adoption services.

(11) Appropriate social services official means the social services official with guardianship and custody of the child, or for a child in the guardianship and custody of a voluntary authorized agency and placed out for adoption, the social services official of the district where the prospective adoptive parent(s) reside(s).

(b) Application for adoption subsidy.

(1) The social services official or voluntary authorized agency responsible for an adoption placement must provide information to foster parent(s) and prospective adoptive parent(s) regarding the adoption subsidy program, including an explanation of the criteria used to determine whether a particular child is hard-to-place or handicapped, at the time a child is identified to a person or persons interested in adopting that child or at the time the foster parent(s) with whom the child is residing are told that a proceeding to free the child for adoption has been commenced.

(i) Prior to placing a child in an adoptive home, or approving foster parent(s) as adoptive parent(s) for a child, the social services official or voluntary authorized agency must document whether the person(s) with whom the child will be placed or the foster parent(s) with whom the child is living will adopt the child with or without an adoption subsidy.

(ii) The official or agency must also document its assessment as to whether or not the child may be currently eligible for an adoption subsidy. If a child does not appear to be eligible for the adoption subsidy and the prospective adoptive parent(s) or the foster parent(s) indicate an inability or unwillingness to adopt the child without subsidy, the social services official or voluntary authorized agency must seek alternative adoptive placement for the child. Efforts to locate adoptive parent(s) willing to accept the adoptive placement of the child without payment of an adoption subsidy must be documented by the case-worker.

(2) At the time of an adoptive placement, the social services official or voluntary authorized agency responsible for placement must provide an adoption subsidy agreement to any person(s) who indicate(s) a desire to apply for an adoption subsidy.

(i) Written notice must be given to any person(s) applying for an adoption subsidy that:

(a) except as specifically provided in this clause, the person(s) applying for an adoption subsidy must submit a completed subsidy agreement and supportive documentation to the social services district or voluntary authorized agency as early as possible but in no event after the date the child's adoption is finalized. The notice must indicate that completed subsidy agreements and supportive documentation may only be submitted after finalization of the child's adoption in cases where:

(1) the adoptive parent can establish that he or she was unaware of any handicapping condition affecting the child at the time the child's adoption was finalized;

(2) a physician submits a written diagnosis of the child's medical condition, certifies that such condition existed prior to the date the child's adoption was finalized, and describes the basis for making each of these findings; and

(3) the child's adoption was finalized on or after January 1, 1982;

(b) if an adoption subsidy is denied or granted in an amount which the applicant determines to be inadequate or inappropriate or if the application for the subsidy is not acted upon within 30 days of filing, such person has the right to a fair hearing pursuant to subdivision (g) of this section.

(ii) In the case of a child in the guardianship and custody of a social services official, but placed out for adoption by a voluntary authorized agency, or in the case of a child in the guardianship and custody of a voluntary authorized agency and placed out for adoption by such voluntary authorized agency, the agency must attach any and all agency documentation relevant to eligibility for an adoption subsidy to the adoption subsidy agreement and must forward completed subsidy materials to the appropriate social services official for review and approval within 15 working days of receipt of the subsidy agreement.

(iii) Within 15 working days of receipt of the subsidy agreement and the documentation provided by the voluntary authorized agency responsible for the adoptive placement or by the adoptive parent(s), the social services official must complete an assessment of eligibility and, unless authorized by the department to approve the agreement, and must forward its recommendation and the completed subsidy materials to the State Adoption Service for review and final approval.

(iv) Within 30 working days of receipt of the subsidy agreement and documentation provided by the voluntary authorized agency, if authorized by the department, the social services official must approve or disapprove the agreement. If the agreement is not approved or disapproved within 30 days of submission, the voluntary authorized agency may submit the agreement to the department for approval or disapproval.

(c) Payments for the care and maintenance of a handicapped or hard-to-place child.

(1) A social services official must make monthly payments, for the care and maintenance of a handicapped or hard-to-place child, to the person(s) with whom the child has been placed out for adoption or by whom the child has been adopted. Such payments must be applied for either prior to adoption, or subsequent to the adoption if the person(s) adopting the child first became award of the child's physical or emotional condition or disability subsequent to the adoption and a physician certifies that the condition or disability existed prior to the child's adoption. All applications for adoption subsidies must be made on forms and reviewed according to procedures as may be established by the department.

(2) Such payments must be made as follows:

(i) In the case of a child in the guardianship and custody or the care and custody of a social services official who is being adopted by the foster parent(s) with whom the child has been boarded, such payment must continue as a foster care payment until the date of the court order finalizing the adoption and must be made in accordance with Part 427 of this Title. Monthly payments for the care and maintenance of the child as an adopted child under the provisions of this subdivision must begin on the date of the court order finalizing the adoption.

(ii) In the case of a child in the guardianship and custody or the care and custody of a social services official who is placed with and is to be adopted by foster parent(s) other than the foster parent(s) with whom the child had been previously boarded and who is otherwise eligible for an adoption subsidy payment, such payment must initially be made as a foster care payment and must be made from the day of placement for adoption to the foster parent(s) with whom the child is placed, provided such placement does not result in a violation of section 378.3 or 378.4 of the Social Services Law and/or section 443.1(j) of this Title. If the placement would result in a violation of either of such sections, the person(s) adopting the child must be approved adoptive parent(s) and payment must be made as an adoption subsidy payment from the date of placement, in accordance with the provisions of subparagraph (iii) of this paragraph. Foster care payments under this provision must be made in accordance with Part 427 of this Title. Except where the provisions of section 378.3 or 378.4 of the Social Services Law and/or section 443.1(j) of this Title require that adoption subsidy payments be made to the prospective adoptive parent(s) prior to finalization of the adoption, such payments must begin upon the date of the court order finalizing the adoption and must be made in accordance with the provisions of this section.

(iii) In the case of a child in the guardianship and custody or the care and custody of a social services official who is freed for and placed for adoption, is otherwise eligible for adoption subsidy payments and is to be adopted by approved adoptive parent(s) who are not also certified or approved foster parent(s), such payment must be made as an adoption subsidy payment from the date of placement with the approved adoptive parent(s).

(iv) In the case of a child in the guardianship and custody of a voluntary authorized agency who is freed for and placed out for adoption, and who is otherwise eligible for an adoption subsidy, an adoption subsidy payment for the care and maintenance of the child will be made from the date the department approves the subsidy agreement submitted for approval if:

(a) an approved home study has been completed; and

(b) a placement agreement has been signed and the child has been placed in the home.

(3) Payments must be made only pursuant to a written agreement between the social services official or agency and the person(s) with whom the child has been placed out for adoption or by whom the child has been adopted. The written agreement must include, but is not limited to, the following:

(i) the date on which the agreement is entered;

(ii) the first name and birth date of the child for whom the payment is to be made;

(iii) the nature of the child's handicap, if any, indicated both in terms of the diagnosing physician and in lay terms; or

(iv) the condition(s) which make(s) the child hard-to-place, as determined from paragraph (a)(3) of this section; and

(v) the family's annual income, as determined from paragraph (9) of this subdivision;

(vi) the amount to be paid monthly for the care and maintenance of the child, and the board rate upon which the amount of payment is based;

(vii) the provisions contained in paragraph (4) of this subdivision relating to payment when the child is out of the home and/or the custody of the adoptive parent(s);

(viii) the conditions under which the agreement may be modified;

(ix) a provision that whenever the applicable board rate increases or whenever a change in the age of an adopted child qualifies such child to receive adoption subsidy payments at an increased rate, the social services official responsible for making adoption subsidy payments will adjust the adoption subsidy payments to reflect such increases; and

(x) such other provisions as the department, the social services official or the adopting parent(s) may agree to.

(4) Where more than one child is placed with the same person(s) for adoption subject to payments for care and maintenance, a separate written agreement must be completed for each child.

(5) The written agreement authorizing monthly payments will remain in effect until the child's 21st birthday. No payments may be made if the social services official determines that the adoptive parent(s) are no longer legally responsible for the support of the child or the child is no longer receiving any support from such parent(s). Such written agreement must state that it will be the responsibility of the adoptive parent(s) to inform the appropriate State or local official when they are no longer legally responsible for the child or no longer providing any support to the child.

(6) The written agreement shall not be affected by amelioration, remission or cure of the handicapping condition, if any.

(7) The amount of the monthly payment must be determined in accordance with paragraphs (11) and (12) of this subdivision.

(8) The income of the person(s) adopting a handicapped or hard-to- place child shall not be considered by the local social services official in determining whether or not to enter into such an agreement.

(9) Once an agreement to provide a subsidy payment is made, the annual income of the person(s) adopting the child will be considered only for the purpose of determining the amount of the monthly payment to be made, according to the provisions of paragraphs (11) and (12) of this subdivision.

(10) Computation of annual income shall be subject to the following provisions:

(i) Only income earned as wages or salary from employment and/or net income from nonfarm self-employment or net income from farm self-employment as defined in section 404.5(b)(5) of this Title shall be considered in computing annual income. The income of persons other than the adopting parent(s) shall not be considered.

(ii) As evidence of income, a social services official may request wage stubs, or the most recent W-2, or an employer's statement of wages, or, in the case of income other than wages or salary, a copy of the adopting person's latest Federal income tax return.

(iii) When a person adopting is 62 years old or older, or will be subject to mandatory retirement from present employment within five years of the date of adoptive placement, such person's income shall be disregarded in computing annual income.

(11) If the annual income of the person(s) adopting a handicapped or hard-to-place child pursuant to the provisions of this section, as determined by the applicable provisions of paragraph (10) of this subdivision, is equal to or less than the applicable State income standard, the monthly payment for care

and maintenance of the adopted child must be 100 percent of the applicable board rate, unless the person(s) adopting voluntarily and, in writing, request and agree to a lower rate.

(12) (i) If the annual income of the person(s) adopting a handicapped or hard-to-place child pursuant to the provisions of this section, as determined by the applicable provisions of paragraph (10) of this subdivision, is greater than the applicable State income standard, a social services district has two options in determining the amount to be paid for care and maintenance of the child. Unless the person(s) adopting voluntarily and, in writing, request and agree to a lower amount, such amount must be either:

(a) 100 percent of the applicable board rate regardless of the annual income of the person(s) adopting; or

(b) an amount less than 100 percent, but not less than 75 percent, of the applicable board rate, as determined in accordance with the following formula. The social services district must:

(1) calculate the annual income of the person(s) adopting pursuant to the applicable provisions of paragraph (10) of this subdivision;

(2) determine what percentage such annual income is of the applicable State income standard; and

(3) use the following schedule to determine the amount to be paid based on the percentage calculated in subclause (2) of this clause:

ADOPTION SUBSIDY PAYMENTS SCHEDULE

Annual income of person(s) adopting; percentage of applicable State income	Amount of adoption subsidy payment standard
Over 100% but not more than 110%	95% of Applicable Board Rate
Over 110% but not more than 120%	90% of Applicable Board Rate
Over 120% but not more than 130%	85% of Applicable Board Rate
Over 130% but not more than 140%	80% of Applicable Board Rate
Over 140%	75% of Applicable Board Rate

(ii) The social services district must use the same option for all subsidized adoptions. If a social services district wishes to change from one option to the other option, the district must inform the department in writing of the intended change at least 30 days prior to the effective date of the change. The district must use the newly selected option in all new subsidy agreements entered into on or after the effective date of the change. Subsidy agreements finalized before the effective date of the change will not be affected by the change.

(13) The department may authorize the social services official to approve or disapprove the written agreement on behalf of the department pursuant to section 453 (2) of the Social Services Law.

(i) The standards for authorization include, but are not limited to, the following:

(a) the social services district must submit a written request to the department requesting authorization to approve adoption subsidy agreements concerning hard-to-place and/or handicapped children;

(b) the social services district must have an adequate number of staff who have been properly trained in the requirements of the federal and state adoption assistance program and the agreement approval process;

(c) the social services district must have a satisfactory and effective system in place to complete the review and approval of written adoption subsidy agreements;

(d) the social services district must assume responsibility for maintaining the necessary files and documentation for federal and State audits and fair hearings, and for providing information to the department related to such audits and hearings; and

(e) the social services district must be willing to assume fiscal responsibility for those cases which the district has been authorized by the department to approve.

(ii) The department may require social services districts to comply with additional standards to ensure that a social services district complies with state and federal adoption assistance requirements, and may revoke the authority of a social service official to approve written adoption subsidy agreements when the social services district fails to comply with the federal or State statutory and regulatory standards relating to the administration of the adoption assistance program.

(14) Except where the social services district has been authorized by the department to approve or disapprove written adoption subsidy agreements, all written agreements for payments for the care and maintenance of handicapped or hard-to-place children must be submitted to the department for approval or disapproval, in accordance with the provisions of title 9 of article 6 of the Social Services Law and this section. A disapproval must be in writing and must state the reasons therefor. If an agreement is not disapproved in writing by the department or the social services district, where the social services district has been authorized by the department to approve or disapprove the written agreement, within 30 days after its receipt, it will be deemed approved except that:

(i) in the case of an agreement submitted pursuant to section 453(d) of the Social Services Law, approval will be granted contingent upon commitment of the guardianship and custody of the child to an authorized agency; and

(ii) in the case of an agreement submitted by a voluntary authorized agency to a social services official, the voluntary agency may submit the agreement directly to the department for approval or disapproval if the agreement is not approved or disapproved by the social services official within 30 days of submission.

(15) Neither the written agreement nor the amount of the payment is subject to an annual review, except as provided for by paragraph (17) of this subdivision. However, the adopting person(s) may request a review of the agreement and/or a change in the amount paid under the agreement. Such review or change may be granted at the discretion of the social services official in accordance with the regulations, and subject to the approval of the department if the agreement was approved by the department, as set forth in paragraph (14) of this subdivision.

(16) The social services official may adjust the monthly payment in accord with the provisions of the schedules in paragraphs (9) and (12) of this subdivision and changes made thereto by the department pursuant to the provisions of section 453(3) of the Social Services Law. Except as provided for by paragraph (17) of this subdivision, any change in the amount of the monthly payment must be made by amendment to the written agreement and must require the consent of the adoptive parent(s) and the approval of the department if the agreement was approved by the department, as set forth in paragraph (14) of this subdivision.

(17) Whenever the applicable board rate increases due to an increase in the board rate, and/or the clothing replacement allowance or whenever a change

in the age of an adopted child qualifies such child to receive adoption subsidy payments at an increased rate, the social services official responsible for making adoption subsidy payments must adjust the adoption subsidy payments to reflect such increases. A review must be conducted by such official to ensure that such adjustments are included in the adoption subsidy payments made to the persons who have entered into adoption subsidy agreements. The official must provide such person(s) with appropriate notice of such adjustments. Such notice will constitute an amendment to the adoption subsidy agreement and must be attached to such agreement. Such adjustments in payments are neither subject to the approval of the department nor subject to the consent of the adoptive parent(s).

(18)(i) Upon the death of the person(s) who adopted the child prior to the 21st birthday of the child, payments made pursuant to this subdivision must continue and must be made to the legal guardian or custodian of the child under the age of 18 upon the issuance of letters of guardianship or order of custody until the child has attained the age of 21. If the guardian or custodian was the caretaker of the child under the age of 18 prior to the issuance of letters of guardianship or order of custody, such payments must be made retroactively from the death of the adoptive parent or parents. All provisions of this section applicable to maintenance payments made to the person(s) who adopted the child will be applicable to maintenance payments made to the legal guardian or custodian of the child.

(ii)(a) Upon the death of the sole or surviving adoptive parent or both adoptive parents after the 18th birthday and before the 21st birthday of the adopted child, where such adoptive parent or parents were receiving adoption subsidy payments at the time of death, such subsidy payments must continue, but must be made to the guardian of the child on behalf of such child, where the child consents to the appointment of a guardian. Such subsidy payments must be made retroactively from the death of the adoptive parent or parents to the appointment of a guardian, and must continue until the 21st birthday of the child. If, however, there is no willing or suitable person to be appointed as guardian, or the child does not consent to the appointment of a guardian, such subsidy payments must be made retroactively from the death of the adoptive parent or parents and must continue to be made until the 21st birthday of the child: (1) through direct payments to the child, if the social services official determines that the child demonstrates the ability to manage such direct payments; or (2) to a representative payee certified by the social services official.

(b) Upon receipt of notification of the death of the sole or surviving adoptive parent or both adoptive parents after the 18th birthday and before the 21st birthday of the adopted child, where such adoptive parent or parents were receiving adoption subsidy payments at the time of death, the social services official must notify the child of (1) the processes available to continue subsidy payments until the 21st birthday of the child including appointment of a guardian under the Surrogate's Court Procedure Act, application to be approved for direct subsidy payments, or the appointment of a representative payee; and (2) the right of the child to be involved in all such processes.

(c) Where the social services official has determined that the child does not demonstrate the ability to manage direct subsidy payments, the social services official must certify payment to a representative payee on behalf of the child. Subsidy payments received by the representative payee must be held and used strictly for the use and benefit of the child. Designation of the appropriate entity or individual and investigation of an individual for certification as a representative payee must be conducted by the social services official responsible for payment of the adoption subsidy pursuant to this section.

(1) The social services official may designate an employee of the social services district to be the representative payee responsible for receipt of the adoption subsidy on behalf of the child only where the official determines that such employee has no conflict of interest in performing the duties and obligations as representative payee. If the child resides in a social services district other than the district responsible for payment of the adoption subsidy, the social services district in which the child resides may be designated the representative payee and a social services official of such district must select an employee of such social services district to be responsible for receipt of the adoption subsidy as the representative payee, only where the official determines that such employee has no conflict of interest in performing the duties and obligations as a payee. Where a voluntary authorized agency has a prior relationship with a child, or where the social services district does not have sufficient or appropriate staff available to perform the functions of the representative payee, the social services district may contract with a voluntary authorized agency as the representative payee on behalf of the child where the social services district determines it would be in the best interests of the child to do so.

(2) The social services official may designate an individual for certification as a representative payee who must perform the functions and duties of a representative payee in accordance with the best interests of the child. In determining whether an individual is appropriate to be certified as the representative payee, the social services official must first consult with the child and must give the child's preferences significant weight. The child's preference must be determinative of the representative payee only where such preference does not conflict with the best interests of the child. Prior to designation of an individual by the social services official for certification as a representative payee, the social services official must:

(i) collect proof of identity and a verifiable social security number of the nominated representative payee;

(ii) conduct an in-person interview of the individual;

(iii) investigate any potential conflicts of interest that may ensue if such individual is certified; and

(iv) determine the capabilities and qualifications of the individual to manage the subsidy payment for the child.

(3) (i) If, after completion of the investigation, the social services official is satisfied that the individual is qualified, appropriate and will serve the best interests of the child, the social services official must certify the selected individual as the representative payee for the child.

(ii) If the 21st birthday of the child occurs while awaiting the certification of a representative payee, the child is entitled to retroactive direct payment of subsidy payments since the death of the adoptive parent or parents after the 18th birthday of the child.

(4) The representative payee must submit reports to the social services official no less than once a year describing the use of the payments in the preceding year. Such reports must be submitted by December 31st of each year. The social services official may also request reports from time to time from the representative payee. If a representative payee fails to submit a report, the social services official may require that the representative payee appear in

person to collect payments. The social services official must keep a centralized file and update it periodically with information including the addresses and social security or tax-payer identification numbers of the representative payee and the child.

(5) The social services official must revoke the certification of a representative payee upon:

(i) determining that the representative payee has misused the payments intended for the benefit of the child;

(ii) the failure of the representative payee to submit timely reports or appear in person as required by the social services official after such failure; or

(iii) the request of the child upon good cause shown.

(6) The social services official must notify the child of the contact information of the representative payee within 5 days of making a decision.

(7) A child may appeal the refusal of the social services official to certify the individual preferred by the child for certification as the representative payee or revoke the certification of a representative payee upon request of the child pursuant to section 455 of the Social Services Law.

(19) The social services official on an annual basis in a written notification must remind the adoptive parents of their obligation to support the adopted child and to notify the social services official if the adoptive parents are no longer providing any support or are no longer legally responsible for the support of the child. Where the adopted child is school age under the laws of the state in which the child resides, such notification must include a requirement that the adoptive parents must certify that the adopted child is a full-time elementary or secondary student or has completed secondary education. For the purposes of this paragraph, an elementary or secondary school student means an adopted child who is:

(i) enrolled, or in the process of enrolling, in a school which provides elementary or secondary education, in accordance with the laws where the school is located;

(ii) instructed in elementary or secondary education at home, in accordance with the laws in which the adopted child's home is located;

(iii) in an independent study elementary or secondary education program, in accordance with the laws in which the adopted child's education program is located, which is administered by the local school or school district; or

(iv) incapable of attending school on a full-time basis due to the adopted child's medical condition, which incapacity is supported by annual information submitted by the adoptive parents as part of this certification.

(d) Payments for nonrecurring adoption expenses.

(1) Nonrecurring expenses means reasonable and necessary adoption fees, court costs, attorney fees, the costs of an adoption study, including health and psychological examinations and consultations, the cost of supervising an adoption placement, transportation costs, the reasonable costs of lodging and food for a child and his or her adoptive parent(s), which are incurred by or on behalf of the adoptive parent(s) and not otherwise reimbursed from other sources, which are directly related to the legal adoption of a child with special needs and which are not incurred in violation of Federal law or the laws of this State or any other state.

(2) As used in this subdivision, a child with special needs means a child who:

(i) the State has determined cannot or shall not be returned to the home of his or her parents;

(ii) is handicapped as defined in paragraph (a) (2) of this section or is hard-to-place as defined in subparagraph (a)(3) (iii) of this section; and

(iii) a reasonable but unsuccessful effort has been made to place the child with appropriate adoptive parents without adoption assistance, except where such an effort would not be in the best interest of the child.

(3) A social services official must make a payment for nonrecurring adoption expenses incurred by or on behalf of adoptive parents in connection with the adoption of a child with special needs through an authorized agency when the final decree of adoption was entered on or after January 1, 1987 or the final decree of adoption was entered on or after January 1, 1986 and before January 1, 1987, but nonrecurring adoption expenses were paid after January 1, 1987. The payment for nonrecurring expenses will be made as a one-time payment, not to exceed $2,000.

(4) Payments for nonrecurring adoption expenses must be made either to the adoptive parent(s) directly, to an authorized agency on behalf of the adoptive parent(s) or to an attorney on behalf of the adoptive parent(s) for the allowable amount of attorney's fees or court costs incurred in connection with a completed adoption. Such payments must also be made when a child is placed from this State by an authorized agency and is adopted in another state, and the adoptive parent(s) are not eligible for nonrecurring expenses in the other state, but are otherwise eligible for nonrecurring expenses in this State.

(5) Except as specifically provided in this subdivision, payment for nonrecurring adoption expenses must be made pursuant to a written agreement signed prior to the final decree of adoption. The exceptions are:

(i) the final decree of adoption was entered on or after January 1, 1987, and prior to June 14, 1989; or

(ii) the final decree was entered on or after January 1, 1986 and before January 1, 1987, but nonrecurring expenses were paid after that date.

(6) Parent(s) who qualify for an exception as set forth in paragraph (5) of this subdivision must sign an agreement and file a claim for nonrecurring adoption expenses before December 14, 1990.

(7) The agreement for payment of nonrecurring adoption expenses maybe part of the adoption subsidy agreement or may be a separate agreement for those who will not receive an adoption subsidy. The agreement for the payment of nonrecurring adoption expenses must include, but is not limited to, the following:

(i) the nature and amount of any payments to be provided for nonrecurring adoption expenses;

(ii) the condition(s) which makes a child "a child with special needs" as defined in paragraph (2) of this subdivision;

(iii) a provision that the payment of nonrecurring adoption expenses will be made as a one-time payment, not to exceed a maximum of $2,000;

(iv) a provision that the agreement will remain in effect if the adoptive parent(s) move to another state; and

(v) a provision for the protection of the interests of the child where the adoptive parent(s) and the child move to another state while the agreement is effective.

(8) Documentation of the nonrecurring adoption expenses, defined in paragraph (1) of this subdivision, must be provided by the adoptive parent(s) to a social services official or authorized agency so that the amount of the payment for nonrecurring adoption expenses may be determined. Such documentation must be in the form of receipts or written verification of services received

and paid for, or services rendered or being rendered but for which payment has not been made. Except for adoptions specified in paragraph (5) of this subdivision, all receipts or verifications must be received by the social services official or authorized agency with whom the adoptive parent(s) have signed an agreement within two years of the date of the final adoption decree.

(9) All written agreements for the payment of nonrecurring adoption expenses must be submitted to the department for approval or disapproval. The procedures contained in paragraph (c) (13) of this section will apply to the approval or disapproval of agreements for the payment of nonrecurring adoption expenses.

(e) Medical subsidy payments.

(1) Any child with respect to whom payments made for care and maintenance under subdivision (c) of this section are federally reimbursable shall be deemed a recipient of aid to families with dependent children for purposes of determining eligibility for medical assistance. Payments for medical care, services and supplies for all such eligible children shall be made under and in accordance with the provisions of the State's program and medical assistance in Articles 3 and 4 of Subchapter E of this Title.

(2) for any handicapped child with respect to whom a payment made under subdivision (c) of this section is not federally reimbursable, the social services official must make payments for medical care, services and supplies subject to the following conditions.

(i) A social services official must make payments, without regard to the financial need of the person(s) with whom the child has been placed for adoption, for the costs of medical care, services and supplies provided to a handicapped child adopted or placed for adoption by the social services official or by a voluntary agency. For the purposes of this subdivision, a handicapped child shall include, but not be limited to, a child with special needs where a social services official has determined that the child cannot be placed with an adoptive parent or parents without medical subsidy because such child has special needs for medical, mental health or rehabilitative care.

(ii) Payments made for medical care, services and supplies for a handicapped child shall be made only pursuant to written agreement between the social services official and the person(s) adopting the handicapped child.

(iii) A written agreement for medical subsidy payments made under the provisions of this subdivision shall remain in effect until the child's 21st birthday, provided that the child continues to reside in the home of the person(s) with whom the agreement is made or remains financially dependent on such person(s), except as may otherwise be provided in this section.

(iv) Medical subsidy payments shall be made only for the costs of such care, services and supplies as may be authorized under the State's program of medical assistance for needy persons according to the provisions of Articles 3 and 4 of Subchapter E of this Title. The amount of such payments shall not exceed the schedules of payments for such care, services and supplies as contained in Article 4 of Subchapter E of this Title.

(v) Medical subsidy payments shall be made only for the cost of care, services and supplies for which the child or the adoptive parent(s) will not receive payment or reimbursement from insurance, medical assistance or other sources.

(vi) Medical subsidy payments may not be limited to the particular condition for which a child was determined to be a handicapped child, but shall be made for all care, services and supplies payable under the State's program of medical assistance of needy persons.

(vii) Payments for medical care, services and supplies for a handicapped child shall be made only where the person(s) adopting the child has/have applied for such payments prior to the child's adoption, provided that an application may be made subsequent to the adoption if the person(s) adopting the child first became aware of the child's condition or disability subsequent to the adoption and a physician certifies that the condition or disability existed prior to the child's adoption.

(viii) Neither the application for, nor the agreement for medical subsidy payments shall require approval by the office of children and family services.

(ix) The agreement for medical subsidy payments shall not be subject to review or change, except that the social services official shall request, at the social services official's discretion, either annually and/or at the submission of any claim, information about medical insurance or other coverage from the adopting person(s) in order to determine compliance with subparagraph (v) of this paragraph.

(x) At the discretion of the social services official, or pursuant to provisions contained in the written agreement for medical subsidy payments, payments for medical care, services and supplies for an adopted handicapped child may be made either to the provider(s) of such care, services and supplies or to the person(s) with whom the agreement is made.

(3) Payments for medical care, services and supplies for a hard-to-place child with respect to whom a payment under subdivision (b) of this section is not federally reimbursable may be made only if any adopting person at the time of adoption is 62 years of age or older or is subject to mandatory retirement from his present employment within five years of the adoptive placement. Such payments shall be subject to the provisions of paragraph (2) of this subdivision.

(4) Upon the death of persons who have adopted the child prior to the 21st birthday of the child:

(i) the payments made pursuant to this subdivision shall continue and shall be made to the legal guardian of the child until the child has attained the age of 21;

(ii) the assistance provided pursuant to this subdivision shall continue in the form of a medical subsidy payment to the legal guardian of the child until the child has attained the age of 21, if the child would otherwise have been eligible for a medical subsidy at the time of the application for an adoption subsidy; and

(iii) provided the child is not eligible for medical assistance, the appropriate social services official shall make medical subsidy payments on behalf of a child who, upon the finalization of the adoption, was receiving federally reimbursable adoption assistance payments. Such payments may be paid to the legal guardian of the child until the child has attained the age of 21, provided the child would otherwise have been eligible for a medical subsidy at the time of the application for an adoption subsidy, or may be paid directly to a provider of medical care, services or supplies rather than to the legal guardian.

(5) All provisions of this section applicable to medical subsidy payments made to persons who adopted the child shall be applicable to medical subsidy payments made to the legal guardian of the child.

(f) Payments to out-of-state adoptive parents.

(1) Payments made pursuant to subdivision (b) or (c) of this section with respect to a child who was adopted within this State but who has been removed legally from this State by his adoptive parent(s) shall remain in effect until the child's 21st birthday. Such payments shall be made to the adoptive parent(s) at the out-of-state address.

(2) A hard-to-place or handicapped child, as defined in this subdivision, may be placed with residents of another state or of the Commonwealth of Puerto Rico, for the purposes of adoption with subsidy. Payments for a child adopted by such residents of another state or of the Commonwealth of Puerto Rico may be made pursuant to the provisions of this subdivision, provided that such payments are made pursuant to a written agreement between the social services official placing the child and making the payment and the adoptive parent(s) resident of such other state or the Commonwealth of Puerto Rico. The written agreement shall be in accord with the provisions of this subdivision. Payments made to adoptive parent(s) resident of another state or the Commonwealth of Puerto Rico shall be made to the adoptive parent(s) at the out-of-state address.

(3) An adoption subsidy agreement shall become void at such time as it is determined by a social services official that a child, on whose behalf payments for care and maintenance and/or medical care are being made pursuant to provisions of this section, was brought into this State for the sole purpose of qualifying the out-of-state adoptive parent(s) for such payments.

(4) A social services official who makes a determination pursuant to paragraph (3) of this subdivision shall advise the adoptive parent(s) of his decision and shall advise the adoptive parent(s) that the determination may be appealed according to the provisions of section 455 of the Social Services Law and Part 358 of this Title. The local determination shall remain in effect unless and until reversed by the department.

(g) Appeals and fair hearings.

(1) Any person aggrieved by the decision of a social services official or an official of the department not to make a payment or by a decision to make the amount of such payment contrary to provisions of title 9 of article 6 of the Social Services Law or this section or by the failure of such official to determine any application made under this section within 30 days after it is filed with such official may appeal to the department and request a fair hearing thereon. A request for a hearing must be made within 60 days after:

(i) receipt of a written notice indicating denial of the subsidy application by the local social services official or the State adoption service;

(ii) receipt of a written notice indicating that an adoption subsidy will be granted in an amount which the applicant determines to be inadequate or inappropriate; or

(iii) the expiration of the 30-day period in which a social services official or an official of the department is required to either approve or disapprove an adoption subsidy application.

(2) A fair hearing under this section may address only the following issues:

(i) whether the social services official or an official of the department has improperly denied an application for payments to be made under this section, including the failure of such official to issue a determination of an application within 30 days of its filing;

(ii) whether the social services official or an official of the department has determined the amount of payment made or to be made in violation of the provisions of this section; or

(iii) whether the social services official or an official of the department has improperly discontinued payments made under an agreement entered pursuant to this section.

(3) The department shall affirm a social services official's denial of an application for payments under this section if it is found that:

(i) the child for whom payments would be made is not a handicapped or hard-to-place child; or

(ii) there is/was another approved adoptive parent or parents who is/was willing to accept the placement of the child without payment under this section within 60 days of such denial and placement of the child with such other parent(s) would not be contrary to the best interests of the child.

(4) At least six working days prior to the scheduled date of the fair hearing, written notice thereof shall be sent to the parties and their representatives.

(5) A party to a hearing may make a request to a hearing officer that the hearing officer remove himself or herself from presiding at the hearing.

(i) The grounds for removing a hearing officer are that such hearing officer has:

(a) previously dealt in any way with the substance of the matter which is the subject of the hearing except in the capacity of hearing officer; or

(b) any interest in the matter, financial or otherwise, direct or indirect, which will impair the independent judgment of the hearing officer; or

(c) displayed bias or partiality to any party to the hearing.

(ii) The hearing officer may independently determine to remove himself or herself from presiding at a hearing on the grounds set forth in subparagraph (i) of this paragraph.

(iii) The request for removal made by a party must:

(a) be made in good faith; and

(b) be made at the hearing in writing or orally on the record; and

(c) describe in detail the grounds for requesting that the hearing officer be removed.

(iv) Upon receipt of a request for removal, the hearing officer must determine on the record whether to remove himself or herself from the hearing.

(v) If the hearing officer determines not to remove himself or herself from presiding at the hearing, the hearing officer must advise the party requesting removal that the hearing will continue but the request for removal will automatically be reviewed by the general counsel or the general counsel's designee.

(vi) The determination of the hearing officer not to remove himself or herself will be reviewed by the general counsel or the general counsel's designee. Such review will include review of written documents submitted by the parties and the transcript of the hearing.

(vii) The general counsel or the general counsel's designee must issue a written determination of whether the hearing officer should be removed from presiding at the hearing within 15 business days of the close of the hearing.

(viii) The written determination of the general counsel or the general counsel's designee will be made part of the record.

(6) The department shall render its decision within 30 days after the fair hearing.

(7) The department may also review, on its own motion, any decision of the social services official. All decisions of the department shall be binding upon the social services district involved, and shall be complied with by the social services official thereof.

(h) Applicability. Notwithstanding any other provision of this section, agreements for the care and maintenance or for medical care of adopted handicapped or hard-to-place children entered into prior to January 1, 1982, shall continue in force and effect as written.

(i) Information services.

(1) Each social services district, through the use of television, radio or newspaper media, shall inform the general public of the availability of adoption subsidy payments for handicapped and hard-to-place children available for adoption.

(2) Each social services district shall disseminate literature and shall make available other informational services regarding the adoption subsidy program to any person making inquiry, application or other expression of interest in adopting a child.

(j) Reimbursement.

(1) Subject to the provisions of this Title and only for payments for the care and maintenance or for medical care of adopted handicapped and hard-to-place children, the department shall pay to each social services district:

(i) the amount of Federal funds, if any, properly received or to be received on account of such payments;

(ii) except with regard to a child who was in the guardianship and custody of a voluntary authorized agency, seventy-five percent of the amount of such payments remaining after first deducting therefrom any Federal funds paid pursuant to subparagraph (i) of this paragraph for a handicapped or hard-to-place child who was in the care and custody of a social services official, where such child is freed for adoption because his or her parent or parents are deceased, or the guardianship and custody of a social services official at the time the child was place out for adoption; provided, however, that when payments for the care and maintenance of a handicapped or hard-to-place child are made to a person or persons residing in a social services district whose board rate exceeds that of the district making such payments, that portion of the payments which exceeds the board rate of the district making the payments is subject to reimbursement by the State in the amount of 100 percent thereof;

(iii) 100 percent of the amount of such payments remaining after first deducting therefrom any Federal funds paid pursuant to subparagraph (i) of this paragraph for a handicapped or hard-to-place child who was in the guardianship and custody of a voluntary authorized agency at the time the child was placed out for adoption, or was placed out for adoption or being adopted after being placed out for adoption by an Indian tribe.

(2) Where agreements for payment require review and/or approval by the department, reimbursement shall be available only for payments made under those agreements which have been submitted to and approved by the department in accordance with the requirements of this section.

(3) No payments shall be made pursuant to this section if the social services official determines that the adoptive parents are no longer legally responsible for the support of the child or the child is no longer receiving any support from such parents.

(k) Claiming. Claims for reimbursement for payments made for adoption subsidies shall be made by each local social services district in the manner and upon such forms as shall be required by the department.

Part 423
Preventive Services Regulations
Section   *(Extracts)*
423.2   Definitions
423.3   Client Eligibility Criteria for Preventive Services
423.4   Service Provision Requirements

§423.2 Definitions.

(a) Preventive services agency means an authorized agency as defined in paragraphs (a) and (b) of subdivision 10 of section 371 of the Social Services Law, or a not-for-profit corporation as defined in paragraph 5 of subdivision (a) of section 102 of the Not-for-Profit Corporation Law, or a public agency that receives prior approval from the department, that provides a program of preventive services as defined herein.

(b) Preventive services shall mean those supportive and rehabilitative services provided to children and their families in accordance with the provisions of this Part for the purpose of: averting a disruption of a family which will or could result in placement of a child in foster care; enabling a child who has been placed in foster care to return to his family at an earlier time than would otherwise be possible; or reducing the likelihood that a child who has been discharged from foster care would return to such care. The following services, when provided for the above-stated purpose and in conformity with this Part, are considered preventive services:

(1) Case management as defined as the responsibility of the local department of social services to authorize the provision of preventive services, to approve the client eligibility determination according to the criteria of section 423.3 of this Part and, to approve in writing, the service plans as defined in Part 428 of this Title.

(2) Case planning is defined as assessing the need for, providing or arranging for, coordinating and evaluating the provision of those preventive services needed by a child and his or her family to prevent disruption of the family or to help a child in foster care return home sooner. Case planning shall include, but not be limited to, referring such child and his or her family to other services as needed, including but not limited to, educational counseling and training, vocational diagnosis and training, employment counseling, therapeutic and preventive medical care and treatment, health counseling and health maintenance services, vocational rehabilitation, housing services, speech therapy and legal services. Case planning responsibility shall also include documenting client progress and adherence to the plan by recording in the uniform case record as defined in Part 428 of this Title and sections 430.8 through 430.12 of this Title that such services are provided and providing casework contacts as defined in paragraph (3) of this subdivision. Case planner means the caseworker assigned case planning responsibility as defined in Section 428.2 (c) of this Title.

(3) Casework contacts as defined as:

(i) Individual or group face-to-face counseling sessions between the case planner, assigned caseworker, as directed by the case planner, or person providing specialized rehabilitative services, supportive services or probation services as defined in section 423.2(f), (g) and (h) of this title and the child and/or family in receipt of preventive services for the purpose of guiding the child and/or family towards a course of action agreed to by the child and/or family as the best method of attaining personal objectives or resolving problems or needs of a social, emotional, developmental or economic nature.

(ii) Individual or group activities with the child and/or the child's parents that are planned for the purpose of achieving such course of action as specified in the child and family's service plan.

(4) Day care services as defined in the Consolidated Services Plan of the department prepared pursuant to section 34-a of the Social Services Law.

(5) Homemaker services as defined in the Consolidated Services Plan of the department prepared pursuant to section 34-a of the Social Services Law.

(6) Housekeeper/chore services as defined in the Consolidated Services Plan of the department prepared pursuant to section 34-a of the Social Services Law.

(7) Family planning services as defined in the Consolidated Services Plan of the department prepared pursuant to section 34-a of the Social Services Law.

(8) Home management services as defined in the Consolidated Services Plan of the department prepared pursuant to section 34-a of the Social Services Law.

(9) Clinical services as defined as assessment, diagnosis, testing, psycho-therapy, and specialized therapies provided by a person who has received a master's degree in social work, a licensed psychologist, a licensed psychiatrist or other recognized therapist in human services.

(10) Parent aide services as defined as those services provided in the home and community that focus on the need of the parent for instruction and guidance and are designed to maintain and enhance parental functioning and family/parent role performance. Techniques may include but are not limited to role modeling, listening skills, home management assistance and education in parenting skills and personal coping behavior.

(11) Day services to children as defined in section 425.1 of this Title shall mean a program offering a combination of services including at least: social services, psychiatric, psychological, education and/or vocational services and health supervision and also including, as appropriate, recreational and trans-portation services, for at least three but less than 24 hours a day and at least four days per week, excluding holidays. If it can be demonstrated that one or more of these services are not needed by the population served, that service may be waived.

(12) Parent training as defined as group instruction in parent skills development and the developmental needs of the child and adolescent for the purpose of strengthening parental functioning and parent/child relationships in order to avert a disruption in a family or help a child in foster care return home sooner than otherwise possible. Parent training may include child-parent interaction groups formed to enhance relationship and communication skills.

(13) Transportation services as defined as providing or arranging for transportation of the child and/or his family to and/or from services arranged as part of the child's service plan except that transportation may not be provided as a preventive service for visitation of children in foster care with their parents and may only be provided if such transportation can not be arranged or provided by the child's family.

(14) Emergency cash or goods as defined as money or the equivalent thereto, food, clothing or other essential items that are provided to a child and his family in an emergency or acute problem situation in order to avert foster care placement.

(15) Emergency shelter as defined as providing or arranging for shelter where a child and his family who are in an emergency or acute problem situation reside in a site other than their own home in order to avert foster care placement.

(16) Housing services defined as rent subsidies, including payment of rent arrears, or any other assistance necessary to obtain adequate housing will be considered preventive services but will only be available to families of children already in foster care if such families satisfy the definition set forth in paragraph (c)(2) of this section and the eligibility standards set forth in sections 430.9(e)(2) and 430.9(f) of this Title. Rent subsidies and/or other assistance necessary to obtain adequate housing may not exceed the sum of $300 per month per family, except as provided in section 423.4(b)(2) of this Part, may not be provided for a period of more than three years, and must be made in addition to any other payments or benefits received by the family.

(i) Such other assistance necessary to obtain adequate housing will include security deposits; finder's or broker's fees; household moving expenses; exterminator fees; mortgage arrears on client owned property which place the family at imminent risk of losing their home; and/or essential repairs of conditions in rental or client owned property which create a substantial health or safety risk.

(ii) Housing services may be provided directly by the local social services district or by a local public agency or private not-for-profit agency or organization through a purchase of services agreement, as prescribed by Part 405 of this Title. The social services district responsible for determining the permanency planning goal of a child or children in foster care must determine whether the family is eligible for housing services and must be the district responsible for the cost of such services. If the family moves out of the housing unit before the three year maximum eligibility period has elapsed, housing services must be terminated, unless the local social services district in which the family is residing determines that housing services must be continued to prevent the child or children from reentering foster care. In such cases, the local social services district in which the family is residing must be responsible for providing housing services to the family for the remainder of the three year period. If the family moves to another state, housing services must be terminated.

(iii) For purposes of this Part, lack of adequate housing will be determined pursuant to the standards set forth in paragraph (e)(2) of section 430.9 of this Title. In no case will a temporary residence in a shelter, including those defined in Part 900 of this Title, a hotel/motel or any other such emergency or transitional residential facility be considered adequate housing for purposes of providing housing services.

(iv) If a rent subsidy is being provided, the sum of the public assistance shelter allowance, or the amount of rent the family is deemed able to pay, and the rent subsidy must not exceed the family's actual rent expenditures for the particular residence.

(a) When the family is not eligible for or in receipt of a public assistance shelter allowance, the amount the family is deemed able to pay will be the highest of the following:

(1) 10 percent of the family's gross monthly income; or

(2) 30 percent of the family's gross monthly income after first deducting $40 for each dependent and any amount paid by the family for the care of children under 13 years of age for that month, but only where such care is necessary to enable the parent or caretaker to be gainfully employed or to participate in an approved program of vocational training or rehabilitation as defined in section 415.2(a)(2) of this Title, and only to the extent such amounts are not reimbursed.

(b) As used in this subparagraph the term:

(1) family includes any person residing in the household to which the child will be discharged, unless such person pays a prorated amount toward rent and utilities. In such a case, the share of rent and utilities payable by such person will be deducted from the actual cost of rent.

(2) dependent includes any member of the family household (excluding foster children), other than the head of the household or such person's spouse, who is under 18 years of age or is a disabled person or is a full-time student.

(c) In no event may the actual cost of rent toward which subsidy may be applied exceed 150 percent of the following fair market rental values:

Metropolitan Counties:

0 Bedrooms	1 Bedroom	2 Bedrooms	3 Bedrooms	4 Bedrooms

Albany-Schenectady-Troy, NY
COUNTY(IES):
Albany, Greene, Montgomery, Rensselaer, Saratoga, Schenectady

309	371	438	551	613

Binghamton, NY
COUNTY(IES): Broome, Tioga

279	335	396	489	549

Buffalo, NY
COUNTY(IES): Erie

282	342	403	504	563

Elmira, NY
COUNTY(IES): Chemung

282	342	403	504	565

Glens Falls, NY
COUNTY(IES): Warren, Washington

291	354	416	520	583

Nassau-Suffolk, NY
COUNTY(IES): Nassau, Suffolk

499	605	712	891	996

New York, NY
COUNTY(IES):   Bronx, Kings, New York, Putnam, Queens, Richmond,
                        Rockland

375	455	535	671	751

Niagara Falls, NY
COUNTY(IES): Niagara

271	328	386	483	541

Orange County, NY
COUNTY(IES): Orange

372	452	531	664	744

Metropolitan Counties:

0 Bedrooms	1 Bedroom	2 Bedrooms	3 Bedrooms	4 Bedrooms

Poughkeepsie, NY
COUNTY(IES): Dutchess

422	513	604	755	846

Rochester, NY
COUNTY(IES): Livingston, Monroe, Ontario, Orleans, Wayne

331	405	477	596	663

Syracuse, NY
COUNTY(IES): Madison, Onondaga, Oswego

292	349	409	511	573

Utica-Rome, NY
COUNTY(IES): Herkimer, Oneida

254	309	363	455	509

COUNTY(IES): Westchester

472	572	674	842	942

Non-Metropolitan Counties:

	0 Bedrooms	1 Bedroom	2 Bedrooms	3 Bedrooms	4 Bedrooms
Allegany	249	298	349	437	490
Cayuga	291	354	416	520	583
Chenango	288	349	411	514	575
Columbia	274	332	392	490	549
Delaware	267	326	383	478	536
Franklin	264	321	377	472	529
Genesee	271	328	387	483	541
Jefferson	284	345	406	507	569
Otsego	267	326	383	478	536
Schoharie	267	326	383	478	536
Seneca	291	354	416	520	583
Sullivan	288	362	414	506	578
Ulster	341	414	488	609	683
Yates	272	330	389	487	543

	0 Bedrooms	1 Bedroom	2 Bedrooms	3 Bedrooms	4 Bedrooms
Cattaraugus	245	297	349	437	490

Chautauqua	261	318	374	468	523
Clinton	278	331	389	483	531
Cortland	298	362	427	534	598
Essex	265	321	377	472	529
Fulton	237	289	339	425	475
Hamilton	264	321	377	472	529
Lewis	284	345	406	507	569
St. Lawrence	271	328	387	483	541
Schuyler	274	332	392	490	549
Steuben	274	332	392	490	549
Tompkins	298	362	427	534	598
Wyoming	272	328	387	483	541

These fair market values may be increased by the department upon issuance of written notice to local social services districts of such changes.

(v) The family's need for housing services, including the need for the specific form of assistance and the amount of any financial assistance being provided, must be reassessed at each assessment and service plan review required pursuant to Part 428 of this Title. When a rent subsidy is being provided, the family's need for such subsidy must be calculated as prescribed in subparagraph (iv) of this paragraph at each reassessment. When, as a result of such reassessment, the case manager determines that the family's needs have changed and the housing services should be modified, reduced, increased or terminated before the three year maximum eligibility period has elapsed, the family must be so notified in writing no later than 30 days prior to the initiation of such action. Such notice must advise the family of its right to request a hearing pursuant to section 423.4(m)(4) of this Part. Housing services must be terminated before the three year maximum eligibility period has elapsed if:

(a) the child or children have returned to foster care, except when such return is due to emergency circumstances based upon a parent service need and foster care is necessary for a specified period not to exceed 30 days;

(b) the local social services district or the family has located adequate permanent housing for the family and continued housing services are not necessary;

(c) the family no longer meets the financial eligibility standard set forth in subparagraph (iv) of this paragraph;

(d) the child is no longer residing in the household;

(e) the family moves out-of-state;

(f) the youngest child discharged from care as a result of the family's eligibility for housing services reaches his/her 18th birthday; or

(g) the family moves out of the original housing unit for which housing services were obtained and the local social services district in which the family currently resides determines that adequate permanent housing is available and continued housing services are not necessary to prevent the child's return to foster care.

(vi) Payments for housing services must be made directly by the local social services district or purchase of service agency to the landlord, mortgage holder, exterminator, or contractor responsible for repairs.

(17) (i) Intensive, home-based, family preservation services are defined as casework services and direct therapeutic services provided to families in order to reduce or avoid the need for foster care placements of children who are in imminent danger of such placements. Intensive, home-based, family preservation services may include arranging on behalf of the families housing assistance, child care, job training, education services, emergency cash grants and basic support needs.

(ii) Caseworkers providing intensive, home based family preservation services must provide at least one-half of their direct services in the family's residence or temporary home, work with not more than four families at any given time and be available to the families 24 hours a day. The caseworkers must be trained in family preservation techniques and must aid in the solution of practical problems that contribute to family stress so as to effect improved parental performance and better resolution of intra-familial conflicts.

(iii) Intensive, home-based, family preservation services may be provided for up to 30 days per family and may be extended for an additional 30 days per family when necessary to maintain the progress already achieved or when the provision of such services for the additional days is necessary to avoid the foster care placement of children.

(18) Outreach activities are defined as those activities designed to publicize the existence and availability of preventive services for parents, caretakers, and children who meet the criteria for the provision of preventive services and to advise such parents, caretakers and children of the availability of such services to meet their needs, alleviate the cause or condition that creates the risk of foster care placement and to assist the family to stay together. Outreach activities may be undertaken to publicize the existence and availability of preventive services for parents, caretakers, and children who have been diagnosed as having acquired immune deficiency syndrome (AIDS), or human immunodeficiency virus (HIV)-related illness or HIV infection, as those terms are defined by the AIDS Institute of the State Department of Health and are contained in directives issued by the department from time to time. These outreach activities are for the purpose of identifying parent service needs and child services needs, as described in sections 430.9(c) (4) and 430.9(c) (5) of this Title.

(19) Respite care and services for families as described in Part 435 of this Title.

(c) (1) Family is defined solely for the purpose of this section as:

(i) the child who is at risk of foster care, his/her parents, or legal guardians, or other caretakers and siblings; or

(ii) a woman who is pregnant as specified in section 430.9(c) (6) of this Title; or

(iii) a child who does not live with his/her parents and needs services to prevent return to foster care; or

(iv) a minor parent in foster care whose child or children are residing with him or her in a foster family home or residential facility.

(2) For the limited purpose of authorizing eligibility for housing services as defined in paragraph (b)(16) of this section, family may only include:

(i) a child in foster care whose permanency planning goal is discharge to parent or relative, together with such child's parent, legal guardian or other caretaker, siblings and own child or children; or

(ii) a child with a goal of discharge to another planned living arrangement with a permanency resource who is to be discharged from foster care prior to his or her 18th birthday or who is placed in trial discharge status after his or her 18th birthday and his or her own child or children.

(d) Mandated preventive services shall mean preventive services provided to a child and his family whom the district is required to serve pursuant to section 430.9 of this Title.

(e) Non mandated preventive services means preventive services defined in paragraphs (b)(1)-(15) of this section provided to a child and his/her family who the district may serve pursuant to section 409-a(2) of the Social Services Law. Non mandated preventive services will not include housing services defined in paragraph (b)(16) of this section or intensive, home-based, family preservation services in paragraph (b) (17) of this section or crisis respite care and services for families defined in paragraph (b)(19) of this section.

(f) Specialized rehabilitative services are defined as assessment, diagnosis, testing, psychotherapy, and specialized therapies provided as a component of a service plan to a child and/or family by a person who has received a master's degree in social work, is a licensed psychologist, is a licensed psychiatrist or other recognized therapist in human services or is a licensed or qualified individual including, but not limited to, a registered nurse or an alcohol or substance abuse counselor.

(g) Supportive services are defined as those services provided as a component of a service plan to a child and/or family including, but not limited to, parent aide services, homemaker services, home health aide services, parent training services, housekeeper/chore services, and home management services.

(h) Probation services are defined as services provided by a probation service that are related to the provision of adjustment services to persons in need of supervision or are included as preventive services pursuant to a contract or agreement with a social services district.

§423.3 Client eligibility criteria for preventive services.

(a) The eligibility criteria for mandated preventive services shall be as defined in section 430.9 of this Title, appropriate provision of mandated preventive services.

(b) Non-mandated preventive services may be provided by a social services district to children and their families when such services are not provided pursuant to subdivision (a) of this section and the child is at risk of foster care or returning to foster care and preventive services would enable the child to be returned home sooner, except that intensive, home-based, family preservation services, as defined in section 423.2(b)(17) of this Part, or respite care and services for families, as defined in Part 435 of this Title, may not be provided as non-mandated preventive services.

§423.4 Service provision requirements.

(a) Preventive services shall be provided according to the needs of the child and his family and according to this section.

(b) Length of service.

(1) Preventive services shall continue only if a new determination is made every six months after the initial application for services that the child will be placed or continued in foster care unless such services are provided and that it is reasonable to believe that by providing such services, the child will be able to remain with or be returned to his family. Documentation for compliance with this subdivision shall be pursuant to section 430.9(g) of this Title, utilization review-standard for the recertification of mandated preventive services.

(2) (i) With the exception of housing services as defined in section 423.2(b) (16) of this Part, the provision of mandated preventive services to children and their families during a foster care placement may not be provided for more than

an average of three months for all children in care within each particular social services district with a goal of return to parents or relatives and no child in foster care may receive preventive services for more than a total of 24 months. Local social services districts that exceed the three-month average must have that portion of expenditures in excess of the average reimbursed as nonmandated preventive services.

(ii) Where housing services are provided in the form of payment of rent or mortgage arrears, such arrears payment must be made directly to the landlord or mortgage holder. The amount of such arrears payment may not exceed $1,800, or the equivalent of six months of housing services at the maximum amount of $300 a month, and in no case may exceed the total amount owed. In cases where an arrears payment relates to a period preceding the date of application for preventive services by more than six months, the authorization period will begin six months preceding the date of application. Where the arrears payment relates to a period preceding the application by less than six months, the authorization date will be the date arrears began to accrue.

(iii) Payments for security deposits, finder's or broker's fees, household moving expenses, exterminator fees, and/or essential repairs of conditions in rental or client owned property which create a substantial health or safety risk, and which are payable in the same month, may be issued in one month but the total amount paid may not exceed an amount equivalent to up to six months of housing services at $300 a month, or $1,800. In such cases the authorization date will be deemed to have commenced on a date six months prior to the date payments were made. Each $300 increment of payment must be included in determining the maximum 36 month eligibility period.

(iv) Whenever $100 or more of a housing subsidy is sought for repairs to rental property, the participating landlord must agree to rent the property to the family for a minimum one-year period commencing on the date housing services are provided.

(v) In cases where adequate housing is located, provided and, if necessary, renovated such that a child could be discharged from care pursuant to this Part, the child must be discharged within two months from the date such housing is made available. Discharge may occur on a trial basis. Where adequate housing is made available and the child is not discharged within the two month period, the reason for the child remaining in care will be deemed to be due primarily to a factor other than housing and housing services will be terminated.

(3) The provision of nonmandated prevention services to children and their families during a foster care placement shall continue only if a new determination is made every six months after the initial application for services that the child will be continued in foster care unless such services are provided and that it is reasonable to believe that by providing such services, the child will be able to be returned to his family.

(4) The provision of housing services as defined in section 423.2(b)(16) of this Part as a preventive service must not exceed a period of 36 months commencing on the date housing services were authorized and provided.

(5) The provision of intensive, home-based, family preservation services must not exceed 30 days except as provided in section 423.2 (b)(17)(iii) of this Part.

(c) Case management and case planning requirements.

(1) Case management, case planning and casework contacts are required for all children and their families in receipt of preventive services.

(i) Case management services shall be provided by the local department of social services. There shall be only one case manager for each family receiving any child welfare services, including foster care, preventive services, child protective services, day care and adoption services.

(ii) Case planning may be provided by a local department of social services or through purchase of service with a preventive services agency.

(a) There shall be only one case planner for each family receiving preventive services.

(b) When a child and his family are receiving preventive services and foster care services or are receiving preventive services and child protective services, there may be more than one case worker assigned to the case.

(c) The local department of social services will designate the agency having case planning responsibility, as well as any other agencies having a role in the case. The agency assigned case planning responsibility will then assign a case planner to the case. Each additional agency with a role in the case will assign caseworker(s) to the case.

(1) The local department of social services will identify responsibilities for each agency with a role in the case, including completion of the uniform case record and provision of casework contacts.

(2) When there is more than one agency with a role in the case, the assigned case planner and assigned caseworker(s) must jointly develop the assessment and service plan and complete the service plan reviews. There must be only one assessment and service plan.

(d) There must be at least 12 casework contacts with a child and/or family in receipt of preventive services within each six-month period of services. The first six-month time period commences at the case initiation date or at the initiation of preventive services; subsequent six-month periods will be calculated from the service plan due date.

(1) For purposes of this Part, casework contacts must be made by the following:

(i) the case planner;

(ii) a caseworker assigned to the case, as directed by the case planner;

(iii) the person providing specialized rehabilitative services as defined in section 423.2(f) of this Part. Such person may be considered to be making casework contacts as defined in section 423.2(b)(3) of this Part when the specialized rehabilitative services are directed by, arranged by or otherwise coordinated by the case planner. Such persons providing specialized rehabilitative services are permitted access to preventive services records only if they are employed by a preventive services agency as defined in section 423.2(a) of this Part or an authorized agency as defined in subdivision (a) of section 371.1 of the Social Services Law or have been granted access to individually identifiable information in such records with the consent of the parent or child pursuant to section 423.7(e) of this Part;

(iv) the person providing supportive services as defined in section 423.2(g) of this Part. Such person may be considered as making casework contacts as defined in section 423.2(b)(3) of this Part when the supportive services are directed by, arranged by or otherwise coordinated by the case planner. Such persons providing supportive services are permitted access to preventive service records only if they are employed by a preventive services agency as defined in section 423.2(a) of this Part or an authorized agency as defined in subdivision (a) of section 371.10 of the Social Services Law or have been granted access to individually identifiable information in such records with the consent of the parent or child pursuant to section 423.7(e) of this Part; and

(v) the person providing probation services as defined in section 423.2(h) of this Part.

(2) (i) At least six of the 12 casework contacts must be made by the case planner, or an assigned caseworker, as directed by the case planner. Four of such contacts must be individual face-to-face meetings with the child and/or his or her family. Two contacts by the case planner or an assigned caseworker, as directed by the case planner, within the six-month period must take place in the child's home.

(ii) No more than two of the remaining six contacts in any six-month period may be made by supportive service providers as defined by subclause (iv) of this clause.

(3) The preventive service casework contacts required by this clause will not apply in cases where housing services are the only preventive service being provided. In such cases, there must be at least one in-home casework contact within the first six months of provision of the housing services, at least one casework contact at the time of each reassessment and one contact 60 days prior to termination of the housing services. Such contacts must consist of efforts to locate other sources of permanent housing for the family and/or other sources of housing assistance which would enable the family to remain in the housing unit for which housing services were obtained. This subclause will not change the casework contact requirements set forth in section 430.12(b) of this Title.

(d) (1) Core services.

(i) Effective October 1, 1984 each local department of social services must ensure that each child and his/her family mandated to receive services pursuant to this Part have the following core services available to them if such services are identified as needed in the child's service plan:

(a) day care;

(b) homemaker services;

(c) parent training or parent aide;

(d) transportation;

(e) clinical services;

(f) respite care and services for families, provided pursuant to Part 435 of this Title, in which a parent, legal guardian, caretaker or child has Acquired Immune Deficiency Syndrome (AIDS), HIV infection or HIV-related illness (as such terms are defined by the AIDS Institute of the New York State Department of Health) and who are mandated to receive preventive services under the parent service need or child services needs standards of section 430.9(c)(4) and (c)(5)(i) of this Title; and

(g) twenty-four hour access to emergency services which means developing a plan for, arranging for or providing emergency services, including cash or the equivalent thereto, goods and shelter when a child is at risk of foster care and such services may prevent placement. The plan may include coordination with income maintenance staff or identification of service agencies within the social services district that provide 24-hour services such as a privately administered telephone hotline.

(ii) Effective December 9, 1988, each local department of social services must ensure that housing services as defined in section 423.2(b)(16) of this Part are provided each eligible child and his/her family.

(2) Any other preventive service specified in section 423.2(b) of this Part may be provided according to the needs of the child and his/her family.

(e) Planning requirements. To ensure that the services listed in subdivision (d) of this section are available to each child and his family mandated to receive the services, each local department of social services shall include in its consolidated services plan:

(1) the number of children and families needing each core service and description of indicators used to determine this estimate;

(2) an assurance that every child and family needing any of the core services have these services provided to them in a timely manner;

(3) description of the organization of preventive services within the local department of social services, including staff available to provide preventive services;

(4) the names and addresses of agencies providing purchased preventive services and the services provided by each agency;

(5) an assurance that efforts are made to coordinate services with purchase of service agencies and other public and private agencies within the district that provide services to children, including the use of referral procedures with these agencies and formal and informal agreements; and

(6) an assurance that a plan has been prepared and staff are aware of procedures for providing or arranging for 24-hour access to emergency services for children who are at risk of foster care as specified in paragraph (d)(6) of this section.

This requirement shall be effective for the 1984-87 Consolidated Service Plan and every three years thereafter. Yearly updates of this information shall be required in a form and manner specified by the department.

(f) Purchase of service contracts. For the purpose of this Part, each purchase of services contract shall include but is not limited to the following:

(1) specification of case planning responsibilities, including responsibility for completion of the uniform case record and casework contacts;

(2) identification of the services to be provided;

(3) an estimate of the number of children and families that will receive each service and the percentage of those children and families that will be mandated and nonmandated;

(4) procedures for referrals between purchase of service agencies and the local department of social services and other public and private agencies within the district that provide services to children;

(5) methods the local department of social services will employ to monitor the effectiveness of the service provided;

(6) outreach responsibilities where applicable;

(7) child protective services reporting requirements;

(8) case management procedures, including:

(i) how the local social services district will authorize the service, approve the client eligibility determination and approve the service plan; and

(ii) procedures for arranging case conferences and service plan reviews;

(9) payment procedures; and

(10) procedures to ensure confidentiality as required by section 423.7 of this Part.

(g) Preventive services in foster care.

(1) Except as noted in paragraph (2) of this subdivision, of the children in foster care, only those children who have a goal of discharge to parent or caretaker and who meet the eligibility criteria of section 430.9(e)(1) of this

Title will be eligible for the mandated preventive services identified in section 423.2(b)(1)-(15) of this Part. Such services must be provided to the family or the child and family together. For each period during which such services are provided, the casework contacts required by section 441.21 of this Title must be met.

(2) Minor parents in foster care, whose own child or children are residing with them in a foster family home or residential facility, where such child or children meet the eligibility criteria of subdivision (c), (e) or (h) of section 430.9 of this Title, will be eligible for mandated preventive services identified in section 423.2 (b) (1)-(18) of this Part. Such services must be provided to the minor parent and his or her child or children for the purpose of keeping the minor parent and his or her child or children together, including facilitating a custody arrangement that maintains or seeks to restore custody of the child or children of the minor parent to such minor parent except when this custody arrangement would place the child or children of the minor parent at imminent risk of abuse or maltreatment. For each period during which such services are provided, the casework contacts required by section 441.21 of this Title must be met.

(3) Non mandated preventive services subject to the eligibility criteria of this section may be provided to any child in foster care whose goal is return home, and these services will not be subject to the limitation that mandated preventive services to children in foster care average no longer than three months as provided for in paragraph (b)(2) of this section. Such services may include any of the services provided in section 423.2(b)(1)-(15) of this Part which the child and family need except that services must be provided only to the family or to the child and family together. Notwithstanding the requirement of this paragraph that non mandated preventive services be provided to the family or to the child and family together, day services may be provided to the child alone. Preventive services must be provided only if the casework contact requirements for children in placement pursuant to section 441.21 of this Title are fulfilled.

(4) Housing services defined in section 423.2(b)(16) of this Part may only be provided to those families and children who satisfy the eligibility criteria of section 430.9(e)(2) and 430.9(f) of this Title.

(h) Preventive services to children immediately after discharge. Mandated and nonmandated preventive services provided to a child for the first three months following discharge from foster care may include any of the services in section 423.2(b) of this Part that the child and his family need except that such services shall be in addition to the following after care requirements: three face-to-face casework contacts, including one home visit, and one case conference with the preventive services agency that shall be provided by a local social services department or by the authorized agency providing the foster care services for the child.

(i) Preventive services to children in receipt of child protective services.

(1) A child and his family who are in receipt of child protective services may receive mandated preventive services if the child is deemed to be at risk of foster care or at risk of returning to care and if the child and family meet one of the eligibility criteria as specified in section 430.9 of this Title, except that the health and safety criteria of section 430.9(c)(1) of this Title shall only apply to indicated cases.

(2) A child and his family who are in receipt of child protective services may receive nonmandated preventive services if the child is deemed to be at risk of foster care or at risk of returning to care.

(3) When a child and his family are receiving both preventive services and child protective services, the child protective services unit of the local department of social services shall be the sole public agency responsible for receiving and investigating or arranging with the appropriate society for the prevention of cruelty to children to investigate all reports of suspected child abuse or maltreatment made pursuant to this Title for the purpose of providing protective services to prevent further abuse or maltreatment to children and to coordinate, provide or arrange for and monitor the provision of those services necessary to safeguard and ensure the child's well-being and development and to preserve and stabilize family life wherever appropriate.

(4) For all indicated child protective services cases, all monitoring requirements as specified by the department shall be followed. When preventive services are purchased by a local district for indicated child protective services cases, the local district shall notify the agency providing services of the local district staff person assigned monitoring responsibility.

(j) Preventive services to adopted children. Preventive services may be provided to adopted children who are at risk of foster care according to the client eligibility criteria specified in section 423.3 of this Part.

(k) Emergency services.

(1) Emergency cash or the equivalent thereto, goods and shelter may be provided if and only if they are directly related to averting or abbreviating a foster care placement. When any such expenditures are included within the Emergency Assistance to Needy Families with Children Program as set forth in Part 372 of this Title, the social services district must make an application within 10 days of the provision of these services. Expenditures for these services may not exceed expenditures allowed under the Emergency Assistance to Needy Families with Children Program.

(2) Before emergency shelter is provided to avert the placement of a child into foster care, social services districts must comply with section 423.5(j) of this Part. Social services districts must first explore a family's eligibility for shelter services or shelter payments under the aid to families with dependent children, home relief, emergency assistance to needy families with children, emergency assistance to aged, blind and disabled persons, or supplemental security income programs as set forth in this Title and, where appropriate, determine eligibility for and provide emergency shelter under such programs. Placement in emergency shelter does not relieve a social services district from assisting the family to obtain permanent housing. This assistance may include, where applicable, providing preventive housing services to those families eligible for such services pursuant to Section 409-a(5)(d) of the Social Services Law in accordance with the provisions of the preventive housing services demonstration program established pursuant to Chapter 165 of the Laws of 1991.

(*l*) Housing services. Housing services, as defined in section 423.2(b) (16) of this Part, may be provided only upon the determination by the case manager that a lack of adequate housing is the primary factor preventing the discharge of the child or children from foster care and that the child or children will be discharged no later than two months after such services have been provided and adequate housing has been made available.

(1) When any of the services provided as housing services pursuant to this section are also available under a public assistance program including aid to families with dependent children, home relief or emergency assistance to needy families with children, the case manager must assure that an application for public assistance is made within 10 days of the determination of eligibility for housing services. However, if the service provided pursuant to the aid to families with dependent children or home relief program would result in recoupment pursuant to section 352.31 (d) of this Title, then housing services must be provided as a preventive service instead of providing such services under the aid to families with dependent children or home relief program.

(2) Whenever housing services are provided as a preventive service to a family in receipt of public assistance or care, including food stamps and medical assistance, the case manager must provide the local public assistance, food stamp and/or medical assistance office with written notice of such provision within 30 days of authorization or modification and not later than 30 days prior to termination of housing services. However, any payment provided as a housing service may not be considered a resource and therefore may not negatively effect the family's eligibility for public assistance, food stamp or medical assistance benefits.

(m) General requirements.

(1) Notwithstanding any provision of this Part and, with the exception of court orders, preventive services shall not be provided to the parents or their children if refused by the parents of the child at risk.

(2) Reasonable efforts shall be made by the preventive services agencies to communicate with the child and his family in their primary language.

(3) Each child and his or her family requesting to apply for services must be informed of available services, eligibility requirements of the services, the provisions of section 423.7 of this Part pertaining to confidentiality and preventive services records, and the right to a fair hearing pursuant to paragraph (4) of this subdivision and Part 358 of this Title.

(4) In accordance with Part 358 of this Title, an applicant for preventive services whose application has been denied or not acted upon within 30 days or a recipient of preventive services whose service has been reduced or terminated by a social services district, shall be entitled to a fair hearing by the department, provided the request is made within 60 days after such action or failure to act.

(5) Each preventive services agency shall keep a record of the number of families applying for or referred for preventive services and a record of whether their applications have been denied and the reasons for such denial.

(6) Preventive services must be provided without regard to income. Fees must be collected for preventive day care services in accordance with the day care fee schedule as published in the Consolidated Services Plan. Fees must be collected for preventive day services pursuant to subdivision (c) of section 425.5 of this Title. In addition, in accordance with the fee schedules established by the department, fees may be collected by a local social services district for the following preventive services: homemaker, housekeeper/chore, clinical services and transportation, if such district establishes a fee schedule and such fee schedule is approved by the department. Such fees must be based on documentation of current family size and monthly gross income. Notwithstanding any provision of this Part, a family that is unable to pay fees is eligible for the service.

(7) Staff and volunteers of agencies providing preventive services shall not engage in discrimination or harassment of families receiving preventive services on the basis of race, creed, color, national origin, age, sex, sexual orientation, gender identity or expression, marital status, religion, or disability. Such agencies shall promote and maintain a safe environment, take reasonable steps to prevent discrimination by staff and volunteers, promptly investigate incidents of discrimination and harassment, and take reasonable and appropriate corrective or disciplinary action when such incidents occur. For the purposes of this section, gender identity or expression shall mean having or being perceived as having a gender identity, self-image, appearance, behavior or expression whether or not that gender identity, self-image, appearance, behavior or expression is different from that traditionally associated with the sex assigned to that person at birth. Gender identity refers to a person's internal sense of self as male, female, no gender, or another gender, and gender expression refers to the manner in which a person expresses his or her gender through clothing, appearance, behavior, speech, or other means.

Part 427
Standards of Payment for
Foster Care of Children

§427.2 Definitions.

As used in this Part:

(a) Foster care of children means all activities and functions provided relative to the care of a child away from his home 24 hours per day in a foster family free home or a duly certified or approved foster family boarding home or a duly certified group home, agency boarding home, child care institution, health care facility or any combination thereof.

(b) Standards of administration for foster care include the following:

(1) intake (study, summary, and information, referral, and assisting and arranging for services to prevent foster care);

(2) placement services (development, implementation and evaluation of placement service plans);

(3) post-placement services (development and implementation of discharge service plans); and

(4) selection, development and supervision of foster care facilities.

(c) Foster child means a person who meets the following criteria contained in following paragraphs (1) through (3) of this subdivision or the criteria contained in paragraph (4) of this subdivision:

(1) Age.

(i) the child is under the age of 18 years; or

(ii) is between the ages of 18 and 21 years and entered foster care before his or her 18th birthday, and has consented to remain in foster care past his or her 18th birthday; and

(a) is a student attending a school, college or university; or

(b) is regularly attending a course of vocational or technical training designed to fit him or her for gainful employment; or

(c) lacks the skills or ability to live independently.

(2) Residential program. The child is cared for away from his or her home 24 hours a day in a foster family free home; a duly licensed, certified, or approved foster family boarding home; a duly licensed or certified group home, agency boarding home, child care institution, or health care facility; or any combination thereof.

(3) Placement. (i) the child's care and custody or guardianship and custody have been transferred to an authorized agency pursuant to the provisions of section 384 or 384-a of the Social Services Law; or

(ii) the child has been placed with a social services official pursuant to article 3, 7, 10, 10-B or 10-C of The Family Court Act.

(4) Minor parent/child case.

(i) the minor parent meets the criteria specified in paragraphs (1) through (3) of this subdivision;

(ii) the child or children of the minor parent reside(s) with the minor parent in a foster family home or residential facility and such child or children are not in the care and custody or custody and guardianship of the local commissioner of social services; and

(iii) the costs of the care of the child or children of the minor parent are combined with the costs of the care of the minor parent.

(d) Foster family boarding home means a residence owned, leased, or otherwise under the control of a single person or family who has been certified or approved by an authorized agency or is used by a local probation department, the State Department of Mental Hygiene or the Office of Children and Family Services to care for children, and such person or family receives payment from the agency for the care of such children. Such home may care for not more than six children, including all children under the age of 13 residing in the home, whether or not they are received for board. However, up to two additional children may be cared for if such children are siblings, or are siblings of a child living in the home, or are part of a minor parent/child unit as defined in section 427.2(s) of this Part, or are children freed for adoption and placed for adoption with the person(s) who have been certified or approved as foster parents. Such home may exceed these limits only to receive or board a child or children returning to that foster family boarding home pursuant to section 443.6 of this Title.

(e) Foster family free home care shall mean care provided to a foster child, at no cost to an authorized agency, by a family other than that of the child's parent, stepparent, grandparents, brother, sister, uncle, aunt or legal guardian for the purpose of adoption or for the purpose of providing care.

(f) Institution means a facility established for the 24-hour care and maintenance of 13 or more children, operated by a child care agency.

(g) Group residence means an institution for the care and maintenance of not more than 25 children, operated by an authorized agency.

(h) Group home means a family-type home for the care and maintenance of not less than seven nor more than 12 children who are at least five years of age, operated by an authorized agency, in quarters or premises owned, leased, or otherwise under the control of such agency; except that such minimum age shall not be applicable to siblings placed in the same facility, nor to children whose mother is placed in the same facility.

(i) Agency boarding home means a family-type home for the care and maintenance of not more than six children operated by an authorized agency, in quarters or premises owned, leased, or otherwise under the control of such agency; except that such a home may provide care for more than six brothers and sisters of the same family.

(j) District foster care apportionment amount means the dollar amount specified by the department, in accordance with subdivision (1) of section 153-e of the Social Services Law, as the maximum amount of expenditures by a local social services district for the care and maintenance of children out of their homes which are eligible for reimbursement by the State and Federal governments.

(k) Excess foster care expenditures means the amount of a district's foster care expenditures which exceed the district foster care apportionment amount.

(*l*) Interim approval means that funds expended before the approval of the application for reimbursement of excess foster care expenditures shall be reimbursed, but that such reimbursement shall be refunded to the State, if approval is denied.

(m) Natural disaster means any occurrence which serves as the basis for an official declaration of a state of emergency by the Governor of the State of New York or the President of the United States.

(n) Application means a written request to the State Department of Social Services for reimbursement of excess foster care expenditures.

(o) Emergency, extraordinary or unforeseen circumstance means any event, condition, or set of events or conditions which are outside the reasonable control of the local social services district and which have not occurred in the years from which data were drawn to develop the district foster care apportionment amount and which have a substantial impact on the district.

(p) Children who are refugees means children who:

(1) are in the care and custody or guardianship and custody of a social services official;

(2) are outside of their country of nationality;

(3) may or may not have any adult relatives in the United States;

(4) have been lawfully admitted to the United States; and

(5) who, because of persecution or fear of persecution on account of race, religion, or political opinion fled from their native countries and cannot return there because of fear of persecution on account of race, religion, or political opinion. Children who are refugees includes children who are unaccompanied refugee minors.

(q) Children who are Cuban/Haitian entrants means children who:

(1) are in the care and custody or guardianship and custody of a social services official; and

(2) have been granted parole status as a Cuban/Haitian entrant (status pending) or granted any other special status subsequently established under the Federal immigration laws for nationals of Cuba or Haiti, or are other nationals of Cuba or Haiti who:

(i) were paroled into the United States and have not acquired any other status under the Federal Immigration and Nationality Act; or

(ii) are the subject of exclusion or deportation proceedings under the Immigration and Nationality Act; or

(iii) have an application for asylum pending with the Immigration and Naturalization Service; and

(iv) have not had a final, nonappealable, and legally enforceable order of deportation or exclusion entered against them. Children who are Cuban/Haitian entrants includes children who are unaccompanied entrant minors.

(r) An unaccompanied refugee minor or an unaccompanied entrant minor means a person who:

(1) has not yet attained his or her 21st birthday;

(2) has no known immediate adult relatives in the United States;

(3) has been lawfully admitted to the United States in parole status; and

(4) is an alien who, because of persecution or fear of persecution on account of race, religion or political opinion fled from his native country and cannot return there because of fear of persecution on account of race, religion or political opinion.

(s) Minor parent/child unit means a family consisting of a foster child or an adopted child who is a minor parent and the child or children of such minor parent residing together in the same foster family home, residential facility or adoptive home.

(t) Supervised independent living program means one or more of a type of agency boarding home operated and certified by an authorized agency in accordance with the regulations of the Office of Children and Family Services to provide a transitional experience for older youth who, based upon their circumstances, are appropriate for transition to the level of care and supervision provided in the program.

(u) Supervised independent living unit means a home or apartment certified in accordance with the standards set forth in Part 449 of this Title by an authorized agency approved by the Office of Children and Family Services to operate a supervised independent living program for the care of up to four youth including their children. Each supervised independent living unit must be located in the community separate from any of the authorized agency's other congregate dwellings.

§427.3 Allowable items of expenditure.

(a) Payments for only the following items are allowable expenditures for the purpose of this Part and State reimbursement for local expenditures:

Salaries
    Administrative
    Social services
    Child care
    Medical--clinical
    Child support
    Maintenance
Fringe benefits and payroll taxes
    Social Security
    Insurance--Life/Health
    Pension and Retirement
    Workers' Compensation/
    Unemployment/NYS Disability
    Postage
    Dues, licenses, permits
    Office supplies
    Subscriptions-publications
Fringe benefits and payroll taxes
    Workers' Compensation
    Transportation and workers expense
    Allowances--children

Allowances--parents
Activities--children
Tuition--children
Related school expense
Outside camp fees
Religious stipends
Purchase of services
Purchase of health services
Food
Clothing
Bedding--linen--uniforms
Supplies and equipment
Supplies and equipment--medical
Rent
Rent--furnishing and equipment
Rent--vehicles
Utilities
Repairs and maintenance--plant
Repairs and maintenance--equipment
Repairs and maintenance--vehicles
Telephone and telegraph
Conference expense
Administrative expense
Staff development
Research activities
Publicity
Audit, legal and advisory fees
Insurance
Interest
Taxes
Uses charges/Property
Plant
    Equipment--Vehicles
    Office
    Other
Boarding home payments--normal
Boarding home payments--special
Boarding home payments-exceptional
Boarding home payments-emergency
Clothing payments--initial regular
Special payments (boarding homes)
Charges from parent organizations

(b) For purposes of allowability in the maximum State aid rate-setting process, the following additional limitations shall apply to the following stated item of expenditures:

(1) Rental costs (including sale and leaseback of facilities).

(i) Related party transactions.

(a) Actual costs for rentals of land, building and equipment and other personal property owned or controlled by organizations or persons affiliated with an authorized agency, or owned or controlled by members, directors, trustees, officers or other key personnel of such authorized agency or their families either directly or through corporations, trusts or other similar arrangements in which they hold more than 10 percent interest in such land, building and equipment or an interest valued at $1,000 or more, whichever is less, are allowable only to the extent that such rentals do not exceed the amount the authorized agency would have received had legal title to the rented items or facilities been vested in it.

(b) Actual charges in the nature of rent between or among authorized agencies or organizations under common control are allowable to the extent such charges do not exceed the normal costs of ownership, such as depreciation, taxes, insurance and maintenance; provided that no part of such costs shall duplicate any other allowed costs.

(ii) Nonrelated party transactions. Rental costs of land, building, and equipment and other personal property are allowable if the rates are reasonable in light of such factors as rental costs of comparable facilities and market conditions in the areas, the type, life expectancy, condition and value of the facilities lease, options available and other provisions of the rental agreement. Application of these factors, in situations where rentals are extensively used, may involve among other consideration, comparison of rental costs with the amount which the institution would have received had it owned the facilities.

(iii) Sales/leaseback transactions. Rental costs specified in sale and leaseback agreements, incurred by authorized agencies through selling plant facilities to investment organizations, such as insurance companies, associate institutions or private investors, and concurrently leasing back the same facilities, are allowable only to the extent that such rentals do not exceed the amount which the authorized agency would have received had it retained legal title to the facilities.

(2) Tuition.

(i) Reimbursement of tuition paid is available at the normal reimbursable rate for children residing in an authorized child care institution who attend a special act school district statutorily affiliated with the child care institution in which they reside.

(ii) State reimbursement of tuition paid is available until July 1, 1979 at the normal reimbursable rate for children who have attended a special act school district which is not statutorily affiliated with the child care institution in which they reside during the period between September 1, 1978 and December 31, 1978. Commencing January 1, 1979, State reimbursement of tuition paid is not available for children who attend a special act school district which is not statutorily affiliated with the child care institution in which they are placed, unless such school placements are approved in advance by the local social services commissioner responsible for their placement, or unless the children are placed into such institution on an emergency basis, in which case approval for such placement must be received from the local commissioner within 60 days after placement if such reimbursement is to continue. Such approvals will remain in effect for the duration of each academic year.

(iii) State reimbursement of tuition paid is available until July 1, 1979 at the normal reimbursable rate for children who have attended a special act school district during the period between September 1, 1978 and December 31, 1978, and who reside in group homes. Commencing January 1, 1979, reimbursement of tuition paid is not available for children who attend a special act school district and who are placed in group homes, unless such school placements are approved in advance by the local social services commissioner responsible for their placement, or unless the children are placed into such group home on an emergency basis, in which case approval for such placement must be received from the local commissioner within 60 days after placement if such reimbursement is to continue. Such approvals will remain in effect for the duration of each academic year.

(iv) State reimbursement of tuition paid for children who attend a special act school district and who reside in group homes shall not include reimbursement for tuition charged by public school districts other than special act school districts.

(c) Special payments (boarding homes)

(1) For purposes of allowability in the maximum State aid rate-setting process, the term special payments, as referred to in subdivision (a) of the section, means those expenditures made on behalf of a child residing in a foster boarding home for items, costs, or services that are approved pursuant either to paragraph (3) or (4) of this section as being necessary for the child but that are not included in establishing rates for board, care and clothing.

(2) Special payments include but, are not limited to expenditures for the following categories of items, costs and services:

(i) special attire for proms, religious observances and graduation, and for circumstances or occasions, such as school attendance or scouting activities, in which uniforms are necessary items of clothing;

(ii) school expenses such as books, activity fees, costs of field trips, club dues, school jewelry, school pictures, art supplies, and yearbooks;

(iii) music, art, and dancing lessons, and the purchase or rental of items needed to take part in such activities;

(iv) gifts for birthdays, holidays and other special occasions;

(v) extraordinary transportation and communication expenses. These expenses include:

(a) transportation provided by the foster parents for visits to the staff of an authorized agency, the foster child's birth parents, siblings who continue to reside with the birth parents, and to siblings who are placed separately with relatives or who are in foster care or adoption homes;

(b) payments to the birth parents, legal guardians, other relatives and significant others, for travel in excess of 50 miles (including the first 50 miles) to visit children in foster care;

(c) the costs of public transportation when it is necessary for school attendance if such costs are not reimbursed by the school district;

(d) other exceptional transportation required by the authorized agency or for agency approved reasons; and

(e) extraordinary telephone costs for communication with birth parents and siblings;

(vi) day care and baby-sitting services when necessary for the care and supervision of a child in foster care;

(vii) special furniture/equipment for the care of children in foster care such as cribs, high chairs, and car seats;

(viii) window guards necessary to protect the safety of a foster child;

(ix) special recreational/hobby expenditures including travel expenses such as lodging, tools and the costs of transportation, entry or use fees, uniforms and materials. These expenditures are limited to $400 per calendar year per foster child;

(x) compensation to a foster parent for the damage to and/or loss of personal property owned by the foster parent that is caused by the foster child in his or her care to the extent not covered by insurance. Requests for such compensation must be submitted in writing to the appropriate social services district in a manner required by such district within 30 days from the date the foster parents become aware of such damage or loss of personal property. The compensation herein provided for is limited to a maximum of $1,000 per foster child per foster boarding home over a two year period from the date of placement in such home. Compensation of less than $25 will not be granted;

(xi) day camp or residential summer camp costs, including registration and transportation expenses. Reimbursement for residential summer camp fees is available for a maximum of two weeks;

(xii) nonmedical needs of a handicapped child, including special equipment or clothing that is not covered by medical assistance, which arise from the child's handicap; and

(xiii) costs of diapers for a child from birth to the date of the child's fourth birthday.

(3) Requests for special payments for items, costs, or services identified in the categories set forth in paragraph (2) of this subdivision must be reviewed and approved by the social services district.

(4) A social services district may wish to make special payments to a foster parent for items, costs or services not otherwise identified among the categories set forth in paragraph (2) of this subdivision. In order to be eligible for State reimbursement for such payments, the social services district must request approval from the department through the appropriate regional office of the Division of Services and Community Development. The regional office will notify the social services district whether the items, costs or services are equivalent to those in paragraph (2) of this subdivision. This approval must be obtained before the payment can be made.

§427.6 Foster family boarding home program—payments and state reimbursement.

(a) Each social services district must establish and submit to the department annually a schedule of rates which it pays to foster family boarding homes for normal, special and exceptional foster care services and clothing replacement provided to children; however, State reimbursement for payments for such care based upon such rates is limited to the maximum provided for in subdivision (b) of this section.

(b) State reimbursement must be made only on actual payments to certified or approved foster parents providing care for children in foster family boarding homes up to the maximum levels established by the department for normal, special and exceptional foster care services and clothing replacement based upon data published by the U.S. Bureau of Labor Statistics, and other generally accepted sources, relating to the cost of raising children.

(c) If approved by the department, social services districts are eligible to receive State reimbursement for payments for special foster care services made on behalf of children who:

(1) are boarded out with foster parents who meet the criteria of subdivision (e) of this section; and

(2) suffer from pronounced physical conditions as a result of which a physician certifies that the child requires a high degree of physical care; or

(3) are awaiting family court hearings on PINS or juvenile delinquency petitions, or have been adjudicated as PINS or juvenile delinquents; or

(4) have been diagnosed by a qualified psychiatrist or psychologist as being moderately developmentally disabled, emotionally disturbed or having a

behavioral disorder to the extent that they require a high degree of supervision; or

(5) are refugees or Cuban/Haitian entrants, as defined in section 427.2(p) and (q) of this Part and are unable to function successfully in their communities because of factors related to their status as refugees or entrants. Such factors include but are not limited to, the inability to communicate effectively in English, the lack of effective daily living skills and the inability of the child to relate to others in the child's community; or

(6) enter foster care directly from inpatient hospital care. Such children are eligible for special foster care services for a period of one year. Eligibility after one year will continue only if the child meets one of the conditions described in paragraph (2), (3), (4), (5) or (7) of this subdivision; or

(7) in the judgment of the local social services commissioner, have a condition equivalent to those in paragraph (2), (3), (4) or (5) of this subdivision. Special payments for foster children who have the equivalent conditions described in this paragraph are approved if:

(i) a list of equivalent conditions has been developed by the local social services commissioner and approved by the department as eligible for special foster care services; or

(ii) individual, child specific requests for special foster care services have been approved by the local social services commissioner. Such child specific requests must be approved by the department within 60 days after approval by the local social services commissioner.

(d) If approved by the department, social services districts are eligible to receive State reimbursement for payments for exceptional foster care services made on behalf of foster children who:

(1) are boarded out with the foster parents who meet the criteria of subdivision (e) of this section; and

(2) require, as certified by a physician, 24-hour-a-day care provided by qualified nurses, or persons closely supervised by qualified nurses or physicians; or

(3) have severe behavior problems characterized by the infliction of violence on themselves, other persons or their physical surroundings, and who have been certified by a qualified psychiatrist or psychologist as requiring high levels of individual supervision in the home; or

(4) have been diagnosed by a qualified physician as having severe mental illnesses, such as child schizophrenia, severe developmental disabilities, brain damage or autism; or

(5) have been diagnosed by a physician as having acquired immune deficiency syndrome (AIDS) or human immunodeficiency virus (HIV)-related illness, as defined by the AIDS Institute of the State Department of Health. Such definitions are contained in directives issued by the department from time to time. Foster children who have tested positive for HIV infection and subsequently tested negative for HIV infection due to seroconversion remain eligible for exceptional services for a period of one-year from the date of the test which indicated seroconversion. Upon expiration of such one-year period, the child's condition must be evaluated and the local social services commissioner must determine the child's continued need for exceptional services in accordance with paragraph (2), (3), (4) or (6) of this subdivision; or

(6) in the judgment of the local social services commissioner, have a condition equivalent to those in paragraph (2), (3), (4) or (5) of this

subdivision. Exceptional payments for foster children who have the equivalent conditions described in this paragraph are approved if:

(i) a list of equivalent conditions has been developed by the local social services commissioner and approved by the department as eligible for exceptional foster care services; or

(ii) individual, child specific requests for exceptional foster care services have been approved by the local social services commissioner. Such child specific requests must be approved by the department within 60 days after approval by the local social services commissioner.

(e) If approved by the department, social services districts are eligible to receive State reimbursement for payments for special or exceptional foster care services made to foster parents who:

(1) provide foster family boarding home care to the foster children described in subdivisions (c) and (d) of this section; and

(2) have demonstrated their ability to care for foster children with special or exceptional conditions through past training and experience in nursing, special education, child care or the completion of or participation in special training provided by an authorized child caring agency or other relevant training and experience; and

(3) actively participate in agency training for foster parents of not less than four hours per year in the case of providers of special foster care services and five hours per year in the case of providers of exceptional foster care services; and

(4) actively participate in case conferences as determined by the authorized agency; and

(5) are able to provide the intensive supervision and interpersonal relationships that are consistent with the child's therapeutic goals. This includes the ability to work with the professionals involved in the treatment plan, such as physicians, nurses, social workers, psychologists and psychiatrists. Foster parents must also be able to accept assistance and guidance in caring for the child.

(f) Where certified or approved foster parents are providing care for a foster child who was eligible for special or exceptional foster care services prior to August 1, 1990 and are receiving a payment for such child which exceeds the amounts established pursuant to this section, State reimbursement will continue to be made at the higher amount so long as the child continues to receive care as a foster child in that foster family boarding home. Such higher payments cannot be made after March 31, 1991 and the rate of payment after such date will be the rate authorized by this section.

(g) State reimbursement through the Department of Social Services is not available for foster care or for bed reservations in any foster family boarding home during any period in which a child is being held therein for detention as defined in section 510-a of the Executive Law.

(h) In the case of a child or children who reside with their minor parents in the same foster family home, and who are not in the care and custody or custody and guardianship of the local commissioner of social services, State reimbursement will be made only for payments made to certified or approved foster parents providing care for such minor parent/child unit.

§427.16 Standards on clothing for children in foster care.

(a) Responsibility of social services districts. For each child in foster care, the social services district shall:

(1) determine clothing needs upon admission to care;

(2) authorize allowances to buy necessary clothing;

(3) authorize special allowances to cover the costs of additional clothing for:

(i) religious ceremonies;

(ii) educational or summer camp activities;

(iii) special physical conditions;

(iv) replacement of clothing that is stolen or destroyed; and

(4) review and evaluate the child's clothing needs with the child, when appropriate, and the foster parent to ensure that:

(i) additional clothing is provided for the child as needed;

(ii) clothing is clean, attractive, and well fitting;

(iii) the child's participation in the planning and the selection of his clothes is consistent with his age and maturity; and

(iv) advance notice is given for special clothing requests.

(b) For each child placed in a child caring agency or institution, the social services district shall provide a clothing allowance only when the negotiated board rate does not include such an allowance.

Part 428
Standards for Uniform Case Records and
Family and Child Assessments and Service Plans
(Extracts)

Section
428.8   Access to Foster Care Records by a Former Foster Child
428.9   Service Plan Review for Foster Care Cases

§428.8 Access to foster care records by a former foster child.

(a) Purpose. This section establishes the standards and process whereby a former foster child may receive access to foster care records from an authorized agency.

(b) Definitions. As used in this section:

(1) Former foster child means a person 18 years of age or older, who has been discharged from foster care on either a trial or final basis and was not adopted.

(2) Foster care record means the following:

(i) health and medical records, including medical histories of the foster child and his or her birth parents, to the extent available, and in accordance with section 373-a of the Social Services Law and section 357.3 of this Title;

(ii) educational records of the foster child;

(iii) social history, assessment and service plan documents and plan amendments in the form and manner required at the time such documents were completed, or which predate uniform case recording requirements pursuant to this Part;

(iv) progress notes;

(v) face sheet or equivalent, and any other documents which identify and describe family members, including but not limited to parents, guardians, siblings and half siblings, and grandparents; and

(vi) placement information pursuant to section 372(1)(e) of the Social Services Law.

(3) Authorized agency includes those entities defined in section 371 (10) (a) and (b) of the Social Services Law.

(c) An authorized agency must grant a former foster child's request for access to his or her foster care record, subject to the provisions of this section. A former foster child is entitled to receive all items in the foster care record as that term is defined in paragraph (2) of subdivision (b) of this section, except for confidential HIV-related information concerning any person other than the former foster child. The former foster child may gain access to child protective services information regarding the former foster child, including reports to the Statewide central register of child abuse and maltreatment in accordance with section 422 of the Social Services Law.

(d) Access by a former foster child to his or her foster care record must be granted in one of the following methods as chosen by the authorized agency:

(1) a summary statement containing the requested information;

(2) a copy of the entire foster care record;

(3) a copy of the portions of the record containing the requested information;

(4) a personal review of the applicable records by the former foster child within the agency facility, when mutually convenient to the authorized agency and the former foster child; or

(5) any combination of the above.

(e) The former foster child must submit a written request detailing the specific information sought and include a copy of a document verifying the identity of the former foster child such as a current valid driver's license or other commonly accepted form of identification which provides proof of the name and date of birth of the former foster child. Nothing precludes the former foster child from requesting all available agency foster care records that pertain to the former foster child.

(f) Upon the receipt by an authorized agency of a written request from a former foster child for information concerning the former foster child, the authorized agency must verify the identity and age of the former foster child by reviewing the submitted identification documentation; the authorized agency must search its foster care records to determine whether a foster care record exists for such a person.

(g) Within 30 days of the receipt of the written request, the authorized agency must provide the former foster child with the requested information or a written explanation of the delay including the date the information will be provided.

(h) An authorized agency may impose reasonable and customary charges, not to exceed the actual costs incurred by the authorized agency, for making copies of and/or mailing case record documents. No charge may be imposed for providing personal review of the records or preparing a summary.

§428.9 Service plan review for foster care and other out-of-home placement cases.

(a) The service plan review must be conducted in accordance with the requirements of section 430.12 of this Title and must be documented in the uniform case record for any child in foster care or any child who was placed by a court in the direct custody of a relative or other suitable person pursuant to Article 10 of the Family Court Act. The term foster care case includes children who are legally free for the purpose of adoption and children not in the care and custody or custody and guardianship of the local commissioner of social services who reside with their minor parents in the same foster family home or residential facility.

(b) (1) Unless such service plan review will occur within 60 days of the date certain for a permanency hearing, a case consultation must be held for each child defined in section 1087 of the Family Court Act in preparation for each permanency hearing held in accordance with Article 10-A of the Family Court Act including in those cases where the permanency hearing will constitute the service plan review. Such case consultation must be documented in the progress notes and the decisions and outcomes must be incorporated into the permanency hearing report. Such case consultation must be conducted no earlier than 60 days, prior to the date certain of the permanency hearing and must be completed with sufficient time to finalize and submit the permanency hearing report at least 14 days before the date certain for the permanency hearing. Participants in the case consultation must include:

(i) the case planner and/or the child's caseworker;

(ii) the child's parent(s), unless the parent has had his or her parental rights to the child terminated or unless it can be documented that one or both of them are unwilling or unable to attend;

(iii) each child who is at least 10 but less than 14 years of age, unless it can be documented that the child is unwilling to attend, or it can be demonstrated that such attendance would not be in the child's best interests;

(iv) each child 14 years of age or older in accordance with the standards set forth in section 428.3(i) of this Title:

(v) members of the case planning team chosen by the child who is 14 years of age or older in accordance with the standards set forth in section 428.3(i) of the Title; and

(vi) the child's foster parent, if the child is in placement in a foster boarding home; the child's pre-adoptive parent, if the child is in such placement; or the relative or other suitable person with whom the child has been placed directly by a court order.

(2) Wherever practicable, the case consultation participants must meet together at the same time, however, at a minimum a face-to-face case consultation must be held separately with each of the required participants.

(3) Efforts must be made to also consult with the case manager; the permanency discharge resource; key providers of service to the child and family; the child's school; in the case of an Indian child, the child's tribe, if known; and any other person identified by the parent(s), however, efforts to involve such additional person(s) must not delay the case consultation or preparation of the permanency hearing report.

(c) The purpose of such case consultation described in subdivision (b) is to assist with the development of the permanency hearing report and to address the following:

(1) review the progress and the status of the child who had been removed from his or her home, including the child's health and education;

(2) review the safety of the child in his or her current environment;

(3) review the appropriateness of the current placement, including whether such placement is the least restrictive environment that can meet the child's needs;

(4) assess whether it would be safe to return the child to his or her home, and assess the level of risk of the likelihood of abuse or maltreatment such return would entail;

(5) review the progress made by each parent toward successful implementation of the service plan and the child's permanency planning goal, unless the parent has had his or her parental rights to the child terminated;

(6) review the reasonable efforts made to assist with the achievement of the child's permanency planning goal;

(7) assess the need for modification or continuation of the current permanency planning goal;

(8) review the current service plan and any barriers to service delivery and assess the need to make modifications to support the safety, permanency and well-being of the child;

(9) review the current visiting plan and assess the need to make modifications to support family relationships;

(10) for a child who is not free for adoption, review the status of the concurrent permanency plan for the child, in the event the child is unlikely to be able to safely return home;

(11) review the status of any permanency discharge resource being considered for the child; and

(12) develop a recommendation as to whether the child needs to continue in placement or be discharged from such placement. If the child will be discharged from placement within the upcoming six months, develop a recommended discharge plan;

(13) for a child completely free for adoption with a goal of adoption, review the status of each adoption milestone, and assess progress toward achievement, as appropriate, including but not limited to recruitment efforts, adoption assistance/subsidy approval and overcoming any other barriers to finalization of the adoption; and

(14) for a child in foster care for whom the permanency planning goal is discharge to another planned living arrangement with a permanency resource, address the steps taken by the authorized agency to ensure that the child's foster parent(s) or the child care facility with whom or in which the child is placed is following the reasonable and prudent parent standard as set forth in section 441.25 of this Title and to ascertain whether the child has regular, ongoing opportunities to engage in age or developmentally appropriate activities, including by consulting with the child in an age-appropriate manner about the opportunities of the child to participate in such activities.

(d) The permanency hearing report, prior to filing with the court, must be developed by the responsible social services district or voluntary agency in accordance with a purchase of services agreement, and in consultation with appropriate district and voluntary staff, including but not limited to the social services district and/or agency attorney.

(e) The permanency hearing report must be prepared in the form and manner as required by OCFS.

(f) The permanency hearing report must be filed with the court and mailed to those parties required by section 1089 of the Family Court Act.

Part 430
Utilization Review for Foster Care
and Preventive Services

§430.9 Appropriate provision of mandated preventive services.

(a) For cases authorized for mandated preventive services for the first time after April 1, 1982, the provision of preventive services shall be considered mandated if one of the following standards, as set forth in subdivision (c), (d),

(e) or (g) of this section is met: the standard for the provision of mandated preventive services to clients at risk of placement; the standard for the provision of mandated preventive services to clients at risk of replacement in foster care; the standard for the provision of mandated preventive services to return children to their parents; or the standard for recertification of mandated preventive services. For cases receiving mandated preventive services before April 1, 1982, the standard for recertification of mandated preventive services, as set forth in subdivision (g) of this section, shall be met. In all other cases, the provision of preventive services shall be considered nonmandated and the decision to provide such services shall be made solely by the local social services district.

(b) General requirements. The appropriateness of the provision of mandated services shall be documented on the forms prescribed by the department in Part 428 of this Title according to the standards for documentation defined under the standards set forth in subdivision (c), (d), (e) or (g) of this section. These include the standard for the provision of mandated preventive services to clients at risk of placement, the standard for the provision of mandated preventive services to clients at risk of replacement in foster care, the standard for the provision of mandated preventive services to return children to their parents, and the standard for recertification of mandated preventive services. In the absence of documentation in the uniform case record, the provision of such services shall be deemed inappropriate.

(c) Standard for the provision of mandated preventive services to clients at risk of placement. The provision of preventive services shall be considered mandated when such services are essential to improve family relationships and prevent the placement of a child into foster care. The circumstances in which preventive services shall be considered essential for these purposes are the following:

(1) Health and safety of child.

(i) Circumstance. One or more children in the family has been subjected by the parents or caretakers within the 12-month period prior to the date of application for services to serious physical injury by other than accidental means, or to the risk of serious physical injury by other than accidental means, or to a serious impairment or risk of serious impairment of their physical, mental or emotional condition as a result of the failure of the parents or caretakers to exercise a minimum degree of care and such action by the parents has resulted in a determination that an allegation of abuse or maltreatment is indicated.

(ii) Documentation. The first uniform case record form required after the date of authorization for preventive services shall contain a description of instances within the 12 months immediately prior to the date on which the program choice "Preventive" is chosen when the child has been harmed emotionally or physically. The required uniform case record form shall contain a description of the type of harm which has resulted or shall indicate that, at the time of application for service, conditions existed which placed the child or siblings in danger of serious emotional or physical harm and contain a description of the type of physical or emotional harm which would have been likely to result from these conditions. The record shall also contain the date of indication.

(2) Parental refusal.

(i) Circumstance. The parents or caretakers have refused to maintain the child in the home or have expressed the intention of surrendering the child for adoption.

(ii) Documentation. The first uniform case record form required after the date of authorization for preventive services shall contain a description of the actions taken by the parents or caretakers which indicate a refusal to maintain the child in the home or shall include the date and a summary of the circumstances of the parents' or caretakers' verbal refusal or expression of intent to surrender the child.

(3) Parent unavailability.

(i) Circumstance. The child's parents or current caretakers have become unavailable due to:

(a) hospitalization;

(b) arrest, detainment or imprisonment;

(c) death; or

(d) the fact that their whereabouts are unknown.

(ii) Documentation. The first uniform case record form required after the date of authorization for preventive services shall contain a description of the reason for the parents' or caretakers' absence from the home, and the expected duration of the absence if the parents or caretakers are living and their whereabouts known. In the event of the death of the parents or caretakers or in the cases in which their whereabouts are unknown, such uniform case record form shall indicate the likelihood of finding a new permanent caretaker or the previous caretaker, and an estimated time in which that will be accomplished.

(4) Parent service need.

(i) Circumstance.

(a) The child is placed at risk of serious physical or emotional harm due to an emotional, mental, physical, or financial condition of the parent or caretaker which seriously impairs the parent's or caretaker's ability to care for the child; or

(b) a parent or caretaker has been diagnosed as having acquired immune deficiency syndrome (AIDS), human immunodeficiency virus (HIV)-related illness or HIV infection, as those terms are defined by the AIDS Institute of the State Department of Health and are contained in directives issued by the department from time to time, and such condition seriously impairs, or exacerbates other conditions which seriously impair, the parent's or caretaker's ability to care for his or her child, and places the child at risk of foster care placement.

(ii) Documentation. The first uniform case record form required after the date of authorization for preventive services must contain:

(a) description of the type of emotional, physical, or mental condition which is impairing the parent's functioning, the functions which are impaired, and instances in which the impairment has seriously harmed the child emotionally or physically or has placed the child in danger of such harm, or a summary of what financial needs, including a lack of adequate housing, impairs the parents' or caretakers' ability to care for the child adequately, and what specific risk to the child exists if such needs are not met; or

(b) a medical report showing a diagnosis by a licensed physician that a parent or caretaker has AIDS, HIV-related illness or HIV infection and a description of how this condition seriously impairs, or exacerbates other conditions which seriously impair, the parent's or caretaker's ability to care for his or her child and places the child at risk of foster care placement. Records which include information regarding AIDS, HIV-related illness or HIV infection must be maintained in accordance with subpart 360-8 and section 431.7 of this Title.

(5) Child services needs.

(i) Circumstances. The child has special needs for supervision or services which cannot be adequately met by the child's parents or caretakers without the aid of intensive services and this results in the child being at risk of foster care placement without such services. This need for services is the result of one of the following:

(a) the child has a diagnosed or diagnosable physical, mental or emotional condition which severely impairs the child's ability to carry out daily, age-appropriate activities; or

(b) the child's behavior, although not dangerous, results in severe management problems in the home, the school or the community;

(c) the child's behavior presents a serious danger to other people or to the child himself; or

(d) the child is the subject of a petition under article 7 of the Family Court Act, or has been determined by the assessment service established pursuant to section 243-a of the Executive Law, or by the probation service where no such assessment service has been designated, to be at risk of being the subject of such a petition, and one of the following conditions applies:

(1) the family would have been eligible for preventive services at some time in the past, if application had been made;

(2) some child in the family has been placed in foster care at some time in the past;

(3) the child's behavior leading to the filing of the petition or to the risk of such filing is similar to the behavior described in clause (b) of this subparagraph but is less severe and this behavior has been exhibited over a period exceeding six months; or

(4) the family, or some member of the family has in the past or is currently receiving services from the social services district, the local mental health or mental retardation agency, the probation service, or the youth board for at least six months. The services which are or have been provided by the social services district must be those services which are set forth in the district's consolidated services plan; or

(e) the child has been diagnosed as having AIDS, HIV-related illness or HIV infection. The condition which results in such diagnosis must impair the child's ability to carry out daily, age-appropriate activities or result in a need for supportive services, other than medical or health-related services, to allow the parents or caretakers to maintain the child in their home.

(ii) Documentation. The first uniform case record form required after the date of authorization for preventive services shall show the services which are to be provided to the child and/or other family members which will prevent the child's placement in foster care and assist in alleviating the behavior or condition or assist the parents or caretakers in dealing with the child's behavior or condition. In addition, such uniform case record form shall contain:

(a) a description of behavior patterns or limitations which illustrate a serious impairment of the child's ability to carry out everyday activities at an age-appropriate level. A diagnosis by a licensed psychiatrist or psychologist, including a permanently certified school psychologist, or by a certified social worker other than the case manager or case planner shall be deemed appropriate documentation for this subparagraph;

(b) a description of repeated instances of behavior within the 12 months immediately prior to the date on which the program choice "Preventive" is chosen in which the child has exhibited behaviors leading to severe management problems in the home, school or community;

(c) a description of instances within the 12 months immediately prior to the date on which the program choice "Preventive" is chosen in which the child has intentionally harmed or attempted to harm other persons or himself, or indicate that a licensed psychiatrist or psychologist, including a school psychologist with a master's degree in psychology, or a certified social worker other than the case manager or case planner has stated in writing that the child presents a serious danger to himself or others; or

(d) a description of the contents of any petition filed, pursuant to article 7 of the Family Court Act, concerning the child, including the allegations made, the date of filing, and the person or persons who filed, or a summary of the determination of the assessment service or the probation service that the child is at risk of becoming the subject of such a petition, and either:

(1) a description of the circumstances in which the family would have been eligible for preventive services in the past, including the standard under which it would have qualified;

(2) a description of the circumstances which led to the placement of any child in the family in foster care, including the dates of placement, which child was placed, and the reason for placement;

(3) a description of instances of behavior similar to that leading to the filing of the petition, extending over a period of at least six months, and presenting a potential for severe management problems in the home, school or community; or

(4) a description of the services received by the family, including the time period during which the services were provided, the family member or members receiving services, the agency providing services, and the reason the services were sought; or

(e) a description of the condition(s) resulting from the child having AIDS, HIV-related illness or HIV infection, and examples of instances in which the condition(s) impairs the child's ability to carry out daily, age-appropriate activities or results in a need for supportive services, other than medical or health-related services, to allow the parents or caretakers to maintain the child in their home. A medical report showing the relevant diagnosis by a licensed physician must also be included as part of the documentation for this subparagraph. Records which include information regarding AIDS, HIV-related illness or HIV infection must be maintained in accordance with subpart 360-8 and section 431.7 of this Title.

(6) Pregnancy.

(i) Circumstance. A woman is pregnant or has given birth and has shown an inability to provide adequate care for her unborn or infant child.

(ii) Documentation. The first uniform case record form required after the date of authorization for preventive services shall indicate whether the woman is pregnant or has given birth and shall include a description of the parental functions which the woman is unable to perform. In addition, such uniform case record form shall show that services are to be delivered to the woman which will assist her in performing these functions.

(d) Standard for the provision of mandated preventive services to clients at risk of replacement in foster care. The provision of preventive services shall be considered mandated when such services are essential to prevent the replacement of a child into foster care. The circumstances in which preventive services shall be considered essential for these purposes include all of the circumstances described in the standard for the provision of mandated preventive services to clients at risk of placement, as set forth in subdivision (c) of this section, and all of the following circumstances.

(1) Family Court contact.

(i) Circumstance. The child is the subject of a juvenile delinquency or persons in need of supervision petition, or has been determined by the Family Court Intake or Family Court Probation Service to be at risk of being the subject of such a petition.

(ii) Documentation. The first uniform case record form required after the date of authorization for preventive services shall include a description of the child's previous placement, and a description of the petition or other disposition by the Family Court, including the date of the petition or disposition.

(2) Unplanned discharge.

(i) Circumstance. The child has been discharged from foster care within the two years immediately prior to the date of application for services and that discharge took place at least three months prior to the anticipated discharge date and without the achievement of all the client goals set forth in the service plan as required by the uniform case record and being pursued at the time of discharge.

(ii) Documentation. The first uniform case record form required after the date of authorization for preventive services shall contain a description of the child's previous placement, including the dates during which the child was in foster care, show the anticipated discharge date at the time of discharge, and describe which client goals could not be met due to the early discharge. If no service plan had been completed during the previous placement, information in the progress notes shall be used to the extent possible.

(3) Recurrence of reason for placement.

(i) Circumstance. The child or the parents or caretakers have exhibited a pattern of behavior or a condition which is substantially similar to one or more of the behaviors or conditions which contributed to the child's previous placement in foster care and which is likely to lead to the necessity of replacement of the child.

(ii) Documentation. The first uniform case record form required after the date of authorization for preventive services shall contain a description of the child's previous placement, including the dates and reason for placement, contain a description of the behavior or circumstances occurring at the time of application for services which are similar to the factors contributing to the original placement, and provide reasons why this behavior or condition is likely to become serious.

(e) Standard for the provision of mandated preventive services to return children to their parents.

(1) The provision of preventive services, other than housing services, will be considered mandated to safely return a child currently in foster care to his/her parents sooner than would otherwise be possible, only if all of the conditions in subparagraphs (i), (ii) and (iii) of this paragraph are met.

(i) Service appropriateness.

(a) Condition. The preventive services provided must be directly related to one or more of the reasons the child is currently in foster care.

(b) Documentation. The most recent assessment and service plan required by the uniform case record must show only preventive services to be delivered to the child and family which relate to one or more documented reasons establishing or maintaining the necessity of the child's placement.

(ii) Discharge plan.

(a) Condition. Discharge of the child from foster care must be anticipated within six months.

(b) Documentation. The required uniform case record form must show the anticipated discharge dates to be in conformance with the standard in subparagraph (i) of this paragraph and must include a service plan for discharge consistent with the goals set forth in the most recent service plan as required by the uniform case record.

(iii) Safety and appropriateness.

(a) Condition. Return to the child's parents or caretakers may only occur where the placement will be safe and appropriate.

(b) Documentation. The most recent assessment and service plan required by the uniform case record must include a written consideration and determination that return of the child to his/her parents or caretakers will be safe and appropriate.

(2) The provision of housing services as defined in section 423.2(b)(16) of this Part, will be considered mandated to discharge a child from foster care to his/her parents or caretakers only if the conditions in subparagraphs (i), (ii) and (iii) of this paragraph are met.

(i) Service appropriateness.

(a) Condition. At the time housing services are authorized, the case manager must determine that the primary factor preventing the discharge of the child from foster care is the family's lack of adequate housing.

(b) Documentation. Such determination can be made only in the following circumstances as documented in the first uniform case record form due after authorization for housing services:

(1) the child has been in foster care at least 30 days and the child can be safely returned to the parents or caretakers if housing services are provided, or the child has been in foster care for any length of time and since the placement date the family has moved to a different residence that is inadequate to house the child and the child can be safely returned to the parents or caretakers if housing services and any other available preventive services are provided;

(2) there is a description of the family's housing situation and a determination has been made that one or more of the following circumstances exist: the family is homeless or is residing temporarily in a shelter, hotel/motel, or other temporary housing; the family is residing in its own home, in a room and board situation or in the home of friends or relatives and that by the addition of the child to be discharged to the family would exceed the capacity of such residence as specified in local law, ordinances, or rules and regulations, would result in eviction or would create an unreasonable and unsafe degree of overcrowding as determined by the case manager; and family has a home, however rent or mortgage arrears places the family at imminent risk of losing the home; the family is residing in a building which is the subject of a vacate order; or the condition of the family's home poses a health and safety risk that would place the children to be discharged at imminent risk of harm; and

(3) where appropriate, there is a description of the home that the family has moved into or will move into in order for the child to be returned, or if a

home has not yet been located the type of home the family will need, in order to provide adequate housing for the child(ren) to be returned safely.

(ii) Discharge plan.

(a) Discharge of the child from foster care must occur no later than two months after housing services are authorized, or paid or, where relevant, adequate housing was located, provided and, if necessary renovated, such that the child could be safely discharged to such housing. Where adequate housing is made available and the child is not discharged from care, the reason for the child remaining in care will be deemed to be due to a factor other than inadequate housing and housing services must be terminated.

(b) Documentation. The uniform case record must document the actual date of discharge, the date that housing services were authorized or paid and, if relevant, the date adequate housing was located, renovated and provided. If the child is not discharged within two months of either the authorization date of such services or the actual provision of adequate housing, the case record must document the specific circumstances which prevented the child's discharge from care, and a termination date no later than two months after either the date of the authorization of housing services or the date adequate housing was made available for the family to move in.

(iii) Safety and appropriateness.

(a) Condition. Return to the child's parents or caretakers may only occur where the placement will be safe and appropriate.

(b) Documentation. The most recent assessment and service plan required by the uniform case record must include a written consideration and determination that return of the child to his/her parents or caretakers will be safe and appropriate.

(f) Standard for the provision of housing services as a mandated preventive service to children with a goal of discharge to another planned living arrangement with a permanency resource.

(1) Service appropriateness.

(i) Condition. The provision of housing services as a preventive service will be considered mandated to discharge a child to another planned living arrangement with a permanency resource only if:

(a) the case manager has determined that housing services, as defined in section 423.2(b)(16) of this Title, are necessary and such services have been authorized; and

(b) the case manager has determined that, at the time housing services are authorized, the child has been in foster care at least 90 days, is prepared for discharge to another planned living arrangement with a permanency resource and can be discharged only if housing services are provided.

(ii) Documentation. The required uniform case record form must include a description of the home that has been located or if none has been located the type of home the child will need in order to be discharged from foster care.

(2) Discharge plan.

(i) Discharge of the child from foster care must occur no later than two months after housing services are authorized, unless an unforeseen circumstance, other than the child's inability to locate adequate housing, occurs and results in the case manager's determination that discharge must be postponed. In such instances, the reason for the child remaining in care will be deemed to be due to a factor other than inadequate housing and housing services must be terminated.

(ii) Documentation. The uniform case record must document the actual date of discharge and the date that housing services were authorized, paid and, if relevant, the date adequate housing was located, renovated and provided. If the child is not discharged within two months of either the authorization date of such services or the actual provision of adequate housing, the case record must document the specific circumstances which prevented the child's discharge from care and a termination date no later than two months after either the date of authorization or the date adequate housing was made available.

(g) Court orders. Notwithstanding any other provision of this section, the provision of preventive services shall be considered mandated when placement of the child in foster care has been ordered by the Family Court but such order has been stayed or reversed upon an appeal or a request for rehearing by the local department of social services. In addition, the provision of preventive services shall be considered mandated when a Family Court orders such services to be provided.

(h) Standard for the recertification of mandated preventive services.

(1) The provision of preventive services, other than those described in paragraph (2) of this subdivision, for a period beyond the initial six-month eligibility period will be considered mandated only if the most recent assessment and service plan required by the uniform case record for the family and the child indicates that not all client goals which are related to the reasons establishing the initial mandate for preventive services and which are currently being pursued have been achieved, or that removal of services at the present time would lead to a deterioration of the progress made.

(2) The provision of housing services as defined in section 423.2(b)(16) of this Title beyond the initial six-month eligibility period will be considered mandated only if the most recent assessment and service plan required by the uniform case record for the family and the child indicates that termination of the housing services would result in the family's inability to maintain or secure adequate housing. In no case may the provision of housing services exceed a period of 36 months commencing on the date housing services were authorized and provided. Housing services may not be provided as a nonmandated preventive service.

(i) Standard for the provision of mandated preventive services for children placed in designated emergency foster family boarding homes.

(1) Standard. The provision of preventive services is mandated if a child is placed in a designated emergency foster family boarding home as defined in section 446.2 of this Title and is expected at the time of placement to return home within 60 days. If the child does not return home within 60 days as initially planned, the continued provision of preventive services may not be considered mandated, unless he or she meets the eligibility requirements of subdivision (e) of this section.

(2) Documentation. The required uniform case record form must show that preventive services are being provided for a child who is expected at the time of placement to return home within 60 days after entering care in a designated emergency foster family boarding home.

(j) Standard for the provision of mandated preventive services as a follow-up service for children discharged from designated emergency foster family boarding home care.

(1) Standard. The provision of preventive services is mandated as a follow-up service for six months, including the time the child was in a designated emergency foster family boarding home care, if a child is returned

home within 60 days after entering designated emergency foster family boarding home care.

(2) Documentation. The required uniform case record form must indicate the child's discharge date from a designated emergency foster family boarding home and the follow-up preventive services to be provided to the child and family.

§430.10 Necessity of placement.

(a) General requirements.

(1) For purposes of this section, the placement of a child in foster care after April 1, 1982, shall be considered necessary if the standard for necessary activities prior to the placement and the standard for placement, as set forth in subdivisions (b)-(c) of this section, are met.

(2) The necessity of a child's placement shall be documented on the forms prescribed by the department in Part 428 of this Title according to the standards for documentation defined under the standard for necessary activities prior to placement and the standard for placement as set forth in subdivisions (b) and (c) of this section. In the absence of documentation in the uniform case record for the standard for placement, the placement shall be deemed unnecessary. To the extent permitted by the Mental Hygiene Law and the regulations of the Office of Mental Health and the Office of Mental Retardation and Developmental Disabilities, social services officials shall obtain copies of the case records and service plans and any updates to such records and plans for children whose care and custody have been transferred to such officials and who are receiving care in facilities operated or supervised by such offices. Such records, plans and updates shall be made a part of the uniform case record. It shall be the responsibility of the district to show that the standard for necessary activities prior to placement has been met, and a failure to provide evidence that this standard has been met shall be deemed equivalent to a failure to meet the standard.

(b) Standard for necessary activities prior to placement. For each foster care placement, the district shall:

(1) provide preventive services to the family and child prior to placement, unless the offer of preventive services has been refused or the placement is the result of a court order or due to the circumstance described as health and safety of the child as defined in paragraphs (c)(1) and (d)(2) of this section or unless the parents or caretakers are dead, their whereabouts unknown, or their absence is anticipated to be longer than six months or the child has been placed in a facility operated or supervised by the Office of Mental Health or Office of Mental Retardation and Developmental Disabilities;

(2) attempt prior to the placement of a child in foster care to locate adequate alternative living arrangements with a relative or family friend which would enable the child to avoid foster care placement, unless the child is placed as a result of a court order or surrender agreement as defined in paragraphs (d)(2) and (c)(2) of this section or the child has been placed in a facility operated or supervised by the Office of Mental Health or Office of Mental Retardation and Developmental Disabilities;

(3) document in the first uniform case record form required after the date of authorization for foster care services that preventive services have been offered and the reasons why they were not able to avert the placement, except when the placement is the result of a court order or due to the circumstances described as health and safety of the child, as defined in paragraphs (d)(2) and (c)(1) of this section, or when a child is placed in a facility operated or supervised by the

Office of Mental Health or Office of Mental Retardation and Developmental Disabilities, or when the child's parents or caretakers are dead, their whereabouts are unknown, or their absence is expected to last longer than six months, and that no adequate alternative arrangements are available except in placements resulting from court orders or surrender agreements, as defined in paragraphs (d)(2) and (c)(2) of this section or when a child is placed in a facility operated or supervised by the Office of Mental Health or Office of Mental Retardation and Developmental Disabilities;

(4) prior to placing in foster care the child or children of a minor parent who is in foster care, attempt to place such child or children in the same foster family home or residential facility without assuming care and custody of the child or children of the minor parent, unless foster care placement is necessitated by a court order as described in paragraph (d) (2) of this section; and

(5) document in the first uniform case record form required after the date of authorization for foster care services that it was not possible to place the child or children of a minor parent in foster care with the minor parent; or why it was necessary to seek care and custody of such child or children despite placing the minor parent and his or her child or children in the same foster family home or residential facility.

(c) Standard for placement. Placement of a child in foster care shall occur when removal from the home is essential for ensuring the child receives proper care, nurturance or treatment. The circumstances in which placement may be considered essential for this purpose are the following:

(1) Health and safety of child.

(i) Circumstance. The child or a sibling has been subjected by the parents or caretakers, within the 12 months immediately prior to the date on which the program choice "Placement" is selected, to serious physical injury by other than accidental means, or to risk of serious physical injury by other than accidental means, or to serious impairment of their physical, mental or emotional condition as a result of the failure of the parents or caretakers to exercise a minimum degree of care.

(ii) Documentation.

(a) The first uniform case record form required after the date of authorization for foster care services shall contain a description of instances within the 12 months immediately prior to the date on which the program choice "Placement" is selected in which the child has been harmed emotionally or physically and the type of harm which has resulted, or shall indicate that at the time of placement conditions existed which placed the child or siblings in danger of serious emotional or physical harm which would have been likely to result from these conditions.

(b) If the child has continued in placement beyond the date the first service plan review is required, the most recent assessment and service plan required by the uniform case record shall indicate that conditions persist which, if the child were to be returned home, would continue to place the child in danger of serious physical or emotional harm. In order to establish a continuing danger to the child, the assessment and service plan shall cite one or more of the following factors: the parents' or caretakers' willingness to maintain regular contact with the child, their behavior during visits, their response to services offered or provided by the district or other involved agencies, their expressed willingness to take the child home and to plan for his or her welfare, the present status of environmental or any other factors which contributed to the original problems which necessitated the placement, and the overall progress of the parent toward the accomplishment of the goals established in the most recent service plan required by the uniform case record.

(2) Parental refusal or surrender.

(i) Circumstance. The parent or caretakers refuse to maintain the child in the home or have voluntarily surrendered the child for adoption.

(ii) Documentation.

(a) The first uniform case record form required after the date of authorization for foster care services shall show that, prior to the placement, the local social services district attempted without success to persuade the parents or caretakers to maintain the child in the home, and offered services to assist in maintain ing the child in the home and that these services were refused. The most recent assessment and service plan required by the uniform case record shall show that the district continues to make such efforts, and that these efforts continue to fail and/or be refused for as long as the child's discharge objective is "return to parents" or until the parents have signed a surrender agreement.

(b) If a surrender has been completed, the assessment and service plan required by the uniform case record shall also:

(1) include a copy of the surrender agreement, or a description of the date and conditions of the agreement;

(2) indicate whether the agreement of any other putative parent is necessary before the child can be adopted;

(3) document efforts beginning within 30 days of the date of the surrender agreement to locate and assess the suitability to care for the child of any other putative parent whose agreement is necessary before the child can be adopted; and

(4) show efforts, if the parent is suitable, to place the child with the parent, if the other parent is unsuitable, to obtain a surrender agreement from this person or as soon as legally appropriate, to initiate an action to terminate this person's parental rights pursuant to section 384-b of the Social Services Law, or if the parent's whereabouts are not known and efforts to locate him or her are unsuccessful, to initiate an action to terminate this parent's rights on the basis of abandonment once he or she has failed to maintain contact with the child or the child's caretakers for a six-month period, pursuant to section 384-b of the Social Services Law.

(3) Parent unavailability.

(i) Circumstance. The child's parents or caretakers are unavailable due to:

(a) hospitalization;

(b) arrest, detainment or imprisonment;

(c) death; or

(d) the fact that their whereabouts are unknown.

(ii) Documentation.

(a) The first uniform case record form required after the date of authorization for foster care services shall contain the reason for the absence of the parents and the expected duration of that absence if the parents or caretakers are living and their whereabouts known, and a summary of the efforts to find an alternative living arrangement for the child, as defined in subdivision (b) of this section.

(b) If the parents or caretakers are living and their whereabouts known, and if the child has continued in placement beyond the date the first service plan review is required, the most recent assessment and service plan required by the uniform case record shall indicate whether any change has occurred in the reason for the parents' or caretakers' absence or in the expected duration of that absence. For parents or caretakers whose whereabouts are unknown, the most recent assessment and service plan required by the uniform case record shall indicate what progress has been made in attempting to locate them. When parental rights have been terminated, no further documentation is required to establish necessity of placement.

(4) Parent service needs.

(i) Circumstance. The child is placed at risk of serious physical or emotional harm due to an emotional, mental or physical condition of the parents or caretakers, which seriously impairs the parents' or caretakers' ability to care for the child.

(ii) Documentation.

• (a) The first uniform case record form required after the date of authorization for foster care services shall contain documentation of the specific type and degree of parental impairment and a summary of instances in which the parental impairment seriously harms the child emotionally or physically or has placed the child in danger of such harm.

(b) If the child has continued in care beyond the date the first service plan review is required, the most recent assessment and service plan required by the uniform case record shall show that the impairment persists and that it would continue to pose a risk of serious emotional or physical harm to the child if he or she were to return home. In order to establish a continuing danger to the child, such assessment and service plan shall cite one or more of the following factors: the parents' or caretakers' willingness to maintain regular contact with the child, their behavior during visits, the adequacy of and their response to services offered or provided by the district or other involved agencies, their expressed willingness to take the child home and to plan for his or her welfare, the present status of the condition which necessitated the placement, and the overall progress of the parent toward the accomplishment of the goals established in the service plan.

(5) Child service needs.

(i) Circumstance. The child has special needs for supervision or services which cannot be adequately met by the child's parents or caretakers, even with the aid of intensive services in the home. This need for services is the result of one of the following:

(a) The child has a diagnosed or diagnosable, physical, mental or emotional condition which severely impairs the child's ability to carry out daily, age-appropriate activities and which presents treatment needs which are too extensive or specialized for the child's parents to be able to maintain the child in the home.

(b) The child's behavior, although not dangerous, cannot be managed in the home, the school, or the community, even with extensive support to the parents and child.

(c) The child's behavior presents a serious danger to other people or to the child himself.

(d) The child is eligible for admission to a facility operated or supervised by the Office of Mental Health or the Office of Mental Retardation and Developmental Disabilities.

(ii) Documentation. The most recent assessment and service plan required by the uniform case record shall show the services which are to be provided to the child which will assist in alleviating the child's behavior or condition.

(a) The first uniform case record form required after the date of authorization for foster care services, shall contain:

(1) a description of behavior patterns which inhibit the child's ability to carry out everyday activities in school, home or community; diagnosis by a licensed psychiatrist or psychologist, including a permanently certified school psychologist, or by a certified social worker other than the case manager or case planner, shall be deemed appropriate documentation for this subparagraph;

(2) a description of repeated instances of behaviors which cannot be managed in the home, the school, or the community, and efforts to ameliorate these problems through the provision of extensive support services; or

(3) a summary of instances within the 12 months immediately prior to the date on which the program choice "Placement" is chosen in which the child has intentionally harmed or attempted to harm other persons or himself, or indicate that a licensed psychiatrist or psychologist, including a permanently certified school psychologist, or a certified social worker other than the case manager or case planner, has stated, in writing, that the child presents a serious danger to himself or others.

(b) If the child has continued in placement beyond the date at which the service plan review is required, the most recent assessment and service plan required by the uniform case record shall indicate that the behavior or condition continues at the present to require services at a level sufficient to justify continued placement, including:

(1) examples or a description of the child's recent behavior which illustrates that the child continues to require the provision of an extensive set of services and that without these services his behavior would be cause for placement; and

(2) the reasons why necessary services or supervision still cannot be provided in the child's home.

(c) If the behavior which led to the placement has stopped or greatly diminished over a six-month period, the most recent assessment and service plan required by the uniform case record shall show which services needed by the child to prevent or diminish the behavior cannot be provided in the home and the reasons why they cannot be provided.

(d) If a child has been placed in a facility operated or supervised by the Office of Mental Health or the Office of Mental Retardation and Developmental Disabilities, documentation in the uniform case record which indicates that the child has been admitted to such facility shall be deemed to fulfill the documentation requirements of this subparagraph.

(6) Pregnancy.

(i) Circumstance. A woman is pregnant or has given birth, and foster care placement would enable the mother and child to remain together and would significantly aid the mother in preparing to assume responsibility to care for her child or in making a decision to surrender the child for adoption.

(ii) Documentation. The first uniform case record form required after the date of authorization for foster care services shall:

(a) indicate whether the woman is pregnant or has given birth; and

(b) contain a description of the parental functions which the woman is unable to perform, as well as the availability of the woman's parents or other relatives as resources.

(d) Notwithstanding any other provisions of this section, reimbursement shall not be withheld for any placement undertaken for the following reasons:

(1) Diagnostic evaluation. The child has been placed in a foster care program for no longer than 90 days specifically for the purpose of conducting

a comprehensive diagnostic evaluation of the child. The first uniform case record form required after placement in the foster care program shall indicate the specific questions to be answered by the evaluation, examples of the child's behavior or problems which necessitate this type of evaluation for this child, the reasons why the evaluation could not be completed while the child remains at home, and a description of the evaluation results when they become available.

(2) Court-ordered placement. The child was placed or remanded to the custody of the Commissioner of Social Services by the Family Court and foster care placement has been ordered by the court pursuant to article 3, 7, 10, 10-B or 10-C of the Family Court Act. Documentation shall include a copy of the court order or a description of the date and condition of the order in the first uniform case record form required after the court-ordered placement.

(e) Notwithstanding any other provisions of this section, reimbursement cannot be withheld for any placement that is continued beyond 90 days where a determination has been made by the case manager and documented in the assessment and service plan required in the uniform case record that the primary factor necessitating continued placement is the family's lack of adequate housing and that preventive services, including housing services as defined in subdivision (16) of section 423.2(b) of this Title, have been authorized to facilitate the child's or children's discharge from care and the child or children will be or have been discharged within two months of the date of authorization of such services or the date adequate housing is made available to the family.

§430.11 Appropriateness of placement.

(a) The type and level of a foster care placement for a particular child shall be considered appropriate for the purposes of this section if the standard for continuity in the child's environment and the standards for appropriate level of placement, as set forth in subdivisions (c) and (d) of this section, are met.

(b) The requirements of this section shall pertain to all children placed in foster care for whom a uniform case record, as described in Part 428 of this Title, is required. The appropriateness of a foster care placement shall be documented on the forms prescribed by the department in Part 428, according to the standards for documentation defined in the standard for continuity in the child's environment and the standards for appropriate level of placement, as set forth in subdivisions (c) and (d) of this section. In the absence of documentation in the uniform case record, the placement shall be deemed inappropriate.

(c) Continuity in the child's environment.

(1) (i) Standard. Whenever possible, a child shall be placed in a foster care setting which permits the child to retain contact with the persons, groups and institutions with which the child was involved while living with his or her parents, and to which the child will be discharged. It shall be deemed inappropriate to place a child in a setting which conforms with this standard only if the child's service needs can only be met in another available setting at the same or lesser level of care. The initial placement of the child into foster care and all subsequent placements must take into account the appropriateness of the child's existing educational setting and the proximity of such setting to the child's placement location. When it is in the best interests of the foster child to continue to be enrolled in the same school in which the child is currently enrolled, the agency with case management, case planning or casework

responsibility for the foster child must coordinate with applicable local school authorities to ensure that the child remains in such school. When it is not in the best interests of the foster child to continue to be enrolled in the same school in which the child is currently enrolled, the agency with case management, case planning or casework responsibility for the foster child must coordinate with applicable local school authorities where the foster child is placed in order that the foster child is provided with immediate and appropriate enrollment in a new school; and the agency with case management, case planning or casework responsibility for the foster child must coordinate with applicable local school authorities where the foster child previously attended in order that all of the applicable school records of the child are provided to the new school.

(ii) Any Indian child who is placed into foster care pursuant to the provisions of section 384, 384-a or 384-b of the Social Services Law or article 3, 7, 10, 10-B or 10-C of the Family Court Act shall be placed in the least restrictive setting which most approximates a family and in which his or her special needs, if any, may be met. Placement in accordance with the order of preference set forth in subdivision (f) of section 431.18 of this Title supersedes other continuity factors in the placement of an Indian child. Any placement made pursuant to this subparagraph shall, in the absence of good cause to the contrary, as defined in section 431.18(f)(2) or (g)(2) of this Title, be made according to the preferences set forth in section 431.18(f) of this Title.

(2) Documentation. The uniform case record, as described in Part 428 of this Title, shall:

(i) show in the first uniform case record form required after the child's placement in his current setting that the child has been placed in a setting which enables him or her to maintain ties to his or her previous school, neighborhood, peers and family members, or show the reasons why such placement was not practicable or in the best interests of the child;

(ii) show in the first visiting plan required by the uniform case record after the child's placement in his current setting that biweekly visits with the parents or significant others are possible or the reasons why a placement was chosen which made such visits impossible;

(iii) show in the first uniform case record form required after the child's placement in his current setting that the child is placed under the supervision of a person or persons of a religious faith the same as that of the child or is placed with an agency, association, corporation, society or institution which is under the control of an incorporated or unincorporated church, as defined in article one of the Religious Corporation Law, representing a religious faith the same as that of the child, or, if that is not possible, show that the child's religious faith will be protected, and preserved in the current setting, or show the reasons why placement was not practicable or in the best interests of the child;

(iv) (Reserved)

(v) for foster care placement involving Indian children, contain documentation which evidences the efforts made by social services districts to comply with the order of preference set forth in subdivision (f) of section 431.18 of this Title. Information concerning efforts by social services districts to comply with the order of preference contained in the case record shall be made available to the Indian child's tribe and the Secretary of Interior upon request;

(vi) if the setting is a foster family home or agency-operated boarding home, document in the first uniform case record form required after the placement of the child in the current setting that a determination has been made of the appropriateness of placing the child with his or her siblings or half-siblings in accordance with the provisions of section 431.10 of this Part;

(vii) the uniform case record must include a written consideration of the safety and appropriateness of the placement;

(viii) if the child has been placed in a foster care placement a substantial distance from the home of the parents of the child or in a state different from the state in which the parent's home is located, the uniform case record must contain documentation why such placement is in the best interests of the child; and

(ix) show in the uniform case record that efforts were made to keep the child in his or her current school, or where distance was a factor or the educational setting was inappropriate, that efforts were made to seek immediate enrollment in a new school and to arrange for timely transfer of school records.

(Eff. 5/18/16)

(3) For purposes of paragraphs (1) and (2) of this subdivision, the term Indian child shall have the meaning which is given to such term by subdivision (a) of section 431.18 of this Title.

(4) Within 30 days after the removal of a child from the custody of the child's parent or parents, or earlier where directed by the court, or as required by section 384-a of the Social Services Law, the social services district must exercise due diligence in identifying all of the child's grandparents, all parents of a sibling of the child where such parent has legal custody of the sibling, and other adult relatives, including adult relatives suggested by the child's parent or parents, with the exception of grandparents, parents of a sibling of the child where the parent has legal custody of the sibling and/or other identified relatives with a history of family or domestic violence. The social services district must provide the child's grandparents, parents of a sibling of the child where such parent has legal custody of the sibling and other identified relatives with notification that the child has been or is being removed from the child's parents and which explains the options under which the grandparents, parents of a sibling of the child where such parent has legal custody of the sibling and other relatives may provide care of the child, whether through foster care or direct legal custody or guardianship, and any options that may be lost by the failure to respond to such notification in a timely manner. The identification and notification efforts made in accordance with this paragraph must be documented in the child's uniform case record as required by section 428.5 (c)(10)(viii) of this Title. For the purpose of this paragraph, a sibling includes a sibling or half-sibling related through blood or adoption.

(d) Standard for appropriate level of placement.

(1) The most appropriate level of placement for each child will always be considered to be the least restrictive and most homelike setting in which the child can be maintained safely and receive all services specified in his or her service plan.

(2) Family foster homes and agency boarding homes. The placement of a child in a foster family home or an agency boarding home shall be considered placement at an appropriate level for the purposes of this section, if the services required in the most recent assessment and service plan required by the uniform case record are available to the child as part of the placement.

(3) Group homes and group residences.

(i) Standard. The placement of a child in a group home or group residence shall be considered placement at an appropriate level of care for the purposes of this section only if:

(a) the child is 10 years of age or older and the necessity of the child's placement is based, in whole or in part, on one or both of the reasons described in paragraphs (c)(5) and (6) of section 430.10 of this Part, as child service needs or pregnancy; and

(b) the services or supervision needed by the child cannot currently be provided in a foster boarding home setting.

(ii) Documentation. The first uniform case record form required after the placement of the child in the current setting shall show the child's age and contain adequate documentation of the necessity of placement, and shall specify the services needed by the child which cannot be provided in a family foster home or agency boarding home.

(iii) Subparagraph (i) of this paragraph notwithstanding, the placement of any child 10 years of age or older in a group home or group residence shall be deemed placement at an appropriate level even when the services or supervision needed by the child which cannot be provided in a foster boarding home setting cannot be specified, if one or more previous placements in family foster homes or agency boarding homes have been terminated due to the child's refusal to stay in the home or the foster parents' refusal is due to the child's behavior. In this event, the first uniform case record form required after the placement of the child in the current setting shall contain a description of the previous placements and the reasons for their terminations.

(iv) Subparagraph (i) of this paragraph notwithstanding, the placement of any child in a group home or group residence shall be deemed placement at an appropriate level if such placement is necessary for the child to remain with his mother and/or siblings. In this event the first uniform case record form required after the placement of the child in the current setting shall indicate:

(a) that the child or his mother requires foster care due to pregnancy, as defined in paragraph (c)(6) of section 430.10 of this Part; or

(b) that one or more siblings requires care in a group home or group residence and that it is in the best interests of the child to maintain him or her with his or her siblings.

(v) Subparagraph (i) of this paragraph notwithstanding, the placement of any child 10 years of age or older in a group home or group residence shall be deemed placement at an appropriate level for the purposes of this section, if the child has been a victim of incest and this is shown in the first uniform case record form required after the placement of the child in the current setting to be one of the reasons for placement.

(vi) Subparagraph (i) of this paragraph notwithstanding, the placement of any child 10 years of age or older in a group home or group residence shall be deemed placement at an appropriate level, if the first uniform case record form required after the placement of the child in the current setting shows that the parents resist placement of the child in a foster family home or agency boarding home, that the group home or group residence would provide better access to the parents than would a foster family home or agency boarding home, that the child's permanency planning goal is discharge to parents, and that the State Commissioner of Social Services or his or her representative has approved placement in this setting.

(4) Institutional placement.

(i) Standard. The placement of a child in an institution, as defined in Part 442 of this Title, other than a group residence, shall be considered placement at an appropriate level for the purposes of this section only if the child is 12 years of age or older and:

(a) the necessity of the child's placement is based, in whole or in part, on one or more reasons described in paragraph (c)(5) of section 430.10 of this Part as child service needs; and

(b) if services or a level of supervision are needed by the child which cannot currently be provided in any other level of care and which can be provided in the institution in which the child is placed.

(ii) Documentation. The first uniform case record form required after the placement of the child in the current setting shall show the age of the child, and contain adequate documentation of the necessity of placement, which services or level of supervision needed by the child cannot currently be provided in any other level of care, and efforts to obtain necessary services or supervision in a less restrictive level of care.

(5) Supervised independent living.

(i) Standard. The placement of a child in supervised independent living shall be considered placement at an appropriate level for the purposes of this section only if the child:

(a) is at least 16 years of age and (1) has been in foster care for at least 90 consecutive days during period immediately preceding the date on which the child entered the program, or (2) is in the care and custody of a social services official but has been discharged from foster care on a trial basis at the time that the child entered the program;

(b) has a permanency planning goal of another planned living arrangement with a permanency resource; and

(c) will be discharged from care within 12 months after placement in the program and has an established service plan for discharge; a child in a supervised independent living program may be discharged from care within 18 months after placement in the program if it is determined that the child would be unable to complete a vocational training or educational program if the child was discharged from the program to an alternative address within 12 months after placement in the program.

(ii) Documentation. The first uniform case record form required after placement of the child in the program must show that the child was at least 16 years of age and was in foster care for at least 90 consecutive days during the period immediately preceding the date on which the child was placed in supervised independent living, or was in the care and custody of a social services official but had been discharged from foster care on a trial basis at the time the child entered such program, that he or she has a permanency planning goal of another planned living arrangement with a permanency resource, and that the anticipated discharge date is no later than 12 months after the placement of the child in supervised independent living, unless the child will be unable to complete a vocational training or educational program if the child was discharged from the supervised independent living program to an alternative address. In such instances the discharge date must be no later than 18 months after the child entered the program, and documentation must be provided that details why the child would be unable to continue in the vocational/educational program if the child was discharged to an alternative address.

(6) Child placed in facilities operated or supervised by the Office of Mental Health or the Office of Mental Retardation and Developmental Disabilities.

(i) Standard. The placement of a child in a facility operated or supervised by the Office of Mental Health or Office of Mental Retardation and Developmental Disabilities shall be considered placement at an appropriate level of care for the purposes of this section only if the child meets the criteria for admission to a facility operated or supervised by the Office of Mental Health or Office of Mental Retardation and Developmental Disabilities.

(ii) Documentation. For children placed in facilities operated or supervised by the Office of Mental Health or Office of Mental Retardation and Developmental Disabilities, the name and location of such facility shall be included in the uniform case record. The inclusion of such information in the case record shall be deemed to fulfill the documentation requirements of this subparagraph.

(e) Court placements. Notwithstanding any other provision of this section, a placement shall not be subject to denial of reimbursement due to inappropriate placement if a court has ordered that the child be placed in that particular setting. The first uniform case record form required after the placement of the child in the current setting shall include either a copy of the court order or a description of the terms of the order. In the event that a utilization review of the case has been completed, and has found that the child's placement does not comply with the requirements of this section, other than that defined in this subdivision, the district shall petition the court for a rehearing of the case within 30 days of the notification to the district that the placement is not appropriate. The district shall submit the finding of the utilization review to the court as documentation for the court review.

(f) Notwithstanding any other provision of this section, the placement of a child under 10 years of age in a group home or group residence and the placement of a child under 12 years of age in an institution other than a group residence shall be deemed necessary and excepted from the age standards, as defined in clause (d)(3)(i)(a) and subparagraph (d)(4)(i) of this section, only if:

(1) the child's service needs, as documented in the first uniform case record form required after placement in such setting require:

(i) sufficient supervision that professional staff are required who are awake and on duty 24 hours per day, where professional staff shall include all those whose primary responsibility is to supervise, teach, provide therapy to, or otherwise deal directly with the children; and

(ii) at least three of the following:

(a) intensive therapy from a licensed psychologist or psychiatrist or a certified social worker;

(b) for a group home or group residence onsite medical staff on a daily basis, and for institutions onsite medical staff at least 16 hours per day;

(c) a licensed speech pathologist;

(d) a licensed physical therapist;

(e) any other licensed or certified therapist;

(f) onsite educational services;

(g) structured recreational therapy; and

(2) the group home, group residence, or institution has been granted written approval to care for children of these ages by the commissioner of the State Department of Social Services or by his or her representative, and the review of the agency's program which precedes this approval includes consideration of the ratio of staff to children in care; or

(3) if the considerations in paragraph (1) or (2) of this subdivision are not met but the placement has been approved by the State Commissioner of Social Services or by his or her representative.

§430.12   Diligence of effort.

(a) A social services district shall be considered to be exercising diligent efforts to achieve the permanent discharge of a child in foster care only if it complies with the requirements for casework activity and documentation contained in this section.

(b) The requirements of this section pertain to all children placed in foster care for whom a uniform case record, as described in Part 428 of this Title, is required and additionally the requirements of paragraph (2) of subdivision (c) of this section pertain to all children placed by a court in the direct custody of a relative or other suitable person pursuant to Article 10 of the Family Court Act. Compliance with these requirements must be documented in the form and manner required by OCFS pursuant to Part 428 according to the standards for documentation defined under the general requirements, the standards for discharge to parents, the standards for discharge to adoption, the standards for another planned living arrangement with a permanency resource, and the standards for discharge to adult residential care, as set forth in subdivisions (c)-(g), respectively, of this section. To the extent permitted by the Mental Hygiene Law and the regulations of the Office of Mental Health and the Office of Mental Retardation and Developmental Disabilities, social services officials must obtain copies of the case records and service plans and any updates to such records and plans for children whose care and custody have been transferred to such officials and who are receiving care in facilities operated supervised by such offices. Such records, plans and updates must be made a part of the uniform case record. It is the responsibility of the district to show that the requirements of this section have been met, and a failure to provide evidence that the requirements have been met is deemed equivalent to a failure to make diligent efforts to achieve the permanent discharge of the child.

(c) General requirements.

(1) Consistency.

(i) Standard. The uniform case record must demonstrate consistency among the service needs identified as contributing to the child's need for placement, the goals or outcomes and services planned for to meet these needs and the services which are provided to the child, members of his or her family, or other significant resource persons. For children who have been placed in facilities operated or supervised by the Office of Mental Health or the Office of Mental Retardation and Developmental Disabilities, the services provided by that facility will be deemed to fulfill the requirements of this subparagraph with respect to the child's service needs.

(ii) Documentation. (a) If the child's placement is deemed necessary, due at least in part to a reason described in paragraphs (c)(1)-(4) of section 430.10 of this Part as health and safety of child, parental refusal or surrender, parent service need, or parent unavailability, and the child's permanency planning goal is return to parents or relatives, the most recent assessment and service plan or risk assessment and service plan required by the uniform case record must contain client goals or outcomes and services tasks or activities to meet these needs;

(b) if the child's placement is deemed necessary due at least in part to reasons described in paragraphs (c)(5)-(6) of section 430.10 of this Part as child service needs or pregnancy, specific client goals or outcomes to meet these needs must be contained in the assessment and service plan or risk assessment and service plan required by the uniform case record;

(c) the assessment and service plan or risk assessment and service plan required by the uniform case record must show that services have been provided according to the service plan for family and child, or that reasonable attempts have been made to provide those services;

(d) information concerning the services which are provided to children in facilities operated or supervised by the Office of Mental Health or Office of Mental Retardation and Developmental Disabilities and which is forwarded by such facilities to the social services district responsible for maintaining the uniform case record must be included in the uniform case record and will be deemed to fulfill the documentation requirements of this subparagraph with respect to the child's service needs;

(e) if a minor parent is in foster care and has residing with him or her his or her child or children, and such child or children are not in the care and custody or custody and guardianship of the local commissioner of social services, the assessment and service plan required by the uniform case record must show that the needs of the child or children of the minor parent have been assessed and that goals or outcomes necessary to meet these needs must be contained in the assessment and service plan required by the uniform case record; and

(f) if the permanency plan for the child is adoption or placement in a permanent home other than that of the child's parent, the uniform case record must document the steps taken to find an adoptive family or other permanent living arrangement for the child; to place the child with an adoptive family, a fit and willing relative, a legal guardian, or in another planned permanent living arrangement; and to finalize the adoption or legal guardianship. At a minimum, such documentation must include child specific recruitment efforts such as the use of State, regional, or national adoption exchanges, including electronic exchange systems. Such documentation must reflect reasonable efforts to place the child in-state or out-of-state in a timely and orderly manner and to finalize the placement of the child.

(2) Service plan reviews.

(i) Standard. A panel of at least two people must participate in the review of each comprehensive family assessment and service plan, each family reassessment and service plan and each child assessment and service plan, if the child is completely legally freed for adoption, as required under section 428.6 of this Title. The panel must include the case planner or the child's caseworker and an administrator or other person not responsible for the case management or delivery of services to that case, nor in the direct line of supervision for that case. The review panel must convene a case conference, with the review panel members and the parent(s) and child present, as required in clauses (a) and (b) of this subparagraph, to review progress made through implementation of the previous service plan, identify issues of concern and suggest modifications that impact on and inform the development of a new service plan for the case. A written statement of the conclusions and recommendations must be developed by the panel, and such report must identify barriers to permanency and any other issues that must be addressed in the new service plan. The service plan review must be held no earlier than 60 days, but no later than 90 days from the date the child was removed from his or her home, or where the child is placed in foster care pursuant to Article 3 or 7 of the Family Court Act, no earlier than 60 days, but no later than 90 days from the date the child was placed in foster care. Subsequent service plan reviews must be held every six months thereafter. A permanency hearing satisfies the requirements for a service plan review if such permanency hearing is held and completed within six months of the previous service plan review.

(a) Efforts must be made to involve the following persons as participants in the development and review of the service plan and in the service plan review:

(1) the child, if he or she is at least 10 but less than 14 years of age, unless there is a documented reason related to the current necessity of placement why the child should not be involved;

(2) the child, if 14 years of age or older, in accordance with the standards set forth in section 428.3(i)of this Title;

(3) the parent(s), unless their rights to the child have been terminated, guardian(s), or, in the case of a child whose permanency planning goal is other than discharge to a parent, the person to whom the child will be discharged;

(4) in the case of an Indian child, the child's tribe if known, and where possible, a qualified expert witness as defined in section 431.18(a)(5) of this Title;

(5) the child's current foster parent, caretaker relative, or pre-adoptive parent presently providing care for the child. Such foster parent, caretaker relative or pre-adoptive parent must be provided with notice of and an opportunity to be heard in any service plan review;

(6) for a child with a permanency planning goal of another planned living arrangement with a permanency resource, any person identified as the permanency resource;

(7) the case manager, case planner's supervisor, and child protective services monitor, if applicable;

(8) key providers of service to the child and family;

(9) members of the case planning team chosen by the child in foster care who is 14 years of age or older in accordance with the standards set forth in section 428.3(i) of this Title:

(10) the attorney for the child; and

(11) any other person the child's parent(s) identifies.

(b) (1) The efforts to involve the participants listed in clause (a) of this subparagraph must include, but are not limited to:

(i) written notice to each participant at least two weeks prior to the service plan review inviting them to attend, giving the date, time and location of the service plan review and in the case of the parent(s), informing them that they may be accompanied by a person(s) of their choice; and

(ii) where possible, face-to-face contact by the case planner with the invited participants who were unable to attend the service plan review no later than 30 days after the date the service plan review was held.

(2) During the face-to-face contact required by item (ii) of subclause (1) of this clause, those invited participants who were unable to attend the service plan review must be given a summary of the service plan for the child and family which at a minimum must include the following:

(i) new or continued goals or outcomes and anticipated completion dates when goals are to be achieved;

(ii) tasks which describe the activities to be completed within the upcoming review period, and the family members and/or the service provider who are to perform each activity;

(iii) an updated visiting plan for children in foster care;

(iv) documentation stating the involvement of the parent, child and any others in the development of the service plan as required by sections

428.3(d) and 428.9 of this Title, and a listing of the participants in the service plan review; and

(v) a review of the previous service plan, which describes the progress in meeting or completing previously stated goals or outcomes and tasks or activities, the participation of family members in the process, and the service provision problems, if any, during the period under review.

Upon presentation of the service plan documents described in subclause (2) of this clause to the invited service plan review participants, the contents will be discussed, or, in the event that such face-to-face contact is not possible, a letter stating that a service plan review was held will be sent to the invited participant(s). The letter must inform the invited participant(s) that a copy of the documents described in subclause (2) of this clause will be made available to them upon request.

(3) For a child in foster care or a child placed by a court in the direct custody of a relative or other suitable person pursuant to Article 10 of the Family Court Act, the parent of the child must be given a copy of the family and child(ren)'s service plan, consistent with article 27-F of the Public Health Law.

(c) A written statement of the conclusions and recommendations from the review or a copy of the service plan shall be made available to all participants, subject to the confidentiality requirements of Part 357 of this Title.

(d) For a child in foster care for whom the permanency planning goal is discharge to another planned living arrangement with a permanency resource, the service plan review must address the steps taken by the authorized agency to ensure that the child's foster parent(s) or the child care facility with whom or in which the child is placed is following the reasonable and prudent parent standard as set forth in section 441.25 of this Title and to ascertain whether the child has regular, ongoing opportunities to engage in age or developmental appropriate activities, including by consulting with the child in an age-appropriate manner about the opportunities of the child to participate in such activities.

(ii) Documentation. The family assessment and service plan or child assessment and service plan if the child is completely legally freed for adoption required by the uniform case record must indicate the names and, where appropriate, the title(s) of the panel members, the names of the invited participants who attended the service plan review and the date of the review. Attendance by the invited participants or their representative will indicate that the two-week notice requirement of clause (i)(b) of this paragraph has been met. When the invited participants do not attend the review the efforts made to involve them in the review and the efforts made pursuant to clause (i)(b) of this paragraph must be documented.

(3) Casework contacts. (i) Standard. Casework contacts with the child, the child's caretakers, the child's parents or relatives, if any, must adhere to the standards mandated in section 441.21 of this Title. When a foster child is placed in a facility operated or supervised by the Office of Mental Health, Office for People with Developmental Disabilities, Office of Alcoholism and Substance Abuse Services or the Department of Health, casework contacts required by this paragraph may be made by appropriate staff from the above referenced State agencies or by appropriate staff who perform like or similar functions under contract with such State agencies where such contacts otherwise satisfy the frequency, location and content requirements set forth in section 441.21 of this Title. *(Eff. 5/18/16)*

(ii) Documentation. The progress notes shall show the extent to which these contacts are occurring pursuant to section 441.21 of this Title, the location of the contacts and the content of the contacts. If such contact is made by appropriate State or contract staff, in accordance with subparagraph (i) of this paragraph, information concerning the date, location, content of the contact and services provided to the foster child must be forwarded by such State or contract staff in the month the contact occurs to the social services district or the voluntary authorized agency case manager, case planner or case worker responsible for maintaining the foster child's uniform case record. This information must then be included in the foster child's uniform case record in accordance with Part 428 of this Title.   *(Eff.5/18/16)*

(4) Education.

(i) Standard. The social services district with care and custody or guardianship and custody of a foster child who has attained the minimum age for compulsory education under the Education Law is responsible for assuring that the foster child is a full-time elementary or secondary school student or has completed secondary education. For the purpose of this paragraph, an elementary or secondary school student means a child who is:

(a) enrolled, or in the process of enrolling, in a school which provides elementary or secondary education, in accordance with the laws where the school is located;

(b) instructed in elementary or secondary education at home, in accordance with the laws in which the foster child's home is located;

(c) in an independent study elementary or secondary education program, in accordance with the laws in which the foster child's education program is located, which is administered by the local school or school district; or

(d) incapable of attending school on a full-time basis due to the foster child's medical condition, which incapability is supported by regularly updated information in the child's uniform case record.

(ii) Documentation. The progress notes for each school age child in foster care must reflect either the education program in which the foster child is presently enrolled or is enrolling; or the date the foster child completed his or her compulsory education; or where the child is not capable of attending school on a full-time basis, what the medical condition is and why such condition prevents full-time attendance. The social services district must update the progress notes on an annual basis to reflect why such medical condition continues to prevent the foster child's full-time attendance in an education program. On an annual basis, by the first day of each October, the education module in CONNECTIONS must be updated with education information about each school age foster child in the form and manner as required by the Office.

(5) Discharge planning.

(i) Standard. For any child 18 or under who is discharged from foster care, the district shall consider the need to provide preventive services to the child and his family subsequent to his discharge.

(ii) Documentation. The uniform case record form to be completed upon discharge of the child shall show either the recommended type of preventive services and the district's attempts to provide or arrange for these services, or the reasons why these services are deemed unnecessary.

(d) Discharge to parents. The following requirements shall pertain to all children in foster care placement whose permanency planning goal is discharge to parents or relatives:

(1) Visiting.

(i) Standard. Districts must plan for and make efforts to facilitate at least biweekly visiting between the child and the parents or caretakers to whom he is to be discharged, unless such visiting is specifically prohibited by court order, or by the transfer of custody agreement, or the child is placed in a facility operated or supervised by the Office of Mental Health or Office of Mental Retardation and Developmental Disabilities or because the placement that was chosen pursuant to the standards expressed in section 430.11 of this Part makes biweekly visitation an impossibility. In the latter case, the district, at a minimum, must, except as herein after provided, plan for and facilitate monthly visits between the parent and the child. In the case of children 13 years or older placed by the court as PINS or juvenile delinquents in an institution less than 100 miles from their homes, and the placement that was chosen, pursuant to the standards expressed in section 430.11 of this Part, makes biweekly visitation impossible, the district, at a minimum, must plan for and facilitate quarterly visits between the parent and the child; however, at the time a service plan for discharging the child is developed, appropriate visits, of a greater frequency than quarterly, between the child and the family must be arranged. In the case of children 13 years or older placed by the court as PINS or juvenile delinquents in an institution 1000 miles or more from their homes, the standards contained in this subparagraph do not apply. At the time the service plan for discharging the child is developed, appropriate visits between the child and the family must be arranged. Any act to limit or terminate visiting for children voluntarily placed in foster care must comply with the requirements set forth in section 431.14 of the Title. The efforts of the districts to facilitate at least biweekly visiting must include:

(a) provision of financial assistance, transportation or other assistance which is necessary to enable biweekly visiting to occur;

(b) follow-up with the parent or relative when scheduled visits do not occur in order to ascertain the reasons for missed visits and to make reasonable efforts to prevent similar problems in future visits. Any act to limit or terminate visiting for children voluntarily placed in foster care must comply with the requirements set forth in section 431.14 of this Title; and

(c) arranging for visits to occur in a location that assures the privacy, safety and comfort of the family members. In no case, except where a family court has ordered supervised visiting, will congregate visits involving members of more than one family satisfy the provisions of this subparagraph.

(ii) Documentation must include:

(a) a visiting plan as required by the uniform case record which includes the planned frequency and location of the visits, the name of the child and the names of the persons who are scheduled to visit the child and any arrangements or assistance necessary to facilitate biweekly or monthly visiting, and if supervised visits are planned, the reasons for such supervision;

(b) indications in the progress notes or in the visiting plan required by the uniform case record of the extent to which visiting has occurred in accordance with the visiting plan and the follow-up efforts which were undertaken when scheduled visiting has not occurred;

(c) indications in the visiting plan required by the uniform case record of the grounds for any attempt to limit or terminate visiting rights, including any documents submitted to the court; and

(d) where appropriate, a statement that the child has been placed in a facility which is operated or supervised by the Office of Mental Health or the Office of Mental Retardation and Developmental Disabilities.

(2) Lack of progress.

(i) Abandonment.

(a) Standard. If a parent evinces an intent to forgo his or her parental rights and obligations, as manifested by his or her failure to visit the child and communicate with the child or agency, although able to do so and not prevented or discouraged from doing so by the agency, so that the child is considered an abandoned child pursuant to section 384-b of the Social Services Law, and no mitigating circumstances exist, then an action to terminate parental rights must be initiated within 60 days of the completion of the assessment and service plan or risk assessment and service plan required by the uniform case record which documents these circumstances.

(b) Documentation. The assessment and service plan or risk assessment and service plan required by the uniform case record must document the evidence of the parent's intent to forgo his or her parental rights and obligations. The progress notes must indicate the date that the petition to terminate parental rights is filed.

(ii) Permanent neglect.

(a) Standard. If a parent has failed for a period of one year to substantially and continuously or repeatedly maintain contact with or plan for the future of the child, although physically and financially able to do so, notwithstanding the agency's diligent efforts to encourage and strengthen the parental relationship when such efforts will not be detrimental to the child so that the child is considered a permanently neglected child pursuant to section 384-b of the Social Services Law, and no mitigating circumstances exist, then an action to terminate parental rights must be initiated within 60 days of the completion of the assessment and service plan or risk assessment and service plan required by the uniform case record which documents these circumstances, as specified in section 431.9 of this Title and section 384-b of the Social Services Law.

(b) Documentation. The assessment and service plan required by the uniform case record must document the lack of contact or the parents' inability to plan for the child and the district's attempts to encourage and strengthen the parental relationship. The progress notes must indicate the date that the petition to terminate rights has been filed.

(iii) Discharge time.

(a) Standard. Every child with a permanency planning goal of return to parents or relatives who has been in care for 15 of the most recent 22 months must be discharged from care or the social services district must comply with the standards for the filing of a petition to terminate parental rights as set forth in section 431.9 of this Title.

(b) Documentation. When the child has been in care for 15 of the most recent 22 months the most recent assessment and service plan or risk assessment and service plan required by the uniform case record must show that the child has been discharged from foster care or that a petition to terminate parental rights has been filed in accordance with the provisions set forth in section 431.9 of this Title, unless the plan shows that the child is in care in the home of a relative; or a compelling reason why it would not be in the best interest to initiate termination proceedings; or that services have not been provided to the family of the child which are necessary for the safe return of the child to his or her family.

(e) Discharge to adoption. The following requirements pertain to all children in a foster care placement whose permanency planning goal is discharge to adoption.

(1) Children not legally free.

(i) Standard. For children who are not legally free for adoption, an action to legally free the child must be initiated within 30 days of the establishment of the permanency planning goal of adoption. The child must be freed within 12 months after the establishment of the permanency planning goal of adoption.

(ii) Documentation. The progress notes must indicate when the action has been initiated and must include copies of the petition and any documents submitted in support of the petition or descriptions of the content of the documents. In addition, the date that the child was freed must be noted in the progress notes. If the case does not meet the standard for freeing the child within 12 months, the district will be considered to be out-of-compliance with the standard unless, at the time of the first recertification after the 12-month period, the assessment and service plan or risk assessment and service plan or risk assessment and service plan required by the uniform case record shows that a petition to terminate parental rights was filed within 120 days of the date the permanency planning goal of adoption was chosen and the delay was caused solely by the court and not by the district or agency caring for the child, or that the court refuses to terminate parental rights.

(2) Children legally free.

(i) Standard. Children who are legally free for adoption but not in an adoptive home must be placed in an adoptive home within six months after the child was freed for adoption. For children in facilities operated or supervised by the Office of Mental Health or the Office of Mental Retardation and Developmental Disabilities, the district will be deemed in compliance with this standard during the time the child remains in the facility. If the child is discharged from the facility to a foster care placement, the time in the facility when the child was legally free will be considered to be part of the total time the child is legally free but not in an adoptive home and the documentation requirements specified below will apply.

(ii) Indian children. An Indian child who is legally free for adoption must, in the absence of good cause to the contrary, be placed in accordance with the preferences set forth in subdivision (g) of section 431.18 of this Title.

(iii) (a) Documentation. The progress notes must indicate when the child was placed in the adoptive home, or if the child was not placed in such home within the time frame stated in the standard. In instances where a handicapped or hard-to-place child was not placed in an adoptive home within six months, the progress notes must indicate that inquiry was made of the adoptive placement registry within three months of the date the child became legally freed and the results of such inquiry. The first assessment and service plan or risk assessment and service plan required by the uniform case record after the six-month period must indicate that an attempt will be made to obtain a subsidized adoptive placement for the child, or record the reason the district believes that subsidy will not be required to complete the adoptive placement before the end of the 12th month. Failure to place the child in an adoptive home within 12 months from the date he or she was freed constitutes non-compliance with this standard, unless the child's permanency planning goal, as recorded on the assessment and service plan or risk assessment service plan required by the uniform case record is other than discharge to adoption, or unless the State Commissioner of Social Services, or his or her representative, has approved a continuation of the efforts to place the child in an adoptive home. Such approval will not be given for more than 12 months without a subsequent review of the case by the State Commissioner of Social Services or his or her representative. If an agreement to adopt the child has been signed by the prospective adoptive parents, and the prospective parents then refuse to maintain the child in the home or otherwise to complete the adoptive process, as documented in the most recent assessment and service plan or risk assessment and service plan required by the uniform case record, the date of that refusal is deemed to be the date on which the child was freed. During the time the child is in a facility operated or supervised by the Office of Mental Health or Office of Mental Retardation and Developmental Disabilities, the documentation requirements of this subparagraph will be deemed to have been met for such child.

(b) Each social services official who places an Indian child in an adoptive home must maintain a record of such placement which evidences the efforts made to comply with the order of preference set forth in subdivision (g) of section 431.18 of this Title. Information concerning efforts by social services districts to comply with the order of preference contained in the case record must be made available to the child's Indian tribe and the Secretary of Interior upon request.

(iv) For purposes of this paragraph, the term Indian child will have the meaning which is given to this term by section 431.18 of this Title.

(3) Children in adoptive placement.

(i) Standard. For children who are legally free, in an adoptive home, but whose adoptions are not yet final, such adoptions must be finalized within 12 months after the child is placed in an adoptive home.

(ii) Documentation. The progress notes must indicate the date of finalization or, if the child's adoption was not finalized in the required time frame, the district will be considered to be out-of-compliance with the standard, unless, at the time of the first recertification after the six-month period, the assessment and service plan or risk assessment and service plan required by the uniform case record shows that the delay was caused solely by the court, and not by the district or agency caring for the child, or that the adoptive parents have delayed finalization.

(f) Another planned living arrangement with a permanency resource. Another planned living arrangement with a permanency resource is a permanency planning goal to assist foster care youth in their transition to self-sufficiency by connecting the youth to an adult permanency resource, equipping the youth with life skills and, upon discharge, connecting the youth with any needed community and/or specialized services. An adult permanency resource is a caring committed adult who has been determined by a social services district to be an appropriate and acceptable resource for a youth and is committed to providing emotional support, advice and guidance to the youth and to assist the youth as the youth makes the transition from foster care to responsible adulthood. The following requirements pertain to all children in a foster care placement whose permanency goal is discharge to another planned living arrangement with a permanency resource and, where indicated, to children deemed to be discharged to another planned living arrangement with a permanency resource or deemed to have a goal of discharge to another planned living arrangement with a permanency resource. For purposes of this subdivision only, a child deemed to be discharged to another planned living arrangement with a permanency resource means a child 16 years of age or older who has resided in foster care for at least 12 months within the past 36 months and who has been discharged to parents or relatives. For the purposes of this subdivision only, a child deemed to have a goal of another planned living arrangement with a permanency resource means a child 16 years of age or older who resided in foster care for at least 12 months within the past 36 months and who has a goal of discharge to parents or relatives or a goal of adoption.

(1) Setting of goal.

(i) Standard. The child is 16 years of age or older, for this goal to be established and it is determined to be in the child's best interests that he or she remain in foster care and not return to his or her parents or be adopted until the child reaches the age of 18. No other child may have a goal of discharge to another planned living arrangement with a permanency resource.

(ii) Documentation. The first assessment and service plan required by the uniform case record at the time of the selection of the permanency planning goal must indicate the reasons for choosing this goal rather than "discharge to parents or relatives" or "discharge to adoption," and must summarize efforts to accomplish either or both of these permanency goals before this goal was selected and document a compelling reason why it would not be in the best interests of the child to be returned home, placed for adoption, placed with a legal guardian or placed with a fit and willing relative.

(2) Preparation for discharge.

(i) Standard.

(a) The district must ensure the provision to all children with a goal of discharge to another planned living arrangement with a permanency resource, or deemed to have a goal of discharge to another planned living arrangement with a permanency resource, of structured programs of vocational training and independent living skills, including at least two days per year of formalized group instruction in independent living skills. Vocational training includes, but is not limited to, training programs in a marketable skill or trade or formal on-the-job training. Children enrolled in secondary education, taking academic courses and receiving at least passing grades which if maintained would lead to graduation prior to the child's 20th birthday, and children enrolled in full-time study at an accredited college or university are deemed to meet the requirement for vocational training. Vocational training must begin at the time the goal of discharge to another planned living arrangement with a permanency resource is selected or deemed to be selected or by the child's 16th birthday, whichever is later, and must continue without interruption until the child is discharged to another planned living arrangement with a permanency resource, unless the child is employed in a paying job for which such child's vocational training has prepared him or her, or is employed in a paying job at an hourly rate which would provide income, if the child was employed on a full-time basis, equal to or greater than 150 percent of the poverty level for a family of one as established by the Federal Department of Health and Human Services, or has passed a test approved or administered by the agency, school, or firm providing the training, or has otherwise successfully completed a course of vocational training as evidenced by a certificate or some other document demonstrating completion. Independent living skills include formalized instruction, including supervised performance in job search, career counseling, apartment finding, budgeting, shopping, cooking, and house cleaning. Instruction in these skills must begin at the time the goal is selected or by the child's 14th birthday, whichever is later, and must continue without interruption until the child is discharged, unless the child has demonstrated competency in all of the above skills, either through a test approved by the department or through an assessment based on observation of the child's performance; in either case, the child's on-going application of those skills must be deemed to meet the standard. The vocational training requirements of this subparagraph cannot apply where the child demonstrates an inability to participate in and benefit from vocational training because of the child's inability to read or compute at an appropriate grade level. Where a child is found to be unable to benefit from such training, remedial education must be provided to prepare the child to participate in and benefit from vocational training. In the case of children who have been placed in facilities operated or supervised by the Office of Mental Health or Office of Mental Retardation and Developmental Disabilities, the services provided by that facility are deemed to fulfill the requirements of the standard contained in this subparagraph.

(b) Subject to the availability of State and Federal funds therefor, the district must ensure that a monthly independent living stipend is regularly provided to each child 16 years of age or older who has, or is deemed to have, a goal of discharge to another planned living arrangement with a permanency resource and who, according to his or her case plan, is actively participating in independent living services. The independent living stipend is to be provided in addition to the regular allowance the child is entitled to receive pursuant to section 441.12(a) of this Title. The purposes for providing an independent living stipend are: to give the child incentive to participate in independent living services, to teach the child to manage money, and to provide the child with a means to accumulate savings to assist him or her in the transition to independent living. The amount of the monthly stipend must be in accordance with the following schedule:

Age	Monthly stipend
16	$20.00
17	25.00
18	30.00
19	35.00
20	40.00

Depending upon the child's financial needs and abilities, the district must pay the entire monthly stipend in one lump sum payment or in two or more smaller payments spread over the month. Stipend payments to the child must be suspended for any period of time that the child, according to his or her case plan, is not actively participating in independent living services. A child placed in a facility operated or supervised by the Office of Mental Health or the Office of Mental Retardation and Developmental Disabilities is not eligible to receive an independent living stipend.

(ii) Documentation.

(a) Each assessment and service plan required under Part 428 of this Title must show the type, location, duration, and intensity of the vocational training and instruction in independent living skills being provided to the child, as well as the level of achievement the child has attained. If the required vocational training and/or instruction in independent living skills has not been provided, the case record must document that the reason for the failure to complete the training was because of the child's unwillingness to cooperate, or the child's employment in a job as referenced in clause (a) of subparagraph (i) of this paragraph, or the child's passing of a test displaying competence in relevant job skills and independent living skills, or the child's inability to participate in and benefit from vocational training because of educational deficiencies. If the reason for the failure to complete the training or instruction is the child's unwillingness to cooperate, the case record must document the efforts made by the district to encourage participation by the child in the training or instruction. Any assessment that the child cannot participate in and benefit from vocational training because of the lack of reading or computation skills must be contained in the uniform case record. The record must contain the date of the assessment of educational deficiencies, a plan of remediation including the remedial services provided to the child and the date of anticipated completion of the plan which under no circumstances may be the same as or subsequent to the date of planned discharge. This plan must be designed to enable the child to participate in and benefit from vocational training. Information concerning the services which are provided to children in facilities operated or supervised by the Office of Mental Health or Office of Mental Retardation and Developmental Disabilities and which is forwarded by such facilities to the social services district responsible for maintaining the uniform case record must be included in the uniform case record and will be deemed to fulfill the documentation requirements of this subparagraph.

(b) Each assessment and service plan, reassessment and service plan review also must show the amount and frequency of the independent living stipend payments made to the child and the child's active participation in independent living services as outlined in the case plan. If the child did not receive an independent living stipend for any period of time, the case record must document the reason the child did not receive a stipend or the reason that the stipend was suspended. Such documentation must include a description of how and why the child was not actively participating in independent living services as outlined in the case plan or that the child was placed in a facility operated or supervised by the Office of Mental Health or the Office of Mental Retardation and Developmental Disabilities.

(3) Discharge.

(i) Standards.

(a) For each child discharged to another planned living arrangement with a permanency resource, the district must identify any persons, services or agencies which would help the child maintain and support himself or herself and must assist the child to establish contact with such agencies, service providers or persons by making referrals and by counseling the child about these referrals prior to discharge. This must include efforts to assist the child to reestablish contacts with parents, former foster parents or other persons significant to the child.

(b) No child can be discharged to another planned living arrangement with a permanency resource, unless such child has received written notice of such discharge at least 90 days prior to the date of discharge and has had the goal of another planned living arrangement with a permanency resource continuously for a six-month period immediately prior to discharge. This notice requirement does not apply where the child has voluntarily departed from the foster care placement without the consent of the district and has been absent from said placement for 60 days.

(c) No child may be discharged to another planned living arrangement with a permanency resource, unless the child has a residence other than a shelter for adults, shelter for families, single-room occupancy hotel or any other congregate living arrangement which houses more than 10 unrelated persons and there is a reasonable expectation that the residence will remain available to the child for at least the first 12 months after discharge. This requirement does not apply to a child who is a member of the military or job corps or who is a full-time student in a post-secondary educational institution or where the child has voluntarily departed from the foster care placement without the consent of the district and has been absent from said placement for 60 days.

(ii) Documentation.

(a) Documentation includes goals or outcomes and services in the service plan and a summary by the district of the efforts made and their results in the assessment and service plan required by the uniform case record.

(b) A copy of the written notice of discharge must be maintained in the case record until the child attains the age of 21, showing the date the child received the notice. In addition, the child's service plans prepared pursuant to Part 428 of this Title must show that the child has had the goal of independent living continuously for a six-month period immediately prior to discharge. If the notice is not received by the child because the child is voluntarily absent from the foster care placement without the consent of the district, the case record must document when the child left the foster care placement, the voluntary nature of the absence of the child, the absence of consent by the district and the efforts made by the district to make contact with the child to encourage the return of the child to the placement.

(c) The plan amendment or service plan required by the uniform case record must include a description of the living arrangements secured for the child, together with an assessment of the permanency of those arrangements. If the child is discharged without the district securing living arrangements for the child, the case record must document that the reason for the failure to secure such arrangement has been that the child is a member of the military or job corps or a full-time student in a post-secondary educational institution or has voluntarily departed from the foster care placement without the district's consent and has been absent from the placement for 60 days.

(4) Post-discharge.

(i) Standards.

(a) Every child discharged to another planned living arrangement with a permanency resource and every child deemed to have been discharged to another planned living arrangement with a permanency resource must remain in a status of trial discharge for at least six months after discharge and must remain in the custody of the local commissioner during the entire period of trial discharge. Trial discharge may continue at the discretion of the district up to the age of 21 if the reassessment and service plan review indicates either the need for continued custody or a likelihood that the child may need to return to foster care. During the period of trial discharge, the district must provide after-care services to the child, including casework contacts with the child, with the number of face-to-face contacts and in-home contacts equal to those required for that child pursuant to subdivision 431.16(c) of this Title during the six months immediately preceding the child's discharge. In addition, after-care services include the provision of services consistent with the service needs of the child identified in the uniform case record which would enable the child to live independently after he or she is discharged from care. In the event that the child becomes homeless during the period of trial discharge, the district must assist the child to obtain housing equivalent to that authorized by clause (c) of this subparagraph. Under no circumstances may a district refer or place a child during the 30-day period following the child's becoming homeless in a shelter for adults, shelter for families, single-room occupancy hotel, or any other congregate living arrangement which houses more than 10 unrelated persons. If appropriate housing is not available within 30 days of the date the child becomes homeless, the district must place the child in a suitable foster boarding home, agency boarding home, group home or institution consistent with section 430.11 of this Part. The provisions of this clause relating to trial discharge do not apply where a court order terminates the district's custody of the child or where the child reaches the age of 21.

(b) After the district's custody of the child has been terminated whether by court order or by the district's own action, the district must maintain supervision of the child until the child is 21 years of age, where the child has been discharged to another planned living arrangement with a permanency resource or is deemed to have been discharged to another planned living arrangement with a permanency resource and has permanently left the home of his or her parents or relatives prior to the termination of the district's custody. Supervision includes at least monthly contact with the child, unless the child has maintained adequate housing and income continuously for the past six months, in which case at least quarterly contacts shall occur, either face-to-face or by telephone. Where monthly contacts are required, face-to-face contacts on a quarterly basis must occur with the remaining contacts being either face-to-face or by telephone. This requirement of quarterly face-to-face contacts does not apply to children living 50 miles outside of the district. In all cases, the district must provide referral to needed services, including income and housing services, with sufficient follow-up efforts to ensure that the child has begun to receive the services for which he or she was referred. The contact requirements of this clause must be satisfied when the child has refused contact or cannot be located during a 60-day period in which two face-to-face or telephone contacts and one in-home contact have not been successful. The contact requirements mandated by this clause must resume when the child is located and desires to cooperate with the district.

(c) Nothing in this subdivision mandates the participation of a child in the status of trial discharge or supervision. Such participation is contingent upon the consent of the child.

(ii) Documentation.

(a) The requirements of the uniform case record, as established in Part 428 of this Title, will apply until the district's custody of the child has been terminated, either by court order or by the district's own action. Each reassessment and service plan review after the child's discharge must show whether the child remains in the custody of the local commissioner, the need for continued custody, the number and location of casework contacts with the child, the child's current living arrangements and service needs including, but not limited to whether the child has become homeless, the services provided during the past six months, including but not limited to housing and income services, and the services to be provided during the next six months. If the required number of casework contacts with the child has not been made, the case record must document that the primary reason for the failure to complete the contacts has been the child's unwillingness to cooperate with the district. The case record must also document the efforts made by the district to make contact with the child and to encourage participation in the district's supervisory functions.

(b) After termination of the district's custody of the child, whether by court order or by the district's own action, progress notes must be maintained which show the number and type of contacts with the child, the services and service providers to whom the child has been referred, and whether the child actually received services. If the required number of contacts with the child has not been made, the case record must document the efforts made by the district to contact the child and to encourage the child to cooperate with the district.

(g) Adult residential care. The following requirements shall pertain to all children in a foster care placement whose permanency goal is discharge to adult residential care.

(1) Setting of goal.

(i) Standard. Discharge to adult residential care shall be the permanency planning goal only for children for whom the necessity of placement is based in whole or in part on the reason described in section 430.10(c)(5) of this Part, as "child service need" and for whom the service needs arise out of a factor other than the child's behavior. For each child with this goal, the district shall consider alternative permanency goals, including "discharge to parents or relatives" and "discharge to adoption" before this goal is chosen, and the Director of Social Services shall review and approve the establishment of this goal.

(ii) Documentation. The assessment and service plan or risk assessment service plan required by the uniform case record must document the specific reasons why this is the most appropriate permanency goal for this child and the reasons why the child should not be discharged to parents or relatives or to an adoptive placement.

(2) Preparation for discharge.

(i) Standard. For each individual discharged to adult residential care, the service plan for discharging the child must include the types of services and programs needed by this individual, specific programs which could meet the individual's needs, and plans and activities to assist the child in making the transition from the present program to the new program. In the case of children in facilities operated or supervised by the Office of Mental Health or the Office of Mental Retardation and Developmental Disabilities, the services provided in preparation for discharge by such facilities to such children shall be deemed to fulfill the requirements of this subparagraph.

(ii) Documentation. Documentation must include goals or outcomes and services in the service plan which will assist with the transition and a summary by the district of the efforts made and their results in the assessment and service plan or risk assessment and service plan required by the uniform case record. Information concerning the services which are provided to children in facilities operated or supervised by the Office of Mental Health or Office of Mental Retardation and Developmental Disabilities and which is forwarded by such facilities to the social services district responsible for maintaining the uniform case record must be included in the uniform case record and will be deemed to fulfill the documentation requirements of this subparagraph.

(h) Court orders. Notwithstanding any other provision of this section, a case shall not be subject to denial of reimbursement due to lack of diligent efforts if a court has ordered that actions be taken which prohibit compliance with the provisions of this section. The first uniform case record form required after the court order shall include either a copy of the court order or a description of the terms of the order. In the event that a utilization review of the case has been completed, and has found that the district's activities do not comply with the requirements of this section, other than that defined in this subdivision, the district shall petition the court for a rehearing of the case within 30 days of the notification to the district that diligent efforts have not been made. The district shall submit the finding of the utilization review to the court as documentation for the court review.

(i) (1) Length of time in care. For Federal fiscal years beginning October 1, 1985 and ending September 30, 1990, the maximum number of children who are in receipt of federally reimbursable foster care maintenance payments pursuant to title IV-E of the Social Security Act and who, at any time during such years, will remain in foster care after having been in such care for 24 months shall not exceed 57 percent of the total number of children who receive such payments during such period.

(2) Social services officials shall monitor their foster care caseloads as often as is necessary to ensure compliance with the provisions of paragraph (1) of this subdivision.

(j) Transition plan. Whenever a child will remain in foster care on or after the child's eighteenth birthday, the agency with case management, case planning or casework responsibility for the foster child must begin developing a transition plan with the child 180 days prior to the child's eighteenth birthday or 180 days prior to the child's scheduled discharge date where the child is consenting to remain in foster care after the child's eighteenth birthday. The transition plan must be completed 90 days prior to the scheduled discharge. Such plan must be personalized at the direction of the child. The transition plan must include specific options on housing, health insurance, education, local opportunities for mentors and continuing support services, and work force supports and employment services. The transition plan must be as detailed as the foster child may elect.

(k) Consumer reports. (1) Standard. Upon attaining the age of 14 years and each year thereafter until discharged from foster care, each child in foster care must receive a copy of any consumer report on such child, as prescribed by the office of Children and Family Services at no cost to the child. The agency with case management, case planning or casework responsibility for the child, as determined by the social services district with legal custody of the foster child, must provide or arrange for the provision of assistance to the foster child, including, where feasible, from any court-appointed advocate, in interpreting and resolving any inaccuracies in the report(s). For the purpose of this subdivision, a *consumer report* means information by a consumer reporting agency bearing on the consumer's credit worthiness, credit standing, credit capacity, character, general reputation, personal characteristics, or mode of living which is used or expected to be used or collected in whole or in part for the purpose of serving as a factor in establishing the consumer's eligibility for:

(i) credit or insurance to be used primarily for personal, family, or household purposes;

(ii) employment purposes; or

(iii) any other purpose authorized by federal law.

(2) Documentation. Documentation must include a copy of any consumer report provided to the child in foster care annually and any assistance provided by the agency to the child in foster care in interpreting the consumer report(s) or resolving any inaccuracies in such report(s).

(*l*) A child in foster care who is leaving foster care by reason of attaining 18 years of age or older and who has been in foster care for six months or more may not be discharged from care without being provided with the following, if the child is eligible to receive such document:

(i) an official or certified copy of the child's United States birth certificate;

(ii) social security card issued by the Social Security Administration;

(iii) health insurance information;

(iv) copy of the child's medical records in accordance with section 357.3 of this Title; and

(v) a driver's license or identification card issued by the State in accordance with the requirements of federal law.

Part 431
Care and Protection of Children

Section   *(Extracts)*

§431.8 Procedures in cases of children absent without consent from foster care placement.

(a) Definition. For purposes of this Part, a child absent without consent is a child who has been placed by an authorized agency in foster care in a certified foster boarding home, an approved relative foster home, or a licensed foster care facility, and who disappears, runs away or is otherwise absent voluntarily or involuntarily without the consent of the person(s) or facility in whose care the child has been placed.

(b) Reporting requirements.

(1) The name of a foster child who is absent without consent from a foster care placement must be reported no later than 24 hours from the time the absence occurs by the foster parent or staff of an agency boarding home, group home, or institution to the authorized agency responsible for supervising the placement of the child.

(2) If the authorized agency receiving the report is a voluntary agency, that agency must also report the child's absence within 24 hours of such absence to the social services district which has custody of the child.

(3) (i) An authorized agency receiving a report of a child in foster care's absence without consent must report the absence to the local law enforcement agency and to the National Center for Missing and Exploited Children immediately, and in no case later than 24 hours after receiving notice of such absence.

(ii) In addition to the requirement set forth in subparagraph (i) of this paragraph, a social services official must report to law enforcement and to the National Center for Missing and Exploited Children immediately, and in no case later than 24 hours of receiving information that following categories of children are missing or abducted:

(a) a child of a family for which the social services district has an open child protective services or open preventive services case;

(b) a child or youth who is receiving federally funded independent living services;

(c) a child under the supervision of the social services district pursuant to a court order; or

(d) a youth over whom the social services district has supervision responsibilities in accordance with section 430.12(f)(4)(i)(b) of this Title.

(iii) An authorized agency receiving information that a child in foster care or a child as referenced in clauses (a)-(d) of subparagraph (ii) of this paragraph has been identified as being a sex trafficking victim, as defined by applicable federal law, must immediately, and in no case later than 24 hours after receiving such information, report such child to law enforcement.

(4) An authorized agency receiving a report of a child's absence without consent must report the absence to the child's biological parents within 24 hours of such absence unless the parents' parental rights have been terminated, the parents have surrendered the child for adoption, or the parents cannot be located.

(5) Where the family court has approved the foster care placement, the local social services commissioner in whose custody the foster child has been placed, or a designated representative, must provide written notice to the family court which approved the petition for foster care of the child's absence without consent within 48 hours of the reported absence.

(6) A report of a child's absence without consent must be reported to the Child Care Review Service no later than seven calendar days of the absence, and must be documented in the uniform case record within 30 days of such report.

(c) Required casework contacts.

(1) When a foster child is reported to an authorized agency as absent without consent, the case manager or case planning supervisor is responsible for ensuring that diligent efforts are made no later than 72 hours after the report of the absence to contact the following persons for any information concerning the child's location:

(i) members of the child's foster family household or the agency boarding home, group home or institution where the child was placed;

(ii) members of the child's biological family and extended family, including relatives within the third degree of the child, where known, or legal guardian of the child;

(iii) the child's school principal, teacher(s) or other appropriate staff at the school last attended;

(iv) close friends of the child, where known;

(v) adults known to be working with the child in recreational or educational activities;

(vi) professional persons involved with the child's development, including, but not limited to, doctors, nurses, psychologists, psychiatrists, or clinical social workers; and

(vii) the administrator or coordinator(s) of the county's runaway and homeless youth services.

(2) If a child who is absent without consent cannot be located after conducting the required casework contacts in accordance with paragraph (1) of this subdivision, and such child remains in the custody of the local social services commissioner, the case manager or case planning supervisor is responsible for ensuring that a continuing effort is made to locate the child. Within each 30 day period following the child's absence, reasonable efforts must be made to obtain information on the child's location as long as the child remains in the custody of the local social services commissioner or until the child is discharged in accordance with paragraphs (f) (2) and (3) of this section. Sources to be contacted for such information must include, but are not limited to:

(i) members of the child's foster family household or the agency boarding home, group home or institution where the child was placed;

(ii) members of the child's biological family and extended family, including relatives within the third degree of the child, where known, or legal guardian of the child;

(iii) the child's school principal, teacher(s) or other appropriate staff at the school last attended;

(iv) the administrator or coordinator(s) of the county's runaway and homeless youth services; and

(v) the local law enforcement agency.

(d) Cooperation with law enforcement agencies.

(1) Information provided to the authorized agency responsible for a child's care which might lead to the location of a child absent without consent from a foster care placement must be transmitted by the authorized agency to the local law enforcement agency within 24 hours after receipt of such information.

(2) The local social services commissioner or an authorized representative may petition the family court having jurisdiction over the foster child for a warrant to return the child who is absent without consent if the child's presence is required at a hearing or proceeding in family court and the local law enforcement agency requires such a warrant before acting to return the child.

(e) Documentation. Information gathered under the provisions of subdivisions (c) and (d) of this section must be documented in the progress notes of the uniform case record for a foster child who is absent from a foster care placement. Such information must include persons contacted, dates of those contacts, and information pertaining to the child's absence.

(f) Case disposition for a foster child absent without consent.

(1) A child who is absent without consent from a foster care placement and who has been determined to be a runaway by the authorized agency responsible for the child's care, must be reported as absent to the Child Care Review Service and payment to the authorized agency for the child's foster care must be suspended no later than seven consecutive calendar days after the child has been absent, in accordance with section 628.3 of this Title.

(2) A foster child 16 years of age or older who is absent without consent from a foster care placement and who cannot be located, or is located and refuses to return after the responsible authorized agency has used diligent efforts for 60 consecutive days in accordance with subdivisions (c) and (d) of this section must be discharged from care if one of the following events occurs:

(i) the local social services commissioner petitions for and the family court grants termination of the local social services commissioner's custody of the child; or

(ii) the court order granting custody of the child to the commissioner expires; or

(iii) a voluntary placement agreement executed pursuant to Section 384-a of the Social Services Law is revoked by order of the court or by expiration of the agreement; or

(iv) the child becomes 21 years old.

(3) A foster child under the age of 16 years who is absent without consent from a foster care placement and who cannot be located after the responsible authorized agency has used diligent efforts for 60 consecutive days in accordance with subdivisions (c) and (d) of this section must be continued as a case in suspended payment after the child has been absent for seven consecutive calendar days in accordance with section 628.3 of this Title. The child's status must be indicated as absent in the Child Care Review Service until the child has been located, or until one of the following events occurs:

(i) the local social services commissioner petitions for and the family court grants termination of the local social services commissioner's custody of the child; or

(ii) the court order granting custody of the child to the commissioner expires; or

(iii) a voluntary placement agreement executed pursuant to Section 384-a of the Social Services Law is revoked by order of the court or by expiration of the agreement; or

(iv) the child becomes 21 years old.

(4) Upon the return to foster care of a child absent without consent, the foster care case must be restored to the status of "active open" in the Child Care Review Service.

(g) Services to be provided following reinstatement in foster care after absence without consent. When a child is returned or returns voluntarily to foster care after being absent without consent, diligent efforts must be made to provide services to the child which will restore the child to a supportive environment. In addition to providing the foster care services required by this Title, an assessment must be made of the need of the child for rehabilitative services. Such services may include, but are not limited to:

(1) remedial educational services;

(2) psychological counseling;

(3) medical services in accordance with section 441.22 of this Title; and

(4) drug and alcohol abuse treatment where available from a public agency. If a determination is made that any such services are needed by the child, referrals to providers of such services must be made and such referrals must be documented in the uniform case record.

(h) Whenever a child in foster care is absent without consent as defined in this section, the authorized agency with either case management or case planning responsibility for the child must:

(i) determine and document in the child's case record the primary factors that contributed to the child running away or otherwise being absent without consent and to the extent possible and appropriate, respond to those factors in the child's current and subsequent foster care placements; and

(ii) determine the child's experiences while absent from care, including screening the child as a possible sex trafficking victim as that term is defined by applicable federal law.

§431.9 Termination of parental rights by local social services agency.

(a) Except as required in subdivision (e) of this section, each social services official must, at six months from removal and every six months thereafter, evaluate the status of the relationship, of each child in direct or purchased foster care with his/her natural family in order to determine whether the interests of the child will be served through termination of the parent's legal rights to guardianship and custody of the child. If it is determined that termination of the rights of the parent(s) would be in the child's best interests, or if, following a Family Court permanency hearing held under Article 10-A of the Family Court Act, there is a court order directing that a proceeding to terminate parental rights be instituted, the social services official must take appropriate steps to promptly initiate essential procedures to terminate parental rights.

(b) In making a determination to terminate parental rights in accordance with subdivision (a) of this section, the social services official must consider:

(1) whether there are indications of parental rejection of the child, which may include the failure of the parent(s) since the child was removed or the most recent permanency hearing to:

(i) request visits with the child;

(ii) cooperate with the agency in planning and arranging visits with the child, although physically and financially able;

(iii) communicate with the child regularly by phone or letter if there is physical or financial inability to visit;

(iv) keep appointments to visit child as arranged;

(v) keep the agency informed as to his or her whereabouts;

(vi) keep appointments with agency staff which may have been arranged to assist the parent with those problems which affect the parent's ability to care for the child;

(vii) use community resources as arranged or suggested by the agency, or ordered by the court, or other involved agencies to resolve or correct the problems which impair parental ability to care for the child;

(viii) demonstrate a willingness and capacity to plan for the child's discharge, including taking what steps are necessary to provide an adequate, safe and stable home and parental care for the child within a reasonable period of time;

(2) whether there are indications that efforts to encourage and strengthen the parental relationship would not be in the child's best interests as evidenced by:

(i) addiction to alcohol or drugs to such a degree that the parent's ability to function in a mature and reasonable manner is impaired, or anti-social behavior to a degree that the parent is frequently incarcerated;

(ii) consistent expressed hostility towards the child or evidence of neglect and/or abuse during periods when the child has visited the parent;

(iii) consistent expressed resistance on the part of a child, judged to be of sufficient maturity and intelligence to make such judgment, to accept visits from the parent, or resistance on the part of a small child without sufficient maturity or judgment who exhibits resistance or defensive behavior; e.g., continual crying when parents visit, bedwetting, compulsive scratching, nervous habits, only evident when child is with parents but not evident in everyday behavior in the foster home;

(iv) the parent's mental illness, manifested by a disorder or disturbance in behavior, feeling, thinking or judgment to such an extent that if the child were returned to the custody of the parent, the child would be in danger of becoming a neglected child as defined in the Family Court Act;

(v) the parent's mental retardation, manifested by impairment in adaptive behavior to such an extent that if such child were returned to the custody of the parent the child would be in danger of becoming a neglected child as defined in the Family Court Act.

(c) If the social services official determines that the interests of the child would be best served by terminating parental rights and petitioning for the guardianship and custody of the child, he or she must:

(1) require that a caseworker on his or her staff, or on the staff of the agency having direct care of the child, interview the parents, parent, or legal guardian in order to discuss the future needs of the child for care, parental affection, safety and security, and determine whether the parent, parents or guardian will voluntarily surrender the guardianship and custody of the child, and accept such surrender as agreed. If such agreement cannot be reached with the parent, parents or guardian, clearly indicate to such parent, parents or guardian the steps which the agency may take or have been ordered to take in order to obtain a court commitment of guardianship and custody;

(2) require that there be documentation in the child's case record of all evidence which indicates the need to ask the court to grant the agency guardianship and custody of the child; and

(3) obtain whatever legal counsel is necessary in order to prepare a petition, which must be presented to the proper court as soon as possible but in no case more than 30 days following a determination that it is in the best interests of the child to terminate parental rights, unless there are serious extenuating circumstances which in the opinion of the local commissioner justify a special extension.

(d) Denying or limiting parental visitation. Prior to or concurrent with the initiation of a proceeding to terminate parental rights, if it is deemed to be in the child's best interests to deny or limit the right of the parent or parents to visit, and if such parent or parents will not voluntarily agree to such a limitation or discontinuance of visiting, a social services official must seek court approval of such decision to limit or deny to the parents the right to visit, provided legal grounds for such action exists under Article 10 or 10-A of the Family Court Act.

(e)(1) a social services district must file a petition to terminate parental rights or if such a petition has been filed by another party, seek to be joined as a party to such petition if one of the following events occurs:

(i) the child has been in foster care for 15 of the most recent 22 months;

(ii) a court of competent jurisdiction has determined the child to be an abandoned child; or

(iii) a court of competent jurisdiction has made a determination that the parent has been convicted of: the murder or voluntary manslaughter of another child of the parent; the attempt, facilitation, conspiracy, or solicitation to commit such a murder or manslaughter, or a felony assault that resulted in serious bodily injury to the child or to another child of the parent.

(2) A social services district is not required to file a petition to terminate parental rights as set forth in paragraph (1) of this subdivision if based on a case by case determination:

(i) the child is being cared for by a relative, provided, however, nothing in this section precludes a social services district from filing a petition to terminate parental rights when such petition is in the best interests of the child.

(ii) the social services district has documented in the case plan available for court review a compelling reason for determining that filing such a petition would not be in the best interests of the child and, for the purposes of this section, a compelling reason would include, but not be limited to:

(a) the child was placed into foster care pursuant to article three or seven of the family court act and a review of the specific facts and circumstances of the child's placement demonstrate that the appropriate permanency goal for the child is either:

(1) return to his or her parent or guardian, or

(2) discharge to another planned living arrangement with a permanency resource;

(b) where adoption is not the appropriate permanency goal for the child;

(c) the child is fourteen years of age or older and will not consent to his or her adoption;

(d) the child is the subject of a pending disposition under article ten of the family court act, except where such child is already in the custody of the commissioner of social services as a result of a proceeding other than the pending article ten proceeding and a review of the specific facts and circumstances of the child's placement demonstrate that the appropriate permanency goal for the child is discharge to his or her parent or guardian;

(e) there are insufficient grounds for filing a petition to terminate parental rights; or

(iii) the social services district has not provided the family of the child, consistent with the time period in the service plan of the child, such services as the social services district deems necessary for the safe return of the child to the child's family, consistent with the provisions of section 430.12 of this Title unless such services are not legally required.

(3) Whenever a social services district determines that a petition to terminate parental rights must be filed in accordance with the provisions of this subdivision, the social services district must also make reasonable efforts to identify, recruit, process and approve a qualified family for the adoption of the child, if such steps have not already taken place.

(4) When a court of competent jurisdiction has made a determination that a child is abandoned in accordance with subparagraph (ii) of paragraph (1) of this subdivision or where a court of competent jurisdiction has made a determination that a parent has been convicted of the criminal offenses set forth in subparagraph (iii) of paragraph (1) of this subdivision, the social services district must file a petition to terminate parental rights or seek to be joined in a pending proceeding within sixty days of such court determination, unless one of the exceptions set forth in paragraph (2) of this subdivision apply.

§431.10 Placement in foster family care of children who are siblings.

(a) Foster children who are siblings or half-siblings must not be unnecessarily separated. The social services district is responsible for ensuring that diligent efforts are made to secure a foster family boarding home or agency boarding home which is willing and able to accept the placement of the siblings together, unless placement together is determined to be detrimental to the best interests of the siblings. Such efforts must be documented in the case record in accordance with section 428.6(b)(6), 428.10(d)(6) or 428.11(b)(4) of this Title.

(b) A social services district may make a decision that minor siblings or half-siblings should be separated only if placement together is determined to be contrary to the health, safety or welfare of one or more of the children after consultation with, or an evaluation by, other professional staff, such as a licensed psychologist, psychiatrist, other physician, or certified social worker. Factors to be considered in making a determination of whether siblings or half-siblings should be placed together must include, but are not limited to:

(1) the age differentiation of the siblings;

(2) the health and developmental differences among the siblings;

(3) the emotional relationship of the siblings to each other;

(4) the individual services needs;

(5) the attachment of the individual siblings to separate families/locations; and

(6) the continuity of environment standards pursuant to section 430.11(c) of this Title. The factors used by social services districts to determine that siblings or half-siblings should be placed apart must be documented in accordance with section 428.6(b)(6), 428.10(d)(6), or 428.11(b)(4) of this Title.

(c) If minor siblings or half-siblings are placed apart in foster family boarding homes and/or agency operated boarding homes on an emergency basis, they must be reunited within 30 days unless the social services commissioner or a designated representative determines it is contrary to the best interests of one or more of the siblings to be placed together, after a careful assessment in accordance with subdivision (b) of this section.

(d) Foster parents must be informed if any child placed with them has siblings or half-siblings, and if so, the location of the siblings or half-siblings.

(e) Authorized agencies are responsible for ensuring that diligent efforts are made to facilitate regular biweekly visitation or communication between minor siblings or half-siblings who have been placed apart, unless such contact would be contrary to the health, safety or welfare of one or more of the children, or unless lack of geographic proximity precludes visitation.

Part 432
Child Abuse and Maltreatment

§432.1 Definitions.

For purposes of this Part, the following definitions shall apply:

(a) Abused child means a child, less than 18 years of age, whose parent or other person legally responsible for his care:

(1) inflicts or allows to be inflicted upon such child physical injury by other than accidental means which causes or creates a substantial risk of death, or serious or protracted disfigurement, or protracted impairment of physical or emotional health or protracted loss or impairment of the function of any bodily organ; or

(2) creates or allows to be created a substantial risk of physical injury to such child by other than accidental means which would be likely to cause death or serious or protracted disfigurement, or protracted impairment of physical or emotional health or protracted loss or impairment of the function of any bodily organ; or

(3) commits, or allows to be committed, a sex offense against such child, as defined in the Penal Law allows, permits or encourages such child to engage in any act described in sections 230.00, 230.25, 230.30 and 230.32 of the Penal Law; commits any of the acts described in section 255.25 of the Penal Law; or allows such child to engage in acts or conduct described in article 263 of the Penal Law; provided, however, that the corroboration requirements contained in the Penal Law and the age requirement for the application of article 263 of such law shall not apply to proceedings under article 10 of the Family Court Act (child protective proceedings).

(b) Maltreated child means a child, less than 18 years of age:

(1) whose physical, mental or emotional condition has been impaired or is in imminent danger of becoming impaired as a result of the failure of his parent or other person legally responsible for his care to exercise a minimum degree of care:

(i) in supplying the child with adequate food, clothing, shelter or education in accordance with the provisions of part 1 of article 65 of the Education Law, or medical, dental, optometrical or surgical care, though financially able to do so or offered financial or other reasonable means to do so; or

(ii) in providing the child with proper supervision or guardianship, by unreasonably inflicting or allowing to be inflicted harm, or a substantial risk thereof, including the infliction of excessive corporal punishment; or by misusing a drug or drugs; or by misusing alcoholic beverages to the extent that he loses self-control of his actions; or by any other acts of a similarly serious nature requiring the aid of the court; provided, however, that where the parent or other person legally responsible is voluntarily and regularly participating in a rehabilitative program, evidence that the parent or other person legally responsible has repeatedly misused a drug or drugs or alcoholic beverages to the extent that he loses self-control of his actions shall not alone establish that the child is a neglected child in the absence of evidence establishing that the child's physical, mental or emotional condition has been impaired or is in imminent danger of becoming impaired as set forth in paragraph (1) of this subdivision; or

(2) who has been abandoned by his parents or other person legally responsible for his care; or

(3) who has had serious physical injury inflicted upon him by other than accidental means.

(c) Person legally responsible for a child includes the child's custodian, guardian, any other person responsible for the child's care at the relevant time. Custodian may include any person continually or at regular intervals found in the same household as the child when the conduct of such person causes or contributes to the abuse or neglect of the child.

(d) Subject of the report means any of the following persons who are allegedly responsible for causing injury, abuse or maltreatment to, or allowing injury, abuse or maltreatment to be inflicted on, a child named in a report to the State Central Register of Child Abuse and Maltreatment:

(1) a child's parent or guardian;

(2) a director, operator, employee or volunteer of a home or facility operated or supervised by an authorized agency, OCFS, or an office of the Department of Mental Hygiene or a family day-care home, a day-care center, a group family day-care home or a school-age child care program;

(3) a consultant or any person who is an employee or volunteer of a corporation, partnership, organization or any governmental entity which provides goods and services pursuant to contract or other arrangement which provides for such consultant or person to have regular and substantial contact with children; or

(4) any other person 18 years of age or older legally responsible for a child, including the child's custodian, guardian and any person responsible for the child's care at the relevant time. Custodian may include any person continually or at regular intervals found in the same household as the child when the conduct of such person causes or contributes to the abuse or maltreatment of the child.

(e) Other person named in the report shall mean and be limited to the following persons who are named in a report of child abuse or maltreatment other than the subject of the report: any child and/or children who are named in a report made to the State Central Register of Child Abuse and Maltreatment and the parent, guardian or other person legally responsible for such child(ren) which parent, guardian or other person legally responsible for such child(ren) have not been named in the report as the person allegedly responsible for causing injury, abuse or maltreatment to such child(ren) or as allegedly allowing such injury, abuse or maltreatment to be inflicted on such child(ren).

(f) Unfounded report means any report made, unless an investigation determines that some credible evidence of the alleged abuse or maltreatment exists.

(g) Indicated report means a report made in which an investigation determines that some credible evidence of the alleged abuse or maltreatment exists.

(h) Public hearing means a hearing held prior to the submission of a local plan in a place and at a time which will allow the maximum number of concerned citizens and professionals to attend. The hearing shall be publicized in a manner which would bring the meeting and its purpose to the attention of the maximum number of agencies and individuals. Notice of such hearings should be publicized at least two weeks in advance through local media and through notices mailed by the local department of social services to appropriate groups, organizations and community agencies. The meeting shall be conducted in such a way as to encourage recommendations from those in attendance.

(i) Rehabilitative service means those services necessary to safeguard and protect the child's well-being and development and to preserve and stabilize family life, including but not limited to preventive services as defined by Part 423 of this Title, and protective services for children as defined by subdivision (p) of this section; provided, however, that no activity relating to the receiving of reports of child abuse and/or maltreatment or the investigation thereof and the determination as to whether or not such a report is indicated or unfounded, or to the family assessment response for such reports, will be considered a rehabilitative service for the purposes of this Part.

(j) Monitoring means the active continued involvement of the social services district's child protective service with those indicated cases of child abuse and maltreatment which are open on the State central register, but where the child protective service worker(s) are not the primary service provider for the case. The purpose of such involvement is to ensure the continued safety of the child(ren) in the case, that risk reduction activities and services are being implemented, and that the service plan is modified when progress has been insufficient.

(k) Monitor shall refer to the employee of the child protective service who is monitoring the services being provided by someone other than the child protective service employee to children named in an indicated case of child abuse and/or maltreatment which is open in the State Central Register and their families.

(*l*) Family and children's services plan shall refer to the case planning requirements of the uniform case record, pursuant to Part 428 of this Title.

(m) Case management shall mean the responsibility of the local social services district to authorize the provision of protective services for children, to approve in writing the child and family services plan, and to approve in writing the reports to be submitted to the State Central Register of Child Abuse and Maltreatment and the filing of such reports to the State Central Register.

(n) Case planning means assessing the need for, providing or arranging for, coordinating and evaluating the provision of protective services for children and all other rehabilitative services provided to children named in abuse and/or maltreatment reports and their families. Case planning includes referring child(ren) and his/her family to providers of rehabilitative services, as needed.

Case planning responsibility also includes recording in the child's uniform case record that such services are provided and that casework contacts, as prescribed by subdivision (o) of this section, are provided. In addition, case planning includes the timely completion of reports required by this Part to be submitted or transmitted to the State central register.

(o) Casework contacts mean face-to-face contacts with a child and/or a child's parents or guardians, or activities with the child and/or the child's parents or guardians, which may include but are not limited to:

(1) facilitating information gathering and analysis of safety factors;

(2) facilitating information gathering and analysis of the inter-relatedness of risk influences and individual risk elements affecting family functioning;

(3) reaching a determination on the allegations reported to the State central register;

(4) providing necessary protection to the child and/or ensuring the provision of such protection;

(5) providing rehabilitative services to reduce risk to the child and/or ensuring the provision of such services;

(6) evaluating the level of progress being made toward achievement of outcomes set forth in the family and children's service plan; and

(7) assessing family needs and strengths and facilitating the provision of services in conjunction with a family assessment response.

(p) Protective services for children mean activities on behalf of children, under the age of 18, who are named in an alleged or an indicated report of abuse and/or maltreatment. The following activities may be considered protective services for children:

(1) identification and diagnosis, including assessment of a child's safety and risk to the child of abuse or maltreatment;

(2) receipt of child abuse and/or maltreatment reports and investigation thereof, including the obtaining of information from collateral contacts such as hospitals, school and police;

(3) making determinations, following investigations, that there is credible evidence of child abuse and/or maltreatment;

(4) receipt of child abuse and/or maltreatment reports and the provision of a family assessment response to such reports, including communicating with the family to identify concerns affecting family stability and assisting them to identify services and resources that will minimize future risk to a child;

(5) providing counseling, therapy and training courses for the parents or guardians of the individual, including parent aide services;

(6) counseling and therapy for individuals at risk of physical or emotional harm;

(7) arranging for emergency shelter for children who are suspected of being abused and/or maltreated;

(8) arranging for financial assistance, where appropriate;

(9) assisting the Family Court or the Criminal Court during all stages of a court proceeding in accordance with the purposes of title 6 of article 6 of the Social Services Law;

(10) arranging for the provision of appropriate rehabilitative services, including but not limited to preventive services and foster care for children;

(11) providing directly or arranging for, either through purchase or referral, the provision of day care or homemaker services, without regard to financial criteria. Programmatic need for such service must have been established as a result of the investigation of a report of child abuse and/or maltreatment

received by the State Central Register and such services must terminate as a protective service for children when the case is closed with the register, pursuant to the standards set forth in section 432.2(c) of this Part;

(12) monitoring the rehabilitative services being provided by someone other than the child protective service worker;

(13) case management services;

(14) case planning services; and

(15) casework contacts.

(q) Documentation file shall mean the memos and procedures compiled by a local district which supports compliance with the statutory and regulatory requirements related to child protective services.

(r) Primary service provider shall refer to a caseworker who is responsible for both case planning and providing casework contact services to children named in indicated abuse and/or maltreatment reports and their families.

(s) Pre-determination means the period between the time a report of suspected child abuse or maltreatment is made and a determination report is submitted or transmitted to the State central register.

(t) Post-determination means the period beginning with the time a report of suspected child abuse or maltreatment is determined to be indicated and the family continues to receive child protective services through the time that the child protective services case is closed.

(u) Caseload means the number of cases to which an individual child protective services worker provides either pre-determination and/or post-determination services or a family assessment response. A case is established through the State Central Register numbering process and is the result of a report of suspected child abuse or maltreatment being made to the State Central Register.

(v) Casework supervision means the provision of guidance and support to a child protective services worker in planning and taking actions with or pertaining to a family in the worker's caseload. Actions supervised include, but are not limited to, the initial steps to be taken in response to a report of child abuse or maltreatment, taking protective custody of a child, developing and carrying out a service plan for a family, and deciding when to close a case.

(w) Risk assessment means an evaluation of elements that pertain to and influence a subject of the report, other persons named in the report and any other children in the household in order to assess the likelihood that such child(ren) named in the report or in the household will be abused or maltreated in the future.

(x) Specialized rehabilitative services means assessment, diagnosis, testing, psychotherapy, and specialized therapies provided as a component of a service plan to children named in an indicated child abuse and/or maltreatment report and their families by a person who has received a master's degree in social work, is a licensed psychologist, is a licensed psychiatrist or other recognized therapist in human services or is a licensed or qualified individual including, but not limited to, a registered nurse or an alcohol or substance abuse counselor. Such service providers may be considered to be making casework contacts as defined in section 432.2(b)(3) of this Part when the specialized rehabilitative services are directed by, arranged by, or otherwise coordinated by the case planner.

(y) Supportive services means those services provided to the children named in an indicated report and/or their families including, but not limited to, parent aide services, homemaker services, or home health aide services, parent training services, housekeeper/chore services; and home management services. Persons providing such services may be considered to be making casework contacts as defined in section 432.2(b)(3) of this Part when the supportive services are directed by, arranged by or otherwise coordinated by the case planner.

(z) Probation services means services provided by a probation service that are related to the provision of protective services.

(aa) Preliminary assessment of safety means an evaluation of safety factors to determine whether the child(ren) named in the report and any other child(ren) in the household may be in immediate danger of serious harm, and, if any child is assessed to be unsafe, undertaking immediate and appropriate interventions to protect the child(ren).

(ab) Controlling interventions are activities or arrangements which protect a child from unsafe situations, behaviors or conditions which are associated with immediate danger of serious harm, and without which the unsafe situations, behaviors or conditions would still be present or would in all likelihood immediately return.

(ac) Legally sealed report means a report made to the State Central Register on or after February 12, 1996, that was determined to be unfounded based on a lack of some credible evidence or a report made to the State Central Register that was assigned to the family assessment response track.

(ad) Family assessment response (FAR) is an alternative child protective response to reports of child abuse and maltreatment in which no formal determination is made as to whether a child was abused or maltreated and which is based on principles of family involvement and support consistent with maintaining the safety of the child. In family assessment response, the family and child protective service jointly participate in a comprehensive assessment of the family's strengths, concerns, and needs, and plan for the provision of services that are responsive to the family's needs and promote family stabilization, for the purpose of reducing risks to children in the family.

(ae) Family assessment response track means the employment of the family assessment response, as established in section 432.13 of this Part, to address a report of alleged child abuse or maltreatment by using family assessment response-specific processes and practices for the assessment of safety, risk, and family strengths and needs and the development and implementation of solution-focused plans to address identified needs.

(af) Investigative track means the employment of child protective service procedures, as established in section 432.2 of this Part, to address a report of alleged child abuse or maltreatment by using methods of investigation, assessment of safety and risk, and determination of such report as indicated or unfounded.

(ag) The Family Led Assessment Guide (FLAG) means a tool used in a family assessment response by all members of the family and child protective service staff to jointly identify the family's individual and family strengths, needs and concerns. The contents of the FLAG are specified by OCFS.

(ah) Wraparound funding means flexible and non-categorical funding used for the short-term provision of goods and services to meet family-identified needs, as part of a plan to support the family's ability to provide adequate care to their children and/or to minimize risk for one or more children in their household. The choice of goods and services is individualized to meet the unique needs of each child and family.

(ai) OCFS refers to the New York State Office of Children and Family Services or any successor state agency of that or any other name that is responsible for the supervision of child protective services in New York State. References to the department also refer to OCFS.

(aj) State Central Register means the New York Statewide Central Register of Child Abuse and Maltreatment or any successor agency that assumes the duties and responsibilities established in section 422 of the Social Services Law. References to the SCR or the register and any variations of that name also refer to the State Central Register.

(ak) CONNECTIONS refers to the computerized electronic system of record that is used for recording child welfare case information in New York State, including information regarding reports of alleged child abuse and maltreatment and the provision of protective services. This term will also apply to any successor reporting system that may be required by OCFS for recording such information.

§432.2 Child protective service: responsibilities and organization.

(a) General.

(1) The local commissioner of each social services district shall establish a child protective service within such district which shall operate as a single organizational unit. The child protective service shall perform those functions assigned to it by title 6 of article 6 of the Social Services Law. No other responsibilities may be assumed by the child protective service, except that the child protective service may provide for, arrange for and coordinate services to children named in a child abuse and/or maltreatment report and their families prior to a determination as to whether some credible evidence exists as to the alleged abuse or maltreatment.

(2) The child protective service shall have a sufficient number of staff with adequate qualifications to fulfill the purpose of title 6 of article 6 of the Social Services Law and shall be organized in such a way as to maximize the continuity of responsibility, care and service of individual workers towards children and families.

(3) Every social services district must provide to the child protective service information available to such district that is relevant to the investigation of a report of child abuse or maltreatment or to the family assessment response to such a report, except where the confidentiality of such information is expressly protected by law.

(b) Responsibilities of the child protective service. (1) The child protective service shall be the sole public organizational entity responsible for receiving and investigating, or arranging with the appropriate society for the prevention of cruelty to children to investigate all reports of suspected child abuse or maltreatment made pursuant to title 6 of article 6 of the Social Services Law, and for either investigating such reports for the purpose of determining if the allegations contained in such reports are indicated or unfounded, or providing or arranging for the provision of a family assessment response to those reports, pursuant to section 432.13 of this Part, for the purpose of assisting the family to assess and address any risk factors for their children. The child protective service shall also be the sole public organizational entity responsible for providing or arranging for and coordinating the provision of those services necessary to safeguard the child's well-being and development and to preserve and stabilize family life wherever appropriate, for abused and maltreated children who are named in a report assigned to the investigative track and for children in a family served through a report assigned to the family assessment response track. Where a child protective service worker is not the primary service provider of an open indicated child abuse or maltreatment case, a child protective service worker shall monitor the provision of the rehabilitative services being provided to children named in abuse and/or maltreatment reports and their families, pursuant to the requirements in paragraph (5) of this subdivision. Where a child protective service contracts with another agency to provide a family assessment response, a child protective service worker shall monitor the provision of assistance to the family named in the report.

(2) Intake. (i) The child protective service shall be responsible for receiving reports of suspected cases of child abuse and/or maltreatment from the State Central Register on a 24-hour, 7-day per week basis. When oral reports are made initially to the local child protective service, the child protective service shall immediately make an oral or electronic report to the State Central Register.

(ii) Each district is required to designate child protective services casework staff who will be responsible for receiving reports of child abuse and/or maltreatment during and after the district's normal business hours. After a district's normal business hours, a child protective service worker may receive notification of the existence of a report of child abuse and/or maltreatment from a third party for the purpose of contacting the State Central Register. The use of after-hours third-party answering services must be approved by OCFS.

(iii) Caseworkers at the local district who are not normally employees of the child protective service may be designated to directly receive reports of suspected child abuse and/or maltreatment from the State Central Register after the district's normal business hours, if the organization and administrative requirements of the single organizational unit, as set forth in subdivision (d) of this section are adhered to.

(iv) Intake procedures shall be clearly delineated in the documentation file. At a minimum, such documentation file shall include:

(a) a copy of the current information provided to the State central register which lists emergency telephone numbers and names of contacts which would be used if contact through the designated on-call procedures could not be made; and

(b) procedures which describe after-hours coverage to be followed as well as letters of agreement with answering services or other local or State agencies or departments which assume any responsibility related to telephone coverage after normal working hours.

(3) Investigation/assessment. (i) The child protective service must commence or cause the appropriate society for the prevention of cruelty to children to commence, within 24 hours after receiving a child abuse and/or maltreatment report, an appropriate investigation or family assessment response for each report of suspected child abuse and/or maltreatment. Within 24 hours of receiving a child abuse and/or maltreatment report, the child protective service, or the appropriate society for the prevention of cruelty to children must conduct a face-to-face contact or a telephone contact with the subjects and/or other persons named in the report or other persons in a position to provide information about whether the child may be in immediate danger of serious harm. In addition, for any report assigned to the investigative track, within one business day of the oral report date, the child protective service must review State Central Register records pertaining to all prior reports involving members of the family, including legally sealed unfounded and family assessment

response reports where the current report involves a subject of the unfounded or family assessment response report, a child named in the unfounded or family assessment response report or a child's sibling named in the unfounded or family assessment response report. Within five business days of the oral report date, the child protective service must review its own child protective service record(s) that apply to the prior reports, including legally sealed unfounded and family assessment response reports where the current report involves a subject of the unfounded or family assessment response report, a child named in the unfounded or family assessment response report or a child's sibling named in the unfounded or family assessment response report. For prior reports in which case records are maintained by another social services district including legally sealed unfounded and family assessment response reports, the child protective service with investigative responsibility must request relevant portions of such record(s) within one business day of the oral report date. The social services district maintaining the case record must provide the inquiring child protective service with the requested pertinent portions of their records within five business days of receiving such request.

(ii) The full child protective investigation must include the following activities:

(a) face-to-face interviews with subjects of the report and family members of such subjects, including children named in the report. If at any time during an investigation the subject of the report or another family member refuses to allow a child protective service worker to enter the home and/or to observe or talk to any child in the household, or if a child in the household cannot be located, the child protective service worker must assess whether it is necessary to seek a court order to obtain access to the child or home or to compel production of the child or whether other emergency action must be taken. The assessment must be made, at a minimum, in consultation with a child protective service supervisor as soon as necessary under the circumstances, but no later than 24 hours after the refusal or failure to locate the child or access the home. When it is assessed that it may be appropriate to seek a court order, legal staff who represent the child protective service must also be consulted, if possible. The assessment and the decision must be clearly documented in the progress notes for the investigation;

(b) obtaining information from the reporting sources and other collateral contacts which may include, but are not limited to, hospitals, family medical providers, schools, police, social service agencies and other agencies providing services to the family, relatives, extended family members, neighbors and other persons who may have information relevant to the allegations in the report and to the safety of the children; provided, however, the name or other information identifying the reporter and/or source of a report of suspected child abuse or maltreatment, as well as the agency, institution, organization, program and/or other entity with which such person(s) is associated must only be recorded or documented in progress notes and such documentation must be recorded in the manner specified by OCFS pursuant to section 428.5(c)(2) of this Title;

(c) within seven days of receipt of the report, conducting a preliminary assessment of safety to determine whether the child named in the report and any other children in the household may be in immediate danger of serious harm. If any child is assessed to be unsafe, undertaking immediate and appropriate controlling interventions to protect the child(ren); the results of each safety assessment must be documented in the case record in the form and manner required by OCFS;

(d) a determination of the nature, extent and cause of any condition enumerated in such report and any other condition that may constitute abuse or maltreatment;

(e) obtaining the name, age and condition of other children in the home; and

(f) after seeing that the child or children named in the report are safe, notifying the subjects and other persons named in the report, except children under the age of 18 years, in writing, no later than seven days after receipt of the oral report, of the existence of the report and the subject's rights pursuant to title 6 of article 6 of the Social Services Law concerning amendment or expungement of the report.

(g) in social services districts approved by OCFS to provide family assessment response, if within seven days of receipt of the report, the child protective service determines pursuant to the criteria in section 432.13(c)(4) of this Part that a report that has been assigned to the investigative track meets the requirements for assignment to the family assessment response track and that such assignment most effectively supports the safety of children named in the report and matches the family's needs, the assignment of the report may be changed to the family assessment response track. The reason(s) for the choice of assignment must be documented in the initial safety assessment.

(iii) Prior to making a determination that a report of abuse and/or maltreatment assigned to the investigative track should be indicated or unfounded, the investigation to be conducted by the child protective service shall include, but not be limited to:

(a) one home visit with one face-to-face contact with the subjects and other persons named in the report so as to evaluate the environment of the child named in the report as well as other children in the same home;

(b) an assessment of the current safety and the risk of future abuse and maltreatment to the child(ren) in the home and documenting such assessment in the form and manner provided by OCFS.

(iv) The child protective service has the sole responsibility for making a determination within 60 days after receiving the report as to whether there is some credible evidence of child abuse and/or maltreatment so as either to "indicate" or "unfound" a report of child abuse and/or maltreatment.

(v) A child protective service supervisor must review and approve the decision to either indicate or unfound the allegation(s) of child abuse and/or maltreatment.

(vi) The child protective service worker shall, in all cases where a child abuse or maltreatment report is being investigated, assess whether the best interests of the child require Family Court or Criminal Court action and shall initiate such action, whenever necessary.

(vii) Such investigation/assessment procedures shall be clearly delineated in the documentation file and shall support the district's assurances which are set forth in the district's consolidated services plan relating to child protective services. At a minimum, such documentation file shall include:

(a) the procedures which describe in detail the processes used for assigning child abuse and maltreatment cases and initiating an investigation of the case within the 24-hour time frame;

(b) if applicable, the interagency agreements entered into with the appropriate societies for the prevention of cruelty to children; and

(c) the procedures regarding notifying subjects and other persons named in a report, except children under the age of 18 years, no later than seven days of the existence of such report and notifying subjects and such other persons of an indicated determination within seven days of such indication.

(4) Providing, arranging for and/or coordinating services. (i) The child protective service shall be responsible for the provision and coordination of rehabilitative services and foster care services, where appropriate, or arranging for the provision and coordination of rehabilitative services and foster care services, where appropriate, to any child who is named in an indicated child abuse and/or maltreatment report and his/her family, including other children in the same household, in order to safeguard and ensure a child's well-being and development and to preserve and stabilize family life whenever appropriate.

(ii) The child protective service may, where appropriate, provide for or arrange for and coordinate services to children named in child abuse and/or maltreatment reports and their families prior to a determination as to whether some credible evidence exists as to the alleged abuse or maltreatment.

(iii) The provision of child protective services shall be limited to any child named in a child abuse and/or maltreatment report or any member of the child's family, including other children in the same home.

(iv) The child protective service worker shall, in all cases where subjects of an indicated abuse and/or maltreatment report refuse to accept rehabilitative services and/or foster care services, assess whether the best interests of the child require Family Court action to compel the subjects of the report to accept rehabilitative services and/or foster care services and shall initiate such action whenever necessary, unless there is insufficient evidence to initiate a Family Court petition to compel involvement in such service(s).

(v) In directly providing services to children named in an abuse and/or maltreatment report and their families, the child protective service worker must ensure:

(a) that any safety response initiated or maintained protects the child from immediate danger of serious harm; and

(b) that services planned and/or provided are likely to reduce the risk related to one or more identified risk elements.

(vi) In cases where the child protective service is the primary service provider to children named in indicated child protective services cases and their families, the child protective service worker must make casework contacts which, at a minimum, consist of at least two separate face-to-face contacts per month with the subject(s) and other persons named in the report, at least one of which must take place in the subject's home. Where the child protective service is coordinating the delivery of rehabilitative services pursuant to subparagraph (viii) of this paragraph, by providers of specialized rehabilitative services, supportive services and probation services as defined by section 432.1(x), (y) and (z) of this Part, such providers may make up to six of the contacts required during a six-month period. However, only contacts made by the case planner or case worker, as directed by the case planner, may be counted as the required in-home contact and only two of the contacts made by other service providers may be made by supportive service providers. For purposes of this subparagraph, the first six month period commences at the case initiation date or at the opening of an indicated child protective service case; subsequent six-month periods will be calculated from the service plan due date.

(vii) In cases where the child protective service is the primary service provider to children named in indicated child protective services cases and their families, the child protective service worker shall be responsible for the case management of the case.

(viii) In cases where the child protective service is the primary service provider to children named in indicated child protective services cases and their families, the child protective service is responsible for identifying, utilizing and coordinating other services in the community and provided by the social services district, to assist in the rehabilitation of individuals named in an indicated child abuse and/or maltreatment report and to reduce risk to children named in such cases. In coordinating the delivery of rehabilitative services, the child protective service worker must ensure that the roles, responsibilities and tasks and activities of all service providers are clearly defined and that the established plan of service is being implemented.

(ix) In cases where the child protective service is the primary service provider to children named in indicated child protective services cases and their families, a child protective service supervisor must review casework decisions made by the child protective service worker. Such review must include, at a minimum, a review of the family and children's services plan for the case and of the information periodically reported to the State central register.

(x) Any child protective service caseworker may provide and arrange for preventive services in addition to protective services for children to his own protective services case, as long as the case is eligible for mandated preventive services pursuant to section 430.9 of this Title and the caseworker is directly providing services to the children named in indicated abuse and/or maltreatment reports and their families.

(xi) Any child protective service caseworker may provide foster care services in addition to protective services for children in his own protective service case, as long as it has been determined that foster care placement was necessary pursuant to department standards set forth in section 430.10 of this Title.

(xii) For those cases under court-ordered supervision, where a child protective service worker is not the primary service provider of a child protective services case, a child protective service worker shall monitor the provision of the rehabilitative services being provided to children named in indicated abuse and/or maltreatment reports and their families, pursuant to the requirements of paragraph (b)(5) of this section.

(xiii) (a) When the family court orders the child protective service to supervise or monitor the respondent(s) and the family involved, pursuant to section 1039 or section 1052(a)(i), (iii), (iv) and (v) of the Family Court Act, the child protective service must undertake all practicable efforts to carry out the provisions of the order. In order to comply with such an order, the child protective service must meet the requirements of subparagraphs (i) through (xii) of this paragraph.

(b) When an order issued pursuant to Family Court Act section 1039 or section 1052(a) appears to be in conflict with other requirements of this section, or is unclear or ambiguous, the child protective service must so advise the court issuing the order and work with the court to resolve the conflict in order to both comply with the order and provide services to the respondent(s) and family involved. Nothing in this paragraph is to be construed as authorizing the child protective service to disregard or fail to comply with any provision of an order issued by a family court.

(c) When a child protective service is ordered to supervise or monitor the respondent(s) and family involved, the child protective service must comply with the applicable notification requirements of the Family Court Act.

(5) Monitoring. (i) The child protective service shall be responsible for monitoring the provision of services, including foster care services, to children named in open indicated abuse and maltreatment reports and their families, when the child protective service worker is not the primary service provider for the case.

(ii) The purpose of monitoring is to ensure the continued safety of the child(ren) that risk reduction activities and services are being implemented in the established plan for services, and that the service plan is modified when progress has been insufficient.

(iii) Monitoring includes, but is not limited to, all of the following tasks:

(a) Preparing or receiving, reviewing and approving the reports required to be submitted to the State central register by section 432.3(c)(4) of this Part, and receiving and reviewing the family and children's services plan as defined in section 432.1 of this Part.

(1) The reports made to the State central register must be consistent with the family and children's services plan in order to establish a unified and consistent plan for all children named in abuse or maltreatment reports and their families.

(2) In reviewing the appropriate section(s) of the family and children's services plan, the monitor has the continuing responsibility to assess:

(i) whether a safety response has been initiated or maintained when necessary, and whether such response protects the child from immediate danger of serious harm;

(ii) whether services planned and/or provided are likely to reduce the risk related to one or more identified risk elements;

(iii) whether the family is cooperating with the other service providers;

(iv) whether the needs of all the children in a household are taken into consideration when formulating a treatment plan; and

(v) whether the best interests of the child require Family Court or Criminal Court action.

(3) If, after the face-to-face contact required in clause (b) of this subparagraph, or after telephone contact with the primary services providers, the monitor is unable to approve the reports required to be submitted to the State central register because of a discrepancy between the content of the family and children's services plan and the content of the plan for protective services which the monitor has determined to be necessary for reporting purposes to the State central register, the monitor must notify his or her supervisor, who will be responsible for ensuring that the issue in question is discussed by all relevant parties at an administrative level for purposes of seeking a final resolution. After the issues have been satisfactorily resolved, the highest level of child protective services staff involved in the resolution must approve the reports to be submitted to the State central register pursuant to paragraph (c)(4) of this section.

(4) In situations where the child protective service and other service units within a social services district are unable to come to an agreement on a plan for care and services, the social services district commissioner must develop procedures for mediation, including the designation of an individual(s) who has the responsibility of approving the family and children's services plan as well as the reports required to be submitted to the State central register. Such

individual is accountable for the decisions resulting from the mediation process. Such mediation process must be approved by the department.

(b) Conducting face-to-face contacts with the primary service provider(s) or, where applicable, other local district staff involved in the case, when a major change in the service plan for the case is being considered. For the purpose of this subparagraph, a major change in the service plan for the case shall be defined as:

(1) consideration of returning a child to his home or to relatives from a foster care placement, or consideration of placing a child into foster care from his present living arrangement;

(2) terminating the provision of mandated preventive services for the case;

(3) consideration of closing the case with the State central register pursuant to the standards in subdivision (c) of this section; and

(4) consideration of initiating a court petition under article 10 of the Family Court Act, or recommending a significant change in a court disposition for a case under such article.

The face-to-face contact may include, but need not be limited to, attendance at the service plan review for children who are presently in foster care who are also named in an open indicated child protective services report. In attending the service plan review, the child protective service monitor may serve as one of the individuals required to attend the service plan review for foster care cases pursuant to section 430.12(c)(2) of this Title.

(c) Direct dialogue with the primary service provider and other service providers, as applicable, either through a face-to-face contact or a telephone discussion, as often as is necessary to ensure continuity of service delivery, but at a minimum of every six months starting from the date that the appropriate case planning services, as defined in section 432.1(n) of this Part, were transferred from the child protective service to a caseworker in another service unit of the local district, or to a caseworker in an agency from which rehabilitative services are purchased. Such direct dialogue shall include informing the primary service provider of investigations of abuse and/or maltreatment reports.

(d) Ensuring that the results of investigations of reports of abuse and/or maltreatment, including any changes in the assessment of future risk of abuse or maltreatment, are incorporated into the formulation of the new treatment plan for the child(ren) and family.

(e) Ensuring that appropriate information exchange exists between the child protective service and other service providers. Completed department reporting forms relative to the child protective services allegations which are contained in the child protective services may be released to authorized agencies having the responsibility for the care and supervision of a child named in a report and to other service providers only if, in the latter case, informed consent is given by the subject(s) of or other persons named in the report.

(6) Fiscal requirements for child protective service.

(i) Activities completed by child protective services casework staff, such as the completion of the appropriate reporting forms to be sent to the statewide central register, the investigation of abuse and/or maltreatment reports and monitoring tasks as prescribed in paragraph (5) of this subdivision, shall be considered activities solely reimbursable as a protective service for children.

(ii) Rehabilitative service, as defined by section 432.1(i) of this Part, may be considered activities reimbursable as a protective service for children, pursuant to the definition of protective services for children contained in section 432.1(p) of this Part.

(c) Case closing on the State central register. (1) Standards for case closing. A case may be closed with the State central register only when the local child protective service has documented compliance with the standards specified in clauses (i)(a), (b) and (c) of this paragraph, as applicable.

(i) General standards for case closing when all rehabilitative services are to be terminated to children named in indicated reports of abuse and/or maltreatment and their families. A case may be closed to the statewide central register only:

(a) if the local child protective service can show that all children in the household are assessed to be safe despite the withdrawal of controlling interventions that may have been provided to protect the children and it is concluded that the risk of future abuse or maltreatment has decreased sufficiently; or

(b) the child protective service has offered rehabilitative services to the children named in indicated abuse and/or maltreatment reports and their families, but such services have been rejected, and the child protective service worker has assessed that it would not be in the best interest of the child to initiate a Family Court petition for a determination that a child is in need of care and protection; or

(c) the child protective service has sought a Family Court order but the court has dismissed such a petition, and it is not in the child's best interest to continue additional Family Court action.

(ii) Standards when one or more children named in abuse and/or maltreatment reports are in foster care. A case may be closed with the statewide central register when one or more children named in abuse and/or maltreatment report(s) are in foster care, if all such children are:

(a) freed for adoption;

(b) continuing in out-of-home placement with a permanency planning goal of another planned living arrangement with a permanency resource or adult residential care; or

(c) it is documented in the family and children services plan that the necessity of foster care for all children who are named in abuse and/or maltreatment report(s) is not presently attributable to the reasons set forth in paragraph (1) or (4) of section 430.10(c) of this Title.

(iii) Standard when one or more children named in abuse and/or maltreatment reports are receiving mandated preventive services. A case may be closed with the statewide central register when one or more children named in abuse and/or maltreatment report(s) are receiving mandated preventive services if all such children are presently at risk of foster care because of reasons which are unrelated to circumstances set forth in paragraph (1) or (4) of section 430.9(c) of this Title.

(2) Necessary activities prior to case closing. (i) In considering the closing of a case with the State central register, the child protective services shall:

(a) review events, correspondence and summary of conversations included in the family and children's case record;

(b) review assessments of the family, including risk analyses, made by all service providers;

(c) review the accomplishments made by the family in achieving the outcomes set forth in the family and children's service plan; and

(d) discuss with the family and children directly, or with other service providers, the family's response to the termination of protective services for children.

(ii) Approval by a supervisor of the child protective services worker must be obtained prior to the case being closed with the State central register.

(3) Documentation of compliance with case closing standards. (i) General. Upon closing a case with the statewide central register, the local child protective service shall provide documentation to the department that the requirements of this subdivision were met. Such documentation shall include notifying the State central register, in a form and manner prescribed by the department, that the standards in this subdivision have been adhered to.

(ii) In documenting that children named in abuse and/or maltreatment report(s) are not placed in foster care due to a circumstance set forth in paragraph (1) or (4) of section 430.10(c) of this Title, the child protective service must document, or ensure that such documentation exists, in a form and manner prescribed by the department, that, if the child were to be returned home, the child would not be in danger of serious physical or emotional harm. In (re)assessing the risk to the child, the child protective service worker must cite one or more of the following factors: the parent's or caretaker's willingness to maintain regular contact with the child, their favorable behavior during visits, their favorable response to services offered or provided by the district or other involved agencies, their expressed willingness to take the child home and to plan for his or her welfare, the present favorable evaluation of safety factors and risk elements which in the past contributed to the original problems which necessitated the placement, and the overall progress of the parent toward achieving the outcomes established in the family and children's service plan.

(iii) In documenting that children named in abuse and/or maltreatment report(s) are not at risk of foster care because of a circumstance set forth in paragraph (1) or (4) of section 430.10(c) of this Title, the child protective service worker must document, in a form and manner prescribed by the department, that such children are not in danger of serious emotional or physical harm, or ensure that such documentation exists. In cases where such danger previously existed, the child protective service worker must document that the emotional, physical or mental condition which had impaired the ability of the child's parents or caretaker to function no longer places the child in danger of serious emotional or physical harm. In addition, if the ability to care for a child had been impaired because of prior financial problems, including a lack of adequate housing, the child protective service worker must document that such impairment no longer places the child in danger of serious emotional or physical harm.

(iv) A child protective service supervisor shall approve, in writing, that the case closing decision has been made in accordance with the requirements of this subdivision.

(d) Use of risk assessment. (1) For child abuse or maltreatment reports that are assigned to the investigative track, risk assessment must be employed by the child protective service when key case decisions are made concerning a child named in the report, including but not limited to, whether controlling interventions which would provide safety and protection to the children, including but not limited to, intensive home based preservation services or foster care placement, must be immediately instituted; whether to keep an indicated case open for the provision of services after the determination of whether the report is indicated or unfounded is made; which outcomes that are intended to facilitate behavior change and/or alter the conditions affecting a family should be developed; whether there is a need to reassess a family's progress toward reducing the risk to children in the family; and whether an open child protective case may appropriately be closed.

(i) Supervisors must, at case conferences with staff and when reviewing case records, examine the caseworkers' use of risk assessment for arriving at key case decisions.

(ii) When a child protective service is the primary service provider, case records must contain documentation that key decisions were reached through consideration of the items described in paragraph (2) of this subdivision. This subparagraph does not apply to a determination that a report is to be indicated or unfounded.

(iii) When a child protective service is monitoring the provision of child protective services, it is responsible for ensuring that the items described in paragraph (2) of this subdivision are considered when making key case decisions.

(iv) Risk assessment activities for reports assigned to the investigative track must be documented in the form and manner required by OCFS pursuant to Part 428 of this Title and clause (b)(3)(iii)(b) of this section. Risk assessment activities for reports assigned to the family assessment response track must be completed and documented in the form and manner required by OCFS pursuant to section 432.13 of this Part.

(e) Administration and organization of the child protective service.

(1) The child protective service of each social services district shall be administered by a person designated by the local commissioner. This person shall have direct administrative control and accountability for the effective provision of the district's child protective service. This person shall be solely responsible for overseeing those functions assigned to the child protective service by title 6 of article 6 of the Social Services Law, and only such other functions which would aid in the rehabilitation of any individual who is named in a child abuse and/or maltreatment report.

(2) The local child protective service shall be comprised of staff of the district who are specifically designated and identifiable as the child protective service of a social services district. A local child protective service for that district may consist of one or more local district workers whose responsibilities may be designated in part, as performing child protective services functions, if such district receives less than 200 reports of abuse and/or maltreatment on an annual basis. Such organizational arrangement must be approved by OCFS.

(3) After-hours coverage. (i) After a district's normal working hours, a child protective service worker may receive notification of the existence of reports of child abuse and/or maltreatment from a third party for the purpose of contacting the State Central Register. Such arrangement cannot be used unless it is approved by OCFS.

(ii) A local district may assign casework staff other than staff of the child protective service to perform the intake and/or the investigation functions during after hours if OCFS has approved a district's after-hours organizational structure. For the purpose of this paragraph:

(a) staff performing child protective service functions shall have the powers and responsibilities assigned by title 6 of article 6 of the Social Services Law for the duration of the time the staff is functioning in the child protective service; and

(b) such staff shall have the background, skill and training as required by paragraph (b)(5) of this section.

(4) Intra/inter-agency agreements. Each local district commissioner shall develop written procedures between the local district's child protective service and other units or bureaus of the district. In addition, each commissioner shall develop written agreements for use between the local district's child protective service and other service providers outside the local district. Such written agreements or procedures shall ensure:

(i) that appropriate information is received by the child protective service from other service units in the social services district and other provider agencies, in a timely manner, including but not limited to documentation of risk assessment activities and any component of the family and children's services plan, as defined by section 432.1(1) of this Part, so as to permit the child protective service to monitor the provision of services to children and families as described in paragraph (b)(5) of this section;

(ii) that the monitor and service providers receive information as to the kind and nature of reports being investigated or assessed in family assessment response, and the determinations of such investigations, except that such information may only be disclosed in conformity with subdivisions 4 and 5 of section 422 of the Social Services Law, subdivision 5 of section 427-a of the Social Services Law, and sections 357.5 and 432.13 of this Title;

(iii) that the child protective service is notified of the time and place of service plan reviews that are held for children in foster care who are named in indicated abuse and/or maltreatment reports open with the State Central Register;

(iv) that the child protective service receives appropriate information from other service providers, including information concerning contacts with children named in an indicated report and their family, to allow for the planning, administration and evaluation of the various components of the child and family services plan, and information concerning contacts with children named in a family assessment response report, to allow for implementation of assistance identified through a FLAG;

(v) that other units or bureaus in the district, and other agencies outside the district, receive information relating to the child protective aspects of the case, so as to facilitate continuity of service provision; provided, however, that the confidentiality restrictions in subdivision 4 of section 422 and subdivision 5 of section 427-a of the Social Services Law are adhered to;

(vi) a formal method of effectuating case planning decisions, when the child protective service and other service units within a local district do not agree on a plan for care, pursuant to the requirements set forth in paragraph (b)(5) of this section;

(vii) the timely and expeditious transfer of cases from the child protective service to other service units within the district or to other service agencies outside the district after the investigation of or family assessment response to the abuse and/or maltreatment report has concluded and such transfer is deemed to be appropriate; and

(viii) that the child protective service staff be notified of any court petition filed pursuant to article 10 of the Family Court Act by any other child protective agency as defined by subdivision (i) of section 1012 of the Family Court Act or by any other person so directed by the court to originate an article 10 proceeding as determined by section 1032 of the Family Court Act. In addition, the child protective service shall be notified of any complaint which initiates Criminal Court action involving subjects of abuse and/or maltreatment reports. Such notice shall occur prior to the time of the filing.

(5) Staffing. (i) Each local child protective service must have sufficient qualified staff to fulfill the purposes of title 6 of article 6 of the Social Services Law. The staffing qualifications in this paragraph apply to all employees hired to work in the child protective service on or after January 1, 1986. These requirements also apply to staff of the local social services district who are transferred from other units to employment in the local child protective service.

(ii) (a) Each child protective service worker, including supervisors, must satisfactorily complete a basic training program in child protective services within the first three months of his/her employment in the child protective service. Such program must be approved by OCFS and must focus on the skills, knowledge and attitudes essential to working in the child protective service. Such training program must include, but need not be limited to: basic training in the principles and techniques of child protective service investigation, including relationships with other investigative bodies; legal issues in child protective service matters; diagnostic assessment of child abuse and maltreatment cases; methods of remediation, treatment and prevention of child abuse and maltreatment; and case management and planning of child protective services cases, including the relationship of the child protective service issues to permanency planning for children who remain at home or who are in out-of-home care.

(b) All persons employed by a child protective service on or after December 1, 2006 must satisfactorily complete six hours of annual in-service training approved by OCFS, beginning in their second year of employment. Pursuant to section 421(5) of the Social Services Law, such annual in-service training shall include, but not be limited to: review of the protocols for identification and investigation of child abuse and maltreatment; any developments in legal, treatment, and prevention issues in child protection; and review and analysis of field experiences of child protective workers.

(c) All persons hired or assigned to be a supervisor by a child protective service on or after April 1, 1986 must satisfactorily complete a course in the fundamentals of supervising and managing child protective practice approved by OCFS, within three months of their employment as a supervisor. Any person employed as a child protective supervisor who has not completed such a course by the effective date of this regulation must satisfactorily complete such a course no later than three months following the effective date of this regulation. The content of such training shall be determined by OCFS, in compliance with paragraph (c) of subdivision 5 of section 421 of the Social Services Law. Additionally, all such supervisors must attend the core training required for child protective services caseworkers, if they have not already done so, and participate in an annual in service training program that is specifically tailored for child protective service supervisors.

(d) Social services districts must maintain documentation verifying compliance with the training requirements of this paragraph and must make this documentation available to OCFS upon request.

(iii) Each non-supervisory child protective service worker must have a baccalaureate or equivalent college degree and/or must have relevant human services experience. Persons employed as supervisory staff of the child protective service prior to the effective date of this regulation must have a baccalaureate or equivalent degree or must have a minimum of one year of experience in child welfare services. Supervisory staff of the child protective service hired on or after the effective date of this regulation must have a baccalaureate or equivalent college degree and a minimum of two years of relevant work experience in child welfare services.

(a) In any instance in which the education or work experience requirements for child protective supervisory staff creates an obstacle to hiring suitable staff, a social services district may request a waiver from OCFS exempting them from this provision. The waiver must be approved by the OCFS commissioner or the commissioner's designee.

(6) (i) Staff review and evaluation. Each local child protective service must establish a procedure to review and evaluate the backgrounds of and information supplied by all applicants for employment in the local child protective service. This procedure must take into account any appropriate collective bargaining agreements and applicable provisions of the Civil Service Law. As part of this procedure, the child protective service must require such applicants to submit all of the following information:

(a) a statement or summary of each applicant's employment history, including but not limited to any relevant child-caring experience;

(b) the names, addresses and, where available, telephone numbers of references who can verify the applicant's employment history, work record and qualifications;

(c) the names, addresses and telephone numbers of at least three personal references, other than relatives, who can attest to the applicant's character, habits, reputation and personal qualifications; and

(d) a sworn statement by the applicant indicating whether, to the best of such applicant's knowledge, the applicant has ever been convicted of a crime in New York State or any other jurisdiction.

(ii) If an applicant discloses in the sworn statement furnished in accordance with subparagraph (i) of this paragraph that he/she has been convicted of a crime, the local child protective service must determine, in accordance with guidelines developed and disseminated by OCFS, whether to hire any such applicant, except that any local child protective service which had guidelines for the review of persons with conviction records in use prior to January 1, 1986 may continue to use the district guidelines in making the required determination. If the service determines it will hire the applicant, the service must maintain a written record, as part of the application file or employment or other personnel record of such person, of the reason(s) why such person was determined to be appropriate and acceptable as an employee.

(iii) Each local child protective service must inquire of OCFS whether any person who is actively being considered for employment or any person who is employed by an individual, corporation, partnership or association which provides goods or services to the local child protective service and who will have the potential for regular and substantial contact with children being cared for by the child protective service is the subject of an indicated report of child abuse or maltreatment on file with the State Central Register. The local child protective service may make such an inquiry to OCFS regarding any current employee or a person who is being considered for use as a volunteer or for hiring as a consultant and who has or will have the potential for regular and substantial contact with children being cared for by the service. An inquiry regarding any current employee may be made only once in any six-month period. Inquiries made pursuant to this paragraph shall be subject to the following provisions.

(a) Prior to making an inquiry to OCFS, the local child protective service must notify, in the form prescribed by OCFS, the person who will be the subject of the inquiry that an inquiry will be made to determine whether such person is the subject of an indicated report of child abuse or maltreatment on file with the State Central Register.

(b) (1) Except as set forth in subclause (2) of this clause, a child protective service may not permit a person hired by the service or a person who is employed by an individual, corporation, partnership or association which provides goods or services to the service to have contact with children in the care of the service prior to obtaining the result of the inquiry required by this subparagraph.

(2) An employee of a child protective service or an employee of a provider of goods and services to the child protective service may have contact with children cared for by the service prior to the receipt by the service of the result of the inquiry required by this subparagraph only where such employee is visually observed or audibly monitored by an existing staff member of the service. Such employee must be in the physical presence of an existing staff member for whom:

(i) the result of an inquiry required by section 424-a of the Social Services Law has been received by the child protective service and the service hired the existing staff member with knowledge of the result of the inquiry; or

(ii) an inquiry was not made because such staff member was hired before the effective date of section 424-a of the Social Services Law.

(c) (1) When the person who is the subject of the inquiry is an applicant for employment, a fee, as established by law, will be charged by OCFS when it conducts a search of its records within the State Central Register to determine whether such applicant is the subject of an indicated report.

(2) The required fee must either accompany the inquiry form submitted to OCFS or, for an inquiry submitted by a social services district, the district may elect to have the fee subtracted from its claims for reimbursement submitted pursuant to section 601.1 of this Title.

(3) Fees must be paid in a manner specified by OCFS to the "New York State Office of Children and Family Services". For social services districts electing to have the fees subtracted from their claims for reimbursement submitted pursuant to section 601.1 of this Title, the fees will be subtracted quarterly to match the number of inquiries made. Personal checks and cash are not acceptable forms of payment.

(d) If, an applicant, employee, or other person about whom the service has made an inquiry is found to be the subject of an indicated report of child abuse or maltreatment, the local child protective service must determine, on the basis of information it has available and in accordance with guidelines developed and disseminated by OCFS, whether to hire, retain or use the person as an employee, volunteer, or consultant or permit the person providing goods or services to have access to children being cared for by the service, except that any local child protective service which had guidelines for the review of persons who are subjects of indicated reports of child abuse or maltreatment in use prior to January 1, 1986 may continue to use the local guidelines in making the required determination. Whenever such person is hired, retained, used or given access to children, the child protective service must maintain a written record, as part of the application file or employment or other personnel record of any such person, of the specific reason(s) why such person was determined to be appropriate and acceptable as an employee, volunteer, consultant or provider of goods with access to children being cared for by the service.

(e) If the local child protective service denies employment or makes a decision not to retain an employee, use a volunteer, hire a consultant, or not permit a person providing goods or services to have access to children being cared for by the child protective service, the service must provide a written statement to the applicant, employee, volunteer, consultant, or other such person indicating whether the denial or decision was based in whole or in part on the existence of the indicated report and, if so, the reasons for the denial or decision. If the denial or decision is based in whole or in part on the existence of such report of child abuse or maltreatment the statement must also include, in the form prescribed by OCFS, written notification to the applicant, employee, volunteer, consultant or other person that:

(1) he/she has the right, pursuant to section 424-a of the Social Services Law, to request a hearing regarding the record maintained by the State Central Register;

(2) a request for such a hearing must be made within 90 days of the receipt of the notice of denial or decision indicating that the denial or decision was based in whole or in part on the existence of the indicated report; and

(3) the sole issue at any such hearing will be whether the applicant, employee, volunteer, consultant, or other person has been shown by a fair preponderance of the evidence to have committed the act or acts of child abuse or maltreatment giving rise to the indicated report.

(f) If in a hearing held pursuant to a request made in accordance with clause (c) of this subparagraph and section 424-a of the Social Services Law, OCFS fails to show by a fair preponderance of the evidence that the applicant, employee, volunteer, consultant, or other person committed the act or acts upon which the indicated report is based, OCFS must notify the local child protective service which made the inquiry to OCFS that, pursuant to the hearing decision, the decision of the service to deny the application, discharge the employee, or not to use the volunteer, not to hire the person as a consultant, or not to permit the person providing goods or services to have access to children being cared for by the service should be reconsidered. Upon receiving such notification from OCFS, the local child protective service should review its decision without considering the indicated report.

(iv) Reimbursement by OCFS will be withheld from a local social services district for the salary of any employee of the local child protective service who does not comply with the background review, educational, experience or training requirements of this paragraph or paragraph (5) of this subdivision.

(f) Local plan for the administration of child protective services.

(1) Pursuant to section 34-a of the Social Services Law and Part 407 of this Title, each local social services district shall prepare and submit to OCFS a multi-year consolidated services plan, hereinafter referred to as the "plan," which shall include information on protective services for children, provided directly or contracted for through purchase of services agreements. The plan shall be updated through the preparation of annual implementation reports, which shall be submitted to OCFS for approval.

(2) The child protective services component of the plan shall include, but not be limited to, the following:

(i) input from consultation with law enforcement agencies, the Family Court, and appropriate public or voluntary agencies;

(ii) a summary of the required public hearing, indicating the composition of the audience, the nature of the testimony given, and the impact the public hearing had in the development of the plan or annual implementation report. The summary shall include documentation that notice of the public hearing was provided at least 15 days prior to the date of the hearing and that such notice specified the time and place for the discussion of the child protective services component. The summary should also include copies of newspaper clippings related to the public hearings;

(iii) an organizational chart of the child protective service, including the total number of professional staff involved in the provision of such services, as well as any anticipated or planned changes in the structure of the child protective service;

(iv) a list of services that would be necessary and appropriate to help fulfill the function and responsibilities of the child protective service which are not available through the district or the community;

(v) information concerning the financing of local protective services for children, including the amount of money allocated for purchasing services from other agencies and the amount of money allocated by the local district for the direct provision of services;

(vi) the legal assurances set forth in paragraph (3) of this subdivision;

(vii) a listing of the sworn police officials of a city police department other than the police department of the City of New York, or of a county, town or village police department or county sheriff's department who have received permission from the local social services district to receive records and reports of child abuse and maltreatment. Such permission may be granted only for records and reports that have been assigned to the investigative track and only when such officer certifies that the records and reports are necessary in order to conduct a criminal investigation of the subject of the report, and that such investigation is reasonably related to the allegations contained in the report;

(viii) a summary of the understanding between the local social services district and the district attorney's office, which outlines the cooperative procedures to be followed by both parties in investigating incidents of child abuse and maltreatment consistent with their respective obligations for the investigation or prosecution of such incidents, as required by law and in accordance with the responsibilities of the child protective service as set forth in subdivision (b) of this section or a summary of the reasons why such an understanding has not been developed in spite of a good faith effort being made to do so; and

(ix) a description of the terms and conditions to be set forth in any written agreement between the local district and a provider or coordinator of services which authorizes redisclosure of child protective services information including records, reports or other information by such service provider or coordinator to other persons or agencies providing services to the child and family.

(3) Legal assurances. Each local district shall include in the child protective services component of its plan assurances that the child protective service is implementing each duty and responsibility assigned to it by title 6 of article 6 of the Social Services Law and this Part. Such assurances shall include, but not be limited to, assurances:

(i) that a separate organizational unit responsible for child protective services operates within the local district according to the requirements specified in this section;

(ii) *(Repealed, 10/22/14)*

(iii) that the State Central Register is kept fully informed and up-to-date concerning the receipt and disposition of reports by the entry of all appropriate reports and information into CONNECTIONS;

(iv) that the appropriate district attorney is immediately informed by telephone of any child who has died as a result of suspected child abuse and/or maltreatment, and that copies of all reports on such children are forwarded to the district attorney's office;

(v) that the appropriate medical examiner or coroner is informed if there is a reasonable cause to suspect that a child has died as a result of suspected child abuse and/or maltreatment;

(vi) that the findings from the medical examiner or coroner are secured on any case where there is reasonable cause to suspect that a child has died as a result of child abuse or maltreatment;

(vii) that telephone notice is provided and a copy of any or all reports of suspected abuse or maltreatment that have been assigned to the investigative track are forwarded immediately to the appropriate district attorney if a prior request in writing for such notice and copies has been received by the child protective service and provided that such request specifies the kinds of allegations concerning which the district attorney requires such notice and copies and provides a copy of the relevant provisions of law;

(viii) that a copy of any or all reports of suspected abuse and/or maltreatment is forwarded to any appropriate duly incorporated society for the prevention of cruelty to children or to any other duly authorized child protective agency, if a prior written request for such copies has been received from such society or agency by the child protective service;

(ix) that the district commences or causes the appropriate society for the prevention of cruelty to children to commence, within 24 hours after receiving a report of child abuse and/or maltreatment, an appropriate investigation or, for approved social service districts, a family assessment response to all reports of suspected child abuse and/or maltreatment. Such investigation or response must meet the requirements of paragraph (b)(3) of this section, or section 432.13 of this Part;

(x) that upon receipt of a report of suspected abuse or maltreatment that is assigned to the investigative track, and after seeing to the safety of the child or children named in the report, but in no event later than seven days after the receipt of the oral report, the local district delivers or mails to the subject(s) and other persons named in the investigative track report, except children under the age of 18 years, a written notification, in such form as required by OCFS, informing them of the existence of the report and of the subject(s)' rights with regard to amendment of information contained in the report; and, upon receipt of a report that is assigned to the family assessment track, and after seeing to the safety of the child or children named in the report, but in no event later than seven days after the receipt of the report, the local district delivers or mails to the parent(s), guardian(s), or other legally responsible person(s) of any child named in the report a written notification, in such form as required by OCFS, informing them of the existence of the report and of the nature of family assessment response; except that, when a new report is received that is consolidated into an open child protective services investigation or family assessment response, the child protective service may provide only verbal notification of the new report to all persons who were notified of the open report unless such person requests written notification;

(xi) that the local district determines, within 60 days, whether a report assigned to the investigative track is "indicated" or "unfounded" and, if "indicated," delivers or mails to the subject(s) and other persons named in the report, except children under the age of 18 years, a written notification, within seven days of the determination, in such form as required by OCFS, informing the subject(s) of their rights to request the commissioner to amend or, for any report received by the State Central Register prior to February 12, 1996, expunge the report and their right to request a fair hearing;

(xii) that upon receipt of written notice from the State Central Register of any expungement or amendment of the record of a report made pursuant to a subject's request or pursuant to a hearing, the local district expunges from or amends as directed all records of the report, and informs, for the same purposes, any other agency or person that received such report or information;

(xiii) that the local district shall take all appropriate measures to protect a child's life and health including, when appropriate, taking or keeping a child in protective custody without the consent of a parent or guardian, if there is reasonable cause to believe that the circumstances or condition of the child are such that continuing in his place of residence or in the care and custody of the parent, guardian, custodian or other person responsible for the child's care presents an imminent danger to the child's life or health;

(xiv) that upon being notified that a child is retained in protective custody, the child protective service staff shall commence a proceeding at the next regular weekday session of the appropriate Family Court, or recommend to the court, at that time, that the child be returned to his parents or guardian;

(xv) that, based upon the investigation and evaluation, the local district offers appropriate services to any child believed to be suffering from abuse or maltreatment and to the child's family, or both, and, in offering these services, explains to the family that the child protective service has no legal authority to compel the family to accept services;

(xvi) that, in those cases in which an appropriate offer of services is refused and the child protective services determines that the best interests of the child require court action, the local district initiates such action or makes a referral to the appropriate district attorney, or both;

(xvii) that the local district assists the Family Court or the Criminal Court during all stages of the court proceeding, in accordance with the purposes of title 6 of article 6 of the Social Services Law;

(xviii) that the local district provides or arranges for, coordinates and monitors rehabilitative services for children and their families on a voluntary basis or under a final or intermediate order of the Family Court according to the standards set forth in paragraphs (b)(1)-(6) of this section;

(xix) that the local child protective service receives, in accordance with title 6 of article 6 of the Social Services Law and paragraph (b)(2) of this section, reports of suspected abuse or maltreatment on a 24-hour, seven-day-a-week basis;

(xx) that, in local districts in which oral reports are made initially to the local child protective service, all reports are immediately upon receipt transmitted orally or electronically to the State Central Register;

(xxi) that the local child protective service has sufficient staff, of sufficient qualifications, to fulfill the purposes of title 6 of article 6 of the Social Services Law, and that with respect to such staff the local child protective service has complied with the background review, educational, experience and training requirements of subdivision (d) of this section;

(xxii) that, when necessary, the commissioner of a local district gives consent for medical, dental, health or hospital services for any child who has been found by the Family Court to be an abused or neglected child or has been taken into or kept in protective custody or removed from the place where such child is residing or who has been placed in the custody of such commissioner, pursuant to section 417 of the Social Services Law or section 1022, 1024 or 1027 of the Family Court Act;

(xxiii) that the local district conducts continuing publicity and education programs for local department staff, persons required to report cases of suspected abuse and maltreatment, and any other appropriate persons, to encourage the fullest degree of reporting of suspected child abuse or maltreatment, and that such educational programs include, but are not limited to, subjects relating to the responsibilities, obligations and powers imposed by title 6 of article 6 of the Social Services Law, as well as the diagnosis of child abuse and maltreatment and the procedures of the child protective services, the Family Court and other duly authorized agencies;

(xxiv) that the local district shall, when notified by a physician, take custody of any child treated by such physician, whether or not additional medical treatment is required, if such physician has reasonable cause to believe that the circumstances or condition of the child are such that the continuation of the child in his place of residence or in the care and custody of the parent, guardian, custodian, or other person responsible for the child's care presents an imminent danger to the child's life or health;

(xxv) that the local district must, when notified by the person in charge of any hospital or similar institution that such person has retained custody of a child because such person has reasonable cause to believe that the circumstances or conditions of the child are such that continuing in his/her place of residence or in the care and custody of the child's parent, guardian, custodian or other person responsible for the child's care presents an imminent danger to the child's life or health, immediately commence an investigation, and, if no further medical treatment is necessary, take all necessary measures to protect the child's life and health, including, where appropriate, taking custody of the child;

(xxvi) that the local district has made a good faith effort to develop a written understanding between the local district and the district attorney's office which specifies the cooperative procedures to be followed by both parties in investigating incidents of child abuse and maltreatment consistent with the respective obligations for the investigation or prosecution of such incidents as otherwise required by law, and in accordance with the responsibilities of the child protective service as set forth in subdivision (b) of this section;

(xxvii) that the local district makes current procedural manuals and service directories available to employees of the district's child protective service, service providers and professionals involved in the prevention of child abuse and maltreatment;

(xxviii) that upon receipt of written notice from the State Central Register that a report received by the State Central Register on or after February 12, 1996 has been "unfounded," the local district immediately seals the report and updates, as appropriate, information regarding such report in other records of the district and informs, for the same purposes, any other agency or person that received such report or any information about such report, or for any report received by the State Central Register prior to February 12, 1996, expunges the report and informs, for the same purposes, any other agency or person that received such report or information about such report. Legally sealed unfounded reports may be made available only to:

(a) OCFS for the purpose of supervising a social services district;

(b) OCFS and local or regional fatality review team members for the purpose of preparing a fatality report pursuant to sections 20 or 422-b of the Social Services Law;

(c) a local child protective service, OCFS, all members of a local or regional multidisciplinary investigative team established pursuant to section 423(6) of the Social Services Law, or the Justice Center for the Protection of People with Special Needs, when investigating a subsequent report of suspected abuse or maltreatment involving a subject of the unfounded report, a child named in the unfounded report, or a child's sibling named in the unfounded report;

(d) the subject of the report; and

(e) a district attorney, an assistant district attorney; an investigator employed in the office of a district attorney; or a sworn officer of the division of state police, or of a city, county, town or village police department or of a county sheriff's office when such official verifies that the report is necessary to conduct an active investigation or prosecution of a violation of subdivision four of section 240.50 of the Penal Law. Information from a legally sealed unfounded report that is relevant to the investigation of the current report may be made a part of a subsequent report involving a subject of the unfounded report, a child named in the unfounded report or a child's sibling named in the unfounded report. Information from the legally sealed unfounded report that is not made part of the subsequent report remains legally sealed.

(xxix) that, upon receiving a written request from the State Central Register for all records, reports or other information maintained by the local child protective service pertaining to an indicated report of child abuse and maltreatment, the local child protective services provides such reports, records or information to the State Central Register within no more than 20 calendar days of receiving the request;

(xxx) that, for those local districts approved for family assessment response, when a report received by the State Central Register has been assigned to the family assessment response track, the local district immediately seals the report and updates, as appropriate, information regarding such report in records maintained by the district and informs the State Central Register, any other agency or person that received such report or any information about such report that the report is legally sealed, in accordance with SSL 427-a(4)(c)(i). Legally sealed family assessment response reports shall be made available only to:

(a) the social services district responsible for the family assessment response track case;

(b) the child protective services staff of a social services district that receives a subsequent report of suspected child abuse and maltreatment involving the same subject or the same child or children named in the family assessment response report. When the subsequent report has been assigned to the investigative track and the family assessment response report, record, or information is relevant to the investigation of the subsequent report of suspected child abuse and maltreatment, such relevant information may be used by the child protective services for its investigation and may be included in th record of the investigation of the subsequent report and used in a related family court action. Information from the family assessment response case that is included in the record of the subsequent report shall then be subject to all laws and regulations regarding confidentiality that apply to the record of the subsequent investigation.

(c) staff of OFCS and persons designated by OFCS, which shall include:

(1) local or regional child fatality review team members, provided that the child fatality review team is preparing a fatality report pursuant to section 20 or 422-b of the Social Services Law;

(2) all members of a local or regional multidisciplinary investigative team established pursuant to section 423(6) of the Social Services Law, when investigating a subsequent report of suspected child abuse or maltreatment involving a member of a family that was part of a family assessment response, provided that only the information from the family assessment response record that is relevant to the subsequent report be entered into the record of the subsequent report, which is to be provided to the multidisciplinary review team or agency; and

(3) citizen review panels, provided that any information obtained shall not be re-disclosed and shall only be used for the purposes set forth in section 371-b of the Social Services Law.

(d) a court, but only while the family is receiving services provided under the family assessment and services track and only pursuant to a court order or judicial subpoena, issued after notice and an opportunity for the subject of the report and all parties to the present proceeding to be heard, based on a judicial finding that such reports, records, and any information concerning such reports and records, are necessary for the determination of an issue before the court. The report must be submitted to the court for inspection and such directions as may be necessary to protect confidentiality, including but not limited to redaction of portions of the record, and to determine any further limits on re-disclosure;

(e) community-based agencies that have contracts with the social services district to carry out activities for the district under the family assessment response track;

(f) providers of services under the family assessment response track; and

(g) the subject of the report;

(xxxi) that the local district authorizes a provider or coordinator of services to which it has referred a child reported to the State Central Register to redisclose child protective services information, including records, reports or other information, to other persons or agencies providing services to the child and the family only if the district has a written agreement with the provider or coordinator of services, which includes the specific agencies and categories of individuals to whom redisclosure by the provider or coordinator of services is authorized and which has been reviewed and approved by OCFS; and

(xxxii) that nothing in article 27-F of the Public Health Law limits a social services official's or agency's responsibility or authority to report, investigate, or redisclose information necessary for the provision or monitoring of child protective services.

(4) Documentation file. Each local district must maintain program information, in the form of a documentation file, which must describe the operations of local child protective services and which provides evidence as to the methods by which the local district adheres to the legal assurances set forth in paragraph (3) of this subdivision, in a format determined by OCFS. Such documentation file must be made available to OCFS upon request.

(5) Procedures for review and approval of the plan and annual implementation report. The procedures for the review and approval of the plan

and the annual implementation report shall be consistent with the procedures cited in Part 407 of this Title.

§432.3 Child protective service: duties concerning reports of abuse or maltreatment.

Such duties shall include the following:

(a) Reporting. (1) Receipt of, in accordance with this Part, with the approved child protective services component of a district's consolidated services plan, and title 6 of article 6 of the Social Services Law, on a 24-hour, seven-day-a-week basis, all reports of suspected abuse or maltreatment; or

(2) Insurance that, if a local reporting system is to be developed and submitted for approval, it fulfill the following requirements:

(i) all reports must immediately upon receipt be transmitted orally or electronically to the State Central Register;

(ii) there must be a single telephone number available 24 hours a day, seven days a week, and the availability of this number must be highly publicized in each social services district;

(iii) the child protective service must be capable of receiving reports from all reporting sources and immediately responding to or causing an appropriate immediate response to be made when necessary according to the provisions of sections 432.2(b)(2) and 432.13 of this Part.

(b) The maintenance of an up-to-date local central register, which shall be separate and distinct from the case record and which shall contain a record of all reported cases of child abuse and maltreatment, including all reports received concerning a particular case, a record of each report written by the local child protective service concerning a particular case, and a record of the final disposition of reports assigned to the investigative track, including services offered and accepted. Reports and information that a local district may access from CONNECTIONS meet the requirements for a local district maintaining its local central register.

(c) Keeping the State Central Register fully informed and up-to-date concerning the handling of reports by:

(1) requiring a written report be submitted, by persons required to report cases of suspected child abuse or maltreatment, to the child protective service within 48 hours after the initial report, and a copy of this report be submitted to the State Central Register by the child protective service;

(2) requiring the child protective service, not later than seven days after the initial report, to send an initial safety assessment to the State Central Register via CONNECTIONS;

(3) requiring the determination of a report assigned to the investigative track to be submitted to the State Central Register via CONNECTIONS at any time it is determined that a case is "unfounded" or "indicated," but in no event later than 60 days after the initial report;

(4) requiring other follow-up reports on such cases at such times as OCFS deems necessary;

(5) requiring a report be submitted to the State Central Register via CONNECTIONS whenever a case is closed;

(6) requiring reports for a family assessment response to be submitted to the State Central Register via CONNECTIONS, as specified in section 432.13 of this Title;

(7) requiring the local child protective service to submit to the State Central Register all records, reports or other information maintained by the service

pertaining to an indicated report of child abuse or maltreatment as expeditiously as possible but within no more than 20 calendar days of receiving a request from the State Central Register for such records, reports or information; and

(8) requiring the child protective service to enter a 24-Hour Fatality Report into CONNECTIONS within twenty-four hours of receiving a report of a child fatality from the State Central Register and to enter a 30-Day Fatality Report into CONNECTIONS no later than 30 days after receiving a report of a child fatality from the State Central Register.

(d) Giving telephone notice and forwarding immediately to the appropriate district attorney any reports in which a child has died as a result of suspected child abuse or maltreatment.

(e) Reporting to the appropriate medical examiner or coroner for his investigation if there is reasonable cause to suspect that a child has died as a result of suspected child abuse or maltreatment.

(f) Securing the findings from the medical examiner or coroner on any case where there is reasonable cause to suspect that a child has died as a result of child abuse or maltreatment.

(g) Providing telephone notice and forwarding immediately a copy of any or all reports of suspected child abuse or maltreatment to the appropriate district attorney if a prior request in writing for such notice and copies has been received by the child protective service and such request specifies the kinds of allegations concerning which the district attorney requires such notice and copies and provides a copy of the relevant provisions of law, provided that only copies of reports that have been assigned to the investigative track may be forwarded and that reports assigned to the family assessment response track shall remain legally sealed.

(h) Forwarding a copy of any or all reports of suspected abuse or maltreatment to any appropriate duly incorporated society for the prevention of cruelty to children or any other duly authorized child protective agency, if a prior request for such copies has been received in writing by the child protective service.

(i) (1) Commencing or causing the appropriate society for the prevention of cruelty to children to commence within 24 hours an appropriate investigation or family assessment response on all reports of suspected child abuse and maltreatment in accordance with the provisions of sections 432.2(b)(3) and 432.13 of this Part.

(2) Request and receive, as provided for in subdivision 1 of section 425 of the Social Services Law, when applicable, from departments, boards, bureaus, or other agencies of the State, or any of its political subdivisions including school districts (as that term is defined in subdivision 2 of section 1980 of the Education Law), and charter schools operated pursuant to article 56 of the Education Law, or any duly authorized agency, or any other agency providing services under the local child protective services plan, such assistance and data as will enable the local child protective service to fulfill its responsibilities properly, including providing such assistance and data to members of a multi-disciplinary team established pursuant to subdivision 6 of section 423 of the Social Services Law when such members accompany a representative of the child protective service. Such assistance and data includes, but is not limited to:

(i) access to records relevant to the investigation of suspected abuse or maltreatment; and

(ii) access to any child named as a victim in a report of suspected abuse or maltreatment or any sibling or other child residing in the same home as the named victim. Such access includes conducting an interview of such child without a court order or the consent of the parent, guardian or other person legally responsible for the child when the child protective service encounters circumstances that warrant interviewing the child apart from family or other household members or the home or household where child abuse or maltreatment allegedly occurred. The representative of the child protective service and other members of a multi-disciplinary team accompanying a representative of the child protective service may be asked to provide their photographic employment identification or, if they lack photographic employment identification, an alternate form of government issued photographic identification, and to identify the child or children to be interviewed, but may not be asked for or required to provide any other information or documentation as a condition of having access to a child or children. Nothing contained herein shall preclude a school, school district or other program or facility operated by a department, board, bureau, or other agency of the state or any of its political subdivisions, or by a duly authorized agency or other agency providing services under the local child protective services plan from authorizing a staff member of the school or other such program or facility to observe the interview of the child, either from the same or another room, at the discretion of the school, school district or other such program or facility. Nothing contained herein shall preclude a school, school district or other such program or facility from requiring that representatives of the child protective service or other members of a multi-disciplinary team accompanying a representative of the child protective service comply with the reasonable visitor policies or procedures of the school, school district or other such program or facility, unless such policies or procedures are contrary to the requirements of this paragraph. *(Eff.11/16/16)*

(j) Upon receipt of a report of suspected abuse or maltreatment that has been assigned to the investigative track, and after seeing to the safety of the child or children named in the report, but in no event later than seven days after the receipt of the oral report, must deliver or mail to the subject(s) and other persons named in the report, except children under the age of 18 years, a written notification in such form as required by OCFS, informing them of the existence of the report and of the subject(s) rights with regard to amendment.

(k) Determining, within 60 days, whether a report that has been assigned to the investigative track is "indicated" or "unfounded"; and

(1) if "indicated," notify the State Central Register by recording that determination in CONNECTIONS and mail or deliver to the subject(s) and other persons named in the report, except children under the age of 18 years, a written notification, within seven days of the "indicated" determination, in such form as may be required by OCFS, informing them of the subject(s) rights in regard to requesting that the report be amended or expunged, and their right to a fair hearing; or

(2) if "unfounded," notify the State Central Register by recording that determination in CONNECTIONS, in accordance with the provisions of section 432.9 of this Part. No notice shall be sent to the subject(s) or other persons named in the report by the district.

(*l*) Taking all appropriate measures to protect a child's life and health including, when appropriate, taking or keeping a child in protective custody without the consent of a parent or guardian if appropriate staff of the child protective service have reasonable cause to believe that the circumstances or conditions of the child are such that continuing in his place of residence or in the care and custody of the parent, guardian, custodian or other person responsible for the child's care presents an imminent danger to the child's life or health.

(m) Upon notification by a physician who is treating a child that the physician has reasonable cause to believe that the circumstances or condition of the child are such that the continuation of the child in his place of residence or in the care and custody of the parent, guardian, custodian, or other person responsible for the child's care presents an imminent danger to the child's life or health, take custody of such child.

(n) Upon notification by the person in charge of a hospital or similar institution that such person has retained custody of a child because such person has reasonable cause to believe that the circumstances or conditions of the child are such that continuing in his place of residence or in the care and custody of the child's parent, guardian, custodian or other person responsible for the child's care presents an imminent danger to the child's life or health, immediately commence an investigation and, if no further medical treatment is necessary, take all necessary measures to protect the child's life and health, including, where appropriate, taking custody of the child.

(o) Upon notification that a child is retained in protective custody, the child protective service shall commence a proceeding at the next regular weekday session of the appropriate Family Court, or recommend to the court at that time that the child be returned to his parents or guardian.

(p) Based on the investigation and evaluation, offer appropriate services to the family or any child believed to be suffering from abuse or maltreatment, or both, or to the family and any child who are part of a family assessment response, and, in offering these services, explain to the family that the child protective service has no legal authority to compel the family to receive services.

(q) In those cases in which an appropriate offer of services is refused and the child protective service determines that the best interests of the child require court action, initiate the action or make a referral to the appropriate district attorney or both.

(r) Assisting the Family Court or the Criminal Court during all stages of the court proceeding in accordance with purposes of title 6 of article 6 of the Social Services Law.

(s) Providing or arranging for, coordinating and monitoring, as authorized by the Social Services Law and by title 6, rehabilitative services as defined in section 432.1 of this Part for children and their families on a voluntary basis or under a final or intermediate order of the Family Court.

(t) Receive, in accordance with section 912-a of the Education Law, from school authorities a report on the examination of a child that has been determined to be using dangerous drugs and, in an appropriate case, to take such action and offer such protective services as are prescribed by this Part. Such report and the results of a subsequent investigation or family assessment response shall not be used for law enforcement purposes.

(u) When necessary, give effective consent for medical, dental, health and hospital services for any child who has been found by the Family Court to be an abused or neglected child or has been taken into or kept in protective custody or removed from the place where such child is residing or who has been placed in the custody of a commissioner of a social services district, pursuant to section 417 of the Social Services Law or section 1022, 1024 or 1027 of the Family Court Act.

§432.4 Education and training.

(a) The commissioner of social services in each social services district must conduct a continuing publicity and education program for local district staff, persons required to report and any other appropriate persons, to encourage the fullest degree of reporting of suspected child abuse or maltreatment and to develop public support for the prevention of child abuse and maltreatment. The program must include, but not be limited to, responsibilities, obligations and powers under this Title, as well as the diagnosis of child abuse and maltreatment and the procedures of the child protective service, the Family Court and other duly authorized agencies.

(b) In the furtherance of its responsibilities under subdivision (a) of this section, each social services district must make current procedural manuals and service directories available to employees of the district's child protective service, service providers and professionals involved in the prevention of child abuse and maltreatment.

§432.5 Obligations of persons required to report.

(a) The commissioner of social services in each social services district is authorized to reimburse any person or official required to report cases of suspected child abuse or maltreatment for expenses incurred in the taking of or causing of photographs to be taken of the areas of trauma visible on a child who is the subject of a report, or, if medically indicated, for a radiological examination of a child.

(b) The commissioner of social services in each social services district shall insure that any photographs or X-ray results taken as a result of the report be sent to the child protective service at the time the written report is sent, or as soon thereafter as possible.

§432.6 Requirements for written notification.

Written notification to the subject(s) or other persons named in a report of suspected child abuse or maltreatment assigned to the investigative track shall be in accordance with language required by OCFS.

§432.7 Access to reports.

The commissioner of social services in each social services district shall insure that any reports made, as well as any other information obtained, reports written or photographs taken concerning such reports, be confidential and shall only be made available to those persons defined under title 6 of article 6 of the Social Services Law, because any person who willfully permits and any person who encourages the release of any data and information contained in the local or statewide register to persons or agencies not permitted by title 6 of article 6 of the Social Services Law shall be guilty of a class A misdemeanor.

§432.8 Penalties for failure to report.

When a commissioner of social services has reasonable cause to suspect that a person has willfully failed to report a case of suspected child abuse or maltreatment, which such person was required to report pursuant to title 6 of article 6 of the Social Services Law, the commissioner shall report the suspected failure to the district attorney.

§432.9 Disposition of unfounded reports.

(a) Upon determining that a report is "unfounded," the local district shall notify the State Central Register, in such form as shall be required by OCFS.

(b) The State Central Register will inform the subject(s) and other persons named in the report, except children under the age of 18 years at the time of notification, that the report was unfounded and the records of the report were sealed, or were expunged if the report had been received by the State Central Register of Child Abuse and Maltreatment prior to February 12, 1996.

(c) Upon written notice from the State Central Register that the records of the unfounded report were sealed in or expunged from the State Central Register:

(1) The local district must immediately seal the child protective services case record in which the report has been maintained; except that, if the report had been received by the State Central Register prior to February 12, 1996, the social services district must immediately expunge the report and all identifying information relating to the report from the local register of child abuse and maltreatment and any other locally maintained child protective services case record.

(2) The social services district must update any other record, including the uniform case record, which it has maintained that makes reference to the report to state that the report was determined to be unfounded and to legally seal such report pursuant to subdivision five of section 422 of the Social Services Law. The social services district must inform any agency or person to which it has provided information concerning the report to update its record for the same purpose. However, if the report had been received by the State Central Register prior to February 12, 1996, other agencies or units must be asked to expunge from any other record, including the uniform case record reports received from the social services district.

(d) The State Central Register may review any or all unfounded determinations made by a local district and affirm any such determination or give notice to the district as to the reasons why its determination of "unfounded" is not affirmed. When reviewing an unfounded determination, the State Central Register may request additional information from the district to support the determination.

(e) Upon notice from the State Central Register that additional information is required to support an unfounded determination, the local child protective services unit shall immediately provide the required information.

(f) Upon written notice from the State Central Register that the report should be "indicated," the district shall comply with the requirements of section 432.3(k) of this Part.

§432.10 Child care review service reporting requirements.

(a) Information on all children who are named in indicated reports of child abuse and maltreatment and who are receiving or have received services as a result of being named in such reports shall be entered and maintained on the child care review service.

(b) The only information which shall be entered and maintained on the child care review service pursuant to subdivision (a) of this section is:

(1) demographic information;

(2) information concerning court-related activities involving the child; and

(3) the following assessment and service plan data elements contained in the appropriate uniform case record forms prepared pursuant to Part 428 of this Title:

(i) plan date;

(ii) plan type;

(iii) child and family service needs;

(iv) service status;

(v) service program choice(s);

(vi) reason(s) for service program choice; and

(vii) permanency planning goal.

(c) Nothing contained in subdivision (a) or (b) of this section shall preclude the entering or maintaining of information related to the provision of foster care and/or preventive services on the child care review service for children who are named in indicated reports of child abuse and maltreatment.

§432.11 Adjournments in contemplation of dismissal.

(a) A social services official, when acting as the petitioner in a child abuse and neglect proceeding which is commenced pursuant to article 10 of the Family Court Act, shall not consent to an order which adjourns such proceeding in contemplation of dismissal if the official determines that such an adjournment would not be in the best interests of the child because the provision of protective services to the child and family during the term of the adjournment would not help to alleviate the circumstances which resulted in the alleged abuse or neglect of the child.

(b) The factors to be considered in making the determination not to consent to an adjournment in accordance with subdivision (a) of this section because the adjournment would not be in the best interests of the child shall include, but not be limited to:

(1) whether the terms of an order which will adjourn a child protective proceeding in contemplation of dismissal will include requirements that the child's parent(s) or guardian(s) avail themselves of rehabilitative services and/or refrain from the types of conduct which relate to the alleged abusive or neglectful behavior that necessitated the filing of a child protective petition;

(2) whether the evidence which a child protective service could introduce in a child protective proceeding to prove that the respondent in such proceeding abused or neglected a child will be available at a subsequent fact-finding hearing which would be held in the event that the conditions of the order issued in contemplation of dismissal in a child protective proceeding were violated;

(3) the seriousness of the alleged incidents of child abuse or neglect;

(4) the likelihood that the child will be abused or neglected after the issuance of an order which adjourns a child protective proceeding in contemplation of dismissal;

(5) the amount of cooperation which the respondent in a child abuse and neglect proceeding is willing to provide to the child protective service to help alleviate the circumstances which resulted in the alleged abuse or neglect of the child; and

(6) whether the terms of an order which will adjourn a child protective proceeding in contemplation of dismissal can be made sufficiently clear so that compliance with its provisions may be adequately monitored by a child protective service.

§432.12 Access by mandated reporters to the findings of an investigation.
(a) A person or official required by section 413 of the Social Services Law to report cases of suspected child abuse or maltreatment must receive, upon request, the findings of an investigation of a report made by that person or official for any report that has been assigned to the investigative track. When the report has been assigned to the family assessment response track, the person or official making the request must be informed that the report has been assigned to a family assessment response, that there is no determination made for a report addressed with a family assessment response, and that such records are legally sealed and confidential.

(b) (1) When a request by such person or official is made at the time of making an oral report of suspected child abuse or maltreatment to the State Central Register, the State Central Register must forward the request to the appropriate child protective service, or where the suspected child abuse or maltreatment occurred in residential child care, to a designated person within OCFS. The request for the findings of an investigation must be forwarded by the State Central Register to the child protective service or OCFS when the report of suspected child abuse or maltreatment is transmitted.

(2) When a request by such person or official is made at any time subsequent to making the oral report of suspected child abuse or maltreatment to the State Central Register, the request must be made by the person or official to the appropriate child protective service or, where the suspected child abuse or maltreatment occurred in residential child care, to a designated person within OCFS.

(3) As used in this section, residential child care means:
(i) foster care provided to a child whose care and custody or custody and guardianship have been transferred to a social services official or OCFS and such care is provided in a group home or child care institution;
(ii) care provided to a child in a facility or program operated or certified by OCFS pursuant to article 19-G or 19-H of the Executive Law, excluding foster family care;
(iii) care provided to a child in the New York State School for the blind or the New York State School for the deaf, pursuant to the provisions of articles 87 and 88 of the Education Law;
(iv) care provided to a child in a private residential school which is within the State and which has been approved by the Commissioner of Education for special education services or programs;
(v) care provided to a child in an institution for the instruction of the deaf and the blind which has a residential component and which is subject to the visitation of the Commissioner of Education pursuant to article 85 of the Education Law;
(vi) care provided to a child through a residential placement with a special act school district listed in chapter 566 of the Laws of 1967, as amended;
(vii) care provided to a child in a residential facility licensed or operated by the Office of Mental Health or the Office For People With Developmental Disabilities, excluding family care homes; or
(viii) care provided by an authorized agency in a residential facility, licensed or operated by the Office of Mental Health or the Office For People With Developmental Disabilities, excluding a family care home, which is located on the same campus of the authorized agency where care enumerated in subparagraph (i) of this paragraph is provided to a child.

(c) Upon receipt of such a request, the local child protective service, or where the suspected child abuse or maltreatment occurred in residential child care, OCFS must release the findings of the investigation, in writing, as follows:

(1) Prior to releasing the findings, the identity of the person or official making the request must be confirmed.

(2) If the request is made prior to the completion of an investigation of a report of child abuse or maltreatment, the released information must be limited to whether the report is indicated, unfounded or under investigation. If a child protective service has not been notified by the State Central Register to seal or expunge a report which the child protective service has determined to be unfounded, the child protective service must indicate that it has recommended to the State Central Register that the report should be unfounded.

(3) If the request is made after the completion of an investigation of a report of child abuse or maltreatment, the released information must be limited to that the report is indicated or unfounded.

(4) The child protective service or OCFS must also include in the written release of the findings of the investigation of a report of child abuse or maltreatment a statement that the information is confidential and that redisclosure of such information is prohibited by section 422 of the Social Services Law.

(5) The child protective service or, for a case of suspected child abuse or neglect which occurred in a residential child care setting, OCFS must file in the record of the investigation of the report a copy of the findings which were released to a mandated reporter pursuant to the provisions of this section. The findings must contain the date of release to a mandated reporter and the name of the mandated reporter to whom the findings were released.

§432.13 Family assessment response.

(a) General.

(1) Description of family assessment response. Pursuant to Social Services Law Section 427-a, the local commissioner of a social services district may establish, with OCFS approval, a differential response program, family assessment response, as an alternative means of responding to certain child protective service reports that allege abuse and maltreatment. In family assessment response, there is an ongoing assessment of the safety of children without a determination of whether the report of alleged abuse or maltreatment should be indicated or unfounded. Reports are addressed by engaging the family in a comprehensive assessment of child safety, risk of subsequent harm, and family strengths and needs. The family assessment response approach seeks to minimize future risk of abuse or maltreatment of a child or children by engaging the family in the development and implementation of solution-focused plans to address identified needs in order to support the family's ability to care for its children.

(2) A family assessment response program established by a social services district shall be part of that district's child protective service.

(3) Responsibilities for a family assessment response. When a report alleging maltreatment of a child is assigned to the family assessment response track, the child protective service must fulfill the following responsibilities:

(i) first establish that children in the family named in the report are safe; and

(ii) provide ongoing assessment of safety and risk, including completion of an initial safety assessment; and

(iii) engage the family in an assessment of: the concerns reported to the State Central Register, any family-identified needs and concerns that may impact the safety or risk of children, and the family's strengths and resources that could be engaged to address the identified concerns; and

(iv) when appropriate, partner with the family to assist the family in obtaining, goods and services that will help the family meet its identified needs regarding care of the children, thereby reducing future risk of abuse or maltreatment of a child or children.

(4) Reports assigned to the family assessment response track are not subject to the requirements of child protective services specified in Title 6 of the Social Services Law and in sections 409-e and 409-f of the Social Services Law. except as specified in Social Services Law sections 422, 426 and 427-a.

(b) Authorization and application to implement family assessment response.

(1) Application and OCFS approval. The commissioner of a social services district that seeks to implement a family assessment response program must submit an application to OCFS that describes, in a manner prescribed by OCFS, its plans for family assessment response. The application must be approved by OCFS before the social services district can implement family assessment response.

(i) Each social services district that has received OCFS approval to implement a family assessment response program must comply with any requirements for family assessment response that may be established by statute, these regulations, or by OCFS.

(ii) OCFS may revoke its approval for family assessment response for any social services district that does not comply with family assessment response requirements established by statute, these regulations, or by OCFS, but only after having first consulted with the district in an effort to assist them to resolve the compliance issues.

(iii) If OCFS revokes its approval for a social services district to provide family assessment response, the district may at any time, after having resolved the issues that resulted in its previous revocation, submit a new application to OCFS requesting, to implement family assessment response.

(2) Family assessment response is optional. The decision by a social services district to apply to establish and implement a family assessment response program is voluntary and optional. The commissioner of a social services district that has established a family assessment response program may terminate that program at any time. The commissioner must immediately notify OCFS of a decision to terminate family assessment response. A social services district that has terminated its family assessment response program may, at any time, submit a new application to OCFS to implement family assessment response.

(3) Applicability. The provisions of this section apply only to those social services districts that have received approval from OCFS to implement family assessment response.

(4) Determination of the size and scope of a family assessment response program. A social services district applying to implement family assessment response must determine the projected size and scope of its family assessment response program, including targeted goals for the number of child protective service reports that it will assign to the family assessment response track, the number of staff members who will work in its family assessment response

program, and the criteria it will use to classify and assign reports to the family assessment response track. After implementing a family assessment response program, a district may reassess and revise these determinations.

(i) A social services district's plans for the size and scope of its family assessment response program that are submitted in its family assessment response application, as well as subsequent chances to those plans, are subject to the approval of OCFS.

(ii) Criteria for screening reports. Districts must establish criteria. which are subject to the approval of OCFS, for the categories of allegations in child protective service reports that the district will or will not accept for potential assignment to the family assessment response track. The criteria must comply with the provisions of subdivision 3 of section 427-a of the Social Services Law, as well as with any additional standards that may be established by OCFS. Changes in a district's criteria are subject to the approval of OCFS.

(a) In order to establish a robust family assessment response program, a district should develop screening criteria for the family assessment response track that include a broad spectrum of cases representing a significant percentage of its child protective service reports.

(b) Child protective service reports regarding a child fatality must be investigated pursuant to Section 20(5) of the Social Services Law and Sections 422-b, 423(6) and 424(5)(a) of the Social Services Law, and must not be assigned to the family assessment response track.

(iii) Written protocol. The social services district must develop and adhere to a written screening protocol for determining initial track assignments. The protocol must protect the safety of children while effectively matching the child protective service to the family's needs. The initial screening protocol must include:

(a) the designation of the types of reports that, upon receipt, the social services district will and will not consider for potential assignment to the family assessment response track;

(b) the designation of the staff responsible for determining, the initial track assignments for new child protective service reports; and

(c) a description of whether and how the social services district will screen reports that are received during on-call hours for potential assignment to the family assessment response track.

(c) Determining the appropriate child protective service track.

(1) Intake procedures. The intake procedures for child protective service reports described in section 432.2(b)(2) of this Part apply to family assessment response cases.

(2) Initial track assignment. When it receives a child protective service report from the State Central Register, a social services district with a family assessment response program, using its written protocol, must identify whether the report is eligible to be assigned to the family assessment response track. make an initial determination about whether to assign the report to the investigative track or the family, assessment response track, and enter the initial track assignment into CONNECTIONS.

(3) Inform the family of family assessment response action. Following the preliminary assignment of a child protective service report to the family assessment response track, child protective service staff must, pursuant to section 432.13(e)(3)(ii) of this Part, provide each parent, guardian or other person legally responsible for the child or children who will be participating in the family assessment response with information that describes and compares

the family assessment response track to the investigative track in order to enable the family to make an informed decision about whether to accept participation in the family assessment response track.

(4) Final determination of track assignment. Not later than seven days after receipt of a report alleging abuse or maltreatment that has been assigned to the family assessment response track, the child protective service must determine whether the case should continue as a family assessment response. The initial track assignment of a report may be changed until it becomes permanent, but no later than seven days following receipt of the report, at the same time that the initial safety assessment must be completed pursuant to section 432.13(d) of this Part.

(i) The child protective service must document in the initial safety assessment the reasons for its choice of track assignment for any report that is permanently assigned to family assessment response or that is initially assigned to family assessment response, but subsequently assigned to the investigative track within seven days of receipt of the report.

(ii) All information entered into the record before the track assignment becomes permanent remains in the record, irrespective of whether the track assignment is changed.

(iii) The decision about track assignment supports the safety of children while effectively matching the child protective service to the family's needs. The determination of the appropriate track assignment must be based on the following factors:

(a) Finding that children are safe. In order for a child protective service report to be assigned to the family assessment response track, the initial (seven day) safety assessment, conducted pursuant to section 432.13(d) of this Part, must include a determination that each child named in the child protective service report or known to be living in the household is safe in the home;

(b) Compliance with State- and locally-designated screening criteria. If a child protective service report is initially assigned to the family assessment response track, and the child protective service determines during its initial safety assessment that conditions in the family's circumstances that were not included in allegations in the report place the case outside of state-mandated or locally determined screening criteria for family assessment response, the child protective service must re-assign the report to the investigative track:

(c) Record review. During the initial safety assessment, the child protective service must review State Central Register records as well as its own child protective records pertaining to all prior reports involving members of the family, as specified in Section 432.2(b)(3)(i) of this Part, and assess whether information in those case records indicates that the family assessment response approach would not be an appropriate response to the current child protective service report; and

(d) Agreement by parents, guardians, and other legally responsible persons.

(1) Participation in family assessment response is voluntary on the part of the family named in the child protective service report. Their agreement to participate in a family assessment response and to cooperate in assessment activities with child protective service staff is necessary in order for the child protective service to confirm the assignment of a report to the family assessment response track. Child protective service workers must provide information about family assessment response to parents, guardians, or other persons legally responsible, pursuant to sections 432.13(c)(3) and

432.13(e)(2)(i) and (ii) of this Part, to inform their decisions about whether to choose to participate in a family assessment response.

(2) If a parent declines assignment of the report to the family assessment response track, the report must be addressed through the investigation track; except that, if one or more persons who are subjects of the report wish to participate in a family assessment response, and the child protective service believes that the family can benefit from a family assessment response despite the refusal to cooperate by a parent, the child protective service may assign the report to the family assessment response track.

(5) Changing the track assignment after seven days.

(i) Seven days after a child protective services receives a report, the assignment of the report in CONNECTIONS to the family assessment response track or the investigation track cannot be changed.

(ii) If more than seven days have passed since the assignment of a report to the family assessment response track, in the following, instances the open family assessment response case must be closed and a new case opened, to be assigned to the investigative track:

a. If while conducting a family assessment response, the child protective service has reasonable cause to suspect child abuse, or the family is not cooperating with the family assessment response assessment and there is reasonable cause to suspect maltreatment of a child, the case is no longer eligible for inclusion in the family assessment response track. The child protective service must make a new report to the State Central Register, which must be assigned to the investigation track, and the open case that was assigned to the family assessment response track must be closed.

b. If a child protective service that is conducting a family assessment response receives a new report alleging child abuse or maltreatment from the State Central Register that contains allegations that do not meet the state's or local district's criteria for inclusion in family assessment response, the child protective service must assign the new report to the investigative track and close the open case that was assigned to the family assessment response track. Allegations from the family assessment response report should be added to the new investigative track report, as appropriate.

(iii) Information in the case record for a family assessment response case that is relevant to a subsequent investigation case may be included in the case record for the investigation track case, pursuant to Social Services Law section 427-a(5)(e)(iii).

(d) Initial safety assessment. Whenever a child protective service receives a report of child abuse and maltreatment that it assigns preliminarily to the family assessment response track, the child protective service must commence an initial safety assessment within 24 hours of receipt of the report to determine whether children named in the child protective service report are safe in their homes. The initial safety assessment must be completed no later than seven days following, receipt of the report, at which time the assignment of the report to the family assessment response track or the investigative track becomes permanent. In order to confirm the assignment of a child protective service report to the family assessment response track, the initial safety assessment must contain a finding, that no child in the home is in immediate or impending danger of serious harm.

(1) Initiation within 24 hours. The child protective service must initiate a safety assessment no more than 24 hours after receiving, a report, by conducting a face-to-face interview or making a telephone contact with one or

more of the following persons who are in a position to provide information on the safety of the child or children:

(i) Source. Whenever possible, child protective service staff should contact the source of the report prior to the first meeting with the family. The source can confirm and possibly expand upon the details of the report or provide impressions of family functioning, strengths, and resources;

(ii) Subject(s) and members of the family. Whenever possible, initial contact with the subject(s) of the report should be by telephone. Child protective services staff should inform the subject(s) about the existence of concerns, initiate the safety assessment and begin engaging the family in the family assessment response process. During the initial contact, the family assessment response worker and the family schedule the first face-to-face meeting.

(iii) Other persons. Child protective workers should interview any other persons who are in a position to provide information about whether any child is in immediate danger of serious harm.

(2) Completing the initial (seven day) safety assessment. The initial safety assessment should be completed using, the following guidelines:

(i) The child protective service conducts the initial safety assessment by assessing, with the family, the physical health and well-being of all of the children in the family, the safety of the children's living conditions and the existence of any other safety factors in the home. All children named in the report or living in the home must be seen and all children who are developmentally capable should be engaged in the assessment process. The child protective service worker applies the safety criteria designated by OCFS to determine if one or more safety factors place a child in immediate or impending danger, and makes a decision regarding the child's safety status.

(ii) The child protective service may obtain information from collateral contacts including, but not limited to, hospitals, family medical providers, schools, police, social services agencies and other agencies providing services to the family, relatives, extended family members, neighbors and other persons who may provide information on the status of the child's safety should that information be needed to determine the presence of safety factors within the family. Family assessment response staff should ask the parents/caretaker for their recommendations regarding collaterals that can supply this information and should not routinely make collateral contacts without first asking the family.

(3) Documenting the safety assessment. Whenever a report alleging maltreatment of a child is initially assigned to the family assessment response track during the seven days following, receipt of the report, the child protective service must enter the initial safety assessment into CONNECTIONS no later than seven days after receipt of the report, in a manner specified by OCFS. The initial safety assessment must specify the track to which the report is assigned following completion of the safety assessment and document the reasons for assigning the report to the family assessment response track or the investigation track, as specified in section 432.13(c)(4).

(4) Ongoing assessment of safety. After completing the initial safety assessment, the child protective service remains responsible for continually monitoring the presence or emergence of safety threats throughout their work with the family, until the family assessment response case is closed.

(e) Conducting the family assessment response.

(1) Use of the family assessment response approach. Immediately upon preliminary assignment of a report to the family assessment response track, the child protective service should apply family assessment response principles in its work with the family and continue to do so until the case is either reassigned to the investigative track, within seven days of receipt of the report, or the case is closed.

(2) Activities implementing the family assessment response. The child protective service's activities in conducting family assessment response must, at a minimum, include the following:

(i) Provide written notification to parents. No later than seven days after receipt of a child protective report that the has been assigned to the family assessment response track, the child protective service must provide written notification to every parent, guardian or other person legally responsible for the child or children named in the report. Written notice is not provided to any other persons.

(a) The child protective service may determine the form of the written notification it provides, but it should be written in plain language.

(b) The notification must inform the person that a report was made to the State Central Register and explain that it is the intent of the social services district to meet the needs of the family without engaging in an investigation by assigning the report to the family assessment response track, and that the child protective service workers who will be assisting the family are mandated reporters and are required to report suspected abuse or maltreatment.

(c) The child protective service must verbally inform the parent, guardian or other person legally responsible about the areas of concern that triggered the report and explain that they must explore those concerns and assess the safety of any child named in the report or living in the household.

(d) If, while a case assigned to family assessment response is open, a subsequent report is received that is consolidated with the open case, the requirement to provide written notification is waived; the child protective service must provide verbal notification of the new report to every parent, guardian or other person legally responsible for the child or children named in the report.

(ii) Provide information about family assessment response. The child protective service must provide the family with information about family assessment response to aid them in making an informed decision about whether to accept assignment of the report to the family assessment response track. Such information should include but is not limited to:

(a) a description of family assessment response that explains how it differs from an investigative response, including that there is no determination made in family assessment response cases. This information must be given to the family verbally; families must also be given written information about family assessment response, such as a brochure;

(b) an explanation of the importance of partnership and cooperation in the family assessment response, including the essential role of meetings between child protective service workers and the family, so that CPS workers and the family are able to jointly assess the children's safety and well-being as well as the family's strengths, risks, and needs;

(c) information regarding the confidentiality of records in family assessment response; and

(d) an explanation that the choice to accept assignment of the report to the family assessment track is voluntary and that the family may choose either family assessment response or assignment to the investigative track.

(iii) Engage the family. Family assessment response workers must work in partnership with the families participating in a family assessment response. Workers should be transparent with families regarding all actions that they take regarding the case. To the extent feasible, child protective service workers should include all family members in discussions, including children who are old enough to express opinions, as well as any other persons who the family would like to include, such as members of the extended family.

(iv) Complete the family led assessment Guide (FLAG). Family assessment response staff must engage the family in an examination of the issues of concern to the child protective service as well as the family's strengths, concerns, and needs. The assessment must be conducted using a Family Led Assessment Guide (FLAG), as specified by OCFS. The family-led assessment should be initiated as soon as possible after receipt of the child protective service report, but no more than 30 days following receipt of the report. The assessment should be conducted in accordance with the principles and practices of family assessment response. Child protective workers must document at least one completed FLAG in CONNECTIONS, as well as any revised versions of the FLAG.

(v) Provide on-going risk assessment. Family assessment response workers must engage with the family in on-going joint evaluation and assessment of the family's progress including periodic assessments of risk to the child or children.

(vi) Focus on solutions. When the FLAG identifies challenges to the family's ability to support the well-being or meet the needs of their child or children, family assessment response workers must offer to work jointly with the family to develop and implement solutions to address their needs.

(vii) Offer needed services. Where appropriate, family assessment response workers must offer assistance to the family in implementing solutions to their identified needs that will be supportive of family functioning, meet the children's needs and reduce risk to children in the family. Assistance may include providing; information on services and supports available in their community, building supportive networks with extended family and community resources, advocating for the family with schools, landlords and others, referring the family to government and privately funded programs, contacting service providers, and paying for goods or services.

(a) No "Application for Services" or signatures. as required in section 404.1(c)(8) of this Title, are necessary in order to provide services in cases assigned to the family assessment response track.

(b) Districts may use child protective, wraparound, or other funding sources to pay for goods and services provided through family assessment response.

(c) The acceptance of services or goods by families who are receiving family assessment response is voluntary.

(viii) Notifying the family of case closing. No more than seven days after closing a family assessment response case record, the child protective service must notify the family, including all subject(s) of the report, that the case has been closed. The notification may be in a form determined by the child protective service, but must be provided in writing and, if feasible, also verbally. The notice must inform the family and subject(s) that the family assessment response report is sealed and that the records will be maintained for ten years after the report was received at the State Central Register. Notices must also inform the subject(s) of the report about the applicable confidentiality provisions and of their right to access the records for the family assessment response.

(3) Closing cases. Family assessment response is a short term child protective service.

(i) The case should be closed if the family is assessed as providing, adequate care for their children, the children are safe, and the family has no requests for services or supports.

(ii) The decision to close a family assessment response case must be made in conjunction with the family, whenever possible.

(iii) When needs have been identified, the family should be given information about available community resources to meet those needs. To the extent possible, a family assessment response caseworker should be present with identified service providers and appropriate family members at their first meeting to introduce them to facilitate a "warm handoff."

(iv) If the family assessment response caseworker believes the family has unmet needs but the family declines additional services, and there is no current maltreatment or immediate danger of serious harm, the case must be closed.

(v) Timeframes. The following timeframes apply to closing a family assessment response case:

(a) A family assessment response case should usually be closed within 60 days.

(b) Addressing family needs may necessitate keeping, a family assessment response case open for up to 90 days. A case that remains open for more than 60 days should be kept open only for the specific purpose of assisting a family to meet specific needs.

(c) If a family requires more assistance in meeting its needs than can be provided within 90 days, the child protective service will assess the family's eligibility for preventive services in accordance with section 430.9 of this Title and, if the family is eligible and consents, open a preventive services case.

(d) In extraordinary circumstances, a family assessment response case may be kept open for more than 90 days. When such an instance occurs:

(1) a family assessment response worker and supervisor must document in progress notes the reason for keeping the case open, including specific goals and steps to achieve those goals; and

(2) a family assessment response worker must make contact with the family no less than once every two weeks during, the period past 90 days, and must document each contact.

(4) Case work contacts. The number of casework contacts must be commensurate with the requirements for completing the family assessment response assessments and for meeting the needs of the family. There are no specific contact requirements for family assessment response except when the family assessment response case is open for more than 90 days, as specified in section 432.13(e)(3)(v)(d) of this Part.

(5) Documentation. Activities conducted as part of a family assessment response case must be documented in CONNECTIONS, in the form and manner prescribed by OCFS. Family assessment response workers must document, at a minimum, the following information in the family assessment response case record:

(i) Essential data relating to the identification of each child and family member;

(ii) Activities undertaken to initiate a safety assessment within 24 hours;

(iii) Findings of the initial safety assessment, including the reasons for assigning the report to the family assessment response track;

(iv) Information from at least one Family Led Assessment Guide (FLAG), based on discussions with the family. as well as any revisions of the FLAG;

(v) Services that were offered to the family and services that were accepted and provided, directly and through contract or other means;

(vi) Findings of periodic risk assessments;

(vii) Evaluations and assessments of progress;

(viii) Ongoing plans for supportive services after the case is closed, if applicable; and

(ix) Factors allowing, for the closing of the case.

(6) Changing the case status from family assessment response track to investigative track.

(i) Reporting suspected abuse. If a family assessment response worker has reasonable cause to suspect that there is child abuse occurring in a family that is part of a family assessment response, the worker must make a report to the State Central Register. The new child protective service report containing allegations of child abuse must be assigned to the investigative track and the family assessment response case must be closed.

(ii) Closing a case clue to lack of cooperation. If a report has been assigned to the family assessment response track following an initial safety assessment and the family later refuses to cooperate with the family assessment response workers in completing the full assessment of strengths and needs and/or in developing or implementing a plan to address family problems or issues and the family assessment response worker has reasonable cause to suspect maltreatment of a child, the child protective service must make a report of suspected maltreatment to the State Central Register. The resulting child protective service report must be assigned to the investigative track and the family assessment response case must be closed.

(f) Administration and organization.

(1) Staffing.

(i) Sufficient staff. Each family assessment response unit must designate sufficient qualified staff whose primary function is to address child protective service reports using the family assessment response approach. to fulfill the purposes of section 427-a of the Social Services Law.

(ii) Education and training requirements.

(a) Every family assessment response worker, including supervisors, must meet the minimum education and training requirements for a child protective service worker specified in section 432.2(e)(5) of this Part.

(b) Every family assessment response worker must complete training in family assessment response, in the form and manner specified by OCFS.

(iii) Other employment requirements for family assessment response. All family assessment response staff are subject to the requirements (employment history, employment and personal references, criminal background attestation, State Central Register database check) for applicants for child protective service staff, pursuant to section 432.2(e)(6) of this Part.

(iv) Supervision of family assessment response.

(a) A child protective service supervisor must review assessments and decisions made by a family assessment response caseworker, including, at a minimum, a review of the progress notes, the initial safety assessment, the complete Family Led Assessment Guide, and the information related to the decision to close the case.

(a) A child protective service supervisor must approve the assignment of a child protective service report to the family assessment response track and the decision to close a case assigned to the family assessment response track.

(v) Case assignment.

(a) Local districts applying to implement family assessment response and those requesting to expand or chance their approved family assessment response program shall develop a plan that describes their program organization, staffing plan, and case assignment process, including how they will support effective practices in providing family assessment response. The plan shall include:

(1) a description of the policy and process for assigning reports to the family assessment response track, including whether family assessment response cases are assigned to child protective services staff who are dedicated exclusively to family assessment response or to staff who provide both family assessment response and investigations;

(2) the number of staff and supervisors that will be assigned to family assessment response cases exclusively, including staff of any community-based agency that will perform family assessment response activities pursuant to 432.13(f)(3);

(3) the number of staff and supervisors that may be assigned to cases in both the family assessment response track and the investigative track; and

(4) if the local district has determined that any child protective service worker may be assigned to cases in both tracks, a description of the measures that will be taken to maintain the integrity of both approaches, including a description of the measures that will be taken to support such staff.

(b) If a local district currently providing family assessment response assigns staff to cases in both the family assessment response track and the investigative track, that district shall, upon the request of OCFS, provide OCFS with a written description of its plans to support both approaches, as described in 432.13(f)(1)(v)(a).

(2) Quality assurance

(i) The social services district shall be responsible for assessing and evaluating the implementation of its family assessment response program, including the provision of services to families served by family assessment response, in order to assure the quality of its service.

(ii) The social services district must comply with any requirements for quality assurance established by OCFS.

(3) Contracting for family assessment response services. A child protective service may allow a community-based agency currently used by the local district for preventive services to perform the activities in section 432.13(e) of this Part that are necessary for assessment and service provision in a family assessment response case. A local social services district that wishes to contract its family assessment response activities to a community-based agency must first receive approval of its arrangement by OCFS. The arrangement between the social services district and the community-based agency must:

(i) adhere to all provisions of section 432.13;

(ii) require that staff at the community-based agency who are assigned to family assessment response meet the minimum education and training, requirements for family assessment response workers. as specified in section 432.13(f)(1)(ii) of this Part;

(iii) require that the community-based agency inform the social services district if such community-based agency determines that a report must be investigated as a case of suspected child abuse or maltreatment. The community-based agency is to be directed to have a staff member make a report to the State Central Register, if no person has yet done so. The social services district shall be responsible for conducting the ensuing child protective service investigation; and

(iv) provide that the local child protective service retains responsibility for the following activities:

(a) conducting the initial safety assessment;

(b) making the decision about whether to assign a child protective service report to the family assessment response track or to the investigative track; and

(c) approving the closing of a family assessment response case.

(4) Annual report. The local district must provide OCFS with such information about family assessment response as is requested by OCFS to be used in the preparation of an annual report on child protective services by OCFS.

(g) Confidentiality of family assessment response records.

(1) The records of a family assessment response report are legally sealed. They will be maintained at the State Central Register for ten years from the date the report was made.

(2) All reports assigned to, and records created as part of, family assessment response, including reports made or written as well as any other information obtained or photographs taken concerning such reports or records, are confidential, as required by SSL 427-a(5)(d), and shall only be made available to:

(i) Staff of OCFS and persons designated by OCFS, which shall include:

(a) local or regional child fatality review team members, provided that the child fatality review team is preparing a fatality report pursuant to section 20 or 422-b of the Social Services Law;

(b) all members of a local or regional multidisciplinary investigative team established pursuant to section 423(6) of the Social Services Law, when investigating, a subsequent report of suspected child abuse or maltreatment involving, a member of a family that was part of a family assessment response, provided that only the information from the family assessment response record that is relevant to the subsequent report be entered into the record of the subsequent report. which is to be provided to the multidisciplinary review team or agency; and

(c) citizen review panels established pursuant to section 371-b of the Social Services Law, provided that any information obtained shall not be re-disclosed and shall only be used for the purposes set forth in section 371-b of the Social Services Law.

(ii) Community-based agencies that have contracts with the social services district to carry out activities for the district under family assessment response.

(iii) Providers of services under family assessment response.

(iv) Any social services district investigating a subsequent report of abuse or maltreatment invoking the same subject or the same child or children named in the report.

(v) The subject of the report. Reports or records must not be provided to any other persons named in the report.

(vi) A court, but only:

(a) while the family assessment response case is open; and

(b) pursuant to a court order or judicial subpoena, issued only after the subject of the report and all parties to the present proceeding have been given notice and an opportunity to be heard. based on a judicial finding that such reports, records, and any information concerning such reports and records, are necessary for the determination of an issue before the court.

(3) When presented with a court order or judicial subpoena, a social services district must submit family assessment response reports, records, and information to the court for inspection and for such directions as may be necessary to protect confidentiality, including but not limited to redaction of portions of the reports, records, and information and to determine any further limits on re-disclosure.

(4) A court shall not have access to sealed family assessment response records, reports, or other information after the conclusion of services provided under family assessment response, except when provided that information pursuant to 18 NYCRR Sections 432.13(g)(5)(iii) and 432.13(a)(5)(iv).

(5) Persons who are given access to legally sealed family assessment response reports must not re-disclose such records, reports, and information except as follows:

(i) OCFS, its designees, and social services districts may disclose aggregate, non-client identifiable information;

(ii) Social services districts, community-based agencies that have contracts to carry out activities for family assessment response, and providers of services under family assessment response may exchange such reports, records, and information as necessary to carry out activities and services related to the same person or persons addressed in the records of a family assessment response case;

(iii) A child protective service may unseal a family assessment response report, record, or information when it is relevant to a subsequent report of suspected child abuse and maltreatment.

(a) The child protective service may use relevant information from the unsealed report or record for purposes of investigation and family court action concerning, the subsequent report and may include such relevant information in the record of the investigation of the subsequent report.

(b) If the social services districts initiates a proceeding under article ten of the Family Court Act in connection with a subsequent report of suspected abuse or maltreatment and there is information in the report or record of a previous family assessment response case that is relevant to the proceeding, the social services district must include such information in the record of the investigation of the subsequent child protective service report and make that information available to the family court and the other parties for use in the proceeding. The family court may consider the information from the family assessment response case that is relevant to such proceeding in making any determination in the proceeding. Such information shall then be subject to all the laws and regulations regarding confidentiality that apply to the record of the subsequent report.

(iv) A subject of a family assessment response report may. at his or her discretion, present information from a legally sealed family assessment response report, in whole or in part, in any proceeding under article ten of the

Family Court Act in which the subject is a respondent. or in any proceeding, involving the custody of, or visitation with, the subject's children, or in any other relevant proceeding. The court may consider any such information provided by the subject in making a determination. However, the court is not authorized to order the subject to produce such report, records, or information, in whole or in part.

Part 433
Abuse, Neglect Significant Incidents Involving Vulnerable Persons
Section   *(In its Entirety)*
433.1   Scope
433.2   Definitions
433.3   Duty to Report
433.4   Investigations and Reports
433.5   Plans of Prevention and Remediation
433.6   Incident Management Program
433.7   Incident Review Committees
433.8   Records
433.9   Death Reporting
433.10   Compliance

§433.1 Scope.
This Part requires the Office of Children and Family Services to establish standards for the protection of persons with special needs pursuant to article 11 of the Social Services Law. Section 488 of the Social Services Law defines a vulnerable person as a person who, due to physical or cognitive disabilities, or the need for services or placement, is receiving services from a facility or provider agency.

§433.2 Definitions.
When used in this Part:

(a) Facility or provider agency means a program or residential facilities operated by the Office of Children and Family Services pursuant to article 19-G of the Executive Law, detention programs, runaway and homeless youth programs, residential facilities for children granted operating certificates pursuant to section 460-b of the Social Services Law, and family type homes for adults.

(b) Custodian means a director, operator, employee or volunteer of a facility or provider agency; or a consultant or an employee or volunteer of a corporation, partnership, organization or governmental entity which provides goods or services to a facility or provider agency pursuant to contract or other arrangement that permits such person to have regular and substantial contact with individuals who are cared for by the facility or provider agency.

(c) Vulnerable person means a person who, due to physical or cognitive disabilities, or the need for services or placement, is receiving services from a facility or provider agency.

(d) Mandated reporter means a custodian or human services professional, but shall not include a service recipient.

(e) Human services professional means a physician; registered physician assistant; surgeon, medical examiner; coroner; dentist; dental hygienist; osteopath; optometrist; chiropractor; podiatrist; resident; intern; psychologist; registered nurse; licensed practical nurse; nurse practitioner; social worker; emergency medical technician; licensed creative arts therapist; licensed marriage and family therapist; licensed mental health counselor; licensed psychoanalyst; licensed speech/language pathologist or audiologist; licensed physical therapist; licensed occupational therapist; hospital personnel engaged in the admission, examination, care or treatment of persons; Christian Science practitioner; school official, which includes but is not limited to school teacher, school guidance counselor, school psychologist, school social worker, school nurse, school administrator or other school personnel required to hold a teaching or administrative license or certificate; social services worker; any other child care or foster care worker; mental health professional; person credentialed by the office of alcoholism and substance abuse services; peace officer; police officer; district attorney or assistant district attorney; investigator employed in the office of the district attorney; or other law enforcement official.

(f) The Justice Center means the Justice Center for the Protection of People with Special Needs established pursuant to article 20 of the Executive Law.

(g) Vulnerable Persons' Central Register means the central register established and operated by the Justice Center pursuant to section 492 of the Social Services Law and which duties include, but are not limited to, receiving reports of allegations of reportable incidents involving persons receiving services provided by a facility or provider agency.

(h) Reportable incident means the following conduct that a mandated reporter is required to report to the Vulnerable Persons' Central Register.

(1) Physical abuse means conduct by a custodian intentionally or recklessly causing, by physical contact, physical injury or serious or protracted impairment of the physical, mental or emotional condition or causing the likelihood of such injury or impairment. Such conduct may include but shall not be limited to: slapping, hitting, kicking, biting, choking, smothering, shoving, dragging, throwing, punching, shaking, burning, cutting or the use of corporal punishment. Physical abuse shall not include reasonable emergency interventions necessary to protect the safety of any person.

(2) Sexual abuse means any conduct by a custodian that subjects a person receiving services to any offense defined in article 130 or section 255.25, 255.26 or 255.27 of the Penal Law; or any conduct or communication by such custodian that allows, permits, uses or encourages a service recipient to engage in any act described in article 230 or 263 of the Penal Law. For the purposes of this definition of sexual abuse a person with a developmental disability who is or was receiving services and is also an employee or volunteer of a service provider shall not be considered a custodian if he or she has sexual contact with another service recipient who is a consenting adult who has consented to such contact.

(3) Psychological abuse means conduct by a custodian intentionally or recklessly causing, by verbal or non-verbal conduct a substantial diminution of a service recipient's emotional, social or behavioral development or condition, supported by a clinical assessment performed by a physician, psychologist, psychiatric nurse practitioner, licensed clinical or master social worker or licensed mental health counselor, or causing the likelihood of such diminution. Such conduct may include but shall not be limited to intimidation, threats, the display of a weapon or other object that could reasonably be perceived by a service recipient as a means for infliction of pain or injury, in a manner that constitutes a threat of physical pain or injury, taunts, derogatory comments or ridicule. Clinical assessment is necessary for substantiation after investigation, but not for reporting a reasonable suspicion.

(4) Deliberate inappropriate use of restraints means the use of a restraint when the technique that is used, the amount of force that is used or the situation in which the restraint is used is deliberately inconsistent with a service recipient's individual treatment plan or behavioral intervention plan, generally accepted treatment practices and/or applicable Federal or State laws, regulations or policies, except when the restraint is used as a reasonable emergency intervention to prevent imminent risk of harm to a person receiving services or to any other person. Restraint includes the use of any manual, pharmacological or mechanical measure or device to immobilize or limit the ability of a person receiving services to freely move his or her arms, legs or body.

(5) Use of aversive conditioning means the application of a physical stimulus that is intended to induce pain or discomfort in order to modify or change the behavior of a person receiving services in the absence of a person-specific authorization by the Office of Children and Family Services. Aversive conditioning may include but is not limited to, the use of physical stimuli such as noxious odors, noxious tastes blindfolds, the withholding of meals and the provision of substitute foods in an unpalatable form and movement limitations used as punishment including but not limited to helmets and mechanical restraint devices.

(6) Obstruction of reports of reportable incidents means conduct by a custodian that impedes the discovery, reporting or investigation of the treatment of a service recipient by falsifying records related to the safety, treatment or supervision of a service recipient; actively persuading a mandated reporter to make a false statement or intentionally withholding material information during an investigation into such a report; or intentional failure of a supervisor or manager to act upon such a report in accordance with governing regulations, policies or procedures; or, for a mandated reporter who is a custodian failing to report a reportable incident upon discovery.

(7) Unlawful use or administration of a controlled substance means any administration by a custodian to a service recipient of a controlled substance as defined by article 33 of the Public Health Law, without a prescription; or other medication not approved for any use by the federal food and drug administration. It also shall include a custodian unlawfully using or distributing a controlled substance as defined by article 33 of the Public Health Law, at the workplace or while on duty.

(8) Neglect means any action, inaction or lack of attention that breaches a custodian's duty and that results in or is likely to result in physical injury or serious or protracted impairment of the physical, mental or emotional condition of a service recipient. Neglect shall include, but is not limited to: failure to provide proper supervision, including lack of proper supervision that results in conduct between persons receiving services that would constitute physical abuse, sexual abuse, psychological abuse, deliberate or inappropriate use of restraints, use of aversive conditioning, obstruction or reports of reportable incidents, or unlawful use or administration of a controlled substance, as defined above; failure to provide adequate food, clothing, shelter, medical, dental, optometric or surgical care, consistent with the rules and regulations governing the same, provided that the facility or provider agency has reasonable access to the provision of such services and that necessary consents to any such medical, dental, optometric or surgical treatment have been sought and obtained from the appropriate individuals; or failure to provide access to educational instruction, by a custodian with a duty to ensure that an individual

receives access to such instruction in accordance with the provisions of this part and of article 65 of the Education Law and/or the individual's individualized educational program.

(9) Significant incident means an incident, other than an incident of abuse or neglect, that because of its severity or the sensitivity of the situation may result in, or has the reasonably foreseeable potential to result in, harm to the health, safety or welfare of a person receiving services and shall include but not be limited to:

(i) conduct between persons receiving services that would constitute abuse as defined in paragraphs (h)(1)-(7) of this section if committed by a custodian; or

(ii) conduct on the part of the custodian, which is inconsistent with a service recipient's individual treatment plan or individualized educational program, generally accepted treatment practices and/or applicable Federal or State laws, regulations or policies and which impairs or creates a reasonably foreseeable potential to impair the health, safety or welfare of a person receiving services, including but not limited to:

(a) unauthorized seclusion, which mean the placement of a person receiving services in a room or area from which he or she cannot, or perceives that he or she cannot leave at will;

(b) unauthorized use of time out, which means the use of a procedure in which a person receiving services is removed from regular programming and isolated in a room or area for the convenience of a custodian, or as a substitute for programming but shall not include the use of a time-out as an emergency intervention to protect the health or safety of the individual or other persons;

(c) except as defined and provided for in paragraph (7) of this subdivision, the administration of a prescribed or over-the-counter medication, which is inconsistent with a prescription or order issued for a service recipient by a licensed, qualified health care practitioner, and which has an adverse effect on a service recipient. For the purpose of this subdivision adverse effect shall mean the unanticipated and undesirable side effect from the administration of a particular medication which unfavorably affects the well-being of the service recipient;

(d) inappropriate use of restraints, which means the use of a restraint when the technique that is used, the amount of force that is used or the situation in which the restraint is used is inconsistent with a service recipient's individual plan, generally accepted treatment practices and/or applicable Federal or State laws, regulations or policies. For the purposes of this clause, restraint shall include the use of any manual, pharmacological or mechanical measure or device to immobilize or limit the ability of a person receiving services to freely move his or her arms, legs or body; or

(e) any other conduct identified in regulations, guidelines or standards established by the Justice Center.

(10) Physical injury and impairment of physical condition shall mean any confirmed harm, hurt or damage resulting in a significant worsening or diminution of an individual's physical condition.

(11) Delegate investigatory entity shall mean a facility or provider agency, or any other entity authorized by the regulations of the Office of Children and Family Services or the Justice Center.

(12) Person receiving services or service recipient shall mean an individual who is an inpatient in a residential facility or who receives services from a facility or provider agency.

(13) Personal representative shall mean a person authorized under state, tribal, military or other applicable law to act on behalf of a vulnerable person in making health care decisions or, for the programs that serve children under the jurisdiction of the state education department or the Office of Children and Family Services, the service recipient's parent, guardian or other person legally responsible for such person.

(14) Abuse or neglect shall mean conduct described in paragraphs (1) through (8) of this section.

(15) Subject of the report shall mean a custodian who is reported to the Vulnerable Persons' Central Register for the alleged abuse or neglect of a vulnerable person.

(16) Other persons named in the report shall mean and be limited to the following persons who are named in a report to the Vulnerable Persons' Central Register other than the subject of the report: the service recipient whose care and treatment is the concern of a report to the Vulnerable Persons' Central Register and the personal representative, if any.

(17) Intentionally and recklessly shall have the same meanings as provided in subdivisions one and three of section 15.05 of the Penal Law.

§433.3 Duty to report.

(a) Reportable incidents as defined in this Part and in section 488 of the Social Services Law shall be reported immediately upon discovery to the Vulnerable Persons' Central Register, in accordance with section 491 of the Social Services Law. Discovery occurs when the mandated reporter witnesses a suspected reportable incident or when another person, including the vulnerable person, comes before the mandated reporter in the mandated reporter's professional or official capacity and provides the mandated reporter with reasonable cause to suspect that the vulnerable person has been subjected to a reportable incident.

(b) Nothing contained herein shall affect or diminish the obligation of persons who are mandated to make reports to the Statewide Central Register of Child Abuse and Maltreatment pursuant to section 413 of the Social Services Law.

§433.4 Investigations and reports.

The Justice Center may refer reports of abuse, neglect and significant incidents to be investigated by the Office of Children and Family Services which may delegate the responsibility of the investigation to the facility or provider agency in which the reported incident is alleged to have occurred. All facilities or provider agencies must conduct any investigations delegated to them by the Office of Children and Family Services or the Justice Center as prescribed by all applicable rules, regulations, guidance and policies of the Justice Center and the Office of Children and Family Services. The investigatory entity shall provide the notice of initiation of investigation in accordance with guidance provided by the Office of Children and Family Services or the Justice Center. The notice of the determination of the investigation shall be issued by the Justice Center.

(a) Abuse and/or neglect investigation findings shall be reported to the Justice Center within 50 days from the date of the Justice Center accepting a report of an allegation of abuse or neglect. Exceptions to the completion of an investigation within 50 days are permitted only with documented good cause, submission of all investigatory information to the Justice Center, and at the approval of the Justice Center.

(b) A facility or provider agency shall commence an immediate and thorough investigation of an alleged report of abuse and/or neglect upon receipt of notice from the Justice Center or the Office of Children and Family Services that such report has been accepted by the Vulnerable Persons' Central Register for investigation.

(c) Appropriate precautions should be made to secure the safety and health of all service recipients if the allegations in the report warrant such measure or if the allegations are of such a nature law enforcement should be notified.

(d) Upon notification that a report of abuse, neglect and/or a significant incident has been made to the Justice Center with respect to a vulnerable person, the director of the facility or provider agency or his or her designee shall evaluate the situation and immediately take appropriate action to protect the health and safety of the vulnerable person involved in the report and of any other vulnerable persons similarly situated in the facility, provider agency or program. Additional action shall be taken whenever necessary to prevent future incidents of abuse, neglect or significant incidents. Any action taken should cause as little disruption as possible to the daily routines of the vulnerable persons in the facility, provider agency or program. The following alternatives shall be considered in determining the course of action that will be taken with regard to a specific incident of alleged abuse, neglect or significant incident:

(i) removal or transfer of the subject of the report, consistent with the policy of the agency's board of directors, appropriate collective bargaining agreement(s) and applicable provisions of the Civil Service Law;

(ii) initiation of disciplinary action against the subject of the report, consistent with appropriate collective bargaining agreement(s) and applicable provisions of the Civil Service Law with respect to state employees only, such action shall be taken only after consultation with the Justice Center;

(iii) increasing the degree of supervision of the subject of the report;

(iv) provision of counseling to the subject of the report;

(v) provision of increased training to staff and volunteers pertinent to the prevention and remediation of abuse and maltreatment;

(vi) removal or transfer of the vulnerable person, consistent with applicable placement procedures, if it is determined that there is a risk to such youth in remaining in that program; and

(vii) provision of counseling to the vulnerable person involved in the report and any other youth, as appropriate.

(e) Investigations shall include an appropriate medical examination of an injured vulnerable person, and a record of the name of the examiner and his or her findings.

(f) Witnesses to the incident shall be identified and interviewed in as private an environment as possible. Interviews of witnesses should be conducted separately by qualified, objective individuals. Interviews of vulnerable persons should be conducted by individuals with an understanding of the vulnerable persons' individual needs and/or capabilities. To the extent possible confidentiality should be maintained, except as otherwise provided by law or regulation, during the course of the investigation.

(g) Investigations shall consist of a review of all pertinent information including but not limited to records, photographs, videos, observations of incident scene, and/or expert assessments.

(h) Investigations shall include the documentation and retention of physical evidence if any, which shall be given to the facility or agency provider's executive or other appropriate person for safeguarding. Such facility or agency provider's executive or other appropriate person should develop a plan and protocol for the safeguarding of any physical evidence received during an investigation and shall keep such evidence in a secure location, as provided for in such plan.

(i) Investigations shall include detailed written documentation of each step taken in the investigative process.

(j) Investigative findings shall be stated in writing referencing the supporting documentation and/or evidence obtained.

(k) Significant incidents shall be investigated and findings reported to the Justice Center and, if the investigation is not conducted by the Office of Children and Family Services, to the Office of Children and Family Services within 60 days from the date of the Justice Center or the Office of Children and Family Services, whichever is applicable, referring a report to a facility or provider agency. Facilities or provider agencies shall follow all applicable regulations, rules, policies and/or guidelines established by the Justice Center and, if the investigation is not conducted by the Office of Children and Family Services, by the Office of Children and Family Services governing significant incidents.

§433.5 Plans of prevention and remediation.

Upon receipt from the Justice Center of a report of abuse or neglect of a vulnerable person or a significant incident, where the Justice Center or the Office of Children and Family Services has determined that it appears likely that a crime may have been committed against a vulnerable person or that there has been a violation of the statutory, regulatory or other requirements related to the care and treatment of individuals receiving services, the director of the program shall consider any appropriate recommendations received from the Office of Children and Family Services and the Justice Center for preventive and remedial action, including legal action, and shall:

(a) Develop and implement a written plan of action to be taken with respect to an individual employee or volunteer to protect the continued health and safety of the vulnerable person in the program and to provide for the prevention of future acts of abuse, neglect or significant incident. Such plan shall also describe the actions taken to address the investigative findings. The plan shall be subject to approval by the Office of Children and Family Services or the Justice Center, as applicable.

(b) In the event an investigation finds a report of abuse, neglect, or significant incident may be attributed in whole or in part to noncompliance with any of the program rules, the regulations of the Office of Children and Family Services or the regulations, policy or guidance of the Justice Center, the facility or provider agency shall develop and implement a plan of prevention and remediation which, at a minimum, shall address each area of noncompliance and indicate how the program will come into compliance. Such plan shall also describe the actions taken to address the investigative findings and shall be subject to the approval and/or continued monitoring by the Office of Children and Family Services and/or the Justice Center.

(c) The plan of prevention and remediation shall be stated in writing and endorsed with the signature of the facility or provider agency's director or other executive with supervisory authority.

(d) The plan of prevention and remediation shall prescribe a monitoring date or interval of monitoring dates should that be deemed appropriate, with the name of the individual or individuals responsible for assessing the efficacy of the remedial action.

§433.6 Incident management program.

Facilities or provider agencies shall establish policies or practices that require the following:

(a) all reportable incidents are identified and reported to the Vulnerable Persons' Central Register in accordance with all applicable laws and regulations;

(b) all reportable incidents are promptly investigated, if such investigation has been delegated to the facility or provider agency for investigation;

(c) individual reportable incidents and incident patterns and trends are reviewed to identify and implement preventative and corrective actions, which may include, but are not limited to staff retraining, appropriate disciplinary action allowed by law or contract, or opportunities for improvement;

(d) information regarding individual reportable incidents, incident patterns and trends, and patterns and trends in reporting and responses to reportable incidents shall be shared consistent with applicable law, with the Justice Center in the form and manner required by the Justice Center or the Office of Children and Family Services as applicable.

§433.7 Incident review committees.

Facilities or provider agencies shall establish an incident review committees pursuant to section 490(1)(f) of the Social Services Law.

(a) Such committee must be composed of members of the governing body of the facility or provider agency and other persons identified by the director of the facility or provider agency including some members of the following: direct support staff, licensed health care practitioners, service recipients and representatives of family, consumer and other advocacy organizations, but not the director of the facility or provider agency.

(b) Incident review committee requirements may be waived by the Office of Children and Family Services upon written application, based on size or the facility or provider agency or other relevant factors. Waivers granted by the Office of Children and Family Services shall be in accordance with rules and regulations issued by the Justice Center.

(c) An incident review committee shall meet regularly to:

(1) review the timeliness, thoroughness and appropriateness of the facility or provider agency's response to reportable incidents;

(2) recommend additional opportunities for improvement to the director of the facility or provider agency, if appropriate;

(3) review incident trends and patterns concerning reportable incidents;

(4) make recommendations to the director of the facility or provider agency to assist in reducing reportable incidents; and

(5) the facility or provider agency shall cooperate with the Justice Center or the Office of Children and Family Services in all investigations and provide access to the facility premises and all records.

(d) Members of the committee shall be trained in confidentiality laws and regulations and shall comply with section 74 of the Public Officers Law.

§433.8 Records.

Records of facilities or provider agencies, as defined in section 488(4) of the Social Services Law, shall be made available for public inspection and copying when such records relate to abuse and neglect of vulnerable persons to the same extent that those records would be available from a state agency. Requests for such records shall be made in writing to the Justice Center. Facilities or provider agencies covered by this subdivision shall cooperate with the Justice Center, including providing any requested records to the Justice Center.

§433.9 Death reporting.

(a) Every director, operator or other person in charge of a facility or provider agency as defined in section 488 of the Social Services Law shall report to the Justice Center:

(i) the death of a vulnerable person, as defined in section 488 of the Social Services Law, who is receiving services from the facility or provider agency;

(ii) the death of a vulnerable person, as defined in section 488 of the Social Services Law, who received service from the facility or provider agency in the last 30 calendar days preceding their death.

(b) The report shall be made in the manner and form as prescribed by the Justice Center.

(c) The report shall be made immediately upon discovery of the death of the vulnerable person, and in no event later than 24 hours after the discovery.

(d) Within five working days of the death of the vulnerable person, a written report must be submitted to the Justice Center in the form and manner prescribed by the Justice Center.

(e) Within 60 working days of the report of the death of the vulnerable person, the facility or provider agency must provide the Justice Center with a copy of the autopsy report regarding the death of the vulnerable person or furnish the Justice Center with a statement that such autopsy is not completed or is otherwise unavailable to the facility or provider agency at that time.

§433.10 Compliance.

All facilities or provider agencies shall comply with all laws, regulations, rules and policies as prescribed by the Justice Center and shall cooperate with all investigations and inquiries made by either the Office of Children and Family Services or the Justice Center, including requests for access to all facilities and programs and all facility or program records.

Part 434
Child Protective Services Administrative Hearing Procedure

§434.1 Scope.
The provisions of this Part apply to the following hearings:
(a) Hearings held pursuant to section 422 of the Social Services Law to determine by a fair preponderance of the evidence whether the record of a report maintained in the State Central Register of Child Abuse and Maltreatment should be amended or expunged and, if such report is indicated, whether the act or acts of child abuse or maltreatment described in such report could be relevant and reasonably related to the appropriateness of the subject to engage in child care employment or to become an adoptive parent, a foster parent or a day care provider.
(b) Hearings held pursuant to section 424-a of the Social Services Law to determine whether the subject of a report of child abuse or maltreatment has been shown by a fair preponderance of the evidence to have committed the act or acts of child abuse or maltreatment giving rise to the indicated report.

§434.2 Definitions.
For purposes of this Part, the following definitions apply:
(a) Abused child means a child as defined in section 412.1 of the Social Services Law.
(b) Appellant means (1) a subject of an indicated report of child abuse or maltreatment who has requested a hearing pursuant to section 422 of the Social Services Law to determine whether the subject has been shown by a fair preponderance of the evidence, as such term is defined in subdivision (i) of section 434.10 of this Part, to have committed the act or acts of child abuse or maltreatment giving rise to the indicated report and whether such act or acts could be relevant and reasonably related to the appropriateness of the subject to engage in child care employment or to become an adoptive parent, a foster parent, or a day care provider, or (2) a subject of an indicated report who has requested a hearing pursuant to section 424-a of the Social Services Law to determine whether the subject has been shown by a fair preponderance of the evidence, as such term is defined in subdivision (i) of section 434.10 of the Part, to have committed the act or acts of child abuse or maltreatment giving rise to the indicated report.
(c) Authorized agency means an agency as defined in section 371.10 of the Social Services Law.
(d) Commissioner means the Commissioner of the New York State Office of Children and Family Services.
(e) Department or Office means the New York State Office of Children and Family Services.
(f) Hearing means a proceeding at which (1) a subject of a report of child abuse and maltreatment may seek relief from a decision of the department to deny a request to amend an indicated report of child abuse or maltreatment maintained by the State Central Register of Child Abuse and Maltreatment, or, for reports received prior to February 12, 1996, amend or expunge an indicated report of child abuse or maltreatment maintained by the State Central Register of Child Abuse and Maltreatment, or (2) it is determined whether a subject committed the act or acts of child abuse or maltreatment giving rise to an indicated report and if so whether such act or acts are relevant and reasonably related to the appropriateness of the subject to engage in child care employment or to become an adoptive parent, foster parent or a day care provider.

(g) Hearing officer means an attorney who is employed by the department and designated and authorized by the commissioner to preside at hearings.

(h) Indicated report means a report of child abuse or maltreatment in which an investigation conducted by the local social services district, the department, or the Commission on the Quality of Care for the Mentally Disabled has determined that some credible evidence of the alleged child abuse or maltreatment exists.

(i) Licensing agency means an authorized agency which has received an application to become an adoptive parent or an authorized agency which has received an application for a certificate or license to receive, board or keep any child pursuant to the provisions of section 376 or 377 of the Social Services Law or an authorized agency which has received an application from a relative within the third degree of the parent or stepparent of a child or the child's legal guardian for approval to receive, board or keep such child or an authorized agency or State or local governmental agency which receives an application to provide day care services in a day care center, family day care home or group family day care home pursuant to the provisions of section 390 of the Social Services Law, or the Department of Health of the City of New York when such department receives an application for a certificate of approval to provide family day care pursuant to the provision of the health code of such city, or a State or local governmental official who receives an application for a permit to operate a camp which is subject to the provisions of article 13-A, 13-B or 13-C of the Public Health Law or the Division for Youth which has received an application for a certificate to receive board or keep any child at a foster family home pursuant to the provisions of section 501(7), 502, or 532-a(3) of the Executive Law.

(j) Maltreated child means a child as defined in section 412(2) of the Social Services Law.

(k) Parties to a hearing means the appellant, the State Central Register of Child Abuse and Maltreatment, the local child protective service, the Commission on Quality of Care for the Mentally Disabled, and the department.

(*l*) Provider agency means an authorized agency, the Division for Youth, juvenile detention facilities subject to the certification of such division, programs established pursuant to article 19-H of the Executive Law, and licensed day care centers, including head start programs which are funded pursuant to title V of the Federal Economic Opportunity Act of 1964, as amended, special act school districts as enumerated in chapter 566 of the Laws of 1967, as amended, and residential schools which are operated, supervised or approved by the Education Department.

(m) Subject of a report means any parent of, guardian of, custodian of or other person 18 years of age or older legally responsible for, as defined in section 1012(g) of the Family Court Act, a child reported to the State Central Register of Child Abuse and Maltreatment, who is allegedly responsible for causing abuse or maltreatment to such child or who allegedly allows such abuse or maltreatment to be inflicted on such child, or a director of or an operator of or employee or volunteer in a home operated or supervised by an authorized agency, the Division for Youth, or an office of the Department of Mental Hygiene or in a family day care home, a day care center, a group family day care home or a day services program, or a consultant or any person who is an employee of or a volunteer in a corporation, partnership, organization or any governmental entity which provides goods or services and has regular and substantial contact with children in residential care who is allegedly responsible for causing abuse or maltreatment or who allegedly allows such abuse or maltreatment to be inflicted on such child.

§434.3 Persons entitled to a hearing.

(a) A subject of a report of child abuse or maltreatment has a right to a hearing pursuant to section 422 of the Social Services Law to determine whether the record of the report in the Statewide Central Register of Child Abuse and Maltreatment should be amended or, if the report was received by the Statewide Central Register of Child Abuse and Maltreatment prior to February 12, 1996, amended or expunged on the grounds that it is inaccurate or is being maintained in a manner inconsistent with title 6 of article 6 of the Social Services Law. The burden of proof at such hearing is on the office, appropriate local child protective service or the Commission on Quality of Care and Advocacy for Persons with Disabilities, as the case may be. The issues at the hearing are:

(1) whether the subject has been shown by a fair preponderance of the evidence to have committed the act or acts of child abuse or maltreatment giving rise to the indicated report, where it has been determined at the administrative review that the act or acts of child abuse or maltreatment giving rise to the indicated report would not be relevant and reasonably related to the employment of the subject by provider agencies or the approval or disapproval of applications which would be submitted by the subject to licensing agencies; or

(2) whether the subject has been shown by a fair preponderance of the evidence to have committed the act or acts of child abuse or maltreatment giving rise to the indicated report and, if there is a finding of a fair preponderance of the evidence, whether such act or acts are, based on guidelines developed by the office, relevant and reasonably related to the employment of the subject by provider agencies, or the approval or disapproval of applications which would be submitted by the subject to licensing agencies.

(b) Any person who has been informed by a licensing or provider agency that he or she has been denied employment, discharged from employment, not used as a volunteer or not hired as a consultant or informed that an application for a permit or license has been denied based in whole or in part on the fact that such person is the subject of an indicated report of child abuse or maltreatment may request a hearing pursuant to section 424-a of the Social Services Law. The request for a hearing must be made within 90 days of the receipt of notice of denial of an application by a provider or licensing agency which indicates that the denial was based in whole or in part on the existence of the indicated report. Any hearing requested under this paragraph must be held within 30 days of the request unless the hearing is adjourned for good cause shown. Any subsequent adjournment for good cause shown must be granted only upon consent of the person who requested the hearing. At any such hearing, the sole question to be decided is whether the subject has been shown by a fair preponderance of the evidence to have committed the act or acts of child abuse or maltreatment giving rise to the indicated report. In such hearings the burden of proof on the issue of whether an act of child abuse or maltreatment was committed is upon the department.

§434.4 Time and place of the hearing.

The hearing must be held at a time and place convenient to the appellant as far as practicable, taking into account circumstances such as the physical inability of the appellant to travel.

§434.5 Notice of the hearing.

All hearings held pursuant to this Part will be scheduled by means of a written notice issued to the appellant and his or her representative, if known, by the department. The notice must include:

(a) the date, time and location of the hearing and a statement informing the appellant of his or her right to a change in the date and place of the hearing where necessary;

(b) a statement of the issues which will be decided at the hearing;

(c) a statement of the manner in which the hearing will be conducted;

(d) a statement of the right of the appellant to be represented by an attorney or other representative;

(e) a statement of the right of the appellant to present evidence on his or her behalf and to produce witnesses;

(f) a statement of the right of the appellant to cross-examine witnesses;

(g) a statement that a verbatim record of the hearing will be maintained;

(h) a statement of the method by which adjournments may be requested and granted; and

(i) a statement of the right of the appellant to review the documents maintained by the State Central Register of Child Abuse and Maltreatment.

§434.6 Hearing officer.

(a) The hearing must be conducted by an impartial hearing officer who is employed by the department for that purpose and who has not been involved in any way with the action in question. The hearing officer has all the powers conferred by law and the regulations of the department to administer oaths, issue subpoenas, require the attendance of witnesses and the production of books and records, rule upon requests for adjournment, rule upon evidentiary matters and to otherwise regulate the hearing, preserve requirements of due process and effectuate the purpose and provisions of applicable law.

(b) A party to a hearing may make a request to a hearing officer that the hearing officer remove himself or herself from presiding at the hearing.

(1) The grounds for removing a hearing officer are that such hearing officer has:

(i) previously dealt in any way with the substance of the matter which is the subject of the hearing except in the capacity of hearing officer; or

(ii) any interest in the matter, financial or otherwise, direct or indirect, which will impair the independent judgment of the hearing officer; or

(iii) displayed bias or partiality to any party to the hearing.

(2) The hearing officer may independently determine to remove himself or herself from presiding at a hearing on the grounds set forth in paragraph (1) of this subdivision.

(3) The request for removal made by a party must:

(i) be made in good faith; and

(ii) be made at the hearing in writing or orally on the record; and

(iii) describe in detail the grounds for requesting that the hearing officer be removed.

(4) Upon receipt of a request for removal, the hearing officer must determine on the record whether to remove himself or herself from the hearing.

(5) If the hearing officer determines not to remove himself or herself from presiding at the hearing, the hearing officer must advise the party requesting removal that the hearing will continue but the request for removal will automatically be reviewed by the general counsel or the general counsel's designee.

(6) The determination of the hearing officer not to remove himself or herself will be reviewed by the general counsel or the general counsel's designee. Such review will include review of written documents submitted by the parties and the transcript of the hearing.

(7) The general counsel or the general counsel's designee must issue a written determination of whether the hearing officer should be removed from presiding at the hearing within 15 business days of the close of the hearing.

(8) The written determination of the general counsel or the general counsel's designee will be made part of the record.

§434.7 Persons who may be present at a hearing; authorization of representative.

(a) The parties to a hearing, their attorneys or representatives, their witnesses and any witness called by the hearing officer may be present at the hearing. Other persons may be admitted upon the hearing officer's discretion. Upon the hearing officer's motion, or upon the motion of either party, potential witnesses may be excluded from the hearing during the testimony of other witnesses.

(b) An individual representing the appellant must have a written authorization signed by the appellant if the appellant is not present.

§434.8 Conduct of the hearing.

(a) A hearing officer must preside at the hearing and must make all procedural rulings. He or she may make an opening statement describing the nature of the proceedings, the issues to be decided and the manner in which the hearing will be conducted.

(b) The hearing officer must exclude testimony or other evidence which is irrelevant or unduly repetitious.

(c) All testimony must be given under oath or affirmation unless the testimony is given by a young child who is unable to understand the meaning of oath or affirmation.

(d) Each party is entitled to be represented by an attorney or other representative of his or her choice, to have witnesses give testimony and to otherwise have relevant and material evidence presented on his or her behalf, to cross-examine opposing witnesses, to offer rebuttal evidence and to examine any document or item offered into evidence.

(e) Technical rules of evidence followed in a court of law will not apply but evidence introduced must be relevant and material.

(f) Copies of the documentary evidence which a social services official, the State Central Register of Child Abuse and Maltreatment or the Commission on Quality of Care for the Mentally Disabled plan to use at the hearing must be provided, if requested, to the appellant or his or her representative who has appropriate written authorization from the appellant for the examination, at a reasonable time before the date of the hearing and at a place accessible to the appellant or the appellant's representative.

§434.9 The record.

(a) The record of the hearing, including the recommendations of the hearing officer, is confidential, but the record may be examined by either party or their representatives at a place accessible to them and at a reasonable time.

(b) The record must include:

(1) all notices, intermediate rulings and all records maintained in the State Central Register of Child Abuse and Maltreatment;

(2) the transcript or recording of the hearing and the exhibits received into evidence;

(3) matters officially noticed;

(4) questions and offers of proof, objections thereto and rulings thereon;

(5) proposed findings and exceptions, if any;

(6) any report rendered by the hearing officer;

(7) any request for disqualification of a hearing officer; and

(8) the hearing decision.

(c) The forms and documents contained in the State Central Register of Child Abuse and Maltreatment relating to an indicated report of child abuse or maltreatment are admissible into evidence at the hearing. A certification by the director of the State Central Register of Child Abuse and Maltreatment or his or her designee that the forms and documents are true and accurate copies of the complete record of the indicated report of child abuse or maltreatment at issue, and that the State Central Register of Child Abuse and Maltreatment is required by law to receive reports of alleged child abuse and maltreatment, is prima facie evidence that such forms and documents comprise the complete record of the indicated report of child abuse or maltreatment at issue. Such forms and documents must be admitted into evidence upon the submission of the required certification to the hearing officer. The admission of such forms and documents must be for the purpose of showing that the forms and documents are those presently maintained at the State Central Register of Child Abuse and Maltreatment in relation to the indicated report of child abuse or maltreatment at issue in the hearing. The admission of such forms and documents will be without regard to the truth or falsity of the contents of any such forms and documents and no implication as to the truth or falsity of the contents of any such forms or documents may be made by the hearing officer solely on the basis of such forms or documents having been admitted into evidence pursuant to this subdivision. Nothing in this subdivision will be construed to require the State Central Register of Child Abuse and Maltreatment to submit into evidence forms and documents not maintained by or at the State Central Register of Child Abuse and Maltreatment at the time of the hearing.

§434.10   Evidence.

In any hearing under this Part:

(a) Proof that the appellant abused or maltreated one child is admissible evidence on the issue of whether the appellant abused or maltreated any other child.

(b) Proof of injuries sustained by a child or proof of the condition of a child which is of such a nature as would ordinarily not have occurred except by reason of the acts or omissions of the appellant is prima facie evidence that the child was abused or maltreated by the appellant.

(c) Any writing, record or photograph, whether in the form of an entry in a book or otherwise, made as a memorandum or record of any condition, act, transaction, occurrence or event relating to a child in a child abuse or maltreatment proceeding by any hospital or any other public or private agency is admissible in evidence as proof of that condition, act, transaction, occurrence or event, if the hearing officer finds that it was made in the regular course of business of any hospital or any other public or private agency and that it was made in the regular course of such business at the time of the act, transaction, occurrence or event, or within a reasonable time thereafter.

(d) Previous statements made by the child relating to any allegations of abuse or maltreatment are admissible in evidence. The testimony of the child during the hearing is not necessary to support a finding of abuse or maltreatment.

(e) Proof of the impairment of emotional health or impairment of mental or emotional condition as a result of the unwillingness or inability of the appellant to exercise a minimum degree of care toward a child may include competent opinion or expert testimony and may include proof that such impairment lessened during a period when the child was in the care, custody or supervision of a person or agency other than the appellant.

(f) A Family Court finding, in a proceeding brought pursuant to article 10 of the Family Court Act, that a child has been abused or neglected is presumptive evidence that the report of child abuse and maltreatment maintained by the Statewide Central Register of Child Abuse and Maltreatment concerning such child is substantiated by a fair preponderance of the evidence if the allegations are the same; however, dismissal or withdrawal of a Family Court petition does not create a presumption that there is a lack of a fair preponderance of the evidence to prove that a child has been abused or maltreated for purposes of this Part.

(g) An appellant may introduce evidence to rebut any presumptions contained in this section.

(h) Some credible evidence is evidence that is worthy and capable of being believed.

(i) Fair preponderance of evidence is evidence which outweighs other evidence which is offered to oppose it.

(j) Relevant evidence is evidence having any tendency to make the existence of any fact that is at issue more or less probable than it would be without the evidence.

§434.11 Decision after the hearing.

(a) Hearing decisions must be made and issued by the commissioner or by a member of his or her staff who is designated by the commissioner to consider the record of the hearing. The decision must be based exclusively on the record of the hearing. The decision must be in writing and must describe the issues, recite the relevant facts and the pertinent provisions of law and department regulations, make appropriate findings, determine the issues, state reasons for the determination, and when appropriate, direct specific action to be taken by any of the parties to the hearing.

(b) For hearings held pursuant to section 424-a of the Social Services Law, a copy of the decision must be mailed to the appellant and his or her attorney or other designated representative within 60 days after the record is closed.

(c) For hearings held pursuant to section 422 of the Social Services Law, a copy of the decision must be mailed to the appellant and his or her attorney or other designated representative within 90 days after the record is closed.

(d) The failure of the department to issue a decision within the time period specified in subdivision (b) or (c) of this section or to mail a copy of the decision to the appellant and/or his or her attorney or other designated representative within such time period will not result in the sealing or expungement of the report maintained in the State Central Register of Child Abuse and Maltreatment.

Part 436
Kinship Guardianship Assistance Program

§436.1 Definitions.

For the purpose of this Part, the following definitions apply:

(a) *Applicable board rate* means an amount equal to the monthly payment that has been made by a social services official, in accordance with section 398-a of the Social Services Law and other provisions of the Social Services Law, for the care and maintenance of the child, while such child was boarded out in the certified or approved foster family boarding home with the prospective relative guardian. Such rate shall reflect annual changes in room and board rates and clothing replacement allowances

(b) *Child* means a person under 21 years of age whose custody, care and custody, or custody and guardianship have been committed to a social services official prior to such person's 18th birthday pursuant to section 358-a, 384, 384-a or 384-b of the Social Services Law or article 3, 7, 10 or 10-C of the Family Court Act.

(c) *Office* means the New York State Office of Children and Family Services.

(d) *Prospective relative guardian* means a person or persons who is related to the child through blood, marriage, or adoption who has been caring for the child as a fully certified or approved foster parent for at least six consecutive months prior to applying for kinship guardianship assistance payments.

(e) *Relative guardian* means a person or persons who was appointed as a guardian or permanent guardian for a child after entering into an agreement with a social services official for the receipt of payments and services in accordance with this Part.

(f) *Social services official* means a county commissioner of social services, a city commissioner of social services, or an Indian tribe with which the office has entered into an agreement to provide foster care services in accordance with subdivision 2 of section 39 of the Social Services Law.

(g) *State income standard* means the most recent Federal income official poverty line (as defined and annually revised by the Federal Office of Management and Budget) updated by the office for a family size of four and adjusted by the office for family size.

(h) *Applicable State income standard* means 275 percent of the State income standard.

(i) *Successor guardian* means a person or persons who is approved by a social services official to receive payments pursuant to this Part, who has been named in the agreement in effect between the relative guardian and social services official for kinship guardianship assistance payments, who shall provide care and guardianship for a child in the event of death or incapacity of the relative guardian, and who has assumed care for and is the guardian or permanent guardian of such child, provided that such person was appointed guardian or permanent guardian of such child by the court following, or due to, the death or incapacity of the relative guardian. Once approved in accordance with this Part, a successor guardian shall be deemed to have the same rights and responsibilities as a relative guardian in relation to any provisions of this Part and any agreement entered into under this Part.

(j) *Prospective successor guardian* means a person or persons whom a prospective relative guardian or a relative guardian seeks to name or names in the original kinship guardianship assistance agreement, or any amendment thereto, as set forth in this Part, as the person or persons to provide care and guardianship for a child in the event of the death or incapacity of a relative guardian, who has not been approved in accordance with this Part.

(k) *Incapacity* means a substantial inability to care for a child as a result of:
(1) a physically debilitating illness, disease or injury; or
(2) a mental impairment that results in a substantial inability to understand the nature and consequences of decisions concerning the care of a child.

(Eff. 5/11/16)

§436.2 Application for kinship guardianship assistance payments.

(a) In addition to the notification provided pursuant to sections 430.11(c)(4) and 443.2(e) of this Title, a social services official must provide information upon request to a prospective relative guardian on the availability and standards of eligibility for the kinship guardianship assistance and for non-recurring guardianship expenses programs. Upon request, the social services official must provide the prospective relative guardian with an application for the kinship guardianship assistance and the non-recurring guardianship expenses programs. Such application must be in a form as prescribed by the Office.

(b) A prospective relative guardian who has been caring for an eligible foster child for at least six consecutive months and who intends to seek guardianship or permanent guardianship of the child may apply to the social services official who has custody, care and custody, or guardianship and custody of the child to receive kinship guardianship assistance and non-recurring guardianship expense payments on behalf of the child, provided, however, such application may not be submitted for a child who was placed into foster care pursuant to Article 10 of the Family Court Act unless both the fact finding hearing held in accordance with section 1051 of the Family Court Act and the first permanency hearing in accordance with section 1089(a)(2) of the Family Court Act for the child had been completed or for all other children in foster care, the first permanency hearing for the child has been completed.

(c) Applications may be accepted prior to issuance of letters of guardianship of the child to the relative guardian pursuant to the provisions of the Family Court Act or the Surrogate's Court Procedure Act.

(d) Within 30 days of the receipt of a completed kinship guardianship assistance and non-recurring guardianship payment application, the social services official must make a determination whether to approve or disapprove the application in accordance with the standards set forth in this Part.

(e) If the decision by the social services official is to disapprove the application, the social services official must provide the prospective relative guardian(s) with written notice of the disapproval, the basis for the disapproval and the right to an administrative hearing in accordance with the standards set forth in section 436.10 of this Part.

§436.3 Eligibility for kinship guardian assistance payments.
(a) A child is eligible for kinship guardianship assistance payments under this Part if the social services official determines the following:
(1) the child has been in foster care for at least six consecutive months in the home of the prospective relative guardian, as defined in section 436.1 of this Part; and
(2) the child being returned home or adopted are not appropriate permanency options for the child; and
(3) the child demonstrates a strong attachment to the prospective relative guardian and the prospective relative guardian has a strong commitment to caring permanently for the child; and
(4) that age appropriate consultation has been held with the child, provided, however, with respect to a child who has attained 14 years of age, that the child has been consulted regarding the kinship guardianship arrangement, and with respect to a child who has attained 18 years of age, that the child has consented to the kinship guardianship arrangement; and
(5) (i) if the child has been placed into foster care pursuant to article 10 of the Family Court Act, that both the fact finding hearing pursuant to section 1051 of the Family Court Act and the first permanency hearing pursuant to section 1089(a)(2) of the Family Court Act have been completed; or
(ii) for all other children in foster care, that the first permanency hearing has been completed.
(b) The financial status of the prospective relative guardian or the prospective successor guardian may not be considered in determining eligibility for kinship guardianship assistance payments.
(c) (1) Notwithstanding any other provision of law to the contrary, a prospective relative guardian and any person over the age of 18 living in the home of the prospective relative guardian who has not already been subject to a national and State criminal history record check pursuant to section 378-a of the Social Services Law, as part of the process of the prospective relative guardian becoming a certified or approved foster parent, must complete such a record check in accordance with the procedures and standards set forth in section 378-a of the Social Services Law prior to the social services official acting upon the application for kinship guardianship assistance.
(2) The social services official must inquire of the office whether each prospective relative guardian and each person over the age of 18 living in the home of the prospective relative guardian has been or is currently the subject of an indicated report of child abuse or maltreatment on file with the Statewide Central Register of Child Abuse and Maltreatment and, if the prospective relative guardian or any other person over the age of 18 residing in the home of the prospective relative guardian resided in another state in the five years preceding the application, request child abuse and maltreatment information maintained by the child abuse and maltreatment registry from the applicable child welfare agency in each such state of previous residence, if such an inquiry and request has not been previously made as part of the process of the prospective relative guardian becoming a certified or approved foster parent.
(3) Notwithstanding any other provision of law to the contrary, prior to a social services official approving a prospective successor guardian to receive payments pursuant to this Part, the social services official must:
(i) complete a national and state criminal history record check of the prospective successor guardian and any person over the age of 18 living in the home of the prospective successor guardian pursuant to section 378-a(2) of the

Social Services Law in accordance with the procedures and standards set forth in such statute;

(ii) inquire of the office in accordance with section 424-a of the Social Services Law whether each prospective successor guardian and each person over the age of 18 living in the home of the prospective successor guardian has been or is currently the subject of an indicated report of child abuse or maltreatment on file with the Statewide Central Register of Child Abuse and Maltreatment; and

(iii) if the prospective successor guardian or any other person over the age of 18 residing in the home of the prospective successor guardian resided in another state in the five years preceding the inquiry, request child abuse and maltreatment information maintained by the child abuse and maltreatment registry from the applicable child welfare agency in each such state of previous residence.

(4) The prospective successor guardian must inform the social services official that has entered into an agreement with the relative guardian for payments under this Part in writing of the death or incapacity of the relative guardian and of the prospective successor guardian's desire to enforce the provisions in the agreement that authorize kinship guardianship assistance payments to him or her in the event of the death or incapacity of the relative guardian.

(5) The clearances required by paragraph (3) of this subdivision must be conducted following receipt by the social services official of the written communication required by paragraph (4) of this subdivision.

(d) If the social services official determines that the child is eligible for kinship guardianship assistance payments and that it is in the best interests of the child for the relative to become the legal guardian of the child, the social services official must enter into an agreement with the prospective relative guardian authorizing the provision of kinship guardianship assistance payments, non-recurring guardianship expense payments, and other services and payments available under this Part subject to the issuance by the court of letters of guardianship of the child to the prospective relative guardian or guardians and the child being finally discharged from foster care to such relative or relatives. In determining whether it is in the best interests of the child for the prospective relative guardian to become the relative guardian of the child, the social services official must determine and document that compelling reasons exist for determining that the return home of the child and the adoption of the child are not in the best interests of the child and are, therefore, not appropriate permanency goals. The determination of best interests made pursuant to this subdivision must be documented in accordance with section 428.5(c)(12) of this Title. A copy of the fully executed agreement must be provided by the social services official to the prospective relative guardian.

(e) The social services district must comply with the case plan documentation requirements set forth in section 428.5(c)(12) of this Title in regard to the administration of the kinship guardianship assistance and non-recurring guardianship expenses programs.

(f) A child remains eligible for kinship guardianship assistance payments under this Part when a successor guardian, as defined in section 436.1(i) of this Part assumes care and guardianship of the child.   *(Eff.5/11/16)*

§436.4 Kinship guardianship assistance and non-recurring guardianship expenses agreement.

(a) Payments for kinship guardianship assistance and non-recurring guardianship expenses must be made pursuant to a written agreement between the social services official and the prospective relative guardian.

(b) The written agreement must specify, at a minimum:

(1) the amount of, and manner in which, each kinship guardianship assistance payment will be provided under the agreement;

(2) the manner in which the payment may be adjusted periodically, in consultation with the relative guardian, based on the circumstances of the relative guardian and the needs of the child;

(3) the availability of independent living services in accordance with section 436.9 of this Part;

(4) the additional services and assistance that the child and the relative guardian will be eligible for under this agreement, which are limited to the additional services and assistance set forth in title 10 of article 6 of this Social Services Law and this Part and the procedures by which the relative guardian may apply for additional services, as needed;

(5) the requirement by the relative guardians to notify the social services official of any changes in circumstances that would impact continued eligibility for kinship guardianship assistance;

(6) the medical coverage available to a child in a kinship guardianship assistance arrangement;

(7) that the social services official will pay the total cost of non-recurring expenses associated with obtaining legal guardianship of the child, to the extent the total cost does not exceed $2,000 in accordance with section 458-c of the Social Services Law and section 436.7 of this Part; and

(8) that the agreement will remain in effect regardless of the state of residence of the relative guardian at any time.

(c) The agreement must be fully executed prior to the issuance of letters of guardianship of the child to the relative guardian in order for the child to be eligible for payments and services under this Part.

(d) The execution of the kinship guardianship assistance agreement, in and of itself, does not qualify a prospective relative guardian to receive kinship guardianship assistance payments.

(e) The granting of letters of guardianship by the court is a process that is separate and distinct from the application for kinship guardianship assistance payments and the execution of the kinship guardianship assistance agreement. The determination of whether to grant a petition by a prospective relative guardian for letters of guardianship is solely within the discretion and authority of the court.

(f) The original kinship guardianship assistance agreement and any amendments thereto executed in accordance with this section may name an appropriate person to act as a successor guardian for the purpose of providing care and guardianship for a child in the event of death or incapacity of the relative guardian. Relative guardians are not required to name a prospective successor guardian as a condition for the approval of a kinship guardianship assistance agreement.

(g) A fully executed agreement between a relative guardian and a social services official may be amended to add or modify terms and conditions mutually agreeable to the relative guardian and the social services official, including the naming of an appropriate person to provide care and guardianship for a child in the event of death or incapacity of the relative guardian.

(h) The social services official must inform the relative guardian of the right to name an appropriate person to act as a successor guardian in the original kinship guardianship assistance agreement or through an amendment to such agreement.

(i) A fully executed agreement between a relative guardian or a successor guardian and a social services official may be terminated if:

(1) a social services official has determined that a relative guardian or a successor guardian is no longer legally responsible for the support of the child; or

(2) following the death or permanent incapacity of a relative guardian, all prospective successor guardians named in such agreement were not approved by the social services district pursuant to this Part. *(Eff.5/11/16)*

§436.5 Payment of kinship guardianship assistance.

(a) (1) Once the prospective relative guardian with whom a social services official has entered into an agreement under section 436.4 of this Part has been issued letters of guardianship for the child by the court and the child has been finally discharged from foster care to such relative, a social services official must make monthly kinship guardianship assistance payments for the care and maintenance of the child.

(2) In the event of death or incapacity of a relative guardian, a social services official must make monthly kinship guardianship assistance payments for the care and maintenance of a child to a successor guardian that has been approved pursuant to this Part.

(3) Following the death or incapacity of the relative guardian, a social services official must approve a prospective successor guardian who is named in the agreement between the relative guardian and a social services official for payments under this Part and who has been awarded guardianship or permanent guardianship of the child by the court unless, based on the results of the clearances required by section 436.3 of this Part, the social services official has determined that approval of the prospective successor guardian is not authorized or appropriate. Provided however, that no approval can be issued pursuant to this paragraph unless the prospective successor guardian has been awarded guardianship or permanent guardianship of the child by the court and the clearances required by section 436. 3 of this Part have been conducted.

(4) Notwithstanding any other provision of law to the contrary, if a prospective successor guardian assumes care of the child prior to being approved pursuant to paragraph (3) of this subdivision, payments under this Part must be made once a prospective guardian is approved pursuant to such paragraph retroactively from:

(i) in the event of death of the relative guardian, the date the successor guardian assumed care of the child or the date of death of the relative guardian, whichever is later; or

(ii) in the event of incapacity of the relative guardian, the date the successor guardian assumed care of the child or the date of incapacity of the relative guardian, whichever is later.

(5) In the event that a successor guardian assumed care and was awarded guardianship or permanent guardianship of a child due to the incapacity of a relative guardian and the relative guardian is subsequently awarded or resumes guardianship or permanent guardianship of such child and assumes care of such child after the incapacity ends, a social services official must make monthly kinship guardianship assistance payments for the care and maintenance of the

child to the relative guardian, in accordance with the terms of the fully executed written agreement.

(b) The amount of the monthly kinship guardianship assistance payment made pursuant to this section must not be less than 75 percent of the applicable board rate nor more than 100 percent of such rate as determined by the social services district in accordance with this section, provided, however, that the rate chosen by the social services district must be equal to the rate used by the social services district for adoption subsidy payments under section 453 of the Social Services Law. The social services official may consider the financial status of the prospective relative guardian or relative guardian only for the purpose of determining the amount of the payments to be made.

(c) Computation of annual income is subject to the following provisions:

(1) Only income earned as wages or salary from employment and/or net income from nonfarm self-employment or net income from farm self-employment as defined in section 404.5(b)(5) of this Title may be considered in computing annual income. The income of persons other than the prospective relative guardian may not be considered.

(2) As evidence of income, a social services official may request wage stubs, or a recent W-2, or an employer's statement of wages, or, in the case of income other than wages or salary, a copy of the prospective relative guardian's latest Federal income tax return.

(3) When the person assuming guardianship is 62 years of age or older, or will be subject to mandatory retirement from present employment within five years of the date of assuming guardianship, such person's income shall be disregarded in computing annual income.

(d) (1) If the annual income of the prospective relative guardian, as determined by the applicable provisions of subdivision (c) of this section is equal to or less than the applicable State income standard, the monthly payment for care and maintenance of the child must be 100 percent of the applicable board rate, unless the prospective relative guardian, in writing requests and agrees to a lower rate.

(2) If the annual income of the prospective relative guardian, as determined by the applicable provisions of this section, is greater that the applicable State income standard, a social services district has two options in determining the amount to be paid for care and maintenance of the child. Unless the prospective relative guardian voluntarily and, in writing, requests and agrees to a lower amount, such amount must be either:

(i) 100 percent of the applicable board rate, regardless of the annual income of the prospective relative guardian; or

(ii) an amount less that 100 percent, but not less than 75 percent, of the applicable board rate, as determined in accordance with the following formula. The social services district must:

(a) calculate the annual income of the prospective relative guardian pursuant to the provisions of subdivision (c) of this section;

(b) determine what percentage of such annual income is of the applicable State income standard; and

(c) use the following schedule to determine the amount to be paid based on the percentage calculated in clause (b) this subparagraph:

KINSHIP GUARDIANSHIP ASSISTANCE PAYMENTS SCHEDULE

Annual income of relative guardian(s) percentage of applicable State income standard	Amount of kinship guardianship assistance payment
Over 100% but not more that 110%	95% of Applicable Board Rate
Over 110% but not more than 120%	90% of Applicable Board Rate
Over 120% but not more than 130%	85% of Applicable Board Rate
Over 130% but not more that 140%	80% of Applicable Board Rate
Over 140%	75% of Applicable Board Rate

The social services district must use the same option for all kinship guardianship assistance cases. If a social services district wishes to change from one option to other option, the district must inform the office in writing of the intended change at least 30 days prior to the effective date of the change. In addition, such change in option must also apply to the district's adoption subsidy payments. The district must use the newly selected option for all new kinship guardianship assistance agreements entered into on or after the effective date of the change. Kinship guardianship assistance agreements finalized prior to the effective date of the change will not be affected by the change.

(e) Kinship guardianship assistance payments must be made to the relative guardian or guardians or to the successor guardian or guardians until the child's 18th birthday or, if the child had attained 16 years of age before the kinship guardianship assistance agreement became effective, until the child attains 21 years of age provided the child is:

(1) completing secondary education or a program leading to an equivalent credential;

(2) enrolled in an institution which provides post-secondary or vocational education;

(3) employed for at least 80 hours per month;

(4) participating in a program or activity designed to promote, or remove barriers to, employment; or

(5) incapable of any of such activities due to a medical condition, which incapability is supported by regularly updated information in the child's case record.

(f) (1) Notwithstanding paragraph (a)(1) and subdivision (e) of this section, and except as provided for in paragraphs (a)(2)-(4) of this section, no kinship guardianship assistance payments may be made pursuant to title 10 of article 6 of the Social Services Law or this Part if the social services official determines that the child is no longer receiving any support from the relative guardian or that the relative guardian is no longer legally responsible for the support of the child, including:

(i) if the status of the legal guardian is revoked, terminated, suspended or surrendered; or

(ii) when the child is removed from the home of the relative guardian or the successor guardian, placed into foster care and the Family Court has approved a permanency planning goal for the child of other than return to the home of the relative guardian or the successor guardian.

(2) Notwithstanding paragraph (a)(1) and subdivision (e) of this section, and except as provided for in paragraph (a)(5) of this section, no kinship guardianship assistance payments may be made pursuant to a successor guardian if the social services official determines that the successor guardian

is no longer legally responsible for the support of the child, including if the status of the successor guardian is terminated or the child is no longer receiving any support from such guardian. A successor guardian who has been receiving kinship guardianship assistance payments on behalf of a child under this Part must keep the social services official informed, on an annual basis, of any circumstances that would make the successor guardian ineligible for such payments or eligible for payments in a different amount.

(3) (i) When there is a failure to respond to the annual notification, pursuant to section 436.6 of this Part, or otherwise when a social services district has reasonable cause to suspect that the relative guardian or successor guardian is either no longer legally responsible for the support of the child or is no longer providing any support for the child, such district may require the relative guardian or successor guardian to submit documentation, as specified by the district, that addresses and verifies the continuing responsibility of the relative guardian or successor guardian to support the child and/or the provision of support of the child by the relative guardian or successor guardian. The relative guardian or successor guardian is required to provide the required documentation in the time period established by the district and to cooperate with the district. In addition, the district may require the relative guardian or successor guardian to meet with district staff in person, by telephone or by other means of communication, as specified by the district, to review the status of the case. The district must take into consideration where the relative guardian or successor guardian resides, the relative guardian's or successors guardian's employment situation and the care needs of the child when determining the time and location of, and the means of communication for, such meeting. If the relative guardian or successor guardian is unable to make the scheduled meeting for reasons beyond the relative guardian's or successor guardian's control, the district must provide the relative guardian or successor guardian with one additional opportunity to meet in accordance with the standards set forth in this paragraph. Failure to provide the requested documentation within the period requested or to meet with district staff as directed may be a ground for termination of the kinship guardianship assistance agreement.

(ii) When determining whether the relative guardian or successor guardian is providing the child with any support for the purposes of this paragraph, the term, any support from the relative guardian or successor guardian, means actual documented use at least 50 percent of such monthly kinship guardianship assistance payments by the relative guardian or successor guardian for the food, clothing, medical, education and/or shelter needs of the child.

(g) The relative guardian or successor guardian who has been receiving kinship guardianship assistance payments on behalf of a child under title 10 of article 6 of the Social Services Law and this Part must keep the social services official informed of any circumstances that would make the relative guardian or successor guardian ineligible for such payments or eligible for payments in a different amount. The relative guardian or successor guardian must notify the social services official in writing within 30 days of any circumstance or event that would impact the continued eligibility of the child for kinship guardianship assistance.

(h) The placement of the child with the relative guardian or successor guardian and any kinship guardianship assistance payments made on behalf of the child under this section must be considered never to have been made when determining eligibility for adoption subsidy payments under title 9 of article 6 of the Social Services Law and section 421.24 of this Title of a child in such legal guardianship arrangement. *(Eff. 5/11/16)*

§436.6 Annual notification.

(a) The social services official, on an annual basis, must remind the relative guardian or the successor guardian of the relative guardian's or successor guardian's obligation to support the child and to notify the social services official if the relative guardian or the successor guardian is no longer providing any support or is no longer legally responsible for the support of the child. Where the child is school age under the laws of the state in which the child resides, such notification must include a requirement that the relative guardian or the successor guardian must certify and provide satisfactory documentation to the district that the child is a full-time elementary or secondary student or has completed secondary education. For the purposes of this section, an elementary or secondary school student means a child who is:

(1) enrolled, or in the process of enrolling, in a school which provides elementary or secondary education, in accordance with the laws where the school is located;

(2) instructed in elementary or secondary education at home, in accordance with the laws in which the child's home is located;

(3) in an independent study elementary or secondary education program, in accordance with the laws in which the child's education program is located, which is administered by the local school or school district; or

(4) incapable of attending school on a full-time basis due to the child's medical condition, which incapacity is supported by annual information submitted by the relative guardian or the successor guardian as part of this certification.

(b) Where the child had attained the age of 16 years before the kinship guardianship assistance agreement became effective and is over the age of 18 but under 21 years of age, the relative guardian or the successor guardian must certify and provide satisfactory documentation to the district that the child is:

(1) completing secondary education or a program leading to an equivalent credential;

(2) enrolled in an institution which provides post-secondary or vocational education;

(3) employed for at least 80 hours per month;

(4) participating in a program or activity designed to promote, or remove barriers to, employment; or

(5) incapable of any of such activities due to a medical condition, which incapacity is supported by regularly updated information in the child's case record.

(c) (1) For the purpose of subdivision (a) of this section, satisfactory documentation of the child's education status means a document executed by an appropriate school official that confirms that the child satisfies one of the standards set forth in paragraphs (a)(1)-(3) of this section.

(2) For the purpose of subdivision (b) of this section:

(i) satisfactory documentation of the child's education status means a document executed by an appropriate school official that confirms that the child satisfies one of the standards set forth in paragraph (b)(1) or (2) of this section;

(ii) satisfactory documentation of the child's employment status means a document executed by the child's employer that confirms that the child satisfies the standard set forth in paragraph (b)(3) of this section; and

(iii) satisfactory documentation of the child's participation in a program or activity designed to promote, or remove barriers to, employment means a document executed by such program or activity that the child satisfies the standard set forth in paragraph (b)(4) of this section.

(d) For any child in receipt of kinship guardianship assistance payments, the relative guardian or the successor guardian must certify to the district whether the child continues to reside in the home of the relative guardian or the successor guardian or, if not, the relative guardian or the successor guardian must inform the district where the child currently resides.

(e) The relative guardian or the successor guardian must return the certification referenced in this section along with required documentation to the social services official within 30 days of receipt by the relative guardian or the successor guardian.   *(Eff. 5/11/16)*

§436.7 Payments for non-recurring guardianship expenses.

(a) A social services official must make payments for non-recurring guardianship expenses incurred by or on behalf of the relative guardian or guardians who have been approved by the social services official to receive kinship guardianship assistance payments, when such expenses are incurred in connection with assuming the guardianship of a foster child. The agreement for the payment of non-recurring guardianship expenses must be reflected in the written agreement set forth in section 436.4 of this Part. In accordance with subdivision (b) of this section, the payments must be made by the social services official either to the relative guardian or guardians directly or to an attorney on behalf of the relative guardian or guardians for the allowable amount of non-recurring guardianship expenses incurred in connection with obtaining such guardianship.

(b) The amount of the payment made pursuant to this section may not exceed $2,000 for each foster child for whom the relatives seek guardianship or permanent guardianship and may be available only for those expenses that are determined to be eligible for reimbursement by the social services official in accordance with this section.

(c) Payments for non-recurring guardianship expenses made by a social services official pursuant to this section must be treated as administrative expenditures under title IV-E of the federal Social Security Act.

(d) As used in this section, non-recurring guardianship expenses mean reasonable and necessary fees, court costs, attorney fees, and other expenses which are directly related to obtaining legal guardianship of an eligible child and which are not incurred in violation of federal law or the laws of this State or any other state.

§436.8 Medical assistance/medical subsidy.

(a) Any child with respect to whom federally reimbursable kinship guardianship assistance payments are made under this Part is eligible for medical assistance under title XIX of the Federal Social Security Act.

(b) In addition, a social services official must make payments for the cost of care, services and supplies payable under the State's program of medical assistance for needy persons provided to any child for whom kinship guardianship assistance payments are being made under title 10 of article 6 of the Social Services Law and this Part who is not eligible for medical assistance under subdivision (a) of this section and for whom the relative or successor guardian is unable to obtain medical coverage through any other available means, regardless of whether the child otherwise qualifies for medical assistance for needy persons. Payments pursuant to this subdivision may be made only with respect to the cost of care, services, and supplies which are not otherwise covered or subject to payment or reimbursement by insurance, medical assistance or other sources. Payments made pursuant to this subdivision may only be made if the relative or successor guardian applies to obtain such medical coverage for the child from all available sources, unless the social services official determines that the relative guardian has good cause for not applying for such coverage, which include that appropriate coverage is not available or affordable.

(c) An application for payments under this section must be made prior to the issuance of letters of guardianship for the child. An approval of an application for payments under this section is not subject to annual review by the social services official, and such approval remains in effect for as long as kinship guardianship assistance payments are being made under this Part for the child. Applications for such payments shall be accepted prior to the issuance of letters of guardianship of the child, and approval thereof may be granted contingent upon such issuance. *(Eff. 5/11/16)*

§436.9 Independent living services.

Any child who leaves foster care for guardianship with a relative after attaining 16 years of age for whom kinship guardianship assistance payments are being made under this Part is eligible:

(a) to receive those independent living services that are made available by the social services district to foster children pursuant to section 477 of the federal Social Security Act; and

(b) to apply for educational and training vouchers made available pursuant to section 477 of the federal Social Security Act, which will be awarded based on the priorities established by the Office and the amount of funds made available therefor.

§436.10 Fair hearings.

(a) Any person aggrieved by the decision of a social services official not to make a payment or payments for kinship guardianship assistance, non-recurring guardianship expenses, the State's medical assistance program in accordance with section 436.8 of this Part or medical subsidy pursuant to title 10 of article 6 of the Social Services Law or this Part, or to make such payment or payments in an inadequate or inappropriate amount, or the failure by a social services official to determine an application under this Part within 30 days after filing, or the failure of a social services district to agree to a prospective successor guardian being named in an agreement or to approve a prospective successor guardian pursuant to section 436.5(a)(1) of this Part, or the decision of a social services district to terminate an agreement pursuant to section 436.4(i) of this Part, may appeal to the office, which must review the case and give such person an opportunity for a fair hearing thereon and render its decision within 30 days of the completion of the fair hearing. All decisions of the office are binding upon the social services district involved and must be complied with by the social services official thereof.

(b) The only issues which may be raised in a fair hearing under this section are:

(1) whether the social services official has improperly denied an application for payments under title 10 of article 6 of the Social Services Law or this Part;

(2) whether the social services official has improperly discontinued payments under this Part;

(3) whether the social services official has determined the amount of the payments made or to be made in violation of the provisions of title 10 of article 6 of the Social Services Law or this Part;

(4) whether the social services official has failed to determine an application under this Part within 30 days of receipt of a completed application;

(5) whether the social services official has improperly denied an application to name a prospective successor guardian in the original kinship guardianship assistance agreement for payments pursuant to this Title or any amendments thereto;

(6) whether a social services official has inappropriately failed to approve a prospective successor guardian; or

(7) whether a social services official has inappropriately terminated an agreement for payments under this Title.

(c) The provisions of section 22(2) and (4) of the Social Services Law apply to fair hearings held and appeals taken pursuant to this section.   *(Eff.5/11/16)*

§436.11   Claiming.

Claims for reimbursement for payments of kinship guardianship assistance and non-recurring guardianship expenses must be made by each social services district in such form and manner and at such times and for such periods as required by the Office.

Part 441
General

§441.1   Applicability.

The provisions of this Article, except as may be otherwise limited, shall apply, in appropriate part or parts, to all child-care agencies, facilities and programs, public and private, subject to visitation, inspection and supervision by the department.

§441.2 Definitions.

For the purposes of this Article:

(a) Child means a person who meets all the following criteria:

(1) Age.

(i) the child is under the age of 18 years; or

(ii) is between the ages of 18 and 21 years and entered foster care before his or her 18th birthday, and has consented to remain in foster care past his or her 18th birthday; and

(a) is a student attending a school, college or university; or

(b) is regularly attending a course of vocational or technical training designed to fit him or her for gainful employment; or

(c) lacks the skills or ability to live independently.

(2) Residential program. The child is cared for away from his or her home 24 hours a day in a foster family free home; a duly licensed, certified, or approved foster family boarding home; child care institution, or health care facility; or any combination thereof.

(3) Placement.

(i) The child's care and custody or guardianship and custody have been transferred to an authorized agency pursuant to the provisions of section 383-c, 384 or 384-a of the Social Services Law; or

(ii) the child has been placed with a social services official pursuant to article 3, 7, 10, 10-B or 10-C of The Family Court Act.

(b) Voluntary authorized agency means any agency, association, corporation, institution, society or other organization which is incorporated or organized under the laws of New York with corporate power or empowered by law to care for, to place out or to board out children, which actually has its place of business or plant in this State and which is approved, visited, inspected and supervised by the department or which shall submit and consent to the approval, visitation, inspection and supervision of the department as to any and all acts in relation to the welfare of children performed or to be performed under the provisions of title 1 of article 6 of the Social Services Law.

(c) Public authorized agency means any local social services commissioner.

(d) Authorized agency means any voluntary authorized agency or any public authorized agency.

(e) Child-care agency means any voluntary authorized agency, any public authorized agency or the State Division for Youth.

(f) Institution means any facility for the care and maintenance of 13 or more children operated by a child-care agency.

(g) Group residence means an institution for the care and maintenance of not more than 25 children operated by an authorized agency.

(h) Group home means a family-type home for the care and maintenance of not less than seven, nor more than 12, children who are at least five years of age, operated by an authorized agency, in quarters or premises owned, leased or otherwise under the control of such agency, except that such minimum age shall not be applicable to siblings placed in the same facility nor to children whose mother is placed in the same facility.

(i) Agency boarding home means a family-type home for the care and maintenance of not more than six children operated by an authorized agency, in quarters or premises owned, leased or otherwise under the control of such agency, except that such a home may provide care for more than six brothers and sisters of the same family.

(j) Foster family free home care shall mean care provided to a child, at no cost to an authorized agency, by a family other than that of the child's parent, stepparent, grandparents, brother, sister, uncle, aunt or legal guardian for the purpose of adoption or for the purpose of providing care.

(k) Foster care shall mean care provided a child in a foster family free home or boarding home, group home, agency boarding home, child-care institution, health-care facility or any combination thereof.

(*l*) (1) Sprinkler system means an approved, automatic system for fire protection purposes, including a network of piping, heat-activated sprinkler heads, a controlling valve and a device for activating an alarm when the system is activated by heat from a fire, which system is connected to a water supply. A sprinkler system must be designed, installed and maintained in accordance with the New York State Uniform Fire Prevention and Building Code in all rooms and spaces throughout a building.

(2) Fire detection system means an approved installation of equipment which automatically activates a fire alarm when the detecting element is exposed to fire, abnormal rise in temperature or the presence of smoke. Smoke-detecting elements must be provided in all exitways, stairways, corridors, bedrooms and other spaces where such equipment is determined by the department architect to be necessary for the safety of the resident children due to the physical nature of the structure and the nature of the resident population. Heat-detecting elements must be provided in attics, kitchens and areas of fire hazard as defined in paragraph (5) of this subdivision. A fire detection system must be designed, installed and maintained in accordance with the New York State Uniform Fire Prevention and Building Code.

(3) A manually operated fire alarm system means an approved system of hand-activated fire alarm boxes, electrically interconnected to fire alarm sounding devices audible throughout a building. Buildings occupied by the hearing impaired must have alarm systems which include flashing lights. A fire alarm system must have an approved back-up power source which is automatically activated upon loss of its primary power source. A fire alarm system must be designed, installed and maintained in accordance with the New York State Uniform Fire Prevention and Building Code.

(4) Approved means approved in writing by the department as adequate for the intended use and meeting the requirements, if any, of the appropriate local authority.

(5) Area of fire hazard means a heating equipment room; a woodworking shop; a paint shop; a storeroom for mattresses, furniture, paints and/or other combustible or flammable materials or liquids; and any other space or room exceeding 100 square feet in floor area where other combustible or flammable materials are regularly stored.

(6) Fire protection systems and equipment means sprinkler, fire detection and fire alarm systems; emergency lighting; exit signs; fire extinguishers; fire, exit and smoke doors with hardware including closers, locks and panic bars; exterior exit stairs and fire escapes; and other special systems and equipment identifiable with fire safety and protection, including, but not limited to, range hood extinguishing systems, emergency shut off valves and switches, fire dampers, smoke vents and fusible links. There must be no modification or replacement of such systems or equipment in buildings or parts of buildings used in the operation of an institution unless such modification or replacement is in accordance with plans approved by the department.

(m) Supervised independent living program means one or more of a type of agency boarding home operated and certified by an authorized agency in accordance with the regulations of the Office of Children and Family Services to provide a transitional experience for older youth who, based upon their circumstances, are appropriate for transition to the level of care and supervision provided in the program.

(n) Supervised independent living unit means a home or apartment certified in accordance with the standards set forth in Part 449 of this Title by an authorized agency approved by the Office of Children and Family Services to operate a supervised independent living program for the care of up to four youth including their children. Each supervised independent living unit must be located in the community separate from any of the authorized agency's congregate dwellings.

(o) Parent advocate means a person who has previously been a recipient of child welfare services, has successfully addressed the issues which brought the family to the attention of child welfare, has been reunified with his or her children, if applicable, and has subsequently been trained as a parent advocate to work within the child welfare system. A parent advocate is employed by or under contract with an authorized agency, or is employed by an agency that is under contract with an authorized agency, for the purpose of providing support and advocacy to parent(s) or relative(s) through a variety of activities, including, but not limited to, engaging parent(s) or relative(s) and assisting them to understand the child welfare and family court process; attending case conferences; coaching for productive visitation between parents and their children in foster care; accompanying parent(s) or relative(s) to court, school, public benefits offices, and health centers; assisting parent(s) in advocating for themselves; providing assistance in accessing community services; facilitating appointments; and working as a liaison between parent(s) or relative(s), caseworkers, foster parents, and other services providers.

§441.4 Policy and policy manuals.

(a) Each child-care agency and facility operated by such agency will maintain, and keep current and available, a manual or manuals which clearly state the policies of such agency with respect to its programs including policies on admission criteria and procedures, psychiatric and medical care, social services, child care, education, religious observance, religious instruction and training, discharge criteria and procedures, discipline and restraint, appropriate custodial conduct, children's rights, room isolation, shelter, clothing, diet, work and recreation, plant maintenance, fire, sanitation and safety.

(b) A separate manual will be maintained by such residential care facility on personnel policies and practices, including a clear delineation of areas of responsibility and delegations of authority. Such manual will contain the following employee/supervisory activities and will describe how each activity set forth below will be implemented.

(1) Supervisors will be responsible for:

(i) orienting employees;

(ii) monitoring employee performance and employee evaluation;

(iii) directly observing staff interaction with children;

(iv) meeting with their employees on a regular basis to discuss the employee's job performance; and

(v) informing employees that use of alcohol or illegal drugs while on duty or the provision of any alcohol or illegal drugs to child(ren) will constitute inappropriate custodial conduct and will constitute grounds for dismissal.

(2) The agency will develop standard employee evaluation forms to be used by supervisors.

(3) Employees will receive a written evaluation from their supervisors at least once a year, and meet with their supervisors to discuss the evaluation.

(c) All policies will be reviewed periodically and modified, as may be appropriate. Copies of all manuals maintained in accordance with this section will be made available to all staff members whose duties and responsibilities the manuals affect.

§441.8 Abuse or neglect of children.

(a) Any abuse or neglect of a child, either as an incident of discipline or otherwise, is absolutely prohibited. Acts of abuse or neglect for children in the care of residential programs are defined by Section 488.1(a)-488.1(h) of the Social Services Law.

(b) All child care agencies shall prohibit the abuse or neglect of any children in their care, shall not tolerate or in any manner condone an act of abuse or neglect by any staff member or by any other person under their control, and shall vigorously and strictly enforce policies against abuse and neglect.

(c) Reports of abuse, neglect, and significant incidents as defined in Section 488 of the Social Services Law and part 433 of this title must be made to the Vulnerable Persons' Central Register as established in Section 492 of the Social Services Law. Persons who must make reports in accordance with this title and the provisions of section 491 of the Social Services Law include any director, operator, employee or volunteer of a facility or provider agency and any consultant or employee or volunteer of a corporation, partnership, organization or governmental entity which provides goods or services to a facility or provider agency pursuant to contract or other arrangement that permits such person to have regular and substantial contact with individuals who are cared for by the facility or provider agency.

(d) Volunteers and employees of all child care agencies and facilities who have child-caring responsibilities will report any suspected incidents of child abuse or maltreatment concerning a family, a foster family boarding home or a day care to the statewide central register of child abuse and maltreatment or cause such a report to be made when such volunteers and employees have reasonable cause to suspect that a child coming before them in their professional or official capacity is an abused or maltreated child. Whenever such person is required to report to the statewide central register of child abuse and maltreatment pursuant to this subdivision, he/she will immediately notify the person in charge of the agency or facility or that person's designee of the alleged abuse or maltreatment of a child.

§441.9 Discipline.

(a) Deprivation of meals, snacks, mail or visits by family, as methods of discipline are prohibited.

(b) Room isolation, as a method of discipline, is prohibited.

(c) Corporal punishment is prohibited.

(d) Solitary confinement is prohibited.

(e) Discipline shall be prescribed, administered and supervised only by adults. Such responsibilities shall never be delegated to children.

§441.10　Work experiences for children.

(a) As part of its services an agency shall provide work experiences which have value by encouraging positive attitudes in children toward work and toward themselves. The particular work experience shall be individualized and related to an evaluation of the child's needs, and shall be appropriate to the child's age, physical strength and readiness to do the task.

(b) Children shall be encouraged to take pride in their group living unit by performing daily tasks.

(c) Major work experiences made available for pay either directly by the agency or through a community resource shall also be encouraged. Within these and other work assignments shall be training components and direct supervision designed to stimulate the child's interest and to offer opportunities for development of skills of benefit to the children. In addition, there shall be constant concern for the rights of the child and the child shall participate in decisions regarding work assignments.

(d) All work shall be performed under the supervision of responsible adults. Work experience shall not supersede academic education, clinical intervention, religious observance, family contact, recreation, community or other activities within the agency's normal program format. All work shall be done in accordance with applicable labor laws.

§441.11　Religion.

(a) Each child care agency shall be responsible for the religious and moral welfare of every child in its care and shall include in its policy manual a positive policy on matters pertaining to religious observance, instruction and training.

(b) Provision shall be made for each child to attend services conducted in his own religious faith and to receive instruction in such faith, unless the parents or surviving parent or legal guardian expressly request otherwise in writing.

(c) In accordance with the provisions of section 373 of the Social Services Law, a child cared for in a family home, agency boarding home or group home shall, when practicable, be under the care and supervision of persons of the same religious faith; other than for temporary or emergency care or under exceptional circumstances, no child shall be boarded by or with persons not of the same religious faith as the child, or placed in an agency boarding home in which the persons caring for the child are not of the same religious faith as the child, but in any case the religious faith of the child must be preserved and protected; if cared for in a voluntary institution, such institution shall, when practicable, be operated by a voluntary authorized agency under the control of persons of the same religious faith as such child. Voluntary authorized agencies that care for children of different religious faiths shall make provision for the protection of the religious faith of each child as required in subdivisions (a) and (b) of this section.

(d) The religion of a child in care shall not be changed, except on the written request of his parents or surviving parent or legal guardian.

§441.12　Money and personal property.

(a) Each child in care shall receive a regular allowance appropriate to age, which shall not be used to meet basic needs. Any money belonging to a child that is kept in custody by an agency shall be kept separate from agency funds, and account shall be kept of such money. Upon the discharge from care, or transfer of any child to the care of another agency, any money belonging to such child shall be turned over to the person or agency authorized to act as custodian of such money, or to the child, as may be appropriate.

(b) An agency shall permit and encourage children to possess personal belongings, in addition to clothing and toilet articles, as may be appropriate.

§441.13   Education.

Child-care agencies:

(a) shall take such steps as may be necessary to make certain that all children in care receive education appropriate to their needs and in accordance with the requirements of the Education Law;

(b) shall maintain an active and direct liaison with any school in which a child in its care is enrolled;

(c) shall make certain that each child in its care receives appropriate educational and vocational guidance.

§441.14   Social services.

(a) Intake.

(1) Each authorized agency shall establish an intake policy, including admission criteria and procedures, and specifying the services and programs offered by such agency and the children served. A copy of the policy shall be submitted to the State Department of Social Services in accordance with requirements upon completion of the annual review, reflecting any change in policy effected by such review.

(2) Except in the case of an emergency placement, an agency shall not accept a child for care until an intake study has been made, either by the placing agency or the receiving agency, and a determination has been made that the placement meets the needs and interests of the child and his family.

(b) Additional requirements applicable to handicapped children in foster care who attain the age of 18.

(1) In order to provide for continuity of services to persons in need, there is established a program of assistance to the parent(s) or guardian of a child who is developmentally disabled as such term is defined in section 1.03 of the Mental Hygiene Law, emotionally disturbed or physically handicapped, who is receiving care in a group home, agency boarding home, or any child care facility operated by an authorized agency with a capacity of 13 or more, and who attains the age of 18 and who will continue in care after the age of 18.

(2) For each such child, the social services official or an authorized agency acting pursuant to a purchase of service agreement with such official for the care of the child shall notify the parent(s) or guardian of the child that foster care payments and services will terminate when the child reaches the age of 21, that assistance in determining services needed after the age of 21 is available from the department and other appropriate State agencies and that, upon the written consent of the parent(s) or guardian, a report containing the child's name, handicapping condition and other information will be forwarded to an appropriate State agency for the purpose of determining and recommending services for the child after the age of 21. Such notice shall be in writing in such form as the department may require and shall be sent to the parent(s) within 30 days of the first service plan review following the child's 18th birthday.

(3) Upon the written consent of the parent(s) or guardian of the child, the social services official or an authorized agency acting pursuant to a purchase of service agreement shall submit a report of the child's condition and possible need for services after age 21 to the Commissioner of Mental Health,

Commissioner of Mental Retardation and Developmental Disabilities, Commissioner of Education, or the Commissioner of Social Services or their designee(s) for the purposes of obtaining a determination and recommendation of needed services in accordance with section 7.37 or 13.37 of the Mental Hygiene Law or subdivision 10 of section 4403 of the Education Law. The social services official or an authorized agency acting pursuant to a purchase of service agreement shall determine which commissioner or designee shall receive the report by considering the child's primary handicapping condition, in accordance with the following criteria:

(i) For a referral to the Commissioner of Mental Health:

(a) the child shall exhibit the presence of an identifiable mental disorder other than mental retardation, developmental disorders, alcoholism, drug dependence or drug abuse; and

(b) the child shall have an IQ above 70.

(ii) For a referral to the Commissioner of Mental Retardation and Developmental Disabilities:

(a) the child shall be diagnosed as having a developmental disability in accordance with the provisions of section 1.03 of the Mental Hygiene Law; and

(b) the child shall have an IQ below 50.

(iii) For any child who meets the criteria of subparagraph (i) or (ii) of this paragraph but who has an IQ between 50 and 70, the report shall be referred to both the Commissioner of Mental Health and the Commissioner of Mental Retardation and Developmental Disabilities identifying the case as being within the dispute range as to IQ and as being submitted to both commissioners for a determination of the need of the child for adult services.

(iv) For a referral to the Commissioner of Education:

(a) the child shall have a disability other than legal blindness which constitutes or results in a substantial handicap to obtaining and/or maintaining a gainful occupation; and

(b) there is a reasonable expectation that vocational rehabilitation services may benefit the individual in terms of employability.

(v) For a referral to the Commissioner of Social Services:

(a) there is a need for adult services as defined in the comprehensive services plan of the department; and

(b) the child shall exhibit none of the criteria in subparagraphs (i) through (iv) of this paragraph.

(4) If the social services official or an authorized agency acting pursuant to a purchase of service agreement determines that the child shall be referred in accordance with the criteria provided in subparagraph (3)(v) of this subdivision, and that these services will be provided by such official, the social services official shall retain the report or the authorized agency shall submit the report to the social services official who shall retain it and perform the services described in subdivision (e) of this section. If, however, the needed services are or will be the responsibility of another social services district, the social services official or authorized agency making the report shall forward such report to such other social services district. The social services official of such other district shall then perform the services required in subdivision (e) of this section.

(5) The content of the report requesting the determination and recommendation of needed services shall be in accordance with the following requirements:

(i) for referral to the Commissioner of Mental Health, the following items shall be included in the report:

(a) a copy of the written consent of the parent(s) or guardian to the submission of a report for the determination and recommendation of needed services;

(b) a copy of the assessment portion of the uniform case record documentation which establishes the child's condition and/or need for services;

(c) a summary of the child's family/social history;

(d) copies of the most recent medical history, general physical examination and any psychiatric or psychological evaluations, which address such areas as:

(1) mental status;

(2) diagnosis;

(3) history of treatment;

(4) medication summary;

(5) assessments of intellectual functioning (IQ) and sensory motor function;

(6) assessment of social-affective functioning;

(7) self-help skills; and

(8) educational/vocational evaluation/summary; and

(e) other records or reports necessary to assist the Commissioner of Mental Health in determining the child's need for services.

(ii) For referral to the Commissioner of Mental Retardation and Developmental Disabilities, the following items shall be included in the report:

(a) a copy of the written consent of the parent(s) or guardian to the submission of a report for the determination and recommendation of needed services;

(b) a copy of the assessment portion of the uniform case record establishing the child's condition and/or need for services;

(c) a summary of the child's family/social history;

(d) copies of the most recent medical history, general physical examination and any psychiatric or psychological evaluations which address such areas as:

(1) mental/developmental status;

(2) diagnosis;

(3) treatment summary, if applicable, including any specialists' reports;

(4) medication summary, if applicable;

(5) assessment of intellectual/cognitive functioning (IQ);

(6) assessment of ADL (activities of daily living) skills;

(7) assessment/report of behavioral problems;

(8) assessment of self-help skills; and

(9) educational/vocational summary; and

(e) other records or reports necessary to assist the Commissioner of Mental Retardation and Developmental Disabilities in determining the need for services.

(iii) For referral to the Commissioner of Education, the following items shall be included in the report:

(a) a copy of the written consent of the parent(s) or guardian to the submission of a report for the determination and recommendation of needed services;

(b) a request to the office of vocational rehabilitation to conduct an evaluation for eligibility determining;

(c) copies of any records or reports in the child's or family's case record relative to the need for services, including any completed educational/vocational summary and the most recent documents showing the child's medical status/medical history, and the nature and diagnosis of the child's handicap and the prognosis for its change or recovery; and

(d) other records or reports necessary to assist the Commissioner of Education in determining the need for services.

(iv) For referral to another social services district, the following items shall be included in the report:

(a) a copy of the written consent of the parent(s) or guardian to the submission of a report requesting the determination and recommendation of needed services;

(b) a copy of the most recent reassessment and service plan review showing the plan for the child's discharge to or need for adult services;

(c) a copy of any medical, psychiatric or psychologic report(s) which establish the need for adult services; and

(d) other records or reports which may assist the local social services official in making the determination and recommendation for needed services.

(6) A copy of any report sent to the Commissioner of Mental Health, Commissioner of Mental Retardation and Developmental Disabilities, Commissioner of Education or their designee(s) or to another social services official who is acting as the designee of the Commissioner of the Department of Social Services shall be submitted to the department at the same time as such report is submitted to such commissioner or social services official. An authorized agency which submits such a report shall also submit a copy of the report to the local social services official with whom the agency has entered into a purchase of services agreement to care for the child.

(7) If the social services official or an authorized agency acting pursuant to a purchase of service agreement is notified by the commissioner of another State agency to which a report was submitted that such agency is not responsible for determining and recommending adult services for a child, the social services official or the authorized agency which is so notified shall forward the report to another commissioner of a State agency authorized to receive such reports whom the social services official or the agency considers responsible for such determination and recommendation; provided, however, that where such official or agency determines that there exists a dispute as to which State agency has the responsibility for determining and recommending adult services for a child, the authorized agency, if it prepared and submitted the initial report, shall submit the report to the appropriate social services official and the social services official may forward such report and the replies of such State agencies to the Council on Children and Families for the resolution of such dispute.

(8) If the social services official or the authorized agency acting pursuant to a purchase of service agreement which originated the report is notified by another social services official to whom a report has been sent pursuant to paragraph (4) of this subdivision that such other official is not responsible for determining or recommending adult services for the child, the social services official or the authorized agency which originated the report shall submit the report to another social services official or the State agency who or which is responsible for determining and recommending adult services for the child;

provided, however, that if there continues to be a dispute as to which social services official is responsible for determining and recommending adult services for the child, the social services official or the authorized agency shall forward the report and the replies of the other social services official(s) to the department for resolution of the dispute or for direction as to which State agency should be sent the report in accordance with the provisions of paragraph (3) or (4) of this subdivision.

(9) Each social services official shall prepare and submit an annual report to the department on October 1, 1985 and thereafter on or before October 1st of each year. Such report shall contain the following without referring to personally identifying information:

(i) the number of cases submitted to each commissioner pursuant to paragraph (3) of this subdivision, including the type and severity of the handicapping condition of such cases;

(ii) the number of cases submitted to other social services officials pursuant to paragraph (4) of this subdivision, including the type and severity of the handicapping condition of such cases;

(iii) the number of reports retained by the official pursuant to paragraph (4) of this subdivision, including the type and severity of the handicapping condition of such cases;

(iv) the number of replies received which deny responsibility for determining and recommending adult services, and from whom received;

(v) the number of cases referred to the department for resolution of disputes between social services officials;

(vi) the number of cases referred to the Council on Children and Families for the resolution of disputes between State agencies; and

(vii) other information requested by the department as necessary for the department and the Council on Children and Families to monitor the need for adult services.

(10) A single compilation of the annual reports received pursuant to paragraph (9) of this subdivision shall be forwarded to the Council on Children and Families by the department.

(c) Additional requirements and services applicable to a handicapped child placed outside New York State.

(1) Purpose. In order to provide adequate continuity of services to persons in need, there is established a program of assistance to the parent(s) or guardian of a child with a handicapping condition who has been placed in a foster care agency, program, facility or institution outside New York State, and who attains the age of 18. For such a child, the social services official shall:

(i) determine whether such child will need services after the age of 21;

(ii) if such need exists, assess the nature of the services required;

(iii) notify the parent(s) or guardian of such child that foster care payments and services will terminate when the child attains the age of 21, that the child will have an apparent need for adult services and that assistance in locating needed services in this State is available from the department and other appropriate State agencies; and

(iv) upon the written consent of the parent or guardian, submit a report on the child's projected need for services after the child attains the age of 21 to the department for planning purposes. These activities will be completed and reported as part of the first service plan review after the child's 18th birthday, in accordance with the provisions of this subdivision.

(2) Determination of need for services. In determining the child's projected need for services after the child attains the age of 21 the social services official shall consider whether the child can be returned to the home of his parent(s) for care, and shall evaluate the child's existing physical and mental condition and his behavioral and treatment needs as an adult. This determination shall include, but not be limited to:

(i) a description of the child's behavioral skills;

(ii) a description of the child's major strengths and weaknesses, including educational/vocational potential; and

(iii) identification of the special needs the child will require when the child attains the age of 21. Other factors relevant to a determination for any individual child may also be considered in making the necessary determination of the needs of the child for adult services.

(3) Assessment of the nature of services to be required. Based on the determination made pursuant to paragraph (2) of this subdivision, the social services official shall assess the nature of the services required. This assessment shall include, but not necessarily be limited to:

(i) an evaluation of the strengths, weaknesses and specific needs identified in the determination process; and

(ii) identification of specific services that appear to be relevant to developing strengths, overcoming or correcting weaknesses, and/or meeting the specific needs of the child.

This assessment shall consider such factors as physical health needs, mental health needs, training needs, including vocational training, rehabilitative needs, recreation needs and any special needs the child will require as an adult. Consideration shall also be given to the requirements of the social services and mental health services systems.

(4) Notification of parent or guardian of the need for services and availability of assistance in obtaining required adult services in this State.

The social services official shall, within 30 days of the completion of the first service plan review following the child's 18th birthday, notify, in writing the parent(s) or guardian of each child who has a handicapping condition and who is placed for foster care in an agency program, facility or institution outside New York State of the following:

(i) that foster care payments and services for such child shall terminate upon the child's 21st birthday;

(ii) whether or not it is anticipated that the child will need services or placement after the age of 21;

(iii) the results of the determination and assessment which the social services official made pursuant to paragraphs (2) and (3) of this subdivision;

(iv) that planning and referral services are available from the department, from the New York State Council on Children and Families and from other State agencies to assist the parents or guardians in locating needed adult services or placement for their child;

(v) the need for the parent(s) or guardian to request such assistance and to consent to the release of the child's records, diagnosis and reports to assist the department and the council in aiding the family and in locating necessary services or placement; and

(vi) that such a request is voluntary and that the disclosure of any records, reports or evaluations shall be strictly confidential and limited solely to the purpose of locating and/or obtaining a relevant placement or services for the child at the time the child attains the age of 21.

The social services official shall include with the information required to be submitted to a child's parent or guardian pursuant to the provisions of this paragraph the appropriate request, consent and release form for forwarding relevant records, reports and evaluations to the department and/or the council.

(5) Local social services official's report to the department. Upon receipt of the written consent from the child's parent(s) or guardian, the local social services official shall compile and forward to the department within 30 days, the following:

(i) a copy of the parent's signed request for assistance and consent to the release of the social services official's report to the department and to the Council on Children and Families;

(ii) the social services official's report, including the determination of the child's need for services after the age of 21 and the social services official's assessment of the services needed, as specified in paragraphs (2) and (3) of this subdivision; and

(iii) copies of relevant case records, including the first service plan review which was completed following the child's 18th birthday, and any other records, reports, evaluations or other material as may be required in accordance with the referral procedures established by the department and the New York State Council on Children and Families.

(6) Department referral to the New York State Council on Children and Families. Upon receipt of the report submitted by a local social services official on behalf of the parent(s) or guardian requesting the assistance of the department and council to locate needed services, the department shall within 30 days of its receipt, forward the request and report, including the parent's consent, to the council in accord with the referral procedures established by the department, in consultation with the council. In addition, the department shall report annually to the council the number of parent(s)/guardians who were notified that their child will require adult services after the child attains the age of 21 and who have not requested assistance or who have not agreed to consent to the release of records or data.

(d) Powers and duties of the commissioner and social services official upon receipt of a report requesting determination and recommendation of adult services.

(1) The powers and duties conferred upon the commissioner by section 398-c of the Social Services Law relating to the determination of the need for and recommendation of adult services in response to reports submitted pursuant to clause (a) of subparagraph (5) of paragraph (b) of subdivision 1 of section 4402 of the Education Law or subdivision 13 of section 398 of the Social Services Law are designated as powers of the local social services official.

(2) Upon receipt of a request for a determination and recommendation for adult services from another social services official, from a committee on the handicapped, through a report he himself retained for determination, or from a report submitted by an authorized agency acting pursuant to a purchase of service agreement, the local social services official acting as the designee of the commissioner shall determine whether the child who is being referred in such report will likely need adult services, as defined in the department's comprehensive services plan, and, if such need will likely exist, develop a recommendation of all appropriate programs authorized or operated by the department or the local district which may be available when the child attains the age of 21. If necessary and appropriate, the social services official may

conduct or cause to be conducted an evaluation of the child to determine if adult services will be necessary. Such determination and recommendation shall be submitted to the parent(s) or guardian of the child in writing as soon as practicable after the receipt of the report but no later than six months before the child attains the age of 21.

(3) If the social services official acting as the designee of the commissioner determines that a child will not require adult services, as defined in the department's comprehensive services plan, the local social services official acting as the designee of the commissioner shall notify the child's parent(s) or guardian in writing of such determination. Such notification shall be given as soon as practicable after receiving the report but no later than six months before the child attains the age of 21.

(4) If the social services official acting as the designee of the commissioner determines that the department is not responsible for determining and recommending adult services for a child, the social services official, acting as the designee of the commissioner, shall promptly notify in writing the committee on the handicapped, multidisciplinary team, social services official or authorized agency which sent the report and the department that such determination has been made. Such determination shall be made as soon as practicable after receiving the report. The notice shall state the reason(s) why the social services official determined that he was not responsible for determining the need for adult services and may recommend another State agency which may be responsible for determining and recommending adult services. Any such recommendation of another State agency shall be based on consideration of the child's primary handicapping condition and shall be in accordance with the criteria set forth in paragraph (c)(3) of this section.

(5) A determination or recommendation for adult services by the department or a local social services official shall not be construed to create an entitlement to adult services.

§441.15 Special services.

Psychiatric, psychological and other essential services shall be made available appropriate to the needs of the children in care.

§441.17 Restraint of children in care.

(a) Definitions. As used in this Part:

(1) Restraint means the containment of acute physical behavior by physical, mechanical, or pharmacological intervention, or room isolation, except that room isolation shall only be permitted in institutions as specified in this Part and section 442.2 of this Subchapter. Restraint as used in Part does not mean time out, confinement of a child to his own room for treatment or disciplinary reasons or use of a locked unit.

(2) Acute physical behavior means only that behavior which clearly indicates the intent to inflict physical injury upon oneself or others or to otherwise jeopardize the safety of any person.

(3) Physical restraint means the use of staff to hold a child in order to contain acute physical behavior.

(4) Mechanical restraints refers to restraining devices used to contain acute physical behavior.

(5) Pharmacological restraint means the use of a chemical agent to contain acute physical behavior by causing an immediate radical suppression of such behavior.

(6) Room isolation means confinement of a child in a room specifically designed and designated for such use in order to control acute physical behavior of that child.

(7) Time out means the removal of a child from a situation that is too threatening or emotionally overwhelming for the child or where the child may lead other children into an uncontrollable state or where the child has exceeded the reasonable limits set by the staff.

(8) Locked unit means a program approved by the department that is contained within a closed unit and is designed to serve a special population.

(9) Discipline means methods for achieving, restoring, and maintaining order and purposefulness through encouragement, guidance, and teaching children to live as socialized beings.

(b) Restraint shall be used without purposely inflicting pain or harm, and only when other forms of intervention are either inappropriate or have been tried and proved unsuccessful. Restraint, including room isolation, will never be used for punishment or for the convenience of staff.

(c) An authorized agency shall not use any method of restraint unless it has submitted its restraint policy to the department and such policy has been approved in writing by the department in accordance with subdivision (d) of this section.

(d)(1) To qualify for approval of its restraint policy by the department, an authorized agency must be in compliance with the provisions of this section and section 442.2 of this Subchapter, if applicable, and maintain a section of the agency's policy manual which clearly states the plan and procedures for the use of restraint. Such a section and the authorized agency's policy on restraint shall include at a minimum the following:

(i) preventive methods and procedures for situations which might lead to the use of restraint;

(ii) appropriate alternatives to restraint;

(iii) the circumstances when restraint might be necessary;

(iv) methods of applying restraint and the rules which must be observed in applying such restraint; and

(v) a description of the training agency staff will receive as required by subdivision (h) of this section.

(2) No changes or modifications in the authorized agency's policy on restraint shall be made without prior written approval of the department. All approved changes shall be recorded in the agency's policy manual. The agency shall conduct its program of restraint in accordance with its approved policy.

(3) The duration of department approval will be for a period of two years. However, department approval may be revoked in whole or in part at any time that an agency is not using restraint in accordance with its approved policy and any other provision of this section and section 442.2 of this Subchapter, if applicable.

(4)(i) Agencies currently using restraint or planning to use restraint shall submit a request for provisional approval to the department in a form and manner prescribed by the department. No agency shall continue to use restraint 90 days after promulgation of these regulations without written provisional approval by the department. Such request shall include the agency's plan for training staff in the use of restraint as required by subdivision (h) of this section. The initial training as required by subdivision (h) must be completed prior to final approval by the department.

(ii) The department shall review the agency's policy on restraint and the agency's plans for training. In addition, the department's architect shall review all rooms used for isolation to determine whether the room(s) meets the requirements of subdivision (h) of section 442.2 of this Subchapter. Within 90 days of receipt of the request for approval, the department shall make a determination as to whether the application is acceptable.

(iii) If the department determines that the application is unsatisfactory, the department shall notify the applicant in writing of the denial of approval and the reasons therefor.

(iv) If the department determines that the applicant is in compliance with the standards and regulations as set forth in this section and section 442.2 of this Subchapter, if applicable, it shall notify the applicant in writing of final approval of the application.

(e) Three months prior to the expiration of the approved restraint policy, authorized agencies shall submit a request for renewal of such policy to the department. The department will review the agency's restraint policy and incident reports and case records of children on whom restraint has been used or who have been placed in room isolation or injured as a result of a restraint incident. The agency will be notified of continued approval of their restraint policy within 90 days from the date the department received their request for renewal. Continued approval will be based upon the agency's continued compliance with this section and section 442.2 of this Subchapter, if applicable, and a showing by the agency of continued need for such policy.

(f) Mechanical restraints. Permissible mechanical restraints consist solely of handcuffs and footcuffs which may be used only when a child is being transported by vehicle and such child constitutes a clear danger to public safety or to himself. In no case may a child be attached to any object in the vehicle. Handcuffs and footcuffs may not be attached to each other. Mechanical restraints must be authorized by a physician and the director of the authorized agency. The term mechanical restraint shall not be construed to include seat belts, shoulder harnesses, or wheelchair locks used in vehicular transportation.

(g) Pharmacological restraint. Pharmacological restraint is permitted only on an order made at the time of the restraint incident by a physician who is familiar with the child and the child's treatment goals, medical history and diagnosis. Such restraint shall only be used after other forms of intervention have been tried and proved unsuccessful, and only for such period as may be necessary to contain acute physical behavior and prevent physical injury to the child or other children. Standing orders are prohibited.

(h) Staff training.

(1) All staff involved in the use of restraint must complete at least six hours of training in the agency's policy concerning:

(i) preventive methods and procedures for situations which might lead to the use of restraint;

(ii) appropriate alternatives to restraint;

(iii) the circumstances when restraint might be necessary; and

(iv) methods of applying restraint and the rules which must be observed in so doing.

(2) All staff involved in the use of restraint must complete such training prior to their use of restraint, except as provided in paragraph (d)(4) of this section and must complete a review of such training every six months following the initial training.

(i) If it appears that a child may have sustained an injury immediately prior to or during the use of restraint, including room isolation, the child shall be examined by a physician or nurse immediately following the period of restraint. A report of such examination shall be kept in the child's medical record.

(j) Following each instance during which restraint is used, a summary of the incident, including efforts made to identify and resolve the problem that led to the use of restraint, the reason restraint was determined necessary and the child's reaction to the use of restraint, shall be recorded and kept in the progress notes of the child's uniform case record.

(k) Each authorized agency shall maintain daily records of the number of children on whom restraints, including room isolation, have been used, including the name and age of each such child and the type of restraint used.

§441.18   Children's privacy rights.

The provisions contained in this section shall apply unless a condition in a court order provides to the contrary. Such condition shall be documented in the child's record.

(a) Mail.

(1) A child in care has an unrestricted right to send mail without prior censorship or prior reading.

(2) A child in care has the right to receive mail without prior reading or prior censorship. However, an authorized child care agency or foster family boarding home may require the child to open the mail in the presence of a staff member or the foster parent if there is reasonable cause to suspect the delivery of contraband (e.g., drugs or weapons).

(3) Nothing contained in paragraphs (1) and (2) of this subdivision shall be construed to permit a child's use of mail for fraudulent, illegal or illicit purposes.

(4) As part of a treatment plan developed or approved by the local social services district caseworker who has case management responsibility for a child, and in consultation with the authorized agency or foster parent, the authorized child-care agency or foster parent may require that a child open mail arriving from a predesignated person in the presence of a staff member or foster parent. Such a situation might arise when it is anticipated that mail from a parent or other person is likely to cause emotional harm to a child, and that such potential harm could be lessened with the presence of a staff member or foster parent. The child shall be informed of this aspect of the treatment plan when it is established and the reason(s) for its implementation.

(b) Telephone.

(1) A child in care shall have the right to receive or refuse any and all calls made to him/her during reasonable hours to be set by the authorized agency or foster parent.

(2) A child in care shall be allowed to call any person of his/her choosing; however, the time, duration and cost of such calls may be restricted by the limits of the authorized agency's or foster family boarding home's policies for access and utilization of the telephone.

(3) Nothing contained in paragraphs (1) and (2) of this subdivision shall be construed to permit a child's use of the telephone for fraudulent, illegal or illicit purposes.

(4) Except at the child's request, neither agency staff nor foster parents shall listen in on a child's phone conversation. An area which affords the child

a reasonable degree of privacy shall be provided for the purpose of receiving and initiating phone calls whenever it is physically possible to provide such an area. It is not, however, required that an authorized agency or foster home have a telephone, except as required by section 442.14 of this Subchapter, nor that it have any specific policy for its utilization beyond what is contained in this subdivision.

(c) Access to attorney and clergy. Nothing contained in subdivision (a) or (b) of this section shall be construed to impede access of a child to either his attorney or his clergyman.

(d) Searches.

(1) Searches of a child's property may be made only when there is reasonable cause to suspect that the child has in his possession one or more of the following: an item(s) which does not belong to him; items, the possession of which by either an adult and/or a child is a crime or offense (e.g., weapons, firearms, controlled substances and marijuana) or articles which the authorized agency or foster parent, subject to the supervision of the authorized agency, may consider to be dangerous or harmful to the child, other children in the home or agency, or to the physical structure. A search may include having a child empty out his/her pockets when there is reasonable cause to believe that a stolen or illegal object may be concealed there.

(2) Only in instances when the conditions of paragraph (1) of this subdivision are present and, in addition, there is reasonable cause to believe that the child or other persons in the facility or home are in imminent danger of serious harm due to that child's intent to use or distribute an object(s) or substance(s) in his/her possession may the child's person be searched. In such situations a search may include asking a child to empty such personal effects as a wallet or purse; removing outer garments such as coat, hat and shoes, garments may be searched carefully (frisked) including pant cuffs, sleeve cuffs and waist bands; and a visual inspection of the mouth, nose and ears may be done. This type of search should be done by a person of the same sex as the child. Strip searches are not permissible.

(3) Only when it is perceived that the safety of children is imperiled, as a result of suspicions that weapons or dangerous articles may be widespread in the facility may an unannounced general search be undertaken of a portion or of the entire facility. Such searches require prior approval from the department's regional office director or his/her designee. If time does not permit receiving such prior approval, notification must be provided to the department at the earliest possible time, but not later than the first business day following the day the search takes place.

(4) Every possible effort must be made to obtain the child's physical presence whenever his room, locker, or possessions are to be searched. If this is impossible because the child is not present and there is reasonable cause to believe that a person(s) at the facility or home will be endangered by awaiting the child's return, the authorized agency or foster parent shall notify the child at the earliest possible time that a search has been made and whether any material has been confiscated.

(5) Except in foster family boarding homes, every search must be authorized by the director of the authorized agency or the director's designee. Every search must have an explanation of the purpose and the results of the search documented both in the child's record and in a separate search documentation log.

§441.22 Health and medical services.

(a) Each authorized agency is responsible for providing comprehensive medical and health services for every foster child in its care.

(b) Assessment and testing of children in foster care for HIV infection. The terms AIDS, HIV infection, HIV-related illness and HIV-related test are defined in section 360-8.1 of this Title.

(1) Assessment for risk factors for HIV infection. Each child in foster care must be assessed for risk factors related to HIV infection and to determine whether the child has the capacity to consent to HIV-related testing. Capacity to consent means an individual's ability, determined without regard to the individual's age, to understand and appreciate the nature and consequences of a proposed health care service, treatment, or procedure, or of a proposed disclosure of confidential HIV-related information, as the case may be, and to make an informed decision concerning the service, treatment, procedure or disclosure.

(2) Timing of the initial assessment.

(i) Each child entering foster care on or after September 1, 1995, must be assessed within five business days of entry into care to determine, based on the child's developmental stage and cognitive abilities, whether it is possible that the child may have the capacity to consent to HIV-related testing.

(a) If it is determined that there is no possibility that the child has the capacity to consent, then within five business days of the child's entry into care the authorized agency also must complete an initial assessment of the child's risk for HIV infection based on the risk factors set forth in this subdivision.

(b) If it is determined that there may be a possibility that the child has capacity to consent, then within 30 business days of the child's entry into care, the authorized agency must: initiate discussions and counseling with the child based on the child's developmental stage and cognitive abilities regarding the behaviors that create a risk for HIV infection and the importance of reducing and preventing such behaviors; complete an assessment of the child's risk for HIV infection using the risk factors set forth in this subdivision; and, determine whether the child has the capacity to consent to HIV-related testing.

(ii) Each child who entered foster care prior to September 1, 1995, must be assessed, at least 60 business days prior to the next periodic medical examination required for the child in accordance with the schedule provided in subdivision (f) of this section or at least 60 business days prior to the child's next required service plan review date, whichever occurs sooner, to determine, based on the child's developmental stage and cognitive abilities, whether it is possible that the child may have the capacity to consent to HIV-related testing.

(a) If it is determined that there is no possibility that the child has the capacity to consent, the authorized agency must complete an initial assessment of the child's risk for HIV infection based on the risk factors set forth in this subdivision at least 30 days before the child's next periodic medical examination or the child's next service plan review date, as applicable.

(b) If it is determined that there may be a possibility that the child has capacity to consent, the authorized agency must initiate discussions and counseling with the child based on the child's developmental stage and cognitive abilities regarding the behaviors that create a risk for HIV infection and the importance of reducing and preventing such behaviors, complete an initial assessment of the child's risk for HIV infection using the risk factors sf forth in this subdivision, and determine whether the child has capacity consent to HIV-related testing at least 30 days before the child's next peric medical examination or the child's next upcoming service plan review date, as applicable.

(3) Assessment standards and risk factors related to HIV infection. The assessments of a child's capacity to consent and of a child's risk for HIV infection must be made by a medical provider or by designated agency staff with basic information and training regarding HIV and AIDS, knowledge of the risk factors associated with HIV infection, the HIV-related testing available and the confidentiality provisions regarding HIV-related information. The assessment of a child's risk for HIV infection must be appropriate for the age and developmental stage of the child and must include a review of the medical and psychosocial history available at the time to determine whether one or more of the following risk factors related to HIV infection exists.

(i) Risk factors in the medical and psychosocial history of the family related to an infant or child and associated with direct perinatal transmission of HIV infection at birth include:

(a) that this child had a positive drug toxicology or symptoms of drug withdrawal at birth;

(b) that this child had a positive test for syphilis at birth;

(c) that a sibling of this child has a diagnosis of HIV infection, initially tested positive for HIV infection but later seroreverted to negative, or died due to an HIV-related illness or AIDS;

(d) that this child has symptoms consistent with HIV infection; or

(e) that this child was abandoned at birth and no risk history is available.

(ii) Risk factors in the medical and psychosocial history of the family related to the child's mother or father, or a sexual partner of the child's mother or father. These risk factors are relevant generally to an infant or young child if they occurred before the child was born and placed the child at risk of HIV infection through perinatal transmission at birth. These risk factors include:

(a) that the individual has a diagnosis of HIV infection, or symptoms consistent with HIV infection, or death due to HIV-related illness or AIDS;

(b) that the individual has or had a male sexual partner who has had sex with another man;

(c) that the individual has a history of sexually transmitted diseases, such as syphilis, gonorrhea, hepatitis B, or genital herpes;

(d) that the individual is known or reported to have had multiple sex partners or engaged in the exchange of sex for money, drugs, food, housing, or other things of value prior to the child's birth;

(e) that the individual is known or reported to inject illegal drugs or share needles, syringes or other equipment involved in drug use or body piercing;

(f) that the individual is known to use non-injection illegal drugs, such as crack cocaine;

(g) that the individual has a history of tuberculosis;

(h) that the individual had a transfusion of blood or blood products between January, 1978 and July, 1985 in the United States of America; or

(i) that the individual had a transfusion of blood or blood products in other country at a time when the blood supply of that country was not ᵊd for HIV infection.

Risk factors related to the child and associated with the child's other means of direct transmission of HIV infection after the . The assessment of these risk factors may include discussions with the child, when appropriate for the age and developmental stage of the child, in addition to the required review of the medical and psychosocial history available at the time. These risk factors include:

(a) that this child has symptoms consistent with HIV infection;

(b) that this child has been sexually abused;

(c) that this child has engaged in sexual activity;

(d) that this child has a history of sexually transmitted diseases, such as syphilis, gonorrhea, hepatitis B, or genital herpes;

(e) that this child is known or reported to have had multiple sex partners or engaged in the exchange of sex for money, drugs, food, housing, or other things of value;

(f) that this child is known or reported to inject illegal drugs or share needles, syringes or other equipment involved in drug use or body piercing;

(g) that this child is known or reported to use non-injection illegal drugs, such as crack cocaine;

(h) that this child has a history of tuberculosis;

(i) that this child had a transfusion of blood or blood products between January, 1978 and July, 1985 in the United States of America; or

(j) that this child had a transfusion of blood or blood products in any other country at a time when the blood supply of that country was not screened for HIV infection.

(4) Procedures relating to HIV-related testing. If a child is determined through the required assessment to have one or more risk factors for HIV infection, designated agency staff must initiate the following process necessary to obtain legal consent for HIV-related testing and to arrange for the HIV-related testing of the child based on the child's case circumstances.

(i) A case involving a child identified as having one or more risk factors for HIV infection and determined to have the capacity to consent to an HIV-related test. In such case, the designated staff must:

(a) inform the child of the results of the assessment of risk factors for HIV infection and counsel the child regarding the benefits of being tested for HIV infection in order to receive medical care and services if an HIV infection is present;

(b) inform the child that arrangements may be made for agency-supervised confidential HIV-related testing and that anonymous testing is available as an alternative;

(c) provide information to the child of the requirements regarding the confidentiality of HIV-related information and the disclosures of confidential HIV-related information to certain persons and entities required by article 27-F of the Public Health Law and section 373-a of the Social Services Law as set forth in paragraph (8) of this subdivision;

(d) after providing the initial counseling and information to the child, ask the child whether he or she will agree to be referred for agency-supervised confidential HIV-related testing or anonymous testing; and

(e) if the child indicates that he or she will agree to be referred for agency-supervised confidential HIV-related testing, request that the child provide the authorized agency with written permission for such a referral and, within 30 business days of receiving such written permission arrange for the HIV-related testing of the child including obtaining the necessary pre-test counseling for the child, written informed consent of the child and post-test counseling for the child in accordance with article 27-F of the Public Health Law; or

(f) if the child indicates that he or she will agree to be referred for anonymous testing, offer to assist the child in obtaining access to an anonymous testing site; or

(g) if the child indicates that he or she will not agree to be referred for agency-supervised confidential HIV-related testing or anonymous testing, continue as part of the on-going casework contracts with the child to discuss the importance of HIV-related testing or seek a court order authorizing HIV-related testing of the child if there is an urgent medical necessity for such testing.

(h) Regardless of whether a child who has the capacity to consent agrees to be referred for HIV-related testing, designated agency staff must continue to provide on-going counseling to the child regarding the importance of preventing and reducing behaviors that create a risk of HIV infection.

(ii) A case involving a child identified as having one or more risk factors for HIV infection and determined to lack capacity to consent to HIV-related testing and whose parents have surrendered the guardianship and custody of the child pursuant to section 383-c or 384 of the Social Services Law or whose parental rights to the child have been terminated pursuant to section 384-b of the Social Services Law. In such case, the designated staff must contact the commissioner of the social services district in whose guardianship and custody the child is placed, or the commissioner's designated representative, who must provide the necessary written informed consent for the HIV-related testing of the child. Upon the issuance of such written informed consent by the commissioner or the commissioner's designated representative, the authorized agency must arrange for the HIV-related testing of the child.

(iii) Any other case involving a child identified as having one or more risk factors for HIV infection and determined to lack capacity to consent to HIV-related testing. In such case, designated staff in the authorized agency must:

(a) inform immediately the parent or guardian of the child regarding the results of the assessment of risk factors related to HIV infection;

(b) recommend the HIV-related testing of the child on the basis that one or more risk factors related to HIV infection exist;

(c) request that the parent or guardian provide the authorized agency within 10 business days with written permission to refer the child for the HIV-related testing;

(d) provide the opportunity for the parent or guardian to meet with agency staff if the parent or guardian objects to such testing in order to discuss the importance of early treatment for a child with HIV infection;

(e) if the parent or guardian of the child who lacks capacity to consent provides the agency with written permission for the child to be referred for HIV-related testing, and the child has been placed in foster care voluntarily by the parent or guardian in accordance with section 384-a of the Social Services Law, or the child has been placed in foster care as a juvenile delinquent in accordance with article 3 of the Family Court Act or as a person in need of supervision in accordance with article 7 of the Family Court Act or as a destitute child in accordance with article 10-C of the Family Court Act, arrange for the HIV-related testing of the child including obtaining the necessary pre-test counseling for the parent or guardian, written informed consent of the parent or guardian, and post-test counseling for the parent or guardian in accordance with article 27-F of the Public Health Law;

(f) if the parent or guardian of the child who lacks capacity to consent does not provide written permission for the child to be referred for HIV-related testing and/or the necessary written informed consent for such testing, and the child has been placed in foster care voluntarily by the parent or guardian in accordance with section 384-a of the Social Services Law, or the child has been placed in foster care as a juvenile delinquent in accordance with article 3 of the Family Court Act or as a person in need of supervision in accordance with article 7 of the Family Court Act or as a destitute child in accordance with article 10-C of the Family Court Act, continue, as part of the on-going casework contacts with the parent or guardian, to discuss the importance of HIV-related testing of the child or seek a court order authorizing HIV-related testing of the child if there is an urgent medical necessity for such testing or if the parent or guardian of the child cannot be located, is incapacitated or is deceased;

(g) if the parent or guardian of the child who lacks capacity to consent provides the agency with written permission for the child to be referred for such testing, and the child has been found by the family court to be an abused or a neglected child pursuant to article 10 of the Family Court Act or has been taken into or kept in protective custody or removed from the place where the child was residing pursuant to section 417 of the Social Services Law or section 1022, 1024 or 1027 of the Family Court Act, the designated staff must arrange for the HIV-related testing of the child including either:

(1) obtaining the necessary pre-test counseling for the parent or guardian, written informed consent of the parent or guardian, and post-test counseling for the parent or guardian in accordance with article 27-F of the Public Health Law; or

(2) contacting the commissioner of the social services district in whose care and custody the child is placed, or the commissioner's designated representative, who must provide the necessary written informed consent for the HIV-related testing of the child;

(h) if the parent or guardian of the child who lacks capacity to consent does not provide written permission for the child to be referred for HIV-related testing within 10 business days of the request and the child has been found by the family court to be an abused or a neglected child pursuant to article 10 of the Family Court Act or has been taken into or kept in protective custody or removed from the place where the child was residing pursuant to section 417 of the Social Services Law or section 1022, 1024 or 1027 of the Family Court Act, the designated agency staff must contact the commissioner of the social services district in whose care and custody the child is placed, or the commissioner's designated representative, who must provide the necessary written informed consent for the HIV-related testing of the child. Upon the issuance of such written informed consent by the commissioner or the commissioner's designated representative, the authorized agency must arrange for the HIV-related testing of the child.

(5) Conducting and timing of the HIV-related testing.

(i) The HIV-related testing may be conducted at designated testing centers or other medical facilities, by licensed medical personnel including medical staff employed by the authorized agency, or in connection with a comprehensive medical examination of the child.

(ii) If the necessary written informed consent for the HIV-related testing of the child has been obtained in accordance with paragraph (4) of this subdivision, the HIV-related testing must occur:

(a) within 30 business days of the child's entry into foster care if the child entered foster care on or after September 1, 1995, and it was determined within five business days of the child's entry into foster care that there was no possibility that the child had the capacity to consent to HIV-related testing; or

(b) within 60 business days of the child's entry into foster care if the child entered foster care on or after September 1, 1995, and it was determined within five business days of the child's entry into foster care that there was a possibility that the child had the capacity to consent to HIV-related testing; or

(c) by or at the time of the child's next scheduled periodic medical examination or the child's next service plan review, whichever occurs sooner, if the child entered foster care before September 1, 1995.

(6) Additional assessments of a child in foster care.

(i) Each service plan review of a child that occurs after the initial assessment of the child pursuant to paragraph (2) of this subdivision must include an assessment by designated agency staff of whether HIV-related testing of the child is recommended based on the child's medical history and any information regarding the child obtained since the initial assessment of the child, the prior service plan review of the child or the prior periodic medical examination of the child, as applicable.

(ii) Each periodic medical examination of a child required pursuant to subdivision (f) of this section that occurs after the initial assessment of the child pursuant to paragraph (2) of this subdivision must include an assessment by designated agency staff of whether HIV-related testing of the child is recommended based on the child's medical history and any information regarding the child obtained since the initial assessment of the child, the prior service plan review of the child or the prior periodic medical examination of the child, as applicable.

(iii) If it is determined at a service plan review or periodic medical examination of the child that HIV-related testing of the child is recommended, the authorized agency must initiate the process set forth in paragraph (4) of this subdivision to arrange for the HIV-related testing of the child. If the necessary written informed consent for the HIV-related testing of the child is obtained, the authorized agency must arrange for the HIV-related testing of the child within 30 business days of the recommendation.

(7) Medical services and counseling. If a child tests positive for HIV infection, the authorized agency must:

(i) arrange for any additional HIV-related testing of the child necessary to verify the existence of HIV infection including obtaining the necessary written informed consent for such additional HIV-related testing in accordance with paragraph (4) of this subdivision;

(ii) refer the child for appropriate medical services; and

(iii) provide or arrange for appropriate psychological and other support services for the child and/or the child's family and/or the child's foster family, as applicable.

(8) Documentation of HIV-related testing of a child in foster care. Information regarding any HIV-related testing of a child in foster care and the results of such testing must be documented in the medical history of the child within the uniform case record in accordance with sections 428.3(b) (4) (ii) of this Title and 441.22(k) (5) of this Part. Such information must be provided only to those persons or entities authorized to have access to HIV-related information concerning the foster child in accordance with subdivision (o) of this section, section 357.3 of this Title, and article 27-F of the Public Health Law, including:

(i) the certified or approved foster parents or prospective adoptive parents of the child in accordance with section 357.3 of this Title and section 373-a of Social Services Law;

(ii) the child, if the child is determined to have capacity to consent as defined in paragraph (1) of this subdivision and in article 27-F of the Public Health Law; and

(iii) the parents or guardian of the foster child, except that, if the child is determined to have capacity to consent, the child's written release for such disclosure must be obtained in accordance with section 360-8.1(g) of this Title before any information concerning the HIV-related test is provided to the child's birth parents or guardian.

(9) Recruitment of families to provide foster or adoptive homes for HIV-infected children. Authorized agencies operating foster boarding home programs or adoption programs must include in their community relations recruitment efforts, as required by sections 421.10 and 443.2 of this Title, information regarding the need for families who are able and motivated to care for HIV-infected foster children when such need is indicated as a result of the assessment and testing required by this subdivision.

(c) (1) Initial medical examination upon admission into foster care. Each child admitted into foster care must be given a comprehensive medical examination within 30 days after admission. When records are available to document that such an examination has been completed within 90 days prior to admission into care, and the authorized agency has obtained such records and determines that the child's health status does not warrant a second comprehensive examination within 30 days after admission into foster care, the local social services district may waive the initial medical examination required by this paragraph.

(2) When an initial medical examination is required, the examination must be comprehensive in accordance with current recommended medical practice, taking into account the age, environmental background and development of the child. Such an examination must include the following:

(i) a comprehensive health and developmental history;

(ii) a comprehensive unclothed physical examination;

(iii) an assessment of the child's immunization status and the provision of immunizations as necessary;

(iv) an appropriate vision assessment;

(v) an appropriate hearing assessment;

(vi) appropriate laboratory testing;

(vii) a dental screening; and

(viii) observation for child abuse and maltreatment which, if suspected, must be reported to the State Central Register of Child Abuse and Maltreatment as mandated by section 413 of the Social Services Law.

Laboratory tests may include complete blood count, urinalysis, tuberculin skin test, X-rays, HIV related tests, where performed in a manner consistent with article 27-F of the Public Health Law, and lead, sickle cell, and venereal disease screening at the direction of a physician when indicated on the basis of the child's age, medical history, environmental background and physical/developmental condition.

(3) The comprehensive medical examination described in paragraph (2) of this subdivision must be completed within 30 days:

(i) after a child is accepted into foster care, unless records are available to document that such an examination has been completed within 90 days prior to admission into care and the initial medical examination is waived by the authorized agency; or

(ii) after a foster child returns to foster care if more than 90 days have passed and the child:

(a) was discharged from care, either on a trial basis or on a permanent basis; or

(b) was absent from care without leave.

(4) The comprehensive medical examination described in paragraph (2) of this subdivision may be conducted at any time at the discretion of the authorized agency when:

(i) there are concerns about a foster child's health when such child returns to care within 90 days after:

(a) being discharged from care, either on a trial basis or on a permanent basis; or

(b) being absent from care without leave; or

(ii) a child is transferred to the care of another agency and the receiving agency determines that a comprehensive medical examination may be necessary to assist in the formulation of the child's service plan.

(d) Prior to accepting a foster child into care in cases of voluntary placement, or within 10 days after admission into care in emergency or court-ordered placements, authorization in writing must be requested from the child's parent or guardian for routine medical and/or psychological assessments, immunizations and medical treatment, and for emergency medical or surgical care in the event that the parent or guardian cannot be located at the time such care becomes necessary. Such authorization must become a permanent part of the child's medical record. If written authorization cannot be obtained from the child's parent or guardian in cases of involuntary placements, the local social services commissioner may provide written authorization where authorized in accordance with section 383-b of the Social Services Law.

(e) Prior to accepting a child into care or within 10 days after admission into care, authorization must be requested from the child's parent or guardian for release of the child's past medical records. If written consent for release of such records cannot be obtained, the local social services commissioner may authorize release of such records. Diligent efforts must be made by the authorized agency to obtain such records by submitting a written request, along with the appropriate authorization, to the various doctors and/or hospitals known to have previously treated the child. When a preschool child is placed in foster care, diligent efforts must be made to obtain the child's birth record from the hospital where the child was born or from another hospital in possession of such record. Upon receipt, such record must be included in the uniform case record.

(f) (1) Each foster child must have complete periodic individualized medical examinations, the results of which must be maintained in the child's uniform case record. Such examinations must be provided according to the following schedule:

(i) for children aged 0-1 year: at 2-4 weeks; 2-3 months; 4-5 months; 6-7 months; 9-10 months;

(ii) for children aged 1-6 years: at 12-13 months; 14-15 months; 16-19 months; 23-25 months; 3 years; 4 years; 5 years; and

(iii) for children aged 6-21 years: at 6 years; 8-9 years; 10-11 years; 12-13 years; 14-15 years; 16-17 years; 18-19 years; and 20 years.

(2) Such examinations must follow current recommended medical practice and be consistent with the needs of the child as determined by the child's physician. Every examination must include the following, as appropriate by age:

(i) a comprehensive health and developmental history;

(ii) a comprehensive unclothed physical examination;

(iii) an assessment of immunization status and provision of immunizations as necessary;

(iv) each periodic medical examination of a child that occurs after the initial assessment of the child for risk factors related to HIV infection in accordance with subdivision (b) of this section, must include an assessment by designated agency staff of whether HIV-related testing of the child is recommended based on the child's medical history and any information regarding the child obtained since the initial assessment of the child, the prior service plan review of the child or the prior periodic medical examination of the child, as applicable.

(v) an appropriate vision assessment;

(vi) an appropriate hearing assessment;

(vii) laboratory tests as appropriate for specific age groups or because the child presents a history or symptoms indicating such tests are necessary;

(viii) dental care screening and/or referral. All children up to age three should have their mouths examined at each medical examination and, where appropriate, should be referred for dental care. All children three years of age or over must have a dental examination by a dentist annually and must be provided with any dental care as needed; and

(ix) observation for child abuse and maltreatment which, if suspected, must be reported to the State central register of child abuse and maltreatment as mandated by section 413 of the Social Services Law.

(g) When the medical examination indicates a condition requiring follow-up care as determined by the child's physician, the agency responsible for the child's care must provide or arrange for such follow-up care as recommended by the child's physician.

(h) (1) Within 60 days of the acceptance into foster care of a child who is eligible for medical assistance, the local social services district must notify in writing the child's foster parent(s), or the institution, group residence, group home or agency boarding home where the child is residing of the availability of child/teen health plan services (C/THP). All families eligible for C/THP services must also be informed in writing at least annually of the availability of such services in accordance with section 508.4(a) of this Title.

(2) The local social services district is responsible for assuring that a current listing of the names and locations of medical providers offering examinations, diagnosis and treatment to children eligible for C/THP is made available to foster parents and to other authorized agencies upon request.

(i) For a foster child placed with a child-caring agency having an established Medicaid per diem rate agreement, C/THP services must be provided in accordance with that agency's per diem rate agreement and may not be claimed separately.

(j) (1) Each authorized agency responsible for the care of a child must inform the foster parent(s) of the comprehensive health history, current health status and health care needs of the foster child when the child is placed in the home, including:

(i) the requirements for type and frequency of medical examinations;

(ii) the agency's procedures for obtaining medical care in cases of suspected illness;

(iii) the agency's procedures for securing emergency medical treatment; and

(iv) information related to whether the child has had an HIV related test or been diagnosed as having AIDS, and HIV related illness or an HIV infection. The terms AIDS, HIV related test, HIV related illness and HIV infection are defined in section 360-8.1 of this Title.

(2) Each authorized agency must inform the foster parent(s) that assistance is available in scheduling appointments with and providing transportation to providers of medical care on behalf of the foster children placed in their care if such assistance is requested.

(k) For each child in foster care, an authorized agency must maintain a continuing individual medical and dental history within the uniform case record, which must include:

(1) Form DSS-711, Child's Medical Record, or copies of a comparable physician's medical record form. Such form must record the results of the initial medical examination and must be maintained as a continuous and permanent medical history for children placed in foster care. For children in the care of a voluntary agency for whom the local social services district has responsibility, the agency must maintain a continuous and permanent medical and dental history, and the local social services district must maintain a current copy of such history in its files.

(2) Form DSS-704, Medical Report on Mother and Infant. Such form must be used to record the child's birth history, as available from the appropriate hospital, for each preschool child placed in foster care, either in the direct care of the local social services district or in the care of voluntary agencies.

(3) Form DSS-3306, Progress Notes. Such form must be maintained in the uniform case record by the agency providing care to a child and must include a summary of activities related to medical and dental appointments, examinations and services, including records of referrals and transportation provided.

(4) Timely entry of the appropriate data related to medical examination appointments.

(5) Documentation that an assessment has been made in accordance with subdivision (b) of this section for risk factors related to HIV infection, and that, if one or more risk factors have been identified, procedures have been followed to obtain the necessary written informed consent and to arrange for the HIV-related testing of the child. Results of such testing must be included in the medical history of the child within the uniform case record.

(*l*) (1) Each foster parent providing care for an adolescent who is 12 years of age or over must be informed in writing within 30 days of placement of the child in the home, and annually thereafter, of the availability of social, educational and medical family planning services for the adolescent in accordance with section 463.2 of this Title.

(2) Each authorized agency, in accordance with section 463.2 of this Title, may, with the prior approval of the local commissioner of social services or upon the delegation of such responsibility by the local social services district, make the offer of family-planning services to all foster children for whom such services would be appropriate and provide such services upon request of the foster child. Such offer may be made orally as long as it is also made in writing.

(m) Upon the transfer of any foster child to the care of another voluntary agency, the agency with which the child was previously placed must provide to the receiving agency a summary of the child's health history and the medical records received from the child's physician.

(n) Medical examination upon discharge from care. Each child discharged from care to another planned living arrangement with a permanency resource must have a comprehensive medical examination prior to discharge, unless the child has undergone such an examination within one year prior to the date of discharge.

(o) Upon a child's discharge from foster care, the local social services district is responsible for ensuring that:

(1) in accordance with section 357.3 of this Title, a comprehensive health history of the child is provided to the child's parent or guardian or to a child, at no cost, if the child is discharged to his or her own responsibility. Such a history must include, but not be limited to, conditions or diseases believed to be hereditary, where known; drugs or medication taken during pregnancy by the biological mother, where known; immunizations received by the child in foster care and prior to placement in care, where known; medications dispensed to the child while in care and prior to placement, where known; allergies the child is known to have exhibited while in care and prior to placement in care, where known; diagnostic tests, including developmental or psychological tests and evaluations given to the child while in care and prior to placement in care, where known; and their results; any follow-up treatment provided to the child prior to placement in care, where known; or provided to the child while in care or still needed by the child; and laboratory tests, including tests for HIV, and the results, where known, except that confidential HIV-related information must not be disclosed to the child's parent or guardian without a written release from the child if the child has capacity to consent as defined in section 360-8.1(a)(8) of this Title and in article 27-F of the Public Health Law. The conditions for the written release authorizing such disclosure are described in section 360-8.1(g) of this Title and in article 27-F of the Public Health Law. The term confidential HIV-related information is defined in section 360-8.1(a)(5) of this Title and in article 27-F of the Public Health Law.

(2) the importance of comprehensive and periodic medical assessments and follow-up treatment is discussed with the child's parents or guardian, or with children discharged to their own care;

(3) assistance is offered to the child's parent(s) or guardian or the child in finding a physician or medical provider organization in an appropriate location through referrals to and/or lists of such medical providers required to be maintained by social services districts in accordance with section 508.6 of this Title;

(4) diligent effort is made to obtain the name and address of the physician or medical organization who will be providing medical services to the child; and

(5) a copy of the child's comprehensive health history is provided to the child's medical provider when identified.

(p) If a foster child is discovered to have an elevated blood lead level, the authorized agency is responsible for notifying the department and the local health department.

Part 443
Certification, Approval and
Supervision of Foster Family Boarding Homes

§443.1 Definitions.

(a) Authorized agency. The term authorized agency refers to an entity defined in paragraphs (a) and (b) of subdivision 10 of section 371 of the Social Services Law.

(b) Certificate. A certificate to board permits an individual to receive remuneration from an authorized agency for the care at board of a child under the age of 18 years, or under the age of 21 years if a student attending a school, college or university or regularly attending a course of vocational or technical training designed to fit him/her for gainful employment, and who entered foster care prior to his/her 18th birthday. Such a certificate may be issued by the public or private authorized agency purchasing such care.

(c) (Reserved)

(d) A letter of approval or approval permits a relative within the second or third degree of the parent(s) or stepparent(s) of a foster child to receive remuneration from an authorized agency for the care at board of a child under the age of 18 years, or under the age of 21 years if a student attending a school, college or university or regularly attending a course of vocational or technical training designed to fit him/her for gainful employment, and who entered foster care prior to his/her 18th birthday. Such a letter of approval shall be issued by the local commissioner of social services or by an authorized agency, only if the home has been approved by the authorized agency as required by this Part.

(e) Foster family home care. Foster family home care is temporary or long-term care of a child whose care and custody or guardianship and custody have been transferred to an authorized agency pursuant to the provisions of section 383-c, 384 or 384-a of the Social Services Law or who has been placed with a social services official pursuant to article 3, 7, 10, 10-B or 10-C of the Family Court Act and who is cared for away from his or her home 24 hours a day in a family home with a foster parent duly certified or approved by an authorized agency or certified or approved by a social services commissioner.

(f) Approved home. An approved home is a home in which temporary or long-term care is provided to a child whose care and custody or guardianship and custody have been transferred to an authorized agency pursuant to the provisions of section 383-c, 384 or 384-a of the Social Services Law or who has been placed with a social services official pursuant to article 3, 7, 10, 10-B or 10-C of the Family Court Act and who is cared for 24 hours a day in a family home with a foster parent who is a relative within the second or third degree to the parent(s) or stepparent(s) of the child and who is duly approved by an authorized agency as required by this Part.

(g) Approved emergency relative foster home. An approved emergency relative foster home is a home in which foster care is provided to a child placed with an authorized agency who is cared for 24 hours-a-day in a family home with a foster parent who is a relative within the second or third degree to the parent(s) or stepparent(s) of the child and which is duly approved by an authorized agency in accordance with section 443.7 of this Part.

(h) Certified emergency foster home. A certified emergency foster home is a home in which foster care is provided to a child placed with an authorized agency who is cared for 24 hours-a-day in a family home with a foster parent who is either a relative other than one who is within the second or third degree to the parent(s) or stepparent(s) of the child or is a nonrelative with a significant prior relationship with the child's family and which is duly certified by an authorized agency in accordance with section 443.7 of this Part.

(i) Relative within the second or third degree. A relative within the second or third degree to the parent(s) or stepparent(s) of a child refers to those relatives who are related to the parent(s) or stepparent(s) through blood or marriage either in the first, second or third degree in the kinship line. A relative within the second or third degree of a parent includes the following:

(1) grandparents of the child;

(2) great-grandparents of the child;

(3) aunts and uncles of the child, including the spouses of the aunts or uncles;

(4) siblings of the child;

(5) great-aunts and great-uncles of the child, including the spouses of the great-aunts or great-uncles;

(6) first cousins of the child, including the spouses of the first cousins;

(7) great-great grandparents of the child; and

(8) an unrelated person where placement with such person allows half-siblings to remain together in an approved foster home, and the parents or stepparents of one of the half-siblings is related to such person in the second or third degree.

(j) Foster family boarding home means a residence owned, leased or otherwise under the control of a single person or family who has been certified or approved by an authorized agency to care for not more than six children, including all children under the age of 13 whether or not they are received for board, except that up to two additional children may be cared for if such children are siblings, or are siblings of a child living in the home, or are children freed for adoption and placed for adoption with the person(s) who have been certified or approved as foster parents. Such home may exceed these limits only to receive for board a child or children returning to that foster family boarding home pursuant to section 443.6 of this Part.

§443.2 Authorized agency operating requirements.

(a) Outreach. Authorized agencies operating a foster family boarding home program must seek to recruit persons with the ability and motivation to serve children in need of a substitute family life.

(b) Inquiries. Authorized agencies operating a foster family boarding home program must:

(1) respond in writing within 10 days to inquiries from persons interested in becoming foster parents and must have a written procedure for doing this.

(2) offer an appointment to each person inquiring about the program or shall arrange for them to attend an orientation meeting about foster family care.

(3) provide application and medical report forms to persons interested in the program at the time of the initial interview or the orientation meetings.

(4) inform persons who express an interest in becoming or who apply to become certified or approved foster parents, that as part of the application process, each applicant and each person over the age of 18 currently residing in the home of the applicant will be required to provide fingerprints in the form prescribed by the Office of Children and Family Services for the purpose of a criminal history record check by the Division of Criminal Justice Services and the Federal Bureau of Investigation in accordance with the provisions set forth in section 443.8 of this Part.   *(Eff. 1/25/17)*

(5) (i) inform persons who express an interest in becoming, or who apply to become a certified or approved foster parent, that the agency must inquire of the Office of Children and Family Services whether any person who applies for certification or approval to be a foster parent and whether any person over the age of 18 who resides in the home of the applicant is the subject of an indicated child abuse or maltreatment report on file with the Statewide Central Register of Child Abuse and Maltreatment and inform such persons that if they, or any other person over the age of 18 who resides in the home of the applicant, resided in another state at any time during the five years preceding the application for certification or approval as a foster parent made in accordance with this Part, the agency will request child abuse and maltreatment information maintained by the child abuse and maltreatment registry from the applicable child welfare agency in each such state of previous residence; and

(ii) inform persons who express an interest in becoming or who apply to become certified or approved foster parents, that as part of the application process, that the agency must inquire of the Justice Center for the Protection of People with Special Needs whether any person who applies for certification or approval as a foster parent and whether any person over the age of 18 who resides in the home of the applicant is listed on the register of substantiated category one cases of abuse or neglect administered by the Justice Center for the Protection of People with Special Needs.

(6) require applicants for certification or approval to complete the forms which are necessary for the agency to inquire of the Office of Children and Family Services and the Justice Center for the Protection of People with Special Needs whether the applicant and any person over the age of 18 who resides in the home of the applicant is the subject of an indicated child abuse or maltreatment report on file with the Statewide Central Register of Child Abuse and Maltreatment and/or is listed on the register of substantiated category one cases of abuse or neglect by the Justice Center for the Protection of People with Special Needs and, where applicable, to request child abuse and maltreatment information from the applicable child welfare agency of the state where the applicant or other person 18 years of age or older resided in the five years preceding the application for certification or approval as a foster parent. This includes foster parents who are completing a new application in the following situations:

(i) an initial application for certification or a letter of approval as a foster parent has been received;

(ii) an application for certification or approval as foster parents has expired because it has been pending for six months or more;

(iii) a previously certified or approved foster home that was closed is to be reopened; or

(iv) a new adult spouse of a foster parent has come into the home and has applied for certification or approval as a foster parent.

(7) inquire of the Office of Children and Family Services and the Justice Center for the Protection of People with Special Needs whether an applicant, and any person 18 years of age or older who resides in the home of the applicant, is the subject of an indicated child abuse or maltreatment report on file with the Statewide Central Register of Child Abuse and Maltreatment and/or is listed on the register of substantiated category one cases of abuse or neglect maintained by the Justice Center for the Protection of People with Special Needs and, if the applicant or other person 18 years of age or older who resides in the home of the applicant resided in another state in the five years preceding the application for certification or approval as a foster parent made pursuant to this Part, request child abuse and maltreatment information maintained by the child abuse and maltreatment registry from the applicable child welfare agency of each such state of previous residence;

(8) determine, on the basis of the information it has available and in accordance with guidelines developed by the Office of Children and Family Services, whether to approve the applicant if an applicant or any person 18 years of age or older who resides in the home of the applicant is the subject of an indicated report of child abuse or maltreatment on file with the Statewide Central Register of Child Abuse and Maltreatment and/or with another state's child abuse and maltreatment registry and/or is listed on the register of substantiated category one cases of abuse or neglect maintained by the Justice Center for the Protection of People with Special Needs, except that any social services district which had guidelines for the review of persons who are subjects of indicated reports of child abuse or maltreatment in use prior to January 1, 1986 may continue to use the district guidelines in making the required determination;

(9) if such an applicant is approved, the agency must maintain a written record, as part of the application file, which sets forth the specific reason(s) why the applicant was determined to be appropriate and acceptable to be certified or approved as a foster parent. If the agency denies the application, the agency must furnish the applicant with a written statement setting forth its reason(s) for the denial, including a statement indicating whether the denial was based in whole or in part on the existence of an indicated report. If the denial is based in whole or in part on the existence of an indicated report of child abuse or maltreatment on file with the Statewide Central Register of Child Abuse and Maltreatment which names the applicant as a subject, the notice of denial must also inform the applicant, in the form prescribed by the Office of Children and Family Services, that;

(i) the applicant has the right, pursuant to section 424-a of the Social Services Law, to request a hearing before the Office of Children and Family Services regarding the record maintained by the Statewide Central Register of Child Abuse and Maltreatment;

(ii) a request for such hearing must be made within 60 days of the receipt of the notice of denial indicating that the denial was based in whole or in part on the existence of the indicated report; and

(iii) the sole issue at any such hearing will be whether the applicant has been shown by a fair preponderance of the evidence to have committed the act or acts of child abuse or maltreatment giving rise to the indicated report;

(10) reconsider its decision to deny the applicant foster care certification or approval which was based in whole or in part on the existence of an indicated report of child abuse or maltreatment whenever the agency is informed by the Office of Children and Family Services that, as a result of a hearing held pursuant

to a request made in accordance with paragraph (8) of this subdivision and section 424-a of the Social Services Law, the Office of Children and Family Services has failed to show by a fair preponderance of the evidence that the applicant committed the act or acts upon which the indicated report is based and that the agency's decision to deny the applicant should be reconsidered. Upon receiving such notification from the Office of Children and Family Services, the agency should review its denial without considering the indicated report.

(11) require a joint application to be submitted by married individuals living in the same household.

(12) utilize the application form to elicit information including, but not limited to the following:

(i) age;

(ii) health;

(iii) physical functioning;

(iv) income;

(v) marital status;

(vi) employment of the applicants;

(vii) information regarding the physical facilities of the prospective foster home;

(viii) the names of those persons who will be sharing living accommodations with the child in foster care, including the names of persons 18 years of age or older living in the home;

(ix) whether any other application for certification or approval has ever been made, whether such application was accepted or rejected and, if rejected, the reasons therefor.

(13) each agency must establish a procedure to review and evaluate the backgrounds of and information supplied by all applicants for certification or approval. As part of this procedure, applicants must be required to submit all of the following information:

(i) a statement or summary of the applicant's employment history, including but not limited to any relevant child-caring experience;

(ii) names, addresses and, where applicable, telephone numbers of references who can verify the applicant's employment history, work record and qualifications;

(iii) names, addresses and telephone numbers of at least three personal references, other than relatives, who can attest to the applicant's character, habits, reputation and personal qualifications and which must be verified in accordance with this section;

(iv) a sworn statement by the applicant indicating whether, to the best of the applicant's knowledge, the applicant or any other person over the age of 18 currently residing in the home has ever been convicted of a crime in New York State or any other jurisdiction. If an applicant discloses in the sworn statement that he/she or any other person over the age of 18 currently residing in the home has been convicted of a crime, the agency must determine, in accordance with guidelines developed and disseminated by the Office of Children and Family Services to the extent consistent with section 443.8 of this Part, whether to approve such applicant. If the agency determines that it will approve the applicant to receive a foster care placement, the agency must maintain a written record, as part of the application and home study file of such applicant, of the reason(s) why the applicant was determined to be appropriate and acceptable to be certified or approved as a foster parent; and

(v) completed fingerprint cards for the applicant(s) and each person over the age of 18 currently residing in the home of such applicant(s). The authorized agency must promptly submit such fingerprint cards to the Office of Children and Family Services for forwarding to the Division of Criminal Justice Services to perform a criminal history record check by the Division of Criminal Justice Services and the Federal Bureau of Investigation. The authorized agency must use the information obtained through the criminal history record check(s) in accordance with section 443.8 of this Part;

(14) acknowledge, within 10 days of receipt of a completed application, receipt of such form and either reject the applicant for home study or accept the applicant for home study. Such acceptance must be conditioned on the submission of an acceptable medical report form.

(15) reject an application for home study only on the basis of information in the application or medical report forms or the criminal history record check or the Statewide Central Register of Child Abuse and Maltreatment check or information provided by another state's child abuse and maltreatment registry or the register of substantiated category one cases of abuse or neglect maintained by the Justice Center for the Protection of People with Special Needs. A person whose application is not accepted must be advised in writing of the reason(s) for rejection;

(16) require that a medical report form must be filed with the agency either prior to or after acceptance for a home study. The completion of the home study required by this Part must be conditioned upon the submission of an acceptable medical report form. The medical report form must cover a physical examination of the applicant(s) conducted not more than one year preceding the date that the application is submitted to an authorized agency, and must include the following:

(i) a written statement from a physician, physician assistant, nurse practitioner or other licensed and qualified health care practitioner as appropriate, regarding the foster family's general health, the absence of communicable disease, infection or illness or any physical conditions which might affect the proper care of a foster child; and

(ii) the result of a tuberculosis screening and additional related tests as deemed necessary within the last 12 months and an additional report of chest X-rays where a physician, physician assistant, nurse practitioner or other licensed and qualified health care practitioner as appropriate, determines that such X-rays are necessary to rule out the presence of current diseases.

(17) if the applicant and the applicant's family have previously completed a medical exam for an adoption study, that medical report will satisfy the requirement of paragraph (16) of this subdivision if the report has been completed within the past year.

(18) unless an application has been rejected prior to submission of the medical report form in accordance with paragraph (16) of this subdivision, within 15 days of receipt of a medical report form an agency must acknowledge receipt of such form and must either accept or reject the applicant for a home study. A person whose application is not accepted based on an unacceptable medical report must be advised in writing of the reasons for such rejection.

(19) treat all reopenings of foster homes that have closed as requests for a new certificate or approval. A new application must be completed regardless of how long the home has been closed. The only exception to this requirement is when a reopening occurs for administrative reasons, i.e., when the home

should not have been closed initially but because it was, a reopening is necessary.

(c) Home Study. Authorized agencies must complete a home study within four months after acceptance of an application unless delays occur as a result of circumstances beyond the control of the agency or unless the schedule for interviews with the applicant is changed by mutual consent of the applicant and the agency representative.

(1) A home study and evaluation of the members of the foster family household or the relative's family household must determine compliance with all of the following criteria for certification or approval:

(i) Age. Each foster parent must be over the age of 21.

(ii) Health. Each member of the household of the foster family must be in good physical and mental health and free from communicable diseases. However, physical handicaps or illness of foster parents or members of their household must be a consideration only as they affect the ability to provide adequate care to foster children or may affect an individual child's adjustment to the foster family. Cases must be evaluated on an individual basis with assistance of a medical consultant when indicated. A written report from a physician, physician assistant, nurse practitioner or other licensed and qualified health care practitioner as appropriate, on the health of a family, including a complete physical examination of the applicant, must be filed with the agency initially and biennially thereafter. Additional medical reports must be furnished upon the request of either the agency worker or the foster parent. Such reports must conform to the standards set forth in this Part.

(iii) Employment. Employment of a foster parent outside the home must be permitted when there are suitable plans for the care and supervision of the child at all times, including after school and during the summer. Such plans must be made part of the foster family record and must receive prior agency approval, unless only one of the two foster parents is working outside the home.

(iv) Marital status. The marital status of an applicant may be a factor in determining whether or not a certification or approval will be granted only as it affects the ability to provide adequate care to foster children. Changes in marital status of certificate and letter of approval holders must be reported to the authorized agency and existing certificates or letters of approval may be revoked and new certificates or letters of approval issued consistent with the best interests of the child.

(v) Character. Each applicant for certification or approval must be required to provide the agency with the names of three persons who may be contacted for references. The agency must seek signed statements from these persons attesting to the applicant's moral character, mature judgment, ability to manage financial resources and capacity for developing a meaningful relationship with children, or utilize in-person interviews attesting to the same.

(vi) Ability and motivation. The agency must explore each applicant's understanding of the role of a foster parent and the applicant's ability, motivation and psychological readiness to be a foster parent in accordance with guidelines issued by the office. The agency also must explore the understanding of the other members of the household about foster care and their concept of a foster child's role in the family.

(2) Authorized agencies must advise applicants at the outset of the home study process that the agency decision to either certify or approve or not to certify or approve them for foster family care will be presented in writing, and

that applicants who are rejected will be offered a personal interview in accordance with the provisions of this Part.

(3) When an authorized agency decides to discontinue a home study or to deny certification or approval upon completion of the home study, it must advise the applicant in writing of the reasons for the agency's decision and must offer an interview to discuss the decision.

(4) A plan to discontinue a home study or to deny certification or approval for foster family care must be reviewed and approved by one or more supervisory level personnel unless the home study was discontinued at the request of the applicant.

(5) When an agency denies an application for certification or approval on the basis, in whole or in part, that the Office of Children and Family Services has notified the agency that the applicant is the subject of an indicated report of child abuse or maltreatment on file with the Statewide Central Register of Child Abuse and Maltreatment, the applicant may request a hearing in accordance with the provisions of this section and section 424-a of the Social Services Law.

(6) An application for certification or approval that has been pending for six months due to failure of the applicant to provide information requested or to cooperate with the approval or certification process will be considered expired. This expiration will require a new application for those prospective foster parents who still seek certification or approval.

(7) (i) When an authorized agency, as defined in section 371(10)(b) of the Social Services Law, denies an application pursuant to section 443.8 of this Part, the authorized agency must provide to the applicant a written statement setting forth the reasons for such denial, including the summary of the criminal history record provided by the Office of Children and Family Services in accordance with this Part. The authorized agency, to the extent authorized by subdivision (d) of section 443.8 of this Part, must also provide a description of the Division of Criminal Justice Services' and Federal Bureau of Investigation's record review process and any remedial processes provided by the Office of Children and Family Services to any prospective foster parents or prospective adoptive parent. If the applicant is disqualified under section 443.8(e) (1)(i)(b) of this Part for a felony conviction of spousal abuse, then the applicant may apply to the Office of Children and Family Services through an administrative hearing held in accordance with section 22 of the Social Services Law for relief from the disqualification based on the ground that the offense was not spousal abuse as that term is defined in section 443.8(i) of this Part.

(ii) When an authorized agency, as defined in section 371(10)(a) of the Social Services Law, denies an application pursuant to section 443.8 of this Part based on the results of a criminal history record check conducted by the Division of Criminal Justice Services, the authorized agency must provide to the applicant a written statement setting forth the reasons for such denial, including the summary of the criminal history record provided by the Office of Children and Family Services in accordance with this Part. The authorized agency, to the extent authorized by section 443.8 of this Part, must also provide a description of the Division of Criminal Justice Services' record review process and any remedial processes provided by the Office of Children and Family Services to any prospective foster parents or prospective adoptive parent. If the applicant is disqualified under section 443.8(e)(1)(i)(b) of this Part for a felony conviction of spousal abuse, then the applicant may apply to the Office of Children and Family Services through an administrative hearing held in accordance with section 22 of the Social Services Law for relief from the disqualification based on the ground that the offense was not spousal abuse as that term is defined in section 443.8(i) of this Part.

(iii) When an authorized agency, as defined in section 371(10)(a) of the Social Services Law, denies an application pursuant to section 443.8 of this Part when directed to do so by the Office of Children and Family Services based on the results of the criminal history record check conducted by the Federal Bureau of Investigation, the authorized agency must provide to the applicant a written statement setting forth the reasons for such denial. The Office of Children and Family Services must also notify the prospective foster parent or other person over the age of 18 who currently resides in the home of the applicant in accordance with the standards set forth in section 443.8 of this Part. If the applicant is disqualified under section 443.8(e)(i)(i)(b) of this Part for a felony conviction of spousal abuse, then the applicant may apply to the Office of Children and Family Services through an administrative hearing held in accordance with section 22 of the Social Services Law for relief from the disqualification based on the ground that the offense was not spousal abuse as that term is defined in section 443.8(i) of this Part. *(Eff.1/25/17)*

(d) Foster parent orientation.

(1) Authorized agencies must orient applicants who have been accepted for a home study or, in the case of relatives who are in the process of a home study, to:

(i) the social, family and personal problems that lead to family breakdown and the need for the placement of children;

(ii) the problems and reactions of children upon separation, and the function and responsibility of the foster family in relation to the child, the natural parents, and the agency staff;

(iii) the agency policy and practice to have defined goals to achieve permanency for each child entering the foster care system;

(iv) the authority of the local social services districts, the Office of Children and Family Services and Family Court to supervise the agency's practice;

(v) the nature of the relationship of agency staff to foster parents and children, including definitions of the function and responsibility of the social workers assigned to the children and their families;

(vi) the payments to foster parents for care and expenses; the definition of foster family care, certification or approval of the home; and

(vii) the rights and responsibilities of a foster parent as defined by a letter of understanding that must be executed at the time of certification or approval.

(e) Training and placement information.

(1) (i) Authorized agencies must provide training to each certified or approved foster parent in a training program approved by the Office of Children and Family Services which will prepare foster parents to meet the needs of children in their care so that the best interests of the children placed by the certifying or approving agency will be met.

(ii) Such training must include knowledge and skills relating to the reasonable and prudent parent standard, as defined in section 441.25 of this Title, for the participation of the child in foster care in age or developmentally-appropriate activities, including knowledge and skills relating to the developmental stages of the cognition, emotional, physical, and behavioral capacities of a child. Such training must also include knowledge and skills relating to applying the standard to decisions such as whether to allow the child to engage in extracurricular, enrichment, cultural, and social activities, including sports, field trips, and overnight activities lasting one day or more, and to decisions involving the signing of permission slips and arranging transportation for the child to and from extracurricular, enrichment and social activities.

(iii) Such training will, as appropriate, help the foster parent to understand the issues confronting children preparing for another planned living arrangement with a permanency resource; and will, to the extent possible, be coordinated with a child's program to develop life skills for the purpose of preparing for another planned living arrangement with a permanency resource.

(iv) Such training must also include information on eligibility for the kinship guardianship assistance and non-recurring guardianship expensed programs, and the medical coverage available to certain relative foster parents under the kinship guardianship assistance program.

(2) Before a child is placed in a foster home, authorized agencies must prepare the foster parent with appropriate knowledge and skills to provide for the needs of the child. Such preparation must be continued, as needed, after the placement of the child.

(3) Authorized agencies shall provide basic information to foster parents about each child who is to be placed in the home. Where a child is placed on emergency basis, such information shall be provided within 30 days of placement. Information shall include, but need not be limited to, the following topics:

(i) the estimated length of time a child may need to be in placement and the assumptions and knowledge on which the estimate is based;

(ii) the health of the child, including the procedure to be followed in obtaining consent for emergency medical treatment in accordance with section 507.5 of this Title and the child's medical history in accordance with the provisions of section 357.3 of this Title;

(iii) handicaps or behavior problems;

(iv) school and educational experiences;

(v) the relationship of the child and the natural parents;

(vi) requirements and plans for visitation of and by the natural family, including probable location of such visits; and

(vii) placement and discharge goals.

(f) Recordkeeping. Authorized agencies must develop a record for each foster parent applicant and each certified or approved foster parent that must include, but not necessarily be limited to:

(1) the application;

(2) medical report(s);

(3) summary of the home study;

(4) interviews with applicants;

(5) personal references;

(6) placement/action record listing the names of children placed in the home, with the dates of the children's placement and removal;

(7) summary of each annual evaluation made pursuant to section 443.10;

(8) physical description of the home, including allocation of space;

(9) summary of agency conference that clarifies the basis for each decision that affects the applicant's status with the agency;

(10) copies of correspondence with the applicant;

(11) reports from the Office of Children and Family Services and the Justice Center for the Protection of People with Special Needs which notifies the agency whether the applicant for certification or approval or other person 18 years of age or older who resides in the home of the applicant is the subject of

an indicated report of child abuse or maltreatment on file with the Statewide Central Register of Child Abuse and Maltreatment and/or is listed on the register of substantiated category one cases of abuse or neglect maintained by the Justice Center for the Protection of People with Special Needs and, where applicable, information from the child abuse and maltreatment registry of another state;

(12) responses from the Office of Children and Family Services regarding the criminal history record check(s) conducted in accordance with section 443.8 of this Part;

(13) if the prospective foster parent is certified or approved, or if the renewal of a certification or approval of an existing foster parent is not denied, notwithstanding that the authorized agency is notified by the Office of Children and Family Services that the prospective or existing foster parent or any other person over the age of 18 who is currently residing in the home of the prospective or existing foster parent has a criminal history record, a record of the reasons why the prospective or existing foster parent was determined to be appropriate and acceptable to receive a foster care placement, provided, however, the authorized agency may not grant or continue certification or approval where a prospective or existing foster parent has been convicted of a mandatory disqualifying crime or where an authorized agency, as defined in section 371(10)(a) of the Social Services Law, has been directed by the Office of Children and Family Services to deny such application for certification or approval or to hold such application in abeyance because of the results of the Federal Bureau of Investigation criminal history record check conducted in accordance with section 443.8 of this Part; and *(Eff. 1/25/17)*

(14) if the application for certification or approval is granted, notwithstanding that the agency is notified by the Office of Children and Family Services, a child welfare agency of another state or the Justice Center for the Protection of People with Special Needs that the applicant or other person 18 years of age or older who resides in the home of the applicant is the subject of an indicated child abuse or maltreatment report on file with the Statewide Central Register of Child Abuse and Maltreatment and/or the child abuse or maltreatment register of another state or is listed on the register of substantiated category one cases of abuse or neglect maintained by the Justice Center for the Protection of People with Special Needs, a record of the reasons why the applicant was determined to be appropriate and acceptable to receive a foster care placement.

(g) Interstate placements.

(1) The provisions of this section apply when the Office of Children and Family Services, through the Interstate Compact on the Placement of Children, receives a request to conduct a home study for the certification or approval of a person or persons in New York as foster parents for the placement of a foster child or children from another state.

(2) Upon receipt of such request, the Office of Children and Family Services will forthwith transmit the request to the social services district in which the prospective foster parent(s) reside for the purpose of conducting a home study and certifying or approving the prospective foster parent(s) in accordance with the standards of this Part.

(3) The social services district must conduct and complete a home study of the prospective foster parent(s) in accordance with subdivision (c) of this section and as defined in paragraph (6) of this subdivision. The social services district may conduct the home study directly or may use a voluntary authorized

agency under contract with the social services district or a voluntary authorized agency under contract with the Office of Children and Family Services to conduct the home study. If the social services district uses a voluntary authorized agency under contract with the Office of Children and Family Services to conduct the home study, the costs of the home study will be charged back to the social services district in which the prospective foster parent(s) reside and such costs are subject to state reimbursement as a foster care service.

(4) Notwithstanding the timeframes set forth in subdivision (c) of this section, the social services district or the voluntary authorized agency must complete the home study and simultaneously return such home study to the Office of Children and Family Services and to the state or local agency which submitted the request set forth in paragraph (1) of this subdivision within 60 days of the receipt of the request by the Office of Children and Family Services. Provided, however, for requests made on or before September 30, 2008, if the social services district or the voluntary authorized agency is not able to complete the home study within 60 days of the receipt of the request because of circumstances beyond their control, including, but not limited to, the failure to receive documentation on background checks or to receive medical forms and if such social services district or voluntary authorized agency requested such documentation at least 45 days before the end of the above referenced 60 day period, the social services district or voluntary authorized agency will have 75 days from the date of the receipt of the request to complete the home study.

(5) Nothing herein requires that the prospective foster parent(s) complete the education or training requirements of this Part for the completion of the home study. Nothing herein requires that the complete certification or approval process otherwise required by this Part be concluded within the timeframes set forth in paragraph (4) of this subdivision.

(6) The term home study means an assessment of the safety and suitability of placing the child in the home of the prospective foster parent(s) based on an evaluation of a home environment conducted in accordance with applicable requirements of this Part to determine whether the proposed placement would meet the individual needs of the child, including the child's safety; permanency; health; well-being; and mental, emotional, and physical development.

(7) Where a social services district proposes to place a foster child with prospective foster parent(s) in another state, the social services district must treat a home study received from another state, Indian tribe or private agency under contract with the other state as meeting the requirements imposed by New York State for the completion of a home study before placing a child or children in the home, unless within 14 days of receipt of the home study, the social services district determines, based on the content of the home study, that making a decision in reliance on the home study would be contrary to the welfare of the child or children.

(h) Inter-county Placements.

(1) Where a social services district proposes to place a foster child with prospective foster parent(s) who reside in another social services district, the prospective foster parent(s) may apply to the social services district in which the prospective foster parent(s) reside for certification or approval as foster parent(s) in accordance with this Part. The social services district in which the prospective foster parent(s) reside is responsible for processing the application and performing the home study in accordance with subdivision (c) of this

section. The social services district may conduct the home study directly or may use a voluntary authorized agency under contract with the social services district or a voluntary authorized agency under contract with the Office of Children and Family Services to conduct the home study. If the social services district uses a voluntary authorized agency under contract with the Office of Children and Family Services to conduct the home study, the costs of the home study will be charged back to the social services district in which the prospective foster parent(s) reside and such costs are subject to state reimbursement as a foster care service.

(2) The social services district in which the prospective foster parent(s) reside or voluntary authorized agency must complete the home study within 60 days of the receipt of the application for certification or approval to be foster parent(s). Provided, however, for requests made on or before September 30, 2008, if the social services district or voluntary authorized agency is not able to complete the home study within 60 days of the receipt of the request because of circumstances beyond its control, including, but not limited to, the failure to receive documentation of background checks or to receive medical forms, and if the social services district or voluntary authorized agency requested such documentation at least 45 days before the end of the above referenced 60 day period, the social services district or voluntary authorized agency will have 75 days from the date of the receipt of the request to complete and forward the home study as noted above.

(3) A social services district or a voluntary authorized agency may not refuse to provide an application or delay or deny a home study to a person seeking certification or approval as a foster parent on the basis that such person is seeking to provide care for a child who is in the custody of another authorized agency.

(i) Confidentiality of Out-of-State Child Abuse and Maltreatment Information. The authorized agency must safeguard the confidentiality of the information received from the applicable child welfare agency in the other state in accordance with subdivision (b) of this section to prevent unauthorized disclosure and the authorized agency is prohibited from using such information for any purpose other than conducting background checks pursuant to this Part.

§443.3 Certification or approval of foster family homes.

(a) Certification and approval. Foster family boarding homes must meet the following health and safety standards and physical plant requirements:

(1) The physical facilities of the foster home or relative foster home must be in good condition and present no hazard to the health and safety of children.

(2) The foster home must be in substantial compliance with all applicable provisions of State and local laws, ordinances, rules and regulations concerning health and safety.

(3) The physical space, construction and maintenance of the foster home and premises must be in good repair and kept in a sufficiently clean and sanitary condition so that the physical well-being as well as a reasonable degree of physical comfort is assured the members of the foster family.

(4) Separate bedrooms are required for children of the opposite sex over seven years of age, unless the children are siblings or half-siblings sharing the same bedroom and the alternative sleeping arrangement is consistent with the health, safety, and welfare of each of the siblings or half-siblings and is necessary to keep the siblings or half siblings placed together in the same foster home.

(5) Not more than three persons may occupy any bedroom where children at board sleep, unless the children are siblings or half- siblings and the occupancy is consistent with the health, safety, and welfare of each of the siblings or half-siblings and is necessary to keep the siblings or half-siblings placed together in the same foster home.

(6) No bed may be located in any unfinished attic or basement.

(7) No child above the age of three years may sleep in the same room with an adult of the opposite sex. Children must not sleep together in the same bed with an adult.

(8) Each child must have sleeping space of sufficient size for the safety, comfort, and privacy of the child. Each child must have a separate bed or crib of sufficient size and cleanliness for the comfort and well being of the child, with waterproof covering, if needed, and suitable bedding adequate to the season. Bunk beds may be used.

(9) There must be an adequate and safe supply of water for drinking and household use. Water from wells, springs or other private sources must be protected against contamination. There must be provision for hot water for washing and bathing.

(10) The dwelling must have window barriers, including window screens, guards and/or stoppers above the first floor of the foster home.

(11) Heating apparatus must be safe and adequate to provide for the reasonable comfort of children in the home.

(12) Adequate bathing, toilet and lavatory facilities must be provided and kept in sanitary condition.

(13) The home must be free from fire hazards and equipped with at least one smoke detector.

(14) No certified or approved foster parent may rent rooms to lodgers or boarders or receive and care for maternity cases, except as part of the foster care program, or receive or care for convalescent cases or conduct any business on the premises which might adversely affect the welfare of children, unless permitted by the authorized agency which certified or approved the home.

(15) All firearms, rifles and shotguns, as defined in section 265.00 of the Penal Law, must be securely stored and must be maintained in compliance with applicable State and local standards regarding the licensing, storage and maintenance of such weapons.

(b) Certified and approved foster parents must execute an agreement with the authorized agency that granted the certificate or letter of approval to operate stipulating that the foster family boarding home parent will:

(1) enable children received at board to mingle freely and on equal footing with other children in the household and in the community, and to be accepted as members of the household and share in its pleasures and responsibilities and to apply the reasonable and prudent parent standard set forth in section 441.25 of this Title;

(2) arrange for children of school age to attend school regularly as required by the Education Law;

(3) never leave children under the age of 10 years alone without competent adult supervision, nor children above that age except as might reasonably be done by a prudent parent in the case of his or her own children;

(4) except as permitted by the appropriate authorized agency, never use a foster family boarding home to care for more than two infants under two years of age, including the foster parents' own children, except in those cases

where the foster parents have demonstrated the capacity to do so and a sibling group would otherwise have to be separated;

(5) provide children with sufficient nutritious, wholesome and properly prepared food, served at regular hours. Foster children must be permitted to eat meals at the table in the same manner as other family members with due consideration to their age and special needs;

(6) keep the clothing of children provided by the agency, parent or foster parent in proper condition of repair and cleanliness; endeavor to provide children with a sufficient quantity of clothing, adapted to seasonal conditions, and of such style and quality as not to distinguish them from other children in the community;

(7) provide for each child at board sufficient individual toilet articles and towels, suitable to the child's age and gender, and individual drawer and closet space;

(8) provide a suitable, well-lighted place for children of school age for home study;

(9) recognize and respect the religious wishes of the natural parents of children in care and endeavor to protect and preserve their religious faith;

(10) endeavor to cooperate with the agency staff in the implementation or review of each child's service or discharge plan and to inform the agency of any incident or event that affects or may affect the child's adjustment, health, safety or well-being and/or may have some bearing upon the current service plan;

(11) provide a family atmosphere of acceptance, kindness and understanding and endeavor to give each child the support, attention and recognition that facilitates adjustment to the home and that promotes the child's normal development;

(12) permit an authorized representative of the agency to enter the home to investigate in good faith a formal complaint regarding care of the foster child;

(13) inform the agency of any changes in marital status, family composition or number of persons residing in the home and any changes in the physical facilities comprising the foster home;

(14) agree to cooperate in facilitating regular biweekly visitation or communication between minor siblings or half-siblings who have been placed apart, unless as determined by the agency such contact would be contrary to the health, safety or welfare of one or more of the children or unless the lack of geographic proximity precludes visitation; and

(15) agree only to redisclose confidential HIV-related information concerning the foster child to persons or entities other than those set forth in article 27-F of the Public Health Law for the purpose of providing care, treatment, or supervision of the foster child boarded out or placed with the foster parent or upon a specific written authorization signed by the commissioner of the social services district or the commissioner's designated representative in accordance with section 2782 of the Public Health Law. Where confidential HIV-related information is disclosed, the following written statement must accompany it:

"This information has been disclosed to you from confidential records which are protected by State law. State law prohibits you from making any further disclosure of HIV-related information without the specific written consent of the person to whom it pertains, or as otherwise permitted by law. Any unauthorized further disclosure in violation of

State law may result in a fine or jail sentence or both. A general authorization for the release of medical or other information is not sufficient authorization for further disclosure."

The terms AIDS, HIV-related test, HIV-related illness, HIV infection and confidential HIV-related information are defined in section 360-8.1 of this Title.

(16) Exceptions applicable solely to approved foster boarding homes. Exceptions to the provisions of this Part, other than statutory requirements, may be proposed by the authorized agency as part of the foster boarding home approval process when the authorized agency determines that such exception is necessary to board a foster child; is in the best interests of the child to effect such boarding arrangement; and is consistent with the health, safety, and welfare of the child. Any exception, however, is tentative only and subject to review and approval by the social services district with legal custody of the foster child who would be boarded out in such home. Such decisions must be made by supervisory staff within the social services district who do not have direct supervisory responsibilities over the case management of the particular foster child. Boarding arrangements will be made contingent on such approval. Upon such review, should it be determined that the exception is not necessary or in the best interests of the child to be boarded, upon notice thereof to the agency, the social services district with legal custody of the foster child who would be boarded out in such home must disapprove the proposed arrangement. All exceptions must be requested in writing by the authorized agency and the social services district must document how the granting of the request relates to the best interests of the child.

(c) The agreement required pursuant to this Part must include the statement of preference of foster parents as required under subdivision 1-a of section 374 of the Social Services Law and a statement of the foster parent's rights regarding removal of a child from a foster family home as provided under section 443.5 of this Title.

(d) A certificate must be issued to persons required to receive such certificate in accordance with section 421.24(b)(2)(ii) of this Title if such persons have had an adoptive home study made in accordance with Part 421 of this Title and such persons have been approved to adopt a handicapped or hard-to-place child.

(e) When a home study has been completed and an authorized agency intends to certify or approve the home, the agency shall:

(1) arrange for the foster parents to review the written report of the home study, exclusive of any statement by or based on material provided by references, with the agency's homefinder;

(2) give foster parents the opportunity to enter their reaction to the evaluation as an addendum to the report; and

(3) arrange for the foster parent and the home finder to sign the evaluation after it has been reviewed and the foster parent addendum has been attached.

(f) A certificate or letter of approval shall be issued to a certified or approved foster home only after the applicant(s) executes the agreement required by this Part.

(g) Maintenance of Register and certificate or letter of approval.

(1) Every person who receives, boards or keeps any child under certificate or letter of approval shall keep a record of each child in a register to be provided by the Office of Children and Family Services. Authorized agencies

shall provide foster parents with the appropriate forms for maintaining a register of the children placed in the home as required by this Part and section 380 of the Social Services Law.

(2) The register and certificate or letter of approval shall be accessible for examination at all reasonable times by the authorized agents of the Office of Children and Family Services, of the authorized agency issuing such certificate or letter of approval, and of any incorporated society for the prevention of cruelty to children. Certificates, letters of approval and registers are the property of the State and not of the person to whom issued, and shall be delivered upon demand to the issuing agency when renewed, discontinued or revoked.

(h) Regular and emergency conferences.

(1) Authorized agencies shall assure foster parents providing care for a child that regular conferences shall, whenever possible, be prearranged and held at a mutually convenient time in the foster boarding home at least every 90 days or at such shorter periods as may be required pursuant to this Subchapter.

(2) Authorized agencies shall arrange for conferences with foster parents regarding acute problems, emergencies or crisis situations whenever necessary to provide services that are responsive to the problems and that protect the best interests of the child.

(3) Authorized agencies shall require foster care workers to explain the purpose of each regular or emergency conference to the foster parent at the beginning of each conference; and, in addition, at each regular conference, identify and discuss concerns of the foster family about the child in placement, obtain an account of the child's placement, relationships and functioning in the home, school and community.

(i) Authorized agencies shall have a written policy and procedure governing decisions to remove a child from a foster family home and also provide each foster parent with a copy of such policy and procedure upon certification or approval and at the time of recertification or reapproval; the provisions shall conform to the requirements of section 431.10 of this Title.

(j) Authorized agencies shall provide each foster family boarding home with a manual that summarizes all current agency policies and procedures that have some direct or indirect bearing upon the role and responsibility of a foster parent.

(k) Authorized agencies shall summarize, in the foster family boarding home record, the action taken pursuant to a decision to remove a child from the home or to a request from a foster family to have the child removed.

(*l*) Authorized agencies shall inform each foster parent of the procedure for obtaining administrative review of any grievance or complaint about the agency policy or practice.

(m) Authorized agencies must establish and maintain a written procedure and practice for advising foster parents of their rights:

(1) to have their application to adopt a child who has been continuously in their care at least 12 months given preference and first consideration over all other applicants as provided by section 383.3 of the Social Services Law;

(2) to intervene, as an interested party, in any court proceeding involving the custody of a child who has been in their care for 12 continuous months or longer;

(3) to be given notice and an opportunity to be heard at all permanency hearings for any foster child in the care of the foster parent.

(n) Authorized agencies must comply with the requirements of sections 378 and 398.6(n) of the Social Services Law regarding the number of children in care and with the requirements of section 373 of the Social Services Law with regard to religious faith.

(o) Restrictions and limitations. Authorized agencies shall not:

(1) permit persons certified or approved to provide care in a foster family boarding home to provide such care for another agency without obtaining the certifying or approving agency's written consent and approval for each child or minor to be boarded. No person shall be certified or approved by more than one authorized agency;

(2) permit use of designated emergency homes for any foster care purpose other than designated emergency foster family boarding home care as defined in section 446.2 of this Title or as an approved respite care and services provider as defined in section 435.2(b) of this Title. An exception may be made by an authorized agency when it determines such exception is necessary to board a child, is in the best interest of the child and is consistent with the health, safety and welfare of other children receiving care in the home. A report on the exception must be made within 15 days of the placement by the agency to the appropriate regional office of the Office of Children and Family Services;

(3) initiate action to remove a child from a placement because of change in family composition or circumstances following certification or recertification, or approval or reapproval unless there has been an evaluation of the effect of the change upon the child or children and it is determined that such change is detrimental to the best interests of the child or such change would produce a violation of this Part, the agreement required by section 443.3(b) of this Part or of any statutory requirement.

(p) Reimbursement. With the exception of foster family free home care as defined in section 441.2(j) of this Title, certified and approved foster care parents must be reimbursed for each such child to whom they provide foster care according to the standards established in Part 427 of this Title.

(q) Foster homes.

(1) Except as provided by this section, no child under the age of 16, in the case of placement by a parent or legal guardian, or under the age of 18, in the case of placement by a public or private authorized agency, shall be placed or received at board for remuneration in a foster home unless such home is certified or approved as provided by the Social Services Law and this Title.

(2) A certificate is not required when children are placed or received at board with relatives within the second or third degree, as set forth in section 443.1(i) of this Part, with legally appointed guardians, at schools and academies meeting the requirements of the Education Law as to compulsory education, and at camps operated for profit for the accommodation of school age children during school vacation periods under permits issued by health officers pursuant to Part 7 of the State Sanitary Code. When a child is placed at board with a relative(s) within the second or third degree, the relative's home must be approved by an authorized agency as required by this Part and a letter indicating such approval must be issued to the approved foster parent(s).

(3) No child shall be placed in a foster home, either free or at board, until such home has been visited and careful inquiry made by the agency proposing to make such placement, or its representatives, and a written report filed in the foster parent's case record describing the conditions and suitability of the home

and compliance with requirements of law, this Title, and the rules of local departments of health and social services.

(r) Applications and forms.

(1) Pursuant to Title 1 of article 6 of the Social Services Law, certificates shall be on forms provided by the Office of Children and Family Services.

(2) Certificates or letters of approval must specify the name and address and the religious faith, if any, of the person to whom issued, and the maximum number of children to be boarded, and the age and sex of the children to be cared for at board; and will be valid only for the residence as occupied at the time of issue. A certificate or letter of approval issued to married individuals living in the same household must be issued in the name of both individuals.

(3) Certificates.

(i) Application for certificate or letter of approval to board children shall be made to the authorized agency from which children are to be received upon a form prescribed by the Office of Children and Family Services, or upon a substantially equivalent form approved by the Office of Children and Family Services.

(ii) The agency shall make a written record of each application.

(iii) Such certificate or letter of approval shall be valid for not more than one year after the date of issue but may be renewed or extended pursuant to the requirements contained in this Part.

(4) Before any certificate or letter of approval may be issued, careful investigation of the applicant, including inspection of the premises to be occupied, shall be made and a written report filed in the agency to which the application is made. The investigation and report shall cover all of the requirements of this Part.

§443.5 Removal from foster family care.

(a) Whenever a social services official or another authorized agency acting on his or her behalf proposes to remove a child in foster family care from the foster family home, he/she or such other authorized agency, as may be appropriate, must notify the foster family parents of the intention to remove such child. This notice must be in writing.

(1) Such notification must be given at least 10 days prior to the proposed effective date of the removal, except where the health or safety of the child requires that the child be removed immediately from the foster family home.

(2) Such notification must further advise the foster family parents that they may request a conference with the social services official or a designated employee of the social services district at which time the foster parents, with or without a representative, may appear to have the proposed action reviewed, be advised of the reasons therefor and be afforded an opportunity to submit reasons why the child should not be removed.

(3) Each social services official must instruct and require any authorized agency acting on the official's behalf to furnish notice in accordance with the provisions of this section.

(4) Foster parents who do not object to the removal of the child from their home may waive in writing their right to the 10-day notice, provided, that such waiver shall not be executed prior to the social services official's or authorized agency's determination to remove the child from the foster home and the receipt by the foster parents of notification of such determination.

(b) Upon the receipt of a request for such conference, the social services official shall set a time and place for such conference to be held within 10 days of receipt of such request and shall send written notice of such conference to the foster family parents and their representative, if any, and to the authorized agency, if any, at least five days prior to the date of such conference.

(c) The social services official shall render and issue his or her decision as expeditiously as possible, but not later than five days after the conference. Written notice of this decision must be sent to the foster family parents and their representative, if any, and to the authorized agency, if any. Such decision shall advise the foster family parents of their right to appeal to the Office of Children and Family Services and request a fair hearing in accordance with section 400 of the Social Services Law.

(d) In the event there is a request for a conference, the child shall not be removed from the foster family home until at least three days after the notice of decision is sent, or prior to the proposed effective date of removal, whichever occurs later.

(e) In any agreement for foster care between a social services official, or another authorized agency acting on his or her behalf, and foster parents, there shall be contained therein a statement of a foster parent's rights provided under this section.

§443.6 **Return to foster family care after interruption in care; return to a family boarding home following placement in a foster care institution.**

(a) Whenever a social services official, or an authorized agency acting on such official's behalf, determines that it is in the best interests of a child to be placed in the foster family home in which the child was last placed, when such child is returning to the foster care system after an interruption in care or returning to a family boarding home following placement in a foster care institution, the local social services district or the authorized agency shall place the child returning to care or returning to a family boarding home with the child's prior foster parent(s).

(b) When placement is made in compliance with the provisions of this section, the local social services official or the authorized agency shall waive the restrictions on the number of children who may reside in a foster family home, notwithstanding subdivisions 3 and 4 of section 378 of the Social Services Law and sections 427.2(d) and 443.3 of this Title.

(c) The following factors must be considered in all determinations as to whether it is in the best interests of the child to place the child with his/her prior foster parent(s) when such child is returning to foster care or returning to a family boarding home following placement in a foster care institution:

(1) certification/approval status of the prior foster parent(s);

(2) length of time in placement with prior foster parent(s) and quality of relationship that developed during the placement;

(3) length of time since placement with the prior foster parent(s);

(4) basis for the child's discharge from placement with the prior foster parent(s);

(5) willingness of prior foster parent(s) to accept returning child;

(6) willingness of child to return to prior foster parent(s);

(7) availability of space in the foster home;

(8) ability of prior foster parent(s) to care for returning child;

(9) proximity to prospective adoptive parents, if return to care was caused by temporary disruption of adoptive placement;

(10) proximity to siblings in care, if applicable; and

(11) compliance with standards for appropriateness of placement and compliance with other applicable Office of Children and Family Services regulations.

(d) In the event a child returning to the foster care system has been placed with foster parent(s) other than the prior foster parent(s), the following factors must also be considered in the social services official's or agency's determination of the best interests of the child:

(1) how well the child is faring in the new placement; and

(2) the impact of removal of the child from the new foster parents and return to the foster parents with whom he/she was last placed.

(e) The local social services district or the authorized agency receiving the child for care or which is placing the child following placement in a foster care institution shall document the basis for determinations which result in placement of the child in a new foster family home, rather than with his/her prior foster parents, in the first assessment summary on the uniform case record after the child is placed in accordance with Part 428 of this Title.

(f) The local social services official or any authorized agency acting on such official's behalf shall institute a supervisory review process to ensure that all cases in which children are returning to care or are returning to a family boarding home following placement in a foster care institution are properly assessed for a determination as to whether it would be in the best interests of the child to be placed with his/her prior foster parent(s).

§443.7 Agency procedures for certifying or approving potential emergency foster homes and emergency relative foster homes.

(a) A potential foster home or the home of a relative of a foster child may be certified or approved as an emergency foster home under the following allowable circumstances:

(1) Allowable circumstances.

(i) a child is removed from his or her own home pursuant to section 1021, 1022, 1024 or 1027 of the Family Court Act or a child is removed and placed into foster care pursuant to article 3, 7, 10, 10-B or 10-C of the Family Court Act or section 384-a of the Social Services Law; or

(ii) a child currently placed in a foster care setting needs to be placed in a foster home and the social services district documents within the uniform case record a compelling reason why such home needs to be certified or approved on an emergency basis;

(2) an eligible relative or non-relative, identified in subdivisions (g) and (h) of section 443.1 of this Part, is identified by the child, child's parent(s) or stepparent(s), the court, a representative of the local district or other interested party, as potentially appropriate to provide foster care to the child or such person or relative volunteers to provide foster care to the child. For the purposes of this section, an eligible non-relative may include, but is not limited to, a child's godparent, neighbor, family friend, or an adult with a positive relationship with the child.

(b) Before placing a foster child with a potential caretaker or eligible relative on an emergency basis the authorized agency must:

(1) secure a signed and dated statement from the potential caretaker or eligible relative indicating the exact relationship to the child and the child's parent(s), that the potential caretaker or eligible relative is willing to provide foster care for the child and an assurance that the potential caretaker or eligible relative understands that the child is in the legal custody of the commissioner of social services and that by accepting responsibility for providing foster care for the child, potential caretaker or eligible relative agrees to comply with

foster care requirements, including, but not limited to those involving the role and authority of the certifying or approving authorized agency and the social services district with legal custody of the child to supervise the placement.

(2) perform a home study of the potential caretaker's or eligible relative's home and family on an expedited basis which assesses the potential caretaker's or eligible relative's home to ensure that there is no apparent risk to the health and safety of the child;

(3) perform a home study of the potential caretaker's or eligible relative's home and family on an expedited basis which assesses the potential caretaker's or eligible relative's family, focusing on the following factors:

(i) the family's relationship with the child and the child's parent(s) or stepparent(s);

(ii) the care provided to other children in the home by the potential caretaker or eligible relative;

(iii) the potential caretaker's or eligible relative's knowledge of the circumstances and conditions that led to the need for the child's foster care placement;

(iv) the past role of the potential caretaker or eligible relative in helping and/or protecting the child from and/or preventing occurrences of abuse or maltreatment of the child; and

(v) the present ability of the potential caretaker or eligible relative to protect the child placed in its home from abuse or maltreatment and the potential caretaker's or eligible relative's ability to understand the need to protect the child from abuse or maltreatment;

(4) explain to the potential caretaker or eligible relative the agency's role and authority to supervise the placement;

(5) obtain information necessary to contact character references pursuant to this Part; and

(6) review agency records to determine whether or not the potential caretaker(s) or eligible relative(s) have a prior history of abuse or maltreatment.

(c) If the home is found suitable after the requirements of subdivision (b) of this section have been completed, it will be certified or approved as an emergency foster home or an emergency relative foster home for 90 days from the date of placement of the child in the home.

(d) The potential caretaker or eligible relative must execute an agreement with the authorized agency within seven days of placement that provides that the potential caretaker or eligible relative will comply with provisions of this Part.

(e) Within seven days of placement, the authorized agency must obtain:

(1) a completed Statewide Central Register database check form, and submit such form to the Office of Children and Family Services pursuant to section 424-a of the Social Services Law and section 443.2(b)(7) and (8) of this Part;

(2) if the applicant or other person 18 years of age or older who resides in the home of the applicant resided in another state at any time during the five years preceding the emergency approval or emergency certification issued pursuant to this section, the documentation necessary to enable the agency to request child abuse and maltreatment information maintained in the child abuse and maltreatment registry from the applicable child welfare agency in each such state of previous residence; and

(3) a completed form to check the register of substantiated category one cases of abuse or neglect, and submit such form to the Justice Center for the

Protection of People with Special Needs pursuant to section 495 of the Social Services Law and section 443.2(b)(7) and (8) of this Part.

(f) On the date of the foster child's placement in the certified or approved emergency foster home or within one business day thereof, the authorized agency must provide a sufficient number of blank fingerprint cards for the foster parent(s) and each person over the age of 18 currently residing in such home and a description of how the completed fingerprint cards will be used upon submission to the authorized agency by the foster parent(s). The foster parent(s) must submit the completed fingerprint cards to the authorized agency no later than two weeks following the receipt of such cards for the purpose of a criminal history record check performed by both the Division of Criminal Justice Services and the Federal Bureau of Investigation.

(g) Emergency foster homes and emergency relative foster homes certified or approved on an expedited emergency basis for 90 days, may continue to provide foster care beyond the 90th day of placement if they are finally certified or approved on or before the end of the 90th day or if the provisions of subdivision (h) of this section apply. For an emergency foster home to receive final certification or approval, all requirements for certification or approval as a foster home as set forth in this Part must be met within 90 days from the date of placement.

(h) Continued placement.

(1) An emergency foster home certified or approved on an emergency expedited basis for 90 days in accordance with this section may continue to provide foster care beyond the 90th day of certification or approval as an emergency foster home when the foster parent has otherwise satisfied all of the requirements for final certification or approval as a certified or approved foster home except for the completion of the Statewide Central Register of Child Abuse or Maltreatment database check process in accordance with section 443.2 of this Part, or the completion of the process to check the register of substantiated category one cases of abuse or neglect maintained by the Justice Center for the Protection of People with Special Needs in accordance with section 443.2 of this Part, or the completion of the criminal history record check process in accordance with section 443.8 of this Part where the certified emergency foster parent or approved emergency foster parent has otherwise complied with the requirements of subdivisions (e) and (f) of this section.

(2) Such certified emergency foster parent or approved emergency relative foster parent may continue to provide foster care until the completion of the Statewide Central Register of Child Abuse and Maltreatment database check process as set forth in section 443.2 of this Part, the check of the Justice Center's register of substantiated category one cases of abuse or neglect as set forth in section 443.2 of this Part and the criminal history record check process as set forth in section 443.8 of this Part or unless the certification or approval is otherwise revoked by the authorized agency for cause in accordance with this Part.

(3) Upon receipt of the result(s) of the Statewide Central Register of Child Abuse and Maltreatment and the criminal history record check(s) from the Office of Children and Family Services and the check of the register of substantiated category one cases of abuse or neglect from the Justice Center for the Protection of People with Special Needs, the authorized agency must make a decision whether to finally certify or approve such emergency foster parent within 60 days of the receipt of such results. If, once the Statewide Central Register of Child Abuse and Maltreatment database check process, the Justice

Center's register of substantiated category one cases of abuse or neglect check process and criminal history record check process are completed, and the authorized agency determines that the home should continue to be certified or approved, a final certification or approval must be issued for the home.

(i) Failure to meet the requirements for certification or approval of the foster home. Except as set forth in this section, if the emergency foster parent(s) or the relative foster parent(s) fails to meet all requirements for approval pursuant to this Part within 90 days from the date of placement, the authorized agency must:

(1) provide notice to the foster parent(s) or relative foster parent(s) within the first 90 days of placement if such requirement(s) for certification or approval as a foster home have not been or cannot be met. Such notice must be provided no later than 20 days prior to the expiration date of the emergency certification or approval and must identify the particular problem(s) that constitute a barrier to certification or approval as a foster home;

(2) revoke a foster parent(s) or a relative foster parent(s) certification or approval pursuant to section 443.12 of this Part if all requirements for approval are not met within the first 90 days from the date of placement;

(3) upon revocation of an approval or certification, remove the child from the home of the relative or foster parent, place such child in a suitable certified foster home or an approved relative foster home, and inform the relative of the right to request a hearing in accordance with the provisions of section 400 of the Social Services Law; and

(4) remove the child from the home of the foster parent or relative pursuant to section 400 of the Social Services Law and section 443.5 of this Part when health and safety risks to the child warrant such removal and place the child in a suitable certified foster home or an approved relative foster home. At the time the child is removed from the home, the relative or caretaker foster parent must be informed of the right to request a fair hearing in accordance with the provisions of section 400 of the Social Services Law.

§443.8   Criminal history record check.

(a) An authorized agency must perform criminal history record checks with the Division of Criminal Justice Services and the Federal Bureau of Investigation regarding any prospective foster parent and each person over the age of 18 who is currently residing in the home of such prospective foster parent before the foster parent is finally approved or certified for the placement of a foster child.

(b) At the time a foster parent applies for renewal of his or her approval or certification, an authorized agency must perform a state and national criminal history record check with the Division of Criminal Justice Services in accordance with subdivision (d) of this section regarding each person over the age of 18, other than a foster parent certified or approved prior to January 11, 2007, who is currently residing in the home of such foster parent who has not previously had such criminal history record checks completed.

(c) With the exception of the requirement that a criminal history record check must be completed by the Federal Bureau of Investigation, the provisions of this section also apply to persons who were certified or approved as foster parents on or before February 11, 1999.

(d) Fingerprinting.

(1) The authorized agency must obtain fingerprints of the prospective foster parent and each other person over the age of 18 who currently resides in the

home of such prospective or existing foster parent in the form prescribed by the Office of Children and Family Services and such other information as is required by the Office of Children and Family Services, the division of criminal justice services and the federal bureau of investigation.

(2) The authorized agency must provide to the applicant sufficient blank fingerprint cards and a description of how the completed fingerprint cards will be used upon submission to the authorized agency.   *(Eff.1/25/17)*

(3) The authorized agency or its designee must promptly transmit such fingerprint cards to the Office of Children and Family Services.

(4) The Office of Children and Family Services will promptly submit the fingerprint cards to the Division of Criminal Justice Services for its full search and retain processing in regard to the state criminal history record check and for the forwarding of the fingerprints to the Federal Bureau of Investigation. The Office of Children and Family Services will also include the applicable fee imposed by the Division of Criminal Justice Services and the Federal Bureau of Investigation.

(5) No part of the fee imposed for the processing of the fingerprints with the Division of Criminal Justice Services or the Federal Bureau of Investigation will be charged to the prospective or existing foster parent or any person over the age of 18 who currently resides in the home of such prospective or existing foster parent who submitted fingerprint cards pursuant to this subdivision.

(6) The Division of Criminal Justice Services and the Federal Bureau of Investigation will promptly provide the Office of Children and Family Services with a criminal history record, if any, on such person.

(7) (i) The Office of Children and Family Services will review the criminal history record information provided by the Division of Criminal Justice Services and the Federal Bureau of Investigation and promptly provide the authorized agency, as defined in section 371(10)(b) of the Social Services Law, with a summary of the criminal history record and notify the authorized agency of the actions that it must take regarding the person as set forth in subdivision (e) of this section.

(ii) The Office of Children and Family Services will review the criminal history record information provided by the Division of Criminal Justice Services and promptly provide the authorized agency, as defined in section 371(10)(a) of the Social Services Law, with a summary of the criminal history record and notify the authorized agency of the actions it must take regarding the person as set forth in subdivision (e) of this section.

(iii) The Office of Children and Family Services will review the criminal history record information provided by the Federal Bureau of Investigation and evaluate such results in accordance with the standards set forth in subdivision (e) of this section. The Office of Children and Family Services will inform the authorized agency, as defined in section 371(10)(a) of the Social Services Law, that the application for certification or approval of the prospective foster parent either: (a) must be denied; (b) must be held in abeyance pending subsequent notification from the Office of Children and Family Services; or (c) that the Office of Children and Family Services has no objection, solely based on the Federal Bureau of Investigation criminal history record check, for the authorized agency to proceed with a determination on such application based on the standards for certification or approval of a prospective foster parent, as set forth in this Part.   *(Eff.1/25/17)*

(e)(1) Except as set forth in this section, the authorized agency must deny an application for certification or approval as a certified or approved foster parent or deny an application for renewal of the certification or approval of an existing foster parent submitted on or after October 1, 2008 or revoke the certification or approval of an existing foster parent when a criminal history record of the prospective or existing foster parent reveals a conviction for:

(i) a felony conviction at any time involving:

(a) child abuse or neglect;

(b) spousal abuse;

(c) a crime against a child, including child pornography; or

(d) a crime involving violence, including rape, sexual assault, or homicide, other than a crime involving physical assault or battery; or

(ii) a felony conviction within the past five years for physical assault, battery, or a drug-related offense.

Notwithstanding any other provision to the contrary, with regard to a foster parent fully certified or approved prior to October 1, 2008, the provisions of this paragraph only apply to mandatory disqualifying convictions that occur on or after October 1, 2008.

(2) The authorized agency must hold the final determination of an application for certification or approval of a prospective or existing foster parent in abeyance whenever the criminal history record of the prospective or existing foster parent reveals:

(i) a charge for a crime set forth in paragraph (1) of this subdivision which has not been finally resolved; or

(ii) a felony conviction that may be for a crime set forth in paragraph (1) of this subdivision. An authorized agency may proceed with a determination of such application, in a manner consistent with this subdivision, only upon receiving subsequent notification from the Office of Children and Family Services regarding the status of such charge or the nature of such conviction.

(3) The authorized agency may deny an application for certification or approval of a prospective foster parent or deny the renewal or reapproval of an existing certification or approval of an existing foster parent, consistent with the provisions of article 23-A of the Correction Law, when:

(i) a criminal history record of the prospective or existing foster parent reveals a charge or a conviction of a crime other than one set forth in paragraph (1) of this subdivision; or

(ii) a criminal history record of any other person over the age of 18 who resides in the home of the prospective or existing foster parent reveals a charge or a conviction of any crime.

(4)   *(REPEALED,Eff.1/25/17)*

(f) (1) When an authorized agency, as defined in section 371(10)(b) of the Social Services Law, denies an application or revokes a certificate or approval pursuant to this section, the authorized agency must provide to the applicant or existing foster parent, to the extent authorized by federal and state law, a written statement setting forth the reasons for such denial or revocation, including the summary of the criminal history provided by the Office of Children and Family Services in accordance with subdivision (c) of this section. The authorized agency must also provide a description of the Division of Criminal Justice Services' and the Federal Bureau of Investigation's record review process and any remedial processes provided by the Office of Children and Family Services to any prospective foster parent. If the applicant is disqualified under clause (e)(1)(i)(b) of this section for a felony conviction of spousal abuse, then the applicant may apply to the Office of Children and Family Services for an administrative hearing in accordance with section 22 of the Social Services Law for relief from the disqualification based on the grounds that the offense was not spousal abuse as that term is defined in subdivision (i) of this section.

(2) When an authorized agency,as defined in section 371(10)(a) of the Social Services Law, denies or revokes a certificate or approval pursuant to this section based on criminal history record information provided to the Office of Children and Family Services by the Division of Criminal JusticeServices, the authorized agency must provide to the applicant or existing foster parent, to the extent authorized by Federal and State law, a written statement setting forth the reasons for such denial or revocation, including the summary of the criminal history provided by the Office of Children and Family Services in accordance with subdivision (c) of this section. The authorized agency must also provide a description of the Division of Criminal Justice Services' record review process and any remedial processes provided by the Office of Children and Family Services to any prospective foster parent. If the applicant is disqualified under clause (e)(1)(i)(b) of this section for a felony conviction of spousal abuse, then the applicant may apply to the Office of Children and Family Services for an administrative hearing in accordance with section 22 of the Social Services Law for relief from the disqualification based on the grounds that the offense was not spousal abuse as that term is defined in subdivision (i) of this section.

(3) Where the Office of Children and Family Services directs an authorized agency, as defined in section 371(10)(a) of the Social Services Law, to deny or revoke a certificate or approval based on the review and evaluation of a criminal history record check by the Federal Bureau of Investigation, the Office of Children and Family Services must also notify the applicant, foster parent or other person over the age of 18 who currently resides in the home of the applicant or foster parent whose criminal history was the basis for the denial or revocation and must provide such prospective foster parent, foster parent or other person a copy of the results of the Federal Bureau of Investigation criminal history check and a written statement setting forth the reasons for such denial or revocation. If the applicant or foster parent is disqualified under clause (e)(1)(i)(b) of this section for a felony conviction for spousal abuse, the applicant or foster parent may apply to the Office of Children and Family Services through an administrative hearing held in accordance with section 22 of the Social Services Law for relief from the disqualification based on the grounds that the offense was not spousal abuse as that term is defined in subdivision (i) of this section. *(Eff.1/25/17)*

(g)(1) When a criminal history record of the foster parent or of any other person over the age of 18 who resides in the home of such foster parent reveals a charge or conviction of any crime, the authorized agency must perform a safety assessment of the conditions in the household. Such assessment must include:

(i) whether the subject of the charge or conviction resides in the household;

(ii) the extent to which such person may have contact with foster children or other children residing in the household; and

(iii) the status, date and nature of the criminal charge or conviction.

(2) The authorized agency thereafter must take all appropriate steps to protect the health and safety of such child or children, including, when appropriate, the removal of any foster child or children from the home. The authorized agency must document the safety assessment and the steps and

actions taken by the authorized agency to protect the health and safety of the child.

(3) Where the authorized agency denies the application or revokes the certification or approval of the foster parent in accordance with the standards set forth in this section, such authorized agency must remove any foster child or children from the home of the foster parent.

(h) Confidentiality.

(1) Any criminal history record information provided by the Division of Criminal Justice Services or the Federal Bureau of Investigation, and any summary of the criminal history record provided by the Office of Children and Family Services to an authorized agency pursuant to this section, is confidential and is not available for public inspection.

(2) Nothing in this subsection prevents an authorized agency, the Office of Children and Family Services or other State agency referenced in paragraph (a) of subdivision two of section 378-a of the Social Services Law from disclosing criminal history information to any administrative or judicial proceeding relating to the denial or revocation of a foster parent's certification or approval or the foster child's removal from the home.

(3) Where there is a pending court case, the authorized agency which received the criminal history record summary from the Office of Children and Family Services must provide a copy of such summary to the Family Court or Surrogate's Court.

(i) For the purposes of this section spousal abuse is an offense defined in section 120.05 or 120.10 of the Penal Law where the victim of such offense was the defendant's spouse; provided, however, spousal abuse does not include a crime in which the prospective or existing foster parent, who was the defendant, has received notice pursuant to this section and the Office of Children and Family Services finds after an administrative hearing held pursuant to section 22 of the Social Services Law, that he or she was the victim of physical, sexual or psychological abuse by the victim of such offense and such abuse was a factor in causing the prospective or existing foster parent to commit such offense.

(j) The authorized agency must inform the Office of Children and Family Services either through CONNECTIONS or any other means so specified by the Office of Children and Family Services when a person is no longer certified or approved as a foster parent.   *(Eff.1/25/17)*

Part 449
Supervised Independent Living Programs

Section   *(Extracts)*
449.1   Definitions
449.4   Requirements for Each Supervised Independent Living Unit

§449.1   Definitions.

For the purpose of this Part:

(a) Authorized agency means one of the entities defined in paragraph (a) of (b) of subdivision 10 of section 371 of the Social Services Law.

(b) OCFS means the New York State Office of Children and Family Services.

(c) Supervised independent living program authorization means written approval issued by OCFS to an authorized agency in accordance with this Part for the operation of a supervised independent living program.

(d) Supervised independent living program means one or more of a type of agency operated boarding home operated and certified by an authorized agency in accordance with this Part to provide a transitional experience for older youth who, based upon their circumstances, are appropriate for transition to the level of care and supervision provided in the program.

(e) Supervised independent living unit means a home or apartment certified in accordance with the standards set forth in this Part by an authorized agency approved by OCFS to operate a supervised independent living program for the care of up to four youth including their children. Each supervised independent living unit must be located in the community separate from any of the authorized agency's other congregate dwellings.

(f) Supervised independent living program certification means a certificate issued by an authorized agency approved to operate a supervised independent living program for the operation of a supervised independent living unit. Such certification is non-transferable and is effective for a one year period.

(g) Youth means a child in the care and custody or the custody and guardianship of the commissioner of a local department of social services or OCFS.

(h) Adult permanency resource means a caring, committed adult who has been determined by a social services district to be an appropriate and acceptable resource for a youth and is committed to providing emotional support, advice and guidance to the youth and to assist the youth as the youth makes the transition from foster care to responsible adulthood.

§449.4   Requirements for Each Supervised Independent Living Unit.

(a) Personnel

(1) Each authorized agency operating a supervised independent living program must establish a procedure to review and evaluate the backgrounds of and information supplied by all applicants for employee, volunteer or consultant positions in the supervised independent living program. This procedure must take into account any appropriate collective bargaining agreement(s) and, in the case of a supervised independent living program operated by a social services official, must also comply with applicable provisions of the Civil Service Law. As part of this procedure, each employee, volunteer or consultant applicant must submit all of the following information:

(i) a statement or summary of the applicant's employment history, including, but not limited to, any relevant child-caring experience;

(ii) the names, addresses and, where available, telephone numbers of references who can verify the applicant's employment history, work record and qualifications.

(iii) the names, addresses and telephone numbers of at least three personal references, other than relatives, who can attest to the applicant's character, habits, reputation and personal qualifications; and

(iv) a sworn statement by the applicant indicating whether, to the best of such applicant's knowledge, the applicant has ever been convicted of a crime in New York State or any other jurisdiction.

(2) Persons caring for youth must be in good physical and mental health, and free from any communicable disease. Physical fitness must be shown by a certificate from a physician at the time of initial employment and annually thereafter.

(3) If an applicant discloses in the sworn statement furnished in accordance with subparagraph (iv) of paragraph (1) of subdivision (a) of this section that he or she has been convicted of a crime, the authorized agency operating the supervised independent living program must determine, in accordance with guidelines developed and disseminated by OCFS, whether to hire the applicant

or to use the volunteer or consultant. If the authorized agency determines it will hire the applicant or use the applicant as a volunteer or consultant who has the potential for regular and substantial contact with youth in the program, the authorized agency must maintain a written record, as part of the application file or employment or other personnel record of such person, of the reason(s) why such person was determined to be appropriate and acceptable as an employee, volunteer or consultant.

(4) Inquiries to the Statewide Central Register of Child Abuse and Maltreatment:

(i) With regard to any person who is actively being considered for employment, or to any individual or any person who is employed by an individual, corporation, partnership or association which provides goods or services to the authorized agency, and who has or will have the potential for regular and substantial contact with youth being cared for by the authorized agency, the authorized agency operating the supervised independent living program must inquire of OCFS whether any such person is the subject of an indicated report of child abuse or maltreatment on file with the Statewide Central Register of Child Abuse and Maltreatment. In addition, the authorized agency may inquire whether any current employee or any person who is being considered for use as a volunteer or for hiring as a consultant and who has or will have the potential for regular and substantial contact with youth who are being cared for by the supervised independent living program is the subject of an indicated report of child abuse or maltreatment on file with the Statewide Central Register of Child Abuse and Maltreatment. An inquiry regarding any current employee may be made only once in any six-month period.

(ii) Prior to making an inquiry pursuant to subparagraph (i) of this paragraph, the authorized agency must notify, in the form prescribed by OCFS, the person who will be the subject of an inquiry that the inquiry will be made to determine whether such person is the subject of an indicated report of child abuse or maltreatment on file with the Statewide Central Register of Child Abuse and Maltreatment.

(iii) Except as set forth in clause (a) of this subparagraph, an authorized agency may not permit a person hired by the authorized agency or a person who is employed by an individual, corporation, partnership or association which provides goods or services to the authorized agency to have contact with youth in the care of the supervised independent living program prior to obtaining the result of the inquiry required by this subdivision.

(a) An employee of an authorized agency or an employee of a provider of goods and services to the authorized agency may have contact with youth cared for by the supervised independent living program prior to the receipt by the authorized agency of the result of the inquiry required by this subdivision only where such employee is visually observed or audibly monitored by an existing staff member of the authorized agency. Such employee must be in the physical presence of an existing staff member for whom:

(1) the result of an inquiry required by section 424-a of the Social Services Law has been received by the authorized agency and the authorized agency hired the existing staff member with knowledge of the result of the inquiry; or

(2) an inquiry was not made because such staff member was hired before the effective date of section 424-a of the Social Services Law.

(iv) When the person who is the subject of the inquiry is an applicant for employment, OCFS will charge a five-dollar fee when it conducts a search of its records within the Statewide Central Register of Child Abuse and Maltreatment to determine whether such applicant is the subject of an indicated report.

(a) The required fee must either accompany the inquiry form submitted to OCFS or, for an inquiry submitted by a social services district, the district may elect to have the fee subtracted from its claims for reimbursement submitted pursuant to section 601.1 of this Title.

(b) Fees must be paid by authorized agency business check, certified check, postal or bank money order, teller's check or cashier's check made payable to "New York State Office of Children and Family Services". Personal checks and cash are not acceptable forms of payment.

(v) If the applicant, employee or other person about whom the authorized agency has made an inquiry is found to be the subject of an indicated report of child abuse or maltreatment, the authorized agency must determine, on the basis of information it has available and in accordance with guidelines developed and disseminated by OCFS, whether to hire, retain or use the person as an employee, volunteer or consultant, or to permit the person providing goods or services to have access to youth being cared for by the authorized agency. Whenever such person is hired, retained, used or given access to youth, the authorized agency must maintain a written record, as part of the application file or employment or other personnel record of such person, of the specific reason(s) why such person was determined to be appropriate and acceptable as an employee, volunteer, consultant, or provider of goods or services with access to youth being cared for by the supervised independent living program.

(vi) If the authorized agency denies employment or makes a decision not to retain an employee, not to use a volunteer, not to hire a consultant, or not to permit a person providing goods or services to have access to youth being cared for by the supervised independent living program, the authorized agency must provide a written statement to the applicant, employee, volunteer or consultant or other person indicating whether the denial or decision was based in whole or in part on the existence of the indicated report and, if so, reasons for the denial or decision. If the denial or decision was based in whole or in part on such indicated report, the statement must also include written notification, in the form prescribed by OCFS, to the applicant, employee, volunteer, consultant or other person that:

(a) He or she has the right, pursuant to section 424-a of the Social Services Law, to request a hearing before OCFS regarding the record maintained by the Statewide Central Register of Child Abuse and Maltreatment;

(b) The request for such a hearing must be made within 90 days of the receipt of the written notice indicating that the denial or decision was based on the existence of the indicated report; and

(c) The sole issue at any such hearing will be whether the applicant, employee, volunteer, consultant or other person has been shown by a fair preponderance of the evidence to have committed the act or acts of child abuse or maltreatment giving rise to the indicated report.

(vii) If, in a hearing held pursuant to a request made in accordance with subparagraph (vi) of this paragraph and section 424-a of the Social Services Law, a decision issued by OCFS finds that there was a failure to show by a fair preponderance of the evidence that the applicant, employee, volunteer, consultant or other person committed the act or acts upon which the indicated report is based, OCFS will notify the authorized agency which made the inquiry that, pursuant to the hearing decision, the authorized agency's decision to deny the application, discharge the employee, not to use the volunteer or consultant, or not to permit the person providing goods or services to have access to youth being cared for by the authorized agency should be reconsidered. Upon receiving such notification from OCFS, the authorized agency should review its denial or other decision without considering the indicated report.

(5)* Review of Applicants:

(i) Each program under this section is required to check applicants for employment and volunteer positions as well as contractors and consultants, with the Register of Substantiated Category One Cases of Abuse or Neglect ("staff exclusion list") maintained by the Vulnerable Persons' Central Register ("VPCR"), as required by section 495 of the Social Services Law, before determining whether to hire or otherwise allow any person to be an employee, administrator, consultant, intern, volunteer or contractor who will have the potential for regular and substantial contact with a service recipient; or before approving an applicant for a license, certificate, permit or other approval to provide care to a service recipient.

(a) If an applicant is listed on the staff exclusion list, a facility or provider agency as defined in section 488 of the Social Services Law shall not hire such a person for a position in which the person would have the potential for regular and substantial contact with a service recipient in any such facility or program or otherwise permit such person to have a position in which the person would have the potential for regular and substantial contact with a service recipient in any such facility or program. Other providers or licensing agencies as defined in subdivision (3) or (4) of section 424-a of the Social Services Law shall determine whether to hire or allow such a person to have regular or substantial contact with a service recipient in accordance with the provisions of subdivision (5) of section 424-a of the Social Services Law.

(b) Any program that is required to conduct an inquiry pursuant to section 495 of the Social Services Law shall first conduct the inquiry required under such section. If the result of the inquiry under section 495 of the Social Services Law is that the person about whom the inquiry is made is on the staff exclusion list and the program is required to deny the application in accordance with Article II of the Social Services Law, the facility or provider agency shall not be required to make an inquiry of the Office under section 424-a of the Social Services Law.

(ii) If an applicant is not listed on the staff exclusion list, then a database check must be completed in accordance with section 424-a of the Social Services Law and this section.

(iii) Each program under this section is required by section 553 of the Executive Law, and subdivision 1 of section 378-a of the Social Services Law, to obtain criminal history background checks for certain prospective employees, or volunteers who will have the potential for substantial, unsupervised or unrestricted physical contact with children or vulnerable persons through the Justice Center as authorized by Article 20 of the Executive Law.

(a) The Justice Center will review and evaluate the criminal history information for any person applying to be an operator, employee, or volunteer for whom a criminal background check is required by law at any facilities or provider agencies as defined in subdivision 4 of section 488 of the Social Services Law that are operated, licensed or certified by the Office of Children and Family Services.

(b) If an applicant has been convicted of a crime, the agency must determine, in accordance with guidelines or regulations developed and disseminated by the Office of Children and Family Services or the Justice Center, whether to hire or use the person as an employee, or volunteer. If the agency determines it will hire or use the person, the agency must maintain a written record, as part of the application file or employment or other personnel record of such person, of the reason(s) why such person was determined to be appropriate and acceptable as an employee, volunteer or consultant.

(iv) A custodian, as defined in section 488 of the Social Services Law, shall be subject to immediate termination if he or she is convicted of any felony or misdemeanor as defined in the Penal Law, that relates directly to the abuse or neglect of a vulnerable person, or is placed on the staff exclusion list.

(v) At the commencement of employment, and annually thereafter, the agency must provide each staff employee a copy of the applicable Justice Center created or approved code of conduct required to read and to acknowledge that he or she has read and understands such code of conduct. Failure on the part of staff to acknowledge the code of conduct can result in disciplinary action including termination, consistent with appropriate collective bargaining agreements.

(b) Physical facility.

(1) A supervised independent living unit must be in an appropriate neighborhood and so located that it is readily accessible to necessary services and adequate transportation.

(2) A supervised independent living unit must be of sufficient size to provide proper accommodations for the youth placed in the unit.

(3) A supervised independent living unit must be kept in clean and sanitary condition and in good repair, and must provide for the reasonable comfort and well-being of the youth.

(4) A supervised independent living unit must be protected by a fire detection system, a sprinkler system, as those terms are defined in section 441.2 of this Title, or a smoke detection system or individual smoke detectors as required by applicable local codes and the New York State Uniform Fire Prevention and Building Code.

(i) Buildings used in whole or in part as a supervised independent living unit must comply with all applicable laws, ordinances, rules, regulations and codes relating to buildings, fire protection, health and safety.

(ii) All areas of fire hazard in the supervised independent living unit must be protected by a sprinkler system or fire detection system, as those terms are defined in section 441.2 of this Title. Areas of fire hazard must be separated from other areas by construction having a fire resistance rating of at least one hour. An area of fire hazard means a heating equipment room; a woodworking shop; a paint shop; a storeroom for mattresses, furniture, paints and/or other combustible or flammable materials or liquid; and any other space or room exceeding 100 square feet in floor area where other combustible or flammable materials are regularly stored.

(iii) Other than quantities of flammable materials necessary for the operation and maintenance of the supervised independent living unit, which must be kept in closed containers in storage cabinets, and fuel oil, which must be kept in oil storage tanks, flammable materials must not be stored in the supervised independent living unit.

(iv) All fire protection systems and equipment must be designed, installed, and maintained in accordance with the New York State Uniform Fire Prevention and Building Code. All fire protection systems and equipment must be inspected according to local and New York State building codes. A written report of such inspections must be kept on file by the authorized agency. All identified defects in systems or equipment must be corrected and re-inspected immediately.

(v) A supervised independent living unit must be free from all conditions that constitute a hazard to the life, health or safety of any person. The following are prohibited:

(a) portable electric space heaters or self-contained fuel-burning space heaters;

(b) solid-fuel-burning, free-standing stoves, except where approved in writing by the authorized agency;

(c) use of fuel-burning or electric "hot plates";

(d) illegal connections for gas appliances;

(e) combustible or flammable containers for ashes;

(f) the accumulation of combustible or flammable materials in any part of the unit;

(g) damaged equipment, furnishings or physical plant, when their condition makes them unsafe for normal use;

(h) broken plumbing or stopped sewers that are not promptly repaired;

(i) exposed steam pipes, heating pipes and radiators and unenclosed heating plants and equipment with which youth may come in contact;

(j) use of materials containing asbestos in any construction, renovation or repair of any supervised independent living program where such construction, renovation or repair occurs on or after July 1, 1993;

(k) any furniture, toys or construction containing lead-based paint;

(l) any lead paint hazard or paint condition conducive to lead poisoning, as such term is defined in 10 NYCRR 67.1. Any building used in whole or in part as a supervised independent living unit occupied by a child six years of age or younger must be inspected to determine if it presents such hazard. The authorized agency must request the local health department to perform such inspection and is responsible for correcting any hazard called to its attention as a result of such inspection. In the event that such request for inspection is rejected by the local health department, the authorized agency must notify OCFS immediately;

(m) extension cords, unless approved in writing by the authorized agency; and

(n) any other condition deemed hazardous by OCFS or the authorized agency.

(vi) Fire extinguishers must be provided in each supervised independent living unit and maintained in accordance with the New York State Uniform Fire Prevention and Building Code. Fire extinguishers must be wall-hung between two feet and four-and-one-half feet above the floor. All staff members and youth must be instructed in the proper operation of extinguishers. In each unit there must be a minimum of one fire extinguisher on each floor, and, additionally, one in the kitchen, one in the laundry room and one outside any heating equipment room.

(vii) A supervised independent living unit must have a minimum of two means of egress from the unit's floor that are readily accessible to the youth. For a window opening to qualify as a means of egress, it must be at least 24 inches high and 20 inches wide with the bottom of the window no higher than three feet eight inches above the floor unless acceptable access is provided by steps or furniture fixed in place. An upper level window, to qualify as a means of egress, must also have a platform outside the window and a stair, permanently affixed to the building, leading to ground level.

(viii) Youth are not permitted above the second story in a building of type 5, wood frame construction (that type of construction in which the walls, partitions, floors and roof are wholly or partly of wood or other combustible materials). Youth of limited mobility are not permitted above the first story in a building of wood frame construction. A building of wood frame construction occupied by youth of limited mobility must be protected by a sprinkler system and the first story must be handicap accessible for youth of limited mobility and accommodate the needs of such youth.

(ix) All exit doors and means of egress, halls and stairs must be well lighted and kept clean, free of obstruction and ready at all times for immediate use. Battery-operated or generator-powered emergency lighting units or systems must be provided and maintained in accordance with the New York State Uniform Fire Prevention and Building Code.

(x) Each supervised independent living unit must be provided with emergency lights, such as flashlights or battery-operated lanterns, in good working order.

(xi) Each supervised independent living unit must have a plan for evacuation of the unit, posted in a conspicuous place on each floor level in the unit. The agency must maintain a diagram of the living unit's floor plan on file.

(xii) Youth and staff must be instructed in how to evacuate the building in which the supervised independent living unit is located. Newly admitted youth, newly hired staff and volunteers must be instructed in evacuation procedures as part of their orientation to the supervised independent living unit. Evacuation procedures must be reviewed quarterly with youth after placement.

(xiii) Electrical wiring and equipment must comply with the New York State Uniform Fire Prevention and Building Code and any other applicable laws, ordinances, rules, regulations and codes. Certification of such compliance is required for all new supervised independent living units prior to opening and a record of such certification of compliance must be kept on file by the authorized agency. OCFS may require recertification of the safety of an electrical system in any supervised independent living unit where the electrical system appears to be unsafe or inadequate, or if new electrical work has been done.

(xiv) Heating, ventilating and other mechanical systems must comply with the New York State Uniform Fire Prevention and Building Code and any other applicable laws, ordinances, rules, regulations and codes and must be designed, installed, located and maintained so that under normal conditions of use such equipment and systems are not a danger to the health or welfare of youth or staff in the building in which the supervised independent living unit is located. Heating plants and equipment must be protected from tampering by youth.

(xv) All shop, maintenance, grounds and farm equipment must be equipped with approved safety devices and must be maintained in safe working condition. Youth must not operate such equipment except under the close supervision of responsible staff members.

(xvi) A minimum of one non-coin operated, single line telephone must be provided and must be accessible at all times in each supervised independent living unit occupied by youth or each youth must be provided with a personal cellular telephone. Emergency telephone numbers for fire, police and medical assistance must be posted in the supervised independent living unit.

(xvii) Each authorized agency must request in writing an annual safety inspection of the buildings in which supervised independent living units are located and all fire protection equipment by local fire authorities and/or the authorized agency fire and casualty insurance carrier who must be requested to give the authorized agency a written report of their findings. An authorized agency is responsible for correcting any hazards called to its attention as a result of such inspection that could affect a supervised independent living unit in the building and for keeping a copy of the report and a written record of the action taken, with date, on file. An authorized agency must keep a copy of the written request for inspection and the response on file and must notify OCFS immediately in the event that such request for inspection is rejected by the local fire authorities or the authorized agency's fire and casualty insurance carriers.

(xviii) An authorized agency must report promptly by telephone to OCFS the occurrence of any fire in any supervised independent living unit, or within any building in which such authorized agency has certified a supervised independent living unit. This report must be made as soon as possible and in no event later than 24 hours after the fire, and the authorized agency must then confirm the occurrence of the fire by a written report to OCFS within 10 working days after the date of the fire. The written report must include:

(a) the date and time of the fire;
(b) the extent of personal injuries;
(c) the extent of property damage;
(d) the probable cause of the fire, if known;
(e) which fire department responded;
(f) whether youth were relocated, and, if so, where;
(g) whether fire and smoke detection and alarm devices or systems operated properly;
(h) whether evacuation procedures were followed;
(i) the location of the fire;
(j) a description of the progress of the fire, the manner in which the fire spread and what efforts were made and methods were used to combat the fire; and
(k) any problems encountered with evacuation procedures, response by the fire department and ability of the fire department to combat the fire effectively.

(xix) All fireplaces and their chimneys in the supervised independent living unit must be inspected and cleaned annually by a qualified person.

(5) There must be an adequate and accessible supply of hot and cold water of safe quality in the supervised independent living unit.

(6) The supervised independent living unit must be effectively screened against flies and other insects.

(7) Temperature in the supervised independent living unit must be maintained at a comfortable level according to New York State Fire Prevention and Building Codes.

(8) Adequate bathing, toilet and lavatory facilities must be provided in the supervised independent living unit, and must be kept in sanitary condition.

(9) Each youth must have a separate bed. Single bedrooms must contain at least 70 square feet. Bedrooms occupied by more than one youth must have 70 square feet plus an additional 50 square feet of floor area per additional youth. There must be at least two feet of space between beds. Youth must not walk through one bedroom to get to another bedroom.

(10) All habitable rooms, except the kitchen, must be no less than seven feet in any dimension. For rooms with sloped ceilings, include only the floor dimensions with a clear ceiling height of five feet or more in this calculation.

One-third of the minimum required floor area of each room must have a ceiling height of seven feet.

(11) The kitchen must have at least three feet of clear passage between counter fronts and appliances or counter fronts and walls.

(12) Every sleeping room occupied by youth must have good natural light and ventilation, and must have one or more windows opening directly to the outside.

(13) No bed may be located in an unfinished attic, unfinished basement or other space commonly used for other than bedroom purposes.

(14) Separate and accessible drawer space for personal belongings, and sufficient closet space for indoor and outdoor clothing, must be available for individual youth.

(15) Supervised independent living units which house parenting youth and their children must comply with the following additional conditions:

(i) No peeling or damaged paint or plaster may be present;

(ii) Access to outdoor play space must be available;

(iii) Radiators and piping accessible to children must be covered or have a barrier to protect children;

(iv) Porches, decks, and stairways must have railings with a barrier to prevent children from falling;

(v) Adequate barriers to prevent children from gaining access to unsafe, dangerous or hazardous areas or devices, such as fireplaces, wood burning stoves, gas space heaters, pools, spa pools, hot tubs, and second floor and above windows, must be provided;

(vi) Protective caps, covers, or permanently installed obstruction devices on all electrical outlets accessible to children must be present;

(vii) All matches, lighters, medicines, drugs, cleaning material, detergents, aerosol cans, beauty aids, and poisonous or toxic materials and plants must be safely stored and must be used in such a way that they will not contaminate play surfaces, food and food preparation areas, or constitute a hazard to children, and other such materials must be kept in a place inaccessible to children;

(viii) Hand bags, backpacks, briefcases, plastic bags, toys and objects small enough for children to swallow must not be accessible to children; and

(ix) Each child must have a separate bed or crib, as appropriate.

(16) Children of different genders above the age of four years may not sleep in the same room, except that a parenting youth may sleep in the same room as his or her children.

(c) Services

(1) Supervised independent living programs must include the following service components to provide youth with opportunities to achieve positive outcomes and make successful transitions to self-sufficiency:

(i) An ongoing support network of consistent adults or families in their lives;

(ii) A diligent and ongoing effort to establish an adult permanency resource for each youth;

(iii) Preventive health care;

(iv) Employment skills/training, and the development of work ethics;

(v) Educational support;

(vi) Housing support;

(vii) Budgeting and financial management skills;

(viii) Shopping, cooking and housecleaning skills;

(ix) Access to community resources/community linkages;

(x) Connections with caring adults, such as mentors;

(xi) Positive youth development;

(xii) Necessary developmentally appropriate services;

(xiii) Preparation for discharge and the transition to adulthood;

(xiv) Parenting skills, child development education and any other child rearing training deemed necessary; and

(xv) Ongoing assessment of life skills competency.

(2) Supervised independent living units that house parent youth and their children must also meet the following criteria:

(i) The staff and parenting youth must maintain current first-aid and CPR training certification.

(ii) The plan for youth in placement must include appropriate childcare for the child.

(iii) No more than two children under two years of age may be cared for in any single supervised independent living unit.

(d) Other conditions for participation in supervised independent living programs to be observed:

(1) Youth who participate in the supervised independent living program must be at least 16 years of age and not more than 21 years of age.

(2) Such youth must have been in a foster care placement for at least 45 consecutive days during the period immediately preceding the date on which the youth entered a supervised independent living program, or must have been in the care and custody or custody and guardianship of a social services official or OCFS and have been discharged from foster care on a trial basis in accordance with the provisions of section 430.12(f)(4) of this Title.

(3) The supervised living program must comply with applicable discharge planning requirements set forth in the Part 428 and 430.12(f) of this Title.

(4) As required by section 428.7 of this Title, a plan amendment must be documented and approved by the social services district with case management responsibility for the child within 30 days of discharge of the child from foster care.

(5) Prior to the transfer of a foster child to a supervised independent living program, the local district which has care and custody or custody and guardianship of the child, or, for a youth in the custody of OCFS, OCFS, must give written approval of the transfer.

(6) Health supervision, medical and dental care must be provided to each youth in accordance with section 441.22 of this Title.

(7) The educational and recreational needs of youth must be met.

(8) Each supervised independent living unit must have facilities that will enable youth to prepare meals. The authorized agency must require that youth maintain sufficient quantities of good quality, properly prepared food specific to the dietary needs of the youth.

(9) Youth must have individual toilet articles and requisites for personal grooming and hygiene, suitable to ages and needs.

(10) Youth must have appropriate seasonal clothing. Clothing must be kept clean and in good repair.

(11) A supervised independent living unit may occupy a house or apartment rented or owned by the authorized agency.

(12) No supervised independent living unit may house more than four youth including their children.

(13) If two or more youth live together in the same unit, they must be of the same gender unless the authorized agency receives approval to place siblings of the opposite gender together by utilizing the waiver process identified in section 449.6 of this Part.

(14) Only persons placed in the supervised independent living program by the authorized agency may reside in a supervised independent living unit.

(15) Supervised independent living programs must be in compliance with all applicable provisions of State and local laws, ordinances, rules and regulations concerning health, safety and nondiscrimination.

Part 466
Implementation and Administration of the Connections System

§466.1 Scope.

The provisions of this Part apply to the implementation and administration of the CONNECTIONS system. This Part establishes standards for the internal and external recording of information in the CONNECTIONS system, the protection of confidential individual identifiable information, the sealing and expungement of information and the security of the system.

§466.2 Definitions.

For the purposes of this Part the following definitions apply:

(a) The CONNECTIONS system means the statewide automated child welfare information system implemented and administered by OCFS pursuant to section 446 of the Social Services Law. The CONNECTIONS system contains, but is not limited to, those data elements required by applicable State and federal statutes and regulations, relating to the provision of child welfare services including foster care, adoption assistance, adoption services, preventive services, child protective services, and other family preservation and family support services.

(b) OCFS means the New York State Office of Children and Family Services, successor agency to the Department of Social Services and the Division for Youth, pursuant to chapter 436 of the Laws of 1997.

(c) A public or private agency means an authorized agency, as defined in paragraphs (a) or (b) of subdivision 10 of section 371 of the Social Services Law; a not-for-profit corporation, as defined in paragraph 5 of subdivision (a) of section 102 of the Not-for-Profit Corporation Law; or a public agency that receives prior approval from OCFS to provide foster care and/or child welfare services.

§466.3 Mandatory use.

Upon issuance of an administrative directive by OCFS indicating that information regarding a child welfare service or services must be entered into the CONNECTIONS system, each social services district or public or private agency providing such service that has access to the CONNECTIONS system must use the CONNECTIONS system for recording the information in the form and manner prescribed by OCFS to satisfy the data requirements for the particular service. Any such administrative directive may require use of the CONNECTIONS system for all or part of the services or information to be documented, and may apply initially to a limited number of social services districts and/or public and private agencies.

§466.4 Confidentiality.

(a) Individual identifiable information contained in the CONNECTIONS system is confidential and may be disclosed only in a manner consistent with applicable statutory and regulatory standards.

(1) Individual identifiable information regarding children in foster care and their families is confidential and access to such information is allowable only pursuant to the standards set forth in sections 372, 373-a, 409-e and 409-f of the Social Services Law and applicable OCFS regulations including sections 357.3, 428.8, 430.12 and 431.12 of this Title.

(2) Individual identifiable information regarding children and families receiving preventive services is confidential and access to such information is allowable only pursuant to the standards set forth in sections 409-e and 409-f of the Social Services Law and applicable OCFS regulations including section 423.7 of this Title.

(3) Individual identifiable information regarding adoption assistance and adoption services is confidential and access to such information is allowable only pursuant to the standards set forth in section 114 of the Domestic Relations Law, sections 373-a and 409-f of the Social Services Law and applicable OCFS regulations including section 357.3 of this Title.

(4) Individual identifiable information regarding child protective services is confidential and access to such information is allowable only pursuant to the standards set forth in sections 422(4), 422(5), 422(6), 422(7), 422-a, 424(4) and 424(5) of the Social Services Law and applicable OCFS regulations including section 432.7 of this Title.

(5) In addition to the standards set forth in paragraphs (1) - (4) of this subdivision, information contained in the CONNECTIONS system is subject to all other applicable federal and State confidentiality standards, including but not limited to, those set forth in Article 27-F of the Public Health Law regarding confidential HIV-related information and section 459-g of the Social Services Law regarding the street address of residential programs for victims of domestic violence.

(b) Consistent with applicable statute and regulation, an employee of OCFS, a social services district or a public or private agency providing child welfare services may have access to client identifiable information contained in the CONNECTIONS system only when access to such information is necessary for the employee to perform his or her specific job responsibilities.

(c) Each social services district and each public or private agency providing child welfare services that has access to the CONNECTIONS system must develop and implement policies and practices to maintain the confidentiality of individual identifiable information contained in the CONNECTIONS system consistent with applicable statutes and regulations including the taking of disciplinary action against any employee who fails to comply with the confidentiality standards set forth in this Part.

§466.5 Sealing and expungement of information.

(a) All individual identifiable information regarding a child and/or family receiving preventive services that are not provided in conjunction with or in addition to child protective, foster care or adoption services must be expunged from the CONNECTIONS system six years after the 18th birthday of the youngest child in the family.

(b) All individual identifiable information regarding a child and/or family receiving child protective services is subject to the sealing and expungement standards set forth in sections 422(5), 422(6) and 422(8) of the Social Services Law and section 432.9 of this Title.

(c) The expungement of individual identifiable information from the CONNECTIONS system includes the elimination of the electronic data and information from the electronic system or the elimination of the electronic data required to access such information.

§466.6 Security.

(a) OCFS, local social service districts, and public or private agencies providing child welfare services that have access to the CONNECTIONS system must establish and maintain a CONNECTIONS security plan addressing the following areas:

(1) Physical security of CONNECTIONS resources;

(2) Equipment security to protect equipment from theft and unauthorized use;

(3) Software and data security;

(4) Telecommunications security;

(5) Personnel Access Control;

(6) Contingency plans for meeting critical processing needs in the event of short or long-term interruption of services;

(7) Emergency and/or disaster preparedness;

(8) Designation of a security manager for OCFS and a security coordinator for the local district or public or private agency; and

(9) A program for conducting periodic security reviews at least once every two years to evaluate physical and data security operating procedures and personnel practices and to determine whether appropriate, cost effective safeguards exist to comply with the areas set forth in this subdivision. A report of each security review and all relevant supporting documentation must be maintained and made available to OCFS upon request.

(b) Each social services district and each public or private agency providing child welfare services that has access to the CONNECTIONS system must immediately report in writing to the State Information Technology staff person designated by OCFS the loss or theft of any CONNECTIONS equipment and any event that may jeopardize the security of the CONNECTIONS system.

TITLE 22
Judiciary

Part 127
Assignment and Compensation of Counsel,
Psychiatrists, Psychologists and Physicians

Section
127.5   Workload of the Attorney for the Child

§127.5 Workload of the attorney for the child.

(a) Subject to adjustment based on the factors set forth in subdivision (b), the number of children represented at any given time by an attorney appointed pursuant to section 249 of the Family Court Act shall not exceed 150.

(b) For representation provided under an agreement pursuant to section 243(a) and (b) of the Family Court Act, the workload standards set forth in subdivision (a) may be adjusted based on such factors as:

(1) Differences among categories of cases that comprise the workload of the office covered by the agreement;

(2) The level of activity required at different phases of the proceeding;

(3) The weighting of different categories and phases of cases;

(4) Availability and use of support staff;

(5) The representation of multiple children in a case;

(6) Local court practice, including the duration of a case;

(7) Other relevant considerations.

(c) The administrators of offices pursuant to such agreements shall be responsible for managing resources and for allocating cases among staff attorneys to promote the effective representation of children and to ensure that the average workload of the attorneys for children in the office complies with the standards set forth in subdivision (a) as modified by subdivision (b).

(d) For representation provided by a panel of attorneys for children pursuant to section 243(c) of the Family Court Act, the Appellate Division may adjust the workload standards of subdivision (a) to ensure the effective representation of children.

(e) The Chief Administrator of the Courts, with respect to representation pursuant to section 243(a) of the Family Court Act, and the Appellate Divisions, with respect to representation pursuant to section 243(b) and (c) of the Family Court Act, shall annually, at the time of the preparation and submission of the judiciary budget, review the workload of such offices and panels, and shall take action to assure compliance with this rule.

This page intentionally left blank.

INDEX

i

INDEX

INDEX

INDEX

INDEX

INDEX

INDEX

INDEX

INDEX

INDEX

INDEX

INDEX

Notes

Notes